The Ribbon

The Ribbon
A Celebration of Life

edited by
the Lark Books staff
and Marianne Philbin

Lark Books
Asheville, North Carolina

Marianne Philbin, editor, is curator at The Peace Museum in Chicago. The Peace Museum, the only museum of its kind, provides peace education through the arts. In 1983, Marianne met Justine Merritt and later organized the exhibition *The Ribbon: A Celebration of Life.*

Don Willcox, text author, has written a number of books on crafts and textiles. He first became interested in The Ribbon after seeing the exhibit at The Peace Museum, which he visited shortly after returning from a pilgrimage to Hiroshima and Nagasaki.

Published in 1985 by
Lark Books
50 College Street
Asheville, North Carolina 28801

First edition
Library of Congress Catalog Card Number: 85-80922
Printed in the United States of America
ISBN 0-937274-24-0

For all of you, all over the world, who made The Ribbon grow
by creating banners,
by sharing your enthusiasm,
by giving your time and your talents.
And especially for you who see The Ribbon
and take encouragement from it.

Nineteen young artists in Doniphan, Missouri, contributed cloth pictures for this colorful banner. Holding the banner (left to right) are Bradley Griffin, Bobbi Staggs, Jonathan Griffin, and Rickie Staggs.

Sister Jovita Schussele moved her treadle machine outdoors to sew a banner. The "war box," created by Kendrew Lascelles, was used in a mime performed at Indiana Ribbon celebrations. Photo: Kevin Swank, *Evansville Courier*.

Towns across the country saw Ribbon previews when banners were sewn together and displayed in parades, museums, schools, and churches.

Foreword

There can be no single spokesperson for a project such as The Ribbon, and in a way, there is no need for one; each Ribbon panel, as you'll see in the following pages, speaks for itself. What I would like to do here, what we want to do through this book, is simply offer an introduction.

The beauty of The Ribbon and the source of its power lie in the fact that it was created by hundreds and hundreds of private citizens from across the United States and around the world. I am simply another participant in this incredible project, another voice asking for peace.

I am introducing the tens of thousands of people who took time away from other pursuits to get involved in The Ribbon; time away from their children, from television, from meetings, to make a banner to add to The Ribbon so that their voices might be added to the chorus of voices crying out for an end to the wildness of military buildups, uncountable bombs, and madness.

I am introducing all those who expressed their creativity, designing and stitching banners, weaving, painting, embroidering, quilting. Some were textile artists skilled in technique; others were children who traced their hands with help from teachers or parents, senior citizens who sat around a quilting frame sharing stories, Cub Scout troops, community groups, church groups, prison inmates, families, students. Perhaps no endeavor in our history has intimately involved more people from more varied backgrounds.

I am introducing the personal statements made through each Ribbon panel. The Ribbon asked a simple question: what do you cherish in life? What can't you bear to think of as being lost forever in nuclear war? The answers are as varied as the participants—picnics, grandchildren, music, videos, hometowns, Shakespeare, puppet shows, trees, football fields, friends, and even "the least of Thy creation," poison ivy . . . Each panel represents a personal statement, and whether it's the artist using symbol, the intimate listing of family members, the humorous image, they are all moving, all magnificent.

Most importantly, they were all made with love. Hundreds of people stopped what they were doing to make a Ribbon panel, to say to the world and every person in it that love is important. They are the embodiment of Dwight Eisenhower's famous words, ". . . I think that people want peace so much that one of these days governments had better get out of their way and let them have it."

The Ribbon is unique and beautiful, and through this book, we hope to introduce you to some of the people who participated and some of the panels they created. To those who did not have a chance to participate, I ask that you read this book, and keep in mind what The Ribbon asks the generals, the politicians and every one of us to remember: that we cherish the earth and all its people, and together, we can put an end to war.

Studs Terkel, radio commentator and author of Working, *recently won the Pulitzer Prize for* The Good War, *an oral history of World War II.*

Justine Merritt's banner was the
beginning of The Ribbon. On it she
embroidered the names of friends and
relatives, loved ones who would be lost
in a nuclear war. Photo: Paul Brezny

Justine Merritt. Photo: David Cornwell,
Rocky Mountain News, Denver, Colorado

Introduction

Back in February of 1982, when Jonathan Schell had just written *The Fate of the Earth* and the national freeze campaign was warming up, I wasn't working for peace and I did not wish to work for peace. Many of my friends were busy working very hard in many different ways, but I maintained a distance, not from them, but from the peace movement.

In February, however, I went on a retreat to pray—literally—for guidance for my life. I had been travelling and writing for a couple of years, but something seemed out of focus. I prayed, I realized later, with a divided heart: half of my heart was very earnestly imploring the Lord to guide me, and the other half of my heart was saying "and make sure you send me to South America" where I thought I wanted to go.

But something happened. One morning, again in prayer, the poem "Gift" was given to me, and even the stubborn, frightened child in me could understand that the path I was to follow led not to South America, but toward working for peace at home.

In the moments and days that came after the writing of the poem, I felt that I would probably do very much what my friends were doing, which was attending peace vigils, writing letters to senators and representatives, letters to the editor, perhaps becoming involved in the campaign for a nuclear freeze. I assumed that I would be doing what might be called "traditional" peace work (and I love that pun, because you see, The Ribbon is traditional "piece" work); I expected to be ringing doorbells and signing petitions, but during the first week of March, it occurred to me to tie a ribbon around the Pentagon. The ribbon I envisioned would be a symbol of peace encircling a symbol of war, and it would be tied around the Pentagon in August of 1985, the fortieth anniversary of the bombings of Hiroshima and Nagasaki.

People asked me later if I ever thought of tying a ribbon around the Kremlin, or the United Nations Building, or the Capitol, but it was always clear to me that it was somehow most important for The Ribbon to go around the Pentagon. I see the Pentagon as a symbol of my nation's violence, and of my own. I wanted The Ribbon to be a gentle reminder to the nation that we love the earth and all its people.

From the beginning, I envisioned The Ribbon as segments of fabric sewn together, with each segment being a symbol of what we cannot bear to think of as lost forever in nuclear war. Like many people, for years after the bombing of Hiroshima, I had been unable to confront the reality of living in a nuclear age, unable to confront my own fears of nuclear war. When I read the newspapers, when I listened to the late evening news before sleep or awoke with the morning TV describing the number of warheads on a Trident submarine, or the plans for the MX missile, or the notion that we can prevail in a nuclear war, I became angry, grief-stricken, terrified. I felt powerless. The idea behind The Ribbon from the beginning was to face that sense of powerlessness.

When I was making my own Ribbon panel, I found that as I would thread my needle, I was confronting the fear, confronting the grief and terror. As I drew the needle up through the cloth, I was praying for peace, and the prayer became an affirmation of life. The very task of creating my panel helped empower me to face the reality of living in a nuclear age.

I faced the reality that the lives of my grandchildren are in jeopardy, Beethoven's melodies are in jeopardy, every shell and flower and bird is in jeopardy, and the planet is as vulnerable as I am. I thought about how many weapons there are, and faced the realization that all this could be lost, not just an apple blossom this spring, but the newest grandchild, who is only six months old. I faced the terror that I might actually survive, that I might "prevail" in such an outrageous act of genocide, and in confronting those realities and turning them into an affirmation of life, I felt less grief-stricken, less afraid, less angry, and more committed than ever to working for peace. In creating my panel for The Ribbon, I felt a great sense of healing, and I think The Ribbon has had a similar effect on many others.

I never doubted that The Ribbon would work. Initially, I think I imagined we'd have 2,000 segments, 40 from each state, and that maybe 1,000 people would help to hold The Ribbon around the Pentagon. I never doubted that it would work, but I could never have dreamed how many people it would touch. There is no way, as I write this now, to know how many will gather on August 4th in Arlington, Virginia but we are planning for 100,000 people. There is no way to know how many segments there will be, but we are estimating close to ten miles of Ribbon.

Tens of thousands of people have become involved in The Ribbon. Participants have come from all over

Most Ribbon participants made their banners to show "What I cannot bear to think of as lost in a nuclear war." For thousands, that means "children." Photo: David Hildebrand

12

the country, from Lopez Island off the coast of Washington State, from the South Bronx, from condominiums in Florida, convents in Indiana, schools in Chicago, farms in Iowa. Persons who call themselves Christians, who call themselves atheists, good witches, Mennonites, Catholic bishops, rabbis, Buddhists, agnostics, persons of every age and color, of every economic background, all saying the same thing: we understand the power of the weapons that are presently on this earth. We understand megatons, we understand silos, we understand submarines that can erase cities. But listen to us. Stop and listen. We love the earth and all its people. We want no part of nuclear war.

It is a terrible, wonderful burden to sit and create a segment for The Ribbon. I embroidered names, because I cannot imagine a world without people. Some wove the colors of the rainbow, unable to imagine a world without color. A young woman I met recently created her panel on some of the things her family loved. The panel includes a tree with children swinging from its limbs, an ice cream cone, a jar of jelly, and in the corner, a wonderfully drawn elephant, because this young woman happens to love elephants. She told me that as she drew the elephant, she cried. She cried not only because she was imagining a world without elephants, but also because she realized that the next time she went to the zoo with her two little boys, each elephant in that zoo would seem incredibly alive, incredibly precious to her, symbolizing all that is wonderful in life.

I think that one of the reasons The Ribbon has touched so many hearts is because the segments represent such an expression of creativity, such an investment of time, and such personal statements. With its palm prints of infants, its footprints of toddlers, its applique of the Golden Gate Bridge or the New York skyline, its quilted pizza or embroidered flowers, we hope that The Ribbon will help political leaders from around the world to realize that perhaps they have misjudged the deep yearning for peace within the people. We hope that The Ribbon will encourage those leaders to move ahead with greater resolve, to move ahead continuously, not always easily, but continuously, toward a planet without nuclear weapons.

I believe that it is happening. I believe that hearts are being touched and changed—which simply means that somewhere, someone is saying, "whoops, I was wrong about that . . . ." Which is saying an awful lot.

We have an opportunity to change and grow, and I want people to remember that for 37 years, from the bombing of Hiroshima and Nagasaki in 1945 until February of 1982, I was one of those people who said don't talk to *me* about nuclear destruction, don't talk to *me* about nuclear war—I don't want to hear it. But I was called to hear it. Sooner or later, we must all hear it. I think The Ribbon has changed other lives as well. All over this nation, people have threaded their fears into prayers for peace, creating something beautiful to affirm the hope present in all our lives.

Justine Merritt

13

Gift

For months —
or is it years?
I have carefully,
I have silently prayed to the Father to spare the ocean's shells;
for the sake of one lovely shell, I've prayed,
do not let the world be destroyed.

For months —
or is it years?
I have prayed carefully,
I have prayed silently to the Father to spare the earth's blossoms;
for the sake of one lovely rose, I've prayed,
do not let the world be destroyed.

For months —
or is it years,
I have carefully prayed,
I have silently prayed to the Father to spare the earth's birds;
for the sake of one grey sparrow's song, I've prayed,
do not let the earth be destroyed.

And for all those months of all those years,
since an August day in a far away Japan,
I've prayed for shells and roses and birds' song
and hid,
because I could not bear to see such a secret sorrow,
hid the image of a baby's ear,
curved, soft;
not as hard as an ocean's shell — a baby's ear —
no protection at all — a baby's ear —
against the wind of a nuclear holocaust.

Hid the image of a child's fingers curved around an adult's hand;
trusting that the adult would take the child safely across a busy street;
a child's fingers,
stronger than the petals of a rose,
but not strong enough to ward off the vaporizing heat of a man-made sun.

Hid,
for thirty-seven years, the sound of children's laughter caught
in a blinding blast;
laughter — no protection at all against a hydrogen bomb.

The shell, the rose, the bird's song
deliberate disguises to hide the babies, the toddlers, the children from the unspeakable.

No wonder we have terrors in our nights,
hiding a planet's extinction in our dreams;
no wonder we wake exhausted at dawns,
unable to comprehend an end
not just of Mozart's melodies but — of ring-around-a-rosie;
unable to comprehend and then,
unable to grieve an end to the Mona Lisa as well as hide-and-seek.

Symphony, rock musician,
Michelangelo and motorcycle racing,
jungle, Antarctica,
beloveds — and enemies all changed to something we cannot glimpse,
nor dare to.

So, I have prayed for four hundred and forty-four months
for shells and blossoms and birds' songs
and only yesterday was strong enough to pray for all the little ones.

We too are the little ones,
asked to protect children from more than busy streets.

We are called,
we are chosen to spread the word;
we are chosen,
we are called to bring the peace. Amen.

> Justine Merritt
> February, 1982
> Denver, Colorado

Corvallis, Oregon, residents perform a "Ribbon dance" after wrapping the Corvallis Arts Center with their segment of Ribbon. Photo: Robert Hunt.

St. Mark's Episcopal Church youth group in Venice, Florida, made four banners for The Ribbon. Photo: Kate Hill Moore.

Frank Neely, Roan Carratu, and Louise Morris work on one of the banners made by their group, Nashvillians for a Nuclear Arms Freeze, in Nashville, Tennessee. Photo: David Hildebrand

Banner-makers in Buncombe County, North Carolina, proudly parade their segment of Ribbon throughout downtown Asheville.

The People

by Don Willcox

To sew, in order to speak, is nothing new to women. Women have been expressing themselves with needle and thread for centuries. Historically the needle has often been the only avenue or voice through which women could connect themselves to each other, to their families, and to the times in which they lived.

The Ribbon is easily the single most gigantic sewing event in human history. No one anticipated how far it would reach when the project first began. The Ribbon grew by word of mouth, and from touch to touch.

The banners which make up The Ribbon are gentle messages. Each banner illustrates the theme "what I cannot bear to think of as lost forever in nuclear war." Made of cloth and sewn or tied together, these soft banners gather in stark contrast to the axioms which are permanently chiseled into marble or welded into inflexible steel. Like the voices expressed on Tibetan prayer flags, like the prayers folded into Japanese paper cranes, the voices these banners represent are vulnerable, impermanent, expressed upon a fragile material. They are voices of the living. They are voices which proclaim our indivisibility, rather than our schisms.

These fragile ribbons of cloth were joined to circle the Pentagon on August 4, 1985, surrounding the military might reputed to be the most powerful on earth. And like the hundreds upon thousands of folded paper cranes strung together at Hiroshima and Nagasaki, the individual Ribbon banners joined together represent harbingers of peace and hope.

Members of the Plowshares group in Madison County, North Carolina, finish work on their Ribbon panels. Photo: Don Willcox

The banners featured in this book are but a small sample of the thousands that make up The Ribbon. The number of labor hours devoted to The Ribbon project is mind-boggling. Apart from the tens of thousands of volunteer hours devoted to organizing, if each segment were to average out at 25 hours of labor, The Ribbon around the Pentagon would represent between one-quarter and one-half million hours of labor, or, if you will, of love.

From an initial mailing to 100 friends and family members on Justine Merritt's Christmas card list, The Ribbon grew to include thousands of supporters in 50 states, as well as participants in Japan, West Germany, the Netherlands, Canada, New Zealand, France, England, the Soviet Union, Guatemala, Peru, and Tanzania. The phenomenon of The Ribbon is proof once again that one individual, when joined by other individuals, can make a difference.

Those involved in The Ribbon have literally stitched, sewn, and tied themselves into a commonality of

purpose from a core of incredible diversity. Ribbon participants have come from a myriad of religious persuasions, political perspectives, and cultural backgrounds. A purpose more important than those differences—unfortunately something even larger than life on earth itself—has embroidered thousands together. What's so extraordinary is that this Ribbon ten miles long has been created through a process of affirmation—by affirming life.

Although there are many who may often have felt that we should wrap, stuff, and tie the windows and doors of the Pentagon permanently shut so that no one ever escapes to unleash destruction, The Ribbon achieved its goal through a more peaceful form of expression. There were frustrations, worries, tears, and even occasional conflicts. But The Ribbon built an extraordinary network.

The Ribbon was not intended as a media event staged by corporate executives, advertising agencies, public relations professionals. It had no pre-planned budget and was affiliated with no single institution or organization. The Ribbon came together because of the work of volunteers, people who got caught up in the project, who learned by doing, who made mistakes. Most were "grassroots" folks who came to The Ribbon with little knowledge of the logistics of networking, issuing press releases, or ordering porta-johns for outdoor events.

A survey conducted by researchers at Texas Woman's University provides some insight into the individuals who helped to create The Ribbon. Gabriella Miller and Carol Cockrell mailed questionnaires to several hundred Ribbon participants, and found that 98% of those who answered the questionnaire were female, usually college educated, more often "liberal" than "conservative," ranging in age from 14 to 85. For 50% of the respondents, this was their first encounter with social issues. Respondents represented the following religious backgrounds: 23% Catholic, 14% Quaker, 27%

Protestant, 32% non-affiliated, and 4% non-Christian.

Two of the questions posed by the survey were: " Why did you join The Ribbon? What does the Ribbon mean to you?" A few of the answers:

"The Ribbon is a positive, loving, benevolent act . . ."

"The Ribbon is a peace project I could participate in. In my small town, I need to approach activism in a careful way; The Ribbon seems pretty non-threatening."

"The Ribbon is a way in which the average person can send a very big message to our government: we want no part of your plans for nuclear war!"

". . . I didn't have anything to say out loud, yet I could say a lot through sewing."

". . .The Ribbon is a dynamic way to handle frustrations and make a statement."

There are hundreds of additional responses. Many, like The Ribbon banners themselves, express an awareness of our vulnerability, and an appreciation of the fragility of life on earth. We have painted, drawn, glued, cut, batiked, sewn, crocheted and embroidered our segments, the participants said. Our stitches have been a means of healing. Our voices are personal. They are private. Our stitches translate helplessness into help, hopelessness into hope. Our stitches move in and out through the fabric of our nation in search of eyes to see and ears to listen. Our stitches offer no periods, no exclamation marks, no beginnings and no ends. Our stitches remain continuing . . . .

It is difficult to determine how many people The Ribbon has involved. Lucille Miller, Justine Merritt's mother, completed the first Ribbon segment in 1982, at the age of 80. By the spring of 1985, Ribbon organizers were expecting nearly 20,000 individual segments to be present at the Pentagon on August 4th.

We are unable, in one book, to share the stories of all those who worked on The Ribbon. We've selected experiences from a few states, believing that these states are representative. They provide a taste of urban, rural, the South, the Far West, the Midwest, and the East.

New York

By the time The Ribbon was scheduled to be wrapped around the Pentagon, there were state coordinators for all 50 states. In New York, the state coordinator was Bette Ann Jaster, a registered nurse and a sister in the Dominican order. Bette Ann had been involved for a number of years with organizations working for peace and social justice. She had worked with Advocacy and Social Service in Harlem, for example, and

Women's Action for Nuclear Disarmament members celebrated completion of their banners by "ribboning" the Federal Building in Sonoma, California. Photo: Robert Kuiper

Meet Your Neighbors, a senior citizens' group in Carrboro, North Carolina, collaborated on this Ribbon panel. Photo: Don Willcox

later with the Dominican Sisters of The Sick Poor in Ossining, New York.

It was in 1983 that Bette Ann first heard about The Ribbon from her sister-in-law, Mary Frances Jaster, one of the Denver-based national coordinators of The Ribbon project. In January of 1985, Bette Ann wrote a proposal to her community requesting permission to devote half a year of full-time commitment to The Ribbon. Her request was approved.

Bette Ann recalls her first meeting with Justine Merritt. "I met Justine at the bus depot in Newburgh, New York. It gave me a quick under-standing of our budget—no frills! Anyway, after an initial experience where Justine and I traveled some 565 miles on behalf of The Ribbon, I was so affected by both Justine and the project that I decided to try to devote myself to it full-time."

By the spring of 1985, Bette Ann had built a network of 32 New York state resource people to help disseminate information on The Ribbon. She raised money as needed. She successfully spread the word across New York state through

speaking engagements, marches, rallies, and other events. The list of groups which supported The Ribbon in New York is extensive and includes Catholics, Methodists, Presbyterians, Congregationalists, Church Women United, Women's International League for Peace and Freedom, Pax Christi, The Rivertown Peace Center, Mid-Hudson Peace Fellowship, a number of colleges, and many public and parochial schools.

To have followed Bette Ann Jaster through one of her typical working days in that period would help one understand the extraordinary diversity of people who found a common language under the umbrella of The Ribbon. One day, for example, began with Bette Ann speaking on the topic of nuclear war to a Brownie troop on East 19th Street in Manhattan, and ended with another talk at The Dwelling Place, a facility for homeless women on 40th Street. Bette Ann remembers an overwhelming response from the approximately 70 women in the room. "They wanted to know where to catch the bus for Washington," she recalls. At last report, The Dwelling Place had contributed four segments to The Ribbon.

One of the individuals Bette Ann encountered while working for The Ribbon was Bill Gillespie, a 34-year-old resident of Newburgh, New York and the father of ten children. A taxi driver who fell victim to unemploy-ment, Bill decided to make positive use of his unexpected free time by becoming involved with the "drop-in" center run by the Newburgh Ministry. It was while visiting the drop-in center that Bill first heard about The Ribbon.

He decided to participate, and contributed three segments. Bette Ann got to know Bill and exhibited his banners in many places. "Bill always wants to know what people say when I tell them that the segments were made by a man," Bette Ann said.

One of Bill Gillespie's Ribbon segments includes a scene with a drawing of a coyote and a text that reads: "Help us . . . I say the poor are endangered species like these animals." In another scene, Bill drew a taxi with a chipmunk as the driver and a rabbit as the passenger. The text reads: "To the White House, Bill!"

Although the majority of Ribbon participants are women, men from all over the country have taken part. In New York, men who contributed to The Ribbon include a number of inmates from the Fishkill Correc-tional Facility, where both Justine Merritt and Bette Ann Jaster were able to speak thanks to a contact with the chaplain there, Fr. Ted Parker.

Justine and Bette Ann spoke to an audience of 45 inmates about The Ribbon, and afterward, 15 of the men offered to make a segment. With the help of friends, Bette Ann supplied the necessary materials. In order to give the inmates an idea of how to proceed, Bette Ann showed

This graceful banner, part of The Ribbon destined for the Pentagon, was painted by Mr. and Mrs. Maruki and signed by the first participants in the Tokyo Ribbon project. Japan, since then, has created its own Ribbon under the leadership of Mari Katabatake (at right), which includes more than 300 banners. Photo: Mr. Negishi

them her own incomplete segment, and then asked them to help by suggesting flowers to be added to her piece. Now that it's completed, Bette Ann feels that the segment was indeed a collaborative effort with the inmates of Fishkill.

Many Ribbon segments involved input from more than one person. Nearly 50 people, for example, contributed in a unique way to the segment made by Maureen and Paul Ciaccio of White Plains, New York. The Ciaccios placed a classified advertisement in *Sojourners* magazine asking readers to support their Ribbon segment by mailing them old, worn socks. The ad worked, and socks began arriving in the mail. Maureen attached names to the socks and incorporated them into her Ribbon segment, which ended up including fragments of socks from some 50 contributors. The theme of the segment was "how wonderful feet are. They take us all over the earth on missions of peace."

Contributors to The Ribbon ranged in age from pre-schoolers to senior citizens. In Scarsdale, New York, one of the members of the

Scarsdale Congregational Church, a woman in her 80's, decided she wanted to make a segment but felt reluctant because she was no longer able to write legibly. She wanted to reproduce a favorite poem, but was concerned about her penmanship. One of the members of her church volunteered to do the calligraphy; she then carefully embroidered around the calligraphy and around the segment borders.

Two days after completing her banner, the woman died. Her Ribbon segment became a part of her memorial service. And it became a part of The Ribbon.

Minnesota

Gail Irish grew up in a politically active Quaker family. She first heard about The Ribbon from a Quaker publication called *The Friendly Woman*. The Ribbon's Denver address was listed in the article, and this prompted Gail to write.

Gail recalls that Justine Merritt wrote back almost immediately, and asked if she'd like to take on some of the organizational responsibilities in Minnesota. Gail says she "resisted." She felt intellectually in tune with the

project, but not yet personally connected.

However, in August of 1984, Justine Merritt showed up in Minnesota, and everything changed for Gail. The two women got to know each other. Gail did a lot of listening, she said later, and recalled that from that point on, the Ribbon became personal. From that point on, Gail was committed.

Not being entirely certain as to how to begin organizing a state, she decided that a good place to start would be to set up an information table at regional events. People were interested, and Gail began to develop a mailing list and contacts. She put up a table at the "Grand Old Days" celebration in St. Paul, and then another table at the Minneapolis "Take Back the Night" march, which focused on the issue of violence against women. The networking continued, and ten months later, the Minnesota contingent included groups from a variety of churches, as well as participants from peace organizations such as WAMM (Women Against Military Madness), WILPF (Women's International League for Peace and Freedom), and the Honeywell Project, opponents of the Minneapolis Honeywell Corporation defense contracts. Gail extended further Ribbon participation to senior citizen groups, elementary public and parochial schools, a women's spirituality group, "Spirit Rising," a Unitarian Universalist Sunday School, as well as dozens of individuals.

On Mother's Day, 1985, her state contingent marched in a Minneapolis Mother's Day parade from Franklin Avenue and Bloomington to Loring Park. On May 26th, some 400 Ribbon segments from Minnesota encircled the Minnesota State Capital in St. Paul.

One of the many interesting groups who contributed to the Minnesota Ribbon project was TANA (Teenagers Against Nuclear Arms). TANA was founded by students at an alternative school called Bello North, which is located about 60 miles south of the Canadian border in Effie, Minnesota. The school functions as a group home, providing a learning experience for 13- to 18-year-olds who have encountered problems with family adjustment, school, drugs, and authority.

One of the teachers at Bello North read about The Ribbon, and talked to her students about the project. Shortly thereafter, three of the students organized Teenagers Against Nuclear Arms, having decided that there was a lack of participation among teenagers in working on nuclear issues. The goals of the organization would be to circulate information, write legislators and form affiliate high school groups

throughout the state. As one of their first projects, members of TANA made a segment for The Ribbon.

North Carolina

Lori Eichel, her husband Jim, and their three children live in Chapel Hill, North Carolina. Lori had lived in Denver at one point, and knew Justine Merritt. Lori's first exposure to The Ribbon came by way of a Christmas card she received from Justine.

Lori is a weaver, and at the time she first heard about The Ribbon, she was a graduate student in textile design at North Carolina State University. The idea of the Ribbon captured Lori's imagination. It soon began even to interfere with her graduate studies, which were eventually set aside so that she could devote more time to The Ribbon project.

Lori became state coordinator, and used every means at her disposal to

spread the word about The Ribbon within her state. She sent out news releases, scheduled speaking engagements, lent out a videotape on The Ribbon to interested groups, participated in street fairs, and talked to hundreds of people.

Organizing in North Carolina led to participation by Church Women United, The Newman Catholic Student Center, Fellowship to Reverse the Arms Race, Sisters of Mercy, The Campus Y, Lockridge Artists Association, The Center for Peace Education, WILPF, SANE, WAND, Plowshares, the North Carolina Peace Network, groups from Jewish, Catholic, Episcopal, Quaker and other congregations, senior citizens groups, artists, schools and others.

Several Ribbon segments were also contributed by the Plowshares group. Organized to foster awareness and action on peace and environmental

In Wangen im Allgau, Germany, Ribbon banners became part of a "Circle of Silence for Peace" during Holy Week. Sigrid Dale, a German-born Detroiter, introduced Wangen residents to The Ribbon during a visit; many then became enthusiastic participants. Photo: Stefan Seufert

21

issues, Plowshares draws its membership from households around Marshall, North Carolina. Activities sponsored by the group include the making of a peace quilt, picnics designed to increase public awareness of environmental issues, and support of various political candidates.

Karol Kavaya, a member of Plowshares, was excited by the idea that through The Ribbon, "hands all across our country would be working positively on one single event." For months before the scheduled event at the Pentagon, Karol said she anticipated the overwhelming vision of actually seeing the Pentagon circled by a moving ring of humanity. Karol's Ribbon segment includes an image of her husband, her dog, and their yard of boxwood trees, because "these are the dearest, most valued parts of my life."

Another group which contributed to The Ribbon in North Carolina was Meet Your Neighbors, a senior citizens group based in Carrboro. Through a program sponsored by Orange Chatham Community

Action, approximately 35 to 40 local senior citizens meet daily to share neighborhood news and a family-style meal at the rock-bottom price of 50 cents. Members of the group collaborated on one banner for The Ribbon, which is divided into 18 squares. Some members were only able to contribute their signatures, while others contributed drawings, stitches and messages. The segment was made from an old bed sheet, and while it was being worked on, it accumulated several coffee stains. The group decided to leave the stains as an additional group "fingerprint."

State Coordinator Lori Eichel said that her commitment to The Ribbon revitalized her belief that individual people can actually effect positive social change.

California

California coordinator Audrey Keller decided to become involved with The Ribbon after reading a newspaper article about Justine Merritt and the project.

One of the first major efforts made to publicize The Ribbon in California

was to arrange for a booth at the 1984 Democratic National Convention. Because of the number of people who converged on San Francisco for the convention, the potential for exposure was enormous. Audrey displayed a number of Ribbon segments in her booth, and received an enthusiastic response.

With help from many other state resource people, California thoroughly celebrated The Ribbon with exhibits, parades, marches and vigils. Audrey's mailing list grew to include 2,000 names, her apartment filled with Ribbon material, her mailbox with inquiries, and her phone nearly rang off its stand.

Approximately 2,000 segments from California became part of the national Ribbon. Among those were a number of banners created by members of the Sonoma County chapter of WAND (Women's Action for Nuclear Disarmament). The WAND chapter decided to adapt the idea of circling the Pentagon to the Sonoma County

Seventh-graders at St. Mary's Cathedral School in Miami, Florida, made several banners as a classroom project. Photo: Sr. Caroljean Willie, S.C.

22

Church Women United's Indiana members contributed more than 600 banners to The Ribbon, displayed here at their 1984 Assembly in Purdue.

Federal Building in Santa Rosa. The group measured the building and calculated that 270 segments were needed. Not knowing what kind of response they would get, WAND put out the call for banners; more than 700 came in.

As the group began to adjust to this overwhelming response, they began to feel that some kind of celebration was in order. Their first thought was to rent public exhibition space, but decided instead to "wrap" a house to raise funds. Noni Verbiscar-Brown, a WAND member, offered to lend her home for the purpose.

To advertise the event, the group made up 200 posters, which were later auctioned off. So many segments of Ribbon were available that two floors of deck were completely wrapped, as well as several walls in the long hallways inside the house. Those who attended made donations toward the nuclear freeze, and from this single event, WAND raised in excess of 5,000 dollars.

The next day, the same 700 segments were used to circle the Sonoma County Federal Building. Carrying the Ribbon around the building required the volunteer help of more than 400 people. Some of the segments had been contributed by classes of school children who made banners as part of school programs directed toward a greater nuclear awareness. Many of the children participated in the Federal Building wrap.

For the finale, a single, symbolic segment of Ribbon was attached to an arch of 60 large, multi-colored helium balloons, and let fly. Participants had been asked to sign the segment before it was sent aloft. No one seems to know exactly what happened to this segment; perhaps this flying rainbow continues to spread the message of peace.

In another part of California, Ribbon segments were also sent skyward, but in a different way. Nearly 2,000 segments were strung together on wire and hung from trees and posts in a winding "sky path" through Lake Merritt Park in downtown Oakland. The sky path was created as part of the annual Festival on the Lake. The California contingent of The Ribbon was invited to the 1985 festival as the featured participant.

To create the sky path, nearly 20 resource people from throughout the state worked to organize "sew-ins" to join the segments together. The central sew-in was held at Lake Merritt United Methodist Church and took place over a period of eight days. Betty Mihalaros, coordinator of the central sew-in, said that participation was "enthused and completely ecumenical," with representatives from many different churches and organizations working together to create The Ribbon.

Bill Thompson, a kindergarten teacher from Redwood City who took an early retirement to work for peace, arranged the installation of the Ribbon in Lake Merritt Park. In addition to the banners that were strung through trees, a number of banners were displayed in a booth set up to disseminate Ribbon information and to provide visitors with an opportunity to make their own Ribbon segments.

Wherever Ribbon banners were displayed, whether in a booth at a street fair such as at the fair in Oakland, or in an exhibit at a gallery such as at The Peace Museum in Chicago, inquiries would follow from hundreds of newcomers who wanted to know how they could participate. State coordinators would often set up special Ribbon-making events to provide an opportunity for people to get involved, or would extend special invitation to specific groups.

In Maryland, for example, State Coordinator Lani Irwin worked with teachers at Prince George's Community College in Largo to organize a Soviet-American Ribbon collaboration involving children from the Soviet Embassy School, and children from the "gifted and talented" program within Prince George's County schools. Some 30 children took part in the collaboration, which was sponsored by the college as part of its week-long program on "Living With Peace on This Planet."

Lani Irwin tacked lengths of muslin in the hallway of the college art department for use as Ribbon segments, and then organized a 3½ hour program around the subject of nuclear war and the peace message of The Ribbon. The program included discussions, music and dance performances by several of the Soviet children, refreshments and a concluding sesssion where all the children made segments for The Ribbon.

Joe Mayer, one of the teachers who helped organize the program, said later, after talking at length with the children, that "there was no extraordinary reaction to the event. The American children halfway expected that the Russian kids would be two-headed monsters. What they found out was that the Russians were pretty much like themselves . . . neat kids who liked Michael Jackson music, and seemed to have similar interests and dreams."

Twelve inmates of the women's section at the Monterey County (California) Jail have contributed segments to The Ribbon. This effort was assisted by the Monterey Catholic Diocese Detention Ministry, and by the Monterey County Jail staff. Each contributor signed the reverse side of her segment, and at the conclusion of the sewing session, the inmates dedicated their Ribbon segments with prayers for peace, and with shared singing.

Group involvement

The Ribbon is a remarkable project that came together because of the deep commitment and personal involvement of hundreds of individuals across the country. One group in particular, Church Women

United (CWU), has made an extraordinary nationwide contribution toward the overall impact of The Ribbon. Members of this group have contributed thousands of banners to The Ribbon.

CWU is an autonomous national movement of nearly half a million Protestant, Roman Catholic, Orthodox, and other Christian women. An ecumenical movement founded in 1941, CWU today includes nearly 2,000 local chapters, or units, representing 50 states, the District of Columbia and Puerto Rico. CWU membership includes a broad spectrum of religious tradition, race, age, economic status, and ethnic background.

The goals of Church Women United include worship, study, and action through service, advocacy, and the empowerment of women.

Once every four years, CWU organizes an Ecumenical Assembly. In July, 1984, this Assembly was held in West Lafayette, Indiana on the campus of Purdue University. Nearly 3,000 women from 50 states and 62 foreign countries (representing 29 denominations) gathered together to celebrate their indivisibility, as well as "to reach for richer and fuller lives, to empower themselves for collective action, and to learn that they could change structures and systems of injustice."

At this 1984 Assembly, the women held continuing prayer vigils for peace, and they dedicated a 1¼ mile length of completed CWU Ribbon. The dedication included the following text: "Peace binds the pieces. Peace supports the pieces. Peace is the strong thread that weaves the fabric of wholeness. If anyone is excluded, the wholeness is imperfect. Peace is the backing of our patchwork quilt."

One of the Assembly speakers described CWU challenges in this way: "Because women do not think of courage in relationship to power, women therefore act from a position of mutuality and respect."

Following the 1984 CWU Ribbon dedication, CWU's support for the Ribbon included appeals for funding, sponsorship, and hands-on participation in many state capital Ribbon walks, the spreading of information locally and nationally, continued prayer vigils for peace both locally and nationally, a number of sew-ins, and an ever-increasing number of banners made by individual CWU members.

International participation

Banners for The Ribbon also came from groups outside of the United States. The churches of Castricum, Holland, a small town on the North Sea above Haarlem, contributed a Ribbon segment featuring a continuous tulip field and measuring nearly 150 feet in length. The idea for this segment grew out of an exchange between the Bethlehem United Church of Christ in Evansville, Indiana, and an ecumenical group of Christian church people in Castricum. The two groups became sister organizations, working together; the idea of the tulip field was contributed by one of the younger members of the Dutch church. His thought was that the tulip, as a symbol of Holland and of nature's beauty, could grow into an unending field. The continuous ribbon of tulips was created by members of several Catholic and Protestant churches in the small Dutch town.

Ribbon segments also came from France, Canada, New Zealand, England, Guatemala, the Soviet Union, Peru and Tanzania, the Federal Republic of Germany, the German Democratic Republic, and Japan. The segments from the Federal Republic of Germany were assembled in Bonn, and displayed in a silent vigil for peace in the main square during the "World Day of Prayer."

The greatest overseas participation is in Japan. Hundreds of banners were made throughout the country, and a Ribbon similar to that made in the United States was created to encircle the A-Bomb Memorial Dome in Hiroshima on August 4th.

Copies of The Ribbon newsletter have been translated into Japanese and circulated to some 30 women's groups. Mari Kitabatake, the young woman who served as Japanese Ribbon Coordinator, helped arrange a relay system to carry Ribbon segments to Hiroshima from outlying prefectures. The relay was scheduled so that all segments would arrive in Hiroshima at approximately the same time.

August 4, 1985

Tying a ribbon around the Pentagon is no simple task. The Center for New Creation in Arlington, Virginia took on the immense responsibility of handling the logistics and the events of August 4th. The primary coordinators were

Joan Urbanczyk and Marie Grosso, two very special women who attended to an extraordinary number of details.

Just to satisfy the police requirements, for example, Joan and Marie worked with the General Services Administration, Pentagon security, the Washington, D.C. police, the Capitol police, the Park Police, the Arlington police, and the Secret Service.

They enlisted the support of the American Red Cross and Physicians for Social Responsibility to help in the area of health and safety. They found nearly 2,000 volunteer marshals, and more than 50 Washington area host groups to help

The Ribbon segment from Castricum, in the Netherlands, features a brilliantly colored field of tulips.

accommodate some of the visiting Ribbon participants. They arranged for tank trucks, water tanks and porta-johns. All summer long, they planned for the arrival of the 100,000 people expected to converge on Washington on August 4th.

State coordinators held sew-ins at the state level in the early part of the summer, and then arranged to transport the segments from each state to Washington. On August 3, a non-denominational religious service for peace was scheduled at Washington Cathedral. On August 4th, after an early morning press reception, the participants were to assemble by state to receive their Ribbon sections and to receive instructions for the day's events.

Ribbon officials who negotiated with the Pentagon were not only granted official permits to assemble and park buses, but were also given a specific route to walk when circling the Pentagon.

Early in the organization process, it was determined that there would be no speeches on August 4th, no celebrity presentations, no "center stage." The focus of the day would be on The Ribbon, and on the participants who expressed their hopes and fears on their banners. Each state contingent would arrive in Washington with a similar understanding of their purpose, which Ribbon organizers described this way:

> We bring The Ribbon,
> the work of thousands of hearts
>   and hands,
> to our nation's capital
> as a gentle reminder
> that we love the earth
> and its peoples.

Our Ribbon is a visible symbol of "all that we cannot bear to think of as lost forever."
By it, we say "no" to nuclear war and to the preparation for war.

We are people of all colors, from many religious and philosophical, cultural and economic traditions.
We come in a spirit of love
and with a deep awareness that all of creation
is intrinsically interconnected.

With us we bring our deepest fears,
expressed in a diversity of ways, and released into a profound hope that we can find another way.

We come to confront the cumulative violence
within ourselves
and our institutions.
We seek a transformation that will nourish
a social, economic, political
and ecological balance
that can ensure a future
for our children and ourselves.

By our presence we affirm the belief
that war is not inevitable
that readiness for war already fractures the peace.

This peace we seek
is much more than the absence of war.
It is rather a peace that is rooted in justice
and imbued with compassion.
It is well-being and harmony,
a restoration of right order among all peoples
and within all of creation.
It is a set of mutual relationships between beings and the earth
in which power is not claimed by the strongest arm
nor security by the largest weapons system.
It is a state that is realized only in the full flowering of each person's potential.

The Ribbon represents our acknowledgment
of each individual's ability
to make a difference
in building this peace.
Through it we declare
that together
we can intercept the forces
convening to annihilate the planet.

The Ribbon has tapped
new sources of creative potential among us.
With it we bring a vision, not a program,
a process that is enabling.
Together
we celebrate our human dignity
and own our vulnerability
in this nuclear age.

Many state coordinators have planned continuing events to follow up the tying of the Pentagon. California coordinators, for example, planned to rush back immediately after the event to participate in a huge parade down Wilshire Boulevard in Los Angeles. A number of state archives have expressed interest in local Ribbon segments, and a sampling of banners from all over the country will be donated to The Peace Museum in Chicago. An exhibition on The Ribbon will also be available for loan to groups and galleries around the country as part of The Peace Museum's Traveling Exhibition series.

Most of the remaining segments will be returned to their appropriate states. Many will more than likely find their way back to their original contributors, like travel-weary celebrities having performed their best and completed their purpose.

The Banners

A visit to The Peace Museum's Ribbon
exhibition inspired Erica Miller-Mahin,
age 8, to create a banner of her own.

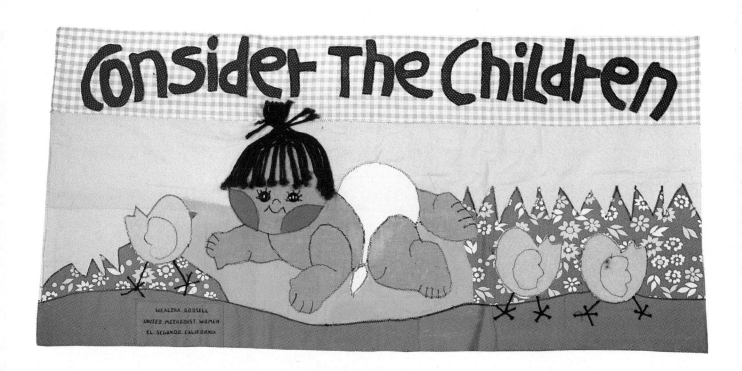

WEALTHA S. GODSELL
El Segundo, California
Consider the Children
Photo: David Hitt

BULBUL
Mountain View, California
The Joy and Healing of Laughter

I chose humor as my theme because laughter dispels tension, it disarms. Laughter is a pleasure and is good for us physically. Laughter is an expression of joy. We learn and remember with laughter. Laughter can bring people together. Laughter is childlike and an expression of delight. With laughter we are reminded that if we take ourselves too seriously life becomes too grim. Laughter reminds us what strange and wonderful creatures we are. I put bells dangling from ribbons because I love the sound of people laughing.
Photo: Paul Brezny

MARY MILNE
Ithaca, New York
Photo: Paul Brezny

SISTERS OF HOLY CROSS
Manchester, New Hampshire

KIM IRWIN
Chapel Hill, North Carolina
Photo: Laura Drey

MARY MILNE
Ithaca, New York
Photo: Paul Brezny

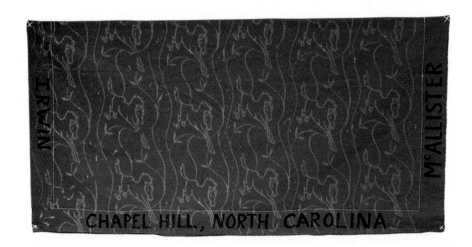

ELLEN SARKISIAN
Cambridge, Massachusetts

Never having spoken out publicly before about the danger of nuclear war, I was moved to express myself in this way after hearing a concert in Boston last spring performed by the Musicians against Nuclear Arms.

Envious of the musicians and performers in the concert who had gifts they could offer in service of this cause, I went through the literature tables looking for ways to express my concern. I had no intention of speaking, writing, or organizing, but when I read about The Ribbon I said to myself, "I will sew." The Ribbon was my way to make a personal statement about a problem that no one knows how to describe or how to solve.
Photo: David Caras

JOAN TANNER KREVY
Watertown, Massachusetts

ANNETTE HOLLAND
Bayside, California

The children on my banner represent our daughters, Elise and Josephine, but they also represent all the children on earth. We live at the edge of a lovely little valley in northwestern California, bordered on the east by the redwood forest and on the west by the ocean. I wanted to suggest something of the beauty of this little corner of the earth, which is now filled with blossoming flowers.

I cannot bear to think how much of life could be destroyed by nuclear war, but I think about it every day. The earth needs a miracle as never before. I hope and pray that one way the miracle will come is through the kind of love that is being expressed in The Ribbon.

My mother, my daughters, my husband and I will all be in Washington, D.C. this August to help carry The Ribbon. May the power of the love that inspires us inspire and transform the world! And may it be in time!
Photo: David Hitt

YUKO KAWATA
Kure, Japan

PAT BROWN
Portola Valley, California
Puppet Shows for Children
Photo: Paul Brezny

ELAINE SHELTON
Denver, Colorado

The jeans, shirt, and arm band are old friends of mine, with me in the 60's in San Francisco and New York where they were my uniform and proud symbols of love, hope, and remembering. Then came 1979: Three Mile Island, the murder of Harvey Milk, Jonestown. The world turned to tears, terror, anger, and pain, so I put my symbols away. In 1982, The Ribbon came into my life and I was going to make a panel, something wondrous. In 1984, the thought came that my old friends should come out and stand with their sisters and brothers. I'm still proud, working on an ongoing dream of world peace and personal and universal enlightenment.
Photo: Paul Brezny

Sent from
The Federal Republic of Germany

Sent from
The Federal Republic of Germany

Sent from
The Federal Republic of Germany

32

Sent from the Federal Republic
of Germany

Sent from
The Federal Republic of Germany

Sent from
The Federal Republic of Germany

HE'S GOT
THE WHOLE WORLD
IN HIS HAND

E.V. ABENDKREIS MARXLOH I DUISBURG BR.DEUTSCHLAND 1984

Sent from
The Federal Republic of Germany

Sent from
The Federal Republic of Germany

Sent from
The Federal Republic of Germany

Frauenkreis der Samariter - Kirchengemeinde
Berlin - Friedrichshain   DDR

Frieden auf Erden   FRIEDEN

E.V. Frauenhilfe-Duisburg-Hassterfeld. 1984.

COMMUNITY OF HOPE
Cincinnati, Ohio

IRENE GILLINGWATER
Prescott, Arizona

JULIE PARMENTER
Sebastopol, California
Harmony in Peace

The Ribbon seemed like such a
wonderful idea that I suggested the
project to my daughter's teacher at
Discovery School, Sebastopol. Each
student did a section for The Ribbon.
My daughter, Julie, is developmentally
disabled. She is a fun loving, happy, and
giving twelve-year-old! Her father was in
the Navy and was subjected to radiation,
as were many servicemen.
Julie's father and I designed her section of
The Ribbon, using the bright colors she
likes, and cut out the felt shapes. Julie's
Discovery School classmates (disabled
and non-disabled) helped her glue the
colored felt shapes on the muslin.
The design shows how different shapes,
sizes, and colors can be together in
harmony. The same is true of people. All
shapes, sizes, abilities, colors, and
nationalities can live together in peace
and harmony.

MARIAN PENA, S.H.F.
Oakland, California
Hold Fast To Dreams

I work in West Oakland with black,
Asian, and Hispanic children. I chose my
theme with them in mind — the places
they live and the dreams they hold for
today and for tomorrow.
Photo: David Hitt

SISTER MARTHA WORDEMAN
Iaeger, West Virginia
Photo: Paul Brezny

MONA BRUMMEL JOHNSTON
Arcata, California
Photo: David Hitt

36

MILDRED STRICKLER
Berea, Kentucky

A good friend from Lexington, Kentucky gently nudged me into the work on my Ribbon section. I was recovering from major surgery when Mary planted the seed. A few days later, I was sketching ideas and chose a simple, straightforward design, "The Human Family Tree," growing out of a world symbolized by the crazy quilt.

MOLLY HART
Cloverdale, California
Understanding—Integration—Peace

"Understanding—Integration—Peace" is a variation on a tapestry theme that deals with the concept of free encounter. The two colored ribbons represent two distinct forces or entities that can freely merge, interweave and co-exist, and yet maintain their individuality and integrity separately. To me this concept depicts the ideal relationship between people, between mankind and nature, between nations. I think the way to peace involves understanding and appreciating our differences, then integrating with others on our common ground.
Photo: Robert Kuiper

LOUISE CHISHOLM
Freeport, Nova Scotia, Canada

I thought a lot about the things I loved best in the world and finally decided on children, butterflies, and rainbows so those are the elements of my design. I am 42, a freelance artist. I have never before been involved in any peace campaign, but I found this one compelling. I have travelled and talked about it in my small part of Canada.
Photo: Paul Brezny

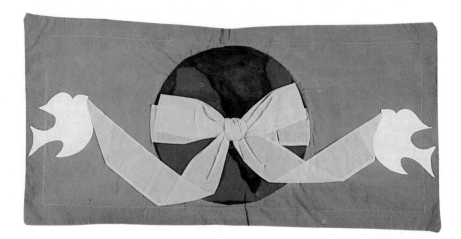

JEAN WALL PENLAND
Asheville, North Carolina

BOWLING GREEN STATE
UNIVERSITY/ART 343
Bowling Green, Ohio

REBECCA LOWE
Portland, Oregon

SUE GORDON
Y.M.C.A.
Tanzania, Africa

ST. MARY'S SCHOOL
Franklin, New Hampshire

DAN A. BARKER
Blodgett, Oregon
American Tanka
Photo: Jim Lind

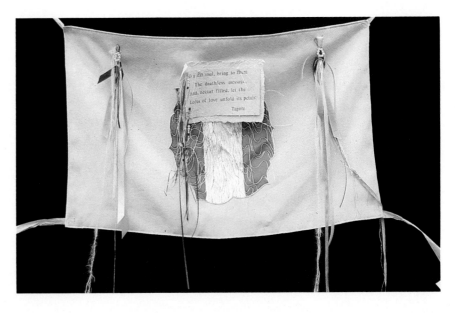

GUILFORD PEACE ALLIANCE
Guilford, Connecticut

The Guilford Peace Alliance began after we had succeeded in bringing about a referendum at our town meeting in May, 1982 (524 in favor, 17 against). We only heard about The Ribbon project recently. We hurried to put our banner together. A number of us sat around the table and talked and created. There was no plan. Each of us did what she or he was moved to do, and gradually we worked and cooperated and put our banner together. It evolved with a wonderful feeling of shared electricity. The twelve of us felt connected with one another and with people all over the world. Our inspiration came partly from the *arpilleras* of Chile.

PATTY ELWIN DAVIS
Ithaca, New York

I am an avid quilter and active member of the Ithaca Textile Arts Guild. Our group adopted the "Frieze" campaign as a 1984-85 project and almost every member, each using her individual craft, contributed a panel to The Ribbon. We are most enthusiastic about the project and feel grateful that such an opportunity was presented to us so that we may express our sentiments on this vital subject in our own media.
Photo: C. Hadley Smith

SHERRY BROWN
North Bangor, New York

In my Ribbon piece, I wanted to tell of all I would miss in the event of a nuclear catastrophe: people, mountains, trees, family, peace. I first became involved in the "no-nuke" movement in 1976, and in April, 1977, was one of 1,404 people arrested in Seabrook, New Hampshire on trespassing charges. I continue to educate friends and acquaintances of the link between nuclear power and nuclear weapons, and the dangers of both. I am a mother of three children, married, and living in a rural area of this beautiful country.
Photo: Shari Weber McMahon

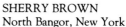

ANN MARIE ANEMA
San Leandro, California

My piece of ribbon explores
  our fragile relationship to
    Peace.
A balance.
A paradox of opposing forces.
The beauty of Earth,
  a jewel in space.
Living playfully in the present
  amidst the insanities.
Love.
  Freedom.
Rejoicing and trusting the spirit of life.
Photo: David Hitt

JOANN LACHENMYER YATES
San Francisco, California

I heard about The Ribbon at a nuclear
freeze meeting in Haight-Ashbury. The
Ribbon seemed like a great idea—a
positive yet simple idea that would
indicate the love of many people. I chose
the Golden Gate Bridge scene because it
obviously represents San Francisco,
which I would miss very much.

KATHLEEN SHEEDER
Philadelphia, Pennsylvania
Photo: Vincent Pietromartere

41

JOAN POOLE HOLBROOK
Chapel Hill, North Carolina
Rainy Day on Planet Earth
Photo: Laura Drey

PATSY EVANS WEISS, ANDREA and
HANNAH EVANS, DEBORAH and
NICOLA SKIDMORE
Palo Alto, California
Photo: David Hitt

WESTERLY FRIENDS
FIRST DAY SCHOOL
West Kingston, Rhode Island
Walk Cheerfully Over the World

Our Friends meeting felt The Ribbon
would be a good project for our First
Day School children. Because we didn't
want to frighten the children or give
them negative images, we asked them *not*
what they would most hate to lose in a
nuclear war, but what they loved most in
this world. We wanted our contribution
to The Ribbon to be a celebration of life,
not a statement of fear. The children,
ages 3-11, named *many* things they loved:
flowers and animals (including dinosaurs,
as you can see!), rainbows and sunshine,
starlight and moonlight, mountains and
seashells, the ocean, the forests, home
and family, good food and good smells,
music, dancing, gymnastics, reading,
running, friends, holidays, laughter,
wintertime, rainy days, the wind . . . so
many things for one small panel!
Photo: Richard Jeffery

DIANE ELLIS, R.D.H., FELIX K. LIAO,
D.D.S. and staff
Providence, Rhode Island
The World's Smiles

This dental office would not want to lose
the big smiles, little smiles, wide smiles,
or healthy smiles, nor the opportunity to
improve smiles.

FRANCISCAN SISTERS
Little Falls, Minnesota

MARY LOU MILLER
Bloomington, Indiana

PEACE LUZON PILIPINAS TO ALL

MANILA

PEACE ON EARTH

THELMA CASE
Republic of the Philippines

Ms. Case is a Methodist missionary working in the Philippines.

BEAVERDAM PRESBYTERIAN CHURCH
Pocomoke, Maryland
Photo: Joe R. Anderson

CHELSEA SAMMEL
Los Altos, California

After three months of psychiatric care and hospitalization, I am just beginning to notice the world around me again and to sense the importance and immediacy of problems other than my own. Seeing the world with a wider vision and feeling I have a place in it has made me want to be a part of preserving it. I know that world peace can be realized, and through more simple means than we've ever thought: a work of art, a song, perhaps a Ribbon.
Photo: David Hitt

Let us all sing the same song

LYNN CABANI-CZEBINIAK
Spencer, New York
Photo: Ann Gefell

ELIZABETH MORGAN
South Wellfleet, Massachusetts

This has been a very exciting project for
me. I am 63, and am extremely emotional
about the current world situation and
prospects of a future for the coming
generations. I've not the energy for
marching anymore, so this was a way for
me to add my voice to the pleas for peace
with all the peoples of the world.

B. SEUFERT
Wangen im Allgau, Federal Republic of
Germany

Pack up
your sorrows...

Bill Thompson
Redwood City CA

WILLARD R. THOMPSON
Redwood City, California
Pack Up Your Sorrows

At 35, I took up the guitar to learn to communicate with music and song to the elementary children I was to teach for 21 years. In the grim reality of life in this nuclear age, music lifts the spirit, carries the word, and supports our collective desire to live in peace.
I dedicate this ribbon to Victor Hara, who sang for peace and freedom until killed by the military in Chile after the death of their democratically elected president, Salvador Allende.
Photo: David Hitt

LORI EICHEL
Chapel Hill, North Carolina
Mother and Child

46

RUTH DONHOWE
St. Paul, Minnesota
Minnesota Wildflowers

This piece represents flowers of the boreal forest of northern Minnesota, which are particular favorites of mine, and are found near our lake cottage as well as in my wildflower garden at home in the city. I am a quilter and a mother of two daughters and a son. The fabrics used are scraps that date back to children's clothing and maternity clothes. Therefore they are literally flowers from my life and work.
Photo: Paul Brezny

NANCY EAMES
Bowling Green, Ohio

ALICE LECK GANT
Anchorage, Alaska
Consider the Flowers

I like improving soil and then improving my living space with the flowers I plant in the modified soil. Nuclear fallout is sure to be bad for my garden and my family—not to mention the gardens and families of others.

47

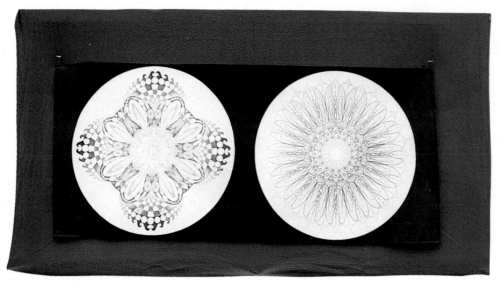

JIM LIND
Falls City, Oregon
Endangered Species Tribute

I am an artist currently working on a watercolor series portraying endangered species. The two mandalas on my panel are reproductions of "Zinging the Blues" (a tribute to the blue whale) and "Neptune's Gray Matter" (a tribute to the California gray whale). With the threat of nuclear destruction, all species are endangered. Our primary global concern should be the elimination of such a threat to all beings who share this planet.

SARAH YOURSHAW
Arlington, Virginia

The development of a sense of security and basic trust in the world is one of the most important tasks of early childhood. My ribbon segment symbolizes the feelings of a young child, tucked into bed by loving hands, hugging his teddy bear, free to dream and to grow up to fulfill those dreams.
This quilt piece is taken from a quilt given to my son Ivan, now 17, when he was born. I used his well-loved bear, a gift for his first Christmas, as the model for this teddy. Ivan and his brother Erik are my hopes for the future.

PATRICIA MARIE SIGLER, O.P.
Akron, Ohio
Photo: Sister Denise Macko, O.P.

BARBARA BLESSING
Kenmore, New York
Photo: Laura Loehr

BOWLING GREEN STATE
UNIVERSITY/ART 343
Bowling Green, Ohio

JUNE STARR, MARY STARR and
DANIEL DUDDE
Asheville, North Carolina
Photo: Laura Drey

CHAPEL HILL, N.C.   NAN G

GOCH

DESTROYED BY BOMBS
7.2.1945

JUSTICE AND PEACE

CHURCH PEACE GROUP GOCH, F.R.S.

NAN GRESSMAN
Chapel Hill, North Carolina
Photo: Laura Drey

Sent from
The Federal Republic of Germany

JILL MARTUZA
Lexington, Massachusetts

My segment depicts the ocean and
beaches and evokes my most pleasant
memories of summers at the beach. To
me, the ocean and shore provoke a sense
of rhythm and peace and harmony which
would vanish forever in a nuclear war.
Photo: David Caras

THE SPIVACK FAMILY
Los Angeles, California

When my daughter and I asked ourselves what we would miss most in nuclear devastation, we decided that *most* of all we would miss each other—our family—including the dog, Garp. So the banner, depicting all of us, happy, in touch with each other, important to each other, was our choice for the subject. We are proud to be a part of The Ribbon.

HOLY FAMILY CHURCH
St. Louis Park, Minnesota

AL SCHREINER
Ridgewood, New Jersey
Photo: Trish Dalto

51

Plum Island

JANET IRONS
Cambridge, Massachusetts

Plum Island is a wildlife refuge on the coast of Massachusetts. I walk along the grey, weathered boardwalks over the salty marshes while the cattails and grasses rustle around me, or stroll along the serene beaches, hypnotized by the simple and elegant patterns made by rocks, shells, sand and seaweed on the shoreline. There, like nowhere else on earth, a tremendous feeling of tranquility washes over me and leaves me at peace with myself and the rest of the world. I would hate for us to lose forever such places of refuge.
Photo: David Caras

J.S. Bach
1685~1985

JUDITH FEITNER
Odessa, New York

CAROL GASKIN
Winlaw, British Columbia, Canada
Seeds, Seeds, Seeds

The piece was inspired by my love of seeds and a long-term fascination with the DNA helix. This was a much easier medium to use for this image than my normal medium which is clay.
Photo: Carol Gaskin

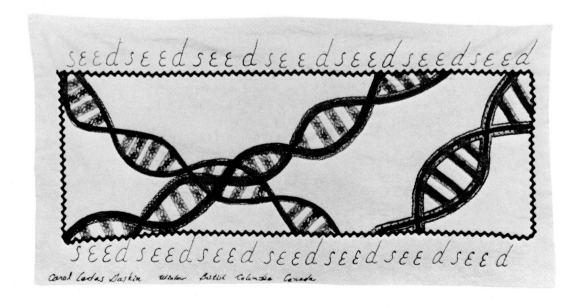

seeds eed seeds eed seeds eed seeds eed seeds eed seeds eed seed

seed seed seed seed seed seed seed seed

Carol Ladas Gaskin   Winlaw British Columbia Canada

PAT HUMBERT
Park Forest, Illinois
All We Are Saying is Give Peace a Chance

LADIES OF THE MORNING
Glen Ellyn, Illinois
Photo: Barbara Matt

JOANNE MILLER
Buffalo, New York
Photo: Laura Loehr

LILLIAN HELDRETH
Negaunee, Michigan

VILLA AUGUSTINA
Gaffstown, New Hampshire

CHURCH WOMEN UNITED
Beatrice, Nebraska

Our Ribbon banner is very symbolic of this area. To the left is the National Homestead cabin which represents our first home. We are striving to preserve our homes and our family units. Prayer begins in the family and in the home where love always dwells. The clear blue sky represents the pure clean air in our environment. Trees provide shade and shelter for us, animals and birds, and they purify the air. In the center of the picture, we placed the dove, the symbol of the Holy Spirit. He is descending on the children and the church. In the center foreground are children of many races, holding hands and walking to the church to pray. If we play together and pray together, there will be peace in the world.

TEXTILE STUDY GROUP
New York, New York

Hands express giving, caring, feeling, creating. Nuclear catastrophe obliterates all of this. In this banner, we are saying that, without our hands, we would lose our ability to reach out to others through our skills. We would be disconnected from others and life. The fabrics reflect the diversity of our group, and the techniques reflect the diversity of the fiber artist's work—applique, knotting, tatting, basketry, weaving and quilting. The name of each participating member is sewn inside of each hand. The patterns are silhouettes of members' hands in various work positions.

NANCY WHITTINGTON
Chapel Hill, North Carolina

This design was inspired by a leaf shape—leaves interlocked. This motif and the colors represent what I would never want to lose—the symmetry of nature and the green and golden colors.
Photo: Laura Drey

MARY CIOFALO
San Francisco, California
Photo: David Hitt

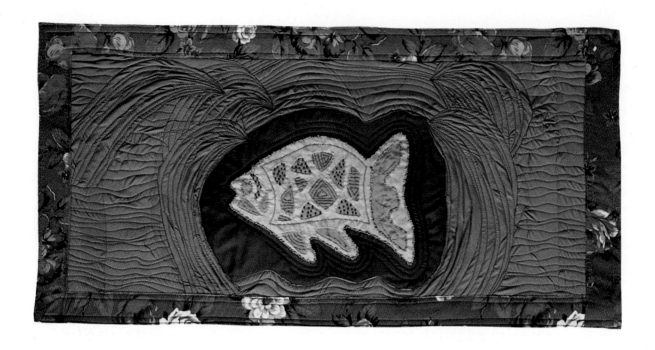

SUSAN ADAMS
Marshall, North Carolina
Photo: Paul Brezny

MARGARET WEINBERGER and
MELANIE BERNING
Bowling Green, Ohio

SELAH MARTHA and
ELLEN HANSEN
Anchorage, Alaska

LEWIS RUBINSTEIN
Poughkeepsie, New York

CAROL OLSON
Auberry, California

I am a silkscreener, designer, and a quiltmaker, and have been at it for about twelve years. When a friend told me about The Ribbon I decided *this* was the thing for me! I was in college in the 60's, and when all the college students were busy demonstrating against the war, I was doing my nails! Although I have a deep commitment to peace, I never seemed to get around to doing anything concrete about it. This Ribbon was the answer. It was the vehicle I could and would use to make my statement and help rid me of a little guilt!
Photo: Jamey Taylor

RACHEL and AGNES BARTON-SABO
Anchorage, Alaska

I am an artist. My design came from one of a series of collages, this one from a meditation on the family. It represents an awakening to psychic, spiritual, intuitive energies for the purposes of living and healing as a family.
Agnes, my daughter, is also an artist. She has her own vocabulary of symbols from hours and hours of drawing and painting. Hearts and rainbows are standard images. I explained the purpose of The Ribbon. She attended the "sew-in" with me where she created this image. (I seamed the edges for her.)

JASON FORSBERG, ALAN FRANK
and RICHARD LARPENTER
ROEPER SCHOOL
Bloomfield Hills, Michigan

MARIAN YOORS
New York, New York

I first heard about the banner project at the Clearwater Hudson Valley revival in 1983. I embroidered a traditional Indian design, the Tree of Life, with the wool I use to weave tapestries to create a joyous banner dedicated to life and all its beauty and peace.
Photo: Cynthia Hoy

LOLA LOITERSTEIN
Schenectady, New York

I want to leave a tranquil world for my grandchildren. The banner depicts my desire for the whole world to dance together without fear of war or famine.

TERESA DOUGHERTY
San Jose, California
The Glory of Earth
Photo: David Hitt

he has made everything beautiful in its time

also he has put eternity into man's mind ECCL 3:11

MARY C. REYES
Lexington, Kentucky

Five years ago, at the age of 51, I discovered that stitchery is what I want most to do in my life. My Ribbon segment expresses an image of what is, to me, one of the most remarkable verses in the Bible, part of which is embroidered on the border. The verse concludes, " . . . yet so that we cannot understand what God has done from the beginning to the end." I had driven to Loretto, Kentucky to hear Justine [Merritt] speak, and on the long, dark drive home, realized that this was my opportunity to try to express the image of the verse.
Photo: Paul Brezny

BEATRICE SCHALL
Chapel Hill, North Carolina
Peace
Photo: Laura Drey

BETTY H. HUNT
Castle Rock, Colorado
Photo: Charles D. Brown

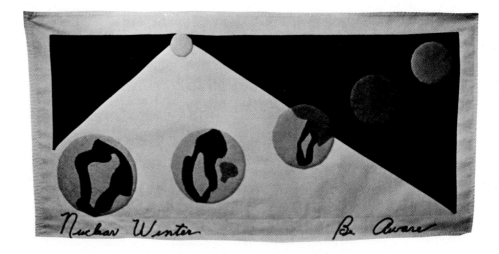

LINDA LEE JONES MARGANIAN
West Bridgewater, Massachusetts
Love is a Flower, Peace is Trees.

My particular banner changed many times during its initial conception, until its present state, which is unfinished: I have yet to do the embroidery of the two words which constitute the theme of my banner—love and peace. I chose a large peace symbol because I spent eight months in England during the protests at Greenham Common and myself participated in the Mother's Day March for Peace, Oxford, England. This symbol has a universal meaning regardless of race, national origin, sex or religion. Then, I decided to depict the things peace allows us to enjoy and put them in the largest openings in the symbol, so to be embraced by the symbol. These are the scene of the ocean at sunset and the mountains during a winter snowstorm. These are my favorite getaway places when I want peace. I wanted to emphasize the role of men and women in creating and maintaining peace, so I made a family out of cloth and painted in the details of clothing, skin, hair, even sneakers. Each child is dressed according to the scenery depicted above it. One child is "going out" to the seashore, and the other is "coming in" from the snowstorm. Deuteronomy 28:6 promises us that "Blessed shalt thou be when thou comest in, and blessed shalt thou be when thou goest out."

SUSAN M. KEMP
Rochester, New York
My Family and The Animals

RONNIE KAMPHAUSEN
Southbury, Connecticut

It took me about a year to decide on a design and several weeks to complete it during the cold Connecticut winter days. The symbolism is apt for me. I am from a family of fisherwomen/men and swimmers. We've experienced the force of the tide and the need to use the current, not go against those natural forces. I personally see weaponry and missiles as anti-life and certainly anti-peace. I wanted to show how underwater missiles can be hidden — fish probably get used to their quiet ways, but we need to be aware of their presence and potential for destruction. The colors seemed appropriate, though the red, white and blue doesn't mean that only U.S. weaponry is my target for concern. I assume the missile depicted could be another country's weapon. I tried to make it "generic," but suggestive of the military.

I am a Quaker and have been raised to value life and peaceful pursuits. I was too young to remember Hiroshima when the bomb went off, but feel its horror today and hope there is never a recurrence.

I have embroidered my maiden name (Peacock, from Baltimore, MD) and my married name (Kamphausen, from Southbury, CT) so as to include my family in the statement and hope for peace in the Ribbon.

I have shared the banner with my Friends meeting in Connecticut. Children in the First Day school of my "home" Meeting in Baltimore have also used the banner for discussion. One young boy took it into Meeting to explain his interpretation of the symbolism. A local peace group in Southbury was inspired to make its own banners. I shared the idea and my effort in a joint religious service on peace with a local Unitarian group. The idea grows...
Photo: Kevin Templeton

COMMITTEE FOR A
NUCLEAR FREEZE
Wellesley, Massachusetts

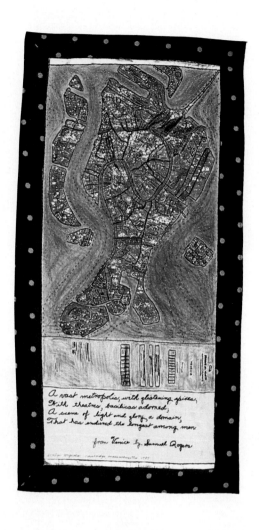

EVELYN VIGNOLA
Cambridge, Massachusetts

I spent three weeks in Italy in 1983; it was my first and only trip outside of the United States. It was an incredible experience, and I had already used Italian tile patterns as a source of inspiration for a quilt. Suddenly, I focused on Venice as the thing I would hate to see lost forever, because the city embodies both natural and man-made phenomena that I so admire.

VICTOR INITIATIVE FOR PEACE
Victor, New York
Photo: Julie Gelfand

NEIGHBORHOOD ARTS PROGRAM
Dayton, Ohio

Our community arts program is particularly involved with social issues. When we heard about The Ribbon project through a local church that was involved, we decided to extend the awareness of The Ribbon and the opportunity to participate to members of the community. We sponsored several workshops, and supplied the material, fabric paints, fabric markers, etc., free of charge. We also coordinated an exhibit of Ribbon sections at the main library in downtown Dayton. We were thrilled to be a part of this project, which crossed age, race, sex and political barriers to address a common concern — through a visual arts medium.

NANCY E. LAKE
Santa Rosa, California

JUDY FREEMAN
Prescott, Arizona

MARGY COATES
Denver, Colorado
Photo: Paul Brezny

CINDY TAYLOR CLARK
Wells, Maine
Twins

MADELINE McMURRAY
Bayside, California
Earth Celebration

Each year at the turning of the equinox
and the solstice, we invite our friends and
their friends to join in a celebration of
the patterns of the earth. In the fall and
spring we gather in the morning to greet
the sun and in the summer and winter we
come together at night to participate with
the longest and shortest days of the year.
Celebrations like these have gone on
throughout all of history all over the
world and speak to us of our place in the
whole of things—the patterns of the
universe. Our actions today repeat and
preserve human history.
Earth celebration and The Ribbon
project serve the same purpose.
Photo: David Hitt

BOBBIE MARKLEY
Hedgesville, West Virginia

SISTERS AT ST. MARY OF
SORROWS PARISH
Buffalo, New York

In November, 1984, our convent
community at St. Mary of Sorrows
Parish opened our home and our hearts
to a family of Salvadoran refugees. This
family lived with us for six months while
their application for political asylum was
reviewed by the Canadian government. In
May, 1985, they moved to Canada and
found the safety and freedom they had
been searching for during the two years
since they left El Salvador. Our banner
depicts our shared hope of peace and
friendship between the United States and
El Salvador, as well as between all
countries with whom we have ideological
differences. Our experience has taught us
that differences can be resolved if both
parties can meet together in openness,
respect and a sincere desire to preserve
life, our most precious possession.
Photo: Ann Oestreich, S.S.J.

ANTOINETTE M. WINTERS
Concord, Massachusetts
Save Life on Earth

Save life on earth. Save life on earth.

JOSEPH, TOBY, ALAN, LANI — HUGHESVILLE MD.

TOBIAS and JOSEPH FELTUS
Hughesville, Maryland

HYDE PARK—
MT. LOOKOUT NEIGHBORS
Cincinnati, Ohio
Photo: Ilona (Nonie)Smith

ERIN FITZ-HENRY
Oneonta, New York

ERIN FITZ-HENRY

BETTY CYPSER
Katonah, New York
Photo: Paul Brezny

MARY BUNKER
Stanford, California

JO BROWN
Portland, Oregon
Photo: Paul Brezny

MARGUERITE PURPURA
Center Moriches, New York
Peace

After working out the details of my banner, I thought about what I would most miss if someone's elbow hits the red button. Personally, life itself. Every moment is an adventure with something new to be discovered in even routine daily tasks. My one regret would be that my daughter would miss out in experiencing her full life and full potential therein.

LIZ LYTLE-RUPP
Richmond, Virginia

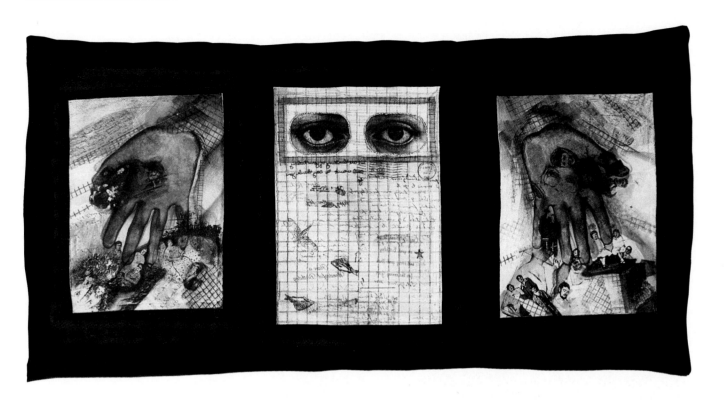

GLORIA WELNIAK
Middleton, Wisconsin
Without Them, I Would Be Dead

My panel, with my eyes seeing the unspeakably tragic destruction of our planet, and my hands "losing" my family and friends, speaks to the transformation of my spirit which occurred as I constructed my panel. For the first time in my life, I saw clearly what was most important to me, what kept me alive these 45 years. This is the first self-portrait I have done in my career and I deeply hope that the world will not be destroyed before I have a chance to construct a second one.

ANNEBERT YOORS
Design by Jan Yoors
New York, New York
Photo: Cynthia Hoy

SHARIE RODY
Falls City, Oregon
Hymn to the Universe

I am portraying people joining in love and peace to create the global harmony message to eliminate the threat of nuclear extinction, to honor nature, and to celebrate the inherent beauty and indomitable quality of the human spirit.
Photo: Jim Lind

PAULINE FARRELL and
RENEE CRUIKSHANK
Cold Spring, New York

ALLIE WALTON
Deerfield, Illinois
War God Losing Power

I did my first "War God Losing Power" in the 60's when I was in a fury over the Vietnam war. As soon as I heard of The Ribbon project in early 1983, I knew it was time to do that War God again since he has clearly not yet lost his power. So I made him smaller and weaker, and fading, with his two gasping serpents. The other pieces are affirming life triumphant.

CHUCK CAVE
Dayton, Ohio

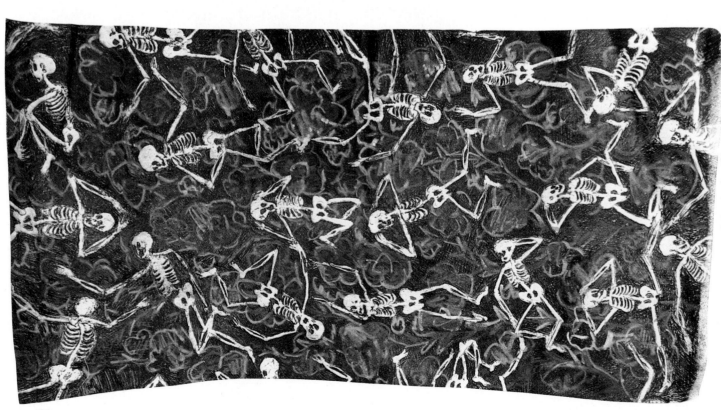

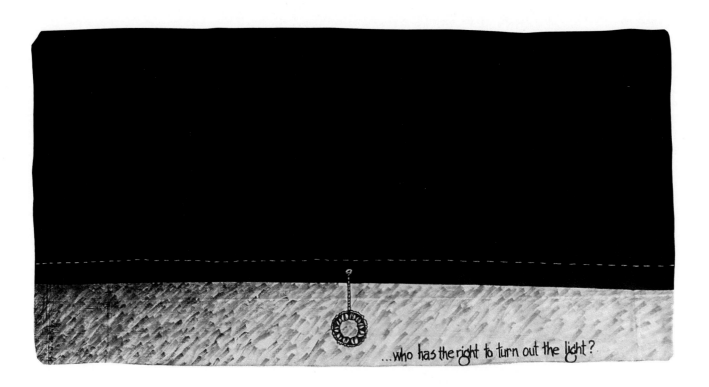

...who has the right to turn out the light?

MARILYN and JACK DA SILVA
Bowling Green, Ohio

CHRISTIAN WOMEN FELLOWSHIP
Oklahoma City, Oklahoma
Photo: Bill Olney

The Stars Are Not As High

Nor Time As Certain

Nor Space As Deep

As Our Dreams for a Peace Full Planet...

MARCIA BEDARD and
CAROL ALDRIDGE
Bowling Green, Ohio

MILISSA O'CONNELL
St. Paul, Minnesota

Let us flood the consciousness of policy-makers in Washington with our message:

> This we know. The earth does not belong to man; man belongs to the earth. This we know. All things are connected like the blood which unites one family. All things are connected. Whatever befalls the earth befalls the sons of the earth. Man did not weave the web of life. He is merely a strand in it. Whatever he does to the web, he does to himself.
>
> Chief Seattle, 1854

SAWYER STERN
Sycamore, Illinois
A Final Look Back

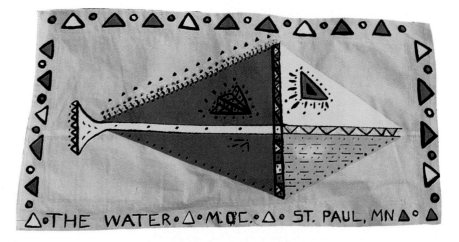

△ • THE WATER • △ • M.O'C. • △ • ST. PAUL, MN △ ° △

HELLO UNIVERSE

OR WILL IT BE GOODBYE ?

TOBIAS FELTUS
Hughesville, Maryland

BETTY MIHALAROS
Oakland, California

I am a former teacher. The children in
my segment represent the children of
Oakland. My dog is under the tree, and
the sheep represents the spinning,
weaving, and knitting aspects of my life. I
enjoy nature as evidenced by the violets,
strawberries, butterfly, rabbit, etc.
Photo: David Hitt

MARGARET and ANDREW
DIRCKSEN
La Grange, Indiana

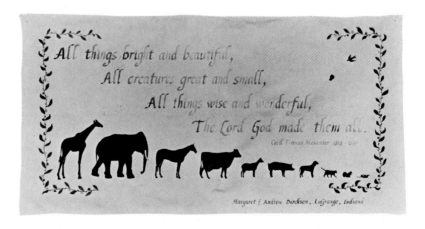

SUSAN DENOV GINEX
Chicago, Illinois

I am a Montessori preschool teacher, and I wanted to include little children in the theme of my segment. When the tulips bloomed early this year and all my preschoolers came to school in shorts and spring dresses, I knew that spring and the yearly rebirth of life were what I wanted on my piece. My husband and children helped with the design and wanted to be included, so their names are on the back.
Photo: Joseph Ginex

ESTELLE TORPY
Rockville, Maryland
Fabric Memories

"Fabric Memories" holds strong personal meaning for my family. The picture shows my son, Brendan, and daughter, Carolyn, flying kites. They are wearing their favorite colors. The number on the hot air balloon was my husband, Dan's, racecar number. I love the freedom represented by the balloon, which was sewn in scraps left over from T-shirts made for a family Fourth of July picnic. The clouds are from my babysitter's prom dress and an angel costume of my mother's. The oldest piece is from the headpiece I wore at my best friend's wedding, and the newest piece is from a jumper of my daughter's. The landscape shows mountains, fields and water. I guess one can tell that I love sunny days outdoors with my family best of all.
Photo: Daniel Torpy

ADDEENE MOORE CIRCLE, FIRST UNITED METHODIST CHURCH
Centralia, Washington

Spring in the Northwest is especially welcomed since our winters *seem* long and gray. As we thought about the "things we could not bear to think of as lost forever," our thoughts turned to the beautiful flowering Japanese cherry trees. They were just beginning to bloom when we started to plan our segment of The Ribbon, so we all agreed that was what we wanted to portray. The blossoms were individually made from pink voile material and we just kept making them all spring and summer!
Photo: Stellajoe Staebler

PENNY DALTO
Ridgewood, New Jersey

To know that there is more than 10 miles of Ribbon is to know that there is love, light, and hope. The kaleidoscope of dreams, prayers, lives, and colors weaving its way around Washington speaks to all. If each one of us becomes actively involved in the pursuit of peace and non-violent conflict resolution in whatever way is comfortable for us, we can, with combined energies, create a climate for change so that our human family may live in harmony with the earth and with each other.
Photo: Trish Dalto

BENEDICTINE SISTERS
Ridgely, Maryland

Our segment tells others that life is a precious gift to be preserved, not destroyed. It is a celebration of life—the life of the youngest member of our community to the lives of the octagenerians. The arthritic hands and failing eyesight of some of the sisters who worked on this segment speak loudly of the cost of life and desire to work for its preservation.
Photo: Rose Greeson

DELORA SIMPSON
Sebastopol, California

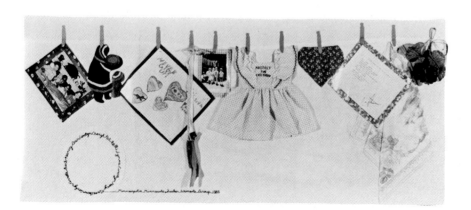

PHYLLIS WARREN
Stoneham, Massachusetts
My Family

JUNE FLESHMAN
Lebanon, Oregon
Photo: Earl Riddle

WOMEN'S GROUP,
MINNEAPOLIS FRIENDS
MEETING
Minneapolis, Minnesota
Love on the Line

The violets and driftwood represent the
beauty of natural things. The
handkerchief represents the caring and
example of a mentor. The poem
represents the flash of creativity. The
heart represents the warmth of love. The
pinafore is the strength of motherhood.
The pictures represent the closeness of
family. The school letter represents the
accomplishment of vocation. The circle
of names is the community of others. As
Quaker women, we know peace is not
the absence of war, but a way of life that
requires constant attention.
Photo: Kelli Fifield

PETER HERMANN
Bowling Green, Ohio

LILA WINSTEAD
Richmond, Virginia

KATHY LOVEN
Big Lake, Minnesota

GERTRUDE MYRRH REAGAN
Palo Alto, California
"Peace spreads like wildflowers"—
an optimistic statement, or is it? No one
needs to tell people that living out their
dreams in peace is better than being
blown up. Unfortunately, war spreads
like wildfire. To encourage peace, we
have to study the dynamics of war and
figure out alternatives to it in order to
protect the flowers, songs, dances,
poetry, and cathedrals of the spirit.
Photo: David Hitt

UNITED METHODIST WOMEN
Pine Bluff, Arkansas

MARIE RUSZKAY
Newark, Delware
U Can't Hug Your Kids with Nuclear Arms
Photo: James B. Dunson, Jr.

Marshall Miller, Oneonta, N.Y. Age 10

MARSHALL MILLER
Oneonta, New York

LIBBY WOODRUFF
Marshall, North Carolina
Photo: Paul Brezny

MILDRED HAYWOOD
Anacortes, Washington
Photo: Paul Brezny

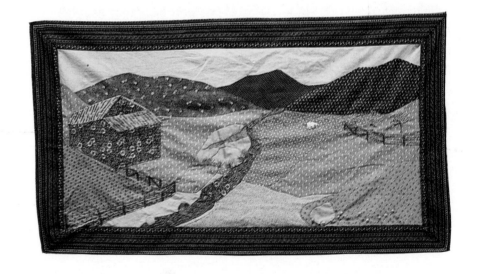

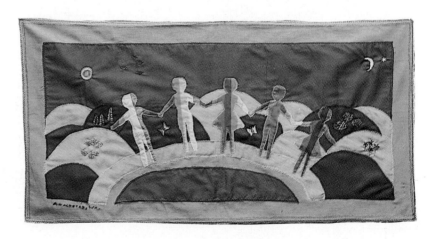

BOWLING GREEN STATE
UNIVERSITY/ART 343
Bowling Green, Ohio

KAREN S. SURBERT
Vancouver, Washington
It Was Good

SALLY CUMMING
Pleasant Ridge, Michigan
Beginnings and Growth

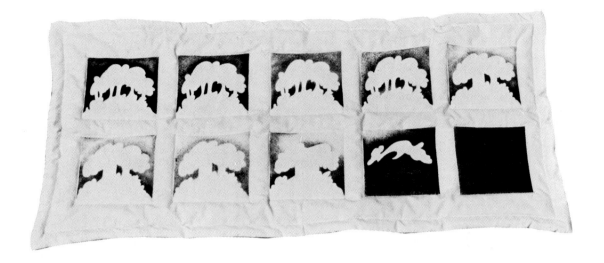

ELIZABETH BAYER
Duxbury, Massachusetts

What a unique and exhilarating experience, to have the opportunity to be part of a national affirmation of life.

SISTERS OF ST. FRANCIS OF THE IMMACULATE CONCEPTION
Peoria, Illinois

JANE WITTER
Portland, Oregon
Photo: Rebecca Lowe-Warren

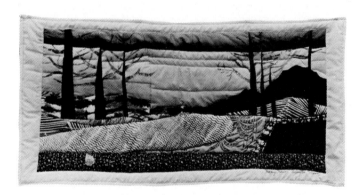

MARCIA GIBBONS
Kittery Point, Maine

NANCY CRASCO
Arlington, Massachusetts

All of the individuals whose names are written in the trees on my banner helped make me what I am today: a teacher, an artist, a quiltmaker. I wish to preserve the natural beauty of our planet for them and their descendants. I love them. I love the outdoors. Please, let us keep both safe.

MARION EVANS
Wilmington, Delaware
Which Kind of Stewards Are We?
Photo: James B. Dunson, Jr.

RIVKAH SWEEDLER
Home, Washington
The World of My Daughters,
Hilary, Marci, and Jesica

We live in Home, Washington, on the
Longbranch Peninsula of Puget Sound.
Of great importance to us is the process
of living and enjoying the bounty of these
woods and beaches without leaving any
permanent scars of destruction. Home
was established in 1896 by a group of
idealistic free thinkers. They believed in
the rights of the individual as long as the
rights of others were also respected. Free
speech, intellectual inquiry, and
education for all ages were greatly valued.
The community existed for 20 years and
was well known throughout the world
among similar free thinkers.

MARTHA'S VINEYARD
FRIENDS MEETING
West Tisbury, Massachusetts
Sailing For Life
Photo: John Angevin

JUDITH TRIPP HARVESTER
West Brookfield, Massachusetts

When my husband and I were first
getting to know each other, we spent
many evenings getting to know the
constellations. We plan to teach our
children when they are old enough. We
will do everything we can not to lose that
opportunity.
Photo: Rebecca Raymond

CHURCH OF THE BRETHREN
GENERAL BOARD
Elgin, Illinois

MARY RUTH HALL and
MARGARET STAFFORD
Bridgewater, Massachusetts
Awakening

The nation and the world will experience an awakening to a new dawn, an awakening like no other; one that will bring understanding, and make real the dream of peace and affection among those societies called human. The cockerel crowing with the rising sun symbolizes that awakening, which each of us must experience within ourselves before the understanding becomes ours, before humanity can awaken to the dream.
Photo: Linda Marganian

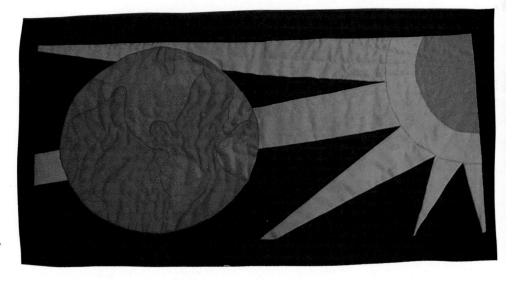

MOLLY SWAIN
Oneonta, New York

BERTHA LOUISE MCKANN
Harbinger, North Carolina

I read about The Ribbon and suddenly
had the gut feeling that I *had* to be a part
of it and commit my idea for others to
see. When I began thinking about what I
would miss the most, I finally arrived at
the basic idea: the earth, our island. If it
dies, so do my dreams. My banner says
that there are no more choices—ever! My
participation in The Ribbon is a cry for
help. That is a demand, not a plea. I see
that we need to be more than "sunshine
soldiers and summer patriots." If we are
not heard, there will be no one left to
record the foolish mistake.

EARLY BIRD SWIMMERS
Needham, Massachusetts

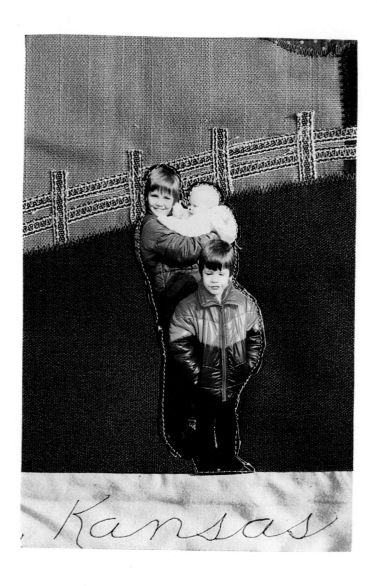

PHYLLIS DETTMER
Leawood, Kansas
Photo: Buck Firth

SUSAN M. CALHOUN
Waldoboro, Maine

My segment shows our farm: the house, flowers, our vegetable garden, which feeds us most of the year, three blue jays, three fish, the lake, and pine trees. My husband, Ken Stewart, our two-year-old son, Nathan, and I are standing in the road to the duck pond. Nathan was born at home, in the house pictured. The name of the farm reflects our interest in Rudolph Steiner's philosophy—anthroposophy—in which he explains that the nature of man is three-fold: physical, spiritual and emotional.
Photo: Paul Brezny

REBECCA DAVIS
Prescott, Arizona

SHERYLLEE K. LOWE
Flossmoor, Illinois

My favorite part of being a homemaker
and mother is preparing and sharing the
holidays with my family and friends, so I
put symbols for our many favorites at the
top of my Ribbon piece. The roses were
used at my in-laws' 50th wedding
anniversary party. The sun is part of my
collection of sun symbols which have
brought lots of pleasure to my life. The
dinner party symbol is from the front of
one of the T-shirts I bought at an exhibit.
It is my favorite symbol of creativity. The
round "friends are special" was made for
me by a friend. I really believe The
Ribbon has provided thousands of
people a way to deal with their fears and
hopes in a wonderful, creative manner.
They have used this safe, unusual outlet
to give of themselves and be part of
something bigger for the world without
risk to their livelihood. Many have told
me that The Ribbon is the first
involvement they have had directly with
the peace movement or the "Freeze."

Sent from
Japan

89

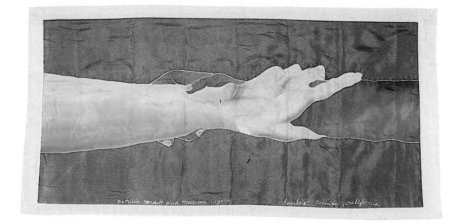

LAUREL HECHT and
ADAM DAIGLER
Ithaca, New York

The left side is the positive side of things;
the right side is the negative. The subject
idea was one of balance, and was made
by two political artists.

PATRICIA ANNE SENNOTT
Arcata, California
Photo: David Hitt

LINDA KAUN
Los Angeles, California

GAIL RANDOLPH
Los Gatos, California
A Mixed Bouquet: Bringing All the Differences Together
I see a pattern in my life of bringing differences together: quilting and patchwork, eclectic home furnishings, mixing clothing styles, bringing together people of many ages and interests, improving communications, and bringing "haves" and "have nots" closer to understanding . . . Particularly, I enjoy the diversity of people and cultures in the world.
Photo: David Hitt

JILL PROVOST
Plattsburgh, New York

This is a drawing of our house where I live, my daddy's car, my sister's and my swing set, and our cats. The grey cat is mine. His name is Fluffer. The orange cat is my sister, Tricia's. His name is Rusty. We named our cats. They will be two years old on July 1, 1985. My mommy and daddy planted the tree on their tenth wedding anniversary. I love my cats, and house and my sister and mommy and daddy. I want us all to live.

JULIA FELTZ, S.S.J.
Buffalo, New York

CHRISTIAN WOMEN FELLOWSHIP
Oklahoma City, Oklahoma
Photo: Bill Olney

PATRICIA P. HARRIS
Bridgeville, Delaware
Lilies of the Field

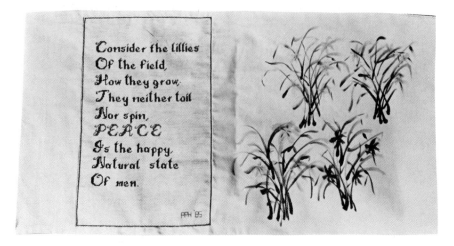

92

CATALINA ZOBEL and
VIRGINIA Z. FERGUSON
Wilmington, Delaware
Photo: James B. Dunson, Jr.

Sent from the Netherlands

TRINITY UNITED CHURCH
WOMEN
Portland, Oregon
Rain
Photo: Earl Riddle

SUZANNE RICHARD
Hinesburg, Vermont
Photo: Susan Lilienthal

MARGARET RUTH DIETZE HART
Dearborn, Michigan
Interdependence

I chose the theme of interdependence for my project because I have become increasingly, continuously aware of the interdependence of all things, all events on earth and in God's universe. It is very exciting to me that human beings can be affected by, and motivated by, ideas expressed by other people who live separated by geography and time. On my holonomy symbol, I have embroidered the names of individuals—some living, some no longer alive in the flesh, some directly known by me, others known through their writings. We are all connected, linked, from past, through present, into the future.
Photo: Paul Brezny

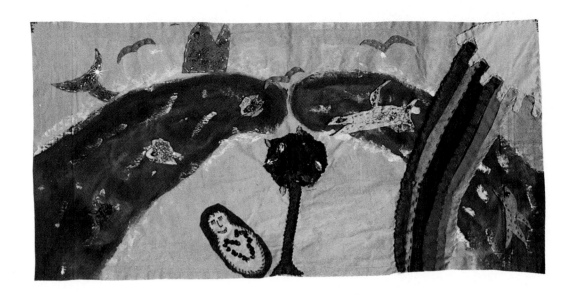

LINDA S. PERRY
Lexington, Massachusetts
Photo: David Caras

Sent from
the Federal Republic of Germany

FRIEDE ALLEN MÜTTERN! KEINE BOMBEN AUF IHRE KINDER! DAS HERZ DER MÜTTER RUFT ALLEN MÄNNERN DER WELT ZU: LÖST ENDLICH EINMAL AUF FRIEDLICHE, DEMOKRATISCHE WEISE DIE WIRTSCHAFTLICHEN PROBLEME! HABT ACHT VOR DER FRUCHTBAREN ERDE! ZEIGT EUCH ALS MENSCHEN! GLAUBT NICHT, DASS IHR MIT EUREM UNRECHT JE EINMAL DEN FRIEDEN BRINGT! H.G.

FRAUENHILFE BRAUNFELS BRD

BUNDESREPUBLIK - DEUTSCHLAND

95

FULTON ELEMENTARY P.T.A.
Minneapolis, Minnesota

This, as well as other pieces of the
Minnesota Ribbon, were part of the
annual Mother's Day march for peace
and justice, held May 11, 1985.
Photo: Kelli Fifield

Sent from the Netherlands

CHRISSY PALATUCCI SMITH
Santa Cruz, California
Let Love Reign

As an artist working in prints and textiles
I often use the heart symbol. Since the
very symbol of a heart denotes love, I
feel that until we learn to love all our
brothers and sisters on earth we will
never be at peace. But peace begins
within. "Love God," "love your
neighbor," these are the only true
commandments, in any language, any
religion, any nation.
Photo: Pat Feary

MARY MAUPIN
Marshall, North Carolina

I am a painter and mother of two boys. My studio is in my home. My husband is a woodworker and carpenter. I am a Quaker, so I have strong feelings of non-violence, from a Biblical perspective. I am involved in our Madison County peace group, Plowshares. Thirty-eight of us made a friendship quilt to be sent to our sister community in the Soviet Union. Many of us are interested in needlework and the arts. Wrapping the Pentagon seems such a wonderful symbol to me, and a perfect way of integrating my painting and my politics.
Photo: Paul Brezny

TOINI KAARTINEN
Spencer, New York
Photo: Ann Gefell

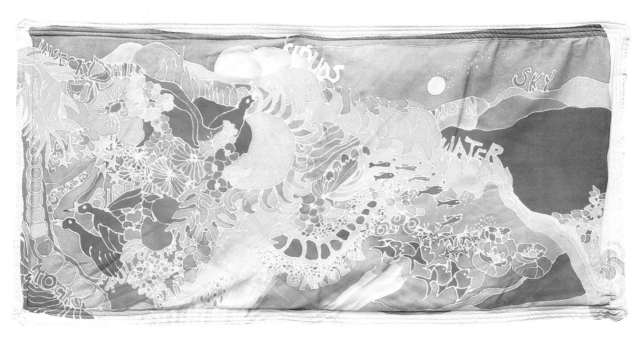

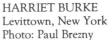

HARRIET BURKE
Levittown, New York
Photo: Paul Brezny

LIESE BRONFENBRENNER
Ithaca, New York
Photo: Mary Milne

Hold back the never ending night!

CAROLYN A. DAHL
Houston, Texas
Ribbon Cows

I could have chosen many subjects for my banner as the whole world looked so precious and fragile when I tried to select what I could not bear to lose in life. My strongest feelings, however, kept returning to a childhood image of peace and security centered on the gentle cow. My Swedish grandfather drew the cow shape that I use in this banner. John Edward traced his drawing onto a piece of wood and whittled a wonderful toy cow. I remember vividly the peace of the room as the wood fire snapped, the coffee heated, and his pocketknife worked the wood while the cold Minnesota wind carved into the snow outside.

Today his frayed drawing and the toy cow are mine, and I trace the shape on beautiful silk. His black and white cow pleased a child, but my cows are colored in hot Texas hues to attract attention for peace. Around the border are those who watch and wait and protect the right of all individuals to peace-filled memories. Threaded together by the ribbon that unites us in this project, we tie our personal symbols and hopes into an ever expanding vision of peace.

98

LOVE... Which Binds All Things Together In Perfect Unity...

COLOSSIANS 3.14-15

FIRST PRESBYTERIAN CHURCH OF PHILIPSTOWN, COLD SPRING, NEW YORK

PAULINE FARRELL and
RENEE CRUIKSHANK
Cold Spring, New York
Love

We volunteered to create a banner
representing our church. After much
discussion and discarding of ideas we
decided that one of the things we would
miss most, in the event of a nuclear
war, is relationships . . . or people. This
evolved into people together, people
united in a common brotherhood
of love. Our banner illustrates this
thought . . . showing people joined
together, and the scripture "Love . . .
which binds all things together in perfect
unity."

DENISE L. SMITH
Chapel Hill, North Carolina

I would miss the children after a nuclear
war. I teach art and help with after-school
care during the week. On Sundays, I
teach elementary children at church. I'm
concerned about man's possible use of
nuclear weapons and what is the most
effective way to prevent their use.
Photo: Laura Drey

LOREE TUCKER-McKENNA
Pendleton, Oregon
Nature Blossoms
Photo: Jim Lind

DIANE WESTGATE
Twain Harte, California

I am a weaver and basketmaker. I found out about The Ribbon through a weaving shop. The invitation to participate was one I could not ignore. I have felt so helpless about the way this country is heading. The idea of writing letters to our representatives seems like a lesson in futility. But joining together with thousands of others to make a permanent statement with fabric was a perfect outlet for my voice. I *needed* to do my share of The Ribbon. It was too important a task to be neglected.

I took the instructions quite literally—what I would hate to think of as being lost forever in a nuclear war. I thought in terms not of a direct hit, but of a nuclear winter. Buildings and objects would remain, but anything with life would not survive. I chose to show things important to me that depend on the atmosphere—plants, animals, people, water. Columbine, one of my favorite wildflowers, seemed the perfect center since its definition, "dovelike", is the symbol for peace. The other choices I included are those I feel most passionate about. Some, due to lack of space or talent, had to be expressed in words. I stitched a basket after my name since I am probably best known for my pine needle baskets. In addition to making them myself, I have taught over 200 people to make them, and in turn many of those have gone on to teach. I am most proud of helping to keep this craft alive and I want it to endure for centuries to come.

DIANE PSOTA
Rohnert Park, California
Sonoma County Hills

Although I was born in New England, California has become *home* to me. The hills in Sonoma County have come to represent California. What would I miss most if there were a nuclear war? The beauty and peace of my home.

NANCY PAPA
Los Gatos, California
Interwoven

I used rainbow colors to illustrate a change, a new possibility forthcoming, one that is brighter and born from darkness. Separate bands relate to individual cultures or the uniqueness of individuals but interwoven to signify our connectedness.
Photo: Paul Brezny

RUTH NORTON
Rochester, New York
Photo: Julie Gelfand

FIRST UNITED METHODIST
SIXTH GRADE
Brighton, Michigan

JANE KAUFMANN
Dover, New Hampshire

BOWLING GREEN STATE
UNIVERSITY SATURDAY
ART PROGRAM
Bowling Green, Ohio

TAFI BROWN
East Alstead, New Hampshire

My banner is made up of blueprint photographs of my neighbors and scenes — animals, landscape, architecture — from my community and environment that I love so much.
Photo: Paul Brezny

LOIS ARDITO
Arlington, Massachusetts
The Fruits of Life's Labour
Photo: David Caras

GIGI BENANTI
Norwalk, Connecticut
Happy Sunny Days

with great help from Ken, _____ and B_____

Continue Goddess, Goddess breast, Breast Milk, Milk Flow, Flow life, life P_____

Woodacre, Marin County

Mother, do you think they'll drop the bomb

by my own hand   Alexandra Genetti

IRIS THOR
Vestal, New York

ALEXANDRA GENETTI
Woodacre, California
History of the World in One Yard

This banner is meant to express the idea that we would not only lose what we have today, but also what has passed: the entire creation—time! I am concerned that a record of history be kept and that all the great art and discoveries of the past remain with us. For now, as far as we know, we are the only keepers of the history of the planet. Time passes, from the big bang to the planets forming around our sun, to the primordial oceans and one-celled life growing into plants and earth and reptiles and mammals and birds and, finally, humans. Cave peoples, Babylon, the first writing and the first history, Egypt along the Nile. Crete with her snake goddess and dolphins. Greece, the Parthenon, Rome, Stonehenge. The Great Wall of China. Buddha under the bodhi tree, Ravenna with Queen Theodosia. Hagia Sophia, Florence and the Renaissance . . . on to San Francisco (near where I live) and my two beautiful children, who want to be a part of ongoing, continuing history. That's what it's really all about . . . CONTINUITY.
Photo: Paul Brezny

DANA IRWIN and SAM MCMILLAN
Asheville, North Carolina
The Luxury of Mere Existence

We are an artist and a poet. Our subject is life. We believe in leading lives of noisy desperation. The alternative is boring. How we became involved with The Ribbon: The idea came up and konked us on the head so hard we couldn't ignore the swelling.
Photo: Sam McMillan

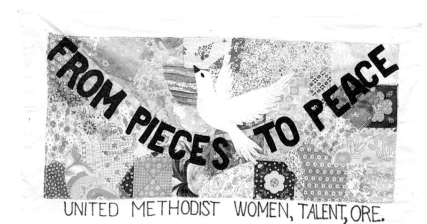

THE CHILDREN OF THE ETHICAL HUMANIST SOCIETY OF LONG ISLAND

SYLVIA H. EINSTEIN
Belmont, Massachusetts
Utopia

I see this small town as a place where all the people and things I care about live together harmoniously. My banner is made from fabric given to me by family and friends, and from fabric with symbols of people, ideas, and things I cannot bear to lose.
Photo: David Caras

UNITED METHODIST WOMEN
Talent, Oregon
Photo: Paul Brezny

ETHICAL HUMANIST SOCIETY
CHILDREN
Westbury, New York

Once at the Long Island Ethical Humanist Society, we met to ponder the question, "Is there anything for which I would die?" Some people said there were various ideals for which they would die; there were some who said they would die if the act would bring world peace; still others felt there was no cause for which they would sacrifice their lives. And yet, on one subject, there was unanimity: all who were parents said they would die for their children. We are born and we live and we give the earth over to the children and the children of the children when we pass on. And so, when considering yet another question—what I cannot bear to think of as lost forever in a nuclear war—again, the answer is, "the children."

First Unitarian Universalist Church School. Rochester, Mn.

We would miss pets, rainbows, flowers and colors.

FIRST UNITARIAN
UNIVERSALIST CHURCH SCHOOL
Rochester, Minnesota

OUR PIECE OF PEACE - KALAMA, WA.

UNITED METHODIST WOMEN

PEGGY EVERST, EMMA STONE,
BETTY NIXON
Kalama, Washington
Our Piece of Peace
Photo: Stellajoe Staebler

KAY NOSLER
Menlo Park, California

A friend told me about the peace Ribbon and gave me the muslin for my banner. There was a sampler in a Danish cross-stitch book that I was going to do some time in the future. I decided that the future was now and the sampler form would be a good way for my family to list what we would not want to have lost forever because of a nuclear war.
The list describes the interests of individual people, my husband Peter, and my son Alexander and myself. It describes a family and the achievements and creations of human beings. It describes our planet earth which makes us special and unique in the universe.
I'm not a marcher or a demonstrator, so this method of expression by way of my medium has meant a great deal to me.
Photo: David Hitt

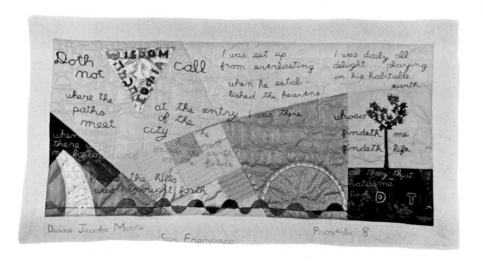

DIANE JACOBS MOORE
San Francisco, California
Proverbs 8

UNITED METHODIST WOMEN
Doniphan, Nebraska
Photo: Sharee Kelly

BARBARA COLBATH
Rochester, New Hampshire
The Winged Creatures
Photo: Susan Bickford

ST. JOHN'S UNITED CHURCH OF
CHRIST SUNDAY SCHOOL
Walnut Creek, Ohio
Photo: Kermit Miller

LAKE SUPERIOR FRIENDS
Marquette, Michigan

We at the Lake Superior Friends Meeting
were looking for a peace project that we,
as a small meeting, could accomplish. In
the tradition of Quakers, The Ribbon
project drew a consensus from the
meeting, but a consensus could not be
reached on a central theme for the
banners. Therefore, each individual
depicted, in his or her own creative way,
what he or she would miss if there were a
nuclear war. The children of the meeting
did their portion as a part of a First Day
School lesson. On March 22, 1985 we
met for a ''Ribbon Bee'' at which time we
sewed our panels together.
Photo: Lillian Heldreth

PAMELA TYRRELL
Shippensburg, Pennsylvania

I was born in Malta and came to the U.S. when I was 10. Seeing the whole world live in harmony has been one of my fantasies since I was a child. Doing this banner gave me a chance to feel part of that reality.

SISTER JACINTA FIEBIG, SISTER BARBARA SHEAHAN and friends
Rapid City, South Dakota
The Black Hills of South Dakota

The spruce trees covering South Dakota's hills look black in the distance; thus, the name of the hills became the Black Hills. Some nuns who live in Rapid City, nestled among the Black Hills, have created this Ribbon segment to express the idea that this beautiful creation of God not be destroyed in war.
Photo: David Hitt

ROSAMOND SORENSEN
Nelson, British Columbia, Canada

...and He saw that it was good. Gen. 1:25

ELSA REICHLE
Muncie, Indiana
Photo: Joan Whitaker

CHURCH WOMEN UNITED
Bloomington, Indiana

EVE MENGER-HAMMOND
Madison, New Jersey

LAURA FRANKENSTEIN
Rochester, New York
Photo: Julie Gelfand

IRIS THOR
Vestal, New York

VIRGINIA RANDLES
Athens, Ohio

I am a fiber artist working on quilts. The Ribbon project was brought to my attention by an article sent to me by my daughter. My immediate response was to consider all life on this earth, and what destruction would mean to any part of it. I simply had to participate by making a segment. I chose the graphic design in patchwork to symbolize my thoughts and feelings. I am deeply moved by the international scope of The Ribbon.
Photo: 2 C Studio

FIRST BAPTIST CHURCH
Chili, New York
Photo: Julie Gelfand

BENEDICTINES FOR PEACE
Chicago, Illinois

Through history, Benedictines have been
noted for being people of peace, so this
time in history calls us to try to be
involved in whatever ways we can in
peacemaking. Our banner depicts our
commitment. As we are a unified
community, we portrayed the lake and
city-scape of the Midwest as one with the
mountains of the West.
Benedictines for Peace is a five-year-old
organization bringing together men and
women who follow the Rule of Benedict.
There are chapters and units all over
North America. Our group numbers 61.
Eight of us Sisters worked on the banner.
Four of us will be at the Pentagon to take
part in the celebration in August.

ST. JOSEPH'S COMMUNITY
Juneau, Alaska

St. Joseph's Convent is a group of five
religious women who work in a variety of
ministries in the Juneau diocese. The
Ribbon piece reflects the beauty and
richness of nature—creation and people
about us—and the gift these are to us.
Photo: David Hitt

113

DIANE WILKINSON
Elgin, Illinois

WINES ELEMENTARY SCHOOL
OPEN CLASSROOM PROGRAM
Ann Arbor, Michigan
Photo: Joanne Leonard

CLAIRE COOPERSTEIN
Chapel Hill, North Carolina
All the Different People
Photo: Laura Drey

114

LAUREEN KENNEDY
Grand Rapids, Michigan

SISTER PAT SCHNAPP
Bowling Green, Ohio

CHRISTIAN WOMEN FELLOWSHIP
Oklahoma City, Oklahoma
Photo: Bill Olney

THE VILLAGE CHRISTIAN CHURCH WOMEN'S GUILD OF OK. CITY OK.

STEFAN SEUFERT
Wangen im Allgaeu, Federal Republic of
Germany

I am presently involved in absolving my
civilian service working for the German
Red Cross. I am also active in Pax
Christi, a Protestant peace group. My
banner depicts the two city gates of
Wangen and the city coat of arms.

Sent from the Federal
Republic of Germany

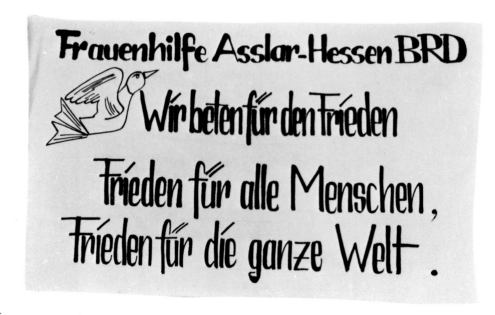

Sent from the Federal Republic
of Germany

JUDITH HERRMANN
Amtzell, Federal Republic of Germany

THE SUZUKI FAMILY
Tokyo, Japan
Photo: Dennis Watson

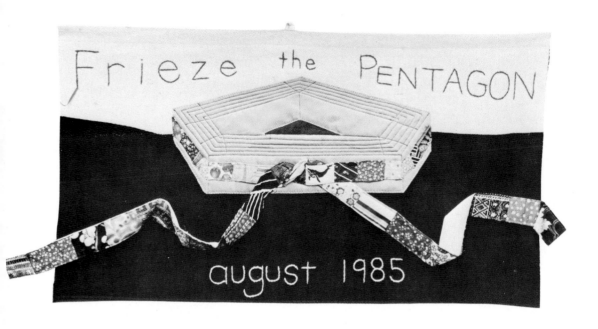

MARY MILNE
Ithaca, New York

Photo: Paul Brezny

ST. MARY'S WOMEN'S GROUP
Long Beach, New York

LAURA and FRIEDA MOLINELLI
Briarcliff, New York

Our Ribbon was created in the hope and prayer for peace and harmony with all of God's creatures and creation. The beauty and freedom of the dolphin is our inspiration. Frieda (Mom) and Laura (daughter) have worked together for peace and freedom in many ways. Laura designed the banner, Mom put it together.

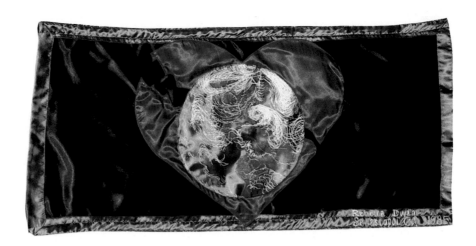

REBECCA WALLACE HANKINS DWAN
Sebastopol, California
Burden of Greed
Photo: Robert Kuiper

LINDA S. PERRY
Lexington, Massachusetts
All the Springs
Photo: David Caras

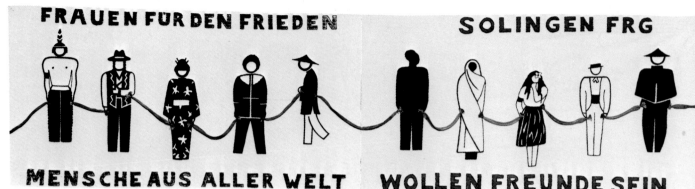

FRAUEN FÜR DEN FRIEDEN SOLINGEN FRG

MENSCHE AUS ALLER WELT WOLLEN FREUNDE SEIN

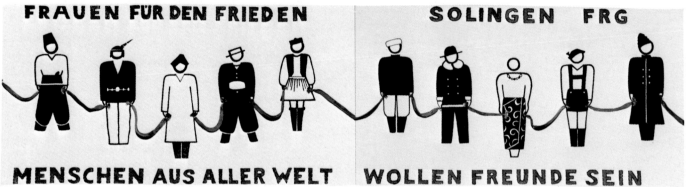

FRAUEN FÜR DEN FRIEDEN SOLINGEN FRG

MENSCHEN AUS ALLER WELT WOLLEN FREUNDE SEIN

Sent from the Federal Republic of Germany

SUGAR CREEK CHURCH SENIOR HIGH SCHOOL STUDENTS
Kettering, Ohio

We took a very specific look at the friends and things we lived with every day. On our banner we express everything from the mundane, like Crest toothpaste, to the musically meaningful, like Van Halen, to the inspirational, like the olympics. Our brainstorming went wild as we included Visa, Mastercard, Lee, Apple Computer, and many, many more. Although some people responded to our banner as commercial, we see the logos representing very real aspects of our lives the way we are living them today . . . aspects of our lives that would certainly be gone if a bomb went off tomorrow.
Photo: Deborah Ridley

BAND AGAINST NUCLEAR DESTRUCTION
Anniston, Alabama

This banner is one of eight made under the auspices of a county-wide grassroots group. Pieces of felt, velveteen, and cotton were cut out with a backing and ironed onto a corduroy panel.

120

MADELYN STARBUCK,
TESS AMSEL, CAROLYN PRESCOTT
Austin, Texas
Friday Afternoon, Austin, Texas

Our Ribbon section developed out of
our ongoing Friday afternoon painting
sessions, and is a jointly executed group
portrait intended to convey a spirit of
camaraderie, warmth, and what Carolyn's
father calls intangible attunement.
Photo: Paul Brezny

CECILIA CHRISTENSEN
Palo Alto, California

The question was asked, "What in life is
most dear to me, that I can't imagine a
world without, a world threatened with
nuclear destruction?"
Color.
A cultural symbol for colorfulness is the
rainbow. Here is my rainbow
representation, the colors of the human
race included, and to paraphrase Ntozake
Shange, my banner is for the human race
which has considered suicide when the
rainbow is enough.

LINDA MILLER
Maumee, Ohio

MAGGIE O'CONNOR
Minneapolis, Minnesota

In November, 1983, I was beside the Mississippi River, filled with despair. Despair that earth could/would survive the onslaught of humankind, and despair that I would be able to conceive a child after months of trying. I began to sing *"llo t'amo, llo rido, llo credo"* which translates, "I love you, I laugh, I believe." I realized I did not believe and that my emptiness in belief was dangerous. I went from the river to my mother's house on an errand. She showed me a magazine editorial about The Ribbon. Immediately, I realized that I believed August, 1985 was too late, and in that realization, knew the danger of my despair. I began work on my Ribbon segment that day. Stitch by stitch, I struggled with the despair; my love of earth and life; my need to believe. As I worked many people saw the piece and wondered why I could spend so much time on something I would give away. The people, from the crustiest street man to the most calm intellectual, were also very moved by the image of wrapping the Pentagon in embroidery of all we don't want to lose in nuclear war. This mixture of puzzlement and appreciation seems interwoven with the struggle that we *can* do something about nuclear war—that we must protect our planet and all it means. Now I feel a belief in our ability to stop nuclear war— piece by piece. As I write this, I am also awaiting the birth of my twins.

JOHN ANGEVIN
Edgartown, Massachusetts
. . . And On and On . . .

GINNY KORANEK
Marshall, North Carolina
Photo: Paul Brezny

Noah Pyles W.A. Vancouver age 10

NOAH PYLES
Vancouver, Washington

**FIRST CHURCH UNITED
METHODIST WOMEN**
Kearney, Nebraska

We would hate to lose all the children of
the world. The tears in the eyes of each
child are tears shed for a life unlived and
a world destroyed.
Photo: Sharee Kelly

STELLA NEIL, R.S.M.
Des Moines, Iowa

I created my banner because of the
inspiration of a good friend, Rosemary
Ronk, R.S.M. Prior to her death,
Rosemary began to work on The
Ribbon. The design symbolized the four
seasons and the cycle of life that comes
from the land—the seeds, the seasons,
and the soil. They make up the normal
cycle of life. The children live out their
own life cycles. All in the fertile state of
Iowa.
Photo: Bob Brammer

123

JAN MYERS
Minneapolis, Minnesota

My portion of The Ribbon started out as a statement about the importance of color in my life. And I mean color in the broadest sense: the infinite variety of experience that has led me to this time and this place. I toyed with the idea of a more embroidered surface, because the first needlework I did, taught to me by my mother, who had died within the past year, was cross-stitch. But I decided that pieced work was really what I needed to do.

When pieced together, it alone did not say enough, so I decided to add the words from Pete Seeger's song about making the garden grow.

The words have very special significance to me on a personal level, because this was the song that my husband and I chose to have sung at our wedding. For us, it expressed our commitment toward maintaining a simplicity in our lives together. Working on our garden, both literally and figuratively, was what we planned to do together, and to hopefully make our contribution to "fertile ground" within the world. When I review Pete Seeger's words, I am still overwhelmed by the way in which he has said so much so simply. I do believe that the roots of peace, as the roots of relationships, must be mulched "deep and low."
Photo: Paul Brezny

MADELAINE KANE
Grand Rapids, Michigan

SHIRLEY RAPOPORT
Muskegon, Michigan
Photo: Philip C. Brautigan

PHYLLIS DETTMER
Leawood, Kansas
Photo: Buck Firth

CHURCH WOMEN UNITED
Delaware Assembly
Dover, Delaware

This piece of The Ribbon was made by
all the women who attended our
assembly in April, 1984. Each woman
was given a piece of the banner and then
placed it on the background with a pin.
Adele Majka sewed the pieces together.
Photo: James B. Dunson, Jr.

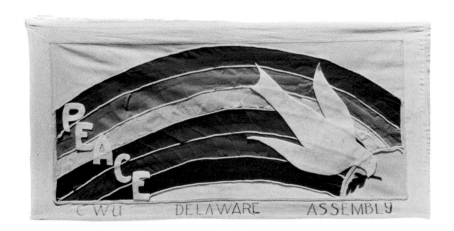

MIMI DIETRICH
Catonsville, Maryland

Please let the children touch the
quilts.

Let my children and my grandchildren
and
my great-grandchildren feel the
warmth
and the comfort and the peace
in a handmade quilt.

Let them touch my quilts, my friends'
quilts,
the artists' quilts, and the pioneers'
quilts.

Let our quilts become antiques for
our
great grandchildren to touch — to
feel
our feelings, our creativity, our
thoughts,
and our lives.

Don't destroy our grandmothers'
quilts.
They are history allowing us to touch
our past.
Give our children a *future* to touch.
Please.
Photo: Bob Dietrich

GLORIA ROSE FORTUNATO
West Springfield, Massachusetts

My banner is for my first child, Michael
Robert. Those items shown are ones that
depict life's wonders. I hope to share this
with Michael, and with the members of
my family. I hope to share a full life with
them all.
Photo: Robert M. Fortunato

126

THE TANGENTS
Wayne, Pennsylvania
Photo: James B. Dunson, Jr.

CHURCH WOMEN UNITED
Oklahoma

Church Women United in Oklahoma
has made 15 segments for The Ribbon.
They have incorporated into their
banners cherished bits and pieces — baby
clothes, grandma's apron, Boy Scout
Eagle award badges — along with their
prayers. Each banner is a handmade
statement: "Let there be peace on earth
and let it begin with me."

ELAINE JAFFE
Silver Spring, Maryland
Sunrise-Sunset

To express creatively what one feels
about nuclear war, a most emotional
topic, is a challenge. How difficult it is to
choose one thing. Everything and
everyone—all are irreplaceable.

127

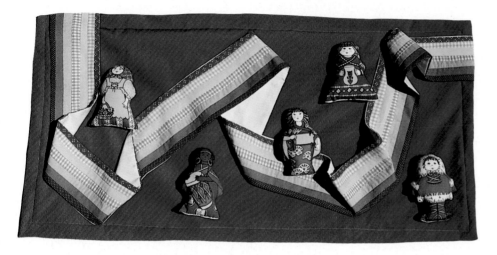

LINDA J. MARGANIAN
West Bridgewater, Massachusetts
Peace in our World

I made dolls for my daughter, depicting women all over the world. I made the rainbow-colored ribbon to symbolize the fact that people of the world don't come all in the same size or color, nor do they speak the same language. The banner is on a background of green to symbolize living things, like growing plants, happy children, all of life dependent on chlorophyll from green plants. The people in the banner and the ribbon connecting them show interdependence of living things on each other, thus symbolizing peace.

SARAH WENTWORTH
Cambridge, Massachusetts

MARY CIOFALO
San Francisco, California
Colors I Love
Photo: David Hitt

JANE RUBEY
Orinda, California
Real Feelings
Photo: David Hitt

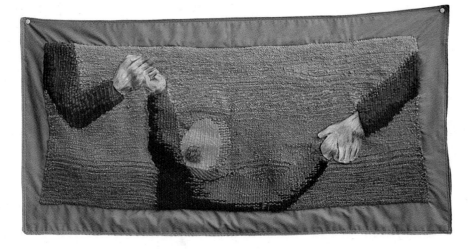

JANICE STEINHAGEN
Mystic, Connecticut

We dream of our children, still
unconceived and still a mystery, their
faces visible only in our imaginations,
and we fear for the world they will face
with us and after us. Just as we blended
our respective skills as weaver and potter
to make our part of The Ribbon, so we
dream of collaborating to create and
nurture our children, to give life and
breath to the abstract reality of our love.
It is the hope of someday seeing the faces
of our children that we celebrate.
Photo: Erich Steinhagen

WINES ELEMENTARY SCHOOL
OPEN CLASSROOM PROGRAM
Ann Arbor, Michigan
Photo: Joanne Leonard

ANYA FIRSZT
Bowling Green, Ohio

FRITZI GALLEY
Arlington, Massachusetts
The Stars Are Waiting

PATTI STEWART
Portland, Oregon
Photo: Rebecca Lowe-Warren

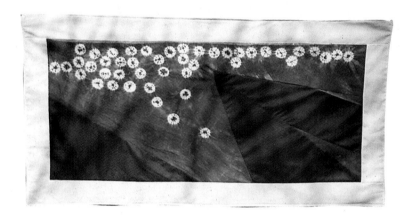

130

Lynda Parkins   Calvary Baptist Church   Newark, Delaware   6/27/84

LYNDA PARKINS
Newark, Delaware
Photo: James B. Dunson, Jr.

MARY RODMAN
Prescott, Arizona

RUTH SANDY
Rochester, New York
Photo: Julie Gelfand

131

LUTHERAN and CATHOLIC
CHURCHWOMEN
St. James, Minnesota

KATHRYN KENNEDY
Illinois

TREVA MARKS
Zionsville, Indiana

The title of my banner, "Exaltavit
Humiles" (let the humble be exalted) is
biblical in origin. However, the idea for
using the eggs of various species of birds
to illustrate the concept came after
reading the poem *Exaltavit Humiles* by
Daniel Berrigan. The last lines of the
poem remind me that we move in, and
by, grace, and that nuclear weapons are
anti-grace for they would destroy those
things which are exalted by God: the eggs
of the sparrow, the jay, the scarlet
tanager, the Baltimore oriole, and the
scissor-tailed flycatcher.

NOELIE DRISCOLL
Bloomington, Indiana

JOAN MICHIE and LEE ANN
HALTER
Rochester, New York
Women Together
Photo: Stephen Hedges

KATHRYN EWERS BUNDY
Charleston, Illinois

133

ELLEN DOHNER LIVINGSTON
Park Forest, Illinois
Nick's Grubbies

ALISA ROSE
Verona, Wisconsin
Koala
Photo: Gloria Welniak

PEACE LINKS/
CHURCH WOMEN UNITED
Norman, Oklahoma

134

GAIL BRUSSOCK
Oak Park, Illinois
Letter and Ribbon to the President

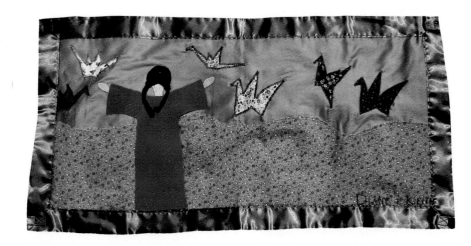

BETH WICKENDEN
Ithaca, New York
Nuclear Family

When I began to work on my Ribbon
piece in the fall of 1984, three concerns
affected the design. One was the season
—its beautiful crisp, clean and vivid color
with long afternoon shadows. The second
was a documentary I had recently seen on
the Vietnam memorial in Washington,
D.C. The image of the soldiers' friends
and families, running their fingers along
their loved ones' names, had a very
powerful impact on me. The incredible
numbers and statistics of war were then
transformed into individuals and
relationships. And lastly, as a mother of
two young children, I wanted to
represent my family and our own joys
and fears.
"Nuclear Family" is not just about my
own personal concerns, but about the
strength and reinforcement of joining
hands and raising voices together to make
a statement about the urgency of peace.
Photo: Lee Melen

DIANE BENJAMIN and
KEITH ALCOCK
Rochester, Minnesota

135

ELIZABETH WHITEFORD-
HOFFMAN
Detroit, Michigan

PAT O'CONNOR
St. Paul, Minnesota

JOY HARDIN and CILLA LAULA
Arcata, California
Photo: David Hitt

CHURCH WOMEN UNITED
Drew County, Arkansas

SANTIAM PEACE COALITION
Portland, Oregon

STEPHANIE MONAGHAN BLOUT
Lexington, Massachusetts

Baby blocks, or building blocks, is a
traditional American patchwork pattern.
It, and the background outline quilting
represent not only the progression of
babies from one generation to another,
but the inherited gifts they could bring to
the world. This Ribbon panel is
dedicated to my grandmother, Grace
Comard Fischetti, who taught me sewing
and the meaning of the words faith, love,
and integrity. I hope I will have the
chance to pass on these precious gifts to
my daughter.
Photo: David Caras

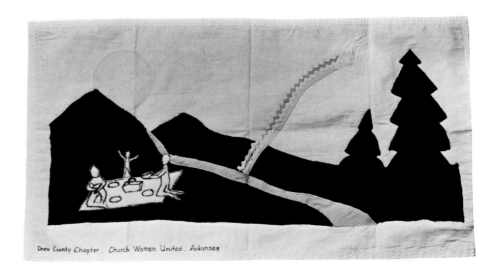

Drew County Chapter Church Women United, Arkansas

everyone is holy

In Memory of Grace Comard Fischetti 1900 - 1985

BABY BLOCKS

FRANCISCAN SISTERS
Sioux City, Iowa

We are a group of Franciscans who minister in northwest Iowa. We are members of our community's justice committee. Our picture on The Ribbon depicts corn, for which Iowa is famous and which feeds the world. We want our fertile soil preserved.

AIKEN PEACE MOVEMENT
Aiken, South Carolina

We are a small ecumenical group that meets each Friday in a public park to pray for peace in a town that feels economically dependent on the nearby nuclear industry. We decided that those things most painful to think about being destroyed in a nuclear war would be the innocent and helpless — all our children and the animals of the world. By allowing this situation to develop, we adults are responsible for our fate.

SHARON KEECH
Chapel Hill, North Carolina
This Fragile Web

My fascination with the interaction of elements and the connectedness of life forms brings me to weaving and forms the basis of my Ribbon segment.
Photo: Laura Drey

138

MARGARET L.D. HATCH
Cornwall-on-Hudson, New York

CATHOLIC INFORMATION CENTER
Grand Rapids, Michigan

LIEVE SEEGER
Rochester, New York
Photo: Julie Gelfand

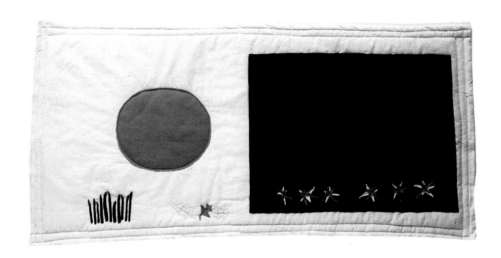

LINDA STENZEL
Las Cruces, New Mexico

PAULINE GRAY
Meridale, New York

JANICE MARDEN
East Rochester, New York

Since I was a small child, I have always had a dream of discovering the most perfect, peaceful and untouched spot on earth. When the pressures of work and school seem more than I can face, I often close my eyes and retreat to this perfect location I have created in my mind's eye. In the event of a nuclear war, I would no longer have the hope of seeing my dream in reality. My picture-perfect scene will be destroyed.
Photo: Julie Gelfand

KATHY YOUNG
Hartsdale, New York

I'm a Presbyterian minister and director of the Presbyterian Criminal Justice Program. The design on my banner is the War Resisters' League civil defense poster combined with the (I believe) Episcopal Peace Fellowship cross/peace symbol. One of my needlepoint pieces was the gift from my denomination to the Russian Orthodox Church's leader in Moscow, which gives me a personal feeling of connectedness with that place. So, taking part in The Ribbon seemed an appropriate continuation for me.

CENTER FOR JUSTICE
Buffalo, New York

We wanted to share our logo and motto with everyone who is celebrating life by participating in The Ribbon project. It is our belief that true and lasting peace will only come about—not through nuclear strength, not by subduing the enemy, not by securing our economic lifestyle—but when justice is a reality; when each person's basic human needs are met, when we live in unity and harmony with each other and with creation, as God intended us to do. It is our hope that "peace through justice" will become your motto, too, and a source of empowerment for you as it is for us. Photo: Ann Oestreich, S.S.J.

141

CHURCH WOMEN UNITED
Oklahoma

MARGE ENMAN
Manchester, New Hampshire

CHURCH WOMEN UNITED
Oklahoma

MONICA, ERICA, ALEX and DANA BICKFORD
Rochester, New Hampshire
Photo: Susan Bickford

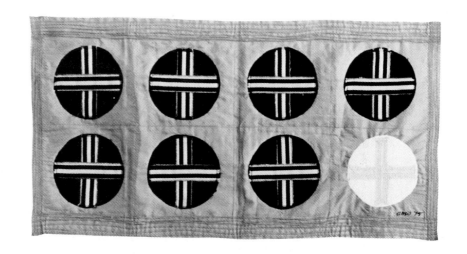

ANTOINETTE M. WINTERS
Concord, Massachusetts
Memento Mori

This design is based on a traditional quilt design, "Circles and Crosses." I was walking in a graveyard and was stricken by the number of young men who died in war. My own son was 2 at the time. I thought this definition of "Memento Mori" was appropriate: "A reminder of man's failures or mistakes."

VIRGINIA LAMING
Brewster, Massachusetts

The isms and ideologies of this world do not matter as much as the way people are treated—with respect and dignity. I am a 67-year-old widow who has lived in many countries and knows from experience that the average person in any place can be friendly and kind, and abhors hatred as much as I do.

143

MARCIA ELLEN WIENER
Port Jefferson, New York

4-H FRIENDS CLUB
Kearney, Nebraska
Photo: Sharee Kelly

ELIZABETH and C. LE ROY
DARLINGTON
South Orange, New Jersey

I am a former high school chemistry teacher, and I feel that the search for peace must be given the highest priority by mankind if the human race and all other forms of life are to survive. Twenty-five years ago, I picketed the Pentagon to protest nuclear testing in the atmosphere. I hope this demonstration will dramatize our yearning for peace.

TRICIA MULLEN
Seekonk, Massachusetts
Cherish

Nuclear war has been an intense fear of mine, especially since my two children were born. I created this felt ribbon with a drive that I've never had before. It became so important for me to be able to express what I really cherish most, my family and friends, fresh, plentiful food, water, and the beauty of God's earth and creatures.

MARILYN LARKIN
San Rafael, California
Marin Hills

I knew from the beginning that I wanted to participate in The Ribbon, and I chose the hills of Marin County, California, as my theme because it is my home, and to me it symbolizes the good earth that is home to all of us.
Guns, missiles, and bombers are tangible, and can be seen, touched, and heard. Thoughts of love and prayers for peace are not, but in The Ribbon they at least become visible.
Photo: David Hitt

KITTY BUZARD
Bowling Green, Ohio

145

ANN INGRAHAM
Eureka, California
Photo: David Hitt

SHIRLEY FREY McCONAHAY
Chapel Hill, North Carolina
Spring From Studio Window
Photo: Laura Drey

SHIRLEY BALDWIN WARING
Hanover, New Hampshire

I am 53, a Quaker, and a pacifist. I am married to Tom Waring, with whom I parent four Norton children and five Waring children, aged 18-35. Yuri is my grandchild; her parents are John Christopher Norton and Mie Kimura Norton of Japan. My shame at the Hiroshima and Nagasaki atomic bombings by my country has intensified beyond words because I now have Japanese family. Yuri is the bridge of healing, for me, between our two countries, which our governments declared enemies. She is also the bridge of love which connects the grandparents, 8,000 miles apart, who do not speak each others' languages, but who are bonded to each other through this beloved child of the two cultures.

146

THE WOMEN OF GRACE UNITED
METHODIST CHURCH
Wilmington, Delware
Photo: James B. Dunson, Jr.

CHURCH WOMEN UNITED
Nebraska City, Nebraska
Photo: Sharee Kelly

FRANCISCAN SISTERS
Rochester, Minnesota

Mt. Jabor ~ Portland ~ Oregon

ANNE L. COOK
Portland, Oregon
Photo: Rebecca Lowe-Warren

BARBARA A. LUX
Palo Alto, California

I chose the hummingbirds to represent all things on earth. The lives of these exquisite, fearless, industrious flying acrobats hang in the balance minute by minute. They expend so much energy beating their wings they must take in an extraordinary amount of food, feeding 50 or more times a day. This means that if they could not feed every 15 or 20 minutes they would perish. I believe all life on earth hangs in balance. We human beings have the ability to protect or destroy this fragile earth, depending on how we use its resources. Also I fear if we do not learn to live in peace with all peoples on earth, all could be lost in a nuclear war.

Sent from the Federal Republic of Germany

Solange die Erde steht, soll nicht aufhören Saat und Ernte, Frost und Hitze, Sommer und Winter, Tag und Nacht.

148

JUDY ROBBINS
Glastonbury, Connecticut
Chief Joseph

Chief Joseph was a Nez Perce Indian chief who led the remnants of his tribe on a harrowing trek toward freedom in Canada, as the whites took by force his beloved homeland, the Wallowa Valley, now Washington and Idaho. Thirty-five miles from the Canadian border, with the relentless, icy breath of winter harsh upon them, they made camp to allow their many sick and wounded to heal. They were discovered and attacked by the cavalry. Forced to surrender, Joseph made this eloquent speech:

> I am tired of fighting. Our chiefs are all killed . . . It is cold and we have no blankets. The little children are freezing to death. My people, some of them, have run away to the hills and have no blankets and no food. I want to have time to look for my children and see how many of them I can find. Maybe I shall find them among the dead. Hear me, my chiefs, my heart is sick and sad. From where the sun now stands, I shall fight no more forever.

Moved among prisons and reservations for years, Joseph was finally returned to the state of Washington to die. The white physician who filled out his death certificate listed the cause of death as a broken heart. This Ribbon segment is for Joseph.

The design is pieced of cotton fabrics in colors and motifs that echo Joseph's heritage. In the center of the pieced section, there is a turtle medallion that I beaded in the traditional manner. The turtle is a symbol of the homeland, the North American continent. This land, our "Turtle Island," is the mother of us all.

In addition to the beaded and pieced areas, I worked satin ribbons into the piece to connect it firmly to The Ribbon project. I also used the words of Joseph. After he had exhausted every possible means to achieve a large-scale peace and failed, he finally vowed at least to maintain his commitment to peace on a personal level. If many of us were to do the same, I believe that a profound shift in consciousness would occur. I believe that one of the functions of The Ribbon is to work toward this consciousness from the level of personal commitment.

FIRST PRESBYTERIAN
CHURCH WOMEN
Harrison, Arkansas
Photo: Offie Lites

WESTSIDE KINDERGARTEN
Morrilton, Arkansas
Photo: Offie Lites

**SECOND UNITARIAN
UNIVERSALIST CHURCH**
Chicago, Illinois

FRIENDS SCHOOL
Cambridge, Massachusetts

This was made by children in Lynette
Tarkington and Ann O'Halloran's Lower
School classroom (grades K - 2). The
children did free-form appliques based
on the theme, "What peace means to
me."
Photo: David Caras

PAMELA BEALS ROCHE
Yuma, Arizona

I am a single parent and use my sewing as
a private magical world to escape to when
the going gets rough. My sewing is a diary
of sorts, all my feelings about life are put
into my various projects. I learned about
The Ribbon while reading a craft
magazine. My banner shows the people of
the world. They are featureless, to
represent many people.
Thank you for helping me make a
pleasant memory.
Photo: Richard Maynard

151

MARIAN V. MEIER
Glen Ellyn, Illinois

While trying to determine what to show on my portion of The Ribbon, I decided it had to be unicorns and butterflies. In January, I was diagnosed as having a malignant tumor. I won't be able to be in Washington, but I hope to attend our state demonstration over Memorial Day weekend in Springfield. It will be a sad time, indeed, when there is no time for thinking of reality and fantasy.

MA—0233)

CONSTANCE LILLY
West Boxford, Massachusetts

The subject of my work is my son, Nathan. The love, innocence, and trust that I have seen in him the first two years of his life have moved me greatly. I have felt connected with the universe. I have seen the magic of human potential. And I have come to understand that someday he will ask me for the truth about nuclear destruction. I will answer him as a mother, an artist, a captain of my own conscience, a peacemaker. I will say, "If we work together, we can make a difference."

ALICE SIEGFRIED
Oneonta, New York

ESTHER LAVERNE
FERGUSON-USHER
Hobart, Indiana
Save the Animals

Most of the animals on this banner are
endangered species. The parrot and
penguin are there just because I like
them. I firmly believe that animals are
just as important in God's scheme of
things as people are. And they are worth
saving. The little verse at the top of the
banner is from an English hymn.
Photo: James J. Swain II

LOUISE VAHLE
St. Paul, Minnesota
Photo: Paul Brezny

CHURCH WOMEN UNITED
Newtown, Connecticut

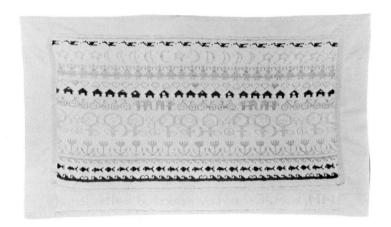

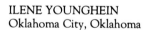

ILENE YOUNGHEIN
Oklahoma City, Oklahoma

I am a 63-year-old grandmother who
thinks there is no hope for the world
unless we stop the proliferation of
nuclear weapons. I have made 85
segments of the Peace Ribbon to date. It
may seem crazy, but not as crazy as
making five or six new atomic bombs a
day or spending 300 billon dollars a year
on defense — more than the world
spends yearly on food and twice that
spent on housing. I have become so
frustrated sending letters to legislators
and the President, that I have turned to
The Ribbon project as an outlet for my
frustration, and because I feel so strongly
for peace.
Photo: Gaylord Younghein

154

THE ONLY UNCONTROLLED GROWTH IS CALLED OBESITY, CANCER, OR OUR MILITARY COSTS

ILENE YOUNGHEIN
Oklahoma City, Oklahoma

are We Sheep Falling for Nat'l Insecurity, That's Not Cheap?

The seas and all therein   JBM '88

JULIA BOOTH MYERS
Walpole, Maine

My husband, Edward, and I have been
involved with the sea for 45 years,
earning our living from it and sailing the
Maine coast as often as time has allowed.
Photo: Art Davison

THE SHIGA FAMILY
Tokyo, Japan

SHIGA FAMILY

TOKYO, JAPAN

JEAN ANNE BAILEY
Beverly, Massachusetts

I began to sketch, searching for a universal symbol, but my doodles kept showing little sketches of cozy moments of the evenings with my husband and cats, of reading and drinking tea from a favorite cup. I realized that the feelings evoked by those moments were the universal statement I was looking for. Universal images of peace and love must be a part of every simple act and moment.

PRESCOTT PEACE NETWORK
Prescott, Arizona

We made our banner at a sewing bee. It shows Prescott's Thumb Butte. We feel it is essential to our survival that we learn to live in peace. We believe that peace is more than the absence of war and that personal and collective action brings change.

ST. SCHOLASTICA PRIORY
Duluth, Minnesota

Acknowledgements

As is always the case with projects of this magnitude, there are literally hundreds of people to thank, and unfortunately, never enough space to do so. Of all the volunteers who donated time to The Ribbon project, however, there are some who should be singled out.

Special thanks go first and foremost to members of the board of directors of The Ribbon: Alice Coleman; Jean Cronin, National Arts Coordinator; Janel Crumb, Colorado State Coordinator; Ramona Elizalde; Bette Ann Jaster, New York State Coordinator; Mary Frances Jaster, National Coordinator; Barbara Michelin, International Coordinator; Lucille Miller, Secretary; Justine Merritt, Founder; Mary Jo Peterson, Treasurer; David Steele; Diane Wilkinson; and Marie Grosso and Joan Urbancyzk from the Center for New Creation.

Working from the Center, Marie Grosso and Joan Urbancyzk took responsibility for organizing the August 4th event at the Pentagon. Their exhausting work ranged from obtaining permits to mapping out a route, to working on publicity with help from colleague Terrell Lamb.

Those who helped provide essential financial support included Jack Race, Mary Reyes, Bob and Sally Cory, Mary and Bob Inger, Archbishop James Casey of the Archdiocese of Northern Colorado, Church of the Brethren, whose support enabled The Peace Museum to produce The Ribbon poster; The Community Cash Flow, whose loan helped to cover the costs of producing Ribbon postcards; the H.C. Gemmer Foundation of Indianapolis, and The Pacific Peace Fund.

Very special help was provided by Janet and Walter Clark. Without their support, there would have been little business conducted on behalf of The Ribbon: the Ribbon office was located in their home.

Perhaps most importantly, special thanks are due to the resource people and state coordinators who made The Ribbon happen across the country. Resource people included Cookie Anderson, the Rev. Charlotte Asher, Marie Baker, Benedictines for Peace, Thomas Bringer, Margie Bronson, Dr. William Buffett, Kathleen Crowley, Barbara Culbertson, Suzanne Davenport, Margo Dodds, Dominican Sisters of the Sick Poor, Eileen Farley, Genesis Farm, Jean Goebel, Barbara Goodwin, Julie Hagood, Sr. Lori High, Dotty Hoppe, Kate Iverson, Fr. John Kiernan, Adele Kushner, Patricia Manion, Gail Merritt, Mary Milne, Sr. Madeleine Perkins, Joan Pope, Sr. Agnes Prendergast, Mary Reyes, Rae Ann Uttermohlen, and Lillian Valencia.

Special thanks to the state coordinators, who devoted thousands of hours to organizing for The Ribbon. They are: Nancy Whitt, Alabama; Judith Haggar, Alaska; Florence Speight, Arizona; Liz Workman, Arkansas; Audrey Keller, California; Sr. Janel Crumb, Colorado; Katherine Rees Hosen, Connecticut; Adele Majka, Delaware; Jennifer Weiss, District of Columbia; Bruce Gagnon, Florida; Bettie J. Durrah, Georgia; Tara Hands, Hawaii; Christians Praying for Peace, and Tom and Jean Richtsmeier, Idaho; Ellen Livingston and Sheryllee Lowe, Illinois; Sr. Karen Durliat, Indiana; Emma Lou Heusinkveld and Miriam Cline, Iowa; Opal May Evans, Kansas; The Kentucky Ribbon Committee and Jennifer Miller, Kentucky; Sandra Thornburg and Dusky Loebel, Louisiana; Sue Calhoun, Maine; Lani Irwin, Maryland; Janet Irons and Abigail Jones, Massachusetts; Judy Loveland and Elaine Morse, Michigan; Gail Irish, Minnesota; Diane Newman, Mississippi; Carol Griesemer, Missouri; Jim Rohrrsen, Montana; Sharee Kelly, Nebraska; The Franciscan Center, Nevada; Jeannine Hasenfuss, New Hampshire; Marie Varley, New Jersey; Sr. Rosella Hehn and Mrs. Ben Sanchez, New Mexico; Bette Ann Jaster, New York; Lori Eichel, North Carolina; Sharon Rezac-Andersen, North Dakota; Mollie Heron and Vivian Kline, Ohio; Lillian Pawlik, O.S.B., Oklahoma; Sharie Rody, Oregon; Joan Pope, Pennsylvania; Diane Ellis, Rhode Island; Mary deGrys, South Carolina; Rose Christensen, South Dakota; Margaret Gregg and Louise Morris, Tennessee; Anita Freeman Davidson, Texas; Susan Lilienthal, Vermont; Judith Whitehead, Utah; Cathy Rowan and community, Virginia; Arline Faruolo, Washington; Denise Stephenson, West Virginia; Gloria Welniak, Wisconsin; Dolly Lewis, Wyoming; Louise Chisholm, eastern Canada; Carol Gaskin, western Canada.

Also of invaluable service were those volunteers who were able to lend technical and professional skills. Legal advice came from Kathy Zelko and Eric Katz; Ron Ludwig volunteered accounting services; and photographers Bernie Mantey and Pat Foster helped to document The Ribbon as it grew and evolved.

Helping to focus national attention on The Ribbon was The Peace Museum, which presented the first major exhibition on the project, and The Chapin Foundation, which helped to bring that exhibit from Chicago to New York.

Others who contributed to the success of The Ribbon included Church Women United, who lent their support from the very beginning; Gabriella Miller and Carol Cockrell who polled participants and did a study of the project; Duane Gall who lent the use of his computer; Pat Hutchinson and Ruth Robinson, the first treasurer and secretary; the Sisters of Loretta who helped distribute hundreds of fliers, Robert and Betsy Tournier, who helped arrange housing for Justine Merritt; Barbara Britten, June and Bill Thompson, Mari Kitabatake, the Japanese coordinator; Andrea Wisneski, Robbie Fanning, the Senior Residents at Tamai Towers in Denver, and the Youth of St. Rose of Lima Church in Denver.

Producing *The Ribbon: A Celebration of Life* in time for the August 4th event at the Pentagon was a task that required long hours and incredible dedication on the part of many people. On behalf of The Ribbon Project, I'd like to extend a very special thank-you to Lark Books staff members Rob Pulleyn, Carol Parks, Nancy Orban, Steve Millard, Dennis Swinehart, and Sandra Soto; and to writer Don Willcox. It was because of their collective vision, drive, commitment and creativity that the book you see was published. Not unlike The Ribbon itself, producing the book was very much a group effort.

Special thanks are also due to Jean Cronin and Mary Frances Jaster, who were spectacularly helpful to us as we prepared this book, suggesting possibilities, supplying information and gathering materials; and of course, to Justine Merritt, whose inspiration kept us all going, and will undoubtedly continue to do so long after August 4th. We are grateful to have had the opportunity to be a part of The Ribbon.

Marianne Philbin

Students and residents of Oneonta, New York, parade their Ribbon segment for a Hiroshima Day Remembrance during the summer of 1984.

Credits

The Ribbon: A Celebration of Life is the product of many talents and a great deal of spirited cooperation among members of the Lark Books staff. Nancy Orban kept the entire organization flowing, loose ends from fraying, and spirits from sagging. Carol Parks oversaw the editing, writing, and promotion. Rob Pulleyn took command of the worrying and worked on production. Steve Millard designed the book and masterminded its production. Dennis Swinehart dealt with schedules, budgets, and falling debris. Sandra Soto set the type, and John Graeter paid the bills. Jill Casey took in the orders, Joan Kosugi kept the computer humming, and Fleta Monaghan and Jeff Britton used their brains and brawn to ship the orders out. Pat Wald functioned as "command central," and Kate Pulleyn lent her sharp proofreader's eye.

Others who worked their magic under our tight deadlines include Capitol Engraving, which did the color separations; Paul Brezny, who photographed many of the banners; Ralph Burns and Brigid Burns, who made the black and white transfers; Cornerstone Printers and Daniels Graphics, which helped in their usual, wonderful ways; and our good printer, Byrd Press, which put all the elements together.

This book couldn't have happened had it not been for the gifts of three people. Don Willcox brought his intelligence, enthusiasm, criticism — and the original idea. Marianne Philbin provided knowledge, wisdom, creativity, and laughter to every aspect of the book. Justine Merritt supplied the silent guidance and set the example for us all.

Lark Books wishes to thank all of you who submitted banners and photographs for this book. We wish we could have included every one of them. We have taken every care to ensure that the information presented here is accurate and that proper credit is given for photographs. If we have inadvertently neglected to credit a photographer, or have misspelled the name of a town, we hope you will extend us your forgiveness.

the Lark Books staff

Banners are paraded in front of the Federal Building in Evansville, Indiana. Photo: Kevin Swank, *Evansville Courier*

CONTEMPORARY NURSING

Issues, Trends, & Management

CONTEMPORARY NURSING

Issues, Trends, & Management

Barbara Cherry, DNSc, MBA, RN, NEA-BC
Professor, Associate Dean and Department Chair for Leadership Studies
Texas Tech University Health Sciences Center
School of Nursing
Lubbock, Texas

Susan R. Jacob, PhD, MSN, RN
Professor and Interim Associate Dean of Academic Affairs
The University of Tennessee Health Science Center
College of Nursing; Education Consultant, Faith Community Nursing
Church Health Center
Memphis, Tennessee

7th EDITION

ELSEVIER

ELSEVIER

3251 Riverport Lane
St. Louis, Missouri 63043

CONTEMPORARY NURSING: ISSUES, TRENDS, & MANAGEMENT, ed 7   ISBN: 978-0-323-39022-4

Notices

Knowledge and best practice in this field are constantly changing. As new research and experience broaden our understanding, changes in research methods, professional practices, or medical treatment may become necessary.

Practitioners and researchers must always rely on their own experience and knowledge in evaluating and using any information, methods, compounds, or experiments described herein. In using such information or methods they should be mindful of their own safety and the safety of others, including parties for whom they have a professional responsibility.

With respect to any drug or pharmaceutical products identified, readers are advised to check the most current information provided (i) on procedures featured or (ii) by the manufacturer of each product to be administered, to verify the recommended dose or formula, the method and duration of administration, and contraindications. It is the responsibility of practitioners, relying on their own experience and knowledge of their patients, to make diagnoses, to determine dosages and the best treatment for each individual patient, and to take all appropriate safety precautions.

To the fullest extent of the law, neither the Publisher nor the authors, contributors, or editors assume any liability for any injury and/or damage to persons or property as a matter of products liability, negligence or otherwise, or from any use or operation of any methods, products, instructions, or ideas contained in the material herein.

Library of Congress Cataloging-in-Publication Data
Contemporary nursing: issues, trends, & management/[edited by] Barbara Cherry, Susan R. Jacob. — Ed. 7.
   p.; cm.
   Includes bibliographical references and index.
   ISBN 978-0-323-39022-4 (pbk.: alk. paper)
   I. Cherry, Barbara, MSN. II. Jacob, Susan R.
   [DNLM: 1. Nursing—United States. 2. Nursing Care—United States. WY 100 AA1]
   610.73—dc23
                                                                                          2012037205

Senior Content Strategist: Sandy Clark
Content Development Manager: Laurie Gower
Senior Content Development Specialist: Lisa P. Newton
Publishing Services Manager: Jeff Patterson
Project Manager: Anne Konopka
Senior Design Direction: Ryan Cook

Printed in China

Last digit is the print number: 9   8   7   6   5   4   3   2   1

Working together
to grow libraries in
developing countries

www.elsevier.com • www.bookaid.org

*To all the student nurses whose curiosity and enthusiasm for nursing
will provide strong leadership for the profession far into the future
and to all practicing nurses who face serious challenges but reap
great rewards for providing high-quality health care for
individuals, families, and communities.*

Being a Nurse Means . . .

You will never be bored,
You will always be frustrated,
You will be surrounded by challenges,
So much to do and so little time.
You will carry immense responsibility
And very little authority.
You will step into people's lives,
And you will make a difference.
Some will bless you.
Some will curse you.
You will see people at their worst,
And at their best.
You will never cease to be amazed at people's capacity
For love, courage, and endurance.
You will see life begin
and end.
You will experience resounding triumphs
And devastating failures.
You will cry a lot.
You will laugh a lot.
You will know what it is to be human
And to be humane.

Melodie Chenevert, RN

CONTRIBUTORS

Jeri Ashley, MSN, RN, AOCNS, CHPN
System Director, Life Planning/Palliative
    Medicine Services
Baptist Trinity Home Care and Hospice
Memphis, Tennessee

Mary Jo Assi, DNP, RN, NEA-BC, FNP-BC
Director, Nursing Practice and Work Environment
American Nurses Association
Silver Spring, Maryland

**L. Antoinette (Toni) Bargagliotti, PhD, RN, ANEF,
    FAAN**
Professor, Loewenberg School of Nursing
The University of Memphis
Memphis, Tennessee

Virginia Trotter Betts, MSN, JD, RN, FAAN
President and CEO
HealthFutures, Inc.
Nashville, Tennessee

Barbara Cherry, DNSc, MBA, RN, NEA-BC
Professor, Associate Dean and Department Chair for
    Leadership Studies
Texas Tech University Health Sciences Center, School
    of Nursing
Lubbock, Texas

**Genevieve J. Conlin, DNP, MEd, MS/MBA,
    RN, NEA-BC**
Director of Nursing
Spaulding Rehabilitation Hospital
Boston, Massachusetts

Charlotte Eliopoulos, PhD, RN, MPH, ND
Executive Director
American Association for Long Term Care Nursing
Glen Arm, Maryland

Debra D. Hatmaker, PhD, RN, FAAN
Executive Director
American Nurses Association
Silver Spring, Maryland

Susan R. Jacob, PhD, MSN, RN
Professor and Interim Associate Dean of Academic
    Affairs
The University of Tennessee Health Science Center,
    College of Nursing
Education Consultant
Faith Community Nursing, Church Health Center
Memphis, Tennessee

Patricia R. Keene, DNP, ACNP-BC, ACHPN
Professor of Nursing
Union University
Germantown, Tennessee

Rebecca R. Keck, DNP, RN, NEA-BC
Senior Associate Dean for Administration
    & Operations; Chief Administrative Officer
Assistant Professor of Nursing
Vanderbilt University School of Nursing
Nashville, Tennessee

Marylane Wade Koch, MSN, RN
Adjunct Faculty, School of Nursing
Austin Peay State University
Clarksville, Tennessee

Robert W. Koch, DNS, RN
Director of Professional Development
West Cancer Center
Memphis, Tennessee

Laura R. Mahlmeister, PhD, MSN, RN
Clinical Professor of Nursing
University of California
San Francisco, California
President, Mahlmeister & Associates
Belmont, California

Rosemary A. McLaughlin, PhD, CNE, RN-NIC
Professor of Nursing
Union University
Jackson, Tennessee

Tommie L. Norris, DNS, RN
Professor & Associate Dean of Evaluation
   and Effectiveness
The University of Tennessee Health Science Center
   College of Nursing
Memphis, Tennessee

Cheryl Peterson, MSN, RN
Senior Director for Nursing Programs
American Nurses Association
Silver Spring, Maryland

Patricia Reid Ponte, DNSc, RN, FAAN, NEA-BC
Senior Vice President for Patient Care Services
Chief of Nursing, Dana-Farber Cancer Institute
Executive Director, Oncology Nursing & Clinical Services
Brigham and Women's Hospital
Boston, Massachusetts

Anna Marie Sallee, PhD, MSN, RN
Adjunct Faculty
Alvin Community College,
Alvin, Texas
Staff Nurse and Educator, Houston Hospice
Houston, Texas

Zoila V. Sanchez, PhD, FNP
Professor of Nursing
Union University
Jackson, Tennessee

Carla D. Sanderson, PhD, RN
Vice President, Institutional Effectiveness and
   Professional Regulation
Chamberlain College of Nursing
Downers Grove, Illinois

Teresa Maggard Stephens, PhD, RN
Clinical Assistant Professor
The University of Tennessee College of Nursing, Knoxville;
   Nursing Research Coordinator
The University of Tennessee Medical Center
Knoxville, TN

Margaret Elizabeth Strong, DNP, RN, NE-BC
Associate Professor, Division of Nursing
Baptist College of Health Sciences
Memphis, Tennessee

Dawn Vanderhoef, PhD, DNP, RN, PMHNP/CS-BC
Assistant Professor and PMHNP Program Director
School of Nursing, Vanderbilt University
Nashville, Tennessee

Elizabeth E. Weiner, PhD, RN-BC, FACMI, FAAN
Senior Associate Dean for Informatics
Centennial Independence Foundation Professor of
   Nursing
Professor of Biomedical Informatics
School of Nursing, Vanderbilt University
Nashville, Tennessee

Kathleen M. Werner, MS, BSN, RN
Director, Performance Improvement
Meriter-UnityPoint Health
Madison, Wisconsin

Tami H. Wyatt, PhD, RN, CNE, ANEF, FAAN
Associate Professor
Chair, Educational Technology & Simulation
Co-Director, Health Information Technology &
   Simulation Center
University of Tennessee, Knoxville, School of Nursing
Knoxville, Tennessee

Carla Mueller, PhD, RN
Professor
Department of Nursing
University of Saint Francis
Fort Wayne, Indiana

Patricia Taylor, RN, MSN-ED
Assistant Professor of Nursing
Kapi'olani Community College
University of Hawaii
Honolulu, Hawaii

At no other time in the history of modern nursing have nurses been presented with such tremendous opportunities to improve health care and advance the nursing profession. By understanding and providing leadership to address the serious issues currently facing the U.S. health care system, nurses can advance health care delivery to promote the health and well-being of each individual in our society. These important issues include patient safety and quality care, health care reform and the uninsured population, nursing workforce challenges, advancing technology, changing legal and ethical concerns, care at the end of life, evolving nursing education trends, rising health care costs, and working within a multicultural society.

WHO WILL BENEFIT FROM THIS BOOK?

The seventh edition of *Contemporary Nursing: Issues, Trends, & Management* is an excellent resource to help nursing students and practicing nurses understand the complex issues facing today's health care systems and implement strategies from the direct patient care level to the national legislative arena that can significantly improve patient care, the health care system, and the nursing profession.

ORGANIZATION

Unit 1: The Development of Nursing

The book opens with a presentation about the exciting evolution of nursing, its very visible public image, and its core foundations, which include nursing education, licensure and certification, nursing theory, and nursing research and evidence-based practice. These opening chapters provide the reader with a solid background for understanding and studying current and future trends.

Unit 2: Current Issues in Health Care

This unit provides a comprehensive overview of the most current trends and issues occurring today in nursing and health care, including health care financing and economics, legal and ethical issues, cultural and social issues, complementary and alternative healing, workplace issues and nursing workforce challenges, collective bargaining

and unions, technology in the clinical setting, end-of-life care, and emergency preparedness. Students, faculty, and seasoned nurses will be challenged to critically examine each of these significant issues that are shaping the practice of professional nursing and the health care delivery system.

Unit 3: Leadership and Management in Nursing

This unit offers a foundation of knowledge in nursing leadership and management, with a focus on the basic skills that are necessary for all nurses, regardless of the setting or position in which they work, to function effectively in the professional nursing role. Chapters examine leadership and management theory and roles, budgeting basics, effective communication, delegation and supervision, staffing and nursing care delivery models, quality improvement and patient safety, and health policy and politics. The updated content in this unit provides the most current information available related to nursing leadership and management and will serve as both a valuable educational tool for students and a useful resource for practicing nurses.

Unit 4: Career Management

The final unit prepares the student to embark on a career in nursing. Making the transition from student to professional, managing time, understanding career opportunities, finding a good match between the nurse and the employer, and passing the NCLEX-RN® examination are all presented with practical, useful advice that will serve as an excellent resource for both students and novice nurses as they build their careers in professional nursing.

LEARNING AIDS

Each chapter in the seventh edition contains the same features that made the previous editions so successful:
- Real-life **Vignettes** and **Questions to Consider** at the beginning of each chapter, which pique the reader's interest in the chapter content and stimulate critical thinking
- **Key Terms** that contain clear and concise definitions of terms that are critical to enhance readers' understanding of the topics and expand their vocabulary related to health care issues

- Integrated **Learning Outcomes** that provide instructors and students with a clear understanding of what behaviors can be expected after a study of the chapter is completed
- **Chapter Overview,** which is an overall perspective and guide to the chapter content
- **Case Studies,** included as appropriate, that apply theory to clinical practice
- **Summary** at the end of each chapter that provides a wrap-up and helps students focus on points to remember
- **References** related to chapter content that help students explore further the issues that were covered

NEW TO THIS EDITION

- Every chapter in the seventh edition has been updated to include the most current and relevant information available. New to this edition is a **Professional/Ethical Issue** in every chapter. These dilemmas present interesting, real-life cases that will test the reader's ability to think critically and apply ethical and professional standards to address issues or concerns the reader will face in his or her nursing practice.

  Additionally, other new and expanded content in this edition includes the following:
- A new chapter on palliative care, one of the newest subspecialties. This chapter describes the benefits, barriers, and challenges of palliative care as well as the role of the palliative care nurse in providing care to patients who are facing serious illness.
- Expanded information on health care reform and the Patient Protection and Affordable Care Act of 2010
- The nursing workforce supply, changing demands, and new employment opportunities for nurses
- Technological advancements and their impact on health care and nursing practice
- Meaningful use criteria for electronic health records
- Implications for nursing practice from the following major reports:
  - *The Future of Nursing: Leading Change, Advancing Health* released by the Institute of Medicine and the Robert Wood Johnson Foundation
  - *LACE (Licensure, Accreditation, Certification, and Education) Consensus Model* for advanced practice registered nurse (APRN) regulation published by the American Association of Colleges of Nursing

  - *Crisis Standards of Care: A Systems Framework for Catastrophic Disaster Response* released by the Institute of Medicine
  - *A Nurse's Guide to the Use of Social Media* released by the National Council of State Boards of Nursing
- The most current legal issues facing nurses
- Technological trends in nursing education, such as e-learning, iPads, and digital messaging

TEACHING AND LEARNING RESOURCES

For Instructors

Instructor Resources on Evolve, available at http://evolve.elsevier.com/Cherry/, provide a wealth of material to help you make your nursing instruction a success. In addition to all of the Student Resources, the following are provided for Faculty:

- **TEACH for Nurses Lesson Plans**, based on textbook chapter Learning Outcomes, serve as ready-made, modifiable lesson plans and a complete roadmap to link all parts of the educational package. These concise and straightforward lesson plans can be modified or combined to meet your particular scheduling and teaching needs.
- **PowerPoint Presentations** are organized by chapter, with more than 1000 slides for in-class lectures. These are detailed and include customizable text and image lecture slides to enhance learning in the classroom or in Web-based course modules. If you share them with students, they can use the note feature to help them with your lectures.
- The **Test Bank** has more than 500 test items, complete with the correct answer, rationale, cognitive level of each question, corresponding step of the nursing process, appropriate NCLEX format, and text page reference(s).
- **Image Collection** includes all the images from the book.

For Students

Student Resources on Evolve, available at http://evolve.elsevier.com/Cherry/, provide a wealth of valuable learning resources. The Evolve Resources page near the front of the book gives login instructions and a description of each resource.

- **Resumé Builder** offers templates and samples of resumés and cover letters.
- **Student Case Studies** provide detailed case studies covering the major content in the chapters.
- **Student Review Questions** assist in preparing for the NCLEX® examination.

Barbara Cherry, DNSc, MBA, RN, NEA-BC, received her diploma in nursing from Methodist Hospital School of Nursing, her BSN from West Texas A&M University, her MBA from Texas Tech University, her MSN from Texas Tech University Health Sciences Center, and her Doctor of Nursing Science from the University of Tennessee Health Science Center. Dr. Cherry's clinical background is in critical care, medical-surgical, and nephrology nursing. Her research is focused on the long-term care nursing workforce and technology. She has more than 25 years of clinical and nursing leadership experience followed by 15 years as a nurse educator and academic administrator. She is currently Professor, Associate Dean and Department Chair for Leadership Studies at Texas Tech University Health Sciences Center School of Nursing in Lubbock, Texas.

Susan R. Jacob, PhD, MSN, RN, received her BSN from West Virginia University, her MSN from San Jose State University, and her PhD from the University of Tennessee, Memphis. Her extensive experience as a clinician, educator, and researcher has been focused in the community health arena, specifically home health and hospice. She has been an educator for more than 30 years and has taught at both the undergraduate and graduate levels. Dr. Jacob's research has addressed the bereavement experience of older adults and enhanced models of home health care delivery. Dr. Jacob, Professor and Interim Associate Dean of Academic Affairs in the College of Nursing at the University of Tennessee, Health Science Center, Memphis, Tennessee, serves as an educational consultant for faith community nursing and schools of nursing preparing for accreditation.

ACKNOWLEDGMENTS

Our contributors deserve our most sincere thanks for their high-quality, timely work that demonstrates genuine expertise and professionalism. Their contributions have made this book a truly first-rate text that will be invaluable to nursing students and faculty and will serve as an outstanding resource for practicing nurses. We extend a special thanks to our reviewers, who gave us helpful suggestions and insights as we developed the seventh edition.

We would like to express our grateful appreciation to the Elsevier staff—Sandra Clark, Senior Content Strategist; Lisa Newton, Senior Content Development Specialist; and Anne Konopka, Project Manager—for their very capable and professional support, guidance, and calm reassurance.

Our deepest appreciation goes to the most important people in our lives—our husbands, Mike and Dick, our families, and our friends. Their enduring support and extreme patience have allowed us to accomplish what sometimes seemed to be the impossible.

TABLE OF CONTENTS

UNIT 4: Career Management

1

*Building on a strong foundation for a bright
future.*

The Evolution of Professional Nursing

Susan R. Jacob, PhD, MSN, RN

ⓔ Additional resources are available online at: *http://evolve.elsevier.com/Cherry/*

PROFESSIONAL/ETHICAL ISSUE

Gretchen Ornish graduated from nursing school last year and became active in the local Nurses Association. She volunteered for the program planning committee because her friend, Beth Aaron, was also on the committee. The committee decided to plan a program for *Nurses Week* that would highlight pioneers in nursing. Beth agreed to pull a list of famous nurses together for the committee. When the committee met to start planning the program Beth presented her list that included Florence Nightingale, Clara Barton, Dorothea Dix, Lillian Wald, Mary Breckenridge, and many others. When Gretchen realized that all of the nurses on Beth's list were white, she suggested that Beth add additional names of nurses such as Mary Seacole, Harriet Tubman, Sojourner Truth, Mary Mahoney, Beverly Malone, and Elizabeth Carnegie. Beth was very reluctant to add other nurses to the list she had already developed, saying that there would not be enough time to feature more nurses than she already had on the list.

She also stated that the names she had already come up with were widely known, and in her opinion the most significant. Gretchen was very disappointed because she remembered so many black nurses of distinction and felt that they should be honored as well. She feared that the program planning committee would be criticized for overlooking some very important black nursing leaders. Gretchen did not want to be part of providing what might be considered a biased program. She voiced her concerns to Beth and the committee, stating that she felt that it would be so much better if a more diverse group of nursing pioneers was highlighted. In spite of Gretchen's concerns Beth convinced the committee to proceed with planning the program to include the list of nursing pioneers she presented.

What are some strategies that Gretchen might use to persuade Beth and the committee to present a more diverse group of nursing pioneers at the Nurses Week program?

1

VIGNETTE

My mother and grandmother who are both nurses were very excited when I decided to pursue nursing as a career. They love to talk about their experiences in nursing school in the 70s and 90s. They shared with me what they were taught about Florence Nightingale and Mary Seacole, trailblazers who began the work of organized nursing. My class on the evolution of nursing covers much of the same history that my mother and grandmother were taught in their nursing programs. However, since the time when they received their education, nursing has evolved into a profession that is focused on meeting the complex needs of the diverse people it serves and preparing providers who can think critically to meet those needs. Nursing education today involves interprofessional experiences and the use of technologies such as vSim and Shadow Health that was *unheard of in their day. Although my grandmother, mother, and I have a lot in common when it comes to our desire to help individuals achieve optimal health outcomes, our nursing education and career opportunities are vastly different.*

Questions to Consider While Reading This Chapter:
1. What were the challenges faced by nurses historically?
2. How has access to care and managed care affected professional nursing practice?
3. What are the challenges facing nurses in the twenty-first century?
4. What areas of nursing specialization enhance patient care?

KEY TERMS

Florence Nightingale (1820 to 1910): Considered the founder of organized, professional nursing. She is best known for her contributions to the reforms in the British Army Medical Corps, improved sanitation in India, improved public health in Great Britain, use of statistics to document health outcomes, and the development of organized training for nurses.

Professional nurse: A specially trained *professional* that addresses the humanistic and holistic needs of patients, families, and environments and provides responses to patterns and/or needs of patients, families, and communities to actual and potential health problems. The professional nurse has diverse roles, such as health care provider, client advocate, educator, care coordinator, primary care practitioner, and change agent (Katz et al, 2009).

LEARNING OUTCOMES

After studying this chapter, the reader will be able to:
1. Summarize health practices throughout the course of history.
2. Analyze the effect of historic, political, social, and economic events on the development of nursing.
3. Describe the evolution of professional challenges experienced by nurses of diverse ethnic, racial, and educational backgrounds.

CHAPTER OVERVIEW

Throughout the pages of recorded history, nursing has been integrated into every facet of life. A legacy of human caring was initiated when, according to the book of Exodus, two midwives, Shiphrah and Puah, rescued the baby Moses and hid him to save his life. This legacy of caring has progressed *throughout the years, responding to psychological, social, environmental, and physiologic needs of society. Nurses of the past and present have struggled for recognition as knowledgeable professionals. The evolution of this struggle is reflected in political, cultural, environmental, and*

We thank Shiphrah A. Williams-Evans, PhD, APRN, BC, for her contribution to this chapter in the 4th edition.

economic events that have sculpted our nation and world history (Catalano, 2012).

Traditionally, society recognized men as healers. Women challenged the status quo and transformed nursing from a mystical phenomenon to a respected profession (Catalano, 2012). Florence Nightingale and Mary Seacole played major roles in bringing about changes in nursing. Using the concept of role modeling, these women demonstrated the value of their worth through their work in fighting for the cause of health and healing. During the twentieth century, nurses made tremendous advancements in the areas of education, practice, research, and technology. Nursing as a science progressed through education, clinical practice, development of theory, and rigorous research. Today nurses continue to be challenged to expand their roles and explore new areas of practice and leadership. This chapter provides a brief glimpse of health care practices and nursing care in the prehistoric period and early civilization and then describes the evolution of professional nursing practice. Box 1-1 summarizes some of the important events in the evolution of nursing.

PREHISTORIC PERIOD

Nursing in the prehistoric period was delineated by health practices that were strongly guided by beliefs of magic, religion, and superstition. Individuals who were ill were considered to be cursed by evil spirits and evil gods that entered the human body and caused suffering and death if not cast out. These beliefs dictated the behavior of primitive people, who sought to scare away the evil gods and spirits. Members of tribes participated in rituals, wore masks, and engaged in demonstrative dances to rid the sick of demonic possession of the body. Sacrifices and offerings, sometimes including human sacrifices, were made to rid the body of evil gods, demons, and spirits. Many tribes used special herbs, roots, and vegetables to cast out the "curse" of illness.

EARLY CIVILIZATION

Egypt

Ancient Egyptians are noted for their accomplishments in health care at an early period in civilization. They were the first to use the concept of suture in repairing wounds. They also were the first to be recorded as developing community planning that resulted in a decrease in public health problems. One of the main early public health problems was the spread of disease through contaminated water sources. Specific laws on cleanliness, food use and preservation, drinking, exercise, and sexual relations were developed. Health beliefs of Egyptians determined preventive measures taken and personal health behaviors practiced. These health behaviors were usually carried out to accommodate the gods. Some behaviors were also practiced expressly to appease the spirits of the dead (Catalano, 2012). The Egyptians developed the calendar and writing, which initiated recorded history. The oldest records date back to the sixteenth century BC in Egypt. A pharmacopoeia that classified more than 700 drugs was written to assist in the care and management of disease (Ellis and Hartley, 2012). As in the case of Shiphrah and Puah, the midwives who saved the baby Moses, nurses were used by kings and other aristocrats to deliver babies and care for the young, older adults, and those who were sick.

Palestine

From 1400 to 1200 BC, the Hebrews migrated from the Arabian Desert and gradually settled in Palestine, where they became an agricultural society. Under the leadership of Moses, the Hebrews developed a system of laws called the Mosaic Code. This code, one of the first organized methods of disease control and prevention, contained public health laws that dictated personal, family, and public hygiene. For instance, laws were written to prohibit the eating of animals that were dead longer than 3 days and to isolate individuals who were thought to have communicable diseases. Hebrew priests took on the role of health inspectors (Ellis and Hartley, 2012).

Greece

From 1500 to 100 BC, Greek philosophers sought to understand man and his relationship with the gods, nature, and other men. They believed that the gods and goddesses of Greek mythology controlled health and illness. Temples built to honor Aesculapius, the god of medicine, were designated to care for the sick. Aesculapius carried a staff that was intertwined with serpents or snakes, representing wisdom and immortality. This staff is thought to be the model of today's medical caduceus.

BOX 1-1   Important Events in the Evolution of Nursing

1751—The Pennsylvania Hospital is the first hospital established in America.

1798—The U.S. Marine Hospital Service comes into being by an act of Congress on July 16. It is renamed the U.S. Public Health Service in 1912.

1840—Two black women, Mary Williams and Frances Rose, who founded Nursing Sisters of the Holy Cross, are listed as nurses in the *City of Baltimore Directory.*

1851—Florence Nightingale (1820-1910) attends Kaiserswerth to train as a nurse.

1854—During the Crimean War, Florence Nightingale transforms the image of nursing. Mary Seacole, a black woman from Jamaica, West Indies, nurses during the same time.

1861—The outbreak of the Civil War causes black women to volunteer as nurses. Among these women are Harriet Tubman, Sojourner Truth, and Susie King Taylor.

1872—Another school of nursing opens in the United States: the New England Hospital for Women and Children in Boston, Massachusetts.

1873—Linda Richards is responsible for designing a written patient record and physician's order system—the first in a hospital.

1879—Mary Mahoney, the first trained black nurse, graduates from the New England Hospital for Women and Children in Boston, Massachusetts.

1881—The American Red Cross is established by Clara Barton.

1886—The Visiting Nurse Association (VNA) is started in Philadelphia; Spelman College, Atlanta, Georgia, establishes the first diploma-granting nursing program for African Americans.

1893—Lillian Wald and Mary Brewster establish the Henry Street Visiting Nurse Service in New York.

1896—The Nurses' Associated Alumnae of the United States and Canada is established.

1898—Namahyoke Curtis, an untrained black nurse, is assigned by the War Department as a contract nurse in the Spanish-American War.

1899—The International Council of Nurses (ICN) is founded.

1900—The first issue of the *American Journal of Nursing* is published.

1901—The Army Nurse Corps is established under the Army Reorganization Act.

1902—School of nursing is established in New York City by Linda Rogers.

1903—The first nurse practice acts are passed, and North Carolina is the first state to implement registration of nurses.

1908—The National Association of Colored Graduate Nurses is founded; it is dissolved in 1951.

1909—Ludie Andrews sues the Georgia State Board of Nurse Examiners to secure black nurses the right to take the state board examination and become licensed; she wins in 1920.

1911—The American Nurses Association (ANA) is established.

1912—The U.S. Public Health Service and the National League for Nursing (NLN) are established.

1918—Eighteen black nurses are admitted to the Army Nurse Corps after the armistice is signed ending World War I.

1919—*Public Health Nursing* is written by Mary S. Gardner. A public health nursing program is started at the University of Michigan.

1921—The Sheppard-Towner Act is passed providing federal aid for maternal and child health care.

1922—Sigma Theta Tau is founded (becomes the International Honor Society of Nursing in 1985).

1923—The Goldmark Report criticizes the inadequacies of hospital-based nursing schools and recommends increased educational standards.

1924—The U.S. Indian Bureau Nursing Service is founded by Elinor Gregg.

1925—The Frontier Nursing Service is founded by Mary Breckenridge.

1935—The Social Security Act is passed.

1937—Federal appropriations for cancer, venereal diseases, tuberculosis, and mental health begin.

1939—World War II begins.

1941—The U.S. Army establishes a quota of 56 black nurses for admission to the Army Nurse Corps. The Nurse Training Act is passed.

1943—An amendment to the Nurse Training bill is passed that bars racial bias.

1945—The U.S. Navy drops the color bar and admits four black nurses.

1946—Nurses are classified as professionals by the U.S. Civil Service Commission. The Hospital Survey and Construction Act (Hill-Burton) is passed.

1948—The Brown Report discusses the future of nursing.

1948—Estelle Osborne is the first black nurse elected to the board of the ANA. The ANA votes individual membership to all black nurses excluded from any state association.

1949—M. Elizabeth Carnegie is the first black nurse to be elected to the board of a state association (Florida).

1950—The Code for Professional Nurses is published by the ANA.

BOX 1-1   Important Events in the Evolution of Nursing—Cont'd

1952—National nursing organizations are reorganized from six to two: ANA and NLN.

1954—The Supreme Court decision *Brown v. Board of Education* asserts that "separate educational facilities are inherently unequal."

1965—The Social Security Amendment includes Medicare and Medicaid.

1971—The National Black Nurses Association is organized.

1973—The ANA forms the American Academy of Nursing.

1974—The American Assembly of Men in Nursing is founded.

1978—Barbara Nichols is the first black nurse elected president of the ANA. M. Elizabeth Carnegie, a black nurse, is elected president of the American Academy of Nursing.

1979—Brigadier General Hazel Johnson Brown is the first black chief of the Army Nurse Corps.

1983—The American Academy of Nursing (AAN) Task Force on Nursing Practice in Hospitals identifies work environment characteristics known to this day as the "Forces of Magnetism."

1985—Vernice Ferguson, an black nurse, is elected president of Sigma Theta Tau International.

1986—The Association of Black Nursing Faculty is founded by Dr. Sally Tucker Allen.

1990—Congress proclaims March 10 as Harriet Tubman Day in the United States, honoring her as a brave black freedom fighter and nurse during the Civil War.

1990—The Bloodborne Pathogen Standard is established by OSHA.

1991—*Healthy People 2000* is published.

1993—The National Center for Nursing Research is upgraded to the National Institute of Nursing Research within the National Institutes of Health.

1994—NCLEX-RN®, a computerized nurse-licensing examination, is introduced.

1996—The Commission on Collegiate Nursing Education is established as an agency devoted exclusively to the accreditation of baccalaureate and graduate-degree nursing programs.

1999—Beverly Malone, the second black president of the ANA, is named Deputy Assistant Secretary for Health, Department of Health and Human Services, Office of Public Health and Science.

1999—The IOM releases its landmark report: To Err Is Human: Building a Safer Health System.

2000—M. Elizabeth Carnegie is inducted into the ANA Hall of Fame. The American Nurses Credentialing Center gives its first psychiatric mental health nurse practitioner examination. *Healthy People 2010* is published.

2001—Beverly Malone is appointed General Secretary, Royal College of Nursing, London. The Health Care Financing Administration (HCFA) becomes the Centers for Medicare & Medicaid Services (CMS).

2002—Johnson and Johnson Health Care Systems, Inc. launches The Future of Nursing, a national publicity campaign to address the nursing shortage.

2002—To address the nursing shortage, the Nurse Reinvestment Act is signed into law by President George W. Bush.

2002—Significant funding is obtained for geriatric nursing initiatives.

2003—The American Nurses Foundation launches an "Investment in Nursing" campaign to deal with the nursing shortage.

2003—The IOM report *Keeping Patients Safe: Transforming the Work Environment of Nurses* is released.

2003—The AACN White Paper on the Role of the Clinical Nurse Leader is published.

2005—The CCNE decides that only programs that offer practice doctoral degrees with the Doctor of Nursing Practice (DNP) title will be eligible for CCNE accreditation.

2005—The NLN offers and certifies the first national certification for nurse educators; the initials CNE may be placed behind the names of those certified.

2006—The AACN approves essentials of doctoral education for advanced nursing practice (DNP) (www.aacn.nche.edu/DNP/pdf/Essentials.pdf).

2007—The Commission on Nurse Certification, an autonomous arm of the AACN, begins certifying clinical nurse leaders (CNLs).

2007—American Nurses Credentialing Center, acquired the Texas Nurses Association's Nurse Friendly Program and renamed it Pathway to Excellence.

2008—The Commission on Collegiate Nursing Education begins accrediting DNP programs.

2010—Healthy People 2020 was launched by the Department of Health and Human Services.

2010—The Patient Protection and Affordable Care Act (Public Law 111-152) is passed.

2010—The Health Care and Education Affordability Reconciliation Act is passed.

2011—The IOM report *The Future of Nursing: Leading Change, Advancing Health* is released.

From AACN, 2003; Carnegie, 1995; Deloughery, 1998; Donahue, 1999; Kalisch and Kalisch, 1995; IOM, 2003; 2011. (http://www.thefutureofnursing.org/IOM.Report).

Hippocrates (460 to 362 BC), considered the "Father of Medicine," paved the way in establishing scientific knowledge in medicine. Hippocrates was the first to attribute disease to natural causes rather than supernatural causes and curses of the gods. Hippocrates' teachings also emphasized the patient-centered approach and use of the scientific method for solving problems (Catalano, 2012).

India

Dating from 3000 to 1500 BC, the earliest cultures of India were Hindu. The sacred book of Brahmanism (also known as Hinduism), the Vedas, was used to guide health care practices. The Vedas, considered by some to be the oldest written material, emphasized hygiene and prevention of sickness and described major and minor surgeries. The Indian practice of surgery was very well developed. The importance of prenatal care to mother and infant was also well understood. Public hospitals were constructed from 274 to 236 BC and were staffed by male nurses with qualifications and duties similar to those of the twentieth-century practical nurse (Ellis and Hartley, 2012).

China

The teachings of the Chinese scholar Confucius (551 to 479 BC) had a powerful effect on the customs and practices of the people of ancient China. Confucius taught a moral philosophy that addressed one's obligation to society. Several hundred years after his death, Confucius' philosophy became the basis for Chinese education and government. Central to his teachings were service to the community and the value of the family as a unit. However, women were considered inferior to men.

The early Chinese also placed great value on solving life's problems. Their belief about health and illness was based on the yin and yang philosophy. The yin represented the feminine forces, which were considered negative and passive. The yang represented the masculine forces, which were positive and active. The Chinese believed that an imbalance between these two forces would result in illness, whereas balance between the yin and yang represented good health (Ellis and Hartley, 2012). The ancient Chinese used a variety of treatments believed to promote health and harmony, including acupuncture. Acupuncture involves insertion of hot and cold needles into the skin and underlying tissues to manage or cure conditions (such as pain, stroke, or breathing difficulty) and ultimately to affect the balance of yin and yang. Hydrotherapy, massage, and exercise were used as preventive health measures (Giger and Davidhizar, 2008). Baths were used to reduce fever, and bloodletting was used to release evil spirits from the body (Ellis and Hartley, 2012).

Rome

The Roman Empire (27 BC to 476 AD), a military dictatorship, adapted medical practices from the countries they conquered and the physicians they enslaved. At the end of the Dark Ages, there were a series of holy wars, including the Crusades. The first military hospital in Europe was established in Rome to care for the injured. Military nursing orders that were made up exclusively of men were developed to care for the injured. They were very well organized and dedicated, and they wore suits of armor for protection with the emblem of a red cross. (Catalano, 2012; Walton et al, 1994). The Romans practiced advanced hygiene and sanitation and emphasized bathing (Ellis and Hartley, 2012).

THE MIDDLE AGES

The Middle Ages (476 BC to 1450 AD) followed the demise of the Roman Empire (Walton et al, 1994). Women began using herbs and new methods of healing, whereas men continued to use purging, leeching, and mercury. This period also saw the Roman Catholic Church become a central figure in the organization and management of health care. Most of the changes in health care were based on the church's emphasis on charity and the sanctity of human life. Wives of emperors and other women considered to be noble became nurses. These women devoted themselves to caring for the sick, often carrying a basket of food and medicine as they journeyed from house to house (Bahr and Johnson, 1997). Widows and unmarried women became nuns and deaconesses. Two of these deaconesses, Dorcas and Phoebe, are mentioned in the Bible as outstanding for the care they provided to the sick (Freedman, 1995).

During the Middle Ages, physicians spent most of their time translating medical essays, and provided little actual medical care. Poorly trained barbers, who lacked any formal medical education, performed surgery and medical treatments that were considered "bloody" or "messy." Nurses also provided some medical care, although in most hospitals and monasteries, female nurses who were not midwives were forbidden to witness childbirth, help with gynecologic examinations, or even diaper male infants (Kalisch and Kalisch, 1986). During the Crusades, which lasted for almost 200 years (from 1096 to 1291), military nursing orders, known as Templars and Hospitalers, were founded. Monks and Christian knights provided nursing care and defended the hospitals during battle, wearing a suit of armor under their religious habits. The habits were distinguished by the Maltese cross to identify the monks and knights as Christian warriors. The same cross was used years later on a badge designed for the first school of nursing and became a forerunner for the design of nursing pins (Ellis and Hartley, 2012).

THE RENAISSANCE AND THE REFORMATION PERIOD

Following the Middle Ages came the Renaissance and the Reformation, also known as the rebirth of Europe (the fourteenth to sixteenth centuries AD). Major advancements were made in pharmacology, chemistry, and medical knowledge, including anatomy, physiology, and surgery. During the Renaissance, new emphasis was given to medical education, but nursing education was practically nonexistent.

The Reformation, which began in Germany in 1517, was a religious movement that resulted in a dissention between Roman Catholics and Protestants. During this period, religious facilities that provided health care closed. Women were encouraged toward charitable services, but their main duties included bearing and caring for children in their homes. Furthermore, hospital work was no longer appealing to women of high economic status, and the individuals who worked as nurses in hospitals were often female prisoners, prostitutes, and alcoholics. Nursing was no longer the respected profession it had once been. This period is referred to as the "Dark Ages" of nursing (Ellis and Hartley, 2012).

During the sixteenth and seventeenth centuries, famine, plague, filth, and crime ravaged Europe. King Henry VII eliminated the organized monastic relief programs that aided the orphans, poor, and other displaced people. Out of great concern for social welfare, several nursing groups, such as the Order of the Visitation of St. Mary, St. Vincent de Paul, and the Sisters of Charity were organized to give time, service, and money to the poor and sick. The Sisters of Charity recruited intelligent young women for training in nursing, developed educational programs, and cared for abandoned children (Ellis and Hartley, 2012).

THE COLONIAL AMERICAN PERIOD

The first hospital and the first medical school in North America were founded in Mexico—the Hospital of the Immaculate Conception in Mexico City and the medical school at the University of Mexico. During this time in the American colonies, individuals with infectious diseases were isolated in almshouses or "pesthouses" (Ellis and Hartley, 2012). Procedures, such as purgatives and bleeding, were widely used, leading to shortened life expectancy. Plagues, such as scarlet fever, dysentery, and smallpox caused thousands of deaths. Benjamin Franklin, who was outspoken regarding the care of the sick, insisted that a hospital be built in the colonies. He believed that the community should be responsible for the management and treatment of those who were ill. Through his efforts, the first hospital, called the Pennsylvania Hospital, was built in the United States in Philadelphia in 1751 (Ellis and Hartley, 2012).

FLORENCE NIGHTINGALE

Florence Nightingale was born in Florence, Italy, on May 12, 1820. The Nightingale family was wealthy, well traveled, and well educated. Nightingale was an intelligent, talented, and attractive woman. From an early age, she demonstrated a deep concern for the poor and suffering. At 25 years of age, she became interested in training as a nurse. However, her family was strongly opposed to this choice and preferred that she marry and take her place in society (Joel, 2006). In 1851, her parents finally permitted her to pursue training as a nurse. At 31 years of age, Nightingale attended a 3-month nursing training program at the Institution of Deaconesses at Kaiserswerth, Germany. In 1854, she began training nurses at the Harley Street Nursing Home and served as superintendent of nurses at King's College Hospital in London (Ellis and Hartley, 2012). The outbreak of the Crimean War marked a turning point in Nightingale's career. In October 1854, Sidney Herbert, British Secretary of War and an old friend of the Nightingale family, wrote to Nightingale and asked her to lead a group of nurses to the Crimea to work at one of the military hospitals under government authority and expense. Nightingale accepted his offer and assembled 38 nurses who were sisters and nuns from various Catholic and Anglican orders (Ellis and Hartley, 2012).

Nightingale and her team were assigned to the Barracks Hospital at Scutari. When Nightingale arrived, she found deplorable conditions. Between 3000 and 4000 sick and wounded men were packed into the hospital, which was originally designed to accommodate 1700 patients. There were no beds, blankets, food, or medicine. Many of the wounded soldiers had been placed on the floor, where lice, maggots, vermin, rodents, and blood covered their bodies. There were no candles or lanterns. All medical care had to be rendered during the light of day (Ellis and Hartley, 2012).

Despite the distressing conditions at the Barracks Hospital, the army physicians and surgeons at first refused Nightingale's assistance. However, within a week and faced with scurvy, starvation, dysentery, and the eruption of more fighting, the physicians, in desperation, called her to help. Nightingale immediately purchased medical supplies, food, linen, and hospital equipment, using her own money and that of the Times Relief Fund. Within 10 days, she had set up a kitchen for special diets and had rented a house that she converted into a laundry (Gill, 2004; Small, 2002). The wives of soldiers were hired to manage and operate the laundry service. She assigned soldiers to make repairs and clean up the building. Just weeks later, she initiated social services, reading classes, and even coffeehouses, where soldiers could enjoy music and recreation (Nies and McEwen, 2011).

Nightingale worked long, hard hours to care for these soldiers. She spent up to 20 hours each day caring for wounds, comforting soldiers, assisting in surgery, directing staff, and keeping records. Nightingale introduced principles of infection control, a system for transcribing physicians' orders, and a procedure to maintain patient records.

Nightingale is credited with using public health principles and statistical methods to advocate for improved health conditions for British soldiers. Through carefully recorded statistics, Nightingale was able to document that the soldiers' death rate decreased from 42% to 2% as a result of health care reforms that emphasized sanitary conditions. Because of her remarkable work in using statistics to demonstrate cause and effect and

improve the health of British soldiers, Nightingale is recognized for her contributions to nursing research (Nies and McEwen, 2011).

Nightingale also demonstrated the power of political activism to effect health care reform by writing letters of criticism accompanied by constructive recommendations to British army leaders. Nightingale's ability to overthrow the British army's management method that had allowed the deplorable conditions to exist in the army hospitals was considered one of her greatest achievements (Nies and McEwen, 2011).

After her return from the Crimea, Nightingale experienced ongoing health problems. Early writers suggest that she retreated to her bedroom for the next 43 years and continued her involvement in health care from her secluded apartment. More recent research, however, indicates a more active involvement (Ellis and Hartley, 2012).

Florence Nightingale's work, from the Crimean War to the establishment of formal nursing education programs, was a catapult for the reorganization and advancement of professional nursing. Nightingale wrote extensively about hospitals, sanitation, health and health statistics (creating the first pie chart), and nursing education. Among her most popular books is *Notes on Nursing* published in 1859.

In 1860, Nightingale established the first nursing school in England, St. Thomas' Hospital of London. By 1873, graduates of Nightingale's nurse training program in England migrated to the United States, where they became supervisors in the first of the hospital-based (diploma) nursing schools: Massachusetts General Hospital in Boston, Bellevue Hospital in New York, and the New Haven Hospital in Connecticut.

Until her death in August 1910, Nightingale demonstrated the powerful effect that well-educated, creative, skilled, and competent individuals have in the provision of health care. She is honored as the founder of professional nursing (Ellis and Hartley, 2012). Nightingale had the means to support her work and the stamina to drive forward in her belief concerning health care. Even though Louis Pasteur's germ theory was not widely known and was very controversial at the time, her theory of environmental cleanliness is still applicable today.

MARY SEACOLE

Mary Seacole was a Jamaican nurse who learned the art of caring and healing from her mother. In her native land of Jamaica, British West Indies, she was nicknamed "Doctress" because of her administration of care to the sick in a lodging house in Kingston (Carnegie, 1995). Seacole learned of the Crimean War and wrote to the British government requesting to join Nightingale's group of nurses. However, she was denied the right to join because she was black. She was confused about this denial because many of the British soldiers had lived in Jamaica, where she had already provided health care to them.

Seacole had previously served as a nurse in Cuba and Panama during the yellow fever and cholera epidemics. She had also conducted forensic studies on an infant who died of cholera in Panama. She felt that her experience would be valuable in treating disease in the Crimean War, and she sailed to England at her own expense. She provided a letter of introduction to Nightingale, which was blocked because Seacole was black, even though she had been trained by British army physicians (Carnegie, 1995).

After several efforts to join Nightingale's group failed, Seacole, who was not a woman of wealth, purchased her own supplies and traveled more than 3000 miles to the Crimea, where she built and opened a lodging house. On the bottom floor of the house was a restaurant, and on the top floor an area was arranged like a hospital to nurse sick soldiers (Carnegie, 1995).

When Seacole finally met Nightingale, the response from the British Army physicians was still the same: "no vacancies" (Carnegie, 1995). However, being denied enlistment did not deter Seacole; she remained faithful and nursed the sick throughout the Crimean War. Her efforts did not go unnoticed by the English people. Long after the war was over, the British government finally honored Seacole with a medal in recognition of her efforts and the services she provided to the sick and injured soldiers.

NURSING IN THE UNITED STATES

The Civil War Period

During the United States Civil War, or the War Between the States (1861 to 1865), health care conditions in the United States were similar to those encountered by Nightingale and Seacole. Numerous epidemics plagued the country, including syphilis, gonorrhea, malaria, smallpox, and typhoid (Nelson, 2001; Oermann, 1997).

The Civil War was initiated by the attack on Fort Sumter, South Carolina, April 17, 1861. At this time, there were no nurses formally trained to care for the sick. However, thousands of men and women from the South and North volunteered to care for the wounded. Hospitals were set up in the field, and transports were put in place to carry the wounded to hospitals (Carnegie, 1995).

Secretary of War Simon Cameron appointed a schoolteacher named Dorothea Dix to organize military hospitals and provide medical supplies to the Union Army soldiers. Dix received no official status and no salary for this position.

Women providing nursing care during the Civil War worked under very primitive conditions. Maintaining sanitary conditions was an overwhelming challenge and often not possible. Greater than six million patients were admitted to hospitals. There were approximately 500,000 surgical cases performed. Unfortunately, there were only about 2000 individuals who served as nurses, far fewer than the number needed to provide adequate care (Fitzpatrick, 1997; Kalisch and Kalisch, 1995). According to records kept at three hospitals, 181 male and female black nurses served between July 16, 1863, and June 14, 1864. White nurses were paid $12 per month; black nurses received $10 per month (Carnegie, 1995).

Three black nurses made particularly important contributions to nursing efforts during the Civil War: Harriet Tubman cared for the sick as a nurse in the Sea Islands off the coast of South Carolina and was later known as the "conductor of the underground railroad." It is also reported that she was the first woman to lead American troops into battle (Carnegie, 1995). Sojourner Truth, known for her abolitionist and nursing efforts, was an advocate of clean and sanitary conditions for patients. She insisted that these conditions were needed for patients to heal. Susie King Taylor, although hired to work in the laundry, served as a nurse because of the growing number of wounded who needed care. Having learned to read and write, which was against the law for blacks at the time, she also taught many of her comrades in Company E to read and write (Carnegie, 1995).

Many other volunteer nurses made important contributions during the Civil War: Clara Barton served on the front line during the Civil War and operated a war relief program to provide supplies to the battlefields and hospitals. Barton also set up a postwar service to find missing soldiers and is credited with founding the American Red Cross (Nies and McEwen, 2011). Louisa May Alcott, who served as a nurse for 6 weeks until stopped by ill health, authored detailed accounts of the experiences encountered by nurses during the war for a newspaper publication titled *Hospital Sketches* (Kalisch and Kalisch, 1995; 2003).

When the Civil War ended, the number of nurse training schools increased. The war had proven the need for more nurses to be formerly trained. These early nursing programs offered little or no classroom education, and on-the-job training occurred in the hospital wards. The students learned routine patient care duties, worked long hours 6 days a week, and were used as supplemental hospital staff. After graduation, most of the nurses practiced as private duty nurses or hospital staff (Lindeman and McAthie, 1990). The first nursing textbook, titled *A Manual of Nursing,* was published in 1876 and was used by the New York Training School for Nurses at Bellevue Hospital (Kalisch and Kalisch, 1995).

During the 1890s, the nationwide establishment of hospitals and nursing schools for blacks gained momentum as black musicians, educators, and community leaders became alarmed at the high rates of morbidity and mortality among black Americans. Because of segregation and discrimination, African Americans had to establish their own health care institutions to provide black patients with access to quality health care and to provide black men and women with opportunities to enter the nursing profession. However. in 1886, John D. Rockefeller, a white philanthropist, funded the establishment of the first school of nursing for black women at the Atlanta Baptist Seminary—now known as Spelman College (Jones, 2004). (See Box 1-2.)

1900 to World War I

In the 1900s, states began to require nurses to become registered before entering practice. By 1910, most states had upgraded education requirements to high school, upgraded training, and required registration before practice (Deloughery, 1998; Donahue, 1999). The Army and Navy Nurse Corps was created in 1901 and 1908, respectively, and an estimated 30,000 nurses served in World War I (Ellis and Hartley, 2012).

Lillian Wald was a pioneer in public health nursing, and is best known for the development and establishment of the first viable practice for public health nurses. The main location for this practice was the Henry Street Settlement House, located in the Lower East Side of New York City. Its purpose was to provide well-baby care, health education, disease prevention, and treatment of patients with minor illnesses. Nursing practice based at the Henry Street Settlement House formed the basis of public health nursing for the entire country. Instead of relying on patients visiting the clinic, public health nurses made their way to the various tenements located around Henry Street (Nies and McEwen, 2011).

Lillian Wald also developed the first nursing service for occupational health. She believed that prevention of disease among workers would improve productivity and was able to convince the Metropolitan Life Insurance Company that her ideas had merit. As a result, nursing agencies, such as those in place at the Henry Street Settlement House, provided skilled nursing services to employees. Another innovation that emerged from this program was the sliding fee scale, by which patients were billed according to their income or their ability to pay. In 1911, Wald chaired a committee formed by members of the Associated Alumnae of Training Schools for Nurses, later to become the American Nurses Association (ANA), and the Society of Superintendents of Training Schools for Nurses, the precursor of the National League for Nursing (NLN). The purpose of the committee was to develop standards for nursing services performed outside of the hospital environment. The committee determined that a new organization was necessary to meet the needs of community health nurses. The result of the committee's recommendation was the formation of the National Organization for Public Health Nursing, whose goals were to establish educational and practice standards for community health nursing (Stanhope and Lancaster, 2012).

The ANA and the NLN are still leading nursing organizations today. The ANA has focused primarily on professional aspects of nursing, and the NLN was the only accrediting body for nursing schools until 1996, when the Commission on Collegiate Nursing Education (CCNE), an autonomous arm of the AACN, was established as an agency devoted exclusively to the accreditation of baccalaureate and graduate degree nursing programs (Ellis and Hartley, 2012).

In 2013 the National League for Nursing Accreditation Commission (NLNAC) changed its name and is now the Accreditation Commission for Education in Nursing (ACEN). This organization accredits practical, diploma, baccalaureate, and graduate degree nursing programs.

World War I and the 1920s

During the early 1900s, the world was rapidly changing and moving toward global conflict. Germany was arming, and the rest of Europe was trying to ignore the threat. "Prosperous" was the word used to describe the U.S. economy. Women were granted the right to vote and were moving into the workforce on a regular basis.

Advancements in medical care and public health were being made. The primary site for medical care moved from the home to the hospital, and surgical and diagnostic techniques were improved. Pneumonia management was the focus of scientific study. Insulin was discovered in 1922, and in 1928 Alexander Fleming discovered the precursor of penicillin, which would eventually be used to successfully treat patients with pneumonia and other infections (Kalisch and Kalisch, 1995). (See Box 1-2.)

Environmental conditions improved, and the serious epidemics of the previous century became nonexistent. Lillian Wald, in *The House on Henry Street,* linked poor environmental and social conditions to prevalent illnesses and poverty and used this information to lead the fight for better sanitation and housing conditions (Nies and McEwen, 2011).

With the outbreak of World War I in 1914, nurses were desperately needed to care for the soldiers who were injured or who suffered from the many illnesses that were a result of trench warfare (Nies and McEwen, 2011). The war offered nurses a chance to advance into new fields of specialization. For example, nurse anesthetists made their first appearance as part of the surgical teams at the front lines. More than 20,000 U.S.-trained nurses served in World War I (Oermann, 1997).

Because many nurses volunteered to provide services during the war, the community health nursing movement in the United States stalled. However, the American Red Cross, founded by Clara Barton in 1882, assisted in efforts to continue public health nursing. The Red Cross nurses originally focused on members of rural communities who were not able to access health care services. As the war continued, however, the Red Cross nurses also moved into urban areas to provide health care services (Stanhope and Lancaster, 2012).

During World War I, the U.S. Public Health Service, founded in 1798 to provide health care services to merchant seamen, was charged with the responsibility to provide health services at the military posts located within the United States. A nurse, which was "loaned" by the National Organization for Public Health Nursing, established nursing services at U.S. military outposts. The responsibilities of the U.S. Public Health Service continued to grow; eventually it was composed of physicians, nurses, and other allied health professionals, who provided indigent care and practiced in community health programs (Stanhope and Lancaster, 2012).

BOX 1-2   Duties of the Hospital Floor Nurse in 1887

In addition to caring for your 60 patients, each nurse will follow these regulations:

1. Daily sweep and mop the floors of your ward; dust the patient's furniture and windowsill.
2. Maintain an even temperature on your ward by bringing in a scuttle of coal for the day's business.
3. Light is important to observe the patient's condition; therefore, each day fill kerosene lamps, clean chimneys, and trim wicks. Wash the windows once a week.
4. The nurse's notes are important in aiding the physician's work. Make your pens carefully; you may whittle nibs to your individual taste.
5. Each nurse on day duty will report every day at 7 AM and will leave at 8 PM except on Sabbath, on which day you will be off from 12 noon to 2 PM.
6. Graduate nurses in good standing with the director of nurses will be given an evening off each week if you regularly attend church.
7. Each nurse should lay aside from each payday a good sum of her earning for her benefits during her declining years so that she will not become a burden. For example, if you earn $20 a month, you should set aside $10.
8. Any nurse who smokes, uses liquor in any form, gets her hair done at a beauty shop, or frequents dance halls will have given the director of nurses good reason to suspect her worth, intentions, and integrity.
9. The nurse who performs her labors, serves her patients and physicians faithfully and without fault for a period of 5 years will be given an increase by the hospital administration of 5 cents per day, providing there are no hospital debts that are outstanding.

Further changes were in store for nursing during World War I. In 1918, the Vassar Camp School for Nurses was established. Its purpose was to provide an intensive 2-year nurses' training program for college graduates. Graduates of the program were given an army reserve commission and would be activated during times of war to meet increased nursing needs. Sponsored by the American Red Cross and the Council of National Defense, the school graduated 435 nurses. The Vassar Camp School for Nurses was a short-lived enterprise. When peace was declared in 1919, the program was permanently disbanded (Snodgrass, 2004; Stanhope and Lancaster, 2012).

In 1921, the federal government recognized the need to improve the health of women and children and passed the Sheppard-Towner Act, one of the first pieces of federal legislation to provide funds to assist in the care of special populations (Nies and McEwen, 2011). This funding provided public health nurses with resources to promote the health and well-being of women, infants, and children.

Following these improvements, the Frontier Nursing Service (FNS) was established in 1925 by Mary Breckenridge of Kentucky. Born into a wealthy family, Breckenridge learned the value of providing care to others from her grandmother. Breckenridge began her career at St. Luke's Hospital School of Nursing in New York. After serving as a nurse during World War I, she returned to Columbia University to learn more about community health nursing. Armed with her new knowledge and a passion to assist disadvantaged women and children, Breckenridge returned to Kentucky and the rural Appalachian Mountains (Stanhope and Lancaster, 2012).

Breckenridge believed that the rural mountain area of Kentucky, cut off from many modern conveniences, was an excellent place to prove the value of community health nursing. She established the FNS in a five-room cabin in Hyden, Kentucky. After overcoming serious obstacles, such as no water supply or sewage disposal, six other nursing outposts were constructed in the rural mountains from 1927 to 1930. The FNS based its hospital in Hyden and eventually attracted physicians and nurses to provide medical, dental, surgical, nursing, and midwifery services to the rural poor. Financial support for the FNS ranged from fees for labor and supplies to funds raised through annual family dues to donations and fundraising efforts. Nurses working for the FNS traveled a 700-square mile area, often on horseback, to provide services to approximately 10,000 patients (Stanhope and Lancaster, 2012).

Breckenridge established an important health care service for rural Kentucky communities. Equally important was her documentation of the results of community health nursing in rural communities. Breckenridge followed the advice of a consulting physician and collected mortality data on the communities before nursing services actually were started. The results were startling; mortality was significantly reduced, and the need for the nursing services was clearly documented. Breckenridge proved that even in appalling environmental conditions without heat, electricity, or running water, nursing services could make a substantial positive impact on the health of the community (Stanhope and Lancaster, 2012). The FNS is still in operation today and provides vital service to the rural communities of Kentucky.

The Great Depression (1930 to 1940)

The U.S. economy prospered during World War I and well into the 1920s. However, after the stock market crash in October 1929, economic prosperity quickly dissipated. Millions of men and women became unemployed. Before the Depression, many people had private duty nurses. However, during the Depression, many nurses found themselves unemployed because most families could no longer afford private duty nurses.

Franklin D. Roosevelt, elected president of the United States in 1932, faced a country in shambles. He responded with several innovative and necessary interventions and ushered in the first major social legislation that had been enacted in U.S. history. Titled the "New Deal," the legislation had several social components that affected the provision of medical care and other services for indigent people across the country (Karger and Stoesz, 2005).

The piece of legislation that had the greatest effect on health care in the United States was the Social Security Act of 1935, which set the precedent for the passage of the Medicare and Medicaid acts that followed in 1965. The main purposes of the 1935 Social Security Act were to provide (1) a national old-age insurance system, (2) federal grants to states for maternal and child welfare services, (3) vocational rehabilitation services for the handicapped, (4) medical care for crippled children and blind people, (5) a plan to strengthen public health services, and (6) a federal-state unemployment system (Karger and Stoesz, 2005).

The passage of the 1935 Social Security Act provided avenues for nursing care, and nursing jobs were created. With funds from the Social Security Act, public health nursing became the major source of health care for dependent mothers and children, the blind, and crippled children. Nurses found employment as public health nurses for county or state health departments (Stanhope and Lancaster, 2010). Hospital job opportunities also were created for nurses, and the hospital became the usual employment setting for graduate nurses.

World War II (1940 to 1945)

The United States officially entered World War II after the bombing of Pearl Harbor in December 1941. At that time, the nursing divisions of all of the military branches had inadequate numbers of nurses. Congress passed legislation to provide needed funds to expand nursing education. A committee of six national nursing organizations, called the National Nursing Council, received one million dollars to accomplish the needed expansion. The U.S. Public Health Service became the administrator of the funds, which further strengthened the tie between the U.S. Public Health Service and nursing (Stanhope and Lancaster, 2012).

The war was considered a global conflict, and nursing became an essential part of the military advance. Nurses were required to function under combat conditions and had to adapt nursing care to meet the challenges of different climates, facilities, and supplies. As a result of their service during World War II, nurses finally were recognized as an integral part of the military and attained the ranks of officers in the army and navy. Colonel Julie O. Flikke was the first army nurse to be promoted to colonel in the U.S. Army and served as Superintendent of the Army Nurse Corps from 1937 to 1942 (Deloughery, 1998; Robinson and Perry, 2001).

Post–World War II Period (1945 to 1950)

The period after World War II was a time of prosperity for the average American. The GI Bill enabled returning veterans to complete their interrupted education. The unemployment rate dropped to an all-time low in the United States. In an effort to provide more areas of employment for the returning men, the federal government mounted a massive campaign to encourage women to return to the more traditional roles of wife and mother. Consequently, numerous women in all professions, including nursing, chose to return to marriage and childrearing rather than continue employment outside the home.

After World War II the Soviet Union began invading and taking over Eastern European countries. With support from China, the North Koreans made a grab for South Korea, resulting in the Korean War. Again, nurses volunteered for the armed services to provide care to patients near the battlefields in Korea. This time they worked in mobile army surgical hospitals, better known as MASH units, where medical and surgical techniques were further refined.

The two decades after World War II saw the emergence of nursing as a true profession. National standards for nursing education were established by the National Nursing Accrediting Service. By 1950, all state boards were participating in the test pool; they continue to do so today. Nursing continued to improve the quality and quantity of educational programs as the number of nursing baccalaureate programs increased and associate degree programs developed in community or junior colleges (Ellis and Hartley, 2012) (Box 1-1).

The end of World War II and the early 1950s marked the beginning of significant federal intervention in health care. The Nurse Training Act of 1943 was the first instance of federal funding being used to support nurse training. The passage of the Hill-Burton Act, or the Hospital Survey and Construction Act of 1946, marked the largest commitment of federal dollars to health care in the country's history. The purpose of the act was to provide funding to construct hospitals and to assist states in planning for other health care facilities based on the needs of the communities. Nearly 40% of the hospitals constructed in the late 1940s and the early 1950s were built with Hill-Burton funds. The hospital construction boom created by the Hill-Burton Act led to an increased demand for professional nurses to provide care in hospitals (Nies and McEwen, 2011). (See Box 1-3.)

It was also in the early 1950s that the National Association of Colored Graduate Nurses (NACGN) went out of existence. This was the organization that fought for integration of the black nurse into the ANA. From 1916 to 1948, black nurses in the South were barred from membership in the ANA because of segregation laws in the Southern states. In the 1940s, the NACGN began to wage an all-out war against discrimination by the

BOX 1-3 **Qualities of Good Nurses During Post–World War II**

1. Tidy and loyal to the hospital and its personnel
2. Compliant with the orders of the physicians and directives of nursing management
3. Always busy
4. If census was low, fold laundry, clean shelves, prepare supplies to be sterilized
5. Ability to get work done no matter how many patients assigned

From Martell LK: Maternity care during the post–World War II baby boom: the experience of general duty nurses, *West J Nurs Res* 96(3):387-391, 1999.

Southern constituents of the ANA. The NACGN chose as its central issue the route to membership in ANA. This issue was raised by the NACGN on the floor at every national convention of the ANA, and it evoked strong opposition from the Southern state constituents. Speaking from the floor of the House of Delegates at the 1946 convention in Atlantic City, a white nurse from Georgia referred to black nurses as "our darkies." Immediately a motion was passed to strike the reference from the record. However, this comment caused an uproar, and the black nurses who were barred from membership in the Southern states started the wheels turning to bypass the states and join ANA directly. This arrangement, known as *individual membership,* was put into effect in 1948. With the establishment of individual membership, black nurses in the South could bypass their states and become members of the ANA. This type of individual membership continued until all barriers had been dropped in the early 1960s (Carnegie, 1995).

Nursing in the 1960s

Federal legislation enacted during the 1960s had a major and lasting effect on nursing and health care. The Community Mental Health Centers Act of 1963 provided funds for the construction of community outpatient mental health centers; opportunities for mental health nursing were expanded when funds to staff these centers were appropriated in 1965 with the passage of the Medicare and Medicaid acts (Nies and McEwen, 2011). Medicaid, Title XIX of the Social Security Act, was enacted and replaced all programs previously instituted for medical assistance. The purpose

of the Medicaid program, which was jointly sponsored and financed with matching funds from federal and state governments, was to serve as medical insurance for those families, primarily women and children, with an income at or below the federal poverty level. Medicaid quickly became the largest public assistance program in the nation.

Health departments employed public health nurses to provide the bulk of the care needed by children and pregnant women in the Medicaid population. Services provided by these nurses included family planning, well-child assessments, immunizations, and prenatal care. A physician assigned as the district health officer supervised the nurses. Without the public health nurses and local health departments, many women and children in the inner city areas and rural communities would have been without access to basic health care.

Another important amendment to the Social Security Act was Title XVIII, or Medicare, passed in 1965. The Medicare program provides hospital insurance, part A, and medical insurance, part B, to all people 65 years of age and older who are eligible to receive Social Security benefits; people with total, permanent disabilities; and people with end-stage renal disease. As a result of Medicare reimbursement, many hospitals began catering to physicians who treated Medicare patients. Medicare patients were attractive to the hospitals because all hospital charges, regardless of amount or appropriateness of services, were reimbursed through the Medicare program (Nies and McEwen, 2011).

As a result of Medicare reimbursement, hospital-bed occupancy increased, which led to increased numbers of nurses needed to staff hospitals. Nursing embraced the hospital setting as the usual practice area and moved away from the community as the preferred practice site. Nursing schools also followed the trend by reducing the number of curriculum hours devoted to community health and concentrated their efforts on hospital-based nursing (Stanhope and Lancaster, 2012).

Another outcome of the Medicare legislation was the home health movement. To receive Medicare reimbursement for home health services, patients had to have (1) home-bound status; (2) a need for part-time or intermittent, skilled nursing care; (3) a medically reasonably and necessary need for treatment; and (4) a plan of care authorized by a physician. Home health agencies were established and began to employ increasing numbers of nurses. The number of home health agencies began to grow in the mid-1960s, and the home health industry continued unprecedented growth into the 1990s as a result of Medicare reimbursement and other influences, including a growing older adult population, advances in medical technology, and public demand for increased access to health care. Home health was one of the first employment settings that provided nurses the opportunity to work weekdays only.

Nursing in the 1970s

The women's movement of the 1970s greatly influenced nursing. Nurses began to focus not only on providing quality care to patients but also on enhancing the economic benefits of the profession. Hospitals were receiving significant reimbursements for patient care; however, nurses' salaries did not reflect an adequate percentage of that reimbursement. Health care costs soared. This increase in health care costs built the framework for mandated changes in reimbursement. Nursing practice and the educational focus remained in the hospital setting.

During this time, nurses played a major role in providing health care to communities and were instrumental in developing hospice programs, birthing centers, and daycare centers for older adults (Nies and McEwen, 2011). Although basic educational programs for nurse practitioners expanded during the 1970s and master's-level preparation was developed as the requirement for graduation and practice, certification was also required to practice as a nurse practitioner. Before this time, only certification was required. State nursing practice acts were amended to provide for monitoring and licensing advanced practice nurses. Men also began to increase in numbers in this female-dominated profession (Ellis and Hartley, 2012).

In 1974, the ANA conducted research in the area of ethnic minorities and submitted a proposal to the National Institute of Mental Health to fund a project to permit minority nurses—African Americans, Hispanics, Asians, and American Indians—to earn PhDs. Of the graduates of the project, the vast majority serves on faculties of universities and are conducting research on factors in mental health and illness related to ethnicity and cross-cultural conflict, thereby fulfilling their commitment to advance the cause of quality health care for people of all ethnicities.

Despite past laxity, the ANA House of Delegates at its 1972 convention passed an affirmative action resolution calling for a task force to develop and implement a program to correct inequities. The house also provided for the position of an ombudsman to evaluate involvement of minorities in leadership roles within the organization and to treat complaints by applicants for membership or by members of the association who had been discriminated against because of nationality, race, creed, lifestyle, color, age, or sex. It was also in the 1970s that the ANA elected its first black president, Barbara Nichols, who served two terms.

Within the structure of many professional organizations is a unit referred to as an *academy*, which is composed of a cadre of scholars who deal with issues that concern the profession and take positions in the name of the academy. The American Academy of Nursing (AAN) was created by the ANA board in 1973. An elected group of highly accomplished leaders across all sectors of nursing (education, research, and practice), it uses the credential FAAN (Fellow, American Academy of Nursing). Through the application of visionary leadership, the intent of the AAN is to transform health care policy through nursing knowledge to optimize the well-being of the American people.

At its convention in Atlantic City in 1976, the ANA launched its Hall of Fame to pay tribute to those nurses who had paved the way for others to follow or who have made outstanding contributions to the profession.

Nursing in the 1980s

The types of patients needing health care changed in the 1980s. Homelessness became a common problem in large cities. Unstable economic developments contributed to an increase in indigent populations (Nies and McEwen, 2011). Acquired immunodeficiency syndrome (AIDS) emerged as a frightening, fatal epidemic.

Runaway health care costs became a national issue in the 1980s. Medicare was still reimbursing for any and all hospital services provided to recipients. In 1983, in an attempt to restrain hospital costs, Congress passed the Diagnosis-Related Group system for reimbursement, better known as the DRG system.

Before 1983, Medicare payments were made to the hospital after the patient received services. Although there were restrictions, the entire bill generally was paid without question. DRGs were implemented to provide prospective payment for hospital services based on the patient's admitting diagnosis and thereby to reduce the overall cost to Medicare. Hospitals now were to be reimbursed one amount based on the patient's diagnosis, not on hospital charges. The system was developed by physicians at the Yale–New Haven Hospital and addressed approximately 468 diagnoses classified according to length of stay and cost of procedures associated with the diagnosis (Nies and McEwen, 2011).

As a result of the DRG reimbursement system, hospitals were forced to increase efficiency and more closely manage hospital services, including the patient's length of stay, laboratory and radiographic testing, and diagnostic procedures. Case management and critical pathways were developed to more efficiently manage patient care, and case management became a new area of specialization for the professional nurse.

Despite the high cost of health care, medicine prospered. Medical care advanced in areas such as organ transplantation, resuscitation and support of premature infants, and critical care techniques. Physician specialization and advances in medical technology flourished. Medical specialties, such as nephrology, cardiology, endocrinology, orthopedics, neurosurgery, cardiovascular surgery, and advanced practices for obstetrics all led to improved health care services and costs in the hospital setting. The advanced technology also led to the development of outpatient surgery units.

Outpatient surgery services blossomed and provided a quick and efficient site for surgery that did not require extended hospital stays. Costs were greatly reduced because of fewer staff members needed for coverage, fewer supplies, and reduced facility costs. Nurses were interested in employment opportunities in outpatient facilities because they afforded a chance to work only during the day with no weekend assignments.

As the concern over increasing health care costs heightened, use of ambulatory services increased and enrollment in health maintenance organizations grew. Advanced nurse practitioners increased in popularity as cost-effective providers of primary and preventive health care. A growing number of nurses moved from the hospital setting into the community to practice in programs, such as hospice and home health. Consumers began to demand bans on unhealthy activities, such as smoking in public. Health education became more important as consumers were encouraged to take responsibility for their own care (Stanhope and Lancaster, 2012). Even the terminology changed; the individual once known as the *patient* became known as the *client*

or *consumer* and was afforded respect as a person who purchases a service.

Public health programs struggled to survive as counties and states cut health department budgets. A landmark study conducted by the Institute of Medicine (IOM) in 1988, titled *Who Will Keep the Public Healthy?* (IOM, 2003) indicated a dismal picture for public health. The study determined that public health had moved away from its traditional role and core functions and that no strategy was in place to bring public health back to its original purpose (Stanhope and Lancaster, 2012). Inadequate funding for public health continues to be a problem; however, it is hoped that soon public health will be restored to its original function and purpose.

Nursing enrollments dropped drastically in the late 1980s. This drop in enrollment occurred as the complexity of health care was rapidly increasing and more nurses were assuming expanded roles. As a result of these trends, a serious national shortage of nurses occurred across all settings (Ellis and Hartley, 2012).

In the late 1980s, several nursing scholars suggested that nursing research be firmly focused on the substantive information required to guide practice, rather than on philosophic and methodologic dilemmas of scientific inquiry. In 1985 the creation of the National Center for Nursing Research at the National Institutes of Health brought with it an increase in federal resources for nursing research and research training (Rebar et al, 2011).

Nursing in the 1990s

The 1990s began with alarm over the state of the U.S. economy. Government statisticians reported an alarming increase in the national debt complicated by slow economic growth. In the early 1990s, average household incomes were stagnating. More women with families entered the workforce to afford the increasing cost of living. More nurses selected jobs in which they could work more hours in fewer days for more money, sometimes sacrificing the fringe benefits, allowing them to work a second job or earn higher pay through shift differential for working evening and night shifts. Creative shifts, such as the 10-hour day, 4-day workweek or the 12-hour day, 3-day workweek became commonplace in health care facilities. Just as in the 1980s, the cost of health care continued to increase with the technologic advancements in medical care. Men were considered a minority in nursing, and salaries were thought to be on the increase as a result of male presence in the profession (O'Lynn and Tranbarger, 2006).

There also were growing concerns in the 1990s about the health of the nation, which prompted the *Healthy People 2000* initiative. Many diseases associated with preventable causes characterized mortality in the United States. In 1990, more than 2 million U.S. residents died from diseases such as heart disease, cancer, cerebral vascular disease, accidents, chronic obstructive pulmonary disease, liver cirrhosis, tuberculosis, and human immunodeficiency virus infection. The inner city became a concern of disparities in these diseases with issues related to access and quality of care (Nies and McEwen, 2011). Factors contributing to these common disease states related to lifestyle patterns, behaviors, and habits (modifiable risk factors). More youth were at risk because of behavior such as smoking cigarettes, using abusive drug substances, eating poorly balanced diets, failing to exercise, having sex with multiple partners, and being subjected to acts of violence. *Healthy People 2000: National Health Promotion and Disease Prevention Objectives* was published in 1991 by the U.S. Department of Health and Human Services as a nationwide effort to help states, cities, and communities identify health promotion and disease prevention strategies to address these health risk problems.

The AIDS epidemic radically changed the process for infection control among health care workers in health care institutions across the nation. Recapping needles, wearing latex gloves, and using isolation precautions were issues that triggered much dialogue and debate among health care workers. Health care workers were mandated to use preventive measures in the form of Universal Precautions; all contact with blood and body fluids from all patients was considered potentially infectious.

Exposure to hazardous materials became a major issue of concern for not only health care workers but also the general public. Chemical and radioactive substances that created dangerous exposure and health risks were increasingly used in the workplace. Employers were held legally accountable for informing their employees of the actual or potential hazards and for reducing their exposure risk through training and the use of protective equipment. The hazardous materials issue was especially important in nursing and medicine, particularly with regard to exposure to carcinogenic chemicals used in drug therapy and in environmental infection control.

In 1990, the increasing costs of Medicaid and Medicare triggered political action for health care reform. Findings of a federal commission appointed to evaluate the American health care system included the following (Chitty and Black, 2014):

- Fifteen percent of the gross national product was related to health care expenditures (this amounts to approximately $1 trillion annually).
- The United States spent more than twice as much as any industrialized nation for health care services.
- Americans were living longer, which indicated a growing demand for home health and nursing home care, in addition to increased Medicare expenditures.

It became apparent that if health care spending continued to increase, the U.S. economy would be in danger of collapse. Thus the health care system moved toward managed care in an attempt to control health care expenditures. The managed care movement has had a tremendous effect on nursing.

The focus of managed care was on providing more preventive and primary care, using outpatient and home settings when possible, and limiting expensive hospitalizations. Massive downsizing of hospital nursing staff occurred, with an increased use of unlicensed assistive personnel to provide care in hospitals. There was an increasing demand for community health nurses and advanced practice nurses to provide primary care services. The nurse of the 1990s had to be focused on delivering health care services that (1) encompassed health risk assessment based on family and environmental factors, (2) supported health promotion and disease prevention, and (3) advanced counseling and health education (Nies and McEwen, 2011).

In June 1993, the National Center for Nursing Research was renamed the National Institute of Nursing Research. Moving nursing research into the National Institutes of Health enhanced the interprofessional possibilities for collaborative investigation. As a result, nursing research grew rapidly during the 1990s. Multiple research programs focused on important health issues, such as health promotion across the lifespan. Nursing research began to inform health care policy through federal commissions and agency programs (Rebar et al, 2011).

In the 1990s, mandatory state licensure authorities (which set practice standards at the level of entering associate-degree graduates) and national nongovernmental bodies (which certify graduate-prepared specialists) forged a partnership. These national certifying agencies were intensely engaged in improving methods for determining the continual competence of certified nurse practitioners within the swift current of health care change. The consumer's voice in the partnership was heard via collaboration with advocacy organizations and the appointment of more public members to licensing, certifying, and accreditation boards. Voluntary credentialing bodies recognized that if they were to serve effectively, they had to engage in active public information campaigns to inform consumers about their health care choices (Buhler-Wilkerson, 2001).

Nursing in the Twenty-First Century

Professional nurses in the twenty-first century are faced with many challenges within the dynamic state of health care. In addition to the issues of access, cost, quality, safety, and accountability in health care, nurses today are challenged by an aging population, a serious nursing shortage, generational differences in an aging workforce with poor prospects for replacements, high acuity and short staffing, conflict in the workplace, expanding technology, complex consumer health values, and an increasingly intercultural society. Nurses have identified numerous areas of concern, including insufficient staffing, inadequate salaries, effects of stress and overwork, violence in the workplace, lack of participation in decision making, and dissatisfaction with the quality of their own nursing care.

Changing duties, responsibilities, and conflicts amid nursing shortages and public concern over patient safety and quality of care characterize present-day practice. These changes require professional nurses to have core competency in critical thinking, communication, interprofessional collaboration, assessment, leadership, and technical skills, in addition to knowledge of health promotion and disease prevention, information technology, health systems, and public policy.

Public funding to schools of nursing needs to be increased to attract and retain nursing faculty. In support of the nursing profession, the U.S. Congress adopted the Nurse Reinvestment Act to provide funds for nursing education, recruitment, and retention programs. President George W. Bush signed the bill into law in August 2002.

In May 2003, the IOM released recommended partnerships of academic institutions, local and state public health departments, community health agencies, and schools of public health to establish training for medical and nursing school curricula. The future of public health in our nation depends on a competent, well-trained public health workforce. A well-trained workforce is in the best interest of all those concerned with maintaining a healthy society (IOM, 2003).

In 2008, the Robert Wood Johnson Foundation (RWJF) proposed a partnership with the IOM to assess and respond to the need to transform the nursing profession. The RWJF and the IOM established a 2-year Initiative on the Future of Nursing. The IOM report released in 2011 had the following four key messages: (1) Nurses should practice to the full extent of their education and training; (2) Nurses should achieve higher levels of education and training through an improved education system that promotes seamless academic progression; (3) Nurses should be full partners with physicians and other health professionals in redesigning health care in the United States; and (4) Effective workforce planning and policy making require better data collection and an improved information infrastructure (IOM, 2011). These recommendations focus on the intersection between the health needs of diverse populations across the lifespan and the actions of the nursing workforce.

In 2010, Congress passed and President Barak Obama signed into law comprehensive health legislation. These laws, the Patient Protection and Affordable Care Act (Public Law 111-148) and the Health Care and Education Affordability Reconciliation Act (Public Law 111-152), are collectively referred to as the Affordable Care Act (ACA). The ACA represents the broadest changes to the health care system since the creation of Medicare and Medicaid programs in 1965. The ACA is expected to provide insurance coverage for 32 million previously uninsured Americans. This new demand on the health care system has significant implications for nursing, the nation's largest health care profession with more than 3 million RNs nationwide. Nurses have the potential to effect significant changes in the health care system that will meet the demand for safe, quality, patient-centered, accessible, and affordable care (IOM, 2011).

AACN's report on the 2013-2014 enrollment in baccalaureate and graduate programs in nursing showed that U.S. nursing schools turned away 78,089 qualified applicants from baccalaureate and graduate nursing programs in 2013 due to budget constraints and insufficient numbers of faculty, clinical sites, classroom space, and clinical preceptors. Budget constraints, an aging faculty, and increasing job competition from clinical sites have contributed to this emerging crisis (AACN, 2014).

A wave of faculty retirements is expected across the United States over the next decade. Master's and doctoral programs in nursing are not producing a large enough pool of potential nurse educators to meet the demand. Higher compensation in clinical and private-sector settings is luring current and potential nurse educators away from teaching. According to the American Academy of Nurse Practitioners, the average salary of a nurse practitioner, across settings and specialties, is $94,050. By contrast, AACN reported in March 2013 that master's prepared faculty earned an annual average salary of $80,690. http://nurse-practitioners.advanceweb.com and http://www.aacn.nche.edu/research.da

SUMMARY

Nursing is a dynamic profession that has evolved into a theory, research, and evidence-based practice. From its unorganized and variably defined beginnings, a profession based on the framework of competence, autonomy, determination, and human caring has developed. The challenges and opportunities have paralleled the path of world history and have brought about significant changes in the profession. From the men who opened the path, to the women who brought dignity and respect to their philosophy of caring, to the pioneers who brought unity to the profession plagued by a history of racism, sexism, and sometimes disgrace, nursing has become recognized as critical to the health of the nation. Despite myriad challenges, the practice of nursing has been distinguished and qualified by the intellect, skill, commitment, and contribution of countless nuns, deaconesses, and individuals such as Seacole, Dix, Barton, Wald, Breckenridge, and Nightingale.

The nursing profession has the capacity to effect far-reaching changes in the health care system. Close proximity to patients and scientific understanding of care across the health care continuum from health promotion to disease prevention to coordination of care give nurses the unique ability to lead in the improvement and redesign of the health care system. Research has linked nursing care to the safety of patients. Nurses will continue to increase knowledge, manage technology, and maintain ethical standards to provide high-quality, patient-centered, safe care to individuals, families, communities, and populations throughout the world.

Nurses are crucial in preventing medication errors, reducing infection rates, and facilitating patients' transition from hospital to home. Significant nursing contributions to creating a quality, patient-centered health care system that is accessible, equitable, evidence based and sustainable will require transforming the work environment, scope of practice, education, and numbers of nurses in the United States.

Through periods of war, socioeconomic change, and health care reform, nurses have played a vital role in initiating change to improve the health care arena. Nurses have provided the integrity to maintain the quality of care in all health care settings. The evolution of the practice from the treatment of disease to health promotion and disease prevention has led the way in determining the type of providers needed to care for patients in the future. This evolution will continue to provide the foundation for the scope of practice, educational curricula, scholarship, and research necessary for nurses to lead and manage the health care environment of the future (Catalano, 2012).

REFERENCES

American Association of Colleges of Nursing (AACN): *Competencies and curricular expectations for Clinical Nurse Leader (sm) education and practice,* 2013 (website). http://www.aacn.nche.edu/cnl/CNL-Competencies-October-2013.pdf. Accessed September 30, 2014.

American Association of Colleges of Nursing (AACN): *Nursing Faculty Shortage Fact Sheet* (website). http://www.aacn.nche.edu/media-relations/fact-sheets/nursing-faculty-shortage. Accessed August 18, 2014.

Bahr L, Johnson B: *Collier's encyclopedia,* vol 18, New York, 1997, Simon and Schuster.

Buhler-Wilkerson K: *No place like home: a history of nursing and home care in the United States*, Baltimore, 2001, Johns Hopkins University Press.

Carnegie ME: *The path we tread: blacks in nursing worldwide, 1854–1994,* ed 3, New York, 1995, National League for Nursing, Jones and Bartlett.

Catalano JT: *Nursing now: today's issues, tomorrow's trends,* ed 6, Philadelphia, 2012, FA Davis.

Chitty KB, Black BP: *Professional nursing: concepts and challenges,* ed 7, St Louis, 2014, Elsevier/Saunders.

Deloughery GL: *Issues and trends in nursing,* ed 3, St Louis, 1998, Mosby.

Donahue MP: *Nursing: the finest art—an illustrated history*, St Louis, 1999, Mosby.

Ellis JR, Hartley CL: *Nursing in today's world: challenges, issues and trends,* ed 10, Philadelphia, 2012, Wolters Kluwer/Lippincott Williams & Wilkins.

Fang D, Li Y, Bednash GD: *2012–2013 salaries of instructional and administrative nursing faculty in baccalaureate and graduate programs in nursing,* Washington, DC, 2013, American Association of Colleges of Nursing.

Fitzpatrick MF: The mercy brigade, Civil War Times Illustrated 36(5):34–40, 1997.

Freedman D: *The Anchor bible dictionary,* New York, 1995, Doubleday.

Giger J, Davidhizar R: *Transcultural nursing: assessment and intervention,* ed 5, St Louis, 2008, Mosby.

Gill G: *Nightingales: the extraordinary upbringing and curious life of Miss Florence Nightingale,* New York, 2004, Ballantine Books.

Institute of Medicine (IOM): Who will keep the public healthy? Educating public health professionals for the 21st century. Workshop summary. In Gebbie K, Rosenstock L, Hernandez LM, editors: *Committee on Educating Public Health Professionals for the 21st Century, 2003, Board on Health Promotion and Disease Prevention, Institute of Medicine of the National Academies,* Washington, DC, 2003, The National Academies Press.

Institute of Medicine (IOM): *The future of nursing: leading change, advancing nurse,* Washington, DC, 2011, The Academies Press.

Joel L: *The nursing experience: trends, challenges and transition,* ed 5, New York, 2006, McGraw-Hill.

Jones ZO: Knowledge systems in conflict: the regulation of African American midwifery, *Nurs Hist Rev* 12:167–184, 2004.

Kalisch P, Kalisch B: *The advance of American nursing,* ed 2, Philadelphia, 1986, JB Lippincott.

Kalisch P, Kalisch B: *The advance of American nursing,* ed 3, Philadelphia, 1995, JB Lippincott.

Kalisch B, Kalisch P: *American nursing: a history,* ed 4, Philadelphia, 2003, Lippincott Williams & Wilkins.

Karger HJ, Stoesz D: *American social welfare policy: a pluralist approach,* ed 5, New York, 2005, Allyn and Bacon.

Katz JR, Carter C, Bishop J, et al: *Keys to nursing success,* ed 3, Columbus, OH, 2009, Pearson/Prentice-Hall.

Lindeman C, McAthie M: *Nursing trends and issues,* Springhouse, PA, 1990, Springhouse.

Nelson S: *"Say little, do much": nineteenth century religious women and care of the sick,* Philadelphia, 2001, University of Pennsylvania Press.

Nies MA, McEwen M: *Community/public health nursing: promoting the health of populations,* ed 5, St Louis, 2011, Elsevier Saunders.

Oermann MH: *Professional nursing practice,* Stamford, CT, 1997, Prentice-Hall.

O'Lynn CO, Tranbarger R: *Men in nursing: history, challenges, and opportunities,* New York, 2006, Springer.

Rebar CR, Gersch CJ, Macnee CL, et al: *Understanding nursing research: using research in evidence-based practice,* ed 3, Philadelphia, 2011, Wolters Kluwer/Lippincott Williams & Wilkins.

Robinson TM, Perry PM: *Cadet nurse stories: the call for and response of women during World War II,* Indianapolis, 2001, Center Nursing Press.

Salzman J, Smith D, West C, editors: *Encyclopedia of African-American culture and history,* vol 3, New York, 1996, Macmillan Library Reference USA, Simon and Schuster Macmillan.

Small H: *Florence Nightingale: avenging angel,* London, 2002, Constable and Robinson.

Snodgrass ME: *Historical encyclopedia of nursing,* Santa Barbara, CA, 2004, Diane Publishing.

Stanhope M, Lancaster J: *Public health nursing; population-centered health care in the community,* ed 8, St Louis, 2012, Elsevier.

Walton J, Barondess J, Locke S: *The Oxford medical companion,* New York, 1994, Oxford University Press.

ADDITIONAL RESOURCES

American Association of Colleges of Nursing (AACN): *The essentials of doctoral education for advanced nursing practice,* 2008, (website). www.aacn.nche.edu.

Carnegie ME: Black nurses at the front, *Am J Nurs* 84(10):1250–1252, 1984.

Reed K, Dennison, P: The Clinical Nurse Leader (CNL)®: point-of-care safety clinician, *The Online Journal of Issues in Nursing* 16(11):, 2011.

Each nurse forms the image of nursing every day.

2

The Contemporary Image of Professional Nursing

L. Antoinette (Toni) Bargagliotti, PhD, RN, ANEF, FAAN

ⓔ Additional resources are available online at: *http://evolve.elsevier.com/Cherry/*

> *"People are always blaming their circumstances for what they are. I don't believe in circumstances. The people who get on in this world are the people who get up and look for the circumstances they want, and if they can't find them, make them."*
>
> *George Bernard Shaw*

PROFESSIONAL/ETHICAL ISSUE

John is asked to join a health care mission trip to a remote area of South Sudan that has no health care. As the only nurse, John will be joining a physician's assistant, a dentist, and multiple laypersons that will "help." They will be taking donated out-of-date medications (fourth-generation antibiotics, vials of multi-dose vaccines) as well as syringes and sterile supplies that were to be discarded because of their age and questionable sterility. When John asks whom he needs to contact in this country about a temporary license to practice, the team assures him that isn't necessary because it would be such "a hassle" and they will only be there for 10 days. There will be minimal water and no electricity in this village.

RESPONSE 1

Because there is no health care, the team reasons that the medications and syringes are probably fine. Following this line of reasoning, John would provide unsafe care that places people at risk who have no idea of the risk that they are taking. There will be no follow-up care or referral resources. Highly sophisticated antibiotics will be introduced into an "antibiotic-naïve" region to people who may not finish a course of treatment because they give the remaining pills to a needy family member or trade them for food.

RESPONSE 2

John reasons that he is violating all of the ANA Code of Ethics and cannot participate in unsafe care that is disrespectful of human rights. He can't practice without a license or the knowledge and consent of the government or bring drugs into the country in suitcases without any permission to do so. Once reconstituted, the vaccines will be unrefrigerated.

VIGNETTE

Mary is a senior nursing student who asks a faculty member, "Why can't we wear different scrubs and jewelry to clinical? Have you seen what nurses wear? I don't know what difference it makes anyway. Patients don't care what we're wearing. They care that we know how to take care of them. You know, two months after we graduate, we'll be wearing what everyone else does. Yes, I know we look better than everyone else does. But why?"

Questions to Consider While Reading This Chapter:
1. How does the image of a nurse differ from that of a physician?
2. How does the nurse's appearance affect the patient's opinion of the quality of care the nurse provides?

KEY TERMS

Antiestablishment: Opposition to the conventional social, political, and economic principles of society.

Art: Any branch of creative work, especially painting and drawing, that displays form, beauty, and any unusual perception.

Literature: All writings in prose or verse.

Media: All the means of communication, such as newspapers, radio, and television.

Stereotype: A fixed or conventional conception of a person or group held by a number of people that allows for no individuality.

LEARNING OUTCOMES

After studying this chapter, the reader will be able to:
1. Describe the image of nursing in art, media, and literature over time.
2. Identify nursing actions that convey a negative image of nursing.
3. Suggest strategies that would enhance the image of nursing.

4. Explain how the IOM *Future of Nursing* report is shaping the image of nursing.
5. Create an individualized plan to promote a positive image of nursing in practice.

CHAPTER OVERVIEW

This chapter describes how the image of nursing has been shaped and suggests strategies that nurses can use to forge a positive public and professional image of their practice. Because nurses have been the subjects of artists, sculptors, and writers for thousands of years, an historic perspective is used to illustrate the contextual background for the evolving image of the profession.

IMAGES OF NURSING

When you imagine a nurse, what mental picture comes to mind? Do you think of *LIFE* magazine's 1942 nurse in a starched white uniform with a cap, the nurses portrayed in Johnson & Johnson's *Campaign for Nursing's Future* (2013), or your colleagues with whom you practiced yesterday? All of them are architects of healing.

The contemporary image of professional nursing in the United States is an ever-changing kaleidoscope created by the 4.18 million men and women of all ages, races, and religious beliefs who have active licensure as registered nurses (RNs). Adding to this multifaceted collage are the numerous snapshots of nurses and nursing as portrayed in television commercials, bumper stickers, art, poetry, architecture, postage stamps, television dramas, television series, movies, newspaper comic strips, stained-glass windows, and statues. Second in size to the profession of teaching, nurses have been alternatively described as either saints or sinners, powerless or powerful, admired or ignored, and, most recently, those who dare to care. Their practice has captured the attention of historians, economists, and sociologists who have studied this unusual group of people.

To whatever your image of nursing is, first add the many heroic nurses who served in Afghanistan and Iraq and in every U.S. war. In July 1775 after the United States established the Continental Army, General George Washington requested the Second Continental Congress to provide one nurse for every 10 patients and one matron for every 100 patients to supervise the care of wounded and sick solders. His confidence was well placed.

In 2007, Captain Maria Ortiz, a 40-year-old clinic nurse manager, became the first nursing casualty in Iraq, dying from mortar fire to her clinic in Baghdad. Captain Jennifer Moreno was a 25-year-old University of San Francisco nursing graduate who was commissioned in the U.S. Army upon graduation. She completed the Army Airborne course and was a medical-surgical nurse who volunteered and was selected from thousands of female officers to a Special Operations Cultural Support team that included multinational, multi-branch soldiers. For the first time, women soldiers were included on these teams of all male Rangers or Green Berets because they could engage with Afghan women to obtain information unavailable to male soldiers. Every mission would be highly dangerous, especially so for women. She is thought to be the first nurse to serve on these teams. Captain Moreno served in Afghanistan with the 3rd Battalion, 75th Ranger Regiment (see Figure 2-1).

FIGURE 2-1 Captain Jennifer Moreno.

In October 2013, while on a night mission that prevented a high-profile suicide attack in Kandahar that would have killed hundreds of civilians, an Afghan woman walked out of the compound detonating her suicide vest, wounding six Rangers. Another insurgent detonated another bomb injuring others. Receiving a staff sergeant's call to help a wounded Ranger and the ground commander's order for everyone to stay put to avoid detonating other bombs, Moreno heeded the call for help and ran through a heavily mined village to rescue wounded Rangers. Her Bronze Star commendation reads: "Disregarding her own well-being, Moreno unhesitatingly moved to assist (the soldiers) upon realizing the severity of the wounds sustained by her fellow teammates. While in transit, Moreno detonated Device No. 5 and was killed in action" (KOMO News, 2013; Army Times, 2014). More than a thread in the rich tapestry of the heroic work of all nurses, Ortiz and Moreno's courage and sacrifice illuminates the timeless commitment of all nurses to save lives and advance health.

Since Florence Nightingale reduced mortality rates from 42% to 2% in a Crimean hospital constructed over an open sewer, nurses have been reformers who use limited resources to address unlimited "wants" for health care. The request for Nightingale's nursing services in the Crimea was born out of newspaper reports about the devastating health care conditions in the Crimean War. However, the outcome that Nightingale and these nurses achieved changed conditions in the British Army, forged a system of nursing education, and continues to strongly influence the profession.

Although nurses have become concerned with their public image and media portrayal, Kalisch and Kalisch's (1995) extensive work outlining the image of nursing in film and media over time permanently etched the image issue into the professional radar screen.

WHY IMAGE IS IMPORTANT

Publicly, concerns about the image of nursing are most often associated with a deepening national and global concern about the evolving nursing shortage. However, the image of nursing has far more serious effects than the numbers of nurses who are not there. RNs, who are 40% of the entire health professional workforce, are the "glue" that binds the health care of many into a more seamless experience for the patient. Safe patient care demands coordination of the armada of health professionals who use many technologies and many handoffs to provide care to a single person in intensive care and other technology-driven areas. How nursing is perceived inside and outside of the health care system directly affects how successful nurses will be in providing and coordinating patient care.

The requirement for health care usually comes unexpectedly and without warning. When patients seek health care in a hospital, they are entrusting their life and well-being to the one person who has 24/7 direct responsibility for their care and their environment—the RN. Unlike their personal physician, with whom patients may have had a long-term relationship, the RN, who is coordinating all of their care, is new to them and changes every 8 to 12 hours. It is important that the public trusts and believes in this nurse and the profession the nurse represents.

REGISTERED NURSE SUPPLY

Between 1983 and 1998, the proportion of the registered nurse (RN) workforce younger than 30 years of age decreased from 30% to 12%, while the average age of working RNs increased 4.5 years from 37.4 years of age to 41.9 years of age. There was a projected shortfall of 20%, or 400,000, RNs expected by 2020. However, Buerhaus and colleagues (2009) reported that the registered nurse supply is growing faster than projected due to the surge in new nurses 23 to 26 years of age who are entering the workforce. The RN shortfall trends have reversed over the past decade, as nursing has become a more attractive career. State and national recruitment incentives as well as growth in both associate degree and primarily baccalaureate programs have positively impacted the projected nursing shortage.

According to the National Council of State Board Reports (2002, 2013), the number of new graduates increased by more than 230% between 2002 (70,692) and 2013 (163,001). Adding to the increases in new nurses is the socioeconomic trend for almost 24% of registered nurses to remain in the workforce full time until the age of 69. Whether this is due to the effects of a sluggish economy or a healthier workforce at older ages, this trend is mirrored among men in other professions as well (Auerbach, Buerhaus, Staiger, 2014). Later retirement ages convert a gradual workforce loss over several years to larger losses at one time when the majority of baby boomers reach 70. The immediate effect of these changes has created surpluses of nurses in California

and other states diminishing the opportunities for new graduates in those areas. To some extent, this leads to a mistaken belief that the shortage has been ameliorated.

Legislative efforts to stem a nursing shortage began in 2002 with the Nurse Reinvestment Act (Public Law 107-205), which provided nursing scholarships, public service announcements promoting nursing as a career, faculty loan cancellation programs, geriatric training grants, and nurse retention and safety enhancement grants. In 2010, the Patient Protection and Affordable Care Act increased the nursing student loan amounts, provided $50 million per year to fund nurse-managed health centers (Title V, Section 330A-1), funded gerontology nursing fellowship programs (Title V, Section 5305), provided up to $40,000 in educational loan repayment for nurse faculty and $80,000 for doctorally prepared nurse faculty, and significantly strengthened Title VIII advanced nursing education grants. Additionally, funding was made available for graduate nursing demonstration grants (Section 5509) to hospitals providing advanced nursing education clinical training to advanced practice nurses (nurse anesthetists, clinical nurse specialists, nurse practitioners, and nurse-midwives).

The projection of a potential nursing shortage will continue to loom large as an image-maker for nursing. According to the U.S. Bureau of Labor, the employment rate of RNs has one of the highest growth rates of employment of all occupations. With an employment rate expected to increase by more than 19%, job production for nurses is projected to grow faster than the average of all occupations (11%) until 2020 (Bureau of Labor Statistics, 2014). The strategies that have been used to ameliorate nursing shortfalls, such as the migration of internationally educated nurses, are insufficient to ameliorate a nursing shortage. Internationally educated nurses (IENs) are 8% of the U.S. working nurse force (Budden et al, 2013). Notably, the 2013 NCLEX-RN pass rate of IENs was 21.4% representing only 1% of newly licensed nurses (National Council of State Boards of Nursing [NCSBN], 2013). Similarly, strategies to entice nurses back into nursing will produce little for a profession that already has 83% of its licensed members in nursing practice and only 3% seeking a nursing position (Budden et al, 2013).

NURSING IN ART AND LITERATURE

Although the way that nursing has been portrayed in art and literature over time may seem to be unrelated to the contemporary image of nursing, the mental image of contemporary nursing is enmeshed with these earliest images.

Art and literature have been the way in which people describe the human condition and cultural values of their time. In these earliest descriptions of nurses and nursing are found the enduring fundamental and essential tensions that exist within the profession today. Found within art and literature is the eternal question asked by those who know they will one day require nursing care, "Can I trust and entrust my life to this nurse?"

Antiquity Image of Nursing

The earliest literary reference to nursing chronicles the actions of two nurse-midwives in approximately 1900 BC in Exodus 1 of the Old Testament, which indicates that the practice of two midwives became the vehicle through which the Israelites, the Jewish race, and the resultant Judeo-Christian heritage survived. From the sixth century until the 1800s, nurses were imaged as untrained servants, soldiers, women of religious orders, or wealthy people performing acts of Christian charity (Kalisch and Kalisch, 1995; Kampen, 1988). These meager artistic renderings of nurses convey images that continue to be familiar to contemporary nurses.

Victorian Image of Nursing

In 1844 when Florence Nightingale was "called" to become a nurse, Charles Dickens immortalized a different kind of nurse through Sairy Gamp, the nurse for whom nursing was endured because of the lack of other opportunities. For Sairy Gamp, a drunken, physically unkempt, uncaring nurse in *The Life and Adventures of Martin Chuzzlewit,* nursing provided a way to profit from the sick and dying. Reflecting the concern of Victorian England for untrained caregivers, Dickens writes Sairy should be advised of the advantages of "a little less liquor, and a little more humanity, and a little less regard for herself, and a little more regard for her patients, and perhaps a trifle of additional honesty."

Fortunately Sairy's literary arrival was followed by Longfellow's portrayal of the heroic Nightingale in *Santa Filomena* (1857). As important as Nightingale was to the improved health care of British soldiers and to the development of modern nursing, the ever-increasing positive images of Nightingale occurred solely because she was able to succinctly demonstrate the aggregate outcomes of nursing practice. Nightingale was one of the earliest users of the emerging body of knowledge called *statistics* and developed the pie chart that remains in common use. Notably, nursing emerged at a time of turbulent social change and reform in Great Britain.

Early Twentieth-Century Nursing

Toward the end of the Nightingale period at the turn of the century, nurses in war settings vividly capture the attention of artists. The most compelling image is George Bellows' 1918 canvas, *Edith Cavell Directing the Escape of Soldiers from Prison Camp* (Donahue, 1910). World War I Germany shocked the world with its 1915 firing squad execution of Edith Cavell, founder of the first nursing school in Belgium, who aided soldiers escaping prison camps. The art of heroic nursing expressed in several famous paintings reflected the reality of World War I nurses who were also the recipients of three Distinguished Service Crosses, 23 Distinguished Service Medals, 28 French Croix de Guerres, 69 British Military Medals, and 4 U.S. Navy Crosses (Donahue, 2010). Notably, American nurses who served in World War I were not commissioned in the military services. One in every three nurses served in World War I.

The 1930s Nurse as Angel of Mercy

On a grander scale, Warner Brothers' film *The White Angel* (1936) chronicled the professional life of Florence Nightingale (Jones, 1988). Endorsed by the American Nurses Association (ANA), *The White Angel* clearly portrayed Nightingale's persistence and head-to-head confrontation with medicine. Anticipating that the medical staff would deny rations for the nurses, she brought provisions for them. When the medical staff locked her out of the hospital, Nightingale sat outside in the snow until patients and soldiers required physicians to admit these nurses. *The White Angel* conveyed to the public that nursing is a holy vocation, nurses have professional credentials, and their career choice is opposed because popular opinion held that women belong at home (Jones, 1988). A subtle inference of the film is that Nightingale was smart enough to overcome the obstacles of medicine.

In 1938, Francis Rich's tall and imposing white limestone statue, *The Nurses Memorial*, sometimes referred to as the *Spirit of Nursing*, was placed in Arlington National Cemetery to honor military nurses. Similarly, Germany's postage stamp issued in 1936 commemorated nursing with a larger-than-life nurse compassionately overlooking people (Donahue, 2010).

The 1940s Nurse as Heroine

Considered to be the most positive movie about nursing, *So Proudly We Hail* is the 1942 story of nurses in Bataan and Corregidor. The film, starring Claudette Colbert, portrayed a small group of nurses rerouted to the Philippines after the attack on Pearl Harbor. Soon cut off from supplies and replacements as the Japanese took over the Philippines, these nurses provided care with few supplies and no staff to the thousands of soldiers in the Philippines. When the last nurses were to be evacuated from the occupied islands, a number of nurses voluntarily stayed behind, made the march to Bataan, and were interned as prisoners of war. Norman's *We Band of Angels: the Untold Story of American Nurses Trapped on Bataan by the Japanese* (1999) tells, via their diaries and interviews, the gritty, difficult, and heroic story of these nurses who served in Bataan.

Nursing was depicted positively on a 1940 Australian postage stamp as a larger-than-life figure looking over a soldier, a sailor, and an aviator; on Costa Rica's 1945 postage stamp of Florence Nightingale and Edith Cavell; and in the 1945 commissioning of the USS *Higbee*, a navy destroyer named in honor of a navy nurse (Donahue, 2010).

After nursing's glorious contributions to World War II, nurses returned home to find low salaries, long hours, too few staff, and too many patients. However, nursing continued to be glamorized through the Cherry Ames book series, the Sue Barton series, and other romance novels.

Nursing in the Antiestablishment Era of the 1960s

Ken Kesey developed the modern version of Sairy Gamp through the character of Nurse Ratched in *One Flew Over the Cuckoo's Nest* (1962). This best-selling novel later became a play and motion picture (1975) that won six Oscars, including Best Picture. Entrusted with the care of the mentally ill, Nurse Ratched, a militaristic nurse in a starched white uniform, was the ultimate power figure that punished patients to cure their psychosis through conformity to a "system" (Jones, 1988). However, the reality of the turbulent period of the 1960s is that nursing was one of President Lyndon Johnson's first salvos in the war on poverty. The Nurse Training Act of 1964 was funded at $250 million ($1.88 billion in 2014 dollars). Although nurses also dramatically shaped the future of health care through the development of coronary care units, intensive care units, hemodialysis, and Silver and Ford's first nurse practitioner program in Colorado, a U.S. Bureau of Labor study indicated that nursing salaries at the time were woefully inadequate in comparison with other, far less trained American workers (Kalisch and Kalisch, 1995).

Nursing in the Sexual Revolution of the 1970s

Media images of the nurse in the 1970s were formed amid a sexual revolution and a growing antimilitary American culture. War would again provide the media backdrop. The 1976 postage stamp, *Clara Maas, She Gave Her Life,* commemorated the 100th birthday of a 25-year-old nurse who died after deliberately obtaining two carrier mosquito bites so that she could continue providing care to soldiers with yellow fever in the Spanish-American War (Donahue, 2010). Her modern-day counterparts would be nurses in *M*A*S*H*, the hit television series that ran from 1972 to 1983.

The nursing profession viewed *M*A*S*H* as professionally destructive because of the negative portrayal of Major Margaret "Hot Lips" Hoolihan and the nurses of the 4077th Army MASH (Mobile Army Surgical Hospital) unit in Korea. The sexual exploits of nurses and physicians and the uncaring Margaret provided few positive images. However, for the American public who were receiving a daily dose of Vietnam footage on nightly news, *M*A*S*H* presented a glimmer of reality.

The continuous front-line exposure to the massive trauma of young men did not immunize the more than 5,000 army nurses who served in Vietnam from caring or from the horrors of what they were seeing. They coped with these horrors with a sense of humor and irreverence toward "the system." These nurses were young (average age of 23), newly graduated (only 35% having 2 years of experience, 60% having less than 6 months experience), and 21% were men. From 15 Army nurses in Vietnam in 1965, their numbers quickly expanded to a maximum of 900 nurses in 1969, who provided care for 5,283 beds (58 patients to 1 nurse), working 12-hour shifts, 6 days a week (West, 2014). Lt. Sharon Lane, who was killed by mortar fire to her nursing ward, was the only nurse killed by direct enemy fire. At the end of the war, Captain Mary Klinker, a flight nurse, was killed when her plane carrying 128 people, mostly Vietnamese orphans, was downed by enemy fire near Saigon (*Women in the Vietnam War,* History Channel).

Nurses serving in Vietnam would later be imaged in the television series *China Beach* (1988-1991).

Nursing in the 1980s to 1990s

The complexities of nursing are realistically described in the play and television movie *Miss Evers' Boys*. Through the character of Miss Evers, the play tells the true story of Nurse Rivers, who was hired to recruit and retain young African-American men into the infamous Tuskegee experiment designed to describe the long-term effects of untreated syphilis. Although the study began in 1932, penicillin became the treatment of choice for syphilis in 1947 in the civilian population. When subjects asked Nurse Evers to obtain the new treatment of penicillin for them and she sought to do so, the physician investigators required her to discourage them from treatment. Subjects were told they would be dropped from the study and forgo the benefits of free treatment, a free ride to the clinic, one hot meal per day, and, in case of dying, $50 for their funeral. Subjects were never told they had syphilis, only that they had "bad blood." The study, which was funded for 40 years by the U.S. Public Health Service, ended in 1972 only because it became publicly known through the press. Ironically, Nurse Evers was the only consistent staff person throughout the 40 years of the study. As the narrator of the story, Nurse Evers introduces non-nurses to the dilemmas of nursing practice during that era and the consequences of misplaced faith and trust in other health care disciplines. Notably an outcome of the Tuskegee study was the requirement for institutional review boards to prevent this from occurring again.

In 1997, three films used war and nursing as a backdrop: *The English Patient, Love and War,* and *Paradise Road*. In all of these films, the nurse is a knowledgeable, nonjudgmental caregiver.

Artistic views of nursing during this period focused on caring. In the *Vietnam War Women's Memorial,* located in Washington, DC, the central figure is the nurse in battle fatigues cradling the head of a soldier for whom she is providing care. Evident in the bronze statue is the fatigue of the nurse and her care for this dying soldier.

Millennial Media

As David Stanley (2008) noted in his review of nurses in film from 1900 to 2007, more recent films with nurses tend to portray them as thoughtful, independent, intelligent professionals. In 2000, 2004, and 2010, the character of Greg Focker, RN, in the movies *Meet the Parents, Meet the Fockers,* and *The Little Fockers,* endures his father-in-law's stereotyped views about men who

are nurses. In the 2001 movie *Pearl Harbor,* nurses were positively portrayed as heroically providing care and order to the chaos following the bombing attack on Pearl Harbor. Although a number of successful television series take place in hospitals, such as NBC's *ER* (1994-2009), ABC's *Grey's Anatomy* (2005-), Fox's *House* (2004-), and NBC's and ABC's *Scrubs* (2001-2010), their central characters are primarily physicians, although much of what is depicted is nursing practice provided by interns and residents. Because the primary storylines, which focus on physicians, portray the physicians negatively, the scriptwriters' neglect of nursing may be professionally helpful to nursing.

The Fox series *HawthoRNe* (2009-2011) featured Christina Hawthorne, a multitasking chief nursing officer with strong administrative and clinical skills who advocated for patients and nurses. However, breaches of nurses' ethical standards, sexual interaction between a patient and nurse, and porous professional boundaries negatively portrayed nursing.

On April 6, 2014, CBS television's *60 Minutes* traveled with two West Virginia nurse practitioners, Teresa Gardner and Paula Meade, in their Health Wagon as they provided primary care to rural Appalachian people who cannot afford health care in six West Virginia counties. Originally begun by Sr. Bernie Kenny from a Volkswagen Beetle, the Health Wagon is now a mobile primary care clinic in a 13-year-old Winnebago van that is funded by federal grants, donations, and the support of pharmaceutical suppliers, who provide needed medications.

Social Media

Nurses have created a new aspect to the media portrayal of nursing through their use of social media, such as Facebook, Snapchat, and Instagram. While designed to provide an asynchronous communication medium among friends, "friending" is now often extended to unknown persons. Nurses and student nurses who have self-identified as nurses or students have posted comments about their practice, managers, or patients (whether named or not) that have created serious professional issues for nursing. Thirty-three state boards of nursing (SBNs) reported receiving complaints about nurses' use of social media, and twenty-six of these SBNs reported having disciplined the licenses of nurses (NCSBN, 2011). Nursing students have been expelled from nursing programs because of both positive and negative postings about patients. The courts have upheld those decisions because of the significant breach of professional boundaries. Regrettably, nurses have "friended" patients and their families, leading to significant professional concerns about maintaining professional boundaries (NCSBN, 2011; Cronquist and Spector, 2011).

With the widespread use of cell phones with cameras, candid pictures and video clips that are amusing to friends are not as amusing to human resource personnel hiring nurses, to nurse managers, or to a courtroom when an error with serious consequences brings the nurse's professional judgment into question. Nurses have been terminated from positions and had their licenses disciplined or removed because they have posted pictures of patients on a social media site. They have been similarly disciplined for receiving patient pictures and not immediately reporting the problem. It is important for the nurse to understand that whatever is posted can be seen by others as well as the intended person and is available to be seen forever. Removing a posting or a picture from a website does not make it unavailable because it remains retrievable (Cronquist and Spector, 2011).

Nurses can positively use electronic social media to share workplace concerns or events that are emotionally charged for support and guidance, but must always be mindful of not providing names, explicit details or patient identifiers, including photos, in order to protect patient and nurse privacy. For more information, review *Social Media Guidelines for Nurses* at https://www.ncsbn.org/347.htm.

Nursing's Response

Nursing students are the future of nursing. And students have taken this responsibility seriously with two similar programs directed toward the image of nursing. In 1993, the National Student Nurses Association (NSNA) (www.nsna.org/activities/nursing.asp) developed the ongoing Image of Nursing program designed to improve and protect the image of nursing. The program logo, "Nursing: Not just a job, a profession," articulated the student perspective on nursing. This program has given annual awards for Image of Nursing projects and provided information to students. An important part of the NSNA Image of Nursing program has been the media surveillance information provided to students. How to contact the television networks, how to most effectively transmit information to them, and sample letters are provided to enable the voices of students to be heard when there is negative nursing media or advertisements (NSNA, 2014). More recently, the NSNA has adopted a policy on social media that includes important examples of boundary violations.

In April 2001, seven graduate students at the Johns Hopkins University School of Nursing founded the Center for Nursing Advocacy (*www.nursingadvocacy. org*), which was rebranded to the Truth About Nursing (*www.truthaboutnursing.org*) in 2008. Designed to monitor and positively influence the portrayal of nurses in all media venues, the organization successfully changed many negative uses of nurses. Skechers, Schick, Dentyne Ice, and the Lung Cancer Alliance all were persuaded to remove "naughty nurse" televised advertisements (Truth About Nursing, 2011).

Media Campaigns for Nursing

In 1990, the Tri-Council of Nursing with funding from the Pew Foundation implemented the Nurses of America (NOA) media campaign to convey to the public that nurses are expert clinicians who are able to interpret technical data in usable ways as well as coordinate and negotiate health care. A strategically important part of the NOA campaign raised consciousness among nurses about the lack of visibility of nursing in the news media. A study of sources quoted by health coverage journalists in *The New York Times, The Los Angeles Times,* and *The Boston Globe* indicated that nurses accounted for only 10 of more than 900 citations, ranking nurses last after patients (Buresch, Gordon, and Bell, 1991). Sigma Theta Tau International's Woodhull study of 20,000 articles published in 16 newspapers, magazines, and other health care publications (1998) indicated that nurses were cited only 4% of the time in the more than 2000 articles about health care (Sigma Theta Tau International, 1998).

Seeking to stem the nursing shortage and enhance the image of nursing, Johnson & Johnson launched a $50 million multiyear media campaign *(Campaign for Nursing's Future)* in 2002 (Johnson & Johnson, 2013). This has included more than 32 million pieces of recruitment posters, brochures, and videos in English and Spanish to junior high schools, career and community centers as well as many television advertisements that are also available on YouTube (www.youtube.com). These have influenced 24% of 18- to 24-year olds to consider nursing as a career. Additionally, there is the Nursing Notes by Johnson and Johnson Facebook fan page that launches two nursing videos per month, a comprehensive website *(Discover Nursing)* with information about nursing, an interactive program *(Your Future in Nursing)* for new graduates, and a Twitter handle (@JNJNursing-Notes) (Johnson & Johnson, 2013). To commemorate the tenth year of this campaign, Johnson and Johnson invited nurses and nursing students to send a picture that became the *Art of Nursing: A Portrait of Thanks Mosaic project*. For every picture they received, Johnson and Johnson donated $1 to the NSNA Foundation Scholarship Fund. Accompanying their marketing campaign for nursing has been the ongoing Promise of Nursing galas that have raised more than $19 million for nursing faculty scholarships for students planning to be nursing faculty in that state (Johnson & Johnson, 2013).

THE ENDURING PUBLIC CONCERN WITH NURSING

Against this backdrop of nursing images that extend from antiquity to the latest news broadcast is the question of the image that nurses will create today.

The Institute of Medicine's Future of Nursing

In 2010, The Institute of Medicine (IOM) issued a landmark report, *The Future of Nursing*, that has significantly impacted the image and future of nursing. This report included four main recommendations: (1) higher levels of nursing education (80% BSN by 2020 and doubling the number of doctorates) through seamless academic progression; (2) removal of barriers to enable nurses to practice to their full scope of practice based on their educational preparation; (3) inclusion of nurses as full partners with physicians and other professionals in redesigning the health care system in the United States; and (4) improved data collection and information infrastructure to facilitate more effective workforce planning and information infrastructure (IOM, 2010). The IOM also recommended nurse residency programs that would be funded by the Secretary of Health and Human Services redirecting all graduate medical education funds from diploma schools to residency programs in rural and critical access areas, a change in accreditation standards to include an assessment of clinical competency, seamless access to higher levels of nursing education that extends beyond an articulation agreement, insuring that nurses engage in life-long learning, and prepare and enable nurses to lead change to advance health. They envisioned nursing preparation for leading change that would occur through the inclusion of leadership and business practices across all nursing curricula and the development of leadership and mentoring programs, as well as the inclusion of nurses on all private, public, and governmental health care boards, executive management teams, and in other strategic leadership roles (IOM, 2010).

What the Public Believes About Nursing

Since 1999, when the Gallup poll began including nursing in its annual December poll on ethics, the public has rated nursing higher than all other professions for every year except 2001, when firemen outranked nursing, which likely represents a response to their work during and after the 9/11 attacks. In the 2014 Gallup poll on ethical professions, 80% of the public rated nurses as the most ethical profession. In 2014, two other medical professions—medical doctors and pharmacists—tie for second place at 65%, with police officers and clergy approaching 50% (Gallup poll, 2014).

THE REALITY OF THE CONTEMPORARY STAFF NURSE

"The reason for the existence of the modern health care institution—the hospital, the nursing home, the mental hospital, the home care agency—is to deliver nursing. If surgery could be done safely and economically on the kitchen table, and if people could survive it, it would be. If diagnosis and management of serious medical illness could be done in office practices in 8.5-minute visits, it would be. If the chronically mentally ill could be taken care of at home, and protected from the world and from themselves, they would be. If the demented, the frail, the paralyzed, the very old could be cared for at home, they would be and it would be a whole lot cheaper because public policy would not contemplate channeling the money to family caregivers: they're supposed to want to do it anyway" (Diers, 1988).

Logically it could be inferred that nurses' satisfaction with the work setting should be high because their practice settings exist to deliver their services, and new practice settings are emerging daily. The public highly values their profession. Nursing's heroic and noble public image has been etched in stone and in stained-glass windows in larger-than-life proportions. The last National Sample Survey of Registered Nurses (NSSR) found that 79.8% of practicing RNs were satisfied with their job and 88.4% were with the same employer in the preceding year (USDHHS, 2010). Among all RNs, nursing faculty are the most satisfied (86.6%). A more recent survey found that 90% of RNs were satisfied with their career choice (AMN Healthcare, 2013).

FACTS ABOUT TODAY'S REGISTERED NURSE

Forty percent of all health care professionals in the United States are registered nurses, making nursing the largest health care professional group. Almost half of all anesthesia providers in the United States are certified registered nurse anesthetists (CRNA) (Rand, 2010) who are the major providers of anesthesia care to rural, medically underserved, and military personnel (American Association of Nurse Anesthetists [AANA], 2014). In many rural hospitals, CRNAs are the sole anesthesia provider (AANA, 2014).

Reflecting the aging population of America, nurses are older, with a mean age of 46 years. However, for the first time in 30 years, the aging of the nursing workforce has slowed because of the influx of new graduates younger than 30 years of age. Although nursing continues to be a female-dominated profession (only 9.6% are male), there are increasing numbers of men entering nursing. Although men were only 5% of the nursing workforce prior to 2000, 11% of new nurses entering the workforce between 2010 and 2013 were men. Men make up almost half (41.1%) of CRNAs (US Census Bureau, 2013), 12% of nurse practitioners (NPs), 7% of nurse managers, and 7% of staff nurses (Budden et al, 2013). Former U.S. Surgeon General Dr. Richard Carmona entered health care as a nurse. Interestingly, men are as equally likely as women to obtain a baccalaureate degree in nursing.

Although nursing is becoming more diverse, minority populations, who make up 37% of the American population, are only 19% of the nursing workforce (Budden et al, 2013). The nursing workforce is 6% African American, 6% Asian, 3% Hispanic, 1% American Indian/Alaska Native, 1% Hawaiian/Pacific Islander, and 1% other. Notably, there are increasing percentages of African American, Asian, and Hispanic nurses (Budden et al, 2013). However, African-American nurses (14.9%) were more likely than white (13.4%), Hispanic nurses (10.5%), or Asian, Native Hawaiian, or Pacific Islanders (8.3%) to obtain graduate education in nursing (USDHHS, 2010).

In 2013, 42% of new graduates entered nursing with a BSN (NCSBN, 2013). Although nurses have entered the profession at different levels of education, when reporting their highest level of nursing education in 2010, the largest percentage (46.6%) have a BSN, followed by nurses with an ASN (37.9%), a master's or doctorate degree (10.6%), or a diploma (6.9%) (USDHHS, 2013a). Extrapolating from these data, 57.2% of all RNs have a minimum of baccalaureate education in nursing (USDHHS, 2013a). However, by 2013, the percentage of nurses with a baccalaureate or higher degree in nursing had increased to 61% (Budden et al, 2013). From 2007 to 2011, the number of master's graduates increased by 60% and doctoral graduates tripled (USDHHS, 2013a).

Slightly more than half (63.2%) of all nurses practice in hospitals; 7.4% in long-term care and extended care facilities; 5.4% in other health care services; and 4.6% in outpatient care settings (USDHHS, 2013b). The majority of nurses (64%) are staff nurses, 4% are nurse managers, 2% are advanced practice registered nurses (APRNS), 2% are faculty, and in the less than 1% category are researchers and nurse executives. Interestingly, 85% of younger nurses (<30 years old) practice in hospitals (Budden et al, 2013).

APRNs (i.e., clinical specialists, nurse practitioners, nurse-midwives, and nurse anesthetists) are 7% of the nursing population. The majority (54%) of APRNs are nurse practitioners (NPs), followed by clinical nurse specialists (CNSs) (30%), CRNAs (12%), and nurse-midwives (4%) (Budden et al, 2013). From 2008 to 2013, the numbers of APRNs increased by 29% with a 33% NP increase, a 46% increase in CRNAs, a 26% increase in CNMs, and a 19% increase in CNSs (Budden et al, 2013).

The demographics of twenty-first century nursing strongly suggest that continued professional success will require attracting more students who are male and who are from ethnic and minority groups. As the data indicate, men are as likely as women, and black nurses are more likely than their white counterparts, to obtain higher degrees. However, there are insufficient numbers entering nursing.

The American Assembly of Men in Nursing (http://aamn.org) is an organization dedicated toward positively influencing the factors affecting men in nursing. The mission of this organization of men and women is to provide a "framework for nurses to meet, discuss, and influence factors, which affect men as nurses" (American Assembly of Men in Nursing, 2014). An important part of their work is their annual meeting, where papers related to men in nursing and men's health is presented. The barriers encountered by men entering nursing have been well documented (Roth and Coleman, 2008). A small study of male nursing students ($n = 29$) older than 25 years of age in a community college program indicated that gender did not interfere with their opportunities as a student, although they did report a lack of locker facilities, absence of male faculty, and a feminine gender bias in nursing textbooks. All subjects described problems in maternity clinical rotation regarding patients who refused their care based on gender. Although describing the event as being uncomfortable for both patients and for themselves, these students believed they had other life experiences that ameliorated any possible negative effects (Smith, 2006). In a qualitative study of men who are nurses, men reported how anomalous it was to be referred to as a "male nurse" because this isn't done in other professions.

CREATING THE IMAGE OF TWENTY-FIRST CENTURY NURSING

The twenty-first century image of nursing is one that nurses create every day as they practice and describe nursing to others. Conceptually, nursing is first and foremost "knowledge work" (Bargagliotti, 2003), regardless of age, gender, ethnic background, ethical perspective, or level of job satisfaction of the nurse. Knowledge workers are people who require specialized education to do work that requires judgment (Drucker, 2002). The knowledge work of nurses counts in terms of human lives and financial costs. When nursing practice is conceptualized as knowledge work in which nursing judgment counts, other images of nursing fade away. Insufficient staffing is not related to an aging workforce on the one hand or a diminished work ethic of a younger generation on the other hand.

Consider the following data about the potential benefits of nursing judgment to patients. A meta-analysis of all mortality/morbidity/nurse staffing studies since 1990 indicated that decreasing the nurse-patient ratio in the evening was accompanied by a 90% increase in mortality and that 47% of deaths from abdominal aortic surgery were due to nursing staffing (Kane et al, 2007). Hospitals with higher percentages of BSN nurses (36%) reported a 19% to 34% lower mortality rate than hospitals with lower percentages (11%). Nurses who worked shifts lasting 12.5 hours or longer were three times more likely to make medication and other procedural mistakes. The data clearly indicate that decreased nurse-patient ratios have been associated with higher rates of mortality, shock, urinary tract infections, sepsis, hospital acquired pneumonia, and failure to rescue, especially among surgical patients (Kane et al, 2007).

Aiken and colleagues' (2011) study of all hospital admissions of four of the largest states in the United States in one calendar year found that simply increasing the level of RNs isn't the sole answer to reducing patient mortality. Rather, it is the educational level of the nurses and a positive work environment of the nurse, along with increasing the numbers of nurses, that matter. A positive work environment was defined as one in which there are positive physician-nurse relationships, management listens to the patient concerns of bedside nurses, nurses are engaged in hospital affairs, and hospitals invest in improving quality and in the continuing educational development of nurses. Nursing education matters because for every 10% increase in the percentage of BSN nurses, mortality rates decreased by 4%. These are cumulative, multiplicative effects. Similarly, increasing nurse-patient ratios in hospitals with positive work environments decreased mortality by 12% and failure to rescue by 14%.

There are tangible ways that the knowledge work of nurses is being portrayed to the public. Kalisch, Begeny, and Neuman (2007) found that nurses were being imaged on the Internet between 2001 and 2004 as intelligent and educated (70%) health professionals who are committed to patient care. Interestingly, they also found that the image of nurses as political advocates for health care diminished on the Internet during this time frame. From a very different perspective, McNamara and colleagues (2012) suggested that a powerful image of the discipline of nursing is found throughout the Internet in the curricula of schools of nursing just as it is for other academic disciplines in universities. Regrettably, many faculties are not cognizant of the image of nursing they are projecting to the public in the way they title the course of study in the making of a nurse.

THE BASICS

At the simplest level, 4.18 million RNs create their image by ensuring that only RNs are referred to as "the nurse." Although the International Council of Nurses reserved the title of "nurse" for the RN in 1985, it is the responsibility of every nurse to ensure that the housekeeper, the untrained caregiver, the nursing assistant, and everyone else is not referred to as "the nurse." Imagine how confusing this is for patients and their families. Ensuring that patient teaching and questions about patient care are referred to "the nurse," rather than the assistant to the nurse, ensures that patients and families receive the best information possible.

A second and equally important image issue is how nurses refer to themselves and what they do. Nurses are not "medical" professionals, do not practice in the "medical field," and do not provide medical care. Physicians provide medical care. Nurses practice nursing and they practice in health care, not medical care. Medicine is not the entirety of all health care, as 4.18 million RNs and a host of pharmacists, occupational therapists, physical therapists, and many other health professionals indicate. Aside from being legally incorrect, it is misleading to the public.

Changing Nurse-Physician Interactions

An enduring mystery and common experience for nurses is how to address a medical problem with the primary customer of the hospital, the physician. Physicians are the revenue generators for hospitals,

and, in exchange for hospital privileges, agree to be self-governing and to abide by a set of medical staff bylaws. All medical staff bylaws include a disciplinary process that begins with the section chief, who is required to address documented patient care problems.

All too often, when nurses practice with a physician whose practice is substandard or who is highly volatile, they believe that this behavior is a nursing problem. Rather it is a medical problem that must be addressed by medicine via their staff bylaws. The problem can only be resolved when nurses disengage, factually document the problem in patient care terms rather than as a personality issue, and forward this in writing to a nurse manager and the appropriate section chief.

Just as nursing's involvement with medical problems is confined to appropriate notification, so should medicine's involvement with nursing be similarly confined. When a physician notifies a nurse about a nursing problem, a more positive answer is, "Thank you. Let me investigate the problem and get back to you." Lengthy detailed discussions are seldom useful. When the nurse makes an error, a simple apology and sincere statement of corrective action is sufficient. Consider the following actual clinical situations (Case Studies 2-1 and 2-2).

CASE STUDY 2-1

A nephrologist complained in a meeting with a nursing service administrator, the chief of medical staff, and the physician liaison that he was not being notified by nursing about his patients and that nurses did not know how to take care of his dialysis patients.

Response 1

Nurse 1 told the nephrologist how well prepared the nursing staff is and that his is the first complaint of this type that has been received. (The problem is denied.) However, she indicated that nursing is short-staffed and that there are a lot of agency nurses. (Two excuses are provided.) She will investigate. (This is the first positive response.) However, without a specific incident and patient, she may not be able to correct the problem. (This is the third excuse.)

Response 2

Nurse 2 carefully took notes and limited her comments to clarifying questions while the physician became

increasingly more derogatory. She concluded that there is a need to investigate and indicated that a written report will be sent to all parties. She thanked the physician for bringing this to her attention.

The nurse's investigation indicated that multiple nurses over time and in different units have telephoned the nephrologist, who loudly announced that they had awakened his baby and abruptly hung up the phone. Second, this is a difficult physician who never has time to discuss his patients when making rounds. Specific examples of unanswered questions were obtained.

The written findings were prepared, and nurse 2 posed only one question: "Since the physician is not able to 'take calls' after 5:30 PM, the patient care issue that concerns nursing is the question of who will be covering his patients."

Outcome: Within 2 weeks, the nephrologist's hospital privileges were quietly rescinded.

CASE STUDY 2-2

The nurses on a pediatric unit thought additional nursing staff was needed.

Response 1

The nurses and nurse manager "make their case" by describing how stressed the nursing staff is to the medical staff and to nursing administration. They insist that they cannot provide safe nursing care with their current level of staffing. Nothing happens.

Response 2

The nurse manager requested data from the pharmacy about the number of medications administered by nurses on this 24-bed unit for a specified period. The data indicated that nurses on the unit had administered 84,000 medications over a 3-month period. The only unit administering more medications was a 96-bed NICU that had administered only 10,000 more medications. Additionally, the laboratory data revealed that the unit usually administered 12 units of blood products per day. This necessitated 48 additional sets of vital signs and assessments per day.

Outcome: Additional nursing staff positions were provided to the unit.

THE LOOK OF NURSING

Somewhere between the gleaming white uniform, hose, shoes, and cap of the past and the Mickey Mouse T-shirts, tattoos, nose rings, and looking as though one were going to a "come as you are" party of the present, there is a professional image for nurses. Fogle and Ream (2014) suggest that nursing attire is now more directed toward the nurse's individual preferences than in projecting a professional image. Nurses have come to realize that the "grunge" look does not encourage anyone to take them seriously and are finding more appropriate ways to express their individuality. The work attire of any professional says to the world how significant the task at hand is to that professional. Notably the wrinkled, mismatched scrubs or tank-top-over-tank-top look is far more appropriate for gardening than the knowledge work of nursing.

When some nurses and nursing students design and wear T-shirts that are sexually demeaning to the profession and to them, there is an economic demand and economic support that is being provided to companies to demean the profession. Hopefully, there might be a more appropriate way to express humor in the future.

More recently, the nursing attire of hospital nurses has become an issue of safety for two important reasons. Patients and families have expressed their concerns about being unable to identify who the nurse is in a hospital. When time may be a critical factor, patients and or family members may relay critical information about a patient's condition to a housekeeper believing that person to be a knowledgeable nurse or waste valuable time asking multiple people if he or she is the nurse (Tolbert and Beilstein, 2010; Fogle and Reams, 2014).

The second safety issue is found in the possible transmission of infectious organisms via nursing clothing that is worn in public places. Appearing in the *Wall Street Journal,* Elizabeth McCaughey (2009), former lieutenant governor of New York and chair of a committee on infectious diseases, published an editorial that began with

> *You see them everywhere—nurses, doctors and medical technicians in scrubs or lab coats. They shop in them, take buses and trains in them, go to restaurants in them, and wear them home. What you can't see on these garments are the bacteria that could kill you.*
>
> *Dirty scrubs spread bacteria to patients in the hospital and allow hospital superbugs to escape into public places such as restaurants.*

Her admonition and warning was later supported by a study that cultured nurse and physician scrubs and lab coats and found pathogenic bacteria on 65% of nursing clothing. Notably, the highest colony counts were found for *Staphylococcus aureus* with a higher colony count for methicillin-resistant *S. aureus* (MRSA) than for methicillin sensitive *S. aureus* (Weiner-Well et al, 2011). When the public sees nurses in scrubs in public places, such as grocery stores, restaurants, and department stores, they are rightfully concerned. This does not improve the image of nurses as knowledgeable, responsible health professionals.

Although inking or tattoos are popular today, many health care organizations have decided that tattoos cannot be made visible to patients. A study of health care providers and medical and nursing students ($n = 513$) found that no respondent group had positive attitudes toward tattooed individuals. Women's attitudes were more negative than those of their male counterparts and were extremely negative toward tattooed professional women. Ironically, this study was done to assess attitudes toward tattooed patients (Stuppy et al, 1998). There are no data that suggest that a tattoo will enhance a professional image.

Collectively, the voices of nurses are heard through nursing professional associations, and nursing is imaged through participation rates in professional organizations. For example, there are approximately 60,000 members of the National Student Nurses Association (NSNA, 2014). Because 163,001 first-time takers took the NCLEX-RN® in 2013 (NCSBN, 2013), it might be estimated there are at least 320,000 to 400,000 registered nursing students in the United States. Where are the other 82% of nursing students?

These rates of participation in NSNA mirror the membership rate in the American Nurses Association (ANA). The influence that nursing could have in health policy and health legislation could be phenomenal if nurses participated more fully in their primary professional organization—the ANA. There are 79 or more specialty nursing organizations; however, the primary professional association is the ANA. At the International Council of Nursing, the national representative for United States is the ANA.

CREATING A NEW IMAGE

Envision a new world where nurses value nursing and image it daily. Nurses take themselves seriously and dress the part. Nurses are highly visible to patients, families, and physicians because they have reclaimed their practice. Nurses are clear about the role boundaries between themselves and those who extend their practice, and others are also. Nurses are "stuck like glue" together. Negative comments about a colleague are made to the colleague and to no one else. Professional nurses recognize that their greatest benefit—and one of the most efficient and powerful uses for their money—is the less than 1% of their salary they spend for membership in the ANA, the National League for Nursing, Sigma Theta Tau International, and their specialty organization. They look forward to annual meetings because such meetings provide an excellent opportunity to meet colleagues and discuss issues and practice innovations.

Because all nursing is valued, nurses recognize the value of caring, health promotion, and health teaching in addition to the value of illness care. They celebrate that nurses save lives every day. In the modern health care climate, nurses supervise assistive personnel and use their authority to ensure that patient care delivery is excellent. Nurses value the caring, nurturing role of the nurse because it is worn with style. To this legacy they add the astute businessperson, researcher, policymaker, legislator, and entrepreneur.

In this new world, nurses believe in nursing, in self, and in their colleagues. When nurses safeguard the image of nursing in local newspapers, television, media dramas, and daily practice, they realize that they play a part in forming the image of nursing on a daily basis.

SUMMARY

This chapter describes the major factors that have influenced the image of nursing and how society has viewed the profession during different periods throughout history. Nursing actions that contribute to a negative view are described, as well as strategies that will lead to the public having a positive view of nursing. Nurses must be convinced that the twenty-first century image of nursing is one that they contribute to every day as they practice and describe nursing to others. Convincing the public that nursing is not just about caring, but is a profession that is based on science, is essential. Everyone can care, but not everyone can be a nurse. When nurses are widely recognized as knowledge workers, their ability to be the architect of healing will be greatly enhanced.

REFERENCES

Aides relieve nursing shortage, *Life* 12(1):32–34, 36,1942.

Aiken LH, Cimiotti JP, Sloane DM, et al: Effects of nurse staffing and nurse education on patient deaths in hospitals with different nurse work environments, *Med Care* 49:1047–1058, 2011.

American Assembly of Men in Nursing (website). http://aamn.org. Accessed July 18, 2014.

AMN Healthcare: *2013 survey of registered nurses*, San Diego, CA: Author (website). http://www.amnhealthcare.com/uploadedFiles/MainSite/Content/Healthcare_Industry_Insights/Industry_Research/2013_RNSurvey.pdf. Accessed July 25, 2014.

Auerbach DI, Buerhaus PI, Staiger DO: Registered nurses are delaying retirement, a shift that has contributed to recent growth in the nurse workforce, *Health Aff* doi: 10.1377/hlthaff.2014.0128: 2014 (website). http://content.healthaffairs.org/content/early/2014/07/23/hlthaff.2014.0128. Accessed July 22, 2014.

American Association of Nurse Anesthetists, 2014: *Certified registered nurse anesthetists at a glance* (website). http://www.aana.com/ceandeducation/becomeacrna/Pages/Nurse-Anesthetists-at-a-Glance.aspx. Accessed July 21, 2014.

American Association of Nurse Anesthetists, 2014: *Value of CRNA care* (website). http://www.aana.com/aboutus/value-of-crnas/Pages/default.aspx. Accessed July 21, 2014.

Associated Press: *Madigan Army nurse killed in action in Afghanistan*, KOMO News.com (website). http://www.komonews.com/news/local/Madigan-Army-nurse-killed-in-Afghanistan-226919901.html. Accessed July 21, 2014.

Bargagliotti LA: Reframing nursing to renew the profession, *Nurs Educ Perspect* 24(1):12–16, 2003.

Budden, JS, Zhong EH, Moulton P, Cimiotti JP: Supplement: The National Council of State Boards of Nursing and the Forum of State Nursing Workforce Centers, 2013 national workforce survey of registered nurses, *J of Nurs Regul* 4(2):S1–S72, 2013.

Buerhaus PI, Auerbach DI, Staiger DO: The recent surge in nurse employment: causes and implications, *Health Aff* 28(4):w657–w668, 2009.

Bureau of Labor Statistics: *Occupational outlook handbook 2014* (website). http://www.bls.gov/ooh/healthcare/registered-nurses.htm#tab-6. Accessed July 19, 2014.

Buresch B, Gordon S, Bell N: Who counts in news coverage of health care? *Nurs Outlook* 39(5):204–208, 1991.

Cronquist R, Spector N: Social media: regulatory concerns and guidelines, *J Nurs Reg* 2(3):37–40, 2011.

Dickens C: *Martin Chuzzlewit*, New York, 1910, Macmillan.

Diers D: *The mystery of nursing: Secretary's Commission on Nursing: support studies and background information*, vol 2, Rockville, MD, 1988, Department of Health and Human Services, pp VIII-1–VIII-10.

Donahue MP: *Nursing: the finest art: an illustrated history*, St Louis, 1910, Mosby.

Drucker P: *Managing in the next society*, New York, 2002, St Peter's Press.

Fagan J: *Executive Producer: 60 Minutes Affordable health care for those still uninsured* [television broadcast], New York, April 6, 2014, CBS News.

Foley C, Reams P: Taking a uniform approach to nursing attire, *Nurs 2014* 44(6):50–54, 2014.

Gallup poll: *Honesty, ethics in professions* (website). http://www.gallup.com/poll/180260/americans-rate-nurses-highest-honesty-ethical-standards.aspx. Accessed January 19, 2015.

Institute of Medicine: *The future of nursing: leading change to advance health*, Washington, DC: The National Academies Press (website). http://www.iom.edu/Reports/2010/the-future-of-nursing-leading-change-advancing-health.aspx. Accessed July 20, 2014.

Johnson & Johnson: *About the Johnson and Johnson campaign for nursing's future* (website). http://www.discovernursing.com/sites/default/files/media/press597939604/Campaign%20for%20Nursing%27s%20Future_Overview_5-22-13.pdf. Accessed April 19, 2015.

Jones AH: The White Angel (1936): Hollywood's image of Florence Nightingale. In Jones AH, editor: *Images of nurses: perspectives from history, art, and literature*, Philadelphia, 1988, University of Pennsylvania Press.

Kalisch BJ, Begeny S, Neuman S: The image of the nurse on the internet, *Nurs Outlook* 55(4):182–188, 2007.

Kalisch PA, Kalisch BJ: *The advance of American nursing*, ed 3, Philadelphia, 1995, Lippincott.

Kampen MB: Before Florence Nightingale: a prehistory of nursing in painting and sculpture. In Jones AH, editor: *Images of nurses: perspectives from history, art, and literature*, Philadelphia, 1988, University of Pennsylvania Press.

Kane RL, Shamliyan T, Mueller C, et al: *Nurse staffing and quality of patient care*, Rockville, MD, 2007, U.S. Department of Health and Human Services, Evidence Report/Technology Assessment, Number 151, Agency for Healthcare Research and Quality Publication No. 07-E005.

Kesey K: *One flew over the cuckoo's nest*, New York, 1962, New American Library/Signet.

Longfellow HW: Santa Filomena, *Atlantic Monthly* 1(11):22–23, 1857

McCaughey B: Hospital scrubs are a germy, deadly mess, *Wall Street Journal*, Jan 8, 2009 (website). http://online.wsj.com/news/articles/SB123137245971962641. Accessed July 20, 2014.

McNamara MS, Fealy GM, Geraghty R: The visibility of the discipline on the websites of academic nursing schools, *Nurs Outlook* 60(1):29–36, 2012.

National Council of State Boards of Nursing: *2002 Nurse licensee volume and NCLEX examination statistics*, Vol 13, 2003, (website). https://www.ncsbn.org/1236.htm. Accessed July 19, 2014.

National Council of State Boards of Nursing: *NCLEX Examination Pass Rates 2013* (website). https://www.ncsbn.org/NCLEX_Stats_2013.pdf. Accessed July 19, 2014.

National Student Nurses Association: *Image of nursing* (website). http://www.nsna.org/ProgramActivities/ImageofNursing.aspx. Accessed December 20, 2011.

National Student Nurses Association: *About us* (website). http://www.nsna.org/AboutUs.aspx. Accessed January 29, 2012.

Norman EM: *We band of angels: the untold story of American nurses trapped on Bataan by the Japanese*, New York, 1999, Random House.

Rajacich D, Kane D, Williston C, Cameron S: If they do call you a nurse, it is always "male nurse": experiences of men in the nursing profession, *Nurs Forum* Jan-Mar 48(1): 71–80, 2013.

Rand Corporation: *Is there a shortage of anesthesia providers in the US?* (website). http://www.google.com/url?sa=t&rct=j&q=&esrc=s&source=web&cd=13&ved=0CC8QFjACOAo&url=http%3A%2F%2Fwww.rand.org%2Fpubs%2Fresearch_briefs%2F2010%2FRAND_RB9541.pdf&ei=SAomT5D3LeLnsQKitNmMAg&usg=AFQjCNH-_IeftYNKscLGHjEigSoQ_4vTig. Accessed January 29, 2012.

Roth JE, Coleman C: Perceived and real barriers for men entering nursing: implications for gender diversity, *J Cult Diversity* 15(3):148–152, 2008.

Seago JA, Spetz J, Alvarado A, et al: The nursing shortage: Is it really about image? *J Healthc Manag* 51(2):96–108, 2006.

Sigma Theta Tau International: *The Woodhull study on nursing and the media: health care's invisible partner*, Indianapolis, 1998, STT Center Nursing Press.

Smith JS: Exploring the challenges for nontraditional male students transitioning into a nursing program, *J Nurs Educ* 45(7):263–269, 2006.

Stanley DJ: Celluloid angels: a research study of nurses in feature films 1900-2007, *J Adv Nurs* 64(1):84–95, 2008.

Stuppy DJ, Armstrong ML, Casals-Ariet C: Attitudes of health care providers and students toward tattooed people, *J Adv Nurs* 27(6):1165–1170, 1998.

The History Channel: *Women in the Vietnam War* (website). http://www.history.com/topics/vietnam-war/women-in-the-vietnam-war. Accessed July 21, 2014.

The last moments of Jennifer Moreno, an Army nurse killed in Afghanistan: *Army Times*. April 29, 2014, (website). http://www.armytimes.com/article/20140429/NEWS/304290068/The-last-moments-Jennifer-Moreno-an-Army-nurse-killed-Afghanistan. Accessed July 21, 2014.

Tolbert C. Beilstein L: Nurses attire: Choosing the right answer, *Nurs Leader* 12(5):55–58, 2010.

The Truth About Nursing (website). http://www.truthabout-nursing.org. Accessed August 28, 2012.

U.S. Census Bureau: *Men in nursing occupations* (website). http://www.census.gov/people/io/files/Men_in_Nursing_Occupations.pdf. Accessed July 21, 2014.

U.S. Department of Health and Human Services: *The registered nurse population: findings from the 2008 national sample survey of registered nurses*, Rockville, MD, 2010, Author.

U.S. Department of Health Resources and Services Administration Bureau of Health Professions National Center for Health Workforce Analysis: *The U.S. nursing workforce: trends in supply and education*, Rockville, MD, 2013a.

U.S. Department of Health and Human Services, Health Resources and Services Administration National Center for Health Workforce Analysis: *The U.S. health workforce chartbook*, Rockville, MD, 2013b.

Weiner-Well Y, Galuty M, Rudensky B, et al: Nursing and physician attire as possible source of nosocomial infections, *Am J Infect Control* 39:555–559, 2011.

West IJ: The women of the Army Nurse Corps during the Vietnam War, *Vietnam War Memorial* (website). http://www.vietnamwomensmemorial.org/pdf/iwest.pdf. Accessed July 19, 2014.

3

Educational diversity promotes access and career development.

The Influence of Contemporary Trends and Issues on Nursing Education

Dawn Vanderhoef, PhD, DNP, RN, PMHNP/CS-BC

ⓔ Additional resources are available online at: *http://evolve.elsevier.com/Cherry/*

PROFESSIONAL/ETHICAL ISSUE

Amy, a pre-licensure nursing student, was in her first year of clinical, and excited to begin her 5-week inpatient psychiatric rotation. Amy was considering becoming a psychiatric nurse, like her father and grandmother, and was looking forward to this clinical rotation, which she was sure would help her make a decision about psychiatric nursing. During her fourth week on the psychiatric unit, Amy was assigned to work with Sandy, an RN on the psychiatric intensive care unit (PIC-U). During morning report, Amy learned that a female patient was placed in four-point restraints about 1 hour before the day shift nurses started. The patient, "Lindsey," was assigned to Sandy, and Amy was interested in working with a very ill psychiatric patient, but also very anxious.

After completion of her 15-minute checks, Sandy asked Amy to stay in the room with the patient while she went to the medication room to prepare Lindsay's medications, and Amy agreed. As soon as Sandy left the room, Lindsay asked Amy if she had her cell phone in her pocket, and Amy felt her face get beat red, heart race, and her palms were sweaty, she did not know how to answer the question because she did have her cell phone

in her pocket. Lindsay noticed Amy's anxiety and asked her to take her cell phone out of her pocket to take a picture of her in restraints so she could show it to her attorney. Lindsay explained how the night shift had mistreated her, and she was abused and needed documentation. She told Amy that it was okay to take the picture, that it would only be used if necessary, and if she didn't need it she could delete the photo. Lindsay made a very logical compelling case for needing a photo, so Amy took out her cell phone and took two photos of Lindsay. Quickly, Lindsay said, "Oh, just text the photos to me at 999-999-9999. Don't worry, you are really being a great help and I know you will make an excellent psychiatric nurse. Once you send me the pictures, you can delete them." Amy hesitated, felt uncomfortable, but sent the pictures to Lindsay.

Amy continued the shift with Sandy, and Lindsay was taken out of restraints and doing much better when Amy left for the day. Lindsay thanked Amy for her care and told her that she was doing much better and would delete the pictures from her cell when she was allowed to get her personal belongs back. Amy said good-bye to Sandy and her assigned patients, and went to post conference. Amy did not tell her nursing instructor or Sandy about the pictures and deleted them from her camera as soon as she got into post conference. Amy was embarrassed that a

We thank Carrie B. Lenburg, EdD, RN, FAAN, for her contribution to this chapter in the first through fifth editions and Susan R. Jacob, PhD, RN, for her contribution to the sixth edition.

psychiatric patient convinced her to take her cell phone out and take pictures, and feared she would be dismissed from the nursing program if she told anyone.

What ethical considerations need to be considered in the clinical example above? What ethical principles can be applied to this case? Provide examples.

VIGNETTE

Three students were having an animated discussion after class.

Mark: *I'm tired of all this lecturing! I just want to DO nursing! Why do we always have to discuss things like EBP and critical thinking? What is it anyway? And we're always having to analyze a situation when it's perfectly clear what needs to be done! I don't get it. Just do what the doc orders or what's in the procedure book. I don't need to keep looking up stuff when I've done it before. Besides, we already have way too much to read for every class!*

Katelyn: *But listen to this. I heard about a student several days ago who really got into trouble because of a big mistake she made. She did just what you said, followed the provider's orders, and gave digoxin to an 80-year-old patient. She had already written a note that he was complaining of anorexia, nausea, and visual disturbances, but she didn't take time to look up "dig" toxicity or to really think things through. And guess what? The patient got into a really bad situation. It was lucky that the nurse practitioner read the note, checked the patient, put the pieces together, and got a stat serum "dig" level. She had to administer Digibind! It was so life threatening and really scary! He's not out of the woods yet. The student said the NP was nice and helped her understand what she should have done, but the instructor pulled her off the unit and gave her a serious dress-down because she had not taken a couple of minutes to analyze the situation, to think about what things are danger signs, or to just look up the meds and the patient's condition at the time—she just followed the provider's orders. I'd be scared to be the one being grilled at the risk management meeting! She may even fail the course.*

Audrey: *That sounds like a good example of what our instructors keep telling us. Nursing is about thinking as well as doing. We can seriously harm a patient if we don't know what actually needs to be done. We have to learn enough so we're competent and know how to use best practices for all kinds of situations, and where to get the information fast. We have to really study resources, use our e-books, and medical software to check things out first, and then figure out what we need to do, and fast. Even if we're busy or just don't want to stop and look up something.*

Katelyn: *Why don't we start our own little study group, to learn how to get a better understanding of each class? Nursing is a lot more than just "doing" skills. We've got to be competent in the thinking that goes with the doing. And, there's got to be a way to organize all this information and learn how to put it together for different situations. Whadaya say? I don't want to get into trouble like that other student! Come on; let's get started on those study questions.*

Questions to Consider While Reading This Chapter:

1. What are the major current trends in society and health care, and how do they influence nursing education and practice?
2. What are the most compelling reasons that nurses require ongoing development and validation of competencies for licensure and continuing practice?
3. What local, state, and national resources and Internet websites are available to learn about the trends and issues that influence nursing education?
4. What are the pros and cons of the many different types of nursing education programs that prepare students for current nursing practice?
5. What educational opportunities exist for graduates of various programs to advance beyond their current preparation, including traditional, mobility, and distance-learning programs?

KEY TERMS

Competency outcomes: The results, or end products, of planned study and experience that are focused on specific abilities required for practice.

Contemporary issues: The problems, changes, and concerns that are current for the present time.

Core competencies: The essential cluster of abilities and skills required for competent nursing practice.

Educational mobility: The progressive movement from one type or level of education to another, often based on flexible, self-directed, or advanced placement options. Examples are progression from diploma preparation to an academic degree, such as RN to BSN or MSN; BSN to doctoral degree; or non-nursing degree to BSN, MSN, or doctoral degree.

Education trends: Shifts in conditions and concerns that emerge from and influence various aspects of society; broad changes in the United States and the world that influence the education and practice of nurses and other providers.

Performance examinations: Standardized evaluation based on objective demonstration of specific required competencies; used in conjunction with written tests of *knowledge about* those abilities. They may require performance in actual or simulated situations, related to physical psychomotor skills or the observable evidence of other skills such as critical thinking, communication, teaching, planning, writing, or analysis and integration of data.

LEARNING OUTCOMES

After studying this chapter, the reader will be able to:

1. Integrate knowledge of 10 current trends and issues in society and health care into a more holistic perception of their influence on nursing education, students, faculty, and nursing practice.

2. Create a personal philosophy and plan for ongoing professional development and practice that integrates knowledge of current trends and issues.

3. Access current information resources from the Internet related to evolving trends and issues as a component of ongoing learning and preparation for practice.

4. Differentiate among various types of conventional, mobility, and new nursing education programs and the issues associated with them.

CHAPTER OVERVIEW

Society as a whole is going through many significant changes, and all of them influence nursing education and health care. Nursing care is becoming more complex, and the role of the registered nurse is more demanding, requiring nurses to be active participants in health care decisions. Nurses need to be effective and efficient in understanding how societal, educational, and health care changes influence health outcomes. Our knowledge, thinking, and a broad array of skills all are critical to the kind of nursing care we provide, and they influence how we respond to changes in patients, families, and communities in times of need. Nurse educators must be vigilant in learning about these changes and integrating trends and changes into nursing curricula. Students also need to be aware of evolving trends and issues and learn how they influence learning and practice.

As American society becomes increasingly diverse and complex, new trends precipitate different issues. This chapter describes 10 contemporary trends that influence the way students (and nurses) learn, become competent practitioners, and meet the needs of patients. Competent nurses integrate these changes into their way of being, to become "thinking" nurses as well as "doing" nurses. Thinking nurses learn to integrate essential knowledge, attitudes, and skills into care that involves best practices and evidence-based practices that promote patient safety and quality care. Some of these trends and related issues include the following: the extreme and rapid changes of technology in patient care and education, significant changes in the demographics of our society, the economic crisis and its consequences, the globalization of knowledge and diseases, the requirement for competent health care providers, the increase in domestic abuse and violence of all sorts, complexity of physical and mental health conditions, ethical issues, and the shortage of nursing faculty and nurses. It also describes the types of nursing education programs, their contribution to the profession, the expansion of innovative nursing programs, degrees and specialties available, and multiple technologic learning methods used. Tables illustrate online resources, important organizations and associations, and some statistics related to types of programs.

INTRODUCTION

New nursing programs, courses, experiences, and changing requirements for the development of clinical skills and critical thinking pave the way for different opportunities for students to prepare for initial and continuing nursing practice in a rapidly changing society amidst a rapidly changing health care delivery system. These trends influence the number and types of nursing programs for basic and experienced students at the undergraduate and graduate levels. Essential differences among basic education programs; innovations in new degree programs, majors, and courses; and mobility and distance-learning programs are reviewed in the context of changes in national organizations and accrediting and regulatory bodies. Students who study and comprehend these trends are better prepared to cope with a rapidly changing nursing education models and health care systems. It is imperative that nursing students at all levels stay abreast of change in nursing education and health care landscape as they become competent health care practitioners and meet the complex needs of patients from diverse multicultural and demographic backgrounds. Lenburg (2008) developed a framework for nursing competency development and evaluation called the Competency Outcomes and Performance Model (COPA). The COPA framework is useful for nursing instructors to use when identifying essential competencies and outcomes for practice, indicators that define competencies, ways to learn competencies, and effective ways to document that learners achieve the competencies. Given the complexities of patient care, and health delivery systems, the COPA framework is useful at all levels of nursing education and within professional nursing practice (Lenburg et al, 2011; Lenburg et al, 2009). Using the COPA framework as a guide, Lenburg identified trends and issues related to nursing education, which are used as the framework to organize this chapter (Table 3-1).

TRENDS AND ISSUES IN CONTEMPORARY NURSING EDUCATION

Knowledge Expansion and Use of Technology and the Internet

With ever-expanding developments in electronic information and communication technology, the volume of information is growing exponentially on a global level. Informatics has become a major part of education and practice (Cipriano and Murphy, 2011). The ability to create, access, and disseminate unlimited information rapidly has enormous benefits. From e-mails to complex research documents and telemedicine across the globe, students are communicating more frequently with more contacts and at Internet speed; multiple digital chat rooms, blogs, and social network systems are used in nursing education (Skiba, 2009). Use of social media has become so common in nursing that guidelines and code of ethics statements are being developed by employers and by national nursing organizations (National Council of State Boards of Nursing [NCSBN], 2012; Prinz, 2011). The use of social media has become a concern for nurses, nursing students, and educators. Using this digital forum to communicate requires an understanding of policies and potential legal implications (Cronquist and Spector, 2011).

Websites allow for rapid access to online and printed material. Digital health-related materials can be updated quickly, allowing educators to create and revise online course content, assignments, and examinations. Using computers for written assignments reinforces the development of effective writing skills and the use of standard protocols required in academic and professional documents. They also help students prepare more effectively for computerized licensure examinations. A study conducted by Brodersen and Mills (2014) found that using the RN-Comprehensive Predictor examination or Exit Evaluation at the end of a basic RN program predicts NCLEX-RN success. However, one study reports that students believe they do not have the

TABLE 3-1 Summary of Trends and Issues That Influence Nursing Education	
Major Contemporary Trends	**Related Issues for Students**
Rapid knowledge expansion; increasing use of technology and informatics in education and practice	1. Choosing the most effective electronic and technology options 2. Information overload; virtually unlimited global resources, global research opportunities, issues 3. Identifying current and accurate information; material rapidly outdated 4. Expanded expectations, limited time, rapid response expected; little time for reflection Expansion of nursing informatics, content and skills development
Practice-based competency; outcomes and evidence-based content	Learning focused on core practice competency outcomes, professional skills beyond technical psychomotor skills; core practice competencies; multiple conflicting versions; which to use? Integration of evidence-based standards, research findings into practice; emphasis on critical thinking, problem solving Changes in standards; ensure patient safety
Performance-based competency: learning and objective assessment methods	Multiple teaching-learning methods: interactive collaborative, in-class and out-of-class projects; problem-based learning; increasing self-responsibility; accountability for learning and competence; interprofessional learning; using electronic devices, media to access resources Competency assessment based on performance examinations, specified portfolio documentation; standards-based assessment methods; emphasis on patient safety
Sociodemographics, cultural, diversity, economic, and political changes	Increased aging population; increasing multicultural, ethnic diversity requires increased learning, respect for differences, preferences, customs; generational issues Immigration conflicts, protests; consequences for access and health care Community, faith-based projects, service-learning projects Social, economic, and political changes influence health care delivery and access to clinical experiences; influence disrespect, conflict, abuse, violence; increased poverty and need Multidimensional content, client care, clinical learning sites
Community-focused interdisciplinary approaches	Interprofessional collaborative learning Diverse alternative health practices, influence of cultures Broad scope of nursing; clinical approach; increasing use of diverse experiences throughout community; continuum from acute care to health promotion; from hospitals to home to rural to global settings Requires more planning, travel time, expenses, arrangements; different skills, communications; critical thinking, problem-solving strategies Multiple teachers, preceptors, staff instructors, part-time, with varying abilities; time constraints
Global Health	Extensive global travel and commerce Illness can arrive on any airplane, ship, or bus and spread throughout the country Threat of epidemics Nurses are connected globally through shared networks and technology
Patient-centered care: engagement, safety, and privacy	All expect value, quality, individual respect, consideration, attention; privacy issues Patient initiatives for involvement and protection; balance standards and preferences Increased litigation, medical-nursing errors; focus on safe, competent patient care Increased individual responsibility, accountability for learning and practice

Continued

TABLE 3-1　Summary of Trends and Issues That Influence Nursing Education—cont'd

Major Contemporary Trends	Related Issues for Students
Ethics and bioethical concerns	Alternative solutions to ethical dilemmas; issues regarding diverse beliefs; disputes regarding biotechnology and bioengineering in health care
	Many gray zones instead of black-and-white absolutes; separate professional practice responsibilities from personal opinions, consequences for competence, and patient safety
	Integrate into professional practice acceptance of the individual's right of choice regarding life and death issues, health care methods; respect, tolerance for patient's decisions, ethical competencies for students
	Standards of quality care, patient's rights issues
Increasing shortage of nurses and faculty	Shortage of staff results in limitations in clinical learning; heavy workload; using preceptors, part-time instructors; less one-to-one help for students; consequences for learning and patient safety
	Shortage of qualified faculty; aging, retiring; increased part-time instructors, clinical staff, national and global problems, influence quality education and future nursing staff; need for increased educational funding
	Students need more clinical learning; more responsibility for self-directed learning, seek assistance from others
	Increased use of simulation; required to validate initial and continuing competence
Disasters, violence, and terrorism	New learning skills required for major natural disaster events; new program options, new courses, and new skills needed for emergency responders
	Violence in society, homes, workplace, schools; abuse against women and children
	Preparedness for terrorism; skills, programs for first responders; increased anxiety, uncertainty
Increasing professional and personal responsibility	Lifelong learning to meet professional expectations; certification requirements
	Increasing competency assessment in workplace
	Changes in standards for quality care practice
	High stress from competing demands of school, home, meeting competency requirements

essential information technology competencies (Fetter, 2009). When providing nursing care, there is an increase in information technology or computer use as part of patient care and nursing workflow process, which does not take away from direct patient care time and allows nurses to access and analyze information (Cornell et al, 2010). Further, the Healthcare Information and Management Systems Society (HIMSS) identified that nurses at all levels of education need health informatics competencies (Sensmeier, 2011). In addition, the Technology Informatics Guiding Education Reform (TIGER, 2007) identified three basic informatics competencies: basic computer competencies, information literacy, and information management. The shift toward competency-based education and evaluation with known informatics competencies for students and faculty will help guide nursing curriculum toward inclusion of clinical and simulated experiences that help students develop basic informatics competency. Students who become competent and literate in the use of computers and other digital devices will be more successful in their programs and in practice.

The Internet creates opportunities for distance-learning students to participate in networks, team projects, and research that expand the understanding of universal health needs and cultural differences. The Internet and changes in perspectives of nurse educators also makes it possible for nursing courses or entire degree programs to be delivered online.

Increasingly versatile smart phones help students, faculty, and nurse's access valuable current information to manage complex patient data and thus reduce emotional stress and error (Jeffries, 2005). Furthermore, smartphone use has been associated in acute care settings to quickly connect the nurse with the provider, allowing critical information to be sent and expeditiously address patient care needs (Whitlow et al, 2014). Learning to access and use digital resources on mobile devices has been found to be more effective when introduced early into the nursing curriculum and embedded throughout the program (Zurmehly, 2010).

These electronic advances, however, generate several issues. With almost unlimited information available, students may actually take more time to navigate online resources than traditional print-based resources and get overly engaged in following links, networking, and using chat rooms. Faculty and students need to work together to promote efficient and effective use of electronic learning tools and networking; reducing overload and frustration requires disciplined focus and clear guidelines and outcomes. Learning from the Internet can help students develop skills in analytic thinking, decision making, and reflective judgment that are essential for selecting valid and reliable resources; these are difficult but essential competencies for evidence-based practice (Zurmehly, 2010). The use of blogs has been cited as a method to increase communication among nursing students and a forum to share medical information (Roland et al, 2011).

The Quality and Safety Education for Nurses (QSEN) project, funded by the Robert Wood Johnson Foundation, identified competencies for nurses to achieve knowledge, skills, and attitudes (KSAs) to become successful health care providers. A QSEN graduate and undergraduate informatics competency highlights the importance of becoming proficient in using information technology (QSEN, 2012). The National Organization of Nurse Practitioner Faculties (NONPF) core competencies also include information technology and information literacy (NONPF, 2012). Nurses, nursing students, and nurse educators must stay abreast of the rapid changes related to nursing informatics and information technology.

Practice-Based Competency Outcomes

One trend that has a powerful influence on nursing education and practice at all levels is the emphasis on competency outcomes and criteria that establish realistic expectations for clinical practice (Cronenwett et al, 2007). The National League for Nursing (NLN) has developed outcomes and competencies for graduates of nursing programs at all levels (LVN, ADN and Diploma, BSN, MS, Practice and Research Doctorate programs). The competencies include four core values, integrated concepts and program outcomes for nursing graduates at all levels: human flourishing, nursing judgment, professional identify, and spirit of inquiry (NLN, 2010). In 2008, the AACN (2008a) released the essentials of baccalaureate education, which serve as a guiding framework to build and transform nursing curriculum.

The NONPF has developed one set of core competencies for all graduating nurse practitioners (NONPF, 2012) Competency outcomes, with related criteria (critical elements), specify expected results, which are the measurable results of time and effort spent in learning. The ability to implement realistic practice-based abilities competently, therefore, is the essential outcome; competence is the target, or the endpoint to be reached, and the purpose of study and education.

The outcomes approach requires a mental shift from trying to memorize voluminous readings and class notes (resulting in frustration and the attitude of "just tell me what I need to know") to actually learning to think like a nurse, to integrate information in problem solving and decision making, and providing competent patient care (DiVito-Thomas, 2005). Typical objectives begin with words like *describe, discuss, list,* or *recognize;* they are directions for learning, not what nurses do. Outcomes convert the meaning of the content objectives to actions that nurses actually do, such as implement, integrate, plan, or conduct. This change in approach can be confusing at first, but by achieving the end-results/outcomes, students are more prepared to meet the competency expectations of nursing practice with more confidence and success (Glennon, 2006; Klein, 2006).

Accrediting and certifying organizations must mandate demonstrated mastery of skills, managerial competencies, and professional development at all levels (Institute of Medicine [IOM], 2012; NONPF, 2012).

Validation of competencies often causes anxiety and stress in some students, faculty, nurses, and others, but they are a major incentive to promote patient safety and effective care (Bargagliotti et al, 1999). Practice competencies to promote patient safety have been studied extensively by nurses and physicians under federal auspices. (See the 2000 report on the website: http://bhpr.hrsa.gov/nursing/nacnep/reports/first/2.htm, and click on the link

Collaborative Education to Ensure Patient Safety.) In response to the Institute of Medicine report (IOM, 2000), the Robert Wood Johnson Foundation funded a national initiative, Quality and Safety in Nursing Education (QSEN), to help nursing programs reorganize curricula to focus on patient safety and quality care (Cronenwett et al, 2007). The QSEN competencies at both the prelicensure (AACN, 2007) and graduate level (AACN, 2012) assess the knowledge, skills, and attitudes of nurses within six areas: patient-centered care, teamwork and collaboration, evidence-based practice, quality improvement, safety, and informatics.

Performance-Based Learning and Assessment

Trends related to learning and evaluation methods are changing fundamentally, due in part to changing technology and the increased focus on patient safety. The emphasis on competency outcomes and criteria for acceptable practice has prompted leaders in nursing education to promote innovative programs and learning methods (IOM, 2012) as well as more interactivity and engagement interspersed with lectures. Passively listening, reading, and passing written tests does not necessarily promote competence in the core performance skills expected in practice. Increased emphasis on critical thinking and learning to integrate principles is more effective than trying to remember "all the content," which often leads students to retreat and just want to pass the test. Competency-based learning creates an entirely different atmosphere that is focused on learning concepts and encourages collaboration between teacher and learner to achieve actual practice competencies (Lasater and Nielsen, 2009).

Practice-based competence uses terms like *interactive learning, collaborative learning,* and *competency-based learning.* This trend requires changes in the roles of teachers and students. The teacher is less a "lecturer" and more a facilitator and coach, providing direction for learning stated outcomes; the student is more actively accountable and responsible for achieving competence in designated knowledge and practice skills.

In this new paradigm, instructors focus on the most essential content; create practice-based case studies and simulations; and set the stage for students to engage in problem solving, critical thinking, and integration of concepts, knowledge, and evidence-based practice (Horan, 2009). Nursing faculty provide feedback and

validation that cannot be gained through books or the Internet. Memorization of basic facts is still important, but it is insufficient when nursing practice emphasizes such skills as assessment, critical thinking, communication, patient teaching, and caring and advocating for patients. The focus on practice competence helps students learn how to access and integrate ever-changing information as required in actual practice, rather than trying to remember "all the content." A recent systematic review of 12 studies on simulation found that six of the studies found gains in critical thinking skills through the use of simulation (Cant and Cooper, 2010). Critical thinking is an essential part of applying evidence-based practice, using research findings to guide actual practice (Ireland, 2008).

A trend in many nursing programs is the development and incorporation of evidence-based practice (EBP) courses, in addition to traditional nursing research courses. Learning about EBP includes evaluation, and translation of evidence into practice. The Academic Center for Evidence-Based Practice (ACE) at the University of Texas San Antonio, which was developed as a center for excellence (http://www.acestar.uthscsa.edu/), provides up-to-date information about evidence-based practice. Additionally, many other universities have developed evidence-based practice centers. In 1997, the Agency for Healthcare Research and Quality (AHRQ) developed an evidence-based practice center program (http://www.ahrq.gov/clinic/epc/).

Simulation, in various forms, is another major performance-based learning strategy. Shadow Health and vSim are technologies that use digital patient simulation to teach critical thinking. Shadow Health offers Digital Clinical Experiences that include concept labs, which are immersive tutorials that illustrate complex nursing subjects. Concept labs include examples of real body sounds and realistic, 3D anatomical body models to compare and contrast normal and abnormal findings. The interactive interface of these concept labs can be used to explore body systems at an in-depth level. These experiences make classroom concepts come to life.

Designed to simulate real nursing scenarios, vSim allows students to interact with patients in a safe, realistic environment, available anytime, anywhere. This technology enables students to develop clinical reasoning skills, competence, and confidence in nursing.

Mannequins have become more essential and incorporate sophisticated computerization to promote more realistic learning and critical thinking (Bruce et al, 2009; Hawkins et al, 2008; Horan, 2009; Rush et al, 2008; Smith-Stoner, 2009a; Wagner et al, 2009). Another form of simulation is the use of standardized patients and telemedicine technology to achieve outcomes. The use of standardized patients has been documented as intimidating to some nursing students; however, this simulated learning experience has the ability to bring emotions to the simulation (Sideras, et al, 2013). More recently, faculty are using web-based broadcast of simulations to increase learning (Smith-Stoner, 2009b). Cited within a systematic review (Cant and Cooper, 2010), the Objective Structured Clinical Examinations (OSCEs) are the most valid assessment measurement in use. The use of standardized patients as a competency-based summative assessment allows faculty to assess mastery of entry level clinical skills, some of which the student may not have access to in the clinical setting. Other interactive learning strategies include portfolio learning (Norris et al, 2012) and peer-to-peer learning (Robinson and Niemer, 2010).

Interactive strategies are even more important when the location of clinical learning is considered. More and more diverse settings are used because these are places where nurses' expertise is needed. In addition to hospitals and extended care facilities, clinical learning often takes place in alternative settings, such as nurse-run clinics in schools, daycare and senior centers, and prisons. Over the past decade, service-learning projects have also helped students learn actual practice skills throughout the community (Bentley and Ellison, 2007; Hunt, 2007). Another form is faith-based learning projects with nurses in churches and congregations. Many interactive clinical-related learning strategies and more traditional clinical assignments increasingly engage practicing nurses as preceptors (Wieland et al, 2007).

The change to competency outcomes and practice-based learning requires changes in evaluation methods that focus on valid, actual performance of required competencies in realistic scenarios; paper-and-pencil tests and inconsistent subjective clinical observations by instructors or preceptors are not adequate. Structured, objective validation of competence requires performance examinations that specify the core skills and related critical elements (the application of mandatory principles) that must be met according to established practice standards. In addition to performance of nursing skills, structured portfolios are used to document other competencies (Norris et al, 2012).

Needless to say, a more interactive approach in clinical and classroom courses is difficult for some students and creates issues; faculty and students have to change traditional habits and expectations of each other. Sometimes students think it is easier just to figure out "what the teacher wants" and "study for the test" rather than engage in learning to think and integrate best practices through teacher-assisted interactive exercises. Such exercises, however, help students learn to make effective decisions, to collaborate in the group process, and manage time and resources. It may cause some anxiety, but performance examinations that require 100% accuracy of the mandatory critical elements (principles) provide more reliable evidence of practice competencies.

Sociodemographics, Cultural Diversity, and Economic and Political Changes

From rural to metropolitan areas throughout the United States, the population is undergoing significant changes in sociodemographic, cultural, and economic composition. These trends generate serious issues and consequences for education, health care, and many aspects of the socioeconomic-political systems. The following brief overview is a framework for learning how these trends and issues affect nursing education and practice.

People are living longer, and the number of the very elderly is increasing more rapidly than other age groups. This means more people live with chronic disease and disability; many live in institutions, substandard conditions, or alone. All are subject to increasing needs for health care and assistance. As a result, nursing and other provider programs have increased geriatric content and clinical experiences; geriatric patients require very different care than younger populations. Since 2000, 13 Hartford Centers for Geriatric Nursing Excellence have been developed to advance the knowledge and care of older adults (http://www.geriatricnursing.org/hcgne/memberinstitutions.asp). Advancing Care Excellence for Seniors, the ACES Project, aims to advance the care of older adults through innovations in nursing education. To learn more about the ACES Project (http://www.nln.org/facultyprograms/facultyresources/aces/index.htm)

- The current political debate about health care reform is concerned about all age groups and, regardless of the outcome, nursing will continue to focus on quality care and competent practice (AACN, 2009d; Holroyd et al, 2009).

- The number of diverse ethnic minorities and illegal immigrants is expanding throughout the United States, with multiple socioeconomic consequences. The diversity often is unwanted and leads to disrespect, intolerance, conflicts, abuse, and violence. The Southern Poverty Law Center is a national organization that promotes tolerance in schools, monitors militant hate groups, and initiates lawsuits against violent offenders (Southern Poverty Law Center [SPLC], 2009). Increasingly, health care providers need to learn about different cultural values and health practices and integrate them into care to the extent possible. They need to incorporate and teach tolerance and understanding of cultural diversity as well as positive health practices (Kersey-Matusiak, 2012). In 2008, the American Association of Colleges of Nursing (AACN, 2008b) developed end-of-program competencies for graduates of baccalaureate nursing programs for integrating cultural competencies into undergraduate education (www.aacn.nche.edu/Education/pdf/competency.pdf). *The Essentials of Baccalaureate Education for Professional Nursing Practice* (2008) mandates the inclusion of culturally diverse nursing care concepts in the curriculum. Professional ethics requires that health care providers separate their personal values and beliefs from their professional responsibilities, even to those whose beliefs are different (*Online Journal of Issues in Nursing [OJIN]*, 2009a; Tippitt et al, 2009). The number of families who become uninsured, jobless, homeless, and survive in poverty is increasing. The economic crisis during the first decade of the twenty-first century has resulted in fewer financial resources for health care and ordinary expenses, and thus more people eat unhealthy diets, go without medicines or treatments, and obtain care in emergency departments. More than half of family bankruptcies are due to overwhelming health care debt. Ehrenreich (2009) describes the incredible cycle of hunger, illness, theft, and incarcerations that poor people experience in the United States (Table 3-1).
- Domestic abuse of women and children and various forms of violence are increasing in homes, schools, and public places (*Stop Violence* website, 2009. The incidence of violence has increased even in nursing schools and in hospitals, including vertical abuse among nurses (American Nurses Association [ANA], 2009c; Thomas and Burk, 2009). Substance abuse, long a pervasive problem in society, has become a serious problem for nursing students and nurses (Monroe, 2009; Substance Abuse and Mental Health Services Administration [SAMHSA], 2012). Substance use disorders have consequences for the safety and health of nurses, patients, and others; the increase in stress and anxiety often triggers violence and mental health and economic problems.
- The United States is experiencing an epidemic of obesity, with major consequences on health and the health care system. It leads to the most prevalent health problems that strain health care facilities and financial resources. It is paramount for health care providers to teach prevention of obesity and its consequences in schools. Learning to help people change their dietary habits is a major role for nurses (OJIN, 2009b) and other health care workers.
- The traditional definition of family has changed, as evident in the number of single individuals living with other singles, single-parent households, and same-sex couples (with and without children). These nontraditional families often have limited finances and lack access to nursing and health care. They also may be resented by those with more traditional values and attitudes. Nurses must learn to respect and provide essential care regardless of differences.
- Disrespect for others, abuse of noisy mobile devices in public, and disregard for common courtesy has changed the nature of social interactions. Nursing students who use class time to send digital messages, use cell phones, or search the Internet are disrespectful of those who want to learn and the teacher who is trying to help them learn. This is part of the larger trend of declining civility and integrity, with increased cheating and falsification in school and work (Anastasi et al, 2009; Tippitt et al, 2009). Such incidents trigger anger and retaliation when excessive. In health care facilities, abuse of patients also is increasing. Nurses often need to mediate health care-related situations,

and effective communication skills are essential (Schlariet, 2009).

- As suggested, an important part of nursing education includes trends in society and the issues that result. Nurses work with those in all aspects of society, and thus, course content and interactive practice-based learning that incorporates these issues is essential. One of the most significant issues for students is learning to distinguish the meaningful differences in beliefs, values, and expectations among patients and their responses to illness, treatments, and caregivers. This is why nursing programs include, and students need to learn from, the areas of study that support effective nursing care, such as sociology, cultural diversity, psychology, ethics, religion, economics, history, and literature. Learning the experiences of diverse peoples, including patients and co-workers, their customs, beliefs, health practices, and expectations not only is interesting but also expands human understanding, tolerance, compassion, and the creativity essential for effective professional practice (SPLC, 2009).

Community-Focused Interprofessional Approaches

The societal trends described here, along with the large-scale economic and political influences to reduce health care costs, may indirectly promote prevention and interprofessional initiatives. Many lay and professional health-conscious groups are working to change the national orientation from "illness care" to more efficient and effective "health care." Another contributing factor is the increasing emphasis on health of the family as a whole and on entire communities and populations. *Healthy People 2010,* as described by Zahner and Block (2006), outlines goals for a broad-based population health set by government agencies (Centers for Disease Control and Prevention [CDC] and Merck Company Foundation, 2007. *Healthy People 2020* has expanded on *Healthy People 2010,* with the current mission cited to identify health care initiatives, increase awareness of health, identify measurable objectives and outcomes, improve practice through evidence, and identify research, evaluation, and data collection methods (http://www.healthypeople.gov/2020/about/default.aspx).

As more citizens live longer and develop acute and chronic illnesses, which can lead to disabilities, nurses work in a widening range of settings; such as acute care facilities, ambulatory clinics, nursing homes, hospices, home care, assisted living facilities, faith-based initiatives, and alternative integrative health care practices (Anastasi et al, 2009). Regardless of the setting, community health care involves an interprofessional team, often coordinated by nurses. Nursing students are positioned to learn from and work with practicing nurses who are in diverse roles to understand the scope and role of a nurse, and to begin to identify an area of nursing interest. Therefore, the concept of community care agencies has changed. Hospitals are only one of many community health care resources, along with wellness and senior centers. The changes in the health care landscape with a focus on preventive care, and community care require a different philosophy of care and competencies that emphasize interprofessional and interagency collaboration. The rapidly changing and expanding health care culture incorporates concepts of shared responsibility for health promotion among individuals, family, community, and multiple care providers. Nursing education is influenced by these trends to promote family and community health and healthy lifestyles, and increased interprofessional learning and collaboration (Holroyd et al, 2009; IOM, 2003).

In response to the paradigm shift to interprofessional care, and providing care following the IOM's six aims for improvement—safe, effective, patient centered, timely, efficient, and equitable (IOM, 2001)—AACN developed core competencies for interprofessional collaborative practice. According to the AACN (2011) report, change is needed in the way health care professionals are trained, increasing didactic and clinical interprofessional collaboration. The four competency domains identified include: values/ethics for professional practice, roles/responsibilities, interprofessional communication, and teams and teamwork (http://www.aacn.nche.edu/education-resources/ipecreport.pdf). Although interprofessional educational experiences are encouraged for all health care disciplines, Delunas and Rouse (2014) cite the importance of preparation of students for interprofessional educational experiences and the need for regular meetings when students are engaged in learning as a member of a health care team.

Global Health

With extensive global travel and commerce, the health community now encompasses the world. Illness can arrive on any airplane, ship, or bus and spread throughout the country. An example is the pandemic of the H1N1 "swine flu," which has spread to every continent and continues to cause illness and deaths. Nurses are on the front line of care and defense and have raised concerns about sufficient protection. Similarly, other infections, such as reemerging strains of tuberculosis (Benkert et al, 2009) and methicillin-resistant *Staphylococcus aureus* (MRSA), spread rapidly and are resistant to treatment; nurses and other providers need to become even more diligent in preventing the spread of organisms (ANA, 2009a). With the recent identification of Ebola hemorrhagic fever in the United States among missionary health care providers, the Centers for Disease Control and Prevention has reevaluated and updated the recommendations for health care providers in settings working with patients who have symptoms of ebola (CDC, 2014), nurses often being at the front line of care.

Consistent with the trend toward global health, nurses are engaged in the global health community through collaborative networks, research projects, and shared publications (Critchley et al, 2009). Programs incorporate global content, and students learn to participate in international health research projects and communication through the Internet and have direct learning experiences in countries abroad (Ramal, 2009). The International Council of Nurses (ICN, 2009) provides many opportunities for students to network and learn from each other; its periodic international conferences are a major resource for students and nurses to promote world health (ICN, 2009; see ICN website and student bulletin board, Icn.ch/news/studnt-network-bulletin/).

These trends challenge students to prepare for a wide spectrum of nursing practice that depends on competencies such as clinical decision making (Flin et al, 2008), communication, collaboration, and leadership. Students need to learn how to manage illness and preventive health care for diverse clients dispersed throughout the community as well as to provide critical care to hospital patients who are sicker and go home quicker. Although very helpful, learning in diverse settings throughout the community presents some issues. For example, dispersed clinical learning requires more planning, travel, expense, and time; learning time is much shorter at each location; community-based group projects take more time; and students have less time with instructors because faculty can be only at one location at a time. In many settings, however, students work only with preceptors or staff who help them gain the competence and confidence they need, but who also have other responsibilities. In addition as students and health care leaders, nurses need to effectively communicate with other health care disciplines, and have a good understanding of their role and scope of practice, to practice at the highest level of their degree and licensure.

Patient-Centered Care: Engagement, Safety, and Privacy

As patients have become more knowledgeable about illness care, health promotion, and the consequences of errors in care, they have become more assertive about their right to competent care and privacy of information. The 2002 Health Insurance Portability and Accountability Act (HIPAA) law mandates protection of an individual's privacy by health care providers and throughout society and has changed many previously careless and harmful practices. The economics and politics of health care and access to comprehensive information via the Internet have promoted more consumer activism through advocacy groups and Internet connections to influence health care policy and standards. Patients use Internet resources, sponsored by the government and private entities, to become more informed about illness and health care. As informed and engaged patients, they are better able to make effective decisions in collaboration with health care providers. This makes critical thinking, communication, and teaching essential nursing competencies. This also means that student nurses need to change their approach from "giving patient care" to "working with the patient and family" as members of the health care team.

Another major issue affecting nursing education is the increasing number and consequences of serious medical errors, as reported in the IOM study (2000). These errors have led to an astonishing number of deaths and an increased number of expensive lawsuits, which further increase the cost of health care and tarnish the belief in the quality of available health care. Nursing faculty, administrators, and regulators therefore are increasingly concerned with ensuring the competence of students and nurses (Finkelman and Kenner, 2009; IOM, 2003). Medical-error issues have precipitated increased requirements for competency-based education and performance assessment in schools of nursing and other health disciplines, in annual employment evaluations, and in agency accreditation criteria, all for patient safety.

Many injuries and deaths in medical institutions are preventable, and Medicare recently decided that it will no longer pay for such preventable incidents, many of which are attributed to nurses. Thus, preventive care is being emphasized even more in nursing education. QSEN, the COPA model, Interprofessional Collaboration, and similar initiatives in every specialty organization are designed to change nursing education and practice to promote competence and patient safety (IOM, 2003; NLN, 2009a).

Ethics and Bioethical Concerns

Another trend affecting nursing education is related to the multicultural, multiethnic population and patients who have different ways of responding to illness, treatment, and care providers. This raises ethical issues of who is "right" and who has the "right to decide." This is particularly relevant for freedom of choice and end-of-life issues (Moulton and King, 2010). As described, one difficult issue, particularly for students and novices, is the ethical necessity to differentiate personal beliefs, values, and preferences from professional practice responsibilities. Many ethical dilemmas require students, nurses, and other providers to accept the values of others and the concept of "a gray continuum of values" instead of the black-and-white interpretations based on one's own beliefs. Some of the most controversial issues relate to the right of individual choice regarding abortion, organ transplant, stem-cell research, preference in sexual partners, and the patient's right to die a dignified death. Other issues emerge from the growing use of alternative health remedies outside the mainstream of traditional Western medicine, such as herbs and acupuncture (Anastasi et al, 2009). Dishonesty among nursing students, nurses, and other professionals is increasingly alarming and threatens patient safety (McCabe, 2009). The *American Nurses Association's Code of Ethics for Nurses with Interpretive Statements* (2001) provides a succinct statement of the ethical obligations and duties of every individual who enters the nursing profession, and is a vailable online at www.nursingworld.org/about/01action.htm#code. Chapter 9 presents a comprehensive discussion about ethics in health care and important issues students should be knowledgeable about for competent nursing practice.

Shortage of Nurses and Faculty

The shortage and aging of nurses and nurse educators is a trend that has precipitated serious issues for students, teachers, and health care consumers (AACN, 2009e; Buerhaus et al, 2009; NLN, 2009b). During the recent recession, nurses older than 50 years of age reentered the hospital workforce (Buerhaus and Auerbach, 2011). These authors assert that when this older hospital workforce retires, a hospital nursing shortage will re-emerge, challenging administration to use the experienced workforce to mentor younger nurses. The current lack of a nursing shortage is likely to be followed by a decrease in available workforce and hospitals, and policymakers need to take note to address this coming trend (Staiger et al, 2012).

Students are assigned to multiple and diverse community clinical settings, some of which may be short-staffed, making it difficult for them to find qualified preceptors. Staff nurses who act as clinical instructors or preceptors may or may not be prepared for these roles or receive adequate orientation. Students, therefore, need to learn to take more individual responsibility and initiative to gain essential core competencies. Online learning environments can be simulated to mimic real-world situations that allow for faculty to evaluate student learning from a distance (Phillips et al, 2010). New methods are created in partnership with agencies to promote more effective clinical learning opportunities for students without overburdening staff.

Often the causative trends related to a shortage of faculty include a limited number of nurses prepared at advanced levels, space limitations, and other administrative constraints. For example, AACN's 2013-2014 report cited that nursing schools in the United States turned away 78,089 qualified candidates due to faculty shortages, lack of clinical sites, and space. Faculty are aging (average age of doctorally prepared faculty is 53.5 years of age) and retiring (average age of retirement is 62.5 years), but the number of prospective qualified replacements is severely limited (AACN, 2012). Some schools are expanding enrollments by using more part-time, adjunct, and clinical faculty and by expanding the use of online courses and simulation. Moreover, the number of students in Master of Science in nursing (MSN) or doctoral programs is not adequate to meet

Education is the ladder to success.

current needs. Nurse leaders and organizations are working vigorously with state and national governments and private entities to reverse these trends by seeking increased funding and promoting recruitment and development efforts nationally (see AACN at http://www.aacn.nche.edu/media-relations/fact-sheets/nursing-faculty-shortage).

The nursing shortage and lack of nursing faculty presents many hardships for students, faculty, and nurses; however, difficult situations promote creative and innovative initiatives and solutions. For example, many organizations and associations have initiated collaborative partnerships to improve education in all types and levels of nursing education; some are statewide or regional arrangements (Kruelen et al, 2008; Murray, 2007). (See Flexible Education, Mobility, and Distance-Learning Programs, p. 56.) The NLN has implemented initiatives to improve nursing education and faculty development (see the AACN and NLN websites for position statements regarding innovations and transitions in nursing education).

Disasters, Violence, and Terrorism

Nurses have always worked in situations emanating from disasters, abuse, and violence in families and communities, and in military conflicts. Domestic violence, especially against women and children, has increased as has violence in the workplace and in schools. Increased violence has precipitated an increased emphasis in nursing education (SAMHSA, 2010) and in state regulations of reporting and responding to violent incidents. Criminal acts and substance abuse have become more common in hospitals, other health care agencies, and in schools of nursing, threatening the safety of patients and staff (ANA, 2009c; Monroe, 2009). As a consequence, criminal background checks are required for all students (and employees) as well as by agencies providing clinical experience. Population expansion, especially in urban areas, and mass disasters, such as hurricanes, floods, and earthquakes have precipitated the need for more nurses to get prepared to function effectively along with other first responders. Adelman and Legg (2009) describe details about preparedness and opportunities for nurses who want to learn more. State boards of nursing and other organizations also provide information. The National Student Nurses Association (2011) has a guideline for disease preparedness, recovery and relief projects (http://www.nsna.org/Portals/0/Skins/NSNA/pdf/Disaster%20Preparedness%20Guidelines%202011_12.pdf).

Since the terrorist attacks on September 11, 2001, in New York City, Washington, DC, and Pennsylvania, more nurses (and all other health care personnel and first responders) are more prepared to respond to acts of terrorism and disaster. Many nursing programs have added courses or even entire programs of study for specialized preparation as first responders, emergency nursing, and flight nursing (ANA, 2006; Adelman and Legg, 2009; Whitty and Burnett, 2009). All nurses will not become first responders, but all nurses and students should gain enough knowledge to know their limitations, who and how to notify, and how they could work with more qualified responders. Chapter 15 also provides more information about disaster preparedness for nurses.

Increasing Professional and Personal Responsibilities

Given the complexity of health care delivery and need for health care team members to work as an interprofessional team, another trend with multiple issues has become evident. Students, teachers, and nurses confront increasing life responsibilities and associated stressful demands on time and resources. Many cope simultaneously with the expansion of information and technology; changing health care systems; more interactive and out-of-class methods of learning; multiple care settings; higher expectations for competence; shortage of nurse preceptors and teachers; and multiple cultural, ethical, and legal aspects of an ever-changing society. Many also are responsible for the care of dependent children and aging parents.

At the same time, contemporary conditions require nurses to keep current through planned ongoing professional development. Complexities in practice, emphasis on reducing errors, and increasing consumer activism increase the need for nurses to document continuing competence for initial licensure, relicensure, and recertification. Changes in state and multistate regulations increasingly focus on the need for initial and continuing competence (IOM, 2009). Many states require continuing education, and some mandate a portfolio approach to validate continuing competence (see websites for NCSBN and specific states, such as California, Kentucky, Oklahoma, and Tennessee).

The high stress levels associated with these professional and personal demands have consequences for one's own health and that of those around them. These issues illustrate how important it is for everyone involved in the educational process to be more caring, understanding, respectful, and helpful to each other. Teachers, students, administrators, staff nurses, employers, family, and friends need to learn a new the meaning of "a caring community" in the context of rapid and complex change.

These trends in society, nursing, and academic programs present issues of how to incorporate this additional knowledge into the already overloaded program of study. The issues for students include knowing how to access and use unlimited information, prioritize learning, implement evidence-based practice, deal with ethical dilemmas professionally, and develop competencies required for effective response to contemporary issues. Above all, students must focus on learning to think critically, reflectively, ethically, and compassionately as essential professional skills (IOM, 2011).

DIVERSITY IN NURSING EDUCATION PROGRAMS

A brief review of the major types of education programs that prepare nurses for licensure and advanced practice sets the stage for summarizing some contemporary trends related to flexible, online, and other distance delivery methods in nursing education. A brief description of the types of programs is provided in Table 3-2.

Licensed Practical or Vocational Nurse Programs

Practical nurse (PN) or vocational nurse (VN) programs provide the shortest and most restricted option for individuals seeking a nursing license. In the United States 1297 PN/VN programs are currently accredited (NLN, 2013). Licensed practical nurse (LPN) programs, named licensed vocational nurses (LVN) in California and Texas, usually are 9 to 12 months in length and may be offered by high school adult education programs, community colleges, vocational and proprietary schools, and hospitals. In 2012, the main reason cited for individuals who were qualified, but not accepted into a PN/VN program was a lack of clinical placement sites for 51% of the applicants (NLN, 2012).

Each state board of nursing sets responsibilities and scopes of practice. The LPN/LVN graduate is required to work under the supervision of a registered nurse (RN) or physician, and the scope of practice focuses on technical nursing procedures. LPNs/LVNs may be employed in hospitals, nursing homes, offices, and other structured settings. Of the diploma nurses who responded to a recent survey, 66% were still employed in nursing and 40% were employed full-time with the highest practice

TABLE 3-2	Types of Nursing Education Programs		
Types of Program and Credential	**Type of Institution**	**Length of Program**	**Purpose and Scope**
Practical or vocational nurse program: prepares for LVN or LPN license	High school, hospitals, vocational-technical schools; some colleges	9 to 12 months	Basic technical bedside care; hospitals, nursing homes, home care, offices in LPN positions
Diploma program: prepares for RN license	Hospitals, some in conjunction with colleges	2 to 3 years	Basic RN positions; hospitals and agency care
Associate degree in nursing: prepares for RN license	Community and junior colleges	2 years; some are 1 year bridge programs for LPN/LVN graduates	Basic technical care in RN positions, primarily in institutions
Bachelor's degree in nursing (BSN): prepares for RN license	Colleges and universities	2 to 4 years (depends on type of option); some are 1- to 2-year mobility options for graduates of PN or ADN programs or accelerated options for second-degree students	Basic professional practice as RN; management, community and public health settings; prepares for graduate school and certification; basic programs are 4 years; mobility options may be only 2 years
Master's degree in nursing (MSN)	Universities	1 to 2 years beyond BSN degree; some offer fast-track options	Advanced clinical practice, management, education, leadership positions
Doctoral degree in nursing	Universities	Varies: PhD, DSN, DNP, DNSc	Advanced nursing for research, clinical practice, education, and leadership positions

setting being in a nursing home, extended care, or assisted living facility (Budden et al, 2013).

In 2010, the highest number of LPN/LVN graduates who took the NCLEX-PN as first time candidates were from the Midwest and Southern Regions of the United States (HRSA, 2013). The workforce analysis found that 66,734 candidates sat for the NCLEX-PN in 2010; however, from 2010-2011, there were a decreased number of individuals who passed the examination. A workforce survey conducted in 2008 found that 5% of individuals who qualified for their first U.S. Nursing License were at the LPN-PN level, but less than 1% of the respondents (n=41,018) reported their highest level of education to be at the LVN-PN level (Budden et al, 2013). In the last decade, the full-time salary for LPNs has increased about $11,500 to an average in 2010 of $39,360 (HRSA, 2013).

Regardless of the increasing complexity of patient care, many individuals choose to begin a career in

nursing as an LPN/LVN. Once licensed, many graduates continue their education in mobility programs to become RNs. Many use "1 plus 1" type programs to earn an associate degree; others use the multiple entry-exit programs (MEEP). Some BSN programs accept LPN graduates based on outcomes of written and performance examinations for advanced placement.

Hospital Diploma Programs

The oldest, most traditional type of program that prepares for RN licensure is the hospital-based diploma program. These programs initially were developed in the United States in the late 1800s in general hospitals in cities such as Boston, New York, Hartford, and Philadelphia and subsequently spread across the country. They followed the Nightingale model and began as training programs taught by physicians, usually only several weeks in length. In time, nurse graduates began developing and teaching courses from the nursing perspective and subsequently obtained additional education as educators and administrators. Ultimately, the length of programs was extended, and by the mid-1900s most programs were 3 years in length and had fairly uniform courses of study and clinical hours.

As the number of hospitals increased, the need for nurses likewise increased, and essentially, every hospital developed its own training program as its main source for nursing staff. At their peak from 1950 to 1960, more than 1300 diploma programs were operational. By 2012, only 59 diploma schools remained (NLN, 2012). Diploma programs now are more similar to associate degree programs, typically 2 years in length; many have arrangements with colleges so that students can simultaneously earn an associate or baccalaureate degree. The American Association of Colleges of Nurses report pre-licensure nursing programs at the diploma level to be less than 10% of all basic RN programs, citing the transition from hospital instruction to college or university instruction (AACN, 2014a).

Associate Degree Programs

In the late 1950s, a very different trend in nursing education emerged in response to social, political, and educational changes in society and to a growing shortage of RNs. During World War II, the need for RNs who were prepared more quickly than in diploma programs became critical; the 2-year Cadet Nurse Corps was developed and proved to be very successful. From this experience, some educators realized that nurses and others could be prepared in less time and still meet RN licensure and practice requirements. After the war, Congress made funds available to publicly fund community colleges that offered 2-year associate degree programs in many technical fields. In addition, military benefits for college tuition allowed thousands of men and women to earn a 2-year college degree and fill jobs needed by burgeoning business and industry.

At the same time, the increasing complexity and expansion of medical care required more and better-prepared RNs. A few nurse educators began to create a new 2-year associate degree nursing program in community colleges, which required college courses in arts and sciences and a more integrated approach to nursing content and clinical learning. These pioneers reasoned that nursing belonged in a college setting, as in other disciplines, to provide a better education for nurses and

to establish more respect and recognition for nursing's contribution to the community's health. As the number of community colleges grew and the need for nurses increased, associate degree nursing (ADN) programs became a logical program for development and expansion.

ADN education is a vivid example of how changes in society influence the evolution of nursing education; it was another significant "first" in nursing and an important part of the evolving professionalization of nursing as a discipline. For the first time, it was possible for all RNs to be educated in a college setting and obtain a college degree. ADN programs were so successful that they became the new career pathway for nurses, and now the majority of practicing RNs are ADN graduates.

In 2012, approximately 1048 ADN programs were operational, which is an increase of 84 programs since 2007. (NLN,* 2013). The majority of the AND programs are found in the Midwestern and Southern regions of the United States (NLN, 2013). Of the qualified applicants to ADN programs, 45% are rejected due to difficulty with placements (NLN, 2013). Study findings (Trofino, 2013) indicate that individuals admitted to ADN programs pass the NCLEX-RN® examination at higher rates based on the following; preadmission math subscores, grades in pharmacology and advanced medical-surgical nursing, and not repeating a nursing course. A recent survey study reported that of the nurses who responded, 11,321 reported ADN as highest level of education, and 85% were employed full time (Budden et al, 2013). The trend of acceptance and growth of ADN programs along with the slowly increasing 4-year BSN programs and progressive mobility options established the educational framework for current nursing education.

Baccalaureate Degree Nursing Programs

In 1924, Yale University offered the first separate department of nursing whose graduates earned the baccalaureate degree. The 28-month program required scientific studies and clinical work and had the prestige and

---

*Slide series from the National League for Nursing Annual Survey of Schools of Nursing, Academic Year 2010–2011. NLN Data View National League for Nursing (2011). Number of Basic RN Programs by Program Type: 2003–2012. NLN Data ViewTM. Retrieved from http://www.nln.org/researchgrants/slides/pdf/AS1112_F01.pdf.

authority of other departments, with its own dean and budget (Kalisch and Kalisch, 1995).

Generic BSN programs typically require 2 years of arts and sciences followed by 2 years of nursing courses. RN to BSN programs are growing in number (AACN, 2012), and the AACN's 2012 survey found that 15,002 students with non-nursing degrees were enrolled in accelerated programs. The demographic of this degree-seeking student, according to AACN is "motivated, older, and has higher academic expectations than traditional entry-level students." As in other programs, BSN courses focus on the care of patients with medical, surgical, pediatric, obstetric, and psychiatric conditions, although course sequencing and names differ considerably from school to school. BSN programs focus more emphasis on the family and community and health promotion and illness prevention; a large part of clinical experience is in diverse community settings. These programs also require courses such as research, management, leadership, and statistics. The average salary of a full time RN in 2010 was $63,944, which is up about $20,000 in the last decade (HRSA, 2013).

In the United States, there are 696 BSN programs, which is up 13 programs in the last 5 years (NLN, 2013). In addition, there are 664 BSN completion programs in the United States, and most of the programs, consistent with BNS programs are in the Midwestern and Southern region of the United States. According to the NLN, of all basic RN programs, 39% of applicants are accepted, 28% are qualified but not accepted, and 33% are not qualified. Of the BSN programs in the United States the most common reason cited for denying an applicant is due to shortage of faculty (38%) followed by having a shortage of clinical placement sites (36%). Graduates of BSN programs take the same NCLEX-RN® licensure examination as diploma and ADN graduates. Most specialty areas require the BSN degree for practice and as preparation for specialty certification. Admission into master's programs usually requires a BSN or other degree.

Master's Degree Nursing Programs

In the 1960s and 1970s, the number of BSN graduates increased; however, in response to the complexity of health care, so did the need for more qualified clinicians, educators, and administrators. The federal government responded with support for the development of MSN and BSN degree programs. Nurse leaders lobbied and obtained federal funding for building construction and increased student tuition. Traineeship and fellowship grants were made available to thousands of RNs that enabled them to earn BSN and advanced degrees to meet these needs. Different MSN program options are available; the most typical are for BSN graduates, although an increasing number are designed for graduates of non-nursing degree programs, called *accelerated* or *second-degree* programs. Second-degree graduate nursing programs, in which graduates do not receive a BSN but are eligible to sit for the NCLEX-RN® licensure examination, are growing in number. It has been cited that students in these programs are self-directed adult learners who pass the RN licensure examination at high pass rates (Miller and Holm, 2011).

Until the late 1960s, MSN programs primarily focused on preparing educators and administrators, but then the curriculum shifted to an overwhelming emphasis on clinical practice. By the 1990s, the negative and the positive consequences of this decision became apparent with more competent clinicians but less well-prepared educators and administrators. Most MSN programs are designed to prepare advanced nurse practitioners and clinical specialists in various specialty areas. The extraordinary and rapid changes in health care since the early 1990s highlighted the cost-effective and quality care benefits of using advanced practice nurses in primary health care and other specialty areas. With intensive and persistent legal activities, nurses won battles to change state laws to permit nurse practitioners to write prescriptions, receive reimbursement for care, and operate independent nurse practices and health centers. As a result of this expanded scope of practice, an increasing number of nurses have obtained MSN degrees and advanced practice certification. Most specialty practice nurses, managers, administrators, and educators now are required to have a master's or doctoral degree. The AACN and NLN offer descriptions and numbers of different types of programs on their websites. Additionally, the consensus model for advanced practice registered nurse (APRN) regulation, which included licensure, accreditation, certification and education was published in 2008 (AACN, 2008c). The Licensure, Accreditation, Certification and Education report was published and outlines four APRN roles: nurse anesthetist, nurse midwife, clinical nurse specialist, and nurse practitioner followed by six population foci. This document provides data to guide nursing licensure, accreditation of programs, certification, and educational programs (https://www.ncsbn.org/7_23_08_Consensue_APRN_Final.pdf). Currently there are 504 master's in nursing programs in the United States (NLN, 2013).

Clinical Nurse Leader

In 2000, the national movement to enhance quality and safety in health care led to discussions between the AACN, nurse executives, and other health care leaders that led to the development of a new nursing role—the clinical nurse leader (CNL). In July 2002, the AACN board created the TFER 2 (Task Force on Education and Regulation). Its focus was the nurse competencies needed in current and future health care systems to improve patient care and what the "new nurse" role might look like. This work resulted in the publication of the White Paper on the Role of the Clinical Nurse Leader (CNL) in 2007 (AACN, 2009a). The CNL is a master's-prepared generalist clinician, not an advanced practice nurse, who oversees the care coordination of a distinct group of patients, evaluates patient outcomes, and has the decision-making authority to change care plans when necessary. The CNL actively provides direct patient care in complex situations, serves as a lateral integrator who provides centralized care coordination for a distinct group of patients, and puts evidence-based care into practice to ensure that patients benefit from the latest innovations. A CNL is a leader in the health care delivery system with expertise in quality improvement and cost-effective resource utilization (Rosseter, 2009). The CNL is not an advanced practice nurse, nor is the CNL prepared in an area of clinical specialty; however, the CNL can consult with a Clinical Nurse Specialist as needed and, further, the CNL can provide evidence-based care to complex patients (Harris et al, 2011). The Commission on Nurse Certification, an autonomous arm of the AACN, began certifying CNLs in 2007. By August 2014, more than 3,000 individuals earned CLN certification, up from more than 1850 individuals in 2012. As of 2014, 94 colleges and universities were offering CNL programs that prepare graduates to sit for the CNL certification examination. The AACN and CNC are recognizing CNL faculty leaders by offering the first ever CNL Educator Vanguard Award, to be awarded at the CNL Summit in 2015 (http://www.aacn.nche.edu/leading-initiatives/cnl/cnl-certification/pdf/DirectoryState2010.pdf).

Doctoral Programs

Changes in society and health care and the trend of needing well-educated nurse leaders and researchers to initiate and lead nursing doctoral programs. The first doctoral program for nurses was developed at Teachers College, Columbia University, and the first nurse graduated in 1932 with a doctor of education degree (EdD). In 1934, New York University offered a PhD program for nurses. More than 30 years elapsed before doctoral programs *in nursing* (instead of *for nurses*) were offered (e.g., the doctor of nursing science degree [DNS or DNSc]).

For the past few decades, three types of doctoral degrees in nursing were available: (1) the doctor of philosophy (PhD) for those interested in research; (2) the DNS or DNSc for those interested in advanced clinical nursing practice; and (3) the doctor of nursing (ND) for those with BS or higher degrees in non-nursing fields who want to pursue a career in nursing leadership. The ND degree, which prepared nurses for basic licensure (NCLEX-RN®), was first offered at Case Western Reserve University in 1979. Shortly after, Rush University, the University of Colorado Health Sciences Center, and others offered this degree. Nursing schools have transitioned and no longer offer the ND.

Beginning in 2000, AACN leaders developed and implemented a new clinical-focused doctoral degree: the doctor of nursing practice (DNP) (AACN, 2014a; see AACN webpage for updated information and statistics). The DNP is conceived as preparation for contemporary advanced nurse practitioners; it is viewed as the clinical equivalent to the research-oriented PhD nursing degree. The AACN has recommended that all advanced practice education programs move from the master's to the doctoral level by 2015. Although the DNP prepares clinicians, and does not formally prepare nurse educators, many individuals who complete a DNP degree frequently shift from practice to a dual role and serve in faculty roles, in addition to clinical roles. In 2014, the AACN reported that from 2012 to 2013 the number of students enrolled in DNP programs increased from 11,575 to 14,688; during the same period, the number of DNP graduates increased from 1,858 to 2,443. Additionally, as of August 2014, 243 DNP programs are enrolling students within 48 states plus the

District of Columbia, with 59 programs in the planning stage, which is up from 217 DNP programs in 2012 (AACN, 2014b).

FLEXIBLE EDUCATION, MOBILITY, AND DISTANCE-LEARNING PROGRAMS

Various and nontraditional mobility programs now are commonplace. The AACN and NLN websites attest to the growing number of programs that offer some form of flexible, alternative program, in addition to position statements on technology in nursing education, distance-learning, and online programs. This well-developed trend is based on the success of these programs, the documented needs of students, the nursing shortage, and the expansion and acceptance of electronic learning technology (Shovein et al, 2005). Distance or mobility programs include those for LPN or LVN to ADN and BSN; diploma and ADN graduates to BSN and MSN; and BSN to MSN and doctoral programs. Almost all use some form of Internet-based courses, and some are entirely online. Some require periods of intensive on-campus classes or assigned clinical experiences with preceptors.

The most controversial but pace-setting distance-learning program in nursing was developed under the New York Board of Regents as "the external degree program." Initially named the NY Regents External Degree Program (NYREDP), it later was renamed Excelsior College. Its ADN program, initiated in 1972, and the BSN, in 1976, were fully accredited by the NLN shortly thereafter, albeit with considerable difficulty. This innovative college provides quality degree programs in many disciplines for adult learners underserved by traditional programs by using assessment methods to document prior learning and theory and performance examinations to validate current knowledge and competence. The nursing programs enroll thousands of students and are accessible regardless of geographic location; the students primarily are LPNs or RNs, some of whom also have other degrees or health-related certificates. Early studies documented their competence in the workplace (Lenburg, 1990). It initiated a master's degree program in 2000 with two specialty options. Over the years, many nursing programs have accepted and modified the distance-learning and assessment approach originally developed by the NYREDP and continued as Excelsior College. The integration of electronic learning technology with assessment methods makes nursing degrees accessible to an increasing number of nurses seeking additional preparation.

Career ladder programs designed as "1 plus 1" or "2 plus 2" options have been offered for many years by some schools and through several statewide programs. Multiple mobility programs are available for LPNs to obtain an ADN degree, such as one offered by the New York Coalition for Education Mobility (2004). RN to BSN programs are available in approximately 600 schools as of 2011 (AACN, 2012). In addition, some 165 programs admit ADN graduates into MSN programs (AACN, 2012). With the shortage of nurses and nurse educators, some schools are finding ways to streamline RN to BSN programs.

Changes in social, political, financial, and philosophic trends; the extensive use of communication and learning technology; verified success from past experiences; and the continuing shortage of nurses have combined to make education mobility and distance-learning opportunities a necessity and a reality nationally and internationally. Whereas the NLN continues to support all levels of education programs, the AACN and other organizations vigorously support the BSN for "entry into practice" and the professionalization of nursing (IOM, 2010). In 2003, the New York State Board of Nursing approved a proposal that would require future graduates of diploma and ADN programs to earn a BSN degree within 10 years to be eligible for renewal of licensure; as of this writing, it has not been passed. The New York Organization of Nurse Executives supports this effort and describes the rationale for it on its website (NYONE, 2006).

In October 2010, the IOM released *The Future of Nursing: Leading Change, Advancing Health,* which provides a blueprint for transforming the nursing profession. A key message of this IOM report was that nurses should achieve higher levels of education and training through an improved education system that promotes seamless academic progression. A variety of innovative strategies that include online education and simulation as well as consortium programs will need to be increased to create a seamless pathway from ADN to BSN, ADN to MSN and BSN-DNP and PhD. This will affect the needed transformation of nursing education (IOM, 2011).

The escalating nursing shortage and the aging of the current nursing workforce and nurse educators have prompted more schools to offer flexible mobility options and types of programs. Some target potentially underrepresented groups, such as men, minority groups, and those with existing academic degrees. The most rapidly growing are the accelerated, fast-track, or second-degree programs, designed for non-nurses with other degrees. In 2011, the AACN reported 235 accelerated BSN programs and 63 accelerated master's programs available at nursing schools nationwide. In addition, 33 new accelerated baccalaureate programs were in the planning stages, and 10 new accelerated master's programs were also taking shape. For a list of accelerated nursing programs, visit http://www.aacn.nche.edu/Education-Resources/APLIST.pdf.

Trends and issues that influence nursing education make it even more important to comply with quality standards that emphasize competency outcomes. Changes in number, diversity, and qualifications of students and shortage of faculty and finances make it necessary to develop more efficient and effective learning strategies for on-campus and distant students. Although mobility and electronic options are more convenient, they present issues. In addition to learning to access multiple digital resources, students also need discipline and determination to pursue courses and clinical learning when a teacher is not physically present or accessible. Regardless of methods, they must achieve required competencies in spite of other responsibilities and learn to integrate critical thinking, reflective judgment, and evidence-based practices in patient care. In contrast to previous decades, organizations and schools now require more creative, responsive programs and expect more documented competence from students and faculty (Box 3-1). Although these trends pose challenges for nursing students, faculties, and employers, they move nursing toward more competent professional practice and improved patient safety (Boyer, 2008).

BOX 3-1 Selected Organizations Relevant to Nursing Education: General Description and Purpose

American Academy of Nursing (AAN)—The organization of leaders in all facets of nursing: practice, education, administration, research, organizations, and government; the think tank of the profession; promotes advancement of all aspects of nursing; and publishes position papers, conference proceedings, and documents to advance nursing.

American Association of Colleges of Nursing (AACN)—The organization of deans and directors of baccalaureate and higher-degree nursing programs: establishes standards for programs concerned with legislative issues that pertain to professional nursing education and publishes the *Journal of Professional Nursing, The Essentials of Baccalaureate Education* (2008), and other related documents pertaining to the BSN and higher-degree education.

American Nurses Association (ANA)—The major national nursing organization concerned with a broad scope of practice issues: standard of practice, scope of practice, ethics, legal, and employment issues; a federation of state nurses associations; and publications relate to an array of practice issues and standards.

Commission on Collegiate Nursing Education (CCNE)—A subsidiary of the AACN with responsibility for establishing and implementing standards and criteria and for accreditation of baccalaureate and graduate degree programs in nursing.

National Council of State Boards of Nursing (NCSBN)—The organization of all state boards: coordinates licensure activities on a national level; creates and administers licensure examinations (NCLEX); develops computerized licensure examinations; and works with other organizations to promote nursing standards and regulations and establish interstate licensure protocols.

National League for Nursing (NLN)—The national organization of nurse educators with long-standing commitment to four types of basic programs (LPN, diploma, ADN, and BSN): includes lay citizens concerned with nursing and health care on its board; has councils for nursing informatics, research in nursing education, wellness centers, and multiple types of print publications; initiated a certification program and examination to certify excellence of nursing educators; and established the Centers for Excellence for nursing programs that meet designated standards.

NLN Accreditation Commission (NLNAC)—Formed in 1997 as a subsidiary of the NLN with responsibility for establishing and implementing standards and criteria and for accrediting all types of schools of nursing.

National Organization of Nurse Practitioner Faculties (NONPF)—An organization of nurse practitioners in multiple specialties: sets national standards and criteria for programs and certification.

National Student Nurses Association (NSNA)—A national organization of statewide student nurse associations: concerned with education and career issues and provides student perspectives to other national nursing organizations.

SUMMARY

Chapter 3 presented 10 major trends and related issues in nursing education programs and an overview of multiple types of nursing programs. They have a significant influence on the content, learning process, and evaluation methods used in all types of programs and have influenced the development of new degrees and majors. Additionally, they have had a remarkable effect on the persistence of various types of programs for entry into practice and on the increasing acceptance of diverse mobility and distance-learning programs. Regardless of the type of program, most students now use the Internet to access courses, electronic databases, and other e-learning resources and integrate evidence-based practice and critical thinking. As students integrate current trends and attempt to resolve issues, they create the trends for the next generation, and are participating in nursing history in the making. The most profound trend in nursing education is learning to learn, to reason, and access relevant resources to solve problems. As Carl Rogers said "The only person who is educated is the one who had learned how to learn and change."

REFERENCES

Academic Center for Evidence Based Practice (website). http://www.acestar.uthscsa.edu/ June 7, 2015.

Adelman DS, Legg TJ: *Disaster nursing: a handbook for practice*, Sudbury, MA, 2009, Jones and Bartlett.

Agency for Health Care Research and Quality: *Evidenced based practice* (website). http://www.ahrq.gov/clinic/epcix.htm. Accessed April 23, 2015.

American Association of Colleges of Nursing: *Position statement: baccalaureate degree in nursing as minimal preparation for professional practice* (website). http://www.aacn.nche.edu June 7, 2015.

American Association of Colleges of Nursing: *Position statement on the practice doctorate in nursing* (website). http://www.aacn.nche.edu/DNP/DNPPositionStatement.htm. Accessed April 23, 2015.

American Association of Colleges of Nursing: *Issues bulletin: accelerated baccalaureate and master's degrees in nursing* (website). http://www.aacn.nche.edu/media-relations/AccelProgsGlance.pdf. Accessed April 23, 2015.

American Association of Colleges of Nursing: *The essentials of baccalaureate education for professional nursing practice*, 2008a (website). http://www.aacn.nche.edu/education-resources/BaccEssentials08.pdf. Accessed April 23, 2015.

American Association of Colleges of Nursing: *Cultural competency in baccalaureate education* (website). http://www.aacn.nche.edu/education-resources/cultural-competency. Accessed April 23, 2015.

American Association of Colleges of Nursing: *Nursing education programs*, 2008b (website). http://www.aacn.nche.edu/Education/nurse_ed/nep_index.htm. Accessed April 23, 2015.

American Association of Colleges of Nursing: *Consensus model for APRN regulation: Licensure, Accreditation, Certification and Education (LACE)*, 2008c (website). http://www.aacn.nche.edu/education-resources/APRNReport.pdf. Accessed April 23, 2015.

American Association of Colleges of Nursing: *The clinical nurse leader: developing a new nurse*, 2009a (website). http://www.aacn.nche.edu/cnl/index.htm. Accessed April 23, 2015.

American Association of Colleges of Nursing: *Clinical nurse leader certification* (website). http://www.aacn.nche.edu/cnl/cnl-certification/pdf/ExamHndbk.pdf. Accessed April 23, 2015.

American Association of Colleges of Nursing: *Degree completion programs for registered nurses: RN to master's degree and RN to baccalaureate programs*, 2009b (website). http://www.aacn.nche.edu/Media/FactSheets/DegreeCompletionProg.htm. Accessed April 23, 2015.

American Association of Colleges of Nursing: *End of life care*, 2009c (website). http://www.aacn.nche.edu/elnec. Accessed April 23, 2015.

American Association of Colleges of Nursing: *Government affairs, nursing policy beat: healthcare reform*, 2009d (website with multiple links to shortage and strategies for change). http://www.aacn.nche.edu/Government/index.htm. Accessed April 23, 2015.

American Association of Colleges of Nursing: *Nursing faculty shortage*, 2009e (website). http://www.aacn.nche.edu/Media/FactSheets/FacultyShortage.htm. Accessed April 23, 2015.

American Association of Colleges of Nursing: *Core Competencies for Interprofessional Collaborative Practice*, 2011 (website). http://www.aacn.nche.edu/education-resources/ipecreport.pdf. Accessed April 23, 2015.

American Association of Colleges of Nursing: *Nursing fact sheet*, 2014a (website). http://www.aacn.nche.edu/media-relations/fact-sheets/nursing-fact-sheet. Accessed April 23, 2015.

American Association of Colleges of Nursing: *Nursing fact sheet*, 2014b (website). http://www.aacn.nche.edu/media-relations/fact-sheets/DNPFactSheet.pdf. Accessed April 23, 2015.

American Association of Colleges of Nursing: *2010-2011 Enrollment and graduations in baccalaureate and graduate programs in nursing,* Washington, DC, 2012, American Association of Colleges of Nursing.

American Association of Colleges of Nursing: *Knowledge, Skills and Attitudes,* 2012 (website). http://www.aacn.nche.edu/faculty/qsen/competencies.pdf. Accessed April 23, 2015.

American Association of Colleges of Nursing: *Competencies,* 2007 (website). http://qsen.org/competencies/.

American Nurses Association: *Bioterrorism and disaster response,* 2006 (website). http://www.nursingworld.org/homepage/menu. Accessed April 23, 2015.

American Nurses Association: *Code of Ethics for Nurses with Interpretive Statements* (website). http://www.nursingworld.org/about/01action.htm#code. Accessed April 23, 2015.

American Nurses Association: *2009 H1N1—Information for nurses,* 2009a (website). http://www.nursingworld.org/HomepageCategory/NursingInsider/Archive_1/2009-NI/July09NI/H1N1-Information-for-Nurses.html. Accessed April 23, 2015.

American Nurses Association: *Nursing ethics: the center for ethics and human rights,* 2009b (website; explore links). http://www.nursingworld.org/MainMenuCategories/EthicsStandards.aspx. Accessed April 23, 2015.

American Nurses Association: *Workplace violence,* 2009c (website). http://nursingworld.org/workplaceviolence. Accessed April 23, 2015.

Anastasi JK, Capili B, Schenkman F: Developing integrative therapies in primary care program, *Nurs Educ* 34(6): 271–275, 2009.

Bargagliotti A, Luttrell M, Lenburg CB: Reducing threats to the implementation of a competency-based performance assessment system, *Online J Issues Nurs,* Vol 4 No 2 September 1999 (website). http://www.nursingworld.org/ojin. Accessed April 23, 2015.

Benkert R, Resnick B, Brackley M, et al: Tuberculosis education for nursing practitioner students: where we are and where we need to go, *J Nurs Educ* 48(5):255–265, 2009.

Brodersen LD, Mills AC: A comparison of two nursing program exit exams that predict first-time NCLEX-RN outcome, Computers, Informatics, *Nursing* 32(8):404–412, 2014.

Bruce SA, Scherer YK, Curran CC, et al: A collaborative exercise between graduate and undergraduate nursing students using a computer-assisted simulator in a mock cardiac arrest, *Nurs Educ Perspect* 30(1):22–27, 2009.

Buerhaus PI, Auerbach DI: The recession's effect on hospital registered nurse employment growth, *Nurs Econ* 29(4): 163–167, 2011.

Buerhaus PI, Auerbach DI, Staiger DO: The recent surge in nurse employment: causes and implications, *Health Aff* 28(4):620–624, 2009.

Budden JS, Zhong EH, Moulton P, Cimiotti JP: Highlights of the national workforce survey of registered nurses, *Journal of Nursing Regulation* 4(2):5–13, 2013.

Cant RP, Cooper SJ: Simulation-based learning in nurse education: systematic review, *J Adv Nurs* 66(1):3–15, 2010.

Centers for Disease Control and Prevention: *Infection prevention and control recommendations for hospitalized patients with known or suspected ebola hemorrhagic fever in U.S. hospital.* Updated July 30, 2014 (website). http://www.cdc.gov/vhf/ebola/hcp/infection-prevention-and-control-recommendations.html. November 15, 2014.

Cipriano PF, Murphy J: Nursing informatics. The future of nursing and health IT: the quality elixir, *Nursing Economic$* 29(5):286–282, 2011.

Cornell P, Riordan M, Herrin-Griffith D: Transforming nursing workflow, part 2 the impact of technology on nursing activities, *J Nurs Adm* 40(10):432–439, 2010.

Critchley KA, Richardson E, Aarts C, et al: Student experiences with an international public health exchange project, *Nurse Educ* 34(2):69–74, 2009.

Cronenwett L, Sherwood G, Barnsteiner J, et al: Quality and safety education for nurses, *Nurs Outlook* 55(3):122–131, 2007.

Cronquist R, Spector N: Nurses and social media: regulatory concerns and guidelines, *J Nurs Reg* 2(3):37–40, 2011.

Delunas LR, Rouse S: Nursing and medical student attitudes about communication and collaboration before and after an interprofessional learning experience, *Nursing Education Perspectives* 35(2):100–105, 2014.

DiVito-Thomas P: Nursing student stories on learning how to think like a nurse, *Nurse Educ* 30(3):133–136, 2005.

Ehrenreich B: *Is it now a crime to be poor?* August 9, 2009, New York Times (website). http://www.nytimes.com/2009/08/09/opinion/09ehrenreich.html. Accessed April 23, 2015.

Finkelman AW, Kenner C: *Teaching the IOM: implications of the IOM reports for nursing education,* Silver Spring, MD, 2009, American Nurses Association.

Flin R, O'Connor P, Crichton M: *Safety at the sharp end: a guide to non technical skills,* Burlington, VT, 2008, Ashgate.

Glennon CD: Reconceptualizing program outcomes, *J Nurs Educ* 45(2):55–58, 2006.

Harris JL, Stanley J, Rosseter R: The clinical nurse leader: addressing health-care challenges through partnerships and innovation, *J Nurs Reg* 2(2):40–46, 2011.

Hartford Institute for Geriatric Nursing: *Centers for Geriatric Nursing* (website). http://hartfordign.org/. Accessed April 23, 2015.

Hawkins K, Todd M, Manz J: A unique simulation teaching method, *J Nurs Educ* 47(11):524–527, 2008.

Health Resources and Services Administration (HRSA) Bureau of Health Professionals. National Center for Health Workforce Analysis: April 2013 (website). http://bhpr.hrsa.gov/healthworkforce/reports/nursingworkforce/nursing-workforcefullreport.pdf. Accessed April 23, 2015.

Holroyd A, Dahlke S, Fehr C, et al: Attitudes toward aging: implications for a caring profession, *J Nurs Educ* 48(7): 374–380, 2009.

Institute of Medicine: *To err is human: building a safer health system*, Washington, DC, 2000, National Academies Press (website). http://www.iom.edu. See also Nursing response at www.aacn.nche.edu. and www.nursingworld.org. Accessed April 23, 2015.

Institute of Medicine: *Crossing the quality chasm a new health system for the 21st century*, Washington, DC, 2001, National Academies Press (website). http://www.iom.edu. Accessed April 23, 2015.

Institute of Medicine: *Health professions education: a bridge to quality*, Washington, DC, 2003, National Academies Press.

Institute of Medicine: *Redesigning continuing education in the health professions*, Washington, DC, 2009, National Academies Press.

Institute of Medicine: *The future of Nursing: Leading change, advancing health*, Washington, DC, 2010, National Academies Press.

Institute of Medicine: *The future of nursing: leading change, advancing health*, Washington, DC, 2011, National Academies Press.

Institute of Medicine: The future of nursing: accomplishments a year after the landmark report (Editorial), *J Nurs Scholarsh* 44(1):1, 2012.

International Council of Nurses (ICN): *Nurs Netw*, 2009 (website). http://www.icn.ch/. Accessed April 23, 2015.

Ireland M: Assisting students to use evidence as a part of reflection on practice, *Nurs Educ Perspect* 29(2):90–93, 2008.

Jeffries PR: Technology trends in nursing education: next steps, *J Nurs Educ* 44(1):3–4, 2005.

Kalisch PA, Kalisch BJ: *The advance of American nursing*, ed 3, Philadelphia, 1995, Lippincott.

Kersey-Matusiak G: Culturally competent care: are we there yet? *Nurse Manag* 43(4):34–39, 2012.

Klein CJ: Linking competency-based assessment to successful clinical practice, *J Nurs Educ* 45(9):379–383, 2006.

Kruelen GJ, Bednarz PK, Wehrwein T, et al: Clinical education partnership: a model for school district and college of nursing collaboration, *J Sch Nurs* 24(6):360–369, 2008.

Lasater K, Nielsen A: The influence of concept-based learning activities on students' clinical judgment development, *J Nurs Educ* 48(8):441–446, 2009.

Lenburg CB: Do external degree programs really work? *Nurs Outlook* 38(5):234–238, 1990.

Lenburg CB: *Changes that challenge nursing education*, TN Nurse, October 2002 (website). http://www.tnaonline.org/Media/pdf/tn-nurse-archive-changes-that-challenge-lenburg2.pdf. Accessed April 20, 2006.

Lenburg CB: The influence of contemporary trends and issues on nursing education. In Cherry B, Jacob S, editors: *Contemporary nursing: issues, trends, and management*, ed 4, St Louis, 2008, Mosby.

Lenburg CB, Abdur-Rahman VZ, Spencer TS, et al: Implementing the COPA model in nursing education and practice settings: promoting competence, quality care, and patient safety, *Nurs Educ Perspect* 32(5):290–296, 2011.

McCabe DL: Academic dishonesty in nursing schools: an empirical investigation, *J Nurs Educ* 48(11):614–623, 2009.

Miller JF, Holm K: Graduate nursing programs for non-nurses: a national perspective, *J Nurs Reg* 2(2):4–9, 2011.

Moulton B, King JS: Aligning ethics with medical decision-making: The quest for informed patient choice, *J Law Med Ethics* 38(1):85–97, 2010.

National Council of State Boards of Nursing: *NCLEX educational program codes* (website). https://www.ncsbn.org/NCLEX_Educational_Program_Codes.pdf. Accessed April 23, 2015.

National League for Nursing: *Number of Basic RN Programs by Program. Type: 20003–2011, NLN DataViewTM*, 2012 (website). http://www.nln.org/research/slides/index. Accessed April 23, 2015.

National League for Nursing: *Public policy agenda 2009-2010: promoting excellence in nursing education to build a strong and diverse nursing workforce*, 2009a (website). http://www.nln.org/governmentaffairs/pdf/public_policy.pdf. Accessed April 23, 2015.

National League for Nursing: *Nursing shortage info*, 2009b (website; many links to nursing shortage information). http://www.nln.org/aboutnln/shortage_info.htm. Accessed April 23, 2015.

National League for Nursing: *Outcomes and competencies for graduates of practical/vocational, diploma, associate degree, baccalaureate, master's, practice doctorate, research doctorate programs in nursing*, 2010 (website). http://www.nln.org/facultyprograms/competencies/outcomes.htm. Accessed March 30, 2011.

National League for Nursing 2013: *National survey of schools of nursing*, Fall 2012 (website). http://www.nln.org/research/slides/index.htm. Accessed March 10, 2013.

National Organization of Nurse Practitioner Faculties: *Domains and core competencies*, 2012, Washington, DC (website). http://www.nonpf.com/displaycommon.cfm?an=1&subarticlenbr=14. Accessed April 23, 2015.

New York Organization of Nurse Executives: *NYONE-ACTION, advancing the profession of nursing* (website). http://www.nyone.org. Accessed September 9, 2006.

New York State Coalition for Educational Mobility: *LPN to ADN articulation model*, 2004 (website). http://www.lpntoadn.info. Accessed August, 2006.

Norris T, Webb S, McKeon L, et al: Using portfolios to introduce the Clinical Nurse Leader to the job market, *J Nurs Adm* 42(1):47–51, 2012.

Online Journal of Issues in Nursing: *Ethics columns and multiple articles*, 1999-2009 (website). http://www.nursingworld.org/ojin. Accessed April 23, 2015.

Online Journal of Issues in Nursing: *Obesity on the rise: what can nurses do?* 2009b (website). http://www.nursingworld.

org/MainMenuCategories/ANAMarketplace/ANAPeriodicals/OJIN/JournalTopics/Obesity-on-the-Rise.aspx. Accessed April 23, 2015.

Phillips B, Shaw RJ, Sullivan DT, et al: Using virtual environments to enhance nursing distance education, *Creative Nursing* 16(3):132–135, 2010.

Prinz A: Professional social networking for nurses, *American Nurse Today* 6(7), 2011 (website). http://www.americannursetoday.com/article.aspx?id=8016&;fid=7086. Accessed April 23, 2015.

Quality and Safety Education for Nurses: *Informatics Competency*, 2012 (website). http://qsen.org/competencies/. Accessed April 23, 2015.

Ramal E: Integrating caring, scholarship and community engagement in Mexico, *Nurse Educ* 34(1):34–37, 2009.

Robinson E, Niemer L: A peer mentor tutor program for academic success in nursing, *Nurse Educ Perspect* 31(5):286–289, 2010.

Roland EJ, Johnson C, Swain D: "Blogging" as an educational enhancement tool for improved student performance: a pilot study in undergraduate nursing education, *New Review of Information Networking* 16(2):151–166, 2011.

Rose JR: Nurse-run clinics offer hope to nation's tired, poor and uninsured, *Adv Nurs* 2009 (website). http://nursing.advanceweb.com/editorial/content/editorial.aspx?cc=204382. Accessed March 30, 2010.

Rosseter R: A new role for nurses: making room for clinical leaders, *Jt Comm Perspect* 9(8):5–7, 2009.

Schlariet M: Bioethics mediation: the role and importance of nurse advocacy, *Nurs Outlook* 57:185–193, 2009.

Sensmeier J: Information technology: transforming nursing practice through technology and informatics, *Nurs Manag* 42(11):20–23, 2011.

Scott ES: Peer-to-peer mentoring: teaching collegiality, *Nurse Educ* 30(2):52–56, 2005.

Shovein J, Huston C, Fox S, et al: Challenging traditional teaching and learning paradigm: online learning and emancipatory teaching, *Nurs Educ Perspect* 26(6):340–343, 2005.

Sideras S, McKenzie G, Noone J, et al: Making simulation come alive: standardized patients in undergraduate nursing education, *Nursing Perspectives* 34(6):421–425, 2013.

Skiba D: Emerging technologies center: teaching with and about technology: providing resources for nurse educators worldwide, *Nurs Educ Perspect* 30(4):129–131, 2009.

Skiba D: Emerging technologies center (see column In Every Issue), *Nurs Educ Perspect*, 2005-2009 (website). http://www.nln.org/newsroom/newsletters-and-journal/nursing-education-perspectives-journal. Accessed April 23, 2015.

Smith-Stoner M: Using high-fidelity simulation to educate nursing students about end-of-life care, *Nurs Educ Perspect* 30(2):115–120, 2009.

Smith-Stoner M: Web-based broadcast of simulations expanding access to learning, *Nurse Educ* 34(6):266–270, 2009.

Southern Poverty Law Center: 2009 (website; information on teaching tolerance and monitoring hate groups). http://www.tolerance.org/. Accessed April 23, 2015.

Staiger DO, Auerbach DI, Buerhaus PI: Registered Nurse labor supply and the recession—Are we in a bubble? *N Engl J Med* 366(16):1463–1465, 2012.

Stop violence against women: a project by the advocates for human rights, 2009 (website). http://www.stopvaw.org. Accessed April 23, 2015.

Substance Abuse and Mental Health Services Administration: *Mental health, United States*, HHS Publication No. (SMA) 12-4681 Rockville, MD, 2010, Substance Abuse and Mental Health Services Administration.

The TIGER Imitative Foundation: *"The TIGER initiative: informatics competencies for every practicing nurse: recommendations from the TIGER collaborative,"* 2007 (website). http://www.thetigerinitiative.org/docs/tigerreport_informaticscompetencies.pdf. Accessed April 23, 2015.

Tippitt MP, Ard N, Kline JR, et al: Creating environments that foster academic integrity, *Nurs Educ Perspect* 30(4): 239–244, 2009.

Trofino RM: Relationship of associate degree nursing program criteria with NCLEX-RN success: What are the best predictors in a nursing program of passing the NCLEX-RN the first time? *Teaching and Learning in Nursing* 8:4–12, 2013.

U.S. Department of Health and Human Services: *Healthy People 2020,* Diabetes: overview (website). http://www.healthypeople.gov/2020/topicsobjectives2020/overview.aspx?topicid=8. Accessed April 23, 2015.

U.S. Department of Labor Occupational Safety and Health Administration: *Guidelines for preventing workplace violence for health care and social service workers*, No. OSHA 3148, Washington, DC, 2003, U.S. Department of Labor Occupational Safety and Health Administration.

Wagner D, Bear M, Sander J: Turning simulation into reality: increasing student competence and confidence, *J Nurs Educ* 48(8):465–467, 2009.

Whitlow ML, Drake E, Tullman D, Hoke G, Barth D: Bridging technology to the bedside using smartphones to improve interprofessional communication, *Computers, Informatics, Nursing* 32(7):305–311, 2014.

Whitty KK, Burnett MF: Importance of instruction on mass casualty incidents in baccalaureate nursing programs: perceptions of nursing faculty, *J Nurs Educ* 48(5):291–295, 2009.

Wieland DM, Altmiller GM, Dorr MT, et al: Clinical transitions of baccalaureate nursing students during preceptored, pre-graduation practicums, *Nurs Educ Perspect* 28(6):315–321, 2007.

Zahner SJ, Block DE: The road to population health: using Healthy People 2010 in nursing education, *J Nurs Educ* 45(3):105–108, 2006.

Zurmehly J: Personal digital assistants (PDAs): review and evaluation, *Nurs Educ Perspect* 31(3):179–182, 2010.

4

Nursing Licensure and Certification

Susan R. Jacob, PhD, MSN, RN

Legal regulations and professional certification ensure safe, competent nursing care.

e Additional resources are available online at: *http://evolve.elsevier.com/Cherry/*

PROFESSIONAL/ETHICAL ISSUE

Russell and Rudy were working PRN in a very busy comprehensive home health agency. The agency had recently experienced high RN turnover and numerous changes in administrative personnel. Mary, the efficient staff person with whom they had worked from the beginning of their employment, resigned 6 months ago, and temporary staff have been sporadically doing her job. Russell and Rudy discussed how they both missed Mary because she always reminded them of important things such as insurance enrollment periods, CPR expiration dates, and the date their nursing licenses were about to expire. Rudy stated, "I'm afraid critical things have been slipping through the cracks lately and going unnoticed since Mary resigned." Russell, who had told Rudy he was way over the limit on all of his credit cards and overdue on many of his bills, responded, "I know my RN license is about to expire, but I have no money to spend on that in the near future, so I am really hoping no one checks up on this detail. Then I might get away with not having a current license for a few months until I can get my financial issues worked out."

How should Rudy respond to Russell?

What are the implications for practicing as an RN without a current nursing license?

VIGNETTE

Three nurses are discussing their nursing practice licenses. Joe Branch, a senior nursing student, is preparing for initial licensure. Mary Stone's license is due for renewal. Carmella Larkin has just moved into the state. As the three are talking about these changes in their practice, Giorgio Gonzales, a nurse practitioner, joins the group. Giorgio recently completed a certification *examination and is interested in becoming certified for advanced practice. All the nurses have a general knowledge of the requirements for licensure and certification but lack the specific information needed to legally practice within the state.*

Mary suggests contacting the state board of nursing. *The nurses agree that this is a sensible idea, and Mary leaves to phone the board of nursing. On returning, Mary informs the group that the answers to all of their questions can be found in the state's* nurse practice act *and accompanying rules and regulations, which can be accessed online. She tells them that the state board of nursing office will also send free copies of both documents to individuals who request them.*

The situation described here is not uncommon. Nurses need specific, current information on licensure and renewal of licensure. The most comprehensive sources for this information are the state nurse practice act and the state board of nursing. These resources provide accurate descriptions of the law governing nursing practice within each state and the U.S. territories.

Every nurse and nursing student will benefit from obtaining a copy of their state's nurse practice act and becoming familiar with its contents.

Questions to Consider While Reading This Chapter:
1. Who establishes the "rules" for nursing practice— the state or the employer?
2. Do graduates from different types of nursing education programs require different types of licenses?
3. If a nurse graduate passes the NCLEX-RN® examination, does this person still need a license?
4. What happens if a nurse's license expires? Can the nurse still practice?
5. Must a nurse complete graduate school and take an examination to be an advanced practice nurse?
6. Are the regulations governing advanced practice the same in all states?

KEY TERMS

Accreditation: Voluntary process by which schools of nursing are approved to conduct nursing education programs.

Accreditation Commission for Education in Nursing (ACEN): Entity that is responsible for the specialized accreditation of nursing education programs, both postsecondary and higher degree, which offer either a certificate, a diploma, or a recognized professional degree (clinical doctorate, master's/post-master's certificate, baccalaureate, associate, diploma, and practical).

Advanced practice nurse (APN): Legal title for nurses prepared by education and competence to perform independent practice.

American Nurses Association (ANA): Professional organization that represents all registered nurses.

American Nurses Credentialing Center (ANCC): An independent agency of the American Nurses Association that conducts certification examinations and certifies advanced practice nurses.

Certification: Process by which nurses are recognized for advanced education and competence.

Commission on Collegiate Nursing Education (CCNE): A subsidiary of the American Association of Colleges of Nursing (AACN) with responsibility for accrediting baccalaureate and higher-degree nursing programs.

Compact state: A term of law. In the context of the Nurse Licensure Compact, a state that has established an agreement with other states allowing nurses to practice within the state without an additional license. The interstate compacts are enacted by the state legislatures.

Continued competency program: A variety of initiatives to ensure nurses' knowledge, skills, and expertise beyond initial licensure.

Grandfathered: Statutory process by which previously licensed persons are included without further action in revisions or additions in nurse practice acts.

International Council of Nursing (ICN): Professional organization that represents nurses in countries around the world.

Licensure by endorsement: The original program whereby nurses licensed in one state seek licensure in another state without repeat examinations. The requirements are included in state nurse practice acts or accompanying rules and regulations.

Mandatory continuing education: Educational requirements imposed by individual states for renewal of a license.

Mutual recognition model: Program developed by the National Council of State Boards of Nursing (2012). The Nurse Licensure Compact program establishes interstate compacts so that nurses licensed in one jurisdiction may practice in other compact states without duplicate licensure.

National Council of State Boards of Nursing (NCSBN): Organization whose membership consists of the board of nursing of each state or territory.

We thank Janet C. Scherubel, PhD, RN, for her contribution to this chapter in the fourth edition.

Nurse practice act: Statute in each state and territory that regulates the practice of nursing.

State board of nursing: Appointed board within each state charged with responsibility to administer the nurse practice act of that state.

Sunset legislation: Statutes that provide for revocation of laws if not reviewed and renewed within a specified time period.

LEARNING OUTCOMES

After studying this chapter, the reader will be able to:

1. Explain the development of licensure requirements in the United States.
2. Summarize current licensure requirements in the context of historical developments.
3. Analyze the various components of a nurse practice act.
4. Discuss mutual recognition model and identify Nurse Licensure Compact states.
5. Describe the development of certification requirements for advanced practice.
6. Identify requirements for certification for advanced practice in different specialties.
7. Use appropriate resources to obtain current information on licensure and certification.

CHAPTER OVERVIEW

To practice nursing as a registered nurse (RN)! That is the goal of every student nurse. A goal achieved through study, clinical practice, and successful completion of the National Council Licensure Examination–Registered Nurse (NCLEX-RN®). This chapter discusses how and why nursing licensure developed, steps necessary to becoming licensed, licensure regulations, and the responsibilities of an RN.

After licensure as an RN, nurses must still maintain and increase their knowledge and skills. Many nurses may wish to specialize in a particular area of nursing and expand their practice. Nurses with these goals may seek certification in a specialty field. This chapter

describes certification, the means to achieve certification, and the organizations that administer certifying examinations. Whether it is licensure or certification, the nursing profession is continually progressing. Legal requirements to practice are continually being revised to ensure the protection of the public. Throughout history and in the current health care environment, nurses face complex issues and new challenges as they seek to increase their competence and ensure the delivery of excellent nursing services to patients. This chapter explores issues related to licensure and certification as well as some of the challenges nurses and students will face.

THE HISTORY OF NURSING LICENSURE

Recognition: Pins and Registries

The aim of caregivers throughout history has been to be recognized and acknowledged for one's skills and achievements. Early caregivers, particularly in the monasteries and convents of the medieval period, were identified by the habits they wore. Frequently, special insignias designated health personnel. During the

Crusades, a large Maltese cross adorned the habits of the Knights Hospitalers of St. John of Jerusalem on the battlefield (Kalisch and Kalisch, 2003). These forms of identification allowed others to recognize their particular skills in caregiving and healing. More recently, nurses around the world wore a readily identifiable symbol of their school of nursing—the nursing cap.

Today, as in the past, the school of nursing pin identifies graduates from a particular school of nursing.

Early in each school's history, the students and faculty crafted the pin. The pin's emblems and text symbolize the philosophy, beliefs, and aspirations of the nursing program. Students receive their own pin at graduation in a special pinning ceremony. Nurses wear their pins proudly as evidence of their achievement, learning, and skill. It is one way in which nurses distinguish themselves as distinct health care providers with a specialized body of knowledge and clinical skills.

Though White Coat Ceremonies have been an important rite of passage at medical schools for more than 20 years, there is a coordinated effort to offer similar events at schools of nursing. In 2014, nursing schools in 43 states plus the District of Columbia were provided financial support and guidance by The Arnold P. Gold Foundation and the American Association of Colleges of Nursing to offer a White Coat Ceremony. This ceremony usually consists of the recitation of an oath, cloaking of students in a white coat, an address by an eminent role model, and a reception for students and invited guests. Students typically also receive their nursing pin at the White Coat Ceremony.

Nursing programs also maintain a record of all graduates. Florence Nightingale started this practice in 1860, when she created a list of graduates of the St. Thomas's School of Nursing in England. This list became known as the "registry" of graduate nurses. The registry of nurses initiated by Nightingale provided institutions, as well as patients, with a system of identifying graduates of particular nursing programs. These lists proclaimed to all the skills and knowledge of graduates. These nurses could then be distinguished from lay practitioners and local citizens who provided care to the ill and infirm. Today nursing programs around the world continue the tradition started by Nightingale and maintain a registry or listing of all graduates of the nursing program. In addition, state and international agencies maintain lists of nurses practicing in their jurisdictions.

Purpose of Licensure

As nursing programs proliferated, variations developed among the programs. Entry criteria differed, and many educational programs were structured to meet specific employer needs. A simple registry of nurse graduates was no longer sufficient to ensure minimal levels of competency in all nurses, regardless of the school in which the nurses were educated. Another system was necessary to distinguish those sufficiently trained to provide nursing care from untrained or lesser-trained individuals. Graduate nurses, physicians, and hospitals met to resolve this confusion. The outcome was criteria for the licensure of nurses in the United States. Then, as now, the primary purpose of licensure was protection of the public.

Early Licensure Activities

U.S. nursing programs developed in much the same manner as was the pattern in England. As early as 1867, Dr. Henry Wentworth Acland encouraged licensure of English nurses. However, it was not until 1896 that attempts were made to license nurses in the United States. Prior to the late 1800s, many hospitals established training programs to prepare nursing staff for their own institutions. The programs varied based on the needs of the hospital, the availability of physicians and nurses for training students, and resources devoted to the training. It became apparent to many nurses that consistent minimum standards to practice across settings were necessary. These standards would provide for safety of the public and improve the mobility of nurses among institutions. A key advocate for these standards was the Nurses Associated Alumnae of the United States and Canada. This organization later became the American Nurses Association (ANA). However, the group met with resistance from hospitals, physicians, and even nurses. The early attempts at nursing licensure failed for lack of broad-based support (Joel, 2006).

Nurses worldwide mounted an extensive educational campaign explaining the purposes and safeguards inherent in licensure. Success was achieved, and in 1901 the International Council of Nurses passed a resolution that each nation and state examine and license its nurses. Several U.S. states responded shortly thereafter. In 1903, North Carolina, New Jersey, New York, and Virginia were the first to institute permissive licensure. The licensure rules were voluntary. These permissive licenses permitted but did not require nurses to become registered.

Under permissive licensure, educational standards were set at a minimum of 2 years of training for nurses. State boards of nursing were established with rules for examinations as well as revocation of the license. Nurses not passing the examination could not use the title of RN. These early regulations served two purposes: first, to protect the public from unskilled practitioners; and, second, to provide legal sanctions to protect the title of RN. The New York State Board of Regents began a registry of nurses successfully completing all requirements. In 20 years, by 1923, all states had instituted examinations for permissive licensure. Each state's licensure examinations varied in content, length, and format and included written, oral, and practice components. The early work in examinations for licensure was the forerunner of today's licensure and certification requirements (Kalisch and Kalisch, 2003).

The early state efforts in licensing nurses were commendable. Nonetheless, there was considerable variability among states in nursing education requirements, the licensure examinations, and the nurse practice acts themselves. The widespread variability in nurse practice acts prompted the ANA (and later the National Council of State Boards of Nursing [NCSBN]) to design model nurse practice acts. The model acts provided a template for states to follow. The first was published in 1915. These model practice acts are revised and updated as nursing practice advances. For example, the NCSBN approved the most recent revision of the model practice act and administrative rules in 2011 (NCSBN, 2014c).

The model nurse practice act is composed of many sections, including a definition of nursing and the scope of practice for the RN, descriptions of advanced practice nursing, requirements for prescriptive authority of nurses, nursing education, compact guidelines, and processes for disciplinary actions against nurses who violate sections of the act. Separate sections of the model act provide guidelines for state boards of nursing and the necessary requirements for entry into practice. The most recent model practice act is available online at the NCSBN website (NCSBN, 2009c).

From these model acts, each state or jurisdiction developed a unique practice act. Although individual states and territories' practice acts address the needs of that jurisdiction, each includes the sections described in the model act. Students and practicing nurses may obtain the nurse practice act for any jurisdiction by contacting that state or territorial board of nursing. Appendix B provides a listing of state boards of nursing addresses and Internet addresses, which also can be found on the Evolve website.

Mandatory Licensure

Once each state had established permissive licensure, the next movement was toward a requirement that all nurses must be licensed. This practice is termed *mandatory licensure*. New York was the first state to require mandatory licensure, although this requirement was not in place until 1947. At the same time, nursing groups moved to standardize nursing licensure testing procedures.

After World War II, the ANA formed the NCSBN. The council was composed of a representative of each state and jurisdiction in the United States. As part of its original activities, the council advocated a standardized examination for licensure. These varied activities culminated in the National League for Nursing, which administered the first State Board Test Pool Examination in 1950. The written examination included separate sections on medical-surgical nursing, maternity nursing, nursing of children, and psychiatric nursing. This format for examination continued for more than 30 years, and many of today's nurses took these examinations.

The next major event in licensure efforts occurred in 1982 with the development of the first NCLEX-RN® examination. The test was revised to include all nursing content within one section of the examination. In addition, the format was changed to present questions in a nursing process format. Just as with previous versions of licensing examinations, the NCLEX-RN® examination has evolved over time. Paper-and-pencil testing was replaced with computerized adaptive testing in 1994. Extensive information on the NCLEX-RN® examination may be found in Chapter 28 of this text.

COMPONENTS OF NURSE PRACTICE ACTS

Each state develops rules and regulations to govern the practice of nursing within that state. These rules are in the nurse practice acts or in its accompanying rules and regulations to administer the act. Many nurse practice acts are patterned after the ANA or the NCSBN model practice acts, and all contain comparable information.

Purpose of Act

Each act begins with a purpose. All nurse practice acts include two essential purposes. First, each act includes statements that refer to protecting the health and safety of the citizens in the jurisdiction. The act describes the qualifications and responsibilities of those individuals covered by the regulations. Likewise, the act delineates those excluded from the practice of nursing. These provisions also serve to ensure protection of the public. The second purpose is to protect the title of RN. The legal title, RN, is reserved for those meeting the requirements to practice nursing. Only those licensed may use the designation of RN. Thus, unlicensed personnel are prevented from using the title RN.

Definition of Nursing and Scope of Practice

In each state or jurisdictional nurse practice act, the practice of professional nursing is defined. The definition of nursing is of utmost importance because it delineates the scope of practice for nurses within the state. That is, each act outlines the activities nurses may legally perform within the jurisdiction. Many states follow the guidelines incorporated in the model practice act, although each is specific and delineates practice within that state or jurisdiction. For example, some states describe nursing as a process that includes nursing diagnosis, whereas other states list broad areas of nursing activities. To avoid becoming outdated, there are no lists of skills or procedures in the acts. As nursing knowledge and practices advance, new techniques are frequently allowable because of the comprehensive nature of the definition of nursing.

Many jurisdictions incorporate definitions of advanced practice nursing within one definition of nursing. In other states, the definitions of advanced practice nursing and the scope of practice for advanced practice nurses are defined separately.

Each state or jurisdiction establishes laws regulating practice within its borders. Therefore, it is imperative for the nurse to know and understand the definition of nursing in the states in which he or she practices. Further, each jurisdiction retains the right to govern practice within that jurisdiction. This right supersedes the presence of a mutual recognition agreement with other compact states. The retention of states' rights is an essential component in the mutual recognition model.

There are other important reasons for becoming familiar with the definition of nursing practice. Frequently, nurses are asked to perform in ways that are beyond the legal definition of nursing. This is illegal, and if the nurse complies, he or she could lose the privilege of practicing nursing. In other situations, labor laws or other statutes affect nurses. Definitions may include or exclude nurses based on their legal definitions of nursing practice. As nursing practice becomes more complex and sophisticated, states may revise their nurse practice acts. Nurses are accountable for knowing the definition and scope of practice within their jurisdictions and practicing accordingly. In order to know and understand the laws regulating their practice, nurses should obtain copies of and become familiar with nurse practice acts for the states or jurisdictions in which they plan to practice.

Licensure Requirements
Entry into practice licensure

A section of each nurse practice act describes the requirements and procedures necessary for initial entry into nursing practice or nursing licensure. An initial requirement in all jurisdictions is graduation both from high school and an accredited nursing program. Candidates for licensure must submit evidence of graduation as defined by each state.

To verify an applicant's graduation from a nursing program, a transcript of coursework, a diploma, or a letter from the dean of the program is frequently necessary. Additional requirements for licensure may include a statement regarding the mental and physical health status of the applicant. Some jurisdictions conduct a review of prior legal convictions. This is especially important in reference to felony convictions. Some states also require declaration of misdemeanors, even those that have been expunged. Other states have appended provisions related to recreational drug abuse and some states require declaration of termination and disciplinary action from a nursing or health care employer. Finally, most states require statements from the school of nursing attesting the eligibility of the candidate for licensure. The requirements for licensure are detailed in each nurse practice act and the accompanying rules and regulations for practice.

In the past, it was customary for nurses to practice in only one state or territory. More than ever, nurses are practicing in more than one jurisdiction, either by their physical presence in that jurisdiction or through technological advances including telephone and computer access to patients across state and territory lines. As laws are continually being revised to reflect the current practice of nursing, it is incumbent on the individual to be cognizant of the current licensure requirements in all states and territories in which he or she intends to practice.

Regardless of individual state requirements, all nurse practice acts require candidates to successfully complete the NCLEX-RN® licensure examination before they can practice. In some states, it is possible to obtain a temporary permit to practice, pending receipt of success on the licensure examination. This practice was especially prevalent in past years because it took several months for results of the licensure examinations to be reported. Now, however, with computer testing and the prompt response from the testing services, the use of temporary permits to practice is becoming less frequent.

Temporary permits are still available for nurses moving from one jurisdiction to another. To obtain a license to practice in another state, the nurse applies for licensure by endorsement. Nurses licensed in one jurisdiction may apply for licensure in a second jurisdiction by submitting a letter to the second state board of nursing. Typically, evidence for the new license is similar to that for initial licensure. In addition, proof of the nurse's current license to practice, as well as any restrictions imposed on the license by the first state, is required. These procedures will continue for all states not participating in the Nurse Licensure Compact (NLC). For those states designated as "compact states," the nurse should contact the state board of nursing to determine the appropriate procedures for initiating nursing practice in that jurisdiction.

Advanced Practice Nursing Licensure

Advanced practice nurses must obtain separate nursing licensure in addition to licensure for entry into practice. State requirements vary; therefore, advanced practice nurses should contact the state board of nursing to determine the criteria and procedures.

Renewal of Licensure

In addition to outlining requirements for initial licensure, each nurse practice act includes the requirements and information necessary to renew one's nursing license. These regulations define the length of time a license is valid, generally from 2 to 3 years, as well as any specific requirements for renewal of licensure.

Mandatory Continuing Education

The nurse will find information on mandatory continuing education requirements for renewal of licensure in the section on license renewal. All nurses are expected to remain competent to practice through various means of continuing education. In 1976, California was the first state to institute mandatory continuing education for renewal of licensure. Since that time, a number of states have instituted requirements of continuing education for renewal of licensure. The number of hours necessary varies depending on the jurisdiction, ranging from 20 to 40 hours over a 2- to 3-year period.

A few jurisdictions require specific continuing education coursework in the areas of health care ethics, the state nurse practice act, or other content specific to that jurisdiction. Clinical course content may be designated for specific health problems, such as sexually transmitted diseases, human immunodeficiency virus/acquired immunodeficiency syndrome, and family violence. In other states, the board of nursing allows the nurse wide latitude in meeting the requirements for renewal of licensure. Details of specific continuing education requirements are found in the nurse practice act and the accompanying rules and regulations.

ROLE OF REGULATORY BOARDS TO ENSURE SAFE PRACTICE

Membership of the Board of Nursing

An important section of every nurse practice act is the designation of a regulatory board of nurses and consumers to administer the act. Frequently, this responsibility is assigned to a state board of nursing. The practice act outlines guidelines for membership on the board. In addition, procedures by which members are appointed to the board of nursing are designated. In most cases, the members are appointed by the governor's office. Interested individuals or organizations, such as the state nurses' association, may submit names to the governor for consideration.

Duties of the Board of Nursing

The responsibilities and duties of the board of nursing are delineated in detail. Specific duties of the board may be outlined in the act itself or in the enabling laws. These enabling administrative statutes are frequently designated as rules and regulations for the practice of nursing. It is through the work of the board of nursing that nursing licenses are granted and renewed and disciplinary action taken when provisions of the act are violated. Just as all nurses need to be cognizant of their nurse practice acts, nurses should also become familiar with the role of the state board of nursing.

A major responsibility of the board of nursing is addressing concerns about a nurse's practice. The review of a nurse's potential malfeasance or violation of the act or other state and federal laws is within the responsibilities of the board of nursing. The nurse practice act describes the due process and procedures for this review. The board of nursing will then assign appropriate disciplinary action. These activities are a key responsibility of the board of nursing. Actions may include restrictions on the license or suspension or revocation of a nurse's license. Just as all nurses need to be cognizant of their nurse practice acts, nurses should become familiar with the role of the state board of nursing.

SPECIAL CASES OF LICENSURE

Military and Government Nurses

There are many nurses whose practice takes them throughout the country on a regular basis. For example, many nurses are members of the military or join the military nursing services after graduation. The Veterans Administration and U.S. Public Health Service employ thousands of nurses who serve in many jurisdictions as well as outside U.S. boundaries. It is not necessary for these nursing personnel to obtain a nursing license in each jurisdiction in which they practice. The graduate takes the NCLEX-RN® examination in one state. Upon successful completion, as an employee of the U.S. government, he or she may practice in other jurisdictions without additional licensure requirements. Nurses should obtain the current requirements for licensure as rules are updated to reflect current practices.

Internationally Educated Nurses

Internationally educated nurses (IENs) have become an integral part of the U.S. registered nurse workforce. Top countries represented by IENs passing the NCLEX-RN® examination in 2010 include Philippines, South Korea, India, Canada, and Nigeria (HRSA, 2013).

Internationally educated nurses are another source of pipeline for the U.S. nursing workforce, especially in times of shortage in domestic supply. Health workforce migration, a critical issue for many years, has received increased attention recently as a result of the 2010 World Health Organization Global Code of Practice on the International Recruitment of Health Personnel ("Global Code"). The Global Code represents an effort to promote ethical principles in the recruitment of international health personnel, with a particular focus on minimizing recruitment from countries experiencing critical shortages (HRSA, 2013).

Internationally educated nurses have met the requirements for practice in those countries. When nurses move to the United States, they must show evidence of completing their original educational program and restrictions of their license. In addition, nurses need to demonstrate competency in English and the ability to take and pass the NCLEX-RN® examination. Foreign nurses take a special examination administered by the Commission on Graduates of Foreign Nursing Schools. The examination is given in English and tests the knowledge required to practice in the United States. Upon successful completion, the foreign nurse graduate may apply for a license to practice in the United States. The intent of these regulations is not to be punitive or obstructive to the nurse. The regulations are yet another example of two key principles: first, the protection of the public and, second, the protection of the title of RN.

International Practice

In a similar manner, nurses licensed in the United States may want to practice in other countries. Nurses interested in these opportunities may contact either the International Council of Nurses or the nursing regulatory board of the country in which they wish to practice. The International Council of Nurses is composed of representatives of organized nursing worldwide. One function of the council is to assist nurses in obtaining licensure in other countries.

Each country has specific laws and regulations governing nursing practice that must guide the practice of the U.S. nurse. Just as a foreign nurse must demonstrate competency to practice in the United States, the U.S. nurse should be prepared to submit documentation on education, NCLEX-RN® examination results, and proof of licensure and practice to officials in the foreign country. Advanced planning and contact with the appropriate regulatory agency will ease the transition for the nurse.

REVISION OF NURSE PRACTICE ACTS

Nurse practice acts, just as other sections of states' codes, are written and passed by legislators. As in any legislative endeavor, many governmental agencies, administrators, consumers, and special-interest groups seek to influence the legislation. These groups become actively involved in developing the accompanying rules and regulations. For example, physicians, dentists, pharmacists, licensed practical nurses, certified nursing assistants, emergency personnel, and physician assistants are just a few health care providers directly affected by the scope and definition of nursing practice. Likewise, organizations such as schools, hospitals, home health agencies, and extended care facilities are vitally concerned with the role of nurses today. Equally important, citizen groups are interested in determining nurses' roles and responsibilities. Because of this, the nurse practice act, as finally passed or amended by the state legislature, represents the aims and concerns not only of nurses but of many individuals and multiple-interest groups.

Review of a state's practice act reveals the influential parties involved in creating the act. Each group participates in defining the scope and practice of nursing and regulations affecting nursing practice within the jurisdiction. Because of these varied interests, it is essential for nurses to understand the practice act and the additional legislation that influences and controls their practice. Further, as proposals to amend the nurse practice act are promulgated at the state level, it is imperative for all nurses to be involved in this process. The resulting laws affect their profession, their practice, and their livelihood.

Sunset Legislation

One example of legislative activity affecting nurse practice acts is sunset legislation. "Sunset laws," found in many states, are intended to ensure that legislation is current and reflects the needs of the public. When sunset provisions are included in a nurse practice act, the act must be reviewed by a specific date. If the act is not renewed, it is automatically rescinded. This review process allows for revisions to update practice acts to be consistent with current nursing practice. Many nurse practice acts contain sunset provisions. It is through these activities that the scope of nursing practice is updated and components, such as the diagnosis of nursing problems, have been incorporated into definitions of nursing. Other changes include changes in requirements for mandatory continuing education for licensure renewal. Equally important, sunset laws have provided the means to define advanced practice nursing and incorporate prescriptive authority for advanced practice nurses. Nurses should determine whether

sunset regulations affect the nurse practice act in the state in which they practice. Likewise, nurses should be aware of, and involved in, activities to amend the nurse practice act.

DELEGATION OF AUTHORITY TO OTHERS

The rapid expansion of an array of health care providers, changes in health care delivery systems, and efforts to control health care costs have led to participation of many types of unlicensed personnel in the provision of health care. These personnel present a challenge to RNs working with them. Questions arise as to who can delegate what activities to which unlicensed provider groups. Guidelines for delegation have been developed by many nursing organizations, including the ANA and NCSBN (NCSBN, 2014b). Although the professional organizations' guidelines are helpful, it is the nurse practice acts of individual states that establish the legal definitions of appropriate delegation practices. Because regulations differ among states, each nurse must identify and understand the regulations for the state in which he or she practices. Chapter 19 presents a detailed discussion of delegation and supervision.

CURRENT LICENSURE ACTIVITIES

Mutual Recognition Model

Efforts to provide common definitions of nursing practice, equivalent educational standards for practice, and uniform testing for entry into practice through the NCLEX-RN® examination have been very successful. Nonetheless, most nurses are still required to apply for licensure in each state in which they practice. With the increased mobility of nurses, the telehealth movement, and the necessity of caring for patients across long distances, state boards of nursing have recognized the need to provide practicing nurses with more than procedures of endorsement of their initial license. This need has led to further changes in nursing licensure.

In 1997, the Delegate Assembly of the NCSBN moved to a new level of nursing regulation. The assembly approved a resolution endorsing a mutual recognition model of nursing regulation. Through this model, individual state boards formed the NLC. The first states to participate in the program were Maryland, Texas, Utah, and Wisconsin. Each year, more states are developing compact laws—to date, over half are NLC states. A listing of current compact states may be found on the NCSBN website (NCSBN, 2014d). Nurses practicing in an NLC state are responsible for following the laws and regulations of each state in which they practice, although they are not required to apply for multiple individual state licenses.

A number of issues associated with mutual recognition concern nurses. On one hand, mutual recognition greatly facilitates interstate practice, telehealth programs, and movement of nurses to areas of shortage. In addition, a national database provides information on individual nurses' practice and disciplinary actions taken against nurses. The database, Nursys (NCSBN, 2014e), supports a key licensure goal—to protect the public health and safety. These advantages have resulted in support for the NLC by many nursing organizations.

On the other hand, concerns relate to monitoring nurses' practice in multiple jurisdictions, nurse privacy, and due process rights. Issues related to disciplinary action in home and distant states are still being resolved. In addition, differences in practice requirements in different states may cause nurses confusion as to their rights and responsibilities. The NLC is increasingly affecting all nurses. Nursing students and graduates must remain apprised of changing conditions. As changes occur frequently in this area, the most comprehensive and current sources of information are the websites for the ANA, the NCSBN, and the state boards of nursing for individual jurisdictions.

Continued Competency

As discussed earlier in the chapter, the primary purpose of nurse licensure is protection of the public. Thus mandatory continuing education was instituted as a strategy to ensure that nurses were competent to remain in practice. These programs have continued for a number of years. However, a growing number of nurses believe that more is required than just attending seminars to demonstrate the degree of competence. Consortiums of nurses in a number of states are examining other alternatives for renewal of licensure. These requirements may include designated numbers of clinical practice hours, portfolios of achievements in clinical practice, or other exemplars of practice. Nurses and students are encouraged to become aware of continued competency initiatives so that they may be prepared for changes in future licensure requirements.

There is increasing concern for patient safety and treatment in today's health care system. Models of continued competency are but one attempt by professional nurses to ensure that patients receive safe, effective nursing care. Another strategy in this quest is establishing programs of certification of advanced practice nurses.

CERTIFICATION

History of Certification

There are distinct differences between licensure and certification. At the most basic level, licensure establishes minimal levels of practice, whereas certification recognizes excellence in practice. Because of this difference, the background, requirements, and practice opportunities for licensure and certification differ markedly.

Just as with the development of nursing licensure, at its inception certification was not legally required; rather, it was voluntary. In an effort to recognize nurses who had completed additional education and demonstrated competency in clinical practice, a number of nursing graduate schools and nursing specialty organizations offered certification programs. In the 1970s and later, advanced clinical courses were designed for nurses as a certificate program. The programs varied in length and content and did not offer a full master's course of study in nursing.

A second distinct difference in licensure and certification pertains to the organizations that grant certification. Whereas licensure is granted and governed by legislation and administered through the state boards of nursing, certification is awarded by nongovernmental agencies. The first field of nursing practice to certify advanced practitioners was nurse anesthesia in 1946. Similarly, in 1961, the American College of Nurse-Midwives began certifying nurse-midwives. As certificate programs developed, it became apparent that program standardization was a necessity. In 1975, the ANA convened a national study group at the University of Wisconsin, Milwaukee, to explore the issue. This meeting was attended by 75 nursing specialty organizations. The report of the group recommended the formation of a central organization for certification of nurses. This report, in conjunction with efforts of many nurses, resulted in the formation of the **American Nurses Credentialing Center (ANCC)**. More than a quarter million nurses in more than 40 areas of specialty practice (Box 4-1) have been certified by the ANCC since 1990. More than 80,000 advanced practice nurses are

BOX 4-1   American Nurses Credentialing Center, Certifying Examinations 2012

Advanced Practice Certification
Acute Care NP
Adult NP
Adult Psychiatric and Mental Health NP
Diabetes Management—Advanced
Family NP
Family Psychiatric and Mental Health NP
Gerontologic NP
Pediatric NP
School NP

Clinical Nurse Specialists
Adult Health CNS
Diabetes Management—Advanced
Adult Psychiatric and Mental Health CNS
Child Adolescent Psychiatric and Mental Health CNS
Gerontologic CNS
Pediatric CNS
Public Community Health CNS
Specialties

Ambulatory Care Nursing
Cardiac Rehabilitation Nursing
Cardiac Vascular Nursing

Case Management Nursing
Certified Vascular Nursing
College Health Nursing
Community Health Nursing
Diabetes Management—Advanced
General Nursing Practice
Gerontologic Nursing
High-Risk Perinatal Nursing
Home Health Nursing
Informatics Nursing
Medical Surgical Nursing
Nurse Executive—Advanced
Nursing Professional Development
Pain Management
Pediatric Nursing
Perinatal Nursing
Psychiatric Mental Health Nursing
Public Health Nurse—Advanced
School Nursing

currently certified by the ANCC. Today, many of their examinations are open to nurses with a variety of educational backgrounds.

In addition to the ANCC, other professional specialty nursing organizations (Box 4-2) offer certification examinations. These organizations have created certification boards that are separate from the parent organization in order to maintain an independent role and to conform to department of education requirements. Nurses may contact these specialty nursing organizations directly for current guidelines and information.

BOX 4-2   Other Nursing Certification Organizations

Advanced Practice Palliative Nurse—National Board for Certification of Hospice and Palliative Nurses (NBCHPN®)
  Clinical Nurse Leader—Commission on Nurse Certification
  Comprehensive Care for DNPs—American Board of Comprehensive Care

All APRNs should be certified through a nationally recognized nursing certifying body and understand that the examinations offered by these certification agencies will be used by state boards to grant APRNs the authority to practice. The lengths to which organized nursing has invested in certification of advanced practice in nursing are further indications of nurses' commitment to protection of the public and the patients they serve.

Certification began as a voluntary effort controlled by professional nursing organizations. State agencies were not involved in the credentialing process. This is still the case, although state nurse practice acts do include requirements for nurses to practice in advanced roles. Thus state practice acts first contained provisions requiring certification for nurse anesthetists and nurse-midwives. With the development of additional advanced practice roles, all states have included requirements of certification in their regulations for advanced practice nurses in all specialty roles.

Purpose of Certification

The purpose of advanced practice laws is, first and foremost, protection of the public. Within the acts are definitions of advanced practice nursing. A number of states further differentiate the advanced practice of nursing by including separate titles for nurse practitioners and clinical nurse specialists. The scope of practice of the advanced practice nurse is well defined. States describe supervisory or collaborative practice with physicians, with differences existing among states as to the regulations governing these relationships. Requirements for practice vary among states. Although many states require a master's degree in the specialty area for practice, this is not the case in all jurisdictions. All states require evidence of certification in the specialty area, and many require periods of practice in the specialty prior to awarding certification status. All states incorporate specific provisions for prescribing medications.

Steps to Certification

The best strategy for nurses wishing to practice in an expanded role is to become informed of specific requirements in their chosen field. The nurse should examine carefully the roles and responsibilities inherent in advanced practice nursing. First, the nurse should contact both the ANCC and the specialty organization in his or her area of practice to determine the education, experience, and examination requirements necessary to become certified. Concurrently, every nurse should contact the state boards of nursing in the state(s) in which he or she wishes to practice and obtain information on legal requirements to practice in those jurisdictions. After gathering the requirements to practice, the nurse will be able to develop a plan of action to complete the necessary advanced coursework, clinical practice requirements, and examinations. Upon completion of the requirements of these agencies, the advanced practice nurse may practice in an expanded role. In addition to the certifying agencies, the nurse may wish to contact other advanced practice nurses. These nurses will serve as valuable colleagues to the new advanced practice nurse.

Current Issues in Certification

Despite tremendous strides in less than 40 years, certification processes for the advanced practice nurse continue to evolve. As with any new endeavor, advances are made in small steps and great leaps.

Nurses in advanced practice face changing educational requirements for licensure and relicensure. Professional and legal issues regarding the scope of nursing practice and the independence of advanced practice nursing must change along with changes in the health care environment. Advanced practice nurses develop professional relationships with their physician colleagues, as do all nurses; however, the advanced practice nurses must define their legal relationships with physician practitioners and other caregivers. These issues are not uncommon to nurses in any practice setting; however, the advanced practice nurse is charting new territory.

A unique challenge to advanced practice nurses is reimbursement for nursing services. As advanced practice continues to expand, nurses have moved from secondary to independent billing for services. Federal regulations allow direct reimbursement for some nursing services, yet state and local practices vary. There are ongoing efforts at the state and national levels to resolve these issues. Advanced practice nurses are in constant communication with their peers and professional organizations. They look to all nurses to become involved in issues facing the advanced practice nurse.

A new issue in advanced practice nursing is emerging. Just as with the historical questions of which group will test and license nurses, the question is surfacing as to which organizations will credential and regulate advanced practice nursing. The NCSBN proposes that it is the appropriate agency to credential as well as license advanced practitioners in their vision for the future (2014a). Nursing professional and specialty organizations are currently responding to their draft proposal. It is incumbent for all nurses and potential nurses to become knowledgeable of this issue and participate in the professional discussions. This issue clearly illustrates the changing practice and regulation of nursing.

The Consensus Model for APRN Regulation, Licensure, Accreditation, Certification, and Education

With over 267,000 advanced practice registered nurses (APRNs) in the United States, APRNs represent a powerful force in the health care system. The Consensus Model provides guidance for states to adopt uniformity in the regulation of APRN roles. The target date to complete that work is 2015. Today, many states have adopted portions of the Model elements but there still may be variation from state to state. APRNs moving from state to state need to ask themselves the following:

Have I met the requirements to practice in this state?

Do I have the appropriate certification required to practice in this state?

Does my training/experience match within the scope of practice required to practice?

As long as regulatory requirements differ from state to state, each state border represents an obstacle to portability—potentially preventing access to professionals and access to care. The *Consensus Model for APRN Regulation* has the potential to harness this power by outlining regulatory requirements in licensure, accreditation, certification, and education that should be adopted by every state.

Visit the Consensus Model toolkit, a compendium of resources for understanding the Consensus Model at aprnconsensus@ncsbn.org.

SUMMARY

Nurse practice acts provide protection of the public and protection of the title of RN. This is accomplished through the development of specific regulations regarding education and examination of competence to practice. Each act contains guidelines for disciplinary action to protect both the public and professional nursing. The nurse practice act of each jurisdiction addresses the needs of the state and the responsibilities of nurses practicing within that state. It is important for all nurses and students of nursing to become familiar with the regulations guiding their own practice.

As health care delivery evolves and nursing practice advances, new issues and initiatives arise. It is imperative to update nurse practice acts so that they remain responsive to the needs of all and allow nurses to practice to the full extent of their education and training. Nurses must be part of this process. Collaboration with professional nursing organizations, state boards of nursing, and individual nurses will enable nursing to continually meet the needs of patients.

REFERENCES

American Nurses Credentialing Center: *Certifications available* (website). http://www.nursecredentialing.org/certification.aspx. Accessed October 1, 2014.

Health Resources and Services Administration (HRSA): *The registered nurse population: findings from the 2013 National Sample Survey of Registered Nurses* September 2010 (website). http://bhpr.hrsa.gov/healthworkforce/rnsurveys/rnsurveyfinal.pdf. Accessed October 1, 2014.

Joel LA: *The nursing experience: trends, challenges, and transitions,* ed 5, New York, 2006, McGraw-Hill.

Kalisch BJ, Kalisch PA: *The advance of American nursing,* ed 4, Philadelphia, 2003, Lippincott.

National Council of State Boards of Nursing: *Advanced practice registered nurses,* 2014a (website). https://www.ncsbn.org/2632.htm. Accessed October 1, 2014.

National Council of State Boards of Nursing: *Delegation: American Nurses Association (ANA) and the National Council of State Boards of Nursing (NCSBN),* 2014b (website). https://www.ncsbn.org/1625.htmwww.ncsbn.org/ Joint_statement.pdf. Accessed October 1, 2014.

National Council of State Boards of Nursing: *Model nursing act and rules,* 2014c (website). https://www.ncsbn.org/Model_Nursing_Act_and_Rules.pdf. Accessed October 1, 2014.

National Council of State Boards of Nursing: *Nurse licensure compact,* 2014d (website). https://www.ncsbn.org/nlc.htm. Accessed October 1, 2014.

National Council of State Boards of Nursing: *Nursys database,* 2014e (website). https://www.nursys.com/LQC/TermsConditionsLQC.aspx. Accessed October 1, 2014.

5

Nursing theory provides the direction for nursing practice and research

Theories of Nursing Practice

Susan R. Jacob, PhD, MSN, RN

ⓔ Additional resources are available online at: *http://evolve.elsevier.com/Cherry/*

"Science is built up with facts, as a house is with stones. But a collection of facts is no more a science than a heap of stones a house."
Jules Henri Poincaré, 1909, French scientist and mathematician

PROFESSIONAL/ETHICAL ISSUE

BSN students Matt, Toni, and Britainy were studying together for their theory class when Matt spoke up and said, "I think all this theory is just a bunch of junk. Nurses in practice don't have time to learn about theories, and they sure don't use them to guide their practice."

Britainy spoke up and said, "My aunt is an RN on the cancer unit at Memorial Hospital and she has told me that on her unit they use Jean Watson's caring theory to guide their interactions with patients." Toni said, "Really? Then maybe there is something to this theory stuff. I think we should take this class more seriously." Britainy agreed and suggested that they divide the material among themselves and meet again the next day to prepare for the upcoming test. Matt said, "You guys can do that if you want, but count me out. My plan is to skim the information and take my chances on the test. I am amazed you two really think we will ever need to know any of this stuff after we graduate. Nursing theory is never going to help me start an IV."

Is there a way for Britainy and Toni to convince Matt he is wrong? If so, how?

How can Britainy and Toni convince Matt to divide the theory material with them to prepare for the upcoming test?

VIGNETTE

When I was a nursing student, it was hard for me to understand why I needed to know anything about nursing theory, but now that I am in practice I see that theories provide a way for me to organize, deliver, and evaluate the care I provide. On our labor and delivery unit, we use Roy's adaptation model to guide our practice as we provide care to laboring moms. The use of this theory allows us to assess how well they are coping and provides guidance as we plan nursing interventions that promote their successful coping.

Questions to Consider While Reading this Chapter:
1. What is nursing theory?
2. How is nursing theory different from the theory of other disciplines?
3. How does theory relate to nursing practice?
4. Why is it important to understand nursing theory?
5. Why is it important for nurses to develop theory?

We thank Margaret Soderstrom, PhD, RN, CS-P, APRN, and Linda C. Pugh, PhD, RNC, FAAN, for their contributions to this chapter in the fourth edition.

KEY TERMS

Concept An idea or a general impression. Concepts are the basic ingredients of theory. Examples of nursing concepts include pain, quality of life, health, stress, and adaptation.

Conceptual model A group of concepts that are associated because of their relevance to a common theme.

Nursing science The collection and organization of data related to nursing and its associated components. The purpose of this data collection is to provide a body of scientific knowledge, which provides the basis for nursing practice.

Nursing theory The compilation of data that defines, describes, and logically relates information that will explain past nursing phenomena and predict future trends. Theories provide a foundation for developing models or frameworks for nursing practice development.

Proposition A statement that proposes the relationship between and among concepts.

Schematic model A diagram or visual representation of concepts, conceptual models, or theory.

LEARNING OUTCOMES

After studying this chapter, the reader will be able to:
1. Differentiate between a science and a theory.
2. Identify the criteria necessary for science.
3. Identify the criteria necessary for theory.
4. Explain a nursing theory and a nursing model.

5. Discuss two early and two contemporary nursing theorists and their theories.
6. Explain the effect of nursing theory on the profession of nursing.

CHAPTER OVERVIEW

Explicit, detailed knowledge is the keystone, the foundation, and the carefully laid support that are critical to the classification of a discipline. In a seminal paper entitled "The Discipline of Nursing" (1978), Donaldson and Crowley note, a discipline "is characterized by a unique perspective, a distinct way of viewing all phenomena, which ultimately defines the limits and nature of its inquiry" (p. 113). Nursing, long ranked an art and a science, is actually quite young in its continuing struggle for professional and public recognition as a matchless, expert, and commanding profession. This notion is readily supported as one marks nursing's ongoing effort to define itself as a distinct discipline that is exclusive from other disciplines, particularly the medical practice model. Only when a substantial body of nursing knowledge is collected, organized, and developed will the profession be defined and its scope of practice differentiated. Key in this accomplishment is the development and practice of nursing theory.

It is important for nurses to study the development of nursing theory because without an idea of where you have been, how can you know how, why, when, or where to go? Nursing theory provides nurses with a focus for research and

practice. You may consider using a theory as similar to using a map that provides direction while making available a variety of ways to get where you are going. As logical as this seems, the worth of studying nursing theorists, their theories, and the role of responsibility these theories contribute toward the evolution of nursing science has been curiously underappreciated. Even more surprising, many of the naysayers are nursing students. Nursing theory is not usually the favorite subject of undergraduates, who would rather learn technical, hands-on skills. Whether this is a maturation issue or an issue of knowledge and experience remains undetermined by nursing faculty and the profession itself.

This chapter in no way reflects the breadth and depth of nursing theorists and their theories. There are many scholarly works devoted to this topic. Instead it is a survey, a general overview; a smattering of nursing theories, with chosen segments intended to assist in providing the idea, the notion, and indeed, the semblance of what a theory is and how it is critical to the profession of nursing. Readers interested in examining the theoretic basis for nursing practice will find resources for further exploration at the end of the chapter.

SCIENCE AND THEORY

Science is a method of bringing together facts and giving them coherence and integrity. Science assists us in understanding how the unique yet related parts of a structure fit and become more than the sum of individual parts. In the opening metaphor, the stones represent the facts, the process of laying the stones represents the science, and the future ideas and new directions represent the theory.

Science is dynamic and static—dynamic in figuring out how a phenomenon happens, static in describing what happens. Scientific inquiry involves five steps: (1) hypothesis, (2) method, (3) data collection, (4) results, and (5) evaluation. These five steps are described in Box 5-1.

"Nursing theory is defined as a conceptualization of some aspect of nursing reality communicated for the purpose of describing phenomena, explaining relationships between phenomena, predicting consequences, or prescribing nursing care" (Meleis, 2012). Theory development functions in a parallel manner to scientific process, although theory generally applies to a more specific area of the larger scientific process. Even though Sigmund Freud and Carl Jung each had their individual theories about the psychology of humans, their theories were focused on specific ideas taken from the entire knowledge base surrounding psychology and psychotherapy and its scientific premise. Similarly, Albert Einstein's theory of relativity was but a fraction of the existing scientific knowledge base of mathematics at the time. Nevertheless, it is an undisputed fact that these theorists changed the thinking of their time and were responsible for the evolution of their philosophic and scientific interests (Anastasi, 1958). For a proposed theory to be accepted as a theory, it must meet the following six criteria: (1) inclusiveness, (2) consistency, (3) accuracy, (4) relevance, (5) fruitfulness, and (6) simplicity. These criteria are further explained in Box 5-2.

The importance of theories in the evolution of science is unquestioned. Nursing has evolved as a profession and a science in a similar manner. Nursing theories have explained, explored, defined, and delineated specific areas. They are foundational to nursing, helping to accumulate further knowledge and give indications of what direction nursing should take to develop the discipline. In practice, nursing theories help nurses by describing, explaining, and predicting everyday experiences. Theories can guide nurses in their assessments, interventions, and evaluations of nursing care.

Beginning with the work of Florence Nightingale in 1860, nursing theorists have taken the vast pool of scientific information available and focused on precise target areas of interest. In so doing, theoretic models have been conceptualized to guide nursing actions, interventions, and implementation. Specific nursing theories are discussed later in the chapter.

BOX 5-1   The Five Steps of the Scientific Process

Hypothesis: Ask the question that is to be the main focus. It usually includes independent and dependent variables.

Method: Decide what data will be collected to answer the question. Decide on and identify the step-by-step procedure that will be used to collect these data. Make sure this process can be easily replicated.

Data collection: Implement the step-by-step procedure that has been determined to answer the question.

Results: On the conclusion of the data collection, statistically identify the outcomes. Establish parameters (e.g., level of significance) that will determine whether the data are relevant.

Evaluation: Examine the results to determine the relevance of outcome data in answering the hypothesis. Determine the significance and identify the potential for future research.

BOX 5-2   Criteria for Theory Acceptance

Inclusiveness: Does the theory include all concepts related to the area of interest?

Consistency: Can the theory address new entities without having its founding assumptions changed?

Accuracy: Does the theory explain retrospective occurrences? Does the theory maintain its capacity to predict future outcomes?

Relevance: Does the theory relate to the scientific foundation from which it is derived? Is it reflective of the scientific base?

Fruitfulness: Does the theory generate new directions for future research?

Simplicity: Does the theory provide a road map for replication? Is it simple to follow? Does it make sense?

Nursing Science

As might be expected, there are several definitions of nursing science (Abdellah, 1969; Jacox, 1974). Although these definitions differ, they generally support the premise that nursing science is a collection of data related to nursing that may be applied to the practice of nursing. These data encompass a vast array of knowledge that spans all of nursing and its diversity. This knowledge guides the practice of nursing to better serve patients through healing, prevention, education, and health maintenance.

Theories, Models, and Frameworks

Researchers use theories and conceptual models as their primary method to organize findings into a broader conceptual context (Meleis, 2012; Reed and Shearer, 2012). Different terms are used in relation to conceptual contexts for research. These terms include *theories, models, frameworks, schemes,* and *maps.* Different writers often use terms differently, resulting in a blurring of distinct terms (Meleis, 2012).

Theory

Theory is generally considered an abstract generalization that presents a systematic explanation about how phenomena are interrelated. Therefore, traditionally, a theory must have at least two related concepts that support the theory (Reed and Shearer, 2012).

Conceptual Model

A conceptual model deals with concepts that are assembled because of their relevance to a common theme. The term *conceptual framework* is used interchangeably with *conceptual model.* Conceptual models, or frameworks, also provide a conceptual perspective regarding interrelated phenomena, but they are more loosely structured than theories. There are many conceptual models of nursing that offer broad explanations of the nursing process. Four concepts basic to nursing that are included in these models are: (1) nursing, (2) person, (3) health, and (4) environment. The various nursing models define these concepts differently, link the concepts in various ways, and emphasize differently the relationships among the concepts. For example, Roy's adaptation model emphasizes the patient's adaptation as a central phenomenon, whereas Martha Rogers emphasizes centrality of the individual as a unified whole. These models are used by nurse researchers to formulate research questions and hypotheses.

The terms *conceptual model* (or *framework*) and *nursing theory* are often used interchangeably. In this chapter, the nursing theories described may also be referred to as conceptual models. The term *model* is also used in reference to a diagram depicting the theory. In this chapter, *model* will refer to a schematic model, which is a diagram or visual representation of the conceptual model or theory.

Nursing Theory

Theory and theoretic thinking guide research and practice. The basic ingredients of theory are concepts. Examples of nursing concepts include health, stress, and adaptation. Propositions are statements that propose the relationship between and among concepts (Meleis, 2012). Theories provide us with a frame of reference, the ability to choose concepts to study, or ideas that are within one's practice. A theory helps guide research, and research helps validate theory.

In the research model, the researcher decides what to study and how and why the area of interest is important to the practice of nursing. In the practice model, the clinician decides what areas to directly assess, when to assess, and which intervention to implement. These decisions may or may not be knowingly based on a model or theory. Regardless, often the outcome supports the notion that behavior replicates a theoretic model, even though the nurse may be unaware that he or she is using a theoretic model in the practice process.

Just as in any other discipline, nursing theory has its own unique language. The words of this language identify linkages between the database of scientific nursing knowledge and the extracted information taken from this source for nursing theory. The interpretation of these words translates uniquely to the theory investigated. This application, or language of nursing theory, is the structure, or framework, from which one understands the theory. Table 5-1 presents the language of nursing theory along with definitions and examples.

Schematic Models

A schematic model is something that demonstrates concepts, usually with a picture. It is a visual representation of ideas. The model depicts concepts and shows how the concepts are related with the use of images, such as arrows and dotted lines (Polit and Beck, 2011).

TABLE 5-1   The Language of Nursing Theory

Term	Definition	Examples
Concept	Labels given to ideas, objects, events; a summary of thoughts or a way to categorize thoughts or ideas	Comfort, fatigue, pain, depression, environment
Conceptual model	A structure to organize concepts (ideas)	Roy's adaptation model
Philosophy	Values and beliefs of the discipline	Watson's philosophy and science of caring
Theory	The organization of concepts or constructs that shows the relationship of the ideas with the intention of describing, explaining, or predicting. The purpose is to make scientific findings meaningful and generalizable. Our goal in science has been to explain, predict, and control.	Self-care, adaptation, caring, behavioral system, unitary man, hierarchy of needs, interpersonal relationships, humanistic, nurse-client transactions

For example, a blueprint is a pictorial demonstration of a particular type of house someone might build. A model airplane is a detailed miniature replication of the original full-sized version. Diagramming a sentence outlines the specific parts (adverb, adjective, verb, subject, object, phrases) that make that particular sentence complete. Similarly, a nursing model gives a visual diagram or picture of concepts. Whether that is a critical pathway, decision tree, medication protocol, or other nursing-related practice, the model allows one to view the interrelated parts of the whole in picture form. A model of a nursing theory does the same thing. From the earliest model, offered by Florence Nightingale, nursing theory has been described and explained using this medium. Schematic models are used for clarifying complex concepts. The language of theory is translated into picture form, offering a comprehensive view, or model, of the theory. The schematic model shows how the concepts are related. A model, like a blueprint of a building, allows one to see the layout, including outlines of all features specific to the theory. Although it is not the same as understanding every little detail about the structure, its intent is to provide an overview, which at a glance is informative and descriptive.

Levels of Theory

Many persons refer to the level of a nursing theory, which can range from broad in scope to a smaller, more specific scope. For example, grand theory is often broad in scope and may describe and explain large segments of human experience. Rogers's theory of unitary man describes the entire nursing process. Other levels include middle-range theory and practice theory, which are smaller in scope and may refer to a specific population, such as Jacob's theory of the grief process in older women whose husbands received hospice care (Jacob, 1996) or to a specific situation, such as Sousa and Zauszniewski's (2005) theory of diabetic self-care management, or Tsai and colleagues' (2003) theory of chronic pain. Another example of a middle-range theory is the theory of unpleasant symptoms (Lenz and Pugh, 2003), which examines symptoms that are influenced by physiologic, psychologic, and situational factors as they relate to performance. The model of this theory is presented in Figure 5-1. Nurses often use these middle-range theories that are smaller in scope and simpler to understand to guide their daily practice.

To better illustrate the application of theory to nursing practice, Case Study Box 5-1 presents a case example of middle-range theory application using Mishel's (1997) uncertainty in illness theory. In examining nursing theories, students may be surprised to discover that they are already using some of the concepts in their individual practices. Nursing theories assist with further defining and organizing these concepts into an underpinning that explains, details, and claims nursing practice as a unique discipline.

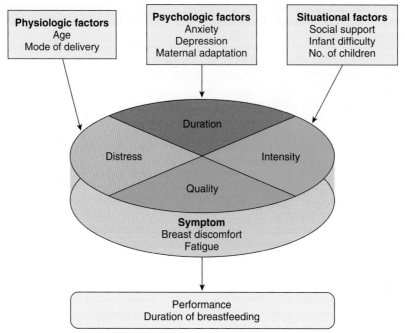

FIGURE 5-1 Theory of Unpleasant Symptoms.

CASE STUDY 5-1   Application of Theory to Practice

Mishel's Uncertainty in Illness Theory

A 9-year-old female client, Christine, is admitted to the pediatric unit for evaluation of a new onset of abdominal pain. The admission diagnosis is intermittent abdominal pain, rule out appendicitis. It is her first time as a patient in a hospital. Her father, who is a surgeon, and her mother, who is a nurse, accompany Christine to the unit. Her mother will stay with her. After talking with the parents, you as the nurse are confident that Christine is well informed, well cared for, and well prepared for her admission. While her parents are speaking with Christine's attending physician in a nearby office, you talk with Christine, who goes from smiling and chatting to bursting into tears. You observe that she is quite upset as she expresses to you that she is afraid because her father told her that if she did need surgery she would not feel anything because she would be asleep. Christine tells you that when she sleeps she wakes up sometimes and that she is sure that if her appendix is "cut out" she will wake up during the operation and it "will hurt a lot." She tells you she has not told her parents she is afraid because they have told her how proud they are that she is so brave. You realize Christine is terrified. Using Mishel's

uncertainty in illness theory, you apply the four-stage framework.

1. *Stimuli frame:* Inadvertently, Christine, who concretely has understood the word *sleep* using her own filter for life experience, has misinterpreted the positive intention of the language used by her father. This misinterpretation has resulted in Christine's negative cognitive schema. Christine notably does not understand "sleep" and its use (or adult misuse, in this case) as a synonym for, or definition of, surgical anesthesia. This is the root cause of Christine's current uncertainty in illness.

   Nursing intervention: Listen carefully and caringly; explain in simple, understandable language what "sleep" means in the context her father presented; initiate, seek, and clarify Christine's concerns and questions; use the term *anesthesia* to differentiate it from *sleep*. Inform and involve her parents in the overall process.

2. *Appraisal stage:* As a result of Christine's concrete experiential interpretation of "sleep," she has applied a negative value to the environmental conditions surrounding her abdominal pain. This is particularly so as it relates to surgical anesthesia.

CASE STUDY 5-1   Application of Theory to Practice—cont'd

Mishel's Uncertainty in Illness Theory

Nursing intervention: Follow up with Christine to make sure she comprehends the newly provided information. Elicit the support of Christine's parents and staff. If there are appropriate postsurgical patients on the unit, have them talk with Christine about their positive anesthesia experience.

3. *Initiation of coping mechanisms:* Christine is 9 years old. Her coping skills are limited to those used in her 9 years of life experience.

Nursing intervention: Check with Christine, and observe verbal and nonverbal cues. Have her verbalize any uncertainties she may be experiencing. Some of this will be influenced by the progress of the illness.

4. *Adaptation:* Dependent on steps 1, 2, and 3

Nursing intervention: As Christine accepts the new information, new schema will follow. Though the

outcome of her abdominal pain may initially be uncertain, her acceptance of the new schema will hopefully result in an increased comfort zone and decreased fear.

Summary: A central tenet of Mishel's theory is the core position that uncertainty in illness must be addressed. If left unheeded, negative perceptions will escalate and clients will suffer. Their quality of life may be affected and positive outcomes may be compromised. Nursing's responsibility in applying Mishel's theory is to reframe the client's perceived loss of control, or uncertainty, and assist the client in developing new skills of assimilation and accommodation. The client will then be able to identify, develop, and master those targets capable of control.

FLORENCE NIGHTINGALE: THE FIRST NURSING THEORIST

If theory means to put concepts in a form in which relationships are described and predictions are made, then Florence Nightingale was the first nursing theorist. Nightingale did not deliberately set out to develop theory; rather her goal was to ease the suffering of soldiers and citizens of England. However, many important influences in her life directed her toward theory development.

- A classic education (philosophy [science], French, Italian, Greek, Latin, the arts, and history)
- Upper-class background, great wealth, and a prominent social life (operas, parties, balls)
- Religion and spirituality (spent much time daydreaming about how she could serve God and experienced four visions from God)
- Era of reform throughout England (Industrial Revolution and dichotomy among the classes)

Despite her wealth and upper-class status, Nightingale was very dissatisfied with life. In 1852, she wrote a monograph titled "Cassandra," in which she pointed out the hopelessness inherent in being a woman in her day. "The family? It is too narrow a field for the development of an immortal spirit. . . . The system dooms some minds to incurable infancy, others to silent misery. Marriage is the only chance [and it is but a chance] offered to women for escape from this death; and how eagerly and how

ignorantly it is embraced" (Nightingale, 1992, pp. 37-38). Her diary writings have been interpreted at times to be suicidal. Often depressed, Nightingale resorted to dreams as an escape from her unhappiness and discontent. Her personality and her lifestyle (dogmatic, practical, a critical observer who was fascinated by numbers and recorded everything she saw and experienced) set her apart. She was self-willed, unhappy, and dissatisfied at times in spite of having beauty, a brilliant social career, and an education of which few men of her day could boast.

She had enjoyed the best of music and art and the companionship of charming and important people. However, in refusing marriage and the round of social gaiety, she was revolting against the restrictions placed on women of her day, and she struggled to be allowed to work in a serious way.

Florence Nightingale eventually convinced her family to allow her to attend nurses' training, and so began her distinguished career in developing professional nursing. Nightingale is well remembered for her significant contributions to professional nursing in the areas of theory of practice, nursing education, scholarship, and statistics. Box 5-3 provides Nightingale's definitions of professional nursing.

Nightingale's Theory of Practice

Nightingale's theory of practice, an environmental adaptation theory, was documented for nurses and laypersons

> **BOX 5-3   Nightingale's Definitions of Nursing**
>
> Nursing is an art—an art requiring an organized, practical, and scientific training.
> Nursing is putting us in the best possible conditions for nature to preserve health—to prevent, restore, or cure disease or injury.
> Nursing is, therefore, to help the patient live.

alike and served as the foundation for the promotion of health. She referred to this theory as the canons of nursing that guided the practice of professional nursing. A description of these canons, or standards, follows.

Ventilation and Warming

In the concept of ventilation and warming, Nightingale is very precise to "keep the air he breathes as pure as the external air without chilling him" (Nightingale, 1859, p. 8). She felt that good ventilation is necessary to carry off noxious elements from a sick person's lungs and skin.

Noise

"Unnecessary noise, or noise that creates an expectation in the mind is that which hurts a patient" (Nightingale, 1859, p. 25). The idea is that the nurse should guard against sudden noise, thoughtless chatter, and whispering in a patient's room, and felt the effect of music may be beneficial.

Variety

Variety is another concept that helps alleviate suffering. Beautiful objects, brilliant colors, cut flowers, perhaps different things to do (e.g., handwork), and even pets may alleviate the boredom felt by those suffering.

Diet

The fourth concept is diet. "Sick cookery should half do the work of your poor patient's weak digestion" (Nightingale, 1859, p. 38). Nightingale reviews some of the common substances (gruel, arrowroot puddings, and egg flip) given to the sick.

Light

"It is the unqualified result of all my experience with the sick that second only to their need of fresh air is their need of light" (Nightingale, 1859, p. 47). Nightingale suggested taking the patient outside for direct sunlight, and keeping rooms well lighted with no bed curtains or dark windows.

Chattering Hopes and Advices

According to Nightingale, "chattering hopes and advices" are attempts by attendants and friends to cheer the patient. Nightingale warns against this because she determines this to be false hope and hollow advice. She clearly appeals, "Leave off this practice of attempting to cheer the sick by making light of their danger and by exaggerating their probabilities of recovery" (Nightingale, 1859, p. 54).

Cleanliness (Health of Houses)

Nightingale's attention to cleanliness takes up a large portion of her book. She writes that health depends on this. Describing the care of bed, bedding, rooms, and walls, she states the exact steps needed to clean each. In addition, she details how to clean the sick person so as to prevent poisoning by the skin. She describes the patient's feeling of well-being after washing and drying. The nurse needs to wash her own hands with friction as well. Some believe that Nightingale's success was based primarily on cleaning up the hospitals.

Because of these significant contributions to nursing and to improving the health of soldiers and citizens alike, Nightingale was highly recognized. Her honors, decorations, medals, and citations may be seen in the United Services Museum in Whitehall, London. She was the first woman to ever receive the British Order of Merit by King Edward VII. One of her biographers (Cook, 1942) said, "she was not only 'The Lady with a Lamp' throwing light into dark places but also a kind of galvanic battery stirring and sometimes shocking the dull and sluggish public to life and action."

SURVEY OF SELECTED NURSING THEORIES

A brief discussion of selected nursing theories follows. The date identified indicates the year in which the theory was first presented. However, most theories have continued to be refined and modified. A summary of the major nursing theorists with a brief description of their theory or conceptual model is presented in Table 5-2, which provides the reader with information to guide further exploration of nursing theory.

A useful nursing theory will make assumptions concerning health problems, environment, behaviors, and target populations that are logical, consistent, research supported, and similar to ones that have proven to be successful in previous programs.

TABLE 5-2   Summary of Major Nursing Theorists and Theory Description

Date and Theorist	Theory Description
Florence Nightingale, 1860	Investigates the effect of the environment on healing.
Hildegard E. Peplau, 1952	Interpersonal relations model explores the interpersonal relationship of the nurse and the client and identifies the client's feelings as a predictor of positive outcomes related to health and wellness.
Faye Abdellah, 1960	Twenty-one nursing problems. Client-centered interventions.
Ida Jean Orlando, 1961	Theory of the nursing process. Deliberate nursing approach that stresses the action of the individual client in determining the action of the nurse; focus is on the present or short-term outcome.
Virginia Henderson, 1966	Definition of nursing. Nursing assists patients with 14 essential functions toward independence.
Myra Estrin Levine, 1967	Conservation model. Four conservation principles of inpatient client resources (energy, structural integrity, personal integrity, and social integrity).
Martha E. Rogers, 1970	Science of unitary human beings: energy fields, openness, pattern, and organization; nurse promotes synchronicity between human beings and their universe or environment.
Betty Neuman, 1970	Systems model: wellness-illness continuum; promotes the nurse as the agent in assisting the client in adapting to and, therefore, reducing stressors; supports the notion of prevention through appropriate intervention.
Dorothea Orem, 1971	Self-care model. Nursing facilitates client self-care by measuring the client's deficit relative to self-care needs; the nurse implements appropriate measures to assist the client in meeting these needs by matching them with an appropriate supportive intervention.
Imogene King, 1971	Goal attainment theory. Goal attainment using nurse-client transactions; addresses client systems and includes society, groups, and the individual.
Sister Callista Roy, 1974	Adaptation model. Client's adaptation to condition using environmental stimuli to adjust perception.
Madeline Leininger, 1977	Theory of cultural care diversity and universality. Transcultural and caring nursing; concepts are aimed toward caring and the components of a culture care theory; diversity, universality, worldview, and ethnohistory are essential to the four concepts of care, caring, health, and nursing.
Jean Watson, 1978	Philosophy and science of caring and humanistic nursing; there are 10 "carative" factors that are core to nursing; this holistic outlook addresses the impact and importance of altruism, sensitivity, trust, and interpersonal skills.
Margaret Newman, 1979	Central components of this model are health and consciousness followed by concepts of movement, time, and space; all components are summative units, described in relationship to health and to each other.
Dorothy E. Johnson, 1980	Behavioral system model for nursing; separates the psychologic and the physiologic aspects of illness; role of the nurse is to provide support and comfort to attain regulation of the client's behavior.
Rosemarie Rizzo Parse, 1981	Theory of human becoming proposes that quality of life from each person's individual perspective should be the goal of nursing practice. Parse first published the theory in 1981 as the "man-living-health" theory; however, the name was officially changed to "the human becoming theory" in 1992 to remove the term *man* after the change in the dictionary definition of the word from its former meaning of "humankind"; individual, by existing, actively participates in creating health according to environmental influences; individual is regarded as an open system wherein health is a process.

Betty Neuman (1970)—The System Model

The system model focuses on the response of the client system to actual or potential environmental stressors and the use of several levels of nursing prevention intervention for attaining, retaining, and maintaining optimal client system wellness. Neuman defines the concern of nursing as preventing stress invasion. If stress is not prevented, then the nurse should protect the client's basic structure and obtain or maintain a maximum level of wellness. Nurses provide care through primary, secondary, and tertiary prevention modes.

Hildegard E. Peplau (1952)—Interpersonal Relations as a Nursing Process: Man as an Organism That Exists in an Unstable Equilibrium

When the client incurs an insult that renders her or him incapable of moving forward because of stressful environmental conditions, anxiety increases. This condition creates a situation wherein the option is to either move in a backward direction or remain on a plateau. Nursing intervention in Peplau's model focuses on reducing the related incapacitating stressors through therapeutic interpersonal interaction. Intervention involves the nurse assisting the client with mutual goal setting. These goals may address exploration of the identified problem, identification of viable options, and implementation of available resources for resolution. The interpersonal nursing process is present and interactive, using associated and appropriate nursing intervention skills, which incorporate the roles of the nurse as resource person, educator, mentor, transfer agent, and counselor. Peplau's model requires that the nurse have self-awareness and insight regarding her or his own behaviors. This awareness may be applied in identifying and working through those behaviors unique to the client's schema. Figure 5-2 presents Peplau's psychodynamic nursing model.

Martha E. Rogers (1970)—Science of Unitary Human Beings: Humans as Energy Fields That Interact Constantly with the Environment

When the client-human unit incurs an insult that renders him or her out of balance with the universe, nursing interventions must be geared toward helping the client-human unit attain an increasing complex balance and synchronicity with the universe. Essential to Rogers's theory is the belief that each being is unique and consists of more than the collective sum of parts, and that each being is constantly evolving in a forward momentum as he or she interacts continually with the surrounding environmental field. Rogers's theory states that a brain integration is necessary to support the notion of human-environmental synergy, using the right side of the brain to recognize every human unit's capacity for imagery, sensation, and emotion and the left side of the brain for language, abstraction, and thought.

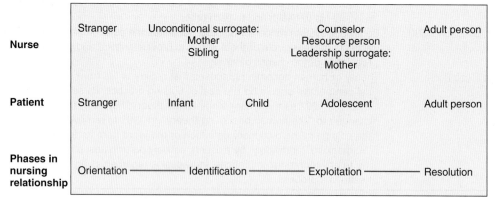

FIGURE 5-2 Peplau's psychodynamic nursing model: Phases and changing roles in nurse-patient relationships. (From Peplau HE: *Interpersonal relations in nursing,* New York, 1952, GP Putnam, p. 54.)

Dorothea Orem (1971)—Self-Care Deficit Model: Self-Care, Self-Care Deficits, and Nursing Systems

When a client incurs an insult that renders him or her incapable of fully functioning, deficient self-care occurs, which makes nursing intervention necessary. The object of Orem's theory is to restore the client's self-care capability to enable him or her to sustain structural reliability, performance, and growth through purposeful nursing intervention. The aim of such intervention is to help the client cope with unmet care needs by acquiring the maximal level of function. This would be to either regain previous function or maximize available function present after the insult, hence restoring a sense of well-being.

Sister Callista Roy (1974)—Adaptation Model: Assistance with the Adaptation to Stressors to Facilitate the Integration Process of the Client

When the client incurs an insult that renders him or her in need of environmental modification, the nurse is the agent of change to assist the individual with this adaptation. By helping the "biopsychosocial" client to modify external stimuli, adaptation will occur. In the case of illness, the outcome is a diminished or absent integration of the constantly changing setting known as the *illness environment* with the constantly changing human, who is interacting with the existing outside surroundings. To attain wellness, adaptation must occur through this integration. The nurse's role is to promote this adaptation by modifying and regulating peripheral stimuli to enable the client's adaptation and integration with a supportive, healing environment. In so doing, the nurse is instrumental in assisting the client with the areas of health and well-being, life worth and value, and self-respect and dignity. Sister Callista Roy's adaptation model is depicted in Figure 5-3.

Madeline Leninger (1977)—Theory of Cultural Care Diversity and Universality

Transcultural nursing and caring nursing concepts are aimed toward caring and the components of a culture care theory; diversity, universality, worldview, and ethnohistory are essential to the four concepts of care, caring, health, and nursing.

Jean Watson (1978)—Theory of Human Caring: Transpersonal Caring as the Fulcrum; Philosophy and Science as the Core of Nursing

When the client incurs an insult that renders him or her in need, the transpersonal process between the client and the nurse is considered a healing nursing intervention. An assumption of Watson's theory is that everyone requires human caring to quell need. Hence, the transpersonal process of "caring," or the caring among nurse, environment, and client, is essential to healing. Caring promotes the notion that every human being strives for interconnectedness with other humans and with nature. The nurse who implements these carative factors is the facilitator in the goal of restoring congruence between the client's perceived self and the existent self through the promotion of health and equilibrium. The expectation is that the client will experience balance and harmony in mind, body, and soul. Harmony, or wellness, will prevail, whereas disharmony, or illness, will be altered, eliminated, or circumvented.

Grand Nursing Theory

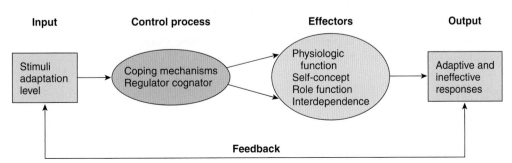

FIGURE 5-3 Roy's adaptation model: The person as an adaptive system. (From Roy C: *Introduction to nursing: an adaptation model*, ed 2, Englewood Cliffs, NJ, 1984, Prentice-Hall, p. 30.)

Margaret Newman (1979, Revised 1986)— Health as Expanding Consciousness

Margaret Newman's theory defines health as "expanding consciousness," or increasing complexity. The theory of health as expanding consciousness was stimulated by concern for those for whom health, defined as the absence of disease or disability, is not possible. Nurses often relate well to people facing the uncertainty, debilitation, loss, and eventual death associated with chronic illness. The theory has progressed to include the health of all persons regardless of the presence or absence of disease. The theory asserts that every person in every situation, no matter how disordered and hopeless it may seem, is part of the universal process of expanding consciousness—a process of becoming more of oneself, of finding greater meaning in life, and of reaching new dimensions of connectedness with other people and the world. (For more information, visit healthasexpandingconsciousness.org/home.)

Merle Mishel (1981, Revised 1990)— Uncertainty of Illness

Uncertainty in illness is frequently a stress-producing incident that is capable of contributing to negative physical and/or psychologic outcomes. Uncertainty exists when the client is unsure about a diagnosed illness. This uncertainty renders the client either incapable of assigning a concrete value to the illness itself or to a predictable outcome. Uncertainty can occur with a client misperceiving a diagnosed illness because of the inadequate information received, the health care provider incorrectly presuming client knowledge, or the health care informant failing to recognize the client's individual unique filtering of provided illness information. Mishel's theory is used in chronic illness and other practice settings. Mishel's model outlines a four-step approach in defining her theory. These include (1) stimuli frame: antecedents generating client uncertainty; (2) appraisal stage: client assignment of a value (positive or negative) to the uncertainty; (3) initiation of coping mechanisms: client ability to develop, improvise, and implement skills to cope with uncertainty; and (4) adaptation: positive client assimilation and accommodation to uncertainty, resulting from effective coping. Mishel's theory establishes a framework that guides nursing practice by assisting nurses to work with clients in establishing interventions that promote positive outcomes.

FUTURE OF NURSING THEORIES AND THEORISTS

At no time in history have so many health care concerns been the primary focus of federal and state legislative agendas. New questions are being asked in the twenty-first century about how health care is being conducted and managed. It is imperative that nurses be on the front lines to provide testimony in response to these queries.

The current nursing shortage, scarce resources, patient safety and medical errors, managed care, Medicare, welfare-to-work plans, confidentiality issues, parity of reimbursement, advanced practice nurses and their scope of practice, mandatory overtime, whistle-blower protection, prescriptive authority, licensure, multistate compacts, telemedicine, and many other policy issues that directly affect nursing practice are coming before the U.S. Congress and individual state legislative bodies for practice-related decisions. The direct effect on nursing cannot be overemphasized.

As nursing continues to operate in an environment of ongoing change, outcome data will be analyzed in an effort to provide quality care and access to that care for all clients in need of health care services. Therefore, one may predict that established nursing theories will be reevaluated and modified accordingly. New theories will be created and developed that may help answer the health care questions of the twenty-first century. Simply put, nursing theories in the twenty-first century will embrace complex environmental changes that incorporate new technologies, such as genetics, computers, noninvasive surgery, robotics, decreasing energy sources, increasing pollutants under a thinning ozone layer, environmental hazards, new diseases, and antibiotic-resistant illness. These changes have already resulted in client needs that differ from those as recent as 5 years ago.

▮ SUMMARY

Let the reader beware. As stated at the beginning of this chapter, the information provided here is in no manner a substitute for a comprehensive analysis of existing nursing theories and theorists. More theories exist than are presented here and, in fact, there are several comprehensive texts that cover these theories in depth. Instead, this chapter offers an overview of theory in the attempt to familiarize readers with the idea of theory. Selected theories are described to that end. Readers should identify nursing theories as ideas that have shaped and continue to shape the nursing profession in practice and research. It is our intention to assist students with understanding that practice and theory are interdependent entities. In other words, practice and theory cannot efficiently or effectively exist one without the other. Like the metaphor at the beginning of this chapter, without the existence of the stones (scientific data), the organization of specific, concentrated yet related areas (theory) could not have happened.

REFERENCES

Abdellah FG: The nature of nursing science, *Nurs Res* 18(5): 393, 1969.

Anastasi A: Heredity, environment, and the question "how?" *Psychol Rev* 65(4):197–208, 1958.

Cook E: *The life of Florence Nightingale*, New York, 1942, Macmillan.

Donaldson SK, Crowley DM: The discipline of nursing, *Nurs Outlook* 26(2):113–120, 1978.

Jacob S: The grief process of older women whose husbands received hospice care, *J Adv Nurs* 24(2):280–286, 1996.

Jacox AK: Theory construction in nursing: an overview, *Nurs Res* 23(1):4, 1974.

Lenz ER, Pugh LC: Theory of unpleasant symptoms. In Smith MJ, Liehr P, editors: *Middle range theory for nursing*, New York, 2003, Springer.

Meleis A: *Theoretical nursing: development and progress*, ed 5, Philadelphia, 2012, Wolters Kluwer/Lippincott.

Mishel MH: The measurement of uncertainty in illness, *Nurs Res* 30(5):258–263, 1981.

Mishel MH: Uncertainty in acute illness, *Annu Rev Nurs Res* 15:57–80, 1997.

Nightingale F: *Notes on nursing: what it is, and what it is not* (commemorative edition), Philadelphia, 1992, Lippincott.

Nightingale F: *Notes on nursing: what it is, and what it is not*, London, 1859, Harrison and Sons.

Polit D, Beck C: *Nursing research*, ed 9, Philadelphia, 2011, Lippincott.

Reed PG, Shearer NBC: *Perspectives on nursing theory*, ed 6, Philadelphia, 2012, Lippincott Williams & Wilkins.

Sousa VD, Zauszniewski JA: Toward a theory of diabetes self-care management, *J Theory Constr Test* 9(2):61–67, 2005.

Tsai P, Tak S, Moore C, et al: Testing a theory of chronic pain, *J Adv Nurs* 43(2):159–169, 2003.

ADDITIONAL RESOURCES

Benner P: *From novice to expert: excellence in power in clinical nursing practice*, Menlo Park, CA, 1984, Addison-Wesley.

Chinn P, Kramer M: *Theory and nursing: integrated knowledge development*, St Louis, 1999, Mosby.

Health as expanding consciousness (website). http://www.healthasexpandingconsciousness.org. Accessed October 1, 2014.

Johnson BM, Webber PB: *An introduction to theory and reasoning in nursing*, Philadelphia, 2001, Lippincott.

King I: *Toward a theory for nursing: general concepts of human behavior*, New York, 1971, John Wiley & Sons.

Kolcaba K, Schirm V, Steiner R: Effects of hand massage on comfort of nursing home residents, *Geriatr Nurs* 27(2):85–91, 2006.

Kolcaba K, Tilton C, Drouin C: Comfort theory: a unifying framework to enhance the practice environment, *J Nurs Adm* 36(11):538–544, 2006.

Leddy S, Pepper J: *Conceptual bases in professional nursing*, Philadelphia, 1998, Lippincott.

Leininger MM: *Transcultural nursing: concepts, theories and practices*, New York, 1978, John Wiley & Sons.

Levine M: The four conservation principles of nursing, *Nurs Forum* 6(1):93, 1967.

Neuman, B. *The Neuman systems model: application to nursing education and practice*. Norwalk, Ct, 1982, Appleton-Century-Crofts.

Newman MA: *Health as expanding consciousness*, St Louis, 2000, Mosby.

Newman MA: *Transforming presence: the difference that nursing makes*, Philadelphia, 2008, FA Davis.

Nicoll L: *Perspectives on nursing theory*, Philadelphia, 1997, Lippincott.

Nightingale F: *Notes on nursing: what it is, and what it is not* (commemorative edition), Philadelphia, 1992, Lippincott.

Nightingale F: *Notes on nursing: what it is, and what it is not*, London, 1859, Harrison and Sons.

Orem DE: *Nursing concepts of practice*, ed 6, New York, 1971, McGraw-Hill.

Parse RR: *Man-living-health: a theory of nursing*, New York, 1981, John Wiley & Sons.

Peplau HE: *International relations in nursing*, New York, 1952, GP Putnam.

Tomey AM, Alligood MR: *Nursing theorists and their work*, ed 6, St Louis, 2006, Mosby.

6

Nursing Research and Evidence-Based Practice

Rosemary A. McLaughlin, PhD, CNE, RN-NIC,
Zoila V. Sanchez, PhD, FNP

Nursing research provides the foundation for evidence-based nursing practice.

ⓔ Additional resources are available online at: *http://evolve.elsevier.com/Cherry/*

ETHICAL/PROFESSIONAL ISSUE

Mary Smith is a 19-year-old female who comes to the health department women's center complaining about vaginal itching, foul smelling discharge, and pain with sexual intercourse. She admits to being sexually active for the last 2 years with multiple partners and a prior history of trichomoniasis infections, twice within the last year. Ms. Smith is on an oral contraceptive pill for the last 2 years and her last menstrual cycle was 4 days ago. Ms. Smith admits that there is family history of cervical cancer. Her mother was diagnosed and treated in 1992 for this condition. Ms. Smith has never had a Pap test. Ms. Smith stated, "The family planning center just did blood work to make sure she was not pregnant and gave me a prescription for oral contraceptive (OC) pills."

As a registered nurse you are aware that family history of cervical cancer needs further inquiry and follow-up.

A vaginal examination is performed by a nurse practitioner, with findings of multiple fleshy, soft, pale-colored growths on the vagina and perianal area. As a nurse you are aware that most cervical cancers are caused by certain oncogenic (cancer-causing) strains of the human papillomavirus. Due to the family history of cervical cancer, you anticipate that the nurse practitioner will follow up with a Pap test on this patient.

However, the current practice guideline recommendations by the American Cancer Society and the American Society for Colposcopy and Cervical Pathology recommend that women younger than 21 should not be screened (Pap test) for cervical cancer or HPV, regardless of whether they are sexually active.

As a nurse, what would you do?

VIGNETTE

I did not understand why I had to take a research class when all I wanted to do was be a staff nurse in a critical care unit. Research? Evidence-based practice? Why are these topics in the nursing program? I have enough to do just learning all the content in my clinical courses. What

do research and evidence have to do with developing my nursing abilities? I trust the faculty, the textbooks, and clinical experience to prepare me for nursing. I'm already getting what I need to know. That was my earlier attitude. Now that I am practicing, I have a new appreciation for nursing research and the evidence it provides for application to practice. I have an entirely different way of addressing clinical questions. I'm starting to ask questions about how I can improve the care I give to patients and how I can be involved in my workplace's efforts to improve care for the patients it serves. I have discovered by purposeful reading in my practice area that research reports and research summaries contain many implications that apply to practice in the critical care unit.

Questions to Consider While Reading this Chapter:
1. How can a desire to read research and evidence-based practice literature in students be facilitated?
2. How does research affect nursing practice?
3. How can nurses motivate colleagues to base their practice on research?

KEY TERMS

Abstract: A brief overview of a research study.

Clinical nurse researcher (CNR): An advanced practice nurse who is doctorally prepared and directs and participates in clinical research.

Clinical nurse specialist (CNS): An advanced practice nurse who provides direct care to clients and participates in health education and research.

Clinical practice guideline (CPG): An evidence-based guide to clinical practice developed by experts in a particular field for direct application in clinical environments.

Control group: Subjects in an experiment who do not receive the experimental treatment and whose performance provides a baseline against which the effects of the treatment can be measured. When a true experimental design is not used, this group is called a comparison group.

Data collection: The process of acquiring existing information or developing new information.

Empirical: Having a foundation based on data gathered through the senses (e.g., observation or experience) rather than purely through theorizing or logic.

Ethnography: A qualitative research method for the purpose of investigating cultures that involve data collection, description, and analysis of data to develop a theory of cultural behavior.

Evidence-based practice: The process of systematically finding, appraising, and using research findings as the basis for clinical practice.

Experimental design: A design that includes randomization, a control group, and manipulation between or among variables to examine probability and causality among selected variables for the purpose of predicting and controlling phenomena.

Generalizability: The inference that findings can be generalized from the sample to the entire population.

Grant: Proposal developed to seek research funding from private or public agencies.

Grounded theory: A qualitative research design used to collect and analyze data aiming to develop theories grounded in real-world observations.

Integrative Research Review (IRR): Methodology that simultaneously synthesizes several experimental and non-experimental research findings to provide a comprehensive understanding of the phenomena of interest.

Meta-analysis: Statistical method of quantitative synthesis of findings from several studies to determine what is known about a phenomenon.

Metasynthesis: Interpretive translations produced from the integration or comparison of findings from qualitative studies.

Methodologic design: Research design used to develop the validity and reliability of instruments that measure research concepts and variables.

Naturalistic paradigm: Holistic view of nature and the direction of science that guides qualitative research.

Needs assessment: Study in which the researcher estimates the resource needs of a group.

Peer-review: A process by which a scholarly work (such as a paper or a research proposal) is checked by a group of experts in the same field to make sure it meets the necessary standards before it is published or accepted.

Practice guidelines: Research-based recommendations stated as standards of practice, procedures, or decision algorithms.

Phenomenology: Qualitative research design employing inductive descriptive methodology to describe the lived experiences of study participants.

Pilot study: Conduct of a smaller version of a proposed study that develops or refines methodology prior to use in a larger study.

Qualitative research: Systematic, subjective approach used to describe life experiences and give them meaning.

Quantitative research: Formal, objective, systematic process used to describe and test relationships and examine cause-and-effect interactions among variables.

Quasi-experimental research: A type of quantitative research study design that lacks one of the components of an experimental design (i.e., randomization, control group, manipulation of one or more variables).

Randomization: The assignment of subjects to treatment conditions in a random manner (determined by chance alone).

Secondary analysis: A research design in which data previously collected in another study are analyzed for different aims than the original study.

State-of-the-science summary: An up-to-date merging of findings from several studies concerning the same topic. The summary identifies limitations and gaps in the understanding of the topic.

Survey: A nonexperimental research design that focuses on obtaining information regarding the status quo of a situation, often through direct questioning of participants.

Triangulation: The use of a variety of methods to collect data on the same concept.

LEARNING OUTCOMES

After studying this chapter, the reader will be able to:

1. Summarize major points in the evolution of nursing research in relation to contemporary nursing.
2. Evaluate the influence of nursing research on current nursing and health care practices.
3. Differentiate among nursing research methods.
4. Critically appraise the quality of research studies using established criteria.
5. Participate in the research process.
6. Use research findings to improve nursing practice.

CHAPTER OVERVIEW

This chapter provides basic knowledge regarding the research process and the ultimate importance of evidence-based nursing practice (EBP). The intent is to inspire an appreciation for nursing research and to show how it can improve nursing practice and how results can be translated into health policy. Nursing research is defined as a systematic approach used to examine phenomena important to nursing and nurses. A summary of major points in the evolution of nursing research in relation to contemporary nursing is presented. A description of private and public organizations that fund research is given, and their research priorities are listed. Major research designs are briefly described, and examples of each are given. Nurses of all educational levels are encouraged to participate in and promote nursing research at varying degrees. Evidence-based practice is the use of the best scientific evidence, integrated with clinical experience and incorporating patients' values and preferences in the practice of professional nursing. The process of locating research and evidence, including practice guidelines is reviewed. Students are introduced to the research process and guided in the process of critically appraising published research and research syntheses. Ethical issues related to research are examined, and historical examples of unethical research are given. The functions of the institutional review board (IRB) and the use of informed consent in protecting the rights of human subjects are emphasized.

DEFINITION OF NURSING RESEARCH

Research is a process of systematic inquiry or study to build knowledge in a discipline. The purpose of research is to develop an empirical body of knowledge for a discipline or profession. Specifically, research validates and refines existing knowledge and develops new knowledge (Burns and Grove, 2010). The results of the research process provide a foundation on which practice decisions and behaviors are laid. Research results create a strong scientific base for nursing practice, especially when deliberately and carefully evaluated for application to specific clinical topics (Melnyk and Fineout-Overholt, 2014).

Nursing research is a systematic approach used to examine phenomena important to nursing and nurses.

Because nursing is a practice profession, it is important that clinical practice be based on scientific knowledge. Evidence generated by nursing research provides support for the quality and cost-effectiveness of nursing interventions. Thus recipients of health care—and particularly nursing care—reap benefits when nurses attend to research evidence and introduce change based on that evidence into nursing practice. The introduction of evidence-based change into the direct provision of nursing care may occur at the individual level of a particular nurse or at varied organizational or social levels.

Research within the realms of nursing education, nursing administration, health services, characteristics of nurses, and nursing roles provides evidence for effectively changing these supporting areas of nursing knowledge (Burns and Grove, 2010). Today, the importance of nursing research to the discipline is recognized; however, much nursing history underlies the current state of acceptance.

EVOLUTION OF NURSING RESEARCH

Nursing research began with the work of Florence Nightingale during the Crimean War. After Florence Nightingale's work, the pattern that nursing research followed was closely related to the problems confronting nurses. For example, nursing education was the focus of most research studies between 1900 and 1940. As more nurses received their education in a university setting, studies regarding student characteristics and satisfactions were conducted. As more nurses pursued a college education, researchers became interested in studying nurses. Questions such as what type of person enters nursing and how are nurses perceived by other groups guided research investigations. Teaching, administration, and curriculum were topics that dominated nursing research until the 1970s. By the 1970s, more doctorally prepared nurses were conducting research, and there was a shift to studies that focused on the improvement of patient care. The 1980s brought nursing research to a new stage of development. There were many more qualified nurse researchers, widespread availability of computers for collection and analysis of data, and a realization that research is a vital part of professional nursing (Polit and Beck, 2014). Nurse researchers began conducting studies based on the naturalistic paradigm. These studies were qualitative rather than quantitative. In addition, instead of conducting many small, unrelated research studies, teams of researchers, often interdisciplinary, began conducting programs of research to build bodies of knowledge related to specific topics, such as urinary incontinence, decubitus ulcers, pain, and quality of life. The 1990s brought increasing concern about health care reform, and now, in the twenty-first century, research studies focus on important health care delivery issues, such as cost, quality, and access. With the developing educational emphasis on the doctorate in nursing practice degree, research emphasis on such patient care foci is gaining momentum, especially in view of the quality gaps highlighted by sentinel reports from the Institute of Medicine (IOM, 2001, 2011).

Increasingly, research findings are being used as the basis for clinical decisions. Evidence-based practice (EBP) can be defined as the process of systematically finding, appraising, and using research findings as a basis for making decisions about patient care (Houser, 2015). The rise of technology and the worldwide access and flow of information have transformed the decision-making processes of practitioners. No longer do nurses and other health care professionals simply compare outcomes of patient care between units in the same hospital; solutions, choices, and outcomes are sought on an international level. Hospitals must show improved outcomes and clinical practice based on current evidence. In recent decades, the nursing discipline is paying greater attention to the necessity of participating in research as evidenced by the maintenance of magnet status for facilities (Wise, 2009).

RESEARCH PRIORITIES

Why set priorities for research in the nursing discipline? Can nurses do research in areas that match personal areas of interest? The answer to the second question is yes, certainly. But nursing exists to provide high-quality nursing care to individuals in need of health-promoting, health-sustaining, and health-restoring strategies. The main outcome of research activity for a nurse is to put the knowledge gained to work in health care delivery. Research priorities, often set by groups that fund research, encourage nurse researchers to invest effort and money into those areas of research likely to generate the most benefit to recipients of care. Research is a costly venture and so nurses engaged in research often match personal interests with funding opportunities available during the planning phase for a proposed investigation.

Two major sources of funding for nursing research are the National Institute of Nursing Research (NINR) and the Agency for Healthcare Research and Quality (AHRQ), which are both funded by federal congressional appropriations. Private foundations and nursing organizations also provide funding for nursing research.

National Institute of Nursing Research

As part of the National Institutes of Health (NIH), the National Institute of Nursing Research (NINR) supports research on the biologic and behavioral aspects of critical health problems that confront the nation. The NINR's focus is designed to advance the "science of health" by encompassing four key themes: symptom science (promoting personalized health strategies); wellness (promoting health and preventing illness); self-management (improving quality of life for individuals with chronic illness); and end-of-life and palliative care (the science of compassion) (NINR strategic plan, 2013).

The areas of research emphasis published by the NINR are useful guides for investigators developing proposals but are not considered to be prescriptive in nature. Investigators bring to bear their own unique expertise and creativity when proposing research in harmony with NINR priority research areas. Recently, the NINR Innovative Questions Initiative was launched to encourage new thinking and creativity in nursing to promote results-oriented innovations. This allowed for identification, discussion, and debate of new research questions (Grady, 2014).

Agency for Healthcare Research and Quality

The Agency for Healthcare Research and Quality (AHRQ) broadly defines its mission as improving "the quality, safety, efficiency, and effectiveness of health care for all Americans" (AHRQ, 2014a). As an agency of the U.S. Department of Health and Human Services, the AHRQ's health-related aims are to reduce the risk of harm by promoting delivery of the best possible health care, improve health care outcomes by encouraging the use of evidence to make informed health care decisions, transform research into practice to facilitate wider access to effective health care services, and reduce unnecessary costs (AHRQ, 2014). Since the inception of the agency in 1989, strategic goals have centered on supporting improvements in health outcomes, strengthening

measurement of health care quality indicators, and fostering access to and cost-effectiveness of health care. The 1999 reauthorizing legislation expanded the role of the agency by directing the AHRQ to:

- Improve the quality of health care through scientific inquiry, dissemination of findings, and facilitation of public access to information.
- Promote patient safety and reduce medical errors through scientific inquiry, building partnerships with health care providers, and establishing centers for education and research on therapeutics (CERTs).
- Advance the use of information technology for coordinating patient care and conducting quality and outcomes research.
- Establish an office on priority populations to ensure that the needs of low-income groups, minorities, women, children, older adults, and individuals with special health care needs are addressed by the agency's research efforts.

The research-related activities of the AHRQ are quite varied, but a recent shift emphasizes a more deliberate translation of research evidence into practice. In a process similar to that used by the NIH, investigators are invited to submit research proposals for possible funding through **grant** announcements. A listing of current areas of the agency's research interests can be found online at www.innovations.ahrq.gov.

The AHRQ actively promotes EBP, partially through the establishment of 14 EBP centers (EBPCs) in the United States and Canada. EBPCs conduct research on assigned clinical care topics and generate reports on the effectiveness of health care methodologies. Health care providers may then use the evidence in developing site-specific guidelines that direct clinical practice. AHRQ also actively maintains the National Guideline Clearinghouse (www.guidelines.gov), a website that makes available to health care professionals a wide array of clinical practice guidelines that may be considered in health care decision making. Another recent addition to AHRQ's initiatives is the Healthcare Innovations Exchange (AHRQ, 2014), which provides a public source of information about innovations taking place in health care delivery. Submitted innovations are reviewed for the quality of achieved outcomes, providing evidence as a foundation for decision making by others who may be searching for or considering similar innovations. Although most AHRQ activities are intended to support health care professionals and institutions, the agency supports health care recipients by designing some information specifically for dissemination to the lay public (AHRQ, 2014).

Private Foundations

Obtaining money for research is becoming increasingly competitive, thus voluntary foundations and private and community-based organizations should be investigated as possible funding sources. Many foundations and corporate direct-giving programs are interested in funding health care projects and research. Computer databases and guides to funding are available in local libraries. In addition, grant-seeking enterprises often purchase subscriptions that allow computer access to enhanced listings of funding foundations that include information about the types of projects those foundations typically fund. Though subscriptions are expensive, costs are often balanced by the efficiency with which suitable funding prospects are identified. An example of such a service is Prospect Research Online (2014) (www.iwave.com).

Private foundations, such as the Robert Wood Johnson Foundation (2014) or the W.K. Kellogg Foundation (https://www.wkkf.org/grantseekers), offer program funding for health-related research. Investigators are encouraged to pursue funding for small projects through local sources or private foundations until a track record is established in research design and implementation leading to securing funding from public sources.

Nursing Organizations

Sigma Theta Tau International (STTI), the American Nurses Association (ANA), and the Oncology Nurses Society (ONS) are a few of the nursing organizations that fund research studies. STTI makes research grant awards to increase scientific knowledge related to nursing practice. STTI supports creative interdisciplinary research and places importance on identifying best practices and benchmark innovations. Awards are made at the international and local chapter levels. The ANA awards small grants through the American Nurses Foundation. Specialty nursing organizations offer grants to support research related to their specialty. For example, the ONS awards grants that focus on issues related to oncology. A list of current nursing organizations offering funding opportunities can be found online at http://nursingworld.org/research-toolkit/Research-Funding.

To summarize, multiple potential sources of funding are available for research projects. The individual or group wishing to conduct research will need to carefully develop a proposal, search for a possible funding source, and submit the proposal. Libraries and the Internet provide ample information about the many foundations and organizations interested in funding research endeavors. Most research institutions establish offices that help in the search and procurement of funding supporting researchers in their work of knowledge building.

COMPONENTS OF THE RESEARCH PROCESS

The research process involves conceptualizing a research study, planning and implementing that study, and communicating the findings. The process involves a logical flow as each step builds on the previous steps. These steps should be included in published research reports so that the reader has a basis for understanding and critiquing the study (Box 6-1).

STUDY DESIGNS

Study designs are plans that tell a researcher how data are to be collected, from whom data are to be collected, and how data will be analyzed to answer specific research questions. Research studies are classified into two basic methods: quantitative and qualitative, two distinctly different approaches to conducting research. The researcher chooses the method based on the research question and the current level of knowledge about the phenomena

---

BOX 6-1   Components of the Research Process

Research is a process that takes place in a series of steps:
1. Formulating the research question or problem
2. Defining the purpose of the study
3. Reviewing related literature
4. Formulating hypotheses and defining variables
5. Selecting the research design
6. Selecting the population, sample, and setting
7. Conducting a **pilot study**
8. Collecting the data
9. Analyzing the data
10. Communicating conclusions

and the problem to be studied. Quantitative research is a formal, objective, systematic process in which numeric data are used. Qualitative research is a systematic approach used to describe and promote understanding of human experiences related to health in a non-numeric fashion. The qualitative approach to research focuses on understanding the human experience as it is lived, thus complementing quantitative methodologies (Polit and Beck, 2014).

Quantitative Designs

Arising from early scientific models for doing research, the nursing discipline directly adopted the quantitative method of conducting research. Thus, quantitative design has traditionally been prevalent in nursing research studies. Deriving meaning from the statistical analysis of numerical data obtained from samples and populations has yielded significant contributions to nursing knowledge. The usual intent of quantitative study is to apply or generalize knowledge from a smaller sample of subjects to a larger population. Quantitative studies usually produce knowledge about very precise topics, creating a need for multiple studies over multiple years before conclusive knowledge is yielded. The most common quantitative designs used in health care research are survey, needs assessment, experimental, quasi-experimental, methodologic, meta-analysis, and secondary analysis. A brief overview of these mostly quantitative study designs is given in Table 6-1. For in-depth understanding of particular methods and their suitability for studying particular phenomena, consult research methods texts.

TABLE 6-1   A Sample of Quantitative Research Methodologies

Method	Description
Survey	Survey research designs are popular in nursing research studies that are designed to obtain information regarding the prevalence, distribution, and interrelationships of variables within a population. This is a useful design when collecting demographic information, social characteristics, behavioral patterns, and information bases.
Needs assessment	Needs assessments are used to determine what is most beneficial to a specific aggregate group. This design can be used by organizations, communities, or groups to establish priorities for their respective client groups (Polit and Beck, 2012).
Methodologic	Methodologic research focuses on the development of data collection instruments, such as surveys or questionnaires. The goal is to improve the reliability and validity of instruments. This work is time-consuming and tedious, but necessary for the implementation of research studies. However, when quality instruments are developed, they can be used in multiple studies.
Meta-analysis	Meta-analysis is an advanced process whereby multiple research studies on a specific topic are reviewed and the findings of these studies are statistically analyzed. Meta-analysis synthesizes quantitative data from multiple similar studies, thus enlarging the power of the results and allowing more confident generalizations than a single study.
Experimental study	Experimental studies, having several subtypes, include the manipulation of one or more independent variables, random assignment to either a control group or treatment group, and observation of the outcome or effect that presumably is a result of the independent variable. Rigor and control of extraneous variables allow researchers to establish cause-and-effect relationships, testing causal relationships (Polit and Beck, 2012).
Quasi-experimental design	A quasi-experimental design is lacking one of the required components of the experimental design. This is a useful design when randomization, a control group, or the manipulation of one or more variables is not possible. Several subtypes exist.
Secondary analysis	Secondary analysis involves asking new questions of data collected previously. The data may have been generated from previous formal research or may have resulted from any prior systematic collection of data. Examples of prior non-research data include the many inevitable records generated as a by-product of health care delivery systems.

Qualitative Designs

Qualitative research is designed for discovery rather than verification. It is used to explore little-understood or ambiguous phenomena rather than to verify a cause and effect. Qualitative methods can be important to the complex study of humans. Concepts that are important to health care professionals often are difficult to reduce in a quantitative way. Interviewing is the main technique used in qualitative methods to explore the meaning of certain experiences to individuals. This method is time-consuming and costly and uses small samples; therefore, generalizations cannot be made from findings. However, when exploring issues such as caregiver burden, it might be more appropriate to interview participants with open-ended questions to get their perspective than to send out a standard questionnaire, thereby broadening the data gathered. The main types of qualitative research designs include phenomenology, ethnography, and grounded theory. Table 6-2 provides brief descriptions of these methods. For a more complete understanding, refer to qualitative research texts.

Although there is a need for qualitative research studies in health care, qualitative one-on-one interviews take time; they must be recorded, typed, transcribed, and analyzed. Data analysis is conducted by the researcher, who then reviews each transcribed interview line by line to group common conceptual meanings. Concepts are combined to describe the experience for the particular group being studied. The researcher cannot assert that findings from a small unique sample would be the same in a large, diverse population. However, findings should be transferable. The researcher should give a thorough description of the sample and setting so that findings could be expected to occur in similar individuals in a similar setting. In addition, triangulation studies may provide the strength needed to increase generalizability of the findings.

Triangulation

Triangulation is the use of various research methods or different data collection techniques in the same study. Triangulation commonly refers to the use of qualitative and quantitative methods in the same study. This method can be useful when data from multiple sources and methods are necessary to provide a holistic understanding of the subject matter.

Pilot Studies

Pilot studies are small-scale studies used to identify the strengths and limitations of a planned larger-scale study. Pilot work is preliminary research that can be used to assess the design, methodology, and feasibility of a study, and typically includes participants who are similar to those who will be used in the larger research study. By performing each step, the researcher can evaluate the effectiveness of the proposed data collection methods to improve and assess the feasibility of the study (Polit and Beck, 2014). Pilot studies can serve to discover preliminary trends in outcomes for a particular agency, personnel, and clients. In fact, many research entities publish the results of pilot studies.

EVIDENCE-BASED PRACTICE AND RESEARCH UTILIZATION

From the beginnings of the nursing research endeavor, nurses have been interested in using nursing research to effectively impact the care of individuals and aggregate groups. Despite other incentives for the conduct of

TABLE 6-2	**A Sample of Qualitative Research Methodologies**
Method	**Description**
Phenomenology	Phenomenology is designed to provide understanding of the participants' "lived experience." This method is a valuable approach for studying intangible experiences, such as grief, hope, and risk taking.
Ethnography	Ethnography is a method used to study phenomena from a cultural perspective. Ethnographers spend time in the cultural setting with the research participants to observe and better understand their experience.
Grounded theory	Grounded theory is designed to explore and describe a social process. This method is used to explore a process that people use to deal with problematic areas of their lives, such as coping with a terminal illness or adjusting to bereavement.

research, none is more powerful for a nurse than the difference that might be made in the lives of individuals and aggregates for the betterment of health. Thus, early emphasis in the 1980s on research utilization has been expanded, with the increasing emphasis on EBP. Though the terms *research utilization* and *evidence-based practice* are related, research utilization has been described as a subset of EBP (LoBiondo-Wood and Haber, 2014). EBP encompasses multiple types of evidence such as research findings, research reviews, and evidence-based theory, and the integration of that evidence with clinical expertise and patient preferences and values (Melnyk and Fineout-Overholt, 2014) (Box 6-2).

In this second decade of the twenty-first century, EBP has become a major driving force in the disciplinary life of clinicians, students, educators, administrators, and policymakers. Discussion on barriers to research utilization and EBP has shifted to how to actively promote implementation of EBP. Extensive work is being done on the best ways to translate research into practice, spawning a new area of health care science called *translation science.*

Eventually, the promise of translation science is to provide guidance on the best ways to incorporate best evidence into health care, including nursing. As an example of translation strategy, White (2011) describes "nurse champions" as key agents in the "timely integration of discovery" into daily practice. Nurse champions will take ownership of a practice project and personally oversee a practice innovation process from discovery to adoption and dissemination. Table 6-2 provides brief descriptions of the steps involved in the EBP process. Whole texts are available that explain the multiple aspects of EBP (Brown, 2014; Larrabee, 2009a; Malloch and Porter-O'Grady, 2010; Melnyk and Fineout-Overholt, 2011), and various models have been proposed that more carefully detail the process of incorporating evidence into practice (Larrabee, 2009b; Newhouse et al, 2007; Stetler, 1994). Within these named resources and many others resides a treasure trove of EBP history, resources, processes, examples, and results.

Advancing Evidence-Based Practice

How does one get started with EBP? A list of strategies for encouraging a climate of EBP is likely to look somewhat different depending on the context of care: Is the context of care delivery a clinic, a hospital, or a conglomerate? A short list of broad strategies suggested by Melnyk and Fineout-Overholt (2014) applies regardless of the setting:

- Assessment of barriers to EBP
- Correction of misperceptions about EBP goals and processes
- Questioning of current clinical practices

Assessment should be as comprehensive as possible in order to identify the knowledge, beliefs, and behaviors that are common in the existing system and to raise the awareness of a need for shifting decision making about clinical care toward a consideration of current best evidence. Misperceptions about EBP may include doubts about the feasibility of EBP initiatives within a busy clinical environment or the idea that EBP is a one-size-fits-all approach to patient care; both of these may be addressed by a learning process. Raising questions about current clinical practices provides a strategy for getting the critical thinking juices flowing about particular clinical practices and problems. Individuals with common interests may form collaborative groups that further strengthen the EBP culture through bonding around specific patient problems and the discovery of evidence-based solutions. The specific tactics, processes,

---

BOX 6-2   Components of Evidence-Based Practice Process

The following is a brief overview of the multistep process involved in evidence-based practice (EBP).

1. Cultivating a spirit of inquiring.
2. Asking a clinical question in the PICOT format (P=population, I=intervention or interest area, C=comparison intervention or group, O=outcome, and T=time).
3. Search for and collect the most relevant best evidence to answer the question. Reliable sources include systematic reviews, pre-appraised literature and studies from **peer-reviewed** journals.
4. Critically evaluate the evidence. Rapid critical appraisal of the findings (evidence) for validity, reliability and applicability, then synthesize that evidence.
5. Integrate the best evidence with one's clinical expertise and patient preferences and values in making a practice decision regarding whether a practice change should be made.
6. Evaluate outcomes of the practice decision or change based on evidence. Outcomes should be measured to determine the positive or negative outcomes of the change.
7. Disseminate the outcomes of the EBP decision or change through presentations or publications so that others can benefit from the process.

and events that undergird an EBP initiative require allocation of resources, creativity, and dedication. Of particular significance to EBP initiatives is the availability of individuals in clinical environments who have the specific responsibility and expertise to understand and translate evidence into practice (Malloch and Porter-O'Grady, 2010).

Nurse Researcher and Evidence-Based Practice Roles

Two nursing roles are specifically focused on research and EBP: the CNS and the CNR.

Clinical Nurse Specialist

The CNS is a registered nurse with graduate preparation in a specialized area of nursing practice and an expert clinician with additional responsibility for education and research. A CNS is in an ideal position to link research to practice by assessing an agency's readiness for research utilization, consulting with staff to identify clinical problems, and helping staff to discover, implement, and evaluate findings that improve health care delivery (National Association of Clinical Nurse Specialists, 2014). CNSs are educated in the research process and can conduct their own investigations and collaborate with doctorally prepared nurses.

Clinical Nurse Researcher

The **clinical nurse researcher (CNR)** should be a doctorally prepared nurse with clinical and research experience. Terminology used to refer to this type of position tends to vary among countries, settings, and agencies. One might see position postings for clinical nurse scientist, nurse scientist, director of nursing research, and others. A CNR can focus either on the conduct or facilitation of research and should possess knowledge of statistics, grantsmanship, evaluation research, and administration. Interpersonal skills, such as patience, flexibility, and approachability, are imperative. A CNR employed by a hospital or home health agency must develop relationships with staff nurses to identify the research questions that staff nurses see as most significant in the particular setting. The CNR is responsible for designing studies and assisting staff nurses with understanding the implications of the study. In addition, the CNR provides guidance to the staff regarding their role in the research process. This role could involve patient recruitment for studies or actual data collection. The CNR also is responsible for disseminating findings of the research not only to staff nurses but also to administrators of the agency so that findings can be incorporated into practice.

The CNR also may need to communicate results to legislators or other policymakers if the results potentially affect health policy. Research evidence is important to policymaking because it provides a logical foundation for policy change. The process of writing brief summaries of evidence or personally testifying about particular topics should be approached carefully. One should know the target audience, the exact policy issue, the background of the issue, and the full range of pertinent evidence (Melnyk and Fineout-Overholt, 2014).

If agencies do not have a CNR, they should be encouraged to develop relationships with researchers in university settings or other agencies. Professors in academic settings are expected to conduct research and often are interested in collaborating with health care agencies that might serve as a site. These agencies often have the patient population that can serve as a study sample. For example, a university professor interested in home health care issues might collaborate with an agency to examine the efficacy of various health care delivery models for patients with congestive heart failure. In today's care environment, it would be essential for the agency to offer care that is the most effective and efficient. Therefore, this collaborative relationship would reward the researcher and the health care agency.

Case Study 6-1 is an illustration of how a CNR led efforts to use research findings to improve practice.

Emerging Roles

In addition to the CNS and CNR, there are emerging role definitions for those of the clinical nurse leader (CNL) and the doctor of nursing practice (DNP). Because of the sparse literature describing role development outcomes, the concrete research and EBP effect of individuals prepared for these roles is yet to be determined. Given the specified role definitions published by the American Association of Colleges of Nursing (AACN, 2014), the CNL and DNP are potential major contributors to the advancement of nursing research and EBP (AACN, 2014). CNLs use quality improvement methods in evaluating individual and aggregate client care and for self-improvement.

Nurses prepared at the DNP level provide leadership for EBP in nursing and translate evidence-based nursing research in their own practice. They are expected to

CASE STUDY 6-1

Mary, a CNR in a medical center, asks the staff nurses on a pediatric oncology unit to identify patient care problems that need to be investigated. The nurses identify pain control as a major problem for the children admitted to the unit. In talking with the nurses on the unit, Mary discovers that the nurses routinely use physiologic measures, such as heart rate and blood pressure, as indicators of pain. Occasionally, the nurses rely on parents' reports, but rarely do they consult the child. Mary conducts a review of the literature to determine proven ways to assess pain in children. In the *Western Journal of Nursing Research,* Mary discovers a meta-analysis of pediatric pain assessment techniques. Findings from this study indicate that self-report tools are appropriate for most children 4 years and older and provide the most accurate measure of children's pain. Mary discovers a pediatric pain interview tool in the literature that she thinks would be practical and feasible for use on the unit. She then writes a utilization memo to the nurse manager citing the problem (inadequate pain control), the research findings documented in the literature, and a suggestion for change in practice (use of the self-report pain assessment) on the pediatric oncology unit. Next, Mary organizes a meeting with the nurses to discuss conducting a pilot study on the unit for the purpose of comparing the effectiveness of the pediatric pain assessment interview tool and their usual procedures for assessing pain in the pediatric oncology patients. Findings from this study are incorporated into practice by documenting the preferred method of pain assessment in the unit's protocol. The change instituted by the pediatric oncology unit is cited in the medical center's accreditation report as an example of how the medical center is meeting standards of care in pain management.

disseminate and integrate new knowledge. Regardless of the official role definition, nurses at the point of care and nursing division leaders increasingly may be called upon to lead and contribute to collaborative research and EBP initiatives at the health care agency level (Larrabee, 2009a).

About the Evidence

In our current health care environment, it is an expectation that practice decisions made from a foundation of evidence are more likely to be clear, rational, and motivational than those decisions made from the foundation of mere authority. Although research evidence forms the backbone of EBP, other evidence types such as patient values and preferences, expert opinion, theory-based information, evidence-based theories, and compiled database information are usefully included in the evidence pool when clinical conditions are at issue (Fawcett and Garity, 2009; Malloch and Porter-O'Grady, 2010; Melnyk and Fineout-Overholt, 2014). Where care is being delivered to an individual, evidence regarding patient assessment and resource availability must also be considered (Melnyk and Fineout-Overholt, 2014).

Locating Published Research and Evidence Summaries for Evidence-Based Practice

The health care literature is continually and rapidly expanding; the task of keeping up with relevant health care information is daunting for all health care professionals. Strategies to facilitate access to research evidence include formulating a clear and concise clinical question, identifying the research design that would best answer the question, and identifying the most appropriate place to look for studies that answer the question.

Many health care practitioners routinely read clinical practice journals but are unfamiliar with research or EBP journals. Computerized databases have aided the process of locating research and evidence summaries relevant to current practice. These databases typically list article information, provide a short summary, identify key words, and include links to similar articles. CINAHL (Cumulative Index to Nursing and Allied Health Literature) Information Systems is an index of selected journal articles about nursing, allied health, biomedicine, and health care. It is an access point for nurses engaged in literature search (www.ebscohost.com/cinahl). MEDLINE (Medical Literature Analysis and Retrieval System Online) is the most comprehensive online resource for national and international medical literature (U.S. National Library of Medicine, 2014). Multiple other useful databases may be available from academic and health care libraries. These databases consist largely of primary or original research studies as well as guidelines and best practices (National Guidelines Clearinghouse; www.guideline.org).

University and public libraries are one of the major access points to these databases and journals that are available online directly from publishers. Because of online availability, novice users may be tempted to limit searches only to those articles that are available online as full text. *This is a serious mistake that any investigator of published literature should avoid.*

The search for literature should be conducted with the intent of procuring all or most of the current articles appropriate to answer the clinical question. A truly comprehensive reading of the literature may include all articles of current and historical relevance to the topic.

Even though nurses may have access to computerized databases to assist with a literature search, they often are unaware of the journals that are entirely devoted to the publication of research studies and the summaries derived from them. Box 6-3 contains a list of research journals and other health-related journals that publish research and evidence summaries.

Other important sources for locating evidence:
- *Clinical practice guidelines* are systematically developed statements to assist practitioner and patient

decisions about appropriate health care for specific clinical circumstances. In the United Kingdom, the Cochrane Collaboration (www.cochrane.org) is an electronic resource for locating high-quality information quickly. This resource has published hundreds of intervention guidelines based on meta-analyses and research reviews of health care practice areas. These guidelines are mainly medical in nature, but not exclusively so.
- Evidence-based nursing (www.evidencebasednursing.com) selects original studies from more than 100 health care journals and presents critical appraisal and summary in brief abstracts. Because this site only includes articles that reviewers have decided meet basic standards of methodological quality, it has a substantially smaller set of articles than health care literature databases.
- The Internet is a useful source of health care information for both health care professionals and consumers. Although the thousands of sites provide ready access to health care information, the potential for harm from inaccurate information is substantial. As a result, it is important to evaluate the quality of web-based materials on the Internet.

Types and Levels of Evidence

Evidence exists in many forms. Perhaps the most obvious form is the journal article describing a single research study. When a particular topic has been studied extensively, the set of research articles available for knowledge building also may be extensive. Prior to the current disciplinary emphasis on EBP, it would have been the responsibility of the reader of these reports to critique each article and decide which, if any, of the research findings could be used in practice (research utilization). Though this technique of logical narrative summary continues to be somewhat useful, more systematic methods have been developed for synthesizing multiple research reports on a single topic. These systematic review methods include meta-analysis (already referred to in the CNR case study) and meta-synthesis, and other forms.

In a meta-analysis, the findings of multiple quantitative randomized controlled trials (RCTs) studies on a single topic are statistically analyzed to produce a summary statistic. A meta-synthesis takes the findings of multiple qualitative studies on a single topic and synthesizes and amplifies the narrative information contained in the reports. An integrated research review (IRR) takes the findings from experimental and non-experimental studies

---

BOX 6-3   Nursing and Health-Related Journals

Nursing

Advances in Nursing Science
Applied Nursing Research
Biological Research for Nursing
Clinical Nursing Research
Evidence-Based Nursing
International Journal of Nursing Studies
Journal of Nursing Scholarship
Journal of Advanced Nursing
Journal of Transcultural Nursing
Nursing Clinics of North America
Nursing Economics
Nursing Research
Nursing Science Quarterly
Qualitative Health Research
Research in Nursing and Health
Western Journal of Nursing Research
Worldviews on Evidence-Based Nursing

Health

American Journal of Public Health
Hastings Center Report
Health Affairs
Health Care Management Review
Health Services Research
Heart & Lung
Journal of Pain & Palliative Care Pharmacotherapy
International Journal of Evidence-Based Healthcare
Journal of Health Economics
Journal of the American Medical Association
New England Journal of Medicine
Oncology Nursing Forum
Social Science and Medicine

on a single topic and are synthesized to provide a comprehensive understanding of the phenomena. The importance of such reviews is that they represent a meticulous integration of the best evidence available at the time the review was conducted and are considered to provide the highest possible evidence according to evidence hierarchies or levels of evidence (Polit and Beck, 2014). Therefore, individuals or agencies with clinical questions are able to consult well-prepared knowledge syntheses for possible application in the practice arena. Figure 6-1 illustrates an evidence hierarchy based on levels of evidence regarding the effectiveness of interventions and/or findings.

With such an array of evidence types, it is not surprising that evidence is viewed as requiring an assessment of just how strong it is. The terms *evidence hierarchy, levels of evidence,* or *strength of evidence* are used to refer to the categorical classifications that have been proposed to rate evidence along a continuum of best evidence to worst evidence. Most rating schemes rate meta-analyses of well-conducted RCTs as best evidence, with other evidence types sitting lower in the hierarchy (Polit and Beck, 2014). One task of the consumer of evidence is to determine the strength of various evidence types used for making decisions about care and care processes.

Clinical Practice Guidelines

A clinical practice guideline (CPG) is an evidence-based guide to clinical practice developed by experts in a particular field for direct application in clinical environments (Polit and Beck, 2014). Like systematic reviews, guidelines gather, appraise, and combine evidence. Guidelines, however, go beyond systematic reviews in attempting to address all the issues relevant to a clinical decision and all the values that could sway a clinical recommendation. Guidelines make explicit recommendations and in some circumstances may be used to define "standard of care." In

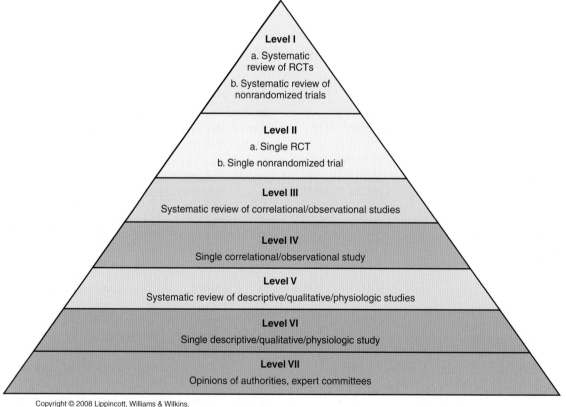

FIGURE 6-1 Quick Guide to an Evidence Hierarchy of Designs for Cause-Probing Questions. (From Polit DE, Beck TC: *Nursing research: Generating and assessing evidence for nursing practice,* Philadelphia, 2011, Lippincott Williams & Wilkins.)

this scenario CPG *may* have legal ramifications. Several court cases have addressed the use of CPGs, but there are no set judicial standards for how these documents may be used and interpreted in individual cases (Moffet and Moore, 2011). This is an evolving discussion because practice guidelines are playing important roles in guiding health care practices. In theory, any professional association, government agency, or health system can produce CPGs: however, practice guidelines are to be researched and driven by evidence. Practice guidelines are based on the consensus of a group of decision makers—ideally experts and front-line clinicians. These groups carefully consider the evidence and decide on the implications therein.

Critical Appraisal

Nurses at all levels of educational preparation should critically read research journal articles and research summary articles. These articles are accepted on a competitive basis and undergo a *blind review* because the reviewers are unaware of who wrote the article. Therefore, readers can assume that experts have scrutinized it for merit and relevance to nursing; however, the reader should critically appraise the findings for validity. This is accomplished through detailed analysis of study design and measurement strategies, and is another layer of evaluation that must be incorporated into appraisal of research evidence for translation. The abstract gives an overview of the study, and the discussion or conclusion provides suggestions for nursing practice based on the findings of the research study. These two sections often are the easiest for the novice to interpret. If sections on methods or statistics are confusing, the reader should consult a CNR to help interpret results.

Pre-appraised evidence such as systematic reviews also require appraisal, but the emphasis is on whether the review provides ample and trustworthy evidence for answering a particular clinical question and the strength of that evidence. The appraisal of various types of research and research summary articles for application to practice is best approached by using defined appraisal guidelines that may be located on the Internet (www.equator-network.org). Careful appraisal may or may not lead one to make a change in practice. If change is implemented, there is an ethical and moral responsibility of the health care provider to evaluate the quality of patient outcomes derived from the change.

Rather than being a simple process of implementing the practice suggestions found at the end of a research report, use of research requires careful and complex analysis, wise implementation, and patient outcome assessment. On the way to becoming seasoned evidence-based nurses, novice nurses should avail themselves of expert guidance from CNRs, CNSs, and other experienced health care professionals. Novice nurses can also develop skills in EBP by reviewing some of the various proposed models for research utilization and EBP.

Clinical practice guidelines can be methodologically weak or strong and thus may yield either valid or invalid recommendations. When considering using a practice guideline as a basis for an agency protocol, or as a guide for providing patient care, health care providers needs to critically assess the credibility, clinical significance, and applicability of the guideline's recommendations. To facilitate the review process there are instruments for appraising the quality of a clinical practice guideline. The Appraisal of Guidelines for Research and Evaluation (AGREE) Instrument is a reliable and valid instrument that evaluates the process of practice guideline development and quality of reporting (Brouwers et al, 2010). AGREE can be accessed at www.agreetrust.org.

Evolution of Evidence-Based Practice: Some Examples

Though much work remains to be done, the potential effect of research on health care knowledge and practice can be demonstrated by two examples.

The use of heparinized saline for flushing capped peripheral intravenous catheters was compared with saline only. Saline only was found to be clinically effective in maintaining patency of peripheral catheters (Goode et al, 1991, 1993) and in neonates (Cook, 2011). As a result of this research, many acute care facilities revised their institutional policies to recommend saline only as a flush for peripheral intravenous catheters.

Pressure ulcers are a significant problem for multiple populations. It should not be surprising that many groups are interested in their prevention and treatment. An online search of the National Guideline Clearinghouse (NGC) yielded multiple clinical guideline statements contributed by groups, public and private, nursing and medical. The national identities of those contributing included New Zealand, Singapore, the United States, and the United Kingdom. In the case of pressure ulcers, a significant amount of research evidence is available for implementing prevention and management strategies.

From these three examples, it can be seen that research evidence can play a significant role in health care practice. However, the process of spreading the "good news" about new or refined practice-related knowledge is a complex one. Researchers must make the knowledge they generate available and understandable. Practitioners must access, interpret, and carefully apply research evidence to the unique contexts presented by individual patients and by patient populations. Different persons and populations need not similarly respond to interventions. Also, there can be honest disagreement among experts about the evidence required to support a practice change. The scientific process may take years to yield enough data to make clinical recommendations and more years to evaluate the effect of evidence-based changes through outcomes research. For instance, peptic ulcer disease was researched for many years before the discovery and acceptance of the presence of *Heliobacter pylori* in the stomach and duodenum (Marshall, 2002). Although these difficulties exist, nursing and other health care disciplines will continue to be held accountable by the public for developing and using the best available evidence for providing health care.

Ethical Issues Related to Research

Institutional Review

In institutional review, a committee called an institutional review board (IRB) or human subjects committee examines research proposals to make sure that the ethical rights of those individuals participating in the research study are protected. Participants must sign an informed consent that explains the study and assures them of their rights, including their right to refuse to participate or to withdraw from the study. Institutions that receive federal funding or conduct drug or medical device research regulated by the U.S. Food and Drug Administration (FDA) are required by federal regulations to establish an IRB. Federally funded studies have to meet strict guidelines to ensure the protection of the human rights of subjects, such as self-determination, privacy, anonymity and confidentiality, fair treatment, and protection from discomfort and harm. The informed consent must include essential study information and statements about potential risks and benefits, protection of anonymity and confidentiality, voluntary participation, compensation, alternative treatment, and specific information on how to contact the investigator (Polit and Beck, 2014).

Historical Examples of Unethical Research

In addition to the institutional review process, a number of codes and regulations have been implemented to ensure ethical conduct in research. The two historical documents are the Nuremberg Code and the Declaration of Helsinki, which were developed in response to unethical acts, such as the Nazi experiments. These experiments occurred in the 1930s and 1940s and included experiments with untested drugs, sterilization, and euthanasia on prisoners of war. These experiments were unethical because they caused grievous harm to the subjects and denied the opportunity to refuse participation (Polit and Beck, 2014).

Another famous incident of unethical research that prompted the need to oversee the conduct of research is the famous Tuskegee syphilis study. This study, which was initiated by the U.S. Public Health Service, continued for 40 years. The study was conducted to determine the natural course of syphilis in African-American men. Many participants were not adequately informed about the purpose and procedures of the study. The subjects periodically were examined but did not receive treatment for syphilis, even after penicillin was determined to be effective. The study was not stopped until 1972, when published reports of the study sparked public outrage (Centers for Disease Control and Prevention, 2014). *Bad Blood* (Jones, 1993), a comprehensive documentary account of the Tuskegee syphilis study, clearly relates the study's adverse effects on research participation by African Americans and on race relations in the United States.

As late as the 1960s, another famous study that violated human rights took place. The Jewish Chronic Disease Hospital in New York was the setting for a study to determine patients' rejection of liver cancer cells. Twenty-two patients were injected with liver cancer cells without being informed that they were taking part in the research. In addition, the physician directing the study did not have institutional approval for a study that had the potential to cause the subject's harm or even death (Murphy, 2004).

In institutions in which IRB approval is not required for non-federally funded programs, the researcher should seek external advice regarding ethical considerations. When IRB approval is an option, researchers should seek it because IRB approval demonstrates scientific rigor to the audience when the research is disseminated either through presentation or publication.

SUMMARY

Educators must prepare health care professionals to have an appreciation of research and to participate in research design implementation and evaluation at the level of their preparation. Practicing nurses of various educational levels actively must seek, develop, and adopt EBP protocols while encouraging affiliated institutions to support this effort. Health care administrators must facilitate an environment that fosters intellectual curiosity and supports research efforts. Collaborative arrangements between health care agencies and universities must be developed for such activities as student projects, continuing education, development of clinical practice guidelines, and research endeavors. Consumers must be educated about the value of health care research, and policymakers must be informed of pertinent findings so that results can be translated into health policy.

REFERENCES

American Association of Colleges of Nursing: *The essentials of doctoral education for advanced nursing practice*, 2014, (website). http://www.aacn.nche.edu/publications/position/DNPEssentials.pdf. Accessed July 23, 2014.

American Association of Colleges of Nursing: *Competencies and curricular expectations for clinical nurse leader education and practice*, 2013, http://www.aacn.nche.edu/publications/white-papers/cnl. Accessed August 27, 2014.

Agency for Healthcare Research and Quality: *AHRQ mission*, 2014a, (website). http://integrationacademy.ahrq.gov/mission. Accessed August 27, 2014.

Agency for Healthcare Research and Quality: *Healthcare innovations exchange*, 2014b, (website). http://www.innovations.ahrq.gov. Accessed May 31, 2014.

Brouwers M, Kho ME, Browman GP, Burgers JS, Cluzeau F, Feder G, Fervers B, Graham ID, Grimshaw J, Hanna S, Littlejohns P, Makarski J, Zitzelsberger L: AGREE II: Advancing guidelines development, reporting and evaluation in healthcare, Can Med Assoc J 182:E839–842, 2010.

Brown S: *Evidence-based nursing: the research-practice connection*, ed 3, Sudbury, MA, 2014, Jones and Bartlett.

Centers for Disease Control and Prevention: *U.S. Public Health Service syphilis study at Tuskegee*, 2011, (website). http://www.cdc.gov/tuskegee/timeline.htm. Accessed July 23, 2014.

CINAHL Information Systems: *Nursing resources from EBESCO* Retrieved from: http://www.ebscohost.com/biomedical=libraies/cinahl-plus=with-full-text. Accessed July 23, 2014.

The Cochrane Collection: *Cochran reviews*, 2014. Retrieved from http:///www.cochrane.org/.

Cook L, Bellini S, Cusson RM: Heparinized saline vs normal saline for maintenance of intravenous access in neonates: an evidence-based practice change, Adv Neonatal Care 11(3):208–215, 2011.

Fawcett J, Garity J: *Evaluating research for evidence-based nursing practice*, Philadelphia, 2009, FA Davis.

Goode CJ, Titler M, Rakel B, et al: A meta-analysis of effects of heparin flush and saline flush: quality and cost implications, Nurs Res 40(6):324–330, 1991.

Goode CJ, Kleiber C, Titler M, et al: Improving practice through research: the case of heparin vs. saline for peripheral intermittent infusion devices, Medsurg Nurs 2(1):23–27, 1993.

Grady, P: Charting future directions in nursing research: NINR's innovative questions initiative, Journal of Nursing Scholarship 46(3):143, 2014.

Houser, J: *Nursing research: Reading, using, and creating evidence*, Burlington, 2015, Jones & Bartlett Learning.

Institute of Medicine: The future of Nursing: Leading change, advancing health. Washington, D.C., 2011, The National Academies Press.

Institute of Medicine: *Report brief: crossing the quality chasm: a new health system for the 21st century*, 2001 (website). https://www.iom.edu/~/media/Files/Report%20Files/2001/Crossing-the-Quality-Chasm/Quality%20Chasm%202001%20%20report%20brief.pdf. Accessed August 27, 2014.

Jones J: *Bad blood: the Tuskegee syphilis experiment*, rev ed, New York, 1993, Free Press.

Larrabee J: *Nurse to nurse: evidence-based practice*, New York, 2009, McGraw-Hill.

Larrabee J: The model for evidence-based practice change, Nurse to nurse: evidence-based practice New York, 2009, McGraw-Hill.

LoBiondo-Wood G, Haber J: *Nursing research: methods and critical appraisal for evidence-based practice*, ed 8, St. Louis, 2014, Elsevier.

Malloch K, Porter-O'Grady T: *Introduction to evidence-based practice in nursing and health care*, ed 2, Sudbury, MA, 2010, Jones and Bartlett.

Marshall, B: The discovery that Heliobacter pylori, a spiral bacterium, caused peptic ulcer disease. In J. Barry & B. Marshall, editors: *Heliobacter pioneers: firsthand accounts from the scientists who discovered heliobacters, 1892–1982*, Oxford, 2002, Blackwell, pp 165–202.

Melnyk BM, Fineout-Overholt E: *Evidence-based practice in nursing and healthcare: a guide to best practice*, ed 3, Philadelphia, 2014, Lippincott Williams & Wilkins.

Murphy TF: *Case studies in biomedical research ethics*, Cambridge, MA, 2004, MIT Press.

National Association of Clinical Nurse Specialists: *Statement on clinical nurse specialists practice and education*, ed 2, http://www.nacns.org/docs/NACNS-statement.pdf. Accessed July 23, 2014.

National Institute of Nursing Research: *NINR strategic plan*, 2013 (website). http://www.ninr.nih.gov/aboutninr/keythemes#.U9AO8vldUxE. Accessed July 23, 2014.

Newhouse RP, Dearholt SL, Poe SS, et al: *Johns Hopkins nursing evidence-based practice model and guidelines*, Indianapolis, 2007, Sigma Theta Tau International.

Polit D, Beck C: *Nursing research: generating and assessing evidence for nursing practice*, ed 8, Philadelphia, 2013, Lippincott Williams & Wilkins.

Prospect Research Online: *iwave information systems,* 2014 (website). www.iwave.com/our-solutions/prospect-research-online. Accessed July 23, 2014.

Rice VH, Stead LF: *Nursing interventions for smoking cessation*, The Cochrane Library Issue 1, Chichester, UK, 2004, John Wiley & Sons, Ltd, Last updated October 21, 2007.

Robert Wood Johnson Foundation: *AbouRWJFus*, 2014a (website). Accessed July 23, 2014.

Robert Wood Johnson Foundation: *What we fund*, 2014b (website). http://www.rwjf.org/en/grants.html#q/maptype/grants/II/37.91,-96.38/z/4. Accessed July 23, 2014.

Shah PS, Ng E, Sinha AK: *Heparin for prolonging peripheral intravenous catheter use in neonates*, The Cochrane Library, Issue 4, Chichester, UK, 2006, John Wiley & Sons, Ltd, Last updated June 1, 2005.

Stetler CB: Refinement of the Stetler/Marram model for the application of research findings to practice, Nurs Outlook 42(1):15–25, 1994.

Titler MG, Kleiber C, Steelman VJ, et al: The Iowa model of evidence-based practice to promote quality care, Crit Care Nurs Clin North Am 13(4):497–509, 2001.

U.S. National Library of Medicine: *Fact sheet MEDLINE*, 2014 (website). http://www.nlm.nih.gov/pubs/factsheets/medline.html. Accessed July 23, 2014.

White CL: Nurse champions: a key role in bridging the gap between research and practice, J Emerg Nurs 37(4):386–387, 2011.

Wise, N.J: Maintaining magnet status: Establishing an evidenced-based practice committee, AORN Journal, 90(2), 205–213, 2009. Doi:10.1016/j.aorn.2009.02.016.

WK Kellogg Foundation: *Grantseekers*, 2014 (website). http://www.wkkf.org/grantseekers. Accessed July 23, 2014.

7

There is a tug of war for the shrinking health care dollar

Paying for Health Care in America: Rising Costs and Challenges

Marylane Wade Koch, MSN, RN

ⓔ Additional resources are available online at: *http://evolve.elsevier.com/Cherry/*

PROFESSIONAL/ETHICAL ISSUE

Susan and Matt Taylor have a 2-year-old daughter, Carmen. Susan worked full time as a nurse in a local clinic until Carmen was born. So far, the Taylors have been able to budget for Susan to work only one day a week so she can stay home and care for Carmen. They downsized to a smaller home and adjusted their spending to address the changes in the economy and rising costs of basic living such as food, gas, and utilities.

The Taylors have health insurance through Matt's employer, a small local business. The premiums and co-pays have increased over the past few years, stressing their tight budget, but they noticed a larger increase in early 2014. Friends and family say that this is due to changes in the insurance market created by the 2014 implementation of the Patient Protection and Affordable Care Act (PPACA).

The Taylors believe that all people should have access to quality health care, and that the PPACA is a major step in the right direction for universal insurance for all American citizens. As a nurse, Susan has been an advocate for those who needed care, with or without insurance. However, the Taylors question why their insurance costs have been affected by the PPACA implementation. Susan did not anticipate that this program might affect her personally, and she is struggling with many questions. Is it fair that the Taylors lifestyle should be affected by these changes? How will the PPACA affect the future of small businesses like Matt's employer? Will Susan need to work more outside the home to cover the additional expenses? Should the Taylors look for a less expensive insurance alternative?

VIGNETTE

As a home care nurse for many years, Callie Thompson's patients were primarily older adults. Knowledge of Medicare coverage guidelines for service was critical to the financial success of the home care agency. Today, in the home care agency, she cares for patients of all ages with varying reimbursement guidelines. These guidelines, which affect the types of services she provides for her patients, differ among managed care organizations (MCOs), government-provided coverage, and insurance companies. When she first took this job, understanding Medicare coverage guidelines was a new challenge. Now even more is required. Callie knows that today's nurse needs extensive knowledge of health care reimbursement guidelines and the economic influences on professional practice to provide quality patient care.

Questions To Consider While Reading this Chapter:

1. Often the role of the professional nurse is influenced by the employer's ability to pay for the costs associated with staffing and providing quality health care services. Is this likely to continue in today's evolving health care environment?

2. What does health care economics and finance have to do with me as I provide patient care?

3. Why do I need to understand health care economics and its implications for my practice? Is that not the role of the finance department or business office at my workplace?

4. With so many variations in health care insurance, I have a hard time understanding my own policy coverage. What role do I have in assisting my patients in understanding their insurance or coverage options? Can being a more informed consumer add value to my practice?

KEY TERMS

Capitation: A method of reimbursing providers (usually primary care providers, such as physicians or nurse practitioners) in which the insurance company pays the provider a set payment each month to provide a defined set of health care services for the patient enrolled in the insurance company's health plan. The payment is typically expressed as a per-member-per-month payment. The defined health care services generally include preventive, diagnostic, and treatment services.

Centers for Medicare & Medicaid Services (CMS): The federal government agency that administers Medicare and Medicaid.

DRGs (diagnosis-related groups): A common method of reimbursement for health care services based on a predetermined fixed price-per-case or diagnosis.

Effectiveness: Production of a desired outcome; taking the right action to achieve the expected result.

Efficiency: The extent to which resources, such as energy, time, and money, are used to produce the intended result.

GDP (gross domestic product): The measure of the total value of goods and services produced within a country; the most comprehensive overall measure of economic output; provides key insight to the driving forces of the economy.

Health Insurance Exchange: Also known as the "Health Insurance Marketplace," an online marketplace for individuals to shop for and purchase health insurance at affordable rates and to identify whether they qualify for cost assistance subsidies to help pay the cost of the insurance; states established health insurance exchanges as a component of the Patient Protection and Affordable Care Act to provide access to affordable health insurance options for American citizens.

Marginal: An economic term that refers to a small or insignificant change in some variable (e.g., the number of medical tests performed).

Medicaid: A jointly sponsored state and federal program that pays for medical services for persons who are elderly, poor, blind, or disabled and for certain families with dependent children who meet specified income guidelines.

Medicare: A federally funded health insurance program for the disabled, persons with end-stage renal disease, and persons 65 years of age and older who qualify for Social Security benefits.

Patient Protection and Affordable Care Act (PPACA): A federal statute enacted in 2010 that requires U.S. citizens and legal residents to have health insurance through comprehensive health care reform; expands health care coverage access to millions of people who were previously uninsured (Kaiser Family Foundation, 2013).

Private health insurance: A method for individuals to maintain insurance coverage for health care costs through a contract with a health insurance company that agrees to pay all or a portion of the cost of a set of defined health care services such as routine, preventive, and emergency health care; hospitalizations; medical procedures; and/or prescription drugs. Typically, the private insurance is provided through an individual's employer with a portion of the cost paid by the employer and a portion paid by the employee. Private insurance policies can also be purchased by individuals but are generally much more expensive than when provided through an employer's group plan.

Prospective payment system: A method of reimbursing health care providers (e.g., physicians, hospitals) in which the total amount of payment for care is predetermined based on the patient's diagnosis; provides for a "set price per diagnosis" payment system; encourages increased efficiency in the use of health care services because providers are reimbursed at a predetermined level regardless of how many services are rendered or procedures performed to treat a particular diagnostic category; the most common method of payment in today's health care system.

Provider: A licensed health care professional (such as a physician or nurse practitioner) or an organization (such as a hospital) that receives reimbursement for providing health care services.

Retrospective payment system: A method of reimbursing health care providers (e.g., physicians, hospitals) in which professional services are rendered and charges are billed based on each individual service provided; also known as the "fee-for-service" payment system. This system may encourage overuse of health care services because the more services rendered or procedures performed, the more revenue received by providers.

Single payer system: A method of reimbursement in which one payer, usually the government, pays all health care expenses for citizens, funded by taxes; decisions about covered treatments, drugs, and services are made by the government. Though the terms universal health care and single payer system are sometimes used interchangeably, universal health care could be administered by many different payer groups; both offer all citizens health insurance coverage.

Third-party payer: An organization other than the patient and the provider (e.g., hospital, physician, nurse practitioner), such as an insurance company, that assumes responsibility for payment of health care charges. An individual's health insurance plan provided by his or her employer is considered a third-party payer.

LEARNING OUTCOMES

After studying this chapter, the reader will be able to:

1. Analyze major factors that have influenced health care access and financing since the middle of the twentieth century.
2. Integrate knowledge of health care resources, access, and financing into managing professional nursing care.
3. Critique the relationship between contemporary economic issues and trends and professional nursing practice.
4. Discuss the implications of the Patient Protection and Affordable Care Act (PPACA) for nursing and health care.

CHAPTER OVERVIEW

In the past several decades, the costs of health care have continued to increase, with economic issues taking a central role in health care decision making. Hospital managers know that for most patients the hospital will receive a predetermined payment, regardless of length of stay and specific treatments. Physicians and nurse practitioners *recognize that the prescribed course of treatment for their patients may be analyzed by a peer review committee; the costs their patients incur may be compared with those of other providers or against cost benchmarks. Businesses require employees to cover larger amounts of their health insurance premiums and/or pay larger deductibles and copayments. Health insurance companies "manage" care, sometimes placing limits on medical care coverage, providers in the network, or on the site of care delivery. The Patient Protection and Affordable Care Act (PPACA) of 2010 added a new dimension to health care financing with comprehensive health care reform and various insurance options for universal coverage of American citizens. These practices are the result of the evolving economics and rising costs of health care.*

The objective of this chapter is to provide an overview of the major economic issues and trends driving changes in health care delivery, how health care is paid for, and how these issues affect nursing practice. The chapter presents information about historical trends in health care finance, the problem of the uninsured and underinsured, allocation of health care resources, methods of paying for health care, the implications of the PPACA, and the effect of health care finance on professional nursing practice.

HISTORY OF HEALTH CARE FINANCING

The high costs of health care did not occur overnight. To understand current health care financing, it is necessary to understand its history (Table 7-1). Historically, several underlying themes have driven health care financing in the United States. Among these are the following:

- The physician's role as being primarily responsible for health care decision making
- The broad objective of providing the "best" possible care to everyone
- The rapidly increasing sophistication and cost of medical technology
- Economic incentives and the fee-for-service payment method that encouraged overuse of health care services

For many years, physician domination in decision making and the fee-for-service payment method were intertwined and contributed to the lack of cost consciousness in health care. Physicians made all decisions about what health care services were needed; costs were rarely discussed between physician and patient, so the cost of care was not considered until bill-paying time. Medical tests or procedures were provided if the physician determined that they offered even marginal aid or diagnostic information.

Beginning in the 1960s, the attitude that "if it might help, do it" flourished as the rapid pace of sophisticated technologies enhanced physicians' abilities to provide treatment. The more tests or procedures physicians performed, the greater their earnings because physicians were paid according to the number of procedures performed or services provided. Instead of attempting to allocate medical resources to the highest medical need, the financial incentive was to provide as much care as possible using the most technically advanced methods of care. Overuse of health services and rapid cost inflation resulted.

Yet consumers of health care remained insulated from cost inflation. Most patients had some form of insurance or third-party payment and did not pay the full cost for their care or even for their health insurance premiums. The full cost of care remained hidden from consumers because costs were subsidized by employers or by taxpayers through such programs as Medicare and Medicaid. Providers had little incentive to contain costs, so the demand for medical care generated "perverse" economic incentives in which providers received more income for using more services with no financial risk for their use of additional resources.

These perverse economic incentives had a drastic effect on the Medicare program. Medicare was established by the U.S. Congress in 1965 to provide health insurance coverage for persons 65 years of age and older who are eligible for Social Security benefits, persons with end-stage renal disease, and the eligible disabled population. By the early 1980s, increased medical usage (increased intensity of care) and high inflation combined with a growing older adult population generated substantial increases in Medicare costs. The rapid growth of Medicare expenditures became a major factor in the federal budget deficit, causing the Centers for Medicare & Medicaid Services (CMS) to rethink the entire Medicare payment system. This led to a revolution in how the government and private insurance companies paid for health care.

Health Care Financing Revolution of the 1980s

The rising cost of health care over the last 40 years is a dangerous trend that poses a significant threat to the U.S.

TABLE 7-1	**Historical Highlights of Health Care Finance**
1847	Massachusetts Health Insurance of Boston offers a group policy.
1861 to 1865	Insurance plans become available during the Civil War.
1890	Individual disability and/or illness policies become available.
1929	First group health coverage is offered for a monthly charge; teachers in Dallas, Texas, contract with Baylor Hospital. This is the beginning of Blue Cross/Blue Shield insurance.
1932	Blue Cross insurance forms.
1934	Hospitals receive payment through Blue Cross, a prepaid health insurance plan to protect hospitals during the Great Depression.
1945	Blue Cross captures 50% of the insurance market.
1946	California Physician Service ensures physician payment through Blue Shield plans.
1950s	Employee benefit packages are initiated to attract workers.
1954	Government disability program with Social Security coverage becomes available.
1965	Medicare and Medicaid programs are created, making comprehensive health care available to millions of Americans.
1977	Health Care Financing Administration (HCFA) is created to manage Medicare and Medicaid separately from the Social Security Administration.
1980 to 1990	Managed care plans emerge.
1983	Hospitals come under diagnosis-related groups (DRGs).
2001 to 2003	The Centers for Medicare & Medicaid Services is created, replacing the HCFA.
2003	Enactment of the Medicare Prescription Drug Improvement and Modernization Act of 2003, the most significant expansion of Medicare since its enactment, including a prescription drug benefit.
2006	Blue Cross/Blue Shield plans cover more than 94 million (1 in 3) Americans. Pay-for-performance is introduced as a model of reimbursement for health care services.
2010	Enactment of the Patient Protection and Affordable Care Act, comprehensive health care reform for universal coverage of Americans. Implementation is scheduled to occur over several years from 2010-2018.

economy. In 1965, annual health care expenditures in the United States were $202 per person; in 2012, the national health expenditures had risen to $8915 per person. Total health care spending increased from $1.3 trillion in 2000 to $2.8 trillion in 2012. National health expenditures as a percentage of the gross domestic product (GDP) was 17.2% in 2012, and is projected to be 19.3% by 2023 (CMS, 2014a). This means for every dollar a person spends buying products or services in the United States, over 17 cents goes to pay for health care. In contrast, health care spending in 2013 in neighboring Canada was expected to reach an all-time high of $21 billion, or $5988 per person, with a health care GDP of 11.2% (Canadian Institute for Health Information, 2013).

To control rapidly rising health care costs, a health care financing revolution began in 1983, when Medicare moved from a retrospective (fee-for-service) reimbursement to a prospective payment system (PPS) based on diagnosis-related groups (DRGs). This shift was critical for hospitals because Medicare is the largest single payer of hospital charges. Under DRGs, each Medicare patient is assigned to a diagnostic grouping based on his or her primary diagnosis at hospital admission. Medicare limits total payment to the hospital to the amount pre-established for that DRG, unlike the previous approach in which hospital patients incurred costs and Medicare reimbursed these charges with a generous payment schedule.

Since 1983, if hospital costs exceed the DRG payment for a patient's treatment, the hospital incurs a loss, but if costs are less than the DRG amount, the hospital makes a profit. Thus, hospitals face a strong financial incentive to reduce the patient's length of stay and minimize procedures performed. Although DRGs originally applied only to hospital payments for Medicare patients, similar reimbursement arrangements were initiated by private insurance companies.

Implementation of the DRG system expanded the role of hospital management, including nurse administrators. First, financial gains were made from careful diagnosis of patients according to their highest potential

DRG classification. Hospital-based utilization management nurses reviewed medical records to determine the most appropriate DRG for patients. Second, hospital record keeping and accounting methodologies were revolutionized by specific Medicare cost accounting procedures. Experienced nurses with business knowledge brought needed technical background and skills to these new accounting and utilization management tasks, expanding opportunities for nurse managers and nurse administrators.

The Development of Managed Care

With the shift to prospective payment under Medicare, private insurance companies followed Medicare's lead and developed managed care. Managed care organizations (MCOs) encompass several different approaches, such as health maintenance organizations (HMOs), preferred provider organizations (PPOs), and point-of-service (POS) plans (Table 7-2). The primary commonality among each of these health plans is that they use some method to review and provide oversight for the use of

TABLE 7-2 **Common Types of Health Insurance Plans in America**	
Fee-for-service (FFS)/ indemnity plan	Member (covered individual) pays a premium for a fixed percentage of expenses covered
	Includes deductible and copayment
	Allows member to choose physician and specialists without restraint
	May only cover usual or reasonable and customary charges for treatment and services, with member responsible for charges above that payment
	May or may not pay for preventive care
PPO (preferred provider organization)	Member (covered individual) pays a premium for a fixed percentage of expense covered
	Includes deductible and copayment
	Member may select physician, but pays less for physicians and facilities on the plan's preferred list
	May or may not pay for preventive care
POS (point of service)	Offered by HMO or FFS
	Allows use of providers outside the plan's preferred list or network, but requires higher premiums and copayments for services
HMO (health maintenance organization)	Member (covered individual) pays a premium
	Has a fixed copayment
	Member must select a primary care physician approved by the HMO
	Member must be referred for treatments, specialists, and services by the primary care physician
	Services outside of "network" must be preapproved for payment
	Plan may refuse to pay for services not recommended by primary care physician
	Encourages use of preventive care
Medicare	Federal health insurance plan for Americans 65 years of age and older and certain disabled persons.
	Member must be eligible for Social Security or railroad retirement
	Part A covers hospital stays and care in skilled nursing facilities (does not cover long-term care)
	Part B requires payment of a premium and covers physician services and supplies
	Carries a prescription drug benefit
Medicaid	Health care coverage for low-income persons who are aged, blind, disabled, or for certain families with dependent children
	Federal program is delivered and managed by each state for eligibility and scope of services offered
	Covers long-term care (i.e., nursing home care) for qualifying individuals
TRICARE: military health insurance (formerly CHAMPUS)	Civilian health and medical health insurance program for military, spouses, dependents, and beneficiaries
	Program offered through Military Health Services System

health care services. In this review process, the patient's medical options are reviewed by a nurse or physician employed by the health insurance company, and a judgment is made as to the necessity of the service being considered. Coverage may be denied for unnecessary, excessive, or experimental procedures, in strong contrast to the previous "if it might help, do it" approach. The goal of managed care is to minimize payment of charges for inappropriate or excessive health care services.

As health care costs rise, the costs for businesses to provide health insurance for employees also rises; these increasing costs are then passed to consumers by increasing the price of the products or services produced by the business. However, health care costs have led to a situation in which U.S. businesses struggle to compete in an international market, where health care costs are significantly lower. Large businesses, such as automobile manufacturers, pushed health insurance companies to decrease the rising costs of health insurance premiums, which led to a move from conventional insurance plans to MCOs. The overall goal of these types of managed care plans is to limit unnecessary health care services and to use the least expensive service when care is needed.

TABLE 7-3 What Health Care Costs	
Typical adult physician office visit	$130-$180
Adult routine physical	$200-$240
Adult emergency room visit	$580-$700
Child office visit	$115-$160
Magnetic resonance imaging (MRI)	$500-$1300
Vaginal delivery of a baby	$9800-$11,000
Cesarean section	$11,500-$12,700
Cardiac catheterization	$6810
Total knee replacement	$22,720
Coronary angioplasty	$19,407
Coronary artery bypass grafting surgery	$39,407
Bone marrow transplant	Autologous $75,000-150,000 Allogeneic $150,000-300,000

Sources:
http://www.bluecrossma.com/blue-iq/pdfs/TypicalCosts_89717_042709.pdf
https://www.healthcarebluebook.com/page_ProcedureDetails.aspx?id=196&dataset=MD
http://nbmtlink.org/resources_support/faq/faq_question8.html

ACCESS TO HEALTH CARE—THE PROBLEM OF THE UNINSURED AND UNDERINSURED

As health care costs continue to rise dramatically in the United States, one major issue that must be addressed is access to health care for the uninsured or underinsured. Prior to the passage of the Patient Protection and Affordable Care Act (PPACA) in 2010, lack of access to health care primarily reflected a lack of insurance coverage, so access was an issue of financial access. The uninsured and underinsured included the working poor employed by small firms without insurance coverage, part-time workers, unemployed persons, and the homeless. The poor are more likely to lack a usual source of care, less likely to use preventive services, and more likely to be hospitalized for avoidable conditions than those who are not poor. See Table 7-3 for the average costs of some health care services and consider these costs in light of a family with an annual income of $25,000 and no health insurance.

The uninsured and underinsured populations generate uncompensated or indigent care costs and bad debt for health care providers. Unpaid costs must be covered by those who do pay so the hospital can continue operating; a process known as *cost shifting*. Providers increase their charges against households and public and private insurers who pay for care to make a contribution for the care of the uninsured population. This increases insurance premiums, making it even more difficult for many households and businesses to afford coverage. The problem of uncompensated care and cost shifting was a major factor leading to health care reform and the passage of the PPACA in 2010.

In 2013, the percentage of the population without health insurance for the entire calendar year was 13.4 percent, or 42.0 million people (U.S. Census Bureau, 2014). In early 2014, "affordable" health insurance became available to the public though health insurance exchanges (also known as the "health insurance marketplace") as a component of the PPACA. As of April 2014, insurance coverage has increased as a result of the PPACA in the following ways (White House, 2014):

- 7.1 million Americans enrolled in a health insurance plan through the PPACA health insurance marketplace

- Approximately 3 million Americans under the age of 26 are now covered under their parents' health insurance plans
- Possibly millions more individuals are covered as a result of expanding Medicaid coverage in many states

Medicaid, a federal health insurance program administered by each state, is intended to improve access to health care for the poor, covering approximately 50.9 million people in 2013 (U.S. Census Bureau, 2013). The PPACA expanded federal Medicaid support to any state that accepted this assistance, allowing those states to increase the number of people who meet the qualifications for Medicaid. Currently, about half of the states in the United States have expanded their Medicaid programs with federal support from the PPACA. The true impact of the PPACA on the percent of the uninsured population remains to be seen and is certainly worth tracking over the next few years! The following section provides a more detailed discussion about the PPACA.

THE PATIENT PROTECTION AND AFFORDABLE CARE ACT

On March 23, 2010, President Barak Obama signed into law the Patient Protection and Affordable Care Act (PPACA) (Public Law 111-148). This comprehensive health care reform plan was designed to expand health insurance coverage to uninsured Americans while controlling costs and improving the quality of health care. In its broadest view, the PPACA is the plan for a comprehensive national health insurance program to provide funding for U.S. citizens and legal residents to secure health insurance beyond the current programs such as Medicare and Medicaid while also providing for provisions to improve the quality of health care and reduce costs. Some key components of the PPACA include the following (Kaiser Family Foundation, 2013):

- Requires U.S. citizens and legal residents to have a qualifying health insurance coverage, or else pay a penalty
- Provides individuals and families at 133% to 400% of the federal poverty level with financial assistance to help make health insurance more affordable
- Requires employers with more than 200 employees to offer health insurance

- Creates state-based health insurance exchanges where individuals and small businesses can purchase qualified coverage at more affordable rates
- Creates a required benefits package for the health insurance plan to be deemed "qualifying health insurance coverage": ambulatory patient services, emergency services, hospitalizations, maternity and newborn care, mental health and substance abuse treatment, prescription drugs, rehabilitative services, laboratory services, preventive and wellness services, chronic disease management, and pediatric services to include vision and oral care
- Eliminates pre-existing condition barriers and annual and lifetime caps to insurance plans
- Provides dependent coverage for children up to age 26 for all individual and group policies
- Requires insurance companies to spend 80% of premiums on medical care, which forces insurance companies to reduce their administrative expenses
- Reduces Medicare payments to some hospitals for hospital-acquired conditions (e.g., falls, decubitus ulcers, infections)
- Establishes the hospital value-based purchasing program in which hospitals are paid based on their performance on quality measures including patient satisfaction
- Reduces Medicare payments to hospitals for preventable hospital readmissions

For a comprehensive summary of the PPACA, visit the Kaiser Family Foundation website at www.kff.org and select Health Reform.

Although the PPACA will take about 10 years to be fully implemented, the Congressional Budget Office (CBO) claims that about 32 million more people will be covered by health insurance by 2019. The full impact of health insurance requirements and costs to individuals, small businesses, and even large employers will not be realized for several years. Additionally, the impact on improving quality and reducing costs as a result of provisions in the PPACA will likely not be fully evident for years to come. Regardless, the PPACA represents the first major effort to reform the U.S. health care system by expanding health insurance coverage to uninsured populations and, just as important, slowing unsustainable health care costs, improving quality, and moving health care to a focus on prevention and population health rather than acute illness treatment.

HOW HEALTH CARE IS PAID

A combination of private and public sources pays for health care services and supplies for individuals in the United States. Most individual health care is paid either by households through direct out-of-pocket payments or by third-party public or private insurers (Table 7-4). Third-party payers include private insurance companies and government health programs, such as Medicare, Medicaid, and the Veterans Administration health system.

Private Insurance

Private insurance accounts for the largest percentage of coverage for health care, with the cost of providing health insurance to employees passed on by the employer to the consumer in the pricing of goods and services. This means that everyone pays a part of the country's health care costs in every purchase made. Individuals still must pay a portion of their health care costs directly from their own pockets, through payments for insurance premiums, deductibles, and copayments.

With managed care products, such as HMOs, PPOs, and POS arrangements, the premium the consumer pays for coverage has continued to rise. In response to these concerns, some companies now offer their employees high-deductible health plans (HDHPs), health reimbursement accounts (HRAs), health savings accounts (HSAs), or a combination of these. These plans offer more flexibility and consumer discretion over their health care dollars and provides a tax-free way to save for future health care needs. These programs may

TABLE 7-4 Health Insurance Coverage in America (2013)

People with health insurance	86.6% of the U.S. population
People without health insurance	13.4% of the U.S. population
Children younger than 19 years of age without health insurance	7.6% of children
People covered by employer insurance plans	53.9% of the U.S. population
People with government insurance	34.3% of the U.S. population (17.3% Medicaid; 15.6% Medicare, other military)

From U.S. Census Bureau: http://www.census.gov/library/publications/2014/demo/p60-250.html

change as the PPACA implementation progresses in the coming years.

Public Insurance: Medicare and Medicaid

Government is the biggest influence in the health insurance market, generating half of hospital revenues and more than one fourth of physician incomes. The largest health insurance program is Medicare. Since its enactment by the federal government in 1965, the population covered by Medicare has doubled. Medicare is an entitlement program based on age or disability criteria, rather than on need. Medicare Part A covers inpatient hospital services, skilled nursing facilities (SNFs), and home health benefits; Medicare does not cover long-term care. Hospital coverage has deductible and coinsurance requirements and some coverage limitations. Medicare Part B covers physician and outpatient services. In January 2006, Medicare added access to a prescription medication benefit, a noted and costly change from previous benefits.

Medicaid is a joint federal-state program to provide health insurance coverage for impoverished families, particularly those with children. Medicaid, along with the Children's Health Insurance Program (CHIP), offers health coverage to almost 60 million Americans. Those eligible for health care services include pregnant women, children and parents, persons with disabilities, and seniors who meet certain income criteria. Each state administers its own Medicaid program within minimal federal income guidelines, so some variances can occur from state to state. The PPACA expanded the minimum income levels for Medicaid eligibility for those under 65 years of age, effective January 1, 2014. However, according to the 2012 Supreme Court ruling on the PPACA, states have the right to opt out of offering the expanded Medicaid coverage. Medicaid is a primary payer of long-term care nationwide. For most states, Medicaid represents the fastest-growing component in the state budget.

Effect of Payment Modes

Various methods of reimbursing providers for health care services have emerged because of rapid growth in health care costs combined with concerns about the safety and quality of health care and implementation of the PPACA. Hospitals can now be rewarded for achieving improved health outcomes and will not be paid for certain medical errors. Payment approaches such as pay-for-performance, "never events," value-based purchasing, and readmission reduction programs focus on aligning reimbursement with patient outcomes. Nurses are at the center of helping hospitals and other health care organizations successfully manage these new payment mechanisms by ensuring that errors are prevented, health outcomes are achieved, and financial rewards are realized.

Pay-for-Performance

Medicare and private insurance companies have shown success with various methods of reimbursing providers based on the quality of care provided with an emphasis on prevention and reducing complications from chronic diseases. Such programs, known as *pay-for-performance,* or *P4P,* provide financial and nonfinancial incentives to promote high-quality care. Hospitals and other providers are rewarded for meeting standards of care for certain conditions such as diabetes, myocardial infarction, pneumonia, and heart failure. The Agency for Healthcare Research and Quality (AHRQ) supports P4P as a way to benchmark and find what does and does not work. Continued research into the value and effectiveness of P4P payment methods is needed as recent studies have raised questions about the comprehensive effectiveness of the P4P approach (Carroll, 2014).

Never Events

To save lives and millions of dollars, Medicare adopted a policy effective October 1, 2008, that it will no longer pay hospitals for the extra costs of treating preventable errors. Commonly referred to as *never events,* Medicare will no longer pay hospitals for the cost of treating medical errors that are largely preventable and have serious consequences for patients. The purpose of the never events payment policy is to eliminate payments for certain medical errors and encourage hospitals to direct resources to preventing errors rather than being paid for them. Never events include hospital-acquired infections, injuries from falls, wrong-site surgery, and mismatched blood transfusions. Nurses have a highly visible and important role to play in preventing such complications and helping to control costs for hospitals.

Value-Based Purchasing

Value-based purchasing (VPB) is CMS reimbursement that rewards inpatient hospitals for providing quality care to include patient satisfaction. The incentives for VBP are based on two domains: (1) the patient experience of care and (2) clinical processes of care. The patient experience of care is based on the hospital's scores on the Hospital Consumer Assessment of Healthcare Providers and Systems (HCAHPS), which is essentially a standardized patient satisfaction survey (see Box 7-1). Clinical process of care measures include such items as discharge instructions for heart failure patients, fibrinolytic therapy received with 30 minutes of hospital arrival for a patient with acute myocardial infarction, and prophylactic antibiotic received within 1 hour prior to surgical incision. In addition to affecting hospital reimbursement, data from the VBP program is used to provide information to the public about hospital quality. Visit the CMS Hospital Compare website at www.medicare.gov/hospitalcompare to learn more about how quality measures are reported to the public. As the reader can easily see, nurses are at the center of addressing the clinical processes of care and the patient experience to enhance the hospital's VBP financial rewards and also its publicly available quality indicators.

Reducing Readmissions

A provision of the PPACA established the *Hospital Readmissions Reduction Program,* which reduces Medicare payments to hospitals with excessive readmissions. A readmission is defined as admission to a hospital within 30 days of a discharge from the same or another hospital (CMS, 2014b). The provision is currently focused on readmissions for acute myocardial infarction, heart failure, pneumonia, chronic obstructive pulmonary disease, total hip arthroplasty, and total knee arthroplasty. Nurses caring for patients with these conditions have a highly important role to ensure effective discharge planning and education so the patient and family are fully prepared to recover at home. New roles for nurses as patient care navigators and transition care providers are

---

BOX 7-1   Components of the HCAHPS Patient Experience Survey

HCAHPS: Hospital Consumer Assessment of Healthcare Providers and Systems
- Communication with nurses
- Communication with doctors
- Responsiveness of hospital staff
- Pain management
- Communication about medicines
- Cleanliness and quietness of hospital environment
- Discharge information
- Overall rating of hospital

rapidly emerging both in community settings and as part of the hospital's services to prevent readmissions. Just as with P4P, never events, and VBP, nurses are again at the center of preventing readmissions and preventing costly financial penalties to the hospital.

IMPLICATIONS FOR NURSES: MANAGING COST-EFFECTIVE, HIGH-QUALITY CARE

Nurses represent a major professional force in the delivery of health care services in the United States and are essential to the delivery of high-quality and efficient health care (Needleman and Hassmiller, 2009). Never has there been greater opportunity to advance the practice of professional nursing and affect health care financial reimbursement. Innovation and excellence in all nursing practice are needed to contain costs while attaining positive, measurable outcomes. As the reader can see from the various methods of reimbursement discussed earlier, nurses are at the center of ensuring positive patient outcomes, maximizing reimbursement and decreasing financial penalties for errors and readmissions. Every setting in which professional nurses practice holds challenges in providing and managing care that is efficient, affordable, and of high quality. Box 7-2 summarizes the trends occurring in health care that affect professional nurses. These trends mandate that nurses have a clear understanding of the economic and financing issues underlying the continually developing roles of nurses.

Care Coordination

One key to improve quality and reduce costs is to ensure health care is coordinated in order to decrease duplication of services and reduce wasted resources. Effective care coordination requires the use of case management and other emerging practice models, such as patient care navigators and transition care coordinators, all with the same goal: to ensure care is delivered in the community through home care, outpatient clinics, and ambulatory care centers at less costly rates and to decrease more expensive hospital-based care. Nurses as care coordinators, case managers, patient care navigators, or transition care coordinators demonstrate cost-effectiveness by ensuring that patients have the resources they need to get effective treatment at the appropriate level of care across the continuum of care.

Expansion of Technology

Improved technology for diagnostic and therapeutic practice is under examination for cost-efficiency versus outcome delivery. Leaders must balance the health contributions of the improved technology and the accompanying costs with issues of quality of life, access to care, risk-benefit analysis, and individual consumer choice.

U.S. consumers have had access to high levels of technology with little concern for costs. Nurses are key players in educating patients and their family members about the cost-to-benefit ratio of certain technologies and can assist in selecting alternative treatment options. One example is found in the increased use of pharmaceuticals; more advanced drugs are marketed with varying degrees of actual documented benefit versus existing, less-expensive drugs. Patients may not trust generic drugs, although they are less expensive. The nurse can be a link to educating patients and the public regarding the potential and implications of using a less expensive drug instead of a more expensive alternative.

BOX 7-2   Economic Issues and Trends

From		To
Illness emphasis	→	Preventive emphasis
Acute care	→	Preventive care, home care
Hospital or institution based	→	Noninstitution based (clinic or home)
Fee-for-service (cost based)	→	Prospective payment and managed care
Physician directed	→	Diverse decision makers and managed care
If it might help, use it	→	Outcomes measurement and cost effectiveness
Independent decisions (practice variation)	→	Protocols and guidelines (best practice)
Local perspective (practice variation, standards, and benchmarking)	→	Global perspective (protocols/guidelines/practice)
Introduction of new technologies (regardless of cost)	→	Outcomes measurement and cost effectiveness
Paper records, medical charts	→	Information systems, computer records

The technology of the Internet offers promise for information and education that allows consumers (or patients) to access health care resources more effectively. Some health care plans offer subscribers free newsletters that highlight ways to prevent disease and to manage chronic illness for improved quality of life and lower costs.

Information technology provides the professional nurse the ability to gather and analyze health-related information and data for improved care. Health care information systems and electronic health records offer many opportunities for managing health care costs. Combining clinical skills with information technology skills can provide a significant advantage to the success of professional nurses because they demonstrate their ability to provide cost-effective outcomes measurement. See Chapter 15 for a more detailed discussion of information technology in the clinical setting.

Consumer Empowerment

Health care customers demand quality health care services at affordable rates. Economic forces motivate the shift toward health promotion and preventive care to achieve cost-effectiveness. This relationship with the consumer emphasizes cost sharing through individual choices in health practices. For instance, the presence of unhealthy personal practices, such as smoking, illegal drug use, or sedentary lifestyle, may lead to a higher insurance rate for an individual. Smokers may pay higher rates and have to be smoke-free for 1 year to qualify for lower rates. Being overweight may cost the subscriber more in premiums because this poses additional health concerns and potential increased health costs. See Box 7-3 for ways to help consumers reduce their health care costs.

BOX 7-3   Ways to Reduce Health Care Costs as a Consumer

- Take good care of yourself. Manage minor illnesses yourself at home.
- Use the Internet to learn more about your health and preventing disease.
- Recognize early warning signs of disease and get prompt treatment from your health care provider.
- Practice preventive health with health screenings and routine self-examinations. Take advantage of free screenings offered at community sites, hospitals, or churches.
- Develop an active relationship with health care providers to improve communication. Ask providers to explain the purpose of all prescribed tests and medications. Become an informed consumer.
- Use emergency care only in emergencies. See your health care provider during office hours.
- Know health risks for lifestyle choices, such as alcohol and drug use, dietary habits, sedentary behaviors, and safety at home and while driving.
- Understand and use the health care benefits of your insurance plan to stay healthy. Take advantage of all preventive benefits offered.
- Choose nonhospital alternatives for treatment whenever possible. Take a conservative approach to health care. Comparison shop for health care alternatives.
- Choose generic drugs whenever possible. Ask your health care provider to prescribe the least expensive drugs that will provide positive outcomes.
- Review your health care bills carefully, and notify the provider and/or facility and/or agency of errors.

From www.missourifamilies.org/features/healtharticles/health38.htm.

SUMMARY

Changes in the U.S. health care system bring new challenges for professional nurses. Health care has moved from an emphasis on illness to an emphasis on wellness and prevention and is shifting from acute care services to preventive and community-based services, such as ambulatory care and home care. Financing of health care services has gone from retrospective, fee-for-service payment systems to prospective payment and managed care and continues to evolve through implementation of the PPACA to expand insurance coverage and new models of financial rewards and incentives (e.g., never events, value-based purchasing, readmission reduction programs) to improve quality and reduce costs. Today, technology is viewed as important to health care delivery, but its value is based on having the appropriate service at the right price.

U.S. leaders and legislators agree that health care costs are too high, but they differ in the best ways to stop the increased cost of health care. Most agree that when citizens practice healthy lifestyles, they require less health care and enjoy a better quality of life. However, what will motivate people to make healthier choices and practice disease prevention?

What do these changes in health care delivery mean to professional nursing? Nursing practice in a cost- and quality-conscious environment is here to stay. Nurses must constantly challenge current practice for quality improvement and cost-effectiveness. Accurate data must be collected to show cost containment and positive patient outcomes. Nurses need to be leaders and have a voice in the ever-changing economic and political environment that determines payment for services. The PPACA can expand the contributions of nursing in many ways. Roles on clinical teams, in administration, with insurance companies, and with the government hold promise for empowered change. Professional nurses can prepare for these evolving careers with a commitment to lifelong learning. Nurses can take the lead by being healthy role models, educating consumers, and encouraging personal responsibility for improved health practices. Managing care brings nurses back to the basics as society recognizes that healthy people are good business.

REFERENCES

Canadian Institute for Health Information: *National health expenditure trends 1975 to 2013,* 2013 (website). https://secure.cihi.ca/estore/productFamily.htm?locale=en&pf=PFC2400. Accessed October 1, 2014.

Carroll, A E: The problem with "Pay for Performance" in medicine, *New York Times,* July 28, 2014. http://www.nytimes.com/2014/07/29/upshot/the-problem-with-pay-for-performance-in-medicine.html?abt=0002&abg=1. Accessed October 1, 2014.

Centers for Medicare and Medicaid Services: *National health expenditure fact sheet,* 2014a (website). http://www.cms.gov/Research-Statistics-Data-and-Systems/Statistics-Trends-and-Reports/NationalHealthExpendData/NHE-Fact-Sheet.html. Accessed October 1, 2014.

Centers for Medicare and Medicaid Services: *Readmission reduction program,* 2014b (website). http://www.cms.gov/Medicare/Medicare-Fee-for-Service-Payment/AcuteInpatientPPS/Readmissions-Reduction-Program.html. Accessed October 1, 2014.

Kaiser Family Foundation: *Summary of Affordable Care Act,* 2013 (website). http://kff.org/health-reform/fact-sheet/summary-of-the-affordable-care-act. Accessed October 1, 2014.

Needleman J, Hassmiller S: The role of nurses in improving hospital quality and efficiency: real-world results, *Health Affairs* 28(4):w625–w633, 2009.

U.S. Census Bureau: *Health insurance coverage in the United States: 2013,* 2014 (website). http://www.census.gov/library/publications/2014/demo/p60-250.html. Accessed October 1, 2014.

U.S. Census Bureau: *Income, poverty, and health insurance coverage in the United States 2012,* 2013 (website). http://www.census.gov/prod/2013pubs/p60-245.pdf. Accessed October 1, 2014.

White House: 7.1 *million Americans have enrolled in private health coverage under the Affordable Care Act, 2014* (website). http://www.whitehouse.gov/blog/2014/04/01/more-7-million-americans-have-enrolled-private-health-coverage-under-affordable-care. Accessed October 1, 2014.

Legal Issues in Nursing and Health Care

Laura R. Mahlmeister, PhD, MSN, RN

Knowledge of the law enhances the nurse's ability to provide safe and effective care.

Ⓔ Additional resources are available online at: http://evolve.elsevier.com/Cherry/

PROFESSIONAL/ETHICAL ISSUE

All health care systems are challenged to provide safe patient care when employees, physicians, or other providers report illness while at work. While health care workers are advised to stay home if they are febrile and have signs of respiratory infection that may be spread to patients and coworkers, anecdotal evidence suggests that workers are in fact pressured to "tough it out" and come to work. The following is a scenario illustrating ethical issues and challenges related to working with sick colleagues.

A pregnant woman arrives in a labor and delivery unit at 6:45 a.m. for a scheduled repeat cesarean delivery. Her obstetrician, Dr. Mary Smith, is on call and planning to perform the surgical birth. The obstetrician is completing her preoperative documentation at the nurses' station. The charge nurse notes that Dr. Smith has obvious symptoms of a severe respiratory illness. She is coughing, sneezing, has copious nasal secretions, and looks quite ill. The charge nurse observes Dr. Smith

drinking about a third of a bottle of a liquid cold and flu remedy and pocketing the rest of the medication in her lab coat. She knows that one of the side effects of the medication is significant drowsiness. She approaches the physician and says, "Dr. Smith, you look quite ill. I am concerned about you and whether you are up to performing surgery this morning. Can we call your partner who scheduled to start at 8:00 a.m. to come in and relieve you?" Dr. Smith responds, "Look, it's just a bad cold. I've taken a large dose of a cold remedy. I will double-mask and use a splash shield. Let's get going. I'm off duty at 8:00 a.m. If we move fast I'll be out of here before then. Call me when the patient's on the table." Dr. Smith then walks into the physician's lounge and reclines on a couch.

Questions: (1) What is the nurse's ethical duty to the patient and coworkers at this time? (2) What danger does allowing Dr. Smith to perform surgery pose to the patient and coworkers? (3) Does the nurse have an ethical duty to the physician?

VIGNETTE

Although the names have been changed to respect patient privacy, this scenario is based on an actual event. Mary Clark is a registered nurse (RN) employed in the emergency department (ED) of a large for-profit hospital. The facility treats clients who are privately insured and individuals with Medicare coverage. Nurse Clark is the assigned triage nurse when Mr. Jones, a 48-year-old patient, walks in for evaluation. He states that he has persistent,

moderate substernal pain that is now radiating laterally toward both shoulders. His skin is pale, he is diaphoretic and is massaging his mid-chest region, stating, "I just wish I could burp up this gas." His vital signs are taken at the triage desk. His blood pressure is 158/88, his pulse is 116 bpm, and respiratory rate is 26 per minute. The oxygen saturation is 98 percent. He reports eating half of a garlic pizza and drinking three beers 1 hour ago. "I'm pretty sure it's just indigestion. This happened before when I ate garlic." Mr. Jones also tells the nurse, "I usually go to the County Hospital right around the corner from my house, but my pain's getting worse and I don't want to drive ten miles across town in rush hour traffic feeling like this. Can the doctor give me an antacid or something?"

Mr. Jones has recently changed jobs and has not yet enrolled in his state's insurance exchange program available under the Affordable Care Act. He tells the triage nurse he is concerned that he will be liable for the cost of the emergency room visit. Nurse Clark directs Mr. Jones to the registration clerk to discuss payment for the emergency room visit, saying, "If you're concerned about payment, you'd better talk to the clerk before we have someone see you. Let me know if you want to be examined." Mr. Jones waits about 10 minutes to see the clerk. He is told that he will be billed for the medical evaluation and care, but he has worsening chest and shoulder pain and is now nauseated. He decides to be examined by the physician. While standing in line at the triage desk to let the nurse know he is feeling much worse and wants to be seen, he collapses, suffering a myocardial infarction. Another patient standing next to Mr. Jones is also injured when Mr. Jones falls to the floor. There is a delay encountered in initiating CPR while a space is made in the busy waiting room, the "crash cart" is brought to the area, and the other patient who has

sustained a broken leg is moved. Mr. Jones has a prolonged and complicated hospital stay. The second patient requires hospitalization for surgical repair of the fracture as well as treatment of her primary complaint (severe migraine headache).

Questions to Consider While Reading This Chapter:
1. What is nurse Clark's legal duty in this situation?
2. What legal principles underlie the nurse's obligations to the patient?
3. What laws, if any, would govern the nurse's decision-making process in this case?
4. Based on Mr. Jones's presenting complaints, a hospital ED protocol required a rapid medical screening examination. In fact, he had yet to be seen 18 minutes after his arrival, when he collapsed. Who would be legally liable for the delay in Mr. Jones's evaluation? The nurse? The registration clerk? The for-profit hospital?
5. Does Mr. Jones bear any responsibility (**contributory negligence**) for the delay in treatment because he waited to ask about the cost of care?
6. Who, if anyone, is accountable for the injury sustained by the other patient waiting to be seen by the triage nurse? The triage nurse? The hospital? Mr. Jones?

KEY TERMS

Accountability: Being responsible for one's actions; a sense of duty in performing nursing tasks and activities.

Advance directives: Written or verbal instructions created by the patient describing specific wishes about medical care in the event he or she becomes incapacitated or incompetent. Examples include living wills and durable powers of attorney.

Breach of duty: Occurs when one person or company has a duty of care toward another person or company, but fails to live up to that standard.

Case law: Body of written opinions created by judges in federal and state appellate cases; also known as judge-made law and common law.

Civil law: A category of law (tort law) that deals with conduct considered unacceptable. It is based on societal expectations regarding interpersonal conduct. Common causes of civil litigation include professional malpractice, negligence, and assault and battery.

Common law: Law that is created through the decision of judges as opposed to laws enacted by legislative bodies (e.g., Congress).

Comparative negligence: A type of liability in which damages may be apportioned among two or more defendants in a malpractice case. The extent of liability depends on the defendant's relative contribution to the patient's injury.

Contributory negligence: A type of liability in which the plaintiff (patient), through his own negligence, contributed to the harm suffered.

Criminal negligence: Negligence that indicates "reckless and wanton" disregard for the safety, well-being, or life of an individual; behavior that demonstrates a complete disregard for another, such that death is likely.

Damages: Monetary compensation the court orders paid to a person who has sustained a loss or injury to his or her person or property through the misconduct (intentional or unintentional) of another.

Defendant: The individual who is named in a person's (plaintiff's) complaint as responsible for an injury; the person who the plaintiff claims committed a negligent act or malpractice.

Disclosure: A process in which the patient's primary provider (physician or advanced practice nurse) gives the patient, and when applicable, family members, complete information about unanticipated adverse outcomes of treatment and care.

Durable power of attorney for health care: An instrument that authorizes another person to act as one's agent in decisions regarding health care if the person becomes incompetent to make his or her own decisions.

Error: A failure of a planned action to be completed as intended or the use of a wrong plan to achieve a specific aim.

Gross negligence: A legal concept that means extreme carelessness showing willful or reckless disregard for the consequences to a person (patient).

Immunity: Legal doctrine by which a person is protected from a lawsuit for negligent acts or an institution is protected from a suit for the negligent acts of its employees.

Liability: Being legally responsible for harm caused to another person or property as a result of one's actions; compensation for harm normally is paid in monetary damages.

Licensing laws: Laws that establish the qualifications for obtaining and maintaining a license to perform particular services. Persons and institutions may be required to obtain a license to provide particular health care services.

Malpractice: Failure of a professional to meet the standard of conduct that a reasonable and prudent member of his or her profession would exercise in similar circumstances that result in harm. The professional's misconduct is unintentional.

Negligence: Failure to act in a manner that an ordinary, prudent person (either a layperson or professional) would act in similar circumstances, resulting in harm. The failure to act in a reasonable and prudent manner is unintentional.

Plaintiff: The complaining person in a lawsuit; the person who claims he or she was injured by the acts of another.

Preventable adverse event: An injury caused by medical management rather than the patient's underlying condition. An adverse event attributable to error is a preventable adverse event.

Punitive damages: Monetary compensation awarded to an injured person (patient) that goes beyond that which is necessary to compensate for losses (e.g., the ability to function, death, income) and is intended to punish the wrongdoer.

Res ipsa loquitur: Legal doctrine applicable to cases in which the provider (e.g., the physician) had exclusive control of events that resulted in the patient's injury; the injury would not have occurred ordinarily without a negligent act; a Latin phrase meaning "the thing speaks for itself."

Respondeat superior: Legal doctrine that holds an employer indirectly responsible for the negligent acts of employees carried out within the scope of employment; a Latin phrase meaning "let the master answer."

Risk management: Process of identifying, analyzing, and controlling risks posed to patients; involves human factor and incident analysis, changes in systems operations, and loss control and prevention.

Sentinel event: As defined by The Joint Commission, an unintended adverse outcome that results in death, paralysis, coma, or other major permanent loss of function. Examples of sentinel events include patient suicide while in a licensed health care facility, surgical procedure on the wrong organ or body side, or a patient fall.

Standard of care: In civil cases, the legal criteria against which the nurse's (and physician's) conduct is compared to determine whether a negligent act or malpractice occurred; commonly defined as the knowledge and skill that an ordinary, reasonably prudent person would possess and exercise in the same or similar circumstances.

Statute or statutory law: Law enacted by a legislative body; separate from judge-made or common law.

Strict liability: A legal doctrine, sometimes referred to as absolute liability, which can be imposed on a person or entity (e.g., a hospital) without proof of carelessness or negligence.

Vicarious liability: Legal doctrine in which a person or institution is liable for the negligent acts of another because of a special relationship between the two parties; a substituted liability.

LEARNING OUTCOMES

After studying this chapter, the reader will be able to:

1. Differentiate among the three major categories of law on which nursing practice is established and governed.
2. Analyze the relationship between accountability and liability for one's actions in professional nursing practice.
3. Outline the essential elements that must be proven to establish a claim of negligence or malpractice.
4. Distinguish between intentional and unintentional torts in relation to nursing practice.
5. Identify causes of nursing error and patient injury that have led to claims of criminal negligence.
6. Incorporate fundamental laws and statutory regulations that establish the patient's right to autonomy, self-determination, and informed decision making in the health care setting.
7. Incorporate laws and statutory regulations that establish the patient's right to privacy and privacy of health records.

CHAPTER OVERVIEW

The preceding vignette highlighted a growing clinical dilemma that nurses and patients face in the complex, ever-changing health care system. Financial considerations may conflict with clinical concerns for patient well-being. In an increasingly complex health care environment, the nurse's ability to make appropriate decisions about the provision of patient care services is assisted by a sound knowledge of the laws governing practice. In the case of Mr. Jones, triage, assessment, medical evaluation, and treatment are regulated by a federal law known as the Emergency Medical Treatment and Active Labor Act (EMTALA) (COBRA, 42 U.S.C. 1395dd). There also may be a specific state law regarding essential care and transport of patients in EDs. Additionally, sections of the state's nurse practice act that describe professional conduct of the RN would assist nurse Clark in managing this clinical problem. With increasing emphasis on patient rights and as well as responsibilities, the impact of patient decisions on outcomes of care often take center stage in an examination of adverse outcomes. Financial concerns, however, may become a secondary consideration for the nurse when he or she has a sound baseline knowledge of health care law.

Each nurse must be able to describe his or her professional duty to the patient or client under the law and associated health care rules and regulations, and recognize legal risks in practice. Knowledge of the law enhances the nurse's ability to provide safe, effective, and humane care in all settings. This chapter examines the legal aspects of nursing practice. The concepts of law, professional accountability, legal liability, negligence, malpractice, and criminal offense are defined. Specific laws or statutes governing nursing practice are also reviewed. The reader is introduced to current, relevant information about case law, also known as common law or judge-made law, as it applies to professional nursing practice. Patients' rights are explored within the context of law and court opinions. Finally, the ongoing reports about medical errors published by organizations such as the Institute of Medicine (IOM), The Joint Commission (TJC), and the Agency for Healthcare Research and Quality (AHRQ) are discussed, and specific strategies to reduce errors and legal risk are detailed.

SOURCES OF LAW AND NURSING PRACTICE

The actions of all individuals are regulated through two systems of principles known as *laws* and *ethics*. Laws enforce a minimal level of conduct by imposing penalties for violations of acceptable behavior (Griffith and Tengnah, 2008). Laws are expressed in terms of "must" and "shall" and are based on a society's interest in prohibiting or controlling certain behaviors. Ethics are described in terms of "should" and "may" and address beliefs about appropriate behaviors within a societal context (Westrick, 2013). Chapter 9 presents an in-depth discussion about nursing ethics. Along with ethics, professional nursing conduct also is regulated by a variety of laws. The two major sources of law are *statutory law* and *common law.* The standards for professional nursing practice are in great part derived from statutory as well as common law. The following section deals with statutory law and describes how it governs and indirectly influences nursing practice.

STATUTORY LAW

The terms *law* and *statute* are used interchangeably in this chapter. Laws that are written by legislative bodies, such as Congress or state legislatures, are enacted as statutes. The previously mentioned law, EMTALA, is an example of a federal statute. Violation of law is a criminal offense against the general public and is prosecuted by government authorities. Crimes are punishable by fines or imprisonment. The list of federal and state statutes that govern nursing practice has multiplied over the past 25 years. Nurses at all levels of practice must develop a greater depth and breadth of knowledge about laws related to patient safety, professional practice, their specific practice setting (e.g., the ED in the case of EMTALA), and health care systems in general. Ignorance of the law is never a defense when a nurse violates a health care statute. A nurse who violates the law is subject to penalties, including monetary fines, suspension or revocation of his or her license, and even imprisonment in some instances (Brown, 2013).

Federal Statutes
Conditions of Participation for Hospitals in Medicare (42 CFR Part 482)

Federal laws, rules, and regulations have a major effect on nursing practice and hospital operations. In the U.S. Code of Federal Regulations (CFR), Title 42 is the principal set of rules and regulations issued by federal agencies regarding public health. Title 42, Part 482, contains the Conditions of Participation for Hospitals in Medicare (CoPs) and is abbreviated in references as "42 CFR Part 482." The CoPs delineate the minimal standards of care required in all health care settings that receive federal reimbursement for treatment of Medicare beneficiaries. Medicare is administered by the Centers for Medicare & Medicaid Services (CMS) and has the authority to establish new rules and regulations to enhance patient safety and quality, and reduce the cost of care. For instance, the CoPs require nurses to develop an individualized written nursing care plan for each

patient and to revise the plan as necessary. Other CoPs mandate that hospitals properly train nurses for their stated roles and responsibilities, provide adequate staff to meet patient needs, and begin discharge planning as soon as possible after the patient's admission to the hospital. Hospitals that are not in compliance with the CoPs may lose their federal funding if the CMS determines the violations place the patient in "immediate jeopardy" of harm. The hospital or units within the hospital may be prohibited from accepting patients until corrective actions are taken to ensure the safety of all patients (Caramenico, 2011). Likewise, nurses engaged in unprofessional conduct that violate CoPs may be barred from employment in hospitals that participate in the Medicare Program. Nurses can access information about the CoPs online and without cost at the CMS website: http://www.cms.gov/Regulations-and-Guidance/Legislation/CFCsAndCoPs/Hospitals.html. The CoPs can be downloaded from the site as a pdf file, *Appendix A of the State Operations Manual.* The *State Operations Manual* delineates each of the 23 CoPs pertaining to hospitals, and provides Interpretive Guidelines for each of the requirements in language that can be easily understood by nurses and consumers of health care.

In 2008, the CMS issued new rules that halt payment to hospitals for treatment of preventable patient complications and injuries, often referred to as "never events." The CMS identified 10 categories of hospital-acquired conditions (HAC) that studies have demonstrated are "reasonably preventable" (CMS, 2008). Box 8-1 lists the 10 categories of adverse events that are subject to nonpayment. The new rules were enacted in 2009 and have already had a significant impact on hospital nursing care through the introduction of evidence-based practices to prevent complications such as falls, infections, and the development of stage III and stage IV pressure ulcers. The major revisions the CMS proposed in the Conditions of Participation for Hospitals in Medicare took effect July 16, 2012. Under the new rules, nurses are required to develop greater expertise in the provision of evidence-based patient care, case management, and discharge planning. Legal concerns have been raised about a possible increase in malpractice claims related to hospital-acquired conditions. It may be more difficult for a hospital to defend a malpractice claim if "strict liability" is applied to these hospital-acquired events. In other

BOX 8-1   **Categories of Hospital-Acquired Conditions Subject to Nonpayment**

1. Foreign object retained after surgery (e.g., instruments, surgical sponges)
2. Air embolism
3. Blood incompatibility (blood transfusion error)
4. Stage III and stage IV pressure ulcer development
5. Falls and trauma
   • Fractures
   • Joint dislocation
   • Intracranial injuries
   • Crushing injuries
   • Burns
   • Electric shock
6. Manifestations of poor glycemic control
   • Diabetic ketoacidosis
   • Nonketotic hyperosmolar coma
   • Hypoglycemic coma
   • Secondary diabetes with ketoacidosis
   • Secondary diabetes with hyperosmolarity
7. Catheter-associated urinary tract infection (UTI)
8. Vascular catheter-associated infection
9. Surgical site infection following:
   • Coronary artery bypass graft—mediastinitis
   • Bariatric surgery
   • Orthopedic procedures
10. Deep vein thrombosis (DVT)/pulmonary embolism (PE)

Source: Centers for Medicare & Medicaid Services (CMS): Medicare program: changes to the hospital inpatient prospective payment system and fiscal year 2009 rates (final rule), 42 CFR Parts 411, 412, 413, 489 (website). http://edocket.access. gpo.gov/2008/pdf/E8-17914.pdf. Accessed January 2009.

words, if the federal government deems the HAC a cause for levying penalties or denying reimbursement, does it constitute negligence *per se*? Case law has yet to determine whether the courts will accept the "strict liability" claim. However, hospitals will still face serious financial losses when hospital-acquired events occur. Beginning in 2015, the Hospital-Acquired Condition (HAC) Reduction Program, mandated by the Affordable Care Act, requires the Centers for Medicare & Medicaid Services (CMS) to reduce hospital payments by 1% for hospitals that rank among the lowest-performing 25% with regard to HACs. Nurses will continue to play a central role in quality improvement activities that reduce the likelihood of revenue loss.

Nursing homes are another highly regulated industry that must meet federal and state requirements to operate. Federal laws have also established rules and regulations to ensure the confidentiality of patients' personal health information (Health Insurance Portability and Accountability Act, or HIPAA). Several federal laws protect the rights of patients who participate as subjects in research by mandating the creation of institutional review boards and an appropriate informed consent process. The Federal False Claims Act makes it an offense to submit a false claim to the government for payment of health care services. Furthermore, the person who reports the false or fraudulent claim (often referred to as a "whistle-blower") is entitled to 15% to 25% of any monetary amount recovered by the federal government if the government wins the case in court. Nurses have been the recipients of these "bounties" in several recent false claim cases in which the federal government recovered several million dollars. The Americans with Disabilities Act (ADA) requires health care entities to provide interpreter services and communication devices when patients are unable to effectively communicate their needs or wishes.

Three federal statutes that nurses must be familiar with and clearly understand are discussed in this section. The list is not comprehensive, but it includes examples of federal laws that directly affect nursing practice. Many federal laws are relevant to specific health care settings (e.g., mental health hospitals, nursing homes, EDs, maternity settings). When nurses are knowledgeable about the federal laws applicable to their area of practice, they are able to more effectively advocate for patients in that setting. Unfortunately, most nurses are unfamiliar with health care law and rely on authorities in their employment setting to know what is legal and therefore permissible. Automatically deferring to administrators or nurse managers about the legality of a particular issue is no longer acceptable behavior for the professional nurse. Each RN must take accountability for knowing the law and understanding how it relates to patient care and nursing practice.

Emergency Medical Treatment and Active Labor Law (COBRA, 42 U.S.C. 1395dd)

This federal statute, often referred to as the "antidumping" law, was enacted in 1986 to prohibit the refusal of care for indigent and uninsured patients seeking medical assistance in an ED (Moy, 2014). This law also prohibits the transfer of unstable patients, including women in labor, from one facility to another. The law states:

> *"All persons presenting for care must receive the same medical screening examination and be stabilized, regardless of their financial status or insurance coverage, before discharge or transfer."*

EMTALA is applicable to people coming to non-ED settings, such as urgent care clinics. It even governs the transfer of patients from an inpatient setting to a lower level of care in some parts of the United States (*Roberts v. Galen of Virginia, Inc., 1997*). Significant penalties can be levied against a facility that violates EMTALA, including a $25,000 to $50,000 fine (not covered by liability insurance). The federal government also can revoke the facility's Medicare contract, and this could result in a major loss of revenue for the institution, or even insolvency. Many legitimate concerns that nurses have about the discharge or transfer of patients could be promptly addressed if the nurse had a solid understanding of EMTALA. A recent case illustrates the importance of understanding EMTALA. In *Love v. Rancocas Hospital* (2006), a woman was transported by ambulance to the ED after losing consciousness at home. She had a history of hypertension and continued to have high blood pressure readings in the ED. The woman also fell off the bed twice while being monitored, but the ED nurse did not report this to the physician. The nurse received a discharge order from the physician and sent the woman home in an *unstable* condition, thus violating the stabilization requirement of EMTALA. The woman returned 2 days later after experiencing a stroke. Understanding EMTALA is not a daunting task for nurses engaged in the triage and medical screening of patients presenting to the ED or obstetric triage department. Nursing journals have published many articles about EMTALA and the nurse's role in upholding this statute (Angelini and Mahlmeister, 2005; Bond, 2008; Caliendo et al, 2004).

Americans with Disabilities Act of 1990 (Public Law No. 101-336, 42 U.S.C. Section 12101)

The intent of this law is to end discrimination against qualified persons with disabilities by removing barriers that prevent them from enjoying the same opportunities available to persons without disabilities. Court cases have established that as a place of public accommodation, a health care facility must provide reasonable accommodation to patients (and family members) with sensory disabilities, such as vision and hearing impairment (*Abernathy v. Valley Medical Center*, 2006; *Boyer v. Tift County Hospital*, 2008). In another case (*Parco v. Pacifica Hospital*, 2007), a nurse was caring for a ventilator-dependent quadriplegic patient who was unable to speak or use his call light. She requested a special pillow that activated the patient's call light when he turned his head, but was told that all the pillows were in use. The patient subsequently experienced three episodes of respiratory distress that he was unable to alert the nurse about, and could only hope that someone would discover his problem before he suffered brain damage or death (Snyder, 2007a). The patient sued for emotional distress and mental anguish. The court affirmed that the ADA requires hospitals to provide assistive devices to patients with communication problems related to a disability. The hospital settled the lawsuit for $295,000.

This statute has relevance for all nurses. As patient advocates, nurses have a legal and ethical duty to provide appropriate patient and family education and to support the process of informed consent. In *Parco v. Pacifica Hospital,* the court noted that it was a basic tenet of nursing practice that patients be given the ability to communicate with caregivers. The health care facility must have a policy that defines how it will meet the client's needs for education and information when there are vision or hearing disabilities. The policy also describes how a nurse can obtain translators and special types of equipment needed to facilitate communication when there are physical disabilities or language barriers.

Patient Self-Determination Act of 1990; Omnibus Budget Reconciliation Act of 1990 (Public Law No. 101-508, Sections 4206 and 4751)

This federal statute is a Medicare and Medicaid amendment intended to support individuals in expressing their preferences about medical treatment and making decisions about end-of-life care. The law requires all federally funded hospitals to give patients written notice on admission to the health care facility of their decision-making rights and policies regarding advance health care directives in their state and in the institution to which they have been admitted. Patient rights under the Patient Self-Determination Act include the right to:

- Participate in their own health care decisions
- Accept or refuse medical treatment
- Make advance health care directives

These choices include collaborating with the physician in formulating "do not resuscitate" (DNR) orders. Facilities must inquire as to whether the patient already has an advance health care directive, and they must make note of this in the patient's medical record. The institution must also provide education to their staff about advance health care directives. The law provides guidance to nurses who often are in the best position to discuss these issues with the patient (e.g., while completing a comprehensive admission assessment). (Legal considerations related to living wills, durable power of attorney, and DNR orders are discussed in "The Law and Patient Rights," the last section of this chapter.)

Health Insurance Portability and Accountability Act of 1996 (Public Law No. 104-191)

The intent of this law is to ensure confidentiality of the patient's health information. Legitimate concerns regarding the uses of and release of medical information, particularly to private entities, such as insurance companies, led to the passage of this law. The introduction of electronic medical records has provided additional impetus for introduction of this legislation. The statute sets guidelines for maintaining the privacy of health data. It provides explicit guidelines for nurses who are in a position to release health information. To maintain confidentiality of the patient's health information, all nurses must have a basic understanding of this federal law. Nurses should also take note that the HIPAA confers whistle-blower protection for individuals who report in good faith any illegal disclosure of patients' health. In 2005 a federal statute, the Patient Safety and Quality Improvement Act, was enacted to allow certain disclosures of patient safety data. The law permits a provider to disclose *nonidentifiable* patient data to a qualified patient safety organization (PSO) for the purpose of analyzing medical errors. The law prohibits an accreditation body, such as TJC, from taking any action against a provider who reports patient safety data to an approved PSO (Public Law No. 109-41).

With the continued increase in the number of nurses using social media such as blogs, social networking sites, video sites, and online chat rooms and forums, a patient's right to privacy is threatened. The National Council of State Boards of Nursing (NCSBN) has published a brochure, "A Nurse's Guide to the Use of Social Media" (NCSBN, 2011a). The publication reviews the benefits and risks of using social media in the workplace or bringing workplace issues to social media sites during free time. The release of private health data, either inadvertent or intentional, is a violation of HIPAA and is punishable by significant fines and a term of imprisonment. It may also result in suspension or revocation of the nurse's license. Civil actions may arise from a violation of patient confidentiality, alleging failure to maintain security of protected patient health data, unprofessional conduct, and violation of hospital policies and procedures that restrict access to patient information on a "need to know" basis. Posting photographs or videotapes of patients, or even ostensibly unidentifiable body parts, is expressly forbidden and also violates the American Nurses Association Code of Ethics for Nurses (2015). Discussing conflicts with managers or coworkers on social networking sites or posting unauthorized photos or videos of professional colleagues opens the nurse to claims of invasion of privacy, slander, intentional infliction of harm, and emotional distress, among other things. Further risks to one's livelihood and future employment as a nurse are presented when the nurse publicly airs dissatisfaction with his or her employer or discusses problems at work that make the employer vulnerable to ridicule or loss of reputation in the community or larger health care arena.

State Statutes

In addition to federal laws, nursing practice is governed by state laws that delineate the conduct of licensed nurses and define behaviors of all health care professionals in promoting public health and welfare.

State Nurse Practice Act and Board of Nursing Rules and Regulations

One of the most important state laws governing nursing practice is a nurse practice act (NPA), which defines the scope and limitations of professional nursing practice. The aim of regulating practice in this manner is to protect the public and make the individual nurse accountable for his or her actions. State legislatures authorize the nurses' licensing board to promulgate administrative rules and regulations necessary to implement the NPA. Once these administrative rules and regulations are formally adopted, they have the same force and effect as any other law.

Although NPAs vary from state to state, they usually contain the following information:

- Definition of the term *RN*
- Description of professional nursing functions

- Standards of competent performance
- Behaviors that represent misconduct or prohibited practices
- Grounds for disciplinary action
- Fines and penalties the licensing board may levy when an NPA is violated

For further exploration, excerpts from three separate state NPAs can be found online (http://evolve.elsevier.com/Cherry/) to illustrate how an NPA defines the scope of practice for nurses.

Surprisingly, many nurses are not even aware that the NPA is a law, and they unknowingly violate aspects of this statute (NCSBN, 2011b). They are not familiar with the administrative rules and regulations enacted by the licensing board. This is an unfortunate lapse because these administrative rules and regulations answer crucial questions that nurses have about the day-to-day aspects of practice and unusual occurrences. For example, the increasing complexity of health care requires effective communication, collaboration, and planning of care among many licensed health team members. Rules promulgated by the Ohio Board of Nursing Section 4723.03, which refer to the competent practice as an RN, direct the nurse in appropriate reporting and consultation.

> *"A registered nurse shall in a timely manner:*
> *Implement any order for a client unless the registered nurse believes or should have reason to believe the order is:*
> *1) Inaccurate*
> *2) Not properly authorized*
> *3) Not current or valid*
> *4) Harmful, or potentially harmful to a client*
> *5) Contraindicated by other documented information; and*
> *Clarify any order for a client when the registered nurse believes or should have reason to believe the order is: [a through e as delineated in (1)]"*
>
> **Ohio Administrative Code,**
> **Section 4723-4-03, E, 2014**

Based on this, an RN in Ohio who does not clarify a questionable order before administering a medication or carrying out the prescribed action is in violation of the law.

Each nurse should own a current copy of the NPA and the licensing board's administrative rules and regulations. The nurse also must know how to access the licensing board online and by telephone in order to clarify issues related to nursing practice. The dramatic changes occurring in health care often lead to uncertainty among nurses about which functions constitute the exclusive practice of registered nursing and which patient care tasks may be lawfully delegated to a licensed practical nurse/licensed vocational nurse (LPN/LVN) or unlicensed assistive personnel. The NPA and licensing board rules and regulations provide essential information that clarifies these important questions. In 2008, the Texas Board of Nursing approved a new rule requiring all nurses to take and pass a Nursing Jurisprudence Exam prior to initial licensure. The examination tests knowledge regarding nursing board statutes, rules, position statements, disciplinary action, and other resource documents accessible on the Texas board website (http://bon.state.tx.us/index.html).

Nurses may also have questions and concerns regarding the legal aspects of floating to unfamiliar units. An NPA provides information regarding the scope of practice, required competencies, and the responsibilities of a nurse who accepts an assignment or agrees to carry out any task or activity in the clinical setting. The NPA broadly defines the practice of registered nursing in accordance with nursing's rapidly evolving functions. In recent years, with the expansion of basic nursing functions and the development of advanced nursing practice, many states have revised their NPAs. Licensing boards also have been authorized in some states to provide guidelines for the development of "standardized procedures." Standardized procedures are a legal means by which RNs may expand their practice into areas traditionally considered to be within the realm of medicine. The standardized procedure actually is developed within the facility where the expanded nursing functions have been approved. It is developed in collaboration with nursing, medicine, and administration. An example of a standardized procedure is a written protocol authorizing a nurse to implement a peripherally inserted venous catheter for patients in the neonatal intensive care unit. The NCSBN provides additional online resources for nurses covering diverse topics, including licensure and regulation (NCSBN, 2011b).

Violations of an NPA

State legislatures have given licensing boards the authority to hear and decide administrative cases against nurses when there is an alleged violation of an NPA or the nursing board's rules and regulations. Nurses who violate the NPA or board's administrative rules and regulations are subject to disciplinary action by the board. Table 8-1 provides a synopsis of the licensing board procedure when a complaint is made about a nurse. Courts have consistently affirmed board of nursing decisions to restrict, suspend, or revoke the nurse's license when nurses have challenged the decision.

Box 8-2 presents the more common grounds for disciplinary action by state boards of nursing. Penalties that licensing boards may impose for violations of an NPA include the following:

- Issuing a formal reprimand
- Establishing a period of probation
- Levying fines
- Limiting, suspending, or revoking a nurse's license

An estimated 10% to 15% of RNs in the United States are chemically dependent (NCSBN, 2011c). The majority of disciplinary actions by licensing boards are

TABLE 8-1 **Licensing Board Procedure When a Complaint is Filed**	
Action	**Consequence**
Complaint is made (initial complaint may be lodged by a telephone call or a letter mailed to the licensing board) by: • Consumer (patient) • Family member • Nurse or nurse manager or employer • Professional nursing organization • State board of nursing • Federal or state authority (i.e., CMS or Department of Health and Human Services)	Sworn complaints must be filed
Licensing board reviews complaint: • Examines evidence • Reviews reports	Insufficient evidence—no action; administrative review scheduled • Nurse notified
Board makes determination	Nurse summoned • Rules of proceeding explained • Witnesses called to testify • Further evidence examined
Licensing board makes decision	Nurse exonerated Nurse guilty of violating the NPA
Board takes disciplinary action	Possible actions • Board issues formal reprimand • Fines levied against nurse • Nurse placed on probation • License suspended or revoked • License not renewed
Nurse may challenge licensing board's actions	Nurse must file appeal in court
Court reviews case (court action is dependent on jurisdiction) • Reviews conduct of proceedings • Reviews board's decision	Licensing board ruling is reversed
Licensing board can appeal ruling	Court reviews case
Court renders a decision *OR*	Licensing board ruling is upheld *OR*
Court renders a decision	Licensing board ruling is overturned Licensing board can appeal to a higher court
Case scheduled for trial	Licensing board ruling is upheld *OR* Licensing board ruling is reversed

CMS, Centers for Medicare & Medicaid Services; *NPA,* nurse practice act.

BOX 8-2   Grounds for Disciplinary Action by State Boards of Nursing

- Practicing without a valid license
- Failure to use appropriate nursing judgment
- Guilty of a felony
- Falsification of records
- Failure to complete nursing documentation
- Incorrect nursing documentation
- Failure to practice in accordance with nursing standards
- Inappropriate behavior or occurrence at work
- Medicare fraud
- Misappropriation of personal items

related to misconduct resulting from chemical impairment, including the misappropriation of drugs for personal use and the sale of drugs and drug paraphernalia to support the nurse's addiction. When a nurse's license is limited or suspended because of problems related to chemical impairment, the ability to practice in the future often is predicated on successful completion of a drug rehabilitation program and evidence of abstinence. An increasing number of state licensing boards have established programs to guide nurses through the process of rehabilitation to re-establish licensure.

Nurse-Patient Ratios and Mandatory Overtime Statutes

Inadequate and often unsafe nurse-patient ratios continue to plague nursing. A growing body of evidence confirms a strong association between nurse-patient ratios and patient outcomes (Konetzka et al, 2013; Zhang and Unruh, 2012; Furukawa et al, 2011). The American Nurses Association (ANA) launched its "Safe Staffing Saves Lives Campaign" in 2008, publishing the results of a poll conducted to examine nurses' perceptions of staffing problems (ANA, 2009a). More than 50% of respondents were considering leaving their current nursing position, and 42% indicated that the reason for leaving was associated with inadequate staffing. Another study surveyed direct care nurses about nursing errors of omission. More than 70% of respondents reported the inability at times to plan and implement required care and intervene in a timely manner. Forty-four percent of respondents missed essential assessments (Kalisch et al, 2012). Eighty-five percent of the nurses indicated that

lack of human resources (nurse and support staff) was the primary reason for omissions in essential components of the nursing process.

Nurse staffing is influenced to some degree by federal law through the Conditions of Participation for Hospitals in Medicare and, increasingly, by state laws. Hospitals risk losing federal Medicare and Medicaid funding for a confirmed pattern of understaffing that has not been properly addressed by managers and administrators. For example, in 2011, the Centers for Medicare & Medicaid Services (CMS) cited several Texas hospitals for understaffing, in part due to increased patient census (Caramenico, 2011). The CMS placed the hospitals in "immediate jeopardy" of losing their funding. Hospital administrators and clinical leaders must prepare a corrective action plan and submit it to the CMS within a specified time when cited by the CMS for safety violations such as unsafe staffing levels. Nurses can positively affect nurse staffing levels when armed with knowledge regarding federal and state laws. When concerns about work-related issues arise (e.g., a reduction in RN staffing, mandatory overtime, or replacement of RNs with LVNs-LPNs or unlicensed assistive personnel), the first question the nurse asks and answers should be, "Is this legal?" (Brooke, 2009). In 1999, California became the first state to enact a law (California Assembly Bill 394) that mandates the establishment of minimum nurse-patient ratios in acute care facilities. The law took effect in January 2004 and set minimum nurse-patient ratios in critical care units, step-down and medical-surgical units, and maternity departments. No other state has followed California's lead in establishing nurse-patient ratios, but by 2014, 14 states had enacted laws that regulate or restrict mandatory overtime for nurses and two states have restrictions established by state regulations (ANA, 2014). The ANA reintroduced the RN Safe Staffing Act for the 2014 session of Congress. It requires hospitals that participate in Medicare to implement staffing plans, which are established by a committee composed of a majority of direct-care nurses for each nursing unit and shift.

An increasing number of lawsuits against health care facilities have set forth claims of corporate negligence for inadequate staffing or "understaffing" when adverse outcomes occur. A jury awarded a $1.7 million verdict against a nursing home for the death of a resident who fell from her wheelchair. Evidence revealed that there was a widespread pattern of understaffing at the nursing home (*Sunbridge Healthcare Corp. v. Penny*, 2005). In 2006, another jury awarded $240,000 in punitive damages (out of a total award of $400,000) against a nursing home because understaffing at the facility was considered an aggravating factor in a patient's death (*Miller v. Levering Regional Healthcare Center*, 2006). The patient was 91 years of age and suffered from Alzheimer's disease. The resident (patient) was left unattended and fell, hitting her head, and subsequently died of her injuries. The court records contained adequate evidence that the facility knew it had a chronic understaffing problem and that the problem directly led to the woman's death (Snyder, 2006). The director of nursing was also found negligent for failing to comply with Medicare guidelines that required the facility to provide sufficient staffing.

Reporting Statutes

The federal government and states seek to protect at-risk individuals (children and older adults) by requiring nurses and other health care providers to report specific types of suspected or actual patient-client injury, abuse, or neglect. Boards of nursing are created to protect the public from unethical, incompetent, or impaired nursing practice. Some states have enacted statutes that *mandate* nurses to report unsafe, illegal, or unethical practices of nursing colleagues or physicians, or administrators of health care facilities that place patients in jeopardy. With these mandates and protections in mind, the following case illustrates the adverse consequences that nurses may still face when reporting and/or whistle-blowing.

A nurse practitioner was contracted to provide health care services to inmates at a county jail in the state of Nevada. During the course of her work, she collaborated with a physician who also treated those incarcerated in the jail. The nurse practitioner, as well as other health care workers providing services in the facility, objected when the physician did not at all times write progress notes when he evaluated and treated the inmates. The primary concern was one of patient well-being, because the nurse and other health care workers relied on the physician's notes to provide safe and effective care. Additionally, the nurse practitioner feared for the health and safety of patients because another physician, the prison's staff psychiatrist, failed to timely assess inmates with psychiatric disorders. The nurse practitioner lodged complaints about

the two physicians through the facility's formal chain of command and was terminated by prison management. The nurse sued her employer claiming wrongful termination under Nevada's whistle-blower protection statute. The nurse's former employer claimed she could not sue for wrongful termination because she did not comply with the state's "generic" whistle-blower law, requiring her to report patient safety concerns directly to a public agency (Nevada State Department of Health). However, the U.S. District Court for the District of Nevada ruled that the fired nurse practitioner had the right to sue her former employer for retaliating against her. The court based its opinion on the state of Nevada's "special" whistle-blower law for health care workers. That special law protected nurses from retaliation (including termination) for internally reporting a situation that could compromise patient safety (*Scott v. Corizon Health*, 2014). The outcome of the nurse's suit against her former employer has not yet been reported in the legal literature.

The nursing literature provides nurses with recommendations and guidelines when considering the duty to report and its consequences (Philipsen and Soeken, 2011; Lachman, 2008). Nurses should be extremely careful to clarify their state's whistle-blower protection law for health care workers before engaging in whistle-blower activities. States vary widely in the requirements that must be met in order for a nurse to claim protection against retaliation for whistle-blowing. A first step requires the nurse to contact the state's board of nursing to determine whistle-blowing requirements established by the licensing board and/or formalized in that state's whistle-blowing protection statute. An increasing number of legal experts advise the nurse to seek the services of an attorney who specializes in reporting and whistle-blowing activities for nurses before making a decision to report (Snyder, 2014).

The types of conduct the boards of nursing require nurses to report vary from state to state. Nurses can access the specific requirements for reporting nurse coworkers at their board of nursing website. Some states require nurses and providers to report victims of domestic or interpersonal violence, whether or not the victim (patient) consents. Nurses can access current information from the state regarding reporting requirements under family or domestic violence statutes. For a list of family violence statutes compiled by the American Academy of

Orthopedic Surgeons (2012), visit http://www.aaos.org/about/abuse/ststatut.asp. Certain specifiable communicable diseases must also be reported to the Centers for Disease Control and Prevention (CDC) such as bubonic plague, anthrax, and botulism. (For the list of reportable diseases, visit http://www.cdc.gov/ncezid/.) State law may also require nurses to report injuries resulting from the use of weapons, attempts to harm oneself, or impaired driving (Mathes, 2014). Nurse managers and administrators are responsible for ensuring that reports made by direct care nurses are forwarded to the appropriate legal authorities. Nurse leaders who fail in this duty may face criminal charges, claims of negligence, and disciplinary action by the nursing board (Hudspeth, 2008).

Child Abuse Reporting Statutes

In 1973, the U.S. Congress enacted the Child Abuse Prevention and Treatment Act, which mandates all states to meet specific uniform guidelines to qualify for federal funding of child abuse programs. All 50 states and the District of Columbia have created laws that require reporting of specific health problems and the *suspected* or confirmed abuse of infants or children. Nurses often are explicitly named within the context of these statutes as one of the groups of designated health professionals who must report the specified problems under penalty of fine or imprisonment. Nurses need not fear legal reprisal from individuals or families who are reported to authorities in suspected cases of abuse. Most legislatures have granted immunity from suit within the context of the mandatory reporting statute. There is also a long history of court decisions shielding the nurse from civil claims by parents or guardians when that report is made in good faith, and in compliance with federal and state laws. The case of *Heinrich v. Conemaugh Valley Memorial Hospital* (1994) upheld this doctrine of immunity. The family of an injured child initiated a lawsuit against a hospital that reported suspected child abuse after a state investigation found them innocent of the charge. The court ruled that the hospital and the physician who made the report in "good faith" were immune from litigation under the Pennsylvania Child Protective Service Law that required reports of suspected child abuse.

It is crucial that nurses understand the requirements of abuse reporting statutes as they apply to their practice setting. For example, ED and pediatric nurses must have in-depth knowledge regarding child abuse reporting laws. Agency policies and procedures in the work setting may provide guidance in regard to reporting duties. If in doubt, the nurse should immediately contact his or her supervisor, an administrator, or the agency's compliance officer (the individual responsible for understanding and ensuring adherence to federal and state statutes) for additional guidance in the matter. In rare situations, when information is not available within the institution, the nurse may consult with the state Department of Health and Human Services or the state nurses' licensing board for guidance and obtaining the reporting statutes. There are serious ramifications for failing to report as required by the state's specific statute, and this could result in criminal charge and claims of negligence.

Institutional Licensing Laws

All facilities (e.g., hospitals, nursing homes, rehabilitation centers) providing health care services must comply with licensing laws promulgated by state legislatures. These laws are created to protect the public and ensure the safe and effective provision of health care services. Specific language usually is contained within health facility licensing statutes regarding the following issues:

- Minimal standards for the maintenance of the physical plant
- Basic operational aspects of major departments (nursing, dietary, clinical laboratories, and pharmacy)
- Essential aspects of patients' rights and the informed consent process

Many state licensing laws mandate minimal levels of education, experience, or credentialing for department administrators, such as nurses, anesthesia personnel, pediatricians, and obstetricians. Several states also require minimum nurse-patient ratios in critical care units and other specialty departments, such as the operating room, nursery, or ED.

Health care redesign and cost-reduction efforts have led to many changes in the way health care services are provided and the settings in which care is rendered. Not all change has been positive, and some redesign schemes have resulted in adverse outcomes for patients (Mahlmeister, 2009a). Investigations by state authorities on reports of patient injuries or death have discovered that in some cases health facilities have operated in violation of existing licensing laws. In the past, direct-care RNs generally could rely on their nurse managers to have a comprehensive knowledge of health facility licensing law and to create policies and procedures that implement and enforce applicable aspects of the law. The trend toward flattened management and reduction in role development for leaders has altered this picture. In an increasing number of settings, nurse managers have been replaced with non-nurse administrators, who may have minimal knowledge of the Conditions of Participation for Hospitals in Medicare and the state health facility licensing laws (Elzer, 2010).

In light of these changes, direct-care nurses should have a working knowledge of current licensing laws as they relate to nursing care and patient care services. The nurse also is guided by the ANA *Scope and Standards of Practice,* which states: "The registered nurse systematically enhances the quality and effectiveness of nursing practice" (ANA, 2010). In many instances, nurses who have serious questions regarding quality of care in their employment setting have been able to resolve these concerns once they have read applicable sections of the health facility licensing law relevant to their setting. Bringing the pertinent section of the law to the attention of managers, administrators, a compliance officer, or the risk management department often is the most effective strategy to resolve problems. In settings in which nurses are represented by union contracts, potential violations of health facility licensing laws may be most effectively addressed through union representatives.

Internet access has allowed nurses to obtain rapid information about current institutional licensing laws. Information can be downloaded and printed quickly. Nurses also can obtain a copy of the health facility's licensing law for their employment setting through the state department or health division of licensing and certification. Other states provide the statute and address questions through the state department of health's divisions of facilities regulations, health facilities inspection, or health quality assurance. The telephone number for this agency can be found in the white pages of the local telephone directory under the heading "State of" (e.g., Michigan). Nurses can call their licensing board or the state nursing association for guidance in reaching the appropriate authority to obtain a copy of the licensing law and to speak to a consultant about concerns.

COMMON LAW

In addition to statutory law, nursing practice is guided by common law, also known as *decisional* or *judge-made*

law. Common law is created through cases heard and decided in federal and state appellate courts. Throughout the years, judge-made law regarding nursing practice has accumulated in the form of written opinions. These opinions eventually contribute to the expected standard of nursing conduct (Mathes, 2014). The body of written opinions about nurses also is known as *nursing case law.* The importance of nursing case law in establishing the current standard of practice cannot be overstated.

One of the most important cases to establish the expected conduct of nurses was *Utter v. United Hospital Center, Inc.* (1977). This West Virginia case affirmed that nurses were required to exercise independent judgments to prevent harm when caring for patients. Before the 1970s, the issue of whether nurses were licensed professionals who made independent judgments was not clearly established. In the Utter case, a patient whose arm was casted had signs and symptoms of compartment syndrome. The affected limb became progressively more edematous and eventually turned black. The nurses failed to activate the chain of command when the primary providers did not respond to their reports and requests for medical re-evaluation. The patient's arm eventually had to be amputated. The court wrote:

> *"Nurses are specialists in hospital care who, in the final analysis, hold the well-being, in fact in some instances, the very lives of patients in their hands. In the dim hours of the night, as well as in the light of day, nurses are frequently charged with the duty to observe the condition of the ill and infirm in their care. If the patient, helpless and wholly dependent, shows signs of worsening, the nurse is charged with the obligation of taking some positive action . . . there was evidence that certain nurses did not fulfill their obligation."*

The duty to prevent harm, known as the nurse's "affirmative duty," has been supported in numerous court decisions. In *Rowe v. Sisters of Pallottine Missionary Society* (2001), a hospital and its ED nurses were found negligent for failing to question a physician's discharge order. A 17-year-old motorcyclist was admitted to the ED for an injury to his left leg. He complained of severe pain in his left knee and numbness in his left foot. The nurses were unable to find a pulse in the left leg or foot. The physician issued a discharge order and gave instructions that included the application of ice and elevation of the affected leg. The next day the man sought emergency care at another hospital for worsening pain and swelling of his leg. An examination revealed a lacerated popliteal artery and dislocated knee. He underwent extensive surgery and suffers permanent impairment of the affected limb. The physician settled the suit against him for $275,000. The jury returned a verdict for the patient in excess of $880,000 and found the nurses negligent for failing to question the discharge order and invoke the chain of command to obtain additional medical consultation and advice.

Every nurse should understand the effect that nursing case law has on his or her current practice. Case law made in appellate court decisions has addressed a range of vital issues related to professional nursing, including the following:

- Nursing malpractice cases
- Questions concerning labor law and collective bargaining
- Lawsuits alleging wrongful termination
- Legal challenges to state board of nursing disciplinary action against a nurse's license
- Legal actions against the nurse instituted by medical licensing boards
- "Practicing medicine without a license" claims
- Lawsuits claiming violation of the nurse's civil rights, including free-speech issues and reasonable accommodation for nurses with disabilities

Efforts should be made by professional nurses to review case law as it is published and discussed in nursing journals. There has been a trend to incorporate "legal advice" columns into many practice journals, and journals often include discussions about nursing case law. There also has been a proliferation of nursing journals dedicated solely to legal issues in nursing practice.

Nurse Managers, in particular, should have knowledge regarding the disposition of cases in their jurisdiction. A risk manager or agency attorney may assist any nurse in understanding how judge-made law in his or her state relates to expectations for nursing practice in the local community. Many medical libraries also subscribe to publications that review federal or appellate court decisions in health care law that are relevant to the local community. Although local jury verdicts do not contribute to common law, it is useful for managers and interested nurses to periodically review published reports of malpractice cases in the state and their immediate community. Medical libraries also often subscribe to a local "jury verdicts" publication. (More information on finding nursing case law is available online at http://evolve.elsevier.com/Cherry/.)

CIVIL LAW

Two major categories of law have been created to deal with conduct that is considered unacceptable—criminal law and civil law. Nurses generally are more familiar with civil law and, in particular, the branch of civil law that deals with torts. Tort law is discussed first, with a discussion of criminal law following.

A *tort* is a civil wrong or injury committed by one person against another person or a property. The wrong results from a breach in one's legal duty regarding interpersonal relationships between private persons. This duty is established through societal expectations regarding interpersonal conduct (Westrick, 2013). Civil suits almost always are brought by one person against another and generally are based on the concept of "fault." The person who initiates the civil lawsuit, the plaintiff, seeks damages for the wrongful behavior from the offending person, known as the defendant. The determination of whether wrongful behavior has occurred usually is determined by a jury, although in certain cases the right to a trial by jury can be waived by the private parties in the suit. In this case, the judge considers the facts and determines the outcome. If the plaintiff succeeds in the civil lawsuit (plaintiff verdict), damages generally are awarded in the form of monetary compensation. Damages may include "hard" damages—financial reimbursement for treatment of injuries, loss of wages, rehabilitation services, or special equipment, and "soft" damages—monetary compensation for pain and suffering, loss of companionship, or mental anguish, among others (Griffith and Tengnah, 2008).

Negligence and Malpractice

There are two types of torts: an unintentional tort (or wrong) and an intentional tort. An unintentional tort is an unintended wrong against another person. The two most common unintentional torts are negligence and malpractice.

Negligence is defined as the failure to act in a reasonable and prudent manner. The claim of negligence is based on the accepted principle that everyone is expected to conduct themselves in a reasonable and prudent fashion. This is true of laypersons, student nurses, and licensed professionals.

A more formal definition of negligence is the failure of a person to use the care that a reasonably prudent and careful person would use under similar circumstances (Mathes, 2014).

Malpractice is a special type of negligence (i.e., the failure of a professional, a person with specialized education and training, to act in a reasonable and prudent manner) (Mathes, 2014). As state NPAs have evolved to reflect the increasing professionalism of RNs, courts have begun to recognize the negligent acts of nurses as malpractice. Evidence of this change in perceptions is apparent in the increasing use of RNs as expert witnesses in malpractice cases.

In general, expert testimony is not needed in cases of "simple negligence," when the actions of the defendant are so obviously careless that even a layperson would recognize the conduct as negligent. In contrast, if the jury does not possess the special knowledge and information that professionals ordinarily have, an expert witness is required to establish whether the person breached the expected standard of care. In this case, the breach in duty is not simple negligence but malpractice.

Elements Essential to Prove Negligence or Malpractice

Although any patient (or surviving family member, in the case of a patient death) may sue the nurse and his or her employer, the following elements must be proved for the plaintiff to succeed in the case.

1. The nurse owed the patient or client a special duty of care based on the establishment of a nurse-patient relationship. When the nurse accepts a patient assignment, it establishes the relationship and requires the nurse to meet his or her duty to the patient. The duty of the nurse is to possess the knowledge and skill that a reasonable and prudent nurse would possess and exercise in the same or similar patient care situation. The duty of the nurse as described is the standard of care. A nurse-patient relationship also may be established through telephone communication in the case of a nurse who performs telephone triage and advice or via computer or audiovisual systems that are being introduced in some health care settings (American Academy of Ambulatory Care Nursing, 2011; American Telemedicine Association, 2014).

2. The nurse has breached his or her duty to the patient or client. Evidence is presented that proves the nurse breached the standard of care. The standard of care is derived from a multiplicity of sources; these are described in Box 8-3.

3. Actual harm or damage is suffered by the patient.

4. There is proximate cause or a causal connection between the breach in the standard of care by the nurse and the patient's injury.
   - No intervening event is responsible for the injury.
   - A direct cause and effect can be demonstrated.
   - In some jurisdictions, the nurse's breach in duty must only be proven to be a substantial cause of the patient's injury.

This last element merits further discussion. The relationship between the nurse's breach in the standard of care and the patient's injury must be established by the plaintiff. To prove proximate cause, there must be a direct causal link. For example, a patient reports that he has an allergy to penicillin and wears a MedicAlert bracelet to that effect. A physician orders penicillin to treat the patient's infection. The nurse fails to check or ask the patient about allergies. The nurse administers the penicillin, and the patient suffers an anaphylactic reaction and dies. There is a direct connection between the nurse's actions and the patient's death. Proximate cause has been established.

One may ask what the physician's liability is in this case. The physician also owes a duty to the patient and may be found negligent for ordering penicillin, if he or she had knowledge of or should have had knowledge of the allergy. However, even in the case of a physician's negligence—"I knew about the penicillin allergy, but forgot"—the nurse has a separate and independent duty to the patient to prevent harm. The nurse must review the patient's medical record for information about allergies, ask the patient about allergies, and check the patient's identification band before administering a drug.

In some jurisdictions, it only is necessary to prove that the nurse's actions were a substantial cause of the injury or harm to prove negligence. For example, in a large teaching hospital, a nurse notes a significant change in a patient's vital signs, suggesting deterioration in his condition. A first-year resident is called to the bedside and made aware of the patient's status. The resident orders the nurse to simply continue observing the patient. The first-year resident remains immediately available in the unit and receives repeated reports of a continued decline in the patient's condition. There is a clear chain of command policy established in the hospital, which takes into

BOX 8-3   Sources That Contribute to the Standard of Nursing Care

Federal Laws
Emergency Medical Treatment and Active Labor Law
Americans with Disabilities Act
Patient Self-Determination Act
Occupational Health and Safety Act
The Patient Safety and Quality Improvement Act

Federal Administrative Rules and Regulations
Rules and regulations for participation in Medicare

Federal Agencies
U.S. Food and Drug Administration
Agency for Healthcare Research and Quality clinical guidelines
National Institutes of Health publications
Centers for Disease Control and Prevention publications
(Morbidity and Mortality Weekly Report)
State Statutes
Nurse practice acts
State reporting statutes
 • Child abuse/elder abuse reporting statutes
 • Domestic violence reporting statutes
 • Health facility licensing laws

State Administrative Rules and Regulations
Licensing board rules

Board of Nursing
Position statements and advisories

Nursing Case Law
Appellate court decisions

Professional Organizations
Standards and guidelines for practice
Nursing journals
Position statements
Technical bulletins and practice resources
Code of ethics

Manufacturer Guidelines
Durable medical equipment
Drugs and solutions
Disposable equipment and supplies

Agency Policies and Procedures
Job descriptions
Agency-specific documents
Nursing care plans
Care maps or critical pathways
Unit- or department-based standards of practice
Medical bylaws

---

account varying levels of skill and expertise of the residents in training. There is also a chain of command policy to deal with unresolved disagreements between health care professionals and nonresponsive providers. Despite the existence of these policies, the nurse does not activate the chain of command.

The patient suffers hypovolemic shock caused by internal bleeding, and this leads to permanent anoxic brain damage. In this case, the nurse's failure to obtain additional medical advice and consultation (a senior resident was physically present and available in the hospital) was a substantial cause of the patient's injury. These two examples illustrate that negligence may constitute a commission (inappropriate penicillin administration) or an omission (failure to activate the chain of command) in care.

Negligence and the Doctrine of Res Ipsa Loquitur

In the majority of cases, a plaintiff must retain a nurse expert witness because the jury does not ordinarily possess the scientific and technologic knowledge necessary to determine the required standard of care. When the negligent act clearly lies within the range of a jury's common knowledge and experience, the doctrine of res ipsa loquitur ("the thing speaks for itself") may be applied. For instance, recent studies have reported close to 5000 foreign objects (instruments, needles, surgical sponges) inadvertently left in a patient's body following surgery each year (Stawicki, 2013). According to the CMS, the costs of removing a retained foreign object after surgery and treating complications of the error is estimated at approximately $60,000 per hospital stay (CMS, 2008). Leaving a surgical instrument in the patient's body after an operation is one case in which the doctrine of *res ipsa loquitur* may apply. It would be obvious to any layperson that it is below that standard of care not to remove a surgical instrument.

Dickerson v. Fatehi (1997) illustrates this point. A woman who underwent neck surgery experienced severe pain in her right arm, hand, and neck after the procedure. Approximately 20 months later, a second surgery was performed to determine the cause of the patient's continued pain. An 18-gauge hypodermic needle with a plastic attachment for a syringe was discovered in her neck and removed. The woman sued the surgeon and nurses involved in the original surgical procedure. The claims against the nurses included a failure to maintain a proper needle count and a failure to ensure the removal of the needle after surgery. The court hearing this case dismissed the suit. On appeal, the Supreme Court of Virginia reversed the lower court's decision and directed the case for trial. The Supreme Court held that in this particular case expert testimony was not necessary to establish the applicable standard of care and that the doctrine of *res ipsa loquitur* applied. A jury would be able to determine whether a reasonably prudent circulating nurse and scrub nurse should have made and reported an accurate needle count.

Gross Negligence

In some cases, the negligent act of the nurse is so reckless and reflects such a conscious disregard for the patient's welfare that it represents gross negligence. When the nurse acts with complete indifference to the consequences for his or her patient, the court may award special damages meant to punish the nurse for the outrageous conduct. These damages are referred to as *punitive damages.* Each state has established standards to determine when punitive damages may be awarded. In *Mobile Infirmary Medical Center v. Hodgen* (2003), the jury awarded $2.5 million in punitive damages (later reduced to $1.5 million) when a new graduate, not yet licensed, administered five times the ordered dose of digoxin. The jury found that the new graduate had been improperly supervised by the novice nurse assigned as her preceptor by the shift charge nurse. The charge nurse was also found liable for failing to properly direct the preceptor in her role responsibilities. The Supreme Court of Alabama found, among other things, that the nurses acted callously and wantonly, the legal threshold that must be crossed before punitive damages can be awarded (Snyder, 2003b).

Claims of Negligence and Student Nurses

Claims of negligence may arise when student nurses provide care. The emphasis on patient safety and reporting preventable adverse outcomes has brought an increasing number of student errors to light (Institute for Safe Medication Practices [ISMP], 2007; Mahlmeister, 2008; Wolf et al, 2009). Because the student is not yet a licensed professional, the faculty member or licensed nurse who is supervising the student is often named in the lawsuit (Brooke, 2009). The state board of nursing may have an advisory or position statement regarding the scope of practice of nursing students, and the duty of the supervising registered nurse supervising the student, to maintain the appropriate level of oversight. Such is the case in California, where the Board of Nursing has promulgated a position statement, "Clinical Learning Experiences: Nursing Students," to guide the supervising nurse in her duty (2008). The agency or hospital in which the student is practicing also may be named under the legal doctrine of vicarious liability. *Dimora v. Cleveland Clinic Foundation* (1996) is a case in point. A student nurse was assigned to care for a patient who had serious difficulty with maintaining her balance and required close supervision when standing, walking, and transferring. The student nurse testified that she knew the patient had an unsteady gait, but still left her unattended on a commode. The patient fell and was injured. The hospital was named in the lawsuit and appealed, claiming the student was not an employee. The Ohio Court of Appeals ruled that a hospital was held to the same legal standard of care for a student nurse's error as for the same error committed by a licensed professional nurse.

Several recent cases reinforce the importance of informing the patient that a student is providing the care, and documenting that he or she agrees to the care. In *Lovett v. Lorain Community Hospital* (2004), a student nurse, under the direct supervision of an instructor, administered Demerol and Vistaril by the intramuscular route and punctured the sciatic nerve. The patient sued the hospital for negligence. A lower court dismissed the initial lawsuit because the student and the instructor were not employees of the hospital. The Ohio Court of Appeals reversed the lower court's decision. The higher court affirmed that a patient may assume that the care he or she receives in a hospital is provided by that institution. The patient can assume that the student and instructor are agents of the hospital, unless the patient has been specifically informed and has agreed to receive care from the student (Snyder, 2004b).

Because a student nurse is not yet a licensed professional, if a lawsuit is filed the alleged claim is usually "ordinary negligence" rather than "professional malpractice." In one case, however, the Michigan Court of Appeals permitted a claim of professional malpractice when a student nurse committed a medication error resulting in the patient's death (*Dennis v. Specialty Select Hospital-Flint*, 2005). In this case, a physician ordered an oral antifungal agent (Nystatin). The student nurse erroneously administered the drug intravenously. The patient died shortly thereafter. The court ruled, among other things, that the student should have possessed the requisite knowledge and clinical judgment to administer the drug safely. The actions of the student were not "ordinary negligence," but "professional malpractice" (Tammelleo, 2005). The court also ruled that both the student nurse and the hospital in which the patient death occurred could be subjected to the claim for malpractice.

Criminal Negligence

Criminal negligence represents a case in which the negligent acts of the nurse (normally an unintentional civil wrong) also constitute a crime. In most states, a nurse can be prosecuted when the conduct is deemed so reckless that the action results in serious harm or death to the patient.

In 1997 two RNs and an advanced practice nurse licensed in Colorado were charged with criminal negligent homicide in the death of a newborn resulting from a medication error (Kowalski and Horner, 1998). In this case, an oil-based form of penicillin was erroneously administered to the infant. The drug was administered at 10 times the physician's prescribed dose. This case, first discussed in the nursing literature in 1998, describes medication dispensing and administration practices that still exist in many U.S. hospitals, placing patients in immediate jeopardy and exposing nurses to claims of criminal negligence. A more recent case that occurred in Wisconsin in 2006 illustrates the ongoing risks for catastrophic medication errors. A labor and delivery nurse inadvertently administered a piggyback solution bag of epidural anesthesia through a peripheral intravenous line. The patient, a 16-year-old female, experienced cardiovascular collapse and died. The error was compounded by a failure to place an identification band on the patient and to use the available point of care bar coding system. In the root cause analysis of this sentinel event conducted at a later date, "multiple latent systems failures" were also identified (Smetzer et al, 2010). The Wisconsin Department of Justice charged the nurse with a felony criminal offense. The charge was eventually reduced to a misdemeanor count of illegally administering prescription medications. The Wisconsin Department of Health and Human Services imposed restriction on the nurse's ability to participate in any capacity in a facility funded by Medicare and Medicare programs for 5 years. The Wisconsin Department of Regulation and Licensing suspended the nurse's license for 9 months, and the hospital terminated her employment. In response to the Wisconsin case, the ANA released a statement opposing charges of criminal misconduct when a registered nurse did not intentionally mean to harm the patient (ANA, 2007). The Association of Nurse Attorneys (TAANA) in collaboration with the American Association of Legal Nurse Consultants (AALNC) also published a Position Paper "Criminal Prosecution of Health Care Providers for Unintentional Human Error" (TAANA, 2011). The organizations strongly oppose criminalization of negligence stating,

> *"The belief that a medication error could lead to felony charges, steep fines, and a jail sentence also can have a chilling effect on recruitment and retention of health care providers—particularly nurses. Its potential impact on patient safety is enormous, sending the wrong message to healthcare professionals about the importance of reporting and analyzing errors."*

The Colorado and Wisconsin, cases should be read by every student nurse and licensed nurse in order to fully appreciate the change in the legal climate in the United States. They reflect the changing perspective of our justice system when negligent acts of health care professionals result in patient death. In the event of an unanticipated patient death, it is more likely that the conduct of basic as well as advanced practice nurses will be scrutinized by the criminal justice system. This shift may in part be a result of the public's increasing awareness of the magnitude of error in health care. It also may stem from consumer demands for greater accountability by health care systems and workers when injury or death occurs. Conservative estimates published by the Institutes of Medicine in 2000 suggested that as many as 98,000 patients die each year as a result of the negligence and malpractice of health care providers (IOM, 2000), and another 90,000 deaths per year are attributed to hospital-acquired infections (CMS, 2011). National data regarding hospital-acquired infections may be accessed at the Centers for Disease Control and Prevention's National Healthcare Safety Network at http://www.cdc.gov/nhsn/. Recent data derived from surveillance activities conducted by the Institute for Healthcare Improvement (IHI) using a new tracking tool, the "Global Trigger Tool," found that the number of adverse events in hospitals may be *ten times greater than previously measured* (Classen et al, 2012). This is an alarming and discouraging finding considering the immense time, money, and effort that have been spent in the last decade to improve patient care outcomes. The findings do, however, provide valuable information.

Other negative consequences that a nurse faces when criminal charges are filed include the loss of his or her job and disciplinary action by the state licensing board. Even when the criminal charges are not supported, the nurse's license can be suspended or revoked and out-of-pocket fines levied by the board if there is evidence of violation of the NPA. An attorney may have to be retained to represent the nurse at considerable personal expense when criminal charges are filed. The nurse's malpractice insurance generally does not cover the attorney's fees in this case. Neither is the nurse's employer obligated to pay the legal fees of a nurse charged with a felony. In the Colorado case, the nurse practitioner was immediately terminated. The two direct-care nurses were permitted to work in nonpatient care areas of the hospital. The costs of the criminal defense of all three nurses were paid by the hospital.

Nursing care that is deemed "deplorable" by the courts may result in disqualification of the nurse's employer from participation in the federal government's Medicare or Medicaid programs. Essentially the facility will be without adequate funding to continue operating, and the nursing staff will lose their jobs. A case in point is *Barbourville Nursing Home v. U.S. Department of Health and Human Services* (2006). During a compliance survey visit to the facility by the DHHS, major infractions of nursing home regulations were discovered. The federal government levied a fine in excess of $24,000 and, because the actions of the nurses placed the patients in immediate jeopardy (e.g., contaminating wounds with feces during dressing changes and inadequate skin care resulting in severe pressure sores), the

nursing home was disqualified from participating in Medicare.

Defenses Against Claims of Negligence

In some cases, a nurse can use certain legal doctrines as a defense against a claim of negligence. These standard defenses are discussed in the next section. In no case may a nurse provide a defense of "only following the provider's orders" against allegations of negligence (ANA, 2010 Snyder, 2007b). The NPA, licensing board rules and regulations, and nursing case law have delineated the nurse's independent duty to evaluate all provider orders before implementing them. In doing so, the nurse must consider two points: (1) is the order lawful, and (2) is the order in this particular patient's best interest?

Each nurse has an absolute duty to take some positive action to prevent harm when orders are inappropriate or incomplete or when the actions of another health care provider endanger the patient's well-being. This principle of affirmative duty is well recognized in law and in ethics. The ANA *Code of Ethics for Nurses* (2015) and the American Medical Association *Code of Medical Ethics* (2011) recognize the central role of nurses in preventing patient harm. A second principle underlying the nurse's legal and professional obligation to address questionable physician's orders or plan of care is patient advocacy (ANA, 2012). The nurse's duty to "speak out" in order to support and protect patients has been reaffirmed by The Joint Commission in its "Speak Up" initiative (TJC, 2013).

In *Columbia Medical Center of Las Colinas v. Bush* (2003), a jury awarded $13.1 million to a patient who suffered permanent brain damage and has no independent motor function or capacity for speech after receiving the wrong medication for a cardiac dysrhythmia. After consulting with a cardiologist, the ED physician ordered verapamil for treatment of the patient's ventricular tachycardia. The ED nurse, who was certified in advanced life support, and her nursing supervisor, who was present, knew the drug was contraindicated for ventricular tachycardia. The two nurses did not question the order and permitted an emergency medical technician (EMT) to give the drug. The patient suffered profound hypotension and cardiopulmonary arrest. The Texas Court of Appeals opined that the nurse and her supervisor had a duty, when they had serious questions about a medication involving extreme risk to the patient, to activate the chain of command to obtain additional medical consultation and advice (Tammelleo, 2004b).

Emergency Situations

Nursing care rendered in a life-threatening emergency may breach the standard of care required under ordinary circumstances. For instance, a woman who is 8 months pregnant arrives in the labor and delivery suite. She is hemorrhaging because of a premature separation of the placenta (abruptio placentae). An emergency cesarean delivery is ordered by the physician. The woman is near death as a result of blood loss. There also are clear signs of fetal distress. To expedite the surgical delivery, the operating room team does not observe the strict aseptic technique normally required during insertion of a Foley catheter into the woman's bladder and forgoes the lengthy abdominal scrub normally performed with an iodine solution.

The mother and infant are brought through the crisis safely, although the woman develops a skin infection at the site of the abdominal incision, which causes noticeable scarring. She also must be treated for a bladder infection, which resolves by discharge on the fourth postpartum day. She sues the nurses and physician. In this case, the defense could argue that the methods used were reasonable and prudent to save the life of the mother and baby. Even a delay of seconds could have resulted in the death of the woman or her infant. Expert witnesses are produced to support the defense assertion that it would breach the standard of care in this particular situation to follow customary procedures in preparing the woman for surgery.

Governmental Immunity

For nurses working in federal or state health care facilities, a defense of governmental immunity may be used. Laws have been enacted that shield individual health care workers employed in federal or (some) state facilities from personal responsibility for damages awarded in malpractice cases. Nurses employed by the Department of Veterans Affairs, the U.S. Public Health Service, the National Aeronautics and Space Administration, and the Department of Defense are shielded from civil suits in the performance of professional duties. This immunity was granted through enactment of specific federal statutes, including the Federal Tort Claims Act of 1946 and the Federal Employees Liability Reform and Tort Compensation Act of 1988. The intent of these laws was to substitute the U.S. government as the defendant in a malpractice suit. The government has waived its sovereign immunity against suit and pays the damages for injuries caused by the negligent acts of health care professionals employed in the aforementioned federal agencies.

State immunity statutes vary. In some instances, individual states have not waived their sovereign immunity from lawsuits. In these cases, the state is *not* substituted for the individual health care provider in malpractice cases. Nurses and physicians are liable for their negligent acts in these states and are personally responsible for damages awarded. It may be imperative in this circumstance for the health care professional to have individual malpractice insurance. The nurse should seek the advice of an attorney to determine whether it would be prudent to purchase malpractice insurance. The state affiliate of the ANA may also be helpful regarding the advisability of purchasing malpractice insurance.

Good Samaritan Immunity

Good Samaritan laws may limit a nurse's liability or shield the nurse from a malpractice claim if the nurse renders assistance in an emergency that occurs outside of the employment setting. Although in most states the nurse owes no legal duty to an accident victim, once the nurse makes a decision to stop and render aid (an ethical decision), a nurse-patient relationship is established. (Some states, including Vermont, Minnesota, and Wisconsin, have enacted "duty to rescue" or "compulsory assistance" laws.) Nurses should contact the state licensing board or the state association of the American Nurses Association to determine if the state in which they are licensed has a "duty to rescue" law.

When the nurse renders care at the scene of an accident, he or she is required to render the standard of care that any reasonable and prudent nurse would render in a similar situation. To prevail in a malpractice suit under the Good Samaritan laws, the plaintiff must prove that the nurse intentionally caused the injury or was grossly negligent. Therefore, each nurse should be familiar with his or her state-specific Good Samaritan statute. Nurses also should be reassured by the fact that the preponderance of malpractice cases that invoke the

Good Samaritan defense are settled in favor of the nurse.

Statutes of Limitation in Malpractice Cases

Each state has established a time limit in which a person may initiate a lawsuit. Although many states have established a time limit of 2 or 3 years from the date of the patient's injury or death in which the plaintiff must sue, statutes of limitation vary widely from state to state. In some jurisdictions, a "termination of treatment" rule exists. It is predicated on the assumption that some injuries result from a series of treatments over time. In this case, the statute of limitation does not begin to run until the treatment ends.

Other rules and regulations govern the "tolling" or running of the statutes of limitation. The court recognizes that an injured party cannot initiate a malpractice case until he or she discovers that some harm was done (discovery rule). This can occur when health care providers actually hide the facts in the case of an injury through fraud, deceit, or concealment, as in the following:

- Fraudulent or misleading entries in the medical record
- Destruction of evidence
- Destruction of the medical record

An Iowa case provides an example of a situation in which the statute of limitations may be extended (*Hanssen v. Genesis Health*, 2011). An orthopedic nurse erroneously gave a patient twice the dose of narcotic pain medication ordered by the physician. The patient became lethargic, experienced breathing problems, and fell twice in the bathroom. After the patient was discharged from the hospital, the orthopedic unit nurse manager wrote a letter to him. In the letter, the manager falsely stated that upon review of his chart, it was discovered that he had not received an incorrect dose of medication, but that he had a sensitivity reaction to the drug. The patient subsequently requested a copy of his complete medical record and decided to file a lawsuit against the nurse and hospital. The suit was filed more than two years after the alleged malpractice, which exceeded Iowa's 2-year statute of limitations. The hospital petitioned the court to dismiss the case based on the tolling of the statute. The court ruled that there were legal grounds for extending the statute because the patient was not aware of the medication error until he received a complete copy of the medical record, at which time he filed a claim.

The statute of limitation also is altered when a foreign object is left in the patient's body. Until the foreign object is discovered, the statute of limitation does not begin to run. States have rules that regulate the tolling of the statute of limitation in cases involving mentally incompetent adults and minors. In the case of an adult patient who is so severely injured that there is a loss of mental capacity, the statute of limitation may not begin to toll until mental competence is regained. The statute of limitation varies in the case of minors and may only expire when the child reaches the age of majority (18 or 21 years of age) (Westrick, 2013).

Each nurse should be familiar with the statute of limitation for his or her state. If the nurse suspects that some form of fraud or deceit has occurred relative to a patient's injury, the agency's risk manager or attorney should be contacted immediately. Major penalties and fines are applicable in cases in which health care providers deliberately deceive the patient or destroy evidence. These acts rise to the level of criminal misconduct and can result in loss of one's professional license and possible incarceration.

Transparency and Disclosure of Error

When errors occur in practice, studies repeatedly confirm that telling the patient (and family) about the mistake (voluntary disclosure) results in far less severe ramifications for the clinicians and health care facility (Hannawa, 2014). In 2001, TJC established a new patient safety care standard requiring that institutions have a process in place to disclose unanticipated outcomes to patients. Disclosure of errors and unanticipated adverse outcomes is a key element of the national patient safety movement. The process of disclosure has been delineated by the National Quality Forum [NQF] in its publication, "Safe Practices for Better Healthcare" (2010). Safe Practice Number 7 states,

> *"Following serious unanticipated outcomes, including those that are clearly caused by systems failures, the patient, and as appropriate, the family should receive timely, transparent, and clear communication concerning what is known about the event"* (p. v).

When an unanticipated outcome occurs, the provider is generally responsible for discussing the situation with the patient and or family members. Other agency representatives may be involved in the disclosure process, including administrators, risk managers, or attorneys (Heimchem et al, 2010). The nurse should not assume responsibility for disclosure before speaking to the provider and agency leaders. It should be determined in advance who will speak with the patient (or family) and how questions and concerns about the patient's condition, subsequent treatment, and the cost of any required care will be addressed (Myers, 2011). Fear that disclosure will lead to a malpractice claim is a significant barrier to voluntary disclosure, despite research findings to the contrary (Hannawa, 2014). In fact, patients sue for many reasons, including withdrawal of health team members after the event, silence, mishandling of information about unanticipated outcomes, delayed communication about adverse events, and anger when they believe they have not been told the truth about events (Kachalia, 2009). If a nurse believes that the patient has not received essential information, concerns are discussed first with the provider. If further clarification is required, the nurse refers to the facility's chain of command or unresolved dispute policy. Research conducted by Shannon and associates (2009) on nurses' perceptions regarding disclosure found that nurses conceived of disclosure as a team event, rather than a physician-patient discussion. Nurses believed they were excluded from the disclosure process. Furthermore, nurses in the study focus groups admitted to routinely and independently disclosing nursing errors that did not involve serious injury, but believed that when systems flaws or team mistakes contributed to the error and injury, the physician should serve as the team leader in the disclosure discussion.

Nursing Malpractice Insurance

With more states recognizing nursing malpractice as a legitimate claim in a civil suit, the question of whether nurses should carry malpractice insurance has become increasingly important. Nursing journals have published a number of articles that either address this question or describe the types of malpractice coverage the nurse should consider; textbooks also discuss the issue of liability insurance (Westrick, 2013). An increasing consensus appears to recommend that all nurses purchase malpractice insurance as a result of changes in the health care system, civil law, and insurance company policies. Legal authors also are quick to note the fallacy

of the assumption that having malpractice insurance increases the risk that the nurse will be targeted in a malpractice case. Lack of coverage will not discourage a lawsuit when there is a legitimate claim. Reasons given for the purchase of malpractice insurance by RNs include the following:

- Expanding functions of RNs and advanced practice nurses
- Floating and cross-training mandates
- Increasing responsibility for supervising subordinate staff
- Failure of some employers to initiate an adequate defense for nurses
- Insurance coverage limits that are lower than the actual judgment made against the nurse in a lawsuit

Other considerations that the nurse must take into account when considering malpractice insurance include whether he or she is employed by the federal government. In this case, the nurse may be shielded from personal liability by federal tort statutes, although some states still uphold the doctrine of "sovereign immunity," making it impossible to sue a state-run medical facility for negligence. In these states, it is a virtual necessity for nurses to purchase malpractice insurance because health care workers become the only available targets in a malpractice case.

Liability

Closely tied to the concepts of negligence and malpractice is that of liability. Liability asserts that every person is responsible for the wrong or injury done to another resulting from carelessness.

Personal Liability

Within the context of nursing practice, the nurse is always accountable for the outcomes of his or her actions in carrying out nursing duties. The rule of personal liability requires the professional nurse to assume responsibility for patient harm or injury that is a result of his or her negligent acts. The nurse cannot be relieved of personal liability by another professional, such as a provider or nurse manager, who asserts, "Don't worry; I'll take responsibility for the consequences."

The principle of personal liability is illustrated in a Connecticut case, *Osiecki v. Bridgeport Health Care Center, Inc.* (2005). A jury found that a nurse caring for a patient with a tracheostomy failed to provide proper tracheostomy care, assessment of breath sounds, and re-evaluation of the patient's pulmonary status at appropriate intervals. The patient died secondary to a pulmonary hemorrhage, and the breaches in the standard of nursing care were found to be a substantial factor contributing to the patient's death. Had the nurse properly assessed the patient and at frequent intervals, early identification of pulmonary congestion would have permitted timely treatment. The surviving spouse was awarded $827,000 for the nurse's negligent actions. In another case, *Janga v. Colombrito* (2011), the nurses caring for a patient receiving anticoagulants were sued individually for his death, which was due to complications of bleeding. The nurses were found negligent for failing to question the order for anticoagulants before a patient underwent a lumbar puncture. There was conflicting testimony about whether or not a physician had issued an order to discontinue the anticoagulants. However, even if the physician did not direct the nurses to stop the medications, the plaintiff's expert witness nurse asserted that they had a duty to recognize that anticoagulants should not be given prior to a lumbar puncture and to advise the physician that they had nevertheless been administered. The court directed the jury to weigh the extent to which the nurses' negligence contributed to the unfortunate outcome. The jury directed the nurses to pay 15% of the monetary award.

In 1989, the ANA summarized the most frequent allegations of negligence leveled against nurses in malpractice cases (Box 8-4). These charges have not substantially changed in the ensuing decades (Nursing Service Organization [NSO], 2009). As nurses assume increasing responsibility for the monitoring and care of patients with complex health problems, the claim of "failure to rescue" is made with increasing frequency (Taenzer et al, 2011). Nurses may be educated to implement effective risk-control strategies that reduce these claims. These personal and system-wide strategies are discussed in the next section.

Many nurses practice under the misconception that they are protected from personal liability when employed by a health care entity, such as a hospital. I have heard nurses say, "Why would a patient sue me personally? I don't have the financial resources of this (hospital, nursing home, home health care agency)!" Nurses can and have been individually

---

> **BOX 8-4 Most Frequent Allegations of Nursing Negligence**
>
> - Failure to communicate and report*
> - Failure to monitor the patient and report significant findings
> - Failure to ensure patient safety
> - Failure to rescue
> - Improper treatment or negligent performance of the treatment
> - Medication errors
> - Failure to follow the agency's policies and procedures
> - Failure to invoke the chain of command/access the line of authority

*The Joint Commission found that communication failures (i.e., reporting, SBAR communication, and shift handoffs) were the number-one contributing cause of medical error and preventable adverse outcomes (*Joint Commission guide to improving staff communication,* Oakbrook Terrace, IL, 2005, The Joint Commission).
Adapted from Nursing Service Organization: CNA Healthpro nursing claims study: an analysis of claims with risk management recommendations 1997-2007, Hatboro, PA, 2008, Nursing Service Organization (website). www.nso.com/pdfs/db/rnclaimstudy.pdf?fileName=rnclaimstudy.pdf&folder=pdfs/db&isLiveStr=Y&refID=rnclaim. Accessed April 2009.

---

named in lawsuits and found negligent. Damages can be levied against the nurse's current assets and future earnings for negligent acts. Furthermore, as Snyder (2003) reports, hospitals have sued nurses to recoup financial losses suffered when they were required to pay damages for the alleged negligence of the nurses named in the malpractice case. Personal liability is illustrated in the case of *Siegel v. Long Island Jewish Medical Center* (2003).

Personal Liability with Floating and Cross-Training

New models of patient care often mandate floating and cross-training of patient care staff to enhance efficiency and reduce staffing costs. These models of care have increased the personal liability of nurses (Westrick, 2013). Professional nurses must be cognizant of state statutes and case law when asked to perform services outside of their usual area of practice. In no case is a nurse permitted to perform tasks or render services when he or she lacks the requisite knowledge and skill to act competently.

The NPA and the administrative rules and regulations of the licensing board provide explicit statutory language regarding a nurse's duty to provide safe and competent care. For example, the Administrative Rules of the Tennessee Board of Nursing (revised, 2011) state:

> *"The Board believes that the individual nurse is responsible for maintaining and demonstrating competence in the practice role whether the recipient of the nursing intervention is the individual, family, community, nursing staff, nursing student body, or other."*
>
> **Tennessee Rules and Regulations of Registered Nurses Rule 1000-01-14: Standards of Nursing Competence**

In addition to the laws governing practice in floating and cross-training situations, an increasing body of nursing case law also defines the limitation of assignments. Appellate court decisions have addressed the issue of when a nurse may safely refuse an assignment to float without the risk of job termination. A landmark case, *Winkelman v. Beloit Memorial Hospital* (1992), addressed the legal issues surrounding floating. The Supreme Court of Wisconsin ruled that under certain circumstances, a nurse had a right to refuse floating assignments without fear of reprisal.

Nurse Winkelman was a skilled maternity nurse who was employed for 16 years at Beloit Memorial Hospital, working exclusively in the nursery. In 1987, the hospital created a policy that required nurses in the maternity setting to float when the patient census was low in their unit. Nurse Winkelman was asked to float to an adult floor dedicated to the care of postoperative and geriatric patients. She notified her immediate supervisor that she did not feel qualified to float to that unit and that attempting to provide care in that setting would place the patients at risk. In her testimony, the nurse said that she was given three choices: float, find another nurse who would float in her place, or take an unexcused absence day. She subsequently went home, and her employer construed her actions as "voluntary resignation of her employment." Nurse Winkelman then filed a complaint for wrongful discharge and breach of contract. A jury verdict was rendered in favor of Nurse Winkelman on the charge of wrongful discharge. The case was appealed and affirmed by the Supreme Court of Wisconsin. The court found that the nurse had identified a fundamental and well-defined public policy in the Wisconsin Administrative Code, which stated that a nurse should not offer or perform services for which he or she is not qualified by education, training, or experience.

The nurse's right to refuse a floating assignment has not been supported in all cases. Courts have affirmed the right of a health care facility to redirect staff to meet the needs of patients. The New Mexico Supreme Court, in *Francis v. Memorial General Hospital* (1986), held that the hospital was not prohibited from discharging a nurse who refused to float when the employer had made a reasonable offer to train the nurse for new responsibilities.

Nurse Francis, a critical care nurse, refused to float to an orthopedic unit, stating he did not feel qualified to care for orthopedic patients. The hospital then offered to provide him with an orientation to the floors where he might float in the future. When he refused the opportunity for orientation, he was terminated. The court upheld his discharge.

Although it is clear that nurses have a legal duty to refuse specific tasks that they cannot perform safely and competently, the prudent nurse should carefully consider the consequences of not floating. Careful negotiation with the nursing supervisor and the team leader making the actual assignment will often result in a satisfactory compromise. The floated nurse should clarify what aspects of professional nursing care he or she can safely carry out and which tasks are beyond his or her current capabilities. A reasonable supervisor will not insist that a nurse attempt to perform a task that he or she has no education, training, or current expertise to implement.

Another important strategy that may reduce the nurse's personal liability is to request that the team leader appoint a resource nurse who is skilled in the care of the patients on the unit. The resource nurse can assist the floated nurse as needed. It also is prudent practice for the floated nurse to enter a note in the medical record naming the resource or support nurse who will be available and responsible to assist with planning and evaluating care. For instance:

> *"Assumed care of Mrs. Jones after report completed. L. Doe, RN, will co-manage patient and assist with procedures, planning, and evaluation of care as needed."*
>
> **J. Smith, RN (Floater)**

An NPA affirms that an RN ultimately is responsible for the quality of care provided to each patient, regardless of who actually is delegated the responsibility of carrying out the task. A claim of negligence may be leveled against the team leader who does not assign a competent "backup" or resource nurse to assist the floater. Only a nurse who is competent in the care of the patients normally treated in the setting (hospital, clinic, or home) can properly supervise a lesser-skilled worker and evaluate the outcomes of care.

Furthermore, TJC requires accredited organizations to ensure that all staff providing patient care, including float staff and agency or registry nurses, are properly oriented to their jobs and the work environment before providing care (TJC, 2014). Chapter 13 provides additional information about floating and accepting assignments.

Personal Liability for Team Leaders and Managers

The concept of personal liability extends to nurses who function as team leaders, supervisors, and upper-level managers. Team leaders, charge nurses, and managers are held to the standard of care of the reasonably prudent nurse employed in that role (Mahlmeister, 2006). Claims of negligence leveled against charge nurses generally surround the following:

- Functioning as a first responder in emergencies
- Triage of patients and allocation of staff and equipment
- Delegation of patient care tasks
- Supervision of orientees, float staff, and subordinates
- Reporting performance deficits in team members
- Supporting or invoking the chain of command process when indicated

Nurse managers and administrators at the upper end of the management ladder also may be held liable for the following:

- Inadequate training
- Failure to periodically re-evaluate staff competencies
- Failure to discipline or terminate unsafe workers
- Negligence in developing appropriate policies and procedures
- Failure to uphold institutional licensing laws and state and federal statutes

The implementation of new models of care that alter staffing patterns and mixes may place managers at the same risk for liability as the health care providers delivering the actual bedside care (Roussel, 2011). The

ANA affirms this view in the *Code of Ethics for Nurses* (2015):

> *"Although nurses in administration, education, and research have relationships with patients that are less direct, in assuming the responsibilities of a particular role, they share responsibility for the care provided by those whom they supervise and instruct." (p. 17)*

The appropriate standard of care is established in the case of team leaders, charge nurses, managers, and leaders by expert nurse witnesses who function in those positions. An increasing body of case law in malpractice suits also is contributing to expectations about team leader and manager conduct. Although nurse managers and administrators generally are well aware of their particular liability risks, direct-care nurses who are relatively unfamiliar with the expanding role of team leaders or charge nurses may be particularly vulnerable to claims of negligence. Health care redesign has resulted in considerable flattening of the chain of command for nursing departments.

In September 2003, the American Organization of Nurse Executives, the American Hospital Association, and other health-related organizations submitted an *amicus curiae* (friend of the court) brief in support of the unique role of the charge nurse (brief *amici curiae*, July 24, 2003). These associations responded to a National Labor Relations Board invitation to file briefs to provide guidance on the meaning of the term *independent judgment* and the scope of discretion required for independent judgment with respect to the charge nurse. The brief asserts that:

> *"The charge nurse's background in the hospital's organization and in nursing practice enables him or her to step in when there is crisis or conflict, quickly to assess the situation and identify needed resources. Charge nurses also direct other employees, sometimes making split-second decisions that can literally be a matter of life or death." (pp. 6-7)*

Team leaders, regardless of their title or designation, have assumed greater responsibility for unit- or department-based functions.

Any RN functioning in the role of team leader or charge nurse should review the following documents from administration:

- Detailed job description for the role, including how responsibilities are limited when the nurse is asked to lead a team or serve as a charge nurse on an unfamiliar floor or department

- Job descriptions for the team members assigned delegated tasks
- Formal period of training and mentoring in the role
- Validated proof of competence before team leading independently
- Guidelines regarding personal patient care assignment when also serving as team leader
- Chain of command model for the facility, department, or unit

Administrators and nurse managers should be aware of landmark case laws regarding incompetent charge nurses and team leaders. A jury directed a verdict in excess of $7 million against a hospital in a 1995 Illinois case, *Holston v. Sisters of the Third Order* (1995).

A charge nurse repeatedly refused a direct-care nurse's requests to personally evaluate a patient whose vital signs were rapidly deteriorating after gastric bypass surgery. The charge nurse also refused to call the patient's physician until the patient experienced cardiopulmonary collapse. Emergency surgery revealed that a central venous pressure catheter had migrated and perforated the cardiac muscle. The patient experienced cardiac tamponade and died approximately 1 week after this critical incident.

This case illustrates the necessity of validating the strong clinical skill of all RNs who are being considered for a leadership role that includes clinical supervision and consultation. Effective risk management of an unresolved clinical problem requires direct-care nurses to consult early and frequently with team leaders or managers. Each consultation with the team leader or manager should be carefully documented in the patient's medical record to demonstrate that appropriate chain of command process has occurred. The employer will likely be named in any lawsuit under the rule of vicarious liability if the team leader or manager offers negligent advice. Vicarious liability is discussed later in this chapter.

Personal Liability in Delegation and Supervision of Team Members

Team leaders and charge nurses who are responsible for delegation and supervision of team members must be absolutely clear about the legality of patient care assignments. They must determine whether it is reasonable and prudent to delegate a particular task based on their knowledge of the worker, the patient's status, and the current conditions in the work setting. The determination of whether a team leader or charge nurse has been negligent in delegating any particular patient care task or supervising

subordinates will be based on these aforementioned considerations.

Mobile Infirmary Medical Center v. Hodgen (2003) is a case in point. A patient with cardiac problems sued after suffering catastrophic physical and mental disabilities when a graduate nurse, not yet licensed, administered five times the ordered dose of digoxin. The shift charge nurse assigned another nurse with only 7 months' experience to act as the graduate nurse's preceptor. The preceptor did not supervise the new graduate when she administered the drug. The jury found all three nurses negligent. The court criticized the shift charge nurse for assigning a novice nurse as a preceptor and for failing to give her explicit directions regarding the level of supervision required in the circumstances. The court also faulted the preceptor, who had never worked with the new graduate, for inadequate supervision. The jury awarded $2.5 million in punitive damages.

Criteria for lawful and safe delegation have been spelled out by state boards of nursing and professional organizations, such as the ANA, the American Association of Critical-Care Nurses, and the NCSBN (AACN, 2004; ANA, 2012; ANA-NCSBN, 2005). These guidelines and a growing body of case law assist the nurse in making decisions about safe delegation of patient care.

In *Williams v. West Virginia Board of Examiners* (2004), the Supreme Court of Appeals of West Virginia upheld the Kentucky Board of Nursing's disciplinary action of an RN. The nurse was responsible for supervising the care of home health aides. Inspectors found numerous violations of the nurse's duty to delegate and supervise care given by the aides. Furthermore, there was evidence that the nurse falsified patients' records, indicating that home health aides were present, when in fact they were absent from the home. The nursing board suspended the nurse's license for 1 year.

Employer Liability

Although a nurse is never relieved of personal liability, the doctrine of vicarious or substituted liability permits a person to also sue the employer for the negligent conduct of nurses within the scope of their employment. Vicarious liability is based on the legal principle of *respondeat superior,* a Latin term that means "let the master answer" (for the actions of subordinates or servants). Because the employer has some control over the worker, the courts have affirmed that the employer may be held responsible for the employee's negligent acts when injury occurs.

In a New York case, *Pedraza v. Wyckoff Heights Medical Center* (2002), a hospital was found liable for the negligence of its nurses when they failed to adhere to the explicit policy it had established that bedrails were to be raised at all times for a particular category of high-risk patients. An 86-year-old patient with Alzheimer's disease was admitted to the hospital for pulmonary problems. Because the woman had Alzheimer's disease, she was classified as high risk for falling, and a fall-injury prevention protocol was to be implemented per hospital policy. A safety alert sign was to be posted above the bed, the patient was to be checked every 2 hours, the bed was to be kept in the lowest position, and all bedrails were to be up at all times. This protocol was not followed. A nurse found the patient face down on the floor in the hallway. One bedrail was down when the nurse had put the patient to bed after ambulating her. The hospital argued, in its defense, that keeping all four bedrails raised amounted to physical restraints and that restraints could not be applied without a physician's order. The court ruled in favor of the injured patient. The court opined that when a hospital employee expressly violates the institution's own internal policy, it is evidence of negligence. A further discussion about the legal aspects related to the use of restraints is presented later in this chapter.

Corporate Liability

Hospitals and other health care facilities have evolved into dynamic systems that coordinate the care provided by a range of health care professionals. As a consequence of these changes, the courts have expanded the concept of corporate negligence in verdicts rendered against health care giants. In *Brodowski v. Ryave* (2005), the Pennsylvania Superior Court ruled that there was sufficient evidence that a systematic breakdown in communication caused an improper diagnosis and led to the patient's admission to a psychiatric unit before a stroke had been ruled out (Passarella, 2005). The patient was not properly treated, is now partially paralyzed, and has brain damage. The "standard of care" required of a health care corporation has been established through these cases but varies from state to state. Some jurisdictions have permitted TJC standards or state department of health licensing laws to define the "corporate standard of care." An agency's own medical bylaws or policies and procedures have been admitted as evidence of the appropriate corporate standard of care. In

Thompson v. Nason Hospital (1991), the court elaborated four duties of a health care corporation:
1. Maintain safe and adequate physical facilities and equipment.
2. Select and retain competent physicians.
3. Oversee the acts of all persons who practice medicine within the facility as they relate to patient care.
4. Formulate, adopt, and enforce rules and policies to ensure quality of care.

The court in the *Brodowski* case based its ruling on the doctrine of corporate liability outlined in the *Thompson* case.

Health care facilities also have been found corporately liable for failing to have adequate numbers of qualified nursing staff assigned on each shift to meet the needs of patients. In a landmark case, *HCA Health Services v. National Bank* (1988), an unattended infant experienced respiratory arrest and suffered permanent anoxic brain damage. The jury rendered a verdict for the plaintiff and awarded $2 million in compensatory damages (for the cost of ongoing care) and $2 million in punitive damages for failing to provide an adequate number of qualified staff.

The current nursing shortage is anticipated to grow in the first decades of this century. Nurses must develop a clear understanding of principles of safe staffing and advocate for appropriate staffing levels. Guidelines published by the ANA (2012) can assist nurses to ensure the efficient use of human resources. Nurses should review position statements published by the Board of Nursing as well as their specialty nursing organizations (e.g., Association of PeriOperative Registered Nurses [AORN] or the Association of Women's Health, Obstetric and Neonatal Nurses [AWHONN]). Staffing guidelines promulgated by these organizations may assist the nurse in articulating concerns and formulating recommendations for improved staffing levels. Another useful strategy is to provide managers and administrators with journal articles that discuss the liability of hospitals when they do not provide sufficient numbers of qualified team members to meet patient needs (Kalisch et al, 2011).

As more nurses become independent contractors, working for temporary staffing agencies, courts have been asked to determine whether a hospital using temporary nursing staff was liable for the acts of an agency nurse (*Ruelas v. Staff Builders Personnel Services, Inc.,* [2001]). An agency nurse was alleged to have abused a patient during administration of an enema. (The precise nature of the abuse was not delineated.) The court affirmed that as a general rule, the employer (in this case, Staff Builders) is legally liable for an employee's wrongful conduct. However, in this case, the agency had no practical or even theoretical right to control how its nurses carried out their clinical responsibilities in a particular setting. Although the agency is responsible for ensuring that the nurse has the requisite license, education, experience, and certifications, the hospital has direct control and supervision of the nurse's actions. Staff Builders was dismissed from the lawsuit.

TJC has developed detailed standards related to the orientation, training, and education of agency (contracted) staff (TJC, 2014). Courts have affirmed that facilities have a duty to provide a targeted orientation for agency nurses. A job-based or unit-based handout, if readily available, can be a useful reference for the agency nurse. A mentor or resource nurse should be provided during the targeted orientation and thereafter as needed when a new task or problem is encountered. Team members should have an opportunity to evaluate the agency nurse and provide written feedback about performance.

REDUCING LEGAL LIABILITY

Risk Management Systems

One of the most powerful allies the nurse has in any health care setting to facilitate positive change and reduce personal and corporate liability is the risk manager. The risk manager is a professional who tracks accidents and injuries that occur in the facility. The job of the risk manager is to establish and strengthen systems within the agency to reduce preventable patient injuries or deaths, and to eliminate the loss of revenues as fines or the payment of damages through the insurance carrier. The risk manager may assist nurse managers in the development of effective policies and procedures to improve practice. The risk manager also is knowledgeable about federal and state administrative rules and regulations affecting health care systems, health care licensing laws, and health care case law. This knowledge is essential to prevent inadvertent violation of health care laws and to reduce claims of negligence and malpractice within the institution.

The IOM report *To Err Is Human* (2000) recommends a proactive approach to risk management. Nurses are encouraged to anticipate the potential for errors, report "near misses," and work closely with the risk manager to reduce preventable adverse events. All health care providers are urged to develop high-reliability operating systems. This concept is derived from the airline and nuclear energy industries. Both have established excellent safety records despite the highly complex and dangerous nature of their operations. The IOM recommends creation of a nationwide mandatory reporting system for collection of information about adverse events and the development of performance standards that focus on patient safety. Nurses will play a central role in this process.

Incident Reports or Unusual Occurrence Reports

Nurses are legally bound to report critical incidents to their nurse managers, agency administration, and the risk manager through a formal intra-agency document titled the "Unusual Occurrence Report" or "Incident Report." Emphasis on patient safety and quality has resulted in renaming of the Incident Report in many health care settings. The document is frequently referred to as the "Unusual Occurrence Form" but is also known by other titles, such as the "Quality Variance Report." This form often is directed to the risk management department through the nurse's immediate manager. The nurse manager has an opportunity to review the written report and begin the process of collecting information and mitigating any identified systems flaws in a timely fashion, depending on the nature of the incident. The report then is forwarded (usually within 24 hours) to the risk manager. If an ongoing problem does not appear to be any closer to resolution as the nurse works through the formal chain of command, the nurse may speak directly to the risk manager for guidance and advice. However, in the usual course of events, the nurse would first address concerns with his or her immediate nurse manager.

Unfortunately, studies indicate that the rate of incident reporting still remains relatively low, particularly among physician providers (USDHHS, 2012). As a condition of participation in the Medicare program, federal regulations require that hospitals develop and maintain a Quality Assessment and Performance Improvement (QAPI) program. To satisfy these requirements, hospitals must "track medical errors and adverse patient events, analyze their causes, and implement preventive actions and mechanisms that include feedback and learning throughout the hospital" (U.S. Office of Inspector General, 2012).

Unfortunately, the report released by the Office of Inspector General (OIG) found that hospital incident reporting systems captured only an estimated 14% of the patient harm events experienced by Medicare beneficiaries. Hospital risk managers, clinical managers, and administrators investigated only those reported events that they considered most likely to lead to quality and safety improvements. Few policy or practice changes were implemented as a result of reported events. Hospital administrators classified the remaining events (86% of all incident reports) as either events that staff did not perceive as reportable (61%) or as events that staff commonly report but did not report in this case (25%). The OIG recommended that the CMS and AHRQ collaborate to create and promote a list of potentially reportable events for hospitals to use, and that the CMS provide guidance to accreditors regarding their assessments of hospital efforts to track and analyze events.

Critical incidents that result in patient injury or death eventually may lead to a malpractice claim. Because state laws vary as to whether the incident report may be "discovered" by the plaintiff's attorney in a lawsuit, it is essential that the nurse follow appropriate procedures when completing and filing this document:

1. The nurse should describe all events objectively and avoid subjective comments, personal opinions about why the incident occurred, or assumptions about events that were not witnessed. For example, if a patient was found lying on the floor at the foot of the bed, the nurse should avoid the statement, "Patient fell out of bed—found on floor." That the patient fell out of bed is an unfounded assumption. The nurse should instead state, "Entered room. Patient discovered lying prone at the foot of the bed. Both upper and lower side rails were raised."

2. The nurse should never note in the patient's medical record that an incident report has been completed and filed. This may alter the protection from discovery normally provided the document in some states. The jury also will be made aware that an incident report has been filed because they have access to nurses' notes submitted in evidence during the trial.

3. The nurse should never photocopy the incident report for his or her personal files. Photocopying an incident report generally is prohibited by agency policy and may be expressly prohibited in writing on the incident report itself. Photocopying the incident report and taking it out of the agency violates patient confidentiality. It may fall into the hands of individuals who are not authorized to read any information about the patient. It may fall into the hands of the plaintiff's attorney, should a lawsuit be filed, with damaging effects on the agency's ability to defend against the claims of negligence.

4. Physicians and advanced practice nurses should not write an order for an incident report to be filed. This brings the existence of an incident report to the attention of the plaintiff's attorney.

5. Report every unusual occurrence or incident. Do not assume that "everyone knows about the problem or event." Box 8-5 lists circumstances under which an incident report should be filed.

BOX 8-5 Circumstances Under which an Incident Report Should be Filed*

- Patient or client injury
- Unanticipated patient death
- Malfunction or failure of durable medical equipment
- Significant or unanticipated adverse reactions to ordered therapy or care
- Inability to meet a patient's need(s), ordered therapy, medications, or treatments after consultation with appropriate nurse mangers or providers. This may be related to:
  - System problems (e.g., pharmacy closed, drug not available)
  - Unresolved problem with order (e.g., incomplete or illegible order)
  - Lack of qualified staff to implement order to provide needed care (e.g., registered nurse [RN] not available to perform task, and law stipulates that only an RN may perform the task
  - Patient or family refusal of care (e.g., request for do-not-resuscitate [DNR] orders)
- Unresolved problems with physical plant that jeopardize patient well-being (e.g., electrical hazard, loose carpet section, delay in repair of essential equipment)
- Unethical, illegal, or incompetent practice that is witnessed or reported
- Patient complaint about provider or health care worker
- Toxic spills, fires, other environmental emergencies
- Violent behavior on the part of family or patient

* This list is not comprehensive but is a representative list of occurrences that should be reported.

INTENTIONAL TORTS IN NURSING PRACTICE

Ordinarily, in the course of carrying out one's nursing duties, breaches in the applicable standard of care are assumed to be unintentional acts. In other words, the nurse did not intend to harm the patient. As noted, this civil wrong is referred to as an *unintentional tort*. An intentional tort is a second category of civil wrong. It involves the direct violation of a person's legal rights. In this case, the nurse intends to perform the offensive act, although normally most nurses do not mean to harm the patient. The following acts are intentional torts:

- Assault
- Battery
- Defamation of character
- False imprisonment
- Invasion of privacy
- Intentional infliction of emotional distress

In the case of intentional torts, the plaintiff does not have to prove that the nurse breached a special duty or was negligent. The duty is implied in law (e.g., the duty to respect a patient's right to privacy). In general, legal remedies for intentional torts include fines and punitive damages, although some intentional torts rise to the level of a criminal act (such as battery) and may result in a jail sentence. Some states, such as California, also have enacted penalties that include a term of imprisonment for willful and malicious breach of confidentiality in releasing information about a patient's human immunodeficiency virus (HIV) status.

Assault and Battery

Patients who agree to treatment or nursing care do not surrender their rights to determine who touches them. Assault is causing the person to fear that he or she will be touched without consent. Battery is the unauthorized or the actual harmful or offensive touching of a person. It is important to note that a charge of battery does not require proof of harm or injury. Nurses engaged in therapeutic procedures may face charges of battery if they touch a patient without consent. It is essential that the nurse ask the patient's permission to proceed before initiating any procedure, particularly those of an invasive nature.

Nurses also should document that the patient has given permission for the treatment or procedure. Consider the following situation:

"A woman in active labor cries out through each contraction. The nurse has a standing order from the obstetrician for administration of an intravenous narcotic should the woman request pain relief. However, the woman refuses, being determined to experience a medication-free birth. As labor progresses, the woman's cries become so loud that other laboring women and visitors in the unit express concern and anxiety. Repeated efforts to assist the woman with breathing and relaxation exercises to reduce her vocalization have failed. The nurse finally says to the patient, "Look, if you don't stop screaming and making those horrible noises, I'm going to give you the pain medication your doctor has ordered, whether you want it or not. You're frightening the other patients!" She repeats this threat several times and in the presence of the woman's family. Although the woman continues to cry out, the nurse does not give the medication. The delivery of the infant is uneventful and without problems. After discharge from the hospital, the patient retains a lawyer, claiming she was threatened with being sedated against her will. She further asserts that the nurse's repeated threats to inject her with a narcotic created an unbearable level of anxiety that interfered with her ability to cooperate with other necessary procedures during the birth. This assertion could result in a charge of negligence or intentional infliction of emotional distress."

In this case, the nurse is charged with assault (i.e., threatening the patient with unauthorized touching). Had the nurse actually carried out her threat of giving the medication, the charge could be expanded to assault and battery. Consequences for the nurse charged with assault may include the following:

- Imposition of fines and punitive damages
- State board of nursing disciplinary action
- Termination by the employer

When battery occurs, the nature of the touching may raise the offense to the level of a crime. In the aforementioned scenario, assume that the nurse decides to give the narcotic against the woman's will. She engages the assistance of a scrub technician to physically restrain the woman so that she can access a vein for the injection. The technician, becoming frustrated with the woman's resistance to the procedure, says, "You're going to be sorry if you don't stop struggling." The technician purposefully hyperextends the woman's arm and says, "There, maybe if it hurts enough, you'll stop this nonsense." A loud snapping sound is heard, and tests indicate that the technician has fractured the woman's arm. The charge of battery in this case may result in more serious ramifications, including punitive damages and a term of imprisonment. Both of these cases are fact-based events known to this author. Unfortunately, similar cases are noted in the nursing and legal literature each month.

Defamation of Character

A person has a right to be free from attacks on his or her reputation (defamation of character). *Libel* is a form of defamation caused by written work. *Slander* refers to an injury to one's reputation caused by the spoken word. Nurses may be subject to a charge of libel for subjective comments meant to denigrate the patient that are placed in the medical record or in other written materials read by others. For example, a patient suffering from extreme pain who requested narcotics frequently was labeled as a "whiner," a "liar," and a "drug seeker" with an "addictive personality." These comments were noted on the medical record, on the nursing Kardex, and in the nurses' notes attached to a clipboard, which was kept on a wall peg outside the patient's room.

The patient subsequently was found to have a severe intraabdominal infection that accounted for the intense pain he experienced. The patient sued for failure of the medical staff to identify and treat the infection. In the process of discovery, the patient, his family, and the attorney he had retained read the defamatory comments about his character. It was a distinct possibility that other family members, coworkers, and the patient's employer who visited may have read these subjective comments on the clipboard. A charge of libel was leveled against the nursing staff.

Nurses also may face charges of slander when they repeat similar types of subjective comments about patients in public places, such as elevators or hospital cafeterias. All patient care staff must be extremely cautious about discussing the patient or their opinions about the patient in public places. Even in report rooms or conference rooms, nurses should consider who in the immediate vicinity could inadvertently overhear the conversation. In all circumstances, only objective, professional language should be used in discussing patients.

False Imprisonment

False imprisonment is defined as the unlawful restraint or detention of another person against his or her wishes. Actual force is not necessary to support a charge of false imprisonment. An adult of sound mind (mentally competent) has a right to refuse any treatment that has previously been agreed to (Mathes, 2014). If he or she refuses, the person may leave the facility (e.g., hospital, rehabilitation center, long-term care facility) whenever he or she chooses. The nurse has no authority to detain the patient, even if there is a likelihood of harm or injury as a result of discontinuing therapy.

The nurse has a duty to immediately notify the provider and appropriate nursing supervisors when a competent patient intends to leave "against medical advice" (AMA) but may not in any way prevent the individual from leaving the facility. Many agencies request that a patient sign an AMA form when they intend to leave in contradiction to the plan of care and despite the absence of a discharge order. The form may provide the facility with a reasonable defense against a malpractice claim if the patient's condition worsens or an injury is sustained and a malpractice claim is filed. A more detailed discussion follows later in this chapter.

Intentional Infliction of Emotional Distress

When the nurse's behavior is so outrageous that it leads to the emotional shock of a patient, the court can compensate the patient for emotional distress. A recent case in the area of maternity nursing illustrates the potential for a claim of intentional infliction of emotional distress. In *Roddy v. Tanner Medical Center* (2003), a woman brought suit against the hospital after she was treated in the ED for a miscarriage at approximately 10 weeks' gestation. While en route to the hospital, Ms. Roddy felt something large extrude from her vagina, and she bled heavily. She reported to the ED nurse that whatever she had passed was still in her underpants with a great deal of blood. Ms. Roddy indicated that the nurse told her she would take whatever she could out of her clothes, and then the nurse placed the soiled clothes in a plastic bag.

Ms. Roddy was subsequently discharged home in stable condition after a gynecologic examination confirmed that she had passed the products of conception. When she returned home and began to remove her clothes from the plastic bag to launder them, the intact fetus dropped to the floor. Ms. Roddy claimed intentional infliction of emotional distress. The court permitted the case to go forward, indicating that there was evidence of "reckless disregard" of the rights of the patient.

Invasion of Privacy

Another basic right is to be free from interference with one's personal life. An invasion of privacy occurs when a person's private affairs (including health history and status) is made public without consent. The nurse has a legal and ethical duty to maintain patient confidentiality, and there may be serious repercussions when the nurse breaches this duty and violates this fundamental patient right.

With the growing use of electronic information systems, issues related to patient confidentiality and invasion of privacy are now being addressed by federal and state legislatures. Statutes, including the federal law HIPAA, have been enacted to control access to electronic health data. Nurses are given passwords to access a patient's electronic medical record. Nurses should never share passwords with colleagues because this increases the risk of unauthorized access to the patient's record. Discussion of patients on social media Internet sites and taking unauthorized pictures of patients with personal electronic devices is a growing area for claims of HIPAA violation and invasion of privacy. The American Nurses Association (2011) and The National Council of State Boards of Nursing (2011) have both published guidelines for nurses with precautionary advice.

In certain circumstances, the law permits divulging information contained in a patient's medical record. These situations include reporting certain communicable diseases, child abuse, and gunshot wounds to the proper authorities. If a nurse is asked to provide information to any sources, the matter should immediately be referred to the agency's administrator or risk manager. In no case should the nurse personally divulge the information or provide copies of the patient's record to another person or agency. Another fact-based case known to this author illustrates the intentional torts of invasion of privacy and intentional infliction of emotional distress. Consider the following situation:

"A nurse works in a physician's office in a small, semirural community. The majority of the town's residents know each other. A patient being treated for several opportunistic infections has an HIV test performed. The nurse also is aware that the patient has been questioned by the physician about his sexual activities and that he has divulged that he is gay and has had unprotected sex with several male partners. When the test results are reported as positive, the nurse calls several close friends (who also know the patient) and reports the finding and information about the patient's sexual conduct. Before the physician informs the patient about his diagnosis, he encounters two of the people who have been told about the HIV test result. They tell him that they know he is gay and infected with the HIV virus. He then discovers that the nurse has informed them about his condition. Suffering from intense shock and emotional pain, the man unsuccessfully attempts suicide."

In this case, the nurse's actions rise to the level of willful, malicious, and intentional infliction of emotional distress. The nurse faces serious charges and, in some states with HIV confidentiality laws, could face a prison sentence for intentionally violating the patient's confidentiality in a manner meant to harm the patient. It is likely that the nurse's license also will be revoked for her actions, and the board may impose a significant fine.

The Nurse and Criminal Law

A crime is an offense against society, defined through written criminal statutes or codes. A criminal act is deemed to be conduct so offensive that the state is responsible for prosecuting the offending individual on behalf of society. Legal remedies for crimes include fines, imprisonment, and, in some states, execution (death penalty). Criminal acts are classified as either minor offenses (misdemeanors) or major offenses (felonies). Misdemeanors that nurses are commonly charged with include the following:

- Illegal practice of medicine
- Failing to report child or elder abuse
- Falsification of the patient's medical record
- Assault and battery and physical abuse of patients

Felony acts may be committed against the federal government and generally involve drug trafficking offenses and, increasingly, fraud in billing for services of Medicare patients. Other serious criminal acts include theft, rape, and murder. A nurse found guilty of a felony generally serves time in prison and usually suffers the permanent revocation of his or her nursing license. Five RNs were indicted on 21 counts, including falsification of records, alteration of forms filed with the state department of health, and tampering with physical evidence in the death of a 97-year-old nursing home patient (Kelley, 2000). The patient died after being fed through a stomach tube attached to an enema bag. The nurses used the enema bag in lieu of the appropriate feeding equipment that was not available. The nursing director was found guilty on three counts, and also surrendered her nursing license.

THE LAW AND PATIENT RIGHTS

Advance Directives

Society now recognizes the individual's right to die with dignity rather than be kept alive indefinitely by artificial life support. As a consequence, the majority of states have enacted "right-to-die" laws. These statutes grant competent adults the right to refuse extraordinary medical treatment when there is no hope of recovery. The term *advance directive* refers to an individual's desires regarding end-of-life care. These wishes generally are made through the execution of a formal document known as a living will. Right-to-die statutes vary from state to state; therefore, nurses must become familiar with their state-specific statute. Agency policies and procedures in the nurse's employment setting also will guide the nurse in an understanding of the patient's rights in this matter.

Living Wills

A living will is a legal document, a type of advance directive, in which a competent adult makes known his or her wishes regarding care that will be provided in the final stages of a terminal illness. A living will generally contains the following:

- Designation of the individual (proxy or surrogate) who is permitted to make decisions once the patient is incapacitated and no longer able to make decisions (often referred to as "decisionally incompetent" or "decisionally incapacitated")

- Specific stipulations regarding what care is acceptable and which procedures or treatments are not to be implemented
- Authorization of the patient's physician to withhold or discontinue certain life-sustaining procedures under specific conditions

Although living wills are legal in every state, they may not be legally binding. In some cases, a proxy is not recognized or sanctioned by the state statute. Living wills have been overturned, particularly when disputes arise among family members or significant others when the terminally ill patient is no longer able to make decisions. A living will may be revoked under any of the following conditions:

- There is evidence that the patient was not competent when the living will was executed.
- The patient's condition is not terminal.
- A state-imposed time for enforcement of the will has expired, and a new living will must be executed.
- The patient's condition has changed substantially, and the stipulations of the will no longer apply.

A living will must be written (in some cases, using a state-specific document), dated, signed, and witnessed. If asked to witness a patient's living will, the nurse should refer the matter to the agency's risk manager. It may not be lawful in a particular state for the nurse to witness this document.

Medical or Physician Directives and DNR Orders

A more specific type of living will that the patient may execute is known as the medical or physician directive. This document lists the desire of the patient in a particular scenario, such as whether he or she would want to be resuscitated if cardiopulmonary arrest occurs. The physician writes DNR orders based on written medical directives dictated by the patient. This medical directive, when properly executed, provides the physician with immunity from claims of negligence or intentional wrongdoing in the patient's death. The physician must also follow any state-specific statute and the agency's policies and procedures before writing a DNR order. Research has discovered a serious lack of uniformity among and within health care facilities in making certain that direct-care nurses and providers are aware of a patient's DNR status. This can result in a significant risk for confusion and error and contribute to claims of negligence.

The nurse has an absolute duty to respect the patient's wishes in the case of DNR orders. A lawfully executed DNR order must be followed. Nurses have been sued for failure to observe DNR orders. Claims against the nurse include battery, negligent infliction of pain and suffering, and "wrongful life" (*Anderson v. St. Francis–St. George Hospital*, 1992). Three problems may arise regarding a DNR order: A physician refuses to comply with the patient's wishes and initiates resuscitation; the patient revokes consent to the DNR order; or a family member demands that the DNR order be rescinded, despite the patient's continued objection to resuscitation (Teno, 2008). If one of these issues arises, the nurse must act promptly to enlist the assistance of the nursing supervisor or a hospital administrator. Remember that a patient may revoke a living will, including a DNR order, at any time.

The agency's ethics committee may be helpful in resolving disagreements between a physician and the patient, or between the family and the patient regarding DNR orders. After notifying the appropriate administrative team members, the nurse should document in detail any comments made by the patient or family regarding a change in DNR status, or comments, actions, or orders issued by a physician who will not respect the patient's stated wishes. The ANA has promulgated a position statement, "Nursing Care and Do Not Resuscitate (DNR) and Allow Natural Death (AND) Decisions (2012), to guide nurses in the legal and ethical dimension of this issue.

Durable Power of Attorney for Health Care

In 1993, the Uniform Health-Care Decisions Act was approved. The Act recognizes an individual's right to make decisions about health care and enables a patient to accept or refuse treatment. The Act is also designed to provide autonomy when making end-of-life decisions. Durable power of attorney is a legal document that authorizes the patient to name the person (the health care proxy) who will make the day-to-day and final end-of-life decisions once he or she is decisionally incompetent. Naming a proxy who is intimately knowledgeable about the person's true wishes is important to ensure that the patient's desires will be carried out when he or she is no longer able to make decisions. Health care law experts recommend that individuals interested in naming a proxy seek legal assistance with executing a **durable power of attorney for health care**.

Nurses may be asked questions about living wills and durable power of attorney for health care by patients and their families. An important aspect of speaking to the patient about these issues is to provide the written materials about **advance directives** that are required under the federal statute, the Patient Self-Determination Act.

Informed Consent

For any patient to make meaningful choices about a particular procedure or treatment, the provider must convey certain material information. Under the doctrine of informed consent, the physician or advanced practice nurse has a duty to disclose information so that the patient can make intelligent decisions. This duty is mandated by federal statute (in the case of Medicare and Medicaid patients) and state law and is grounded as well in common law. In the case of routine as well as specialized care, the primary provider must disclose the following:

- Nature of the therapy or procedure
- Expected benefits and outcomes of the therapy or procedure
- Potential risks of the therapy or procedure
- Alternative therapies to the intended procedure and their risks and benefits
- Risks of not having the procedure

This duty to disclose rests with the provider and cannot be delegated to the RN. When the nurse has reason to believe that the patient has not given informed consent for a procedure, the provider should be immediately notified. In no case should the nurse proceed with initiating any part of the therapy that he or she is responsible for implementing. The patient's questions or concerns should be documented in the medical record to indicate why there has been a delay in carrying out the procedure (Mahlmeister, 2009b). If the nurse is responsible for witnessing the patient's signature on a consent form for the specified procedure, this process also should be deferred until the provider has had an opportunity to clarify the patient's questions.

A variety of negligence claims arise out of the informed consent process. The provider may be alleged negligent for failure to obtain informed consent. Court decisions generally have upheld the provider's duty to obtain informed consent and have dismissed cases that have claimed hospitals and its nurses were negligent for "failing to obtain informed consent." With adoption in some states of the corporate negligence doctrine, an increasing number of appellate courts have ruled that hospitals and nurses may be liable for failure to ensure that informed consent was given to the provider (*Karibjanian v. Thomas Jefferson University Hospital,* 1989; *Keel v. St. Elizabeth Medical Center,* 1992). Nurses have a duty to discuss concerns about informed consent with the primary provider. Should the nurse be unable to resolve the issue, the chain of command should be invoked to clarify questions or concerns.

In some cases, timely notification of a nursing manager may be essential to prevent violation of the patient's right to give consent. The following scenario provides a case in point. An RN is circulating in a surgical case intended to clean a severe leg wound. The consent form signed by the patient explicitly lists "wound debridement" as the procedure to be performed. On beginning the procedure, the surgeon asks for additional instruments, indicating that the wound is so infected that the leg will have to be amputated below the knee. Because the patient has received general anesthesia and is unable to give consent, and the consent form itself does not authorize an amputation procedure, the nurse must question the surgeon's intention to remove the leg. If the surgeon refuses to discuss the matter, or again requests the instruments necessary for the procedure, the nurse must obtain immediate assistant from her supervisor and if possible, the medical administrator (chief of surgery). The instruments for surgical amputation should not be placed on the sterile table, and in compliance with intraoperative communication standards, all other team members should be alerted that there is an unresolved question about the procedure, and that a manager or administrator is on the way to evaluate the surgical plan.

Communication Barriers and Informed Consent

Health care organizations that receive federal funds are required to meet the language access provision of the Culturally and Linguistically Appropriate Services (CLAS) Standards for Health. The standards were issued in 2001 by the U.S. Department of Health and Human Services (USDHHS) and were substantially enhanced in 2011 in collaboration with the USDHHS Office of Minority Health (2011) and the National Partnership for Action to End Health Disparities. (For more information see http://minorityhealth.hhs.gov/npa.)

The standards require that the hospital or health facility must do the following:

- Offer and provide free and timely language assistance services, including bilingual staff and interpreter services at all points of contact at all hours of operation.
- Provide verbal and written notices (in the individual's preferred language), of the right to receive language assistance services.
- Ensure competence of language assistance provided by interpreters and bilingual staff.

Family and friends should *not* be used as interpreters except at the care recipient's request. The duty to ensure appropriate communication is also established by the ADA (discussed previously). When an interpreter is used to facilitate communication, the nurse should document this process. The medical record should contain the name of the interpreter, the topic of the educational session, or substance of the informed consent discussion, and the patient's questions and consent, if given (Smith, 2007).

TJC Comprehensive Accreditation Manual for Hospitals (2014) requires the facility to respect a patient's right to and need for effective communication. Written materials, including consent forms and discharge instructions, should be available in the patient's preferred language. Educational materials should be culturally sensitive, and at a reading level that recognizes literacy limitations. TJC (2008) provides detailed information and guidance for development of a central office to coordinate all communication services, including the availability of interpreters fluent in medical terminology for informed consent discussions between the provider and patient. Language access also includes access to interpreters skilled in signing for hearing-impaired patients and materials in Braille for vision-impaired individuals.

A New Jersey case (*Borngesser v. Jersey Shore Medical Center* [2001]) illustrates the duty to provide an interpreter before informed consent is given for an invasive procedure. A female patient was admitted to the hospital with severe cardiac disease. She was also completely deaf and mute. Notes in the medical record stated, "Patient deaf and dumb and difficult to assess." The nurses established a diagnosis of "Sensory deficit: hearing impaired" and recorded that it was difficult to communicate with the patient. Providers and nurses documented continued difficulty with assessments, patient education, and obtaining informed consent. The patient's 17-year-old daughter was not deaf and could sign, but was not a trained medical interpreter. Ms. Borngesser subsequently died due to her severe cardiac disease and associated complications. Her daughter sued the hospital, claiming that the facility failed to make reasonable accommodation for her deaf and mute mother. *There were no claims of medical or nursing negligence.* The Superior Appellate Court of New Jersey affirmed that the case against the hospital could go forward. The court stated, among other things, that when a hearing-impaired patient is asked to give informed consent, the hospital has a duty to ensure that communication is effective by providing an interpreter fluent in American Sign Language (ASL).

The unique legal requirements related to informed consent in minors is a complex issue. All 50 states and the District of Columbia explicitly allow a minor to consent to testing and treatments for sexually transmitted diseases, except HIV testing and treatment. All other statutes regarding informed consent in adolescents vary widely from state to state (Tillett, 2005). As noted earlier, when dealing with minors, the nurse must use agency resources, including social workers, managers, administrators, and risk managers when facilitating an appropriate informed consent process between the provider and adolescent or older child.

The Right to Refuse Diagnostic Testing, Treatment, and Care

As noted, an adult of sound mind has a right to refuse any treatment that has previously been agreed to. A Connecticut Supreme Court decision affirmed the fundamental right of adults to refuse medical treatment. In the case of *Stamford Hospital v. Vega* (1996), a woman who hemorrhaged after the birth of her infant refused blood on the grounds that it violated her beliefs as a Jehovah's Witness. The hospital obtained an emergency court order authorizing the facility to administer blood. The woman survived and was discharged in good health. Although it was a moot point (the blood already had been given), the family appealed the initial court decision authorizing the blood transfusion. The Supreme Court decided to hear the case and reversed the lower

court's decision, stating the hospital did not have a right to substitute its decision for that of the patient.

If a patient who is under the nurse's care refuses treatment, the nurse has a duty to notify the primary provider. The same principles pertaining to the informed consent process apply to situations when the patient refuses care. The physician or advanced practice nurse should provide the patient with information about the consequences, risks, and benefits of refusing therapy. The provider also must explore any alternative treatments that may be available to the patient. Hospitals have a right to seek a judicial review when patients refuse specific types of lifesaving treatments, but current case law falls squarely in favor of the patient's right to self-determination.

Leaving Against Medical Advice

A common allegation made when a patient self-discharges against medical advice (AMA) and is subsequently injured is that the patient was not fully apprised of the risks inherent in leaving the facility. If a patient intends to leave the facility without a written order, the nurse must act promptly to notify the provider. When circumstances suggest that the person may suffer immediate physical harm, the nurse must clearly articulate the dangers inherent in leaving. This precautionary statement is reserved for situations in which the life and limb of the patient are at risk and the appropriate providers (physicians or advanced practice nurses) are not available to address the direct and indirect consequences with the patient. The nurse should document all these actions and any communication with the aforementioned parties.

If the primary provider has not arrived before the patient leaves, the nurses' notes should reflect the specific advice given the patient, which should include the fact that leaving the facility could:

- Aggravate the current condition and complicate future care
- Result in permanent physical or mental impairment or disability
- Result in complications leading to death
- In the case of a competent elder, prompt notification of the immediate family also would be a reasonable and prudent action.

Lyons v. Walker Regional Medical Center (2000) is a case in point. An ED nurse was found negligent for failing to warn a patient who was leaving AMA that his laboratory results indicated a state of diabetic ketoacidosis, a condition that could be lethal. When the "panic" value laboratory findings were displayed on the computer, the nurse did not bring the results to the physician or patient's attention. Instead, she directed the unit secretary to complete the patient's discharge paperwork. The patient left, and he died 3 days later.

A study of patient characteristics associated with discharge AMA has found that low socioeconomic status, substance abuse, sickness within the family, underlying (and often untreated) psychiatric disorders, anger and anxiety about the admission diagnosis, and lack of effective communication with team members correlated with self-discharge (Alfandre, 2009). Nurses and providers should collaborate to address immediate patient concerns, communicate a time-limited plan of care, and advocate for appropriate consultations (e.g., psychiatry, social work, pastoral services, pain management) to reduce the likelihood of patient self-discharge.

Almost all health care facilities have an AMA form that patients are asked to sign when they decide to refuse or discontinue ordered therapy or intend to leave the facility. The value of the document in countering a claim of negligence should the patient or family later sue will depend in great part on the quality of the nurse's charting.

Nurses have also been charged with a variety of offenses when unlawfully detaining patients, including assault, battery, and false imprisonment (Snyder, 2001). These charges generally arise when well-meaning nurses try to prevent the patient from carrying out his or her intent. Actions that lead to a claim of false imprisonment include applying restraints, refusing to give the patient his or her clothes or access to a telephone, intimidating the patient by assigning a security person to guard his or her room, and sedating the patient against his or her will. As can be expected, in addition to civil penalties, the nurse faces disciplinary action by the licensing board when charges of false imprisonment are reported.

Use of Physical Restraints

One last but equally important area of patient rights to be discussed is the right of a competent adult to be free of restraint. Even patients with mental illness cannot be incarcerated or restrained without due process, and the institution must have the treatment and rehabilitation services necessary to reintegrate the individual into society (Iyer and Levin, 2007). Restraint of any kind is a form of imprisonment, and the reasonable and prudent nurse will closely adhere to all laws, rules, and policies pertaining to the use of restraints. The goal when restraints are clinically indicated is to use the least restrictive restraint and only when all other strategies to ensure patient safety have been exhausted. Patients may never be restrained physically or chemically because there is not enough staff to properly monitor them. Nurses have a legal and ethical duty to report institutions or individuals who violate patient rights through unlawful restraint.

As noted, one of the most common allegations leveled against nurses is a failure to ensure patient safety. Nurses in many practice settings must balance the right of patients to unrestricted control of their bodies and movements against the need to keep vulnerable patients safe from harm. The use of seclusion, chemical restraints, and physical restraints, including vests, mittens, belts, and wrist restraints, is governed by federal and state statutes and accrediting bodies, such as TJC. Many nurses do not realize that even bedrails and chair trays fall under the category of physical restraints; these articles may not be used indiscriminately.

Violation of restraint statutes and the administrative rules and regulations promulgated to enact these laws can result in stiff penalties. The institution can lose its Medicare contract (decertification) and TJC accreditation, effectively putting it out of business. Patients and family members may initiate civil suits for unlawful restraints, resulting in monetary damages if the plaintiff succeeds in the suit. Charges of assault, battery, and/or false imprisonment may be leveled against nurses who use restraints improperly. Claims of negligence may arise from improper monitoring of the patient who has been appropriately placed in restraints in compliance with applicable laws and hospital policy.

Careful nursing documentation is essential when restraints are applied. The patient's mental and physical status must be assessed at regular and frequent intervals as prescribed by law and the agency's policies. The chart must reflect these assessments and the frequency with which restraints are removed. Neurovascular and skin assessments of limbs or other body parts covered by the restraints also must be entered in the medical record. Written physician orders for restraints must be timed and dated, and renewal of orders must be accompanied by evidence of medical evaluations and nursing reassessments.

Based on the aforementioned information, some nurses are under the misconception that current law prohibits restraining patients until a written order is obtained. Nurses may lawfully apply restraints in an emergency, when in their independent judgment no other strategies are effective in protecting the patient

from harm. The physician must be contacted promptly to discuss the patient's condition and the need to restrain and to obtain an order for temporary continuance of restraints. The nurse is guided in the decision to restrain by knowledge of the laws, the agency's policies and procedures, qualifications of the staff, and conditions on the unit or in the department.

SUMMARY

Professional nursing practice is governed by an ever-widening circle of federal and state statutes and is constantly evolving in great part because of an accumulating body of nursing case law. The law provides guidance for every aspect of practice and can assist the nurse in managing the complexities of practice in a rapidly changing health care system. Knowledge is power, and the nurse who possesses a sound understanding of the law as it pertains to professional practice is empowered.

This chapter has reviewed the major sources and categories of law influencing nursing practice. The reader has been introduced to the doctrines of civil and criminal law that affect all nurses. The chapter has explored issues related to the legal rights of patients who are served by professional nurses. As patient advocates, all nurses should keep these fundamental rights uppermost in their minds as they attempt to provide safe, effective, quality care in all settings.

REFERENCES

Abernathy v. Valley Medical Center, WL 3754792 (W.D. Wash., 2006).

Alfandre D: "I'm going home": discharges against medical advice, *Mayo Clin Proc* 84(3):255–260, 2009.

American Academy of Ambulatory Care Nursing: *Scope and standards of practice for professional telehealth nursing,* ed 5, Pitman, NJ, 2011, American Academy of Ambulatory Care Nursing.

American Association of Critical-Care Nurses: *AACN delegation handbook,* ed 2, Aliso Viejo, CA, 2004, American Association of Critical-Care Nurses.

American Medical Association: *Code of medical ethics,* Chicago, 2010–2011, 2011, American Medical Association.

American Nurses Association: *Mandatory Overtime. Policy and Advocacy.* http://www.nursingworld.org/MainMenu Categories/Policy-Advocacy/State/Legislative-Agenda-Reports/MandatoryOvertime. Accessed August 14, 2014.

American Nurses Association: *Code of ethics for nurses (2015),* Washington, DC, 2001, American Nurses Association.

American Nurses Association: *Social networking principles toolkit,* 2011. http://www.nursingworld.org/socialnetworkingtoolkit. Accessed December 10, 2013.

American Nurses Association: *Principles of delegation,* 2012. www.nursingworld.org/MainMenuCategories/ThePracticeof

ProfessionalNursing/workplace/PrinciplesofDelegation. aspx. Accessed October 14, 2011.

American Nurses Association and National Council of State Boards of Nursing: *Joint statement on delegation,* 2005 (website). www.ncsbn.org/Joint_statement.pdf. Accessed June 2007.

American Nurses Association: *Assuring patient safety,* December 8, 2006. http://www.nursingworld.org/MainMenuCategories/Policy-Advocacy/Positions-and-Resolutions/ANAPositionStatements/Position-Statements-Alphabetically/Copy-of-AssuringPatientSafety-l.pdf.

American Nurses Association: *The American Nurses Association comments on the Wisconsin Department of Justice decision to pursue criminal charges against an RN in Wisconsin,* 2007. http://ana.nursingworld.org/FunctionalMenu Categories/MediaResources/PressReleases/2006/CriminalChargesAgainstanRNinWisconsin.aspx. Accessed December 14, 2011.

American Nurses Association: *Safe staffing saves lives,* 2009a. http://www.safestaffingsaveslives.org/WhatIsANADoing/StateLegislation/StaffingPlansandRatios.GM5Editor.html. Accessed September 26, 2011.

American Nurses Association: *Nursing: scope and standards of practice,* ed 2, Washington, DC, 2010, American Nurses Association.

American Nurses Association: *Nursing Care and Do Not Resuscitate (DNR) and Allow Natural Death (AND) Decisions. ANA Position Statement*, 2012. http://www.nursingworld.org/MainMenuCategories/EthicsStandards/Ethics-Position-Statements/Nursing-Care-and-Do-Not-Resuscitate-DNR-and-Allow-Natural-Death-Decisions.pdf. Accessed on April, 15, 2014.

American Nurses Association: *American Nurses Nationwide State Legislative Agenda Reports*, 2011–2012. http://ana.nursingworld.org/MainMenuCategories/ANAPoliticalPower/State/StateLegislativeAgenda.aspx. Accessed August 30, 2012.

American Association of Critical-Care Nurses: *Ethics in Acute & Critical Care Nursing*, 2012. http://www.aacn.org:88/wd/practice/content/ethicmainpage.pcms?menu=practice. Accessed March 02, 2014.

American Society for Healthcare Risk Management: *Risk management pearls on disclosure of adverse events*, Chicago, 2006, American Society for Healthcare Risk Management.

American Telemedicine Association: *Telehealth nursing*, 2014. http://www.americantelemed.org/docs/default-document-library/fact_sheet_final.pdf?sfvrsn=2. Accessed March, 22, 2014.

Anderson v. St Francis–St George Hospital, 614 NE 2d 841 (OH, 1992).

Angelini D, Mahlmeister L: Liability in triage: management of EMTALA regulations and managing obstetric risks, *J Midwifery Womens Health* 50(6):472–478, 2005.

Barbourville Nursing Home v. USDHHS, No 05-3421, 6 Cir 04/06/2006 (F3d-KY).

Blaney B: *Texas doctor pleads guilty in retaliation case*, Monday November 7, 2011, Deseret News. http://www.deseretnews.com/article/700195546/Texas-doctor-pleads-guilty-in-retaliation-case.html. Accessed January 3, 2012.

Bond P: Implications of EMTALA on nursing triage and ED staff education, *J Emerg Nurs* 34(3):205–206, 2008.

Borngesser v. Jersey Shore Medical Center, 774 A. 2d 615 (N.J. App. Ct., 2001).

Boyer v. Tift County Hospital. WL 2986283 (M.D. Ga., 2008).

Brief amici curiae American Hospital Association: *American Organization of Nurse Executives, American Society for Healthcare Human Resources Administration, Michigan Health and Hospital Association in response to the National Labor Relations Board's July 24, 2003 Notice and Invitation to File Briefs*, Filed Sept 22, 2003, United States of America before the National Labor Relations Board.

Brodowski v. Ryave, 885 A.2d 1045 (PA Supr Ct. 2005).

Brooke P: When can you say no? *Nursing* 39(7):43–47, 2009.

Brown A: Nurses and noncompliance, *Nurse Leader* 11:46–47, 2013.

Caliendo C, Millbauer L, Moore B, et al: Obstetric triage and EMTALA regulations. Practice strategies for labor and delivery nursing units, *AWHONN Lifelines* 8(5):442–448, 2004.

California Department of Consumer Affairs: *Clinical learning experiences of nursing students*, California Board of Registered Nursing. http://www.rn.ca.gov/pdfs/regulations/npr-b-66.pdf. November, 2008. Accessed December 20, 2011-2008.

Caramenico A: *Patient safety violations endanger hospital federal funds*, August 31, 2011, FierceHealthcare. http://www.fiercehealthcare.com/story/patient-safety-violations-endanger-hospital-federal-funds/2011-08-31. Accessed September 1, 2011.

Centers for Medicare & Medicaid Services: *Hospital-acquired conditions*, 2008. https://www.cms.gov/pf/printpage.asp?ref; http://www.cms.gov/Medicare/Medicare-Fee-for-Service-Payment/HospitalAcqCond/index.html?redirect=/HospitalAcqCond/06_Hospital-Acquired_Conditions.asp Accessed January 7, 2012.

Centers for Medicare & Medicaid Services: *National Healthcare Safety Network report. Data summary for 2010, device-associated module*, 2010. http://www.cdc.gov/nhsn/pdfs/datastat/nhsn-report_2010-data-summary.pdf. Accessed January 13, 2011.

City of Irving v. Pak, 885 SW 2d 189 (Tex., 1994).

Classen D, Resar R, Griffin F, et al: 'Global Trigger Tool' shows that adverse events in hospitals may be ten times greater than previously measured, *Health Affairs* 30(4):581–589, 2012.

Columbia Medical Center of Las Colinas v. Bush, WL 22725001 WW3d (Tex., 2003).

Convalescent Services, Inc. v. Schultz, 921 SW 2d 731 (Tex. App, 1996).

Dennis v. Specialty Select Hospital—Flint, WL 2402454 NW2d (Mich., 2005).

Dickerson v. Fatehi, 84 SE 2d 880 (Va., 1997).

Dimora v. Cleveland Clinic Foundation, 683 NE 2d 1175 (Ohio App, 1996).

Educational Review Systems, Inc: *Prevention of retained sponges and towels following surgery: independent study guide*, Dublin, OH, 2008, Cardinal Health. http://www.cardinal.com/education/documents/pdf/CE-Prevention%20of%20Retained%20Sponges%20and%20Towels.pdf. Accessed January 9, 2011.

Edwards JR, Peterson KD, Mu Y, et al: National Healthcare Safety Network report, data summary for 2006 through 2008, *Am J Infect Contr* 37(10):783–805, December 2009.

Elzer R: Guide to CMS compliance, *J Healthcare Management* 55(2):77–80, 2010.

Francis v. Memorial General Hospital, 726 P 2d 852 (N.M., 1986).

Furukawa M, Ragu T, Shao B: Electronic medical records, nurse staffing, and nurse-sensitive patient outcomes: evidence from the national database of nursing quality indicators, *Med Care Res Rev* 68(3):311–331, 2011.

Hannawa A: Disclosing medical errors to patients: effects of nonverbal involvement, *Patient Educ Couns* 94:310–313, 2014.

Hanssen v. Genesis Health, WL 665318 (Iowa Appel. Ct., 2011)

HCA Health Services v. National Bank, 745 SW 2d 120 (Ark., 1988).

Heimchen L, Richards M, McDonald T: Does routine disclosure of medical error affect patients' propensity to sue and their assessment of provider quality? Evidence from survey data, *Med Care* 48(11):955–961, 2010.

Heinrich v. Conemaugh Valley Memorial Hospital, 648 A 2d 53 (Pa., 1994).

Holston v. Sisters of the Third Order, 650 NE 2d 985 (Ill., 1995).

Institute for Safe Medication Practices: *Error-prone conditions that lead to student nurse-related errors,* :ISMP Safety Alert! 2007. (website).www.ismp.org/Newsletters/acutecare/articles/20071018.asp. Accessed July 2008.

Institute of Medicine: *To err is human: building a safer health system,* Washington, DC, 2000, National Academies Press.

Janga v. Colombrito, S.W. 3d WL6146197 (Tx. Appel. Ct. 2011).

Johannessen v. Salem Hospital, 336 Or 211, 82 P3d 139 (Ore., 2003).

Justin and Michelle Malovic v. Santa Monica Hospital Medical Center, Los Angeles County Superior Court, Case No SC019 167 (Calif., 1995).

Kachalia A: *Disclosure of medical error,* January 2009, Agency for Healthcare Research and Quality. http://www.webmm.ahrq.gov/perspective.aspx?perspectiveID=70. Accessed January 3, 2012.

Kalisch BJ, Tschannen D, Lee H, Friese CR: Hospital variation in missed nursing care. *American Journal of Med Qual,* 2011 Jul-Aug;26(4):291–9. doi: 10.1177/1062860610395929. Epub 2011 Jun 3.

Karibjanian v. Thomas Jefferson University Hospital, 717 F Supp 1081, 1083–1084 (ED Pa., 1989).

Keel v. St Elizabeth Medical Center, 842 SW 2d 869 (Ky., 1992).

Kelley T: *Death at a nursing home leads to indictment of five,* Nov 7, 2000, New York Times, p. B–1.

Konetzka R, Park J, Ellis R; Abbo E: Malpractice litigation and nursing home quality of care, *Health Serv Res* 48 (6 Pt 1):1920–1938, 2013.

Kowalski K, Horner M: A legal nightmare: Denver nurses indicted, *MCN Am J Matern Child Nurs* 23(3):125–129, 1998.

Lachman VD, Murray JS, Iseminger K, Ganske K: Doing the right thing: Pathways to moral courage, *The American Nurse* 7(5), 2012.

Lachman VD: Whistleblowing: role of organizational culture in prevention and management, *Dermatol Nurs* 20(5):394–396, 2008.

Loren DJ, Garbutt J, Dunagan WC, et al: Risk managers, physicians, and disclosure of harmful medical errors, *Jt Comm J Qual Patient Saf* 36(3):101–108, 2010.

Love v. Rancocas Hospital, WL1541052 (Distr Ct New Jersey, 2006).

Lovett v. Lorain Community Hospital, WL239927 N.E. 2d. (Ohio, 2004).

Lyons v. Walker Regional Medical Center, 791 So. 2d 937 (Ala., 2000).

Mahlmeister L: Best practices in perinatal nursing: professional role development for charge nurses, *J Perinat Neonatal Nurs* 20(2):122–124, 2006.

Mahlmeister L: Best practices in perinatal nursing: collaborating with student nurses to ensure high-reliability, *J Perinat Neonat Nurs* 22(1):8–11, 2008.

Mahlmeister L: Best practices in perinatal care: maintaining safe and cost-effective staffing models during the current economic downturn, *J Perinat Neonat Nurs* 23(2):111–114, 2009.

Mahlmeister L: Best practices in perinatal nursing: partnering with patients to enhance informed decision-making, *J Perinat Neonat Nurs* 20(2):122–124, 2009.

Mathes, M: *Nurse's Law,* Indianapolis, 2014, Sigma Theta Tau International.

Miller v. Levering Regional Healthcare Center, S.W. 3d. WL1889883 (Mo. App. Ct., 2006).

Mobile Infirmary Medical Center v. Hodgen, So 2d, WL 22463340 (Ala., 2003).

Moy M: *The EMTALA answer book,* Gaithersburg, Md, 2014, Aspen.

Myers V: When something goes wrong: How to disclose error, *American Nurse Today* 8(10):2011. http://www.americannursetoday.com/article.aspx?id=8302&fid=8276#. Accessed December 7, 2011.

National Council of State Boards of Nursing: *Nursing pathways for patient safety,* Chicago, 2010, National Council of State Boards of Nursing.

National Council of State Boards of Nursing: *A nurse's guide to the use of social media,* Chicago, 2011a. http://www.ncsbn.org/NCSBN SocialMedia.pdf. Accessed January 4, 2012.

National Council of State Boards of Nursing: *What you need to know about nursing licensure and boards of nursing,* Chicago, 2011b. https://www.ncsbn.org/Nursing License.pdf. Accessed November 12, 2011.

National Council of State Boards of Nursing: *Substance use disorder in nursing,* Chicago, 2011c. https://www.ncsbn.org/Working_with_Others.pdf. Accessed November 2, 2011.

National Quality Forum: Safe practices for better health-care—2010 update. Executive summary, Washington, DC, 2011, National Quality Forum. http://www.quality forum.org/Publications/2010/04/Safe_Practices_for_Better_Healthcare_%E2. Accessed November 15, 2011.

Nursing Service Organization: *CNA Healthpro Nursing Claims Study: an analysis of claims with risk management recommendations 1997-2007*, Hatboro, PA, 2009, Nursing Service Organization. http://www.nso.com/pdfs/db/rnclaimstudy.pdf?fileName=rnclaimstudy.pdf&;folder=pdfs/db&isLiveStr=Y&refID=rnclaim. Accessed September 24, 2011.

Osiecki v. Bridgeport Health Care Center, Inc., 2005 WL 1331225 (Conn. Super, May 12, 2005).

Parco v. Pacifica Hospital, WL 2491516 (Supr Ct. Los Angeles County, Calif., 2007).

Passarella G: *Hospital faces trial on corporate negligence claim*, October 31, 2005, *Legal* Intelligencer. http://thelegalintelligencer.typepad.com/tli/gina-passarella/. Accessed November 13, 2011.

Pedraza v. Wyckoff Heights Medical Center, NYS2d, 2002 NY Slip Op 22094, 2002 WL 1364153 (N.Y. Sup, June 4, 2002).

Philipsen NC, Soeken D: Preparing to blow the whistle: a survival guide for nurses, *J Nurse Pract* 7(9):740–746, 2011.

Roberts v. Galen of Virginia, Inc, 111 F 3d 405 (6 Cir, 1997).

Roddy v. Tanner Medical Center, 585 SE 2d 175 (Ga., 2003).

Roussel L: *Management and leadership for nurse administration*, Boston, 2011, Jones & Bartlett.

Rowe v. Sisters of Pallottine Missionary Society, WL 1585453 SE 2d (W.Va., 2001).

Ruelas v. Staff Builders Personnel Services, Inc., 18 P 3d 138 (Ariz. App, 2001).

Sehgal N, Wachter R: Identification of inpatient DNR status: a safety hazard begging for standardization, *J Hosp Med* 2(6):366–371, 2007.

Scott v. Corizon Health, 2014 WL 1877431 (D. Nevada, May 9, 2014)

Shah R, Lander L: Retained foreign body during surgery in pediatric patients: a national perspective, *J Pediatr Surg* 44(4):738–742, 2009.

Shannon S, Foglia MB, Hardy M, et al: Disclosing errors to patients: perspectives of registered nurses, *Jt Comm J Qual Patient Saf* 35(1):5–12, 2009.

Siegel v. Long Island Jewish Medical Center, NYS 2d NY Slip Op 17790 WL 22439814 (N.Y., 2003).

Singleton v. AAA Home Health, Inc., WL 1693814, So 2d (La., 2000).

Smetzer J, Baker C, Byrne F, et al: Shaping systems for better behavioral choices: Lessons learned from a fatal medication error, *Jt Comm J Qual Patient Saf* 36(4):152–163, 2010.

Smith L: Documenting use of an interpreter, *Nursing* 37(7):25, 2007.

Snyder E: Chain of command: court rules nurses should have gone over doctor's head, *Leg Eagle Eye Newslett Nurs Profession* 8(2):1, 2000.

Snyder E: Automatic blood pressure cuff: nurses ignored the patient, committed battery, *Leg Eagle Eye Newsletter Nurs Profession* 9(4):1, 2001.

Snyder E: Digoxin overdose: $1.5 million punitive damages, *Leg Eagle Eye Newslett Nurs Profession* 11(12):1, 4–5, 2003.

Snyder E: Student nurse/instructor: court discusses host hospital's legal liability, *Leg Eagle Eye Newslett Nurs Profession* 14(3):4, 2004.

Snyder E: Understaffing, fall, no neuro assessment, epidural hemorrhage, death: nurses faulted, *Leg Eagle Eye Newslett Nurs Profession* 14(8):6, 2006.

Snyder E: Disability discrimination: Quad on ventilator could not communicate with his caregivers, *Leg Eagle Eye Newslett Nurs Profession* 15(10):1, 2007.

Snyder E: Medication ordered is contraindicated: court discusses nurse's legal responsibilities, *Leg Eagle Eye Newsletter Nurs Profession* 15(1):1, 2007.

Snyder E. Whistleblower: Court upholds nurse's rights, *Leg Eagle Eye Newslett Nurs Profession* 23(2):6, 2014.

Stamford Hospital v. Vega, 674 A 2d 821 (Conn., 1996).

Sunbridge Healthcare Corp. v. Penny, SW3d, 2005 WL 562763 (Tex. App, March 11, 2005).

Taenzer A, Pyke J, McGrath S: A review of current and emerging approaches to address failure to rescue, *Anesthesiology* 115(2):421–431, 2011.

Tammelleo A: Wrong drug ordered: nurses must intervene, *Nurs Law Regan Rep* 45(1):1, 2004.

Tammelleo A: Nurse manager subjected to disciplinary action, *Nurs Law Regan Rep* 45(2):1, 2004.

Tammelleo A: Student nurse gives antibiotic IV—death results, *Nurs Law Regan Rep* 46(5):1, 2005.

Texas Nurses Association: *Texas Nurses Association establishes legal defense fund to support nurses indicted for being patient advocates*, 2009. http://www.texasnurses.org/displaycommon.cfm?an=1&subarticlenbr=538#2. Accessed October 2010.

The American Association of Nurse Attorneys (TAANA) and the American Association of Legal Nurse Consultants (AALNC): *Criminal Prosecution of Health Care Providers for Unintentional Human Error. TAANA – AALNC Position Paper*, August, 2011. http://www.taana.org/position_papers#cphcpuhe. Accessed December 08, 2014.

The Joint Commission: Promoting effective communication—language access services in health care, *Jt Comm Perspect* 26(2):8–11, 2008.

The Joint Commission: *Advancing Effective Communication, Cultural Competence, and Patient-and Family-Centered Care*, 2012, The Joint Commission. http://www.jointcommission.org/Advancing_Effective_Communication/. Accessed December 04, 2014.

The Joint Commission: *Comprehensive accreditation manual for hospitals*, Oakbrook Terrace, IL, 2014, The Joint Commission.

The Joint commission: *Speak up initiatives,* Oakbrook Terrace, Il, 2014, The Joint Commission. http://www.jointcommission.org/speakup.aspx.

Thompson v. Nason Hospital, 591 A 2d 703, 707 (Pa., 1991).

Tillett J: Adolescents and informed consent, *J Perinat Neonatal Nurs* 19(2):112–121, 2005.

Unruh L, Zhang L: Nurse staffing and patient safety in hospitals: new variable and longitudinal approach, *Nursing Research* 61(1):3–12, 2012.

U.S. Department of Health and Human Services Office of Minority Health 2011: *National Partnership for Action to End Health Disparities*, 2011. U.S. Office of Inspector General (OIG). http://minorityhealth.hhs.gov/npa. Accessed October 25, 2013.

U.S. Department of Health and Human Services: *Hospital incident reporting systems do not capture most patient harm.* January, 2012. U.S. Office of Inspector General (OIG). http://oig.hhs.gov/oei/reports/oei-06-09-00091.pdf. Accessed January 25, 2012.

Utter v. United Hospital Center, Inc., 236 SE 2d 213 (W.Va, 1977).

Westrick S: *Essentials of nursing law and ethics*, Sudbury, MA, 2013, Jones and Bartlett.

Williams v. West Virginia Board of Examiners, S.E. 2d WL1432298 (W.Va., 2004).

Winkelman v. Beloit Memorial Hospital, 483 NW 2d 211 (Wis., 1992).

Wolf ZR, Hicks RW, Altmiller G, et al: Nursing student medication errors involving tubing and catheters: a descriptive study, *Nurse Educ Today* 29(8):681–688, 2009.

Woods J, Rozovsky F: *What do I say? Communicating intended or unanticipated outcomes in obstetrics*, San Francisco, 2003, Jossey-Bass.

Ethical dilemmas are the puzzles of life.

9

Ethical and Bioethical Issues in Nursing and Health Care

Carla D. Sanderson, PhD, RN

ⓔ Additional resources are available online at: *http://evolve.elsevier.com/Cherry/*

PROFESSIONAL/ETHICAL ISSUE

Nursing students are introduced to the ethical and legal implications of the profession of nursing during the foundational nursing course offered early in their nursing program.

The most dreaded course in the entire nursing curriculum is now Adult Health Nursing. For the first time in your nursing program, your grade point average in the course is only two points above passing. There is so much to learn, so many concepts to put together, so many possible ways to think through test questions, and, in fact, your professor has told you that you are over-thinking the answers.

The last unit test is in 5 days: the Unit 4 examination. So much is riding on your ability to do well. You need to score higher than you have on any Adult Health unit examination to date, yet the Unit 4 examination has the reputation for being the hardest of all, with the lowest scores of the semester.

As you begin to organize your study plan for the test, a friend sends a text to tell you that his friend has a copy of an old Adult Health-Unit 4 examination. He invites you to his apartment that evening, where a group of six to eight students will be reviewing for the examination with the copy in hand.

Your nursing program has made it very clear that no copies of prior exams are available or appropriate for use. You know how important it is to be competent in Unit 4 materials, to possess the independent reasoning ability to pass the examination unaided. In fact, you know that knowing the Unit 4 material could easily be a matter of life and death for a patient who will someday soon be in your care.

And what about those six to eight other nursing students? What if they are able to pass the test without developing the knowledge needed to give safe, competent care?

What are you to do? Do you attend the review with your classmates? Do you determine that it is more important to pass this test and get through nursing school, thinking you can worry about truly learning the material later? Do you have any responsibility over the actions of your classmates? What is your moral and ethical responsibility over the wrongdoing of others?

VIGNETTE

Joe Smith has accepted a position as the nurse manager in a very busy urban emergency department, which serves patients from diverse cultures. Among Joe's many responsibilities is developing the 24-hour, 7-day–week work schedules of the department's nursing workforce in which he has 10 unfilled positions. Another responsibility is implementing the hospital's policy of offering all patients, regardless of cultural beliefs, the right to an advance directive for end-of-life care. At the same time, Joe must ensure that each patient who enters the emergency department receives appropriate high-quality care from competent professional care providers who respect and respond to patients' individual needs and desires. With these responsibilities come challenges, sometimes so significant that the nurse manager is faced with an ethical dilemma.

Questions to Consider While Reading This Chapter:
1. How will ethical and bioethical issues in nursing and health care affect my professional nursing practice?

2. What ethical theories and principles serve as a basis for nursing practice?
3. How am I to think about ethical dilemmas with moral integrity and consistency with my belief system?
4. What goals can I establish to move me toward excellence in moral and ethical reasoning?
5. How can I assist patients and families who face difficult ethical decisions?

KEY TERMS

Accountability: An ethical duty stating that one should be answerable legally, morally, ethically, or socially for one's activities.

Autonomy: Personal freedom and the right of competent people to make choices.

Beneficence: An ethical principle of compassion and patient advocacy, stating that one should do good and prevent or avoid doing harm.

Bioethics: The study of ethical problems resulting from scientific advances.

Code of ethics: A set of statements encompassing rules that apply to people in professional roles.

Deontology: An ethical theory stating that moral rule is binding.

Ethical sensitivity: The capacity to decide with intelligence and compassion, given uncertainty in a care situation, with an additional ability to anticipate consequences and the courage to act (Weaver et al, 2008).

Ethics: Science or study of moral values.

Ethics acculturation: The didactic and experiential process of developing ethical reasoning abilities as a part of ongoing professional preparation.

Fidelity: The agreement to keep promises and commitments, based on the virtue of caring.

Justice: The equal and fair distribution of resources, regardless of other factors.

Nonmaleficence: An ethical principle stating the duty to not inflict harm.

Paternalism: Based on the health care provider's belief about what is in the best interest of the patient, he/she chooses to reveal or withhold patient information such as diagnosis, treatment, or prognosis.

Rights of conscience: The civil right that protects conscientious health care providers against discrimination, allowing them the right to act according to the dictates of their conscience.

Utilitarianism: An ethical theory stating that the best decision is one that brings about the greatest good for the most people.

Values: Customs, ideas of life, and ways of behaving that society regards as desirable.

Veracity: An ethical duty to tell the truth.

LEARNING OUTCOMES

After studying this chapter, the reader will be able to:
1. Integrate basic concepts of human values that are essential for ethical decision making.
2. Analyze selected ethical theories and principles as a basis for ethical decision making.
3. Analyze the relationship between ethics and morality in relation to nursing practice.

4. Use an ethical decision-making framework for resolving ethical problems in health care.
5. Apply the ethical decision-making process to specific ethical issues encountered in clinical practice.

CHAPTER OVERVIEW

In a nursing education program, nursing students begin to embrace the complexities and profound opportunities that are characteristic of the profession of nursing. Prelicensure nursing education is only an introduction to a discipline in which there are no knowledge boundaries. The abundance of nursing practice information is evident from a quick glance across the nursing textbook selections in the campus or online bookstore.

Most of that information addresses the "how-to" aspects of nursing care. The scientific aspects of nursing care are evolving more rapidly than ever as a host of nurse researchers delve into questions about the safe, competent, and therapeutic aspects of professional nursing care. As quickly as nursing science produces new nursing knowledge, how-to information is shared through professional journals, textbooks, and Internet resources. The scientific aspects of care evolve constantly through how-to research.

A myriad of potential questions surpass the how-to body of knowledge that is inherent in the profession of nursing. Everywhere in today's health care delivery system are potential questions of another nature—the "how should" questions, which are challenging and sometimes evolve into ethical dilemmas. The "how should" questions that the emergency department nurse manager faces may sound something like the following:

- *How should I determine the competency of an acutely ill 80-year-old patient who comes to the emergency department without an advance directive? Is her competency intact? How should I determine whether she is capable of giving an informed advance directive?*
- *How should I act if her decision for her own end-of-life care is not consistent with what her family wants for her? Or how should I respond if the family, because of cultural beliefs, will not even allow information about end-of-life care to be shared with their loved one?*
- *How should I view the care of this 80-year-old patient? Is an emergency resuscitation effort for an 80-year-old considered ordinary and routine, or is it considered extraordinary and heroic?*
- *How should I respond to her if, in the course of efforts to stabilize her, she calls me in to ask me whether she is dying?*
- *How much of the truth is warranted?*
- *How should I decide when the availability of one-on-one trauma care beds becomes threatened and the decision must be made to move someone out of one bed to make room for this 80-year-old woman whose condition is rapidly deteriorating?*
- *Is the life of this 80-year-old woman any less significant than that of the 40-year-old father of four who has just been admitted after a tragic car accident?*
- *How should I react when another health care provider on duty devalues the significance of her life?*
- *How should I feel when this 80-year-old patient is entered into a research study designed to test a new drug for flash pulmonary edema from congestive heart failure that has previously only been tested on a younger population?*
- *How should I make staffing assignments when the number of nurses on a given shift is insufficient to provide effective and adequate emergency department care to all?*
- *How should I respond when one of the few nurses reporting to work on a given day refuses to accept the care of patients because of inadequate staffing?*
- *How should I react when presented with situations that test my own sense of conscience and moral integrity?*

This chapter introduces the nursing student to a different aspect of nursing care—the "how should" aspect or, as it is more appropriately called, the ethical aspect. Ethics is a system for deciding, based on principles, how one should think and what should be done. With the goal of developing excellence in moral and reasoning ability, the nursing student begins a career-long process of ethics *acculturation. This process allows the professional nurse to practice with an increasing level of understanding that goes beyond the scientific and moves toward a more complete and whole understanding of human existence.*

NURSING ETHICS

Nursing ethics is a system of principles concerning the actions of the nurse in his or her relationships with patients, patients' family members, other health care providers, policymakers, and society as a whole. A profession is characterized by its relationship to society. The results of a 2014 Gallup poll on professional honesty and ethics indicate that the public ranks nursing as the most ethical of all professions, and has for almost two decades (http://www.gallup.com/poll/180260/americans-rate-nurses-highest-honesty-ethical-standards.aspx) (Rifkin, 2014). Codes of ethics provide implicit standards and values for the professions. A nursing code of ethics was first introduced in the late nineteenth century and has evolved through the years as the profession has evolved and as changes in society and health care have come about. Current dynamics, such as the Patient Protection and Affordable Care Act, the emerging genetic interventions associated with therapeutic and reproductive cloning, debates about securing stem cells for research and treatment, evolving legal definitions of *family,* ongoing questions about euthanasia and assisted suicide, and escalating threats to the effective delivery of health care as a result of significant nursing shortages, now being called *ethical climate in the workplace,* bring nursing's code of ethics into the forefront (Boxes 9-1 and 9-2).

BIOETHICS

Nursing ethics is part of a broader system known as *bioethics.* Bioethics is an interdisciplinary field within the health care organization that has developed only in the past 50 years. Whereas ethics has been discussed since there was written language, bioethics has developed with the age of modern medicine, specifically with the development of hemodialysis and organ transplantation. New questions surface as science and technology produce new ways of knowing. Think of the questions that come from stem cell research, sexual reassignment, and reproductive-assisting technologies such as donor insemination, *in vitro* fertilization, removal of unused zygotes, surrogate parenting, organ transplantation, and funding for end-of-life care. Bioethics is a response to these and other contemporary advances and challenges in health care. It is difficult to imagine a time when answers will be more plentiful than bioethical questions.

Dilemmas for Health Professionals

Physicians, nurses, social workers, psychiatrists, epidemiologists, clergy, philosophers, theologians, researchers, and policymakers are joining through interprofessional initiatives to address ethical questions, difficult questions, and right-versus-wrong questions. As they seek to deliver quality health care, these professionals debate situations that pose dilemmas. They are confronting situations for which there are no clear right or wrong answers. Because of the diverse society in which health

> **BOX 9-1** **American Nurses Association Code of Ethics for Nurses**
>
> - The nurse practices with compassion and respect for the inherent dignity, worth, and unique attributes of every person.
> - The nurse's primary commitment is to the patient, whether an individual, family, group, community, or population.
> - The nurse promotes, advocates for, and protects the rights, health, and safety of the patient.
> - The nurse has authority, accountability, and responsibility for nursing practice; makes decisions; and takes action consistent with the obligation to promote health and to provide optimal care.
> - The nurse owes the same duties to self as to others, including the responsibility to promote health and safety, preserve wholeness of character and integrity, maintain competence, and continue personal and professional growth.
> - The nurse through individual and collective effort, established, maintains, and improves the ethical environment of the work setting and conditions of employment that are conducive to safe, quality health care.
> - The nurse, in all roles and settings, advances the profession through research and scholarly inquiry, professional standards development, and the generation of both nursing and health policy.
> - The nurse collaborates with other health professionals and the public to protect human rights, promote health diplomacy, and reduce health disparities.
> - The profession of nursing, collectively through its professional organizations, must articulate nursing values, maintain the integrity of the profession, and integrate principles of social justice into nursing and health policy.

Reprinted with permission from American Nurses Association: *Code of ethics for nurses with interpretive statements,* Silver Spring, MD, 2015, Nursebooks.org, American Nurses Association. Available online at http://www.nursesbooks.org/Main-Menu/Ethics/Code-of-Ethics.aspx.

care is practiced, there are at least two sides to almost every issue faced.

Every specialization in health care has its own set of questions. Life and death, the margin of viability, quality of life, design of life, one life offering cure for another, right to decide, informed consent, medical confidentiality, and alternative treatment issues prevail in every field of health care from maternal-child to

---

BOX 9-2 International Council of Nurses Code of Ethics for Nurses

- The fundamental responsibility of the nurse is fourfold: to promote health, to prevent illness, to restore health, and to alleviate suffering.
- The need for nursing is universal. Inherent in nursing is respect for life, dignity, and rights of humans. It is unrestricted by considerations of nationality, race, creed, color, age, sex, politics, or social status.
- Nurses render health services to the individual, the family, and the community and coordinate their services with those of related groups.

Nurses and People

- The nurse's primary responsibility is to those people who require nursing care.
- The nurse, in providing care, promotes an environment in which the values, customs, and spiritual beliefs of the patient are respected.
- The nurse holds in confidence personal information and uses judgment in sharing this information.

Nurses and Practice

- The nurse carries personal responsibility for nursing practice and for maintaining competence by continual learning. The nurse maintains the highest standards of nursing care possible within the reality of a specific situation.
- The nurse uses judgment in relation to individual competence when accepting and delegating responsibilities.

- The nurse, when acting in a professional capacity, should at all times maintain standards of personal conduct that reflect credit on the profession.

Nurses and Society

- The nurse shares with other citizens the responsibility for initiating and supporting action to meet the health and social needs of the public.

Nurses and Coworkers

- The nurse sustains a cooperative relationship with coworkers in nursing and other fields.
- The nurse takes appropriate action to safeguard the patient when his or her care is endangered by a coworker or any other person.

Nurses and the Profession

- The nurse plays a major role in determining and implementing desirable standards of nursing practice and nursing education.
- The nurse is active in developing a core of professional knowledge.
- The nurse, acting through the professional organization, participates in establishing and maintaining equitable social and economic working conditions in nursing.

From International Council of Nurses: *ICN code for nurses: ethical concepts applied to nursing,* Geneva, 2005, Imprimiéres Populaires.

---

geriatric care; from acute episodic to intensive, highly specialized care; and from hospital-based to community-based care. Questions about the economics of nursing care and the use of technologies in the diagnosis and treatment of illness abound. In every aspect of the nursing profession lies the more subtle and intricate questions of how this care should be delivered and how one should decide when choices are in conflict.

Many nursing students do not consider health care and the practice of nursing in terms of the personal, truthful, honest, faithful (i.e., keeping promises to patients), qualitative, and subjective side; rather, they look at it only in terms of the technical, quantitative, and objective side. Yet there are distinctively subjective factors that influence the way patients are actually treated, or at least the way they perceive their treatment, that go beyond the data-driven aspect. In many ways, advanced technology has changed the face of health care and

created the troubling questions that have become central in the delivery of care.

Dilemmas Created by Technology

Advances in health care through technology have created new situations for health care professionals and their patients. For the very young and old and for generations in between, illnesses once leading to mortality have become manageable and are classified as high-risk or chronic illness. Although people can now be saved, they are not being saved readily or inexpensively. Care of the acutely or chronically ill person sometimes creates hard questions for which there are no easy or apparent answers. Mortality for most will be a long, drawn-out phenomenon, laced with a lifetime of potential conflicts about what ought to be done.

Even the nature of life itself and the technical manipulation of DNA are under investigation. Health care professionals who adhere to an exclusively scientific or technologic approach to care will be seen as insensitive and will fail to meet the genuine needs of the patient; needs that include assistance with these more subjective concerns, such as how to think about the many advanced care choices laid before them.

THE ETHICS OF CARE

The very nature of the profession of nursing is the obligation and responsibility to care (Beauchamp et al, 2009). The ethic of care involves the nurse fulfilling the caring task by seeking the best way to care for each patient, one patient at a time, thus fulfilling a moral imperative to alleviate suffering by taking action. According to the *Code of Ethics for Nurses,* "The measures nurses take to care for the patient enables the patient to live with as much physical, emotional, social, and spiritual well-being as possible," and "The nurse respects the worth, dignity and rights of all human beings irrespective of the nature of the health problem" (ANA, 2001). Caring defines nursing, as curing often defines medicine (Lachman, 2012).

Today's professional nurse will be deemed competent only if he or she can promote well-being through the scientific and technologic aspects of care and has the ability to deal effectively with the ethical problems encountered when respecting the rights of those being cared for. A competent nurse is an ethically sensitive nurse (Weaver et al, 2008) who can deal with the human dimensions of care that include a search for what is good and right as well as for what is accurate and efficient. The previously listed "how should" questions are just as important as the how-to questions surrounding day-to-day decision making in the emergency department or the care of the 80-year-old patient introduced previously. As the nurse seeks to understand the how-to aspects of nurse management and patient care, he or she also must seek to understand more about respecting the rights of patients.

Answering Difficult Questions

Care that combines human dimensions with scientific and technical dimensions forces some basic questions:
- What is safe care?
- What effect might a patient's cultural preferences have on safe care?
- When staffing is inadequate, what care should be accepted or refused?

- What are other barriers to ethical practice brought about by the workplace environment?
- What does it mean to be ill or well?
- What is the proper balance between science and technology and the good of humans?
- Where do we find balance when science will allow us to experiment with the basic origins of life?
- What happens when the proper balance is in tension?
- What happens when tension exists between personal beliefs and values and institutional policy or patient desires?

No tension is created in the effort to save the life of a dying healthy adolescent or set the broken leg of a healthy older adult. Science and the human good are not in conflict here. No conflict exists when there is a competent nursing staff, sufficient in number to provide quality care. However, what is the answer when modern medicine can save or prolong the life of an 8-year-old child but the child's parents refuse treatment based on religious reasons? Or what is the answer when modern medicine has life to offer a 30-year-old mother in need of a transplanted organ but the woman is without the financial means to cover the cost of the treatment? What is the answer when a family refuses to allow the physician to share news of a terminal illness with their grandmother? What is the answer when new discoveries allow some would-be parents to choose biologic characteristics of children not yet conceived? What is the answer when the emergency department is full of acutely ill patients and there are too few nurses expected for the next shift? At one end of the spectrum lies the obvious; at the other there is often only uncertainty. Health care professionals in everyday practice often find themselves somewhere between the two.

Balancing Science and Morality

If nursing care is to be competent, the right balance between science and morality must be sought and understood. Nurses must first attempt to understand not just what they are to do for their patients but who their patients are. They must examine life and its origins, in addition to its worth, usefulness, and importance. Nurses must determine their own values and seek to understand the values of others.

Health care decisions are seldom made independently of other people. Decisions are made with the patient, the family, other nurses, and other health care providers. Nurses must make a deliberate effort to recognize their own values and learn to consider and respect the values of others.

The nurse has an obligation to present himself or herself to the patient as competent. The dependent patient enters a mutual relationship with the nurse. This exchange places a patient who is vulnerable and wounded with a nurse who is educated, licensed, and knowledgeable. The patient expects nursing actions to be thorough because total caring is the defining characteristic of the patient-nurse relationship. The nurse promises to deliver holistic care to the best of his or her ability. The patient's expectations and the nurse's promises require a commitment to develop a reasoned thought process and sound judgment in all situations that take place within this important relationship. The more personal, subjective, and value-laden situations are deemed to be among the most difficult situations for which the nurse must prepare.

VALUES FORMATION AND MORAL DEVELOPMENT

A value is a personal belief about worth that acts as a standard to guide behavior; a value system is an entire framework on which actions are based and is the backbone to how one thinks, feels, and takes action. Perhaps many nursing students come to the educational setting with a strong backbone and an intact value system. No doubt anyone living in these times has faced many situations in which important choices had to be made. The challenges faced in this generation are too numerous to avoid difficult choices. Values have been applied to those decisions. Yet often people do not take time to seriously contemplate their value system, the forces that shaped those values, and the life and worldview decisions that have been made based on them.

Examining Value Systems

To become a competent professional in every dimension of nursing care, nurses must examine their own system of values and commit themselves to a virtuous value system. A clear understanding of what is right and wrong is a necessary first step to a process sometimes referred to as *values clarification,* a process by which people attempt to examine the values they hold and how each of those values functions as part of a whole. Nurses must acknowledge their own values by considering how they would act in a particular situation.

Diane Uustal was one of nursing's first leaders to describe the role of values clarification in the decision-making process of the nurse. A values clarification process (Uustal, 1992) is an important learning tool as nursing students prepare themselves to become competent professionals. The deliberate refinement of one's own value system leads to a clearer lens through which nurses can view ethical questions in the practice of their profession. A refined value system and worldview can serve professionals as they deal with the meaning of life and its many choices. A worldview provides a cohesive model for life; it encourages personal responsibility for the living of that life, and it prepares one for making ethical choices encountered throughout life. Tools to assist the reader in values clarification can be found online (http://evolve.elsevier.com/Cherry/).

Forming a worldview and a value system is an evolving, continuous, dynamic process that moves along a continuum of development often referred to as *moral development.* Just as there is an orderly sequence of physical and psychologic development, there is an orderly sequence of right and wrong conduct development. Consider an adult of strong physical prowess and strong moral character. With each biologic developmental milestone there is a more mature, more expanded physical being; likewise with each life experience that has choices between right and wrong, there is a more mature, more virtuous person.

Learning Right and Wrong

The process of learning to distinguish right and wrong often is described in pediatric textbooks. Donna Wong describes such development in children (Hockenberry and Wilson, 2010). Infants have no concept of right or wrong. Infants hold no beliefs and no convictions. although it is known that moral development begins in infancy. If the need for basic trust is met in infancy, children can begin to develop the foundation for secure moral thought. Toddlers begin to display behavior in response to the world around them. They will imitate behavior seen in others, even though they do not comprehend the meaning of the behavior that they are imitating. Furthermore, even though toddlers may not know what they are doing or why they are doing it, they incorporate the values and beliefs of those around them into their own behavioral code.

By the time children reach school age, they have learned that behavior has consequences and that good behavior is associated with rewards and bad behavior with punishment. Through their experiences and social interactions with people outside their home or immediate surroundings, school-age children begin to make choices about how they will act based on an understanding of good and bad. Their conscience is developing, and it begins to govern the choices they make (Hockenberry and Wilson, 2010).

The adolescent questions existing moral values and his or her relevance to society. Adolescents understand duty and obligation, but they sometimes seriously question the moral codes on which society operates as they become more aware of the contradictions they see in the value systems of adults.

Adults strive to make sense of the contradictions and learn to develop their own set of morals and values as autonomous people, sometimes referred to as developing a moral compass. They begin to make choices based on an internalized set of principles that provides them with the resources they need to evaluate situations in which they find themselves (Hockenberry and Wilson, 2010).

Understanding Moral Development Theory

Perhaps the most widely accepted theory on moral development is the now classic theory developed by Lawrence Kohlberg (1971). Kohlberg theorizes a cognitive developmental process that is sequential in nature with progression through levels and stages that vary dramatically within society. At first, morality is all about rules imposed by some source of authority. Moral decisions made at this level (preconventional) are simply in response to some threat of punishment. The good-bad, right-wrong labels have meaning, but they are defined only in reference to a self-centered reward-and-punishment system. A person who is in the preconventional level has no concept of the underlying moral code informing the decision of good or bad or right or wrong.

At some point, people begin to internalize their view of themselves in response to something more meaningful and interpersonal (conventional level). A desire to be viewed as a good boy or nice girl develops when the person wants to find approval from others. He or she may want to please, help others, be dutiful, and show respect for authority. Conformity to expected social and religious mores and a sense of loyalty may emerge.

Not all people develop beyond the conventional level of moral development. A morally mature individual

(postconventional level), one of the few to reach moral completeness, is an autonomous thinker who strives for a moral code beyond issues of authority and reverence. Integrative thinking is required to move toward having the critical components necessary to make moral judgments. The morally mature individual's actions are based on principles of **justice** and respect for the dignity of all humankind and not just on principles of responsibility, duty, or self-edification (Kohlberg, 1971).

Moving Toward Moral Maturity

The rightness or wrongness of the complex and confounding health care decisions that are being made today depends on the level of moral development of those professionals entrusted with the tough decisions. Moving toward the level of moral maturity required for sound ethical decision making is, for most, a learning endeavor that requires a strong commitment to the task. Nurses must commit themselves to such learning, to a process called **ethics acculturation** across the span of their career. The issues will only get more complex and confounding as new advances are introduced; the commitment to the development of moral and ethical reasoning is imperative. The desired outcomes as a result of ethics acculturation across the years are integrity, personal growth, practical wisdom, and effective problem solving on behalf of patients and their families (Weaver et al, 2008). These are the qualities that are characteristic of an ethically sensitive and morally mature person.

As a matter of the civil rights afforded to all members of United States society, health care professionals have been afforded **rights of conscience** to practice their own convictions about what is right and ethical care. Rights of conscience have been brought in to focus primarily over the debate on abortion and euthanasia. Historically there has been much liberty given to professionals in choosing to participate in care they believe in, and refusing to participate in care they may find ethically unsound. The current debate on health care reform has sparked discussion on threats to continued rights of conscience for practitioners as federal funding for abortion has been allocated. Professional nurses must be ready to take up the challenge of debating the matter of whether or not the right to act according to conscience should continue to be a part of one's civil rights. Doing so will require careful examination of one's inner sense of right and wrong, the principles and motivations that govern one's actions and thoughts, and one's system of internal accountability for actions taken.

The development of values and value-based behavior is essential for professional nursing. The American Association of Colleges of Nursing (AACN) has delineated five essential values that are described in Table 9-1. The study and examination of these nursing values is a worthwhile endeavor for the nursing student. Students who seek to become morally mature health care providers will appraise the values of the nursing profession and strive to find a comfortable union of those values with their own.

The complexity of today's healthcare environment may lead to value conflicts and the potential for what is referred to as moral distress that comes from knowing the morally right thing to do but not being able to do it because of constraints outside one's control. Moral courage refers to being able to stand up for what is right, taking action based on ethical principles and

protecting ethical values such as honesty, integrity, fairness, respect, responsibility, empathy, compassion, and courage, regardless of the possible consequences taking action might present (Murray, 2010). Moral courage can be developed by simulating ethical dilemmas that students and nurses can process together. The study of ethical theory and ethical principles can guide the dialogue when processing dilemmas and provide a basis for moving forward as a morally courageous professional nurse.

ETHICAL THEORY

Ethical theory is a system of principles by which a person can determine what should and should not be done. Although there are others, utilitarianism and deontology are the Western world's most frequently sited theories as foundational for processing ethical dilemmas.

TABLE 9-1 Essential Nursing Values and Behaviors

Essential Values	Attitudes and Personal Qualities	Professional Behaviors
Altruism—concern for the welfare of others	Caring, commitment, compassion, generosity, perseverance	Gives full attention to the client when giving care; assists other personnel in providing care when they are unable to do so; expresses concern about social trends and issues that have implications for health care
Autonomy—right to self-determination	Respectfulness, trust, objectivity	Provides nursing care based on respect of patients' rights to make decisions about their health care; honors individual's right to refuse treatment
Human dignity—respect for inherent worth and uniqueness of individuals and populations	Consideration, empathy, humaneness, kindness, respectfulness	Values and respects all patients and colleagues, regardless of background
Integrity—acting in accordance with an appropriate code of ethics	Moral, ethical, and legal professional behavior	The nurse is honest and provides care based on an ethical framework that is accepted in the profession
Social justice—acting in accordance with fair treatment regardless of economic status, race, ethnicity, age, citizenship, disability, or sexual orientation	Courage, integrity, morality, objectivity	Acts as a health care advocate; allocates resources fairly Reports incompetent, unethical, and illegal practices objectively and factually

From American Association of Colleges of Nursing: Essentials of baccalaureate education for professional nursing, Washington, DC, 2008, American Association of Colleges of Nursing.

Utilitarianism

Utilitarianism is an approach that supports what is best for most people, rooted in the assumption that an action or practice is right if it leads to the greatest possible balance of good consequences or to the least possible balance of bad consequences. For instance, the utilitarian approach would be at work if the government made a decision to forgo Medicare funding treatment for patients 90 years of age and older with a diagnosis of Alzheimer's disease, and redistribute Medicare funding to other Medicare-eligible individuals with a greater likelihood of benefit to longevity or quality of life. Utilitarian ethics are noted to be the strongest approach used in bioethical decision making. An attempt is made to determine which actions will lead to the greatest ratio of benefit to harm for all persons involved in the dilemma.

Deontology

Deontology is an approach that is rooted in the assumption that humans are rational and act out of principles that are consistent and objective and compel them to do what is right. Ethics are based on a sense of a universal principle to consistently act one way. For instance, the deontological approach would be at work if a decision is made to resuscitate and provide mechanical ventilation to a 23-week, otherwise viable fetus, despite ability to pay for care and availability of newborn intensive care beds. In bioethical decision making, moral rightness is the act that is determined not by the consequences of the actions it produces, but by the intentions and moral qualities intrinsic to the act itself. Deontological theory claims that a decision is right only if it conforms to an overriding moral duty and wrong only if it violates that moral duty. All decisions must be made in such a way that the decision could become universal law. Persons are to be treated as ends in themselves and never as means to the ends of others.

ETHICAL PRINCIPLES

Perhaps the most useful tool for the morally mature professional nurse is a set of principles, standards, or truths on which to base ethical actions. Common ground must be established between the nurse and the patient and family, between fellow nurses, between the nurse and other health care providers, and between the nurse and other members of society. Such common ground can be established by adhering to a set of principles that can move everyone involved toward understanding and agreement.

The practice of ethics involves applying principles to the two ethical theories described—utilitarianism and deontology—or to other theories that are described elsewhere. Principles can permit people to take a consistent position on specific or related issues. If the principles, when applied to a particular act, make the act right or wrong in one situation, it seems reasonable to assume that the same principle, when applied to a new situation, can have the same result.

Three principles have proven to be highly relevant in bioethics: (1) autonomy, (2) beneficence and nonmaleficence, and (3) veracity. These principles do not form a complete moral framework. One principle may be relevant to a situation, whereas the others are not. Yet these principles are sufficiently comprehensive to provide an analytic framework by which moral problems can be evaluated.

Autonomy

Autonomy, the principle of respect for a person, is sometimes labeled as the primary moral principle. This concept holds that humans have incalculable worth or moral dignity not possessed by other objects or creatures. There is unconditional intrinsic value for everyone. People are free to form their own judgments and whatever actions they choose. They are self-determining agents, entitled to determine their own destiny.

If an autonomous person's actions do not infringe on the autonomous actions of others, that person should be free to decide whatever he or she wishes. This freedom should be applied even if the decision creates risk to his or her health and even if the decision seems unwise to others. Concepts of freedom and informed consent are grounded in the principle of autonomy.

Although the principle of autonomy may seem basic and universal, there are times when this principle may be in conflict. For instance, in some male-dominated or patriarchal cultures, the family leader's rights may override the individual and autonomous rights of a family member. In this situation, action based on the moral principle of autonomy may perpetuate conflict.

Beneficence and Nonmaleficence

In general terms, to be *beneficent* is to promote goodness, kindness, and charity. A different yet related principle is *nonmaleficence*, which is a duty not to inflict harm. In ethical terms nonmaleficence is to abstain from injuring others and to help others further their own well-being by removing harm and eliminating threats, whereas *beneficence* is to provide benefits to others by promoting their good. The beneficence-nonmaleficence principle is largely a balance of risk and benefit. At times, the risk for harm must be weighed against the possible benefits. The risk should never be greater than the importance of the problem to be solved.

Although it may seem natural to promote good at all times, the most common bioethical conflicts result from an imbalance between the demands of beneficence and those acts and decisions within the health care delivery system that might pose threats. For instance, it is not always clearly evident what is good and what is harmful. Is the resuscitation effort of the 80-year-old woman good or harmful to her overall sense of well-being? How much beneficence is there in supporting someone toward a peaceful death? What is the balance between beneficence and nonmaleficence in an understaffed emergency department? Is it better to do as much good as you can with the limited resources you have or to refuse to assume care in an effort to prevent harm that can come from being understaffed?

Veracity

Most contemporary professionals believe that telling the truth in personal communication is a moral and ethical requirement. If there is the belief in health care that truth telling is always right, then the principle of veracity can itself pose some interesting challenges.

In the past, truth telling was sometimes viewed as inconvenient, distressing, or even harmful to patients and families. In fact, the first American Medical Association Code of Ethics in 1847 contained such a message:

> "The life of a sick person can be shortened not only by the acts, but also by the words or the manner of a physician. It is, therefore, a sacred duty to guard himself carefully in this respect, and to avoid all things that have a tendency to discourage the patient and to depress his spirits."

The belief that the truth could at times be harmful was held for many years. Only recently, with the shift from a provider-driven system to a consumer-driven system, has the history of silence begun to break. With this shift have come interesting questions. Is the provider-patient relationship generally understood by both parties

to include the right of the provider to control the truth by withholding some or all of the relevant information until an appropriate time for disclosure? How much deception with patients is morally acceptable in the communication of a poor or terminal prognosis?

Difficult questions surface, but at the heart of the principle of veracity is trust. Health care consumers today expect accurate and precise information that is revealed in an honest and respectful manner. A few generations ago, the trust factor may have been such that it was acceptable for providers to share parts of truth or to distort the truth in the name of beneficence. Today, however, for trust to develop between providers and patients there must be truthful interaction and meaningful communication. The moral conflict that results from being less than truthful to patients is too troublesome for today's practitioner. The deontological theory of the health care provider having a duty to tell the patient the truth has taken precedence over the fear of harm that might result if the truth is revealed.

The challenge today is to mesh the need for truthful communication with the need to protect. Health care providers must lay aside fears that the truth will be harmful to patients and come to the realization that more often than not, the truth can alleviate anxiety, increase pain tolerance, facilitate recovery, and enhance cooperation with treatment. With a pledge toward human decency, health care providers must commit themselves to truth telling in all interactions and relationships.

ETHICAL DECISION-MAKING MODEL

Theories provide a cognitive plan for considering ethical issues; principles offer guiding truths on which to base ethical decisions. Using these theories and principles, it seems appropriate to consider a system for moving beyond a specific ethical dilemma toward a morally mature and reasoned ethical action.

Many ethical decision-making models exist for the purpose of defining a process by which a nurse or another health care provider actually can move through an ethical dilemma toward an informed decision. Box 9-3 depicts one ethical decision-making model.

Situation Assessment Procedure

Identify the ethical issues and problems. In the first step of assessment, there is an attempt to find out the

BOX 9-3   Situation Assessment Procedure

- Identify the ethical issues and problems.
- Identify and analyze available alternatives for action.
- Select one alternative.
- Justify the selection.

From Wright RA: The practice of ethics: human values in health care, New York, 1987, McGraw-Hill.

technical and scientific facts and the human dimension of the situation—the feelings, emotions, attitudes, and opinions. A nurse must make an attempt to understand what values are inherent in the situation. Finally, the nurse must deliberately state the nature of the ethical dilemma. This first step is important because the issues and problems to be addressed are often complex. Trying to understand the full picture of a situation is time-consuming and requires examination from many different perspectives, but it is worth the time and effort to understand an issue fully before moving forward in the assessment procedure. Wright (1987) poses some important questions that must be addressed in this first step:

- What is the issue here?
- What are the hidden issues?
- What exactly are the complexities of this situation?
- Is anything being overlooked?

Identify and Analyze Available Alternatives for Action

In the second step, a set of alternatives for action is established. The second step is an important step to follow. Because actions are based most commonly on a nurse's personal value system, it is important to list all possible actions for a given situation, even actions that seem highly unlikely. Without deliberately listing possible alternatives, it is doubtful that the full consideration of all possible actions will take place. Wright's (1987) questions for the second step are as follows:

- What are the reasonable possibilities for action, and how do the different affected parties (patient, family, physician, nurse) want to resolve the problem?
- What ethical principles are required for each alternative?
- What assumptions are required for each alternative, and what are their implications for future action?
- What, if any, are the additional ethical problems that the alternatives raise?

Select One Alternative

Multiple factors come together in the third step. After identifying the issues and analyzing all possible alternatives, the skillful decision maker steps back to consider the situation again. There is an attempt to reflect on ethical theory and to mesh that thinking with the identified ethical principles for each alternative. The decision maker's value system is applied, along with an appraisal of the profession's values for the care of others. A reasoned and purposeful decision results from the blending of each of these factors.

Justify the Selection

The rational discourse on which the decision is based must be shared in an effort to justify the decision. The decision maker must be prepared to communicate his or her thoughts through an explanation of the reasoning process used. According to Wright (1987), the justification for a resolution to an ethical issue is an argument wherein relevant and sufficient reasons for the correctness of that resolution are presented. Defending an argument is not an easy task, but it is a necessary step to communicate the reasons or premises on which the decision is based. A systematic and logical argument will show why the particular resolution chosen is the correct one. This final step is important to advance ethical thought and to express sound judgment. Wright's formula for the justification process is as follows:

1. Specify reasons for the action.
2. Clearly present the ethical basis for these reasons.
3. Understand the shortcomings of the justification.
4. Anticipate objections to the justification.

Usefulness and Application of the Situation Assessment Procedure

A procedure or model for ethical decision making is useful for individuals and groups alike. The more subtle and tenuous issues that arise in health care often are resolved within the context of the patient-provider relationship that exists between two people. Dilemmas resulting from questions about truth telling, acknowledging uncertainty, paternalism, privacy, and fidelity are examples of issues that may be resolved between as few as two people.

Questions that are more encompassing often are addressed in group settings. Institutional ethics committees now are common within health care agencies. The purpose of the committee is to provide ethics education, aid in ethical policy development, and serve as a consultative body when resolution of an ethical dilemma cannot be reached otherwise. Although institutional ethics committees do not make legal decisions that are the province of the patient, the family, or the health care provider, a model such as the situation assessment procedure can be a useful procedure to guide the thinking of a group that has been asked to provide counsel.

More and more nurses are finding themselves facing ethical dilemmas as members of hospital administration teams or policymaking bodies within professional organizations or governmental bodies. Nurses contribute a highly relevant perspective to discussions and decisions about safe and effective care in these times of change. The situation assessment procedure can be applied to the decision-making process when procedures and policies are being developed to address conflicting variables.

Thus application of the situation assessment procedure can occur on two levels. The procedure is applicable to the daily practice level of ethical decision making as patients and providers make choices between right and wrong actions. The procedure is equally applicable to the policymaking level where professionals come together to consider right and wrong choices that affect society as a whole. Professional organizations including the American Nurses Association (ANA) have established committees, such as the Ethics and Human Rights Committee, which allow nurses to meet to set policy for the practice of nursing. Inherent in the policy formation are questions that affect patient care. The situation assessment procedure can be applied to difficult questions that arise in any setting in which the nurse is responsible for or contributes to ethical decision making.

BIOETHICAL DILEMMAS: LIFE, DEATH, AND DILEMMAS IN BETWEEN

Bioethical dilemmas are situations that pose a choice between perplexing alternatives in the delivery of health care because of the lack of a clear sense of right or wrong. It is imperative that every nursing student consider the potential dilemmas that might arise in a given practice setting. Concepts of life and death are central to nursing's body of knowledge, but a discussion of these concepts is incomplete unless the threats of conflict also are explored. A nursing student must not assume that conflict is rare or that it is to be dealt with primarily by other professionals on the health care team. Conflict must be addressed as the concepts of life and its origins, birth, death, and dying are addressed. However, conflict must also be addressed in the many varied situations that come up day after day in the practice of professional nursing.

Life

Entire textbooks are written to address the potential conflict that surrounds questions about the beginning of life. The most significant conflict that will be recorded in the historical accounts of the twentieth century will be the debate about when life begins. The abortion conflict became central in 1973 when the Roe v. Wade decision was made. Although the legal aspects of abortion have been resolved in courtrooms in the United States, the bioethical concerns continue to be debated over 40 years later. The bioethical abortion conflict has been debated using ethical theories and principles, value systems, rights issues, questions regarding the nature of choice, and so on. Answers acceptable to society as a whole have not materialized; thus, the right or wrong of abortion continues to rest with each person. Despite clear, generalizable answers to the abortion question, nurses serving in health settings for women and children must be prepared to face this morally laden issue.

Closely akin to the abortion question are newer questions about reproduction. Genetic screening, genetic engineering, stem cell therapy, and cloning are newer, highly advanced, and sophisticated techniques that bring with them the most ethically entangled questions ever encountered; the entire Human Genome Project with its rapidly developing advances represents the greatest challenge to date. Definitions of family, surrogacy, and other related issues also bring ethically entangled questions. Moving beyond the question about when life begins, health care providers must now address their patients' questions about the right or wrong of designing life itself through the manipulation and engineering of DNA or the right and wrong of new parenting models. Twenty-first-century science has created a whole new dimension of bioethics.

Genomic applications in healthcare, and the ethical implications surrounding them, are becoming increasingly relevant to the day-to-day delivery of care to patients, The National Institute of Health provides a resource in understanding the ethical implications of genomics, the Genetics/Genomics Competency Center (G2C2). Nurses can learn how to apply ethical principles when deliberating genetic/genomic issues related to decision-making, privacy, confidentiality, and informed consent, as well as process situations when patients' beliefs and values influence genomic care choices, and find resources for resolving ethical dilemmas (www.g-2-c-2.org).

The End of Life

The second most debated conflict in health care involves the issue of death and dying. Since the development of lifesaving procedures and mechanical ventilation, questions about quality of life and the definition of death have escalated. With advances in health care, it has become unclear what is usual care and what is heroic care. The purpose and quality of life of a person in a vegetative state continue to be debated and even legislated, as seen in the nationally broadcasted court action in Florida in 2003. Health care providers regularly contend with questions of cerebral versus biologic death in their dealings with patients and families.

The United States is now experiencing the aging of its largest segment of the population, and is facing ethical dilemmas related to the limited resources available to care for them. There is growing concern in the public square about the expenses associated with prolonging the dying process, which often also prolongs suffering. Euthanasia and assisted suicide present the newest ethical questions surrounding the dying process, though the American Nurses Association has an official statement in opposition to these activities (http://nursingworld.org/MainMenuCategories/EthicsStandards/Ethics-Position-Statements/Euthanasia-Assisted-Suicide-and-Aid-in-Dying). The morally courageous nurse must be prepared to recognize his or her own attitudes, feelings, values, and expectations about death in order to take ethical action for the good of the dying patient.

Dilemmas In Between

Life and death dilemmas receive the most attention through the media and in real-life drama played out in the news and on television and theater screens. However, a host of other questions make up most ethical decision-making activities for the professional nurse in the practice of today's health care. Between questions of life and death are questions of existence, reality, individual rights, responsibility, informed consent, cultural competence, equality, justice, ability to pay, and fairness. Added to these are an unlimited number of other questions that arise from the human dimension of caring.

It is in these ordinary day-to-day situations that many professionals find the most important and troublesome questions to an ethic of caring. Basic notions of individual and social justice are viewed in terms of fairness and what is deserved. A person has been treated justly when he or she has been given what is due or owed. Any denial of something to which a person has a right or entitlement is an act of injustice.

The Right to Health Care

Handling injustice has been a part of nursing since the days of Florence Nightingale, and has been at the forefront of the implementation of the Patient Protection and Affordable Care Act as individuals, businesses, and the legislature debate providing quality health care for the many without sacrificing the basic rights of the few. What basic right to health care do people have? Is each person entitled to the same health care package? Should ability to pay affect the specific level of entitlement? Resolutions to such questions have been based largely on the doctrine of justice, which states that like cases should be treated alike and equals ought to be treated equally. Such issues grip at the core of nursing practice wherein access to health care and a respect for human dignity are paramount. Justice becomes a bioethical issue at the point that it affects whether, when, where, and how a patient will receive health care. Americans have different values, beliefs, and priorities about how to surmount the injustices. Nurses must consider how their practice relates to injustice in health care and address factors that work against individual well-being and societal health (Sorrell, 2012). The opportunity for true health care reform will challenge nurses and the entire nation to consider the important ethical issues of justice.

Allocation of Scarce Resources

The issues of organ transplantation and the allocation of scarce resources flow from the doctrine of justice. The problem of scarce medical resources is becoming more common. Which people in need of transplantation should receive organs when available organs are in shorter supply than the number of people who could benefit from them? The justice question is applicable to this situation. The utilitarian view argues that the allocation decision should be framed so as to serve the greatest good for the greatest number of people affected. Should the selected recipient be the man with the largest, most loving family who does the greatest work for society? Or should a more universal law be applied? Should the people in need of organ transplantation be placed on a first-come, first-served list, or should they be entered into a lottery? Distributive justice, or taking into consideration the needs, interests, and wishes of each patient, cannot alone answer allocation dilemmas. Who has the more meaningful life? Who has the best prognosis? Who can pay? As unjust as it may seem to some, these are the kinds of questions responsible parties must answer regarding the allocation of scarce resources. And what about the fact that nurses themselves are scarce resources? What about the challenge of the nurse's autonomous right to refuse to work in understaffed settings? Whose rights come first?

Ethical Challenges

What about the doctrines of justice and freedom and the need for human experimentation and biomedical research? What about animal experimentation? It is accepted that human and animal experimentation is necessary for the progression of health care knowledge, but what about the risk for harm and the moral imperative that providers should, above all, do no harm? What about specifically problematic aspects of research, such as the use of institutionalized or imprisoned research subjects or the practice of research on a viable fetus? Memories of harmful medical research and human experimentation, such as the Nazi atrocities and the Tuskegee incident, have resulted in governmental regulations involving the use of human subjects in medical research. The Nuremberg Code is a set of provisions for research that must be followed for the federal government to approve research. Institutional review boards are established within research institutions for the purpose of overseeing that the degree of risk to the subject is minimized, if not eliminated. Human experimentation tests the principles of autonomy and respect for personhood.

The Challenge of Veracity

Everyday issues that test the principle of veracity are the concepts of alternative treatment and acknowledging uncertainty. It is the nature of health science that new knowledge must come forth to abolish less effective dogma. However, new ignorance comes along with these new discoveries. Which treatment among two or more is best for a patient in a specific situation? Which of the new drugs should be used? Should every patient be subjected to every possible form of diagnostic evaluation? Should this patient be treated with surgery, medication, or both? How do the economics of treatment costs factor in to the decision? And most important, should the patient be made aware of all of these questions and various options for his or her care? Can patients comprehend medicine's esoteric knowledge, in general, and its accompanying certainties and uncertainties, in particular? Is disclosure of uncertainty ultimately beneficial or detrimental?

Acknowledging uncertainty is difficult for today's health care provider. As never before, it seems that providers need to present themselves as confident, knowledgeable, and sensitive to patients who may see them as arrogant, dogmatic, and insensitive. Acknowledging uncertainty may be worth the effort. For the diagnostician, it may lighten the burden by absolving him or her of the responsibility for implicitly making decisions for which there may be conflicting answers. For the patient, knowing about the uncertainty may give him or her a greater voice in decision making and, in the event of treatment failure, may leave him or her better informed and more trustful of the caregiver. It seems that disclosure of uncertainty is ultimately beneficial to both parties. In fact, full disclosure and open communication through a commitment to veracity could prevent many everyday ethical situations. Optimal health care results from an exchange between patient and provider with open communication about the patient's wants and needs and the provider's judgment and advice. All too often, time is not taken for open communication, and the exchange becomes one in which the patient listens to what the all-knowing and wise provider says about his or her needs. In this scenario, it is easy for the provider to assume a paternalistic attitude in the delivery of health care.

The Challenge of Paternalism

Paternalism is an action and an attitude wherein the provider tries to act on behalf of the patient and believes that his or her actions are justified because of a commitment to act in the best interest of the patient. Paternalism is a reflection of the "father knows best" way of thinking. The phenomenon of paternalism presumes, in the name of beneficence, to overlook the patient's right to autonomy. Thus, in the process of attempting to act in the best interest of the patient, paternalism involves actions not based on the patient's choices, wishes, and desires. Paternalism interferes with a patient's right to self-determination and occurs when the provider believes that he or she can make a better decision than the patient.

Whereas it must be recognized that some cultures are highly paternalistic, the most common belief and value system in North America views paternalism as a threat to the patient-provider relationship. Every provider must guard against actions and attitudes that are paternalistic. Perhaps in the past, paternalism was associated with the white-coat image of the physician as a sovereign god. Today paternalistic actions and attitudes can be found among nurses, pharmacists, physical therapists, occupational therapists, social workers, clergy, or anyone who assumes the image of the all-knowing in the delivery of care. A current threat to a healthy patient-provider relationship is the emergence of entrepreneurship in medicine, in which health care providers are called on to be business managers. The bottom-line financial realities can be threats to safe care.

The healthy patient-provider relationship is based on the open communication described previously, wherein patient choice and respect for personhood are deemed just as important as scientific knowledge and sound health care advice. In paternalistic cultures when the patient is denied knowing "the truth" about his diagnosis or choices for care, it is a challenge for health care providers to know when to give the patient information or have discussions in spite of the family's wishes. The provider-patient relationship is built on trust when the right to confidentiality and privacy become ethical and legal obligations.

The Challenge of Autonomy

The provider-patient relationship makes way for the crucial legal concept of informed consent, which stipulates that the patient has the right to know and make decisions about his or her health. These decisions take the form of consent or refusal of treatment. Based on the principle of autonomy, the consent process must be voluntary and without coercion; the fully informed patient must clearly understand the choices being offered.

Informed consent dilemmas evolve from questions about whether patients are competent to make informed decisions and whether there are family members or surrogates to make these decisions by proxy. Difficult questions are posed for health care providers by the need for informed consent from minors, confused older adults, persons in emergency situations, and persons who are mentally compromised, imprisoned, inebriated, or unconscious. The burden of informed consent lies with the physician in most circumstances, although the nurse frequently is responsible for aspects of informing and obtaining consent.

In the latter part of the twentieth century, another crucial concept of consent was introduced. Advances in technology and the potential to keep people alive for extended periods have brought about legislation aimed at giving people choices about end-of-life decisions while they are still healthy and well enough to make informed decisions. The opportunity for people to make advance directives is now common and is even a requirement for admission to hospitals and other health care agencies that receive federal dollars. People are not required to decide, but must be given an opportunity to do so. Ideally the health care community will provide such an opportunity while the patient is well, perhaps in a community setting, such as a public library or community center. Health care professionals, such as nurses and other health care educators, have an ethical obligation to educate the public about the use of advance directives. These opportunities can serve as excellent means of educating patients not only about advance directives but also about their rights in general, changes in health care delivery and managed care, and the role of the various health care providers. These are excellent opportunities to educate the public about the scope of practice of today's professional nurse.

The Challenge of Accountability

A host of specific ethical issues exists within the practice of nursing itself. Professional nursing is a complex profession that is unlike most others. The accountability factor in the practice of nursing is such that a keen sense of responsibility and personal integrity are necessary qualities for every practicing nurse. It is the nurse's ethical obligation to uphold the highest standards of practice and care, assume full personal and professional responsibility for every action, and commit to maintaining quality in the skill and knowledge base of the profession. Failure to meet such obligations places the patient-nurse relationship at risk.

Failure to be accountable for one's own actions causes damage to the healthcare team, causing rifts, blame, and potentially shifting work/responsibilities and patient care between shifts. In other words, lack of accountability can negatively affect quality patient care and team building. In health professions in which the safety and health of society are at stake, the obligation of professionals to police the practice of their colleagues is important.

There are public and legal official policing bodies, such as the state board of nursing, for matters of public record and formal conviction. However, there are countless situations in which the official policing body will never be involved, and the obligation to denounce a harmful action or potentially threatening situation falls to a fellow member of the profession. Sometimes known as *whistle-blowing,* the obligation to denounce is based on the fact that to remain silent is to consent to the action or threatening situation. Whether denouncing a chemical impairment, negligence, abusiveness, incompetence, or cruelty, the obligation is a moral one based at least in part on the principle of beneficence.

Every person bearing the title of nurse must aspire to maintain himself or herself as a professional of integrity who is willing to blow the whistle on those whose actions are irresponsible and harmful. If this is not the case, the wrong will continue, and the harm to others will escalate. In the end, the profession as a whole will suffer, and the well-being of society will be diminished.

▌ SUMMARY

Professional nurses must take up the ethic of caring and be prepared to face any number of potential ethical conflicts in the day-to-day practice of their profession. They must realize that each situation is different and that recognizing this uniqueness demands that responsible parties seek a loving and humane solution to every situation that poses an ethical dilemma. When the answer remains clouded, the decision maker must choose the most appropriate action, given the situation, based on a variety of potentially applicable principles.

To think that dilemmas, such as the ones described here, are unlikely or far removed is to think that the surgery patient will not be troubled by pain or the trauma patient by anxiety or the cancer patient by fear. Ethical conflict is inherent in the practice of nursing and is played out in every practice setting every day. The challenge is not to escape the conflict but to meet it with expectancy and preparedness.

If the profession of nursing is the discipline of human caring, relationships are the foundation of safe practice, ethical practice. Those seeking a career in nursing must realize the multifaceted aspects of the profession. They also should appreciate the rich and diverse opportunities that will be afforded them. Braced with scientific knowledge and the resources for critical examination of health and illness, the professional nurse is provided access to life's most intimate and precious encounters. Perhaps more than any other health care provider, a sensitive and caring nurse is invited to join patients who are experiencing the most intense moments of their lives. Nurses are given the opportunity to embrace patients in their joy over the birth of a child or the good news of a successful surgery, or chemotherapy treatment for cancer. They also are privileged to support patients and their families during the trials of waiting for the outcome of a tragic head injury or the last breath in a life devastated by terminal illness. To all of this, nurses are invited.

With such privilege comes responsibility. The purpose of this chapter is to introduce nursing students to the idea that ethical conflict in health care abounds and to increase students' awareness of their role in resolving conflict. It is important for professional nurses to have a basic knowledge of the ethical thinking enterprise described in this chapter and realize that there are other resources for committed professionals to draw on in an effort to stay abreast of the issues they are likely to face in their practice. Resources include the National Science Foundation's Hastings Center; the Center for Health and Human Dignity; the Institute of Society, Ethics, and the Life Sciences; the Kennedy Institute Center for Bioethics; and the ANA Committee on Ethics and Human Rights. These groups prepare position statements and write papers on specific ethical dilemmas arising from today's health care practice. Learning centers, libraries, and websites generally provide access to these resources.

Bioethics and ethical decision making are philosophic enterprises. Many activities in nursing practice require an actual skill that involves training, practice, and technique development. For example, nursing students are introduced to the principles of intravenous line insertion while in a campus laboratory setting. They may have an opportunity to practice starting an intravenous line in a simulated setting before actually assuming the responsibility for starting one on a patient. The first few times that students insert an intravenous line, their effort is based on a deliberate thinking through of each step and each principle of asepsis, circulation and blood flow, and positioning. In time, the principles of starting an intravenous line become a well-developed technique and skill activity. The same process can be used when developing one's capacity for a critical thinking activity.

This chapter has presented a vignette describing a nursing management situation laden with potential for ethical conflict within patient care. As nursing students move through their educational experience, they will be assigned to care for many different kinds of patients. Every nursing management and patient care situation has the potential of presenting an ethical dilemma. As students are faced with ethical decisions, they refine their decision-making skills. Each time they reflect on ethical theories or consider ethical principles, they develop critical thinking ability. In time, the professional nurse is able to incorporate what he or she has learned into a morally mature personal code of ethics. At this point, there is a liberating joy that comes from knowing that competence in professional nursing practice goes beyond technique and skill to include the ability to reason life's most difficult and challenging questions and all for the benefit of another human being. Although it is not as easy as it may sound, it is well worth the effort.

Girded with truth, nurses must commit themselves to take a bold stance for what is right and against what is wrong. Nurses should feel empowered through their roles as primary patient advocates to voice their morality in the face of a new century that promises sweeping changes in health care delivery. Nurses must speak in support of patient choice and self-determination in the era of managed care. They must speak against the moral wrong of understaffed practice trends wherein patient safety is jeopardized. Nurses must monitor legislation that affects health care and study current issues, such as assisted suicide and cloning. Professional nursing embodies a commitment to not just think and act wisely in the administration of therapeutic nursing interventions, but also to think and act in accordance with specified values and basic principles of right and wrong. Nursing is making a commitment to all of the above.

REFERENCES

American Nurses Association Center for Ethics and Human Rights: *Position Statement–Euthanasia Assisted Suicide and Aid in Dying*, April, 2013. http://www.nursingworld.org. Accessed July 15, 2015.

Beauchamp, TL, Childress, JF: *Principles of biomedical ethics*, ed 6, Oxford, England, 2009, Oxford University Press.

Hockenberry MJ, Wilson D: *Wong's nursing care of infants and children*, ed 9, St Louis, 2010, Mosby.

Kohlberg L: *Stages of moral development as a basis for moral education*, 1971, Center for Moral education, Harvard University, pp 42–53, 86–88.

Lachman, V: Applying the Ethics of Care to Your Nursing Practice, *Ethics, Law and Policy* 21(2):112–115, 2012.

Liptak, Adam : In Florida Right-to-Die Case, Legislation Puts the Constitution at Issue Published: October 23, 2003, New York Times. http://www.nytimes.com/2003/10/23/national/23STAY.html?pagewanted=print.

Murray, J.S: Moral courage in healthcare: acting ethically even in the presence of risk, *OJIN: The Online Journal of Issues in Nursing* 15(3), 2, 2010.

Rifkin, R: *Americans Rate Nurses Highest on Honesty, Ethical Standards. Social Issues*, 2014. http://www.gallup.com/poll/180260/americans-rate-nurses-highest-honesty-ethical-standards.aspx. Accessed December 18, 2014.

Sorrell, J., (November 9, 2012) Ethics: The Patient Protection and Affordable Care Act: Ethical Perspectives in 21st Century Health Care *OJIN: The Online Journal of Issues in Nursing* Vol. 18 No. 1. DOI: 10.3912/OJIN.Vol18No02EthCol01.

Uustal D: *Values and ethics in nursing: from theory to practice*, ed 4, Greenwich, RI, 1992, Educational Resources in Nursing and Holistic Health.

Weaver K, Morse J, Mitcham C: Ethical sensitivity in professional practice: concept analysis, *J Adv Nurs* 62(5):607–618, 2008.

Wright RA: *The practice of ethics: human values in health care*, New York, 1987, McGraw-Hill.

10

Clients deserve culturally competent care.

Cultural Competency and Social Issues in Nursing and Health Care

Susan R. Jacob, PhD, MSN, RN

ⓔ Additional resources are available online at: *http://evolve.elsevier.com/Cherry/*

PROFESSIONAL/ETHICAL ISSUE

Yei Wu, a 64-year-old Chinese female, was admitted to the emergency room (ER) with a temperature of 103°F, severe nausea and vomiting, and uterine bleeding. She was brought to the ER by her 36-year-old son, who had found her lying on the floor in her home when he went to visit her earlier in the afternoon. Because Yei speaks no English, her son provided the necessary information for admittance to the hospital. When the attending physician heard the charge nurse,

Chandra, request an interpreter, he interrupted her by saying that an interpreter would not be needed because the bilingual son could provide interpretation. Chandra remembered learning in her cultural competence training that family members should only be used for interpretation as a last resort.

What avenues should Chandra explore for interpretation services? What are the potential risks of having family members interpret for the patient?

VIGNETTE

When my instructor taught the session on cultural differences, she stressed the high alcoholism rates of American Indians. I began to fear that my instructor and fellow classmates would stereotype me because of my American Indian background. However, no one in my family drinks alcohol because we belong to the Mormon Church, where drinking is not accepted. I wish the instructor had stressed the importance of not stereotyping.

Questions to Consider While Reading This Chapter:

1. What preconceived ideas do you have about the following cultural groups: Hispanic, Appalachian,

   Moroccan, black/African American, South African, and Chinese?
2. What strategies can you implement to overcome prejudice?
3. How can nurses provide effective care to different cultural groups who each have a unique set of beliefs about illness?
4. How can nursing research affect the attitudes and beliefs of health professionals in regard to minority and marginalized populations?

KEY TERMS

Acculturation: The process of becoming adapted to a new or different culture.

Assimilation: The cultural absorption of a minority group into the main cultural body.

Biculturalism: Combining two distinct cultures in a single region.

Cultural humility: Incorporates a lifelong commitment to self-evaluation and self-critique, to redressing the power imbalances in the patient-clinician dynamic, and to developing mutually beneficial and advocacy partnerships with communities on behalf of individuals and defined populations (Tervalon and Murray-Garcia, 1998).

Cultural sensitivity: Experienced when neutral language, both verbal and nonverbal, is used in a way that reflects sensitivity and appreciation for the diversity of another (American Academy of Nursing Expert Panel on Cultural Competence, 2007).

Culture: Shared values, beliefs, and practices of a particular group of people that are transmitted from one generation to the next and are identified as patterns that guide thinking and action.

Enculturation: Adaptation to the prevailing cultural patterns in society.

Ethnicity: Affiliation resulting from a shared linguistic, racial, or cultural background.

Ethnocentrism: Believing that one's own ethnic group, culture, or nation is best.

Marginalized population: A subgroup of the population that tends to be hidden, overlooked, or on the outer edge.

Minority: An ethnic group smaller than the majority group.

Prejudice: Preconceived, deeply held, usually negative, judgment formed about other groups.

Stereotyping: Assigning certain beliefs and behaviors to groups without recognizing individuality.

Transculturalism: Being grounded in one's own culture, but having the skills to be able to work in a multicultural environment.

Worldview: Perspective shared by a cultural group of general views of relationships within the universe. These broad views influence health and illness beliefs.

LEARNING OUTCOMES

After studying this chapter, the reader will be able to:

1. Integrate knowledge of demographic and sociocultural variations into culturally competent professional nursing care.
2. Provide culturally competent care to diverse client groups that incorporates variations in biologic characteristics, social organization, environmental control, communication, and other phenomena.
3. Critique education, practice, and research issues that influence culturally competent care.
4. Integrate respect for differences in beliefs and values of others as a critical component of nursing practice.

CHAPTER OVERVIEW

The United States has always been represented by a culturally diverse society. However, the volume of cultural groups entering our country is increasing rapidly. Professional nurses must provide care to persons of various cultures who have different values, beliefs, and perceptions of health and illness. This chapter explores cultural phenomena, including environmental control, biologic variations, social organization, communication, space, and time in relation to major cultural groups. It also examines different views toward health, illness, and cure. Federally defined minority groups, which include African Americans or blacks, Asians, Hispanics, and American Indians, are emphasized, although the needs of marginalized populations, such as the homeless, refugees, and older adults also are addressed. The need for diversity in the health care force is explored, and strategies for recruiting and retaining minorities in health care are suggested. Strategies that nurses can use to increase their own cultural competence also are given.

POPULATION TRENDS

The demographic and ethnic composition of the U.S. population has experienced a marked change in the past 100 years. The United States always has been a multicultural society, although changes in immigration laws have increased the number of cultural groups entering the United States (Stanhope and Lancaster, 2014). Minority groups have grown faster than the population as a whole. If migration trends continue, by the mid–twenty-first century minority populations will outnumber the white population. Approximately 1 in every 3 Americans will be an ethnic minority. In some U.S. cities, the number of persons from diverse cultural groups is increasing at such a rapid pace that minorities constitute more than half the population. The nation will be more racially and ethnically diverse, as well as much older, by midcentury, according to 2013 projections released by the U.S. Census Bureau. Minorities, now roughly one third of the U.S. population, are expected to become the majority in 2042, with the nation projected to be 54% minority in 2050. By 2023, minorities will comprise more than half of all children.

The growth in the number and proportion of older adults is unprecedented in the history of the United States. Two factors—longer life spans and aging baby boomers—will combine to double the population of Americans aged 65 years or older during the next 25 years to about 72 million. By 2030, older adults will account for roughly 20% of the U.S. population (Centers for Disease Control, 2013).

Along with the dramatic aging of the U.S. population during the next several decades will be significant increases in racial and ethnic diversity. In 2010, 80% of adults aged 65 years or older in the United States were non-Hispanic white. By 2030, that percentage will have declined, and older non-Hispanic white adults will make up 71.2% of the population, whereas Hispanics will make up 12%, non-Hispanic blacks nearly 10.3%, and Asians 5.4%. By 2050, the racial and ethnic diversity of older U.S. adults will have changed even more profoundly. Older non-Hispanic white adults, long deemed the "majority population," will account for only about 58% of the total population aged 65 or older, a decline of more than 20% from 2010. During the same period, the proportion of older Hispanics will almost triple—from 7% in 2010 to nearly 20% in 2050. The proportion of older Asian Americans will more than double during 2010-2050, from 3.3% to 8.5%, and the proportion of older African Americans will increase from 8.3% to 11.2%. Language barriers, reduced access to health care, low socioeconomic status, and differing cultural norms can be major challenges to promoting health in an increasingly diverse older population (Centers for Disease Control, 2013).

This demographic change introduces many interrelated social, economic, political, educational, and health problems. The fact that people are living longer allows more opportunity for the development of chronic illness. Social isolation and depression that result from losses of friends and family will present a challenge for mental health care providers. Primary care providers will be faced with identifying risks to independence and health for the aging population (Stanhope and Lancaster, 2014). Health care providers must guard against issues of ageism, assuming that health issues and levels of cognition are the same for every senior adult.

Federally Defined Minority Groups are:

- Asian American
- Black or African American
- Hispanic or Latino
- Native Hawaiian and other Pacific Islander
- American Indian and Alaska Native

The populations within the federally defined minority groups have grown faster than the population as a whole. In 1970, minority groups accounted for 16% of the population. If current trends continue, the U.S. Census Bureau (2010) predicts that by 2025 minorities will account for more than 55% of the population, thus making up a majority of the total population for the first time (U.S. Department of Health and Human Services [USDHHS], 2010; National Institutes of Health National Heart Lung and Blood Institute). (Visit www.nhlbi.nih.gov/about/factbook/chapter4.htm for more information.) Although tremendous strides have been made in improving health and longevity in the United States, statistical trends show a disparity in key health indicators among certain subgroups of the population. There is a racial gap between blacks and whites of 5.6 years, with average life expectancy of 78 years for whites and 72.7 years for blacks. The infant mortality rate for blacks is twice that of whites (Nies and McEwen, 2011). Although the ranking of health problems according to excess deaths differs for minority groups, the six causes of death that are a priority are cancer, heart disease and stroke, chemical dependency, diabetes, homicide and accidents, and infant mortality (Nies and McEwen, 2011).

Marginalized Populations

Not only should the concern for culturally competent care focus on ethnic minorities and populations with a different heritage than European Americans, but it should consider the needs of *marginalized* populations (Meleis et al, 1995), which live on the periphery or in between. Examples of such populations include lesbian, gay, bisexual and transgender, older adults, veterans, recently arrived immigrants (e.g., from Russia, Afghanistan, and Rwanda), and groups that have been in this country for some time (e.g., from South America and the Middle East) who are less visible than the federally defined minorities (Lenburg et al, 1995). Their lives and health care needs often are kept secret and are understood only by them. Marginalized populations usually have extreme insights about their health care needs, although they often seem voiceless. This is in part a result of the different ways in which they both communicate and are silenced. It also may be because they feel even more peripheral or shut out from mainstream society when they are ill or experiencing a crisis.

ECONOMIC AND SOCIAL CHANGES

Changing world economics have had profound consequences, such as increased joblessness, homelessness, poverty, and limited access to health insurance and health care. Anxiety, hopelessness, depression, and despair commonly affect the individuals in our society who find themselves suddenly without a job and sometimes even without a home as a result of economic downsizing. These conditions often are associated with increased stress-related symptoms, substance abuse, violence, and crime (Lenburg et al, 1995). Dramatic changes in technology and specialization in the health care field have made health care costs skyrocket. Therefore, not everyone can afford health care services. More minorities lack health insurance than the general population (Nies and McEwen, 2011). Higher costs and lower wages for minority groups make it difficult to rise out of poverty (Stanhope and Lancaster, 2014).

Poverty

Most families with racially or ethnically diverse backgrounds have a lower socioeconomic status than does the population at large. Blacks, Hispanics, and American Indians have much higher rates of poverty than non-Hispanic whites and Asians. The median family income of Asians is slightly higher than that of non-Hispanic whites and is consistent with Asians' high levels of education and the higher percentage of families with two wage earners. However, opportunities for education, occupation, income earning, and property ownership that are available to upper- and middle-class Americans often are not available to members of minority groups (Stanhope and Lancaster, 2014).

Poverty rates are important indicators of community well-being and are used by government agencies and organizations to allocate need-based resources. The American Community Survey (ACS) 5-year data allow for the analysis of poverty rates by race and Hispanic origin for many levels of geography. Poverty rates are also presented for selected detailed race and origin groups in the cities and towns with the largest populations of these groups. For the nation and selected places, poverty rates are summarized for detailed Asian groups with populations of 750,000 or more, detailed Native Hawaiian and other Pacific Islander groups with populations of 25,000 or more, and detailed Hispanic groups with populations of 1 million or more (Macartney et al, 2014).

According to the 2007-2011 American Community Survey (ACS), 42.7 million people, or 14.3% of the U.S. population, had income below the poverty level. By race, the highest national poverty rates were for American Indians and Alaska Natives (27.0%) and blacks or African Americans (25.8%). Native Hawaiians and other Pacific Islanders had a national poverty rate of 17.6%. For the Asian population, poverty rates were higher for Vietnamese (14.7%) and Koreans (15.0%), and lower for Filipinos (5.8%). Among Hispanics, national poverty rates ranged from a low of 16.2% for Cubans to a high of 26.3% for Dominicans (http://www.census.gov/library/publications/2013/acs/acsbr11-17.html).

The poor also suffer more than the population as a whole for nearly every measure of health. Substantial disparities remain in health insurance coverage for certain populations. Among the nonelderly population, approximately 30.7% of Hispanic persons have the highest uninsured rates of any racial or ethnic group within the United States. For blacks, the percentage of uninsured in 2010 was 20.8%. Lack of health care coverage has major implications for health (U.S. Census Bureau, 2011). For more information, visit U.S. Census Bureau: *Income, poverty, and health insurance coverage in the United States,* 2011 (website). (www.census.gov/prod/2011pubs/p60-239.pdf.)

Minority members of society often live in poverty. This social stratification leads to social inequality. For instance, it is widely known that school systems and recreational facilities vary significantly between the inner city and the suburbs (Nies and McEwen, 2011). Residential segregation, substandard housing, unemployment, poor physical and mental health, and poor self-image are part of the cycle of poverty. This inequality is especially disturbing as it relates to health care. The United States has a history of providing the highest quality health care to those with the highest socioeconomic status and the worst health care to those with low socioeconomic status. Social, economic, and health problems have led to heated debates about the philosophy, scope and costs, and sources of funding for health care and insurance programs.

VIOLENCE

Changing economic and social conditions have contributed to the increasing level of violence in our society. Statistics indicate that homicide is the second leading cause of death among Americans 15 to 24 years of age and the leading cause of death among black males 15 to 34 years of age (Nies and McEwen, 2011). Businesses, schools, restaurants, playgrounds, and churches have become common settings for random acts of violence (Lenburg et al, 1995). Unemployment is associated with violence because it is an expectation in our society that people should be productive and gainfully employed. The inability to secure or hold a job may lead to feelings of inadequacy, guilt, and frustration, which in turn can precipitate acts of violence. Although the increasing

incidence of violence affects all segments of society, women, children, older adults, and culturally vulnerable groups are especially at risk. Unemployment rates among young minority men in the United States are consistently high (Stanhope and Lancaster, 2014). This group also has the highest rate of violence, with homicide being a major problem for young black males. The differing rates of violence among races are more likely a result of poverty than race (Stanhope and Lancaster, 2014).

Intimate partner violence (IPV), formerly known as *domestic violence,* is the single greatest cause of injury to women 15 to 24 years of age. IPV crosses all ethnic, racial, socioeconomic, and educational lines. It includes battering, resulting in physical injury, psychological abuse, and sexual assault (Nies and McEwen, 2011).

Societal changes have increased the tension between the empowered culturally dominant groups and the less visible vulnerable groups. This tension and behavioral response to tension has major implications for health care delivery and the education of nurses and other health care professionals (Lenburg et al, 1995).

ATTITUDES TOWARD CULTURALLY DIVERSE GROUPS

The range of attitudes toward culturally diverse groups can be viewed along a continuum of intensity, as illustrated in Figure 10-1 (Lenburg et al, 1995).

The extreme negative manifestation of prejudice is hate in its many violent and nonviolent forms. Contempt is somewhat less intense, but is problematic because it is so widespread and undermines many aspects of society. Tolerance reflects a more neutral attitude that accepts differences without attempting to convert them; it is the minimal-level attitude essential in democratic societies. Respect for diversity is manifested in behaviors that integrate differences into positive interactions and relationships. Respect is a demonstration

| Hate | Contempt | Tolerance | Respect | Celebration |

FIGURE 10-1 A continuum of intensity of the range of attitudes toward culturally diverse groups. (From American Academy of Nursing: *Promoting cultural competence in and through nursing education: a critical review and comprehensive plan for action,* Washington, DC, 1995, American Academy of Nursing.)

of the inherent worth of the individual, regardless of differences. The most positive attitude is portrayed as a celebration (or affirmation) of the positive merits of cultural differences (e.g., the value added to life experiences by multiple perspectives, traditions, rituals, foods, and art forms). The combination of ignorance of other cultures and arrogance about one's own culture fosters disrespect and hate. The deliberate attempt to discover and apply the positive benefits of cultural variation promotes respect and a celebration of the value of diversity, whereas perpetuating prejudice fosters narrow-mindedness and contempt. By integrating these perspectives as part of professional role behavior, educators can help students prepare for culturally competent practice in communities of diversity.

DIVERSITY IN THE HEALTH CARE WORKFORCE

Need for Diversity in the Health Care Workforce

Members of some cultural groups are demanding culturally relevant health care that incorporates their beliefs and practices (Nies and McEwen, 2011). Consumers are becoming much more aware of what constitutes culturally sensitive and competent care and are less willing to accept incompetent care (Douglas et al, 2011). There is a lack of diversity and ethnic representation of health care professionals, and there is limited knowledge about values, beliefs, experiences, and health care needs of certain populations, such as immigrants, older adults, and gays and lesbians. Each of these groups has a unique set of responses to health and illness.

Stereotypes should be trashed.

Nurses make up the largest segment of the workforce in health care delivery. Therefore they have an opportunity to be proactive in changing health care inequities and access to health care (Douglas et al, 2011). The changing health care system must reflect the community, and, as health care moves into the community, it is vital that partnerships be formed between health care providers and the community. For these partnerships to become a reality, minority representation in all health professions is vital. Factors inhibiting minority members from attaining a career in nursing include inadequate academic preparation, especially in the sciences; financial costs; inadequate career counseling; lack of valuing the role of nursing by some cultures, and better recruitment efforts by other disciplines (Loftin et al, 2012).

Current Status of Diversity in the Health Care Workforce

According to the U.S. Census Bureau, individuals from ethnic and racial minority groups accounted for more than one third of the U.S. population (37%) in 2012. With projections pointing to minority populations becoming the majority by 2043, professional nurses must demonstrate a sensitivity to and understanding of a variety of cultures to provide high quality care across settings.

Diversity within the nursing workforce—in terms of race/ethnicity and sex—is desirable because it can improve both access and care quality for minorities and medically underserved populations. Nursing has historically been dominated by white females, and as Figure 10-2 shows, the nursing workforce is still predominantly white. However, over time, the proportion of racial/ethnic minorities has been increasing. Black/African Americans, Asians, and Hispanics/Latinos make up greater proportions of the RN population, whereas whites have declined from more than 80% in 2000 to about 75% in the ACS (2008 to 2010).

According to a 2013 survey conducted by the National Council of State Boards of Nursing (NCSBN) and the Forum of Nursing Workforce Centers, nurses from minority backgrounds represent 19% of the registered nurse (RN) workforce. Considering racial/ethnic backgrounds, the RN population is 83% white/Caucasian; 6% black/African American; 6% Asian; 3% Hispanic; 1% American Indian/Alaska Native; 1%

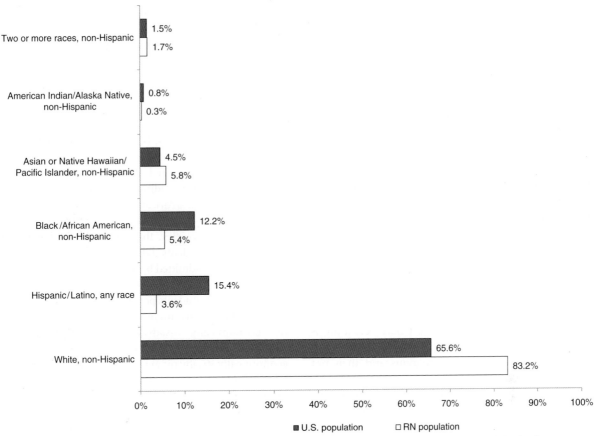

FIGURE 10-2 Distribution of registered nurses and the U.S. population by racial/ethnic background, 2008. (From Chart 11, HRSA 2010. The Registered Nurse Population: Initial Findings from the 2008 National Sample Survey of Registered Nurses, March 2010.)

Native Hawaiian/Pacific Islander; and 1% other nurses.

A survey conducted by the U.S. Census Bureau in February 2013 found that men now compose 9.6% of all RNs. When looking at specific nursing roles, the highest representation by men was in nurse anesthetist positions (41%).

According to the National Sample Survey, RNs from minority backgrounds are more likely than their white counterparts to pursue baccalaureate and higher degrees in nursing. Data show that although 48.4% of white nurses complete nursing degrees beyond the associate degree level, the number is significantly higher or equivalent for minority nurses, including black/African American (52.5%), Hispanic (51.5%), and Asian (75.6%) nurses. RNs from minority backgrounds clearly recognize the need to pursue higher levels of nursing education beyond the entry-level. (http://bhpr.hrsa.gov/healthworkforce/rnsurvey/initialfindings2008.pdf.)

According to AACN's report on *2013-2014 Enrollment and Graduations in Baccalaureate and Graduate Programs in Nursing*, nursing students from minority backgrounds represented 28.9% of students in entry-level baccalaureate programs, 30% of master's students, and 26.9% of students in research-focused doctoral programs. In terms of gender breakdown, men made up 11.4% of students in baccalaureate programs, 10.3% of master's students, 8.7% of research-focused doctoral students, and 11.3% of practice-focused doctoral students. Though nursing schools have made strides in recruiting and graduating nurses that reflect the patient population, more must be done before equal representation is realized. The need to attract diverse nursing students is paralleled by the need to recruit more faculty from minority populations. Few nurses from racial/ethnic minority groups with advanced nursing degrees pursue faculty careers. According to 2013 data from AACN's annual survey, only 13.1% of full-time nursing school faculty come from minority backgrounds, and only 5.5% are male. (http://www.aacn.nche.edu/media-relations/fact-sheets/enhancing-diversity.)

Recruitment and Retention of Minorities in Nursing

It is clear that we have been slow in preparing nurses to be reflective of our population, just as we have been unaware of the need for culturally sensitive patient care and sometimes less than welcoming to students different from the preponderant population (Loftin et al, 2012). Recruitment and retention of students from minority populations must not be separated. In other words, recruitment programs must have retention as their primary focus because there is no point in recruiting minorities into nursing programs and then not helping them succeed.

Before World War II, the only known effort to recruit minority students into nursing on a national scale was made by the National Association of Colored Graduate Nurses (NACGN), which had had recruitment of blacks into nursing as one of its objectives since its inception in 1908. During World War II, the federal government set into motion a mechanism to produce additional nursing personnel by financing basic nursing education. This was done through the Cadet Nurse Corps. The corps had a number of recruiters, two of whom were black. These two nurses confined their recruiting to 82 black/African American colleges and universities. By the end of the war, 21 black/African American nursing schools had participated in the corps, and more than 2000 black nurses had acquired their basic nursing education through this mechanism.

After the war, national recruitment efforts for black nurses reverted to the NACGN, an organization that voted itself out of existence in 1949 and was dissolved in 1951. However, individual black/African American schools in the North and South continued to recruit. In the South, law segregated the nursing schools, and in the North they were segregated by custom. In 1954, the unanimous Supreme Court decision—*Brown v.*

Board of Education—asserted that "separate educational facilities were inherently unequal," making racial segregation in public schools unconstitutional. This decision was interpreted to mean that all kinds of educational discrimination would be considered, including nursing.

It was around the time of the Brown decision that schools of nursing were being accredited by national standards, and many schools, both black/African American and white, just did not measure up to the standards. As a result, many schools closed. With integration permitting black students to be admitted to formerly all-white schools, quality black/African American schools had difficulty attracting enough students, and many of the schools closed. However, the white schools that began admitting black students did not admit the number that would have been admitted by the black/African American schools. For example, many white schools admitted only one or two black students per class.

In the late 1960s, many efforts were made to help the economically disadvantaged in this country. Although not all people of minority groups are economically disadvantaged, the vast majority of disadvantaged people are members of ethnic minority groups. Nursing too became concerned about the disadvantaged and began concerted efforts to recruit more members of minority groups into nursing schools. The Sealantic Fund, one of the Rockefeller Brothers' funds, was one of the first foundations that helped minorities enter nursing school. Sealantic funded projects in 10 universities in different parts of the country to recruit students from minority groups and help them achieve success. The best example of an ongoing project, funded by the division of nursing since 1971, is the National Student Nurses Association's breakthrough in nursing to accelerate the recruitment of minorities, including men.

In 1997, the American Nurses Foundation published a report of a project it had funded, titled "Strategies for Recruitment, Retention and Graduation of Minority Nurses in Colleges of Nursing." Through survey and interview analysis, Hattie Bessent and a cadre of knowledgeable leaders investigated the most effective approach to increase the nursing profession's representation of minority nurses (Bessent, 1997). Members of Chi Eta Phi, a national black/African American nursing society with chapters throughout the country, serve as mentors to minority nursing students. As mentors, sorority members provide intellectual and inspirational stimulation along with counseling.

In 1997, the AACN published a position statement stating that diversity and inclusion had emerged as central issues for organizations and institutions. The AACN encouraged leadership in nursing to respond to these issues by finding ways to accelerate the inclusion of groups, cultures, and ideas that traditionally had been underrepresented in higher education.

As the demographics of the population rapidly changed in the twenty-first century, there were numerous strategies to recruit and retain minority nursing faculty, students, and practicing nurses in the profession to better reflect the population demographics. Just as contributions of diverse cultural groups were increasingly valued, the profession began to value the need for diversity in their students and faculty and view this diversity as strength.

Strategies for Recruitment and Retention of Minorities in the Health Care Workforce

All national nursing organizations, the federal Division of Nursing, hospital associations, nursing philanthropies, and other stakeholders within the health care community agree that recruitment of underrepresented groups into nursing is a priority for the nursing profession in the United States. For more information, visit http://www.aacn.nche.edu/media-relations/fact-sheets/enhancing-diversity.

Nursing shortage reports, including those produced by the American Hospital Association, the Robert Wood Johnson Foundation (RWJF), The Joint Commission, and the Association of Academic Health Centers, point to minority student recruitment as a necessary step to addressing the nursing shortage. For more information on these reports, visit http://www.aacn.nche.edu/diversity-in-nursing.

A lack of minority nurse educators may send a signal to potential students that nursing does not value diversity or offer career ladder opportunities to advance through the profession. Students looking for academic role models to encourage and enrich their learning may be frustrated in their attempts to find mentors and a community of support. Academic leaders are working to address this need by working to identify minority faculty recruitment strategies, encouraging minority leadership development, and advocating for programs that remove barriers to faculty careers.

There also is a need to increase the number of nurse educators and researchers who are from diverse, marginalized, and vulnerable populations. Raising consciousness involves increasing the level of awareness of nurses and other health care professionals about the issues surrounding diversity. This can be accomplished by encouraging participation in forums related to different aspects of various cultural phenomena, such as environmental control, communication, and health beliefs. Such forums might be offered by state and local professional nurses' organizations and health care facilities.

Another successful strategy for recruiting and retaining minorities in education and clinical practice is matched mentoring, which involves matching same-culture mentors either in the same institution or different institutions. A different mentoring strategy involves teaching and modeling by nurses who have been trained in cross-cultural care. Cross-cultural nursing consultants in the care of specific groups are available to agencies, professional groups, licensing bodies, and individual nurses. (Organizations should contact the Transcultural Nursing Society at www.tcns.org to obtain the names of consultants in the field of transcultural nursing.)

Audiovisual media should be used to teach the importance of human health conditions cross-culturally. Video conferencing can provide international links for students and faculty who cannot travel. Students from various cultures can share their clinical experiences. One of the greatest benefits is the discovery that thinking, values, and decision making differ in various cultures. Collaborative arrangements should be encouraged between colleges and universities so that exchange programs can be offered to students. Such exchanges can provide firsthand in-depth experience with a culture that is different from their own. Interactive media can be used to gain a clearer perspective than can be obtained through the print medium on particular cultures.

Strategies such as mentoring by the same-culture professional are effective in recruiting and retaining minorities in nursing. In addition, the value of workshops, continuing education programs, and the use of consultants to promote culturally competent care should not be overlooked.

CULTURAL COMPETENCE

Health professionals, educators, and health care systems must all respond to the consequences of increasing cultural diversity for the future well-being of all populations. The worldwide shortage of nurses and the global immigration of both nurses and populations have heightened the need to educate nurses to deliver culturally competent care for increasingly diverse populations regardless of geographic location. The Standards of Practice for Culturally Competent Nursing Care: 2011 Update provide universally applicable guidelines for use by nurses around the globe to guide clinical practice, research, education, and administration. The recipient of the nursing care described in these standards is assumed to be an individual, a family, a community, or a population (Douglas et al, 2011). These 12 standards (Table 10-1) can serve as a guide and resource by emphasizing cultural competence as a priority.

Lenberg and colleagues (1995) suggest that it is essential that nurses take responsibility to:

- Be sensitive to and show respect for the differences in beliefs and values of others.
- Take responsibility to inquire, learn about, and integrate beliefs and values of others in professional encounters.
- Take responsibility to try to change negative and prejudicial behaviors in themselves and others.

In light of societal changes, responsible persons at all levels in education and health care delivery systems acknowledge the need to reassess the influence of culture on achieving expected health outcomes. There is an imperative need for nurse educators, administrators, students, and others to promote sensitivity to, acceptance of, and respect for the rights of all individuals within the context of their cultural orientation and society as a whole. Nurses must be culturally competent because:

- The nurse's culture often is different from the client's culture.
- Care that is not culturally competent may be more costly.
- Care that is not culturally competent may be ineffective.
- Specific objectives for persons in different cultures need to be met as outlined in *Healthy People 2020.*
- Racial and minority groups experience profound disparities in health and health care.

- Nursing is committed to social justice, providing safe quality care to all.
- Nurses are expected to respond to global infectious disease epidemics.
- Achieving cultural competence should be our goal, although it may take most of us a lifetime to attain. However, we can all aspire to achieve **cultural humility**, which incorporates a lifelong commitment to self-evaluation and self-critique, to redressing the power imbalances in the patient-clinician dynamic, and to developing mutually beneficial and advocacy partnerships with communities on behalf of individuals and defined populations (Tervalon and Murray-Garcia, 1998). If we acquire cultural humility we should also demonstrate **cultural sensitivity** that shows appreciation of the diversity of others.

CULTURAL COMPETENCE IN NURSING EDUCATION

Since the 1960s, there has been a united effort to include concepts sensitive to cultural diversity in nursing education. The National League for Nursing (NLN) and the AACN have made this requirement mandatory for accreditation. In 2008, the AACN developed five end-of-program competencies for graduates of baccalaureate nursing programs as well as a faculty toolkit for integrating these competencies into undergraduate education. *The Essentials of Baccalaureate Education for Professional Nursing Practice* (2008) mandates the inclusion of culturally diverse nursing care concepts in the curriculum with attention to cultural, spiritual, ethnic, gender, and sexual orientation diversity. The following five competencies serve as a framework for integrating cultural content into existing curricula:

1. Apply knowledge of social and cultural factors that affect nursing and health care across multiple contexts.
2. Use relevant data sources and best evidence in providing culturally competent care.
3. Promote achievement of safe and quality outcomes of care for diverse populations.
4. Advocate for social justice, including commitment to the health of vulnerable populations and the elimination of health disparities.
5. Participate in continuous cultural competence development.

TABLE 10-1 **Standards of Practice for Culturally Competent Nursing Care: 2011 Update**

Standard	Description
Standard 1: Social Justice	Professional nurses shall promote social justice for all. The applied principles of social justice guide nurses' decisions related to the patient, family, community, and other health care professionals. Nurses will develop leadership skills to advocate for socially just policies.
Standard 2: Critical reflection	Nurses shall engage in critical reflection of their own values, beliefs, and cultural heritage to have an awareness of how these qualities and issues can affect culturally congruent nursing care.
Standard 3: Knowledge of cultures	Nurses shall gain an understanding of the perspectives, traditions, values, practices, and family systems of culturally diverse individuals, families, communities, and populations they care for, as well as a knowledge of the complex variables that affect the achievement of health and well-being.
Standard 4: Culturally competent practice	Nurses shall use cross-cultural knowledge and culturally sensitive skills in implementing culturally congruent nursing care.
Standard 5: Cultural competence in health care systems and organizations	Health care organizations should provide the structure and resources necessary to evaluate and meet the cultural and language needs of their diverse clients.
Standard 6: Patient advocacy and empowerment	Nurses shall recognize the effect of health care policies, delivery systems, and resources on their patient populations and shall empower and advocate for their patients as indicated. Nurses shall advocate for the inclusion of their patient's cultural beliefs and practices in all dimensions of their health care.
Standard 7: Multicultural workforce	Nurses shall actively engage in the effort to ensure a multicultural workforce in health care settings. One measure to achieve a multicultural workforce is through strengthening of recruitment and retention effort in the hospital and academic setting.
Standard 8: Education and training in culturally competent care	Nurses shall be educationally prepared to promote and provide culturally congruent health care. Knowledge and skills necessary for assuring that nursing care is culturally congruent shall be included in global health care agendas that mandate formal education and clinical training, as well as required ongoing, continuing education for all practicing nurses.
Standard 9: Cross-cultural communication	Nurses shall use culturally competent verbal and nonverbal communication skills to identify client's values, beliefs, practices, perceptions, and unique health care needs.
Standard 10: Cross-cultural leadership	Nurses shall have the ability to influence individuals, groups, and systems to achieve outcomes of culturally competent care for diverse populations.
Standard 11: Policy development	Nurses shall have the knowledge and skills to work with public and private organizations, professional associations, and communities to establish policies and standards for comprehensive implementation and evaluation of culturally competent care.
Standard 12: Evidence-based practice and research	Nurses shall base their practice on interventions that have been systematically tested and shown to be the most effective for the culturally diverse populations that they serve. In areas where there is a lack of evidence of efficacy, nurse researchers shall investigate and test interventions that may be the most effective in reducing the disparities in health outcomes.

Douglas M, Pierce J, Rosenkoetter M, et al: Standards of practice for culturally competent nursing care: 2011 update. *J Transcult Nurs* 22(4): 318, 2011.

The AACN, in collaboration with leading foundations and stakeholders, has taken the following steps to enhance diversity in nursing education:

In April 2008, the RWJF joined with the AACN to launch the RWJF New Careers in Nursing Scholarship Program. This program is designed to alleviate the nation's nursing shortage by dramatically expanding the pipeline of students from minority backgrounds in accelerated nursing programs. Scholarships are awarded to entry-level nursing students with preference given to students from groups underrepresented in nursing or from a disadvantaged background. For more information, see http://www.aacn.nche.edu/news/articles/2008/rwj.

The AACN and the Johnson & Johnson Campaign for Nursing's Future launched the Minority Nurse Faculty Scholars Program in 2007. In addition to scholarship funding, the program also features mentorship and leadership development components to ensure successful completion of graduate studies and preparation for a faculty role. For more information, see http://www.aacn.nche.edu/studnts/scholarships/minority.

In 2013, AACN and the RWJF initiated the Doctoral Advancement in Nursing (DAN) Project to enhance the number of minority nurses completing PhD and DNP degrees. DAN's expert committee has developed a white paper featuring student recruitment and retention strategies that can be used by schools of nursing; comprehensive approaches to leadership and scholarship development for students; suggestions for model doctoral curriculum; and more. For more information, see http://www.newcareersinnursing.org/dan.

In April 2008, the RWJF joined with the AACN to launch funding for Nursing Workforce Development Programs, including funding for Nursing Workforce Diversity Grants. This program provides funding for projects to increase nursing education opportunities for individuals from disadvantaged backgrounds, including racial and ethnic minorities underrepresented among registered nurses.

CULTURAL BELIEF SYSTEMS

A value is a standard that people use to assess themselves and others. It is a belief about what is worthwhile or important for well-being. There is a tendency for people to be "culture bound" (i.e., to assume that their own values are superior, sensible, or right to that of

---

BOX 10-1   Anglo-American and Other Cultural Values

Anglo-American	Other Cultural Values
Personal control over the environment	Fate
Change	Tradition
Time dominates	Human interaction dominates
Human equality	Hierarchy, rank, status
Individualism, privacy	Group welfare
Self-help	Birthright inheritance
Competition	Cooperation
Future orientation	Past orientation
"Action-goal," work orientation	"Being" orientation
Informality	Formality
Directness, openness, honesty	Indirectness, ritual, "face"
Practicality, efficiency	Idealism, theory
Materialism	Spiritualism, detachment

---

others.). Cross-cultural health promotion requires the nurse to work with clients without making judgments as to the superiority of one set of values over another. Box 10-1 provides a comparison of Anglo-American values and those of more tradition-bound countries.

Each culture has a value system that dictates behavior directly or indirectly by setting norms and teaching that those norms are right. Health beliefs and practices tend to reflect a culture's value system. Nurses must understand the patient's value system to foster health promotion.

CULTURAL PHENOMENA

Giger and Davidhizar (2008) have identified six cultural phenomena that vary among cultural groups and affect health care. These phenomena are environmental control, biologic variations, social organization, communication, space, and time orientation.

Environmental Control

Environmental control is the ability of members of a particular culture to control nature or environmental factors. Some groups perceive humans as having mastery over nature; others perceive humans to be dominated by nature, and still other groups see humans as having a harmonious relationship with nature (Stanhope and Lancaster, 2014). People who perceive that they have mastery over nature believe that they can overcome the natural forces of nature. Such individuals would expect positive results from medications, surgery, and other treatment modalities. Persons who believe that they are subject to the forces of nature or that they have little control over what happens to them may not be compliant with treatments because they believe that whatever happens to them is part of their destiny. Blacks and Mexican Americans are most likely to subscribe to this view. Persons who hold the harmony with nature view, such as Asians and American Indians, believe that illness represents a disharmony with nature. These clients may see medication as relieving only the symptoms and not curing the disease. Therefore, they are more likely to rely on naturalistic remedies, such as herbs or hot and cold treatments, to affect a cure (Stanhope and Lancaster, 2014). Included in this concept are the traditional health and illness beliefs, the practice of folk medicine, and the use of traditional and nontraditional healers. Environmental control plays an important role in the way clients respond to health-related experiences and use health resources (Stanhope and Lancaster, 2014).

Biologic Variations

Biologic variations, such as body build and structure, genetic variations, skin characteristics, susceptibility to disease, and nutritional variations, exist among different cultures. For example, babies who are born in Western culture weigh more than non-Western babies. Other common variations include skin color, eye shape, hair texture, adipose tissue deposits, shape of earlobes, and body configuration (Stanhope and Lancaster, 2014). For example, blacks have denser bones than whites, which may account for the low incidence of osteoporosis in the black population. The size of teeth varies among cultures, with whites having the smallest, followed by blacks, Asians, and American Indians. Larger teeth can cause protruding jaws, a condition common in blacks, which does not represent an orthodontic problem (Nies and McEwen, 2011).

Laboratory values for some tests also vary among cultural groups. For example, serum cholesterol levels essentially are the same for blacks and whites at birth. During childhood, the levels are higher in blacks, but they are lower than in whites in adulthood. This finding is interesting because of the high morbidity and mortality from cardiovascular disease in blacks (Nies and

McEwen, 2011). The maternal mortality rate of blacks is three times that of whites; occurrence of stomach cancer is twice as high among black men as white men; and occurrence of esophageal cancer is three times more common among blacks than the general population. Japanese Americans have a lower incidence of cardiovascular and renal disease than the general population, but a higher incidence of stress-related diseases, such as ulcers, colitis, psoriasis, and depression. American Indians have a higher incidence of streptococcal sore throat and gastroenteritis than the general population. American Indian women have the highest incidence of diabetes (Nies and McEwen, 2011).

Mexican Americans have higher rates of obesity and diabetes than the general population, although they have lower rates of cardiovascular disease. The Mexican American population has a pattern of less use of preventive services, including prenatal care, immunizations for children, and vision, hearing, and dental care (Nies and McEwen, 2011).

Social Organization

Social organization refers to the family unit (nuclear, single-parent, or extended family) and the religious or ethnic groups with which families identify. *Family* is defined differently across cultures. For instance, in the black/African American culture, family often includes people who are unrelated or distantly related. Families depend on the extended family for emotional and financial support in times of crisis. Mothers and grandmothers play important roles in black families and are involved in decision making, especially as it relates to health (Stanhope and Lancaster, 2014).

Communication

Communication differences include language differences, verbal and nonverbal behaviors, and silence. Language can be the greatest obstacle to providing multicultural care. If the client does not speak the same language as the nurse, a skilled interpreter is mandatory (Douglas et al, 2011). Comfort with direct eye contact during communication is an area that varies among cultures. Although some cultures, such as European Americans, value direct eye contact as a sign of attention, other cultures, such as black/African American or American Indian, may view direct eye contact as rude behavior.

In the Asian culture, it is considered important behavior to agree with those in authority. This aspect of the

Asian culture has important implications for the nurse who is involved in patient education. The patient may seem compliant and nod his or her head as in agreement with the nurse's instruction even when the instruction is not clear or when the patient has no intention of carrying out the instruction (Stanhope and Lancaster, 2014).

Anglo-Americans tend to be informal in their style of communication, whereas other cultures may prefer a more formal style. Health professionals should not assume that a first-name basis is appropriate for client relationships. With any client, terms of endearment such as "honey" or "dear" are unacceptable and can be interpreted as disrespectful, derogatory, or condescending. The best solution to the challenge of different communication styles and preferences is always to ask the client how he or she prefers to be addressed.

If the nurse and the client do not speak the same language, an interpreter should be consulted. An interpreter can help the nurse establish rapport with the client and explain concepts to the patient that are foreign to the nurse. When interpreters are needed, they should be selected carefully. Adult family members or friends are possible choices, as are bilingual staff and community volunteers. Nurses should be aware that some ethnic groups consider it a breach of confidentiality to have a stranger interpret, whereas certain individuals may not want other family members or friends to know the specifics of their medical condition.

The nurse also should be careful to consider the different dialects spoken in the same country and the culture's view of women and children. Children should not be used as interpreters because of the subject matter and because of certain cultural views of authority. Many cultures view adults as having more authority than children. In many cultures, women would not be acceptable interpreters because of the cultural view of women.

Nurses should be aware of the possibilities for interpreter services. A language line can be accessed 24 hours a day, 7 days a week by calling 1-800-528-5888 and asking for the language you want. A live translator comes on the line to serve you in any one of 77 languages. You can conference call, use two phones on the same line, or simply pass the phone back and forth to the person with whom you wish to converse. For more information, visit www.languageline.com.

Health care facilities may get a reasonable subscription rate that is less costly than the individual rate for these services.

Space

Space refers to people's attitudes and comfort level regarding the personal space around them. There are vast cultural differences in the comfort level associated with the distance between persons. Anglo-American nurses tend to feel comfortable with an intimate zone of 0 to 18 inches. This usually is the distance between the nurse and the patient when the nurse performs certain parts of a physical assessment, such as an eye or ear examination. Entering this zone could be uncomfortable for clients and nurses who have not had time to establish a trusting relationship. This discomfort would be increased for persons whose culture is not comfortable at all with such a limited space. For instance Asians frequently believe that touching strangers is inappropriate; therefore, they have a tendency to prefer more distance between themselves and others, particularly health professionals whom they have not previously known. On the other hand, Mexican Americans tend to be comfortable with less space because they like to touch persons with whom they are talking (Stanhope and Lancaster, 2014).

Time

Time orientation is the view of time in the present, past, or future. Present-oriented persons enjoy what they are experiencing at the moment and only move on to the next event or activity "when the time is right." Punctuality and "watching the clock" are definitely part of Western culture, but many cultural groups, such as American Indians, do not view time in the same way. This difference in time orientation can have implications for the present-oriented professional in the work setting, who may always be late for work without thinking it is an important issue. In addition, there are implications for health teaching. For example, when teaching medication schedules to a patient, it would be important to consider how that individual views time.

Clients who view the past as more important than the present or the future may focus on memories of the past. For instance, the Vietnamese may take actions that they believe are consistent with the views of their ancestors and look to their ancestors for guidance (Giger and Davidhizar, 2008). In Asian culture, time is viewed as being more flexible than in Western culture, and being on time or late for appointments is not a priority (Stanhope and Lancaster, 2014).

People who are future oriented are concerned with long-range goals and health care measures that can be taken in the present to prevent illness in the future. These persons plan ahead in scheduling appointments and organizing activities. They may be seen as having "distant" or "cold" personalities because they are not always engaged in communication at the moment because they may be thinking about their plans for the future. Persons who are oriented more to the present may be late for appointments because they are less concerned with planning ahead (Table 10-2).

TABLE 10-2	**Variations Among Selected Cultural Groups**			
	Black/African Americans	**Asians**	**Hispanics**	**American Indians**
Verbal communication	Asking personal questions of someone met for the first time is seen as improper and intrusive	High respect for others, especially those in positions of authority	Expression of negative feelings is considered impolite	Speak in a low tone of voice, and expect that the listener will be attentive
Nonverbal communication	Direct eye contact in conversation often is considered rude	Direct eye contact among superiors may be considered disrespectful	Avoidance of eye contact usually is a sign of attentiveness and respect	Direct eye contact often is considered disrespectful
Touch	Touching another's hair often is considered offensive	Not customary to shake hands with persons of the opposite sex	Touching often is observed between two persons in conversation	A light touch of the person's hand instead of a firm handshake often is used when greeting a person
Family organization	Usually have close extended-family networks; women play key roles in health care decisions	Usually have close extended-family networks; emphasis may be on family needs rather than individual needs	Usually have close extended-family networks; all members of the family may be involved in health care decisions	Usually have close extended-family networks; emphasis tends to be on family rather than on individual needs
Time	Often present-oriented	Often present-oriented	Often present-oriented	Often present-oriented
Alternative healers	"Granny," "root doctor," voodoo priest, spiritualist	Acupuncturist, acupressurist, herbalist	Curandero, espiritualista, yerbo	Medicine man, shaman
Self-care practices	Poultices, herbs, oils, roots	Hot and cold foods, herbs, teas, soups, cupping, burning, rubbing, pinching	Hot and cold foods, herbs	Herbs, corn meal, medicine bundle
Biologic variations	Sickle cell anemia, mongolian spots, keloid formation, inverted T waves, lactose intolerance, skin color	Thalassemia, drug interactions, mongolian spots, lactose intolerance, skin color	Mongolian spots, lactose intolerance, skin color	Cleft uvula, lactose intolerance, skin color

Data from Giger J, Davidhizar R: *Transcultural nursing,* ed 4, St Louis, 2004, Mosby.
Spector R: *Cultural diversity in health and illness,* ed 5, Upper Saddle River, NJ, 2000, Prentice-Hall.
Payne K: Culturally valid testing: a proactive approach. In: Taylor O, editor: *Nature of communication disorders in culturally and linguistically diverse populations,* San Diego, 1986, College Hill Press.

PRACTICE ISSUES RELATED TO CULTURAL COMPETENCE

Health Information and Education

According to the Task Force on Black and Minority Health, minority populations are less knowledgeable about specific health problems than are whites. Blacks and Hispanics receive less information about cancer and heart disease than do nonminority groups. Blacks tend to underestimate the prevalence of cancer, give less credence to the warning signs, obtain fewer screening tests, and are diagnosed at later stages of cancer than are whites. Hispanic women receive less information about breast cancer than do white women. Hispanic women are less aware that family history is a risk for breast cancer, and less than 30% have heard of breast self-examination. Successful programs to increase public awareness about health problems are being offered to minority groups, but efforts must be continued to reach more of the population. Families, churches, employers, and community organizations need to be involved in facilitating behavior changes that will result in healthier lifestyles. Education programs have the greatest effect on diseases that are affected by lifestyle, such as hypertension, obesity, and diabetes. For example, if patients with diabetes could improve their self-management skills, complications could be prevented, saving human suffering and health care dollars (Nies and McEwen, 2011).

Education and Certification

Increasingly more universities and colleges offer graduate programs in transcultural, cross-cultural, and international nursing. Many nurses have not been exposed to transcultural nursing in their basic education program. Therefore, the availability of graduate study in this area often is an unrecognized possibility.

Transcultural nursing is the study of differences and similarities of various cultural health values and beliefs among different ethnic and minority groups. The Transcultural Nursing Society has been certifying nurses in transcultural nursing since 1988. Certification as a certified transcultural nurse is based on oral and written examinations and evaluation of the nurse's educational and experiential background. Certification has increased recognition of transcultural nursing as a legitimate nursing specialty. Transcultural nurses are interested in finding universal care for clients that will improve, maintain, and restore health and improve client satisfaction.

International Marketplace

Nurses trained in the United States work, teach, and consult in hundreds of foreign countries on every continent. They often are recognized as international pacesetters and are viewed as "commodities for import" by both the more developed countries and the less developed third- or fourth-world nations. Nurses can make a difference in the health outcomes of people all over the world. Technology has enhanced global communication and facilitated travel. As nurses help solve emerging health problems in countries throughout the world, they are the most valuable assets of the health care system. They will be called on to design, implement, and evaluate international projects, educational endeavors, and research with an intercultural focus. Therefore, it is important that nurses understand the intercultural issues related to our global society (Nies and McEwen, 2011).

Nursing Literature

The number of journal articles about culturally diverse clients, transcultural nursing research, international nursing, and the inclusion of transcultural concepts in nursing curricula has increased considerably since the 1950s. The *Journal of Transcultural Nursing* is a refereed journal that was first published in 1989. This journal was created to advance transcultural nursing knowledge and practices. The *Journal of Transcultural Nursing* focuses on theory, research, and practice dimensions of transcultural nursing and provides a forum for researchers. Other journals that address cultural issues include the *Western Journal of Medicine: Cross Cultural Issues,* the *Journal of Cultural Diversity,* the *Journal of Multicultural Nursing,* the *International Journal of Nursing Studies,* the *International Nursing Review,* and the *Journal of Holistic Nursing.* Nurse authors also need to be encouraged to publish articles related to clients' cultural views and health care needs in nursing specialty and practice journals that are more widely read by nurses who actually are providing care on a daily basis to clients from diverse cultures.

Although research articles on transcultural issues are becoming a common feature in health care journals, there is a need for additional research that examines individual behavioral responses to normal life processes, such as pregnancy, birth, death, and human growth and development. There also is a need for well-designed studies that explore the biologic, psychologic, sociologic, and spiritual differences within, between, and among cultural groups (Douglas et al, 2011). Dr. Madeline Leininger created the theory of culture care diversity and universality to guide transcultural research. Even though numerous research studies have been conducted on cultural diversity issues, a significant time gap often exists between the identification of findings and publication of results. The limited dissemination of research findings inhibits widespread acceptance of new interventions that could improve health care practices of culturally diverse populations. Computer information technology and online networks help narrow this gap and distribute research findings in a timely manner (Douglas et al, 2011).

Responsibility of Health Care Facilities for Cultural Care

Nursing policies should reflect openness to including extended family members and folk healers in the nursing care plan, provided their presence is not harmful to the client's well-being. For example, Hispanic clients may want the support of a curandero (a native healer), espiritualista (spiritualist), yerbo (herbalist), or sabador (equal to a chiropractor). Blacks may turn to a hougan (voodoo priest or priestess) or "old lady." American Indians may seek assistance from a shaman or medicine man. Clients of Asian descent may want the services of an acupuncturist or bonesetter. In some religions, spiritual healers may be found among the ranks of the ordained and may be called *priest, bishop, elder, deacon, rabbi, brother,* or *sister* (Nies and McEwen, 2011). Most hospital chaplaincy programs have access to religious representatives available for patients of various religions.

Clients may need to consult with their support persons and folk healers before making medical decisions. Nurses must respect the client's right to privacy and allow time for the client to interact with his or her spiritual or cultural healers. Nurses must respect unconventional beliefs and health practices, and work with clients to develop a plan of care that builds on their beliefs and incorporates nontraditional health practices that are not harmful. These nontraditional healers should be received with respect and provided privacy to

enable the healers to interact with their patients (Nies and McEwen, 2011).

Health care facilities should provide resources for nurses and other health care professionals to assist with the culture-specific needs of clients. Health care facilities should have a list of interpreters fluent in the major languages spoken by persons typically using the organization. Translators who have knowledge of health-related terminology are more effective than those who do not. Gender, birth origin, and socioeconomic class need to be considered when selecting a translator. Gender is an important consideration because many cultures prohibit discussion of intimate matters between women and men. Birth origin of the client and translator should be determined because often there are many dialects spoken within the same country, depending on the particular region (Stanhope and Lancaster, 2014). Differences in socioeconomic class between client and interpreter can lead to problems of interpretation.

Clinical nurse specialists (CNSs) in transcultural nursing should be added to the staff of institutions serving large numbers of culturally diverse individuals. The transcultural CNS could be a role model to the staff in delivery of culturally sensitive and competent care, provide in-service education to staff related to cultural differences, and conduct research related to cultural and social issues. In addition, consultants should be used to deal with specific cultural issues.

Continuing education programs for nurses should be offered by health care institutions. Programs should focus on promoting awareness of the nurses' own culturally based values, beliefs and attitudes, cultural assessment, biologic variations of cultural groups, cross-cultural communication, and culture-specific beliefs and practices related to childbearing and childrearing, death and dying, issues of mental health, and cultural aspects of aging.

Recommended Standards for Culturally and Linguistically Appropriate Services (CLAS)

Culture and language have a considerable effect on how patients access and respond to health care services. To ensure equal access to quality health care by diverse populations, the Office of Minority Health in the Department of Health and Human Services developed guidelines for health care organizations. In its report, *Assessing Cultural Competence in Health Care: Recommendations for National Standards and an Outcomes*

Focused Research Agenda, the following standards are recommended:

- Promote and support the attitudes, behaviors, knowledge, and skills necessary for staff to work respectfully and effectively with patients and each other in a culturally diverse work environment.
- Have a comprehensive management strategy to address culturally and linguistically appropriate services, including strategic goals, plans, policies, procedures, and designated staff responsible for implementation.
- Utilize formal mechanisms for community and consumer involvement in the design and execution of service delivery, including planning, policymaking, operations, evaluation, training, and, as appropriate, treatment planning.
- Develop and implement a strategy to recruit, retain, and promote qualified, diverse, and culturally competent administrative, clinical, and support staff members that are trained and qualified to address the needs of the racial and ethnic communities being served.
- Require and arrange for ongoing education and training for administrative, clinical, and support staff in culturally and linguistically competent service delivery.
- Provide all clients with limited English proficiency (LEP) access to bilingual staff or interpretation services.
- Provide oral and written notices, including translated signage at key points of contact, to clients in their primary language informing them of their right to receive interpreter services free of charge.
- Translate and make available signage and commonly used written patient educational material and other materials for members of the dominant language groups in service areas.
- Ensure that interpreters and bilingual staff can demonstrate bilingual proficiency and receive training that includes the skills and ethics of interpreting as well as knowledge in both languages of the terms and concepts relevant to clinical or nonclinical encounters. Family or friends are not considered adequate substitutes because they usually lack these abilities.
- Ensure that the clients' primary spoken language and self-identified race or ethnicity are included in the health care organization's management information system as well as any patient records used by provider staff.

- Utilize a variety of methods to collect and use accurate demographic, cultural, epidemiologic, and clinical outcome data for racial and ethnic groups in the service area. Become informed about the ethnic and cultural needs, resources, and assets of the surrounding community.
- Undertake ongoing organizational self-assessments of cultural and linguistic competence; integrate measures of access, satisfaction, quality, and outcomes for CLAS into other organizational internal audits and performance-improvement programs.
- Develop structures and procedures to address cross-cultural ethical and legal conflicts in health care delivery and complaints or grievances by patients and staff about unfair, culturally insensitive, or discriminatory treatment; difficulty in accessing services; or denial of services.
- Prepare an annual progress report documenting the organizations' progress with implementing CLAS standards, including information on programs, staffing, and resources.

CULTURAL ASSESSMENT

Cultural Self-Assessment

The first step to becoming a culturally sensitive and competent health care provider is to conduct a cultural self-assessment. The nurse should engage in a cultural self-assessment to identify individual culturally based attitudes about clients who are from a different culture. Cultural self-assessment requires self-honesty and sincerity and reflection on attitudes of parents, grandparents, and close friends in terms of their attitudes toward different cultures. Through identification of health-related attitudes, values, beliefs, and practices, the nurse can better understand the cultural aspects of health care from the client's perspective. Everyone has ethnocentric tendencies that must be brought to a level of consciousness so that efforts can be made to temper the feeling that one's own culture is best. Box 10-2 shows a cultural self-assessment guide adapted from Swanson and Nies (1997) for the nurse who is not black but is caring for a black client.

Cultural Client Assessment

After the nurse performs a cultural self-assessment, he or she should obtain a cultural assessment for the client.

BOX 10-2 Cultural Self-Assessment

- How do your parents, grandparents, other family members, and close friends view people from racially diverse groups?
- What is the cultural stereotype of blacks/African Americans?
- Does the cultural stereotype allow for socioeconomic differences?
- Have your interactions with black/African Americans been positive? Negative? Neutral?
- How do you feel about going into a predominantly African American neighborhood or into the home of a black/African American family? Are you afraid, anxious, curious, or ambivalent?
- What stereotypes do you have about black men, women, and children?
- What culturally based health beliefs and practices do you think characterize blacks/African Americans? How are these different from your own culturally based health beliefs and practices?

From Swanson J, Nies M: *Community health nursing: promoting the health of aggregates*, ed 2, Philadelphia, 1997, Saunders.

Nursing assessments in institutional and community settings should include the gathering of data pertinent to cultural beliefs and practices. Cultural assessments lead to culturally relevant nursing diagnoses and give direction to effective nursing intervention. Basic cultural data include ethnic affiliation, religious preference, family patterns, food patterns, and ethnic health care practices. Cultural assessments should be used as an adjunct to other patient assessments. These data will give the nurse sufficient information to determine if a more in-depth assessment of cultural factors is needed. A major reason that cultural assessments are performed is to identify patterns that may assist or interfere with a nursing intervention or treatment regimen (Douglas et al, 2011). The nurse needs to find out if the client's beliefs, customs, values, and self-care practices are adaptive (beneficial), neutral, or maladaptive (harmful) in relation to nursing interventions. For example, if a Mexican American client who is diagnosed with hypertension insists on taking garlic instead of an antihypertensive, this could be harmful. If the client agrees to take the garlic in addition to the antihypertensive, this would

be a neutral practice. An adaptive or beneficial practice would include daily exercise in addition to the garlic and antihypertensive.

In the case of Southeast Asians, dermal practices, such as cupping, pinching, rubbing, and burning, are a common part of self-care. The dermal methods are perceived as ways to relieve headaches, muscle pains, sinusitis, colds, sore throats, diarrhea, or fever. Cupping involves placing a heated cup on the skin; as it cools, it contracts, drawing what is believed to be toxicity into the cup. A circular ecchymosis is left on the skin. Pinching may be at the base of the nose or between the eyes. Bruises or welts are left at the site of treatment. Rubbing or "coining" involves rubbing lubricated skin with a spoon or a coin to bring toxic "wind" to the body surface. A similar practice is burning, which involves touching a burning cigarette or piece of cotton to the skin, usually the abdomen, to compensate for "heat" lost through diarrhea (Nies and McEwen, 2011). These practices nurture the client's sense of well-being and security in being able to do something to correct disturbing symptoms. In most cases, the practice would be considered adaptive (beneficial) or neutral. However, if the client had a clotting disorder, the practices would pose a threat to physical integrity and therefore be considered maladaptive (harmful) (Nies and McEwen, 2011).

Cultural Client Nutrition Assessment

A cultural nutrition assessment should be obtained for clients who are minorities. It is necessary to assess the client's cultural definition of food. For example, certain Latin American groups do not consider greens to be food. Therefore, when asked to keep a food diary, these individuals would not list greens, which are an important source of vitamins and iron. Frequency and number of meals, amount and types of food eaten, and regularity of food consumption are other important factors to consider.

Among Asian Americans, dietary intake of calcium may appear inadequate because this group usually has a low rate of consumption of dairy products. However, they commonly consume pork bone and shells, thus taking in adequate quantities of calcium to meet minimum daily requirements. In cultures in which obesity is a problem, it is helpful for the nurse to have an idea of food preferences to help the client select low-calorie, low-fat foods. Asians tend to prefer spicy foods that may lead to the high incidence of stomach cancer, ulcers, and gastrointestinal bleeding (Purnell and Paulanka, 2009).

Nurses should avoid cultural stereotyping as it relates to food because all Italians do not necessarily like spaghetti, nor do all Chinese like rice. However, knowing the clients' food preferences makes it possible to develop therapeutic interventions that do not conflict with their cultural food practices (Stanhope and Lancaster, 2014).

Cultural Beliefs About Sickness and Cures

It also is important for the nurse to consider the nontraditional beliefs of sickness and cure of various cultures. For example, there are diseases that are not classified as Western culture diseases. For different cultural groups, they are real diseases for which the group has medicines and treatments. Examples of such diseases include mal ojo, susto, bilis, and empacho.

Mal ojo ("evil eye") is thought to be caused by persons giving admiration. For example, Hispanic clients may believe in mal ojo in which a child becomes ill as a result of excessive attention from a stranger (Nies and McEwen, 2011). For example, a stranger who lovingly admires a Mexican American baby by looking into the baby's face actually can cause mal ojo. An infant who has mal ojo sleeps restlessly, has fever and diarrhea, and may ultimately die. Treatment consists of rubbing the body with an egg for three consecutive nights. The egg is broken and left under the bed overnight. In the morning, if the egg appears to be cooked, then mal ojo was definitely the cause of the illness. For protection, mothers often adorn their children with red yarn around their wrists or amulets that usually are a deer's eyes (Nies and McEwen, 2011).

Susto, or fright sickness, is an emotion-based illness that is common among Mexicans. An unexpected fall, a barking dog, or a car accident could cause susto. Symptoms include colic, diarrhea, high temperature, and vomiting. Treatment involves brushing the body with "ruda" for nine consecutive nights. The brushing is performed to allow the spirit that has been removed by the disease to return to the body. The treatment often is accompanied by burning candles and saying prayers in the home or church (Nies and McEwen, 2011).

Bilis is a disease brought on by anger. It primarily affects adults and commonly occurs a day or two after a fit of rage. If untreated, bilis can cause acute nervous tension and chronic fatigue, although herbal remedies usually are effective (Giger and Davidhizar, 2008).

Empacho is a disease that can affect children or adults and is caused by food particles becoming lodged in the intestinal tract, causing sharp pains. To manage this illness, the afflicted person lies face down on the bed with his or her back bared. The curer pinches a piece of skin at the waist, listening for a snap from the abdominal region. This is repeated several times in hope of dislodging the material. Empacho usually is not a serious disease (Nies and McEwen, 2011).

It is important to determine how culturally diverse clients define health and illness and whether their health beliefs and practices differ from the norm in the Western health care delivery system (Spector, 2008). For example, the Chinese often find many aspects of Western medicine distasteful. They cannot understand why so many diagnostic tests are necessary and tend to believe that a "good" physician has the ability to diagnose by thoroughly examining the client's body. Chinese clients dislike painful procedures, such as the practice of drawing blood. In their culture, blood is seen as the source of life for the entire body, and the Chinese believe that it is not regenerated. They have a deep respect for their bodies and prefer to die with their bodies intact. Therefore it is not uncommon for the Chinese to refuse surgery that would be mutilating to the body (Spector, 2008). Health represents a balance within the body, mind, and spirit. It is strongly affected by the family and community. Spector (2008) suggests a model for assessing health traditions (Box 10-3).

Spector (2008) also has developed a guide that can be used to assess clients' personal methods for maintaining, protecting (preventing illness), and restoring health (Table 10-3).

BOX 10-3 Health Traditions Assessment Model

Maintaining Health

Physical	Are there special clothes one must wear; foods one must eat or not eat, or combinations to avoid; exercises one must do?
Mental	Are there special sources of entertainment; games or other ways of concentrating; traditional "rules of behavior"?
Spiritual	Are there special religious customs; prayers; meditations?

Protecting Health and Preventing Illness

Physical	Are there special foods that must be eaten after certain life events, such as childbirth; dietary taboos that must be adhered to; symbolic clothes that must be worn?
Mental	Are there special sources of entertainment, games or other ways of concentrating; traditional "rules of behavior?"
Spiritual	Are there special religious customs, superstitions, amulets, oils, or waters?

Restoring Health

Physical	Are there special folk remedies; liniments; procedures, such as cupping, acupuncture, and moxibustion?
Mental	Are there special healers, such as curanderos, rituals, folk medicines?
Spiritual	Are there special rituals and prayers, meditations, healers?

From Spector RE: *Cultural diversity in health and illness,* ed 6, Upper Saddle River, NJ, 2008, Prentice-Hall.

TABLE 10-3 Assessment Guide for Personal Methods to Maintain, Protect (Prevent Illness), and Restore Health

	Physical	Mental	Spiritual
Maintain health	Are there special clothes you must wear at certain times of the day, week, or year? Are there special foods you must eat at certain times? Do you have any dietary restrictions? Are there any foods that you cannot eat?	What do you do for activities, such as reading, sports, or games? Do you have hobbies? Do you visit family often? Do you visit friends often?	Do you practice your religion and attend church or other communal activities? Do you pray or meditate? Do you observe religious customs? Do you belong to fraternal organizations?
Protect health or prevent illness	Are there foods that you cannot eat together? Are there special foods that you must eat? Are there any types of clothing that you are not allowed to wear?	Are there people or situations that you have been taught to avoid? Do you take extraordinary precautions under certain circumstances? Do you take time for yourself?	Do you observe religious customs? Do you wear any amulets or hang them in your house? Do you have any practices, such as always opening the window when you sleep? Do you have any other practices to protect yourself from "harm"?

Continued

TABLE 10-3   Assessment Guide for Personal Methods to Maintain, Protect (Prevent Illness), and Restore Health—cont'd

	Physical	Mental	Spiritual
Restore health	What kinds of medicines do you take before you see a doctor or nurse? Are there herbs that you take? Are there special treatments that you use?	Do you know of any specific practices your mother or grandmother may use to relax? Do you know how big problems can be cared for in your community? Do you drink special teas to help you unwind or relax?	Do you know any healers? Do you know of any religious rituals that help to restore health? Do you meditate? Do you ever go to a healing service? Do you know about exorcism?

From Spector RE: *Cultural diversity in health and illness,* ed 6, Upper Saddle River, NJ, 2008, Prentice-Hall.

SUMMARY

In a society as diverse as the United States, health care cannot come in one form to fit the needs of everyone. Culture has a powerful influence on one's interpretation of health and illness and response to health care. All clients have the right to be understood and respected, despite their differences. They have the right to expect health care providers to acknowledge that their perspectives on and interpretations of health are legitimate. Health care professionals must make a commitment to increase their knowledge, sensitivity, and competence in cultural concepts and care. Perhaps no other group in the health profession has recognized the effect of cultural diversity on outcomes of health care more than nursing. Nurses always have supported the concept of holistic care. By understanding the client's perspective, the nurse can be a better advocate for the client. With increased knowledge, sensitivity, respect, and understanding, therapeutic interventions can be maximized to promote the highest quality of health for clients in our multicultural society.

REFERENCES

American Academy of Nursing: *Diversity, marginalization, and culturally competent health care issues in knowledge development*, Washington, DC, 1995, American Academy of Nursing.

American Association of Colleges of Nursing: *The Essentials of baccalaureate education for professional nursing practice*, Washington, DC, 2008, American Association of Colleges of Nursing.

American Association of Colleges of Nursing: *Enhancing Diversity in the Workforce*, 2014 (website). http://www.aacn.nche.edu/media-relations/fact-sheets/enhancing-diversity. Accessed October 13, 2014.

American Academy of Nursing Expert Panel on Cultural Competence: *American Academy of Nursing standards of cultural competence*, Washington, DC, 2007, American Academy of Nursing Expert Panel on Cultural Competence.

American Academy of Nursing Expert Panel on Culturally Competent Health Care: Culturally competent health care, *Nurs Outlook* 40(6):277–283, 1992.

American Association of Colleges of Nursing (AACN): *Policy Brief: The Changing Landscape: Nursing Student Diversity on the Rise*. Retrieved from: http://www.aacn.nche.edu/government-affairs/.Student-Diversity-FS.pdf. Ethnic Minorities. Accessed July 15, 2015.

American Nurses Association: *Promoting cultural competence in and through nursing education: A critical review and comprehensive plan for action*, Washington, DC, 1995, American Nurses Association.

Bessent H: *Strategies for recruitment, retention and graduation of minority nurses in colleges of nursing*, Washington, DC, 1997, American Nurses Foundation.

Centers for Disease Control and Prevention: *The State of Aging and Health in America*, Atlanta, GA, 2013, Centers for Disease Control and Prevention, US Department of Health and Human Services. http://www.cdc.gov/aging. Accessed October 13, 2014.

Douglas M, Pierce J, Rosenkoetter M, et al: Standards of practice for culturally competent nursing care: 2011 update, *J Transcult Nurs* 22(4), 317–333, 2011.

Fang D, Li Y, Arietti R, Bednash GD: *Enrollment and graduations in baccalaureate and graduate programs in nursing (2013-14)*, Washington, DC, 2014, American Association of Colleges of Nursing.

Giger JN, Davidhizar RE: *Transcultural nursing: assessment and intervention*, ed 5, St Louis, 2008, Mosby.

Health Resources Service Administration: *The registered nurse population: findings from the 2008 National Sample Survey of Registered Nurses*, Washington, DC, 2010, U.S. Department of Health and Human Services.

Lenburg CB, Lipson JG, Demi A, et al: *Promoting cultural competence in and through nursing education: a critical review and comprehensive plan for action*, Washington, DC, 1995, American Academy of Nursing.

Loftin C, Newman S, Dumas B, et al: *Perceived barriers to success for minority nursing students: An integrative review*, International Scholarly Research Notices Published online, May 30, 2012. doi: 10.5402/2012/806543.

Macartney S, Bishaw A, Fontenot K: *U.S. Census Bureau. Poverty rates for selected detailed race and Hispanic groups by state and place, 2007–2011*. Report Number: ACSBR/11-17, February 2013. http://www.census.gov/library/publications/2013/acs/acsbr11-17.html. Accessed October 13, 2014.

Meleis A, Isenberg M, Koerner J, et al: *Diversity, marginalization, and culturally competent healthcare issues in knowledge development*, Washington, DC, 1995, American Academy of Nursing.

National Council of State Boards of Nursing: The National Council of State Boards of Nursing and The Forum of State Nursing Workforce Centers, National Workforce Survey of RNs, *Journal of Nursing Regulation*, 4(2): S1–72, 2013.

Nies M, McEwen M: *Community/public health nursing: Promoting the health of populations*, ed 4, St Louis, 2011, Elsevier.

Purnell L, Paulanka B: *Guide to culturally competent healthcare*, ed 2, Philadelphia, 2009, FA Davis.

Spector R: *Culture care: guide to heritage assessment and health traditions*, ed 7, Upper Saddle River, NJ, 2008, Prentice-Hall.

Spector R: Cultural diversity in health and illness/culture care: guide to heritage assessment health. In Spector R, editor: *Cultural diversity in health and illness*, ed 7, Upper Saddle River, NJ, 2008, Prentice-Hall.

Stanhope M, Lancaster J: *Public health nursing: population-centered health care in the community*, ed 8, St Louis, 2014, Mosby.

Sullivan LW: *Missing persons: minorities in the health professions: a report of the Sullivan Commission on diversity in the healthcare workforce*, Washington, DC, 2004, The Sullivan Commission.

Swanson J, Nies M: *Community health nursing: promoting the health of aggregates*, ed 2, Philadelphia, 1997, Saunders.

Tervalon M, Murray-Garcia J: Cultural humility versus cultural competence: a critical distinction in defining physician training outcomes in multicultural education, *J Health Care Poor Underserved* 9(2):117, 1998.

U.S. Census Bureau: *Income, poverty, and health insurance coverage in the United States*, 2011 (website). http://www.census.gov/prod/2011pubs/p60-239.pdf. Accessed October 14, 2014.

U.S. Department of Commerce, United States Census Bureau: *The older population: Census briefs*, Washington, DC, 2010, U.S. Department of Commerce, United States Census Bureau (website). http://www.census.gov/prod/cen2010/briefs/c2010br-09.pdf. U.S. Government Printing Office. Accessed April 2012.

U.S. Department of Health and Human Services: *National Institutes of Health and National Heart Lung and Blood Institute* (website). http://www.nhlbi.nih.gov/about/factbook/chapter4.htm. Accessed April 2012.

U.S. Department of Health and Human Services: *Public Health Service: Healthy People 2000*, Washington, DC, 1990, U.S. Government Printing Office.

U.S. Department of Health and Human Services: *Public Health Service: Healthy People 2020*, Washington, DC, 2010, U.S. Government Printing Office.

U.S. Department of Health and Human Services: *The 2008 HHS Poverty Guidelines*, Washington, DC, 2008, U.S. Government Printing Office.

ADDITIONAL RESOURCES

Kersey-Matusiak G: Culturally competent care: are we there yet? *Nurs Manage* 43(4):34–39, 2012.

Lipson J, Dibble S: *Culture and clinical care*, ed 2, San Francisco, 2005, University of California School of Nursing.

11

Complementary and Alternative Healing

Charlotte Eliopoulos, PhD, RN, MPH, ND

Consumers are seeking natural remedies; nurses have a responsibility to be aware of the potential effects.

(e) Additional resources are available online at: *http://evolve.elsevier.com/Cherry/*

PROFESSIONAL/ETHICAL ISSUE

Mr. Jensen is a 50-year-old man who has been diagnosed with a rare liver cancer that is typically fatal within 1 year. His oncologist has recommended a form of chemotherapy that cannot offer a cure, but could possibly slow the cancer's spread and offer a few added months of life to Mr. Jensen.

Mr. Jensen, accompanied by his wife, are meeting with the oncologist, who is your employer and whom you are assisting. Mr. Jensen informs the oncologist that after giving it thought, he has decided against the chemotherapy. "I saw what my brother went through with his chemo for lung cancer and I don't want to do the same," Mr. Jensen states. "My wife found this natural health practitioner who offers some kind of touch therapy and uses herbal blends. I've seen him a couple

of times now and have to tell you, I feel great so I'm going that route," he adds.

The oncologist is noticeably annoyed and responds, "You are wasting your time and money on that foolishness. If anything is going to help you it is what medicine has to offer, so I'd think about scheduling your next chemotherapy. The nurse will help you with that." He then exits the room.

Mr. and Mrs. Jensen appear upset and somewhat confused. You heard what the oncologist recommended and understand that there is no evidence supporting the effectiveness of the natural healing methods, yet you also know that the chemotherapy offers no cure and does carry risks and side effects. What do you do?

VIGNETTE

Ruth Jeffers is a registered nurse (RN) who works in a rehabilitation unit of a community hospital. Many of the clients on this unit suffer from chronic musculoskeletal pain. Ms. Jeffers has noted that a growing number of clients have a history of independently using acupuncture, nutritional supplements, and other alternative and complementary healing therapies to improve their symptoms. Although they report beneficial results, most do not tell their physicians that they are using these therapies.

Last year, Ms. Jeffers completed a course in the use of therapeutic touch and has used this therapy to promote

relaxation and pain control with friends and family with considerable success. She is aware of many positive reports on the benefits of these unconventional approaches. She believes therapeutic touch and some other complementary healing therapies could benefit clients on the rehabilitation unit and informally introduces the topic to the team with whom she works. With the exception of one nurse who states that she believes these therapies are associated with the occult and wants no part of them, the nursing staff is enthusiastic and eager to implement complementary therapies. The physical and occupational therapists believe that complementary therapies could prove helpful to clients but that only therapists within their departments, not nursing, should provide these. The physician on the team opposes the use of all alternative and complementary therapies, stating, "I'm not about to put my license on the line for these unproven ideas."

Questions to Consider While Reading this Chapter:
1. What is the best course of action for Ruth Jeffers, RN, if she really believes that complementary and alternative therapies could benefit clients on the unit?
2. What would a hospital need to do to prepare for the inclusion of complementary and alternative therapies in its existing services?
3. What are some of the potential obstacles to introducing complementary and alternative therapies into a conventional setting?
4. What discipline(s) should be responsible for providing and/or coordinating or supervising the practitioners who provide complementary and alternative therapies in the hospital?

KEY TERMS

Biologically based treatments: Herbal therapies, individual and orthomolecular biologic therapies, special diets.

Complementary and alternative medicine (CAM): Healing philosophies, practices, and products that are outside of what Western society considers mainstream medicine and are not typically taught in the educational programs of physicians, nurses, and other health professionals.

Conventional medicine: Western style of medicine practiced in the United States; also called allopathic medicine.

Energy therapies: Qi gong, Reiki, therapeutic touch, healing touch, magnet therapy.

Manipulative and body-based methods: Chiropractic, massage, and related techniques (e.g., manual lymph drainage, Alexander technique, Feldenkrais method, pressure point therapies, Trager psychophysical integration), osteopathy.

Mind-body interventions: Aromatherapy, art therapy, biofeedback, dance therapy, hypnosis, imagery, meditation, music therapy, prayer, qi gong, progressive relaxation, self-help support groups, tai chi, yoga.

Movement therapies: Alexander technique, Feldenkrais method, Rolfing, Trager psychophysical integration.

Natural products: Herbal therapies, individual and orthomolecular biologic therapies, special diets.

Whole medical systems: Ayurvedic medicine, traditional Chinese medicine, traditional healers (e.g., Native American, shamans), environmental medicine, homeopathy, naturopathy.

LEARNING OUTCOMES

After studying this chapter, the reader will be able to:
1. Describe various complementary and alternative healing practices.
2. Identify how to effectively incorporate effective complementary and alternative therapies into care.
3. Provide patient education regarding uses, limitations, and precautions associated with selected complementary and alternative healing practices and products.

CHAPTER OVERVIEW

This chapter presents an overview of complementary and alternative medicine (CAM) therapies and products, which have gained popularity in Western society and are being integrated into health care. As increasing numbers of consumers and clinical settings become interested in and actually use CAM therapies, nurses must become knowledgeable about the uses, limitations, and precautions associated with these new practices and products. Professional nurses have an obligation to understand such practices and products to advise patients and effectively incorporate pertinent therapies into patients' care. Nurses who have knowledge and skills in this area are in key positions to empower patients for self-care that complements conventional medicine.

USE OF COMPLEMENTARY AND ALTERNATIVE HEALING METHODS

Complementary and alternative healing methods (CAM) include healing philosophies, practices, and products that fall outside what Western society considers mainstream (conventional) medicine and that are not typically taught in the educational programs of physicians, nurses, pharmacists, and other health professionals.

The past few decades have seen CAM progress from a fringe movement to highly popular, widely used therapies that are being integrated into conventional care. According to a nationwide government survey, approximately 38% of U.S. adults 18 years of age and older and approximately 12% of children use some form of CAM, and most are paying for these services out of their own pockets (National Center for Complementary and Alternative Medicine [NCCAM], 2014a).

Rather than emerging from the leadership of health care professionals, the growing popularity of CAM has been consumer driven. Several factors contribute to consumers' desire for CAM:

- *Dissatisfaction with the conventional health care system:* The impersonal nature of health care has grown with costs. Shorter hospital stays, several months' waiting periods to see a physician, hurried staff that barely have time to provide basic care, and horror stories of the adverse effects of medications are causing consumers to look for alternative approaches that are safer, less costly, and more responsive and personalized than conventional health care.
- *Increased empowerment of consumers in the health care system:* The Internet and growing assertiveness of consumers in all areas has affected health care. Consumers expect to have a voice in their care-planning activities and be able to utilize all available options for health promotion and disease management, including therapies outside mainstream medicine.
- *Unwillingness to "grin and bear" the effects of diseases:* Today's consumers are less willing than previous generations to live with symptoms that alter their lifestyles or to passively accept a terminal diagnosis and wait to die. They want options and to be empowered to do everything conceivable to promote the best possible quality and quantity of their lives, and they are willing to look to alternative healing measures to do so.
- *Shrinking world:* The rapid pace and ease of information sharing have enabled individuals to learn about diverse practices of cultures throughout the world.
- *Growing evidence of effectiveness:* The body of research supporting the effectiveness of alternative therapies increases almost daily. People hear testimonials from friends and family about the way they have been helped by acupuncture, herbs, and other forms of CAM. In addition, the media regularly report these findings, contributing to consumers' awareness of the body of evidence.

CAM practices and products are consistent with the values, beliefs, and philosophic orientations toward health held by many people (NCCAM, 2014a). With rare exceptions, consumers prefer natural approaches that afford them an active role in their care over high-tech interventions that relegate them to a passive, obedient role. They want to connect with their health care providers, have their individuality recognized, and gain education and skills to effectively make decisions and direct their care. Increasingly, consumers are seeking measures to enhance not just their bodies, but also their minds and spirits. The quality of their lives is equally if not more important to the quantity of years they live. Consumers often discover that CAM promotes many principles of holistic care that they value, such as individual empowerment, self-care, attention to all facets of one's being, and a high quality of life.

PRINCIPLES UNDERLYING ALTERNATIVE HEALING

A wide range of healing therapies are encompassed in CAM, yet most share some common principles:

- *The body has the ability to heal itself.* Most conventional medicine works from the premise that the elimination of sickness requires an intervention "done to" the body (e.g., giving medications, surgery). In CAM, there is the assumption that the body has the potential to heal itself. Complementary and alternative healing therapies enhance the body's ability to self-heal.

- *Health and healing are related to a harmony of mind, body, and spirit.* The mind, body, and spirit are inseparable; what affects one affects all. Healing and the improvement of health demand that all facets of a person be addressed, not merely a single symptom or system.
- *Basic, positive health practices build the foundation for healing.* Good nutrition, exercise, rest, stress management, and avoidance of harmful habits (e.g., smoking) are essential ingredients to health maintenance and the improvement of health conditions. Practitioners of healing therapies are more likely than conventional practitioners to look at total lifestyle practices rather than the diseased body part.
- *Approaches to healing are individualized.* The unique composition and dynamics of each person are recognized in CAM. Practitioners of healing therapies explore the underlying cause of a problem and customize approaches accordingly. It is rare in CAM to find a standing protocol that treats everyone with similar conditions alike.
- *Individuals are responsible for their own healing.* People can use a wide range of therapies, from conventional prescription drugs to herbal remedies, to treat illness. However, it is the responsibility of competent adults to seek health advice, make informed choices, gain necessary knowledge and skills for self-care, engage in practices that promote health and healing, and seek help when needed. Clients are responsible for getting their minds, bodies, and spirits in optimal condition to heal rather than look externally for a physician or nurse to heal them.

A holistic philosophy, promotion of positive health habits, and the client's responsibility for facilitating his or her own health and healing are common threads among healing therapies.

OVERVIEW OF POPULAR CAM HEALING THERAPIES

Hundreds of healing therapies are practiced throughout the world, with varying degrees of evidence to support their effectiveness. As the use of these therapies grew in the United States, the National Institutes of Health (NIH) established the Office of Alternative Medicine in 1992 to evaluate these complementary and alternative practices and products. In 1998, the Office of Alternative Medicine became a freestanding center within the NIH and was named the National Center for Complementary and Alternative Medicine (NCCAM). NCCAM has categorized CAM into several major fields of practice (Box 11-1); the center supports research and serves as a clearinghouse for information on alternative practices and products.

Consumers' growing use and the increased integration of CAM therapies into conventional care place a demand on nurses to become familiar with these therapies. Some of the frequently used CAM therapies are discussed in the following sections.

Acupuncture

Practiced in China for more than 2000 years, acupuncture is a major therapy within traditional Chinese medicine. It is based on the belief that there are invisible channels throughout the body, called *meridians*, through which energy flows. This energy is called *qi* (pronounced "chee") and is considered the vital life force. It is believed that illness and symptoms develop when the flow of energy becomes blocked or imbalanced. Health is restored when the energy becomes unblocked; this is achieved by stimulating acupuncture points on the meridian(s) affected (Figure 11-1).

The acupuncturist typically begins the treatment by taking a history, examining the tongue, and evaluating

---

BOX 11-1 Categories and Examples of Alternative and Complementary Therapies

Alternative medical systems: Acupuncture, Ayurveda, homeopathy, naturopathy, traditional Chinese medicine

Biologically based therapies: Herbal therapies, individual and orthomolecular biologic therapies, supplements

Mind-body interventions: Art therapy, biofeedback, dance therapy, deep breathing, guided imagery, humor therapy, hypnotherapy, imagery, meditation, music therapy, prayer, progressive relaxation, qi gong, self-help support groups, tai chi, yoga

Manipulative and body-based methods: Acupressure, chiropractic, Feldenkrais method, massage, osteopathy

Energy therapies: Qi gong, Reiki, healing touch, therapeutic touch

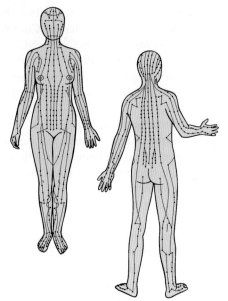

FIGURE 11-1 Acupuncture Meridians. (From Eliopoulos C: *Integrating alternative and conventional therapies,* St Louis, 1999, Mosby.)

pulses. Based on where the acupuncturist assesses the energy imbalance to be, he or she places needles at specific points. The placement of the needles may have no obvious relationship to the area of the body that is symptomatic. Sometimes the acupuncturist applies heat to the acupoints by burning a dried herb on the top of the needle or skin; this procedure is known as *moxibustion.* Electroacupuncture, a process in which a small current of electricity is applied to the tip of the needle, is another means of stimulating acupoints.

Pain relief is the most common reason people seek acupuncture treatment, and research supports its effectiveness for this problem (Ahadian et al, 2006; American Society of Anesthesiologists Task Force on Chronic Pain Management, 2010; Berman et al, 2010; Haigh, 2009; Koog et al, 2014; Last and Hulbert, 2009; Niemtzow, 2013; Selva et al, 2013; Wang et al, 2009). The use of acupuncture for dental pain and chemotherapy-induced nausea and vomiting also has been supported by research. There is some evidence that acupuncture can be of help for nicotine withdrawal, asthma, stroke rehabilitation, carpal tunnel syndrome, and a growing list of other conditions.

Insurance companies vary in their coverage of acupuncture, so it is best for clients to call their individual insurer for determination of benefits. State health departments can be consulted for licensing requirements for acupuncturists in a given state.

Ayurveda

Although it recently has gained popularity because of the writings and lectures of Deepak Chopra, Ayurveda has existed in India for more than 5000 years. Ayurveda means "the science of life" and is a system of care that promotes spiritual, mental, and physical balance. Noninvasive approaches are used to achieve balance and include yoga, massage, diet, purification regimens, breathing exercises, meditation, and herbs.

Individuals are believed to have distinct metabolic body types called *doshas,* which are *vata, pitta,* and *kapha* (Table 11-1). Signs of illness occur when the delicate balance of the doshas is disturbed.

The treatment to restore balance is influenced by the body type a client possesses and could include the following:

- Cleansing and detoxification
- Palliation
- Rejuvenation through special herbs and minerals
- Mental hygiene and spiritual healing

Currently, there is no process for licensing or certifying Ayurvedic practitioners. Because some of the treatments have the potential to cause complications

TABLE 11-1 **Ayurvedic Metabolic Body Types**	
Type	**Characteristics**
Vata	Unpredictable, moody, vivacious, hyperactive, imaginative, intuitive, impulsive, fluctuating energy levels, slender, prominent features and joints, eats and sleeps at varying times throughout day, prone to insomnia, PMS, cramps, and constipation
Pitta	Predictable, orderly, efficient, perfectionist, intense, passionate, short-tempered, medium build, follows routine schedule, warm skin, prone to heavy perspiration, thirst, acne, ulcers, hemorrhoids, and stomach problems
Kapha	Relaxed; graceful; tendency toward procrastination; affectionate; forgiving; compassionate; sleeps long and deeply; cool, pale, and oily skin; eats slowly; prone to high cholesterol, obesity, allergies, sinusitis

(e.g., dehydration from cleansing enemas, herb-drug interactions), finding a reputable trained practitioner is important. There is a need for continued research as scientific evidence for the effectiveness of Ayurvedic practices varies, and more rigorous research is needed to determine which practices are safe and effective.

Biofeedback

Biofeedback is a technique in which the client is taught to alter specific bodily functions (e.g., heart rate, blood pressure, muscle tension). The client uses various relaxation and imagery exercises to affect desired responses. Machinery, such as electroencephalograms, electromyelograms, and thermistors, are used to measure and offer feedback about the function that the client is trying to alter. As the client becomes familiar with ways to successfully alter bodily responses, the equipment may no longer be necessary.

There are many conditions for which biofeedback can offer benefit, including urinary incontinence, anxiety, stress, irritable bowel syndrome, neck and back pain, and cardiac arrhythmias.

Chiropractic Medicine

Chiropractic medicine is a popular and widely accepted CAM therapy in the United States perhaps because it was developed here and has been practiced for more than a century. Chiropractors are licensed in every state, and most insurance companies will pay for chiropractic treatments.

Chiropractic medicine is based on the belief that misalignments of the spine, called *subluxations,* put pressure on the nerves, leading to pain and disruptions in normal bodily function. The misalignment is treated by manipulation and adjustment of the spine. Typically, the chiropractor's hands do the alignment, although chiropractors increasingly are using heat, electrical stimulation, and other treatments.

Dietary Supplements

The past advice that vitamin and mineral supplements are unnecessary if one is eating well has been replaced with the recommendation that everyone should take a daily vitamin and mineral supplement. This shift in thinking has resulted from the realization that many people do not consume the proper nutrients through their diets. Pollutants, stress, and other factors that are more common today than in previous generations heighten the body's need for added protection. Also,

unlike our ancestors, who consumed produce that was picked the same day, we tend to eat more processed foods and produce that may have been in transit for several days before reaching us; therefore, the foods we consume contain fewer vitamins and minerals. Given these factors, the National Research Council of the National Academy of Sciences is re-evaluating the need to increase the recommended dietary allowances (RDAs).

Specific dietary supplements are thought to be beneficial for specific health conditions. However, too much of a good thing could prove harmful, and high doses of vitamins and minerals can lead to serious complications (Altizer et al, 2014; Consumer Reports, 2012; Guallar et al, 2013 Huang et al, 2006; Whitworth, 2006). For example, high doses of folic acid can mask a vitamin B_{12} deficiency (a cause of dementia), and calcium in excess of 2500 mg/day can cause kidney stones and impair the body's ability to absorb other minerals. In addition, because new research may disprove earlier claims about supplements, nurses need to keep abreast of new findings so that they can use supplements wisely and educate consumers to do the same.

Herbs

Plants have been used for medicinal purposes for nearly as long as humans have inhabited the earth. It is estimated that as many as 70,000 plant species have been used at one time or another by various cultures for medicinal purposes (PDR Staff, 2013; Pharmaceutical Press Editorial, 2013; Thomson Healthcare, 2007). Botanical medicine was a mainstream practice in the United States until the early nineteenth century, when medicine's shift toward a more scientific approach caused drugs to be viewed more favorably than herbs. But in the 1960s, when the movement toward natural health began to grow, interest in herbal products increased. The use and sales of herbal remedies have grown significantly since.

In reality, herbs are not that foreign to conventional medicine. Many modern drugs are derived from plants, including the following:

- Atropine from *Atropa belladonna*
- Digoxin from *Digitalis purpurea*
- Ipecac from *Cephaelis ipecacuanha*
- Reserpine from *Rauwolfia serpentina*

With more than 20,000 herbs and related products on the market, staying current of uses, dosage, interactions, and adverse effects is a near impossibility. However, nurses would be wise to become familiar with some of the most commonly used herbs (Box 11-2) and know where to obtain information on other herbs when needed. Because of consumers' widespread use of herbs, questions regarding use of all supplements and education to ensure safe use are significant nursing responsibilities.

Homeopathy

Homeopathy is a branch of medicine developed in the late eighteenth century by Samuel Hahnemann. It was widely practiced in the United States until the early 1900s, when modern (i.e., conventional) medicine discredited it as being unscientific and ineffective.

BOX 11-2 Facts About Commonly Used Herbs

Chamomile

Uses: Sedative effect, calming an upset digestive tract, healing mouth ulcers caused by chemotherapy or radiation.

Cautions: Because it contains coumarin, it could affect coagulation, although clinical studies have not demonstrated this to date; if the client is using an anticoagulant and chamomile, monitor. People are more likely to experience allergic reactions to chamomile if they are allergic to related plants in the daisy family, which includes ragweed, chrysanthemums, marigolds, and daisies.

Echinacea

Uses: Stimulates the immune system to treat or prevent colds, flu, and other infections.

Cautions: Although immunosuppressive effects with long-term use are inconclusive at present, best to limit to short-term use. Should not be used in people with autoimmune diseases. People are more likely to experience allergic reactions to echinacea if they have asthma or are allergic to related plants in the daisy family, which includes ragweed, chrysanthemums, marigolds, and daisies. Gastrointestinal side effects are common.

Feverfew

Use: Relief of migraines (although more evidence is needed).

Cautions: Contraindicated for clients with allergies to ragweed and other members of the Compositae family. People who have used feverfew for an extended period may have headaches, difficulty sleeping, nervousness, and joint and muscle stiffness when they stop taking it. Women who are pregnant should not use feverfew because it may cause the uterus to contract, increasing the risk of miscarriage or premature delivery.

Garlic

Uses: Lowers blood pressure; reduces "bad" cholesterol; stimulates immune system; heart tonic; antioxidant.

Cautions: Close monitoring necessary if taken by person using an anticoagulant because it can prolong bleeding time.

Ginger

Uses: Antiemetic. Studies are mixed on whether ginger is effective for nausea caused by motion, chemotherapy, or surgery. Research is being conducted on ginger's benefit for rheumatoid arthritis, osteoarthritis, or joint and muscle pain.

Caution: Few side effects are linked to ginger when it is taken in small doses. Powdered form can cause gas, bloating, heartburn, and nausea.

Ginkgo Biloba

Use: Believed to increase circulation to the brain and improve cognitive performance in persons with dementia; however, research has not shown ginkgo to be effective in improving memory or cognitive function.

Cautions: Close monitoring necessary if taken by person using anticoagulant because it can prolong bleeding time; can reduce effectiveness of anticonvulsants. Should not be used by people who have fragile blood vessels and a tendency to easily bleed. Side effects of ginkgo may include headache, nausea, gastrointestinal upset, diarrhea, dizziness, or allergic skin reactions. More severe allergic reactions have occasionally been reported. Fresh (raw) and roasted ginkgo seeds should be avoided as they can cause serious adverse effects due to containing high amounts of ginkgotoxin (which is only present in small amounts in standardized ginkgo leaf extracts that do not pose the same risk).

Ginseng

Uses: Improves resistance to stress; immune stimulant; general stimulant. Some studies have shown that Asian ginseng may lower blood glucose and have possible beneficial effects on immune function.

Cautions: Can cause breast tenderness in some menstruating women. Asian ginseng may lower blood sugar levels;

BOX 11-2 Facts About Commonly Used Herbs—cont'd

this effect may be seen more in people with diabetes. Therefore, people with diabetes should use extra caution with Asian ginseng, especially if they are using medicines to lower blood sugar or taking other herbs, such as bitter melon and fenugreek, which are also thought to lower blood sugar. The most common side effects are headaches and sleep and gastrointestinal problems.

Green Tea

Uses: Laboratory studies suggest that green tea may help protect against or slow the growth of certain cancers, but studies in people have shown mixed results. Some evidence suggests that the use of green tea preparations improves mental alertness, most likely because of its caffeine content. There are not enough reliable data to determine whether green tea can aid in weight loss, lower blood cholesterol levels, or protect the skin from sun damage.

Caution: There have been some case reports of liver problems in people taking concentrated green tea extracts, but this problem does not seem to be connected with green tea infusions or beverages. Although these cases are very rare and the evidence is not definitive, experts suggest that concentrated green tea extracts be taken with food, and that people should discontinue use and consult a heath care practitioner if they have a liver disorder or develop symptoms of liver trouble, such as abdominal pain, dark urine, or jaundice. Green tea and green tea extracts contain caffeine, which can cause insomnia, anxiety, irritability, upset stomach, nausea, diarrhea, or frequent urination in some people. It also contains small amounts of vitamin K, which can make anticoagulant drugs, such as warfarin, less effective.

Lavender

Uses: Treatment of anxiety, restlessness, insomnia, and depression. Studies have shown mixed results. Most commonly used in aromatherapy. Some early results from research shows lavender oil when combined with other herbal oils can aid in preventing hair loss in persons with alopecia areata.

Caution: Can cause drowsiness. Topical use of diluted lavender oil or use of lavender as aromatherapy is generally considered safe for most adults. However, lavender oil can be poisonous if taken orally, and applying lavender oil to the skin can cause irritation. There have been reports that topical use can cause breast growth in young boys.

Saw Palmetto

Uses: Thought to improve symptoms with benign prostatic hypertrophy; however, research concluded that it was not more effective than placebo.

Caution: Saw palmetto appears to be well tolerated by most users. It may cause mild side effects, including stomach discomfort.

Soy

Uses: May slightly lower levels of LDL ("bad") cholesterol when taken daily. Some studies suggest that soy isoflavone supplements may reduce hot flashes in women after menopause; however, the results have been inconsistent.

Caution: Minor stomach and bowel problems such as nausea, bloating, and constipation are possible. The safety of long-term use of soy isoflavones has not been established. Soy's possible role in breast cancer risk is uncertain. Until more is known about soy's effect on estrogen levels, women who have or who are at increased risk of developing breast cancer or other hormone-sensitive conditions (such as ovarian or uterine cancer) should be particularly careful about using soy and should discuss it with their health care providers.

St. John's Wort

Uses: Short-term treatment of mild to moderate depression. Although some studies have reported benefits for more severe depression, others have not; for example, a large study sponsored by NCCAM found that the herb was no more effective than placebo in treating minor, moderate, or major depression.

Cautions: Can cause photosensitivity, particularly in fair-skinned individuals; contraindicated when other antidepressants are used. Other side effects can include anxiety, dry mouth, dizziness, gastrointestinal symptoms, fatigue, headache, or sexual dysfunction. Can interact with antidepressants, birth control pills, cyclosporine, digoxin, indinavir (and possibly other drugs used to control HIV infection), irinotecan (and possibly other drugs used to treat cancer), seizure-control drugs (e.g., dilantin and phenobarbital), and warfarin and related anticoagulants.

Valerian

Use: Sedative, but there is not enough evidence from well-designed studies to confirm this. Safe to use for short periods of time (4 to 6 weeks).

Caution: Can cause mild side effects, such as headaches, dizziness, upset stomach, and tiredness the morning after its use. Do not use with barbiturates.

Homeopathy remained popular in other parts of the world, however, and recently has regained popularity in our country.

The origin of the word *homeopathy* helps in understanding this therapy. In Greek, the word *homos* means "similar," and *pathos* means "suffering." At the foundation of homeopathy are the laws of *similars*, the *minimum dose*, and *cure* (Box 11-3).

Although the reason for their effectiveness is not fully understood, homeopathic remedies have been shown to be effective for a variety of conditions. People use homeopathy for a range of health concerns, from wellness promotion and disease prevention to the treatment of diseases and conditions such as allergies, asthma, chronic fatigue syndrome, depression, digestive disorders, ear infections, headaches, and skin rashes (NCCAM, 2014b).

The ideal way to use homeopathic remedies is to have a homeopath prescribe a customized remedy based on individual characteristics and symptoms. However, homeopathic practitioners are not plentiful, so the next best thing is to buy over-the-counter preparations that are labeled for their intended purpose (e.g., arthritis, headache, hay fever, cold).

Hypnotherapy

Although the use of trance states for healing purposes dates back to primitive cultures, hypnotherapy was not approved as a valid medical treatment until the 1950s. This mind-body therapy is now widely and successfully used for a wide range of conditions, including chronic pain, migraines, asthma, smoking cessation, and irritable bowel syndrome.

The process of hypnosis begins by the therapist guiding the client into a relaxed state and then creating an image that focuses attention to the specific symptom or problem that needs to be improved. The client must be in a state of deep relaxation to be receptive to a posthypnotic suggestion. Most people are capable of being hypnotized if they are willing.

Imagery

Imagery is the process of creating a "picture" (image) in the mind that can cause a specific bodily response. Although hypnosis uses imagery, in hypnosis an image and suggestion are presented to the person, whereas in imagery the person creates an image on his or her own. The process of imagery begins by the client establishing a desired outcome (e.g., to relieve stress, enhance circulation, reduce blood pressure). The nurse or other practitioner assists the client in creating an image that helps to achieve the outcome (e.g., the nurse may describe how the blood circulates through the body, help the client develop an image of how cancer cells can be eliminated, or suggest that the client think of a peaceful place where cares can "melt away") and guides the client in reaching a relaxed state. As an alternative to having someone guide him or her through an imagery exercise, a client can learn the process from books or use commercially prepared audiotapes.

Imagery is not a difficult mind-body healing therapy to master and can be easily implemented in virtually every practice setting.

BOX 11-3   Principles Underlying Homeopathy

Law of similars: This law builds on the idea of prescribing remedies that produce symptoms similar to those of the illness being treated. This is the same principle on which vaccines are based. In homeopathy, a dilute preparation is made from a plant or other biologic material; the more dilute the preparation, the higher its potency. The solution typically is added to a sugar tablet or powder for oral use or to a lotion or ointment for external use.

Law of minimum dose: This law, also known as the *principle of dilutions,* states that the lower the dosage of the substance, the greater its effectiveness. In preparing homeopathic remedies, substances are diluted and shaken vigorously; a portion of that substance is then diluted and shaken. This procedure is repeated to the point that the final substance is so dilute that no molecules of the original plant or substance remain. This process, referred to as *potentization,* is believed to transmit some form of information or energy from the original substance to the final diluted remedy. It is believed that the substance has left its imprint or "essence," which stimulates the body to heal itself (this theory is called the "memory of water").

Law of cure: This is the principle used to evaluate the effectiveness of a remedy. If the treatment is successful, symptoms should travel from vital to less vital organs of the body, move from within the body outward, and disappear in reverse order of appearance. If symptoms do not follow this sequence, a new or additional treatment is used. In homeopathic medicine, a worsening of symptoms after a remedy is given is considered a positive sign that healing is taking place.

Magnet Therapy

Although a mainstream therapy in Germany and Japan, the use of magnets has only recently become popular in the United States. The most common uses of magnet therapy are for pain and wound healing.

The mechanism by which magnets work is not completely understood and is being investigated. It is believed that magnets relieve pain by creating a slight electrical current that stimulates the nervous system and consequently blocks nerve sensations. Magnets are hypothesized to speed wound healing by dilating vessels and increasing circulation to an area. Distributors of magnet products make additional claims about the health benefits of magnets, ranging from improving attention deficit disorder to boosting the immune system, although these benefits are yet to be proved.

Magnets come in a variety of forms, strengths, and prices. There are magnet disks that can be strapped to limbs, magnet mattresses that one can sleep on, and magnet jewelry. To be effective for therapeutic purposes, the magnet should have a strength of at least 500 gauss (which is about eight times stronger than the magnets used for attaching things to your refrigerator door).

Preliminary scientific studies of magnets for pain have produced mixed results (NCCAM, 2014c). Overall, there is no convincing scientific evidence to support claims that magnets can relieve pain of any type.

Some studies, including a recent National Institutes of Health (NIH) clinical trial for back pain, suggest the possibility of a small benefit from using magnets for pain. However, the majority of rigorous studies have found no effect on pain. More research on magnets for pain is needed before reaching any firm conclusion.

Persons with pacemakers should not use magnets, and, because the effects of magnets on fetal growth are not fully understood, they should not be applied to the abdomen of a pregnant woman.

Massage, Bodywork, and Energy Therapies

Massage for healing purposes has been used for thousands of years to maintain health. Many people today receive regular massages as an important component of their self-care to aid in stress management. In addition to promoting relaxation, massage can be beneficial for reducing edema, promoting circulation and respirations, and relieving pain, anxiety, and depression.

Massage is the manipulation of soft tissue by rubbing, kneading, rolling, pressing, slapping, and tapping movements. The term *bodywork* is applied to the combination of massage with deep-tissue manipulation, movement awareness, and energy balancing. Touch therapies include techniques in which the hands of the nurse or therapist are near the body, in the client's energy field. Examples of various types of massage, bodywork, and touch therapies are described in Box 11-4.

BOX 11-4   Types of Massage, Bodywork, and Touch Therapies

Alexander Technique
Teaches improved balanced, posture, and coordination by using gentle hands-on guidance and verbal instruction

Feldenkrais Method
Teaches movement re-education by using gentle manipulations to heighten awareness of the body; believes each person has an individualized optimal style of movement

Healing Touch
A multilevel energy healing program that incorporates aspects of therapeutic touch with other healing measures

Reflexology
Application of pressure to pressure points on the hands and feet that correspond to various parts of the body

Reiki
A therapy that uses techniques to direct universal life energy to specific sites

Rolfing (Structural Integration)
Use of manual manipulation and stretching of body's fascial tissues to establish balance and symmetry

Swedish Massage
Most prevalent form of massage that uses long strokes, friction, and kneading of muscles

Trager Approach
Use of gentle, rhythmic rocking and touch to promote relaxation and energy flow

Because therapeutic touch (TT) is a popular alternative healing therapy among nurses, it deserves some discussion. TT became popular in nursing in the 1970s with the work and research of Delores Krieger (Krieger, 1979; Nurse Healers Professional Associates, 2014). Krieger advanced the theory that people are energy fields and that obstructed energy could be responsible for unhealthy states. She proposed that the nurse could draw on the universal field of energy and transfer this energy to the client. This incoming energy could help the client mobilize his or her own inner resources for healing and help unblock the client's obstructed energy.

In TT, there is little direct physical contact between the practitioner and the individual being treated. Rather, TT is an energy-based therapy; the nurse enters the client's energy field to assess and treat energy imbalances.

In the first step of TT, the nurse centers herself or himself and focuses on the intent to heal (this is sometimes referred to as *healing meditation*). During this phase, the nurse quiets the mind and prepares physically and psychologically to connect with the client. This is considered a crucial step in the process to enable the nurse to be fully present in the moment with the client. This is followed by the nurse passing his or her hands over the client's body to assess the energy field and mobilizing areas in which energy is blocked or sluggish by directing energies to that area. TT is used to reduce anxiety, relieve pain, and enhance immune function.

Healing touch (HT) is an energy therapy that is an offshoot of TT. It combines additional healing approaches to the basic ones of TT to open energy blockages, seal energy leaks, and rebalance the energy field. There is a six-level educational program for HT. The Healing Touch International website (http://www.healingtouchinternational.org/) offers a full description of their program in addition to a bibliography of recent research related to this therapy.

Reiki is a practice in which the Reiki practitioner (of which there are several levels) channels energy to others using a series of hand positions. It is believed that healing energy flows through the hands without the need for any special skills. Like other forms of energy work, Reiki is believed to be useful for pain management, wound healing, stroke rehabilitation, and general relaxation; however, research is insufficient to suggest that Reiki is an effective treatment for any condition. Despite the limited research supporting its effectiveness (Lee et al, 2008), the low risk of side effects, affordability,

and desire of a person to utilize this therapy makes an ethical case for its use (Ferraresa et al, 2013).

With the use of healing energy therapies, nurses need to be aware that some individuals may feel spiritual distress if they receive healing energy because they may be concerned about what and who the source of the energy is. For example, a Christian who believes that healing comes directly from Jesus Christ may react negatively to receiving healing energy that is drawn from a vague universal force. Assessing spiritual beliefs, explaining the therapy clearly, and obtaining consent before offering the treatment are useful.

Meditation and Progressive Relaxation

Meditation, the act of focusing on the present moment, has been used for centuries throughout the world. This practice gained considerable attention in the United States in the 1970s when Harvard Medical School cardiologist Herbert Benson published research on the relaxation response (Benson and Beary, 1974). Benson reported that after 20 minutes of meditation, participants' heart rates, respirations, blood pressure, oxygen consumption, carbon dioxide production, and serum lactic acid levels decreased. This led to meditation being used for a variety of conditions, including stress, anxiety, pain, and high blood pressure.

Progressive relaxation is another exercise that shares some of the same benefits as meditation. Typically a person learns to guide himself or herself through a series of exercises that relax the body, such as tightening and relaxing various muscle groups. Many audiotapes are available in bookstores and health food stores that offer scripts to guide meditation and progressive relaxation exercises.

Naturopathy

An intense interest in natural cures in Europe during the nineteenth century led to the development of spas that offered natural treatments to promote health and healing. Soon the movement spread to the United States, and in 1896 the American School of Naturopathy was founded. Naturopathic physicians and treatment facilities using natural cures became popular in the early part of the twentieth century. For example, John Kellogg ran such a facility in Battle Creek in which he subsequently became famous for the natural breakfast cereals that he used. As time progressed, medications and high-tech interventions caused naturopathy to pale by comparison; however, as consumers seek more natural approaches, this form of alternative medicine is making a comeback.

Naturopathy is based on the principle that the body has inherent healing abilities that can be stimulated to treat disease. Naturopathic physicians assess and treat the cause of the disease rather than merely alleviate symptoms. They help clients identify unhealthy practices, encourage healthy lifestyle habits, and guide them in managing health problems using natural approaches, such as herbs, homeopathic remedies, diet modifications, dietary supplements, and exercise.

There are a limited number of accredited schools of naturopathic medicine (e.g., Bastyr University, Southwest College of Naturopathic Medicine and Health Sciences, and National College of Naturopathic Medicine). A handful of states license naturopaths and require that they must have graduated from an accredited program. However, there are many individuals practicing as naturopaths who have obtained their education and experience through other means or who practice in states that do not require licensure; thus learning about the credentials of a naturopath before receiving services is beneficial for clients.

Prayer and Faith

Many people consider their faith to be an integral part of their total being rather than a therapy, but now there is scientific evidence supporting the therapeutic benefits of faith and prayer in health and healing. Hundreds of well-conducted studies have revealed that people who profess a faith, pray, and attend religious services are generally healthier, live longer, have lower rates of disability, recover faster, have lower rates of emotional disorders, and otherwise enjoy better health states than those who do not (Barnum, 2006; O'Brien, 2007; Tuck and Anderson 2014; University of Maryland Medical Center, 2011). Not only do the faith and religious practices of individuals themselves affect health and healing, but research also supports the benefit of intercessory prayer.

Nurses need to appreciate that many people believe in the healing power of prayer and may expect their health care providers to join them in prayer if requested. This does not suggest that nurses or other health professionals should be forced into prayer if it is contrary to their beliefs; rather, if there is no objection from either party, prayer by the client and health care provider can be used as a valuable healing measure.

Tai Chi

Tai chi is another practice from traditional Chinese medicine used to stimulate the flow of qi, the life energy. It is a combination of exercise and energy work that looks like a slow, graceful dance using continuous, controlled movements of the arms and legs. There is a specific sequence of steps to follow in doing tai chi, but fortunately there are many inexpensive videos that can be used, in addition to classes that are offered to aid people in learning this practice.

Tai chi has some demonstrated benefits, including reduction of falls, improved coordination in older adults, and improved function in persons with arthritis (Adler and Roberts, 2006; Jahnke et al, 2010; NCCAM, 2014d; Yang et al, 2014). Many people find that tai chi helps to reduce stress and promotes a general sense of well-being.

Yoga

Yoga has changed from a mystical form of Hindu worship practiced more than 5000 years ago to what is now known as a system of exercises involving various postures, meditation, and deep breathing. The word *yoga* means "union"; the union of body, mind, and spirit is achieved through yoga. Research suggests that yoga has many beneficial effects, such as reducing stress, improving mood and sense of well-being, decreasing heart rate and blood pressure, increasing lung capacity, improving flexibility, and promoting relaxation (NCCAM, 2014e). Yoga can be adapted to any level and capability so that it can be easily used.

There are many other alternative healing modalities, and new ones are appearing regularly. Some may be safe and effective but lack sufficient experience or clinical research to support their claims; others may be worthless and merely an attempt to sell a product or service. Discretion is crucial. Assistance in gaining objective information regarding CAM therapies can be obtained from the NCCAM website (www. nccam.nih. gov) or by calling 1-888-644-6226.

NURSING AND COMPLEMENTARY AND ALTERNATIVE MEDICINE THERAPIES

A Holistic Approach

The use of natural or "alternative" healing measures is hardly new to nursing. From Florence Nightingale (1860), who wrote about the importance of creating an environment in which natural healing could occur, through contemporary nurse theorists who discuss human and environmental energy fields (Hover-Kramer, 2011; Meleis, 2006; Rogers, 1975), nurses have long realized that healing quite effectively occurs in ways not encompassed within the conventional biomedical system. Nursing also has promoted many of the same principles evident in CAM, particularly care of the body, mind, and spirit. In fact, this is the essence of holistic nursing (Box 11-5). Nurses must ensure that the integration of CAM into their practice is done within a holistic paradigm to truly make them healing therapies and not merely disconnected procedures within an already fragmented health care system.

Facilitating Use of Complementary and Alternative Medicine

Nurses need to integrate CAM into their nursing practice. This begins during the assessment process by

exploring clients' use of CAM practices and products. Because it is not unusual for clients to use these without the knowledge of their physicians, nurses may be the first health professional with whom clients have discussed this issue. Factors to assess include the following:

- CAM practices and products being used and their sources
- Appropriateness of use of CAM practices and products
- Side effects and risks associated with use of CAM
- Conditions for which CAM currently is not used that could benefit by its use

Through the assessment process, nurses may identify the need to educate clients about the appropriateness of the CAM products and practices they are using. For example, a client with a pacemaker who uses magnets needs to be advised against continuing this practice; likewise, a client who drinks ginseng tea at bedtime requires an explanation that his insomnia may be the result of the stimulant effects of the herb. There may be situations in which nurses identify that specific conditions could benefit from the use of CAM therapies. As client advocates, nurses could bring this to the attention of the physician and other members of the health care team and make recommendations accordingly.

Nurses traditionally have been responsible for the coordination of client care. As CAM therapies are integrated into conventional care, nurses are the logical professionals to oversee the various parts and ensure that they are working in harmony for the client's benefit.

Nurses can learn to use many alternative healing measures to enhance nursing care. Among these are acupressure, aromatherapy, biofeedback, imagery, massage, and therapeutic touch. Nurses should seek whatever additional education and training are required to gain competency in these therapies and ensure compliance with state licensing laws.

Integrating Complementary and Alternative Medicine Into Conventional Settings

Nurses can demonstrate leadership in helping conventional clinical settings integrate CAM therapies. In fact, nursing's holistic orientation and traditional coordination responsibilities make nurses logical for this role. Let us look at the way in which one nurse accomplished this (Case Study 11-1).

BOX 11-5   Beliefs Guiding Holistic Nursing Practice

- The uniqueness of each individual is honored.
- Health is a harmonious balance of body, mind, and spirit.
- The needs of individuals' bodies, minds, and spirits are assessed and addressed in the caregiving process.
- Health and disease are natural parts of the human experience.
- Disease is an opportunity for increased awareness of the interconnectiveness of body, mind, and spirit.
- Individuals have the capacity for self-healing; the nurse facilitates this process.
- Nurses empower individuals for self-care.
- Individuals' cultural values, beliefs, and practices are honored and incorporated into the caregiving process.
- Individuals have a dynamic relationship with their environment; the environment is part of the healing process.
- Nurses, through their presence and being, are tools of the healing process.
- Nurses engage in self-care and an ongoing process of unfolding inner wisdom.
- Nurses can learn about holistic nursing and network with holistic nurses through involvement in the American Holistic Nurses Association; learn more by visiting the AHNA website (www.ahna.org).

CASE STUDY 11-1

Becky Blake, RN, recently joined the nursing staff in a combined coronary care and step-down unit. It did not take her long to note the expert technical skill of her colleagues, who could read monitors in a flash and respond to emergencies without missing a beat. The skill, efficiency, and organization of the nursing staff were evidenced by the lack of medication errors, infections, and pressure ulcers, coupled with the lowest length of stays of comparable hospital units in the area.

Yet there seemed to be something missing. Clients and their families often showed signs of anxiety and fear that were not addressed. Familiar faces reappeared as some clients were re-admitted because they failed to alter lifestyle habits that contributed to their conditions. The same nursing staff who cared for people with hearts damaged by the effects of smoking, poor diet, and stress were guilty of the same unhealthy practices themselves.

It came to a head for Ms. Blake one morning when she was at a bedside changing an intravenous bag and checking equipment. The client, a man in his fifties, pulled at her arm, looked Ms. Blake in the eyes, and tearfully said, "How do you think I'm going to do? I've been awake all night wondering if I'll be able to do my job, take care of my wife, see my grandkids grow up, do the things I like to do." For the first time, Ms. Blake saw beyond the body in the bed to a human being experiencing considerable emotional distress—distress that was hardly beneficial to his condition. "We have managed to get this man's heart repaired," she thought, "but we have not begun to help him heal the emotional and spiritual pain that this illness created." This began a journey for Ms. Blake of discovering measures to help clients that went beyond the conventional treatments that were regularly prescribed.

Ms. Blake found a local network of holistic nurses and began attending their meetings. Through this group, she learned of the difference between healing and curing and the importance of addressing the needs of body, mind, and spirit. She also heard nurses discussing their own need to be nurtured and committed to positive self-care practices. She met nurses who shared how they were using alternative healing practices and who led her to resources from which she could learn more.

In the months that followed, Ms. Blake attended several workshops and learned how progressive relaxation, meditation, therapeutic touch, and aromatherapy could be used to benefit the clients on her unit. As her understanding of holism grew, she recognized that stress reduction and improved health habits for her coworkers were sorely needed.

After planting seeds through informal discussions and sharing of articles, Ms. Blake requested a formal meeting with the interdisciplinary team on the unit. In this meeting, she described her areas of concern, which included the need to:

- Address clients' emotional and spiritual needs more effectively.
- Promote improved health habits of the staff.
- Develop practices that would reduce stress for clients, their families, and staff.

The staff concurred with these needs and expressed a desire to take actions to address them. Ms. Blake offered some suggestions:

- Coordinate with the staff development instructor to have classes offered on progressive relaxation, imagery, meditation, therapeutic touch, and stress reduction.
- Form an ad hoc committee to develop guidelines, policies, and procedures on how these healing therapies could be safely and legally implemented.
- Begin to include healing therapies into the care plans.
- Arrange for the nutritionist to offer classes to staff on healthy eating.
- Add healthy snacks to the break room.
- Coordinate with the housekeeping and maintenance departments to introduce aromatherapy diffusers, plants, and piped-in music in the unit.
- Develop a system to remind staff to use stress reduction measures throughout their shift.
- Collaborate with the nutritionist, social worker, spiritual care counselor, and nursing clinical resources to provide group sessions for clients and their families on topics such as coping with illness, stress management, and promoting healthy lifestyle habits.
- Request the quality improvement coordinator to monitor and evaluate the effect of these interventions.

It did not take long for the effects of these new approaches to be realized. Clients requested fewer sedatives and analgesics. Surveys of clients and families revealed higher levels of satisfaction. Staff sick days were reduced, and there seemed to be a greater sense of team spirit and cooperation. Soon staff in other parts of the hospital began requesting that similar interventions be implemented in their units.

Using Complementary and Alternative Medicine Competently

As increasing numbers of consumers and clinical settings are interested in or actually using CAM therapies, nurses are challenged to become knowledgeable about the uses, limitations, and precautions associated with these new practices and products. Maintaining a resource library and becoming familiar with websites to stay current are beneficial measures.

Nurses must become familiar with cultural factors that can influence acceptance and use of alternative healing practices. For instance, some individuals may object to energy therapies (e.g., TT, HT) on the grounds that they associate these therapies with occult practices, or they may have anxiety about meditation because they believe evil spirits could invade their minds. As comforting as a massage can be, some people who come from cultures that believe it is inappropriate to touch a person of the opposite sex could become distressed with this measure. Knowledge and sensitivity to personal and cultural preferences are essential.

Legal Considerations

The use of CAM could present some legal issues for which nurses need to be concerned. As growing numbers of practitioners of healing therapies advocate for recognition and separate licensure, some of the healing therapies once considered part of nursing care may require separate licensure. Such is the case with massage. In some states, nurses may not provide a massage unless they are licensed as massage therapists. Acupressure and biofeedback are among the other areas in which the nurse could be challenged if not licensed. Nurses need to clarify the therapies that fall within the realm of nursing practice and take a proactive role in ensuring that other disciplines do not attempt to limit them.

Another legal concern for nurses in the growing arena of CAM is the question of to whom the nurse is responsible when practicing CAM therapies. New, nonconventional practice settings are developing. For example, a nurse may be employed in a setting in which there is an acupuncturist, hypnotherapist, and homeopath. Some questions that could arise include: Who supervises the nurse? Can these therapists delegate responsibilities to the nurse? How does the nurse ensure that in such a practice setting diagnoses are not being made or treatments being prescribed that are beyond the scope of the CAM practitioners? Nurses need to begin to consider the implications of new practice models and develop clear practice guidelines that ensure a legally sound practice.

SUMMARY

An opportunity exists for nursing to demonstrate leadership in the integration of CAM with conventional care. Representing the largest number of health care professionals, nurses can have a significant effect on implementing CAM throughout the health care system. Nurses' historical holistic orientation to care enables them to ensure that the integration of CAM and conventional services is done in a manner that addresses the client's body, mind, and spirit. Without such coordinated efforts, there is the risk that these new therapies will merely be additional ingredients in an already fragmented system of care. Nurses have shown that they can coordinate and promote comprehensive care like no other discipline. Therefore, nursing is the logical discipline to be the hub of the wheel of integrative services.

REFERENCES

Adler PA, Roberts BL: The use of tai chi to improve health in older adults, *Orthop Nurs* 25(2):122–126, 2006.

Ahadian FM, Braun JC, Schulteis G: Quantitative assessment of acupuncture analgesia using a human experimental pain model: a randomized, crossover pilot study, *Med Acupunct* 17(3):12–15, 2006.

Altizer KP, Nguyen HT, Neiberg RH, Quandt SA, Grzywacz JG, et al: Relationship between nonprescribed therapy use for illness prevention and health promotion and health-related quality of life, *Journal Appl Gerontol* 33(4): 456–473, 2014.

American Society of Anesthesiologists Task Force on Chronic Pain Management: Practice guidelines for chronic pain management: an updated report by the American

Society of Anesthesiologists Task Force on Chronic Pain Management and the American Society of Regional Anesthesia and Pain Medicine, *Anesthesiology* 112(4): 810–833, 2010.

Barnum B: *Spirituality in nursing*, ed 2, New York, 2006, Springer.

Benson H, Beary JZ: The relaxation response, *Psychiatry* 37(1):37–46, 1974.

Berman BM, Langevin HM, Witt CM, et al: Acupuncture for chronic low back pain, *N Engl J Med* 363:454–461, 2010.

Consumer Reports: Vitamins and supplements: 10 dangers that may surprise you, *Consumer Reports* 77(9):18–23, 2012.

Ferraresi M, Clari R, Banino E, Boero E, Crosio A, et al: Reiki and related therapies in the dialysis ward: an evidence-based and ethical discussion to debate if these complementary and alternative medicines are welcomed or banned, *BMC Nephrology* 14:129, 2013. http://www.biomedcentral.com/1471-2369/14/129. Accessed August 9, 2015.

Guallar E, Stranges S, Mulrow C, Appel LJ, Miller ER: Enough is enough: Stop wasting money on vitamin and mineral supplements, *Annals of Internal Medicine* 160(2):850–851, 2013.

Haigh C: Acupuncture reduced frequency and pain intensity of primary migraine or tension-type headaches, *Evid Based Nurs* 12(2):47, 2009.

Hover-Kramer D: *Healing touch: Essential energy medicine for yourself and others.* Boulder CO, 2011, Sounds True.

Huang HY, Cabalerro B, Chang S, et al: The efficacy and safety of multivitamin and mineral supplement use to prevent cancer and chronic disease in adults: a systematic review for a National Institutes of Health State-of-the-Science Conference, *Ann Intern Med* 145(5):372–385, 2006.

Jahnke R, Larkey L, Rogers C, et al: A comprehensive review of health benefits of qigong and tai chi, *Am J Health Promot* 24(6):e1–e25, 2010.

Koog YH, Lee JS, Wi H: Clinically meaningful nocebo effect occurs in acupuncture treatment: A systematic review, *Journal of Clinical Epidemiology (Online)*. April 25, 2014. http://www.jclinepi.com/article/S0895-4356(14)00089-4/abstract. Accessed August 9, 2015.

Krieger D: *The therapeutic touch*, Englewood Cliffs, NJ, 1979, Prentice-Hall.

Last AR, Hulbert K: Chronic low back pain: evaluation and management, *Am Fam Physician* 79(12):1067–1074, 2009.

Lee MS, Pittler MH, Ernst E: Effects of reiki in clinical practice: a systematic review of randomized clinical trials, *Int J Clin Pract* 62(6):947–954, 2008.

Meleis AI: *Theoretical nursing: development and progress*, ed 4, Philadelphia, 2006, Lippincott.

National Center for Complementary and Alternative Medicine: *The use of complementary and alternative medicine in the United States*, 2014a, (website). http://nccam.nih.gov/news/camstats/2007/camsurvey_fs1.htm. Accessed June 2014.

National Center for Complementary and Alternative Medicine: *Homeopathy: an introduction*, 2014b. http://nccam.nih.gov/health/homeopathy/. Accessed June 2014.

National Center for Complementary and Alternative Medicine: *Magnets for pain*, 2014c. http://nccam.nih.gov/health/magnet/magnetsforpain.htm. Accessed June 2014.

National Center for Complementary and Alternative Medicine: *Tai chi*, 2014d. http://nccam.nih.gov/health/taichi/introduction.htm. Accessed June 2014.

National Center for Complementary and Alternative Medicine: *Yoga for health*, 2014e. http://nccam.nih.gov/health/yoga/introduction.htm. Accessed June 2014.

Niemtzow RC: Medical acupuncture: Past, present, and future. *Medical Acupuncture* 26(6):371–372, 2013.

Nightingale F: *Notes on nursing*, London, 1860, Harrison.

Nurse Healers Professional Associates: *TT facts*, 2011. http://therapeutic-touch.org/int-contacts/tt-facts/. Accessed May 2014.

O'Brien ME: *Spirituality in nursing: standing on holy ground*, ed 3, Sudbury, MA, 2007, Jones & Bartlett.

PDR Staff: *PDR for Nonprescription Drugs, Dietary Supplements, and Herbs*, ed 34, Houston, TX, 2013, PDR Network.

Pharmaceutical Press Editorial: *Herbal Medicines*, ed 4. Gurnee, IL, 2013, Pharmceutical Press.

Rogers M: *An introduction to the theoretical basis for nursing*, ed 3, Philadelphia, 1975, FA Davis.

Selva O, Martinez Z, Sola I, Stojanovic Z, Urinona T, Bonfill C: Efficacy and safety of needle acupuncture for treating gynecologic and obstetric disorders: An overview, *Medical Acupuncture* 25(6):386–397, 2013.

Thomson Healthcare: *PDR for herbal medicines*, ed 4, Montvale, NJ, 2007, Thomson Reuters.

Tuck I, Anderson L: Forgiveness, flourishing, and resilience: the influence of expressions of spirituality on mental health recovery, *Issues in Mental Health Nursing* 35(4):277–282, 2014.

University of Maryland Medical Center: *Spirituality*, 2011. http://www.umm.edu/altmed/articles/spirituality-000360.htm. Accessed August 5, 2011.

Wang SM, Dezinno P, Lin EC, et al: Auricular acupuncture as a treatment for pregnant women who have low back and posterior pelvic pain: a pilot study, *Am J Obstet Gynecol* 201(3):271, 2009.

Whitworth A: Micronutrients: to supplement, or not to supplement? *J Natl Cancer Inst* 98(4):230–232, 2006.

Yang G, Wang L, Zhang Y, Liu J: Clinical research evidence of tai chi: a systematic literature review, *Journal of Alternative and Complementary Medicine* 20(5):A62–70, 2014.

ADDITIONAL RESOURCES

Ali A, Scoulios N, Ten N, Kanodia A: A national assessment of the usage, cost, and reimbursement of unconventional medical laboratory tests, *Journal of Alternative and Complementary Medicine* 20(5):A3–A4, 2014.

Balch J, Stengler M: *Prescription for natural cures: a self-care guide for treating health problems with natural remedies including diet, nutrition, supplements, and other holistic methods*, Hoboken, NJ, 2011, Wiley.

Bauml J, Xie S, Farrar J, Bruner, Stricker CD, Bowman M, DeMichele A, Mao J: Expectancy in real and sham acupuncture: Does believing make it so? *The Journal of Alternative and Complementary Medicine* 20(5):A9, 2014.

Bauer R: *Mayo Clinic guide to alternative medicine*, ed 2, New York, 2010, Time.

Caspi O, Baranovitch O: When science meets medical tradition: what is needed for a dialogue on integrative medicine? *J Altern Complement Med* 15(5):579–583, 2009.

Conners MS, Altshuler L: *The everything guide to herbal remedies*, Avon, MA, 2009, Adams Media.

Elder CR: Integrating naturopathy: Can we move forward? *Permanente Journal* 17(4):80–83, 2013.

Eliopoulos C: *Invitation to holistic health: a guide to living a balanced life*, ed 3, Boston, 2014, Jones & Bartlett.

Fontaine KL: *Complementary & alternative therapies for nursing practice*, ed 3, Upper Saddle River, NJ, 2010, Prentice Hall.

Furlan A, van Tulder MW, Cherkin DC, et al: Acupuncture and dry-needling for low back pain, *Cochrane Database Syst Rev* 25(1):CD001351, 2005.

Kabat-Zinn J: *Coming to our senses: healing ourselves and the world through mindfulness*, New York, 2006, Hyperion.

Kalauokalani D, Cherkin DC, Sherman KJ: A comparison of physician and nonphysician acupuncture treatment for chronic low back pain, *Clin J Pain* 21(5):406–411, 2005.

Kawas CW: Medications and diet: protective factors for AD? *Alzheimer Dis Assoc Disord* 20(Suppl 2):S89–S96, 2006.

Kotskirilos V, Vietta L, Sali A: *A guide to evidence-based integrative and complementary medicine*, New York, 2011, Churchill Livingstone.

Lim CY, Takano A, Yang S, Lee P: Ayurvedic medicine and the lung, *Respiration* 87(5):428–431, 2014.

Lind BK, Diehr PK, Grembowski DE, et al: Chiropractic use by urban and rural residents with insurance coverage, *J Rural Health* 25(3):253–258, 2009.

Mantle F, Tiran D: *A–Z of complementary and alternative medicine: a guide for health professionals*, New York, 2009, Churchill Livingstone.

Micozzi MS: *Fundamentals of complementary and alternative medicine*, St Louis, 2011, Saunders.

National Center for Complementary and Alternative Medicine: *Herbs at a glance*. http://nccam.nih.gov/health/herbsataglance.htm. Accessed August 2011.

Patz S: Holistic assessment person centered care, *Beginnings* 34(1):10–11 , 2014.

Schiller C, Schiller D: *The aromatherapy encyclopedia*, Laguna Beach, CA, 2009, Basic Health Publications.

Selin H, editor: *Medicine across cultures: history and practice of medicine in non-Western cultures (Science across cultures: the history of non-Western science)*, Norwell, MA, 2010, Kluwer.

Sublet CM: Adding to the evidence base: streamlining biofeedback for urge incontinence, *Urol Nursing* 34(1):27–28, 2014.

Xu J, Murray F: *Magic needles: feel younger and live longer with acupuncture*, Laguna Beach, CA, 2011, Basic Health Publications.

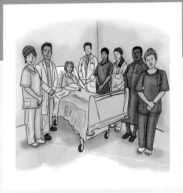

12

Palliative care: A team concept.

Palliative Care

Jeri Ashley, MSN, RN, AOCNS, CHPN,
Patricia R. Keene, DNP, ACNP-BC, ACHPN

ⓔ Additional resources are available online at: *http://evolve.elsevier.com/Cherry/*

PROFESSIONAL/ETHICAL ISSUE

Mrs. P. is an 85-year-old widowed female admitted to the hospital with end-stage Parkinson's disease, which was diagnosed 5 years ago. Her family reports that she has had three falls in the past 2 weeks and during the past 6 months has lost 20 pounds. The weight loss is more than a 10% body weight loss. She scores 40% on the Palliative Performance Scale and was recently diagnosed with right lower lobe pneumonia. The family states that she is having difficulty communicating her needs and is having dysphagia. It was thought that her recent pneumonia was secondary to aspiration. Two of her daughters want to start enteral feedings via a percutaneous endoscopic gastrostomy tube. When asked about advance directives, the family reports that she does not have any. A third daughter indicates that she would not want artificial nutrition and that they had talked about it. The other two daughters are concerned that she will starve to death.

As the RN on the palliative care team, what steps will you take to help the family come to consensus about whether or not to provide artificial nutrition?

Schwarz and Tarzian (2009) demonstrate a method of analyzing situations that are ethically challenging. (See Table 12-1.)

VIGNETTE

Christine Glover is a 32-year-old divorced female who has been undergoing aggressive cancer chemotherapy for 4 years. Her physician has just informed her that her disease continues to spread in spite of these therapies. He tells her that there are two primary options: a Phase I clinical trial or hospice care. She longs to see her young children settled in with her parents before she dies, but she suffers with constant pain, intermittent nausea, and gravitates between anxiety and deep periods of depression, which she hides as best as she can from her family. She struggles between the two options of care, but doesn't know what questions to ask related to treatment. How does she tell her children? How does she prepare her parents for the role of parenting their grandchildren? How can she prepare herself for what lies ahead? She feels the depression enveloping her again.

Questions to Consider While Reading this Chapter
1. What patient experiences have you had related to serious illness?
2. What do you think is important to include in serious illness/end-of-life discussions?
3. Have you considered how you would like to live during serious illness?
4. Have you completed your advance directive?
5. How can nursing research affect end-of-life care?

KEY TERMS

Advance care plan: A process for eliciting a patient's values and preferences concerning current and future health care decisions. This plan is used to establish a patient's goals of care during serious illness.

Advance directive: A document in which a person with decision-making capacity gives permission about future medical care and/or designates the person to make decisions for him/her if decision-making capacity is impaired or lost.

Cost avoidance: These are the savings in total costs per admission or per day saved by hospitals when palliative care consultations are implemented.

Decision-making capacity: The ability of one to make decisions about their health care. They must be able to understand the facts, appreciate the alternatives that may exist, and to communicate these decisions to the health care team.

Disease trajectory: The decline that is seen as a particular disease progresses.

Double effect: In the care of seriously ill and dying patients, the intent of any treatment is to relieve pain and suffering—not to hasten the patient's death; however, the patient's death is a foreseeable potential effect of the treatment. An example would be escalating doses of morphine to relieve a patient's pain with the double effect of depressing respirations, resulting in death.

End-of-Life Nursing Education Consortium (ELNEC): A national project funded by the Robert Wood Johnson Foundation.

Foreseeing: The use of subjective and objective data to predict a patient's disease trajectory.

Foretelling: The gathering and integration of information about disease trajectory that reflects the complete medical condition versus a single disease.

Hospice care: This is not only a type of care but also a philosophy of care that focuses on comfort for the patient and family at the end of life. It includes management of physical emotional, and spiritual needs. Care is provided by a team that includes a physician, nurse practitioner, nurse, social worker, nursing assistant, chaplain, and a volunteer.

Informed consent: Permission given by a patient or caregiver to treat a medical condition with understanding of the risks/benefits of a medical procedure, costs that may accrue, and alternative therapies.

Interprofessional team: A group of professionals that work together to provide comprehensive care to the patient/family. Members of the team may include physician, nurse practitioner, nurse, social worker, chaplain, and nursing assistant.

Palliative care: Care that seeks to improve the quality of life of patients who are facing serious illness. It includes pain and symptom management and support by a team in making health care decisions.

Patient Self Determination Act (PSDA): A federal law that requires health care institutions to give patients a copy of their decision-making rights, determine if the patient has advance directives, and assist them in completing them. The PSDA promotes patients making their own decisions about the health care they want to receive or refuse.

Prognostication: A physician's prediction about the course and outcome of a disease, often made with consideration of survival, symptoms, function, and quality of life with or without treatment.

Withdrawing treatments: This is the removal of a life-sustaining treatment that has already been instituted.

Withholding treatments: This is abstaining from beginning a life-sustaining treatment.

LEARNING OUTCOMES

After studying this chapter, the reader will be able to:

1. Describe the palliative care model and its effectiveness today.

2. Summarize the key elements and issues of palliative care.

3. Integrate palliative care knowledge and skills into the professional nursing role.

CHAPTER OVERVIEW

"Someone should tell us, right at the start of our lives that we are dying. Then we might live life to the limit, every minute of every day. Do it! I say. Whatever you want to do, do it now! There are only so many tomorrows."

Pope Paul VI: Italian Pope, 1897-1978

Palliative care is one of the newest subspecialties. The focus of palliative care is to give comfort to patients with serious illness. It can begin with the diagnosis of a serious illness and continue to the death of the patient, followed by continued support provided to the family. The purpose of this chapter is to describe the benefits, barriers, and challenges of palliative care as well as to discuss the role of the palliative care nurse.

TABLE 12-1 Steps to Analyze Situations Seen as Ethically Challenging and to Explore the Context in Which These Situations Have Risen

Steps to Analyze Ethically Challenging Situations	Context of the Situation
1. Review the overall situation—identify what is going on in this case.	1. Mrs. P. has a disease that is end stage (Parkinson disease).
2. Identify the ethical dilemma(s).	2. Mrs. P. no longer has capacity and is non-verbal. There are no advance directives. Daughters are in disagreement regarding mother's wishes for health care.
3. Gather all relevant facts, about the patient and the contextual situation, including: • Significant medical and social history • Involved family • Decision-making capacity • Existence of advance directives—written, appointed, or verbal—and any pertinent institutional policies • Surrogate or health care agent if decision-making capacity is absent	3. The patient has a history of decline that began 4 years earlier, culminating to her present state. She does not have decision-making capacity. She did tell one daughter that she did not want a feeding tube.
4. Identify the parties or stakeholders involved in the situation, including those who will be affected by the decision(s) made.	4. Stakeholders include the patient and three daughters.
5. Identify relevant legal data, including both state and federal laws.	5. There is no relevant legal data.
6. Identify religious or cultural issues.	6. No religious or cultural beliefs contribute to this case.
7. Identify specific conflicts of ethical principles or values. Identify and consider nursing guidelines and the profession's code and position statements.	7. Ethical principles involved are: autonomy, beneficence, maleficence, and double effect.
8. Identify possible options, their purpose, and their probable consequences to the welfare of the patient. Identify and make use of interdisciplinary and institutional resources, including ethics committee, social workers, chaplains, and other experienced colleagues.	8. Options include feeding tube placement, artificial hydration. Risks of providing artificial nutrition and hydration (ANH) include aspiration, third spacing of fluids, diarrhea/constipation.
9. Identify practical constraints to decisions making, including institutional, legal, organizational, and economic.	9. The team recognized patient is unable to participate in the decision-making process. The daughters reported that they wanted what was best for their mother.
10. Review and evaluate the situation after action has been taken—debrief and support the staff.	10. The decision was made not to start fluids or place a feeding tube. The patient was offered food and fluids orally until she was unable to swallow. She was allowed to die a natural death.

From Schwarz, JK and Tarzian, AJ. Ethical aspects of palliative care. In Matzo M, Witt Sherman D, eds. *Palliative Care Nursing: Quality Care to the End of Life*. New York: Springer Publishing Company, 119-141, 2010.

INTRODUCTION

The world of health care is constantly changing; yet for Western health care, the growth and advancement of new and innovative treatments is mind-boggling. And with these new therapies comes an increasing emphasis on care and rehabilitation of those with serious illness. Today, we live longer; by 2030 20% of the American population will be over 65 years old (Meier et al, 2010).

A question may come to the minds of nurses: "What is the quality of this patient's life?" Hospice is the specialty of interprofessional team members who care for the patient and family who are facing end of life. This care includes aggressive pain and symptom control; affirmation of life while teaching the natural process of the dying; spiritual and psychological care and treatment of the patient and family as the unit of care. But consider the patient who faces serious illness and still has life-sustaining treatment options available. This patient might not elect hospice as a Medicare benefit because he continues to seek cure. The reality becomes that the patient continues with aggressive therapies, but needs the same intensive care that hospice provides to the seriously ill who are at life's end.

Palliative care was coined by Dr. Balfour Mount in 1974. It comes from the Latin root word *pallium*, which referred to an outer garment that cloaked a person. This suggests that palliative care "covers" or "cloaks" the symptoms of serious illness, providing comfort and relief. Palliative care recognizes the same needs, stressors, symptoms, and suffering that a hospice patient might endure but supports and enhances the best quality of life during time of diagnosis, treatment, and life with serious illness.

The World Health Organization defined palliative care in 1990:

> *"Palliative care is an approach that improves the quality of life of patients and their families facing the problem associated with life-threatening illness, through the prevention and relief of suffering by means of early identification and impeccable assessment and treatment of pain and other problems, physical, psychosocial and spiritual."* (Sepúlveda et al, 2002)

The Hospice and Palliative Nurse Association (HPNA) has developed standards of practice for registered nurses. HPNA defines a palliative nurse as one who:

- Provides age-appropriate culturally, ethically, and spiritually sensitive care and support.
- Maintains a safe environment.
- Educates patients/families to identity appropriate settings and treatment options.
- Ensures continuity of care and safe transitions to the next appropriate setting.
- Coordinates care across settings and among caregivers.
- Manages information and protects confidentiality.
- Communicates promptly and effectively.

However, nurses must recognize that the stress, suffering, and symptom burden of patients living with serious illness touches us all—in all settings and in all specialties. Stjernswärd and colleagues (2007) recognize that palliative care should be seen as a public health issue and as such all health care clinicians would do well to become palliative care generalists. As stated in the American Nurses Association *Code of Ethics for Nurses,* "Nursing care is directed toward meeting the comprehensive needs of patients and their families across the continuum of care. This is particularly vital in the care of patients and their families at the end of life to prevent and relieve the cascade of symptoms of suffering that are commonly associated with dying" (American Nurses Association, 2001). As each nurse and other health care providers increase their awareness of symptoms, stress, and suffering experienced during serious illness and gain skill in communication and distress management, patients and families will be cared for with dignity, respect and the celebration of our own humanness.

THE NATURAL COURSE OF SERIOUS ILLNESS

As a patient's health declines, decisions about care must be made. With the initial diagnosis, palliative care can help guide therapy. With disease progression to an end-stage condition, hospice is an option of care. Prior to palliative care, the care model showed disease progression and then death. The palliative care continuum model of care (Figure 12-1) begins comfort care at the time of diagnosis, where early in the disease process, therapies are aggressive but as the disease progresses comfort care increases. Included in this model is the

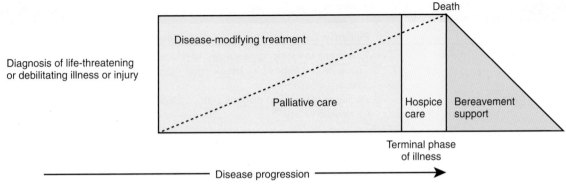

FIGURE 12-1 Model for Palliative Care. (From A National Framework and Preferred Practices for Palliative and Hospice Care Quality: A Consensus Report, *by the National Quality Forum, 2006, Washington, DC. Copyright 2015 National Quality Forum. Reproduced with permission.*)

introduction of **hospice care** and bereavement services. Dame Cicely Saunders is credited as founding the modern-day hospice, St. Christopher's in London, England. In the United States, Florence Wald, dean of Yale School of Nursing, is credited with opening the Connecticut Hospice in 1974.

As patient decline occurs, palliative care or hospice care becomes the focus. Frequently the terms are used synonymously, which is incorrect because they differ. Both offer comfort care to the patient with serious illness, but in hospice care the disease is considered end stage with progression to death. Finestone and Inderwies (2008) discuss the benefits of hospice, one of which is to support both the patient and family. Support includes physical assistance but also emotional, psychological, and spiritual support. Hospice is underutilized by much of the population and its lack of use can be due to cultural beliefs, lack of understanding, fear, or decreased availability. Table 12-2 demonstrates a comparison of hospice and palliative care services.

Prognostication

Patients with serious illness question the time they have until death. Predicting one's death is not a simple task. Research shows that when physicians prognosticate, they are optimistic in predicting survival up to as much as 300% (von Gunten, 2014). Physicians are faced with the task of telling a patient that their time to live is limited. This is difficult not only because of medical complexity, but emotions come into play when there has been a patient-physician relationship. When looking at disease progression, the terms foreseeing and foretelling come into play. Foreseeing is the scientific part of

predicting, whereas foretelling is the art. Foreseeing uses objective data to aid in the prediction. The disease process is distinguished by its severity and ability to be cured. Laboratory and diagnostic findings help to track the progress of the disease—is it improving or getting worse? Current functional status of the patient, including a history of falls, can be helpful for predicting as well. When looking at functional status, cognitive ability and the ability to perform activities of daily living are reviewed (Downing, 2011).

There are a number of tools used to help with **prognostication.** The Palliative Performance Scale (PPS) (Table 12-3) and Karnofsky Scale (Table 12-4) are two such tools. The PPS is a more general tool that identifies functional decline and scores it. Scores are an indication about disease progression to death. The Karnofsky Scale is more appropriate for the patient with a cancer diagnosis.

It is helpful to compare the patient's status at 12 months, 6 months, and 1 month, as well as the current status. The patient's ability to perform activities of daily living, a change in appetite, weight loss, anorexia/cachexia, and/or dysphagia all help paint the picture of serious illness with decline. Laboratory findings and diagnostic test results can also help validate the presence of serious illness. For example, by examination of laboratory data, one is able to assess the extent of organ decline.

After gathering the objective and subjective data, a meeting with the patient and family is imperative. With family being defined by the patient, a family conference is invaluable. A group meeting allows everyone to hear the same thing at the same time from the health care provider. There is less room for misinterpretation as

TABLE 12-2 Comparison of Hospice and Palliative Care Services

Component	Palliative Care	Hospice
Focus of Care	To address the specific needs of patients and families experiencing serious illness	To address the specific needs of the dying patient and their family.
Onset of Care	Begins at the time of diagnosis of a serious illness	Begins with a prognosis of 6 months of less ("Would I be surprised if the patient died in 6 months or less?")
Medicare Benefit	Physicians (MDs) and nurse practitioners may bill	Yes
Beneficiary Entitled to Levels of Care	No specific levels of care	Yes Routine home care, respite care, general inpatient care, continuous care
Settings Where Care Delivered	All inpatient settings, outpatient, private practice, home care (note: in the Memphis community, most care delivered within hospitals)	Home, nursing home, residential, hospice, inpatient (on designated unit or designated beds)
Interprofessional Team Approach	Yes	Yes
Supplies and Symptom Management Medications Covered	No	Yes
Therapies Limited	No Yes Palliative care is delivered side-by-side with aggressive treatment and therapies.	Therapies with significant burden but may prolong life are restricted
Quality Components Include Safety, Timeliness, Patient-Centered Care, Beneficial/Effective Care, Equity Efficiency	Yes	Yes
Expertise on Pain and Symptom Management	Yes	Yes
Appropriate at Any Age	Yes	Yes
Effective Initiation of Life Planning	Most effective	Effective if discussions occur prior to hospice or if earlier referrals to hospice

information is presented at a level understood by the patient and family. There must be time for questions. Information given must be realistic, but should not take away hope.

There are different types of hope: hope for a cure; hope for more time; hope for no pain; hope for a good death. Physicians may shy away from specific time frames. What is helpful is if the patient/family can understand the "usual course of the illness." Some disease states follow a more predictable pattern—for example, metastatic cancer. On the other hand, deaths due to heart failure, emphysema, or dementia are not as easily predicted. With these disease states, it is helpful to review with the patient and family the decline that has already occurred. Plotting it on paper shows the decline and makes it more real. This discussion of prognostication does not end with one meeting, but is ongoing as the disease progresses toward the end of life. Additionally, education is ongoing throughout the disease process for the patient/family.

Two Roads to Death

Ferris and colleagues (2003) describe two roads to death: the usual road and the difficult road. The usual

TABLE 12-3   Palliative Performance Scale

%	Ambulation	Evidence of Disease	Self-Care	Intake	Level of Consciousness
100	Full	Normal No disease	Full	Normal	Full
90	Full	Normal Some disease	Full	Norma	Full
80	Full	Normal with effort Some disease	Full	Norma or reduced	Full
70	Reduced	Can't do normal job or work Some disease	Full	As above	Full
60	Reduced	Can't do hobbies or housework Significant disease	Occasional assistance needed	As above	Full or confusion
50	Mainly sit/lie	Can't do any work Extensive disease	Considerable assistance needed	As above	Full or confusion
40	Mainly in bed	As above	Mainly assistance	As above	Full or drowsy or confusion
30	Bed bound	As above	Total care	Reduced	As above
20	Bed bound	As above	As above	Minimal	As above
10	Bed bound	As above	As above	Mouth care only	Drowsy or coma
0	Death	—	—	—	—

From Anderson F, Downing GM, Hill J, et al: Palliative performance scale (PPS): a new tool. *J Palliat Care* 12(1):6, 1996. Copyright: Institut universitaire de gériatrie de Montréal.

TABLE 12-4   Karnofsky Performance Status Scale

Score	Criteria	Definition
100	Normal, no complaints, no evidence of disease	Able to carry on normal activity and to work, no special care needed
90	Able to carry on normal activity, minor symptoms	
80	Normal activity with some symptoms	
70	Cares for self, unable to carry on normal activities	Unable to work; able to live at home and care for most personal needs; various degrees of assistance needed
60	Requires occasional assistance, cares for most needs	
50	Requires considerable assistance and frequent care	
40	Disabled, requires special care and assistance	Unable to care for self; requires equivalent of institutional or hospital care; disease may be progressing rapidly
30	Severely disabled; hospitalized but death not imminent	
20	Very sick; active supportive care needed	
10	Moribund; fatal processes are progressing rapidly	
0	Death	

From Callin SE, Bennett MI. Assessment of mobility. In Walsh TD, Caraceni A, Fainsinger R, et al, editors: *Palliative medicine*, Philadelphia, 2009, Saunders.

road is what most would describe as a peaceful death, in which the patient begins sleeping more and being less and less responsive. They progress to a comatose state and die. Caregivers describe the death as peaceful and comfortable. The difficult road, on the other hand, is one of restlessness with increased confusion and frequently with hallucinations. To avoid the difficult death, health care providers must view not only the physical aspects of patient care but also the emotional, spiritual, and psychosocial aspects. Physical pain can be medicated; however, emotional/spiritual pain is complicated and medications cannot always erase it. Health care providers must be open to listening and encouraging the patient to deal with difficult issues while they are able to do so.

When death occurs, it can be verified by the absence of heartbeat and respirations, pupils that are fixed and dilated, and absent corneal reflex. Other signs that are seen include a change in skin color and temperature. Frequently, eyes do not close completely and the jaw may remain open. Urine and stool may also be expelled. Depending on the setting, the patient is pronounced deceased by a nurse or physician.

Criteria for Palliative Care

For most institutions, a physician's order is required for hospice/palliative care services. Patients can be referred on admission as well as during their hospital stays. On admission, patients who have had multiple hospitalizations over a relatively short period of time for the same condition (e.g., heart failure, urinary tract infection, sepsis) should be considered. Things that may trigger a palliative care consult include (Weissman and Meier, 2011):

- Receiving a positive response by asking the "surprise" question: "Would I be surprised if this patient died within 6 months to a year?"
- Patients with multifaceted care such as ventilator support, parenteral feedings, and assistance with functional needs
- A patient's place of residence is a long-term care facility (e.g., nursing home)
- The age of the patient
- Cognitive impairment
- Metastatic cancer
- Current or past enrollment in hospice care
- A patient without an advance care plan

Throughout a hospital stay, other triggers can indicate the need for a palliative care consult. These triggers may include the patient's desire to change health care providers, patient or family request for palliative care, or dissension about therapy/treatments that being offered. Other triggers may include a prolonged stay in the intensive care unit or symptoms that have not been controlled. Palliative care can assist with decisions about long-term use of feeding tubes, need for tracheostomy, dialysis, left ventricular assist device placement, automatic implanted cardioverter-defibrillator (AICD) placement, and other life-prolonging therapies.

Palliative care can assist patients and their families with decision making regarding goals of care. For example, the initial intent of therapy may have been cure, but the disease was found to be widespread. The focus could then change to comfort. The patient may hear, "there is nothing more we can do," but there is always care to be provided. It is the focus of the care that changes: quality of time may now be the focus rather than the quantity.

KEY ELEMENTS OF PALLIATIVE CARE

Eight Elements of End-of-Life Nursing Education Consortium

End-of-Life Nursing Education Consortium (ELNEC) is a project that started in February 2002 with a grant from the Robert Wood Johnson Foundation at City of Hope by Bettye Ferrell. The ELNEC core curriculum identifies eight modules: nursing care at the end of life, pain management, symptom management, ethical/legal issues, cultural considerations, communication, loss/grief/bereavement, and final hours. The goal of this project was to improve palliative care. Now there are curricula for pediatrics, critical care, oncology, veterans, geriatrics, and advanced practice nursing. The newest model is integrating palliative oncology care into the Doctor of Nursing Practice. The ELNEC program went international in May 2008, again with the goal of educating nurses (www.aacn. nche.edu/ELNEC).

Eight Domains of National Consensus Project

The National Consensus Project (NCP) for Quality Palliative Care, which began in 2001, is a task force of organizations that strives to improve palliative care.

The organizations involved include: American Academy of Hospice and Palliative Medicine (AAHPM), Center to Advance Palliative Care (CAPC), Hospice and Palliative Care Nurses Association (HPNA), National Hospice and Palliative Care Organization (NHPCO). NCP identifies eight practice domains for palliative care to follow.

Domain 1: Structure and Processes of Care. This domain describes the use of the interprofessional team to work together assessing and planning care with patients and families.

Domain 2: Physical Aspects of Care . This domain emphasizes the use of validated tools for assessment and the treatment of physical symptoms.

Domain 3: Psychological and Psychiatric Aspects of Care. This domain stresses the need to address assessment and treatment of psychiatric concerns and diagnoses. Included also in this domain are the requirements of a bereavement program.

Domain 4: Social Aspects of Care. This domain's focus emphasizes engaging patients and families in the patient's care and taking advantage of their strengths. The team social worker begins this process.

Domain 5: Spiritual, Religious, and Existential Aspects of Care. This domain focuses on involving the chaplain in the plan of care throughout the **disease trajectory.** Spiritual and religious practices are encouraged as a means to obtain comfort.

Domain 6: Cultural Aspects of Care. This domain focuses on the inclusion of cultural aspect when providing care and states that the interprofessional team should be culturally competent.

Domain 7: Care of the Patient at the End of Life. This domain emphasizes communication and physical signs and symptoms of the dying process. Again patient/families/interprofessional team should be involved with scrupulous assessment and management of pain and other symptoms. Ongoing education for families about the dying process is of utmost importance.

Domain 8: Ethical and Legal Aspects of Care. This addresses advance care planning and ethical/legal aspects. Advance care planning is seen as something that is ongoing and may change throughout the disease course. This domain reaffirms that ethical issues are frequent and must be addressed. The identification of complex legal and regulatory issues of palliative care is also addressed in this domain. (For more information, see www.nationalconsensusproject.org/NCP_Clinical_Practice_Guidelines_3rd_Edition.pdf.)

BENEFITS OF PALLIATIVE CARE

Palliative care can be viewed as both a model of care and a philosophy of serving our patients. It is built of multiple components as expressed in the End-of-Life Nursing Education Consortium (ELNEC) curriculum (www.aacn.nche.edu/ELNEC).

- The family is the unit of care and the patient defines family.
- The role of the nurse as an advocate is vital to the care of patients and their families.
- Culture is honored as an important aspect of the patient/family.
- Palliative care further carries an important focus to special populations such as the vulnerable, the prisoner, or the substance abuser.
- Serious illness affects all systems of care. Put another way: where there are patients, there are patients who are suffering needlessly.
- Sensitivity to the reality of financial issues that impact quality of life is critical.
- Palliative care is not just confined to cancer and AIDS, but to all life-threatening illnesses.
- The interprofessional care of the patient/family is integral to high quality palliative care.

To understand the benefits of palliative care, one must grasp the depth and breadth of symptoms, stress, and suffering of serious illness. This section will examine a broad overview of these concepts; however, the reader is encouraged to continue to pursue more in-depth knowledge.

The numbers speak for themselves. We now live in a time of unprecedented numbers of older Americans who are living with chronic illnesses. In 2010, there were 403 million people aged 65 years or older, 12 times the number in 1900 (U.S. Census Bureau, 2014). Additionally, a baby born in the United States can expect to live to 78 years old (U.S. Census Bureau, 2014). And with this longer life span comes an expectation that all illnesses can be treated, as many successes in public health and medical care have shown (Meier et al, 2010). However, "the sheer numbers of the elderly with chronic disability means an unprecedented number will experience prolonged functional dependency and frailty" (Meier et al, 2010). Approximately 57% of Americans age 80 years and older report a severe disability (Meier et al, 2010). Individuals with five or more chronic illnesses account for 66% of Medicare spending and are the largest consumers of health care (Meier et al, 2010).

Technology is more refined than ever before. These technologies offer the ability to prolong life, but they do not consistently restore life to its former level of quality. Many Americans live with one or more chronic illnesses, such as heart failure, chronic obstructive pulmonary disease, stroke, cancer, and dementia. And while these persons are living longer, many suffer from these illnesses that limit their life (Meier et al, 2010). Furthermore, degenerative diseases have replaced communicable disease as the leading causes of death in the United States. Today, 54% of Americans die in acute care facilities surrounded by strangers and suffer from prolonged chronic illnesses and, in many cases, receiving futile treatment that may result in financial burden for the family (Grant and Dy, 2012).

The stress, symptoms, and suffering experienced in chronic illness by both the patient and family also exact a tremendous burden. In 1995, the SUPPORT study (Study to Understand Prognoses and Preferences for Outcomes and Risks of Treatment) "demonstrated a lack of communication between patients, families, and health care providers about goals of care, a significant pain burden in seriously ill patients, and discrepancies between patient preferences for care and the aggressive care received" (SUPPORT Principal Investigators, 1995). This study became the impetus for increasing research and education in palliative care at the end of life.

Pain and Symptom Management

Pain and symptom management and communication are commonly recognized aspects of quality care for persons with serious illness. Dr. Nathan Cherny (2010) best describes the impact of unrelieved pain in his description related to cancer:

> "Unrelieved pain is incapacitating and precludes a satisfying quality of life; it interferes with functioning and social interaction, and is strongly associated with heightened psychological distress. It can provoke or exacerbate existential distress, disturb normal processes of coping and adjustment, and

augment a sense of vulnerability contributing to a preoccupation with the potential for catastrophic outcomes. Persistent pain interferes with the ability to eat, sleep, think, interact with others, and is correlated with fatigue in cancer patients."

In palliative care, the prevalence of pain varies by diagnoses and demographics (Smith et al, 2010). And the fear of unrelieved pain expressed by patients and families is often reflective of what they have experienced (American Geriatrics Society, 2009). The experience of pain for the individual patient has multiple dimensions and includes such factors as the meaning of pain, knowledge of pain and pain management, expectation and goals of pain management, cultural beliefs, and the support received from family and others.

Pain is further complicated by the presence of other symptoms that can occur during serious illness: dyspnea, insomnia, constipation, nausea and vomiting, anxiety, depression, delirium, and fatigue. These symptoms seriously affect quality of life and may limit functional activity to the detriment of the patient's overall well-being. Through comprehensive assessment and management of patient and family, palliative care is able to improve quality of life as evidenced by these benefits:

- Relief of suffering
- Optimization of function
- Promotion of healing and comfort
- Fostering of appropriate hope
- Genuine coordination of care at times of transitions between health care providers
- If anticipated, patient and family are given opportunity and assistance in exploring and preparing for hospice.

Suffering

In 1982, Dr. Eric Cassel published one of the earliest articles on suffering to enter the medical literature, and it opened discussions about suffering for professionals. In his article, he defines suffering as "a state of severe distress associated with events that threaten the intactness of a person" (Cassel, 1982). Suffering is the experience of a person, whereas pain and other symptoms are the result of physical body or organ changes. Suffering and pain can coexist together, although one can be present without the other. However, "the transition from pain to suffering can occur when pain is unrelieved and out of control or when the source of pain in unknown. The persistence of pain and uncertainty therefore can increase suffering" (Matzo and Sherman, 2015).

Relieving a patient's and family's suffering is central to the work of palliative care. Spiritual and existential distress is prevalent but also goes underrecognized in the hospice and palliative care populations (Pulchalski et al, 2009). Excellent pain and symptom management become the foundation for relief of suffering because active symptomatology can dominate a patient's life. However, once physical symptoms are resolved or controlled, spiritual assessment can reveal areas of loss, such as loss of hope, loss of meaning, loss of value, or loss of relationships (Quill et al, 2010). Once discovered, practical strategies including counseling are methods to relieve this suffering.

Family Caregiving

Family caregivers also benefit from palliative care services. The National Alliance for Caregiving defines a family caregiver as "someone who is responsible for attending to the daily needs of another person. He or she is responsible for the physical, emotional, and often financial support of another person who is unable to care for himself or herself due to illness, injury or disability" (National Alliance for Caregiving, 2013). The average period of caregiving is 4.6 years, with 31% of caregivers involved in caregiving for greater than 5 years. Weekly, the average time of caregiving is 20.4 hours, with females providing more caregiving time than male caregivers (National Alliance for Caregiving in collaboration with AARP, 2009). The stresses of caregiving are multifactorial, including compassion fatigue with neglect of their own needs and health (Family Caregiver Alliance, 2006a), role changes with stress (Dumont et al, 2008; Herbert et al, 2009), and the development of depression and other emotional complications (Family Caregiver Alliance, 2006). Matzo and Sherman (2015) define four general areas where strategies can successfully affect caregiving:

1. Setting realistic goals
2. Having difficult discussions
3. Finding help
4. Negotiating expectations

These strategies begin with a comprehensive family assessment, including an assessment of family strengths and weaknesses.

BARRIERS TO PALLIATIVE CARE

Four significant barriers form the basis for the growth and progress of palliative care for the future. First is the lack of a general understanding by health care professionals as well as the consumers of the role and nature of palliative care. In many communities across the United States, palliative care is synonymous with hospice or terminal care of the dying. With that strong linkage, patients and families and often health care providers believe "it's just not time yet," that is, "I'm not dying yet." The lack of recognition of the true nature of palliative care prevents patients and families from obtaining the care they need to address whole person needs. Further, the lack of recognition of the negative impact of a disease condition on the whole person results in distress—physically, socially, psychologically, and spiritually. The denial of death in our American culture also affects the lack of acceptance of palliative care. Woody Allen has been quoted as saying, "I don't want to achieve immortality through my work. I want to achieve it by not dying." Combine this "stigma of death with widely held beliefs that modern medicine and hospitals can perform miracles in the battle against death, the hospitals and nursing homes have become the dominant site for gravely ill, dying people"(Meier, et al, 2010) with more than 70% of deaths in the United States occurring in an institution (Meier et al, 2010).

The second barrier to the growth and progress of palliative care is the limited numbers of palliative care trained professionals. While there has been remarkable growth of palliative care programs in the last 15 years, "these numbers have not matched the number of trained clinicians to lead and staff these programs" (Meier et al, 2010). Dr. Meier (2010) further reports, "A number of strategies have been employed to improve medical and nursing education in palliative care, including the pursuit of subspecialty status for palliative medicine and nursing advocacy for changes in undergraduate and graduate accreditation standards; and numerous philanthropically funded efforts to train mid-career physicians and nurses."

The third barrier to palliative care growth and progress is the question, "How is palliative care paid for?" Although palliative care providers do bill Medicare and other payers for the care they deliver, the reimbursement is for time-intensive care and not procedural services. This reimbursement fails to cover the salaries of the professionals, much less the overhead expenses for running a business. As a result, the recent growth in hospital palliative care services has been financed "not by fee-for-service reimbursement to hospitals and providers but rather by hospitals operating budgets" (Meier et al, 2010). But first, these hospitals and their administrators must be persuaded of the value during economic times of decreased reimbursement. R. Sean Morrison and colleagues analyzed administrative data from eight hospitals with established palliative care teams from 2002 to 2004 and matched these patients to patients receiving usual care. "The palliative care patients who were discharged alive had an adjusted net savings of $1696 in direct costs per admission and $279 in indirect costs per day including significant reductions in laboratory and intensive care unit costs compared with usual care patients" (Morrison et al, 2008).

Communication is the fourth barrier, and it is a vital part of patient care; however, at the end of life it can be detrimental if poorly done. Patients and their families deserve appropriate information to help them make difficult decisions. As patients and families face serious illness, conversations must be kept simple. Trying to tell everything is overwhelming. Unfortunately, health care providers have not been educated in the delivery of difficult news.

COMMON CHALLENGES

Providing quality palliative care is not perfect and there are struggles. As a patient declines, they may no longer be safe to live alone and they frequently report increased falls. Inability to adequately manage medications may also be a challenge. Memory loss may be a contributing factor related to safety. Giving up their independence can be devastating for patients. In a qualitative study, Smucker and colleagues (2014) described safety concerns from 17 hospices in 13 states. Hospice workers described harm from falls and uncontrolled symptoms, especially pain. Some of the factors identified as contributing to the safety issues included patients living alone and/or cognitively impaired, cognitively impaired caregivers, and caregivers with their own physical limitations. These barriers

related to patient safety and independence need to be addressed.

Another common challenge is treating the patient for the family's sake. Families may want intravenous fluids, antibiotics, and other therapies. It is not easy helping them understand that these can be more of a burden than help and may hasten death. Frequently, the family/caregiver is not considering the best interest of the patient during decision making.

Withholding or withdrawing food and fluids or treatments is a challenge for palliative care providers. Withholding and withdrawing have both ethical and legal components. The principle of autonomy comes into play, and the individual ultimately has the right to refuse or accept a therapy. Ideally, the patients should speak for themselves, but unfortunately this may not be the case. Advance directives, if present, can speak for the patient and their wishes. When therapies are considered, a timeframe should also be discussed and the question asked, "Will the therapy be time sustaining or life prolonging?"

Families view food and fluids as an essential. They fear the patient will starve to death when food or fluids are withheld or not started. In truth, patients frequently stop eating gradually as they age or their disease progresses. Patients will say "I'm not hungry" or "Food just doesn't taste good anymore." Families fear their loved one is being starved by the health care provider. It is the progression of the disease that has caused decreased intake of food and fluids. Health care providers do not withhold nutrition from those patients who still want to eat. The introduction of artificial nutrition is just that: artificial! It is helpful to discuss the benefits and burdens of intravenous fluids and feeding tubes and the purpose of these therapies. While both serve a useful purpose in the acute care setting for individuals whose prognosis is good, in the setting of an individual who has a terminal illness, they are a burden. Historically, prior to the advent of intravenous therapy or tube feedings, patients ate and drank as long as they were able. When feeding became a burden, families continued to care for them, offering food and fluids, but not forcing them. The patient was allowed to die naturally. Further, it has not been found that artificial feedings prevent aspiration or increase wound healing (McDonald and Lesage, 2006).

PROFESSIONAL ISSUES IN PALLIATIVE CARE

As mentioned earlier, primary palliative care is integral to care provided by a professional nurse. The Hospice and Palliative Nurses Association's (HPNA) Scope and Standards of Practice identifies the following specific areas of expertise for hospice and palliative care nurses (Dahlin and Glass, 2007).

1. Clinical judgment
2. Advocacy and ethics
3. Professionalism
4. Collaboration
5. Systems thinking
6. Cultural competence
7. Facilitator of learning
8. Communication

Certification

Currently, there are three levels of certification for the palliative care nurse. At the generalist level is the CHPN designation—certified hospice palliative nurse; for the palliative nurse administrator is the CHPA—certified hospice palliative administrator. The hospice palliative advanced practice nurse usually has specialty training or certification in palliative care. The advanced level certification is the ACHPN—advanced certified hospice palliative nurse.

At the institutional level, palliative care programs can now achieve recognition for high-quality palliative care through The Joint Commission. This voluntary certification is based on the National Consensus Project for Quality Care and the National Quality Forum's National Framework and Preferred Practices for Hospice and Palliative Care.

Quality Assessment and Improvement

The National Hospice and Palliative Care Organization (NHPCO) is a hospice and palliative care national organization committed to social change for the care of patients at the end of life. As part of their mission, they are committed to the improvement of multiple areas of quality, including patient-centered measures related to management of pain within 48 hours of admission, avoiding unwanted hospitalizations, avoiding unwanted CPR, and patient safety. In the area of bereavement, a survey has been designed to evaluate bereavement service and completed by family members or primary caregivers. A post-death survey is completed by family members of hospice patients regarding their perceptions about the quality of the care given to their loved ones at end of life. Lastly, a staff job satisfaction survey has been designed specifically for hospice field staff.

The Center to Advance Palliative care (CAPC) is the nation's leading resource for palliative care program development. It provides multiple learning opportunities to assist health care institutions in building hospital programs from strategic planning, to funding, to operations, and sustainability. CAPC is a national organization dedicated to increasing the availability of quality palliative care service for people facing serious, complex illness. They have multiple references and resources available including information on quality assessment and improvement.

Research

Research in palliative care is lacking, in part because it is a relatively new subspecialty, but also palliative researchers are faced with numerous ethical quandaries (Chen et al, 2014). Palliative care research must meet the same rigor as other disciplines, and barriers can include lack of funding, lack of staff, and lack of trained researchers. Obtaining subjects can also be a barrier, especially when there is poor understanding of palliative care by patient/families as well as health care providers. Because patients have life-limiting diseases, they may die before a study can be completed.

Ethical Concerns

Ethical challenges arise when the ethically appropriate course of action or range of choices is unclear, or when there are competing ethical claims that may not be reconcilable (Berlinger et al, 2013). For purposes of this chapter, the following four areas will be briefly examined: advance care planning, double effect, medically futile care, and palliative sedation.

Advance Care Planning

In December 1991, all hospitals, nursing facilities, hospice programs, and health maintenance organizations that serve Medicare or Medicaid patients were mandated to provide new patients with written information describing their rights under state law to make decisions about medical care, including their right of execute a living will or durable power of attorney for health care (Berlinger et al, 2013). This was the **Patient Self Determination Act (PSDA)** of 1991. The living will or **advance care plan** outlines the decisions for health care when one is unable to speak or decide. These documents were intended to foster communication between the doctor and the patient and at the same time, respect the patient's right to autonomy. Ethical dilemmas can arise because an **advance directive** "requires a person to predict accurately the final illness and what medical interventions might be available to postpone death and living wills require physicians to make decisions on the basis of their interpretation of the document, rather than a discussion of treatment options with a person acting on behalf of the patient" (Meier et al, 2010). The suggested solution now in practice is for the patient to appoint a health care agent or appointed decision maker who can speak on their behalf with detailed knowledge of their health care wishes.

Double Effect

Day to day, nurses face issues related to beneficence and nonmaleficence, or do no harm. This principle becomes particularly important with seriously ill or dying patients who are often in a weakened condition, frail, frightened, and vulnerable. Nurses often become distressed when being requested to give opioid therapy in an actively dying patient. Although these medications are intended to relieve pain and symptoms such as dyspnea, they also have a foreseeable risk to hasten death by respiratory depression.

Nash and Nelson (2012) have explained that according to the rule of double effect, an action with two possible effects—one good and one bad—is ethically acceptable if these four conditions are satisfied:

- The good effect has to be intended and therefore is not morally wrong.
- The bad effect is not intended but can be foreseen; that is, causing respiratory depression can result in death.
- The bad effect cannot be the means to the good effect. In this example, pain relief is not achieved by ending a patient's life.
- The symptom must be severe enough to warrant taking risks; that is, administering this dose at this time is needed to relieve the pain.

Palliative Sedation

At times in palliative care and particularly in patients receiving hospice care, patients will present with intolerable symptoms that cannot be controlled by standard methods of pain management. Examples of symptoms that become intolerable include dyspnea, pain, and delirium with agitation. To appropriately manage these symptoms, palliative sedation can be considered. Palliative sedation is the use of sedating medications to relieve refractory or intolerable symptoms when other pharmacologic measures have failed. Education and **informed consent** discussion for the patient and/or the patient's decision-maker includes the purpose of therapy, the expected outcomes, and how the patient and symptoms will be monitored. In consideration of the stress that family members are under during episodes of palliative sedation, continuing education and explanation of the patient's condition and status are important. Further, nursing and the interdisciplinary team require around-the-clock monitoring to ensure that symptoms are controlled, that limited numbers of breakthrough episodes are occurring, and that the need for increased medications are identified promptly.

Medically Futile Care

A medically futile treatment is a treatment option that offers no possibility of physiologic benefit related to diagnosis, prognosis, and the current medical condition. Ethically, a physician is not obligated to provide such a treatment; however, the physician should be aware of any state laws relevant to these decisions.

When decisions of medical futility are being made, a patient/family meeting is a critical strategy to ensure that all pertinent parties are involved in the decision-making process. These relevant parties include the physician, the patient and/or decision maker, the family, and members of the interdisciplinary team. Often, members of the hospital-based ethics committee are also involved.

The first step is to establish common ground of mutual understanding of the patient's condition. This process will involve the members of the interdisciplinary team asking open-ended questions to the patient/family to clarify that information is indeed understood. Once common ground is established, the next step is to determine and verbalize the patient's and family's expectations of treatment and the goals that they wish to achieve. Once clarified, the physician explains the treatment options and in the case of futile treatments, he/she explains why a treatment cannot provide benefit. Lastly, the team will clarify the questions and misconceptions, and once these are clarified to the satisfaction of the patient/family, there is the explicit stating of the medical plan of action for everyone present to hear.

LEGAL CONCERNS

Right to Refuse Treatment

"The right to refuse is the belief that medical care is optional for adults with appropriate capacity" (Berlinger et al, 2013). The landmark cases of Quinlan and Cruzan and others have established that patients have a legal right to refuse life-sustaining medical treatment.

In April 1975, 21-year-old Karen Ann Quinlan suffered an anoxic brain injury. Her medical care included a tracheostomy, artificial ventilation, and a feeding tube with artificial nutrition and hydration. Her condition was later diagnosed as persistent vegetative state, at which time her father sought to be appointed by the courts as her legal guardian so that he could discontinue her respirator that assisted her breathing. Karen's physician refused to do so because this was not in accordance with medical standards of the day. After years and multiple court battles, the ventilator was removed and she died several years later of an infection. The outcome of this woman's experience was the endorsement by the legal system of the use of hospital ethics committees to review decisions to withdraw life-sustaining treatments.

The second young woman to affect decisions to refuse medical treatment was Nancy Cruzan. She was 25 years old in January of 1983 when she was seriously injured in a motor vehicle accident. She was treated at the accident site and en route to the hospital to restore her breathing and heartbeat and was admitted in a coma. A gastrostomy tube was inserted with her husband's permission. She was diagnosed as being in a persistent vegetative state.

Over time, her parents requested that the artificial nutrition and hydration be discontinued, but the hospital refused to do so without a court order. Once more, a series of court interventions were sought, including involvement of the United States Supreme Court. The legal outcome of this series of legal events was the court stated that "incompetent patients need certain protections given when they cannot exercise their right of refusal"; therefore, it was appropriate at the state level "to impose additional safeguards in the form of the clear and convincing evidence standard in light of its interest in preserving life" (Nash and Nelson, 2012).

After this decision, the Cruzan family petitioned the state court in Missouri to grant the request to discontinue the artificial nutrition and hydration. This was approved, and Nancy Cruzan died shortly thereafter. This case affects us today by the increased interest in advance care planning and health care decision makers and also "generated support for the Patient Self-Determination Act" of 1991 (Nash and Nelson, 2012).

◼ SUMMARY

"You matter because you are you, and you matter to the end of your life. We will do all we can not only to help you die peacefully, but also to live until you die."

Dame Cicely Saunders, 1918-2005: nurse, social worker, physician, founder of modern-day hospice.

With the advancement of medical therapies comes the task of deciding when enough is enough. New therapies and devices are seen as a means of extending life by both the medical profession and patients. Unfortunately, this extension of life does not always carry with it quality of life. Difficult decisions arise when the disease has taken over. Health care providers must help patients and their families with these decisions as they face them or as they progress toward death, and comfort and quality of life must be the priority.

REFERENCES

American Geriatrics Society: American geriatric society clinical practice guidelines: pharmacological management of persistent pain in older persons, *Journal of the American Geriatric Society* 57(8):1331–1346, 2009.

American Nurses Association: *Code of ethics for nurses with interpretive statements*, 2001. http://www.nursingworld.org/MainMenuCategories/EthicsStandards/Codeof EthicsforNurses/Code-of-Ethics.pdf. Accessed July 21, 2014.

Berlinger N, Jennings B, Wolf SM: *The hasting center guidelines for decisions on life-sustaining treatment and care near end of life*, ed 2, New York, 2013, Oxford University Press.

Callin SE, Bennett MI: Assessment of mobility, In Walsh TD, Caraceni A, Fainsinger R, et al, editors: *Palliative Medicine*, Philadelphia, 2009, Saunders.

Cassel EJ: The nature of suffering and the goals of medicine, *New England Journal of Medicine* 306(11):639–645, 1982.

Chen E, Riffin, C, Reid C, et al: Why is high-quality research on palliative care so hard to do? Barrier to improved research from a survey of palliative care researchers, *Journal of Palliative Medicine* 17(7):782–787, 2014.

Cherny NI: Pain Assessment and cancer pain syndromes, In Hanks G, Cherny NI, Christakis NA, et al, editors: *Oxford Textbook of Palliative Medicine*, New York, 2010, Oxford University Press.

Dahlin C, Glass E: *Hospice and palliative nursing: scope and standards of practice*, Silver Spring, Maryland, 2007, Hospice and Palliative Nurses Association and American Nurses Association.

Downing CM: "Who knows" 10 steps to better prognostication, In Emanuel L, Librach SL, editors: *Palliative Care: Core skills and clinical competencies*, St. Louis, 2011, Saunders.

Dumont I, Dumont S, Mongeau S: End of life care and the grieving process: family caregivers who wave experienced the loss of a terminal phase cancer patient, *Qualitative Health Research* 18(8):1049–1061, 2008.

End-of-Life Nursing Education Consortium (ELNEC): *Core curriculum*, 2013. http://www.aacn.nche.edu/ELNEC. Accessed June 30, 2014.

Family Caregiver Alliance: Caregiver assessment: principles, guidelines, and strategies for change, Report from a Consensus Development Conference, vol I, *Family Caregiver Alliance*, 2006. http://www.caregiver.org/caregiver/jsp/content/pdfs/vl_consensus.pdf.

Ferris F, von Gunten C, Emanual L: Competency in end-of-life care: last hours to life, *Journal of Palliative Medicine* 6(4):605–613, 2004, 2003.

Finestone A, Inderwies G: Death and dying in the US: the barrier to the benefits of palliative and hospice care, *Clinical Interventions in Aging* 3(3): 595–599, 2008.

Grant M, Dy SL: *UNIPAC #1: The hospice and palliative care approach to serious illness*, ed 4, Glenview, Illinois, 2012, American Academy of Hospice Palliative Medicine.

Herbert RS, Schulz R, Copeland, VC, et al: Preparing family caregivers for death and bereavement: insights from caregivers of terminally ill patients, *Journal of Pain and Symptom Management* 37(1): 3–12, 2009.

Matzo M, Sherman DW editors: *Palliative care nursing: quality care at the end of life*, ed 3, New York, 2015, Springer Publishing Company.

McDonald A, Lesage P: Palliative management of pressure ulcers and malignant wounds in patients with advanced illness, *Journal of Palliative Medicine* 9(2): 285–296, 2006.

Meier DE, Isaacs SL, Hughes RG: *Palliative care: transforming the care of serious illness*, ed 3, San Francisco, 2010, Jossey-Bass.

Morrison RS, Penrod JD, Cassel JB: Cost savings associated with US hospital palliative care consultation programs, *Archives of Internal Medicine* 168(16):1783–1790, 2008.

Nash RR, Nelson LJ: *Ethical and legal issues*, Glenview, Illinois, 2012, American Academy of Hospice and Palliative Medicine.

National Consensus Project for Quality Palliative Care: *Clinical practice guidelines for quality palliative care*, 2009. http://NationalConsensusProject.org. Accessed July 18, 2015.

National Consensus Project for Palliative Care: http://www.nationalconsensusproject.orgon. July 15, 2014.

National Alliance for Caregiving: *Care for the family caregiver: a place to start*, 2013. http://www.caregiving.org/data/emblem_cfC10_Final12.pdf on June 20, 2014.

National Alliance for Caregiving in Collaboration with AARP: *Caregiving in the US*, 2009. http://www.caregiving.org/pdf/research/caregivingUSAllAgesExecSum.pdf.

National Quality Forum: *A national framework and preferred practices for palliative and hospice care quality: a consensus report*, 2006. http://www.qualityforum.org/Publications/2006/12/A_National_Framework_and_Preferred_Practices_fot_Palliative_and_Hospice_Care_Quality.aspx. Accessed July 1, 2015.

Pulchalski C, Ferrell B, Verani R, et al: Improving the quality of spiritual care as a dimension of palliative care: the report of a consensus conference, *Journal of Palliative Medicine* 12:885–904, 2009.

Quill TE, Holloway RG, Shah MS, et al: *Primer of palliative medicine*, ed 5, Glenview, Illinois, 2010, American Academy of Hospice and Palliative Medicine.

Schwarz JK, Tarzian AJ: Ethical aspects of palliative care. In Matzo M, Sherman DW, editors: *Palliative care nursing: quality care to the end of life*, New York, 2010, Springer Publishing Company.

Sepúlveda C, Marlin A, Yoshida T, et al: Palliative care: The world health organization's global perspective, *Journal of Pain and Symptom Management* 24(2):91–96, 2002.

Stjernswärd J, Foley KM, Ferris FD: The public health strategy for palliative care, *Journal of Pain and Symptom Management* 33(5):486–493, 2007.

Smith AK, Stijacic CI, Knight SJ, et al: The epidemiology of pain during the last 2 years of life, *Annals of Internal Medicine* 153(9):563–569, 2010.

Smucker D, Regan S, Elder N, et al: Patient safety incidents in home hospice care: the experiences of hospice interdisciplinary team members, *Journal of Palliative Medicine* 17(5):540–544, 2014.

SUPPORT Principal Investigators: A controlled trial to improve care for the seriously ill hospitalized patients: the study to understand prognoses and preferences for outcomes and risks of treatment, *Journal of the American Medical Association* 264(20):1591–1598, 1995.

US Census Bureau: *65+ in the United States: 2010*, Washington, DC, 2014, US Government Printing Office.

von Gunten C: Prognosis: how long do we wait for the doctor? *Journal of Palliative Medicine* 7(6):634–635, 2014.

Weissman D, Meier D: Identifying patients in need of a palliative care assessment in the hospital setting: A consensus report from the center to advance palliative care, *Journal of Palliative Medicine* 14(1):17–23, 2011.

Wilner LS, Arnold R: *The palliative performance scale. Fast facts and concepts*, November 2004, 125. http://www.eperc.mcw.edu/EPERC/FastFactsIndex/ff_125.htm. Accessed July 1, 2014.

13

Workforce Advocacy for a Professional Nursing Practice Environment

A changing workplace requires nurses to embrace workforce advocacy to ensure quality health care delivery.

Mary Jo Assi, DNP, RN, NEA-BC, FNP-BC, Cheryl Peterson, MSN, RN, Debra D. Hatmaker, PhD, RN, FAAN

Ⓔ Additional resources are available online at: *http://evolve.elsevier.com/Cherry/*

PROFESSIONAL/ETHICAL ISSUE

Victoria Larson graduated from nursing school last year and has worked in the postpartum unit of Southwest Regional Hospital since graduating and passing the NCLEX. The postpartum unit uses couplet care in which the mother and baby are in the same room and cared for by one nurse. Over the last several months, Victoria has gained a great deal of confidence in caring for the mothers and babies together; however, she knows she still needs many more years of experience to become the expert nurse she aspires to be. Today, when Victoria arrives on the unit for her 7 AM to 7 PM shift,

she becomes alarmed when she sees that the charge nurse has assigned her to six mother-baby sets. The typical assignment is three mother-baby sets but occasionally the nurse may be assigned four mother-baby sets when staffing is low. But six sets seems very unreasonable to Victoria, and she does not believe she can safely take care of this number of new mothers and babies. What options, if any, does Victoria have regarding this assignment that she believes to be unsafe? Discuss how she should approach the situation with her supervisor and what questions she should ask.

VIGNETTE

As a new graduate, 26-year-old Elena Gonzalez is searching for her first position as a registered nurse (RN) in a large metropolitan city. As part of her education, she learns about the importance of a nurse's role in advocating for a workplace conducive to delivering safe and effective quality health care. She also understands that the workplace is filled with complex issues—nursing shortages, staffing issues, potential exposure to bloodborne diseases—affecting the nurse, the patient, the organization, and the profession. Elena receives offers from various organizations. However, she wisely chooses not to accept a job on its "face value" and decides to investigate her opportunities more thoroughly. Using the Internet, she searches the

websites of hospitals in her target area. She is looking for the answers to questions such as:

- *Are any organizations within my area recognized as Magnet® hospitals?*
- *Which organizations have shared governance models?*
- *What is the content and length of orientation for new nurses?*
- *What is the organization's philosophy regarding staff mix designations?*
- *Does the organization have a conflict resolution process?*
- *What is the organization's turnover rate, and what is the average time that nurses are employed in the organization?*

Answers to these questions can be found on health care organizations' websites or from their nurse recruiters or nurse educators. Armed with answers to these and other questions, Elena decides to accept a position with a large tertiary care center that she believes has created an environment most supportive of ensuring the delivery of quality patient care. However, she knows that with the acceptance of this position, her role as a workforce and patient advocate has not ended; rather, it has only just begun.

Questions to Consider While Reading this Chapter:
1. What workforce advocacy strategies can Elena use to promote quality patient care and a safe work environment?
2. What is the value of shared governance to Elena's individual nursing practice?
3. If Elena becomes concerned about floating assignments, what questions can help guide her decision about accepting such assignments?
4. What online resources are available to help Elena learn more about important workplace issues and workforce advocacy?
5. How can Elena gain increased marketability of her nursing expertise?

KEY TERMS

Patient advocacy: The nurse and the nursing profession's powerful voice at the local, state, and national levels in supporting policies that protect consumers and enhance accountability for quality by promoting safer health care systems. Patient advocacy is a cornerstone of the nursing profession, and patients depend on nurses to ensure that they receive quality care. Workforce advocacy is a component of patient advocacy.

Workforce advocacy: An array of services and tools designed to help nurses promote an optimal professional work environment and support their professional and personal development. Elements of workforce advocacy include staffing, workflow design, personal and social factors, physical environment, and organizational factors.

Workplace issues: An array of complex issues nurses face in the workplace on a daily basis. These complex issues affect the nurse, the patient, the organization, and the profession. Examples include the nursing shortage, adequate staffing levels, errors in health care delivery, and violence in the workplace.

LEARNING OUTCOMES

After studying this chapter, the reader will be able to:
1. Identify issues that affect the practice of professional nursing in the health care workplace.
2. Identify available resources to assist in improving the workplace environment.
3. Define the role of nurses in advocating for safe and effective workplace environments.
4. Describe workforce strategies that support efficient and effective quality patient care, and promote improved work environments for nurses.

CHAPTER OVERVIEW

In today's modern health care system, nurses are faced with many workplace issues. These complex issues affect not only the nurse but also the patient, the organization, and the profession. This chapter attempts to identify a few select critical issues facing nurses and the nursing profession, including the nursing shortage, appropriate staffing, patient safety and advocacy, and workplace rights and safety. Workforce advocacy is defined, and its specific strategies are highlighted. To be successful and accountable professionals, nurses must recognize current issues and know where to seek support for workforce advocacy.

PROMOTING WORKFORCE ADVOCACY AND A PROFESSIONAL PRACTICE ENVIRONMENT

Professional nurses are experiencing involvement and control in the work environment that was unheard of 20 years ago. Important research is validating the contribution and value of registered nurses (RNs) in the following areas:

- Preventing hospital readmissions (McHugh and Ma, 2013; Tubbs-Cooley et al, 2013)
- Decreasing adverse events and shorter length of stay (Lucero et al, 2010; Martsolf et al, 2014)
- Decreasing patient mortality (Aiken et al, 2009; Blegen et al, 2011; Needleman et al, 2011)

Within this context of the important contributions that nurses make to patients, hospitals, and health care in general, we find nurses challenged to deliver care against all kinds of barriers and with dwindling resources. Nurses' strong commitment to patient care and their role as patient advocates often place them in direct conflict with those who have more control, such as physicians and administrators. How a nurse reacts to such conflicts within the workplace and continues to advocate to improve patient care is a necessary focus for the profession—a focus called *workforce advocacy.*

As we visit Elena Gonzalez 6 months after she assumed her new position, we find that she has become involved in advocating for a safe work environment. Elena and the other nurses working on the medical unit are concerned because there is a limited amount of safe patient handling equipment available. Their patients often have mobility issues, and the nurses are worried about suffering musculoskeletal injuries when transferring and repositioning patients. Where will they find information about ergonomic safety and other workplace safety issues? Are there regulations that require hospitals to implement safety measures to protect their staff against debilitating musculoskeletal injuries? What legal rights do nurses have to demand safe patient handling equipment? Is there an avenue to work with hospital administrators to decrease the costs associated with unsafe practices and to move toward a user-friendly work environment? All of these questions are related to workforce advocacy.

For over a century, the American Nurses Association (ANA) and its state affiliates have advocated for the professional nurse and quality patient care. Through research, continuing education, and knowledge sharing among today's nursing community, ANA offers powerful resources to

nurses seeking to overcome workforce challenges and realize opportunities. In 2003, ANA's commitment to workforce advocacy was advanced with the creation of services and tools designated to help individual nurses self-advocate in their professional and personal development (Box 13-1).

BOX 13-1 Workforce Advocacy Ecosystem Model

Staffing: Refers to job assignments including the volume of work assigned to individuals, the professional skills required for particular job assignments, the duration of experience in a particular job category, and work schedules

Workflow design: Pertains to on-the-job activities of health care workers, including interactions among workers and the nature and scope of the work

Personal and social factors: Refer to individual and group factors, such as stress, job satisfaction, and professionalism, in addition to skills that may be underdeveloped in the nursing population, such as financial literacy

Physical environment: Includes aspects of the workplace, such as light, aesthetics, and sound. These elements will be crucial to address the needs of a maturing workforce and offer solutions to health care employers

Organizational factors: Structural and process aspects of the organization as a whole, such as the use of teams, divisions of labor, shared beliefs, and an increasing leadership capacity among nurses

Adapted from Hickam DH, Severance S, Feldstein A, et al: *The effect of health care working conditions on patient safety,* Evidence Reports/technology Assessments No. 74 (website). http://www.ncbi.nlm.nih.gov/books/NBK36875/ (AHRQ Publication No 03-E031, Rockville, MD, Agency for Healthcare Research and Quality, April 2003; www.ahrq.gov).

BOX 13-2 Five Opportunities and Challenges for Workforce Advocacy Programs

1. Identify mechanisms within health care systems that provide opportunities for RNs to affect institutional policies.
   - Shared governance
   - Participatory management models
   - Magnet® hospital recognition
   - Statewide staffing regulations
2. Develop conflict resolution models for use within organizations that address RNs' concerns about patient care and delivery issues.
   - Identification of the reporting loop
   - Appointment of a final arbiter in disputes
3. Seek legislative solutions for workplace problems by reviewing issues of concern to nurses in employment settings and introducing appropriate legislation, such as the following:
   - Whistle-blower protection
   - "Safe harbor" peer review

- Support for rules outlining strong nursing practice standards
4. Develop legal centers for nurses that could provide legal support and decision-making advice as a last recourse to resolve workplace issues.
   - Provide fast and efficient legal assistance to nurses
   - Earmark precedent-setting cases that could affect case law and health care policy
5. Provide RNs with self-advocacy and patient advocacy information, such as the following:
   - Laws and regulations governing practice
   - Use of applicable nursing practice standards
   - Conflict resolution and negotiation techniques
   - State and national reporting mechanisms that allow RNs to report concerns about health care organizations and/or professionals

American Nurses Association: *Five opportunities/challenges for workforce advocacy programs.* Adapted from the Texas Nurses Association: Workplace advocacy program (website). http://www.nursingworld.org/MainMenuCategories/ThePracticeofProfessional Nursing/workforce/Workforce-Advocacy/Opportunities-for-Advocacy-Programs.html.

Five opportunities and challenges for workforce advocacy programs are highlighted in Box 13-2. Other examples of workforce advocacy and specific workplace issues are discussed in the following sections.

NURSING SHORTAGES AND WORKFORCE CHALLENGES

The nursing profession has a long history of cyclic shortages, which have been documented since World War II. The most recent shortage in the early 2000s was eased by the downturn in the U.S. economy that occurred in the mid- to late 2000s (Thrall, 2009). This easing in the shortage was largely due to many retired nurses re-entering the workforce because of economic pressures, nurses who had planned to retire who were holding on to their positions, some nurses working part-time who had taken full-time positions, and hospitals treating fewer patients because many people were delaying procedures or not seeking care due to loss of insurance (American Hospital Association, 2008; Buerhaus, 2008).

The focus on the nursing shortage beginning in the early 2000s generated many positive results: an unexpected number of young people entered the nursing workforce from 2002 to 2009, causing faster growth in the supply than anticipated. During this same time period, the number of full-time RNs 23 to 26 years of age increased steadily, by 62%—a rate of growth that has not been seen since the 1970s (Auerbach et al, 2011). Despite this positive sign of stabilization, workforce analysts caution nurse educators, policymakers, employers, and other stakeholders that considerably more progress is needed if the country is to meet the fast-growing needs for professional nurses at a time when the population is aging, more people are living with chronic conditions, and implementation of the Patient Protection and Affordable Care Act (ACA) has the potential of covering an additional 32 million Americans, and 40% of RNs are rapidly approaching retirement age (McMenamin, 2014). Continuing attention to the nursing workforce is necessary in order to encourage young people to remain interested in nursing.

Future RN Employment Opportunities

Professional nursing is the largest U.S. health care occupation according to the Bureau of Labor Statistics (U.S. Department of Labor, 2014). Employment of registered nurses is expected to grow by 19% from 2012 to

2022, much faster than the average for all occupations. Thousands of job openings will result from:

- The need to replace experienced nurses who leave the occupation, especially with one third of the nursing workforce older than 50 years of age (Health Resources and Services Administration [HRSA], 2013)
- Technologic advances in patient care that result in more patients accessing the health care system and needing more specialized care
- Increasing emphasis on preventive care
- The rapid growth in the older population, who are much more likely than younger people to need nursing care
- An increased emphasis on employment opportunities for nurses in case management and care coordination such as Advanced Practice Registered Nurses (APRNs) including Family Nurse Practitioners, Pediatric Nurse Practitioners, and Adult-Gerontology Acute Care Nurse Practitioners

Employment will not grow at the same rate in every setting—hospital employment will grow more slowly because many procedures and care are shifting to outpatient and home health settings, more sophisticated procedures can safely be done outside the hospital, and home health and long-term care facilities will see employment growth due to the aging population.

Current projections suggest that the United States will need to produce 1.1 million new RNs by 2022 to fill newly created jobs and replace a legion of soon-to-be retirees; however, the employment market is showing mixed signals. There have been layoffs by some hospitals at the same time that "registered nurse" ranks as the most advertised position nationwide. Health care employers must confront the reality of an aging population and increased access to care due to health care reforms while there is a "graying" of the nursing workforce. Planning for an adequate workforce will remain one of the most critical challenges of the new century. The following sections take a closer look at the challenges faced to ensure an appropriate supply of nurses to meet the nation's health care needs.

Health Care as a Challenging Work Environment

In examining nursing shortages, it is important to consider the nurses' work environment. In a comparison of three national random sample surveys of RNs, areas identified as negatively affecting nursing satisfaction

were: (1) opportunities to influence decisions about workplace organization; (2) recognition of accomplishments and work well done; (3) opportunities for professional development and advancement; and (4) opportunities to influence decisions about patient care (Buerhaus et al, 2009). In a 2013 job satisfaction and career plans survey of RNs, results showed that 90% of nurses stated they are satisfied with their career choice (AMN Healthcare, 2013). Despite the high level of career choice satisfaction, respondents were less optimistic about their current jobs: only 73% said they are satisfied, 51% said they worry that their jobs are affecting their health, 35% said they often feel like resigning, and 33% indicated that they may not be working in their current jobs in 1 year. With the improving economy, approximately 23% of nurses age 55 and older plan to dramatically change their work life in the very near future. Workplace challenges as indicated by this survey charge health system leaders to redesign work environments so that they are able to attract, retain, and develop the best RN workforce.

Nursing School Enrollments and Recruitment

Numerous efforts were undertaken over the past decade to recruit more students into nursing—efforts that have been largely successful. Professional nursing associations and health care companies educated the public regarding the shortage and the benefits of a nursing career. The Johnson & Johnson *Campaign for Nursing's Future*, a multiyear $30 million national initiative, was designed to enhance the image of the nursing profession, recruit new nurses and nurse faculty, and help retain nurses currently in the profession (Johnson & Johnson, 2014). Unfortunately, even when attempts to recruit more people into nursing have been successful, most schools and universities find themselves unable to expand their nursing programs to accept the qualified applicants because they are faced with a serious shortage of nursing faculty. National and statewide efforts have resulted in increases in nursing school enrollments for 13 consecutive years, yet these increases will not balance out the impending wave of RN retirements or employment changes as the economy recovers (American Association of Colleges of Nursing [AACN], 2014a).

Along with the need to recruit into the profession, nursing must continue to examine the ways in which new nurses are introduced into the nursing work culture. Adequate orientation, mentoring, and preceptor programs are essential to introduce and retain new nurses.

Educational Preparation

During past shortages, employers have hired RNs regardless of their degree preparation. The current and projected demands for RNs require not simply more RNs, but more RNs of the right type and right educational and skill mix to handle increasingly complex care demands. Demand has intensified for more baccalaureate-prepared nurses with critical thinking, leadership, quality improvement, case management, and health promotion skills, who are capable of delivering care across a variety of health care settings. Demand has also increased for experienced RNs; for nurses in key clinical specialties, such as critical care, emergency department (ED), operating room, and neonatal intensive care; and for master's- and doctoral-prepared RNs in advanced clinical specialties, teaching, and research.

In October 2010, the Institute of Medicine (IOM, 2011) released its landmark report, *The Future of Nursing: Leading Change, Advancing Health,* initiated by the Robert Wood Johnson Foundation, which called for increasing the number of baccalaureate-prepared nurses in the workforce to 80% by 2020 (the current workforce has only 55% of RNs prepared at the baccalaureate or graduate degree level [HRSA, 2013]). This and other evidence-based recommendations contained in the report state that to respond "to the demands of an evolving health care system and meet the changing needs of patients, nurses must achieve higher levels of education" (IOM, 2011).

Faculty Shortages

One of the most critical problems facing nursing and nursing workforce planning is the aging of nursing faculty (AACN, 2014b). AACN's 2013 survey of baccalaureate nursing programs showed only a 2.6% enrollment increase from 2012 to 2013, marking the lowest growth over the past 5 years. The shortage of faculty is contributing to the current nursing shortage by limiting the number of students admitted to nursing programs. AACN reported that 79,659 qualified applicants were turned away from baccalaureate and graduate nursing programs in 2012, and an insufficient number of faculty was a major reason cited by schools for not accepting all qualified applicants (AACN, 2014b). Faculty salaries continue to be a major contributor to the faculty shortage. Academic institutions, especially those faced with budget cuts, generally cannot compete with nonacademic employers when it comes to salary benefits for faculty.

Nurse Retention

Past nursing shortages have demonstrated that the retention of professional nurses is a key to any organization's success. The ability of an organization to retain nurses primarily depends on the creation of an environment conducive to professional autonomy. Nurses want to work in an environment that supports decision making and effective nurse-physician relationships, which are critically important to patient safety. Although some progress has been achieved, RNs' perceptions of the hospital workplace environment demonstrate need for improvement (Brewer et al, 2012; Buerhaus et al, 2009; Unruh and Nooney, 2011). In two studies of newly licensed RNs, a number of workplace environment issues affected turnover and retention: sprains and strains, including back injuries (Brewer et al, 2012), inadequate orientation, high patient load, and floating between patient care units (Unruh and Nooney, 2011).

Aging Workforce and Retention

As the nation works to increase the supply of professional nurses through education, strategies must be developed to retain the older, expert professional nurse. The following statistics detail the extent of the aging workforce issue (Budden et al, 2013; HRSA, 2013):

- In 2013, more than half (53%) of RNs working in nursing were age 50 or older.
- In terms of nursing faculty, 72% teaching full-time were age 50 or older—only 14% were younger than age 40.

There has been little research to test the effectiveness of recruitment and retention strategies with older nurses. In a qualitative study of influences on the older nurse to continue bedside practice, the authors found that the most pervasive and difficult experiences for older nurses involved dealing with stress, frustration, constant change, physical and mental declines, and dealing with intergenerational conflict (Spiva et al, 2011). Despite the challenges, the nurses in this study found positive aspects of and meaning in being a nurse—through the recollection of earlier and happier memories, making a connection with patients, and cherishing the preciousness of caring for patients and families. Suggestions on ways to keep older nurses practicing include better ergonomics and health care facility design to decrease the time nurses spend walking and reduce the physical demands of their work with aids such as mechanical lifts, decentralized supply storage, and better lighting at the bedside (Bleich et al, 2006).

Although many organizations have added on-site daycare and sick care for children of younger nurses, organizations may need to consider adding adult daycare to assist older nurses who are caring for aging parents. Creative staffing plans with shorter shifts and identified respite periods may help extend the work life of aging nurses. Technology has provided many workplace accessories that reduce the physical demands on nurses that can result in injury or stress, especially to aging nurses.

The American Organization of Nurse Executives (AONE, 2010) has developed *Guiding Principles for the Aging Workforce* that encourage health care facilities to develop benefits that will entice the older nurse to stay in the organization, such as flexible work schedules, programs involving both experienced and newer nurses to promote knowledge transfer, environmental modifications with an emphasis on injury prevention, and phased retirement or rehiring post-retirement. Organizations that strategically plan for an aging workforce will be best positioned to deliver quality health care to their customers.

Emerging Workforce Recruitment and Retention

In addition to planning for retention of an aging workforce, health care is challenged to become the employer of choice for the younger emerging workforce. A number of studies have focused on the work and management expectations of today's young worker who expects balance and perspective in the workplace. In a study focused on Generation Y nurses (those born after 1980), recognition was reported as a key motivator. The younger nurses identified their needs as stability, flexible work schedules, recognition, opportunities for professional development, and adequate supervision (Lavoie-Tremblay et al, 2010). Elena, the young nurse described at the beginning of the chapter, will be searching for opportunities to gain advanced training, education, and certification as she seeks to make herself more marketable in her professional nursing role. She expects feedback on her performance to help refine her skills and build her confidence. She also expects her manager to take a personal interest in her, to know her name, and to help her build a competitive portfolio. Many managers are unaware of these expectations in emerging workforce employees and contribute to their hastened exit from the workplace by not attending to their personal and career needs.

Nursing Salaries

RN salaries show a consistent pattern in alignment with nursing shortages. The hospital RN shortages of the 1960s, 1970s, 1980s, and early 1990s were transitory until wage increases brought the demand and supply of RNs into equilibrium. Unfortunately, during the 1990s nursing salaries remained flat—low salaries definitely contributed to the nursing shortage. Another concern with nursing salaries is the small opportunity for significant salary increases as nurses gain more experience.

Fortunately, a sharp increase in RN wages occurred in 2002 and 2003. This increase reflects the acceleration in demand for RNs that occurred from 2001 to 2004. Since then, the average staff nurse wages have only kept up with inflation. The Bureau of Labor Statistics (U.S. Department of Labor, 2014) reports the median salary for a registered nurse was $66,220. The best paid 10% of RNs made more than $96,320, whereas the bottom 10% earned less than $45,630. In 2012, the highest median salaries were earned by nurses working in government, hospitals, and home health care.

Work Environment

In the late 1990s, studies focused on the work environment as a significant contributor to the difficulty in recruiting and retaining RNs (Nolan et al, 1999). Primary factors for nurse turnover were workload and staffing patterns. Other issues identified were insufficient supply of qualified managers and experienced staff, increased market demand, and inappropriate staffing. The importance of addressing the work environment is clear—efforts at increasing the overall supply of nurses are unlikely to be successful if retention strategies are not developed.

Most health care employers now understand the importance of directing their attention to improving the workplace. Nursing school enrollments are at capacity, and it is vitally important to retain nurses in an effort to boost overall supply. New research has shown the positive impact of a healthy work environment on staff satisfaction, retention, improved patient outcomes, and organizational performance (Aiken et al, 2009; Sherman and Pross, 2010). In a study exploring the mechanism by which reducing patient-to-nurse ratios improves outcomes, Aiken and colleagues (2011) found that decreasing the number of patients per nurse improved mortality and failure to rescue, predominantly in hospitals rated as having a good work environment. Hospitals with a poor work environment derived no benefit from reducing patient-to-nurse ratios.

Several national initiatives have been undertaken to promote positive and safe work environments for nurses. In one of the first efforts, the Nursing Organizations Alliance, a coalition of more than 65 national nursing organizations, developed its *Principles and Elements of a Healthful Practice/Work Environment* (Nursing Organizations Alliance, 2004), which provides a framework for organizations to improve nurses' work environments. The American Association of Critical Care Nurses promotes a "healthy work environment" as one of their three major advocacy issues and developed standards along with measurement tools (AACN, 2014). The Joint Commission also noted more than a decade ago: "if the staffing levels and work environments are not safe for the nurses, they will not be safe for the patients" (The Joint Commission, 2002).

SAFE STAFFING

Many nurses across the country are concerned about the inadequacies of staffing to meet patient care needs. In a survey of almost 220,000 RNs from 13,000 nursing units in over 550 hospitals and a response rate of 70%, nurses reported that 54% of nurses in adult medical units and emergency rooms do not have sufficient time with patients; overtime has increased during the past year with 43% of all RNs working extra hours because the unit is short-staffed or busy; and inadequate staffing affected unit admissions, transfers, and discharges more than 20% of the time (ANA, 2014a).

A landmark study by Aiken and colleagues (2002) found that in hospitals with fewer nurses per patient, surgical patients were more likely to experience higher death rates from failure to rescue (insufficient nursing care) and death from complications. The same study also found that nurses working in institutions plagued by insufficient staffing and workforce shortages were more likely to experience emotional exhaustion and greater job dissatisfaction. Subsequent research has reinforced the importance of appropriate nurse staffing and positive patient outcomes.

However, many questions still exist about how to quantify appropriate staffing and how to appropriately use unlicensed personnel to assist in the delivery of care to patient populations who are more acutely ill, who require high-tech care, and whose lengths of stay are being reduced to keep costs in check. Federal regulations require hospitals to "have adequate numbers of licensed registered nurses, licensed practical [vocational] nurses, and other personnel to provide nursing care to all patients as needed" (U.S. Department of Health and Human Services, 2011, § 482.23). With such nebulous language, it has been left to the states to ensure that staffing is appropriate to meet patients' needs safely. Three general approaches to ensure sufficient nurse staffing have been utilized at the state level (ANA, 2013a):

- Require hospitals to have a nurse-driven staffing committee to create staffing plans that reflect the needs of the patient population and match the skills and experience of the staff. ANA endorses this approach through its *Principles for Nurse Staffing, Second Edition,* which provides recommendations on optimal staffing and requires nurses to be an integral part of the nurse staffing plan development and decision-making process (ANA, 2014b). Such an approach provides for flexible staffing levels that can account for the intensity of patient needs, number of admissions, discharges and transfers during a shift, level of experience of nursing staff, layout of the unit, and availability of resources (e.g., ancillary staff, technology) (ANA, 2013a). As of 2013, seven states require hospitals to have staffing committees responsible for plans and staffing policy—Connecticut, Illinois, Nevada, Ohio, Oregon, Texas, and Washington.
- Require facilities to disclose staffing levels to the public and/or a regulatory body. As of 2013, five states require some form of disclosure/public reporting—Illinois, New Jersey, New York, Rhode Island, and Vermont.
- Enact legislation to mandate specific nurse-to-patient ratios. As of 2013, California continued to be the only state with specified nurse-to-patient ratios.

Under the California rules, one nurse will not care for more than five patients in medical-surgical units, four patients in specialty care and telemetry units, and three patients in step-down units. Research studying the effectiveness of California's staffing law showed that California hospitals increased nurse staffing levels over time significantly more than did comparison state hospitals; however, findings related to patient safety measures were mixed, with significantly decreased rates associated with failure to rescue and significantly increased rates of infections due to medical care in some California hospitals than in comparison state hospitals; and there were no statistically significant changes in either respiratory failure or postoperative sepsis (Mark et al, 2013).

As nurses consider staffing, they will be faced with many decisions, including how to determine appropriate staffing when considering an RN position, how to promote safe staffing in their own setting, and even being faced with a patient care assignment that they feel to be potentially unsafe. When considering a position, nurses should ask the questions regarding safe staffing in Box 13-3. Resources to help nurses' decision making relative to adequate staffing and mandatory overtime are included in Box 13-4. Box 13-5 identifies questions

---

BOX 13-3 Questions to Ask About Safe Staffing Before Accepting Employment

1. Who is the chief nursing officer, to whom does she or he report, and does she or he have authority over staffing?
2. Who controls the staffing budget?
3. Is the level of staffing an active and ongoing discussion in the organization, and do staff nurses have input?
4. Does the organization have a shared governance model?
5. When, where, and how is staffing input obtained from staff nurses?
6. How do ratios in the organization compare with recommendations of national and regional organizations, such as the American Organization of Nurse Executives and the American Association of Critical-Care Nurses?
7. What is the content and length of orientation for new nurses?
8. What is the philosophy regarding staff mix designations?
9. What is the frequency of floating to other nursing units?
10. What are the criteria used by the organization in determining competency of cross-trained staff?
11. What resources does the organization use to supplement staff during peak census?
12. If concerns arise about the adequacy of staffing, where and to whom is it appropriate to voice those concerns?
13. How are overtime, on-call time, and cancellation of regularly scheduled shifts handled?
14. Does the organization mandate overtime? If so, can the staff nurse refuse to participate without repercussions?
15. What is the turnover rate, and what is the average longevity of staff nurses?
16. What opportunities for advancement exist in the organization, such as clinical ladders or other systems of recognition?
17. Where does the organization expect discussions about staffing or practice issues to take place?
18. Is there a conflict resolution process in place?

American Nurses Association: *Questions to ask about safe staffing before accepting employment* (website). http://www.nursingworld.org/MainMenuCategories/ThePracticeofProfessionalNursing/workforce/Workforce.Advocacy/Questions.to.Ask.html Accessed September 2014.

BOX 13-4 Resources for Decision Making Related to Adequacy of Staffing and Mandatory Overtime

Guidebooks

ANA Principles for Nurse Staffing, 2nd Edition—directs RNs on how to determine the level of nurse staffing for any setting. It focuses on patient acuity systems, the basics of workload measurement, patient classification, unlicensed assistive personnel, the role of professional judgment, and the development of principles.

ANA's Principles for Delegation—provides the principles and guidelines for delegation of tasks to others. Its purpose is to define relevant principles and provide RNs with practice strategies when delegating patient care to nursing assistive personnel. It also covers needed definitions and the essentials of care provision and related nurse education.

Principles for Nursing Documentation—focuses on managing the increasingly complex requirements of documenting patient care activities in both paper and electronic formats.

These three documents are available as a *Principles for Practice* set at *www.nursesbooks.org*.

Other Resources

ANA's Nurse Staffing website:
> *http://www.nursingworld.org/MainMenuCategories/ThePracticeofProfessionalNursing/NurseStaffing*

ANA's Position Statements Regarding Workplace Advocacy
> *http://nursingworld.org/positionstatements*

BOX 13-5 Questions to Ask in Making the Decision to Accept a Staffing Assignment

1. *What is the assignment?*

   Clarify the assignment. Do not assume. Be certain that what you believe is the assignment is indeed correct.

2. *What are the characteristics of the patients being assigned?*

   Do not just respond to the number of patients; make a critical assessment of the needs of each patient, his or her age, condition, other factors that contribute to special needs, and the resources available to meet those needs. Who else is on the unit or within the facility that might be a resource for the assignment? Do nurses on the unit have access to those resources? How stable are the patients, and how long have they been stable? Do any patients have communication and/ or physical limitations that will require accommodation and extra supervision during the shift? Will there be discharges to offset the load? If there are discharges, will there be admissions, which require extra time and energy?

3. *Do I have the expertise to care for the patients?*

   Am I familiar with caring for the types of patients assigned? If this is a float assignment, am I cross-trained to care for these patients? Is there a buddy system in place with staff who are familiar with the unit? If there is no cross-training or buddy system, has the patient load been modified accordingly?

4. *Do I have the experience and knowledge to manage the patients for whom I am being assigned care?*

   If the answer to this question is no, you have an obligation to articulate limitations. Limitations in experience and knowledge may not require refusal of the assignment but rather an agreement regarding supervision or a modification of the assignment to ensure patient safety. If no accommodation for limitations is considered, the nurse has an obligation to refuse an assignment for which she or he lacks education or experience.

5. *What is the geography of the assignment?*

   Am I being asked to care for patients who are in proximity for efficient management, or are the patients at opposite ends of the hall or on different units? If there are geographic difficulties, what resources are available to manage the situation? If my patients are on more than one unit and I must go to another unit to provide care, who will monitor patients out of my immediate attention?

6. *Is this a temporary assignment?*

   When other staff are located to assist, will I be relieved? If the assignment is temporary, it may be possible to accept a difficult assignment, knowing that there will soon be reinforcements. Is there a pattern of short staffing, or is this truly an emergency?

7. *Is this a crisis or an ongoing staffing pattern?*

   If the assignment is being made because of an immediate need on the unit, a crisis, the decision to accept the assignment may be based on that immediate need. However, if the staffing pattern is an ongoing problem, the nurse has the obligation to identify unmet standards of care that are occurring as a result of ongoing staffing inadequacies. This may result in a request for "safe harbor" and/or peer review.

8. *Can I take the assignment in good faith? (If not, you will need to get the assignment modified or refuse the assignment.)*

   Consult your individual state's nurse practice act regarding clarification of accepting an assignment in good faith. In understanding good faith, it is sometimes easier to identify what would constitute bad faith. For example, if you had not taken care of pediatric patients since nursing school and you were asked to take charge of a pediatric unit, unless this were an extreme emergency, such as a disaster (in which case you would need to let people know your limitations, but you might still be the best person, given all factors for the assignment), it would be bad faith to take the assignment. It is always your responsibility to articulate your limitations and to get an adjustment to the assignment that acknowledges the limitations you have articulated. Good faith acceptance of the assignment means that you are concerned about the situation and believe that a different pattern of care or policy should be considered. However, you acknowledge the difference of opinion on the subject between you and your supervisor and are willing to take the assignment and await the judgment of other peers and supervisors.

American Nurses Association: *Questions to ask in making the decision to accept a staffing assignment* (website). http://www.nursingworld.org/MainMenuCategories/ThePracticeofProfessionalNursing/workforce/Workforce-Advocacy/Questions-in-Decision-to-Accept-Staffing-Assignment.html.

to help the staff nurse in making a decision to accept an assignment. These questions are designed to help the staff nurse think critically about the assignment so, if there is a problem, the nurse can be clear in telling the manager what makes her or him uncomfortable with the assignment.

Floating and Mandatory Overtime

As concerns about nursing shortages ebb and flow so too does the use of floating and mandatory overtime as strategies for addressing immediate nurse staffing issues. When the availability of nursing staff tightens, employers may (1) require that professional nurses "float" to other patient care units for which they have little or no orientation, experience, or support and (2) implement mandatory overtime and/or mandatory on-call requirements. Particularly with regard to mandatory overtime, such strategies can be challenging given research findings that nurses' work schedules are associated with patient mortality. For example, pneumonia deaths were significantly more likely in hospitals where nurses reported schedules with long work hours and lack of time away from work (Trinkoff, et al, 2011). In addition, findings related to nursing fatigue and sleep deprivation found that nurses are more likely to report clinical decision regret, which occurs when their behaviors do not align with professional nursing practices standard or expectations (Scott et al, 2014).

Nurses believe that an employers' ability to mandate last-minute overtime or to use peer pressure as a negative motivator relieves the employers' sense of urgency to find safer and more appropriate staffing. Although nurses are fully cognizant and concerned about inadequate staffing, they may also be resentful that they bear the personal, professional, and legal burden for this problem by having to work overtime. While the growing research on overtime and medical errors has caused many facilities to drop their use of mandatory overtime and even limit hours of voluntary overtime, it continues to be a concern. Excessive and recurrent use of overtime, at times used as a staffing strategy, has made it necessary for states to pursue legislation limiting its use. See the ANA website at www.nursingworld.org for more information and resources on mandatory overtime.

PATIENT ADVOCACY AND SAFETY

Patient advocacy is a cornerstone of the nursing profession, and patients depend on nurses to ensure that they receive proper care. Although nurses have always advocated for their patients, it has only been during the past 30 years that the recognized role of the nurse as patient advocate has begun to clearly emerge. Today's health care systems have created an environment in which errors and adverse events are attributed to complex systems and complicated uses of technology. This complex environment demands that the nursing profession

Professional nurses are struggling to deliver patient care against all kinds of barriers and with dwindling resources.

assert its powerful voice in the role of patient advocate by supporting public policies that protect consumers and enhance accountability for quality by promoting safer health care systems.

Patient Safety

A major IOM report on patient safety, *To Err Is Human* (Kohn et al, 2000), focused a great deal of attention on patient safety when it reported that between 44,000 and 98,000 patients die in U.S. hospitals each year from preventable medical errors. Subsequently, the IOM released its report, *Keeping Patients Safe: Transforming the Work Environment of Nurses* (Page, 2004), which examined patient safety from the perspective of the work environment in which nurses provide patient care. The report provided evidence of the critical role nurses have in the health care system and found that the typical work environment of nurses is characterized by many serious threats to patient safety. These and other IOM reports have had a major impact on clinical care and encouraged quality and safety programs such as the National Database of Nursing Quality Indicators, and the Quality and Safety Education for Nurses (QSEN) project.

The National Database for Nursing Quality Indicators (NDNQI) is a national nursing quality measurement program that enables hospitals to compare measures of nursing quality against national, regional and state norms for similar units and hospitals. NDNQI was initially started under ANA as a tool for nursing quality measurement, novel research and collaborative learning through data collection at the nursing unit level that allows for empirical linkages between nursing care and patient outcomes. Indicators such as patient falls, physical restraints, nosocomial infections, nursing care hours provided per patient day, and RN satisfaction surveys are used for quality improvement, reporting requirements (e.g., The Joint Commission [TJC], Magnet Recognition Program®), staff retention efforts, budget allocation, and research.

Recognizing the need to strengthen nurses' competencies in the science of patient safety and quality, the QSEN project was developed to prepare nurses with the knowledge, skills, and attitudes necessary to continuously improve the quality and safety of the health care systems in which they work (QSEN Institute, 2012). QSEN faculty developed pre-licensure and graduate-level quality and safety competencies for nurses in the core competencies recommended by the IOM (2003): patient-centered care, interprofessional teamwork and collaboration, evidence-based practice, quality improvement, safety, and informatics. The QSEN competencies are presented in more detail in Chapter 22. The QSEN website provides an abundance of resources about these six competencies: www.qsen.org.

Whistle-Blower Protection

Nurses want the assurance that if they are acting within the scope of their practice, they will be able to speak up for their patients through appropriate channels without fear of retaliation. State and federal whistle-blower protection legislation seeks to prohibit health care organizations from retaliating against nurses when the professional nurse in good faith discloses information or participates in agency investigations. Specifically, whistle-blower protection protects nurses who speak out about unsafe situations from being fired or subjected to other disciplinary actions by their employers.

An example of how whistle-blower protection promotes workplace advocacy is illustrated by a case in Texas. Two Texas nurses filed a complaint against a physician citing unsafe medical practice. The case in a small, rural county made national headlines in 2009 when the two nurses were charged with violating the law by sending an anonymous letter to the state medical board that expressed their concern about the physician's practice at the hospital. After receiving a complaint of harassment from the physician, the sheriff's department initiated an investigation that resulted in criminal charges against both nurses, and they were fired from their hospital positions. Charges against one of the nurses were dropped. The second nurse endured a 4-day trial and was found not guilty. The nurses filed a federal civil suit against their accusers alleging violation of civil rights, among other violations, and won a $750,000 settlement. ANA and Texas Nurses Association strongly supported the nurses, raising alarm about the criminal charges and the fact that the results from this case could have a potentially chilling effect on future nurse whistle-blowers. Ultimately, the county sheriff, county attorney, and hospital administrator were charged and received jail sentences for their roles in trying to silence the two nurses. The physician for whom the nurses brought forward the complaint plead guilty, receiving 60 days in jail and 5 years of probation. In addition, he paid a $5,000 fine and surrendered his medical license. The criminal convictions of all those involved in prosecuting the nurses sends a powerful message in support of whistle-blower protection. Box 13-6

BOX 13-6   *Things to Know About Whistle-Blowing*

- If you identify an illegal or unethical practice, reserve judgment until you have adequate documentation to establish wrongdoing.
- Do not expect those that are engaged in unethical or illegal conduct to welcome your questions or concerns about this practice.
- Seek the counsel of someone you trust outside of the situation to provide you with an objective perspective.
- Consult with your state nurses association or legal counsel if possible before taking action to determine how best to document your concerns.
- Remember that you are not protected in a whistle-blower situation from retaliation by your employer until you blow the whistle.
- Blowing the whistle means that you report your concern to the national and/or state agency responsible for regulation of the organization for which you work or, in the case of criminal activity, to law enforcement agencies as well.
- Private groups, such as The Joint Commission or the National Committee for Quality Assurance, do not confer protection. You must report to a state or national regulator.
- Although it is not required by every regulatory agency, it is a good rule of thumb to put your complaint in writing.
- Document all interactions related to the whistle-blowing situation, and keep copies for your personal file.
- Keep documentation and interactions objective.
- Remain calm, and do not lose your temper, even if those who learn of your actions attempt to provoke you.
- Remember that blowing the whistle is a very serious matter. Do not blow the whistle frivolously. Make sure you have the facts straight before taking action.

American Nurses Association: *Things to know about whistle-blowing,* 2011e (website). http://www.nursingworld.org/MainMenuCategories/ThePracticeofProfessionalNursing/workforce/Workforce-Advocacy/Whistle-Blowing.html.

provides an overview of things to know about whistle-blowing. Nurses should check with their state nurses association to assess the status of whistle-blower protection in their state.

NURSE AND WORKPLACE SAFETY

Nurses are battling to provide safe, quality care for patients in an environment that is inherently dangerous. The occupational safety and health of nurses is an ongoing concern for individual nurses as well as professional nursing associations because of numerous hazards that exist in the health care workplace. See the Centers for Disease Control and Prevention website for detailed information about current health hazards that exist in the healthcare workplace: www.cdc.gov/niosh/topics/healthcare. The following sections will focus on four key hazards: bloodborne pathogens, ergonomic injuries, workplace violence, and fatigue.

Exposure to Bloodborne Pathogens

Nurses and other health care professionals are at major risk for exposure to bloodborne diseases, including hepatitis B, hepatitis C, and human immunodeficiency virus–acquired immunodeficiency syndrome (HIV-AIDS).

In 1991, the Occupational Safety and Health Administration (National Institute for Occupational Safety and Health, 2014) issued the bloodborne pathogens standard to protect health care workers from this risk. The standard was revised by the Needlestick Safety and Prevention Act of 2000 (CDC, 2010). The law requires the use of safer needle devices to protect from sharps injuries. Additionally, the law requires employers to solicit the input of nonmanagerial employees responsible for direct patient care who are potentially exposed to sharps injuries in the identification, evaluation, and selection of effective engineering and work-practice controls. This law also requires employers to maintain a sharps injury log to contain, at a minimum, the brand of device involved in the incident, the department or work area where the exposure incident occurred, and an explanation of how the incident occurred.

Despite this legislation, safer practices related to handling of sharps have not been universally adopted. A decade after the law was enacted, one study demonstrated a 6.5% increase in sharps injuries in operation room settings (Jagger et al, 2010). And though the federal legislation requires that nurses and other direct care workers help evaluate and select safe needle devices, a 2011 survey reported that 43% of nurses who had access to safe needle devices did not know if nurses were involved in the selection process, and 19% reported that nurses were not involved (ANA, 2014a). See the ANA website at www.nursingworld.org for more information and resources about needlestick safety.

Ergonomic Injuries

The most recent data from the U.S. Department of Labor indicate that individuals working in health care experienced musculoskeletal disorders (MSDs) that resulted in days away from work at a rate 56% higher than all private industries, second only to the transportation and warehousing industry (U.S. Department of Labor, 2013). Nursing is ranked second after industrial work for physical workload intensity. Nurse aides, orderlies, and attendants reported the highest incidence of MSDs and were ranked second in overall MSDs requiring days away from work, with RNs ranked fifth (U.S. Department of Labor, 2013).

The extent of MSDs among the U.S. nursing workforce is distressing because it is estimated that 12% of nurses leave the profession annually due to back injuries, and more than 52% complain of chronic back pain (Gallagher, 2013). Two decades of research have demonstrated that use of a single approach (e.g., engineering controls, administrative changes, or worker training) to reduce the incidence of MSDs has been ineffective. There has been a shift toward evidence-based practices such as a comprehensive program that creates no-lift policies, secures appropriate safe patient handling and mobility technology, and trains staff on usage, with a comprehensive tracking system of MSD injuries that includes ongoing evaluation of the program.

Over the past decade, ANA has led major initiatives aimed at reducing workplace injuries, including the *Safe Patient Handling and Mobility Interprofessional National Standards* (ANA, 2013b). The standards, developed by an interprofessional work group of subject matter experts, outline the role of employers and health care workers in safe patient handling and mobility. See http://nursingworld.org/Safe-Patient-Handling-and-Mobility for detailed information about the standards. As of 2014, eleven states have adopted legislation to implement safe patient handling programs in health care facilities (ANA, 2013b). Federal legislation has been introduced to Congress intended to create a national occupational safety and health standard to reduce injuries to both patients and health care workers (Government Printing Office, 2013).

Experts strongly suspect that workplace injuries are highly underreported. Nurses have cited various reasons for not reporting workplace injuries. According to ANA's *2011 Health and Safety Survey* (ANA, 2014a), 68% of nurses who did not report their injuries chose not to do so because they didn't think the injury was significant. Other common reasons were being too busy (14%) and not having anyone to cover them (26%). In other surveys, nurses and other employees have indicated that they did not report injuries that occurred on the job due to fear of repercussions such as disciplinary action, stigmatization as a complainer, harassment, denial of opportunities for promotion, and even termination of employment (U.S. House of Representatives, 2008).

Every organization should have specific policies concerning reporting of workplace injuries and illness. ANA provides a number of resources and information concerning nurses' health and safety rights. The Occupational Safety and Health Administration's (OSHA) recordkeeping standard requires employers to keep a log of workplace injuries and to keep the OSHA 300 Log available to employees and their representatives (OSHA, 2013). The OSHA standard also prevents discrimination against employees who report a work-related injury, illness, or fatality.

Workplace Violence and Incivility in the Workplace

A summary of research by the National Institute for Occupational Safety and Health (2014) found that health care workers have almost five times the risk of experiencing a violence-related workplace injury requiring time off from work than individuals in the overall workforce. This does not include trauma experienced from verbal and less severe physical abuse. It is important to recognize that the spectrum of workplace violence also includes peer-to-peer lateral violence defined as acts of incivility or bullying behavior between colleagues or by someone in a higher level of authority. These behaviors, which include covert or overt acts of verbal and nonverbal aggression, have been reported to result in psychological distress severe enough to cause some nurses to leave the profession (Dellasega, 2009; Dillon, 2012).

Reports in the literature underscore the fact that underreporting of workplace violence is very common and may stem from the perception by health care workers that physical and verbal abuse is just "part of the job." Data obtained from nurses (RNs/LPNs) in a major population-based study showed a rate of physical assaults at 13.2 per 100 nurses per year and at a rate of 38.8 per 100 nurses per year for non-physical violent events (threat, sexual harassment, verbal) (Nachreiner et al, 2007). In the first national study of ED nurses and perceptions of workplace violence, investigators determined that violence against ED nurses is prevalent (Gacki-Smith et al, 2009). More than 25% of nurses who participated in this study reported experiencing physical violence more than 20 times in the past 3 years, and almost 20% reported experiencing verbal abuse more than 200 times during the same period. Another study found that more than 50% of nurses who responded to the survey were fearful of being physically injured at their workplace, but unprepared to handle violent behavior should it be directed toward them from a patient, family member, visitor, or coworker (Speroni et al, 2014). Greater than 25% of nurse respondents in this study said they had never received any training about workplace violence prevention.

Nurses in all settings must proactively advocate for interventions that ensure personal safety and a safe work environment. Workplace violence prevention programs must include a zero tolerance for workplace violence, verbal and nonverbal threats, or actions; ensure that no employee who reports or experiences workplace violence faces reprisals; have detailed record keeping to assess risk and measure progress; develop a comprehensive plan for maintaining security in the workplace; demonstrate management commitment from leadership; and provide periodic employee education about violence prevention in the workplace. ANA has developed a number of resources to combat the issue of bullying and violence in the workplace (ANA, 2014c).

Fatigue

Because the nature of health care can be physically and emotionally taxing, and require 24/7 scheduling in some settings, nursing can be a challenging profession. Nurses may work long and variable hours forgoing adequate rest and sleep, resulting in fatigue. Restorative sleep is critical to the health of the nurse and to ensure that the nurse can provide the highest quality patient care possible (Rogers et al, 2004; Trinkoff et al, 2011).

Inadequate sleep is known to negatively affect performance and mood and may result in an increase in risk-taking behavior, impairment of communication skills, and deficits in short-term and working memory (Killgore et al, 2012). In addition to the increased risk for work-related errors, the effects of fatigue on the health and well-being of the nurse are well-documented. Shift work and long hours have been linked to a multitude of health-related disorders, including diabetes, cardiovascular disease, depression, sleep disturbances, and physical injuries (Bae and Fabry, 2014; Bannai and Tamakoshi, 2014).

In 2013, ANA convened a professional issues panel that included nurses from all areas of the professional nursing community to address the safety and health issues related to nurse fatigue (ANA, 2014d). The resulting position statement outlined responsibilities of both nurses and employers, and included a substantive list of recommendations ranging from limitation of hours worked (to no more than 40 hours in one week and 12 hours in one shift), to elimination of mandatory overtime, and redesign of work schedules to minimize the occurrence of fatigue in the workplace (ANA, 2014d). Both the nurse and the employer have ethical responsibilities to ensure the safety and well-being of those who work in health care settings and the patients they care for. The nurse must take the steps necessary to ensure that he or she has adequate rest prior to the start of a work shift, and the employer must develop and maintain policies and procedures that support a healthy work environment and adequate rest.

Advocating for a Safer Workplace

ANA has emerged as a leader in health care worker health and safety, working in collaboration with other nursing organizations, including the American Association of Occupational Health Nurses, the Association of periOperative Registered Nurses, the Emergency Nurses Association, and labor unions representing health care workers. These organizations advocate for administrative controls, such as adequate staffing and health and safety committees; engineering controls, such as ventilation and safer needlestick devices; and personal protective equipment, such as respirators and synthetic gloves that will prevent exposure to hazardous substances and/or prevent illness or injury from unavoidable exposure. Although the health care industry can be a dangerous place to work, many of the risks are avoidable and dangerous exposures preventable. The following sections detail widely recognized models to promote excellent, safe environments for professional nursing practice.

MAGNET RECOGNITION PROGRAM®

One of the most successful nurse retention models focuses on standards for professional nursing practice that promote quality, excellence, and service. The

American Academy of Nurses, an ANA affiliate, undertook a national study of 163 acute care hospitals in the early 1980s to identify the factors associated with retaining qualified nurses during a nursing shortage (McClure et al, 1983). This landmark study identified 41 hospitals that shared common factors attributed to a 'magnet' environment: one that could attract and retain nurses even in the midst of a critical nursing shortage. Factors deemed to be critical influencers of nurse job satisfaction and turnover rates in the acute care setting included quality of leadership and exemplary management style, organizational structures that support nursing autonomy and career development, and an emphasis on professional practice excellence and quality of patient care. As a result, the ANA's credentialing arm, the American Nurses Credentialing Center (ANCC), used the findings from the study to create the Magnet Recognition Program®, which included best practice standards, originally titled the 14 Forces of Magnetism, to improve nurse satisfaction, the work environment of nurses, and reduce turnover rates.

As the Magnet Recognition Program® evolved, it sought to combine the strengths of the original study with quality indicators identified by the ANA and the standards of nursing practice as defined in the ANA's *Scope and Standards for Nurse Administrators* so that both quantitative and qualitative factors of nursing services were measured. The 2014 Magnet Recognition Program® continues to evolve, with a growing emphasis on quality outcomes in health care.

With its link between quality patient care and nursing excellence, the Magnet Recognition Program® has reached a coveted level of prestige within the nursing community and among acute care facilities. Research has consistently shown that Magnet® hospital nurses have higher levels of autonomy, more control over the practice setting and better relationships with physicians (Aiken et al, 2000; Aiken et al, 2008; Aiken et al, 2009; Armstrong et al, 2009; Wade et al, 2008; McHugh et al, 2013; Kramer et al, 2011). Magnet hospitals have also demonstrated lower mortality rates (McHugh et al, 2013). Magnet status is now seen as the single most effective mechanism for providing consumers and nurses with comparative information, the gold standard for quality nursing care. Nurses advocating for a strong workplace should advocate for their hospital to achieve Magnet status. For more information about the *Magnet Recognition Program®*, go to www.nursecredentialing.org/magnet.

PATHWAY TO EXCELLENCE® RECOGNITION PROGRAM

In 2003, the Texas Nurses Association (TNA) began work to positively affect nurse retention by improving the workplace for nurses and established the Texas Nurse-Friendly Program for small/rural hospitals. The program was designed to improve both the quality of patient care and professional satisfaction of nurses working in small and rural hospitals in Texas. To be responsive to a national market for this program, TNA sold the rights to the Nurse-Friendly Program to the ANCC in 2006. ANCC revised the standards to meet national criteria and renamed the program Pathway to Excellence®. Pathway practice standards were developed based on evidence-based practices and expert nurse input that promote and support a positive practice environment (ANCC, 2012). This recognition may be earned by acute-care and long-term care organizations that meet Pathway® standards for implementation of specific structures and processes designed to create a positive work environment (ANCC, 2012). For more information about the Pathway to Excellence® Program, go to www.nursecredentialing.org/pathway.

SHARED GOVERNANCE

Introduced in the 1970s, shared governance has been identified by RNs as a key indicator of excellence in nursing practice (Brody et al, 2012). The concept of professional practice models, such as shared governance, has attracted the attention of nursing in response to maintaining nursing job satisfaction, quality care, and fiscal viability.

The importance of shared governance is that such models provide an organizational framework for nurses in direct care to become committed to nursing practice within their organizations. The implementation of such models allows nurses to have an active role in decision making by providing maximal participation and accountability for the outcomes of those decisions. Shared governance models render a structure and an environment that empowers staff to make care decisions. Shared governance results in more than job satisfaction for nurses; it includes as equally important increased efficiency and better patient outcomes. Magnet Recognition Program® standards support the formation of a formal shared governance or decision-making model that promotes participation from nurses in all levels of practice regarding clinical practice decisions, quality improvement, and ongoing professional development.

Not all health care organizations have shared governance models. In these organizations it is important that nurses have access and input to the various organizational structures that are in place where decisions that affect the nurse and patient are made. Nurses need to be integral members of such organizational structures as quality improvement and ethics committees. Staff nurses need to know who their representatives are and how to access such committees. Box 13-7 identifies questions that should be asked about shared governance or participatory management models when nurses are trying to identify the organization that would be most conducive to the delivery of quality nursing care.

Regardless of the presence of shared governance models, all organizations should provide nurses with access to conflict resolution procedures that define the processes they should follow if they are in disagreement with the organization. Examples of such processes include open-door policies, ombudsman programs, or dispute-resolution processes. When seeking dispute resolution, the nurse may use a third party or resources internal to the organization to assist in the resolution. Some states have processes that can assist in resolving patient care or professional issues. These processes include peer review, safe harbor, and mandatory reporting.

BOX 13-7   Questions To Ask About Shared Governance Models

- Are nurses encouraged to participate in shared governance?
- How do nurses become involved in the shared governance process?
- What is the ratio of staff nurses to managers involved in shared governance within the organization?
- Is adequate work time allowed to participate in governance councils?
- How does the organization communicate shared governance decisions with staff nurses?
- How did shared governance improve nursing care delivery in the organization?
- Do nurses feel shared governance within their organization is beneficial to their practice?
- Does the organization have outcomes data related to shared governance?
- If so how have those data affected changes in nursing practice?

American Nurses Association: *Questions to ask about shared governance models* (website). http://www.nursingworld.org/MainMenuCategories/ThePracticeofProfessionalNursing/workforce/Workforce-Advocacy/Questions-to-Ask-About-Shared-Governance-Models.html.

SUMMARY

This chapter has covered a variety of significant workplace issues and identified workforce advocacy strategies for a nurse to use to improve the workplace environment and quality of patient care. A rapidly changing health care environment, significantly affected by an aging workforce and a nursing shortage, creates a challenge for all nurses. Nurses must be aware of the issues facing the profession and know where to seek assistance, information, and resources to address workplace issues. Working together with the resources of organizations such as the American Nurses Association, nurses can create a workplace that promotes career satisfaction and quality patient care.

REFERENCES

Aiken LH, Clarke SP, Sloane DM, et al: Hospital nurse staffing and patient mortality, nurse burnout, and job dissatisfaction, *JAMA* 288(16):1987–1993, 2002.

Aiken LH, Clarke SP, Sloane DM, et al: Effects of hospital care environment on patient mortality and nurse outcomes, *J Nurs Adm* 39(Suppl 7-8):S45–S51, 2009.

Aiken LH, Cimiotti JP, Sloane DM, et al: Effects of nurse staffing and education on patient deaths in hospitals with different nurse work environments, *Med Care* 49(12):1047–1053, 2011.

Aiken LH, Havens D, Sloane D: The Magnet Nursing Services Recognition Program: a comparison of two groups of magnet hospitals, *Am J Nurs* 100(3):26–34, 2000.

Aiken LH, Buchan J, Ball J, et al: Transformative impact of Magnet designation: England case study, *J Clin Nurs* 17(24):3330–3337, 2008.

American Association of Colleges of Nursing: *Nursing Shortage Fact Sheet*, Washington DC, 2014a, American Association of Colleges of Nursing (website). http://www.aacn. nche.edu/media-relations/fact-sheets/nursing-shortage. Accessed September 2014.

American Association of Colleges of Nursing: *Nursing faculty shortage fact sheet*, Washington DC, 2014b (website). http://www.aacn.nche.edu/media-relations/fact-sheets/ nursing-faculty-shortage. Accessed September 2014.

American Association of Critical Care Nurses: *AACN's Healthy Work Environments Initiative*, 2014 (website). http://www.aacn.org/wd/hwe/content/hwehome. pcms?menu=hwe. Accessed September 2014.

American Hospital Association: *New report details impact of economic downturn on patients and hospitals*, 2008 (website). http://www.aha.org/presscenter/ pressrel/2008/081119-pr-econimpact.shtml. Accessed September 2014.

American Nurses Association: *2011 ANA health and safety survey*, 2014 (website). http://www.nursingworld. org/2011HealthSurveyResults.aspx. Accessed August 2014.

American Nurses Association: *Nurse Staffing*, 2014 (website). http://www.nursingworld.org/MainMenuCategories/ ThePracticeofProfessionalNursing/NurseStaffing. Accessed September 2014.

American Nurses Association: *Bullying and workplace violence*, 2014 (website). http://www.nursingworld.org/ Bullying-Workplace-Violence. Accessed August 2014.

American Nurses Association: *Nurse Fatigue*, 2014d (website). http://www.nursingworld.org/MainMenuCategories/ WorkplaceSafety/Healthy-Work-Environment/Work-Environment/NurseFatigue. Accessed December 2014.

American Nurses Association: *Nurse staffing plans & ratios*, 2013a (website). http://www.nursingworld.org/ MainMenuCategories/Policy-Advocacy/State/ Legislative-Agenda-Reports/State-StaffingPlansRatios. Accessed September 2014.

American Nurses Association: *Safe patient handling and mobility*, 2013b (website). http://nursingworld.org/ Safe-Patient-Handling-and-Mobility. Accessed August 2014.

American Nurses Credentialing Center: *ANCC American Nurses Credentialing Pathway to Excellence®*, 2012 (website). http://www.nursecredentialing.org/pathway. Accessed August 2014.

American Organization of Nurse Executives: *AONE Guiding Principles for the Aging Workforce*, 2010 (website). http:// www.aone.org/resources/PDFs/AONE_GP_Aging_ Workforce.pdf. Accessed September 2014.

AMN Healthcare: *Survey of registered nurses: Generation gap grows as healthcare transforms*, 2013 (website). http://www. amnhealthcare.com/industry-research/2147484433/1033/. Accessed September 2014.

Armstrong K, Laschinger H, Wong C: Workplace empowerment and Magnet hospital characteristics as predictors of patient safety climate, *J Nurs Care Qual* 24(1):55–62, 2009.

Auerbach D, Buerhaus P, Staiger D: Registered nurse supply grows faster than projected amid surge in new entrants ages 23-26, *Health Aff* 30(12):2286–2292, 2011.

Bae S, Fabry D: Assessing the relationships between nurse work hours/overtime and nurse and patient outcomes: Systematic literature review, *Nursing Outlook* 62(1):138–156, 2014.

Bannai A, Tamakoshi A: The association between long working hours and health: A systematic review of epidemiological evidence. *Scandinavian Journal of Work, Environment & Health* 40(1):5–18, 2014.

Blegen M, Goode C, Spetz J, et al: Nurse staffing effects on patient outcome: safety-net and non-safety-net hospitals, *Med Care* 49(4):406–414, 2011.

Brewer C, Kovner C, Greene W, et al: Predictors of actual turnover in a national sample of newly licensed registered nurses employed in hospitals, *J Adv Nurs* 68(3):521–538, 2012.

Brody AA, Barnes K, Ruble C, et al: Evidenced-based practice councils: potential path to staff nurse empowerment and leadership growth, *J Nurs Adm* 42(1):28–33, 2012.

Budden J, Zhong E, Moulton P, Cimiotti J: Highlights of the national workforce survey of registered nurses, *Journal of Nursing Regulation* 4(2):5–14, 2013.

Buerhaus P: Current and future state of the U.S. nursing workforce, *JAMA* 300(20):2422–2424, 2008.

Buerhaus P, Staiger D, Auerbach D: *The future of the nursing workforce in the United States: data, trends, and implications*, Sudbury, MA, 2009, Jones & Bartlett.

Centers for Disease Control: *Needlestick safety and prevention act 2000*, 2010 (website). http://www.cdc.gov/sharpssafety/ pdf/Neelestick%20Saftety%20and%20Prevention%20Act. pdf. Accessed August 2014.

Dellasega C: Bullying among nurses, *Am J Nurs* 109(1):52–58, 2009.

Dillon B: Workplace violence: Impact, causes, and prevention, *Work* 42:15–20, 2012.

Gacki-Smith J, Juarez AM, Boyett L, et al: Violence against nurses working in US emergency departments, *J Nurs Adm* 39(7-8):340–349, 2009.

Gallagher S: *Implementation guide to the safe patient handling and mobility interprofessional national standards*, Silver Spring, MD, 2013, American Nurses Association.

Government Printing Office: *113th Congress 1st session H.R. 2480, nurse and healthcare worker protection act of 2013*, 2013 (website). http://www.gpo.gov/fdsys/pkg/ BILLS-113hr2480ih/pdf/BILLS-113hr2480ih.pdf. Accessed August 2014.

Bleich MR, Connolly C, Davis K, et al: *Wisdom at work: the importance of the older and experienced nurse in the workplace*, Princeton, NJ, 2006, Robert Wood Johnson Foundation.

http://www.rwjf.org/files/publications/other/wisdomatwork. pdf. Accessed January 15, 2015.

Health Resources and Services Administration: *The U.S. Nursing Workforce: Trends in Supply and Education*, 2013, (website). http://bhpr.hrsa.gov/healthworkforce/reports/ nursingworkforce/nursingworkforcefullreport.pdf. Accessed September 2014.

Institute of Medicine: *The Future of nursing: leading change, advancing health*, Washington, DC, 2011, National Academies Press.

Institute of Medicine: *Health professions education: A bridge to quality*, Washington, DC, 2003, National Academies Press.

Jagger J, Berguer R, Phillips E, et al: Increase in sharps injuries in surgical settings versus nonsurgical settings after passage of national needlestick legislation, *Journal of the American College of Surgeons* 210(4):496–502, 2010.

Johnson & Johnson: *Campaign for nursing's future*, 2014, (website). http://www.discovernursing.com/. Accessed September 2014.

Killgore WD, Grugle NL, Balkin TJ: Gambling when sleep deprived: Don't bet on stimulants, *Chronobiology International* 29(1):43–54, 2012.

Kohn L, Corrigan J, Donaldson M: To err is human: building a safer health system, Washington, DC, 2000, National Academies Press.

Kramer M, Maguire PAT, Brewer BB: Clinical nurses in Magnet hospitals confirm productive, healthy unit work environments, *Journal of nursing management* 19(1): 5–17, 2011.

Lavoie-Tremblay M, Leclerc E, Marchionni C, et al: The needs and expectations of Generation Y nurses in the workplace, *J Nurs Staff Dev* 26(1):2–8, 2010.

Lucero R, Lake E, Aiken L: Nursing care quality and adverse events in U.S. hospitals, *J Clin Nursing* 19(15-16): 2185–2195, 2010.

Mark B, Harless D, Spetz J, Reiter K, Pink G: California's minimum nurse staffing legislation: Results from a natural experiment, *Health Services Research* 48(2): 435–454, 2013.

Martsolf G, Auerbach D, Benevent R, et al: *Examining the value of inpatient nurse staffing: An assessment of quality and patient care costs*, AHRQ, June 9, 2014 (website). http://www.academyhealth.org/files/2014/monday/ martsolf.pdf. Accessed September 2014.

McClure M, Poulin M, Sovie MD, et al: *Magnet® hospitals: Attraction and retention of professional nurses: Task Force on Nursing Practice in Hospitals, American Academy of Nursing*, ANA publ., (G-160):i-xiv, 1-135, 1983.

McHugh MD, Kelly LA, Smith HL, et al: Lower mortality in magnet hospitals, *Medical Care* 51(5):382, 2013.

McHugh MD, Ma C: Hospital nursing and 30 day readmissions among Medicare patients with heart failure, acute myocardial infarction and pneumonia, *Medical Care* 61(1):52–59, 2013.

McMenamin P: Projected job growth in states by 2022: Demand for services, retirements drive need for 1.1 million more nurses, *The American Nurse*, July/August 2014, p 13.

Nachreiner NM, Gerberich SG, Ryan AD, McGovern PM: Minnesota nurses' study: perceptions of violence and the work environment, *Industrial Health-Kawasaki* 45(5):672, 2007.

National Institute for Occupational Safety and Health, Centers for Disease Control and Prevention: *NIOSH Workplace safety and health topics: health care workers*, 2014 (website). http://www.cdc.gov/niosh/topics/healthcare. Accessed August 2014.

Needleman J, Buerhaus P, Pankratz V, et al: Nurse staffing and inpatient hospital mortality, *N Engl J Med* 364(11):1037–1045, 2011.

Nolan M, Lundh U, Brown J: Changing aspects of nurses' work environment: a comparison of perceptions in two hospitals in Sweden and the UK and implications for recruitment and retention of staff, *J Nurs Res* 4(3):221–233, 1999.

Nursing Organizations Alliance: *Principles and elements of a healthful practice/work environment*, 2004 (website). http://www.aone.org/resources/leadership%20tools/PDFs/ PrinciplesandElementsHealthfulWorkPractice.pdf. Accessed September 2014.

Occupational Safety and Health Administration: *Bloodborne pathogens and needlestick prevention*, 2014 (website). https://www.osha.gov/SLTC/bloodbornepathogens/index. html. Accessed August 2014.

Occupational and Safety and Health Administration [OSHA]: *OSHA injury and illness recordkeeping and reporting requirements*, 2013 (website). https://www.osha. gov/recordkeeping/. Accessed August 2014.

Page A, editor: *Keeping patients safe: transforming the work environment of nurses, Institute of Medicine*, Washington, DC, 2004, National Academies Press.

Quality and Safety Education for Nurses Institute: *Project Overview*, 2012 (website). http://qsen.org/about-qsen/ project-overview/. Accessed September 2014.

Rogers AE, Hwang W, Scott LD, et al: The working hours of hospital staff nurses and patient safety, *Health Affairs* 23(4):202–212, 2004.

Scott LD, Arslanian-Engoren C, Engoren MC: Association of sleep and fatigue with decision regret among critical care nurses, *Am J Crit Care* 23:13–23, 2014.

Sherman R, Pross E: Growing future nurse leaders to build and sustain healthy work environments at the unit level, *OJIN* 15(1), 2010 (website). http://nursingworld.org/ MainMenuCategories/ANAMarketplace/ANAPeriodicals/ OJIN/TableofContents/Vol152010/No1Jan2010/ Growing-Nurse-Leaders.html. Accessed September 2014. DOI: 10.3912/OJIN.Vol15No01Man01.

Speroni K, Fitch T, Dawson E, et al: Incidence and cost of nurse workplace violence perpetrated by hospital patients or patient visitors, *Journal of Emergency Nursing* 40(3): 218–228, 2014.

Spiva L, Hart P, McVay F: Discovering ways that influence the older nurse to continue bedside practice, 2011 (website). http://www.hindawi.com/journals/nrp/2011/840120/. Accessed September 2014.

The Joint Commission: *Health care at the crossroads: strategies for addressing the evolving nursing crisis*, Oakbrook Terrace, IL, 2002, The Joint Commission on Accreditation of Healthcare Organizations.

Thrall TH: The return of the RNs, *Hosp Health Netw* 83(4): 22–24, 2009.

Trinkoff AM, Johantgen M, Storr S, et al: Nurses' work schedule characteristics, nurse staffing, and patient mortality, *Nursing Research* 60(1):1–8, 2011.

Tubbs-Cooley H, Cimiotti J, Silber JH, et al: An observational study of nurse staffing ratios and hospital readmission among children admitted for common conditions, *BMJ Qual Saf* 22(9):735–742, 2013.

Unruh L, Nooney J: Newly licensed registered nurses' perceptions of job difficulties, demands and control: Individual and organizational predictors, *J Nurs Manag* 19(5): 572–584, 2011.

U.S. Department of Health and Human Services, Centers for Medicare and Medicaid Services: *§482.23 Condition of participation: nursing services*, 2011, (website). http://www.gpo.gov/fdsys/granule/CFR-2011-title42-vol5/CFR-2011-title42-vol5-sec482-23/content-detail.html. Accessed September 2014.

U.S. Department of Labor, Bureau of Labor Statistics: *Occupational outlook handbook (2014-2015)*, 2014, (website). http://www.bls.gov/ooh/healthcare/registered-nurses.htm. Accessed September 2014.

U.S. Department of Labor, Bureau of Labor Statistics: *Injuries, illnesses, and fatalities*, 2013, (website). http://www.bls.gov/iif/. Accessed August 2014.

U.S. House of Representatives: *Hidden tragedy: underreporting of workplace injuries and illnesses*, 2008 (website). http://democrats.edworkforce.house.gov/hearing/hidden-tragedy-underreporting-workplace-injuries-and-illnesses. Accessed August 2014.

Wade GH, Osgood B, Avino K, et al: Influence of organizational characteristics and caring attributes of managers on nurses' job enjoyment, *J Adv Nurs* 64(4):344–353, 2008.

14

Collective Bargaining and Unions in Today's Workplace

Barbara Cherry, DNSc, MBA, RN, NEA-BC

Collective bargaining is a method to achieve power-sharing in the workplace.

ⓔ Additional resources are available online at: *http://evolve.elsevier.com/Cherry/*

PROFESSIONAL/ETHICAL ISSUE

Samuel Lennon is a registered nurse in the cardiovascular lab at University Hospital. He is currently experiencing extreme stress and internal conflict because the nurses are going through a union organizing effort. What he thought would be a fairly easy process to vote in a **union** to represent the nurses with a strong voice to improve their nurse-to-patient ratios has turned into a tension-filled, adversarial situation. Before the union efforts started, Samuel had a good relationship with his nurse manager; now they are pitted against each other because they both have very different perspectives about unions. He is also feeling tension and distrust with the same nurses he had supportive working relationships with only a few weeks ago; but they are now against each other because of opposing views about unions. His once collegial relationships with the pharmacists and physical therapists on his unit have also become strained. Samuel is now having a great deal of self-doubt about the unionizing efforts and especially what some of his colleagues perceive to be the potential for patient abandonment in the event of a **strike**. Samuel's greatest concern is how this very difficult situation is affecting patient care. *How can Samuel resolve his feelings and ethical concerns about the unionizing effort yet remain true to the original goals of unionization?*

VIGNETTE

Addison Mitchell graduated in June from nursing school. She passed the NCLEX® examination and can now call herself a registered nurse (RN). As she drives to the hospital on the first day of her new job, she is feeling a sense of pride and joy, mixed with sheer fright, as she realizes that this is the world-class place she has chosen for her first job. She had always dreamed of working at this hospital, and she will now have a chance to become a seasoned nurse at one of the finest hospitals in the country.

Addison is realistic enough to know that her feelings of joy may not last as her new job is likely to be very stressful, but she is unaware that she is on the verge of walking into a challenging situation. As she enters the drive leading to
the hospital parking area, picketers are there with signs about unfair working conditions and she quickly learns that nurses are involved in organizing to be represented by a union. As Addison walks to the building with her new name tag that reads "Registered Nurse," she is approached by a person asking her to sign a card. Addison states, "I'm sorry. I'm new here. I need to get my feet on the ground, and then I will be happy to talk to you about the card." Addison begins to feel very anxious because she does not have a good understanding of union organizing efforts or the issues the nurses at the hospital are facing.

Addison does not yet know that she will be approached many times in the coming days by coworkers who will tell her how she should feel and what she should do. She has much to consider before making a decision between two alternatives that she does not fully understand.

Questions to Consider While Reading this Chapter:

1. What questions should the nurse ask about collective bargaining and labor relations?
2. What does signing a card mean, and what questions should Addison ask before signing?
3. How can Addison establish good relationships with both nurse managers and staff nurses in an atmosphere in which collective bargaining has put these two groups in adversarial positions?
4. What skills and information will Addison need to navigate and make effective decisions in this hospital?
5. What provisions in a union contract are in a patient's best interest as well as a nurse's?
6. What resources are available to Addison to help her learn more about labor and management issues occurring in the hospital?

KEY TERMS

Arbitration: The process of negotiation sanctioned in the United States by the National Labor Relations Board. It is the method used for formal talks between management and labor within modern business, industry, or service organizations. Binding arbitration means that all parties must obey the arbitrator's recommendations.

Collective bargaining: The process whereby workers organize under the representation of a union in order to share a degree of power with management to determine selected aspects of the conditions of employment.

Grievance: A term associated with a negative workplace event that results in an allegation by an employee that he or she has not been treated fairly and equitably. Grievances can occur in union and non-union settings. In a union setting, a grievance generally arises when two parties, such as an employee and a manager, interpret contract provisions differently. Grievances often involve job security or safety, which is a union priority, or job performance or discipline, which is a management priority.

Industrial unionism: A type of union in which there is a single union for all workers in a corporation. For example, all people who work in an automobile manufacturing company may be grouped together under the United Auto Workers (UAW). It is possible that the industrial union, with its massive numbers of union members, is the strongest possible collective group.

Labor: A group composed of those who work for others to receive a salary.

Management: The group of people within a business or company who plan, organize, lead, or control the activities of employees who have agreed to work to receive a salary.

Mediation: A form of settling disputes that involves a trained person who listens to all parties and makes recommendations. Such mediation is generally not legally binding.

Occupational unionism: A type of union in which each occupation within a given company has separate unions; these occupational groups might join others of like work across boundaries and across the country. White-collar workers coming from a background of higher education and some measure of job security tend to prefer occupational unionism and organizing with like-minded professionals. In general, nurses prefer occupational unionism.

Picketing: A form of protest in which people (called picketers) congregate outside a place of work or location where an event is taking place. Often this is done in an attempt to dissuade others from going in ("crossing the picket line"), but it can also be done to draw public attention to a cause.

Right-to-work laws: Statutes enforced in 22 U.S. states, mostly in the southern and western United States, allowed under provisions of the Taft-Hartley Act, which prohibit agreements between unions and employers that make membership or payment of union dues or "fees" a condition of employment, either before or after hiring.

Secret ballot elections: To establish a union in a workplace, a majority of employees must express support for the union. The employees prove majority through a secret ballot election conducted by the National Labor Relations Board.

Strike: A work stoppage caused by the refusal of a large portion of employees to perform work; usually takes place to enforce demands relating to employment conditions or to protest unfair labor practices. Sympathy strike occurs when one union stops work to support the strike of another union.

Unfair labor practices: Actions that interfere with the rights of employees or employers as identified under the National Labor Relations Act. An unfair labor practice can be something as simple as suspicion by an employee that he or she was assigned to an unpopular task unfairly, or it can be as complex as the identification of a pattern of many employees receiving discriminatory treatment in the workplace

because of being union supporters. Unfair labor practices are a frequent source of either strikes or the initiation of union activity within a setting.

Union: A group of workers who band together to accomplish goals related to conditions of employment.

Union shop: Refers to a worksite that requires all new employees in a specific work group to join the union. Dues will be deducted automatically from employees' paychecks as defined in the facility's contract.

LEARNING OUTCOMES

After studying this chapter, the reader will be able to:

1. Use terms associated with collective bargaining correctly in written and oral communications.
2. Examine key events in the historical development of collective bargaining and unions.
3. Recognize questionable labor or management practices in the workplace.

4. Analyze collective bargaining as a method to achieve power sharing in the workplace.
5. Evaluate current conflicts and controversies associated with collective bargaining by professional nurses.

CHAPTER OVERVIEW

Collective bargaining is a very complex and often an emotionally charged issue. Because the future of nursing may be influenced by our collective and individual efforts to be fairly represented and to have a voice in the conditions of our work, it is important to understand the costs and benefits of collective action, as well as the motives of those who

would represent nursing. This chapter attempts to present a balanced view of collective bargaining and unionization in the hope that students, staff nurses, and nurses in managerial positions will use the information to make effective decisions when confronted with collective bargaining issues.

DEVELOPMENT OF COLLECTIVE BARGAINING IN AMERICA

Early Activities

During the late nineteenth century, when the Industrial Revolution was a force throughout North America, a cadre of thinkers arose who believed that workers needed to join together to protect themselves from circumstances such as long work hours, child labor, and unhealthy factory conditions. These early groups sought such basic conditions as safety in work situations, adequate pay for hours worked, and the right not to be arbitrarily dismissed. This banding together of workers to accomplish goals was termed *trade unionism*. This technique was successful in many instances and remains with us today.

Federal Legislation

As a result of these early efforts at unionization, Congress passed the National Labor Relations Act (NLRA) in 1935. Under the terms of the NLRA, employees were given the right to self-organize, to form labor unions, and to bargain collectively. As part of the 1935 NLRA, the National Labor Relations Board (NLRB) was established to implement provisions of the NLRA. The NLRB is an independent federal agency that continues to play a vital role in labor-management relations and, working through 26 regional offices in major U.S. cities, they conduct union elections and prosecute unfair labor practices.

With employees' rights protected by federal legislation, collective bargaining now occurs in companies across the country. Employees can legally organize themselves into units recognized under terms of the NLRA without fear of being fired for belonging to a union or for participating in union activities, such as collective bargaining. Typical goals in collective bargaining activities are to establish reasonable working conditions and formal agreements between employees and management for wages and health and retirement benefits.

However, exemptions to the 1935 NLRA were established for nonprofit companies. This meant that employees of nonprofit hospitals such as nurses were not protected under the NLRA and therefore were not legally protected for participation in collective bargaining activities. Hospitals' employees may have been excluded from protection by the NLRA because it was believed that services provided were so essential that organizing activities would be contrary to the public's interest. Eventually, in 1974 legislation allowed for the inclusion of nonprofit hospitals in coverage under provisions of the NLRA. Nurses could form collective bargaining units. The 1974 amendments also included the requirement for a 10-day written notice of the intent to picket or to strike. This notice would allow the health care facility time to prepare and would protect the relative health and safety of the public.

Development of Collective Bargaining in Nursing

Formal unionization in nursing began in 1946 when the American Nurses Association (ANA) endorsed collective bargaining as a way to gain economic security and influence employment issues for nurses. While the ANA worked to pave the way for collective bargaining, it also struggled with its role in representing nurses who were part of unions as well as nurses who did not support unionization. To help resolve ANA's role in representing different interests of nurses, a national nurses union – United American Nurses (UAN)—was established as an ANA affiliate to create an independent voice for union nurses. In 2009, the UAN dropped its affiliation with the ANA and merged with the California Nurses Association/National Nurses Organizing Committee and the Massachusetts Nurses Association to form National Nurses United.

Today, approximately 18% of the nation's registered nurses (RN) are members of unions (Department of Professional Employees, 2012). National Nurses United (NNU) is the largest union in the United States, representing over 185,000 registered nurses (NNU, 2014). Other unions that represent nurses include state affiliates of the ANA, Service Employees International Union, and the American Federation of State, County and Municipal Employees.

THE COLLECTIVE BARGAINING PROCESS

Collective bargaining is a method of equalizing power. As such, it involves negotiation and administrative agreements between employees and employers. Because the individual employee, or even a small group of employees, has limited power to bargain with the employer, the idea of banding together in a union gives the employees a stronger voice to negotiate with management. The goals of collective bargaining are achieved by imposing rules regarding how employers must treat employees represented by a union. The union movement in the United States is involved with strengthening a worker's position in the relationship between management and labor.

Nurses and nurse managers need to understand the steps involved in the union organizing and election process, as well as what are considered appropriate or inappropriate management responses and labor responses. Since union organizing involves power sharing and sometimes a temporary sense of distrust between direct-care nurses and management, it can become an anxious and emotional process. Knowing allowable patterns for the process of union organizing can help alleviate some stress.

The following discussion is an overview of the general steps in the union organizing process based on information taken from the *Basic Guide to the National Labor Relations Act* (NLRB, 1997). The reader will see that careful attention is given to ensuring fairness for employer, employees, and the unions that may be involved in an election to determine if employees agree to unionize.

The Preformal Period in Union Organizing

The goal of collective bargaining is the equalization of power between labor (e.g, direct-care nurses) and management. To initiate collective bargaining activities, an organizing drive is instituted by union forces who attempt to create an official NLRB-sanctioned bargaining unit in a particular institution. The bargaining unit is either accepted or rejected through an election process in which non-management employees (direct-care nurses) vote. If accepted, the bargaining unit will be made up of union members who are workers at the unionized facility and will be designed to protect the workers against arbitrary treatment and unfair labor practices.

A union organizing drive may be initiated when nurses in a particular health care facility contact a union because they feel a need for help in negotiating with their employer. The stimulus for this initial contact is usually not frivolous. There is typically a pervasive feeling among the nurses on a particular unit or in the health care facility as a whole that working conditions are unsatisfactory and that there is no possibility of making improvements under the existing management circumstances.

It is helpful at this point to examine what is to be gained by those petitioning the NLRB for an election for union representation. For a group of nurses, a newly formed union will:

- Have the power to make certain demands of the employer, especially regarding salary, benefits and nurse-to-patient ratios.
- Provide some degree of political power on a local level.
- Require nurses to pay dues to the union.
  For the union organization, a newly formed union will:
- Give the union additional power by adding more members and more bargaining units, especially if the union is part of a larger national union.
- Increase monetary support for the union through dues paid by nurses. The additional money can be used to pay union officials' salaries, organize other bargaining units, or contribute to political causes or candidates.

Once a union has been contacted by nurses and told that there is some interest in establishing a collective bargaining unit, union forces try to determine whether efforts to organize the majority of nurses in the facility will be successful. This determination is made through a process of "signing cards." Union authorization cards help the union organizer, a person who works for the union, to decide whether there is enough interest in unionization on the part of nurses employed in the facility. Once signed by the nurse, the union authorization card designates the union as his or her bargaining agent. The signed authorization card is legally binding on the

employee, despite any claims the union may make to the contrary. *It is very important for the nurse to understand that his or her signature on a union authorization card is automatically authorizing the union to serve as his or her legal representative.*

If 30% of employed nurses sign cards, signaling an interest in representation by the union, the employer and the NLRB are officially notified, and the employer must refrain from anti-labor action, such as firing those who favor the union (NLRB, 1997). If 50% plus 1 of the nurses who are eligible (non-management nurses) to vote respond in the affirmative to accept union representation, then nurses in the facility become represented by the union and are unionized.

Right-to-Work Laws

An important exception to note here is that there are 24 states with **right-to-work laws** that allow employees to work without being compelled to join the union. A nurse in a right-to-work state can choose not to become a union member yet receive the benefits resulting from the union contract. Thus, in right-to-work states, union-member nurses may work alongside non-union member nurses, possibly creating tension between the two groups. The 24 right-to-work states are Alabama, Arizona, Arkansas, Florida, Georgia, Idaho, Indiana, Iowa, Kansas, Louisiana, Michigan, Mississippi, Nebraska, Nevada, North Carolina, North Dakota, Oklahoma, South Carolina, South Dakota, Tennessee, Texas, Utah, Virginia, and Wyoming.

Allowable Actions during the Union Organizing Effort

To follow the process effectively, a nurse should be aware of details of what is and is not allowed and what is and is not likely to occur during union organizing efforts. When a specific union, such as National Nurses United, initiates organizing activities in a particular facility, an organizer goes to the facility. The organizer, who may also be called a *business agent* or *field representative,* is then responsible for developing and implementing plans to ensure success of the unionizing effort.

To form a core support group in the facility, the organizer locates respected leaders in the workplace. Meetings are then held at nonwork settings such as homes or restaurants to gain initial information about grievances and workplace inequities. These later are used as a basis for campaign literature. To gain additional supporters, discussion and card signing takes place in areas in the actual facility: locker rooms, bathrooms, lunch areas, lounges, and less visible work areas. Most recently, e-mail and social media—Twitter and Facebook—are being used very effectively as a source for union organizers to communicate with employees (Carlson, 2014).

As the union drive surfaces to gain management's attention, organizers begin to distribute cards more openly. At this point, the union organizer sends a registered letter to the employer with the names of employees on the organizing committee. Management will probably have already become aware of organizing activities through clues such as employee behavior changes during this period. There will be times when individuals seem distracted or when there is an increase in the number or aggressive quality of complaints about workplace conditions. Conversely, there may be a feeling of distancing between labor and management and an air of unnatural silence among employees.

Although peaceful strikes and **picketing** may occur for the purpose of publicity or seeking recognition, the NLRB prohibits certain behaviors during the pre-election period. The **union** may not:

- Inflame racial prejudices
- Lie about loss of jobs if the union loses the election
- Forge documents or signatures
- Meet or distribute literature in work areas during work times
- Hold meetings within 24 hours of an election

During the pre-election period, **management** may not:

- Solicit spying
- Photograph employees engaged in union activities
- Visit employees in their homes
- Lie about what will happen if the union is the victor in an election
- Question employees about their preferences regarding union activity

The Election Process

There are several steps in the election process. Either the union or the employer must petition the NLRB for an election. Once this petition is made, the request is passed along to the regional NLRB director. Within 48 hours, the union must submit proof of its claim that 30% of eligible nurses are interested in forming a collective bargaining unit. Eligible nurses are generally considered to be those nurses who are engaged in patient care and are not in management positions. Normally, for a 10-day period, literature will be distributed to eligible employees. The union and the employer may circulate literature; however, both sides must cease activities within 24 hours of the election.

On the day actually designated for the election, the three parties (the NLRB, union representatives, and employer representatives) meet to review the list of those eligible to vote. The three parties then count ballots and, in case of a true tie, a victory for the employer is declared. However, any votes in dispute will be set aside for a later recount. Objections must be made within 5 working days after the election and may be made on the grounds of problems with the conduct of the election or unfair labor practices.

Post Election

After the election, in the case of a union victory, federal law guarantees workers the right to collectively bargain and strike. Nurses may subsequently change a bargaining agent or remove the union representation by having 30% of nurses sign cards. An election would follow, requiring a vote of 50% plus 1 in favor of the change (NLRB, 1997).

The NLRA mandates that under the rules of collective bargaining, meetings between management and labor will be held at reasonable times for the purpose of conferring in good faith. Mandatory topics include wages; the establishment of rules about the use of labor, such as hours of work and nurse-to-patient ratios; individual workers' rights; resolution of grievances; and methods of enforcement, interpretation, and administration of the union agreement. Negotiations between union and management occur in cycles following the initial year of collective bargaining. Negotiations are held before a contract is ratified (approved) by both union and management and again just before the contract expires. While this discussion provides a general overview of the union election process, readers are encouraged to visit the NLRB website (www.nlrb.gov) for more detailed information about the union election process.

Principles to Guide Fairness During Union Organizing

In an unprecedented collaboration between a major U.S. health care employer and unions, a set of guiding principles was established to ensure a fair process for union organizing efforts. The principles, which can serve as a guide for employers and unions across the country, will help ensure that health care employees are able to make informed decisions regarding unionization without undue influence or pressure from either side. Based on the seven principles, employers as well as unions should agree in writing how they will (Catholic Healthcare Association of America, 2009):

- Demonstrate respect for each other's organization and mission
- Provide workers with equal access to information from both sides
- Adhere to standards for truthfulness and balance in their communications
- Create a pressure-free environment
- Allow workers to vote through a fair and expeditious process
- Honor employees' decision regardless of the outcome
- Create a system for enforcing these principles during the course of an organizing drive

UNIONS AND PROFESSIONAL NURSING

Professionalism versus Unionization

Nurses in the workplace are buffeted by cost cutting, nursing shortages, shuffled duties, concerns about patient safety and quality care, and hospital reorganizations that bring job insecurity and uncertainty. Despite these difficult working conditions, it is often problematic for nurses to come to grips with their feelings related to the emotionally charged issues associated with unionization. Many nurses may be reluctant to become involved with what they view as trouble-making groups who exaggerate the issues just to win the contest against the adversary, which is management. It is difficult to reconcile feelings of professionalism and service with the perceived union connotations of strife and discord.

In addition, when nurses try to update their thoughts about unionization through reading, it becomes difficult to find objective reading material. Few experienced authorities on collective bargaining can remain neutral or objective. It is difficult to read about unionization without encountering biased language and the attempt to paint one side or the other in extremely unflattering terms. This doesn't help in clearing away the fog of conflict surrounding unionization decisions for nurses.

Questions to Answer

Four major questions need to be answered as nurses consider unionization.

1. Are there relevant gains to be made for the nursing profession and for improved patient care through collective bargaining—or is this a myth?
2. Should nurses, who frequently are called on to supervise the work of others, be classified for collective bargaining purposes as management or labor?
3. Will nurses be too reluctant to strike? This is one of the most powerful tools that a union has at its disposal. There is concern that strikes by nurses could negatively affect patient care and destroy the public's image of nursing. More importantly, the strike is contrary to nursing ethics and licensure to do no harm and avoid patient abandonment.
4. How will nursing unions affect the interprofessional team, which is essential for quality patient care (e.g., physical therapy, dietary, pharmacy)? Will the nursing collective bargaining contract create inequities for other departments?

These questions are addressed in more detail in the following sections.

Gains for the Nursing Profession and Patient Care?

When considering unionization, nurses need to seriously reflect on issues that affect the practice of professional nursing and on the patient care environment beyond what unions typically address during negotiations (wages and benefits, work hours, worker safety, and resolution of grievances). The primary triggers that spark interest in being represented by a union often are forgotten in the challenges confronted by nurses during the union organization process. Consider the following issues that may trigger a group of nurses to seek union representation:

- Physicians not seeing critical patients in a timely manner, putting patients at risk
- Lack of administrative support for collegial, professional relationships among nurses, physicians, and other interprofessional team members
- Inadequate patient hand-off procedures causing errors, frustration, interdepartmental conflicts, and delay in care

- Nursing staff continuing education and unit specific competencies not adequately addressed
- Self-scheduling designed around staff needs, not patient and unit needs

Nurses are cautioned that gains in wages and benefits may be achieved through unionization, but the nursing practice environment may suffer. A survey of more than 3500 RNs in Minnesota found that nurses who were members of collective bargaining units had higher satisfaction regarding wages, but they had overall lower job satisfaction than their nonmember counterparts; nonmembers had significantly higher satisfaction regarding professional relationships, work setting, supervision, patient care, and overall job satisfaction (Pittman, 2007). In a larger study using the National Sample Surveys of Registered Nurses for 2004 and 2008, union representation was negatively associated with job satisfaction (Seago et al, 2011). The authors of this study point out that causes for this finding may be that union nurses could be more vocal about expressing their concerns, or the dissatisfaction may have led to the unionization.

Another professional practice issue to consider is that open dialog between nurses and their managers regarding patient care issues and concerns is limited in a unionized facility. For example, the manager cannot discuss performance issues or concerns with a nurse directly; the union representative must serve as the intermediary between the nurse and the manager. This added layer to address the nurse's performance creates increased costs to the facility for both management time and legal expense.

When faced with union organizing efforts, nurses need to carefully consider all factors including the professional practice environment. Box 14-1 presents a list of questions the nurse should ask when confronted by a union organizing effort.

Promoting a Positive Work Environment

Regardless of whether the nurse works in a union environment, there are several strategies he or she can use to develop and encourage sound relationships between management and labor and promote a positive work environment:

- Assess your knowledge of the labor laws and practices in your area, and seek to understand the unique culture of the facility; seek help before union activity begins or grievances are filed.

> **BOX 14-1   Questions To Ask When Confronted by a Union Organizer**
>
> - What measures has the union successfully used to improve quality of care and promote national patient safety goals?
> - Will the union guarantee in writing that it will be getting employees a specified wage increase and better benefits or be liable to employees if it doesn't?
> - How much are union dues? What portion of union dues goes to paying union salaries?
> - Are there special union assessments, and, if so, how much are they and how often will they be imposed?
> - What are the consequences if employees violate the union constitution and/or bylaws?
> - Will the union guarantee in writing that employees will not be permanently replaced during an economic strike?
> - Will the union pay wages to employees if they are called on to strike?
> - Will union members be expected to picket at other unionized facilities in the event of a strike or an informational picket?

- Understand what protections are already in place through laws and regulations to protect your rights as a nurse in your state (e.g., whistle-blower protection; staffing regulations; safe patient handling laws).
- Identify and be proactive in situations in which the nurses or leaders disrespect others, ignore serious staff and patient care concerns, or neglect appropriate communication and follow-up.
- Participate in education and training that will improve your labor relations skills in union and non-union environments.
- Be proactive in solving issues that compromise patient care; embrace your role in achieving timely outcomes that truly improve care.
- Develop an understanding of and respect for the healthcare facility's financial challenges and become part of the solution for more cost-effective care.

Management or Staff?

One of the difficult issues for nursing in relation to collective bargaining is that in the eyes of the NLRB certain nurses are singled out as management or supervisory personnel and are not allowed NLRA protection, which applies only to non-management employees. Charge nurses and shift supervisors have traditionally been considered part of management rather than labor. But what about nurses who routinely supervise others who act merely as extenders of care? Are these nurses acting exclusively on behalf of the company that employs them, or are they routinely carrying out their responsibilities as a professional nurse?

The definition of *manager* or *supervisor* is problematic even in non–health care settings. In nursing, things become even more complicated. Most experienced RNs are involved in some type of supervisory or management work. For example, most staff nurses who ordinarily provide bedside care have been called on to be in charge of a particular nursing unit for a particular working shift. Does this mean that the nurse should no longer be considered non-management?

Another trend that has an effect on decisions about supervisory status is the increasing use of unlicensed personnel in health care workplaces. More nurses could now be classified as supervisory because they direct the activities of unlicensed workers. In 1994, in *NLRB v. the Health Care and Retirement Corporation,* the U.S. Supreme Court ruled that nurses do indeed direct the work of others and therefore are not eligible for protection under the NLRA. This case was important to the nursing profession because had the ruling been upheld, it would have dramatically lowered the numbers of nurses who could act as "laborers" and engage in collective bargaining. However, in 1997 the decision of the U.S. Court of Appeals for the Ninth Circuit helped clarify this point. The court ruled that RNs who performed charge nurse duties were not management and therefore were eligible for collective bargaining protection. In another case, *Providence Alaska Medical Center v. NLRB,* the ruling recognized that the judgment used by RNs in assigning patients and coordinating patient care was part of their professional role rather than part of any statutory supervision as defined by the NLRA.

Beyond the issue of recognizing who is management and who is staff, there is the uncomfortable prospect of pitting nurse managers against their colleagues in the workplace. A definite schism occurs when managers and staff are placed on opposite sides of the table. Bad feelings arise. For example, a nurse manager represents management but is not insulated in an executive office. In addition, the nurse manager must often assume duties routinely performed by staff nurses in the event of a strike. This can lead to lingering negative feelings even after the strike is resolved.

Techniques frequently used by nurse managers to maintain smooth and efficient job performance in their work settings may be relatively ineffective when unionization or collective bargaining initiatives occur. For example, the nurse manager who believes that open communication in both upward and downward directions is useful for problem solving may become frustrated during unionization initiatives. Union tactics may involve coaching nurses at staff levels to use the "silent treatment" and not cooperate with nurse managers' attempts to communicate.

To Strike or Not?

Strikes can have very powerful effects. The economic effect of a strike can best be understood by noting that hospitals become concerned over lost revenues when the average daily census drops only a few percentage points. Hospitals could possibly have to turn away patients because of a strike and could lose that market share permanently, resulting in long-term losses to the hospital. Thus strikes or the threat of a strike can be effective in gaining concessions (e.g., salary increases, better benefits) from management in an effort to avoid the strike completely or to end it as soon as possible. However, it is important to note that in some states, collective bargaining contracts may contain "no strike" clauses prohibiting the collective bargaining unit from having the power of the strike.

Nursing is a trusted profession, and for many nurses, the strike is a symbol of negative behavior. To safeguard nursing's image and allow for hospitals to react effectively in safeguarding patient care, a 10-day notice of intent to strike is required. On receipt of such notice, the NLRB attempts to mediate, and the hospital is encouraged to decrease census and halt elective admissions. Schedules are developed for covering the emergency department, operating room, and intensive care areas.

As nurses are confronted with making decisions about unionization, it is important to consider the many issues that will affect their personal economic welfare, their practice environment, and the quality of patient care they are able to provide. There are no easy answers as the issues and challenges vary depending on each organization's unique set of circumstances. To successfully negotiate unionization initiatives and make good decisions, nurses are encouraged to learn more about collective bargaining and unions.

Nursing Unions and Interprofessional Teamwork?

Nurses may be the only professional occupation in a health care setting to be represented by a union (i.e., occupational unionism). Unfortunately, having unionized nurses working alongside employees such as pharmacist and therapists, who are not represented by a union, may create ill will between the two groups. The benefit package for nurses represented by a union can be different—and likely better—than the benefit package for other employees. As employment and practice issues arise, nurses have union representation as their go-between to work with management, whereas other disciplines work directly with management to resolve issues. The union contract for nurses' benefits will increase the overall costs to the organization forcing the organization to cut in other areas not controlled by the union, such as benefits for non-unionized health professionals. Imagine how the relationship between two professionals might be strained if the nurse represented by the union has more paid time off and more frequent salary increases than a colleague she works with on a daily basis; plus the non-nursing professional knows that the cost of the union contract may be the reason he is not able to get a salary increase. Relationships between interprofessional team members is a very important consideration as nurses consider unionization!

SUMMARY

This chapter has provided a history and overview of the collective bargaining process and addressed some important issues for nurses to consider as they face questions regarding unionization. These important issues include the role of unionization in addressing the professional practice environment and quality care, the questions surrounding management versus labor in collective bargaining, and the controversy of the strike as a strategy to gain concessions from the employer. The role of unions in the future of health care may hinge on cooperation versus conflict, on relative productivity gains in union versus non-union facilities, and on success of human relations practices in union as well as non-union workplaces. Nurses live in a new era in health care and will need to continue to grow in their knowledge regarding unions and collective bargaining.

REFERENCES

Carlson, J: 2014 likely to be busy year for unions, *Modern Healthcare* 44(3):8, 2014.

Catholic Healthcare Association of America: *Respecting the just rights of workers: guidance and options for Catholic health care and unions*, 2009. Retrieved 07/19/2014 from http://old.usccb.org/sdwp/national/respecting_the_just_rights_of_workers.pdf.

Department of Professional Employees, AFL-CIO: *Nursing: A profile of the profession*, 2012. Retrieved 07/19/2014 from http://dpeaflcio.org/programs-publications/issue-fact-sheets/nursing-a-profile-of-the-profession/.

National Labor Relations Board: *Basic guide to the National Labor Relations Act*, Washington, DC, 1997, U.S. Government Printing Office.

National Nurses United: *About us*, 2014. Retrieved 08/03/2015 from http://www.nationalnursesunited.org/pages/19.

Pittman J: Registered nurse job satisfaction and collective bargaining unit membership status, *J Nurs Adm* 37(10):471–476, 2007.

Seago JA, Spetz J, Ash M, et al: Hospital RN job satisfaction and nurse unions, *J Nurs Adm* 41(3):109–114, 2011.

Information Technology in the Clinical Setting

Tami H. Wyatt, PhD, RN, CNE, ANEF, FAAN,
Teresa Maggard Stephens, PhD, RN

Electronic health records offer nurses and other team members information when, where, and how they need it.

ⓔ Additional resources are available online at: *http://evolve.elsevier.com/Cherry/*

PROFESSIONAL/ETHICAL ISSUE

Katherine is a recent RN-BSN graduate working in the post-anesthesia care unit of a small, community-based hospital. She receives a new patient and begins reviewing the patient's history and medication orders. This patient, a 68-year-old male with multiple comorbidities, has just returned from a hernia repair procedure. Katherine notes he has multiple drug allergies, and she is unfamiliar with one of his prescribed pain medications. She uses her smartphone to access a drug database to check for any interactions and/or contraindications. As she is reviewing this information, her shift supervisor enters the room and demands that she put her cell phone away. Katherine explains what she is doing and expresses her concern over the prescribed medications. The supervising nurse tells Katherine that it is not her responsibility to look up medications, nor is it her job to question a doctor's orders. She continues to inform Katherine that it is against hospital policy for nurses to use a cell phone during work hours. Discuss how Katherine might address this situation in a professional manner considering the use of smartphones as knowledge support is becoming more widely accepted in health care settings.

VIGNETTE

Victoria Ellis is finally living her dream. After four hard years in school, Victoria is working at a university medical center. Although she graduated from a well-respected nursing program, she is apprehensive about her new role, especially documenting care and accessing pertinent information. In nursing school, all of her clinical experiences were in facilities that used *electronic health records (EHRs)*, but Victoria had limited access to the EHRs. She could not log on to the system herself, she couldn't chart, and she could only access limited screens such as lab values, assessment information, and vital signs. Victoria learned in school that EHRs are a vital information technology tool in health care today, but based on her limited experience, an EHR seems like it is nothing more than a paper chart on a computer. So, what's all the hype about EHRs, *information technology*, and health care?

Questions to Consider While Reading this Chapter:

1. What are the potential benefits of electronic health records to nurses, other health care providers, and patients?
2. What are the barriers to a universal U.S. health information technology infrastructure?
3. What is meant by "meaningful use" of EHRs?
4. How might advanced point-of-care technology influence health care at the bedside?
5. How does health information technology affect consumer health?

Thanks to Leslie H. Nicoll, PhD, MBA, RN, and Cynthia K. Russell, PhD, APN, for their contributions to this chapter in previous editions.

KEY TERMS

Decision support tools: Software programs that process data to produce or recommend decisions by linking with an electronic knowledge base controlled by established rules for combining data elements; the knowledge base and rules mimic the knowledge and reasoning an expert health professional would apply to data and information to solve a problem.

Electronic health record (EHR): The longitudinal electronic record of patient health information generated by one or more encounters in any care delivery setting; has the ability to support other care-related activity such as evidence-based decision support, quality management, and outcomes reporting (American Health Information Management Association [AHIMA], 2012).

EHR (electronic health record) interoperability: EHR systems that have ability to share and transfer patient data seamlessly across health care systems and settings in a standardized manner that protects the reliability, confidentiality, privacy, and security of the information.

EHR "meaningful use": A defined set of EHR capabilities and standards that EHR systems must meet to ensure that their full capacity is realized and for the users (hospitals and physician/provider practices) to qualify for financial incentives from Medicare.

Health information technology: The use of various forms of technology to improve the quality of health services to individuals and communities.

Information technology: The hardware and software that enable information to be stored, retrieved, communicated, and managed.

Point-of-care technology: Technologies that allow real-time data retrieval, documentation, and decision support at the bedside or wherever direct care is provided.

LEARNING OUTCOMES

After studying this chapter, the reader will be able to:

1. Describe key attributes of electronic health record systems and their influence on patient safety and quality care.
2. Explain "meaningful use" criteria as applicable to electronic health records.
3. Critique various types of point-of-care technology and their use in the clinical setting.
4. Assess how future trends in technology will affect health care delivery.
5. Use established criteria to evaluate the content of health-related sites found on the Internet.

CHAPTER OVERVIEW

Today's clinical setting is undergoing an explosion in technology used by all health care providers. Yesteryear's clinical settings used telephones, fax and copy machines, and slow computers that primarily stored patients' contact and billing information. Today you are likely to see voice communication systems, handheld computers or tablets, smartphones, robotic pharmacy dispensaries, and fast computers that contain patients' electronic health records (EHRs). These records present data in graphs, tables, and charts that may reveal a different story than words and numbers alone. Transforming patient data into meaningful bits of information is merely one advantage of health information technology (HIT). These data can also be shared with other facilities, creating a comprehensive patient record, which can reduce duplicate services and tests and create continuity in care. In this chapter, you will explore the important role of HIT in today's clinical environment, the adoption rate of this technology in select countries, barriers and opportunities with advanced HIT, and ways to educate consumers about health information on the Internet.

HEALTH INFORMATION TECHNOLOGY ACROSS THE GLOBE

Health information technology (HIT), or technology used to promote the health and well-being of patients and the community, has rapidly increased as technology has advanced. These advancements have led to a new era, the information age. Persons living in the information age demand more sharing of and access to knowledge that was once held only by those in positions of authority. Technology advancements have influenced all sectors of civilization across the globe including health care, even in developing countries that have limited access to health care. For example, the U.S. National Library of Medicine (NLM) provides access to many resources, which are sometimes free. These resources are not limited to the United States, and therefore all countries, including developing countries, have access to information. In 2009, the NLM was accessed daily between 1 and 1,000 times by individuals in sub-Saharan Africa (Royall and Lyon, 2011). Expansion of the Internet is also responsible for promoting access to health resources such as health care websites, medical videos, health promotion games, and images.

Advancements in the widespread use of HIT first occurred in European countries. Germany initiated a universal HIT process in 1993, followed by Norway in 1997, and the United Kingdom in 2002. Around the same time, Canada and Australia both initiated efforts to standardize electronic documentation procedures. Denmark achieved 100% EHR adoption by primary care doctors in 2009 (Protti and Johansen, 2010). Clearly, the United States is watching and learning from the progression and transformation of health care in countries that have universally adopted HIT throughout their health care systems.

Health Information Technology in the United States

For more than a decade, it has been known that HIT in the United States—specifically EHRs—can reduce costs and improve patient care quality and safety (Chaudhry et al, 2006; Walker et al, 2005). The United States is currently challenged to universally implement EHRs across all settings, from hospitals to ambulatory care settings to home health agencies and nursing homes. For EHR systems to have the greatest impact on cost and quality, they must be interoperable with the ability to exchange information across systems and settings in a standardized manner that protects the reliability, confidentiality, privacy, and security of the information.

Within the United States, there are two major influences on the adoption of EHRs, the federal government and America's health insurance plans; both of these entities can set certain requirements regarding EHRs as a condition of payment for services. According to President George W. Bush, "by computerizing health records, we can avoid dangerous medical mistakes, reduce costs, and improve care" (State of the Union Address, January 20, 2004). To this end, President Bush established a goal to have universal EHR adoption in the United States by 2014. President Barack Obama supported this initiative and allocated $25.9 billion of the American Recovery and Reinvestment Act funds to EHR adoption (U.S. Department of Health and Human Services [DHHS], 2014). As a result, a modest growth in adoption of EHRs has occurred.

Measuring adoption rates of EHRs in the United States has been a challenge because it was dependent on self-reporting. However, the Centers for Medicare & Medicaid Services (CMS) now offers incentive programs for providers—hospitals and physician/provider practices—that qualify and adopt certified EHRs that meet meaningful use criteria. Therefore, the CMS now has a process to register providers using EHRs because they may qualify for incentive payments. According to the Centers for Disease Control (2014), 78% of office-based physicians use some form of EHRs. Approximately 80% of hospitals implemented EHRs by 2013 (Jayanthi, 2014).

ELECTRONIC HEALTH RECORDS

An EHR is a system that captures, processes, communicates, secures, and presents data about the patient. In addition to capturing patient data, other components of an EHR include clinical rules, literature for patient education, evidence-based practice guidelines, and payer rules related to reimbursement. When these elements work together in an integrated fashion, the EHR becomes much more than a patient record—it becomes a knowledge tool. The system is able to integrate information from multiple sources and provide decision support; thus the EHR serves as the primary source of information for patient care and quality improvements in the health care system.

Key Functions of the EHR

The Institute of Medicine (IOM) (2003) recommends that EHR systems offer the following eight functionalities: (1) health information and data capture; (2) results/data management; (3) provider order entry management; (4) clinical decision support; (5) electronic communication and connectivity between providers, the health care team, and patients; (6) patient support; (7) administrative process support; and (8) reporting and population health management. Table 15-1 provides more detailed information about these core functionalities.

Two specific functionalities recommended by the IOM—clinical decision support and computerized provider order entry (CPOE)—are frequently mentioned in the literature as essential to improve the quality and safety of health care (IOM, 2003; Smith, 2004). Clinical decision support contributes to safety and quality by providing automatic reminders about preventive practices, such as immunizations, drug alerts for dosing and interactions, and electronic resources for data interpretation and clinical decision making.

CPOE is defined as the "process by which the physician or another health care provider, such as a nurse practitioner, physician's assistant, or physical or occupational therapist, directly enters orders for client care into a hospital information system" (Hebda and Czar, 2009). CPOE contributes to safety and quality by eliminating lost orders and illegible handwriting; generating related orders automatically (e.g., a laboratory test needed to monitor a specific medication); monitoring for duplicate or contradictory orders; and reducing time to fill orders (Hebda and Czar, 2009; IOM, 2003). CPOE functions also contribute to medical error prevention through the following (Bates and Gawande, 2003):

- Improved communication
- More readily accessible knowledge
- Requirement for key pieces of information (such as the dose of a drug)
- Assistance with calculations
- Accuracy checks performed in real time
- Assistance with medication monitoring
- Decision support
- Rapid response to, and tracking of, adverse events

In addition to providing the core functions as noted earlier, the EHR must be efficient and offer additional support that is dependent on each institution or facility and the type of services that are provided (e.g., ambulatory or inpatient services). For example, an inpatient facility EHR needs to integrate with nursing services, pharmacy, operating room management systems, and laboratory information systems, to name a few. To view sample screens from an EHR, see Figures 15-1 and 15-2.

EHR Data Management

A fully functional EHR is a complex system. Consider a single data element (datum), such as a person's weight.

TABLE 15-1 **Core Functionalities for EHR Systems As Recommended by the Institute of Medicine (2003)**	
Health information and data	Information to make sound clinical decisions, such as past medical history, laboratory tests, allergies, current medications, and consent forms
Results management	Electronic reports of laboratory results and radiology procedures with automated display of previous results; electronic consultation reports
Order entry and order management	Computerized provider order entry with or without decision support to eliminate lost orders and illegible handwriting, generate related orders automatically, monitor for duplicate or contradictory orders, and reduce time to fill orders
Decision support	Enhance clinical performance by providing reminders about preventive practices, such as immunizations, drug alerts for dosing and interactions, and clinical decision making
Electronic communication and connectivity	Electronic communication between health care team members and other care partners, such as radiology and laboratory personnel, and connectivity to the patient record across multiple care settings
Patient support	Computer-based patient education and home monitoring where applicable
Administrative processes	Scheduling systems, billing and claims management, insurance eligibility, and inventory management
Reporting and population health management	Meet public and private sector reporting requirements at the federal, state, and local levels; address internal quality improvement initiatives

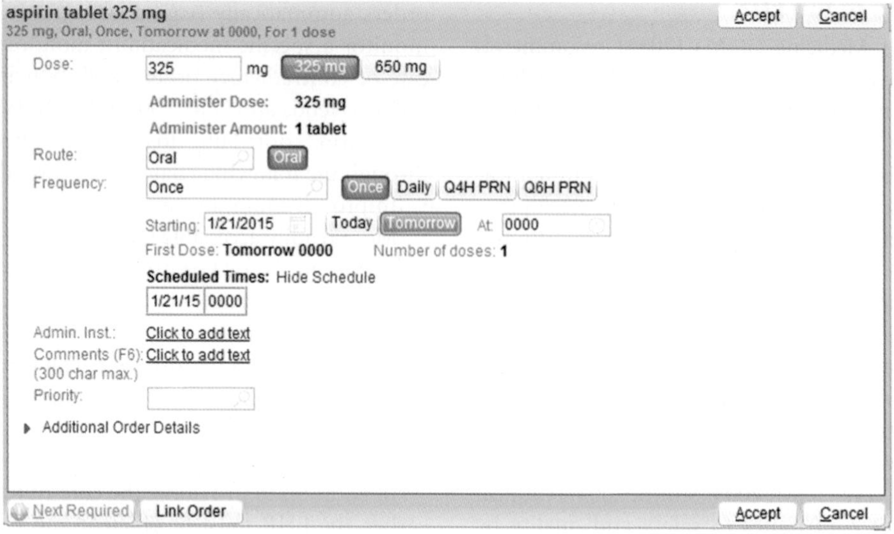

FIGURE 15-1 Selected Screen from a Patient's EHR. (Courtesy of Epic.)

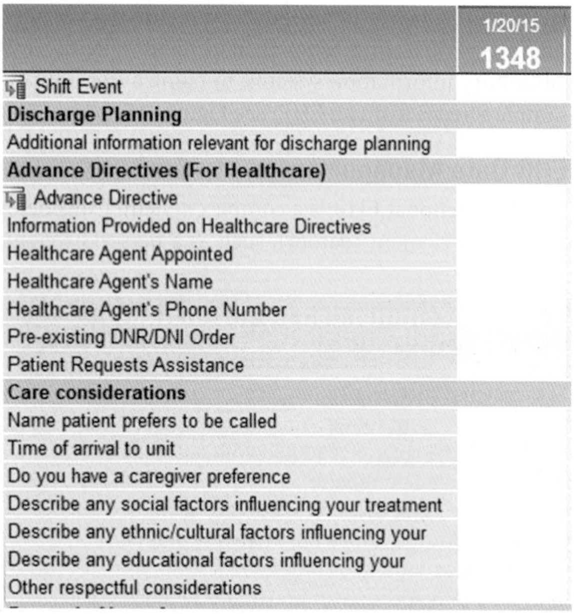

FIGURE 15-2 Selected Screen from a Patient's EHR. (Courtesy of Epic.)

The system must be able to capture, or record, the weight, then store it, process it, communicate it to others, and present it in a usable format, such as a bar graph or chart. All of this must be done in a secure environment that protects the patient's confidentiality and privacy. The complexity of these issues and the development of the necessary systems help explain why adoption of fully functional EHR systems is slow.

Data Capture

Data capture refers to the collection and entry of data into an EHR. The origin of the data may be local or remote from patient-monitoring devices, directly from the individual recipient of health care, and even from others who have information about the recipient's health or environment, such as relatives, friends, and public health agencies. Data may be captured by multiple means, including key entry, pattern recognition (e.g., voice, handwriting, or biologic characteristics), and medical device transmission.

Storage

Storage refers to the physical location of data. In EHR systems, health data need to be distributed across multiple systems at different sites. For this reason, common access protocols, retention schedules, and universal identification are necessary.

Access protocols permit only authorized users to obtain data for legitimate uses. The systems must have backup and recovery mechanisms in the event of failure. Retention schedules address the maintenance of the data in active and inactive form and the permanence of the storage medium. A person's identity can be determined by many types of data in addition to common identifiers, such as name and number. Universal identifiers or other methods are required for integrating health data of an individual distributed across multiple systems at different sites.

Information Processing

EHR functions provide for effective retrieval and processing of data into useful information. These include decision support tools, such as alerts and alarms for drug interactions, allergies, and abnormal laboratory results. Reminders can be provided for appointments, critical path actions, medication administration, and other activities. The systems also may provide access to consensus- and evidence-driven diagnostic and treatment guidelines and protocols. The nurse could integrate a standard guideline, protocol, or critical path into a specific individual's EHR, modify it to meet unique circumstances, and use it as a basis for managing and documenting care. Outcome data communicated from various caregivers and health care recipients themselves also may be analyzed and used for continual improvement of the guidelines and protocols. Data may also be downloaded into statistical software programs for more sophisticated analysis for research purposes.

Information Communication

Information communication refers to the interoperability of systems and linkages for exchange of data across disparate systems. To integrate health data across multiple systems at different sites, identifier systems (unique numbers or other methodology) for health care recipients, caregivers, providers, payers, and sites are essential. Local, regional, and national health information infrastructures that tie all participants together using standard data communication protocols are key. There are hundreds of types of transactions or messages that must be defined and agreed to by the participating stakeholders. Vocabulary and code systems must permit the exchange and processing of data into meaningful information. EHR systems must provide access to point-of-care information databases and knowledge sources, such as pharmaceutical formularies, referral databases, and reference literature.

Security

Computer-based patient record systems provide better protection of confidential health information than paper-based systems because such systems incorporate controls designed to ensure that only authorized users with legitimate uses have access to health information. Security functions address the confidentiality of private health information and the integrity of the data. Security functions must be designed to ensure compliance with applicable laws, regulations, and standards. Security systems must ensure that access to data is provided only to those who are authorized and have a legitimate purpose for its use. Security functions also must provide a means to audit for inappropriate access. Three important terms must be clearly understood:

- *Privacy* refers to the right of an individual to keep information about him or herself from being disclosed to anyone else. If a patient has had an abortion and chooses not to tell a health care provider this fact, the patient would be keeping that information private.
- *Confidentiality* refers to the act of limiting disclosure of private matters. Once a patient has disclosed private information to a health care provider, that provider has a responsibility to maintain the confidentiality of that information and not reveal the information to others who do not have a legitimate need to know.
- *Security* refers to the means to control access and protect information from accidental or intentional disclosure to unauthorized persons and from alteration, destruction, or loss. When private information is placed in a confidential EHR, the system must have controls in place to maintain the security of the system and not allow unauthorized persons access to the data (Computer-Based Patient Record Institute [CPRI], 1995).

Information Presentation

The wealth of information available through EHR systems must be managed to ensure that authorized caregivers (including nurses) and others with legitimate uses have the information they need in their preferred presentation form. For example, a nurse may want to see data organized by source, caregiver, encounter, problem, or date. Data can be presented in detail or summary form. Tables, graphs, narrative, and other forms of information presentation must be accommodated. Some users may need only to know of the presence or absence of certain data, not the nature of the data itself. For example, blood donation centers draw blood for testing for human immunodeficiency virus, hepatitis, and other conditions. If a donor has a positive test result, the center may not be given the specific information regarding the test, but only general information that a test result was abnormal and that the donor should be referred to an appropriate health care provider.

EHRs and "Meaningful Use"

The American Recovery and Reinvestment Act of 2009 directed the "meaningful use" of EHR systems for hospital and physician practice settings and provided for financial incentives from the CMS to providers who adopt and use EHRs that meet the meaningful use standards. "Meaningful use" refers to a complex set of capabilities and standards to be met by EHR use in a series of three stages over several years. The first stage, year 2011-2012, forms the foundation for electronic data capture and information sharing and includes five priorities (HealthIT.gov, 2015):

1. Improve quality, safety and efficiency, and reduce health disparities.
2. Engage patients and their families in their health care.
3. Improve care coordination.
4. Improve population and public health.
5. Ensure adequate privacy and security protections for personal health information.

Stage 1 meaningful use criteria primarily address the capture of health information, access to comprehensive patient health data, exchange of clinical information among the health care team, and reports for quality improvement and public reporting requirements. Stage 2 criteria, effective in 2014, focus on continuous quality improvement at the point of care and structured information exchange (for example, the electronic exchange of diagnostic test results) (U.S. Federal Register, 2012). Recommendations for Stage 3, which were released in 2013, are designed to improve patient outcomes and continue the objectives and goals from Stages 1 and 2. It is anticipated that Stage 3 will be implemented in 2016 (HealthIT.gov, 2014).

In order for providers (hospitals and physician/provider practices) to qualify for the EHR incentive program through CMS, their EHR must be certified as a meaningful use EHR by an independent agency. To date, there are six agencies that certify EHRs: (1) SureScripts, LLC, (2) ICSA Labs, LLC, (3) SLI Global Solutions, (4) InfoGard Laboratories, Inc., (5) Certification Commission of Health Information Technology (CCHIT), and (6) Drummond Group, Inc. (U.S. DHHS, 2013).

To further stimulate the adoption of EHRs, the CMS mandates that to qualify for Medicare and Medicare reimbursement beginning in 2015, facilities must (CMS, 2012):

• Demonstrate the use of an EHR in a meaningful manner
• Demonstrate that the EHR exchanges health information across settings to improve health care
• Submit information on quality measures to HHS

As we can see through discussion of the stages of meaningful use, the full capacity of EHRs has not been realized. This may be due in part to barriers that impede the universal adoption of EHRs in the United States.

Opportunities and Barriers to Adoption of EHRs in the United States

Clearly, the movement toward meaningful use EHRs along with financial incentives is designed to promote universal adoption of EHRs in the United States. This creates not only opportunities but also some barriers for independent health care providers. Meeting the guidelines for meaningful use EHRs is strenuous and often costly for community-based ambulatory services and small rural inpatient centers. Nonetheless, federal dollars have been allocated to this endeavor, and incentive money is available for facilities and providers that meet the criteria for meaningful use.

Interoperability, the ability to share and transfer patient data seamlessly from one provider to the next, is quite possibly the greatest barrier to the successful implementation of a universal system of EHRs in the United States. Market competition has been identified as one barrier to universal adoption and interoperable EHRs in the United States. The development of EHRs began in the 1960s (Jacques, 2011), which has led to 50 years of market competition among many different technology companies to build the most comprehensive, robust, and competitive EHRs. While this has contributed to the advancement of EHR technology, it impedes the ability to build an infrastructure in which EHRs are compatible—or interoperable—with one another.

The power of sharing data across health care settings surpasses the benefits to an individual patient. Obviously, patients benefit when their different providers have access to the same comprehensive patient record. Shared records promote continuity of care across systems and potentially reduce costs by eliminating duplicate diagnostic testing and services. Moreover, much can be learned when data are shared across systems. Aggregate data from such systems can be evaluated and predict outcomes in a particular population, disease, complication, or extended hospital stay. The ability to predict outcomes from data entered across systems is termed *mining data* or *examining trends* and can be highly beneficial to examine population health outcomes.

EHRs and the Health Insurance Portability and Accountability Act

Because of the increase in number of EHRs in the 1990s and the anticipated penetration of EHRs in health care, experts advocated for standardized protocols and clinical practice guidelines to ensure privacy and security. The Health Information Portability and Accountability Act (HIPAA) was signed into law in 1996. HIPAA regulations focus on the privacy and security of patient data, including standard formats for transmitting electronic patient information. By April 2005, health care institutions had to comply with federal HIPAA regulations.

The HIPAA requires that all organizations and facilities that gather or collect personal health information (PHI) are required to name an individual as a privacy officer and develop policies and procedures to ensure the privacy and security of PHI. The protection of PHI extends to every employee, new hire, and patient. Those found in violation of HIPAA regulations may be subject to criminal penalties and civil monetary penalties.

POINT-OF-CARE TECHNOLOGY

With advancing technologies and the movement toward universal use of EHRs, there is a greater demand for HIT at the point of care. This means HIT directly at the bedside or within close proximity to the area where services are delivered. Point-of-care technology is no longer nonessential but is paramount to deliver safe, efficient, high-quality patient care while accessing patient data and evidence-based guidelines. The technology must provide access to past and current patient data, references, policies, procedures, and evidence-based literature to guide clinical decisions at the point of care. A variety of technology tools support point of care decision making and documentation, such as handheld computers, tablets, and smartphones.

It is nearly impossible to visit a health care facility or office and not see small handheld computers or tablets. Tablets are thin, lightweight computers with about a 7- to 9-inch screen. Tablets often have a touch screen or require a stylus to write and select items on the screen. These small devices are as robust as laptops or desktop computers but are more convenient for on-the-go health care providers. These systems have wireless Internet capability so that patient information and other resources can be accessed anywhere, anytime, within the confines of the firewall-protected health care environment to maintain privacy, security, and confidentiality of the data.

Small laptops also allow providers to access pertinent information at the point of care. These laptops are usually secured to a mobile cart, hence, names like *computer on wheels (COWs), mobile point-of-care (MPOC),* and *computer at bedside (CAB).*

Another device that promotes evidence-based clinical decision making at the point of care is a smartphone. These palm-sized computers can store medical applications and access health care journals, calculators, databases, and more through their wireless capabilities. One of the greatest advantages of smartphones is the convenient and quick access to references and tools that were not easily accessible until now. For example, nurses can teach patients about tracking their health by using tools on smartphones or display pictures that show proper procedures. A variety of applications are available for managing chronic disease, diet, exercise, and lifestyle choices (Wyatt and Krauskopf, 2012).

Point-of-care technology is an essential component of nursing as it shifts from a practice that relies on memory to one that emphasizes continuous use of as-needed resources. This means that nurses must transform from being technical experts to knowledge workers and rely on the ever-increasing and reliable computer memory versus the overburdened and fallible human memory. Computer-based alerts and reminders provided by point-of-care technology are helpful in detecting and preventing potential adverse drug events related to drug-drug interactions and abnormal lab values. As today's health care environment focuses on safe, efficient, effective, and high-quality care, access to patient data, standardized protocols, and clinical practice guidelines through point-of-care technology should be considered one of the essential tools of patient care.

Telehealth

A discussion about technology at the point of care would be incomplete without mentioning telehealth. It is the use of telecommunications technology to assess, diagnose, and, in some cases, treat persons who are at a distance from the health care provider. Nurses, physicians, radiologists, psychiatrists, and others use this technology via telephone, computers, interactive videos, and teleconferencing. In many instances, telehealth makes possible the delivery of health care services to underserved populations, such as rural communities, older adults, or prisoners that may have difficulty accessing necessary services. Demonstrated benefits of telehealth include improved quality of care, enhanced continuity of care, increased availability of experts, improved access to care, improved decision making and time savings, and higher-quality records related to the incorporation of digital information (Hebda and Czar, 2009).

The home care arena is seeing significant changes as a result of telehealth. Telehome care devices used to be as simple as blood pressure cuffs. Today, devices such as automated blood pressure monitors, glucose testing meters, peak flow meters, pulse oximeters, weight scales, and two-way digital transport systems are used. The devices offer data recording, audible alarms or reminders, and data uploading, in addition to reports on disease progression and trends. They are used for diverse patient populations, including persons with heart failure, hypertension, diabetes, asthma, chronic obstructive pulmonary disease, cystic fibrosis, depression, and bipolar disorder.

These advancements in technology that enhance and improve health care delivery systems are only as effective as the persons who consume the technology; namely, health care personnel and patients. Without the skill set to use point-of-care technologies, EHRs, and telehealth, patients will not benefit from the advanced technology. Further, patients must possess skills to evaluate and critique technologies and information that influence their health.

INFORMATION LITERACY FOR NURSES

The Association of College and Research Libraries (ACRL) defines information literacy (IL) as the "set of skills needed to find, retrieve, analyze, and use |information" (ACRL, 2013a). It is dangerous to assume that nurses can rely on memory alone when practicing in a complex and dynamic health care environment; therefore, IL skills are necessary for the provision of safe and quality care, as well as evidence-based practice. The IL skills that equip the nurse in the timely retrieval of information necessary to plan, deliver, and evaluate evidence-based care also support independent lifelong learning. Additionally, many leading organizations, including the Institute of Medicine and accrediting bodies, promote the use of technology by nurses at all levels of practice to prevent errors, to enhance care coordination and communication, and to support clinical decision making.

Unfortunately, there is great discrepancy in the levels of IL skills possessed by both new and experienced nurses. As a result, many nurses will turn to less reliable sources (e.g., co-workers) for critical information. Like critical thinking, IL is a concept that must be emphasized within both academic and practice settings. This includes removing barriers to accessing online information at the point of care and providing ongoing training to nursing staff to increase these competencies (Carter-Templeton et al, 2014).

The ACRL published the Information Literacy Competency Standards for Nursing in 2013. These standards are based on the nursing profession's fundamental values of evidence-based practice and translational research. According to these standards, the information-literate nurse is one who: (1) defines and articulates the need for information, (2) accesses needed information effectively and efficiently, (3) critically evaluates the procured information and its sources, and as a result, decides whether or not to modify the initial query and/or seek additional sources and whether to develop a new research process, (4) individually or as a member of a group, uses information effectively to accomplish a specific purpose, and (5) understands many of the economic, legal, and social issues surrounding the use of information and accesses and uses information ethically and legally (ACRL, 2013b).

CONSUMER HEALTH INFORMATION TECHNOLOGY

Web 2.0 tools such as social media, collaboration sites, interactive websites, and Internet bulletin boards or blogs encourage individuals to be more involved and knowledgeable about their own health. The information that patients and families glean from such sites can be a challenge for providers because as patients are better informed, health care providers are required to answer more directed questions. Further, the health care provider must inform patients how to be good consumers of health information. Because the providers are the experts, it is the provider's responsibility to ensure that patients are well informed about how to evaluate content and protect the privacy of others while engaged in discussion either via the Internet or other forms of wireless connection.

Most recently, health consumers are turning to social media for information about health promotion such as healthy eating, exercise, and ways to reduce stress (Thielst, 2011). Consumers often access YouTube, Facebook, Twitter, and LinkedIn to learn more about health,

health prevention, and health promotion. These sites are designed to widely share information and experiences with others. There are pros and cons to this free open-source sharing. Web 2.0 tools are designed to allow any Internet user to become an author of content. With the growing number of Internet users, content is also expanding exponentially so that one can find information about virtually anything, including the most obscure illnesses, home remedies, procedures, and medications. Because of this, information accessible on the Internet may not necessarily be accurate or created by experts. Consumers of information on the Internet, especially health information, must be knowledgeable consumers and evaluate the credibility and accurateness of the source. The following section provides valuable information about how to find and evaluate web-based information.

Finding Information on the Internet

Effective and efficient Internet searching is a must in today's information-overloaded society. Purposeful use of a variety of strategies can improve search results. (Table 15-2 provides an example of these search strategies).

- Quick and dirty searching can be useful if you're looking for information in an unfamiliar area. Type your search term into a search engine such as Google (www.google.com). Review your results to see which ones sound most promising.
- Advanced searching allows you to set specific limits on your searches. For instance, at Google's advanced search (www.google.com/advanced_search), you can limit your searching to educational (.edu), organizational (.org), or governmental (.gov) domains, as well as by language, file type, and date. Another advanced search option is www.googlescholar.com, where you are more likely to find information related to research and evidence-based practice. Limiting your searches in this way can help ensure that your results are more credible, authoritative, useful, and current.
- Brute force is a method of searching where you type in what you think might logically be a web address and see what happens. Sometimes you'll receive an error message, but sometimes you find precisely what you're looking for.
- Link searching can be helpful once you find a relevant website. Explore links from the site you find that connect to other relevant sites.
- Professional associations and societies are a good starting point for professionally oriented information. Scientific and research information usually requires literature resources that can be found in scholarly databases, such as MEDLINE or the Cumulative Index to Nursing and Allied Health Literature (CINAHL).

It is important to be persistent and purposeful in searching. No one search strategy or search engine will work for all purposes every time. Although search engines have improved over time, it can still be a challenge to find what you need on the Internet.

TABLE 15-2 Illustration of Search Strategy Effectiveness*

Type of Search	Site	Results
Quick and dirty	www.google.com	54,200—majority of results were newspaper articles and general websites and articles that list never events but do not provide useful information
Advanced	www.google.com/advanced_search	For .gov = 1830 For .org = 6520 For .edu = 406
Brute force	Searched "www.neverevents.com"	Page returned that said "Page coming soon"
Link searching	Using the .gov advanced search: • First result is Centers for Medicare & Medicaid Services (CMS) • Second result is the Agency for Healthcare Research and Quality (AHRQ)	From first result—no links From second result—many helpful links, including: • What's New in Never Events • Editor's Picks for Never Events including those from the AHRQ, journal articles, books/reports, newspaper/magazine articles, tools/toolkits, and web resources

*The term being explored is *never events,* which Medicare considers to be preventable errors for which Medicare will no longer reimburse organizations if they occur.

Evaluating Information Found on the Internet

As you access information on the Internet, it is imperative that you perform a critical evaluation of what you have obtained. The Internet is open to anyone with access to a computer and material that looks official may actually be posted by persons without formal education in an area.

Some of the information you access may also contain inaccuracies. The affiliation of a website is important to note immediately: *.edu* is an educational institution; *.org* is a nonprofit organization; *.com* is a commercial enterprise; *.net* is an Internet service provider; *.gov* is a governmental body; and *.mil* is military. There are several forms that can

TABLE 15-3 **Website Evaluation Form**						
Website title: Web URL: Date visited: Brief description of the contents of the site:						
Criteria and Types of Evidence	**How Criterion is Met**			**Rating**		
		1 Low	2	3	4	5 High
1. Authority with regard to topic—Who is responsible for the site? Author of site (individual or institutional affiliation, organization) Credentials, expertise, experience Contact information (name, e-mail, postal address) URL type suggests reputable affiliation						
2. Objectivity—Is the purpose of the site clear, including any particular viewpoint? Statement of purpose and scope Intended audience Information presented as factual or opinion, primary or secondary in origin Criteria for inclusion of information Disclosure of sponsorship or underwriting						
3. Accuracy—Is the information accurate?						
4. Currency—Is the information current? Facts compare with related print or other online sources Links provided to quality web resources						
5. Usability—Is the site well designed and stable? Site organization logical and easy to maneuver Content readable by intended audience Information presented is error free (spelling, punctuation) Readily identifiable link back to the institutional or organizational home page Site reliably accessible Pages loaded quickly						
Subtotal for each of the five criteria						
ASSESSMENT OF WEBSITE						
Rating based on the total number of points: 5-9 points: poor 10-14 points: fair 15-19 points: good 20-25 points: excellent	Your personal assessment—Would you recommend this site? Why or why not?					

Courtesy Kent State University Libraries and Media Services, Kent, OH. http://www.library.kent.edu/files/webevalform.pdf

assist you in your evaluation. Table 15-3 shows a website evaluation form from Kent State University that offers five criteria and examples of the types of evidence that should factor into your rating of a website.

FUTURE HEALTH INFORMATION TECHNOLOGY TRENDS

With technology advancing at warp speed, it is difficult to imagine the future, but some of our current technologies offer some insight about the possibilities. To better understand how technology will shape health care, let us review some of the ways technology is currently shaping our lives.

- Social media will no longer be a source of informal content. Social media will develop into social platforms with more legitimate data sources than websites (Accenture, 2014).
- Cloud computing (e.g., applications and data stored and accessed through the Internet) will dominate the computing world (Accenture, 2014).
- Improved technologies will help detect and sense emotions or how patients feel, which improves care (Fierce HealthIT, 2013).
- Telemedicine and mobile health will extend care to the home environment after hospital discharges (Fierce HealthIT, 2013).

- Gaming will continue to expand health technologies by promoting health maintenance, physical activity, and cognitive skills that may lead to improved health behavior (Informationweek, 2014).
- Smart watches will continue to expand their features and become as ubiquitous as smartphones (Forbes. com, 2014).
- Mobile technologies that promote health (mHealth) will continue to advance allowing patients and providers to communicate routinely (Jayanthi, 2014).
- Sensors and wearable health monitoring technologies will continue to expand, offering more options to continuously assess individuals (Jayanathi, 2014).

Security is paramount for health care data. Future health information technologies will integrate more biometric technology for authentication and security. Biometric technologies use human characteristics, such as fingerprints, retinas, irises, voices, and facial patterns, to authenticate or grant access to data or information. More and more health care information systems are including biometric options to provide an additional layer of security. It is almost incomprehensible to imagine health care in 2020 when one considers the evolution in technology and how technology has shaped health care since the invention of the stethoscope.

SUMMARY

As a profession, nurses must understand and manage information technology, promote the meaningful use of EHRs, and teach patients how to use health information wisely. As the largest group of organized health care professionals in the United States, nurses have a responsibility to patients and society to continually improve and refine their competencies and knowledge base related to HIT. Findings of multiple studies confirm that nurses in every role and at each level of education and practice exhibit large gaps in knowledge and competencies for information technology.

Technology is an essential resource for nurses in their important role of tracking, interpreting, and improving

quality of care, in addition to translating research into practice. Technology continues to change and evolve at an ever-increasing pace. Be a lifelong learner. Take in-person or online classes. Arrange groups in your place of employment to learn more about health information technology in the clinical setting. Review the resources that are available to you, and evaluate them to ensure they are valid, current, and based on evidence. If the resources are not valid, take action within your facility to replace outdated or inaccurate resources. If the sources are valid, integrate them into your everyday practice.

REFERENCES

Accenture: *Accenture Technology Vision*, 2014. http://www.accenture.com/microsites/it-technology-trends-2014/Pages/tech-vision-report.aspx. Accessed January 15, 2015.

American Health Information Management Association: *Resources: Glossary of terms*, 2012. http://www.myphr.com/healthliteracy/glossary.aspx. Accessed September 15, 2014.

Association of College and Research Libraries: *Introduction to information literacy*. 2013a. http://www.ala.org/acrl/issues/infolit/intro. Accessed September 2014.

Association of College and Research Libraries: *Information literacy competency standards for nursing*. 2013b. http://www.ala.org/acrl/standards/nursing. Accessed September 15, 2014.

Bates DW, Gawande AA: Patient safety: improving safety with information technology, *N Engl J Med* 348(25):2526–2534, 2003.

Bush GW: *The White House, Remarks by the president in state of the union address*, Washington, D.C, 2004, Office of the Press Secretary. http://millercenter.org/president/speeches/detail/4542. Accessed September 15, 2014.

Carter-Templeton H, Patterson R, Mackey S: Nursing faculty and student experiences with information literacy: A pilot study, *Journal of Nursing Education and Practice* 4(1):208–217, 2014.

Centers for Disease Control and Prevention (2014): Use and characteristics of electronic health record systems among office-based physician practices: United States, 2001-2013, *NCHS Data Brief* 143, January 2014. http://www.cdc.gov/nchs/data/databriefs/db143.htm. Accessed September 15, 2014.

Centers for Medicare & Medicaid Services: *Medicare and Medicaid electronic health record incentive program*, 2012. https://www.cms.gov/EHRIncentivePrograms. Accessed September 15, 2014.

Chaudhry B, Wang J, Wu S, et al: Systematic review: impact of health information technology on quality, efficiency, and costs of medical care, *Ann Intern Med* 144(10):742–752, 2006.

Computer-Based Patient Record Institute: *Guidelines for establishing information security policies at organizations using computer-based patient records: work group on confidentiality, privacy and security*, Schaumburg: IL, 1995, Computer-Based Patient Record Institute.

Fierce HealthIT: *4 innovation trends shaping healthcare trends*, 2013. http://www.fiercehealthit.com/story/4-innovation-trends-shaping-healthcares-future/2013-11-12. Accessed September 15, 2014.

Forbes.com: *Smart watches, Google glass, and the wearable technology chocolate box*, 2014. http://www.forbes.com/sites/rajsabhlok/2013/12/05/smartwatches-google-glass-and-the-wearable-technology-chocolate-box/. Accessed September 15, 2014.

HealthIT.gov: *Meaningful Use Definition & Objectives*, 2015. http://www.healthit.gov/providers-professionals/meaningful-use-definition-objectives. Accessed May 15, 2015.

HealthIT.gov: *Stage 3 Recommendation Task Force Report. Nationwide Roadmap to Interoperability*, 2014. http://www.healthit.gov/facas/sites/faca/files/muwg_stage3_draft_rec_07_aug_13_.v3.pdf. Accessed September 15, 2014.

Hebda T, Czar P: Handbook of informatics for nurses & healthcare professionals, ed 4, Upper Saddle River, NJ, 2009, Pearson-Prentice Hall.

Information week: *3 trends are reshaping healthcare IT*, 2014. http://www.informationweek.com/healthcare/leadership/3-trends-are-reshaping-healthcare-it/d/d-id/1113460. Accessed September 15, 2014.

Institute of Medicine of the National Academies: *Key capabilities of an electronic health record system: Letter report*, Washington, DC, 2003, The National Academies Press. http://www.nap.edu/openbook.php?record_id=10781. Accessed September 2014.

Jacques LB: Electronic health records and respect for patient privacy: a prescription for compatibility, *Vanderbilt J Ent and Tech Law* 13(2):441–462, 2011.

Jayanthi A: 10 biggest technological advancement for healthcare in the last decade, *Becker Hospital Review* 2014. http://www.beckershospitalreview.com/healthcare-information-technology/10-biggest-technological-advancements-for-healthcare-in-the-last-decade.html. Accessed September 15, 2014.

Protti D, Johansen I: Widespread adoption of information technology in primary care physician offices in Demark: a case study, *The Commonwealth Fund*, 2010. http://www.commonwealthfund.org/Publications/Issue-Briefs/2010/Mar/Widespread-Adoption-of-Information-Technology-in-Primary-Care-Physician-Offices.aspx. Accessed September 15, 2014.

Royall J, Lyon B: Sea-change or change challenge? Health information access in developing countries: The U.S. National Library of Medicine experience, *Afr Health Sci* 11(3):457–463, 2011.

Smith C: New technologies continue to invade healthcare: What are the strategic implications/outcomes? *Nurs Adm Q* 28(2):92–98, 2004.

Thielst CB: Social media: ubiquitous community and patient engagement, *Front Health Serv Manage* 28(2):3–14, 2011.

U.S. Department of Health and Human Services: *Health IT Adoption Programs*, 2014. http://www.healthit.gov/policy-researchers-implementers/health-it-adoption-programs. Accessed September 15, 2014.

U.S. Department of Health and Human Services: *The Office of the National Coordinator of Health Information Technology, ONC-authorized testing and certification bodies*, 2013. http://healthit.hhs.gov/portal/server.pt?open=512&mode=2&objID=3120. Accessed September 15, 2014.

U.S. Federal Register: *Medicare and Medicaid Programs; Electronic Health Record Incentive Program—Stage 2*, 2012. https://www.federalregister.gov/articles/2012/03/07/2012-4443/medicare-and-medicaid-programs-electronic-health-record-incentive-program-stage-2. Accessed September 15, 2014.

Walker J, Pan E, Johnston D, et al: The value of health care information exchange and interoperability, Health Aff Online, Supplement Web Exclusives: W5–10–18, Jan-Jun 2005.

Wyatt TH, Krauskopf PB: E-health and nursing: using smartphones to enhance nursing practice, *Online J Nurs Inform* 16(2), 2012. http://ojni.org/issues/?p=1706. Accessed September 15, 2014.

16

Partnering to respond to disaster.

Emergency Preparedness and Response for Today's World

Rebecca R. Keck, DNP, RN, NEA-BC,
Elizabeth E. Weiner, PhD, RN-BC, FACMI, FAAN

ⓔ Additional resources are available online at: *http://evolve.elsevier.com/Cherry/*

PROFESSIONAL/ETHICAL ISSUE

Jeannette Fraser, RN, worked in the emergency department (ED) of a major hospital system when, during her shift in the ED, an explosion occurred at a large factory near the city. As soon as the hospital determined that a disaster occurred with multiple injuries, the hospital's emergency operations plan (EOP) was activated. Fortunately, less than 1 month before the explosion, Jeannette had participated in a large-scale disaster drill conducted by the hospital in partnership with agencies from across the city, including the fire department, the police department, and the city's emergency operations center. Although extremely anxious, Jeannette knew exactly what to do and went to work in her assigned role to triage victims who were coming into the ED. Jeannette knew that the entire hospital staff was more successful in managing the disaster and helping victims because of the well-coordinated EOP that was in place. Recently, Jeannette moved to another state and accepted a nursing position in the outpatient clinic of a large academic medical center. As part of her orientation, Jeannette asks her supervisor about the facility's EOP and the supervisor replies, "I am sure we have a written plan in the policy manual, but I really don't know much about it. This is a very safe community, so we don't need to worry about anything happening here. And besides, if something did happen, the victims would go to the hospital, and it would not affect us." This response from her supervisor leaves Jeannette feeling very concerned and wondering if she should get involved in helping the clinic understand the importance of having a good EOP that is coordinated with the hospital and other community agencies. Think about Jeannette's situation as you consider the following questions:

- In the event of a major disaster, is it conceivable that victims might go to an outpatient or community-based clinic for treatment?
- What are some strategies Jeannette can use to convince the clinic managers about the importance of having an up-to-date EOP in place?
- When might nurses in an ambulatory clinic be considered "first responders"?
- What local, state, and/or federal resources are available to help communities develop EOPs?

VIGNETTE

Jane Wolverton works as a staff nurse on a medical-surgical unit at the Culverton General Hospital. She is in a patient's room giving an intravenous (IV) medication when the news program announces that there has been a major explosion at a chemical plant. The plant has 400 workers, including her husband.

Questions to Consider While Reading this Chapter:

1. How do we prepare for mass casualty events that will overwhelm the resources of our health facility?
2. How do we plan for a catastrophic event to ensure that the response offers the best care possible given the resources at hand? How are response efforts coordinated so that the needs of the local area are met?
3. How do hospitals organize themselves to manage disaster situations while continuing to communicate with other external agencies?
4. How does the response differ when the hospital suffers damage and cannot function normally?
5. Where can I find current information about this ever-changing area?

KEY TERMS

Active shooter: An individual actively engaged in killing or attempting to kill people in a confined and populated area; in most cases, active shooters use firearms and there is no pattern or method to their selection of victims.

All-hazards approach: A process approach for all sectors to prepare for any emergency or disaster that may occur.

Biologic agents: Microorganisms or toxins from living organisms with infectious or noninfectious properties that produce lethal or serious effects in plants and animals.

Chemical agents: Solids, liquids, or gases with chemical properties that produce lethal or serious effects in plants and animals.

Comprehensive emergency management: A broad style of emergency management, encompassing prevention, preparedness, response, and recovery.

Consequence management: Measures to protect public health and safety, restore essential government services, and provide emergency relief to governments, businesses, and individuals affected by the consequences of terrorism.

Containment: Limitation of an emergency situation within a well-defined area.

Credible threat: Situation in which the Federal Bureau of Investigation (FBI) determines that a terrorist threat is credible and confirms the involvement of a weapon of mass destruction (WMD) in the developing terrorist incident.

Crisis management: Measures to identify, acquire, and plan the use of resources needed to anticipate, prevent, and/or resolve a threat or act of terrorism.

Crisis standards of care: A substantial change in usual health care operations and the level of care it is possible to deliver, which is made necessary by a pervasive (e.g., pandemic influenza) or catastrophic (e.g., earthquake, hurricane) disaster. This change in the level of care delivered is justified by specific circumstances and is formally declared by a state government, in recognition that crisis operations will be in effect for a sustained period.

Disaster condition: A significant natural disaster or man-made event that overwhelms the affected state, necessitating both federal public health and medical care assistance.

Emergency: As defined in the Stafford Act, any occasion or instance for which, in the determination of the president, federal assistance is needed to supplement state and local efforts and capabilities to save lives and protect property, public health, and safety; includes emergencies other than natural disasters.

Emergency Management Assistance Compact (EMAC): An organization authorized by the U.S Congress through which a state impacted by a disaster can request and receive assistance from other member states quickly and efficiently (EMAC, 2014).

Incident command system (ICS): A multiagency operational structure that uses a model adopted by the fire and rescue community. The ICS can be used in any size or type of disaster to control response personnel, facilities, and equipment.

Lead agency: As defined by the FBI, the federal department or organization assigned primary responsibility to manage and coordinate a specific function—either crisis management or consequence management. Lead agencies are designated on the basis of their having the most authority, resources, capabilities, or expertise relative to accomplishment of the specific function.

Major disaster: As defined under the Stafford Act, any natural catastrophe (including any hurricane, tornado, storm, high water, wind-driven water, tidal wave, tsunami, earthquake, volcanic eruption, landslide, mudslide, snowstorm, or drought) or, regardless of cause, any fire, flood, or explosion in any part of the United States that in the determination of the President causes damage of sufficient severity and magnitude to warrant major disaster assistance under the Stafford Act to supplement the efforts and available resources of states, local governments, and disaster relief organizations in alleviating the damage, loss, hardship, or suffering caused thereby.

Mass casualty incident (MCI): A disaster situation that results in a large number of victims who need the response of multiple organizations.

Mitigation: Those activities designed to alleviate the effects of a major disaster or emergency or long-term activities to minimize the potentially adverse effects of future disasters in affected areas.

Pandemic: Outbreak of disease that affects populations worldwide; for example, pandemic influenza causes serious illness worldwide.

Preparedness: Activities that build capability and capacity to address potential needs identified by the threat and vulnerability study.

Recovery: Activities designed to return responders and the facility to full normal operational status and to restore fully the capability to respond to future emergencies and disasters; activities traditionally associated with providing federal supplemental disaster relief assistance under a presidential major disaster declaration.

Response: Activities to address the immediate and short-term effects of an emergency or disaster.

Response includes immediate actions to save lives, protect property, and meet basic human needs.

Scene assessment: The act of reviewing the location of an event to look for information that might help to determine treatment options.

Technical operations: Actions to identify, assess, dismantle, transfer, dispose of, or decontaminate personnel and property exposed to explosive ordnance or weapons of mass destruction (WMD).

Terrorist incident: As defined by the FBI, a violent act or an act that is dangerous to human life, in violation of the criminal laws of the United States or of any state, and intended to intimidate or coerce a government, the civilian population, or any segment thereof in furtherance of political or social objectives.

Triage: Process of prioritizing which patients are to be treated first; first action in any disaster response.

Weapon of mass destruction (WMD): As defined by Title 18, US Code 2332a, (1) any destructive device as defined in section 921 of this title, [which reads] any explosive, incendiary, or poison gas, bomb, grenade, rocket having a propellant charge of more than 4 ounces, missile having an explosive or incendiary charge of more than one quarter ounce, mine or device similar to the above; (2) poison gas; (3) any weapon involving a disease organism; or (4) any weapon designed to release radiation or radioactivity at a level dangerous to human life.

LEARNING OUTCOMES

After studying this chapter, the reader will be able to:

1. Describe the interaction between local, state, and federal emergency response systems.
2. Examine the roles of public and private agencies in preparing for and responding to a mass casualty event.
3. Compare and contrast chemical, biologic, radiologic, nuclear, and explosive agents and treatment protocols.
4. Access resources related to disaster preparedness on the Internet.
5. Communicate effectively (using correct emergency preparedness terminology) in regard to a mass casualty incident.
6. Describe the need for personal preparedness for individuals and households.

CHAPTER OVERVIEW

The purpose of this chapter is to describe the various components of our nation's local, state, and federal National Response Framework and how these components interrelate in the event of a mass casualty incident (MCI). The *problems associated with natural or terrorist disasters when the health care system is damaged or rendered ineffective because of the event are reviewed. The kinds of agents that may be used in a terrorist attack are described along with the activities and response systems related to the preimpact and impact phase of a disaster. Readers will be particularly interested to note how standard triage and patient care priorities change when care is provided during an MCI. Additionally, readers are encouraged to closely review the list of key terms to understand and be able to use emergency preparedness terminology and explore the online resources about emergency preparedness and disaster management found throughout the chapter.*

THE NATIONAL IMPERATIVE FOR EMERGENCY PREPAREDNESS

During the past two decades, we have seen many mass casualty events on U.S. soil, some from natural disasters and some as a result of terrorist attacks. Examples of terrorist attacks include the bombing of the Murrah Federal Building in Oklahoma City in 1995 the attacks on the U.S. embassies in Kenya and Tanzania in 1998; the attack in 2000 on the U.S.S. *Cole,* an American warship refueling in Yemen; and the anthrax scare in 2002. None of these events, however, had the same effect as the events of September 11, 2001, when the United States experienced devastating, well-coordinated attacks in New York City and Washington, DC, that led to the deaths of more than 3000 people.

More recent events have kept the threat of terrorism alive. The Boston Marathon bombings in 2013 killed three people and injured an estimated 264 others who were treated in 27 local hospitals (Kotz, 2013). This event vividly demonstrated the need to have coordinated efforts between first responders: law enforcement/fire, medical and mental health services, emergency management, and related local and federal agencies. Recent brutal beheadings of journalists by Islamic extremists remind all of us that the ever-changing world is difficult to protect.

The disasters unfolding in this century are frequently associated with global instability, economic decay, political upheaval and collapse of government structure, violence and civil conflicts, famine, and mass population displacements (Veenema, 2003). The growing complexity and nature of disasters create considerable challenges for individuals responsible for disaster planning and related response. The need for formalized plans for preparedness, mitigation, response, recovery, and evaluation is essential to minimizing the impact to individuals and society at large. Nurses serve in vital roles in planning development and overall response.

Although a great deal of attention has been focused on preparing for an MCI related to a terrorist attack, the United States has suffered major damage from natural disasters. Hurricane Katrina has become the classic example of massive system failure in emergency response. Most of the destruction was due to storm surge, and further flooding took place in New Orleans as the levee system catastrophically failed. Although the death toll from this event did not reach the level seen at the World Trade Center, the damage to the health care systems in the affected areas was substantial. It became evident very quickly that the response systems in place could not be effective in dealing with the destruction of the health care infrastructure, and, in fact, the health care agencies themselves were sites of mass casualties. The extensive need for immediate and long-term shelters for large numbers of victims also highlighted the need for nurses to have knowledge and skills in how to meet the needs of victims with psychological and chronic diseases in a sheltered environment. The Institute of Medicine was called upon to convene a group of experts in 2009 (reconvened in 2011) to address the issues related to the community response to major disasters (Hanfling et al, 2012).

Emergency management plans must address adequate response systems that can be used regardless of the cause of the MCI. A more reasonable approach has been the movement to plan and improve responses to a variety of hazards, called an all-hazards approach. Nurses have traditionally received disaster education as a part of community health content within nursing education programs as it related to natural disasters; however, the education has been focused on responding to a disaster site of victims when the health care system is still intact. The same is true for other health care professional education programs. In addition, they have not routinely received education related to biologic, chemical, nuclear, explosive, or radiologic hazards. It is imperative that all health care providers become knowledgeable about how to provide care for victims of all types of hazards and in situations where the health care system itself has been damaged, destroyed, or has no contact with the other parts of the community.

It is recognized by all federal agencies that the most serious knowledge deficit for health care providers is in the area of bioterrorism attacks and pandemic flu events. Unlike the other hazards, these situations place the health care providers in a position of being first responders. Traditionally, first responders to emergencies have been the law enforcement, firefighters, and emergency medical technicians who respond with ambulances. In a biologic event (covert or natural transmission), however, victims will first appear in emergency departments, physicians' offices, nurse-managed clinics, or even in school health care settings. Health care professionals need to be able to identify symptoms, patterns of similar events, and other irregularities. If they fail to recognize or report significant events, a biologic event could go unrecognized until it is of epidemic proportions.

The same principles of responding to a bioterrorist event are pertinent for coping with a natural biologic outbreak, such as a pandemic flu event or severe acute respiratory syndrome (SARS). It is these types of diseases and exposures that are becoming the target of education for not only the health care community but also the general community at large to cooperate to prevent spread of a disease that would eventually become pandemic and a mass casualty event.

THE BASICS OF EMERGENCY PREPAREDNESS AND RESPONSE

Nurses have significant experience in dealing with natural disasters and are familiar with the work of the Red Cross in bringing disaster relief to affected areas. A disaster condition is defined as a significant natural disaster or man-made event that overwhelms the affected state and necessitates both federal public health and medical care assistance (Federal Emergency Management Agency [FEMA], 2014a). The disaster condition must be of significant impact to warrant federal resources. Understanding the responsibilities of the multiple agencies that respond to a disaster is imperative to be able to communicate with patients, families, and other health care providers.

In some situations, the number of victims is so large that multiple organizations will be called to respond. When casualties occur at this level, the event is termed a mass casualty incident (MCI) or *mass casualty event (MCE)*. Although the situation may be unfamiliar for some nurses, it is important to remember that the nursing fundamentals practiced in other settings and during smaller crises are generally still applicable. Traditionally, triage that is practiced in most health care agencies categorizes patients into low risk, intermediate care, and critically ill (those who need immediate care to save their lives). With such large numbers, however, there is a paradigm shift to change priorities into doing the greatest good for the greatest number of people. Care is given to those patients who have the greatest chance of survival. This type of triage typically places nurses in ethical situations in which they experience discomfort, particularly if patients are triaged and tagged to receive only pain management rather than typical extensive treatment that might be provided during normal health care conditions. Furthermore, the public responds to the visible tags placed on patients and can provide added stress when calling out to health care providers to provide further care.

Community disaster plans need to clearly define the care processes to be used when the needs shift from that of one patient to the needs of the populations (Hanfling et al, 2012). Nurses may also find themselves in positions in which there is a lack of necessary resources, and they will then have to come up with creative solutions. Powers (2010) describes examples of such adaptability by the Australian team in the Maldives post-tsunami 2004, with such actions as using rigid plastic drink bottles as sharps containers at each patient's bed area and using the large, rigid containers used to transport medical supplies as privacy screens and walls between treatment areas. Busby and Witucki-Brown (2011) described such actions and decisions by nurses and other responders as developing situational awareness about MCIs.

Terrorism has created the need for us to prepare against a variety of different agents. A standardized nomenclature has been developed for five categories using the acronym CBRNE, which stands for **c**hemical, **b**iologic, **r**adiologic, **n**uclear, and **e**xplosive. Table 16-1 describes the similarities and differences related to the CBRNE agents and provides information about treatment protocols for each agent.

TABLE 16-1	**CBRNE Agents**			
Agents	**Action**	**Advantages**	**Disadvantages**	**Treatment**
Chemical	Agents injure or kill through variety of means: vesicant, nerve, blood, respiratory	Spread easily through air; cause immediate effects; require decontamination	Less toxic than biologic agents; need to be used in large quantities; subject to dispersion by wind; terrorists need to protect themselves; require trained HAZMAT teams	Dependent on agent used; in some cases have agent-specific medications; require decontamination; require use of personal protective equipment by personnel
Biologic	Disease-causing organisms (bacteria, viruses, toxins)	Available; small quantities can have large effect; spread through large areas; can remain in air or on surfaces; difficult to prepare against	Delayed effects; production hazardous to terrorists; difficult to develop	Dependent on agent used; most cause flu-like symptoms; plague and smallpox most contagious; timing of specific treatment critical; in some cases can have vaccinations
Radiologic	Ionizing radiation able to strip electrons from atoms, causing chemical changes in molecules; expression may be delayed; radiation depends on time, distance, shielding, and quantity of radioactive material	Available; psychological effect likely to be substantial; often used in conjunction with explosive devices ("dirty bombs")	Delayed effects of radiation materials; difficult to shield against	Dirty bomb causes immediate effects (radiation burns, acute poisoning) and long-term effects (cancer, contamination of drinking water); decontamination must occur before patient care can be safely provided by the health care worker
Nuclear	Depends on yield of nuclear weapon, but consists of blast range effects, thermal radiation, nuclear radiation, and radioactive fallout	Requires decontamination; contamination can remain for many years; psychological effect likely to be substantial	Large, heavy, and dangerous weapons; hazardous to terrorists; expensive and difficult to make weapons of this type	Symptomatic treatment of thermal burns, shrapnel injuries, and radioactive fallout; depends on distance from source and time of exposure
Explosive	Most common method for terrorists; capable of violent decomposition; pressure, temperature changes and propellants cause injury and/or death	Available materials to construct explosive device; large devices can be placed in abandoned vehicles; smaller devices can be placed on bodies of persons willing to commit suicide by igniting the device	Volatile ingredients could cause premature explosion of device, thus creating danger for terrorists; government agencies have improved training and processes for identifying incendiary devices	Symptomatic; often requires treatment for burns

PHASES OF DISASTER

Powers (2010) describes three phases of the disaster continuum: preparedness, relief response, and recovery. In the preparedness phase, activities are focused on planning, preparedness, prevention, and warning. After the impact, all efforts are directed to responding to the disaster, initiating the emergency management system, and mitigating the effects of the hazard. During the recovery phase, which usually begins 72 hours after the disaster and may continue for 2 to 3 years, a network of activities is designed to enhance rehabilitation and reconstruction. Evaluation of the disaster preparedness and response plan is a major activity that needs to be included in the recovery phase. It is important for nurses to understand the phases of a disaster, described in the following sections, to know what actions are necessary in each phase.

Preparedness Phase

In January 2001, The Joint Commission's disaster preparedness standards were modified to introduce the concepts of emergency management and community involvement in the management process. These modifications call for accredited organizations to take an "all-hazards" approach to disaster planning—reviewing, analyzing, and addressing all hazards that are determined to be credible and serious threats to the community. Following the terrorist attacks on September 11, 2001, The Joint Commission (TJC) made an additional modification to the standard requiring organizations to communicate and coordinate with each other (TJC, 2013).

Every disaster, regardless of the cause, begins as a local event. Each locale has the responsibility for responding to the emergencies within its community first. Thus the heaviest burden falls on the local community when a mass casualty occurs. Assistance from state and federal levels is appropriated when the local system is unable to provide the necessary level of care. It is imperative, then, that communities plan for the services that will be needed in a time of disaster and train the providers within each agency about responding to all hazard types of MCEs. Efforts must be directed toward the interrelationship of roles and responsibilities of the agencies and services that will be needed at the time of a disaster. Key elements of a community preparedness program should include the following:

- Assessing the community for risks and determining the types of events that may occur
- Planning the emergency activities to ensure a coordinated response effort
- Building the capabilities that are necessary to respond to the consequences of the events

There must be agreements between agencies within the community and between neighboring communities for such entities as emergency response units, hospitals, long-term care facilities, clinics, and health departments to be able to provide mutual aid and transfer of people and materials during a time of disaster. The IOM report (Hanfling et al, 2012) emphasizes that integrated planning for coordinated response by state and local governments, emergency medical services, health care organizations and health care providers in the community is critical to successfully responding to disasters.

Agreements should be in place that address issues related to credentialing health care providers who may be shared among institutions. The Medical Reserve Corps (MRC) was initiated in 2002 to improve the health and safety of communities across the country by organizing and utilizing public health, nursing, medical, and other volunteers to serve their communities. There are currently 993 MRC units and 207,783 volunteers throughout the United States and its territories (Division of the Civilian Volunteer Medical Reserve Corps, 2014). Part of the requirements for membership in the MRC is to complete an emergency response curriculum. Several of the MRC units are associated with universities (Culley, 2010).

The MRC is the responsibility of the local area, with many states receiving funding to establish the network of volunteers. They function as a way to locally organize and utilize volunteers who want to donate their time and expertise to prepare for and respond to emergencies and promote healthy living throughout the year. MRC volunteers supplement existing emergency and public health resources. There are situations (such as Hurricane Katrina) that local units deployed outside of their region to respond to the additional needs that were not being met. (Visit *http://www.medicalreservecorps.gov* for more information about how to volunteer to participate in the MRC system.)

Plans and contracts also need to be developed with school systems, YMCAs, or other large facilities to provide shelter for large numbers of victims. The interface with volunteer agencies, such as the Red Cross, also needs to be arranged. Each agency should have a well-developed emergency operating plan (EOP) that includes its responsibilities and capabilities for responding to an MCE, an identified chain of command, and a plan for interaction with other community agencies. Agency personnel should be knowledgeable about their role in the EOP and receive education concerning the ways to respond to all types of hazards.

Several federal-level programs are designed to assist communities in planning their emergency response to an MCE and to provide assistance during a time of disaster. Agency and community EOPs should outline their relationship with the federal system. The National Response Framework is a guide to how the nation conducts an all-hazard response—from the smallest incident to the largest catastrophe—using a comprehensive, national, all-hazards approach to domestic incident response (FEMA, 2014b). Figure 16-1 illustrates the relationship among local, state, and federal response systems. Following is a description of the key components of the federal response system.

Metropolitan Medical Response System

The Metropolitan Medical Response System (MMRS) builds a cadre of specialty trained responders and equipment. The system is coordinated with area and statewide planning systems and integrates the efforts of all of the emergency response teams. The MMRS includes plans for expanding hospital-based care, enhancing emergency medical transport and emergency department capabilities, locating specialized pharmaceuticals to respond to an MCE, managing

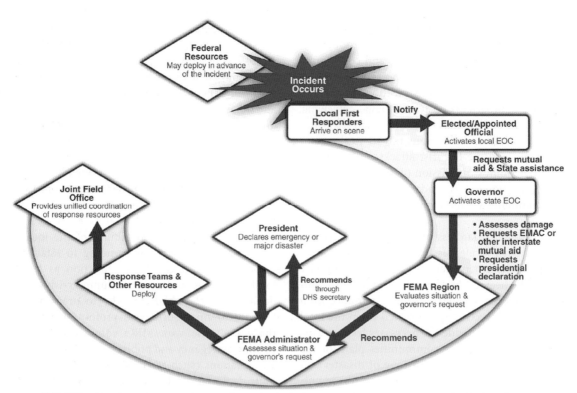

FIGURE 16-1 Emergency response flows from the community to the state to the federal level. (From FEMA: National response framework, 2008 (website). www.fema.gov/pdf/emergency/nrf/nrf-overview.pdf.)

mass fatalities, and providing mental health care for the community, victims, and health care providers. Scenarios designed to test the effectiveness of the MMRS in the community in providing an integrated response to an MCI are conducted on a regular basis.

National Disaster Medical System

The National Disaster Medical System (NDMS) is a federally coordinated system that augments the nation's medical response capability during times of major peacetime disasters and to provide support to the military and the Department of Veterans Affairs medical systems in caring for casualties evacuated back to the United States from armed conventional conflicts overseas (U.S. Dept. of Health and Human Services [USDHHS], 2014a). The National Response Framework utilizes the NDMS under Emergency Support Function #8, Health and Medical Services, to support the federal medical response to major emergencies and federally declared disasters including national disasters, major transportation accidents, technologic disasters, and acts of terrorism. For more information about becoming involved in NDMS visit http://www.phe.gov/Preparedness/responders/ndms.

Disaster Medical Assistance Teams

Disaster Medical Assistance Teams (DMATs) are regionally organized teams of health care professionals and administrative staff designed to be the rapid-response component to support local medical care needs until federal resources can be deployed; DMATs can be sent into areas outside their own regions to assist in providing care for ill or injured victims at the location of a disaster or emergency. DMATs provide triage, medical or surgical stabilization, and continued monitoring and care of patients until they can be evacuated to locations where they will receive definitive medical care. Specialty DMATs can also be deployed to address, for example, mass burn injuries, pediatric care requirements, and chemical injury or contamination. For more information about DMATs, visit http://www.phe.gov/Preparedness/responders/ndms/teams.

Commissioned Corps

The Commissioned Corps emergency response teams are managed by the Office of the Surgeon General and are part of the U.S. Public Health Service. These teams are an additional asset capable of responding in times of extraordinary need when the public health needs exceed the ability of the local or state agencies. The Commissioned Corps comprises more than 6500 health care professionals that can be deployed to respond to a disaster, either as a large group or in small numbers to support the disaster medical assistance team's (DMAT) effort. For more information, visit http://www.usphs.gov.

Strategic National Stockpile

The Centers for Disease Control and Prevention (CDC) host a Strategic National Stockpile (SNS) that has large quantities of medicine and medical supplies to protect the American public if there is a public health emergency severe enough to cause local supplies to be depleted. The SNS has a national repository of antibiotics, chemical antidotes, antitoxins, IV administrations, airway supplies, and other medical-surgical items. A 12-hour "push-pack" of supplies can be deployed within 12 hours of the decision to activate the SNS. The community emergency plan should include procedures to receive the push package. Follow-up pharmaceutical or medical supplies can be shipped within 24 to 36 hours if required. This supply can be tailored to the specific needs of the event if the needs are known at that time (CDC, 2014a).

Community emergency operating plans must include strategies for the community's interaction with these various state and federal response teams and systems to efficiently use the services and materials provided for mass casualty response. Hospital EOPs should include descriptions of the federal responses and how they will be incorporated into the emergency operations. Developing community "crisis standards" was the focus of the IOM reports of 2009 and 2011, which outline the critical components that need to be in place at each level (Hanfling et al, 2012).

Though not formally part of emergency operations, individuals and households play an important role in the overall emergency management strategy. They can contribute by reducing hazards in and around their homes, preparing emergency supply kits and household emergency plans, and monitoring emergency communications carefully. The Ready government website provides additional disaster response information and can be found at *www.ready.gov*.

Relief Response Phase

Response Activities

Response activities are first initiated during the impact phase of disasters. These activities begin at the time of the event and are focused on providing the first emergency response to victims of the disaster, stabilizing the situation, and providing adequate treatment for the victims. This phase requires the interaction of emergency responders from fire and police departments, emergency medical services, hazardous materials teams, health care agencies, health departments, and other agencies to be able to triage, provide assistance, and stabilize the scene. Typically, the first unit responding establishes an incident command post from which to coordinate the activities. However, as other units arrive and as the cause of the incident becomes known, one of the law enforcement agencies may assume control if there is suspicion of a crime before the establishment of a community-based emergency operations center (EOC).

National Incident Management System

Emergencies breed chaos, and it is essential to bring order to the situation for an effective response. The National Incident Management System (NIMS) provides a systematic proactive approach to guide departments and agencies at all levels of government, nongovernmental organizations, and the private sector to work seamlessly during disaster situations (FEMA, 2014c). The system is designed to expand from one person or agency performing all roles to having hundreds of people involved in the process. An efficient NIMS requires a hierarchic chain of command led by the incident manager or commander. Assigned personnel who refer to a specific job action sheet consistently follow job assignments. An NIMS will be established at the scene of the disaster and include representatives of all agencies needed to provide the emergency services.

At the time of a mass casualty, each hospital system will initiate its emergency response plans. Structures may vary from hospital to hospital, but most are using the system called the hospital incident command system (HICS). The assumption is that in a time of crisis, communication will be improved if all disaster responders begin from a common structure. The HICS defines responsibilities, reporting channels, and common terminology for hospitals, fire departments, local governments, and other agencies (California Emergency Medical Services Authority, 2014). The HICS can be customized for organizations of varying sizes. (The HICS 2014 Guidebook can be downloaded online at no charge at http://www.emsa.ca.gov/disaster_medical_services_division_hospital_incident_command_system.)

Regardless of the structure of the NIMS, the ultimate aim is to coordinate the safe and effective response of emergency resources to an incident. In the HICS, there is only one incident commander, supported by clearly identified levels in the command structure. The hierarchy of command is important so that there is no confusion as to who reports to whom or about who is managing the incident. The chain of command is established to allow for communication to flow from the top down or the bottom up. (FEMA provides online training modules about the incident command system for hospitals and health care providers at http://training.fema.gov/EMIWeb/IS/is100HCb.asp.)

Personal Protection and Safety

Personal protection and safety are important regardless of the situational factors causing an MCI. What is important to note, however, is that situational factors dictate how to be personally protected and safe. Protecting the lives of emergency responders takes precedence over other incident issues because if emergency responders are exposed or injured, they will not be able to provide care to others.

Because of the varied routes of exposure from CBRNE agents, personal protective equipment (PPE) must be designed to impede the most vulnerable route(s), thereby blocking the agent from entering the body. Specially designed PPE is available in a variety of levels, each level designed to meet specific protection needs:

- *Level A* provides a totally encapsulated chemical resistant suit, including supplied air. As a result, maximum respiratory and skin protection is provided. In addition, this level of equipment is used to provide protection against liquid splashes or in situations in which agents are still unidentified.
- *Level B* provides a chemical splash–resistant suit with hood and self-contained breathing apparatus (SCBA). It provides maximum respiratory protection but less skin protection than level A equipment.

- *Level C* equipment is chemical-resistant clothing with a hood and an air-purifying respirator. The respirator can remove all anticipated contaminants and concentrations of chemical materials, thus providing adequate protection against airborne biologic agents and radiologic materials.
- *Level D* protection may consist of a uniform or scrubs and is appropriate when it has been determined that no respiratory or skin hazard is present.

Although each level provides some protection, it is important to understand the limitations of all PPE. Typically, first responders to community emergencies are firefighters, police, and emergency medical technicians. These professionals have traditionally been trained in the effective use of PPE and can be a good community resource. In addition, hospital infection control personnel can be an excellent resource for the use of PPE. As health care providers assume the care of patients who may have been contaminated, it is important to note whether they have been decontaminated and require no further protective equipment or what additional level of protection is required.

Communication Within the Health Care Facility

At the initial time of the event, when news stories are first breaking, staff, patients, and families may hear of the incident before the EOP and HICS have been initiated. In this case, it is crucial for the facility information officer to take charge of communicating with the news media and for administrators to initiate a plan to communicate within the health care facility. Crisis intervention strategies to prevent group panic must be instituted immediately. Communication officers need to:

- Determine the effects the crisis will have on the audience.
- Speak clearly and simply about the facts.
- Be direct, honest, and to the point.
- Reassure and calm the audience.

Regular updates of information (every 30 minutes) need to be planned and distributed to all hospital units as quickly as possible. Patients and families need to be informed of measures that will be taken with the initiation of the EOP, such as early discharge or relocation of less ill patients to other areas of the hospital or to other facilities. Family members may not be able to leave the hospital to return home; arrangements will need to be made to care for them, including providing medications that they take regularly.

LESSONS LEARNED FROM MASS CASUALTY INCIDENTS

Although preparation for all types of causes of MCIs (natural or man-made) is necessary, nurses must understand the actions needed when the health care agency is damaged and how health care providers must function during these times. Issues related to use of personnel, rotation and resting of personnel, use of family or volunteers, methods of evacuation, and care of hospital staff and families must be included in emergency preparedness preparations and education. Alterations in the standard of care during an MCI need to be understood. Hospitals are viewed by the community and employees as places of safe haven when a disaster strikes. Incoming staff will be limited, and decisions about how care will be provided must be made. Places to provide rest and measures to encourage staff to rest should be determined early in the MCI. Mechanisms for staff to contact their families or significant others should be initiated as soon as possible. Arrangements need to be made for the care of children, other dependents, and pets for those staff members who will be staying at the hospital for extended periods.

In addition, measures need to be included to provide information to the staff for those who are not able to locate their family because of the disaster. The role of the information liaison office of the HICS is most important for this function. In addition to these considerations, mass causality incidents have the potential to create widespread civil unrest and violence that may follow in the immediate time frame following the event. Safety/security resources, if available, should be put in place as quickly as possible. Personal safety and the safety of others must remain at the forefront in response efforts. This is particularly true for vulnerable populations such as women, children, elderly, and those with disabilities.

Staff need to be prepared to cope with power outages and damage to the institution. All hospitals are equipped with emergency generators, and most hospital staff members assume that these will be operational. Emergency plans and drills need to include scenarios of how to adapt care if the generators are not functioning. It is important that the staff delivering care have the skill set to know how they will function in these situations. Lessons learned from previous disasters emphasize the necessity to include the care delivery staff in this level of detail. Some examples of decisions that had to be made were how to do the following:

- Deliver medications when the usual pumps were not functioning.
- Decide what medications would be given when the medication supply was depleted.
- Provide ventilation and suctioning without electricity.

Nurses and staff on the nursing units need to be prepared for these situations. Preparing unit-based scenarios for discussion can be helpful in preparing for an MCI.

Japan is perhaps the most well-prepared country in the world for any disaster, yet the experience of the Great East Japan earthquake in March 2011 caused Japanese authorities to understand that past assumptions and lessons learned were not particularly valid (Yamamoto, 2011). This was a compound disaster beginning with an earthquake with a magnitude of 9.0, resulting in a devastating tsunami with a consequent nuclear crisis involving the release of radioactive materials into the environment. Earlier, it had been recommended to prepare a 3-day supply of food and other necessities to survive a disaster. However, during this event, responders learned that this was not enough; it took 1 to 2 weeks before there was enough food and water to go around, and even shelters ran short of food and supplies. Shelters also had to take care of community patients, yet they did not have adequate medical supplies.

BIOLOGIC CAUSES OF MASS CASUALTY

Pandemic Influenza

Nurses also need to be prepared to respond to MCIs that result from biologic agents. Although terrorist dissemination of biologic agents was initially the focus of emergency preparedness efforts following the World Trade Center attack, the natural dissemination of biologic agents such as influenza has been the priority for disaster preparedness efforts for communities.

A pandemic influenza is a global outbreak that occurs when a new influenza virus emerges in the human population, causing serious illness and death as it spreads worldwide. The United States has had three previous pandemic flu experiences: In 1918, 50 million died worldwide and 675,000 died in the United States; in 1957, 1 to 2 million died worldwide and 70,000 died in the United States; and in 1968, 700,000 died worldwide and 34,000 died in the United States (USDHHS, 2014b).

Tracking and predicting pandemic flu is an important component of the response to this potential serious threat to the nation's health. The most up-to-date information for flu tracking and reporting is now found on the CDC and WHO websites. Health care providers are directed to these websites to determine the flu outbreaks in their own areas and those within the region, country, and the world. Although most people believe that flu transmission is a local problem, it has become a global issue with the amount of international travel and transmission.

It is important to note that in 2009, when the H1N1 flu virus reached global proportions and was declared an international flu pandemic, academic and pharmaceutical communities united to develop and produce a vaccine within months of its initial detection. The H1N1 vaccine was demonstrated to be effective in diminishing the transmission of the flu. Interestingly, although the H1N1 flu vaccine was readily available, many people did not avail themselves to receive the vaccine. Research indicated that there were cultural differences in the value placed on receiving the flu vaccine, as well as many people viewed that their chance of developing the disease was small or the side effects of the disease outweighed the benefits of the vaccine (Seale et al, 2011).

It needs to be emphasized that while antivirals might be helpful in the event vaccines are not available in the early stages of a pandemic, the current supply of antiviral medication is grossly inadequate to meet our projected needs if all of the population chooses to utilize these medications. Depending on the type of virus or bacteria, it is estimated that as a result of production limitations, new vaccines may not be available until 4 to 6 months after the pandemic actually starts. Unfortunately, regular flu shots are designed for a specific strain of flu and thus will not provide immunity to the various types of flu such as H5N1 or H1N1.

The CDC and the WHO have developed surveillance mechanisms to determine phases of pandemic alert, which include decisions on when to move from one phase to another. The CDC has also developed competencies for response to a pandemic flu epidemic. Visit the WHO influenza website at www.who.int/topics/influenza or the CDC website at http://www.cdc.gov/flu/professionals for more information.

As with other MCEs, planning is aimed at saving the largest number of people. It is likely that flu varieties would strike nearly simultaneously in many different geographic regions and cause multiple waves of disease lasting 4 to 6 weeks in communities. Thus, local communities need to make their plans self-sufficient because other areas will be dealing with the same problem. Control methods include isolation, quarantine, and restrictions. Limitations include suspension of large public gatherings, school closures, and social distancing. The term *social distancing* refers to the attempt to keep people as far apart as possible to limit the possibilities of spreading germs.

The most frequently recommended type of social distancing that has proved to be effective for H1N1 virus has been keeping people suspected of the illness at home until 24 hours after the fever has subsided. Health care providers are advised to treat patients symptomatically without encouraging them to come to offices or emergency departments. Many health care facilities set up separate screening facilities for those who have flu-like symptoms.

Health care providers need to take the time to become familiar with their institutions' preparedness plan. Most will have a plan specific to the threat of pandemic flu. Know what your role is, how you would be notified, and where and how you would report if an emergency is declared.

Being prepared means that you and your family need to be prepared as well. Practice good health hygiene, and follow the general principles of sound public health. Teach family members how to cover their mouths when coughing, how to appropriately dispose of used tissues, and how and when to wash their hands. Develop contingency plans to address school and business closures, unavailability of public transportation, and disruption in social activities. Grocery stores and gas stations may not be open during their typical hours. That means that personal stockpiling of food and medications would help you and your family get through this event with minimal contact with others. Ideally, the goal is to keep the number of people infected within range of existing medical capabilities.

For current information regarding the status of any pandemic flu, visit www.flu.gov for updates in the United States. Planning guides are available for federal, state, business, local, and individuals at this website. Global updates can be found at the WHO website (http://www.who.int/influenza).

Ebola

A more recent world threat is the 2014 Ebola epidemic, affecting multiple countries in West Africa. Symptoms of Ebola include: fever, severe headache, muscle pain, weakness, diarrhea, vomiting, abdominal pain, and unexplained hemorrhage (CDC, 2014b). The infection can be spread through direct contact with blood or body fluids of a person ill with Ebola, objects contaminated with the virus, or infected animals. Although the risk of an Ebola outbreak in the United States is very low, the CDC and partners are taking precautions to prevent this from happening. The Emergency Operations Center has been activated, and teams of public health experts have been sent to West Africa in an effort to control the transmission of the disease before it hits pandemic proportions. For the most current information about Ebola, visit the WHO website at http://www.who.int/csr/disease/ebola/en/.

MANMADE CAUSES OF MASS CASUALTY: ACTIVE SHOOTER EVENTS

The federal government defines an active shooter as "an individual actively engaged in killing or attempting to kill people in a confined and populated area, typically through the use of firearms" (Federal Bureau of Investigations [FBI], 2013a). The FBI (2013b) analyzed 160 active shooter incidents from 2000 through 2013 to look for common elements that might guide law enforcement officials in more effective prevention and response efforts. In the 160 events, 486 individuals were killed and 557 were wounded. This represents an average of 11.4 incidents annually from 2000 to 2013, with an average of 6.4 incidents annually from 2000 to 2006 and an average of 16.4 events annually from 2007 to 2013 (FBI, 2013b).

Active shooter events can take place in a wide variety of locations including schools, health care facilities, and office settings. The U.S. Department of Homeland Security (2008) offers these recommendations for response to an active shooter:

1. Evacuate (RUN)

   If there is an accessible escape path, attempt to evacuate the premises. Be sure to:
   - Have an escape route and plan in mind
   - Evacuate regardless of whether others agree to follow
   - Leave your belongings behind
   - Help others escape, if possible
   - Prevent individuals from entering an area where the active shooter may be
   - Keep your hands visible
   - Follow the instructions of any police officers
   - Do not attempt to move wounded people
   - Call 911 when you are safe.

2. Hide Out (HIDE)

   If evacuation is not possible, find a place to hide where the active shooter is less likely to find you. Your hiding place should:
   - Be out of the active shooter's view
   - Provide protection if shots are fired in your direction (e.g., an office with a closed and locked door)
   - Try not to trap yourself or restrict your options for movement

   To prevent an active shooter from entering your hiding place:
   - Lock the door
   - Blockade the door with heavy furniture

   If the active shooter is nearby:
   - Lock the door
   - Silence your cell phone and/or pager
   - Turn off any source of noise (e.g., radios, televisions)
   - Hide behind large items (e.g., cabinets, desks)
   - Remain quiet

   If evacuation and hiding out are not possible:
   - Remain calm
   - Dial 911, if possible, to alert police to the active shooter's location
   - If you cannot speak, leave the line open and allow the dispatcher to listen.

3. Take Action Against the Active Shooter: (FIGHT)

   As a last resort, and only when your life is in imminent danger, attempt to disrupt and/or incapacitate the active shooter by:
   - Acting as aggressively as possible against him/her
   - Throwing items and improvising weapons
   - Yelling
   - Committing to your actions

Recognizing the increased active shooter threat and the swiftness with which active shooter incidents unfold, there is increased emphasis on the importance of training and exercises. It is important, too, that training and exercises include not only an understanding of the threats faced, but also the risks and options available in active shooter incidents.

SUMMARY

Preparing for an MCE requires a complex set of activities. All nurses need to be aware of the emergency response system at the local, state, and federal levels and how to interface with the systems. They should be involved in developing and evaluating the emergency response plans for their health care agencies and communities. Consider Jane in the opening vignette. Her understanding of the resources available in the community's emergency response system will help her better cope with the disaster facing her family and the hospital where she works. Just as in Jane's situation, disaster can strike anytime, and preparation for an effective emergency response is absolutely critical to ensure the very best outcome for everyone involved. Nurses are well positioned to serve in leadership roles within health care agencies during the time of a disaster because of their excellent skills in communication and collaboration.

REFERENCES

Busby S, Witucki-Brown J: Theory development for situational awareness in multi-casualty incidents, *J Emerg Nurs* 37(5):444–452, 2011.

California Emergency Medical Services Authority: *Disaster medical services: hospital incident command system (HICS)*, 2014 (website). http://www.emsa.ca.gov/disaster_medical_services_division_hospital_incident_command_system_resources. Accessed September 30, 2014.

Centers for Disease Control and Prevention: *Strategic national stockpile*, 2014a (website). http://www.cdc.gov/phpr/stockpile/stockpile.htm. Accessed September 30, 2014.

Centers for Disease Control and Prevention: *2014 Ebola outbreak in West Africa*, 2014b (website). http://www.cdc.gov/vhf/ebola/outbreaks/2014-west-africa/index.html. Accessed September 29, 2014.

Culley JM: The role of the Medical Reserve Corps in nursing education, *J Nurs Educ* 49(12):708–711, 2010.

Division of the Civilian Volunteer Medical Reserve Corps: *About the Medical Reserve Corps*, 2014 (website). https://www.medicalreservecorps.gov/pageViewFldr/About http://www.medicalreservecorps.gov/HomePage. Accessed September 30, 2014.

Emergency Management Assistance Compact: *EMAC*, 2014 (website). http://www.emacweb.org/. Accessed September 30, 2014.

Federal Bureau of Investigation: Critical Incident Response Group, "Active Shooter Event: Quick Reference Guide," 2013a (website). http://www.fbi.gov/about-us/cirg/active-shooter-and-mass-casualty-incidents. Accessed September 30, 2014.

Federal Bureau of Investigation: *A study of active shooter incidents in the United States between 2000-2013*, 2013b (website). http://www.fbi.gov/news/stories/2014/september/fbi-releases-study-on-active-shooter-incidents. Accessed September 30, 2014.

Federal Emergency Management Agency: *The disaster process and disaster aid programs*, 2014a (website). http://www.fema.gov/disaster-process-disaster-aid-programs. Accessed September 30, 2014.

Federal Emergency Management Agency: *NRF resource center*, 2014b (website). http://www.fema.gov/national-response-framework. Accessed September 30, 2014.

Federal Emergency Management Agency: *National incident management system*, 2014c (website). http://www.fema.gov/national-incident-management-system. Accessed September 30, 2014.

Hanfling D, Altevvoght BM, Viswanathan K, et al: *Crisis standards of care: A systems framework for catastrophic disaster response*, 2012 (website). http://www.iom.edu/Reports/2012/Crisis-Standards-of-Care-A-Systems-Framework-for-Catastrophic-Disaster-Response.aspx. Accessed Jan 15, 2015.

Kotz, Deborah: "Injury toll from Marathon bombs reduced to 264," *The Boston Globe,* April 24, 2013 (website). http://www.bostonglobe.com/lifestyle/health-wellness/2013/04/23/number-injured-marathon-bombing-revised-downward/NRpaz5mmvGquP7KMA6XsIK/story.html. Accessed September 30, 2014.

Powers R: Introduction to disasters and disaster nursing. In Powers R, Daily E, editors: *Disaster Nursing International*, Cambridge, NY, 2010, Cambridge University Press, pp 1–11.

Seale H, Kaur R, Wang Q, et al: Acceptance of a vaccine against pandemic influenza A (H1N1) virus amongst healthcare workers in Beijing, China, *Vaccine* 29(8):1605–1610, 2011.

The Joint Commission: *New and revised requirements address emergency management oversight*, 2013 (website). http://www.jointcommission.org/assets/1/18/JCP0713_Emergency_Mgmt_Oversight.pdf. Accessed September 30, 2014.

U.S. Department of Health and Human Services: *National disaster medical system*, 2014a (website). http://www.phe.gov/Preparedness/responders/ndms/teams/Pages/dmat.aspx. Accessed September 30, 2014.

U.S. Department of Health and Human Services: *Flu.gov*, 2014b (website). http://www.flu.gov/pandemic/about/index.html. Accessed September 30, 2014.

U.S. Department of Homeland Security: *Active shooter: How to respond*, 2008 (website). http://www.dhs.gov/xlibrary/assets/active_shooter_booklet.pdf. Accessed September 30, 2014.

Veenema TG: Essentials of disaster planning. In Veenema TG, editor: *Disaster nursing and emergency preparedness for chemical, biological, and radiological terrorism and other hazards*, New York, 2003, Springer Publishing Company, pp 3–30.

Weiner E, Slepski LA: Informatics solutions for emergency planning and response. In Saba VK, McCormick KA, editors: *Essentials of nursing informatics,* New York, 2011, McGraw-Hill, pp 513–524.

World Health Organization: *Avian influenza in Egypt, 2006* (website). http://www.who.int/csr/don/2006_12_27a/en/index.html. Accessed September 30, 2014.

World Health Organization: *Current WHO phase of pandemic alert*, 2014 (website). http://www.who.int/influenza/preparedness/pandemic/h5n1phase/en/. Accessed September 30, 2014.

Yamamoto A: Experiences of the Great East Japan earthquake March 2011, *Int Nurs Rev* 58(3):332–334, 2011.

17

Nursing Leadership and Management

Barbara Cherry, DNSc, MBA, RN, NEA-BC

As a leader and manager, the nurse will coordinate many aspects of care delivery.

ⓔ Additional resources are available online at: *http://evolve.elsevier.com/Cherry/*

PROFESSIONAL/ETHICAL ISSUE

Marybeth Rodgers graduated from nursing school 5 years ago and worked at a renowned academic medical center in a busy medical-surgical unit since graduation. She recently took a job as a staff RN in a small community hospital closer to her home to reduce her commute time and give her more time with her family. Marybeth was very confident in her skills and knowledge to care for adult medical-surgical patients because of her experience over the past 5 years, but she knew she would have a lot to learn in this new setting. After a few weeks working on her new unit in the community hospital, she began to sense one of her nurse colleagues being resentful toward her. Initially the nurse was refusing to help her when she had questions, but she has now begun to openly criticize Marybeth with statements such as "I guess you think you are smarter than everyone else because you worked at that academic medical center downtown," and "I think you are just lazy and don't want to think for yourself; after all, you had all those medical students to think for you." Marybeth senses that she is being talked about by the other nurses and is being excluded from some conversations. She is coming to deeply regret her decision to move to the community hospital; she is having trouble sleeping and now dreads coming to work every day. Marybeth is deeply concerned about reporting the situation to the nurse manager because she knows that the nurse who is causing the problems has worked on the unit for many years and seems well-liked by the supervisor and other nurses. What are Marybeth's options for addressing this situation? What does the ANA Code of Conduct tell us about a nurse's ethical obligation to support colleagues? What resources can Marybeth access to learn more about disruptive behaviors and how to handle them?

VIGNETTE

Nancy Brown, a new registered nurse (RN), has accepted a position in a busy outpatient dialysis unit. During nursing school, Nancy worked in the facility as a patient care technician, and she is confident in her clinical skills because of this experience. Mary, the nurse manager of the dialysis unit, has scheduled Nancy to attend the new-nurse orientation. Although Nancy thinks to herself, "I know what the RNs do around here; I'd like to jump right in without attending orientation," she readily accepts the assignment.

The nurse manager begins the orientation program with a discussion about the mission of the organization and the RN's responsibility to ensure that quality patient care is provided in a safe and cost-effective manner. As Nancy progresses through the orientation program, her confidence quickly fades. She becomes overwhelmed as she listens to a description of her new responsibilities as an RN. The RN's duties involve much more than the expected physical assessment, identifying nursing diagnoses, and developing and implementing care plans. Some of Nancy's many new responsibilities as a staff RN are to:

- *Supervise patient care technicians, and manage assignments and supply use for a group of patients.*
- *Meet with the interprofessional team including the social worker, dietitian, nephrologist, nurse manager, and the patient and family to develop the patient's care plan, and then follow up to coordinate and implement the plan.*
- *Serve on a task force charged with developing and implementing a new training and mentoring program for patient care technicians.*
- *Perform chart audits to review nursing documentation, identify problems, develop recommendations, and report to the quality management committee.*

As Nancy is trying to assimilate the information being presented, she almost fails to hear Mary say that within 6 months of employment, all staff RNs are expected to begin orientation for the charge nurse position to provide backup coverage. At the end of the orientation, Nancy has a new perspective about professional nursing practice—it seems to be as much about managing the delivery of patient care as actually giving the care!

Questions to Consider While Reading this Chapter:
1. What skills will assist Nancy as she begins her new role as a staff RN with many leadership and management responsibilities?
2. Why is it important for the nursing staff to understand the mission and values of the organization to provide direct patient care?
3. What type of team-building skills will help Nancy as she learns to work with the interprofessional team and coordinate the patient's plan of care with a diverse group of health professionals?
4. What resources are available to help Nancy learn and enhance her management and leadership skills?

KEY TERMS

Authority: The legitimate right to direct others given to a person by the employer through an authorized position, such as manager or administrator.

Health care organization: Any business, company, institution, or facility (e.g., hospital, home health agency, ambulatory care clinic, health insurance company, nursing home) engaged in providing health care services or products.

Leadership: The act of guiding or influencing people to achieve desired outcomes; occurs any time a person attempts to influence the beliefs, opinions, or behaviors of an individual or group (Hersey and Blanchard, 1988).

Management: Coordination of resources, such as time, people, and supplies, to achieve outcomes; involves problem-solving and decision-making processes.

Organizational chart: A visual picture of the organization that identifies lines of communication and authority.

Productivity: The amount of output or work produced (e.g., home visits made) by a specific amount of input or resources (e.g., nursing hours worked).

Resources: Personnel, time, and supplies needed to accomplish the goals of the organization.

LEARNING OUTCOMES

After studying this chapter, the reader will be able to:
1. Relate leadership and management theory to nursing leadership and management activities.
2. Differentiate among the five functions of management and essential activities related to each function.
3. Integrate principles of patient-centered care and customer service in professional nursing practice.
4. Implement effective team-building skills as an essential component of nursing practice.
5. Implement the nursing process as a method of problem solving and planning.
6. Apply principles and strategies of change theory in the management role.
7. Discuss implications of leadership and management challenges of the twenty-first century.

CHAPTER OVERVIEW

During nursing school, students are often more concerned with developing clinical knowledge and skills and are less concerned with management and leadership skills. However, immediately after graduation the new nurse is placed in many situations that require leadership and management skills—managing a group of assigned patients, serving on a task force or committee, acting as team leader or charge nurse, or supervising unlicensed assistive personnel and licensed vocational or practical nurses. In addition to providing safe, evidence-based, high-quality clinical care, the challenges for RNs today are to manage nursing units that are constantly admitting and discharging higher-acuity patients, motivate and coordinate a variety of diverse health professionals and nonprofessionals, embrace change to develop work environments that are safer and more conducive to professional nursing practice, and manage limited resources and shrinking budgets.

Regardless of which position or area the nurse is employed, the health care organization will expect the professional nurse to have leadership and management skills, including the following:

- *Make good clinical decisions based on safety, quality, cost, legal, and ethical aspects of care.*
- *Promote evidence-based practice. (See Chapter 6.)*
- *Promote patient safety and quality improvement in the work environment. (See Chapter 22.)*
- *Coordinate patient care activities for the interprofessional team.*

- *Promote staff satisfaction, patient satisfaction, and overall unit productivity.*
- *Create and sustain trust between and among managers and staff.*
- *Actively manage the process of change through good communication, staff involvement, training, sustained attention, and measurement and feedback.*
- *Provide leadership to maintain compliance with governmental regulations and accreditation standards.*

As the reader can easily visualize, leadership and management activities are a primary responsibility for the RN. In fact, professional nursing within a health care organization has as much to do with managing the delivery of care as it does with actually providing that care. This chapter presents key leadership and management concepts that will guide the nurse to grow and develop in this important aspect of the professional practice role.

Throughout this chapter, the term organization *is used to refer to the hospital, home health agency, post–acute care facility, long-term care facility, ambulatory clinic, managed care company, or any other area in which a nurse might be employed to practice professional nursing. Legal and ethical issues are a critical component of nursing management, although it is not within the scope of this chapter to discuss these issues. The reader is encouraged to review Chapter 8 regarding legal issues and Chapter 9 regarding ethical issues.*

LEADERSHIP AND MANAGEMENT DEFINED AND DISTINGUISHED

Leadership Defined

Leadership occurs any time a person attempts to influence the beliefs, opinions, or behaviors of a person or group (Hersey and Blanchard, 1988). Leadership is a combination of intrinsic personality traits, learned leadership skills, and characteristics of the situation. The function of a leader is to guide people and groups to accomplish common goals. For example, an effective nurse leader is able to inspire others on the health care team to make patient-centered care an important aspect of all care activities.

It is important to note that even though leaders may not have formal **authority** granted by the organization, they are still able to influence others. The job title "nurse manager" will not make a nurse a leader. Today's complex health care environment requires that *every* nurse—regardless of his or her role or setting—provide leadership to advance excellence in nursing practice and patient care.

Management Defined

Management refers to the activities involved in coordinating people, time, and supplies to achieve desired outcomes and involves problem-solving and decision-making processes. Managers maintain control of the day-to-day operations of a defined area of responsibility to achieve established goals and objectives. Managers plan and organize what is to be done, who is to do it, and how it is to be done. A manager will have:

- An appointed management position within the organization with responsibilities to perform administrative tasks such as planning staffing, performing employee performance reviews, controlling use of supplies and time, and meeting budget and productivity goals
- A formal line of authority and accountability to ensure that safe and effective patient care is delivered in a manner that meets the organization's goals and standards

Leadership versus Management

Although leadership and management are intertwined and it is difficult to discuss one without the other, these concepts are different. Leadership is the ability to guide or influence others, whereas management is the coordination of resources (time, people, supplies) to achieve outcomes. People are led, whereas activities and things are managed. Leaders are able to motivate and inspire others, whereas managers have assigned responsibility for accomplishing the goals of an organization. A good manager should also be a good leader, but this may not always be the case. A person with good management skills may not have leadership ability. Similarly, a person with leadership abilities may not have good management skills. Leadership and management skills are complementary; both can be learned and developed through experience, and improving skills in one area will enhance abilities in the other.

Power and Authority

Leadership and management require power and authority to motivate people to act in a certain way. Authority is the legitimate right to direct others and is given to a person by the organization through an authorized position, such as nurse manager. For example, a nurse manager has the authority to direct staff nurses to work a specific schedule. Power is the ability to motivate people to get things done with or without the legitimate right granted by the organization. The primary sources of power are (Hersey et al, 1979):

- *Reward power* comes from the ability to reward others for complying and may include such rewards as money, desired assignments, or acknowledgment of accomplishments.

- *Coercive power,* the opposite of reward power, is based on fear of punishment for failure to comply. Sources of coercive power include withheld pay increases, undesired assignments, verbal and written warnings, and termination.
- *Legitimate power* is based on an official position in the organization. Through legitimate power, the manager has the right to influence staff members, and staff members have an obligation to accept that influence.
- *Referent power* comes from the followers' identification with the leader. The admired and respected nurse is able to influence other nurses because of their desire to emulate her.
- *Expert power* is based on knowledge, skills, and information. For example, nurses who have expertise in areas such as physical assessment or technical skills, or who keep up with current information on important topics will gain respect from others.
- *Information power* is based on a person's possession of information that is needed by others.
- *Connection power* is based on a person's relationship or affiliation with other people who are perceived as being powerful.

An individual may also have informal power resulting from personal relationships, being in the right place at the right time, or unique personal characteristics, such as attractiveness, education, experience, drive, or decisiveness. By understanding the authority of an assigned position and the sources of formal and informal power, the nurse will be better able to influence others to accomplish goals.

Formal and Informal Leadership

Both formal and informal leadership can exist in every organization. Formal leadership is practiced by the nurse who is appointed to an approved position (e.g., nurse manager, supervisor, director) and given the authority to act by the organization. Informal leadership is exercised by the person who has no official or appointed authority to act, but is able to persuade and influence others. The informal leader, who may or may not be a professional nurse, may have considerable power in the work group and can influence the group's attitude and significantly affect the efficiency and effectiveness of workflow, goal setting, and problem solving.

The nurse manager must learn to recognize and effectively work with informal leaders. Informal leadership may be positive if the informal leader's purpose is congruent with that of the nursing unit and organizational goals. For example, the informal leader of a patient care group may be highly supportive of a new nursing care delivery model being implemented on the unit, and as a result, the other team members will be more willing to accept the change. However, an informal leader who is not supportive of the nursing unit's goals can create an uncomfortable work environment for the nurse manager and the entire team. Following are some strategies the nurse manager can use to work with informal leaders:

- Identify the informal leaders in the work team, and develop an understanding of their source of power. (See sources of power in the previous section.)
- Involve the informal leaders and other staff members in decision-making and change-implementation processes.
- Clearly communicate the goals and work expectations to all staff members.
- Do not ignore an informal leader's attempt to undermine teamwork and change processes. Coaching and counseling the person and setting clear expectations may be required.

LEADERSHIP THEORY

Understanding the development and progression of leadership theory is a necessary building block for developing leadership and management skills. Researchers began to study leadership in the early 1900s in an attempt to describe and understand the nature of leadership. The following sections review a few key leadership theories. Readers are encouraged to learn more about leadership and management theories, especially as they advance in their nursing career.

Leadership Trait Theory

Early leadership theory centered on describing the qualities or traits of leaders and has been commonly referred to as *trait theory* (Stogdill, 1974). Leadership trait theory was based on the assumption that leaders were born with certain leadership characteristics. Traits found to be associated with leadership include intelligence, alertness, dependability, energy, drive, enthusiasm, ambition, decisiveness, self-confidence, cooperativeness, and technical mastery (Stogdill, 1974). Although trait theories have been important in identifying qualities that distinguish today's leaders, these theories have neglected the interaction

between other elements of the leadership situation. Trait theories also have failed to recognize that leadership traits can be learned and developed through experience. However, by keeping in mind these traits associated with effective leadership, the new nurse can identify areas in which he or she should improve and develop.

Transformational Leadership

In a contemporary concept of leadership, Burns (1978) identified and defined transformational leadership. Burns contends that there are two types of leaders: (1) the transactional leader, who is concerned with the day-to-day operations of the facility and (2) the transformational leader, who is committed to organizational goals, has a vision, and is able to empower others with that vision. The transformational leader is able to guide employees to feel pride in the work of the organization and to inspire them to be actively engaged to achieve the mission and goals of the organization. Transformational leaders spend time teaching and coaching, seek differing perspectives when faced with problems to solve, and seek new ways to improve the work environment. Box 17-1 compares characteristics of Burns's (1978) transformational and transactional leadership styles.

Studies have reported that nurse managers who demonstrate more transformational leadership characteristics achieve higher levels of staff satisfaction and work group effectiveness (Bormann and Abrahamson,

---

BOX 17-1   Comparison of Transformational and Transactional Leaders

Transformational Leaders	Transactional Leaders
• Identify and clearly communicate vision and direction	• Focus on day-to-day operations and are comfortable with the status quo
• Empower the work group to accomplish goals and achieve the vision	• Reward staff for desired work ("I'll do X in exchange for you doing Y.")
• Impart meaning and challenge to work	• Monitor work performance, and correct as needed *or*
• Are admired and emulated	• Wait until problems occur, and then deal with the problem
• Provide mentoring to individual staff members based on need	

2014; Casida and Parker, 2011; Failla and Stichler, 2008; Moneke and Umeh, 2013). The implication for nurse managers is that transformational leadership is very effective in increasing staff satisfaction and work effectiveness. The reader is encouraged to read more about transformational leadership and to seek out transformational leaders as mentors. However, it is important to note that even the most effective transformational leader will fail without possessing the day-to-day management skills of transactional leaders (Bass et al, 1987).

LEADERSHIP SKILLS

Three major types of skills are required for effective leadership (Hersey and Blanchard, 1988):

1. Technical skills—for nurses, this includes clinical expertise and nursing knowledge.
2. Human skills—the ability and judgment to work with and lead people in a compassionate, caring way.
3. Conceptual skills—the ability to understand the complexities of the overall organization and to recognize how and where one's own area of management fits into the overall organization.

At the staff nurse level of management, a considerable amount of technical skill and clinical expertise is needed because the nurse generally is involved in direct supervision of patient care and may be required to help train and mentor nurses. As one advances from lower levels to higher levels in the organization, more conceptual skills are needed. Box 17-2 provides examples of technical, human, and conceptual practices required for nurse leaders.

MANAGEMENT THEORY

Behavioral theories emerged to explain aspects of management based on behaviors of managers, leaders, and followers. Three prevalent management behavior styles were identified by Lewin (1951) and White and Lippit (1960): authoritarian, democratic, and laissez-faire. Box 17-3 presents characteristics of these management styles, which vary in the amount of control exhibited by the manager and the amount of involvement that the staff has in decision making. At one extreme, the autocratic manager makes all decisions with no staff input and uses the authority of the position to accomplish goals. At the opposite extreme is the laissez-faire manager, who provides little direction or guidance and will forgo decision making. Democratic management is also often referred to as *participative* management because of its basic premise of encouraging staff members to participate in decision making.

Depending on the situation, the nurse manager may need to use different types of management styles. For example, autocratic management might be appropriate in an emergency situation, such as treating a patient in cardiac arrest. However, in structuring the weekend call schedule for a home health agency, a participative style of management would be more effective.

Today's health care system requires the use of a democratic or participative management style that involves the staff in patient safety, quality improvement, and patient-centered care. Health care settings are driven to become increasingly cost-effective while continuing to improve

---

BOX 17-2 Effective Leading and Managing: Technical, Human, and Conceptual Practices

Technical Practices
- Keep your own clinical skills and knowledge current.
- Act as a willing expert resource and teacher for clinical problems, contribute to sound clinical judgment and critical thinking.

Human Practices
- Maintain honesty and integrity in work and relationships—trust is essential for effective leadership.
- Create a teaching and learning environment—earn a reputation for exceptional teaching and mentoring.
- Develop and role model a commitment to excellence.
- Create an open, nonthreatening environment—share information, keep staff informed, and encourage them to discuss issues.

- Become a proactive problem solver—knowing how to solve problems is more important than knowing all the answers.
- Maintain a confident, positive outlook—identify areas in which you are weak, and seek help to learn and grow.

Conceptual Practices
- Make a commitment to support the mission, vision, and goals of the organization.
- Accept the realities of complex health care systems, which are under pressure to improve patient safety and quality while reducing costs.
- Understand the needs of external customers (patients, families, physicians, referring facilities) and internal customers (staff, administrators, and other departments).

BOX 17-3 Management Styles

Autocratic/Authoritative	Democratic/Participative	Laissez-Faire
• Determines policy and makes all decisions • Ignores subordinates' ideas or suggestions • Dictates the work with much control • Gives little feedback or recognition for work • Makes fast decisions • Successful with employees with little education or training	• Encourages staff participation in decision making • Involves staff in planning and developing new ideas and programs • Believes in the best in people • Communicates effectively, and provides regular feedback • Builds responsibility in people • Works well with competent, highly motivated people	• Does not provide guidance or direction • Unable or unwilling to make decisions • Does not provide feedback • Initiates little change • Communicates by memos or e-mail • May work well with professional people

---

quality, customer satisfaction, and positive patient outcomes. Staff directly involved in the challenges presented by patient care often can suggest the most workable, practical solutions.

Organizational Theory

Just as leadership and management theories have evolved to provide a framework for understanding leadership and management, organizational theory has evolved to provide a framework for understanding complex organizations. A brief review of systems theory and chaos theory can provide the reader with insight into the value of using organizational theory to understand management processes within today's dynamic, complex health care organizations.

Systems Theory

The systems theory views the organization as a set of interdependent parts that together form a whole (Thompson, 1967). The interdependent nature of the parts of the organization suggests that anything that affects the functioning of one aspect of the organization will affect the other parts of the organization. Open systems suggest that the organization is affected not only by internal changes among any of its parts, but also external environmental forces that will have a direct influence on the organization and vice versa—the internal forces will affect the external environment. In contrast to open systems theory, closed systems theory views the system as being totally independent of outside influences, which is an unrealistic view for health care

Leadership, management, and organizational theories provide the building blocks for effective nursing management practices.

CASE STUDY 17-1

The hospital in which William Scoggins, RN, works has reduced the number of RNs employed by the hospital and now requires that the remaining RNs work overtime "at the request of administration." The quality of patient care, patient safety, and the individual nurses' professional practice and personal health have been negatively affected by this change. William and his fellow RNs seek advice from their state nurses association about their professional responsibility to work mandatory overtime. The state nurses association is responding to the situation, which is occurring more frequently across the state and nation, by proposing legislation to mandate nurse-patient ratios and limits to mandatory overtime. The state government may now require hospital administrators to respond to the need for increased staffing levels.

organizations. To be successful, today's health care organizations must be able to continually adapt to internal and external changes.

Consider the example in Case Study 17-1 to help explain systems theory. As internal forces in one department (hospital administration) mandated changes that affected another area (RNs and patient care), internal forces (RNs) pushed for changes from the external environment (state nurses association and state government). The external environment may now force changes to the organization (hospital administration).

Systems theory has provided nurses with a framework to view nursing services as a subsystem of the larger organization and to realize the interrelatedness and interdependence of all the parts of the organization. The nurse will be wise to consider open systems theory and the effect a change in one area will have in another area, internal as well as external to the organization.

Chaos Theory

Chaos theory is a more recently developed organizational theory that attempts to account for the complexity and randomness in organizations. Despite the implications of the word *chaos*, the theory actually suggests that a degree of order can be attained by viewing complicated behaviors and situations as predictable. Nurse managers may wish for balanced and steady work environments, but in reality they are dealing with, what seems at best, a chaotic system. Chaos theory says that variation is a normal part of managing health care systems. Based on

chaos theory, a nurse manager knows that staff absences as a result of illness, sick children, and family emergencies are a fact of life, which require the nurse manager to have backup plans in place in the event that staff members "call in" and are unable to report for their assigned shift. Other examples of variation in health care are cultural diversity, a constantly fluctuating patient census, and staffing shortages. Until nurses understand that these variations are a normal, predictable state in the organization and should be planned for, they may continue to experience excessive anxiety with the daily events that occur in health care organizations (McGuire, 1999).

MANAGEMENT FUNCTIONS

Classic theories of management suggest that the primary functions of managers are planning, organizing, and controlling (Stogdill, 1974). Leaders in nursing management have added two more functions to this list and now recognize five major management functions (Figure 17-1) as necessary for the management of nursing organizations: (1) planning, (2) organizing, (3) staffing, (4) directing, and (5) controlling (Marquis and Huston, 2014). These management functions are interrelated; different phases of the process occur simultaneously, and the processes should be circular, with the manager always working toward improving the quality, patient safety, and staff and customer satisfaction. Because understanding these five management functions is essential for success as a nurse, they will be discussed in further detail.

Planning

Planning is the first management function and involves several steps: (1) identify goals and objectives to be achieved; (2) identify resources needed (e.g., people, supplies, equipment); (3) determine action steps; and (4) establish a timeline for the action steps and goal achievement. All management functions are based on planning. *Without effective planning, the management process will fail.* Effective planning requires the nurse to understand the organization's mission, philosophy, strategic plan, goals, and objectives.

Mission and Philosophy

The mission statement, the foundation of planning for any organization, describes the purpose of the organization

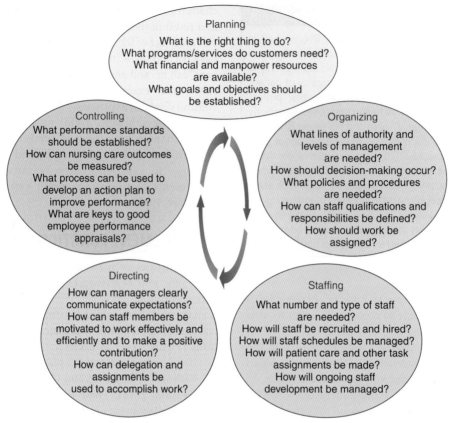

FIGURE 17-1 Management Functions.

and the reason it exists. Most health care organizations exist to provide high-quality patient care, but emphasis may be on different concepts, such as research, teaching, preventive care, spiritual care, or community service. The philosophy is the set of values and beliefs that guides the actions of the organization and thus serves as the basis of all planning. New nurses should be aware of the mission and philosophy of the employing organization and understand the relationship between their own personal value system and that of the organization. Box 17-4 provides an example of an organization's mission and philosophy statement.

Strategic Planning

Strategic planning is long-range planning (extending 2 to 5 years into the future) and results from an in-depth analysis of (1) the business, community, regulatory, and political environment outside the organization;

(2) customer and patient needs; (3) technology changes; and (4) strengths, problems, and weaknesses internal to the organization. The purposes of strategic planning are to:

- Identify strategies to respond to changes in customer needs, technology, health care legislation, the business environment, and the community.
- Dedicate resources to important services and new programs.
- Eliminate duplication, waste, and underused services.
- Establish a timeline for goal achievement.

The strategic plan is a written document that details organizational goals, allocates resources, assigns responsibilities, and determines timeframes. Development of the strategic plan is generally coordinated by upper-level managers who engage employees at all levels in the strategic planning process. Consider the example in Case Study 17-2.

The mission of Community Hospital is to provide high-quality, cost-effective health services that patients and families recommend, employees are proud of, and the community values.

The philosophy and values of Community Hospital are:

- Commitment to professional and individual excellence, with support for personal and professional growth.
- Ethical and fair treatment for *all* through a commitment to relationships based on fairness and trust with our patients and our employees.
- Teamwork is consistently demonstrated as we work together to provide ever-improving quality care.
- Compassion is our highest priority; we will always provide care and comfort to people in need with respectful and dignified treatment at all times.
- Innovation in service delivery is accomplished by investing in the development of new and better ways to deliver health care.

CASE STUDY 17-2

Gina DellaValle, RN, nurse manager for the Quality Care Home Health Agency, noticed that the office had been receiving several calls per week for skilled nursing care for pediatric oncology patients. The agency did not provide services for pediatric patients. Gina reported the situation to the administrator. Gina soon was involved in gathering information about the number of home health agencies that offered pediatric oncology care, the standards of nursing care recommended for pediatric oncology patients, how pediatric oncology patients were receiving home care, how many pediatric patients in the area might need such services, and what reimbursement was available for such services. Within the next few months, the management team for Quality Care Home Health Agency decided that as part of the agency's strategic plan, a program for pediatric oncology services would be developed.

Goals and Objectives

Goals and objectives state the actions necessary to achieve the strategic plan and are central to the entire management process. Goals should be measurable, observable, and realistic. Objectives are more specific and detail how a goal will be accomplished with an established target date.

Goals and objectives serve as the manager's road map. Organization-wide goals are established in the strategic planning process, and then unit goals that support the organization-wide goals are developed. Nurse managers should be able to clearly articulate both the organization-wide goals and the goals of the nursing unit. Additionally, goals and objectives must be communicated to everyone who is responsible for their attainment. Consider the example in Case Study 17-3.

Operational Planning

The nurse manager is most likely to be responsible for operational planning or the short-range planning that

CASE STUDY 17-3

Michele Walker, RN, recently has been appointed as nurse manager in a 150-bed long-term care facility. The mission and philosophy of the organization is to "respect the dignity and worth of the individual and to provide care that will help restore the individual to the best possible state of physical, mental, and emotional health while maintaining his or her sense of spiritual and social well-being." Kenneth Cole, Administrator, has asked Michele to develop a set of goals that she views as priorities to accomplish in the next year. After gathering data about resident needs, costs, and staffing levels and meeting with the medical director, direct-care staff, and staff members in rehabilitation therapy, social services, dietary, and maintenance, Michele develops the following goals: (1) increase by 25% over 12 months the level of satisfaction related to emotional well-being and socialization expressed by residents and family members on the quarterly quality of life satisfaction survey; this will be accomplished by increasing coordination of care activities among nursing, therapy, and social services; (2) reduce resident falls by 50% over 6 months through the implementation of an evidence-based guideline for falls prevention; and (3) increase by 30% in 12 months the number of nursing staff who achieve national certification as a gerontologic nurse through the American Nurses Credentialing Center. To accomplish this goal, the facility will offer certification review courses over the next 6 months. Together Michele and Kenneth review the goals, agree that they fit with the overall organizational plan, and address the needs identified in Michele's facility assessment activities.

encompasses the day-to-day activities of the organization. For example, short-range planning for a medical-surgical unit in a hospital might include maintaining an overall patient-to-staff ratio of 5:1, with 70% of the staff being RNs. As part of accomplishing organizational goals and objectives, the nurse manager involved in operational planning must be concerned with the:

- Number, acuity, type and location of patients to be cared for
- Qualifications and competencies of nursing and other health care staff
- Type and amount of supplies and other physical resources available
- Allocation of resources (e.g., staff, supplies, time) to meet budgetary goals

The nurse manager also must plan for a variety of other activities, such as staff development, regulatory compliance, and quality improvement and patient safety projects. (See Chapter 22.)

Organizing

Organizing is the second management function. At the organizational level, organizing is necessary to establish a formal structure that defines the lines of authority, communication, and decision making within an organization. The formal organizational structure helps define roles and responsibilities of each level of management. The **organizational chart** provides a visual picture of the organization and identifies lines of communication and authority. All nurses should be familiar with the organizational chart of their employing institution. Organizing also involves developing policies and procedures to help outline how work will be done and establishing position qualifications and job descriptions to define who will do the work.

At the unit level, the nurse manager must determine how to best organize the work activities to meet goals. Organizing involves:

- Using resources (e.g., staff, supplies, time) wisely
- Assigning duties and responsibilities appropriately
- Coordinating activities with other departments
- Effectively communicating with subordinates and superiors to ensure a smooth workflow.

Models for staffing and organizing the delivery of patient care are discussed in Chapter 21.

Staffing

Staffing is the third management function. The provision of health care is labor-intensive, with a workforce that is made up of people with a variety of education and skill levels (e.g., professional nurses, physicians, pharmacists, social workers, therapists, dietitians, licensed vocational or practical nurses, technicians, and unlicensed assistive personnel). Hiring and managing staff to accomplish the work of the institution are important functions for all levels of managers.

Marquis and Huston (2014) have described steps in the staffing function as follows:

1. Determine the number and type of staff needed based on goals and budget requirements.
2. Recruit, interview, select, and assign personnel based on job description and performance standards.
3. Get new employees off to a good start by offering excellent orientation, training, and socialization programs.
4. Implement an ongoing staff-development program to ensure that employees at all levels have opportunities to develop personally and professionally and to enhance knowledge and skill levels.
5. Implement creative and flexible scheduling based on patient care needs, employee needs, and **productivity** requirements.

The staffing process most likely will prove to be one of the most time-consuming and challenging functions for the nurse manager; however, it is probably the nurse manager's most important job. Little can be accomplished without the right people properly trained to do the work in an environment that promotes collegial, productive relationships among the health care team.

Nursing leaders are highly concerned with recruiting and retaining a talented RN workforce. Factors positively associated with RNs' work satisfaction are presented in Box 17-5. These factors are based on research studies and provide managers with information about how they can increase nurse satisfaction and thus reduce nursing turnover and improve recruitment and retention efforts. Staff schedules (days and shifts staff are assigned to work) and patient assignment schedules (patient care assignments for which each staff member is responsible during his or her workday) are key to nurse satisfaction, recruitment, and retention.

While meeting staff and patient scheduling needs, the nurse manager must meet organizational staffing and productivity goals. Productivity is the amount of work produced through the use of a specific amount of resources and is measured as output divided by input.

BOX 17-5   Factors Influencing Nurses' Job Satisfaction and Dissatisfaction

Sources of Satisfaction	Sources of Dissatisfaction
• Leader who inspires vision and excitement and serves as a role model for exemplary nursing practice • Collaborative decision-making among team members • Fairness of the workload and salary • Thanks and positive recognition • Open communication and being informed • Guidance, mentorship, and opportunities for professional development and advancement • Challenging work and responsibility to control job performance and be involved in decisions • Support for good nurse-physician relationships • Pleasant work environment with high group cohesion, a sense of team camaraderie, and respectful relationships among staff and physicians, peers, administrators, and other departments • Adequate staffing • Help from managers during stressful times • Ongoing feedback about performance • Agreeable working hours, flexibility in scheduling, and benefits including paid time off and premium pay	• Supervisors who are uninvolved and unsupportive • Poor communication and unclear expectations • Vague, inconsistent rules and regulations • No thanks or recognition • Not being informed about changes • No commitment to professional development • Lack of involvement in decision making • Uncooperative physicians; no support for addressing inappropriate or disruptive behaviors • No help from managers during crisis • Inadequate feedback about performance • Excessive workload negatively affecting quality and increasing stress for the nurse

From Cowden T et al: Leadership practices and staff nurses' intent to stay: a systematic review, *J Nurs Manag* 19(4): 461-477, 2011.
Perrine JL: Strategies to boost RN retention, *Nurs Manage* 40(4):20-22, 2009.
Wieck KL et al: What nurses want: the nurse incentives project, *Nurs Econ* 27(3):169-201, 2009.
Wisokzkey S: Will they stay or will they go? Insight into nursing turnover, *Nurs Manage* 42(2):15-17, 2011.
Hairr DC, Salisbury H, Johannsson M, Redfern-Vance N: Nurse staffing and the relationship to job satisfaction and retention. *Nurs Econ* 32(3):142-7, 2014.
Moneke N, Umeh OJ: How leadership behaviors impact critical care nurse job satisfaction. *Nurs Manage,* 44(1):53-5, 2013.
Dotson MJ, Dave DS, Cazier JA, Spaulding TJ: An empirical analysis of nurse retention: what keeps RNs in nursing? *J Nurs Adm* 44(2):111-6, 2014.

For example, the number of nursing hours worked over a 24-hour period divided by the patient census is a standard productivity measurement used by many hospitals. From a practical perspective, the nurse caring for eight medical-surgical patients during one shift has a higher productivity ratio than the nurse caring for only five patients of similar acuity. Other examples of productivity measurements include number of home visits completed or number of procedures performed. Productivity is a method of measuring and tracking the amount of labor costs as compared with the amount of work produced and is a factor in staffing decisions.

Directing

Directing is the fourth management function. After managers have planned what to do, organized how to do it, and staffed positions to do the work, they must direct personnel and activities to accomplish goals. Directing involves issuing assignments and instructions that allow workers to clearly understand what is expected, in addition to guiding and coaching workers to achieve planned goals. Directing requires the nurse manager to:

- Clearly communicate performance expectations.
- Create a motivating climate and team spirit.
- Model expected behaviors.
- Facilitate feedback.

Communicating Performance Expectations

It is the manager's responsibility to monitor how well staff are performing their jobs. The first step is to ensure that staff clearly understand job expectations. Does the staff member know what problems and issues should be reported to the supervisor and how and to whom to report? Does the staff member know how to perform clinical procedures correctly or how and where to seek help when necessary? Does the nurse clearly understand the expectations for documenting clinical care? Does the nurse know how and when to report to physicians and/or involve other members of the interprofessional team? Is the staff member able to meet patient care needs for the number of patients assigned during a typical shift? Does the nurse know how to communicate effectively with patients as well as family members? These questions represent only a sample of issues that the nurse manager will consider when striving to communicate performance expectations.

Communicating performance expectations is an ongoing process that begins in new-employee orientation and continues throughout the term of employment. An important step in communicating expectations is to directly observe employees performing their jobs; through direct observation, the manager can identify strengths and weaknesses and determine areas where performance expectations need to be addressed. The next step is to communicate expectations in a respectful two-way process in which the manager seeks first to understand the staff member's perspective, feelings, and knowledge about the issue and then to clarify the expectations in a nonjudgmental, nonthreatening way. The final step is to determine issues that may be preventing the employee from meeting performance expectations and work with that employee to develop a mutually agreed-upon plan so that he or she can achieve expectations.

Creating a Motivating Climate

Motivation is the inner drive that compels a person to act in a certain way. The amount and quality of work accomplished by a person are a direct reflection of his or her motivation. A great deal of research has been undertaken to better understand human motivation. Most researchers will agree that motivation is complex and involves a combination of extrinsic, or external, rewards, such as money, benefits, and working conditions, in addition to intrinsic, or internal, needs for recognition, self-esteem, and self-actualization. Box 17-5 summarizes factors that influence nurses' job satisfaction and dissatisfaction.

Positive encouragement and support from the nurse manager are essential to create a motivating work climate.

An effective method to demonstrate encouragement and support is a technique known as "management by walking around" in which the nurse manager literally walks around the unit with the primary purpose of interacting positively with the staff. Just as it implies, management by walking around allows the nurse manager to interact with many different staff on a day-to-day basis, promote quality patient care, and build positive relationships with not only staff but also patients, families, and the interprofessional team.

Positive reinforcement in the form of a sincere "thank you, you did a good job" is one of the most powerful yet most often underused motivational resources available to the manager. To be effective, positive reinforcement should (1) be specific with praise given for a particular task done well or goal accomplished; (2) occur as close as possible to the time of the achievement; (3) be spontaneous and unpredictable (praise given routinely tends to lose its value); and (4) be given for a genuine accomplishment (Peters and Waterman, 1982). Management by walking around puts the manager in a position to observe the employee's work performance and offer immediate praise for a job well done.

Role Modeling

Positive role modeling is another effective tool the nurse can use to create a positive team spirit and promote high-quality patient care. Positive role modeling simply means that the nurse performs the job in such a way that he or she demonstrates ideal performance as a professional nurse; others hopefully will follow the example. Obviously, nurses must be role models for excellence in patient care; similarly, nurses must also model caring and respectful relationships with the entire interprofessional health care team along with an enthusiastic attitude to promote camaraderie and team spirit. If relationships between nurse leaders and their staff are not mutually respectful and caring, it is doubtful that staff will be inclined to establish caring, therapeutic relationships with their patients (Forman, 2006).

Several other skills are essential as nurses function in the directing role, including effective communication and conflict management skills (see Chapter 19), delegation skills (see Chapter 20), and team-building skills (discussed in section Team Builder). The nurse is challenged to create a climate that will generate nurse satisfaction and motivate them to accomplish goals.

Controlling

The purpose of controlling, the fifth management function, is to ensure that employees accomplish goals while maintaining a high quality of performance. Controlling requires the nurse manager to:

- Establish performance or outcome standards.
- Determine action plans to improve performance.
- Evaluate employee performance through performance appraisals and feedback.

Establishing Performance Standards

Performance standards describe a model of excellence for work activities and serve as the basis of comparison between actual and desired work performance. For example, performance standards in an ambulatory outpatient clinic might include that (1) every patient is informed about all lab results within 48 hours, whether normal or abnormal, and (2) all diabetic patients must remove their shoes and socks for a complete foot examination each time they come to the clinic. Nurses can draw on several resources for establishing performance standards, such as:

- Written organizational policies and procedures
- Standards for the practice of professional nursing developed by the American Nurses Association (ANA) and published in *Nursing: Scope and Standards of Practice* (ANA, 2010a)
- Standards for professional nursing specialty practices, such as *Home Health Nursing: Scope and Standards of Practice* (ANA, 2014) and *Gerontological Nursing: Scope and Standards of Practice* (ANA, 2010b)
- Evidence-based practice guidelines

Nurses should continually look for ways to improve individual, team, and organizational performance to achieve established standards of care. Chapter 22 provides more discussion about performance standards and presents an excellent process for measuring performance and planning for improvement.

Evaluating Employee Performance

Evaluating employee performance occurs through the formal annual evaluation process and through frequent feedback and coaching provided to employees. A manager should never wait until the annual performance review to discuss problems or deficiencies with a staff member. Consistent day-to-day feedback and coaching about job performance clarifies expectations, improves

the quality of work, and allows the manager to correct problems before they become serious. Feedback and coaching can occur in brief, spontaneous interactions or in planned sessions with the employee. Box 17-6 presents useful tips for effective coaching.

Ongoing documentation about an employee's job performance is an essential management responsibility. Each health care organization has specific policies related to documentation of employee performance and annual performance evaluations. The result of routine performance evaluations should be mutual goal setting designed to meet the employees' training, educational, and professional development needs.

The management functions of planning, organizing, staffing, directing, and controlling provide the nurse

---

BOX 17-6 Tips for Effective Coaching

- Discuss situations in a neutral way—avoid judgmental language that will put the other person on the defensive.
- Encourage the other person to provide his or her perspective about the situation (e.g., "What did you think about your exchange with that physician?").
- Encourage the person to reflect on his or her performance through open-ended questions, such as:
  - What are your main concerns?
  - What would you like to see happen next?
  - What can you learn from this situation?
  - What is confusing to you?
  - What are some things you could do differently next time?
- Be specific and provide clear examples when possible (e.g., "Next time you are dealing with a difficult family member, consider...").
- Share your own experiences if they are relevant and might help.
- Be sincere. Provide coaching and feedback with the clear intent of helping the person improve.
- Be realistic. Focus on factors that the person can control.
- Thank the employee for listening.
- Ask for feedback from your coworkers, subordinates, and peers about your own performance, and listen when it is offered.

From Grensing-Pophal L: Give-and-take feedback, *Nurs Manage* 31(2):27-28, 2000.
Harvard Business Essentials: *Manager's toolkit: the 13 skills managers need to succeed*, Boston, 2004, Harvard Business School Press.

with a practical set of skills to guide the implementation of management activities. The new nurse will be challenged to maintain the different stages of management that occur in the span of just 1 day. In addition to managing different phases of the process occurring simultaneously, the nurse also must function in many different management roles described in the following section.

ROLES OF THE NURSE LEADER AND MANAGER

Nurses assume various roles as they function in leadership and management positions. The first step toward being an effective nurse leader is to clearly understand the job description, roles and responsibilities, and policies and procedures related to the position in which you are employed or assigned. The following discussion presents information about roles that a nurse will assume in any position.

Patient Satisfaction and Customer Service Provider

Over the past few years, patient satisfaction has moved to the forefront of the nurse's agenda. Nursing shortages, reduced length of stay, more complex patient needs, and national concerns about the quality and safety of patient care have contributed to this growing concern about patient satisfaction. With the advent of health care reform, patient satisfaction is now tied directly to financial rewards for hospitals. Medicare reimbursement rewards inpatient hospitals for providing quality care to include patient satisfaction based on the hospital's scores on the Hospital Consumer Assessment of Healthcare Providers and Systems (HSAHPS), which is a standardized patient satisfaction survey that addresses seven core dimensions:

- Communication with nurses
- Communication with doctors
- Responsiveness of hospital staff
- Pain management
- Communication about medicines
- Cleanliness and quietness of hospital environment
- Discharge information

From how quickly call lights are answered to the extent of family support provided, nurses are challenged to meet a wide spectrum of patient needs to include promoting good communication with the health care team and the patient and family. The complex health care environment has created a competitive marketplace in which home health agencies, hospitals, ambulatory clinics, and even hospice agencies compete for patients. To survive and thrive in this competitive environment, the nurse must keep patient satisfaction and customer service, which includes safety and quality care, first and foremost as the motivator of all plans and activities.

Team Builder

A team is a group of people organized to accomplish the necessary work of an organization. Teams bring together a range of people with different knowledge, skills, and experiences to meet customer needs, accomplish tasks, and solve problems. Team members may include unit secretaries, nursing assistants, social workers, dietitians, therapists, physicians, licensed vocational or practical nurses, and RNs. A team should have clearly defined goals and should be empowered to make decisions within its realm of responsibility. Team building should create synergy. Synergy is the ability of a group of people working together to accomplish significantly more than each person working individually.

Bringing people together to work as a group does not necessarily make them a team. To create synergy, teams must have defined goals and objectives, a commitment to work together, good communication, and a willingness to cooperate. Team members should be encouraged to communicate with one another to identify effective work division and solutions to problems so that synergy is accomplished. The nurse, as team builder, must serve as a role model to encourage and help develop team principles of respect, cooperation, commitment, and a willingness to accomplish shared goals. As a role model for team members, the nurse should do the following:

- Show respect for all members of the team and value their input.
- Clearly define team goals. ("What do we want to accomplish?")
- Clearly define the decision-making authority within the realm of the team.
- Encourage team members to develop a sense of stewardship (or ownership) for the success of the team.
- Exhibit a personal commitment to team goals.
- Encourage team members to willingly help one another.

- Provide the resources necessary to accomplish goals (e.g., time for team meetings, information, supplies).
- Teach members to exchange constructive feedback for the purpose of meeting team goals.
- Provide relevant and timely feedback to the team.

The leader's behaviors have a significant effect on the behaviors of the team. The nurse as leader must have an astute self-awareness of his or her own emotional patterns and an understanding that negative moods can have a negative influence on relationships with staff members. Learning to recognize and manage one's emotional patterns and negative moods is an important step in team building. The nurse manager who is enthusiastic, caring, and supportive can generate those same feelings among all team members.

Resource Manager

Resources include the personnel, time, and supplies needed to provide patient care and operate the organization. Resources cost money and always will be in limited supply. Unfortunately, no health care organization can afford the luxury of an unlimited number of staff or supplies to accomplish the required work. With health care facilities' focus on cost containment, it is essential that nurses develop an understanding of and expertise in resource management.

Each of the management activities of planning, organizing, staffing, directing, and controlling come into play in the role of resource manager. The nurse needs to learn and develop skills in the following areas:

- Planning for the necessary resources (primarily staff and supplies) to manage the unit
- Organizing the resources to meet identified goals
- Staffing appropriately as determined by patient needs and the budget plan
- Directing to maintain resource allocations within budgetary guidelines
- Controlling by analyzing financial reports and making adjustments where necessary

Budget and financial reports are the primary tools for resource management. Because budget and financial management is a very minimal part of the nursing school curriculum, nurses need to take initiative for on-the-job training about the organization's budget and financial management processes. Nurses are encouraged not to be unsettled by financial and budget reports and conversations and instead to get involved. Do not be afraid to say "I don't understand. Please explain."

Review budget and financial reports, ask questions, talk to seasoned nurse managers, talk to the organization's finance department staff, and even consider taking an accounting or finance course at the local college. Understanding financial and budget management is one of the most useful and powerful tools you can have as a nurse leader. Another resource is Chapter 18 of this text, which provides more detailed information about budgets.

Decision Maker and Problem Solver

Problem solving and decision making are essential skills for professional nursing practice. Not only are these skills required in clinical patient care, they also are vital components of effective leadership and management. The nurse leader is continually engaged in decision making while managing the work unit. Problem solving is focused on solving an immediate problem and includes a decision-making step.

Nursing Process as a Guide for Decision Making and Problem Solving

The nursing process, familiar to nurses for addressing patient care needs, can be applied to all management activities requiring decision making and problem solving. The nursing process as a problem-solving process using assessment, analysis and diagnosis, planning, implementation, and evaluation has proven effective to manage the complex decisions required in nursing practice.

Assessment. During the assessment stage, it is important for the nurse to separate the problem from the symptom by gathering information about the problem or situation. It often is appropriate to involve others—especially those close to the situation—who may be able to provide a different viewpoint or information the manager lacks. For example, the nurse manager who is concerned about increasingly high absenteeism among the staff needs to investigate the situation carefully. What is causing the absenteeism? Are there problems on the unit creating an unhappy work environment? Are several staff members coincidentally having personal problems? Are absentee policies being unfairly administered? The nurse manager must correctly assess and diagnose the problem before developing solutions.

Analysis and diagnosis. During the analysis stage, decision makers use information gathered in the assessment phase to identify the specific problem to be solved. At this stage, managers must also decide whether the situation is important enough to require intervention and whether it is within their authority to intervene.

Planning. During the planning stage, the goal is to identify as many options as possible and then objectively weigh the options as to possible risks and consequences and positive and negative outcomes, including patient outcomes and staff satisfaction as key considerations. The decision maker should be flexible, creative, and open to suggestions from other staff and peers when reviewing options. Avoid preconceived ideas or rigid thinking such as "there is only one way to do this job" or "that's the way we have always done it." It is also important to remember that decisions made with input from those who will be affected by the decision are more likely to result in positive outcomes. Cost, quality, and legal and ethical aspects of care also should be carefully considered.

Implementation. The implementation stage should include effective communication, delegation, and supervision. (See Principles of Change presented later in this chapter.) It is important for the nurse to show positive support for the decision outcome and to encourage cooperation and support among all staff. Persons higher in the organizational structure may mandate some decisions, and although not able to control that decision, the nurse can influence a positive outcome.

Evaluation. The evaluation stage is necessary to ensure that the implemented plan effectively resolved the problem or the decision situation. Considerable time and energy may be spent on identifying the problem, generating possible options, and selecting and implementing the best solution. However, time for follow-up evaluation must also be allocated. It is important to establish early (during the planning stage) how and what evaluation and monitoring will take place, who will be responsible, and when it will be accomplished.

Staff input should be included in each stage of the decision-making problem-solving process. Additionally, the nurse might seek help from others who are more experienced and knowledgeable in specific areas. Even the most experienced nurses will not be able to effectively solve every problem, nor will any nurse have all the answers. The key is to understand and incorporate the decision-making problem-solving process into all activities; know when and how to access resources; and learn and improve as successes and failures are experienced.

Change Agent

This text frequently has referred to the changing health care environment, and true to that concept, change is an inevitable occurrence in health care. Whether working with individuals, groups, or the entire organization, the professional nurse is certain to be involved in managing change. The nurse as the change agent is responsible for guiding people through the change process. To successfully engage in change, the nurse must first be willing to confront the demand for change; staff cannot be expected to embrace change if their nurse leader has not done so.

People often feel threatened by change and may react, especially at first, with resistance and hostility. Change that is carefully planned and implemented slowly with all people continually informed and involved will be more successful in reaching the desired outcome (or change). Change will often create a wide range of feelings among staff and managers including fear, achievement, loss, pride, stress, and dissatisfaction. The successful change agent will understand the very real nature of these emotions and manage the change process such that all involved will experience at least some degree of success and pride in the outcome.

In his classic work on change, Lewin (1951) identified the following rules that should be followed when change is necessary:
1. Change should be implemented only for good reason.
2. Change should always be planned and implemented gradually.
3. Change should never be unexpected or abrupt.
4. All people who may be affected by the change should be involved in planning for the change.

Change may be indicated for several reasons, including solving an identified problem, implementing a new program, improving work efficiencies, or adjusting to new mandates by regulatory agencies. Even though a strong reason for change may exist, it almost always will be met with some resistance. Resistance is demonstrated by refusing to cooperate with a course of action or showing active opposition to the change. The effective change agent recognizes that resistance is a natural response to change and does not waste time or energy attempting to eliminate it. Instead, the effective change agent identifies and implements effective change strategies to overcome resistance.

Stages of Change

Effective change strategies can be developed through the three classic stages of change identified by Lewin (1951). These stages are:

1. *Unfreezing stage*—The change agent promotes problem identification and encourages the awareness of the need for change. People must believe that improvement is possible before they are willing to consider change. The change agent's responsibilities are to:
   - Gather information about the problem.
   - Accurately assess the problem.
   - Decide if change is necessary.
   - Make others aware of the need for change.

2. *Moving stage*—The change agent clarifies the need to change, explores alternatives, defines goals and objectives, plans the change, and implements the change plan. The change agent's responsibilities are to:
   - Identify areas of support and resistance.
   - Set goals and objectives.
   - Include everyone affected in the planning.
   - Develop an appropriate change plan with target dates.
   - Implement the change plan.
   - Be available to help, support, and encourage others through the process.
   - Evaluate the change, and make modifications if necessary.

3. *Refreezing stage*—The change agent integrates the change into the organization so that it becomes recognized as the status quo. If the refreezing stage is not completed, people may drift into old behaviors. The change agent's responsibilities are to:
   - Require compliance with the changed processes.
   - Find ways to engage the staff to support the change.
   - Adopt new policies that may be required to support the change.
   - Support and encourage others until the change is no longer viewed as new but as part of the status quo and is well integrated into daily work.

In alignment with Lewin's (1951) three stages of change (i.e., unfreezing, moving, and refreezing), involvement and education are key to successful change.

Involvement

The importance of involving all individuals, groups, or departments affected by the change cannot be overstated. Involvement includes clear, two-way communication and a concerted effort to garner information and feedback from all affected parties about the need for change. The effective change agent will understand that a change in one area almost always will affect another group or department (remember systems theory?).

Education and Training

Education and training also are important components of effective change. People must have appropriate education and training to understand and comply with new policies, procedures, work processes, duties, or responsibilities. Early in the change process, the change agent must consider the training needs of all individuals, groups, and departments. Education and training can reduce fear of the unknown and allow the staff to feel prepared and comfortable with taking on new or different responsibilities.

Clinical Consultant

Staff members look to the nurse leader as a resource for clinical advice. For example, the nurse leader is frequently called on to assess difficult or unusual patient cases and guide the staff nurse to make appropriate nursing judgments. In this role, the nurse serves as a role model for excellence in nursing care and clinical judgment and provides ongoing training and education.

Staff Developer

The nurse should be ever mindful of the need for learning and training opportunities to enhance professional and personal growth for all employees he or she supervises. Accessing resources and planning staff development activities that meet the needs of individual staff members, including RNs, LPNs or LVNs, nursing assistants, and clerical staff is a very important role for the nurse.

Mentor

As the nurse develops into an effective leader, he or she should accept the responsibility to act as a mentor to new nurses, helping them develop effective leadership and management skills. Mentorship is key to developing our future nurse leaders and managers.

Corporate Supporter

The nurse, as a corporate supporter, has a responsibility to embrace the mission, goals, and objectives of the employing organization. In this role as corporate supporter, the nurse is a professional representative for the organization and is committed to supporting and accomplishing organizational goals.

CREATING A CARING AND RESPECTFUL ENVIRONMENT

Perhaps the most important responsibility for the nurse is to create an environment of caring—caring for patients, families, and other staff members. Staff members who feel that their manager sincerely cares about them and the work they do are able to pass that feeling of caring on to their patients and other customers. Caring for the staff members can be demonstrated by the following:

- Offering sincere positive recognition for both individuals and teams
- Praising and giving thanks for a job well done
- Spending time with staff members to reinforce positive work behaviors
- Meeting the staff members' personal needs whenever possible, such as accommodating scheduling needs for family events
- Providing guidance and support for professional and personal growth
- Maintaining a positive, confident attitude and a pleasant work environment

Staff members who feel their work is valued and they are respected and cared about as individuals are able to further contribute to a positive, caring environment in which to provide excellent patient care. Creating a caring environment in the highly technical, fast-paced, and extremely stressful settings in which nurses work can be a significant challenge. However, it is a challenge that is at the heart of nursing if we are to promote the very best in patient care. As Benner (1999) has observed, "Failing to attend to caring practices will continue to fuel a technical cure approach to health care rather than attend to illness prevention, care of the chronically ill and health promotion. Sometimes care itself is the most significant outcome, as well as the most significant means to cure, healing and health."

Addressing and Preventing Bullying

Unfortunately in today's workplace, disruptive behaviors, also referred to as bullying or lateral violence, are all too common among nurses, physicians, managers, and others. Bullying is defined as the "repeated, unreasonable actions of individuals directed toward an employee (or employees) which are intended to intimidate, degrade, humiliate or undermine; or which create a risk to the health or safety of the employees" (Washington State Department of Labor and Industries [WSDLI], 2011). Examples of bullying behaviors include unwarranted or invalid criticism, unjustified blame, profane or disrespectful language, being gossiped about or being the target of rumors, being yelled or shouted at in a hostile way, being sworn at or verbally abused, being assigned undesirable work differently from the rest of your colleagues, and being "put down" or humiliated in front of others (WSDLI, 2011).

The negative effects of bullying are significant. Nurses who are the victims may have problems with their physical health (e.g., sleep disturbances, depression, musculoskeletal problems); feelings of self-blame, reduced self-esteem, and work-withdrawal (WSDLI, 2011). The extreme result of bullying for nurses is that they may leave the profession completely. Bullying causes distress and low morale among other staff, lower productivity and higher costs for the organization, and may also lead to patient safety and quality concerns.

Nurses must provide the leadership to STOP bullying in the workplace. Nurses, especially new nurses, must understand that under no circumstances should such bullying behaviors be tolerated. Managers have the ultimate responsibility to ensure that such behaviors will not be tolerated and will be immediately addressed and stopped. Following are some important steps to address bullying from an individual level (WSDLI, 2011):

- Recognize that bullying is occurring
- Realize that the victim is NOT the source of the problem
- Recognize that bullying is about control and has nothing to do with the victim's performance
- The victim should keep a record of the nature of the bullying (dates, times places, what was said or done and who was present)
- Obtain documents that contradict the bully's accusations against the victim

Actions that employers can take to prevent bullying include implement and enforce zero-tolerance anti-bullying policies; be sure everyone is aware of what bullying is and encourage reporting; and create a code of conduct signed by all employees that defines professional, respectful behaviors. The reader is encouraged to learn more about bullying from articles in nursing journals and the book *Bullying in the Workplace: Reversing a Culture* published by the American Nurses Association.

SPECIAL LEADERSHIP CHALLENGES IN THE TWENTY-FIRST CENTURY

As leaders and managers in the U.S. health care delivery system, nurses will face daunting challenges in this new era of health care reform. Such challenges include reducing health care costs, implementation of the Patient Protection and Affordable Care Act (see Chapter 7 for detailed information), and ongoing concerns about the safety and quality of care. The Institute for Healthcare Improvement (IHI) provides all health care leaders with clear guidance to focus on its *Triple Aim*: (1) improve the patient experience of care to include both quality and satisfaction; (2) improve the health of populations; and (3) reduce health care costs (IHI, 2014). Nurses across all settings and all positions are in the perfect position to significantly influence improvements in these three areas on a day-to-day basis. Three national initiatives provide nurses with the framework for making significant changes to address the Triple Aim:

- *A Proclamation for Change: Transforming the Hospital Patient Care Environment* (Hendrich et al, 2009): This report provides a set of evidence-based recommendations to address inefficiencies that threaten patient safety and to improve retention of the nursing workforce. This proclamation has been endorsed by major health care systems across the nation as well as by professional and consumer organizations. It can be accessed online at http://www.rwjf.org/en/library/research/2009/06/a-proclamation-for-change.html.

- *Keeping Patients Safe: Transforming the Work Environment of Nurses* (Institute of Medicine [IOM], 2003): This book makes a strong connection between the nurse's work environment, patient safety, and quality outcomes. Although released over a decade ago, it is still highly relevant to today's nurses. Nurses are challenged to lead implementation of changes and impart significant improvements in hospitals, nursing homes, home health agencies, ambulatory clinics, and all other settings across the continuum of care. Consider accessing this book online to review and think about how you as an individual nurse and working with your colleagues can turn the book's recommendations into action.

- *The Future of Nursing: Leading Change, Advancing Health* (IOM, 2010): This report provides key recommendations to guide the advancement of the nursing profession in recognition of the vital role that nurses play in realizing safe, cost-effective, high-quality health care across the nation. Access this report online at (http://www.iom.edu/Reports) to gain a better understanding of its recommendations and how to contribute to the advancement of the nursing profession and health care.

SUMMARY

In every area of health care, the professional nurse is expected to provide leadership and management expertise to help manage complex and ever-changing health care organizations. The multifaceted set of theories, functions, roles, and skills presented in this chapter may at first seem overwhelming to the novice nurse. However, by learning and understanding the principles and concepts involved, the graduate nurse can become a successful nurse leader and manager.

Leadership, management, and organizational theories provide a framework on which to build effective nursing management practices. Although there is no one "best" leadership theory, professional nurses should maintain an awareness of their own behavior and how the key elements of the leadership situation influence outcomes.

The management functions of planning, organizing, staffing, directing, and controlling provide the nurse with a defined, practical set of skills to guide management activities. Professional nurses can apply these management functions to perform effectively in various management roles, including customer service provider, team builder, resource manager, change agent, clinical consultant, staff developer, mentor, and corporate supporter.

Developing effective leadership and management skills is an ongoing process that continues throughout one's career as a professional nurse. Nurses in management positions should routinely analyze personal strengths and weaknesses in each of these management roles and identify areas in which learning and development are needed- Box 17-7 provides resources for individual assessments of leadership styles. Modeling effective nurse managers and reading relevant professional journal articles and books can increase leadership and management knowledge and skills. Management and leadership roles are challenging and exciting and present a wonderful opportunity to grow professionally and personally.

BOX 17-7 **Resources for Individual Leadership Assessments**

Consider the following excellent resources for conducting personal leadership assessments and identifying opportunities to build your own leadership skills:

- *The Leadership Challenge with LPI: Leadership Practice Inventory,* by James M. Kouzes and Barry Z. Posners (Jossey-Bass Publisher)

- *Strength Finders 2.0,* by Tom Rath with access code for online assessment (Gallup Press)
- *The New Leadership Challenge: Creating the Future of Nursing,* with online leadership assessments, by Sheila C. Grossman & Theresa M. Valiga. (FA Davis Publisher)

REFERENCES

American Nurses Association: *Home health nursing: scope and standards of practice,* ed 2, Washington, DC, 2014, American Nurses Association.

American Nurses Association: *Nursing: scope and standards of practice,* ed 2, Washington, DC, 2010a, American Nurses Association.

American Nurses Association: *Gerontological nursing: scope and standards of practice,* Washington, DC, 2010b, American Nurses Association.

Bass BM, Avoliio BJ, Goodheim L: Biography and the assessment of transformational leadership at the world-class level, *J Manage* 13(1):7–19, 1987.

Benner P: Nursing leadership for the new millennium: claiming the wisdom and worth of clinical practice, *Nurs Healthcare Perspect* 20(6):312–319, 1999.

Bormann L, Abrahamson K: Do staff nurse perceptions of nurse leadership behaviors influence staff nurse job satisfaction? The case of a hospital applying for Magnet® designation, *J Nurs Adm* 44(4):219–225, 2014.

Burns J: *Leadership,* New York, 1978, Harper & Row.

Casida J, Parker J: Staff nurse perceptions of nurse manager leadership styles and outcomes, *J Nurs Manag* 19(4):478–486, 2011.

Cowden T, Cummings G, Profetto-McGrath J: Leadership practices and staff nurses' intent to stay: a systematic review, *J Nurs Manag* 19(4):461–477, 2011.

Dotson MJ, Dave DS, Cazier JA, Spaulding TJ: An empirical analysis of nurse retention: what keeps RNs in nursing? *J Nurs Adm* 44(2):111–116, 2014.

Failla KR, Stichler JF: Manager and staff perceptions of the manager's leadership style, *J Nurs Adm* 11(38):480–487, 2008.

Forman H: From cheerleader to patent processor, *J Nurs Adm* 36(7/8):346–350, 2006.

Grensing-Pophal L: Give-and-take feedback, *Nurs Manage* 31(2):27–28, 2000.

Harvard Business Essentials: *Manager's toolkit: the 13 skills managers need to succeed,* Boston, 2004, Harvard Business School Press.

Hairr DC, Salisbury H, Johannsson M, Redfern-Vance N: Nurse staffing and the relationship to job satisfaction and retention, *Nurs Econ* 32(3):142–147, 2014.

Hendrich A, Chow MP, Goshert WS: A proclamation for change: transforming the hospital patient care environment, *JONA* 39(6):266–275, 2009.

Hersey P, Blanchard K: *Management of organizational behavior: utilizing human resources,* ed 4, Englewood Cliffs, NJ, 1988, Prentice-Hall.

Hersey P, Blanchard K, Natemeyer W: Situational leadership, perception and impact of power, *Group Organ Stud* 4(4):418–428, 1979.

Institute of Healthcare Improvement: *The Triple Aim,* 2014 (website). http://www.ihi.org/Engage/Initiatives/TripleAim/pages/default.aspx. Accessed October 15, 2014.

Institute of Medicine: *The future of nursing: leading change, advancing health,* Washington, DC, 2010, National Academies Press.

Institute of Medicine: *Page A: Keeping patients safe: transforming the work environment of nurses,* Washington, DC, 2003, National Academies Press.

Lewin K: *Field theory in social sciences,* New York, 1951, Harper & Row.

Marquis BL, Huston CJ: *Leadership roles and management functions in nursing,* ed 8, Philadelphia, 2014, Wolters Kluwer/Lippincott.

McGuire E: Chaos theory: learning a new science, *J Nurs Adm* 29(2):8–9, 1999.

Moneke N, Umeh OJ: How leadership behaviors impact critical care nurse job satisfaction, *Nurs Manage* 44(1):53–55, 2013.

Perrine JL: Strategies to boost RN retention, *Nurs Manage* 40(4):20–22, 2009.

Peters T, Waterman RH: *In search of excellence,* New York, 1982, Harper & Row.

Stogdill RM: *Handbook of leadership: a survey of theory and research,* New York, 1974, The Free Press.

Thompson JD: *Organizations in action,* New York, 1967, McGraw-Hill.

Washington State Department of Labor and Industries: *Workplace bullying and disruptive behavior: What everyone needs to know,* 2011 (website). http://www.lni.wa.gov/safety/research/files/bullying.pdf. Accessed Jan 25, 2015.

White RK, Lippit R: *Autocracy and democracy: an experimental inquiry,* New York, 1960, Harper & Row.

Wieck KL, Dols J, Northam S: What nurses want: the nurse incentives project, *Nurs Econ* 27(3):169–201, 2009.

Wisokzkey S: Will they stay or will they go? Insight into nursing turnover, *Nurs Manage* 42(2):15–17, 2011.

18

Budgeting Basics for Nurses

Barbara Cherry, DNSc, MBA, RN, NEA-BC

The budget serves as the financial guideline that enables the clinical team to provide quality patient care.

e Additional resources are available online at: *http://evolve.elsevier.com/Cherry/*

PROFESSIONAL/ETHICAL ISSUE

Claire Ramsey, RN, works in the critical care unit of a large academic medical center. A new staffing policy for the hospital has been implemented and requires that nurses are either sent home or their shift cancelled in advance if the patient census is low. The nurse must either take paid time off to receive pay for the cancelled shift or can choose not to be paid for the cancelled shift. One of Claire's colleagues, Jonathan, is very vocal about his dislike of this policy and expresses to others that the hospital is "cheating" the nurses by cancelling shifts; he vocalizes about how unfair management is because, as he points out, the managers' shifts are never cancelled, and the hospital has "plenty of money" regardless of the number of patients on the unit. Claire is becoming uncomfortable with Jonathan's discussions because it

seems to be leading to low morale and dissatisfaction among some of the nurses. She really likes her job and does not want to see the unit morale deteriorate over a policy that she herself does not understand and that she believes is not well understood by many other nurses, including Jonathan.

- Discuss the reasons from a budgeting perspective why the shift cancellation policy was implemented for this hospital.
- What steps can Claire take to help her and her colleagues learn more about the staffing policy and why it was implemented?
- How should Claire respond to Jonathan when he begins to vocalize his objections about the policy to her?

VIGNETTE

Justine Scott, RN, sat in the staff meeting being led by the nurse manager for the cardiac telemetry unit where she has worked for the last 6 months since graduating from nursing school. As Justine listened to the nurse manager discuss the unit's budget, she felt like she was hearing a foreign language. The nurse manager discussed "variances for labor and supply costs that were most likely due to increased patient acuity and patient census above budgeted levels." The nurse manager explained the importance of accurately identifying reasons for the budget variances to ensure appropriate resources are allocated to their unit to

support quality patient care. The nurse manager then requested input from the staff nurses regarding their observations about supply usage and overtime costs and how they might be better controlled. In the final topic for the staff meeting, the nurse manager requested input from the staff on "equipment needs to be considered as the unit's capital budget request is developed." As a new nurse, Justine noticed that staff meetings seemed to center more on discussions regarding the "budget" rather than clinical issues. She realized that the budget must be extremely important to support patient care and resolved to learn more about budgets, the financial terminology used by her nurse manager, and what she could do as a staff nurse to support the nurse manager in this seemingly important area of nursing practice.

Questions to Consider While Reading this Chapter:
1. Who should be concerned about unit or departmental budgets?
2. What is the primary purpose of developing a unit or departmental budget?
3. How can nurses and nurse managers improve clinical care with better budgeting skills?
4. What resources are available to help nurses learn more about budgets in the health care setting?

KEY TERMS

Budget: Financial plan for the allocation of the organization's resources and a control for ensuring that results comply with the plan.

Budget assumptions: Statements that reflect issues affecting the future performance of the organization; used as the framework for developing the budget; budget assumptions address questions such as the following: Are supply prices likely to increase or decrease? What salary range will ensure that the organization is able to recruit and retain quality employees? What are the competitors offering in terms of new services? Is the patient census likely to increase or decrease over the next year?

Capital expenditures: Amount spent on items that will have long-term (greater than 1 year) value to an organization. Typically includes property and equipment.

Expense: An event or item that requires the outlay of money for purchase or the incurrence of a liability for future payment; major expenses for health care organizations include salaries, medical supplies and equipment, and facility maintenance.

Fiscal year: A 12-month period used for calculating annual (yearly) financial reports in business; the fiscal year does not have to constitute the calendar year (January to December) but may be any 12-month period (e.g., August through July) established and maintained consistently by the business.

Full-time equivalent (FTE): The number of hours worked or paid that is equal to that expected of a full-time employee working a 40-hour work week; annual work hours for 1 FTE equal 2080 hours, and monthly work hours equal 173.33 hours. One FTE position may be occupied by one employee working full time or shared by two or more employees working part time.

Incremental budgeting: An approach to budget development that extrapolates from the prior period's budget and adjusts for future growth or decline in revenues or expenses to determine the budget for the next period.

Revenue: Money that a health care organization receives in exchange for providing health care or other related services through normal business activities; synonymous with income.

Salaries, wages, and benefits (SWB): Budget category that typically includes direct payment for hours worked, bonuses, accrued vacation, health benefits, employer portion of payroll taxes, and workers' compensation.

Supplies: Materials used in performing tasks within the organization. Typically includes clinical disposables, pharmaceuticals, and office supplies.

Variance: The difference between the planned budget and the actual results.

Variance analysis: The process of analyzing the differences in the planned budget results and the actual results; involves quantitative and qualitative analysis.

Zero-based budgeting: An approach to budget development that begins as though the budget were being prepared for the first time.

LEARNING OUTCOMES

After studying this chapter, the reader will be able to:

1. Understand the basic terminology of budgeting in the health care industry.
2. Contribute to the budget development process for a nursing or clinical department.
3. Contribute to the capital budget development process for a nursing or clinical department.
4. Explain aspects of monitoring financial performance against an operational budget.
5. Understand the overall role of nursing in a health care organization's budget process.

CHAPTER OVERVIEW

The budget serves as the financial guideline that enables a health care organization to achieve its goal of providing high-quality patient care services. Just as nurses learn about clinical guidelines for the care of patients with various diseases, it is also essential that nurses have a working knowledge of the guidelines that ensure the organization is able to operate in a stable financial environment through effective budget management. As nurses advance into supervisory and management positions, they will have financial responsibility for a business unit of a health care organization and must be competent in the financial

aspects of operating that unit. Additionally, the focus on cost and quality initiatives in today's health care settings requires that even staff nurses have a basic understanding of the budget. "The education and evolution of nurses as business managers is critical to building a strong RN workforce" (Talley et al, 2013). This chapter introduces the basic concepts of budgeting in health care organizations, but for a deeper understanding of budgeting, nurses are encouraged to continue to build their knowledge by using a health care finance text and/or other resources suggested at the end of the chapter.

WHAT IS BUDGETING?

As a nursing student, you are probably more aware of budget concepts than you realize. When you decided to become a registered nurse (RN), you had a goal to graduate from nursing school within a specified time period. You had to make a budget plan by predicting your expenses for that period, such as tuition, books, and living expenses. You also predicted your revenue from sources such as student loans, part-time jobs, savings, or parental or spousal support. After predicting your expenses and your revenues, you most likely planned your budget for how much you could spend on a weekly or monthly basis during this time and eventually achieve your goal of graduating from nursing school. Similarly, health care organizations develop budgets for a specified period by determining what goals they want to achieve, predicting expenses and revenues, then planning the annual budget and monitoring it on a monthly basis. For example, a hospital may plan its annual budget to maintain staffing and supplies to operate its current number of beds, provide a raise for all staff, and open a new outpatient surgical center.

Basically the health care organization's budget is a document that details how financial resources will be allocated to ensure that the organization is able to conduct its daily business and achieve strategic goals. The budget itemizes the organization's predicted expenses and expected revenues for a given period of time. More important, budgets require ongoing attention to ensure that the organization's financial needs are met. Just as nursing students most likely have to make decisions to adjust their budgets during nursing school to meet unexpected changes in revenues or expenses, the health care organization invariably experiences the same challenges during the year. Thus the budget becomes a dynamic action plan that guides the allocation of resources and expenditures and influences the nurse manager's decision making on a day-to-day, week-to-week, or month-to-month basis.

Budgets perform four basic functions to make certain the organization can achieve its strategic goals and permit continued operations from an economic point of view. The four budgeting functions are: (1) planning, (2) coordinating and communicating, (3) monitoring progress, and (4) evaluating performance. The following sections describe each of these important budgeting functions.

Planning

Planning is the most important function of the budgeting process. During the planning phase, managers first decide on the goals to achieve for a specified period and identify resources (e.g., staff, supplies, equipment) needed to achieve those goals. Next, they predict revenues and expenses based on those goals and budget assumptions to use in planning the budget. Budget assumptions allow the managers to answer various questions that will have an effect on the budget, such as the following:

- What should nursing salaries be in the coming year to reward and retain nurses, and to remain competitive with other health care organizations in the area?
- How will new services being offered by other health care organizations in the area affect our organization?

Budgets are most often developed for a 1-year period based on predicted amounts of services. For example, hospitals will predict patient census for the coming year and then allocate funds for nursing salaries based on this predicted census.

Consider the following example: The hospital management team has decided to establish a chest pain center as part of the emergency department (ED). In planning the annual budget for the ED and its new chest pain center, the managers have developed the following assumptions:

- The chest pain center will see 12 patients every 24 hours. Of the 12 patients, 75% of the daily census (8 patients) are patients directed from the current ED census, and 25% (4 patients) are patients new to this hospital.
- Four beds will be dedicated to the chest pain center and will require remodeling of an underused section of the current ED.
- The chest pain center will be staffed with RNs dedicated to the center.

The management team has planned to include the following expenses in the annual budget for the new chest pain center: salaries for nurses and support staff, supplies, monitoring equipment, equipment maintenance, funds for marketing the new program, and funds to remodel an area in the current ED for the program. Managers also need to think about the other areas that will be affected by the new chest pain center, such as the

cardiac catheterization suite, echocardiogram, laboratory, electrocardiogram (ECG), and materials management, which all deserve budgetary consideration as a result of the wide-reaching effect of this seemingly small service expansion.

Historically, nursing has had limited input into fiscal (or financial) planning and development of the organization's budget. Administrators with no nursing background and little understanding of nursing values, beliefs, and care requirements traditionally made decisions about resource allocations related to nursing. Today, participating in the budget process to determine resource allocation is a fundamental responsibility of nurse leaders. Involving staff nurses in the budget planning is also highly recommended. Managers and staff who participate in budget planning are more likely to be cost-conscious and appreciate how their unit should function to meet the overall financial goals.

Coordinating and Communicating

Although not commonly associated with budgets, coordination and communication are very important functions of budgeting. The budget process, by necessity, requires that many different groups within an organization come together to discuss the resources necessary to accomplish the goals of a business unit. Therefore, think of the budget process as the best opportunity to discuss concerns about resource allocation with the organization's leaders who are capable of resolving issues.

Consider the new chest pain center described earlier. To plan how the center will establish itself as a center of excellence for emergency care of patients with chest pain, nurses and physicians with experience in caring for chest pain patients must offer input about equipment and supply needs, room layout and design, staffing models, electronic medical record needs, and support staff; the financial officer needs to offer input about reimbursement rates and other financial considerations related to caring for this population; the hospital marketing staff needs to offer input about how the program can be advertised to inform the community about the new service; and other hospital administrators and department managers need to offer input as to how this new center will affect other areas of business both inside and outside the hospital. Just as coordination and communication among these many groups and departments are essential to develop and manage the budget for the new chest pain center, such coordination and communication are also essential for developing and managing the budgets for all units within the hospital.

Monitoring Progress

Monitoring progress is one of the most vital functions of the budget—and the function that the nurse manager will be most involved with on a daily basis. It is through the comparison of actual performance against expected, or budgeted, performance that an organization measures the effectiveness of its budget. Ongoing monitoring of the budget allows timely corrective action or, if the budget plan is right on target, the knowledge that no adjustments are required.

Consider our chest pain center again. The budget was developed on an anticipated volume of 12 patients every 24 hours, and staffing was implemented to serve this volume of patients. At the end of its first month of operation, the nurse manager reviews the budget information and sees that the actual patient volume is averaging only 8 patients per 24 hours, and the associated revenue for the center is approximately 70% of the planned revenue. The nurse manager has several issues to consider: Does staffing need to be reduced to better reflect the number of patients being treated by the center? Are the patients being seen of higher acuity and thus require a higher intensity of nursing care? Is the low volume a reflection of the new program that is not yet widely appreciated in the community, and as its reputation grows, will the volume also grow? If no immediate changes are made, how will the reduced revenue affect the financial status of the center? Fortunately, the nurse manager can consult others involved in developing the budget to address these important issues and make decisions to ensure the success of the center.

The difference between the planned budget and the actual results is called a *variance*. A **variance** is favorable when the results are better than expected, or it is unfavorable when the results are worse than expected. The lower than planned revenue in the chest pain center is an example of an unfavorable variance. *Variance analysis*, the process by which deviations from budgeted amounts are examined, is discussed in more detail later in the chapter.

Evaluating Performance

Budget results can also be used as part of the manager's performance evaluation, including the staff bonus structure

for some hospitals. Evaluating the manager's performance based on budget results is becoming more widely used because of the growing trend toward accountability and compliance in the business world. By looking at the budget results for a given period, an evaluator can determine the manager's overall success in achieving goals. Nurse managers are frequently evaluated based on their effectiveness in managing nursing overtime costs and supply use, both of which are reflected in the nursing unit's budget. Performance evaluations based on budget results can motivate managers to effectively control budgets and will serve as a basis for salary decisions and career advancement for the manager. Even though the manager is the captain of the unit and is ultimately accountable for the unit's budgetary performance, a lack of staff ownership and involvement in the unit's operation usually leads to problems for the manager.

TYPES OF BUDGETS

The three types of budgets for which a nurse manager typically has responsibility are operational, labor, and capital budgets. The components of these budgets are presented in Box 18-1 and are discussed in more detail in the following sections.

Operational Budget

The operational, or operating, budget represents revenues and expenses for an operational unit, such as a product line, unit, department, or overall organization. The chest pain center previously discussed is considered

BOX 18-1	**Three Types of Budgets**
Operating budget	Allocates funds for daily expenses, such as salaries, utilities, repairs, maintenance, and patient care supplies
Labor budget	A subset of the operating budget; allocates funds for salaries, overtime, benefits, and staff development and training
Capital budget	Allocates funds for construction projects and/or long-life medical equipment, such as cardiac monitors, defibrillators, and computer hardware

a product line; an example of a nursing unit is the intensive care unit or medical-surgical unit; an example of a department is dietary or human resources. Whereas the product line, unit, department, and overall organization have designated operational budgets, each operational unit has similar categories of expenses and revenues. The expenses in the operational budget are those necessary to operate on a daily basis, and the revenues are those paid to the organization from various payer sources (Box 18-2). (See Chapter 7 for more information about sources of payments for health care services.)

Labor Budget

The labor budget is a subset of the operational budget. Its purpose is to provide detailed documentation of salaries, wages, and benefits with respect to the operational unit. Factors that affect the personnel budget include salary rates, overtime, benefits (e.g., paid time off, health insurance), staff development and training, and employee turnover. The labor budget is virtually always the largest expense item in an operational budget for a health care organization because nurses and nursing support staff (e.g., nursing assistants, unit secretaries, transportation staff) compose the greatest percentage of the workforce (Goetz et al, 2011). The labor budget is also used to provide managers with a productivity metric, which is the amount of work produced (i.e., hours of nursing care per patient-day) by a specific amount of input or resources (i.e., nursing hours worked).

The productivity metric is necessary to give managers a measurement of the number of nursing hours worked in comparison with the amount of patient care provided. Low productivity (high nursing hours worked with low patient census) is not desirable because it means higher staff salaries combined with lower revenues for patient care services. High productivity (high patient census with low nursing hours) means that there are fewer staff to take care of more patients and they may not be able to provide safe, quality patient care. Most health care organizations have a recommended productivity measure that allows for a balance between financial efficiency and quality and safety of patient care. To achieve this balance, nursing must be at the table to ensure that the discussion about quality and safety is voiced along with productivity and financial efficiency.

One of the primary difficulties encountered in managing the labor budget is accurately predicting future staffing needs. Because budgets are based on a predicted amount of services (i.e., patient census), variances between actual staffing levels and budget levels occur if the facility experiences an unanticipated increase or decrease in patient services. Another concern related to the budget and labor expense is balancing the patient acuity, or degree of patient illness, with the nurse-to-patient ratio.

An important aspect of labor budgeting is understanding the 12-month historical trend for labor hours and patient-days. As a general rule, organizations expect nurse managers to control the number of worked hours versus the actual salary expense. Wage levels, benefit costs, and other related expenses are typically controlled at the leadership level. The operational aspect of scheduling staff (measured in worked hours) to meet the needs of patient volume (measured by patient census) is best controlled and budgeted at the unit or departmental level.

Capital Budget

The capital budget represents funds allocated for construction projects and major equipment purchases (e.g., cardiac monitor, defibrillator, computer hardware). The capital budget is developed separately from the operating budget because capital purchases usually require multiple years to pay out. The main requirements for a purchase or acquisition to be considered as part of the capital budget is that it has a useful life expectancy of more than 1 year and it costs more than a minimum dollar amount established by the organization, typically $500 to $2000.

BOX 18-2 **Examples of Typical Expenses and Revenues for a Health Care Organization**

Expenses	Revenues
• Salaries	• Payments from
• Benefits (paid time off; health insurance)	• Medicare
	• Medicaid
• Patient care supplies	• Private insurance
• Overhead expenses	• Individuals (self-pay)
• Utilities	• Grants
• Administrative costs	• Charitable or philanthropic donations
• Maintenance	
• Housekeeping	

The term *capital* simply refers to the funds used to purchase long-term investments, such as major medical equipment, computer systems, or newly constructed buildings. A capital budget item is an expensive purchase that will be used by the organization for many years. Capital budget items are often referred to as *capital assets, long-term investments, capital investments,* or *capital acquisitions.* These capital assets are treated differently from the operating budget expense because of their multiyear value. Because capital purchases are often considered investments, they are scrutinized more carefully during the budgeting process.

Planning capital budget requests will test the nurse manager's long-range planning skills. The nurse manager must be able to look down the road from 1 year to several years in advance to identify capital budgeting needs and to bring those needs to the attention of senior management. The unit or department need for a capital purchase must be weighed against the financial implications when considering the organization's entire capital budget. The nurse manager has a critical role in helping to plan the capital budget, justify priorities, and ensure that the needs of the facility and patients are met. In addition, nursing staff are vital to a successful capital planning process because their "frontline" equipment needs must be made known to management for purchase consideration.

Budget Methods

There are two basic methods for budgeting: the *incremental* approach and the *zero-based* approach. Both approaches have particular strengths and weaknesses and both are completely sound approaches in most situations.

Incremental Budgeting

The incremental approach is the most commonly used budgeting method, primarily because it is relatively simple to apply to most circumstances. The incremental approach is simply a forward trend of current or recent performance with adjustments for future growth or decline in revenues or expenses. For example, the nursing unit's budget would be based on the actual costs from the previous budget period with a small increase for planned salary raises and an increase in the cost of supplies. It is also possible that the incremental budget might include a decrease in all expenses.

Zero-Based Budgeting

Zero-based budgeting is used far less frequently than incremental budgeting. This method builds a budget from the assumption of no volume and no resources allocated; in other words, it is developed as though the budget were being prepared for the first time. Each budget cycle begins with a critical review of budget assumptions and proposed revenues and expenditures. Then core resources necessary for one unit of service are identified, and from there resource allocation is determined on a variable basis tied to volume.

Again, consider the chest pain center example. If the nurse manager is developing a zero-based budget, he or she would start each new budget planning cycle by doing the following:

- Determining the revenue and expenses for caring for one chest pain patient
- Predicting the average patient volume for the center
- Calculating the total revenues and expenses for the budget period

In developing the budget, the nurse manager understands that whereas one nurse is necessary to care for one patient, that nurse may also be able to care for two or three other patients at the same time. Thus the cost of nursing salaries is variable based on the volume of patients being treated in the center.

This process works somewhat differently with nonvariable departments, such as nursing administration and human resources, which are non–revenue-generating departments (i.e., departments that do not provide a billable health care service). In nonvariable departments, expenses do not vary based on patient volume. Such departments do not base their budgets on a variable volume of patient visits, but rather on a set core of expenses to run the department. Their expenses are allocated to revenue-generating departments.

DEVELOPING A BUDGET

Developing a budget is actually a continual process. Organizations are constantly making projections for future budgets, implementing current budgets, and analyzing month-to-month variances in relation to the budget. The current budget usually covers a 12-month period, also known as the organization's *fiscal year*. The development of the budget for the new fiscal year occurs a few months ahead of the start of the new fiscal year so that the budget can be developed and approved at all levels before it becomes effective. For example, if the hospital's fiscal year is from September 1 to August 31, then budget development for the new fiscal year will begin sometime in early summer—or perhaps even earlier depending on the size and complexity of the organization. Large health systems usually begin the budget process much earlier than smaller systems or single facilities as a result of the number of approval layers.

Health care organizations usually have a defined procedure in place for budget development. This defined procedure tells managers if the budget development will use the incremental method, zero-based method, or some other method defined by the organization. Organizations may also define if they use a "top-down," "participatory," or "iterative" approach to budgeting. In the top-down approach, upper management sets budget goals and imposes those goals on the rest of the organization. In the participatory approach, the people responsible for achieving the budget goals are included in goal setting. The iterative approach is a combination of the top-down and the participatory approach, with upper management defining strategic goals and then unit leaders developing their operating budgets to incorporate their individual goals in conjunction with the organization's strategic goals.

One key to understanding budgets is to know the *unit-of-service* on which costs and revenues are based. "Patient-days" is the common unit-of-service for inpatient facilities; patient visits or visits by categories (short, intermediate, long) are the units-of-service for ambulatory clinics and home health agencies. Budgets are then developed based on the units-of-service predicted for a given period. For example, the nurse manager in a hospital intensive care unit will base his or her budget on the average number of days that patients will be on the unit over the course of 12 months. The director of the home health agency will base his or her budget on the number of home visits that will be made during a 12-month period. The unit-of-service may vary depending on the organization, setting, and financial policies; thus it is essential that the nurse understands the unit-of-service in the area in which he or she is employed.

Following are the basic steps for developing a budget:

1. Review the organization's strategic plan to identify goals and objectives for the organization, department, or defined operational units. The budget is developed to accomplish these goals and objectives.
2. Set budget assumptions on which to base budgeting decisions. Budget assumptions address issues that affect the future performance of the organization and address questions, such as: Are supply prices likely to increase or decrease, and by what percent? What salary range will ensure that the organization is able to recruit and retain quality employees? What will the cost of the health insurance plan be in the coming year? What are the competitors offering in terms of new services? Is the patient census likely to increase or decrease over the next year? Budget assumptions should be developed by a team of managers from different departments and areas of expertise to be certain consideration is given to all issues that will affect the budget.
3. Gather information about past results, and use the information in combination with budget assumptions to set reasonable expectations about future performance.
4. Predict the units-of-service that will be provided during the budget period.
5. Project expected revenues based on the units-of-service.
6. Project expenses based on the units-of-service. Determine expenses for the labor budget first, based on the predicted units-of-service and the number of FTEs needed to provide the predicted service volume. Each full-time employee is considered one FTE, or 2080 hours per year (40 hours per week). In some organizations, nurses are scheduled for three 12-hour shifts each week, 36 hours per week or 1872 hours per year, and are considered 0.9 FTE. After determining units of service and related FTEs, other expenses are fairly straightforward to project.

Developing the budget is generally a process that involves many discussions among many different managers, from finance to nursing. It is important that nursing have a strong and knowledgeable voice in the budget process so that nursing and patient care needs are appropriately addressed. Box 18-3 lists hints to improve your budgeting skills.

BOX 18-3 **Hints to Improve Your Budgeting Skills**

- Understand your organization's budgeting process. What guidelines do you need to follow? What is the timing of the budget process? What key managers can serve as a resource to help you understand the budget process?
- Learn your department's unit of service and exactly how it is defined.
- Build a relationship with a finance person in the organization, and collaborate routinely on improvement projects; invite finance staff to your unit meetings, and ask to participate in theirs; communicate regularly.
- Review financial reports with the finance person to make sure you are correctly interpreting the reports.
- Understand each line in your budget. If you do not know what something means or where a number comes from, find out.
- Have ongoing discussions with your management team throughout the budgeting process. The more you participate in the planning process, the better you will understand the budget and your responsibilities related to it.
- Learn your organization's capital budgeting process and what qualifies a purchase as a capital expenditure.
- Do not look for excuses when performing below budget. Instead look for new opportunities to exceed budget.

VARIANCE ANALYSIS

The primary use of a budget is to evaluate the progress of the department or unit. Variance analysis is the process by which deviations from budgeted amounts are examined by comparing actual performance results against expected, or budgeted, performance. Through this process, variances are evaluated on a quantitative and qualitative basis. Quantitative analysis focuses on numerical variances to the budget. In other words, are you over or under budget for labor (employee salaries), supply usage, or revenue generated? See Table 18-1 for a sample budget and variance report.

Qualitative analysis of budget variances focuses on reconciling the underlying assumptions on which the budget was based with current conditions. In many cases, the operating environment for a department or unit changes in ways that the budget assumptions are rendered invalid. For example, a unit may be budgeted for nurse staffing at 5 hours per patient-day based on a given patient acuity level. Then the hospital gets a new physician group that attracts large numbers of patients with significantly higher acuity levels, and these patients are admitted to this unit. The labor used increases to 7 hours per patient-day based on the new acuity level. This sort of qualitative change can make budgets difficult, if not impossible, to adhere to without modification. Nurse leaders in the clinical department or unit are best positioned to determine why variances have occurred because variances are almost always related to a clinical issue, such as the one just described.

Variance information typically is presented by means of certain standard reports. Labor budget variances are usually presented on a pay-period basis and provide information on performance against the budgeted standard. Overall budget variances will be presented on a monthly, quarterly, or annual basis and typically provide information to compare current performance against budget and current performance against the previous year's performance (see Table 18-1).

COST CONCEPTS RELATED TO BUDGETING

When considering the budget, it is necessary to have a basic understanding of how much health care services cost and how to predict changes in costs. Consider this question: How much does it cost to provide nursing care to one patient for one 12-hour shift? Unfortunately, the answer is not simple because many factors affect how much something costs. An important step to understand costs is to review the primary types of costs that accountants consider when determining the cost of services in a health care setting:

- *Service unit or unit-of-service:* The basic measure of the product or service being produced. The unit-of-service varies by the health care setting and type of service being provided. Examples include patient-days (hospital), home care visits (home health agency), patient visits (outpatient clinic), and operating room time (outpatient surgical center).
- *Direct costs:* Costs that can be traced directly to the production of the unit-of-service. Examples include

TABLE 18-1 Sample Budget and Variance Report

Hometown General Hospital: Department Performance Analysis—Med-Surg for Period Ending 09/20/2015

	Prior Year	CURRENT MTD (MONTH)			CURRENT YTD (YEAR-TO-DATE)			PRIOR YEAR	
	Actual 9/14	Actual 9/15	Budget 9/15	MTD Var (Variance) 9/15	Actual 9/15	Budget 9/15	YTD Variance 9/15	Prior Year 9/14	Prior Year Variance
GROSS REVENUE									
Inpatient revenue	1,276,525	1,300,122	1,322,904	−22,782	11,087,012	12,575,946	−1,488,934	12,733,822	−1,646,810
Outpatient revenue	0	0	0	0	0	0	0	0	0
Other revenue	0	0	0	0	0	0	0	0	0
Total gross revenue	1,276,525	1,300,122	1,322,904	−22,782	11,087,012	12,575,946	−1,488,934	12,733,822	−1,646,810
OPERATING EXPENSES									
Total productive labor	241,270	293,541	257,954	35,587	2,375,340	2,419,097	−43,757	2,376,009	−669
Total nonproductive labor	29,012	40,031	37,352	2679	359,759	359,453	306	328,128	31,631
Employee benefits and taxes	40,372	38,483	41,133	−2650	366,203	401,616	−35,413	398,766	−32,563
Total SWB (salaries, wages, and benefits)	310,653	372,055	336,439	35,616	3,101,302	3,180,166	−78,864	3,102,903	−1601
Supplies	25,687	20,506	22,628	−2123	193,223	213,853	−20,630	219,267	−26,044
Medical and clinical fees	0	0	0	0	0	0	0	0	0
Contracted department and other fees	298	0	41	−41	506	371	135	929	−424
Repairs and maintenance	0	0	20	−20	0	184	−184	242	−242

Utilities and telephone	0	0	0	0	0	0	0	0	0
Rent, lease, and equipment rental	0	0	0	0	1485	0	1485	0	1485
Other controllable expenses	883	1232	953	279	8617	8,741	−124	14,041	−5424
Other noncontrollable expenses	0	0	0	0	0	0	0	0	0
Total operating expenses	337,520	393,792	360,081	33,711	3,305,132	3,403,315	−98,183	3,337,382	−32,249
Gross margin	939,005	906,330	962,823	−56,493	7,781,880	9,172,631	−1,390,751	9,396,440	−1,614,561
Gross margin percentage	73.56	69.71	72.78	−3.07	70.19	72.94	−2.75	73.79	−3.6
Department patient-days	841	853	871	−18	7283	8280	−997	8384	−1101
Average daily census	28	28	29	−1	27	30	−4	31	−4
Observation days	1.67	3.5	5.5	−2	41.54	49.38	−783	48.17	−6.63
Total department patient-days	842.67	856.5	876.5	−20	7324.54	8329.38	−1,004.83	8,432.17	−1,107.62

The budget report shows dollar performance comparing actual revenues and expenses to budgeted revenues and expenses for the same month of the prior year, current month, current YTD, and the annual totals and variances for the prior year. YTD is the totals for the prior months plus the current month in the fiscal year. The department has spent $33,711 (shaded in green) more than budgeted for expenses for the current month, but for the current YTD, the department has spent less than budgeted for expenses by $98,183 (shaded in yellow).

nursing care and supplies to provide direct patient care. The important concept to remember about direct costs is that they vary with the volume of services. As the patient census increases, the need for additional nursing care and supplies also increases.

- *Indirect costs:* Costs that are incurred as a result of the organization's operating expenses but are not directly related to providing the unit-of-service. Examples include salaries for administrative personnel and expenses for security, housekeeping, utilities, and building maintenance. Indirect costs are sometimes referred to as *overhead.*
- *Full cost:* The total of all costs associated with a unit-of-service and includes direct and indirect costs.
- *Fixed costs:* Costs that do not change as the unit-of-service volume changes. For example, administrative salaries do not change regardless of the patient census on the nursing units. The important point to remember about fixed cost is that they remain steady regardless of the change in units-of-service (e.g., patient-days). As the units-of-service increase, the greater the number to share fixed costs. Conversely, as the units-of-service decrease, the fewer number to share fixed costs. An organization's finance leaders are always interested in increasing volume to provide additional revenue to help cover fixed costs.
- *Variable costs:* Costs that vary directly with changes in the volume of units-of-service. For example, in an ambulatory clinic, the cost of immunizations varies directly with the number of patients who receive immunizations.

This list provides only a basic introduction into cost terminology; it does not provide a comprehensive range of cost accounting terminology and concepts. However, it does demonstrate the complexity of assessing and managing costs.

IMPROVING THE COST AND QUALITY OF CLINICAL CARE

Nurses face challenging situations given the nursing shortage, the rise of the national patient safety agenda, the focus on evidence-based practice, and the increasing acuity of patients in all settings from hospitals to home health agencies to nursing homes. At the same time, organizational leaders are faced with challenging economic times, declining reimbursements, and increasing costs in all areas. Changes to improve quality and reduce costs must be made! How can nurses collaborate with organizational leaders and financial managers to make a difference? Nurses are at the front lines of health care and are key to enhancing the *value* of health care, with value being the combination of quality plus cost (Porter, 2010). Nurses can truly affect the quality and cost of care in significant ways:

- As discharge advocates, nurses can ensure appropriate discharge instructions and proper follow-up—especially for patients with one or more chronic conditions such as congestive heart failure and diabetes—to reduce costly readmissions to the hospital and significantly reduce costs (Berry et al, 2011; Jack et al, 2009).
- As advocates for evidence-based practice, nurses can engage in robust evidence-based quality improvement projects that will lead to improved patient outcomes and significantly lower costs by reducing the occurrence of complications such as pressure ulcers, falls, and central-line infections (Goetz et al, 2011).
- As advocates for efficient operations, nurses must be proactive in evaluating staffing patterns and care delivery models along with delegating non-nursing tasks to ancillary personnel to ensure high-quality care and reduce unnecessary costs (Hader, 2009).
- As advocates for appropriate supply usage, nurses can become involved in identifying the most cost-effective medical-surgical supplies that can replace more expensive products (Goetz et al, 2011).

As nurses step up to the challenge of enhancing the *value* of health care—improved quality and lower costs—they must be able to measure and document their contributions. Only by understanding the basics of budgeting and costs can nurses demonstrate their contributions toward reduced readmissions, reduced complications, reduced never events, reduced length of stay, improvements in supply use costs, and overall lower costs per patient combined with increased quality.

SUMMARY

The financial well-being of health care organizations—and the value of health care—rests largely in the hands of the clinical team, with the budget serving as the financial guideline that enables the clinical team to provide quality patient care and achieve strategic goals. This chapter has reviewed the four major functions of the organization's budget: planning, communicating and coordinating, monitoring progress, and evaluating performance. Elements of the three basic types of budgets—operational, labor, and capital—have been described along with the two primary approaches to budgeting—incremental and zero-based. The nurse's role in affecting the organization's financial performance by being an advocate for proper patient discharges and follow-up, evidence-based practice, efficient operations, appropriate supply use, and preventing complications and hospital-acquired conditions is also reviewed.

The reader is cautioned that this chapter merely provides a general overview of budgeting basics to serve as a framework on which nurses can continue to build their knowledge of health care finance and budgeting. As nurses advance into supervisory and management positions, it is essential that they further develop their skills and knowledge in budgeting through personal study, working with mentors, attending classes, reading books and journals, and joining professional organizations that promote health care finance and budget knowledge.

REFERENCES

Berry D, Costanzo DM, Elliott B, et al: Preventing avoidable hospitalizations, *Home Health Nurse* 29(9):540–549, 2011.

Goetz K, Janney M, Ramsey K: When nursing takes ownership of financial outcomes: achieving exceptional financial performance through leadership, strategy and execution, *Nurs Econ* 29(4):173–182, 2011.

Hader R: Tightening the belt in 2009, *Nurs Manage* 40(1):6, 2009.

Jack BW, Chetty VK, Anthony D, et al: A reengineered hospital discharge program to decrease re-hospitalization: a randomized trial, *Ann Intern Med* 150(3):178–187, 2009.

Porter ME: What is value in health care? *New Engl J Med* 363(26):2477–2481, 2010.

Talley LB, Thorgrimson DH, Robinson NC: Financial literacy as an essential element in nursing management practice, *Nursing Economics* 31(2):77–82, 2013.

19

Effective Communication and Conflict Resolution

Anna Marie Sallee, PhD, MSN, RN

How is your message being received?

Ⓔ Additional resources are available online at: *http://evolve.elsevier.com/Cherry/*

"The greatest problem of communication is the illusion that it has been accomplished."
George Bernard Shaw

PROFESSIONAL/ETHICAL ISSUE

Altah is recent RN graduate who works on an active medical-surgical floor in a large hospital in a university town. She has observed a colleague using the computer system to look up information on acquaintances who have been hospitalized at the facility—even from previous years. One night she observes the RN looking up personal health information on a hospitalized athlete who plays at the university and is a local/regional celebrity. Altah knows the nurse's actions are unethical and illegal. However, she recognizes the nurse is well liked by both their co-workers and the administrative personnel at the hospital. She is vibrant and friendly and has many years of experience. Altah, however, is new to nursing and still on a high learning curve. As a single mother of two, she struggled to finish nursing school and support her family, accruing significant educational loans in the process. She is fearful that if the hospital administration feels forced to make a choice, she may lose her job. She struggles with whether to report the nurse or stay silent and hope that someone else will take action.

What ethical principles are in conflict here? Do you believe Altah's fears regarding her personal job security could be legitimate? What communication techniques will be important for Altah use in this situation? Discuss possible options for Altah.

VIGNETTE

Stacy Shannon, RN, the charge nurse on 4-East, receives a telephone call from the secretary in the emergency department (ED) to inform Stacy that a patient is ready for transfer. Stacy was expecting this patient, but had not anticipated the transfer would occur so soon and had not yet informed the nurse who would be assigned to the patient. The ED secretary explains that there are many patients waiting to be seen in the ED and it is becoming increasingly chaotic. Stacy replies that she will locate the nurse who will be assigned to the patient and facilitate the transfer as soon as possible. As Stacy goes down the hallway to locate this particular nurse, she learns that the nurse has left the unit on a short break and is expected back within 10 minutes.

Stacy calls the ED secretary to arrange for the transfer to occur in 20 minutes. To her surprise, she finds out that the patient has left the department and is being brought to 4-East immediately. Within a few moments, the patient and ED nurse arrive. The ED nurse states that he wants to give report on this patient quickly because he needs to return to the ED right away. Stacy assists him in transferring the patient to a bed and making the patient as comfortable as possible.

As Stacy completes this process, the nurse who was on break returns to the unit, learns that she has a new patient she did not expect, and immediately has to receive report from the ED nurse. Stacy notes through both body language and tone of voice that the interaction between the two nurses is less than cordial.

Within 10 minutes Stacy receives a telephone call from the ED charge nurse, who wants to discuss this incident. Negative comments are made about the 4-East nurse who left the unit "unannounced" and that "there is a concern for patient safety." How can Stacy best facilitate a positive outcome in this situation?

Questions to Consider While Reading this Chapter:
1. What communication strategies should Stacy use to respond to the accusations being made by the ED charge nurse and to help resolve the conflict?
2. What strategies can Stacy use to build a trusting relationship between her and the ED charge nurse?
3. What positive communication techniques could have prevented this situation from occurring?
4. What nonverbal cues might Stacy have observed between the two nurses during the report exchange?
5. Should Stacy have intervened when she observed the interaction between the two nurses? If so, how?
6. What strategies can Stacy implement to increase the communication skills of her staff?

KEY TERMS

Active communication: A participatory form of communication that promotes change.

Active listening: The process of hearing what others are saying with a sense of seriousness and discrimination.

Conflict: An experience in which there is simultaneous arousal of two or more incompatible motives.

Filtration: Unconscious exclusion of extraneous stimuli.

Information: The data that is meaningful and alters the receiver's understanding.

Interpretation: Receiver's understanding of the meaning of the communication.

Negative communication techniques: Behaviors that block or impair effective communication.

Perception: The manner in which one sees reality.

Positive communication techniques: Behaviors that enhance effective communication.

LEARNING OUTCOMES

After studying this chapter, the reader will be able to:
1. Outline factors that can influence the communication process.
2. Communicate effectively with diverse intergenerational and interdisciplinary team members.
3. Apply positive communication techniques in diverse situations.
4. Recognize negative communication techniques.
5. Evaluate conflicting verbal and nonverbal communication cues.
6. Examine constructive methods of communicating in conflict situations.
7. Respond to inappropriate use of logical fallacies in communication.
8. Develop professional social media interaction behaviors.

CHAPTER OVERVIEW

Effective communication is a foundational component of professional nursing practice. The development of effective communication skills can only enhance each nurse's professional image while building strong relationships with both patients and colleagues. Understanding communication processes and principles is required for nurses to interact professionally with patients, families and significant others, nursing peers, managers, student nurses, physicians, other members of the interdisciplinary team, and the public. Nurses communicate through a variety of media, including the spoken and written word, demonstration, role modeling, and on occasion, public appearances. The exchange of ideas and feelings is hardly limited to verbal communication. There are many types of nonverbal communication that are often as meaningful as, and in many instances more meaningful than, audible expression. Because communication is such a complex process, there are infinite opportunities for sending or receiving incorrect messages. All too frequently, communication is *faulty, resulting in misperceptions and misunderstandings. This chapter reviews the communication process and components, communication styles, and principles of effective communication in professional nursing, including special communication issues.*

OUR PROFESSION SPEAKS

"Nurses must be as proficient in communication skills as they are in clinical skills."

Standard 1, Standards for Establishing and Sustaining Health Work Environments, American Association of Critical Care Nurses (2005)

"No longer considered to be simply a patient's right, effective communication is now accepted as an essential component of quality care and patient safety."

The Joint Commission (2010)

THE COMMUNICATION PROCESS

"The human voice is the most beautiful instrument of all, but it is the most difficult to play."

Richard Strauss

Communication is a process requiring certain components. There must be a sender, a receiver, and a message. Effective communication is a dynamic process: with a response (feedback), the sender becomes the receiver, the receiver becomes the sender, and the message changes. The method of delivery influences the effectiveness of communication. In addition, communication is affected by many subcomponents, both environmental and in the mind of the communicators. When communication with another person occurs, verbally or nonverbally, a typical pattern develops that includes the actual message being sent, the receiver's belief or interpretation of that message, and the reaction to the message.

Think about the communication activities that occur in the health care setting. There is often much to communicate in a limited period of time and sometimes during very high stress situations. In addition to the actual message, personal goals or hidden agendas can influence the way a message is delivered and/or received. Because of this, it is very important to understand the many elements that influence the communication process.

Interpretation

Interpretation of information can be influenced by such factors as context, environment, precipitating event, preconceived ideas, personal perceptions, style of transmission, and past experiences. Because of the interaction of these factors, the sender's message may mean to the receiver something that was entirely unplanned or unexpected by the sender (see Fig. 19-1).

Context and Environment

Context refers to the entire situation relevant to the communication, such as the environment, the background, and the particular circumstances that lead to the discussion. Environment can denote physical surroundings and happenings and the emotional conditions involved in the communication.

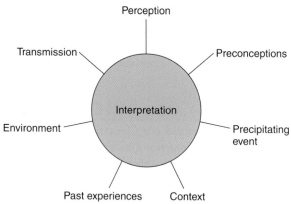

FIGURE 19-1 Factors Influencing Interpretation of Messages.

Precipitating Event

Precipitating event refers specifically to the event or situation that prompted the communication. Precipitating event is a specific single event, whereas context describes the whole ambiance of the situation with the inclusion of multiple circumstances that have led to the precipitating event.

Preconceived Ideas

Preconceived ideas are conceptions, opinions, or thoughts that the receiver has developed before the encounter. Such ideas can dramatically affect the receiver's acceptance and understanding of the message.

Style of Transmission

Style of transmission involves many aspects of the manner of conveyance of the message. Transmission styles include aspects such as open or closed statements or questions, body language, method of organizing the message, degree of attention to the topic or to the receiver, vocabulary chosen (professional jargon versus language a layperson could easily understand), and intonation.

Past Experiences

Each person comes to any type of communication, whether it is friendly conversation, informational lecture, staff meeting, performance evaluation, or any other possible scenario, with baggage in terms of past experiences. Because past experiences are a variety of positive, neutral, and negative events, the influence that the experiences can and will have on communication may be positive, neutral, or negative. **The importance of recognizing that any reaction from the receiver may be biased by previous experiences cannot be overstated.** An astute sender will begin to investigate such a possibility if the receiver reacts in an unexpected or inappropriate manner to information that was not expected to produce such a response, which may range from nonresponse to overly vehement response.

Personal Perceptions

Personal perceptions can have a profound effect on the quality of communication. Perception is awareness through the excitation of all the senses. Perception can be described as all that the person knows about a situation or circumstance based on what each of the senses—taste, smell, sight, sound, touch, and intuition—discover and interpret.

Filtration

The most concise delivery of information is subject to some amount of filtration. Think of the process as similar to washing vegetables in a colander. A large amount of water is poured over the produce. Some of the water comes quickly through the colander holes; some water drips through more slowly; and some water hangs on the contents or settles in the solid portions of the colander and never filters through. If people were not able to filter out a portion of the stimuli that bombard them daily, the clutter would be unmanageable! At the same time, however, it is possible to filter out some part of intended communication that is essential to facilitate understanding.

Feedback

Feedback, simply put, is the response from the receiver. However, as with all communication, feedback is a dynamic process. As the receiver interprets and responds to the original message, the sender begins the same process of feedback to the receiver. Because of this circular property, the process frequently is referred to as the *feedback loop* (van Servellen, 1997). As with the original message, feedback is not confined to verbal responses alone. Both communicants constantly assess nonverbal communication as well. Feedback is formed based on all the components of interpretation and filtration.

VERBAL VERSUS NONVERBAL COMMUNICATION

"What you do speaks so loud that I cannot hear what you say."

Ralph Waldo Emerson

"The most important thing in communication is hearing what isn't said."

Peter F. Drucker

Verbal Communication

Verbal communication is the most common form of interpersonal communication and involves talking and listening. An important clue to verbal communication is the tone or inflection with which the words are spoken and the general attitude used when speaking. Suzette Haden Elgin refers to the "tune the words are set to" (1993). The key to the true meaning of a statement may be contained in the emphasis placed on a specific word. Consider how differently the following phrase could be perceived based on the inflection or the emphasis on the wording:

- You are going to **bed.**
- **You** are going to bed.
- You **are going** to bed.

With an emphasis on *bed,* the first phrase most likely will be perceived as an inquiry. The second phrase might imply that you are going to bed, but no one else is. The last phrase, an imperative (or command), gives the impression of increased emotion, such as anger or frustration.

Another element central to verbal interaction is the concept of attitude. Being aware of and learning to understand the concept of attitude is key to effective communication. Attitude involves a predisposition or tendency to respond in one way or another. Often the attitude that accompanies a verbal interaction, which can be positive or negative, is much more meaningful than the actual words spoken. Although we may hear "attitude" in a person's tone of voice, it is most often communicated loud and clear through nonverbal communication.

Nonverbal Communication

"Oops! Did I just roll my eyes out loud?"

Facebook Posting

Nonverbal communication involves many factors that either confirm or deny the spoken word. Facial expression, the presence or absence of eye contact, posture, and body movement all project a direct message. Indirect nonverbal messages might include dressing style, lifestyle, or material possessions. Never presume that external trappings and physical presentation do not influence the quality of communication. Preconceived ideas and expectations interpret input from all such sources, often on an almost subconscious level.

Consider the following scenario: Rhonda, a young wife and mother, was admitted to the ED with significant abdominal pain. As the nurse inquires about her symptoms, Rhonda repeatedly glances at her husband, Tommy, before she answers. Although she denies any pain at this time, you observe that she guards her stomach, has a "clenched" jaw line, and does not make eye contact with you. As you assess and question Rhonda, Tommy often interrupts with comments such as, "She's just fine. It was only a stomach ache, and it's gone this morning, isn't it, dear?" Which message seems more likely to be true—the verbal or the nonverbal? How will you address the nonverbal cues? As you read the remainder of this chapter, consider strategies that you can use to enhance communication between this husband and wife.

The inability to make eye contact may be construed to mean that the speaker is shy, scared, or not telling the truth. The judgment of which condition is the correct one is based on all the factors that feed into the receiver's interpretation—perception, preconceptions, precipitating event, context, past experiences, environment, and transmission. Faced with the many opportunities for incorrect interpretation, is it any wonder that misunderstandings occur?

An important concept to remember is that when the verbal message and the nonverbal message do not agree, the receiver is more likely to believe the nonverbal message. In 1971, Albert Mehrabian (1981) conducted a seminal study on nonverbal communication in which he found that most communication is 55% nonverbal, 38% vocal signals (such as tone, pitch, or pace), and **only 7% the actual words we say**. Mehrabian's study has significantly influenced our understanding of the "silent messages" we send. In fact, body language is often the most trusted indicator for conveying feelings, attitudes, and emotions (Borg, 2011) because it so often comes from our subconscious—which is much less likely to deceive! Nonverbal language includes such things as dress, posture, facial expression, eye contact, body movements, body tension, spatial distance, touch, and voice.

Kim Holland (2013) states eloquently: "Patients see our hearts through our eyes. It takes an incredible amount of professionalism to appear relaxed, make eye contact and help our patient know—for that brief moment—we are with them." Body positioning toward the patient, a relaxed stance, a gentle touch, and an open face will signal your total presence.

An understanding of the importance prescribed to body language and other nonverbal clues to the intent of the message explains the advantage of face-to-face communication whenever possible. Although a telephone conversation supplies verbal messages, intonation, and feedback, other signals are missing such as facial expression, body position, and environmental clues. The perils inherent in written and electronic communication will be discussed later in this chapter.

POSITIVE COMMUNICATION TECHNIQUES

Effective communication involves a positive exchange of ideas between or among individuals. The successful communicator will strive to demonstrate openness, availability, and acceptance both verbally and nonverbally. The following are some of the many techniques that will help achieve positive communication style.

Developing Trust

Trust between the nurse and the patient is essential to good communication and often must be cultivated. Factors that enhance the development of trust include openness on the part of the nurse, honesty, integrity, and dependability. These can be achieved by doing the following:

- Communicating clearly in language that laypersons can understand
- Keeping promises
- Protecting confidentiality
- Avoiding negative communication techniques such as blocking and false reassurance
- Being available to the patient

The need for trust in the health care setting is not limited to the nurse-patient relationship, but rather pervades all working relationships. Care is more effective when the nursing team and the interprofessional team share the essential element of trust.

Using "I" Messages

The use of "I" messages is a fundamental component in acceptable communication. Consider the following exchange.

Laura: "You make me so mad, Donald."

Donald: "I don't mean to make you mad."

Laura: "Well, you do. You never think about how I feel. You know I hate it when you leave a patient's room as cluttered as 103."

Donald: "You don't have the vaguest idea what went on here last night! That's what I hate about you—always

so quick to judge. You are so critical. You must think that you are perfect!"

When a comment starts with "you," most commonly the receiver's defenses will promptly go on alert. The use of "you" in such a context sounds—and most probably is meant to be—accusatory. Notice how the emotions quickly escalate to anger. Also notice that although the receiver initially tries to sound conciliatory, he soon begins to respond in a similar accusatory form. Instead of using accusatory and defensive language, the sender should frame the comment in terms of how it makes her or him feel. Consider this alternative:

Laura: "Donald, I feel so upset when I find a cluttered room like 103 at the beginning of my shift. I feel as if I am behind when I start."

The difference is obvious. When "I" messages are used, they become less likely to sound accusatory. By using such an opening, the sender allows the receiver to respond to the true message rather than start to mount a defense. It allows for more effective communication because the receiver is more likely to offer an explanation such as the following:

Donald: "I'm really sorry about room 103, Laura. I guess the wheel that doesn't squeak doesn't get oiled, as they say. Our shift started last night with a patient coding right after he arrived from the emergency room. There was no family here. It took forever to find them and then to support them through the shock. About the time things settled down, the patient in room 110 coded. It was quite a night."

In this instance, the "I" message enhances communication by giving Donald the opportunity to address the real concern. In addition, if Laura is truly astute, she has a wonderful opportunity to support her colleague by voicing appreciation for the working circumstances of his shift. Most people respond gratefully to recognition and commiseration. The exchange could build collegiality between the two coworkers and perhaps between the two shifts.

Establishing Eye Contact

As mentioned previously, the avoidance of eye contact can be interpreted in a number of different ways. A person who does not make eye contact may be thought to be shy, scared, insecure, preoccupied, unprepared, or dishonest—the list could go on and on. None of these qualities is likely to be appreciated in a primary caregiver. By making direct eye contact, the nurse gives undivided attention to the patient, and the patient is likely to feel valued and understood by the nurse. Eye contact in essence says, "I am wholly available to you. What you are saying is important to me."

Eye contact is equally important in communication with coworkers and other members of the interprofessional team. This quality is lost in telephone conversations or written communications.

Keep in mind, however, that the use of direct eye contact is a Western value. In some cultures, avoidance of eye contact is considered more appropriate social behavior. By careful observation, the nurse quickly will recognize whether direct eye contact is interpreted as inappropriate or disrespectful. Nurses must make every effort to be sensitive to the cultural values of the client and their coworkers to enhance effective communication.

Keeping Promises

Little else can destroy the fragile trust developing in any interpersonal relationship as quickly as making and then breaking promises. Inherent in the concept of promise keeping are the qualities of honesty and integrity. Once a commitment is made, every effort must be expended to fulfill the expectation. Sometimes the request is impossible to satisfy. If this happens, the nurse must explain the situation or circumstances. The fact that the patient understands the nurse has made an effort to meet his or her needs or desires often is more important than whether the goal is accomplished. If the nurse responds, "I'll check on that," and then finds the request impossible to fulfill, but never returns with an explanation, the lack of dependability perceived by the patient (or colleague) will surely drive a wedge into the relationship.

Expressing Empathy

Empathy is the ability to mentally place oneself in another person's situation to better understand the person and to share the emotions or feelings of that person. Empathy is not feeling sorry for another; rather, it is understanding the experiences of the other person, and it is integral to the therapeutic relationship. The nurse is able to perceive and address the needs of the patient without becoming so emotionally involved as to become inappropriately immersed in the situation.

Using Open Communication

Certain styles of phrasing questions and statements lend themselves to obtaining more information. For example, suppose Chris asks Mr. Barrow, "Do you know where you are?" and Mr. Barrow responds, "Yes." Can Chris assume that Mr. Barrow knows he is in the hospital? Not necessarily. Chris may be surprised to hear a completely unexpected response if he rephrases the inquiry:

Chris: "Mr. Barrow, tell me where you are."

Mr. Barrow: "Why, I'm in the honeymoon berth of the *Titanic*, of course. Have you seen my lovely bride?"

Using open-ended questions or statements that require more information than "yes" or "no" can help gather enough facts to build a more complete picture of the circumstances. Questions or statements that are phrased to require only one- or two-word responses may miss the mark entirely.

Clarifying Information

Both communicants have a responsibility to clarify anything not understood. The sender should ask for feedback to be certain the receiver is correctly interpreting what is being said. The receiver should stop the sender anytime the message becomes unclear and should provide feedback regularly so that misinterpretation can be identified quickly. Such phrases as "What I hear you saying is . . . " or "I understand you to mean . . . " help to communicate to the sender what is being perceived. Other techniques of clarification include using easily understood language, giving examples, drawing a picture, making a list, and finding ways to stimulate all the senses to enhance the ability to understand.

Being Aware of Body Language

Body positioning and movement send loud messages to others. The nurse can imply openness that facilitates effective communication by awareness of body position and movement. In addition to eye contact, effective communication is enriched through an open stance, such as holding one's arms at the side or out toward the patient, rather than crossed, or leaning toward the patient as if to hear more clearly, rather than away from the patient.

Using Touch

Most people have a fairly well-defined personal space. It is important for the nurse to be sensitive to each patient's personal preference and cultural differences in terms of touch. However, for many people, a gentle touch can scale mountains in terms of demonstrating genuine interest and concern. A pat on the back, a hand held, a touch on the shoulder—these are all behaviors that indicate availability and accessibility on the part of the nurse.

NEGATIVE COMMUNICATION TECHNIQUES

Several negative communication techniques have been alluded to in the previous discussion. Closed communication styles, such as asking yes-or-no questions or making inquiries or statements that require other single-word answers, potentially limit the response of the person and may prevent the discovery of pertinent facts. Closed body language can also hinder effective communication. Crossed arms, hands on the hips, avoidance of eye contact, turning away from the person, and moving away from the person all impose a sense of distance in the relationship. Three other techniques that are detrimental to good communication are termed *blocking, false assurances,* and *conflicting messages.*

Blocking

Blocking occurs when the nurse responds with noncommittal or generalized answers. For example:

"Nurse, I've never had surgery before. I'm afraid I might not ever wake up." Mr. Clayton is twisting the bed sheet as he speaks.

"Oh, Mr. Clayton, many people feel that way. It'll be okay." Makayla Butler, RN, smiles brightly, pats his hand, picks up the dirty linen bag, and bounces out of the room.

Does Mr. Clayton feel reassured? Not likely. Will he be inclined to broach the subject with Makayla again? Probably not. Makayla has incorporated some important aspects of positive communication into her response—cheerfulness and touch—but she has not truly communicated. She has effectively blocked Mr. Clayton's attempt to get the reassurance he wanted from her. He may be too intimidated to ask anyone else, assuming that his fear is invalid.

By generalizing in this way, Makayla has trivialized Mr. Clayton's concerns. He is not "many people." He needs to be validated as an individual experiencing a legitimate feeling. Makayla can validate his fear and put

it into perspective at the same time with a different approach.

Makayla: "What makes you think you might not wake up, Mr. Clayton?"

Mr. Clayton: "Well, my wife's cousin's husband had surgery about 25 years ago, and he never woke up."

Makayla: "What kind of surgery did he have?"

Mr. Clayton: "Uh, it was some kind of heart surgery, and he had another heart attack on the table and died right there."

Makayla: "It sounds like his condition was critical going into surgery."

Mr. Clayton: "Yes, ma'am. He'd been sick for a long time."

Makayla: "It's not uncommon to feel afraid of having anesthesia, especially if you have never had surgery before. There are rare cases in which complications do occur during surgery. That's why we put the disclosures on the consent form, so that you will know just what the risks are. Thankfully, though, most surgeries are without such drastic problems. Although your gallbladder certainly has made you uncomfortable, you are otherwise in good health. The tests that were done before surgery, like the chest radiograph and the laboratory work, show that you are healthy and should do well with the anesthesia. That drastically decreases the chance for complications in your case. I will be glad to answer any other questions you have or to ask the anesthetist to come and talk with you some more."

Makayla has validated Mr. Clayton's feeling as legitimate, provided an explanation with reasonable reassurances, and offered to explore the issue with him further or to have someone else talk with him.

Some things are difficult to talk about with another person. The dying patient may want to talk about how he or she feels, ask questions, or perform a life review. A nurse who is uncomfortable with such topics may consciously or unconsciously block communication through generalizations or closed responses. Avoidance of the blocking technique requires a good understanding of oneself. If unable to provide the open communication the patient obviously needs, the nurse should access other personnel who are more comfortable in the situation.

False Assurances

False assurances are similar to blocking and have about the same effect. When someone is trying to get real answers or express serious concerns, an answer such as "Don't worry" or "It'll be okay" sends several unintended messages. Such answers can be interpreted by the patient as placating or showing a lack of concern or a lack of knowledge of the situation. The patient might even conclude that the nurse is being neglectful through trivialization of an issue that is important to him or her. At the very least, the nurse has neither recognized the need the patient has expressed nor provided validation.

Conflicting Messages

Conflicting messages also have been alluded to in the previous discussion. If a person professes pleasure at seeing someone but draws back when that person extends a hand of greeting, the nonverbal message speaks more loudly than the words spoken. If a nurse enters a room and goes through the routine greeting by rote (even with a smiling face and a bouncing step), a patient can quickly perceive this and consider the nurse less approachable.

The nurse's statement that the patient's condition is important to the nurse followed by failing to answer the call bell in a timely manner or by forgetting to bring items promised to the patient sends a double message. Such behavior can leave the patient confused, frustrated, or angry. Carrying through with a commitment, no matter how unimportant it may seem, is a premier method of saying to the person, "You are important to me."

Logical Fallacies

Logical fallacies are related to an individual's culture, gender, background, and personal experiences and are barriers to meaningful communication. Individuals often cannot separate moods, thoughts, and perceptions, for they become interconnected in one continuous evaluation process, involving feeling, thinking, and responding. In times of increased stress, as is common in health care settings, it is more likely that people will employ faulty thinking that affects the communication process. Recognition of distortions and faulty logic will promote effective communication and reduce confusion or even prevent conflict. Following are examples of logical fallacies that are frequently encountered. Visit the following website to learn more about other types of logical fallacies that can impede effective communication: *http://www.nizkor.org/features/fallacies/*

Ad Hominem Abusive

Ad hominem abusive is an argument that attacks the person instead of the issue. The speaker hopes to discredit the other person by calling attention to some irrelevant fact about that person. Perhaps a nurse has just had a disagreement with a physician about lab results that were not properly reported. The nurse makes the following comment to colleagues: "She thinks she's so smart just because she's a doctor." What does that have to do with the disagreement? Nothing. It is an unwarranted attack on the doctor. Does it accomplish the purpose? Very likely, the group will be influenced by the disparaging comment. They may also become angry at the physician, who had legitimate cause to be upset about not receiving lab results. Ultimately, the issue of unreported lab values is lost in the personal attack against the physician.

Appeal to Emotion

Appeal to emotion is an attempt to manipulate other people's emotions in order to avoid the real issue. For example, consider Deb Engles, RN, who has repeatedly failed to document patient care properly. She has been called into the nurse manager's office to discuss the incident and receives a written warning. She comes out tearful. It is obvious to her colleagues that she has been reprimanded. She begins to discuss the problem and makes the following statements: "I am the first person in my family to even go to college. I'm a single parent, and I've worked so hard to get where I am. Our manager doesn't care anything about that. She just wants to pass out written warnings to cover herself. She doesn't care about us as individuals." After a bit of this type of talk, the entire staff is probably becoming angry with the nurse manager—who may feel bad that she had to give the written warning because she does indeed care about her staff. However, Deb has successfully deflected the attention away from the real issue, failure to document properly, which was legitimately addressed.

Red Herring

Red herring is the introduction of an irrelevant topic in order to divert attention away from the real issue. Two nurses, Brian and Nikoah, are having an argument regarding Brian's failure to complete his assigned tasks. Brian states, "It's not my work that you're really mad about. It's that I'm a guy. You just don't like male nurses." Nikoah then begins to defend herself, denying any prejudice against male nurses. The focus of the argument has been turned from the real issue, Brian's failure to complete his assigned tasks, to a situation in which Nikoah is on the defensive about her opinion of male nurses.

Understanding cognitive distortions and logical fallacies should help the nurse recognize the difference between legitimate and faulty reasoning. A clear understanding and use of sound logic will help health care providers resolve problems and stay focused on the true issues.

LISTENING

> "Nature has given men one tongue and two ears, in token that we should listen twice as much as we speak."
>
> **Epictetus**

Listening certainly is as important an element in clear and effective communication as any other component. Many distracters contribute to poor listening habits. Framing an answer while the other person is still talking interferes with receiving the entire message. Environmental disturbances can provide major disruption. A crying baby, a call light buzzing, or multiple concurrent conversations in a busy nurses' station are a few of the interruptions that jumble the simplest of instructions. Preexisting concerns or worries can block absorption of conversation because of the preoccupation. Attempts to continue work-in-progress leads to inattention. Ineffective engagement or peculiar mannerisms on the part of the speaker can be distracting. A person who does not make eye contact, shuffles through papers while talking, or overuses hand movements actually can deter communication. Listening involves three purposeful steps: *Hearing* is listening enough to know what was said. *Understanding* is processing the information you heard. *Judging* is making a decision about what you heard. Does it make sense? Do you believe it? Can you respond appropriately to it (Pearson Education, 2014)?

A number of techniques can be used by the receiver to facilitate the ability to listen:

- Give undivided attention to the sender by moving to a quieter area to avoid distractions and stopping the speaker to clarify any points not understood.
- Provide feedback in terms of the perceived meaning of the message by rephrasing in the receiver's own words.
- Give attention to positioning so you are facing the sender and making eye contact.
- Note nonverbal messages, such as body language, and respond to them.
- Finish listening before you begin to speak.

If you have accomplished each of these steps, you have engaged in active listening. Active listening will dramatically improve the likelihood of receiving the correct message. Equally important, active listening implies a respect for the speaker and communicates a regard for what the speaker has to offer. The nonverbal message that active listening delivers is, "I value you, and what you have to say is important to me."

WRITTEN AND ELECTRONIC COMMUNICATION

> "Clear, accurate, and accessible documentation is an essential element of safe, quality, evidence-based nursing practice."
>
> **American Nurses Association (2010)**

> "I admire machinery as much as any man, and am as thankful to it as any man can be for what it does for us. But, it will never be a substitute for the face of a man, with his soul in it, encouraging another man to be brave and true."
>
> **Charles Dickens**

Charles Dickens referred to the brand new telegraph when he admired machinery. Little could he imagine the advances of electronic communication over the decades. But his message is as appropriate today as in the late 1800s. Nothing quite replaces face-to-face communication and the accompanying nonverbal cues. However, written and electronic communication do open valuable new levels of connection and information exchange.

Health care in the United States is rapidly moving to computer-based electronic health records (EHRs) to impact higher-quality patient care. By 2013, approximately 80% of hospitals implemented EHRs (Jayanthi, 2014) and 78% of office-based physicians use some form of EHRs (Centers for Disease Control, 2014). Unique issues impact the transition to the EHR. Perhaps the most positive aspect is in improved communication among health care providers within the institution as well as between geographically distant sites, which results in prompt and knowledgeable care for individual patients. On the negative side is concern about maintaining patient confidentiality and privacy, an expectation that must be met with diligent attention to appropriate system management and careful individual protection of information, passwords, and other access sources for the EHR.

As communication moves into the cyber environment with the use of the EHR, e-mail and attachments, intranets, chatrooms for clinical discussions/meetings, and into the realm of social media (see discussion later in this chapter), the style of health care recording is changing. Nurses' electronic clinical notes often comprise detailed checklists, which are designed to address a myriad of potential findings and streamline time spent charting. However, most checklist pages include a box for additional comments/explanations, and charting programs include some vehicle for a narrative entry. The following discussion is just as applicable to electronic charting as to pen-and-paper charting…perhaps even more so. By their very nature, checklists do not allow for the unexpected or aberrant event. As tempting as it may be to confine the nursing record to the checklists, some occurrences simply cannot be adequately described without a narrative entry.

Accuracy

Absolute accuracy is paramount in recording legal documentation. For the nurse, this most specifically applies to the nursing notes or any other entry in the patient's chart. Every effort should be made to report concisely, descriptively, and truthfully. To write "Patient walked today" is not adequate. A more concise and descriptive entry reads, "Patient walked to the nurses' station and back three times this shift, a total distance of 96 yards." (Many hospitals have distance measures marked in the hallway for this purpose.)

Consider the following situation: Cody Johnson, RN, entered the patient's room and found her agitated and speaking loudly into the telephone as she twisted her hair with her free hand. She was crying and periodically pounded the bedside table with her fist. Later, the patient told Cody that she had been talking with her mother. Would it be appropriate for Cody to chart, "Patient became very angry with her mother while talking on the telephone." No. The nurse must be diligent not to include personal judgments or quantify the patient's emotional state in such terms.

More accurately, Cody could chart, "Patient found crying while talking on the telephone in a loud tone to her mother. Patient was twisting her hair and hitting bedside table with her fist." The information is descriptive and states exactly what Cody observed factually without any judgmental conclusions. If, however, the patient had said, "My mother makes me so mad," Cody could have charted the statement as a direct quote (enclosed in quotation marks).

Attention to Detail

In addition to absolute accuracy, written documents should be descriptive. As mentioned in the previous section, information should be quantified whenever possible. How many feet did the patient walk? How many times was the patient out of bed? How many cubic centimeters of fluid did the patient drink? Precisely what did the patient say?

Words can be used to depict a verbal picture of a wound, rash, bruise, or any type of injury or situation. Illustrative terms can create a mental image for the person reading the notes, memo, or other communication. Descriptive categories can include measurement, color, position, location, drainage, or condition when speaking of a physical condition; or time, setting, people present, issues, or goals discussed; or direct quotes when speaking of a meeting, conference, evaluation, or other interchange. Consider the differences between the following written communications:

- "1000: Dressing change completed. Site healthy."
- "1000: Dressing change completed. Edges of 4-inch surgical wound approximated, no drainage noted. Skin pink without any redness or edema."

The second entry allows the reader to "see" the wound mentally and follow the progress of healing, even when unable to be present at the time of the dressing change. A good rule when describing any kind of break in skin integrity—whether from a stabbing, a surgical wound, an intravenous line, and so on—is to describe color, drainage, and presence or absence of edema.

Consider the written communication in Box 19-1. What does this message really tell the nurse manager? Not much—only that there is some kind of perceived problem between Lucas and the students. The nurse manager does not know based on the information provided if the problem is "real," if it is based on a bias of Jessica's or a student bias, if the problem has

---

BOX 19-1 Incomplete E-Mail Message

E-Mail Message Date 12/18/2015

To:	Bonnie Thompson, RN, BSN, Nurse Manager
From:	Jessica Lindsay, RN, BSN, Charge Nurse
Subject:	Student precepting

I have had lots of complaints about Lucas Alfred's treatment of students. I do not think he should be assigned as a preceptor anymore and do not plan to do so from now on.

BOX 19-2 Descriptive, Thorough E-Mail Message

E-Mail Message Date 12/19/2015

To:	Bonnie Thompson, RN, BSN, nurse manager
From:	Jessica Lindsay, RN, BSN, charge nurse
Subject:	Student precepting

Today (Monday, August 18) at 0710 I observed what appeared to be an animated conversation between Lucas Alfred, RN, and John Roberts, a student nurse from North Hills University. As I moved toward them, I heard Lucas say loudly, "Well, you better stay with me because I am not going to come looking for you all day. I know how lazy students are." I asked Lucas, "Is there a problem?" He replied, "Oh, no problem. I just hate having students, that's all. They're more trouble than they're worth." I asked Lucas, "Would you prefer that I reassign the student?" He shrugged his shoulders and walked away. I suggested to the student that I assign him to another nurse for the day. He responded, "I'd really appreciate that. Mr. Alfred has let me know since I arrived that he didn't want to work with me."

Because this group of students has been on the unit 2 days per week for the past 3 weeks, I spoke to the other students who had worked with Lucas and asked them how things had gone. The other three students who have worked with him reported similar experiences.

I would like to arrange a time to meet with you and Lucas to address this problem.

---

occurred more than once, if an interpersonal communication problem or misunderstanding exists, or if obvious mistreatment of a student or students has occurred.

Now consider the written communication in Box 19-2. Carefully constructing a factual message of this length is more time-consuming initially, but it will save a lot of frustration in the long run. The nurse manager now has a clear picture of what has occurred and knows that an ongoing problem exists. Most appropriately, Jessica will speak to Bonnie about the problem, even if only briefly. However, a written account of the incident must be submitted and should be composed promptly while the facts are freshly remembered. Additionally, written communication often is the first source of contact because the nurse manager is not likely to be immediately available on all shifts.

The skill of writing concisely yet descriptively must be developed. Over some time, nurses build a repertoire of phrases and illustrative terminology that are useful and effective. Often, when a nurse is stumped as to how to express a situation, she or he will ask a colleague, "How would you write . . . ?" Accessing the experience and expertise of nursing peers is productive in terms of problem solving while also demonstrating respect for the colleague.

Thoroughness

The message examples in the previous section also illustrate the need for thoroughness. In addition to being descriptive in terms of the incident, Jessica's message in Box 19-2 reported her interview with other nursing students. By doing so, Jessica is thorough in describing and reporting the extent of the problem she has discovered. Providing such completeness of information helps to prevent communication breakdown. Anticipating and answering relevant questions before they are asked exemplifies thoroughness and clarifies communication.

Conciseness

Written communication must be concise. The message must state the necessary information as clearly and as briefly as possible. Consider the message written in Box 19-3. Whew! Extraneous details tend to confuse more than clarify. An inherent dilemma often develops as the nurse attempts to determine how to be descriptive and concise at the same time. One must determine what facts are pertinent to enable the reader to understand the true message. When in doubt and when appropriate, the writer can ask another party to read the message and provide feedback to the writer as to what the reader believes the message means. However,

BOX 19-3   Unclear, Rambling E-Mail Message

E-Mail Message Date 12/18/2015

To: Bonnie Thompson, RN, BSN, Nurse Manager
From: Jessica Lindsay, RN, BSN, Charge Nurse
Subject: Student precepting

Today at about 0730 (it may have been earlier because I don't remember whether the breakfast trays had been served or not), I observed what appeared to be an animated conversation between Lucas Alfred, RN, and John Roberts, SN, a student nurse from North Hills University. I thought they might be arguing, but I couldn't tell for sure, so I decided to go over and see what the conversation was about. It really seemed like Lucas was angry because he was talking loudly and not smiling and neither was the student smiling, and I heard Lucas say, "Well, you better stay with me because I am not going to come looking for you all day. I know how lazy students are." Well I could just imagine how that made the student feel, so I asked, "Is there a problem?" even though it was pretty obvious that something was wrong. Lucas said, "Oh, no problem. I just hate having students, that's all. They're more trouble than they're worth." I asked Lucas, "Would you prefer that I reassign the student?" He shrugged his shoulders and walked away. Well I don't know for sure about the student, but I really thought that was rude. I suggested to the student that I assign him to another nurse for the day. He responded, "I'd really appreciate that. He has let me know since I arrived that he didn't want to work with me." Well I know how that would make me feel—to be a student and be treated that way.

The same group of students has been on the unit 2 days a week for the past 3 weeks (maybe a month, I'm not sure, and some of them may have been here on makeup days too), so I talked to other students who had worked with Lucas and asked them how things had been going. They said he'd acted the same way to them. We need to talk to him.

the right to confidentiality and privacy of the people involved must be observed. This basic principle applies to patients, families, students, members of the health care team—to all persons. Consequently, the nurse must be as judicious in handling written material in a confidential matter, as with any other form of communication.

Electronic Communication

"When speaking aloud you punctuate constantly—with body language. Your listener hears commas, dashes, question marks, exclamation points, [and] quotation marks as you shout, whisper, pause, wave your arms, roll your eyes, wrinkle your brow. In writing, punctuation plays the role of body language. It helps the readers hear the way you want to be heard."

Russell Baker

More and more communication is computer-based using e-mail, text messages, chatrooms, file attachments, and other electronic modes. The computer-based written record can be somewhat more transient than other written documents. For example, e-mails are often read and then deleted. However, remember that communication via the computer can be saved and is often retrievable even after deletion. As with any form of written communication, computer-based interaction loses nonverbal cues. Therefore, it is important for the sender to elicit feedback and/or for the receiver to ask for clarification if the meaning of the communication is not clear.

COMMUNICATION STYLES

Communication is influenced by a myriad of individual characteristics learned over a lifetime. However, communication specialists generally recognize four basic communication styles: (1) assertive, (2) aggressive, (3) passive, (4) passive-aggressive (Rose, 2007).

Assertive Communication

The healthiest form of communication is the assertive style. Assertive individuals pronounce their basic rights without violating the rights of others. Assertive communicators are honest and direct while valuing and respecting other individuals' views and seeking a win-win solution without the use of manipulation or game-playing. Assertiveness includes active listening and reflective feedback so that other individuals recognize that their opinions are valued as the assertive communicator seeks to find an acceptable solution without compromising his or her own needs.

Assertive communication requires self-confidence and the ability to set limits rather than succumbing to pressure to avoid disappointing or hurting others at the expense of one's own needs and expectations. While it is the most effective style of communication, healthy assertiveness is difficult for many people to develop. Therefore, assertive communication is the style most people use least (Angelfire, 2009).

Aggressive Communication

Aggressive communicators make decisions for themselves and others with the intent of always coming out the winner. Aggressive individuals want their needs met exclusively and immediately, using guilt, hurt, anger, and a repertoire of other manipulation tools. Aggressiveness may include honesty but in a hurtful, manipulative way. Aggressive individuals commonly feel superior to others and behave in very controlling ways. Persons with whom they communicate often feel humiliated, defensive, resentful, and hurt. Aggressive behavior often leads to and certainly escalates conflict.

Passive Communication

Passive communicators are the polar opposite of aggressive communicators. They allow others to make decisions for them in the hope of avoiding confrontation or difficult situations. Passive communicators are typically inhibited, indirect, and self-denying because they feel that is the safe route. If they win in a situation, it is purely by chance, typically because they happen to share the opinion of the more aggressive person in the exchange. Passive individuals are dishonest because they would rather succumb than state their true feelings or needs.

Passive-Aggressive Communication

Passive-aggressive communicators combine the worst of both styles. These individuals avoid direct confrontation while manipulating others in order to achieve their personal goals. They appear to be honest but "come in the back door" by undermining other individuals through gossip, pouting, playing the victim, and other manipulative behaviors that create or escalate conflict. They win in situations by making other individuals look bad.

SPECIAL INFLUENCES ON COMMUNICATION

Development of truly effective communication necessitates understanding various circumstances that influence communication. In addition to the concepts discussed up to this point, characteristics exist that might impede efficacious exchange of information. Issues such as gender

differences, generational differences, cultural diversity, and dissimilarities in the professional approach of the various health care disciplines all contribute to disparate understandings and interpretations.

Communication and Gender Differences

A significant clarification must be made regarding communication between men and women. The information about gender differences resulting from socialization (although based on research and many years of observations and writings) are generalizations and should be viewed from that perspective. Attributes described do not necessarily apply to all persons or all of the time. Nevertheless, a plethora of observations indicate that men and women solve problems, make decisions, and communicate from different perspectives based on socialization that begins shortly after birth. Typically, boys are taught to be tough and competitive; girls are taught to be nice and avoid conflict. Dr. Pat Heim (1995) suggests, "Playing team sports boys learn to compete, be aggressive, play to win, strategize, take risks, mask emotions, and focus on the goal line." Regarding girls' play, Dr. Heim comments, "Relationships are central in girls' culture and therefore they learn to negotiate differences, seek win-win solutions, and focus on what is fair for all instead of winning."

Some progress has been made over the years since Heim made these comments and as women move into more lateral working situations, but the problem of gender communication style differences persists. Booher (2012) echoes these thoughts in light of today's work environment: "Little did we know that the communication differences we experienced as children on the playground would move from the classroom to the boardroom. Neither men nor women are better communicators. They're just different."

For the most part, women work toward compromise, even when it means relinquishing some of the original goal. Often, women use indirect channels such as questions to guide a conversation toward the point they want to make. Preserving relationships is usually of paramount importance to women. The role of peacemaker and nurturer has been a traditional expectation of women throughout the ages.

Generally, men work toward winning. Traditional role expectations of men have included provider and protector. Men learn early in life how to focus on goals and move aggressively toward accomplishment. Team sports teach men that relationships are not destroyed in the "battle" (Heim, 1995). Consequently, men have been socialized to behave assertively when such performance is needed in pursuit of the goal and then move on without loss of friendships. Women have been socialized that assertive behavior will endanger relationships and that conflict should be avoided to preserve friendships.

Men typically use communication as a tool to deliver information, whereas women value the process of communication itself as an important part of the relationship. Therefore in an effort to improve communication, men might try spending more time in discussion, and women might try to phrase comments more succinctly. Consider the following conversation.

Nurse: "Dr. Vernon, this is Holly Michaels, RN. I'm calling to talk to you about Mrs. Guevara. She says she's having more pain and feels a little dizzy. I've given her pain medicine as soon as I can each time. She says she's a little nauseated. Her husband's in the room, and he says she feels worse too. She did not sleep much last night and has not been able to nap today."

Physician: "I have patients to see. Just give me the facts."

Nurse: "Okay, she has received her medication every 4 to 5 hours this shift. I do not know if she needs a higher dose or just needs the medication more frequently, or maybe we should try a different medicine."

Physician: "What are her vitals? Does she have any drug allergies?"

Nurse: "Just a second, and I'll get the chart."

Physician: "Confound it, when you get your act together, call me back."

Dr. Vernon slams down the telephone.

Consider the many communication styles and concepts illustrated by the previous conversation. Preparedness, conciseness, contributing environmental conditions (patients waiting), and even courtesy are issues that could be more competently addressed. The fact that the conversation is occurring by telephone instead of in person also is a factor responsible for the lack of eye contact and the lost potential for additional information through other body language. Telephone conversations are a fact of life in health care. Careful planning and preparation of what will be said will facilitate effective information exchange. In the professional setting especially, men are more prone to favor brief, concise information exchange. In the professional setting, women still tend to prefer verbal problem solving as the situation is discussed. Knowledge of the gender differences in communication style could have altered the nurse's telephone call in the following manner.

"Dr. Vernon, this is Holly Michaels, RN, from Fairmont General calling about Mrs. Guevara in room 496. She has been receiving her pain medication exactly every 4 hours and continues to complain of incisional pain. She currently is complaining of slight dizziness and nausea, although she has had no emesis. Her blood pressure is 135/86; pulse 112; and respirations 24, which are higher than they have been running. Her temperature is 98.8° F. She has no drug allergies. How would you like to change her orders?"

Holly has prepared the information the physician will need and communicates it in an orderly fashion.

Communication and Generational Differences

In recent years, much attention has been focused on the fact that our society has at least four distinct generational groups. They are variously described as follows:

- Silents/Traditionalists/Veterans—born before the mid-1940s
- Baby Boomers—born between the mid-1940s and the mid-1960s
- Generation X—born between the mid-1960s and 1980
- Generation Y/Millennials—born between 1981 and 2000
- Homeland Generation or Homelanders—variously described as born since 9/11/01 or 2000 (CBS News, 2010; Newburn, 2009; *Nurse Educator*, 2009).

Awareness of generational differences and the accompanying differences in communication styles is important from two perspectives—communication with the patients/families and communication with each other.

Traditionalists

Members of this oldest surviving generation follow the rules, valuing authority, formality, and the chain-of-command. They take pride in accomplishment, are strong decision makers, and have a good sense of self. Tradition is important to them, making them more likely to make decisions based on what has or has not worked in the past. Appearance and respect are important to them. Therefore, they appreciate communication in a more formal style, appropriate dress, and displays of respect. They may be off-put by multiple tattoos, earrings, and various styles of scrubs or other health care attire. They are more likely to respond to formal communication than to the casual or direct approach in a spontaneous setting. "Younger nurses can decrease mistrust that appearance may initiate by verbally affirming their commitment to nursing and to patient care" (Nurse Educator, 2009). This approach is particularly important to the older patient.

Baby Boomers

Baby Boomers grew up in an era of prosperity that formed their worldview, values, and work ethic. Although they questioned political policy, authority, and social mores, they ultimately embraced work as a definition of self-worth, adopting a strong work ethic, becoming goal-directed, and experiencing the accompanying struggle with work–personal life balance. These attributes lead to an expectation of similar commitment from younger generations. Effective communication with Baby Boomers includes direct information in a personable approach, a formal plan, and acknowledgement of value, purpose, and respect. Such communication style is equally applicable with either coworkers or patients.

Generation X

The milieu that Gen Xers experienced during their formative years was fraught with insecurity. The breakdown in many of the traditional security sources previous generations enjoyed helped create a generation of independent problem solvers. The increase in divorces; the prevalence of AIDS, gangs, and abortions; and the exposure of corrupt government officials and policies created an unstable societal environment in which individuals who could meet challenges, recognize and respond to opportunity, and become comfortable with diversity excelled. Xers value autonomy in their work, decision-making, and life choices, but at the same time value the team and teamwork. While they may appear to move too quickly and be insensitive having grown up in a technology-based society, they are capable of fierce commitment to tasks they value. Allow these individuals to be highly involved in decision making regarding health care—whether they are the providers or the recipients.

Millennials

This is the most diverse and globally thinking generation in the workforce, in large part thanks to technology that provides unfettered access to global issues and occurrences. Many come from or are close to "nontraditional" families and have witnessed unparalleled violence within the borders of our country (e.g., Columbine shootings, 9/11). Their comfort with technology and diversity are hallmark characteristics. They value inclusion, team effort, and collective action, and they are quite adaptable to rapid change. Because they are focused on cohesiveness and peer orientation, they value immediate feedback. Such activities as "huddles"—periodic and end-of-shift briefings that allow the team to "stay informed, review work, make plans, and move ahead rapidly" (Institute for Healthcare Improvement, 2014)—work particularly well with this group of communicators.

Homelanders

The line between Millennials and Homelanders is blurry, starting with the choice of years for transition from one to the other. Influences on these individuals include the cascade of occurrences within our borders starting with 9/11 as well as continuously burgeoning technology. The year 2008, with "the recession and the election of the nation's first black president" (CBS News, 2010) is heralded as a seminal year in the development of this group not quite at working age but approaching it quickly. Akin to Traditionalists, this generational group is growing up in a time of financial and political insecurity at home and globally. They are not likely to take prosperity for granted. They are comfortable with multitasking, diversity, and technology like no one before them. Homelanders are expected to pursue a college education as a matter of necessity as the gap between those who are financially sound and those who are not continues to widen. It remains to be seen how they will relate in the workplace or in the role of health care recipient, but we can expect articulate, motivated, tech-savvy individuals coming of age in the near future.

Communication and Cultural Diversity

Although Chapter 10 is devoted to cultural and social issues, it is important to highlight cultural issues specific to communication. Sensitivity to cultural differences is an integral part of the nurse's responsibility. Many cultural beliefs are tightly interwoven with strong religious convictions. Societies throughout the world depend as strongly or even more strongly on a variety of alternative healing sources as on medical science. Some people rarely have an opportunity to interface with medical science as it is known in developed countries.

The obvious difficulty is a potential language barrier. Even if the person speaks English as a second language, the preponderance of slang terms and colloquialisms can confound a literal translation. Additionally, the stress associated with illness and possibly hospitalization only adds to the potential for misunderstanding and frustration. Fortunately, most communities have interpreters willing to translate in the health care setting. The variety of language interpreters (including sign language for the deaf) available even in smaller communities is surprising.

Many forms of communication do not carry the same meanings in various cultures. In some instances, direct eye contact is to be avoided if possible. Touch, also considered a positive communication technique in Western culture, may be perceived as a serious invasion of privacy. Some gestures considered innocuous in one culture may represent vulgarity in another. Some cultures strictly adhere to paternalism; unless the male head of the family agrees to a procedure or treatment, the family member will refuse under any circumstance. Although many people share a sense of modesty, some cultures experience a greater feeling of violation at having to expose certain body parts than do others. The consumption of certain foods, the use of blood or blood products—the possibilities of culturally diverse practices are endless. The prudent nurse must become knowledgeable of the specific cultural practices in the region of her or his employment. (See Chapter 10 for further discussion of communication issues related to culture.)

Interprofessional Team Communication

The interprofessional team is composed of a variety of disciplines approaching health care from the unique perspective of the theories and therapies of their individual professions. Consider the variety represented by nurses, physicians, dietitians, respiratory therapists, pharmacists, occupational therapists, physical therapists, psychologists, and social workers. Then add to the mosaic the sublevel of specialists: cardiologists, endocrinologists, oncologists, orthopedists, clinical nurse specialists, recreational therapists, nurse anesthetists, nurse practitioners, and nurse scientists. RNs with varied educational backgrounds (diploma, associate degree, bachelor or Master of Science in nursing) and licensed vocational nurses are often found in the same unit with similar assignments. Now add managers, administrators, unlicensed assistive personnel, clerical staff, accountants, and housekeeping, to name a few. Also consider cultural and generational differences among health care professionals and workers. Is it any wonder that communication disasters occur?

All of the positive communication techniques previously discussed must be used to clearly understand another's perception. Listening is an essential tool for determination of the intended message as seen from the unique perspective of the other discipline. Frequent clarification and a sense of "safety" are paramount as people explore the meanings that each person attributes to the situation and the discipline-specific suggested solutions. Realization that the fundamental goal of all health care professionals and of ancillary staff is to provide quality patient care should facilitate positive communication.

Confidentiality and Privacy

No discussion of communication is complete without reference to issues of confidentiality and privacy. Breach of confidentiality and the patient's right to privacy through careless gossip has ethical and legal ramifications. Thoughtless conversation in the elevator, the cafeteria, the parking lot, or any other public place has created heartache for the patient and the health care provider alike.

Other sites where communication about confidential or personal patient issues needs to be controlled include the nurses' station, any desks or tables along the halls, and the utility rooms. Such locations are not often viewed as "public" places, but many people pass by these areas and overhear information. Exchange of patient information should occur only between persons with the need and right to know and should take place in private areas.

SOCIAL MEDIA—WARNING! WARNING! WARNING!

" . . . the inherent nature of social networking invites the sharing of personal information or work experiences that may reflect poorly on a nurse's professionalism."

American Nurses Association, Principles for Social Networking and the Nurse

Social Media: Good and Bad

Social media sites have burgeoned in the last decade, connecting health care professionals across the country and globally. Health care–related sites, chatrooms, blogs, forums, and video sites provide an unparalleled opportunity to network, share, and problem-solve health care issues.

"Nurses can positively use electronic media to share workplace experiences, particularly those events that are challenging or emotionally charged . . ."
National Council of State Boards of Nursing [NCSBN], 2011

The professional value of social media comes with a very serious caveat. The patient retains his or her right to confidentiality and privacy in every medium. Not only must nurses be very careful in not using a patient's name, but they must be thorough in avoiding any other type of identifying information. Such information may include geographical location, facility name, room number, or the patient's age, gender, and diagnosis combined with any of these data.

Nurses, like most of our society, are connected in their personal lives to multiple online social media sources such as Facebook, Twitter, and various blogs. Sitting at home alone with a computer may create a sense of privacy, but nothing could be further from the truth. Postings intended for immediate family or friends and protected by the site privacy policy are not infallible. Anything posted online exists forever on a server somewhere, even if it is deleted from the site. This information is forever discoverable in a court of law and can be used in a trial (NCSBN, 2011). Friends might find your story so touching or endearing that they repost to their friends, and the story takes on a life of its own with no available control of dissemination on your part.

A good example of the unintended outcome of a moment's misjudgment is presented in NCSBN's (2011) social media guidelines. A nursing student took a picture of a minor child (with permission) and posted it to her Facebook page with a comment about his bravery during his illness and how much she loved her chosen profession. Although she did not identify the patient by name, the patient's room number was visible in the photo. The patient and his hospital were identified by others viewing the post. Ultimately, the hospital was charged with a HIPAA violation, the nursing program was barred from the clinical site, and the student was expelled. Nursing board actions against the student could include the following:

- Unprofessional conduct
- Unethical conduct
- Moral turpitude

- Mismanagement of patient records
- Revealing a privileged communication
- Breach of confidentiality (NCSBN, 2011)

The nursing student's actions also violated state and federal law, putting her at jeopardy of "both criminal and civil penalties, including fines and possible jail time" (NCSBN, 2011).

Certainly it was never the student's intent to behave unethically, creating this cascade of events. As a profession, we are held to a very high ethical standard to protect our clients' confidentiality. We must be very attentive to our actions.

Another issue that has appeared is the use of texting for communication of patient information among health care providers. According to The Joint Commission (2012), this practice is not acceptable. The receiving individual is not able to verify unequivocally the identity of the person sending the text. There is no way to make a copy of the original message to place in the permanent record. Anything that is sent electronically has the potential to be inadvertently misdirected and/or intercepted.

Proper use of social media can open venues of learning, career advancement, mentoring, and networking, enhancing the global perspective in your nursing career. Use this opportunity wisely and with consideration of the permanence, wide visibility (beyond anything you may intend), and potential impact of your postings.

Online Etiquette

Interactions online are guided by the same sense of decency that any other style of communication dictates. Here are some simple rules:

- Be nice. Be ethical. Don't say anything to someone online that you wouldn't say in a face-to-face conversation, and certainly don't fan the flame of conflict or anger.
- Remember the TMI (too much information) concept. Don't give more personal information than others want to hear.
- Write with clarity. Reread what you've written to determine whether it is clear or if it might be interpreted differently from what you intended.
- Respect others, including their privacy.
- Use discretion. Postings online live forevermore in cyber space.
- Obey copyright laws.

UNDERSTANDING AND MANAGING CONFLICT

The Nature of Conflict

A major goal of communication is to establish understanding and cooperation with others. However, much of our social environment is characterized by interactions that involve conflict, misunderstanding, and a failure to communicate. When more than one person is involved in the interaction, a potential exists for disagreement and misunderstanding. When the interaction becomes stressful, taking on a competitive, hostile, or oppositional nature, it can be classified as conflict (Mayer, 2000). Conflicts stemming from differences in goals or desires are not good or bad. The two fundamental bases for conflict are information (one person has information that another does not have, or two individuals have different sets of information) and perception (people see things differently based on their unique belief systems). Despite the discomfort, disparate points of view can result in constructive behavior and positive outcomes.

Conflict, like stress, can have both beneficial and detrimental consequences to an individual. Some of the benefits that may arise from conflict include: (1) recognize talents and innovative abilities; (2) identify an outlet for expression of aggressive urges; (3) introduce innovation and change; (4) diagnose problems or areas of concern; and (5) establish unity (Mayer, 2000). Harmful consequences of prolonged conflict can include a negative effect on emotional and physical well-being, an emphasis on personal welfare over that of the group, a diversion of time and energy from important goals, financial and emotional costs, and personal fatigue.

Most of us experience abundant opportunities for conflict, which may be related to the fact that we bring to our relationships an accumulation of attitudes, beliefs, opinions, and habits. Thus conflict is normal and is not necessarily something to avoid. Although uncomfortable, conflict signals the presence of diverse points of view, which can spark creativity, nourish growth, and strengthen relationships. Maintaining an environment supportive of professional, clear, and sensitive communication enables individuals to fight more productively, with less hurt, and with a greater chance of resolving differences and disagreements. Characteristics of environments that support professional communication are as follows (Gibb, 1961):

- *Empathy:* Feeling what the other person is feeling and seeing the situation as they see it; entails believing that the other person's feelings are valid, legitimate, and justified.
- *Equality:* All participants in the process are equal; respect for individual differences is apparent, and people are comfortable expressing themselves freely and openly.
- *Openness:* Feelings and thoughts are stated directly and honestly; no attempt is made to hide or disguise the real object of disagreement.
- *Positiveness:* Entails capitalizing on agreements and using them as a basis for approaching disagreements and impasses; conflict is viewed as positive, and individuals involved express positive feelings for each other and the relationship.
- *Supportiveness:* Feelings are expressed with spontaneity rather than with strategy; requires flexibility and a willingness to change personal opinions and positions.

Adopting these communication attitudes and using the positive communication strategies previously discussed can prevent most episodes of conflict in the workplace. However, situations are bound to arise in which the nurse will need to know how to handle a conflict situation and achieve a positive resolution.

Conflict Resolution

People's ability to connect with one another, especially during times of conflict, depends on their capacity to tune into the subtle messages that reveal how a message is actually being received. We seldom create conflict intentionally. Rather, it occurs because we may not be aware of how our own behavior contributes to interpersonal problems. Because interpersonal communication is fragile, there may be barriers to an effectual and meaningful process. Successful resolution to conflict begins to occur when people are aware of their own and others' feelings and emotions and believe that these concerns are relevant and respected.

The first step in conflict resolution is to recognize how individuals manage conflict. The most common conflict resolution styles include the following:

- *Avoidance:* One person uses passive behaviors and withdraws from the conflict; neither person is able to pursue goals.
- *Accommodation:* One person puts aside his or her goals to satisfy the other person's desires.

- *Force:* One person achieves his or her own goals at the expense of the other person.
- *Compromise:* Both people give up something to get partial goal attainment.
- *Collaboration:* Both people actively try to find solutions that will satisfy them both.

Self-awareness of one's usual conflict resolution style will go far in helping to understand how one's own behavior contributes to disagreements. For example, if an individual nurse recognizes avoidance as his or her common style of dealing with conflict, then it would be important for that nurse to review the communication strategies presented in this chapter to identify specific techniques that can be used to develop a more collaborative style of conflict resolution.

Remember, don't make it personal or take it personally. Use "I" rather than "you" messages to avoid defensive responses. Keep the focus on the issue, not personalities. Do not create an environment in which other individuals respond defensively in order to protect themselves. Do not

respond to conflictive situations as a personal attack—even if it feels like one. Focus and refocus on the issue or behavior rather than the individual.

Another—and very important—step in conflict resolution is active listening (Axelrod and Johnson, 2003). Although many of us are apprehensive or reticent when communicating during times of conflict, active listening can reduce the emotional charge from the situation so that both parties can deal with their differences and assist in resolving the conflict. Some excellent active listening techniques and examples are provided in Table 19-1.

Finally, the principle that underscores all successful conflict resolution is that all people involved must view their conflict as a problem to be solved mutually so that each has a sense of winning or discovering options that are acceptable to all. Although this is an easy principle to understand, it can be challenging to put into practice. If both people can remain open, honest, and respectful of the other person's position, feelings of resentment may be minimized. Box 19-4 presents some

TABLE 19-1	**Active Listening Techniques**		
Technique	**Why Done**	**How Done**	**Example**
Paraphrase the content of the message	Shows that you are listening, checking meaning, and interpreting the content	Restate the basic ideas and facts in your own words	"What I hear you saying is that you weren't consulted" or "So, you weren't consulted about this?"
Reflect the emotion of the message	Shows understanding of how the person feels; reflects what is observed rather than what is heard; helps the other person evaluate his or her own feelings after hearing them expressed by someone else	Listen to voice tone, and watch for nonverbal cues that indicate feelings; listen to what the person tells you he or she is feeling; state back how you perceive the feeling	"So you are angry about what happened?"
Open questioning	Obtains more information and avoids any assumptions about what the other person is thinking; encourages the other person to talk	Ask questions that begin with "what," "how," "when," and "where"; use questions that begin with "why" cautiously	"What happened after you spoke with her?"
Acknowledging	Conveys that you appreciate the other person's perspective; acknowledges his or her worth and actions	Acknowledge the value of the person's issues and feelings (shows appreciation for his or her efforts and actions)	"That must be very frustrating."
Summarizing	Reviews progress; pulls together important ideas and information; establishes a foundation for further discussion	Restate the central ideas and feelings you have heard	"So basically what is most important to you is . . . "

Continued

TABLE 19-1 Active Listening Techniques—cont'd

Technique	Why Done	How Done	Example
Framing	Communicates your message in a way the other person will be more open to hearing; increases the opportunity of meeting his or her goals	Present your message in a hopeful, nonjudgmental, and open-ended way; point to common ground and away from differences	"I think it would be best to speak to your supervisor directly about these issues, because she is more directly involved with implementation than I am; what do you think about this idea?"
Reframing	Helps others see their concerns in a new light; broadens the meaning of an issue to identify needs or interests; diffuses negative feelings; establishes a focus for resolution	Recognize underlying needs; reword concerns from negative to neutral or positive, past to future, problem to opportunity	"It sounds as if you would like more direct communication to resolve concerns."

From Axelrod L, Johnson R: *Successful resolution*, Vancouver, BC, 2003, The Neutral Zone. Used with permission from The Neutral Zone, Vancouver, BC.

BOX 19-4 Professional Response to Verbal Conflict

1. Maintain an open and empathetic tone of voice.
2. Maintain eye contact (keeping cultural differences in mind). This may be difficult, but it conveys to the other party that you are confident and competent.
3. Maintain an open body stance with your hands at your side or open toward the person (but not invading the other person's space). Do not cross your arms, tap your foot, wag your finger, or perform any body language that is commonly associated with anger.
4. Do not physically back away unless you perceive you actually are in physical danger. By standing your ground, your carriage will convey the message of assurance.
5. Be aware of your own values, beliefs, and cultural perspectives.
6. When a conversation is obviously escalating, move to a more private location.
7. Listen actively and carefully without criticizing or being defensive.
8. Focus on the problem or issue, not the person(s) involved.
9. Use "I" messages that state your thoughts, feelings, and beliefs in an open and clear manner.
10. Use nonjudgmental, noninflammatory language, such as "It seems to me . . . ."
11. Establish ground rules to maintain a safe environment for dialogue, such as only one person speaks at a time; the other listens.
12. Offer explanations, but do not make excuses.
13. Be redundant, summarize, and convey the same idea in more than one way.
14. Try to understand the intended meaning of what other people are saying.
15. Identify ideas that clarify your own issues, concerns, and are helpful to identify solutions.
16. Avoid unhelpful responses to conflict, such as arguing, sarcasm, moralizing, disbelief, contradiction, criticism, ridicule, and threats.
17. Use metaphors and analogies as gentle ways to create and maintain rapport.
18. Maintain a positive context by stating what you want, and avoid stating what you do not want.
19. Repeat, or play back, what you believe you are hearing.
20. If you say you will take care of something, report something, or change something, do it. Then seek out the person to whom you made the commitment and report your action and the result. Little else will go as far as demonstrating that you are dependable and want to work toward a solution.
21. In more difficult situations, consider using a neutral facilitator who understands his or her role.

basic strategies that can augment a professional response to conflict. The principles listed are remarkably effective in cases of conflict and will help the nurse present herself or himself as a confident and competent professional who will not react to inappropriate behavior in like form, but also will not withdraw from the issues. As always, the focus should be kept on the delivery of quality patient care.

SUMMARY

In today's health care environment, where high stress levels are all too common and patient safety, quality care, and financial constraints are everyday concerns, nurses play a vital role in promoting a productive work environment in which trust and rapport among the health care team members is common and all are working toward the same goal—delivery of safe, timely, efficient, effective, and patient-centered health care. Professional, clear, and sensitive communication provides the foundation for creating such supportive, effective health care environments.

The first step toward developing a professional communication style is understanding the many complex and varied factors that influence the communication process, such as gender, cultural, generational, and interdisciplinary differences, each of which present many challenges for the nurse who must strive to understand and to be understood. The second step is adopting positive communication techniques, which include developing trust, using "I" messages, establishing eye contact, keeping promises, feeling empathy, using an open communication style, clarifying information, and being aware of body language. The third step is for each nurse to reflect on his or her use of negative communication techniques, such as blocking, false assurances, conflicting messages, logical fallacies, and cognitive distortions that may interfere with effective relationships with patients and coworkers. Recognizing—then avoiding—the use of these negative communication techniques is essential if the nurse is to move toward a more professional communication style. The next step in developing a professional communication style is learning to address and resolve conflict in a positive way. Role playing with trusted colleagues using the conflict resolution techniques discussed in this chapter can help the nurse become more adept at managing conflict.

Demonstrating a professional, clear, and sensitive communication style is essential to the professional nursing skill set. As the foundation for effective, supportive work environments and excellent patient care, professional communication must be one goal every nurse strives to achieve.

REFERENCES

American Association of Critical Care Nurses: *Standards for establishing and sustaining healthy work environments*, 2005 (website). http://www.aacn.org/wd/hwe/docs/hwestandards.pdf. Accessed October 5, 2014.

American Nurses Association: *Principles for nursing documentation*, Silver Spring, MD, 2010, Nursesbooks. http://nursesbooks.org/Main-Menu/eBooks/Principles/eBook-Principles-for-Nursing-Documentation.aspx. Accessed January 25, 2015.

American Nursing Association: *Principles for social networking and the nurse*, 2013 (website). http://www.nursingworld.org/socialnetworkingtoolkit. Accessed October 5, 2014.

Angelfire: *Styles of communication*, 2009 (website). http://www.angelfire.com/az2/webenglish/commstyles.html. Accessed October 11, 2014.

Axelrod L, Johnson R: *Successful resolution*, Vancouver, BC, 2003, The Neutral Zone.

Booher D: *Gender benders: gender negotiation communication style differences*, 2012 (website). http://www.negotiations.com/articles/gender-bender/. Accessed October 11, 2014.

Borg J: *Body language: how to know what's really being said*, Dorchester, Dorset, UK, 2011, Dorset Press.

Centers for Disease Control and Prevention: Use and characteristics of electronic health record systems among office-based physician practices: United States, 2001-2013, *NCHS Data Brief* 143, January 2014 (website). http://www.cdc.gov/nchs/data/databriefs/db143.htm. Accessed September 15, 2014.

CBS News: *Generation X (and Y) are history: what's next*, 2010. (website). http://www.cbsnews.com/stories/2010/06/10/business/main6568258.shtml. Accessed October 11, 2014.

Elgin SH: *Genderspeak: men, women, and the gentle art of verbal self-defense*, New York, 1993, John Wiley & Sons.

Gibb J: Defensive communication, *J Comm* 11:141–148, 1961.

Heim P: Getting beyond "she said, he said," *Nurs Admin Q* 19(2):6–18, 1995.

Holland K: *Importance of body language in nursing communication*, 2013 (website). http://www.nursetogether.com/career/career-article/itemid/2427.aspx. Accessed October 5, 2014.

Institute for Healthcare Improvement: *Huddles*, 2014 (website). http://www.ihi.org/knowledge/Pages/Tools/Huddles.aspx. Accessed January 25, 2015.

Jayanthi A: *10 biggest technological advancement for healthcare in the last decade*, Becker Hospital Review, 2014 (website). http://www.beckershospitalreview.com/healthcare-information-technology/10-biggest-technological-advancements-for-healthcare-in-the-last-decade.html. Accessed September 15, 2014.

Mayer B: *The dynamics of conflict resolution*, San Francisco, 2000, Jossey-Bass.

Mehrabian A: *Silent messages: implicit communication of e motions and attitudes*, Beverly, MA, 1981, Wadsworth.

National Council of State Boards of Nursing: *A nurse's guide to the use of social media*, 2011 (website). https://www.ncsbn.org/NCSBN_SocialMedia.pdf. Accessed October 11, 2014.

Newburn J: *Generational communication styles*, 2009 (website). http://www.networksolutions.com/smallbusiness/2009/05/generational-communication-styles-part-2-of-our-generational-marketing-series-by-jessie-newburn/. Accessed October 11, 2014.

Nurse Educator: *Generational conflict in nursing: how to relate to colleagues from multiple generations*, 2009 (website). http://journals.lww.com/nurseeducatoronline/Fulltext/2009/01000/Generational_Conflict_in_Nursing__How_to_Relate_to.12.aspx. Accessed October 11, 2014.

Pearson Education: *Infoplease: homework center-listening skills*, 2014 (website). http://www.infoplease.com/homework/listeningskills1.html. Accessed October 11, 2014.

Rose J: *Communication styles*, 2007. (website). http://trainingpd.suite101.com/article.cfm/communication_styles. Accessed October 11, 2014.

The Joint Commission: *Advancing effective communication, cultural competence, and patient- and family-centered care: a roadmap for hospitals,* Oakbrook Terrace, IL, 2010, The Joint Commission (website). http://www.jointcommission.org/assets/1/6/ARoadmapforHospitalsfinalversion727.pdf. Accessed October 11, 2014.

The Joint Commission: *Standards FAQ details: texting orders*, 2012 (website). http://www.jointcommission.org/standards_information/jcfaqdetails.aspx?StandardsFaqId=401&ProgramId=1. Accessed October 11, 2014.

van Servellen G: *Communication skills for the healthcare professional: concepts and techniques*, Gaithersburg, MD, 1997, Aspen.

20

Delegation—linking together for better patient care.

Effective Delegation and Supervision

Barbara Cherry, DNSc, MBA, RN, NEA-BC,
Margaret Elizabeth Strong, DNP, RN, NE-BC

ⓔ Additional resources are available online at: *http://evolve.elsevier.com/Cherry/*

PROFESSIONAL/ETHICAL ISSUE

Nicole Adams, RN, has taken a position as the new charge nurse for a 24-bed medical-surgical unit at a long-term acute care and rehabilitation hospital. Nicole is excited about this new opportunity but is apprehensive because this is her first position as a charge nurse. After completing the hospital's orientation program, Nicole reports to her unit for her first official day as charge nurse. She is immediately approached by an LPN, who says, "I have worked here for 8 years and I always can take care of everything. I will complete all of the patient assessments and let you know about anything you might need to follow up with." Nicole is alarmed about this statement but knows she must handle the situation carefully to ensure she follows safe delegation practices while also developing a good working relationship with the LPN. Discuss what elements of delegation Nicole should consider in this situation and what the best approach with the LPN might be.

VIGNETTE

Glenda Miller, BSN, RN, is the charge nurse on a medical-surgical floor of a hospital. She has just received report from the 7 pm to 7 am shift and is about to make assignments for the 7 am to 7 pm shift. The philosophy of the unit is that the registered nurse (RN) coordinates all patient care. Today on this 12-bed unit there are eight patients and four empty beds. The nursing staff consists of Ms. Miller, one RN, one licensed practical nurse, one nursing assistant, and one unit secretary. The following interprofessional team members are available for specific patient care needs: a respiratory therapist, physical therapist, occupational therapist, speech therapist, medical social worker, nutritional support nurse, and chaplain. The patients are medically complex with extensive nursing care needs, including psychosocial and emotional support. The patients are described to Ms. Miller as follows:
502: Mr. A. is ventilator dependent with an infection that requires IV antibiotics every 12 hours. He
needs to be out of bed in a chair twice a day. He has a stage I sacral decubitus ulcer and a PEG tube with bolus feedings. He is very hard of hearing, tries to speak, and becomes very frustrated and uncooperative.
503: Mrs. B., age 77, is on day 2 of 40 days of antibiotics for osteomyelitis. She is dehydrated with a central line in her right subclavian and on TPN. She needs to be out of bed and ambulated in the room. She receives a respiratory treatment every 4 hours and needs assistance with a.m. care. Her daughter is at her bedside and is very upset that her mother may need to go to a nursing home.
504: Mr. C., age 52, is to be discharged to a rehabilitation hospital today. Discharge records need to be prepared for the transfer. The family is at his bedside and is extremely anxious.

507: Mr. D., age 64, has TPN infusing into a left subclavian catheter and is on multiple antibiotics. He has vancomycin-resistant Enterococcus in his urine and a stasis ulcer on his left leg that requires Pulsavac every day.

508: Mr. E., age 72, is a ventilator-dependent patient who will start weaning this am. He is on continuous tube feedings and IV antibiotics and needs to be assessed for a PICC line. He is to begin ambulation in the hall twice a day per physician's orders. He also needs to have a pharyngeal speech evaluation scheduled.

509: Mrs. F., age 66, is 3 days post CVA and unable to move her right extremities. She has an IV infusing via her left arm. Her blood pressure is 170/100. She needs total care with personal hygiene and feeding. The physician just ordered range-of-motion exercises every day. Her husband is at her bedside crying continually and asking, "What am I going to do now?"

510: Mr. G., age 52, has been off the ventilator for the past 24 hours and is doing very well. He continues on respiratory treatments every 4 hours. His TPN is being decreased, and his PEG feedings are increasing. He has glucose monitoring ordered every 4 hours, an indwelling urinary catheter to gravity drainage, and IV antibiotics every 12 hours. He needs to be out of bed, ambulating in the hall with assistance. If he stays off the ventilator, he will be discharged in 5 days. The family needs to find a nursing home for him; however, the family has not visited Mr. G. since his admission 18 days ago.

511: Mr. H., age 49, is a new admission that will be coming from ICU sometime during the shift.

In addition to the tasks mentioned, routine activities of taking vital signs, giving scheduled medications, updating care plans, and answering call lights must be assigned. When reviewing the tasks to be accomplished, Ms. Miller must consider several issues to make safe and effective assignment and delegation decisions.

Questions to Consider While Reading this Chapter:
1. Which of the above tasks must the RN perform as required by your state's nurse practice act?
2. Which of the above tasks can be delegated to the nursing assistant?
3. How can the training, skills, and competencies of the licensed practical nurse (LPN) or licensed vocational nurse (LVN) and nursing assistant be determined?
4. How can other members of the interprofessional health care team contribute most effectively to meet patients' needs?

KEY TERMS

Accountability: In the context of delegation, accountability means bearing responsibility for both the action and inaction of the nurse and those to whom he or she delegates tasks (National Council of State Boards of Nursing [NCSBN], 2005).

Assignment: The distribution of work that each staff member is responsible for during a given work period; when making assignments, the RN supervisor directs a staff member to do something that he or she is authorized to do and is within the staff member's scope of practice and/or job description (American Nurses Association [ANA] and NCSBN, 2014).

Competency: The ability of an individual to perform defined behaviors proficiently by demonstrating the appropriate knowledge, skills, attitudes, and professional judgment required for a specific role or setting.

Delegation: Transferring to a competent staff member the authority and responsibility to perform a selected nursing task that the staff member would not normally be allowed to perform; the RN retains accountability for the delegated task (ANA and NCSBN, 2014).

Supervision: The active process of directing, guiding, and influencing the outcome of an individual's performance of an activity or task (ANA, 2012).

Unlicensed assistive personnel (UAP): An unlicensed individual who is trained to function in an assistive role to the RN by performing patient care activities as delegated by the nurse; may include nursing assistants, clinical assistants, orderlies, health aides, or other titles designated within the work setting.

LEARNING OUTCOMES

After studying this chapter, the reader will be able to:

1. Evaluate the effect of changes in the current health care system on nurse staffing patterns and responsibilities.
2. Outline six topic areas that the professional nurse should consider when making delegation decisions.
3. List nine essential requirements for safe and effective delegation.
4. Incorporate principles of delegation and supervision in professional nursing practice to ensure safe and legal patient care.

CHAPTER OVERVIEW

The safe and effective delivery of patient care is the fundamental goal of every health care organization. To accomplish this goal cost-effectively, teams of diverse professionals and assistants are used to deliver care. Because the RN is most often responsible for coordinating care provided by the various team members, he or she must clearly understand and be able to effectively use the management processes of delegation and supervision to ensure
high-quality, safe patient care. This chapter highlights issues that influence staffing patterns and delegation and supervision processes. The chapter also discusses the RN's role and responsibility in delegating to and supervising staff members, including unlicensed assistive personnel (UAP) and LPNs or LVNs, and it provides useful guidelines for establishing a safe and effective delegation and supervision practice.

DELEGATION AND SUPERVISION IN THE HEALTH CARE SYSTEM

In today's complex health care environment, nursing must be knowledge-based not task-based. Nurses are accountable to provide "culturally sensitive, safe, timely, efficient, patient-centered, equitable, and effective nursing care for consumers in a variety of settings across the continuum of health care" (ANA, 2012). Several factors influence staffing patterns and the provision of patient care across multiple health care settings from hospitals to home health. First, reduced reimbursement from Medicare, Medicaid, and private insurance companies has led to cost-cutting measures. Second, the Patient Protection and Affordable Care act has lessened the number of the uninsured, so more people are seeking health care from primary care providers. Third, the consumer is now paying a higher co-pay for care and is demanding that care is provided in an effective and efficient manner. Fourth, the strong focus on safety and quality is requiring health care systems to make rapid changes for continual improvement. Fifth, advances in medical technology are causing a sharp increase in the cost of providing care. Finally, an increase in patient acuity and complex treatments contribute to health care environments struggling to address multiple complex priorities with dwindling resources. Using unlicensed

assistive personnel (UAP), such as nursing assistants and patient care technicians, is one strategy to increase cost-effectiveness of providing patient care.

As the use of UAP increases, the RN is obligated to delegate more tasks to a person who does not have clearly defined parameters for education, training, job responsibilities, and role limitations. The RN must know that the profession defines the scope and standards of practice, while the state nurse practice acts define the legal parameters for nursing practice (ANA, 2012). It is important that the RN work closely with nonclinical administrators and managers to make sure they understand that the nursing process cannot be delegated to anybody other than the RN.

In support of the role of UAP in delivering patient care, the Joint Statement on Delegation (ANA and NCSBN, 2014) states, "There is a need and a place for competent, appropriately supervised, unlicensed assistive personnel in the delivery of affordable, quality health care." As health care facilities continue to seek more cost-effective ways to provide care, RNs must learn new ways of managing care and delegating tasks.

WHAT IS DELEGATION?

Delegation is a legal and management concept that involves assessment, planning, intervention, and evaluation.

Delegation as defined by the American Nurses Association (ANA, 2010) is "the transfer of responsibility for the performance of an activity from one individual to another while retaining accountability for the outcome." Although RNs can transfer the responsibility and authority for the performance of an activity, they remain accountable for the overall nursing care. When delegating tasks, the nurse should understand the delegatee's competencies, communicate succinctly, offer clear guidelines in advance, monitor progress, and remain accountable for the final outcomes of care.

Delegation is a two-way process in which the RN requests that a qualified staff member perform a specific task. When delegating, the RN delegator is accountable for the following:

- The act of delegation
- Supervising the performance of the delegated task
- Assessment and follow-up evaluation
- Any intervention or corrective actions that may be required to ensure safe and effective care
  The delegatee is accountable for the following:
- His or her own actions
- Accepting delegation within the parameters of his or her training and education
- Communicating the appropriate information to the delegator
- Completing the task

Delegation is a management strategy that when used appropriately can ensure the accomplishment of safe and effective patient care. "All decisions related to delegation and assignment are based on the fundamental principles of protection of the health, safety, and welfare of the public" (Duffy and McCoy, 2014).

WHAT SHOULD AND SHOULD NOT BE DELEGATED?

Unfortunately, there is no easy answer as to what can and cannot be delegated. The answer varies, depending on the (1) nursing practice acts and other applicable state laws, (2) patient needs, (3) job descriptions and competencies of staff members, (4) policies and procedures of the health care organization, (5) clinical situation, and (6) professional standards of nursing practice. To establish a safe, effective delegation practice, the RN must seek guidance and integrate information regarding each of these areas as discussed in the following paragraphs

State Nurse Practice Acts

Each state's nurse practice act provides the legal authority for nursing practice, including delegation. However, each state's nurse practice act expresses delegation criteria differently, and the criteria often are not clearly spelled out in the act, or they may be presented in various parts of the act. It is absolutely essential that every RN be familiar with his or her state nurse practice act and know the delegation criteria contained within the act. Johnson (1996) has identified 10 essential elements related to delegation criteria in nurse practice acts, as follows:

1. Definition of delegation
2. Items that cannot be delegated
3. Items that cannot be routinely delegated
4. Guidelines for the RN about what can be delegated
5. Description of professional nursing practice
6. Description of LPN or LVN and nursing assistive personnel roles
7. Degree of supervision required
8. Guidelines for decreasing the risks associated with delegation
9. Warnings about inappropriate delegation
10. Restricted use of the word *nurse* to licensed nurses only

Although not every state's nurse practice act contains all 10 elements, the RN can use this list to assist in understanding delegation criteria in his or her own nurse practice act and apply the information to enhance delegation activities. Box 20-1 presents policies common to many nurse practice acts.

If the nurse practice act does not provide clear direction regarding delegation, the state board of nursing may be able to offer guidance. The board of nursing may have developed definitions, rulings, advisory opinions, or interpretations of the law to provide guidance regarding delegation activities. Many state boards of nursing may also have practical tools available, such as delegation decision trees or delegation checklists. Figure 20-1 is a delegation decision tree recommended by the NCSBN and provides an excellent framework for the four steps in the delegation process—assessment and planning, communication, surveillance and supervision, and evaluation and feedback.

Most states also have a practice act to govern practice by LPNs or LVNs. Because the practice of LPNs or LVNs varies significantly from state to state, RNs

From Johnson SH: Teaching nursing delegation: analyzing nurse practice acts, *J Contin Educ Nurs* 27(2):52-58, 1996.

BOX 20-1 **Policies Common to Many State Nurse Practice Acts**

- Only nursing tasks can be delegated, not nursing practice.
- The RN must perform the patient assessment to determine what can be delegated.
- The LPN or LVN and UAP do not practice professional nursing.
- The RN can delegate only what is within the scope of nursing practice.
- The LPN or LVN works under the direction and supervision of the RN.
- The RN delegates based on the knowledge and skill of the person selected to perform the delegated tasks.
- The RN determines the competency of the person to whom he or she delegates.
- The RN cannot delegate an activity that requires the RN's professional skill and knowledge.
- The RN is accountable and responsible for the delegated task.
- The RN must evaluate patient outcomes resulting from the delegated activity.
- Health care facilities can develop specific delegation protocols, provided they meet the state board delegation guidelines.
- Delegation requires critical thinking by the RN.

---

should know the LPN or LVN practice act in the state in which they practice and understand the LPN or LVN's legal scope of practice. The delegation decision tree presented in Figure 20-1 is also applicable to delegation to LPNs and LVNs. State law generally does not define practice by UAP, although such practice should be governed by the health care organization's policies.

Patient Needs

When deciding to delegate, the RN must remember that tasks can be delegated, but nursing practice cannot. The functions of assessment, evaluation, and nursing judgment cannot be delegated. In general, the more stable the patient, the more likely delegation is to be safe. However, it also is important to remember many tasks that can be delegated may also carry with them a nursing responsibility. Taking vital signs on a physiologically stable patient after a cerebrovascular accident (CVA) could be delegated to the UAP, but the task presents an opportunity for the RN to assess the patient's cognitive functioning. In the vignette presented at the opening of this chapter, Ms. Miller should not delegate any care for the newly admitted patient until the nursing assessment is complete.

Job Descriptions and Competencies

The RN who is delegating has the responsibility of knowing the background, skill level, training received, and job requirements of each person to whom tasks are delegated. The job description provides important information about what a staff member is allowed to do and delineates the specific tasks, duties, and responsibilities required of the person as a condition of employment. Job descriptions generally comply with state laws and the health care organization's standards of care. However, in all cases, legal requirements related to delegation supersede any organizational requirement or policy.

The RN should be aware of what type of education and training the person received to function as described in the job description. The RN should also know what kind of orientation is provided to new employees. In the opening vignette, the LPN's job description most likely would include duties such as "perform dressing changes" and "administer oral medications," but Ms. Miller also should know the LPN's knowledge and skill level for the population of patients on the unit.

In addition to requiring job descriptions for care providers, health care organizations also require employees to demonstrate that they are competent to perform certain technical procedures and to apply specific knowledge to safely care for patients. Written documentation of those skills and knowledge for which the employee has demonstrated competency is maintained in the employee's personnel file. Most health care organizations require employees to undergo annual competency training for aspects of care unique to the population of patients generally being cared for in the nursing unit. Box 20-2 provides an example of annual competencies to be demonstrated by nurses in a family practice ambulatory care clinic. Various regulatory and accrediting agencies, such as The Joint Commission (TJC), require written documentation of staff competencies.

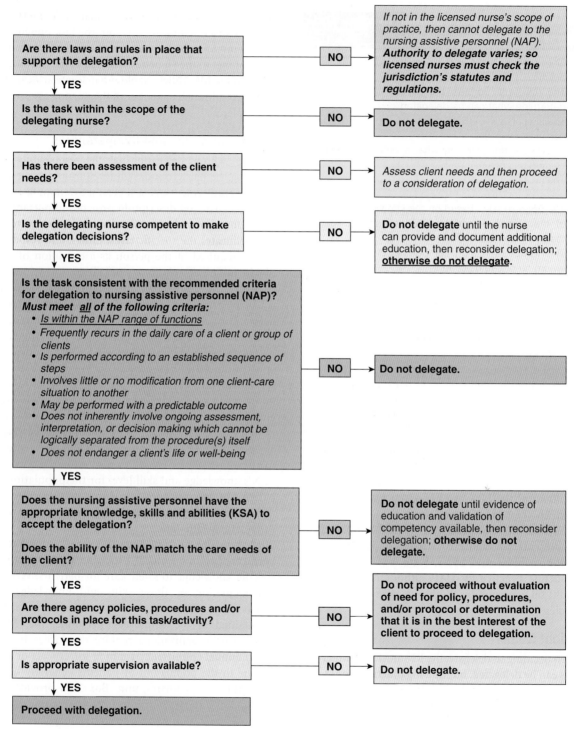

FIGURE 20-1 Decision Tree for Delegating to Nursing Assistive Personnel. (From the Joint Statement on Delegation, American Nurses Association and National Council of State Boards of Nursing. Available online at https://www.ncsbn.org/Delegation_joint_statement_NCSBN-ANA. pdf. Used with permission from the American Nurses Association and the National Council of State Boards of Nursing, 2006.)

Organizational Policies and Procedures

When delegating, the RN should comply with the specific skill requirements designated in the organization's written policies and procedures, which usually describe the supervision required for a specific task and how problems or incidents should be reported and documented. Again it is important for the nurse to remember that the legal requirements related to delegation supersede any organizational requirement or policy. The RN should also know the organization's general standards of care, such as infection control, and ensure that the delegatee has the necessary knowledge and skills to comply with the standards. In the opening vignette, Ms. Miller should be aware of the hospital's policy regarding the orientation process. All clinical staff members should have received training about the unit's infection control, emergency, and safety procedures.

Clinical Situation

Each delegation opportunity presents the RN with a variety of considerations, including the delegatee's current workload and the complexity of the task in relationship to the patient. Does the staff member realistically have time to accomplish the task? Is the staff member familiar with characteristics of the patient population (e.g., pediatrics or geriatrics) and with the task to be performed? Is the RN able to provide the appropriate level of supervision? Other considerations include the availability of resources, such as supplies and equipment.

Professional Standards of Nursing Practice

Professional standards of nursing practice, as established by professional nursing organizations, exist to guide the RN in providing patient care. According to the ANA (2010), "The Standards of Professional Nursing Practice are authoritative statements of the duties that all registered nurses, regardless of role, population, or specialty, are expected to perform competently. The standards are subject to change with the dynamics of the nursing profession, as new patterns of professional practice are developed and accepted by the nursing profession and the public." To practice safe delegation, the RN should be familiar with the standards of practice outlined in the ANA's *Nursing: Scope and Standards of Practice* (2010) and with the standards for any specialty area in which the RN practices. See Appendix A on the Evolve website (http://evolve.elsevier.com/Cherry/) for a list of most of the specialty nursing organizations in the United States.

As an accepted standard of care, the RN should use professional judgment to determine activities that are appropriate to delegate based on the concept of providing safe and effective patient care and protecting the public. In delegation, the RN considers the following:

- Assessment of patient condition
- Capabilities of the nursing and assistive staff
- Complexity of the task to be delegated
- Amount of clinical oversight (supervision) the RN will be able to provide
- Staff workload

"The registered nurse *cannot* delegate responsibilities related to making nursing judgments except to another qualified registered nurse" (Badzek, 2008). Examples of responsibilities include:

- Initial nursing assessment and any subsequent assessment that requires professional nursing knowledge, judgment, and skill
- Determination of nursing diagnoses, establishment of nursing care goals, development of the patient plan of care, and evaluation of the patient's progress with the plan of care
- Any nursing intervention that requires professional knowledge, judgment, and skill. Box 20-3 presents a list of questions to assist the nurse in making delegation decisions.

BOX 20-3   Questions to Guide Delegation Decision-Making

A. State nurse practice act
1. Is the task within the RN's scope of practice?
2. Does the nurse practice act address delegation of the task?
3. Does the task to be delegated require the exercising of nursing judgment?
4. Is the RN delegator willing to accept accountability for the performance of the delegated task?

B. Job description and competencies
1. Does the RN delegator understand the nature of the task and have the knowledge, skills, and competency required to perform the task?
2. Does the delegatee have the appropriate education, training, skills, and experience to perform the task?
3. Is there documented or demonstrated evidence that the delegatee is competent to perform the task?
4. Does the delegatee perform the task on a routine basis?
5. Is the delegatee familiar with the patient population?

C. Organizational policies and procedures
1. What skill level and level of supervision are required for the task as stated in the organization's policy/procedure manual?
2. What is the policy or procedure for documenting tasks and reporting results, observations, problems, or unusual incidents?
3. Does the delegatee have the necessary knowledge and skills to comply with general standards of care, such as infection control?

D. Clinical situation and task
1. Is adequate supervision by the delegator available?
2. Are adequate resources available, including supplies and equipment, to the delegatee?
3. What is the delegatee's current workload? Does the person realistically have time to perform the task?
4. How complex is the task? Does it frequently recur in the daily care of patients? Does it follow a standard and unchanging procedure?

E. Patient needs
1. Has the nursing assessment and plan of care been completed by the RN?
2. What is the patient's clinical, physiologic, emotional, cognitive, and spiritual status?
3. Is the patient's condition considered stable?
4. What is the potential for change in the patient's condition as a result of the delegated task?
5. Can the patient's safety be maintained with delegated care?

F. Professional standards of nursing practice
1. What specific standards of nursing practice apply to the specific situation?
2. Does the delegated task include health counseling, teaching, or other activities that require specialized nursing knowledge, skill, or judgment?

DEVELOPING SAFE DELEGATION PRACTICES

For the RN to make safe, effective delegation decisions, a good understanding of what should and should not be delegated based on the previous discussion is required. However, safe delegation decisions require more! The RN also must know the patient, the staff members to whom he or she is delegating, and the tasks to be performed. The RN must provide for effective outcomes by clearly communicating expectations, supporting and appropriately supervising the delegatee, evaluating the outcomes, and reassessing the patient after the delegated task is completed. Following is a brief discussion about these essential requirements for safe and effective delegation.

Know the Patient

A nursing assessment must be completed before delegation—know the level of care required by the patient, considering his or her clinical, physiologic, emotional, cognitive, and spiritual status. Is the patient's condition considered stable? Generally, the more stable the patient the more likely delegation is to be safe. What is the potential for change in the patient's condition as a result of the delegated task? If there is moderate to high risk that the task will result in a change in the patient's condition, delegation should not be considered. Can the patient's safety be maintained with delegated care? The answer to this question must be a firm "yes" for delegation to be considered.

Know the Staff Member

Before the task is delegated, the delegatee must have the skills and knowledge necessary to perform the task, as evidenced by the person's job description, training program, and documented competencies. Experience and past job performance should also be considerations. Is the staff member knowledgeable and trained to perform the task? Does the staff member perform the task routinely? Select the right person for the right task. It is very helpful for the RN to be involved in development of job descriptions, training programs, and competency documentation for staff members.

Know the Task(s) to be Delegated

The RN delegator must be competent and skilled in performing any task he or she is considering delegating, and the task must be in the RN's scope of practice. Routine, standardized tasks that are performed according to a standard and unchanging procedure and have predictable outcomes are the safest to delegate. These routine tasks are most likely to have been documented in the staff member's competencies and may require fewer directions and less supervision. Complex tasks or activities that pose a high risk for patient complications or unpredictable outcomes should be examined closely before delegation is considered.

Explain the Task and Expected Outcomes

The RN should explain the delegated task, what must be done, and the expected outcomes. If necessary, outline the task in writing. Failure to effectively communicate what is expected may result in unsatisfactory performance, errors, and possible harm to the patient. Directions should be provided clearly and concisely. Demonstration and return demonstration by the delegatee or other in-service education may be required. The delegated task is acceptable only when the staff member understands the task and is adequately prepared to carry it out.

Expect Responsible Action from the Delegatee

When the staff member accepts and understands the task, he or she should then be allowed to perform the task. The staff member becomes responsible for his or her own actions and is obligated to complete the task as mutually agreed. It is important to note that the delegatee cannot delegate the task to another person; for example, if the RN delegates a task to a nursing assistant, that nursing assistant cannot ask another nursing assistant to perform the task. The RN should provide appropriate supervision, but should not intervene in task performance unless assistance is requested or an unsafe situation is recognized. Interfering with the delegatee's task will negate his or her responsibility and obligation. The RN should expect responsible actions, give authority, and retain accountability.

Assess and Supervise Job Performance

Supervising job performance provides a mechanism for feedback and control. Job performance is assessed by making frequent rounds, observing, and communicating (e.g., ask about progress, and determine whether there are any questions or concerns). Determine the appropriate level of supervision. The RN should be available to the delegatee if there are any questions or unexpected problems. Supervise in a positive and supportive manner to reassure the staff member that his or her work is important and appreciated. Intervene immediately if the task is not being performed in a safe and appropriate manner. Poor performance must be documented and reported to the nurse manager. Never ignore poor performance. When a mistake is made, use it as a learning opportunity for all staff involved.

Evaluate and Follow Up

Once the task is complete, evaluate the staff member's performance and reassess the patient to ensure that the expected outcomes were achieved. Follow up with any interventions that may be required based on the patient's care outcomes or the delegatee's job performance. Appropriate evaluation and follow-up will ensure a positive outcome for both patient and staff member. Box 20-4 presents some important steps to remember after the decision to delegate has been made.

Understand High-Risk Delegation

The RN often expresses concern about legal liability—"putting my license on the line"—when delegating to unlicensed staff members. How does the RN know whether he or she might be at risk when delegating? In ANA's *Principles of Delegation* (2012), eleven principles provide guidance and help inform the RN's decision-making regarding delegation:

1. Nursing profession determines scope and standards of practice.

BOX 20-4   From Deciding to Delegate to Actual Delegation: Steps to Remember

A. Communicate effectively.
   1. The delegatee accepts the delegation and accountability for carrying out the task correctly.
   2. The RN delegator provides clear directions to the delegatee, including what specific task is to be performed, for whom the task is to be done, when the task is to be done, how the task is to be performed, what data are to be collected, and any patient-specific instructions.
   3. The RN delegator clearly communicates expected outcomes and timelines for reporting results.
B. Provide appropriate supervision.
   1. Monitor performance to ensure compliance with established standards of practice and organizational policies and procedures.
   2. Obtain and provide feedback.
   3. Intervene if necessary.
   4. Ensure proper documentation.
C. Evaluate and reassess.
   1. Reassess the patient.
   2. Evaluate the performance of the task and the delegatee's experience.
   3. Reassess and adjust the overall plan of care as needed.

---

2. RN is responsible and accountable for provision of nursing practice.
3. RN directs care and determines the appropriate utilization of resources when providing care.
4. RN may delegate task but not the nursing process itself.
5. RN must consider the agency policies and procedures, the knowledge and skills, training, diversity awareness, and experience of person being delegated to.
6. RN decision to delegate is based on the RN's judgment related to care complexity, the availability and competence of the person accepting the delegation and the type and intensity of supervision required.
7. RN acknowledges that delegation involves the concept of mutual respect.
8. Nurse leaders are accountable for systems to access, monitor, verify, and communicate ongoing competency requirements in areas related to delegation.
9. The agency is accountable to provide sufficient resources to enable appropriate delegation.
10. The agency is accountable for ensuring the RN has access to documented competency information for the staff to whom the RN will be delegating tasks.
11. Agency policies regarding delegation are developed with active participation of RNs.

One method to avoid high-risk delegation and simplify the delegation process is referred to as the Five Rights of delegation (ANA and NCSBN, 2014):

1. *The right task:* Delegated tasks must conform to the established guidelines.
2. *The right circumstances:* Delegate tasks that do not require independent nursing judgment.
3. *The right person:* Delegate to someone who is qualified and competent.
4. *The right direction and communication:* Give clear explanation about the task and expected outcomes, and indicate when the delegatee should report back to the RN.
5. *The right supervision and evaluation:* Invite feedback to assess how the process is working and how to improve the process. Also evaluate the patient's outcomes and results of the tasks.

RNs can prevent being placed into unsafe, risky delegation situations by adhering to the safe delegation practices recommended in this chapter. Consider the legal case in which an elderly patient was admitted to the hospital and died shortly after admission by aspiration of food after the nursing assistant left a turkey sandwich on the table for the patient to eat (Legal Eagle, 2010). The patient's family sued the hospital for wrongful death, the nurse was ruled negligent and the family won the case. In this situation, the nurse was informed by the admitting physician that the patient had dysphagia, a swallowing disorder, and needed to be supervised while eating. Unfortunately, the nurse failed to meet the standards of nursing care by not supervising the patient's eating herself or ensuring that the nursing assistant clearly understood the risk involved for a patient with dysphagia and had the skills necessary to respond to an emergency. This legal case could have been prevented had this nurse practiced the principles and strategies for safe delegation present in this chapter. For an example demonstrating excellence in delegation practice in a home health care setting, see Case Study 20-1.

CASE STUDY 20-1   Excellence In Delegation Practice

Amy Laurence, RN, works for a home health care agency. Ms. Laurence manages a caseload of 35 patients and makes between 8 and 10 skilled nursing visits a day. Several of Ms. Laurence's patients need assistance with activities of daily living, such as personal hygiene and mobility. Ms. Laurence assigns these tasks to the home health aides (HHAs) with whom she has worked with over the past 6 to 12 months. From her ongoing evaluation of patient outcomes and supervision of these aides, she knows they are skilled and proficient in performing their assigned tasks.

Five of Ms. Laurence's patients are newly diagnosed with diabetes and need extensive assistance with monitoring blood glucose levels and administering insulin. The home health care agency where Ms. Laurence works has recently adopted a diabetic delegation policy. This policy allows HHAs that have been specifically trained and certified to perform glucose testing and give insulin from prefilled, labeled syringes. Ms. Laurence actively participates in the training classes to certify HHAs in diabetic care.

In caring for her patients with diabetes, Ms. Laurence does extensive diabetic teaching with each of her patients and sees them weekly to assess their learning, monitor their physiologic status, evaluate and adjust their individualized plans of care, and provide ongoing education and support as needed. During the weekly visits, Ms. Laurence fills and labels the exact number of insulin syringes with the correct doses of insulin to last the week. Ms. Laurence is then able to delegate the daily insulin administration and glucose monitoring to the HHAs certified in diabetic care. During the initial delegation process, Ms. Laurence makes supervisory visits to each patient's home to ensure that the HHA is performing the tasks correctly and has been carrying them out according to the patient's plan of care. To provide appropriate supervision of these delegated tasks, Ms. Laurence plans her weekly skilled nursing visits to coincide with the HHA's daily visit. During these visits, Ms. Laurence observes each HHA perform the glucose testing and insulin administration and reinforces any specific training needed. Following these supervisory visits, Ms. Laurence is confident that the HHAs are competent to perform the delegated tasks.

In this case, Ms. Laurence is following all of the criteria essential for safe delegation in her state. She is adhering to the agency's policy, which also is in line with the state board of nursing rules for delegation in a home health care setting. She has actively participated in the training programs for the HHAs and provided clear direction during the initial delegation process. Ms. Laurence provides ongoing patient assessment, care evaluation, and supervision of the HHAs. In performing appropriate delegation, Ms. Laurence is able to focus her energy on skilled nursing services, such as providing patient education, assessing and monitoring patients' physiologic condition, and coordinating the care for the interprofessional home health care team.

SUPERVISION

Supervision is defined by the ANA (2012) as "the active process of directing, guiding and influencing the outcome of an individual's performance of a task." Supervision may be categorized as on-site, in which the nurse is physically present or immediately available while the activity is being performed; or off-site, in which the nurse has the ability to provide direction through various means of written, verbal, and electronic communication (Duffy and McCoy, 2014). On-site supervision generally occurs in the acute care or ambulatory care settings where the RN is immediately available. Off-site supervision may occur in home health care practice, community settings, and long-term care facilities.

Hansten and Jackson (2009) have identified levels of supervision based on the task delegated and the education, experience, competency, and working relationship of the people involved:

- **Unsupervised:** One RN is working with another RN in a collegial relationship, and neither RN is in the position of supervising the other. Each RN is responsible and accountable for his or her own practice. However, the RN in a supervisory or management position (e.g., team leader, charge nurse, nurse manager), as defined by the health care organization, will be in a position to supervise other RNs.

- **Initial direction and/or periodic inspection:** The RN supervises a licensed or unlicensed caregiver, knows the person's training and competencies, and has developed a working relationship with the staff member. For example, the RN has been working with the nursing assistant for 6 months and is comfortable in giving initial directions for a delegated task and following up with the assistant once during the shift.

- **Continuous supervision:** The RN has determined that the delegatee will need frequent to continual support and assistance. This level of supervision is required when the working relationship is new, the task is complex, or the delegatee is inexperienced or has not demonstrated an acceptable level of competence.

ASSIGNING VERSUS DELEGATING

Assigning tasks is not the same as delegating tasks. Assignment, as defined by the ANA, is "the distribution of work that each staff member is responsible for during a given work period" (2012). An assignment designates those activities that a staff member is responsible for performing as a condition of employment and is consistent with the staff member's job position and description, legal scope of practice, and training and educational background. The staff member assumes responsibility and is accountable for completing the assignment.

Assignment Considerations

Assigning groups of patients to various care providers, including UAP and LPNs or LVNs, is not appropriate. For example, UAP cannot be assigned to a patient or group of patients, but rather should be assigned to an RN. Typical assignments for UAP include passing trays, assisting patients with activities of daily living, transporting patients, stocking supplies, and completing delegated tasks for the RN. The LPN or LVN may be assigned specific patients for whom to perform care, but the RN remains responsible for all nursing practice activities, including patient assessment, care planning, and patient teaching.

The RN is also responsible for assignments made to personnel in the clinical setting. Several factors should be considered when making assignments.

- **Patient's physiologic status and complexity of care:** Are vital signs unstable? Is the patient's condition changing rapidly? Does the patient have multisystem involvement? Does the patient need extensive health education? Does the patient need extensive emotional support? What technology is involved in the care (e.g., cardiac monitor, intravenous pump, patient-controlled analgesia pump)? Patients with more unstable physiologic status or complex care requirements need a higher level of skilled care.

- **Infection control:** To what extent are isolation procedures required? Which patients could be adversely affected as a result of cross-contamination? For example, a new patient is admitted with a history of night sweats and chronic cough. The results of a sputum culture are pending. Another patient on the unit was admitted with complications resulting from chemotherapy. The same caregiver should not be assigned to a potentially infectious patient and an immunosuppressed patient.

- **Degree of supervision:** What level of supervision, direct or indirect, is required based on staff members' education, experience, skill level, and competence? Is the appropriate supervision available? The on-call RN who works an occasional weekend may require more supervision than the LPN who has worked in the unit full time and has demonstrated competence in caring for the patient population on the unit.

Note that the most experienced skilled staff members should not be exclusively assigned to the most complex, difficult cases. Assignments should be used as a staff development tool. Assigning a less experienced nurse to a more complex patient, but at the same time increasing the level of supervision, increases that nurse's skill level, competence, and confidence while maintaining safe, effective patient care.

Working with Interprofessional Health Care Team Members

Other health professionals who are members of the interprofessional health care team, including respiratory therapists, physical therapists, occupational therapists, speech therapists, nutritionists, medical social workers, and chaplains, are very valuable in helping meet patient care needs. In the vignette, Ms. Miller will need to coordinate the efforts of each of the interprofessional team members available to her unit to accomplish the many and varied tasks needed by the patients for whom she is responsible and accountable. For example, the respiratory therapist monitors all patients on ventilators and assists in the weaning process. The medical social worker provides valuable assistance to identify family support and assists with nursing home placement for Mr. G. The speech therapist can work on communication techniques with Mr. A., the ventilator-dependent patient who becomes very frustrated when he tries to speak.

BUILDING DELEGATION AND SUPERVISION SKILLS

Effective delegation is an underlying quality for the success of working with others efficiently and being able to provide safe, cost-effective care to patients. Delegating can be very difficult, especially for the novice nurse. Some of the struggles the nurse has are the fear of being disliked, fear of making a mistake, inexperience in working with UAP or LPNs or LVNs, lack of confidence, and lack of knowledge of the delegation process itself. Because delegation and supervision involve interactions between two people, the RN needs to develop strong interpersonal skills and a supportive work environment to guarantee an effective delegation situation. Following are management skills RNs need to develop to become proficient at delegation and supervision.

Communicate Effectively

Clear communication is the key to successful delegation. The first step toward effective communication is for the RN to know exactly what needs to be done and what outcomes are expected. What is the specific task to be done? For whom is the task to be done? When is the task to be done? How is the task to be performed? What is the expected outcome? What feedback is expected? Why does the task need to be done in a certain way?

Maintaining self-control and confidence is an important communication skill. New RNs often have expressed concern about delegating to more seasoned LPNs or LVNs or UAPs. "I have been working here for 12 years, and I do not need you telling me what to do" might be a typical response directed to the new RN. The RN's correct response is to maintain composure and confidence and remain positive. "I really appreciate your experience and knowledge, and I need you to help our team and patients by . . . [describe the task clearly]."

It also is important to listen carefully to the delegatee's response. Did the delegatee appear to listen and understand the directions? Did he or she appear to be hesitant to accept the task? Angry? Uninterested? Frustrated? If a delegation action elicits a negative response from the delegatee, ask for feedback using open-ended, nonthreatening statements, such as, "You seem unsure about performing this task." Always provide an opportunity for the delegatee to ask questions. The positive communication techniques discussed in Chapter 18 provide additional guidelines for the reader to enhance delegation skills.

Create an Environment of Trust and Cooperation

Staff members will report problems more quickly if they know that the reaction from the supervisor will be nonthreatening and nonjudgmental. When mistakes occur, the person should not be blamed or criticized, but rather the supervisor should look for root causes and system issues, such as inadequate training or an excessive workload. Encouraging staff members to report and discuss problems is an excellent method of improving patient care and maintaining a helpful, supportive attitude. Just as the RN establishes trust and rapport with patients, he or she should strive for the same type of supportive relationships with staff members.

Provide Feedback and Follow-Up Evaluation

The delegation process is not complete until the RN reassesses the patient and adjusts the plan of care as indicated. The RN also should provide honest feedback to the delegatee about his or her performance. An easy, although often overlooked, delegation skill is to praise good performance. Often more difficult for the RN, and sometimes ignored, is the duty to address poor job performance.

The RN should tell the staff member about mistakes in a supportive manner—in private—with a focus on "learning from mistakes." However, if the staff member performs in an inappropriate, unsafe, or incompetent manner, the RN must intervene immediately and stop the unsafe activity, document the facts of the performance, and report to the supervisor. In addition, the RN should request additional training or other appropriate action for the staff member to ensure that patient safety is protected. The RN has a professional responsibility to intervene appropriately when poor performance is observed.

SUMMARY

Effective delegation and supervision are essential skills for the professional nurse in any practice role or setting, especially with the increased use of UAP to provide health care services. Although there is no definitive list of what can and cannot be delegated, the RN is guided to safe, effective delegation and supervision through an assessment of (1) the clinical situation; (2) patient needs; (3) the job descriptions and competencies of the assistive and vocational or practical nursing personnel; (4) the health care organization's policies and procedures; (5) nurse practice acts and other regulations and applicable state laws; and (6) professional standards of nursing practice. This chapter presents information to assist the RN with delegation decisions and also discusses effective delegation and supervision skills, including communicating effectively, creating an environment of trust and cooperation, and providing feedback and follow-up evaluation. These activities and skills provide the tools the RN needs to provide safe and legal delegation in practice.

REFERENCES

American Nurses Association: *Principles for delegation*, Silver Spring, MD, 2012, American Nurses Association.

American Nurses Association: *Nursing: scope and standards of practice*, Washington, DC, 2010, American Nurses Association.

American Nurses Association and National Council of State Boards of Nursing: *Joint statement on delegation*, 2014 (website). https://www.ncsbn.org/Delegation_joint_statement_NCSBN-ANA.pdf. Accessed September 20, 2014.

Badzek LA: Provision four. In *Guide to the Code of Ethics for Nurses: Interpretation and application*, Silver Spring, MD, 2008, Nursebooks.org.

Duffy M, McCoy SF: *Delegation and you*, Silver Spring, MD, 2014, American Nurses Association, Nursebooks.org.

Hansten RI, Jackson M: *Clinical delegation skills: a handbook for professional practice*, ed 4, Sudbury, MA, 2009, Jones and Bartlett.

Institute of Medicine: *Keeping patients safe: transforming the work environment of nurses*, Washington, DC, 2004, National Academies Press.

Johnson SH: Teaching nursing delegation: analyzing nurse practice acts, *J Contin Educ Nurs* 27(2):52–58, 1996.

Legal Eagle Eye Newsletter for the Nursing Profession: *Patient chokes, dies: Nurse ruled negligent, delegated supervision of patient to aide*, 18(1), 2010, (website). http://www.nursinglaw.com/jan10ang7.pdf. Accessed September 20, 2014.

National Council of State Boards of Nursing: *Working with others: a position paper*, 2005 (website). http://www.ncsbn.org/Working_with_Others.pdf. Accessed January 31, 2015.

21

Staffing and assigning work are two of the nurse manager's most important and challenging roles.

Staffing and Nursing Care Delivery Models

Barbara Cherry, DNSc, MBA, RN, NEA-BC

e Additional resources are available online at: *http://evolve.elsevier.com/Cherry/*

PROFESSIONAL/ETHICAL ISSUE

LaMicha Hogan, RN, staff nurse in a pediatric unit, is becoming concerned about quality of care issues on her unit. When she first came to work in this unit 18 months ago, she was very impressed with the quality of care the patients received and the camaraderie among the nurses. Team nursing was fully implemented and all nurses supported each other and the families to ensure the pediatric patients received the best care possible. She was thrilled to have become part of such a great team and able to provide excellent care to her patients. Over the last few months, patient acuity and patient census has increased but the number of nurses on the unit has not changed. In response to the increased workload, charge nurses have started making patient care assignments based on tasks rather than on the team nursing model, explaining to the staff nurses that assignments by task is a much more

efficient way to get the work done. Some of LaMicha's colleagues have expressed dissatisfaction with their ability to provide good nursing care and they are also noticing more complaints from family members. LaMicha believes that the shift away from the team nursing model, along with the increased patient volume and acuity, has led to fragmented care and a loss of the team spirit once so prevalent among the nurses. What can LaMicha do as a staff nurse to help find a resolution to the staffing concerns? What data might be available to staff nurses to assess patient outcomes and patient and nurse satisfaction for a quantifiable analysis of the staffing situation? Who should be involved in evaluating and making decisions about staffing and nursing care delivery models? How can LaMicha approach the charge nurses and/or the nurse manager to help address the situation?

VIGNETTE

As a student nurse, John Knox noticed during rotations through the different clinical areas that the registered nurses (RNs) had various types of responsibilities and duties. On the medical-surgical units, RNs supervised a group of licensed practical nurses (LPNs) and nursing assistants who provided direct patient care, and the RNs performed patient assessments, care planning, and education. In the critical care unit, RNs provided all the care required by the patient with little help from any other caregivers. In the obstetric unit, two

RNs worked as a team to provide care to laboring mothers. In the outpatient health clinic, each RN was assigned to perform specific tasks; one nurse was assigned to do all diabetic teaching, and another was assigned to triage all telephone calls from patients. Some of the clinical areas used a mostly RN staff, whereas other clinical units had a variety of staff, from RNs to nursing assistants. John had many questions about why care delivery was very different in the different clinical sites.

Questions to Consider While Reading this Chapter:

1. Why is the RN's work assignment different in different units—obstetrics, critical care, medical-surgical, and the outpatient clinic?
2. Who decides how many nurses and other personnel are needed to staff a clinical site?
3. How do nurse managers on nursing units decide how assignments will be made?
4. Who has responsibility and authority for making patient care assignments?

KEY TERMS

Clinical pathway: Clinical management plans that specify the optimal timing and sequencing of major patient care activities and interventions by the interprofessional team for a particular diagnosis, procedure, or health condition and are designed to standardize care delivery (Coffey et al, 2005); clinical pathways may also be called critical paths, practice protocols, or care maps.

Clinical practice guidelines (CPG): Recommendations for appropriate treatment and care for specific clinical circumstances; guidelines are developed though a systematic process to integrate the best evidence for treating specific medical conditions and assist health care providers to make decisions about appropriate treatment (Institute of Medicine [IOM], 1990).

Nursing care delivery model: Also called care delivery system or patient care delivery model; details the way work assignments, responsibility, and authority are structured to accomplish patient care; depicts which health care worker is going to perform what tasks, who is responsible, and who has the authority to make decisions.

Patient acuity: Indication of the amount and complexity of care required for any particular patient; high acuity indicates a need for more intense, complex nursing care as compared with lower acuity,

which indicates a need for moderate, less complex nursing care.

Patient classification system: Method used to group or categorize patients according to specific criteria and care requirements and thus help quantify the patient acuity, or amount and level of nursing care needed.

Patient outcome: A measurable condition that results from interventions by the health care team; a change in a person's health after treatment; outcomes may be positive such as improved mobility or improved lab values or negative such as infections, falls, or death.

Staff mix: Combination of categories of workers employed to provide patient care (e.g., RNs, LPNs, or licensed vocational nurses [LVNs], and unlicensed assistive personnel [UAP]).

Staffing: Ensuring that an adequate number and mix of health care team members (e.g., RNs, LPNs or LVNs, UAP, clerical support) are available to provide safe, quality patient care.

Unlicensed assistive personnel (UAP): An unlicensed individual who is trained to function in an assistive role to the RN by performing patient care activities as delegated by the nurse; may include nursing assistants, clinical assistants, orderlies, health aides, or other titles designated within the work setting.

LEARNING OUTCOMES

After studying this chapter, the reader will be able to:

1. Outline key issues surrounding staffing for a health care organization.
2. Evaluate lines of responsibility and accountability associated with various types of nursing care delivery models.
3. Analyze the advantages and disadvantages of nursing care delivery models in relation to patient care in various settings.
4. Integrate essential components of the critical pathway model into patient care planning.
5. Differentiate among several nursing care delivery models by evaluating their defining characteristics.
6. Explain the purpose and components of nursing case management.
7. Summarize criteria to be considered in developing future models of nursing care delivery.

CHAPTER OVERVIEW

Of all the nurse's varied and complex roles, staffing and assigning work is probably the most challenging and certainly the most important to the delivery of safe, quality patient care. Charge nurses may spend up to 90% of their time on staffing issues (Institute for Staffing Excellence and Innovation, 2013). Staffing ensures that an appropriate number and level of staff members are available to provide care; assigning is the method used to divide work tasks

among the various staff members. This chapter presents a brief introduction to staffing and its surrounding issues, such as acuity levels and staff satisfaction. A description follows of various nursing care delivery models, which details how work assignments are structured. Also discussed are telehealth and case management as nursing care delivery models, in addition to the use of clinical pathways and clinical practice guidelines.

STAFFING

Staffing can be defined as the activities required to ensure that an adequate number and mix of health care team members (e.g., RNs, LVNs or LPNs, UAP, clerical support) are available to meet patient needs and provide safe, quality care. Important research is validating the contribution and value of RNs to improving patient outcomes, reducing complications and length of hospital stay, and preventing premature mortality (Blegen et al, 2011; McHugh & Ma, 2013; Needleman et al, 2011; Tubbs-Cooley et al, 2013). Two major reports—*Keeping Patients Safe: Transforming the Work Environment of Nurses* (Institute of Medicine [IOM], 2004) and *The Future of Nursing: Leading Change, Advancing Health* (IOM, 2011)—have strongly affirmed nurses' essential roles in achieving quality patient care and safety. For nurses to have the greatest opportunity to achieve safe, quality care, staffing systems must (1) address individual and aggregate patient care needs; (2) incorporate clinical competencies of nurses and other team members to provide care to specified patient populations; (3) reflect the value of RNs as vitally important to the organization; and (4) provide nurses time to exercise professional judgment and acknowledge that patient needs can change from moment to moment (ANA, 2012). While appreciating the overall value of the RN in providing patient care, several specific considerations regarding staffing are reviewed related to (1) patient needs, (2) nursing characteristics, and (3) organizational needs and the practice environment.

Staffing and Patient Needs

Primary considerations for staffing a specific nursing unit are the number of patients; the level of intensity of care required by those patients (commonly referred to

as patient acuity); contextual issues, such as architecture, geography of the environment, and available technology; level of preparation and experience of the staff members providing the care; and the quality of the nurses' work life (ANA, 2012). Knowing only the number of patients that require care is an ineffective way to plan staffing because of the wide range of care requirements needed by individual patients. To account for the diverse care needs and quantify the intensity of care required by a group of patients, nurses use various patient classification systems.

Patient Classification Systems

Patient classification systems group or categorize patients according to specific criteria and care needs and thus help quantify the amount and level of care needed, referred to as the *acuity level.* The higher the acuity level, the more intense and complex the patient's nursing care needs. For example, patients may be grouped in such categories as "uncomplicated postpartum" or "ventilator dependent." These two groups of patients require very different levels and amounts of care and therefore are categorized at different acuity levels. Imagine the many different kinds of patients treated by a health care facility, and you can begin to picture the complexity of patient classification systems. Electronic patient classification systems that extract data from the electronic health record and determine patient acuity scores are now available to streamline the method of managing patient acuity.

Because of this complexity and the differences in patient populations across different health care facilities, patient classification systems vary from organization to organization. However, the ANA (2012) has recommended that the following physical and psychosocial factors be considered when determining the intensity of care required for any group of patients:

- Age and functional ability
- Complexity of care needs
- Communication skills
- Cultural and linguistic diversities
- Severity and urgency of the admitting condition
- Scheduled procedures
- Ability to meet health care requisites
- Availability of social supports
- Other specific needs identified by the patient and by the RN

Understanding the intensity of care required by individual patients and groups of patients based on these factors is the first step in developing effective patient classification systems and planning for appropriate staffing levels. The second step is knowing the level of preparation, skill, and experience of the staff members who are available to provide patient care.

Level of Staff Preparation and Experience

It is of critical importance that the staff members available to provide patient care have the educational preparation, skill, clinical judgment, and experience necessary to meet patient care needs. Another consideration in staffing is the clinical competencies that are required to care for the population being served as well as the nurse's competency with technology and clinical interventions (ANA, 2012). In recognition of the importance of nurse competencies in staffing, the American Association of Critical Care Nurses (AACN) recommends the AACN Synergy Model for Patient Care (AACN, 2014). Staffing systems based on the Synergy Model match patient needs and nurse characteristics to achieve ideal patient outcomes. The nurse who is responsible for making staffing decisions must be aware of each individual staff member's educational level, competencies, experience, skill, and training. Ideally, clinical support from experienced RNs should be available to support and advance the skills of those RNs and other staff members with less experience.

Staffing and Staff Satisfaction

Nurses who are satisfied with their work generally provide higher quality, more cost-effective care. Staffing systems should address the quality of work life for the nursing staff as equally important as the quality of patient outcomes. Attention to staff schedules is a major

responsibility for the nurse manager, especially in light of the 24-hour/day, 365-day/year staffing needs in many health care facilities. Creative staffing options are available to meet the varied needs of staff members, including the following:

- 10-hour shifts, 4 days per week
- 12-hour shifts, 3 days per week
- Combination of 8-hour and 12-hour shifts
- Premium pay or part-time staff for weekend work
- Job sharing, flextime, and/or staff self-scheduling

Each of these options has various advantages and disadvantages. For example, long shifts over consecutive days may result in clinical errors when nurses become fatigued (Barker and Nussbaum, 2011; IOM, 2004). Self-scheduling is a popular staffing technique in which the responsibility for staffing the unit is delegated to the employees on the unit who work collectively to design the schedule based on pre-established staffing criteria and some guidance from the manager. No one scheduling system has proven to be best overall for staff satisfaction. However, staffing methods that gain staff input and enhance staff autonomy seem to be a major key to staff satisfaction (Wieck et al, 2009).

Staffing and Organizational Needs

The three basic organizational needs that are significantly affected by staffing are: (1) financial resources, (2) licensing regulations and The Joint Commission (TJC) or other accreditation standards, and (3) customer satisfaction.

Financial Resources

Productivity, the ratio of the amount of outputs produced (e.g., home visits) to the specific amount of input (nursing hours worked), is the measure of staffing efficiency. Because staff salaries are by far the largest expense for any health care organization, productivity—or the efficient use of staff—has a direct effect on the organization's bottom line. Fortunately, even though RNs represent the highest-paid staff in a facility, research has yet again demonstrated the value of RNs in improving patient outcomes and increasing hospital profitability (Anderson et al, 2011; Dall et al, 2009; McCue et al, 2003). However, it is important to remember that most health care organizations continue to function under tight financial constraints, making efficient management of staff essential to ensure the organization's financial solvency. The nurse manager is accountable for appropriately managing staffing to stay within budgetary guidelines for the following:

- Numbers of staff working at any given time to provide care to a given number of patients
- Staff mix, the combination of types of workers present to provide patient care e.g., RNs, LVNs or LPNs, and UAP)

Licensing Regulations and Accreditation

Health care facility licensing agencies, such as a state health department, and accreditation agencies, such as TJC, address minimum staffing levels. However, TJC and most state licensing agencies do not impose mandatory staffing ratios. These agencies do look for evidence that patients receive adequate care, which can only occur with adequate staffing. They also require documentation of staff training and competency to care for the organization's specific patient population. Licensing regulations for long-term care facilities stipulate minimum RN coverage for the unit, but do not mandate specific nurse-to-patient ratios.

State legislative bodies and professional organizations have addressed staffing in various ways. In 1999, California became the first state to enact legislation requiring hospitals to meet minimal staffing standards. Rather than mandating staffing ratios, the ANA recommends staffing committees that develop unit-specific staffing plans with input from direct care RNs and based on various factors including nurse experience and education, patient numbers, patient acuity, and patient outcomes. The National Database of Nursing Quality Indicators (NDNQI) serves as a resource for data on nurse-sensitive outcomes, including patient falls, catheter-associated urinary tract infections, and nurse turnover and job satisfaction. Such data can serve as a powerful influence for nurses to advocate for safe staffing. States that have enacted legislation reflecting the ANA staffing model include Texas, Oregon, Illinois, Connecticut, Ohio, Washington, and Nevada (ANA, 2014).

Customer Satisfaction

Perhaps most critical to an organization's success in a competitive health care environment is customer (patient) satisfaction. The key to customer satisfaction is the patient's personal interaction with the organization's employees. "Interactions with patients and their families have remarkably strong effects on clinical outcomes, functional status, and even physiologic

measures of health" (Kenagy et al, 1999). With the advent of health care reform, patient satisfaction is now tied directly to financial rewards for hospitals. Medicare reimbursement rewards inpatient hospitals for providing quality care to include patient satisfaction. Appropriate staffing with well-trained, competent, professional nurses is essential to ensure patient satisfaction and allow hospitals to gain the financial rewards of high patient satisfaction.

This section has provided the reader with a brief introduction to staffing issues, such as scheduling options, patient classification systems, productivity and staff mix, and the RN's contribution to improved patient outcomes. These issues related to staffing in a health care organization are much more complex than may appear from this introduction. The reader, especially the person interested in entering nursing management, is encouraged to learn more about staffing and these related issues.

NURSING CARE DELIVERY MODELS

Nursing care delivery models, also called *care delivery systems* or *patient care delivery models,* detail the way task assignments, responsibility, and authority are structured to accomplish patient care. The nursing care delivery model describes which health care worker is going to perform what tasks, who is responsible, and who has the authority to make decisions. The basic premise of nursing care delivery models is that the number and type of caregivers are closely matched to patient care needs to provide safe, quality care in the most cost-effective manner possible.

The four classic nursing care delivery models used during the past six decades are: (1) total patient care, (2) functional nursing, (3) team nursing, and (4) primary nursing. Efforts to continually improve both the quality and cost-effectiveness of patient care have resulted in variations to these four classic models. Examples of variations include modular nursing and the partnership model (or coprimary nursing). Other types of nursing care models include patient-centered care, telehealth nursing, and case management. As the health care system continues to evolve in the twenty-first century with a focus on rapid patient turnover in acute care settings, extensive use of outpatient and community-based settings, and evidence of the RN's valuable role in patient safety and improved outcomes, the need for new models of nursing care delivery is emerging. Thus considerations for future care delivery models also are presented.

Total Patient Care

The oldest method of organizing patient care is total patient care, sometimes referred to as *case nursing*. In total patient care, nurses are responsible for planning, organizing, and performing all care, including personal hygiene, medications, treatments, emotional support, and education required for their assigned group of patients during the assigned shift. A diagram of the total patient care model is shown in Figure 21-1.

Advantages of the total patient care model are as follows:

- The patient receives holistic, unfragmented care by only one nurse per shift.
- At shift change, the RN who has provided care and the RN assuming care can easily communicate about the patient's condition and collaborate about the plan of care

FIGURE 21-1 The Total Patient Care (case method) Delivery Model.

- The nurse maintains a high degree of practice autonomy.
- Lines of responsibility and accountability are clear.

Disadvantages of the total patient care model are as follows:

- The number of RNs required to provide total patient care may simply not be available because of nursing shortages or financial constraints.
- The RN performs many tasks that could be performed by a caregiver with less training at a lower cost.

Today the total patient care method is commonly used in the hospital's critical care areas, such as intensive care units and postanesthesia care units, where continuous assessment and a high degree of clinical expertise are required at all times. This method is less widely used in other patient care settings as health care organizations move to more efficient, interprofessional team approaches to patient care, allowing RNs to concentrate on aspects of care essential to good patient outcomes, such as providing patient teaching and evaluating the patient's response to the plan of care.

Functional Nursing

In the functional nursing method of patient care delivery, staff members are assigned to complete certain tasks for a group of patients rather than care for specific patients. For example, the RN performs all assessments and care planning, and administers all intravenous medications; the LVN or LPN gives all oral medications; and the assistant performs hygiene tasks and takes vital signs. An RN makes the assignments and coordinates the care. A diagram of the functional nursing care model is shown in Figure 21-2.

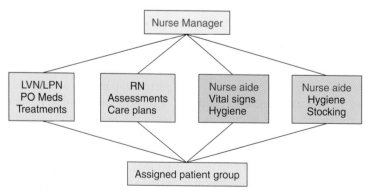

FIGURE 21-2 The Functional Nursing Care Delivery Model.

Advantages of the functional nursing model are as follows:

- Patient care is provided in an economic and efficient manner because less-skilled, lower-cost workers are used in areas where task completion is the focus.
- A minimum number of RNs is required to supervise and to perform strictly nursing duties.
- Tasks are completed quickly, and there is little confusion about job responsibilities.

Disadvantages of the functional nursing model are as follows:

- Care may be fragmented, and the possibility of overlooking priority patient needs exists because several different workers focus only on performing specific patient care tasks.
- The patient may feel confused because of the many different individuals providing different aspects of care.
- Caregivers may feel unchallenged and unmotivated when performing repetitive functions.

Although the functional nursing model is considered efficient and economical, the patient is treated by many caregivers who are not able to give personalized care because they are focused on performing a task, not on meeting patient needs. This model may not fit well in the new health care system, which focuses on customer service. However, functional nursing care delivery is still appropriate in some care settings such as the operating room.

Team Nursing

In team nursing, the RN functions as a team leader and coordinates a small group (generally no more than four or five) of ancillary personnel to provide care to a small group of patients. As coordinator of the team, the RN must know the condition and needs of all the patients assigned to the team and plan for individualized care for each patient. The team leader also is responsible for encouraging a cooperative environment and maintaining clear communication among all team members. The team leader's duties include assessing patients and planning care, assigning duties, directing and assisting team members, giving direct patient care, teaching, and coordinating patient activities. A diagram of the team nursing model is shown in Figure 21-3.

Advantages of the team nursing model are:

- High-quality, safe and effective care can be provided with a relatively high proportion of support staff and/or UAP.

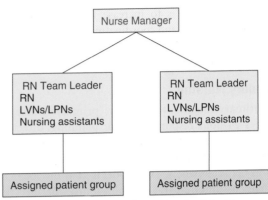

FIGURE 21-3 The Team Nursing Model.

- Each team member participates in decision making and contributes his or her own special expertise in caring for patients.

Disadvantages of the team nursing model are as follows:

- Continuity of care may suffer if the daily team assignments vary and the patient is confronted with many different caregivers.
- The team leader may not have the leadership skills required to effectively direct the team and create a "team spirit."
- Insufficient time for care planning and communication may lead to unclear goals and fragmented care.

Team nursing is an effective, efficient method of patient care delivery and has been used in most inpatient and outpatient health care settings. However, for team nursing to succeed, the team leader must have strong clinical skills, good communication skills, delegation ability, decision-making ability, and the ability to create a cooperative working environment. In an attempt to overcome some of its disadvantages, the team nursing design has been modified many times since its original inception, and variations of the model are evident in other methods of nursing care delivery, such as modular nursing.

Modular nursing, sometimes referred to as pod nursing (Friese et al, 2014), is a modification of team nursing and focuses on a smaller team assigned to a geographic location in the nursing unit. The nursing unit is divided into modules or districts, and the same team of caregivers is assigned consistently to the same geographic location. The concept of modular nursing calls for a smaller group of staff providing care for a smaller group of patients. The goal is to increase the involvement of the RN in planning and coordinating care. To maximize efficiency, each designated module should contain all the supplies needed by the staff to perform patient care.

Primary Nursing

In primary nursing, the RN, or "primary" nurse, assumes 24-hour responsibility for planning, directing, and evaluating the patient's care from admission through discharge. This model differs significantly from the total patient care model in that the "primary nurse" assumes 24-hour responsibility for directing the patient's plan of care. While on duty, the primary nurse may provide total patient care or delegate some patient care tasks to LPNs or LVNs or UAP. When the primary nurse is off duty, care is provided by an associate nurse who follows the care plan established by the primary nurse. The primary nurse, who has 24-hour responsibility, is notified if any problems or complications develop and directs alterations in the plan of care. A fundamental responsibility for the nurse in the primary nursing model is to maintain clear communication among all members of the health care team, including the patient, family, physician, associate nurses, and any other members of the health care team. A diagram of the primary nursing model is shown in Figure 21-4.

Advantages of the primary nursing model are:
- One-to-one relationships between nurse and patient support relationship-based care.
- Nurses are able to practice with a high degree of autonomy and feel challenged and rewarded.

Disadvantages of the primary nursing model are:
- Implementation may be difficult because the primary nurse is required to practice with a high degree of responsibility and autonomy.

- A high degree of clinical judgment and critical thinking is necessary to address clinical problems and to communicate effectively with the health care team.
- The RN may not be willing to accept the 24-hour responsibility required in primary nursing.
- The number of nurses required for this method of care may be difficult to recruit and prove to be more costly for the organization.

The primary care nursing model lends itself well to home health nursing, hospice nursing, oncology nursing and long-term care settings in which the patient requires nursing care for an extended period. Primary nursing may be more difficult to provide in acute care settings, where stays are short and the nurse may see the patient for only 1 or 2 days. Because the concept of primary nursing is sound, some organizations have modified this nursing care model and implemented partnership models that use a wider staff mix.

Partnership Model

The partnership model, sometimes referred to as *coprimary nursing*, is a modification of primary nursing. This model was designed to make more efficient use of the RN, who delegates nonprofessional tasks to the partner, thus providing more time for the RN to address professional demands, such as assessment and patient education. In the partnership model, the RN is partnered with an LVN, LPN, or UAP, and the pair work together consistently to care for an assigned group of patients.

Advantages of the partnership model are as follows:
- The model is more cost-effective than the true primary care nursing system because fewer RNs are needed.
- The RN can encourage the training and growth of his or her partner.

FIGURE 21-4 The Primary Nursing Model.

- The RN can perform the nursing duties, and the partner can perform the nonnursing tasks.

Disadvantages of the partnership model are as follows:

- The RN may have difficulty delegating to the partner.
- Consistent partnerships are difficult to maintain based on varied staff schedules.

PATIENT-CENTERED CARE

Patient-centered care has been a core nursing value since the beginning of professional nursing; however, it is receiving renewed attention for all health professionals as a result of the IOM's focus on safety and quality in health care (Mitchell, 2008). The IOM (2001) defines patient-centered care as "providing care that is respectful of and responsive to individual patient preferences, needs, and values and ensuring that patient values guide all clinical decisions." Delivering patient-centered care means that nurses, physicians, and other health professionals partner with patients and families to ensure that health care decisions respect patients' wants, needs, and preferences and patients have the education and support they need to make decisions and participate in their own care (IOM, 2001).

Patient-centered care is more a philosophy of care rather than a typical nursing care delivery model as discussed in the previous sections. However, because patient-centered care has become a core focus in today's health care organizations, it needs to be incorporated as an essential component of any nursing care delivery model. Practical methods for engaging in patient-centered care are to include patients, families, and significant others in:

- Developing care plans and discharge plans.
- Participating in shift-change or other hand-off reports.
- Receiving education they need to make informed decisions.
- Establishing "family advisory councils" to engage patients and families in decision making and care improvements (Ponte et al, 2003).
- Incorporating user-friendly technology to support patient/family education and active engagement in care.

The nurse, as coordinator of the interprofessional team, is responsible for making the patient and family an integral part of the team, keeping the patient involved in decision making, and promoting an environment respectful of patient's wants, needs, and preferences.

CASE MANAGEMENT

Case management is a model of care in which an RN case manager coordinates patient care with the goal of focusing attention on the quality, outcomes, and cost of care throughout an episode of illness and to assist the patient to move through the continuum of care. Case managers may be employed by health insurance companies to guide care for health plan members or they may be employed by hospitals to coordinate a patient's care throughout the course of an illness. Hospital nurse case managers manage a caseload of patients from preadmission (or onset of illness) to discharge (or resolution of illness). Although case managers generally do not perform direct care duties, they assume a planning and evaluative role and collaborate with the interprofessional health care team to ensure that goals are met, quality is maintained, and progress toward discharge is made. For example, the nurse case manager coordinates arrangements to move the patient from acute care to rehabilitation to home health to independent living, as determined by patient needs. See Case Study 21-1 for an example of case management.

Case Management Related to Other Nursing Care Delivery Models

Nursing case management in a health care facility supplements nursing care and does not take the place of the nursing care delivery model in place to provide direct patient care. For example, if a hospital's medical-surgical unit uses a team nursing approach to patient care, a system of case management also might be in place to assist with coordinating the patient's total care through discharge. Case management is not needed for every patient in a health care facility and generally is reserved for the chronically ill, seriously ill or injured, and long-term, high-cost cases.

Newer Models of Case Management

As health care reform focuses on moving care from expensive acute care settings to less costly community and home settings, newer care models with a foundation in case management are emerging. The first such model is the use of *Patient Navigators*. First conceptualized in

CASE STUDY 21-1   Functions of a Case Manager

Following is a case study to demonstrate the functions of the case manager:

Mr. Smith, 58 years of age, was diagnosed with lung cancer 1 year ago. He has been in Medical Center Hospital with multiple complications for more than 3 weeks. Debra Welch, RN, the case manager assigned to Mr. Smith's case, is working with the patient, family, physician, other members of the health care team, and the insurance company to determine a timely, cost-effective discharge plan. Debra has performed a comprehensive health assessment and understands the patient's condition and the available support systems. The physician, patient, family, and health care team agree that Mr. Smith's prognosis is grave, and the treatment plan should be for palliative care only. Pain management is most important at this stage of the disease. Mr. Smith has a strong desire to go home, and his wife and adult daughter are willing to share the responsibility for home care. Debra also has identified the family's need for emotional support to deal effectively with the terminal illness.

After contacting Mr. Smith's insurance company, Debra learns that the company does not provide home health or hospice benefits, but that the patient could be transferred to a subacute facility for continued care. Knowing Mr. Smith's strong desire to go home and the support systems in place, Debra identifies all the costs for home care (hospital bed, bedside commode, oxygen, wheelchair, and hospice support with pain management) and reports the comparative costs of home care versus subacute care to the insurance company. By demonstrating that home care is less expensive than inpatient, subacute care, Debra is able to negotiate successfully a payment for home care from Mr. Smith's insurance company.

As case manager, Debra's next responsibilities are to coordinate Mr. Smith's discharge and to arrange for home services needed, including hospice care and medical equipment. The home plan of care is developed by the health care team. Debra communicates the plan of care to the home care providers to ensure unfragmented care. As a result of case management, Mr. Smith and his family are able to go home with continued support and a smooth transition of care.

---

cancer treatment, patient navigators help "people 'navigate' through the maze of doctors' offices, clinics, hospitals, outpatient centers, insurance and payment systems, patient-support organizations, and other components of the health care system" (National Cancer Institute, 2009, para 1). The use of patient navigators has been expanded to better manage patients with chronic diseases such as diabetes and hypertension (Esperat et al, 2012). Patient navigator responsibilities include helping patients access resources such the community food bank and free medication programs, making home visits to assess the home environment and implications for chronic disease management, and communicating with other members of the health care team to support appropriate care decisions.

A second model emerging as an important role for the RN is in *transitional care*. As patients with complex care needs move across different levels of care and between multiple providers, communication may be rushed and inadequate, resulting in medication errors, lack of follow-through on key referrals, duplicative testing, inconsistent patient monitoring, and overall poorer patient outcomes (National Transitions of Care Coalition, 2011). Health care systems are recognizing the value of nurses to facilitate safe and effective transitions for chronically ill patients to ensure good communication across settings and providers, appropriate follow-up, clear understanding of the prescribed medication regimen, assistance with referrals for needed resources such as transportation or medications, and most important, encouraging patients and families to take an active role in their health care. Nurse case managers, patient navigators, and transitional care nurses all have similar goals—to work across the maze of health care entities to ensure patients receive the best care possible at the lowest cost with the resources they need to be successful in managing their own care to the extent possible.

CLINICAL PATHWAYS

Clinical pathways, also called *critical paths*, *practice protocols*, *patient care protocols*, or *care maps*, are clinical management plans that specify major patient care activities, interprofessional interventions, and desired outcomes within a specified time period for a particular diagnosis or health condition. The advantage of the clinical pathway is that it provides a means of standardizing care for patients with similar diagnoses and defines key processes and patient goals in the day-to-day management of care. A similar but different term, clinical practice guidelines (CPG), guide broader decision making and focus on the decisions to perform a procedure or service. For example, a clinical practice guideline would be used to determine if a patient diagnosed with prostate cancer should undergo radiation treatment based on his specific cancer diagnosis, age, and other comorbidities. The clinical pathway would guide the care provided to a cancer patient currently undergoing radiation therapy. Clinical pathways are usually developed within the health care facility and are based on broader clinical practice guidelines. Because clinical pathways dictate the type and amount of care given, they have financial implications for the health care facility.

In essence, the clinical pathway can be viewed as a road map the patient and health care team should follow to guide the patient's care management and recovery. As the patient progresses along the path, specified goals should be accomplished. If a patient's progress deviates from the planned path, a variance has occurred and the interprofessional team members must create an action plan to address the problem or issue. Clinical pathways were developed in response to the need to identify quality, cost-effective care plans to reduce the patient's length of stay in the hospital. Accreditation agencies such as TJC may stipulate that certain health care facilities use clinical pathways to meet accreditation standards.

Components of Clinical Pathways

Components of a clinical pathway include physical assessment guidelines, laboratory and diagnostic tests, medications and procedures, safety and self-care activities, nutrition requirements, patient and family education, discharge planning, and milestones the patient should achieve through the progression of care. Many clinical pathways also address triggers, which are events that identify potential or actual variations in the patient's response to the planned interventions. Common uses for clinical paths in acute care settings are for the treatment of community-acquired pneumonia, common surgical procedures such as total hip or knee replacement, and stroke or transient ischemic attack.

Clinical pathways may be developed by a team in the organization to include representatives from nursing, medicine, therapy, pharmacy, and dietary. Professional medical and nursing associations and the Agency for Healthcare Research and Quality (AHRQ)

(www.guidelines.gov) are excellent sources for currently recommended clinical practice guidelines.

CHOOSING A NURSING CARE DELIVERY MODEL

The nursing care delivery models presented in this chapter can be integrated into a variety of health care settings, including acute care, long-term care, ambulatory care, home care, and hospice. The organizational structure, patient needs, and staff availability influence which delivery system will be used.

Acute care settings may use different types of care delivery models for various patient care units. Emergency departments often use functional approaches to care because emphasis is on efficient assessment and immediate treatment. Team nursing frequently is used in medical-surgical units, whereas total patient care is common in critical care units. One study found that more than 50% of staff from 26 hospitals reported using two or three nursing care delivery models, sometimes over the course of one shift (Kramer and Schmalenberg, 2005).

In long-term care settings, such as nursing homes, skilled nursing facilities, and rehabilitation settings, patients remain in the care settings for extended periods. Therefore, the care delivery models may be structured differently than in the acute setting. Because of its economy and efficiency, functional nursing may be used for daily care tasks, whereas a form of primary care nursing is used for assessment, care planning, and evaluation.

The variety of ambulatory care settings continues to grow as health care moves out of the more expensive inpatient settings to the less costly outpatient settings. Outpatient surgery centers, minor emergency clinics, outpatient cancer centers, outpatient dialysis units, outpatient birthing centers, health clinics, and physicians' offices are examples of ambulatory care settings. The nursing care delivery model used in ambulatory settings varies widely, depending on the type of patients being treated and their particular needs. For example, in outpatient dialysis units, a combination of functional and primary care nursing usually works well. Patient care technicians are assigned to perform specific patient care functions, such as dialysis machine setup and treatment initiation, whereas the RN is assigned primary nurse responsibilities for a group of patients to ensure effective assessment, care planning, and care coordination with the interprofessional team. Telephone nursing is becoming increasingly important as a method of care delivery in ambulatory settings.

Home health agencies often use a variation of the primary care model. Although in home care the RN does not provide 24-hour care, he or she is responsible for the patient's needs for a 24-hour period and will coordinate intermittent care provided by others, including the home health aide and therapists involved in the patient's care. In the home health setting, the RN may also function in the role of case manager for his or her assigned patients.

In every care setting, nurses should carefully evaluate the nursing care delivery model to ensure safe, efficient, and effective patient care. When evaluating nursing care delivery models, the following questions should be asked:

- Is patient safety ensured while achieving optimal patient satisfaction and patient outcomes in a timely, cost-effective manner?
- Is patient-centered care being provided with significant involvement of patients and families?
- Are nurses, physicians, and other health team members satisfied with the safety and quality of care they are able to provide?
- Does the system allow for implementation of the nursing process in a timely and efficient manner?
- Does the system facilitate communication among all members of the health care team?

FUTURE NURSING CARE DELIVERY MODELS

Without a doubt, the ways in which nursing care is delivered over the next 20 years will change dramatically as a result of the following factors:

- Rapid technologic advances in medical care with less invasive procedures for disease treatments
- Fast-paced patient turnover in acute care settings; the rapid discharge and admission cycle is now referred to as "churning" and is estimated to range from 25% to 70% on a typical medical-surgical unit (Spader, 2008)

- Evidence of the RN's value in promoting patient safety and quality of care
- Strong focus on patient satisfaction, safety and outcomes of care
- Consumers' demands for instant access to care and information
- Need to engage patients and families to become active partners to address their own health care needs

Because acute care settings now admit only the most seriously ill or injured individuals with a focus on stabilization and transition, the traditional models of nursing care may no longer apply. In the past, nurses provided care based on comprehensive knowledge of the patients' needs, which were learned by caring for the patients over an extended period. Now nurses may have an entirely new group of patients to care for every shift or even more than once during a shift. Identifying effective models of care to support the rapid transition of patients from one setting to another will be a continuing challenge for nurses and health care organizations.

Nurses in outpatient and community-based settings are challenged with similar problems in attempting to address (1) patients' demands for instant access to care and information, and (2) patients' needs for support and education to address lifestyle and personal choices that may affect their health.

Relationship-based care must also be considered as part of the care delivery model in high-tech fast-paced environments where nurses struggle to provide care that is consistent with nursing values of compassion, caring, and healing. Manthey (2003) translated relationship-based care to mean that "regardless of how high-tech, short-term, or financially driven the health system becomes, no one can tell nurses they cannot practice within a conceptual framework of 'intentional presence in a therapeutic relationship with the patient,' where the outcome is competent care that is oriented toward empowering patients to accept responsibility for living their lives with maximum health."

█ SUMMARY

Managers of health care organizations are concerned that patient care is delivered in the most efficient and cost-effective method possible and that staffing is appropriate to ensure safe, high-quality care and

contributes to staff satisfaction. For this reason, nursing care delivery models have undergone tremendous change throughout the past decade and will continue to evolve as organizations look for ways to improve patient safety and outcomes in complex health care systems that are challenged by reduced reimbursement and the need to reduce costs, rapidly advancing technology, rapid patient turnover, and consumer demand for instant access and information. Regardless of changes that are certain to occur, the RN will retain responsibility to evaluate nursing care delivery models to ensure that patient care is delivered safely and efficiently, that caregivers are competent and legally qualified to perform the duties they have been assigned, and that high-quality, safe, patient-centered care and staff satisfaction are maintained.

REFERENCES

American Association of Critical Care Nurses: *The AACN Synergy Model for Patient Care*, 2014 (website). http://www.aacn.org/wd/certifications/content/synmodel.pcms?menu=certification. Accessed October 10, 2014.

American Nurses Association: *Principles for nurse staffing*, ed 2, Silver Spring, MD, 2012, American Nurses Association.

American Nurses Association: *Safe staffing*, 2014 (website). http://www.rnaction.org/site/PageNavigator/nstat_take_action_safe_staffing.html?ct=1. Accessed October 10, 2014.

Anderson EF, Frith KH, Caspers B: Linking economics and quality: developing an evidence-based nurse staffing tool, *Nurs Admin Q* 35(1):53–60, 2011.

Barker LM, Nussbaum MA: Fatigue, performance and the work environment: a survey of registered nurses, *J Adv Nurs* 67(6):1370–1382, 2011.

Blegen M, Goode C, Spetz J, et al: Nurse staffing effects on patient outcome: safety-net and non-safety-net hospitals, *Med Care* 49(4):406–414, 2011.

Coffey RJ, Richards JS, Remmert CS, et al: An introduction to critical paths, *Qual Manag Health Care* 14(1):46–55, 2005.

Dall TM, Chen YJ, Seifert RF, et al: The economic value of professional nursing, *Med Care* 47(1):97–104, 2009.

Esperat MC, McMurry L, Du F, et al: Transformacion para salud: A patient navigation model for chronic disease self-management, *Online J Issues Nurs* 17(2):1, May 2012.

Friese CR, Grunawalt JC, Bhullar S, et al: Pod nursing on a medical/surgical unit: Implementation and outcomes evaluation, *J Nurs Adm* 44(4):207–211, 2014.

Institute for Staffing Excellence and Innovation: *Staffing Education at the Tip of Your Finger!* 2013 (website). http://www.onnursingexcellence.com/staffing.html. Accessed October 12, 2014.

Institute of Medicine, Field MJ, Lohr KN, editors: *Clinical practice guidelines: directions for a new program*, Washington, DC, 1990, National Academies Press.

Institute of Medicine: *Crossing the quality chasm: a new health system for the 21st century*, Washington, DC, 2001, National Academies Press.

Institute of Medicine: *Keeping patients safe: transforming the work environments of nurses*, Washington, DC, 2004, National Academies Press.

Institute of Medicine: *The Future of nursing: leading change, advancing health*, Washington, DC, 2011, National Academies Press.

Kenagy JW, Berwick DM, Shore MF: Service quality in health care, *JAMA* 281(7):661–665, 1999.

Kramer M, Schmalenberg C: Revisiting the essentials of magnetism tool: there is more to adequate staffing than numbers, *J Nurs Adm* 35(4):188–198, 2005.

Manthey M: Primary nursing, *J Nurs Adm* 33(7/8):369–370, 2003.

McHugh MD, Ma C: Hospital nursing and 30 day readmissions among Medicare patients with heart failure, acute myocardial infarction and pneumonia, *Medical Care* 61(1):52–59, 2013.

McCue M, Mark B, Harless D: Nurse staffing, financial performance, and quality of care, *J Health Care Finance* 29(4):54–76, 2003.

Mitchell PH: Patient-centered care—a new focus on a time-honored concept, *Nurs Outlook* 56(5):197–198, 2008.

National Cancer Institute: *What are patient navigators?* 2009. (website). http://crchd.cancer.gov/pnp/what-are.html. Accessed October 14, 2014.

National Transitions of Care Coalition: *Improved transitions of patient care yield tangible savings*, 2011 (website). http://www.ntocc.org/portals/0/TangibleSavings.pdf. Accessed October 14, 2014.

Needleman J, Buerhaus P, Pankratz V, et al: Nurse staffing and inpatient hospital mortality, *N Engl J Med* 364(11):1037–1045, 2011.

Ponte PR, Conlin G, Conway JB, et al: Making patient-centered care come alive: achieving full integration of the patient's perspective, *J Nurs Adm* 33(2):82–90, 2003.

Spader C: Rapid turnover: admission RNs make fast-paced admits/discharges less stressful for everyone, *NurseWeek* Aug 11:32–33, 2008.

Tubbs-Cooley, H, Cimiotti, J, et al: An observational study of nurse staffing ratios and hospital readmission among children admitted for common conditions, *BMJ Qual Saf* 22(9):735–742, 2013.

Wieck KL, Dols J, Northam S: What nurses want: the nurse incentives project, *Nurs Econ* 27(3):169–201, 2009.

22

Quality Improvement and Patient Safety

Kathleen M. Werner, MS, BSN, RN

Nurses are building bridges to patient safety and quality care.

ⓔ Additional resources are available online at: *http://evolve.elsevier.com/Cherry/*

PROFESSIONAL/ETHICAL ISSUE

Christine Hamilton, RN, works in the cardiac step-down unit at large teaching hospital. Christine graduated from nursing school 6 months ago. She has been managing her own patient assignment for the last few months, but she continues to work closely with her mentor, an experienced RN who has worked on the unit for 15 years. Recently, Christine has become concerned about a pattern on the unit of the nurses ignoring alarms on medical devices. She knows that the purpose of the alarms is to alert caregivers about changes in patient conditions, but she also knows that alarms that don't work correctly can be a nuisance and pull nurses away from other important work. Her greatest concern is that ignoring alarms might result in patient harm. To make the situation more complicated, Christine does not feel comfortable in discussing her concerns with her mentor because she has overheard her mentor tell other nurses that there are times when it is okay to ignore alarms. How should Christine begin to address this situation with her colleagues or supervisor? Discuss how this safety concern might be addressed through the quality-improvement process.

VIGNETTE

It was the third postoperative day for Mrs. Slattery in room 918 on the general surgical unit of Metro Hospital. As she arrived for her day shift, Suzanne Harper, RN, was eager to care for this patient. Suzanne had been with Mrs. Slattery every day since her admission and was looking forward to helping her prepare for discharge. Suzanne carried out the routine morning care and did a thorough assessment of Mrs. Slattery. Much to Suzanne's dismay, Mrs. Slattery was not her usual, upbeat self and was less cooperative than normal, stating: "I just don't have much energy. I know I should get up and walk, but I just don't feel like it." Suzanne also noted that Mrs. Slattery's temperature was higher than normal, so she alerted the surgical house staff during rounds. Mrs. Slattery had blood drawn for a CBC and a urine sample was collected.

Within the hour, the answer to Mrs. Slattery's sudden lack of energy and enthusiasm became known—she had developed a urinary tract infection (UTI), most likely as the result of having an indwelling catheter placed during surgery that still remained. Mrs. Slattery would not be going home until the catheter was removed and treatment of the infection was well under way. Suzanne experienced the wisdom of "hindsight" by noting that the catheter should have been removed by postoperative day two. Due to the surgeon's failure to write an order to discontinue the indwelling catheter in a timely manner—as well as Suzanne's failure to bring this to the provider's attention—Mrs. Slattery was now experiencing a setback in her recovery.

Suzanne began to reflect on the number of times this may have occurred with other patients. She also began to consider the implications from the lack of a consistent and standardized way to track the dwell time of urinary catheters. As in Mrs. Slattery's situation, acquiring a urinary tract infection could cost $12,000 to $20,000 in additional expenses for the hospital; it means additional care and treatment with an extended length of stay that is not paid by Mrs. Slattery's insurance company because the catheter-associated UTI would be deemed an event that should have been prevented. Multiply this cost by just ten additional patients, and suddenly the catheter-associated UTI becomes a significant financial burden for the organization. More important, patients experience discomfort and increased fatigue and run the risk for developing even more complications because of their decreased willingness or ability to cooperate with their postoperative care.

The next week, Suzanne approached her nurse manager and expressed concern about the delays in discontinuing indwelling urinary catheters, which created the potential for catheter-associated UTIs. Suzanne's nurse manager thanked her for the feedback and expressed similar interest in resolving this problem. Infection prevention staff members had already been in preliminary conversations with Suzanne's manager about the increased risk of infection and were willing to work collaboratively with the nursing staff and physicians to find a solution to this problem. Suzanne eagerly volunteered to participate in a quality improvement team that was charged with standardizing the care processes for discontinuation of urinary catheters to assure compliance with removal by postoperative day two for 100% of all patients.

The team met regularly for several weeks and gained a clear understanding of why both physicians and nurses lost "track of time" with respect to removal of these catheters. This was accomplished though the creation of a detailed picture of what typically occurred in documenting postoperative orders by the surgical staff and the routine care implemented by nursing personnel. Breakdowns in this process for assuring completeness of all necessary orders were identified, and the team began working on constructive ways to prevent these breakdowns in the future. The team worked with information technology experts to incorporate the indwelling catheter discontinuation order in an electronic order set easily accessible for all physicians. Furthermore, if the discontinuation order was not documented, an electronic alert would be sent to the attending surgeon to remind him or her to either complete the order or document the rationale for not doing so. Likewise, nursing staff would receive an electronic "best practice alert" reminding them to check the orders for this purpose.

Over time, with ongoing monitoring of the ordering practices and the catheter-associated UTI rates, significant progress was made to the point that infection rates are now nearly zero. Suzanne knows that the proper steps are in place to guarantee that this successful infection reduction effort will be sustained through the thoughtful process that was developed. When her patients are ready for discharge, there will be no setbacks caused by situations that could otherwise have been prevented. Suzanne feels like she is a vested part of this success.

Questions to Consider While Reading this Chapter:
1. What key principles of quality improvement are demonstrated in the vignette?
2. What quality improvement tools did Suzanne and the team most likely use to identify the causes for catheter-associated UTIs?
3. What resources are available to help Suzanne and others in her organization learn more about improving the quality of health care?

KEY TERMS

Cause-and-effect diagram: Tool that is used for identifying and organizing possible causes of a problem in a structured format. It is sometimes called a fishbone diagram because it looks like the skeleton of a fish.

Clinical indicators: Measurable items that reflect the quality of care provided and demonstrate the degree to which desired clinical outcomes are accomplished.

Customer: Individual or group who relies on an organization to provide a product or service to meet some need or expectation. It is these customer needs and expectations that determine quality.

Failure mode and effects analysis (FMEA): A systematic process for identifying potential design and process failures before they occur, with the intent to eliminate them or minimize the risk associated with them.

Flowchart: Picture of the sequence of steps in a process. Different steps or actions are represented by boxes or other symbols.

HAC: Hospital-acquired condition. A term used to indicate an unintended and typically adverse patient-acquired condition occurring as a result of being cared for in a hospital.

IOM: National Academy of Sciences Institute of Medicine; a nonprofit organization with a mission of advancing and disseminating scientific knowledge to improve human health. The institute provides objective, timely, authoritative information and advice concerning health and science policy to the government, the corporate sector, the professions, and the public.

The Joint Commission (TJC): A national agency that conducts surveys of inpatient and ambulatory facilities and certifies their compliance with established quality standards.

Never events: Serious adverse events during an inpatient stay that should never occur or are reasonably preventable through adherence to evidence-based guidelines. The Centers for Medicare and Medicaid Services, through revisions in coverage and payment policies, provide hospitals with financial incentives to reduce the occurrence of never events.

Pareto chart: A graphic tool that helps break down a big problem into its parts and then identifies which parts are the most important.

Process: A series of linked steps necessary to accomplish work. A process turns inputs, such as information or raw materials, into outputs, such as products, services, and reports. Clinical processes are a series of linked steps necessary for the provision of patient care.

Process variation: The differences in how the steps in a work process might be accomplished and/or the variables that may affect each step in the process. Variation results from the lack of perfect uniformity in the performance of any process. Understanding variation in a process is necessary to determine the direction that improvement efforts must take.

Quality improvement (QI): Framework for taking action to systematically make changes that lead to measurable improvements in health care services for patients, staff and organizations; quality is determined by the needs, expectations, and desired health outcomes of individuals and populations.

Root cause analysis (RCA): Method of problem solving that helps to identify how and why an event occurred. RCA is defined by TJC (2013) as a "process for identifying the factors that underlie variation in performance, including the occurrence or possible occurrence of a sentinel event. A root cause analysis focuses primarily on systems and processes, not individual performance" (p. SE-2).

Run chart: Graph of data in time order that helps identify any changes that occur over time; also called a time plot. A run chart that has a centerline and statistical control limits added is known as a control chart.

Sentinel event: Defined by TJC (2013) as an "unexpected occurrence involving patient death or serious physical or psychological injury or the risk thereof. Serious injury specifically includes loss of limb or function. The phrase 'or the risk thereof' includes any process variation for which a recurrence would carry a significant chance of a serious adverse outcome. Such events are called sentinel because they signal the need for immediate investigation and response" (p. SE-1).

Standardization: Approach to process improvement that involves developing and adhering to best-known methods and repeating key tasks in the same way, time and time again, until a better way is found, thereby creating exceptional service with maximal efficiency.

LEARNING OUTCOMES

After studying this chapter, the reader will be able to:

1. Apply principles of quality improvement to the role of the professional nurse.
2. Analyze the basis for the increasing emphasis on health care quality and medical errors.
3. Analyze the role of health care regulatory agencies and how they have embodied the principles of quality improvement.
4. Discuss the role process improvement can play in ensuring patient safety and improving quality in the health care system.
5. Describe the tools and skills necessary for successful quality improvement activities.
6. Discuss the professional nurse's role in promoting patient safety.

CHAPTER OVERVIEW

Although Suzanne Harper's story depicted in the vignette seems credible and would be a logical way for any organization to begin addressing customer concerns, far too often this has not been the case. Hospitals and other health care organizations have been slow to recognize the necessity of a true customer perspective and to emphasize quality and safety in a proactive manner. The intention of this chapter is to make the reader aware of the pressing nature of the nation's quality health care crisis and to address the following questions:

- *What is quality in health care?*
- *Who determines the degree to which quality is evident in our health care system?*

- *How can work processes be redesigned to improve quality?*
- *What do the potential answers to the first three questions mean in relationship to professional nursing accountability?*

The responses to these questions, particularly in relation to nursing's commitment to become involved with quality improvement and to participate in its implementation, provide the elements of hope in determining and implementing sustainable, positive improvements in the design and delivery of health care.

THE URGENT CASE FOR QUALITY IMPROVEMENT IN THE U.S. HEALTH CARE SYSTEM

In an alarming 2000 report by the Institute of Medicine (IOM), titled *To Err Is Human: Building a Safer Health System,* authors extrapolated and summarized data from two major studies and concluded that up to 98,000 patients die each year from preventable medical errors, confirming that poor quality of care is a major problem in the United States (IOM, 2000). An updated estimate, developed from studies that were published from 2008 to 2011, validated these original IOM statistics (James, 2013). Contributing factors cited in the original IOM report included the following:

- Overuse of expensive invasive technology
- Underuse of inexpensive care services
- Error-prone implementation of care that could harm patients and waste money

Following this report, the IOM released *Crossing the Quality Chasm: A New Health System for the 21st Century* (2001) to define a vision for improving the quality of our nation's health care. This report states:

> "The U.S. health care delivery system does not provide consistent, high quality medical care to all people. Americans should be able to count on receiving care that meets their needs and is based on the best scientific knowledge—yet this frequently is not the case. Health care harms too frequently and routinely fails to deliver its potential benefits. Indeed,

between the health care that we now have and the health care that we could have lies not just a gap, but a chasm" (p. 1).

The quality chasm report details a number of factors that have contributed to this chasm, including the unprecedented advancement of science and technology, growing complexity of health care, changing public health care needs, and a poorly organized and uncoordinated health care delivery system. Indicators from recent reports indicate just how wide the quality chasm is between what we know is good care and what is current practice:

- On average, 30% of Americans failed to receive recommend care in 2010; fortunately, however, this has improved somewhat from 34% in 2005 (Agency for Healthcare Research and Quality [AHRQ], 2013).
- On average, patients are subjected to at least one medication error each day with extremely high costs to patients, families, health care professionals, hospitals, and insurance companies (IOM, 2007).

The quality chasm report details six guiding aims for improvement that should be adopted by every individual and group involved in the provision of health care, including health care professionals, public and private health care organizations, purchasers of health care, regulatory agencies and organizations, and state and federal policymakers. These six guiding aims are collectively referred to by the acronym STEEEP. Individually, these aims are for health care to be (IOM, 2001):

- *Safe:* Preventing injuries to patients from the care that is intended to help them

- *Timely:* Reducing waits and sometimes harmful delays for both those who receive and those who give care
- *Effective:* Providing services based on scientific knowledge to all who could benefit, and refraining from providing services to those not likely to benefit
- *Efficient:* Preventing waste, including waste of equipment, supplies, ideas, and energy
- *Equitable:* Providing care that does not vary in quality because of personal characteristics, such as gender, ethnicity, geographic location, and socioeconomic status
- *Patient centered:* Providing care that is respectful of and responsive to individual patient preferences, needs, and values and ensuring that patient values guide all clinical decisions

To help establish a framework for accomplishing the significant redesign of the health care system, the authors of the quality chasm report formulated a set of 10 simple rules to guide improvement initiatives. Professional nurses must serve as role models for all health care professionals, caregivers, and administrators in practicing the following 10 rules (IOM, 2001):

1. Care is based on continuous healing relationships. Patients should receive care whenever they need it and in many forms, including face-to-face visits, via the Internet, telephone, and other means as needed.
2. Care is customized according to patient needs and values. The system should be designed to meet the most common needs, but should also be responsive to individual choices and preferences.
3. The patient is the source of control. Patients should be given the necessary information and opportunity to exercise the degree of control they choose over health care decisions that affect them.
4. Knowledge is shared, and information flows freely. Patients should have unfettered access to their own medical information and to clinical knowledge, with clinicians communicating effectively and sharing information.
5. Decision making is evidence based. Patients should receive care based on the best available scientific knowledge, and care should not vary illogically from clinician to clinician or place to place.
6. Safety is a system property. Patients should be safe; reducing risk and ensuring safety require greater attention to systems that help prevent and mitigate errors.

7. Transparency is necessary. The system should make available to patients and families information that allows them to make informed decisions, including information describing the system's performance on safety, evidence-based practice, and patient satisfaction.
8. Needs are anticipated. The system should anticipate patient needs rather than simply react to events.
9. Waste is continually decreased. The system should not waste resources (e.g., supplies, health professionals' time and energy) or patient time.
10. Cooperation among clinicians is a priority. Clinicians should actively engage in collaboration and communication to ensure an appropriate exchange of information and coordination of care.

The remainder of this chapter provides the reader with a set of principles and skills necessary to implement improvements and move toward a system of health care that is safe, timely, effective, efficient, equitable, and patient centered.

PRINCIPLES OF QUALITY IMPROVEMENT

Many buzzwords describe activities associated with quality improvement (QI). The most prevalent are total quality management (TQM), continuous quality improvement (CQI), continuous process improvement, statistical process control, and performance improvement (PI). The terms themselves are not as important as the principles they embody: assessment and improvement of work processes while focusing on what customers want and need. In the example of Suzanne and her patient, the work process is completing postoperative orders that include timely removal of an indwelling urinary catheter. The customer in this situation would be Suzanne's patient, who wants to recover from surgery without complications so that she can go home as soon as possible. Essentially the cornerstones of QI are quality, scientific approach, and "all one team" (Joiner, 1994).

Quality

To provide a better appreciation of the importance of these three QI cornerstones, a customer's perspective of quality must be considered, including the personal interactions they experience with an organization's personnel in addition to the products or services they receive. The products or services provided to the customer are not made up of just the physical items or a one-time experience that the customer encounters, but rather of all the services that go with it. Organizations actually provide a "bundle" of products and services to customers to satisfy some need. If the service and product or outcomes together are perceived as a good value, a loyal customer following will be established. Or as in the case presented in the vignette, Suzanne's patient might view the entire hospital stay negatively because of the delay in discharge due to a preventable complication.

Scientific Approach

The scientific approach, the second cornerstone of QI, emphasizes that to make significant improvements in an organization's processes, decisions must be based on sound, valid data, and the people managing the processes must have a clear understanding of the nature of variation in processes. Remember that a process is a series of linked steps necessary to accomplish work. For example, the steps necessary to complete a new medication order, from the time the order is received until the medication is administered to a patient, is a process. Understanding variation—the differences in how the steps in the process might be accomplished and/or the variables that may affect each step in the process—is necessary to identify the direction that improvement efforts must take.

Two types of variation in processes can occur: common cause variation and special cause variation. Processes that demonstrate common cause variation are stable, predictable, and statistically in control. Processes that demonstrate both common cause and special cause variation are unstable, unpredictable, and not in statistical control. The actions that should be taken to implement improvements under each type of variation are significantly different.

The best way to understand common cause and special cause variation is to use Suzanne's example again. Suzanne's team members collected data over time regarding the number of times patients' surgeons failed to write postoperative orders that included discontinuation of urinary catheters. Overall, the number of missed orders showed variability because of numerous factors associated with this process, one example being the total number of patients with postoperative orders on any given day. The team recognized the total number of postoperative patients as common cause variation and realized that to decrease the occurrence of missing elements within these orders, the overall process would need to be studied to determine the best ways to change

the postoperative care processes, regardless of the total volume of patients.

The team was also aware of a significant physician learning curve associated with the automation of electronic order sets, with two surgeons who did not complete the required training session prior to when the system went "live." The failure to document the catheter discontinuation order under these circumstances was considered to be special cause process variation, one of extreme impact, but related to a clearly identified single source. If the team had modified the overall documentation process based solely on the special cause factor, the underlying problem most likely would not have been improved for the long term.

All One Team

Effective team functioning is the third QI cornerstone, which embodies the principles of believing in people; treating everyone in the workplace with dignity, trust, and respect; and working toward win-win situations for all customers, employees, shareholders, suppliers, and perhaps even the broader community as a whole. For people to work this way, they must believe it is in their best interest to cooperate; they need to be more concerned with how the system as a whole operates rather than optimizing their own contributing area. In other words, all team members must rely more on cooperation and less on competition.

Suzanne's example is one that demonstrates the following three principles of QI:

1. Quality: Suzanne began to consider the patient as the one who would define the quality of her hospital stay. She recognized that the perceived quality of the entire hospital stay could suffer if the prevention of complications could not be improved.

2. Scientific Approach: Suzanne was supported organizationally by her manager, who provided the opportunity for Suzanne to collaborate with other key members of the health care team to better understand the current status of catheter-associated UTIs through analyzing data and examining variations in the process. This group's work led to a clearer understanding of the interrelationship of the processes across multiple health care professionals, which together affected the overall timeliness of urinary catheter discontinuation and enabled the group to make the necessary improvements to achieve the desired result.

3. "All One Team": Managers in Suzanne's hospital had faith in the people who were working on the catheter-associated UTI team. These people were recognized as those who had the best understanding of how the postoperative care processes were happening and where the system was breaking down.

ADVANCING QUALITY THROUGH REGULATION AND ACCREDITATION

Today, almost all healthcare regulatory and voluntary accrediting agencies require QI in some form. The Centers for Medicare and Medicaid Services (CMS), which administers the U.S. Medicare program, has "conditions of participation" for its quality foundation, and most state licensing authorities also have required QI standards. The Joint Commission, an organization that offers voluntary accreditation for healthcare settings, has a strong focus on quality standards as discussed in the following sections.

The Joint Commission

The Joint Commission (TJC) was one of the first accreditation agencies to embrace QI principles as an accreditation requirement in hospital-based settings. Health care organizations voluntarily seek TJC accreditation to demonstrate that they have achieved a "gold seal of approval" by following the quality and safety standards established by TJC. Today, TJC accredits more than 20,500 health care organizations, including hospitals, ambulatory clinics, and long-term care facilities (TJC, 2014). TJC standards address the organization's level of performance in key functional areas such as patient safety, patient rights, patient treatment, and infection control. The TJC accreditation system not only focuses on an organization's ability to provide safe high-quality care, but also requires evidence of actual performance and continued improvement. Health care organizations that are accredited by TJC receive a deemed status to automatically meet foundational approval from CMS.

Core Measures: National Hospital Quality Measures

In 1997, TJC introduced ORYX®, a performance measurement and improvement initiative, as part of the accreditation process. The ORYX® measurements were intended to support organizations in their quality improvement efforts as well as supplement their accreditation process. In 2002, as part of the ORYX® initiative, accredited hospitals began collecting data on standardized "core" performance measures, and by 2004, TJC and CMS worked together to align current and future measures common to both organizations. These standardized measures are now referred to as National Hospital Quality Measures and can be found on the Joint Commission website at http://www.jointcommission.org/performance_measurement.aspx. The performance data for hospitals across the country are now publicly reported on the TJC website at Quality Check (www.qualitycheck.org) and through the CMS Hospital Compare website (www.medicare.gov/hospitalcompare/).

The National Hospital Quality Measures now have an added level of significance beyond the public reporting aspect. These measures, in concert with patient feedback and other select clinical outcome measures, are being used increasingly in programs designed to "pay for performance" in moving health care payments away from simply paying for the provision of services to paying based on the quality process and outcomes associated with those services.

As part of the Patient Protection and Affordable Care Act of 2010, CMS was authorized to begin its "Value-Based Purchasing" program whereby hospital inpatient Medicare payments are reduced annually (from 1% in the first program fiscal year of 2013 up to a maximum of 2% by fiscal year 2017). Hospitals may earn back the reduced payments or even exceed the original payment amount based on their performance results. Other commercial insurance carriers and state agencies are beginning to deploy similar strategies in their payment agreements. For more information on Value-Based Purchasing, visit the Quality Initiatives section of the CMS website (www.cms.gov/Medicare).

It is especially important for nurses to be knowledgeable about the National Hospital Quality Measures and Value-Based Purchasing because they are in the unique position of supporting the overall management of patient care throughout the length of stay in the facility, working collaboratively with other health care professionals to initiate changes, and monitoring ongoing effectiveness of the care provided. For more information, nurses are encouraged to visit the Performance Measurement section of the TJC website (www.jointcommission.org).

CLINICAL INDICATORS AND PROCESS IMPROVEMENT TOOLS AND SKILLS

The basic foundation of the monitoring and evaluation process required by QI principles is in the use of **clinical indicators**, measurable items that reflect the quality of care. Just like the National Hospital Quality Measures previously referenced, clinical indicators are aspects of clinical care that can be measured to show the degree to which care is or is not implemented as it should be. Indicators focus on clinical actions or outcomes of clinical care; indicators should not focus on procedures that support clinical care. For example, replacing the intravenous (IV) solutions on the IV supply cart as they are used is a procedure that supports clinical care. Administering the correct IV solution at the correct rate as prescribed is appropriate clinical care. Both items are measurable, but only the latter is truly a clinical indicator. Indicators are not meant to define quality, but rather to point the way to assessment of areas in which quality issues may be present.

How do process improvement skills and tools fit with clinical indicators? Clinical indicators help to identify the goals of quality improvement, whereas process improvement skills and tools support the quantitative understanding of key work processes. There are several different methods used by healthcare facilities for quality improvement and process improvement, including Lean methodology, Lean Six Sigma, and failure mode and effects analysis (Frankel et al, 2009). The tools described within this section (e.g., flow charts, Pareto charts) are all used in each of these various methods of quality improvement. It is not within the scope of this chapter to address these specific improvement strategies, but it is important to note that all improvement models generally have the following in common:

- Analyzing and clearly understanding the process
- Selecting key aspects of the process to improve
- Establishing "trial" targets to guide improvement measures
- Collecting and plotting data
- Interpreting results
- Implementing improvement actions and evaluating effectiveness

Various tools, such as **flowcharts**, Pareto charts, cause-and-effect diagrams, and run charts, may be used to accomplish each of these six steps. It will become increasingly necessary for professional nurses to understand improvement models and to develop the ability to apply these tools.

Flowcharts

The analysis of a work process usually is initiated through construction of some sort of flowchart or flow diagram. These are indispensable tools in mapping out what actually occurs during the process versus what is intended. There are several different types of flowcharts, each of which is valuable in its own way. A top-down flowchart simply lists the main steps and substeps of a process in a linear fashion (Figure 22-1). A deployment flowchart maps out the steps of a process under headings that designate the people or departments who carry out each step. This type is especially helpful when dealing with processes that cross multiple areas or caregivers and when there is a need for common understanding of what the process is doing as a

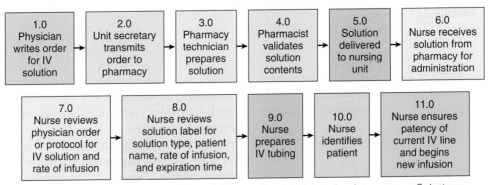

FIGURE 22-1 Top-Down Flowchart of Process for Administering Intravenous Solutions.

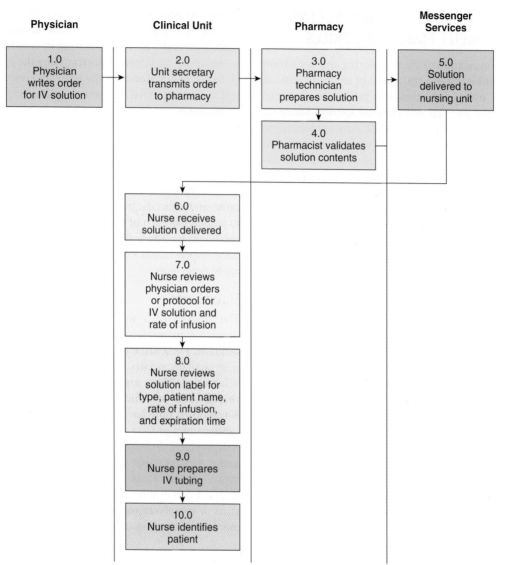

FIGURE 22-2 Deployment Flowchart of Process for Administering Intravenous Solutions.

whole (Figure 22-2). As illustrated in Figures 22-1 and 22-2, top-down and deployment flowcharts can be used to view the process of administering the correct IV solution at the correct rate.

Pareto Charts

In selecting key aspects on which to focus within the process, a Pareto chart may be an appropriate tool. By collecting data on presumed or known problems in a given process, areas of focus or concentration can be achieved. This tool itself is a type of bar graph, with the height of bars reflecting the frequency with which events occur or the effect events have on a process problem. The bars are arranged in descending order so that the most commonly occurring problems are readily visible. Figure 22-3 is based on the Pareto principle, which proposes that 80% of process or system problems are generated from only 20% of the possible causal factors. Therefore, by focusing on the significant few causes, a much broader effect can be achieved in improvement efforts.

Cause-and-Effect Diagrams

Cause-and-effect diagrams are other worthy tools that can help determine potential sources of a problem. These diagrams are lists of potential causes arranged by categories to show their potential effect on a problem. The categories usually are broad, with subsequent levels of detail to illustrate what "might cause" the effect in question. This diagram sometimes is referred to as a fishbone diagram because it resembles a fish skeleton when complete. Cause-and-effect diagrams (Figure 22-4) are useful when the major problem areas have been localized using the Pareto chart.

Run Charts

Measuring data over time to evaluate patterns in process variation typically is suited for tools such as run charts and control charts. Run charts, also known as time plots, are graphs of data points as they occur over time. Valuable information can be obtained regarding process variation by studying the trends in the run chart. A control chart is a slightly more sophisticated tool in helping distinguish between common and special cause variation. A control chart is basically a run chart with statistical control limits added (Figure 22-5).

Through use of these tools, results can be analyzed with interpretations subsequently guiding appropriate improvement actions. Once improvements are initiated, ongoing monitoring follows to evaluate the effectiveness of the changes implemented.

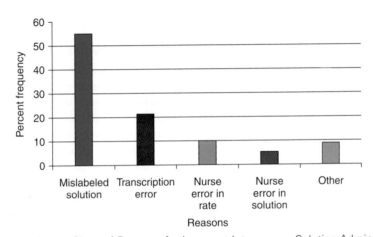

FIGURE 22-3 Pareto Chart of Reasons for Incorrect Intravenous Solution Administration.

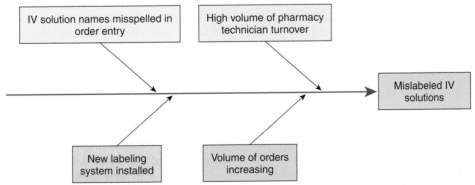

FIGURE 22-4 Cause-and-Effect Diagram of Mislabeled Intravenous Solutions.

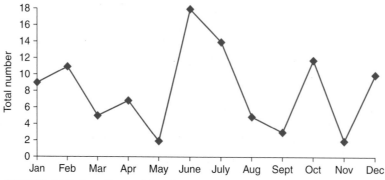

FIGURE 22-5 Run Chart of Number of Mislabeled Intravenous Solutions.

UNDERSTANDING, IMPROVING, AND STANDARDIZING CARE PROCESSES

Standardized processes, otherwise referred to as best known methods or best practices, when effectively managed, have shown to be the foundation for improvements in all areas of business today, but especially in the clinical care setting. There is a typical resistance to standardizing practices, especially when they involve providing patient care and services, but the realistic effect of care without standardization must be considered in the following context as described by Joiner (1994):

- Most employees receive little training on how to do their jobs. Instead the majority are left to learn by watching a more experienced employee.
- Most employees have developed their own unique versions of any general procedures they witnessed or were taught. They think, "My way is the best way."
- Changes to procedures happen haphazardly; individuals constantly change details to counteract problems that arise or in hopes of discovering a better method. Tampering is rampant.

Each of the quality improvement cornerstones could easily be applied to caregiver situations. At first glance, it would be assumed that all care practices are based on scientific evidence and research, and although many are, others exist simply because that was how the practitioner originally was educated. Those practices that are research based, even though they represent best known methods, may still not be widely practiced and therefore result in lack of standardization.

During the past few years, a number of methods have been used in health care settings for the purpose of supporting standardization of care processes. Clinical guidelines, critical pathways, and clinical protocols or algorithms are standardization methods that are more prevalent and familiar. Although these terms sometimes are used interchangeably, the following is offered as a context in which to understand their potential differences.

Clinical Pathways or Critical Pathways

A clinical pathway or critical pathway typically defines the optimal sequencing and timing of interventions by physicians, nurses, and other interprofessional team members when providing care for a patient with a particular diagnosis or procedure, such as a patient who is hospitalized for a coronary artery bypass graft. These pathways typically are developed through collaborative efforts of the interprofessional team that includes physicians, nurses, pharmacists, and others to improve the quality and value of the patient care provided. Among the most obvious benefits of using clinical pathways are (1) reduction in variation of the care provided, (2) facilitation and achievement of expected clinical outcomes, (3) reduction in care delays and ultimately lengths of stay in the inpatient setting, and (4) improvements in cost-effectiveness of the care delivered while maintaining or increasing patient and family satisfaction.

Clinical Protocols or Algorithms

Clinical protocols or algorithms are different from clinical pathways because they represent more of a decision path that a practitioner might take during a particular episode or need. For example, common algorithms exist for treatment of hypertension, provision of both basic and advanced life support, and general diagnostic screening (Figure 22-6).

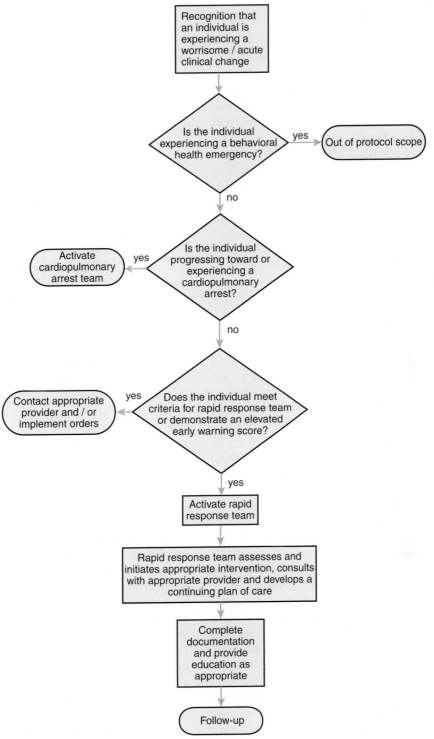

FIGURE 22-6 Clinical Algorithm–Health Care Protocol: Rapid Response Team.

BREAKTHROUGH THINKING TO IMPROVE QUALITY

Just as standardization is critical to the foundation of health care improvement, so is the notion of break-through thinking and swift application of best-known methods for practice. The premise behind break-through thinking and its resulting action is threefold: (1) substantial knowledge exists about how to achieve better performance than currently prevails; (2) strong examples already exist of organizations that have applied that knowledge and broken through to sub-stantial improvements; and (3) the stakes are high and relevant to the most crucial strategic needs of health care (Berwick, 1997).

The Institute for Healthcare Improvement (IHI), a voluntary organization formed to assist leaders in all health care settings actively involved in improving qual-ity, recommends a QI model developed by Langley and colleagues (2009) and composed of two parts. Part one asks three fundamental questions:

1. What are we trying to accomplish?
2. How will we know that a change is an improvement?
3. What changes can we make that will result in im-provement?

Part two uses a sequence of steps, starting with developing an action plan based on the three ques-tions, taking actions to test the plan, making refine-ments as needed, and implementing the resulting changes in real work settings. This is known as a plan–do–check–act (PDCA) cycle (Figure 22-7). For more in-depth information, visit the IHI website at www.ihi.org.

PATIENT SAFETY

Nowhere is the need for QI more evident than in the area of health care errors. As discussed previously, the IOM report *To Err Is Human: Building a Safer Health System* (2000) placed the issue of medical mistakes and patient safety on the pages of many national newspapers, on the agendas of health care governing boards, and at the forefront of federal gov-ernment legislation. In response to the focus on pa-tient safety and the need for data to better understand the priority concerns, several national initiatives were implemented and are discussed in the following sections.

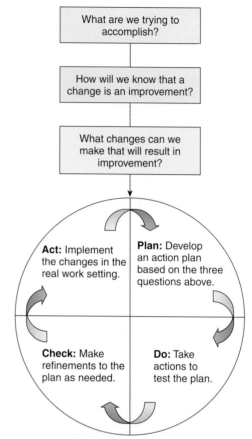

FIGURE 22-7 Institute for Healthcare Improvement (IHI) Quality Improvement Model.

Institute for Safe Medication Practices

An outcome of the patient safety and QI movement was establishment of the Institute for Safe Medication Prac-tices (ISMP), a nonprofit organization that is now well known as an education resource for the prevention of medication errors. The ISMP provides independent, multidisciplinary, expert review of errors reported through the U.S. Pharmacopeia–ISMP Medication Errors Reporting Program (MERP). Through MERP, health care professionals across the nation voluntarily and confidentially report medication errors and hazard-ous conditions that could lead to errors. The reporting process is simple and easily accessible by clinicians. All resulting information and error-prevention strategies are shared with the U.S. Food and Drug Administration (FDA).

The ISMP has also developed *Medication Safety Self Assessments®* to allow nurses and other health care professionals to assess the medication safety practices in their work setting. The self-assessments contain items that address the use of medications in the clinical setting, use of high-alert medications, and system improvements and safeguards that the ISMP has recommended in response to analysis of medication errors (ISMP, 2014). The assessments are publically available on the ISMP website at www.ismp.org/selfassessments.

Role of Regulatory and Accrediting Agencies to Promote Patient Safety

The leaders of regulatory agencies (e.g., CMS) and accrediting agencies (e.g., TJC) have developed standards and programs for to promote patient safety. Three such programs are discussed in the following sections.

Sentinel Event Standard

As one response to the increasing emphasis on patient safety, TJC established its sentinel event standard in 2000. This standard, which continues today, requires organizations to carry out designated steps to fully understand the

factors and systems associated with adverse patient events, given that certain defining characteristics have been confirmed. The steps revolve around a "root cause analysis," which is a direct application of the quality improvement principles and methods defined earlier in this chapter. The intention behind the root cause analysis is to understand the systems at fault within the organization so that improvements can be determined and implemented to prevent any future occurrences. TJC allows organizations some latitude in determining the policy for disclosure of these events to the commission.

National Patient Safety Goals

The purpose of TJC's national patient safety goals is to help accredited organizations address specific areas of concern in regards to patient safety. These goals are based on ongoing analyses of reported sentinel events and the identified root causes of these events. An annual review of these goals generally results in modification of existing goals and the creation of new ones, as evidenced in the published list for 2014, which now includes a goal for improving the safety of clinical alarm systems (Box 22-1).

BOX 22-1 2015 National Patient Safety Goals

1. Improve the accuracy of patient and resident identification.
   - Use at least two patient or resident identifiers when providing care, treatment, and services.
   - Eliminate transfusion errors related to patient misidentification.
2. Improve the effectiveness of communication among caregivers.
   - Report critical results of tests and diagnostic procedures on a timely basis.
3. Improve the safety of using medications.
   - Label all medications, medication containers, and other solutions removed from original containers including medications in syringes, cups, and basins.
   - Reduce the likelihood of patient harm associated with the use of anticoagulant therapy.
   - Maintain and communicate accurate patient and resident medication information.
4. Improve the safety of clinical alarm systems.
   - Make improvements to ensure that alarms on medical equipment are heard and responded to in a timely manner.

5. Reduce the risk of health care–associated infections.
   - Comply with either the current Centers for Disease Control and Prevention (CDC) hand hygiene guidelines or the current World Health Organization (WHO) hand hygiene guidelines.
   - Implement evidence-based practices to prevent health care–associated infections caused by multidrug-resistant organisms in acute care hospitals.
   - Implement evidence-based practices to prevent central line–associated blood stream infections.
   - Implement evidence-based practices for preventing surgical site infections.
   - Implement evidence-based practices to prevent indwelling catheter-associated urinary tract infections.
6. The organization identifies safety risks inherent in its patient population.
   - Identify patients at risk for suicide.
7. Universal protocol for preventing wrong site, wrong procedure, wrong person surgeries.
   - Conduct a preprocedure verification process.
   - Mark the procedure site.
   - Perform a time-out before the procedure.

Adapted from The Joint Commission, 2015. Reprinted with permission. http://www.jointcommission.org/assets/1/6/2015_HAP_NPSG_ER.pdf.

> **BOX 22-2   Never Events: The Centers for Medicare and Medicaid Services Listing of Hospital-Acquired Conditions for 2014**
>
> - Foreign body retained after surgery
> - Air embolism
> - Blood incompatibility
> - Pressure ulcers stages III and IV
> - Falls and trauma: fracture, dislocation, intracranial injury, crushing injury, burn, other injuries
> - Catheter-associated urinary tract infections
> - Vascular catheter-associated infection
> - Manifestations of poor glycemic control
> - Surgical site infection, mediastinitis, following coronary artery bypass graft
>
> - Surgical site infection following certain orthopedic procedures
> - Surgical site infection following bariatric surgery for obesity
> - Surgical site infection following cardiac implantable electronic device
> - Deep vein thrombosis and pulmonary embolism following certain orthopedic procedures
> - Iatrogenic pneumothorax with venous catheterization

The Centers for Medicare and Medicaid Services. Hospital acquired conditions. 2014. (website) http://www.cms.gov/Medicare/Medicare-Fee-for-Service-Payment/HospitalAcqCond/Hospital-Acquired_Conditions.html

Never Events

In 2006, CMS began to investigate ways that Medicare could help decrease or eliminate the occurrence of never events—serious and costly errors in health care delivery that should never happen. Examples of such events include wrong site surgery or mismatched blood transfusions, which can cause serious injury or death to the patient and result in increased costs to Medicare. CMS worked with the National Quality Forum (NQF) to identify hospital-acquired conditions that were determined to be reasonably preventable and for which the additional cost of hospitalization for treating these conditions should not be paid. Box 22-2 presents the most current list of hospital-acquired conditions for which Medicare will no longer make additional payments for treatment.

Beginning in the CMS fiscal year 2015, reimbursement penalties will be applied to hospitals performing in the bottom quartile nationally for a selected subset of the hospital acquired conditions. The initial penalty will be up to 1% of an organization's baseline annual Medicare reimbursement. As with Value-Based Purchasing, this program is a result of the Patient Protection and Affordability Act of 2010.

THE PROFESSIONAL NURSE AND PATIENT SAFETY

For nurses, the challenge starts with making patient safety improvement and error reduction not just an organizational priority, but a personal one as well. This means adopting a state of mind that recognizes the complexity and high-risk nature of modern health care, implementing standardized best practices, and working to eliminate never events. Two significant nursing functions that most closely effect patient safety, quality of care, and resulting outcomes are as follows:

1. Monitoring for early recognition of adverse events, complications, and errors
2. Initiating deployment of appropriate care providers for timely intervention and response and rescue of patients in these situations

A critical factor in supporting a nurse's ability to carry out these two functions is nurse staffing. Although defining the appropriate level of staffing is a matter of debate, there is widespread recognition that a strong linkage exists between patient outcomes and nurse staffing (Aiken et al, 2008; Lucero et al, 2010; Martsolf et al, 2014; McHugh and Ma, 2013; Tubbs-Cooley et al, 2013). Chapter 13 presents a thorough discussion about strategies nurses can use to promote quality care and a safe work environment.

Nursing Quality Indicators

The governing body of the American Nurses Association (ANA) established the National Database of Nursing Quality Indicators (NDNQI) in 1998 as part of the ANA's safety and quality initiative. This national database program collects designated indicators (Box 22-3) that strongly affect patient clinical outcomes for two major purposes: (1) to provide comparative data to

---

BOX 22-3 The National Database of Nursing Quality Indicators (NDNQI)

Nursing Staff Skill Mix:
  Registered Nurses (RNs)
  Licensed Practical/Vocational Nurses (LPN/LVNs)
  Unlicensed Assistive Personnel (UAP)
Nursing Hours per Patient Day
RN Education/Certification
Nurse Turnover
RN Survey:
  Practice Environment Scale
  Job Satisfaction Scales
Patient Falls/Injury Falls
Hospital/Unit-Acquired Pressure Ulcers
Physical/Sexual Assault
Pain Assessment/Intervention/Reassessment Cycles
Peripheral IV Infiltration
Physical Restraints

Healthcare-Associated Infections:
  Catheter-Associated Urinary Tract Infection
  Central Line-Associated Bloodstream Infection
  Ventilator-Associated Pneumonia
  Ventilator-Associated Events

New Clinical Measures in 2014
Falls in Ambulatory Settings (now available)
Pressure Ulcer Incidence Rates from Electronic Health
  Records (now available)
Nursing Care Hours in Emergency Departments,
  PeriOperative Units, and Perinatal Units
Skill Mix in Emergency Departments, PeriOperative
  Units, and Perinatal Units
Hospital Readmission Rates

From www.nursingquality.org. accessed 06/22/2015.

---

health care organizations to support QI activities and (2) to develop national data to better understand the link between nurse staffing and patient outcomes. The NDNQI is unique in that it is the only national nursing quality measurement program that allows comparison measures of nursing quality among national, regional, and state hospitals of similar type and size, from the unit level perspective. As of 2014, 2000 hospitals have joined the database with quarterly reports now being provided to these organizations for analysis of their own care processes and support systems as related to nurse staffing (ANA, 2014).

Interprofessional Teamwork

Equally critical in its effect on patient safety is the work environment that supports the interdependence and effective communication among nurses and other health care professionals. Most nurses and other clinical staff assume they already work in teams; however, teamwork concepts are infrequently taught in health professional educational programs. Patient care is dependent on effective interprofessional communication to support the coordination of activities that promote efficiency and safety. One strategy to improve interprofessional teamwork is TeamSTEPPS (Team Strategies and Tools to Enhance Performance and Patient Safety). TeamSTEPPS was developed by the AHRQ and the U.S. Department of Defense as an evidence-based teamwork system

aimed at optimizing patient outcomes by improving communication and teamwork skills among health care professionals. Comprehensive information about TeamSTEPPS, including readiness assessments and training materials, is available online at *http://teamstepps. ahrq.gov.*

QSEN (QUALITY AND SAFETY EDUCATION IN NURSING) COMPETENCIES

This chapter has examined the vital need to transform today's health care systems to improve quality and safety for patients. Nurses are emerging as leaders in this transformation and as such, need to incorporate into their nursing practice the six competencies recommended by the IOM (2003) as essential for all health professionals:
- Patient-centered care
- Teamwork and collaboration
- Evidence-based practice
- Quality improvement
- Safety
- Informatics

To support nursing education around these six competencies, the national *Quality and Safety Education for Nurses* (QSEN) project was created through support from the Robert Wood Johnson Foundation (Cronenwett et al, 2009). In support for the importance of these six competencies to nursing practice, they have been incorporated into nursing education standards and the nurse licensure examination (American Association of Colleges of Nursing, 2008; Smith et al, 2007) so that all nurses will be held accountable for being competent in these six areas.

While these six competencies may seem familiar to nurses, it is important to understand them as intended by the IOM so that all disciplines (e.g., nursing, medicine, pharmacy) have the same frame of reference for incorporating the competencies into practice. Table 22-1 presents each competency with its definition and a sample of knowledge, skills, and attitudes related to the competency. The QSEN website (www.qsen.org) is a good resource with extensive information about each competency including annotated bibliographies, peer-reviewed teaching strategies, and instructional videos. Readers are encouraged to visit the QSEN website to learn more about these competencies, which are essential to today's nursing practice.

TABLE 22-1 QSEN Competencies

PATIENT-CENTERED CARE

Definition: Recognize the patient or designee as the source of control and full partner in providing compassionate and coordinated care based on respect for patient's preferences, values, and needs

Knowledge	Skills	Attitudes
Integrate understanding of multiple dimensions of patient-centered care	Elicit patient values, preferences, and expressed needs as part of clinical interview	Value seeing health care situations "through patients' eyes"
Describe how diverse cultural, ethnic, and social backgrounds function as sources of patient, family, and community values	Communicate patient values, preferences, and expressed to other members of health care team	Respect and encourage individual expression of patient values, preferences, and expressed needs

TEAMWORK AND COLLABORATION

Definition: Function effectively within nursing and interprofessional teams, fostering open communication, mutual respect, and shared decision making to achieve quality patient care

Knowledge	Skills	Attitudes
Describe one's own strengths, limitations, and values in functioning as a team member	Demonstrate awareness of one's own strengths and limitations as a team member	Acknowledge one's own potential to contribute to effective team functioning
Describe examples of the effect of team functioning on safety and quality of care	Follow communication practices that minimize risks associated with hand-offs among providers and across transitions in care	Appreciate the risks associated with hand-offs among providers and across transitions in care

EVIDENCE-BASED PRACTICE (EBP)

Definition: Integrate best current evidence with clinical expertise and patient/family preferences and values for delivery of optimal health care

Knowledge	Skills	Attitudes
Demonstrate knowledge of basic scientific methods and processes	Participate effectively in appropriate data collection and other research activities	Appreciate strengths and weaknesses of scientific bases for practice
Discriminate between valid and invalid reasons for modifying evidence-based clinical practice based on clinical expertise or patient/family preferences	Consult with clinical experts before deciding to deviate from evidence-based protocols	Acknowledge own limitations in knowledge and clinical expertise before determining when to deviate from evidence-based best practices

TABLE 22-1 QSEN Competencies—cont'd		
QUALITY IMPROVEMENT		
Definition: Use data to monitor the outcomes of care processes and use improvement methods to design and test changes to continually improve the quality and safety of health care systems		
Knowledge	**Skills**	**Attitudes**
Describe strategies for learning about the outcomes of care in the setting in which one is engaged in clinical practice	Seek information about outcomes of care for populations served in care setting	Appreciate that continual quality improvement is an essential part of the daily work of all health professionals
Describe approaches for changing processes of care	Design a small test of change in daily work	Appreciate the value of what individuals and teams can do to improve care
SAFETY		
Definition: Minimizes risk of harm to patients and providers through system effectiveness and individual performance		
Knowledge	**Skills**	**Attitudes**
Examine human factors and other basic safety design principles as well as commonly used unsafe practices	Demonstrate effective use of technology and standardization practices that support safety and quality	Value the contributions of standardization/reliability to safety
Discuss potential and actual effect of national patient resources, initiatives, and regulations	Use national patient safety resources for own professional development and to focus attention on safety in care settings	Value relationship between national safety campaigns and implementation in local practices and practice settings
INFORMATICS		
Definition: Use information and technology to communicate, manage knowledge, mitigate error, and support decision making		
Knowledge	**Skills**	**Attitudes**
Identify essential information that must be available in a common database to support patient care	Navigate the electronic health record	Value technologies that support clinical decision making, error prevention, and care coordination
Describe examples of how technology and information management are related to the quality and safety of patient care	Respond appropriately to clinical decision-making supports and alerts	Value nurses' involvement in design, selection, implementation, and evaluation of information technologies to support patient care

Source: abbreviated from Cronenwett L et al: Quality and safety education for nurses, *Nurs Outlook* 55(3):122-131, 2007.

ROLE OF PROFESSIONAL NURSES IN QUALITY IMPROVEMENT

There are lessons for all nurses from one of the original patient safety and quality improvement mentors, Florence Nightingale. Nightingale used data to support her efforts to reduce the incidence and spread of infections in the patient wards she was accountable for during the Crimean War. What resulted from her work was a broader shift in the culture of health care at that time.

What can result from the current emphasis on quality and patient safety is a new cultural shift in health care with "building health care systems that do no harm" increasingly being the shared value and goal of all those involved in patient care delivery. Nurses are in the perfect position to lead this cultural change. Quality improvement should not be considered a separate function within the role of care provider, but rather an ongoing part of the professional role for all health care professionals.

SUMMARY

For today's graduating nurses, the challenge is to find whatever means are available to refine the knowledge and skills fundamentally necessary to enter a partnership with all other interprofessional team members in the ongoing improvement of health care. Just as essential to professional nursing practice as knowing, for instance, the symptoms of diabetic ketoacidosis or how to give an injection, is understanding the basic principles of QI, process improvement, and variation; using clinical indicators, process improvement tools, and standardized care processes; and addressing patient safety in every aspect of care. Every nurse should enter practice accepting accountability for the quality of care provided by the health care organization and taking a leadership role to implement improvements to achieve health care that is safe, timely, effective, efficient, equitable, and patient centered.

REFERENCES

Agency for Healthcare Research and Quality: *National healthcare quality report, 2013*, Publication No. 14-0005, May 2014, AHRQ. (website). http://www.ahrq.gov/research/findings/nhqrdr/index.html. Accessed January 25, 2015.

Aiken LH, Clarke SP, Sloane DM, et al: Effects of hospital care environment on patient mortality and nurse outcomes, *J Nurs Adm* 38(5):223–229, 2008.

American Association of Colleges of Nursing: *The essentials of baccalaureate education for professional nursing practice*, Washington, DC, 2008, American Association of Colleges of Nursing.

American Nurses Association: *Quality improvement solutions from ANA*, 2014, NDNQI. (website). http://www.nursingquality.org/#intro. Accessed January 25, 2015.

Berwick D: The breakthrough series, *Qual Connect* 6(2):11, 1997.

Cronenwett L, Sherwood G, Gelmon S: Improving quality and safety education: the QSEN leaning collaborative, *Nurs Outlook* 57(6):304–312, 2009.

Frankel A, Leonard M, Simmonds T, et al: *The essential guide for patient safety officers*, Oakbrook Terrace, IL, 2009, Joint Commission Resources.

Institute of Medicine, Kohn L, Corrigan J, Donaldson M, editors: *To err is human: building a safer health system*, Washington, DC, 2000, National Academies Press.

Institute of Medicine: *Report brief: crossing the quality chasm: a new health system for the 21st century*, 2001. (website). http://www.nap.edu/html/quality_chasm/reportbrief.pdf.

Institute of Medicine, Greiner AC, Knebel E, editors: *Health professions education: a bridge to quality*, Washington, DC, 2003, National Academies Press.

Institute of Medicine: *Preventing medication errors: quality chasm series*, 2007. (website). http://www.nap.edu/catalog.php?record_id=11623. Accessed January 25, 2015.

Institute for Safe Medication Practices: *ISMP self assessments*, 2014. (website). http://www.ismp.org/selfassessments. Accessed September 22, 2014.

James, John T: A new, evidence-based estimate of patient harms associated with hospital care, *J Patient Saf* 9(3):122–128, 2013.

Joiner BL: *Fourth generation management*, New York, 1994, McGraw-Hill.

Keers RN, Williams SD, Cooke J, Ashcroft DM: Causes of medication administration errors in hospitals: a systematic review of quantitative and qualitative evidence, *Drug Safety* 36(11):1045–1067, 2013 Nov.

Langley GJ, Nolan KM, Nolan TW, et al: *The Improvement Guide: A Practical Approach to Enhancing Organizational Performance*, ed 2, San Francisco, 2009, Jossey-Bass.

Lucero R, Lake E, Aiken L: Nursing care quality and adverse events in U.S. hospitals, *J Clin Nursing* 19(15-16): 2185–2095, 2010.

Martsolf G, Auerbach D, Benevent R, et al: *Examining the value of inpatient nurse staffing: An assessment of quality and patient care costs*, June 9, 2014, AHRQ. (website). http://www.academyhealth.org/files/2014/monday/martsolf.pdf. Accessed January 25, 2015.

McHugh MD, Ma C: Hospital nursing and 30 day readmissions among Medicare patients with heart failure, acute myocardial infarction and pneumonia, *Medical Care* 61(1):52–59, 2013.

Smith E, Cronenwett L, Sherwood G: Current assessments of quality and safety education in nursing, *Nurs Outlook* 55(3):132–137, 2007.

The Joint Commission: *Sentinel events*, 2013. (website). http://www.jointcommission.org/assets/1/6/CAMH_2012_Update2_24_SE.pdf. Accessed September 22, 2014.

The Joint Commission: *About the Joint Commission*, 2014. (website). http://www.jointcommission.org/about_us/about_the_joint_commission_main.aspx. Accessed September 24, 2014.

Tubbs-Cooley H, Cimiotti J, Silber JH, et al: An observational study of nurse staffing ratios and hospital readmission among children admitted for common conditions, *BMJ Qual Saf* 22(9):735–742, 2013.

Westbrook J, Woods A, Rob M, et al: Association of interruptions with an increased risk and severity of medication administration errors, *Arch Intern Med* 170(8): 683–690, April 26, 2010.

23

Nurses must be powerful, informed advocates for health policy that improves health and health care!

Health Policy and Politics: Get Involved!

Virginia Trotter Betts, MSN, JD, RN, FAAN,
Barbara Cherry, DNSc, MBA, RN, NEA-BC

ⓔ Additional resources are available online at: *http://evolve.elsevier.com/Cherry/*

PROFESSIONAL/ETHICAL ISSUE

Tashauna Banks works in a very busy outpatient surgical center where the nurses often stay past the end of their shift to care for patients who are not yet stable enough to go home. Tashauna and other nurses in the center typically work over 50 hours per week. While the pay is very good, Tashauna is often so fatigued, especially at the end of the week, that she is concerned about making mistakes that might harm her patients. Tashauna also knows that two of her colleagues work as agency nurses on their days off from the surgical center, which means they may be working up to 65 to 70 hours per week. Tashauna has begun to notice that nurse fatigue is a problem in their surgery center, negatively affecting the nurses' motivation and energy levels. She also notices lapses in attention to detail and what sometimes seems to be slow reaction to urgent situations. She becomes very concerned as she realizes that fatigue could have extremely serious legal ramifications if a medical error caused by fatigue leads to patient harm.

When visiting with some of her nurse friends who work at the local medical center, Tashauna learns that nurse fatigue is a concern there as well. Tashauna and her nurse friends discuss their responsibility to make good decisions when agreeing to work overtime and using the *Code of Ethics for Nurses* as a guide. After the discussion with her friends, Tashauna is motivated to take action to address the problem of nurse fatigue both in her own work setting as well as at a broader level through the state nurses association. She understands that together, nurses can have a powerful voice to affect change both in the work setting and at the state and national policy level.

- What resources are available for Tashauna and her colleagues to learn more about nurse fatigue?
- How can the *Code of Ethics for Nurses* guide nurses to make balanced decisions about their work hours?
- What responsibility do the managers in health care organizations have to address nurse fatigue and keep nurses and patients safe?
- Discuss steps Tashauna can take to begin to address the problem of nurse fatigue in her own work setting and through the state nurses association.

VIGNETTE

Juan Hernandez is one of only four registered nurses (RNs) now staffing the 7 AM to 7 PM shift in a 12-bed medical intensive care unit (MICU) as two RN colleagues have just transferred to positions in the hospital's rapidly growing case management service. The chief nursing officer *(CNO) and MICU nurse manager are actively recruiting permanent RNs for the vacant positions but have not been successful as yet. Temporary service RNs and nursing assistive personnel are filling in within the staffing mix. Juan is aware that all posted openings for RNs throughout* his hospital system now include "BSN preferred" as a descriptor following the hospital's recently announced plans for achieving Magnet® Hospital status.

When Juan begins to inquire about the issues in hiring BSN-prepared nurses, he is both relieved and alarmed by what he hears. First, the hospital administrators clearly support his position that adequate numbers of permanently employed, well-educated RNs are essential to provide high-quality, safe patient care. The hospital's rapidly evolving care models and driving force to succeed on the Magnet journey require giving a preference to nurses with a BSN or above. However, an underlying complicating issue for health care organizations in Juan's state and region is that the numbers of nurses with the needed education and credentials simply are not adequate to meet the demand, and hiring is taking much longer than in the past, which further complicates issues of safety, quality, and continuity of care in Juan's MICU.

Juan calls his state nurses association (SNA) to discuss his concerns and to learn more about the nursing workforce trends. Through that call, he discovers that other nurses and hospitals across the United States are facing many of the same dilemmas. Meeting nurses' current professional responsibility to provide and advocate for safe care for patients is colliding with the larger national and employer issues of securing an increased number of better educated, more broadly skilled nurses to meet the rapidly evolving

expectations in complex care systems whose future depends on a focus on patient quality, safety, and satisfaction. Therefore, Juan makes a commitment to engage in discussions about policy and political strategies that are needed now to promote and protect models of care that will facilitate professional nursing practice; promote development of a highly educated nursing workforce to meet his state's and region's needs; and ensure his ability to grow in his own professional career as the health care system expects and rewards new knowledge, skills, abilities, and credentials for RNs.

Questions to Consider While Reading this Chapter:

1. What types of local, state, and federal health policies affect Juan's nursing practice?
2. What are the major steps in health policy development that Juan must understand in order to engage in policy improvements for the nursing workforce and his own professional career?
3. How can Juan relate his knowledge of the nursing process to an effective plan for policy development related to improving the nursing workforce and his own professional career?
4. What types of grassroots political strategies can Juan use to ensure that policymakers hear his interests and concerns about quality, safe patient care, and the supply of professional nurses?

KEY TERMS

Constituent: A citizen who has the opportunity to vote for candidates in elections for representation at the local, state, and federal level.

Constituent/State Nurses Association (C/SNA): The professional organizational unit member of the American Nurses Association that represents all professional nurses within a state or territory or other defined organizational entity or boundary—also known as the state nurses association (SNA).

Grassroots lobbying: Personal advocacy by individual constituents—everyday citizens—in support of a problem/position/option related to a policy issue.

Health policy: A set course of action undertaken by governments or health care organizations in order to achieve a particular health outcome. Private health policy is made by health care organizations, such as hospitals, whereas public health policy refers to local, state, and federal legislation,

regulation, and court rulings that govern health care within a certain arena.

Lobbying: Acting to persuade, educate and/or convince policymakers to respond positively to a particular position on an issue or to follow a particular course of legislative, regulatory, or funding activity.

Platform: The statement of principles and policies of a political party, candidate, or elected official.

Policymaker: A local, state, or federally elected or appointed official who can propose and directly affect legislation, regulations, or programs that can become actualized.

Regulation: Rules used to implement legislation and translate concepts into actions that can be put into practice.

Stakeholders: Individuals, groups, or organizations who have a vested interest in and may be affected by policy decisions and actions being taken, and thus may attempt to influence those decisions and actions.

LEARNING OUTCOMES

After studying this chapter, the reader will be able to:

1. Differentiate between policy and politics.
2. Discuss the roles of the legislative, administrative, and judicial levels of government.
3. Differentiate among federal, state, and local governments and their roles in governing and influencing health care and nursing.
4. Identify three policy issues of significant consequence to nurses and nursing.
5. Demonstrate knowledge needed to be a responsible and informed politically active nurse.
6. Use diverse technologic resources to obtain information about current health policy developments and political issues.

CHAPTER OVERVIEW

*Perhaps at no other time in the history of the nursing profession has there been such an imperative for strong, involved, informed nursing leadership. The challenges currently faced by the U.S. health care system—ongoing and serious patient safety issues; a shortage of appropriately educated and geographically dispersed nursing and other essential health professionals; complex, high-tech work environments; a fragmented delivery system; an aging population; and dramatic overall health care system changes in response to passage and implementation of The Patient Protection and Affordable Care Act—confront the health and well-being of patients, families, and communities across the country. Nurses can no longer simply move forward and participate in the delivery of patient care without also addressing these larger issues that affect the whole of the health care system. Frequently, these critical issues can be understood, addressed, and resolved only through the **policy process**. Without a doubt, legislation, regulation, and health policy directly affect how health care is delivered and how the health care system responds to the very real challenges and opportunities it faces.* **Nurses must get involved now** *in the policy process and provide strong leadership among the health care professions to ensure evolution to an efficient, effective health care system that promotes and protects the health and well-being of each person in our society.*

This chapter explores the effect of governmental roles, structures, and actions on health care policy and demonstrates how participation in the policy process can shape the U.S. health care system. Local, state, and federal legislative concerns including the involvement of professional nursing organizations in policy and politics are discussed. The nurse's very important role in the policy process and involvement in political advocacy and campaigns is described. This chapter provides the reader with a basic understanding of policy development and political processes, tools to gain political savvy, and methods for getting politically involved.

NURSES' INVOLVEMENT IN HEALTH POLICY AND POLITICAL ACTION

Nurses' involvement in policy and politics has become considerably more important in recent years for the following reasons:

- State and federal governments play an increasingly important role in health care, especially as federal and state governments and multiple private players embark on implementation of *The Patient Protection and Affordable Care Act (PPACA)*, which was signed into law in 2010.
- Nursing practice is directly affected by health policy development, which is, in turn, affected by the political action of citizens—nurses and many others.
- National attention on nurses and nursing has intensified—our numbers, education, scope of practice, and overall value to the health care system.

Decisions affecting the health care system, patient care, and the nursing profession will be made with or without the input of nurses. As the reader will see from health policy examples provided throughout this chapter, patient care and nursing practice are highly political endeavors with health policy determining the types of care systems in place and how that care is paid for. Thus, it is absolutely essential that nurses become actively engaged in the policy process and use effective political action to successfully achieve the development of health policies that are reflective of nursing's perspective on the preferred future for the profession and for health and the health care delivery system in the United States.

WHAT IS HEALTH POLICY?

Health policy is a set course of action(s) undertaken by governments or health care organizations to obtain a desired outcome. Private health policy is made by health care organizations, such as hospitals, and includes those policies instituted to govern innumerable employer/ employee practices and processes in the delivery of the health care services provided within the organization. A hospital's specific plan to report errors in patient care is an example of private health policy. Public health policy refers to local, state, and federal legislation, regulations, and resource allocation related to health, health care service delivery, coverage, workforce, and reimbursement. The mandatory requirement for licensure to practice professional nursing is an example of public health policy. There is a close link between private and public policy in that the policies of health care organizations must conform to (and are actually frequently developed and implemented to comply with) a public policy. Although it is vital that the RN be an informed participant in policy development at one's employing health care organization, this chapter focuses on the development of public or governmental health policy, which will be referred to simply as *health policy*.

Health Policy at the Local, State, and Federal Level

Health policies may be developed and implemented at the local, state, or federal level, and they apply to all residents within the jurisdiction of the respective governmental authority. Local health policy applies only to those people who are residents of that local community, whereas health policy enacted at the federal level applies to all residents in the United States.

Local Health Policy

At the local level, many cities or counties offer a variety of health care services to meet the needs of their residents. For example, as part of a city's health policy, free or reduced-rate immunizations may be offered to all children in the community. Allocating funds to employ RNs as school nurses in public schools is another example of local health policy. A more comprehensive (and thus perhaps more controversial) policy is a community's requirement for tobacco-free public areas such as restaurants and office buildings. Local health policy varies considerably across the United States, with some

communities funding an extensive variety of health programs and others offering very limited health services or none at all. However, even the smallest communities are involved to some extent in health policy through partnerships with their state government to provide public health programs such as safe drinking water, enforcement for seat belt and child restraint laws, and emergency medical systems.

State Health Policy

Health policy at the state level has a powerful influence on the health and safety of each state's residents. In addition to its lead role in governing nursing and other health professions' scope, practice, and performance through the state's professional practice acts, each state also has innumerable health policies that may not be visible. These policies include maintaining a safe meat supply through livestock inspections; ensuring safe food storage, preparation, and serving in restaurants; and ensuring that health care facilities provide safe, quality care through regulatory compliance. Only when these activities fall short of preventing problems—as in cases of *Escherichia coli* (*E. coli*) outbreaks—do most residents of the state realize the critical nature of these health policies.

State health policy also involves paying for some individual health care services. The Medicaid program is funded through a blend of state and federal funds, and is a health insurance program for health care services for eligible people at (or below) a specific income level and other designated categories (as defined by a combination of federal and individual state standards). Most states also have a state Children's Health Insurance Program (CHIP) that provides health insurance coverage to uninsured children who do not qualify for the state Medicaid program. The CHIP is funded through a partnership between federal and state governments. State and federal governments are also the prime sources of funding for public mental health and substance abuse services, long-term care services for older adults and disabled persons, and health care services for prisoners.

A key piece of the PPACA is the opportunity for state development and implementation of State Health Insurance Exchanges (SHIEs). A SHIE is a set of state-regulated and standardized health care plans from which individuals may purchase health insurance eligible for federal subsidies; such plans offer affordable and credible coverage that meet national standards for covered services with individual state benchmarks. The critical role that states are playing in accepting or rejecting the Medicaid Expansion provisions of the PPACA is among the most significant health policy issues of the decade as these states' decisions affect millions of poor and very vulnerable citizens.

Federal Health Policy

State government and state health policies have an enormous effect on people's health and safety. Likewise, the federal government plays a vitally important leadership role in the health of Americans, including passage of the PPACA by the 111th Congress. The federal government's role in health care includes significant funding for health and disease prevention and research; supplemental funding for education for health professionals, including nurses and physicians; and paying for individual health care services through Medicare, Medicaid, CHIP, Veterans Administration, and Indian Health Services care systems.

Federal health policies have played and continue to play a pivotal role in shaping nursing practice. The first federal policy to provide funding for nursing services was the Sheppard-Towner Act of 1921. This act, passed by Congress despite objections from the American Medical Association (AMA), provided states with matching funds to establish prenatal and child health centers staffed by public health nurses. The goal of the act was to reduce maternal and infant mortality rates by teaching women about personal hygiene and infant care. Eventually, this highly successful program was discontinued when the AMA successfully persuaded Congress that physicians should perform these health activities (Starr, 1982), but these services were later reinstated (and continue today) within Title V of the Social Security Act of 1935.

Another example of federal legislation that has significantly influenced the context of nursing practice over the past 6 decades was the Hill-Burton Act of 1950. This act provided funding to local communities that resulted in a boom in the construction of hospitals across the country. As the number of hospitals increased rapidly, so did the need for nurses to staff them. Thus, the professional nurse's historic role shifted from community and public health settings to be predominately in hospital/acute care settings over the last 6 decades. Other key federal legislation has affected nursing practice through expanding Medicare and Medicaid reimbursement directly to advanced practice nurses and implementing policies and programs to expand the nursing supply through enhancing access to nursing education at all levels of nursing from BSN to DNP and PhD. Table 23-1 provides some historic examples of how health policy enacted at the federal level affected

TABLE 23-1 Examples of Health Policies that have Influenced Professional Nursing Practice

Legislation	Influence on Professional Nursing Practice
Nurse practice acts and registration of nurses were established (1910).	Established scope of practice and minimal educational requirements for nurses; implemented by most states.
Sheppard-Towner Act (1921) funded prenatal and child health centers staffed by public health nurses.	First federal policy to provide funding for nursing services.
Hill-Burton Act (1950), also known as the Hospital Survey and Construction Act, provided federal funding for hospital construction.	Caused a boom in hospital construction, shifting nurses' primary employment setting from public health to hospitals.
Nurse Training Act (1964) Public Law 88-581 (78 Stat. 908) provided enhanced funding for collegiate nursing programs.	Expanded university education for nurses, and laid the groundwork for the development of APRNs.
Medicare program (1965) provided funding for health care services for older adults and the disabled.	Led to an increased number of hospitalized older adults and an increased need for nurses in acute care settings.
Renal Disease Program (1972) provided funding for dialysis treatments and renal transplants for patients with kidney failure.	Led to the development of a new area of nursing practice that is now a recognized specialty—nephrology nursing.
Diagnosis-related groups (DRGs) (1983) changed Medicare reimbursement to hospitals from a fee-for-service method to a fixed-fee method.	Forced hospitals to reduce patients' lengths of stay, cut costs, and initially reduce staff, including nurses; led to the development of new nursing roles—nursing case management and utilization review.

Continued

TABLE 23-1 Examples of Health Policies that have Influenced Professional Nursing Practice—cont'd	
Legislation	**Influence on Professional Nursing Practice**
Balanced Budget Amendment (1997) Title 42 Sect 4511 CFR 410.75 and 410.76 provided for direct reimbursement of nurse practitioners and nurse clinical specialists, regardless of geographic location following state NPAs requirements for scope and practice.	Expanded the practice opportunities for advanced practice registered nurses (APRNs), and further increased the importance of political action at the state level to remove barriers to APRN practice such as medical supervision or other unwarranted limitations on scope and independence.
Medicare Modernization Act (Medicare Part D) (2003) PL 108-173 117 Stat 2066 added a prescription drug benefit for Medicare enrollees.	Provides needed access to medications for Medicare enrollees, and calls attention to cost-and-effectiveness outcome from policymakers, requiring nurses to stay alert to proposed legislation and to advocate for appropriate benefits for the nation's older adults.
Mental Health Parity and Addictions Equity Act (MHPAEA) 2008 PL 110-343 Sect 511 removed discrimination in insurance coverage and benefits for mental illnesses and substance abuse disorders.	Greatly increases access to a continuum of mental health/substance abuse services, and puts pressure on developing a nursing workforce with sufficient numbers and knowledge to address these illnesses as integrated with other chronic illnesses and as specialty services.

nursing practice and health care. Current policy issues affecting nursing practice and health care are addressed later in this chapter.

HOW IS HEALTH POLICY DEVELOPED?

The development of health policy at the state or federal level is a complex, dynamic process that occurs in the following three ways (Chaffee et al, 2013):

- Enactment of legislation and the accompanying rules and regulations that carry the weight of law
- Administrative decisions/directives made by various governmental agencies of the executive branch
- Judicial decisions that interpret statutes, regulations, and settle legal disputes/conflicts within society

Numerous players (individuals and groups) are involved in developing health policy including: elected officials and their staffs; officials/staff of executive branch governmental agencies; individual experts in a health-related area; citizens who may be affected by a health problem; stakeholders, such as corporate representatives, who may be affected by a health problem or policy; and representatives from special interest groups who have a particular focused interest in one or more policy options. As a special interest group representing the interests of 3.1 million professional nurses throughout the United States, the American Nurses Association

(ANA) carries a strong voice and high visibility in influencing health policy and nursing practice. At the state level, the C/SNAs of the ANA are the policy voice of the nursing profession with state governors and legislatures.

The development of health policy involves all three branches of government: executive, legislative, and judicial. A basic knowledge of the functions of the three branches of government is necessary to understand health policy development. Table 23-2 presents a brief review of the three branches of the federal government and their differing roles in health policy. Although most state governments parallel the structure and functions of the federal government, there are differences among states. Each nurse is encouraged to learn about the governmental structure of his or her state. In addition to understanding the branches of government, nurses also need to understand the influence of legislation and regulation on health policy as discussed in the following sections.

Legislation and Health Policy Development

The development of health policy refers to the steps through which a health issue moves from being a societal problem to becoming an actual health program that can be funded, implemented, and evaluated. The legislative process is fundamental to the movement from a

TABLE 23-2 The Three Branches of the Federal Government

	Executive	Legislative	Judicial
Composition	Office of the President and 15 executive departments (State, Treasury, Defense, Agriculture, Energy, Housing and Urban Development, Justice, Commerce, Education, Health and Human Services, Interior, Labor, Transportation, Veterans Affairs, and Department of Homeland Security)	Senate and House of Representatives, known collectively as Congress, with 535 elected members	U.S. Supreme Court, federal district courts, and U.S. circuit courts of appeals
Role in Health Policy	Recommends legislation and promotes major policy initiatives Implements laws and manages programs after they have been passed by Congress through regulation, oversight, and presidential funding priorities Writes regulations that interpret statutes (laws) Has the power to veto legislation passed by Congress	Possesses the sole federal power to enact legislation and to tax citizens and allocate federal spending Able to originate and promote major policy initiatives Power to override a presidential veto	Judicial interpretations of the Constitution or various laws may have a policy effect Resolves questions regarding agency regulations that may affect policy
Restrictions to Power	Unable to enact a law without the approval of Congress (legislative branch)	U.S. Supreme Court may invalidate legislation as unconstitutional	Unable to recommend or promote legislative initiatives

public problem to a public solution: a public plan, program, or service. Although there are many problems related to health care and nursing practice, problems that will attain policy solution status are those that are brought to the attention of a policymaker who is willing to take definitive action through legislative, regulatory, or funding processes.

Generally, interested individuals or citizens' groups approach policymakers either with a problem to be solved or suggest a policy option to a health problem that they have identified. However, policymakers may also become aware of problems through their personal experiences or that of their constituents and take on solutions development action independently. At the federal level, only members of Congress can introduce legislation. The Congressional member who introduces a specific piece of legislation becomes the prime sponsor of that legislation. Legislation is introduced by a member of Congress after careful analysis of the problem, which likely includes the following:

- Public perception of the problem
- Definition of the problem

- Societal consequences of action or inaction and the number of people affected by the problem and/or the options for resolution
- Degree of support and opposition from other members of Congress, special interest groups, business leaders, and the general public, especially their constituents

After the problem is thoroughly analyzed and a decision is made to move forward with a policy solution, the sponsoring Congressman drafts the legislation and Congressional staff translates the option into legal, technical, and constitutional language that the Congressman then introduces through the appropriate process. Only then does the health problem addressed by a policy option/solution become a bill—a proposed legislative policy solution. Visit http://www.votesmart.org/education/how-a-bill-becomes-law to review all the necessary steps for how a bill becomes law.

Although the legislative process to enact a new law appears to be simple and straightforward, it is actually very complex and convoluted, with only a fraction of introduced legislation actually making it through the final process to become law. In the 112th U.S. Congress (2011 to 2012), 10,439 bills were introduced, but only 283 of those actually became public law (Congressional Record, 2013). In other words, only 2.7% of bills introduced in the 112th Congress actually became public law!

Once a bill becomes a law (a public policy), implementation falls to the jurisdiction of one of the departments under the executive branch of government. (See Table 23-2.) At the federal level, most health-related policies fall under the jurisdiction of the U.S. Department of Health and Human Services (DHHS) and its related agencies. The agency that will administer the law develops the regulations to implement the law. Implementation of new legislation can often be very different from what was originally intended when Congress debated and passed the bill. It is extremely important that supporters of any new law take steps to ensure that its advocates and the legislative policymakers implement the law as intended. This important caution leads us to the discussion about regulation and health policy.

HEALTH POLICY THROUGH REGULATION

The regulatory arena is an important but often overlooked area of policy that significantly affects nursing practice. An understanding of regulatory authority and processes provides nurses with the knowledge necessary to become involved and more successfully influence the future of nursing. *Regulation* refers to the written set of rules issued by the executive branch agency that has responsibility for administering a law. Because regulations carry the force of the law, they directly shape the implementation of health policy. Thus, it is very important that regulations reflect the intent of the law as enacted by the legislative body. Once the proposed regulations are developed, they must be published and open to public comment for a specified length of time before being adopted as final rules. As regulations are being developed by the government agency, public hearings are held to allow interested individuals and groups to comment on the draft content of the regulations and to suggest amendments or substitutions. At this stage, nurses can and must play an influential role in shaping the final regulations by writing to the regulatory agency or speaking at public hearings. Informed comments are critical for the development of administrative law. Each comment received must be considered and responded to before final regulations are issued. The time interval between the interim and final rules is critical for assessing the effect of the proposed rules and requires concerted nursing vigilance and action to react to the proposed rules either positively or negatively. Final published regulations carry the force of the law and will dictate how the law is actually implemented.

At the federal level, the proposed (or interim) regulations are published in the *Federal Register*. The *Federal Register* (located online at https://www.federalregister.gov) is the best source of information about proposed new rules as well as proposed changes to existing rules for federal programs. It is printed each day and contains complete directions about where to send comments in addition to the deadlines for the public comment period. Most states have a parallel publication (e.g., *Texas Register*) with information about proposed rules and regulations at the state level for state legislation. It cannot be overemphasized that supporters of any new law must be vigilant and involved in the development of rules and regulations long after the legislation has passed and been adopted as law to ensure its implementation as planned and supported.

A great deal of thoughtful, focused effort goes into the development of health policy—from the time a public health problem is identified; a legislative solution is conceived; a bill is passed; and a health policy is actually implemented through regulation and funding. By understanding and becoming involved in these processes, nurses can protect and influence nursing practice and create and shape positive change throughout the health care system.

HEALTH POLICY AND POLITICS: A KEY CONNECTION

Many people may view politics as somewhat "shady" activities that occur in and around federal, state, and local governments to influence the outcomes of candidate elections and/or the passage of legislation. Chaffee and colleagues have defined politics as "the process of influencing the allocation of scarce resources" (2013). Politics can also be defined as the process used to influence decisions and exert control over policy, circumstances, and events. As the reader will see, "influence" is the common denominator in any definition of politics. Political influence can be achieved through many methods, including the following:

- Campaign activity and contributions
- Knowledge
- Relationships
- Information/data
- Talent
- Perceived control over large groups of votes

Florence Nightingale was the consummate political nurse. She understood how to use data and expert knowledge to influence the British Parliament to allocate funds to reform British military hospitals and substantially improved the health conditions for the troops through changes in sanitary practices (Nightingale, 1859).

Politics is a necessary part of the policy process. Multiple interest groups (such as, government officials, special interest groups, and corporate leaders) are all competing to achieve their potentially different policy goals/outcomes. The process becomes even more interesting when the varied and increasingly polarized agendas of the Democratic, Republican, and emerging independent parties are added to the mix. Groups and individuals who have a stake in the fate of a piece of legislation or the election of a candidate use political strategies to obtain their desired outcome(s). Thus it is through *effective* political action that nurses can positively influence legislative and regulatory decisions and the development of health policies that will affect nursing practice and the health of Americans in a positive way. Following is a discussion of how nurses can get involved in the political process and use effective political strategies to influence health policy.

Health Policy and the Nursing Process

The first step for nurses to get involved in health policy development and politics is to learn to recognize nursing and health care issues that are amendable to and/or require policy action. During nursing school, students learn the nursing process as the foundation for professional nursing practice. Once nursing students graduate, they appreciate the nursing process as the basis for making sound clinical judgments. As nurses commit to being more policy focused and politically active, they will find that applying the nursing process is a natural and comfortable approach to identifying and taking

on broader professional and health care issues. Just remember the following:

1. *Assessment:* collecting information and understanding the information are important first steps for approaching policy issues
2. *Analysis and diagnosis:* analyzing the information and identifying the fundamental issue or underlying problem that needs to be addressed
3. *Planning:* developing options for an effective policy plan involves input from many sources and perspectives
4. *Implementation:* Implementing a policy requires political action and a set of strategies and strategic interventions.
5. *Evaluation:* assessing evidence that determines the success (or not? and the why or why not?) of the intervention

Nurses' ability and inclination to observe, use data, analyze it from a variety of perspectives and then make a plan prior to taking action make them "naturals" for policy activity and involvement. Policy work is challenging, important, and, in so many instances, fun and exciting and should become a part of the professional nurse's skill set.

GRASSROOTS POLITICAL STRATEGIES

Grassroots political strategies are actions taken at the local level to influence policymakers. Nurses as political constituents have a right (and a responsibility!) to petition, lobby, or persuade policymakers to ensure that their interests and concerns are heard. Such advocacy actions (frequently referred to as *lobbying*) provide individuals and groups who are stakeholders in a particular issue an opportunity to be heard. The lobbying process also provides policymakers with needed information from health experts upon which to base their decisions. Following are various methods through which nurses can be effective grassroots participants/players:

- Registering to vote and voting in *all* elections
- Joining professional nursing organizations with policy advocacy agendas
- Working on political candidates' campaigns
- Meeting with policymakers or their staff members
- Attending and speaking up at "meet the candidates" town hall meetings
- Communicating with policymakers by e-mail, fax, and telephone

Register to Vote and Vote in All Elections

Voting is a must for *every* nurse. However, voting is not enough. *Informed voting* is necessary to enhance nurses' political power to ultimately improve the health of patients and the care that they receive. Becoming informed involves reading legislative newsletters and finding out about policymakers' backgrounds, voting records, and current party and candidate platforms. Discussing your findings on these issues with nurse colleagues and others in the community enhances everyone's understanding of candidates and their positions and facilitates informed voting. Nurses must participate in identifying and electing "nurse-friendly" candidates and then become candidates and policymakers themselves.

Join a Professional Nursing Organization

Another must for the professional nurse seeking to make a policy difference is to join a professional nursing organization. The value of the ANA, its C/SNAs and its organizational affiliates, is that, *together,* the nursing profession is much more powerful than any individual RN speaking alone. Within a professional collective, nurses know more, have more resources, and are able to pool their strengths and direct resources toward "winning" the health policy competition and thus ensuring a more "nurse-friendly" public policy.

The ANA is the foremost recognized professional nursing organization for federal health and nursing public policy. The ANA speaks for all professional nurses, regardless of specialty. All nurses should consider ANA membership as one of their fundamental professional investments. Nurses who choose to also be a member in a specialty organization that represents their focus arena of nursing practice have the additional advantage of receiving clinical and health policy information related to that specialty.

Because professional nursing organizations monitor public policy and offer avenues for their members to learn about health policy, they serve as an invaluable resource for reliable information related to policy issues and policymakers. Joining a professional nursing organization that has a political action committee (PAC) can help develop the necessary skills to understand and participate in political issues and elections and provide nurses increased access to policymakers.

A PAC is an arm of a corporation, association, or union formed to provide support and resources either to work toward the election or reelection of policymakers who support the organization's overall goals or to persuade a policymaker to support a certain policy. Not all professional nursing organizations have PACs, but those that do so may choose to endorse a specific candidate for office. Endorsement simply means that, in a particular political race, the nursing organization selects a particular candidate to support because of that candidate's platform or record supporting specific issues or policy goals. Although endorsement does not mean that everyone in the organization *must* vote for the selected person, it does mean that the organization has carefully screened the candidate, and the nurse can be reasonably sure that, if elected, the candidate will support the organization's preferred outcomes and interests. Nursing organizations are looking for health-friendly and nurse-friendly candidates who will champion laws and programs to improve health and nursing.

Work in Political Candidates' Campaigns

Most political candidates are not health professionals and do not fully understand health-related issues. By becoming involved in political campaigns, nurses can (and should) educate and inform candidates about health care issues. Other activities that the nurse may undertake on behalf of the candidates include assisting in writing health care position statements, working in campaign offices, attending local debates, displaying the candidates' political buttons, signs, and stickers and participating in fundraising events. Nurse supporters may also write letters/e-mails to and/or call other nurses in the region to tell them about their support of the candidate and to ask for their vote. Having nurse-friendly candidates win and become nurse-friendly policymaking officials is critical to achieving nursing's policy agenda.

Visit with Policymakers and their Staff Members

Personal visits to policymakers and their staff members can be one of the most effective methods of advocacy for or against a health care policy. Nothing is more effective in communicating nursing's position on an issue than face-to-face contact between a group of well-informed nurses and a policymaker and his or her staff. Face-to-face meetings provide a great opportunity for nurses to educate policymakers about health care issues while enhancing the image of the nurse as an informed, trustworthy constituent. Policymakers are very interested in information that will increase their knowledge about health care and help them develop options for future health care policy. Tips to prepare for a personal visit with policymakers are available in the online *RN Activist Tool Kit* on the American Nurses Association website (www.nursingworld.org).

Participate in "Meet the Candidates" Town Hall Meetings

A strategy that nursing associations can use to determine which candidate(s) to endorse is to invite all candidates running for a particular office to a town hall meeting to discuss their positions and platforms directly with nurses. Town hall gatherings with nurses allow the candidates to talk about their platform to a group of interested likely voters and afford nurses an opportunity to voice their experiences, opinions, and concerns about health care issues and assess the candidates' views. Box 23-1 provides the correct titles to use when addressing state elected officials.

Hosting a meet-the-candidates town hall meeting can be an exciting activity for student nurses and faculty. Just as in preparing for a personal visit to a policymaker, nursing students should also prepare carefully to host a town hall meeting:

1. Before the town hall meeting, become familiar with each candidate's background, including his or her voting record on health policy issues, party affiliation, major contributors, personal occupation, family information, and hobbies. This information can provide insight into the candidate's positions on issues.
2. Identify current issues that would be relevant for discussion with the candidates. Collect and review information related to the issues and then prioritize the issues. Time may not be sufficient to discuss all of the issues of interest.

---

3. Prepare to give concise examples of how the issue affects the individual, community, health care consumers, and other members of the nursing profession. Be prepared to debate the pros and cons of health positions that may arise.
4. Plan the agenda for the meeting to allow ample time for discussion.
5. After introductions are made, listen carefully as each candidate presents his or her campaign platform, and then be prepared to clearly and concisely discuss the issues with relevant examples. Real-world stories put a human face on health policy issues.
6. At the conclusion of the meeting, provide the candidate with contact information (names, addresses, telephone numbers, and e-mail addresses) for key members of your group.

Communicate with Policymakers Through E-mail, Fax, and Telephone

Contacting policymakers through letters, e-mail, fax, and telephone can be effective if properly planned and implemented. The timing of the communication is important; it should be made early before policymakers publically commit to a certain policy option. It is easier to persuade an undecided policymaker than it is to get him or her to switch positions. A second very effective step is to send a follow-up communication immediately before the vote on a particular bill is scheduled. Information about voting schedules can be obtained online in most states and certainly from your SNA.

Because of the security slowdowns that may affect delivery, U.S. mail to Congress and the White House may be subject to delay, making letters a less effective means of communicating with federal policymakers. Using e-mail or sending a fax is really the best way to make sure your voice will be heard in a timely way to make a difference. Guidelines for communicating with policymakers include the following (ANA, 2014):

1. *Be brief.* Short, direct e-mail and faxes are the most effective.
2. *Be specific.* Deal with just one subject or issue in the communication; state your topic clearly in the first paragraph. The subject of an e-mail message should contain the number of the bill to which you are referring in the message. For example, "In Opposition to Senate Bill 123" immediately focuses the reader. The message itself should be just a few short lines to relay a clear and strong message related to the issue. Brief

---

BOX 23-1 **Speaking with the Governor, Lieutenant Governor, Legislators, or Staff**

Governor: Governor (last name)
Lieutenant Governor: Lt. Governor (last name)
Speaker of the House: Mr. Speaker or Madam Speaker
Senator: Senator (last name)
Representative: Representative (last name) or Mr. or Ms. (last name)
Staff: Mr. or Ms. (last name)

examples of how the issue/policy affects the policymaker's constituents are often most persuasive.

3. *Be personal.* Communication is most effective when it reflects your personal experiences and presents your views in your own words; mass-produced letters, e-mails, and faxes do not carry as much weight as a communication that you have written/modified in your own words.

4. *Provide your name and address.* Policymakers pay most attention to communications that come from their constituents—the very people who may be voting for or against them in their next election. So it is important to let them know if you are from their district. Include contact information so that the elected official may respond to your concerns.

5. *Be persistent.* Communicate often, especially if the policymaker is undecided on an issue.

Telephone calls are usually taken by a staff member; ask to speak to the staff person assigned to the bill or issue for which the call is being made. After introducing yourself, give a brief and simple message, such as "Please tell Senator or Representative [name] that I support/oppose [bill number]." You may briefly state your reasons for supporting or opposing the bill and ask for the policymaker's position on the bill. Conclude the call by leaving your name, telephone number, and address; if appropriate ask for a written response to your telephone call.

Rosters of state legislators can be found online in most states. The roster contains contact information for each policymaker and usually includes information about his or her committee memberships. Contact information for members of the U.S. House of Representatives is available online at www.house.gov. This site includes committee memberships and links to individual representatives' websites. Similar information for U.S. senators is also available online at www.senate.gov.

THE AMERICAN NURSES ASSOCIATION

The ANA is the professional nursing organization representing the nation's entire RN population—approximately 3.1 million RNs. The ANA is composed of 51 C/SNAs plus other direct membership categories that represent state and U.S territory nursing associations and includes key corporate affiliated entities such as the American Nurses Credentialing Center (ANCC), the American Nurses Foundation (ANF), the American

Academy of Nursing (AAN), and over 35 specialty organizations such as the American Psychiatric Nurses Association and the American Association of Critical-Care Nurses. A complete list of ANA-affiliated organizations and links to their websites can be found on the ANA website at www.nursingworld.org.

Through legislative, regulatory, and political activities, the ANA has taken firm and visible positions on a huge variety of health policy issues of great importance to the nation and to the profession. A few of these include: Medicare and Medicaid passage and then significant reforms over time including APRNs' direct reimbursement in these plans; patients' rights; the importance of safe workplaces and safe health devices and practices such as safe needles, safe patient handling, and whistleblower protection for health care workers; adequate reimbursement for health care services; access to health care; and, most recently, comprehensive health care reform. Most important, it is the ANA members—the state nurses associations—that carry forward on the policy and political activities for health policy and nursing practice, roles, and reimbursement within a given state. A tremendous amount of health policy development and implementation occurs within state boundaries and, in order for the nursing profession's voice to be heard, SNA membership and participation is a **must** because very few of the specialty nursing organizations have a state presence for policy and political activity. Students are encouraged to spend time browsing the ANA website at www.nursingworld.org to learn more about this nursing organization so important to us all.

Nurses Strategic Action Team

Nurses are the largest group among the health care disciplines, and there can be great power in numbers. In addition to numbers, professional nurses have the respect of the public as a "best" source of unbiased, truthful information about health policy issues as reflected in national Gallup polling (Gallup, 2013). Nurses are impressive in their collective abilities to mobilize and take effective grassroots action in shaping national health care policy through the Nurses Strategic Action Team (N-STAT). N-STAT is an ANA program that unifies nurses' political voices across the country to enact measures to benefit health care for everyone and to defeat measures that would have serious negative effects on the health care system. N-STAT is composed of thousands of nurses around the United States who stay informed on issues and contact their legislators about pending issues. Through legislative updates, N-STAT keeps members up-to-date on key bills as they move through the legislative process. Through action alerts, members are informed about when e-mails, telephone calls, and faxes will have the most effect. N-STAT makes the political process less intimidating by keeping nurses informed of political issues and providing strategies for making their opinions known. For more information and to sign up as a member of N-STAT, visit www.rnaction.org. At this website, be sure to look for information about NPAL and how you can become even more involved as a Nurse Political Action Leader.

CURRENT HEALTH POLICY ISSUES

Policy issues come and go as societal, health care, and public needs, demands, and priorities ebb and flow. However, several policy topics bear watching over the next decade—health care reforms using the frames of implementation of the PPACA and Medicare's drive for value through health care safety and quality, and enhancing/shaping the health care workforce. The critical importance of these topics will keep them on the policy agenda for many years to come.

Health Care Reform

Health care reform is the general term used to refer to health policy initiatives to effect significant changes in how health is promoted and health care is accessed, delivered, and paid for in the United States. Many Americans, consumer groups, and health care organizations such as the ANA, as well as vocal individuals including many professional nurses have long supported bold and comprehensive health care reforms for the Nation to address critical health problems facing our Nation and its citizens. Nurses know first-hand that the health care system has been facing serious issues for decades. These issues include a growing uninsured population, barriers in access to care, health care disparities, rapidly rising costs, health professional shortages (e.g., nurses, primary care physicians, mental health and substance abuse clinicians), concerns about quality and safety, and a system focused on illness care rather than one that promotes health and wellness. The U.S. health enterprise has yielded poor outcomes with unsustainable costs—it is neither patient focused nor value based.

After decades of efforts to incrementally "fix" the failing U.S. model, historic comprehensive health care reform became a reality with passage of the PPACA in 2010. Access to quality care services and the ability to obtain/maintain affordable, credible health insurance coverage were perhaps the most significant of the prior system inequities that were addressed through the 2010 health care reform legislation. In 2010, prior to the full implementation of the PPACA, 49.9 million Americans—just over 16.3% of the population—were without health insurance coverage for a full year (U.S. Census Bureau, 2011) and, after the Great Recession (2007-2009), the uninsured numbers rose to 21% for adults aged 19 to 64 (Sommers et al, 2014). Lack of health insurance is perhaps the greatest barrier to accessing health care services and has a tremendous negative effect on an individual's overall health status. Studies have consistently found that the uninsured receive less than adequate health care. Consider the following findings (Kaiser Family Foundation, 2012):

- More than 50% of the uninsured have no regular source of health care.
- Uninsured individuals are twice as likely to delay or ignore needed care, resulting in conditions being diagnosed at a later, more acute stage.
- Uninsured individuals are less likely to receive preventive care services; are more likely to be hospitalized for avoidable conditions; and are more likely to use the emergency department for nonemergency care—a delivery setting which is neither cost nor clinically effective.

The lack of health insurance also has serious financial consequences for individuals and families as well. More than 60% of bankruptcies in the United States are related to illnesses, medical causes, or medical debt (Himmelstein et al, 2009). The uninsured populations also generate uncompensated or indigent care costs and bad debt for health care providers requiring providers to increase charges to public and private insurers and making health coverage more costly for all including U.S. businesses and corporations.

The comprehensive nature of the PPACA system reform required a multiyear implementation period of its many provisions with many of its major health insurance provisions and protections set for implementation in 2014. Among these included the Federal or State Health Insurance Marketplace with premiums supports; Medicaid expansion for persons under

133% of poverty without arbitrary categorical restrictions or standards among states; a set standard for 10 essential benefits that all Qualified Health Plans (QHPs) must include, such as preventive and rehabilitation services, hospital services, emergency and lab services, ambulatory services, mental health and substance abuse services at parity, prescription drugs, maternity, and newborn and pediatric services (HealthCare.gov, 2014).

In the first years of PPACA implementation (2010-2014), the following were implemented rather smoothly:

- Increasing access and providing insurance protections such as elimination of co-pay/deductibles for preventive services
- Elimination of pre-existing condition barriers and annual and lifetime caps to insurance plans
- Allowing young adults up to age 26 to stay on parents' plans
- Increasing reimbursement to primary care providers such as APRNs
- Educational mechanisms to rapidly grow the primary care workforce

As year 1 of enrollment in the health insurance marketplace concluded, the PPACA has had remarkable positive impact by decreasing rate of uninsured persons ages 19 to 64 from 20% to 15% and has been especially effective in minority populations as the rate of uninsured Hispanics ages 19 to 64 fell from 36% to 23% (Sommers et al, 2014).

The PPACA will continue to challenge the nation's health policy, services, and related industry leaders and providers for years to come because of its broad reach, its implications for innovative population and patient-centered care models, and new reimbursement schemes based on value not volume and outcomes not interventions. As rules and regulations are developed and published to implement the PPACA, nurses and professional nursing organizations must have a strong and united voice to ensure that the PPACA will positively affect access to care, cost and quality of care, and ultimately the U.S. population health status as intended by the policymakers. Getting to the policy table with a voice will be required to ensure that nursing education, practice, and reimbursement are not overlooked.

The ANA will play a strong role to influence implementation of health care reform arising from the PPACA and its accompanying rule making along with the reshaping of the health system delivery through the influence of the Centers for Medicare & Medicaid (CMS) by regulation and funding initiatives. The ANA document *Health System Reform Agenda* released in 2008 (www.nursingworld.org) reaffirmed the four areas of health care reforms that have historically been deemed essential to the nursing profession: access to care, quality of care, cost of care, and workforce development.

More recently, ANA leaders worked with other key national nursing organizations to develop a set of reform principles and recommendations supported by organized nursing to serve as an expert resource/reference for federal policymakers and their staff. The principles and recommendations address (1) the supply of RNs, APRNs, and nursing faculty; (2) the full utilization of advanced practice nurses to provide comprehensive, cost-effective, and high-quality care; (3) the use of care coordination models and reimbursement to improve quality outcomes and reduce costs for patients and the overall health enterprise; (4) increased emphasis on wellness and health promotion strategies; and (5) implementation of a nationwide health information system (Gonzales, 2009). At each meeting of the ANA Membership Assembly since 2010, those policy priority principles have been reaffirmed, and ANA has frequently and forcefully advocated for them with President Obama, U.S. Department of Health and Human Services, and CMS.

It is vitally important that nurses pay particular attention to evolving developments about the PPACA and other national and state health care reforms. The ANA/SNAs provide the professional venue for nurses to stay current—and become involved—as health care reform moves toward implementation in our country. Comprehensive health system change will not be smooth or seamless or without continuing controversy, but it is critical. Through informed participation in health care reform initiatives, nurses can advocate for their profession and the safety, quality, value and availability of health and nursing care for all Americans.

The IOM Future of Nursing Report

In 2010, the Institute of Medicine (IOM) issued a report calling attention to the essentiality of nursing in the success of reforming the U.S. health care system. In its 2010 report, *The Future of Nursing: Leading Change, Advancing Health*, the IOM had four major recommendations:

- Nurses should practice to the full extent of their education and training.
- Nurses should achieve higher levels of education and training through an improved education system that promotes seamless academic progression.
- Nurses should be full partners, with physicians and other health care professionals, in redesigning health care in the United States.
- Effective workforce planning and policymaking require better data collection and information infrastructure.

In furtherance of these objectives, the IOM report recommended that the proportion of nurses in the United States who hold at least a bachelor's degree be increased from its current level of 50% to 80% by 2020.

Since the *Future of Nursing* report was released in 2010, extensive progress has been made in implementation of its recommendations through a national initiative entitled *Future of Nursing Campaign for Action*. As part of the campaign, coalitions at the state and local levels are driving action and policy change to transform nursing and health care. For example, the Indiana Action Coalition has created opportunities for nurses and physicians to join together to improve patient access to care. The campaign is monitoring its progress through measurable indicators in its "Dashboard" project. The dashboard indicators as of 2014 include (Future of Nursing Campaign for Action, 2014):

- Percentage of employed nurses with baccalaureate degree in nursing or high degree
- Total fall enrollment in nursing doctorate programs
- State progress in removing regulatory barriers to care by nurse practitioners
- Number of required clinical courses and/or activities at top nursing schools that include both RN students and other graduate health professional students
- Percent of hospital boards with RN members

Becoming involved in the *Campaign for Action* at your local or state level is an excellent opportunity to affect health care policy and drive transformation in your own area. Detailed information about the campaign and resources to help you get involved are available at www.campaignforaction.org.

Other Nursing Policy Initiatives

Extensive data about numbers of nurses by education and demographic distribution have been, and continue to be, collected and analyzed, thus providing policymakers and nursing advocates with the information needed to identify the underlying multifaceted problems of the supply, utilization, and the professional knowledge and skills that make a difference in patient outcomes by setting. In addition, a nursing workforce with the needed knowledge, skills, and authority has a tremendous effect on population health, health care quality, costs, and value and thus requires that effective policy interventions be developed and implemented that promotes such an environment for professional nursing.

The PPACA contains a number of provisions to increase the supply of nurses with ever-advancing degrees, knowledge, and skills through accelerated nursing programs with the expectation that nurses in increased numbers and with enhanced educational credentials increase access to quality care services. A number of health care reform initiatives in the PPACA are predicated on APRNs filling a range of new roles in primary care, prevention, and care coordination. Under the PPACA, hospitals' Medicare payments will be tied to scores on patient safety, quality outcomes including how frequently patients have to be readmitted to the hospital, and patient satisfaction surveys. Achieving such measures are exactly what nurses do best. All professional nurses will be expected to know more and do more to achieve these national expectations of hospital and health system performance.

Nurses need to stay alert for new and proposed legislation and its amendments that will affect nursing care, patient safety, and health care quality. Nurses can review and track the progress of proposed bills at the federal level on the Library of Congress's "Thomas" website (www.thomas.gov). Simply enter the bill number or key words from the bill, and use the search button to find information about a particular piece of legislation. It is absolutely essential that nurses stay actively engaged in tracking these important pieces of legislation and advocating for passage of legislation that will improve access to care; access to nurses; and improvements in the nursing workforce, patient safety, quality of care, and the work environment of nurses.

▌ SUMMARY

Nurses must be powerful advocates for health care for all and for their profession. By understanding the policy and political processes presented in this chapter, nurses can make significant contributions to the development of health policies that promote a healthier society. A basic professional responsibility is to be involved in professional nursing organizations and to be politically active in supporting meaningful health policies. Just as the first politically active nurse, Florence Nightingale, used expert knowledge to shape health policy to make a difference, so can **we make a difference** in the lives of people we care for, in our own lives, and in the future of our profession.

REFERENCES

American Nurses Association: *Activist Tool Kit: Activist Resources: Tips: contacting your member of Congress*, 2014. (website). http://www.rnaction.org/site/PageServer?pagename=nstat_activist_toolkit#activist-resources. Accessed September 19, 2014.

Chaffee MW, Mason DJ, Leavitt JK: A framework for action in policy and politics. In Mason DJ, Leavitt JK, Chaffee MW, editors: *Policy and politics in nursing and health care*, ed 6, Philadelphia, 2013, Saunders.

Congressional Record: *Bill summary & status for the 112th Congress*, 2013. (website). http://www.congress-summary.com/B-112th-Congress/Laws_Passed_112th_Congress_Seq.html. Accessed September 19, 2014.

Gallup: *Honesty/ethics in professions*, 2014. (website). http://www.gallup.com/poll/1654/honesty-ethics-professions.aspx. Accessed September 24, 2014.

Gonzales R: Headlines from the hill: Health system reform: Where is nursing? Where are you? *Am Nurse Today* 4(7):18, 2009.

HealthCare.gov: *Essential health benefits*, 2014. (website). https://www.healthcare.gov/glossary/essential-health-benefits/. Accessed January 25, 2015

Himmelstein DU, Thorne D, Warren E, et al: Medical bankruptcy in the United States, 2007: results of a national study, *Am J Med* 122(8):741–746, 2009.

Institute of Medicine: *The future of nursing: leading change, advancing health*, Washington, DC, 2010, National Academies Press.

Kaiser Family Foundation: *Kaiser Commission on Medicaid and the uninsured: the uninsured and the difference health insurance makes*, 2012. (website). http://www.kff.org/uninsured/upload/1420-10.pdf.

Future of Nursing Campaign for Action: *Dashboard Indicators*, 2014. (website). http://campaignforaction.org/dashboard.

Nightingale F: *Notes on hospital*, West Strand, London, 1859, John W. Parker and Sons.

Sommers BD, Musco T, Finegold K, et al: Health reform and changes in health insurance coverage in 2014, *N Engl J Med* 371:867–874, 2014. DOI: 10.1056/NEJMsr1406753.

Starr P: *The social transformation of American medicine: the rise of a sovereign profession and the making of a vast industry*, New York, 1982, Basic Books.

U.S. Census Bureau: *Income, poverty, and health insurance coverage in the United States*, 2011. (website). http://www.census.gov/prod/2011pubs/p60-239.pdf.

Moving from student to professional can be frightening; plan your strategies.

24

Making the Transition from Student to Professional Nurse

Tommie L. Norris, DNS, RN

ⓔ Additional resources are available online at: *http://evolve.elsevier.com/Cherry/*

PROFESSIONAL/ETHICAL ISSUE

Lauren, a new nurse, just graduated with her BSN and interviews with the nurse manager. She comes with questions and asks, "Tell me about the culture of your unit?" The nurse manager describes the culture as "accepting, diverse, and dynamic." Lauren is excited to have such a culture to begin her nursing career. She attends new employee orientation for 3 days and looks forward to beginning her career on her first nursing unit. She arrives 30 minutes early and enters the nursing lounge. She scans the lockers to determine if one is available. She notices several of the night shift nurses watching, so she asks, "Do we have assigned lockers or should I just chose one that is empty?" One nurse rolls her eyes and mumbles, "New BSN nurses think they deserve what we have worked for." Lauren hopes she didn't understand her correctly and waits for her preceptor to arrive. She shares with the preceptor her concern with choosing a locker and what she thought she heard from the night nurse. Lauren's preceptor replied, "Never mind her. She is always like that. She doesn't like anyone, especially new nurses with a BSN." Lauren takes report the following day from the night nurse and was told that the "patient is monitoring her own blood sugar" and did not report lab values ordered at midnight. Lauren was surprised when she found the results from the lab posted from the previous night noting that the patient's blood sugar was actually 400 mg/dL. When she reported this again to her preceptor, she was told, "Sometimes the night nurse forgets to check lab results." Lauren senses anxiety and wonders if she can ever work under these conditions.

1. Was Lauren being targeted for horizontal violence?
2. Was information being purposefully withheld?
3. What are the signs of horizontal violence?
4. Should Lauren report the night nurse to the nurse manager?

VIGNETTE

Every nurse has experienced the transition from student to professional nurse. Why can't we learn from our experiences and help our future nurses have a positive first impression of nursing? The cost alone of the revolving door for new nurses should be enough for organizations to reconsider not only how novice nurses are orienting to the facility but also what proactive measures are in place to ensure that experienced nurses stay rather than leave due to violence or burnout.

413

Questions to Consider While Reading this Chapter:

1. What could educators incorporate into the curriculum to decrease the "reality shock" of transition from student to professional nurse?
2. What could employers of novice nurses do during the orientation phase to help nurses learn the ropes of their organization, which may differ somewhat from the learning environment?
3. What strategies should novice nurses use to gain self-esteem and prove themselves capable of having the required skills while still needing help with specific tasks and skills that come with experience?
4. Should professional nurses form official teams to look at the role of mentoring as one means of transitioning novice nurses into the profession?
5. What could orientation for new employees include to help novice nurses be proactive in preventing or reacting to violence at work?

KEY TERMS

Biculturalism: The merging of school values with those of the workplace.

Compassion fatigue: The gradual decline of compassion over time as a result of caregivers being exposed to events that have traumatized their patients.

Horizontal hostility (also known as *lateral hostility*): Disruptive behaviors that "intimidate, demean, undermine, or exclude another nurse" (Anno et al, 2013). Eye-rolling, badgering, belittling, or withholding information are examples.

Intuition: Extracting clues from one's subconscious so decisions are based on a holistic view of the patient and surroundings.

Mentoring: A mutual interactive method of learning in which a knowledgeable nurse inspires and encourages a novice nurse.

Novice nurse: A nurse who is entering the professional workplace for the first time; usually occurs from the point of graduation until competencies required by the profession are achieved.

Preceptor: An experienced professional nurse who serves as a mentor and assists with socialization of the novice nurse.

Reality shock: Occurs when a person prepares for a profession, enters the profession, and then finds that he or she is not prepared.

Role model: A person who serves as an example of what constitutes a competent professional nurse.

Socialization: The nurturing, acceptance, and integration of a person into the profession of nursing; the identification of a person with the profession of nursing.

Transition: Moving from one role, setting, or level of competency in nursing to another; change.

Transition shock: The abrupt shock associated with moving from student to professional nurse associated with doubt, confusion, disorientation, and loss (Duchscher, 2009).

Trust: is having confidence that your peers in the workplace have good intentions toward you.

Workplace violence: Sexual harassment and abusive acts from patients or coworkers that can be physical, verbal, and emotional and lead to a hostile work environment. It has been suggested that identifying workplace violence is difficult due to its subjectivity by the recipient.

LEARNING OUTCOMES

After studying this chapter, the reader will be able to:

1. Compare and contrast the phases of reality shock with the phases of transition shock.
2. Differentiate between the novice nurse and the expert professional nurse.
3. Design strategies to ease the transition from novice nurse to professional nurse.
4. Differentiate between compassion fatigue and burnout.
5. Make the transition from novice nurse to professional nurse.

CHAPTER OVERVIEW

According to the Merriam-Webster dictionary (www. merriam-webster.com), transition is defined as "change" or the "passage from one state, place, stage, or subject to another." As nurses prepare to enter the profession and make the transition from student to registered nurse (RN), they move not only from one role to another, but also from the school or university setting to the workplace. Transition is a complicated process during which many changes may be happening at once. The novice

nurse tries to juggle all these changes while continuing a life outside of nursing (e.g., as mother, father, husband, wife, daughter, son, active church leader, or community volunteer).

To help students gain an understanding of the issues involved in the transition from the student role to that of the professional nurse, this chapter discusses the various stages of reality shock. Strategies that may alleviate this shock and ease the transition are also suggested.

REAL-LIFE SCENARIO

The first impression the novice nurse has of his or her chosen profession is valuable and sets the stage for entry into nursing. This first impression occurs during the transition phase from student to professional. Consider Case Study 24-1.

REALITY SHOCK

Novice nurses are described as feeling as though they are isolated and vulnerable (Iheduru-Anderson, 2014). When the expert student moves into the novice nurse role, uncertainty takes over, and the support of classmates and the nursing instructors is gone. This time

---

CASE STUDY 24-1

Rachel Stevens had wanted to be a nurse for as long as she could remember. As a child, she donned a pretend laboratory jacket and set to work providing care to teddy bears and dolls. She softly spoke to her pretend patients, explaining that she was a nurse and would make everything better. After graduation from high school, Rachel entered nursing school and visualized her dream coming true. She was a high achiever and received comments from her instructors, such as "shows evidence of applying the nursing process to the clinical environment," "psychomotor skills improving," and "becoming more autonomous." Her patients complimented her nursing abilities and caring attitude. Finally, Rachel graduated from nursing school, passed the national licensure examination, and accepted her first position as an RN. She proudly entered the hospital and felt confident that she would be a caring nurse and assist patients to achieve their highest level of health.

The hospital provided a 2-month orientation period. The first week consisted of classes to explain benefits, safety education, Standard Precaution protocols, and computer classes. Rachel loved her new job. The next step in her employment was orientation to the medical-surgical unit where she would be working. The nurse manager welcomed her to the unit and introduced her to the staff. Because all the seasoned nurses wanted to transfer to

the day shift, Rachel was hired to work the evening shift, which had a higher nurse-patient ratio than the day shift. Rachel proudly sat through the shift report, jotting down reminders that were stressed by the previous shift, such as "The patient in room 200 needs a blood glucose test drawn at 6 PM," and "the patient in room 215 is to receive a unit of blood." Rachel's assignment consisted of six patients. The charge nurse encouraged Rachel to ask if she had any questions. The nursing assistants hurried to complete their tasks. Rachel reread her assignment and entered the first room. "Hello, my name is Rachel Stevens, and I'll be your nurse tonight." She assessed her patients and reviewed their medication sheets. No medications were due until 6 PM, so she began researching those medications with which she was not familiar. At 5:30 PM, the charge nurse informed Rachel that the only other nurse on the floor would be going for dinner and that Rachel should respond to her patients during her absence. Rachel was a little nervous about the responsibility, but positively acknowledged the assignment.

Moments later, Rachel was paged to respond to a newly admitted patient who was assigned to the nurse on break. As soon as Rachel entered the room, the patient complained of nausea and began vomiting. Rachel assessed and comforted the patient and reviewed the

Continued

medication record for orders related to antiemetics. The physician had not ordered medication for nausea, so Rachel quickly telephoned his office to report the patient's condition. She received an order to insert a nasogastric tube and place to suction. Rachel was anxious; she had only inserted one such tube with her instructor's assistance. She gathered supplies and reentered the patient's room. She measured for correct placement and was just positioning the patient when she received a page that the blood had arrived for the other patient, and the laboratory assistant could not obtain a blood culture ordered on yet another of Rachel's patients.

After numerous unsuccessful attempts to insert the nasogastric tube, Rachel became more anxious and requested assistance from the charge nurse. The charge nurse replied, "I'm admitting a new patient and can't help you. Don't you know how to insert the nasogastric tube?" Rachel explained that she had made numerous attempts, and the patient was continuing to vomit. Rachel returned to the patient's room and attempted again

to insert the tube. The nurse originally assigned to the patient returned to the floor; however, neither the secretary nor the charge nurse informed Rachel of the new admission with orders, so she proceeded to care for her other patients. Finally, Rachel again requested help, and the charge nurse inserted the tube to the relief of Rachel and the patient. Now the medications were late, she had forgotten to check the patient's blood sugar, and she had not completed the charts. "Where are my notes?" Oh, well, she would just have to remember. Finally, at 10 PM, 1 hour before the shift ended, Rachel sat down to chart. She took out scrap paper and began writing her notes, but what time did she start the blood? She became more and more anxious. The clock continued to advance to 11 PM, and Rachel was still charting. "You need to give the shift report to the oncoming shift," said the charge nurse. Rachel complied and 15 minutes later returned to her charting. At 1 AM, Rachel left the unit feeling depressed and incompetent.

marks the end of one era as a student and the beginning of a new era in a nursing career.

Novice nurses often suffer what Kramer (1974) describes as *reality shock,* which is the result of inconsistencies between the academic world and the world of work. Reality shock occurs in novice nurses when they become aware of the inconsistency between the actual world of nursing and that of nursing school. As the novice nurse enters the new profession, reality shock begins. The excitement of passing the licensure examination quickly fades in the struggle to move from the student to the staff nurse role. Reality shock leads to stress and burnout (Caliskan and Ergun, 2012), which can threaten the well-being of new nurses and result in exhaustion, "irritability, detachment, and cynicism" (Profit et al, 2014), and ultimately absenteeism and turnover (Laschiger et al, 2012). The National Council of State Boards of Nursing (NCSBN) (2015) states that 25% of new nurses leave their position within the first year, which has a substantial impact on employers because the average cost to replace the nurse can be more than $64,000. New nurses were found to experience higher levels of stress during the first 3 to 6 months after employment, which were thought to be risk factors for patient safety and errors. The NCSBN reports that 50%

of novice nurses fail to recognize life-threatening complications, and 40% report having made a medication error. An Institute of Medicine (IOM) report recognized the need to assist novice nurses in their transition to practice (2011). The four phases of reality shock, *honeymoon, shock or rejection, recovery,* and *resolution,* first described by Kramer in 1974, continue to be recognized in novice nurses today.

Honeymoon Phase

During the honeymoon phase, everything is just as the new graduate imagined. The new nurse is in orientation with former school friends or other new graduates who often share similarities. Many novice nurses in this phase are heard making the following comments: "Just think; now I'll get paid for making all those beds," or "I'm so glad I chose nursing; I will be a part of changing the future of health care."

Shock (Rejection) Phase

Then orientation is over, and the novice nurse begins work on his or her assigned unit. This nurse receives daily assignments and begins the tasks. "But wait. I've only observed other nurses hanging blood. Where is my instructor?" Now the shock or rejection phase comes into play. The nurse comes into contact with conflicting viewpoints and different ways of performing skills, but lacks the security of having an expert available to explain uncertain or gray areas. Novice nurses describe this phase as similar to "sink or swim" and describe feeling alone (Horsburgh and Ross, 2013). Although students had thought themselves fully prepared, in reality they were not. During this phase, the novice nurse may be frightened or react by isolating him or herself. Feelings of discomfort are experienced, and the inexperienced nurse often wonders whether the other nurses care about the patients. After going home from a shift, the new nurse may experience feelings of rejection and a sense of lack of accomplishment. The novice nurse may reject the new environment and have a preoccupation with the past when he or she was in school. A need to contact former instructors, call schoolmates, or visit the nursing school may occur. Others may reject their school values and adopt the values of the organization. In this way, they may experience less conflict (Kramer, 1974); however, there are drawbacks to this approach as well.

During this phase, Kramer (1974) suggests that novice nurses must ask themselves two important questions:

1. What must I do to become the kind of nurse I want to be?
2. What must I do so that my nursing contributes to humankind and society?

Dealing with the shock phase can be approached in many different ways. Some common approaches for dealing with it are reviewed in the following sections. After that, each nurse must decide which method best allows the previous two questions to be answered.

Natives

Many nurses choose to go "native" (Kramer, 1974). That is, they decide they cannot fight the experienced nurses or the administration, thus they adopt the ways of least resistance. These nurses may mimic other nurses on the unit and take shortcuts, such as administering medications without knowing their action and side effects and the associated nursing responsibilities.

Runaways

Others choose to "run away." They find the real world too difficult. These new nurses may choose another occupation or return to graduate school to prepare for a career in nursing education to teach others their "values in nursing." Perkins (2010) describes wondering why she was tolerating poor working conditions, but states she found little hope in finding a better environment in other hospitals. This resulted in beginning graduate school after 8 months of practice.

Rutters

Some adopt the attitude that "I'll just do what I have to do to get by," or "I'm just working until I can buy some new furniture." These nurses are called *rutters*. They consider nursing just a job.

Burned Out

These nurses bottle up conflict until they become burned out. Kramer (1974) describes the appearance of these nurses as having the look of being chronically constipated. In this situation, patients may feel compelled to nurse their nurse. New graduates are not immune to burn out; they enter "energized" but quickly lose interest in the profession (Turner, 2014). High nurse-to-patient ratios with scant ancillary support staff make for an impossible transition (Perkins, 2010), leading to burnout. When there is a chasm between the novice nurse's expectations and the desire of the health care facility to meet these expectations, this void is fundamental to burnout (Fearon and Nicol, 2011). Some common symptoms of burnout include fatigue, negativity in personal relationships, difficulty sleeping, excessive stress, anxiety, vulnerability to disease, depression, and alcohol or substance abuse (Mayo Clinic, 2014). The more intelligent, hard-working nurses are the most prone to burnout; if you exhibit these symptoms, remember that they can be reduced.

Compassion Fatigue

Not to be confused with burnout or transference, compassion fatigue is the gradual decline of compassion over time as a result of caregivers being exposed to events that have traumatized their patients (Figley, 2001). Even experienced nurses, who commonly have a great deal of empathy working in environments where patients suffer trauma, may develop a reaction in which they have a decrease in compassion. Exposure to traumatic events experienced by their patients may result in compassion fatigue. Nurses who work in emotionally charged environments, such as hospice, emergency departments, and mental health settings, are likely to experience this reaction. Intensive ongoing losses such as those in oncology care make nurses vulnerable to burnout and compassion fatigue (Babbel, 2014). The balance between caring too much or having apathy is difficult to achieve (Compassion Fatigue Awareness Project, 2013). Nursing students are also at risk for compassion fatigue and need to find ways to "disconnect" from work or school (Olin, 2012). The compassion fatigue process is depicted in Figure 24-1.

Loners

These nurses create their own reality. They adopt the attitude of "just do the job and keep quiet." These nurses may prefer night shifts, during which they often are "left alone."

New Nurse on the Block

These nurses change jobs frequently. They go from the hospital setting to community health to the physician's office. They are always new in their setting and therefore adopt the attitude of "teach me what you want; I'm new here."

Change Agents

These nurses care enough to work within the system to elicit change. They frequently visit the nurse manager or head nurse to suggest change or a better way. They keep the welfare of the patient at the forefront. Unfortunately, Kramer (1974) refers to these nurses as "bicultural troublemakers." These nurses are able to incorporate the agency's values while simultaneously remaining true to their own professional beliefs. They are viewed as always wanting to make changes but also have innovative ideas that benefit the profession and/or agency.

Recovery Phase

Usually the first sign that a nurse has entered the recovery phase is the return of his or her sense of humor or desire to succeed. The novice nurse begins to understand the new culture to a certain degree, thus there is less tension and anxiety, and healing begins. The nurse in this phase may comment, "I'll hang that blood, and I'll bet I can infuse it before 8 hours this time."

Resolution Phase

The resolution phase is the result of the shock phase combined with the novice nurse's ability to adjust to the new environment. If the nurse is able to positively work through the rejection phase, he or she grows more fully as a person and a professional nurse during the resolution phase. Work expectations are more easily met, and the nurse will have developed the ability to elicit change.

Most novice nurses experience each phase of reality shock (honeymoon, shock or rejection, recovery, and resolution); however, the degree of shock is individualized. For example, the new graduates who complete their clinical rotation during school in the same institution as they choose to begin their career may suffer reality shock to a much lesser degree because they already may be familiar with the environment, staff, and overall personality of the nursing unit. However, many students choose another institution for various reasons, such as

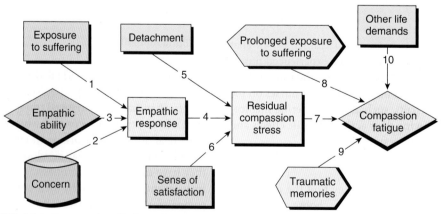

FIGURE 24-1 Compassion Fatigue Process. (From Figley CR (2001): *Compassion fatigue: an introduction* [website]. www.giftfromwithin.org/html/cmpfatig.html. Accessed December 2006.)

better hours, better pay, or less travel time to work. Nurses who choose to work in an institution different from the one in which they worked as student nurses may experience a higher degree of shock. This does not imply that all nurses should work in the institution where they received their clinical educational experience. The staff in the institution where novice nurses were educated may continue to see them as only "student nurses," which simply presents another barrier for novice nurses to overcome.

Zerwekh and Claborn (2013) suggest nurses complete a reality shock inventory to make them more aware of how they feel about themselves and the situation at present. The higher the score, the better the nurse's attitude. It might be helpful to take the test at different times throughout one's career or when trying to decide whether a career change would be advantageous (Box 24-1).

CAUSES OF REALITY SHOCK

Many nurses are familiar with the term *culture shock*. Culture shock occurs when people are immersed into a culture different from their own with norms that are unfamiliar and uncomfortable. This is exactly what happens in reality shock. Patient-centered nursing is prioritized in nursing school, whereas in the workforce it is the management of tasks and timelines. This disconnect may lead the novice nurse to feelings of failure because of the inability to provide holistic care. Furthermore, novice nurses who require additional time to complete skills/tasks are often ridiculed rather than supported (Norris, 2010). First, consider how students were taught to think in nursing school. When they prepared a care plan that took all night to complete, how were they to view the patient? Nursing schools teach holistic nursing, or rather "wholistic" nursing, in which students are

---

BOX 24-1 Reality Shock Inventory

Respond to the following statements with the appropriate number.

1—strongly agree
2—agree
3—slightly agree
4—slightly disagree
5—disagree
6—strongly disagree

1. _____ I think often about what I really want from life.
2. _____ Nursing school and/or my work has brought stresses for which I was unprepared.
3. _____ I would like the opportunity to start anew, knowing what I know now.
4. _____ I drink more than I should.
5. _____ I often feel that I still belong in the place where I grew up.
6. _____ Much of the time my mind is not as clear as it used to be.
7. _____ I am experiencing what would be called a crisis in my personal or work setting.
8. _____ I cannot see myself as a nurse.
9. _____ I must remain loyal to commitments, even if they have not proven as rewarding as I had expected.
10. _____ I wish I were different in many ways.
11. _____ The way I present myself to the world is not the way I really am.
12. _____ I often feel agitated or restless.
13. _____ I have become more aware of my inadequacies and faults.
14. _____ I often think about students or friends who have dropped out of school or work.
15. _____ I am still finding new challenges and interest in my work.
16. _____ My own personal future seems promising.
17. _____ There is no sense of regret concerning my major life decision of becoming a nurse.
18. _____ My views on nursing are as positive as they ever were.
19. _____ I have a strong sense of my own worth.
20. _____ My sex life is as satisfactory as it has ever been.

Scoring

To compute your score, reverse the number you assigned to statements 1, 3, 9, 10, 11, and 19. For example, if you responded to a statement with a 1, your score for that statement would be a 6. Likewise, 2 would become a 5; 3 would become a 4; 4 would become a 3; 5 would become a 2; and 6 would become a 1. Total the numbers. The higher your score, the better your attitude. The range is 20 to 120.

From Zerwekh J, Claborn JC: *Nursing today: transition and trends,* ed 5, Philadelphia, 2006, Saunders.

taught to look at the patient as a whole and even incorporate the family and significant other into the care plan. However, in the workforce, nurses may function with a partial-person approach (Kramer et al, 2013): different members of the health care team divide the patient care into parts.

Partial-Task Versus Whole-Task System

This type of health care, in which different members of the health care team divide the patient care into parts, is termed the *partial-task system* and only requires partial knowledge (Kramer, 1974). For instance, one nurse may be assigned to administer all medications, whereas another may be assigned to dressing changes. The nursing assistant aids with personal hygiene and grooming; the physical therapist provides range-of-motion exercises, and the respiratory therapist teaches pulmonary hygiene techniques. There are many other nursing care delivery models in which the role of the RN varies considerably. The partial-task system just described is also congruent with the model known as "functional nursing," which places a high emphasis on completion of tasks. It is an efficient method when working with large numbers of patients, but the nurse cannot provide holistic care within such a system (Huber, 2013). With functional nursing and the partial-task system, the nurse is seen as only part of the care picture, but the RN is the central organizer and responsible for follow-through on all care given by other members. This type of system is popular because fewer professional staff members are required, and it is frequently used on the

evening and night shifts when staffing is considerably less. This type of partial-task system encourages loyalty to the organization because it forces the nurse to focus on task completion and productivity. The nurse ensures that all tasks are carried out, but is not the sole provider of care. A simple checkmark often assesses quality, with initials being placed by completed tasks (Box 24-2).

Most novice nurses are more comfortable with the whole-task system because it is more consistent with what they were taught in school. The whole-task system requires complete knowledge and encourages loyalty to the profession. The nurse provides total patient care, which incorporates physical, emotional, spiritual, and cultural components. The model of nursing care consistent with the whole-task system is primary nursing, in which the nurse is responsible for all the needs of the patient (Huber, 2013). This model provides increased satisfaction for the patient and the nurse. However, because of the need to use an increasing number of lower-salaried employees and the shortage of RNs, few institutions continue to use this model.

Evaluation Methods

Another inconsistency between the school and work environment is the means of evaluation (Kramer, 1974). The school environment evaluates care from the "correct step" aspect, whereas the evaluation phase in the work environment is based on whether components of care were completed according to established policies and procedures. Were all the steps carried out in a logical, correct, and efficient way? This is exemplified in Case Study 24-2.

BOX 24-2 **Whole-Task and Partial-Task Checklists**			
Whole-Task Checklist		**Partial-Task Checklist**	
(Completed By Same Nurse)		(Completed by Different Members of the Health Care Team)	
Initials	*Task*	*Initials*	*Task*
TN	✓ Nursing history	SJ	✓ Nursing history
TN	✓ Nursing assessment	TN	✓ Nursing assessment
TN	✓ Patient education	BC	✓ Patient education
TN	✓ Medication teaching	CS	✓ Medication teaching
TN	✓ Bed made	CS	✓ Bed made
TN	✓ Intake and output recorded	SJ	✓ Intake and output recorded
TN	✓ Dressing changed	SJ	✓ Dressing changed
TN	✓ IV fluids hung	CS	✓ IV fluids hung
TN	✓ Patient turned	BC	✓ Patient turned

Think back to your first days in the nursing skills course. Can you remember the hours of practice you spent in learning the six "rights" of medication administration and technique of parenteral medication administration? Remember the stress you felt when the instructor observed you drawing up and administering your first intravenous (IV) push medication? How much error did the instructor allow? Probably not much. This is not to say that you should become lax in your tolerance for error. For example, it is never acceptable to have errors in the six "rights" of medication administration. You must and will develop your own system and quality check for performing nursing care. Nursing texts often list supplies followed by a flow diagram for procedures in which each step is listed. Let us go back to the resuscitation scenario: even basic and advanced life support courses focus on algorithms that direct the care of the patient step by step. Always remember that patient safety comes first.

The transition from student to professional nurse is difficult, and changes in the health care environment have only added to the strain. Socialization and caring relationship with colleagues are key to a nurse's ability to transition or to just "survive" at the clinical level (Martin and Wilson, 2011). Often new nurses are greeted with open hostility rather than being welcomed (Anno et al, 2013; Iheduru-Anderson, 2014). Nursing administrators may not support the novices' need to learn and may expect them to perform at the same level as experienced nurses. Unfortunately, the novice nurse may become bewildered and discouraged.

FROM NOVICE TO EXPERT

Benner (1984) described the following five stages through which novice nurses proceed to become clinically competent:

- **Stage 1:** The nurse has few experiences with clinical expectations, and skills are learned by rote; this stage usually occurs while completing the nursing educational requirements.
- **Stage 2:** Exemplifies advanced beginners who are able to perform adequately and make some judgment calls based on experience; most novice nurses enter the workforce during this stage.
- **Stage 3:** Includes competent nurses who are able to foresee long-range goals and are mastering skills.
- **Stage 4:** Includes proficient nurses who view whole situations rather than parts and are able to develop a solution.
- **Stage 5:** Includes expert nurses for whom intuition and decision-making are instantaneous.

During these five stages of transition from novice to expert, nurses are most likely to experience stress. Stressors common to novice nurses include the following:

- Unrealistic expectations: Novice nurses are expected to care for a standard patient workload as soon as orientation is completed (Martin and Wilson, 2011) or placed in specialized units (Caliskan and Ergun, 2012)
- Stressful work environments: Patient ratios are unrealistic (Feng and Tsai, 2012; Perkins, 2010).
- Powerlessness: Novice nurses are not heard when suggesting changes to improve workflow, but often are blamed when things go wrong (Perkins, 2010).

SPECIAL NEEDS OF NOVICE NURSES

The following skills have been identified as needing further refinement in novice nurses. However, it is important to remember that a novice nurse's "need for support does not end with orientation (Smith, 2007). Discussion about each of these areas follows.

- Interpersonal skills and communication skills (University Alliance, 2014) (Clinical skills/judgment (Maguire (2013)
- Organizational skills (Smith, 2007)
- Delegation skills (Huber, 2013)
- Priority-setting skills (Huber, 2013; Nelson, 2010)
- Assertiveness skills
- Dealing with horizontal violence (Khadjehturian, 2012)
- Intuition

Interpersonal Skills

Most physicians, administrators, and nurse managers expect the novice nurse to immediately develop interpersonal skills that they take for granted. These feelings probably are rooted in the past when nurses in training spent most of their time on units caring for patients and received little theoretic information or content in the classroom setting. They had time to get to know the members of the health care team and felt comfortable interacting with them. It is difficult for many people, including novice nurses, to be comfortable with interpersonal skills at work when they feel incompetent and inadequate as a member of the interprofessional health care team. They are often uncomfortable making rounds, clarifying orders, and participating in interprofessional team conferences. However, effective communication is critical. For nurses, it is especially important so they can communicate with other members of the health care team, patients, and coworkers in a fast-paced environment (University Alliance, 2014). For example, consider the novice nurse who receives the following order from the patient's physician: "Give Tylenol as needed for pain." The unit secretary transcribes the order and hands the chart to the new nurse, stating, "You will need to clarify this order: I can't take the new order." Feelings of fear and uncertainty invade the novice nurse as he or she practices what to say to the physician. This fear and sense of insecurity can lead to the novice nurse avoiding future contact with the physician, thus compromising patient safety.

"Can you clarify the Tylenol order on your patient?" Or possibly, "How much Tylenol did you want your patient to have?" or maybe "Hey stupid, can't you write your orders using the six 'rights'?"

Well, perhaps the conversation would go as follows:

"Dr. Jones, this is the student nurse. I mean the nurse taking care of your patient. I don't understand your order. I mean can you clarify how much Tylenol you want me to take? I mean how much Tylenol do you want the patient to have?"

The inexperienced nurse hangs up, feeling ineffective, and the physician questions the nursing care the patient is being given.

Before asking the physician to clarify the order, it is a good idea to practice what will be said and even write it down so as not to forget. Then, when face to face with the person, state the facts simply and allow time to consider the correct answer. A smile during the exchange in conversation might provide the receiver with a little more patience. Gaps in communication may also occur between the experienced staff and the novice nurse because staff are so familiar with the routines that they may leave out information, making the novice unable to complete the task. Novice nurses need to develop interpersonal communication skills by building self-confidence (Pfaff et al, 2014).

Clinical Skills

Novice nurses Novice nurses often feel unprepared to perform clinical skills in the "real world" (Kramer et al, 2013). Practice increases the effectiveness, efficiency, and correctness of performing skills. However, until the nurse has experience, there are actions the novice nurse can take. For example, it is wise to be familiar with the procedure manual on the unit. Also, during the orientation phase the novice nurse should ask for a mentor to observe or assist with procedures for which there is a lower comfort level or a lesser degree of experience, to role-model excellent communication skills, and to answer the mentee's questions. It is important to remember that practice does make "perfect" or at least competent. Every new nurse needs a confidant— someone to share ideas and validate assumptions (Smith-Trudeau, 2014). Remember, no one was born with a Foley catheter in one hand and the set of directions engraved in memory.

Organizational Skills

The novice nurse may lack organizational skills. This lack of proficiency may be exaggerated by feelings of being "overwhelmed" by the new environment. Typically, student nurses are responsible for a limited number of patients, and although they must answer for their care, they typically are not responsible for as many patients as they will be assigned as new nurses. Someone is usually with students to offer suggestions on how to organize their time. The instructor might question: "Now what do you plan to do, and what supplies will you need to accomplish the task?" New nurses might consider asking these same questions. If unsure, the procedure book lists not only the steps to follow but also the supplies that will be needed. List specific time-limited tasks. Avoid scheduling time so tightly that a slight delay causes chaos. Planning and prioritization skills were seen as areas of concern of newly graduated nurses (Huber, 2013). Chapter 25 offers valuable tips on getting organized, setting priorities, and managing time.

Delegation Skills

Most students have limited exposure to delegation. Uncertainty or feeling uncomfortable with delegation may be a result of the characteristics of the personnel to whom one is delegating. Consider the licensed practical nurse, the nursing assistant, or other non-licensed staff. Often these personnel are older and more experienced; therefore, the new nurse might feel intimidated when delegating to these individuals. Novice nurses should familiarize themselves with policies concerning which tasks can be performed by which category or level of health care provider. The question "Who can perform this task other than myself?" should be considered. Because of the broad span of responsibility for most nursing jobs, it is impossible for one person to complete all the work alone (Huber, 2013). Delegation relies on **trust** and leadership skills, both of which may be deficient in the novice nurse. Chapter 19 presents a comprehensive overview of delegation.

There are also times when the novice nurse should decline to accept a delegated responsibility because he or she may not be competent to perform the task even though it is within his or her scope of practice. Remember that patient safety is always the priority. Show your willingness to learn, and ask someone to demonstrate the task. By simply stating, "I would appreciate you demonstrating the procedure and allowing me to observe, and when the next opportunity arises I would like for you to observe me completing the procedure."

Priority-Setting Skills

Priority setting is a skill that all nursing students must demonstrate. The difference between nursing school and the workplace is that serious consequences occur if prioritizing is not done effectively in the workplace. Flanagan (1997) suggests asking the following questions when prioritizing:

- Will patients be jeopardized if this task is not done?
- Is this task a priority because of time deadlines?
- What other personnel can perform this task?
- Do safety concerns make this task a priority?
- What will be the consequences if this task is postponed?
- What are the legal issues related to the priority of the task?

Many novice nurses need help in organizational skills. Novice nurses may derive more satisfaction from performing technical skills, such as starting an intravenous (IV) drip, than from cognitive skills, such as developing a plan of care. Once they are comfortable with basic skills, they move on to critical thinking skills. Nelson (2010) describes novice nurses as feeling overwhelmed-they must plan for multiple patients and feel a sense of urgency and stress. She stresses that preceptors must have patience and understanding as they rely on experienced nurses for advice and support.

How many people make to-do lists? Many make grocery lists, lists of bills to be paid, or lists of important dates. The same should be done for work—tasks are crossed off as they are completed. At the end of the day, consider what time was spent in unproductive ways, what caused interruptions, and what could have been done to save time. The same list may cue the novice nurse of a "forgotten" task or intervention. Huber (2013) also suggests determining the urgency of the problem, which allows for prioritization.

Assertiveness Skills

Students are often naive when they are told by recruiters, "Come work for us; we offer a 6-month orientation, and you can ask for an extension if you feel uncomfortable. You will not be placed in charge, and only after a full year's experience will you be allowed to independently care for patients requiring advanced technology, such as ventricular assist devices." Students may be misled into feeling that they are "advanced" in their learning and moving ahead of all the others if they agree to shorten their orientation or if, after only 6 months, they take on the responsibility of caring for patients with special equipment.

However, after 6 months, even though novice nurses are becoming more competent and confident, they lack the experience to make instantaneous decisions based on intuition. Unfortunately, novice nurses are often employed on the night shift working with nurses with the same or less experience. As newer novice nurses (those who graduated the following semester) are hired, the more experienced novice nurses may even be expected to serve as a preceptor. Faculty should invite recent graduates to speak to classes concerning expectations after employment. Faculty should also inform students that they will move through many stages during the next year, and that they should take full advantage of this learning opportunity.

VIOLENCE AT WORK

When you think of dangerous occupations, law enforcement and military careers may come to mind. However, nursing is one of the most dangerous professions in America (Fink, 2013). Nursing is a "high stress job" that provokes acts of workplace violence among coworkers (Dahlby and Herrick, 2014). Half of all emergency room nurses report being a victim of violence (Fink, 2013). Student nurses are also leading recipients of vertical or nurse-to-student violence, which perpetuates the cycle of lateral violence continuing in nursing. According to Longo (2011), the American Nurses Association (ANA) (2001) reported that the majority (56.9%) of student nurses have been threatened or experienced verbal violence while in the clinical setting. The ANA's continuing education module *Navigating the Work Environment: Embracing a Zero Tolerance for Bullying* is a resource for any nurse who has experienced or wants to be prepared for horizontal violence. Box 24-3 shows four types of workplace violence identified by Wild Iris Medical Education (2014).

The Florida Nurses Association (2014) describes horizontal violence and bullying as being prevalent in the nursing profession. Horizontal violence includes such acts as withholding patient information, exclusion, belittling, refusing to assist, badgering, displaying errors for others to observe, eye-rolling, and criticizing colleagues for following rules. Hubbard (2014) suggests horizontal violence leads to increased stress and job dissatisfaction, which can lead to missed work days. He also suggests bullying can have a negative influence on retention and recruitment of nurses. New graduates are at risk, and it is estimated that 60% of new graduates will leave their first position due to horizontal violence, and 50% will actually leave the professional altogether. Horizontal violence can also increase the likelihood of nursing care error.

The Joint Commission issued a sentinel event alert in response to a growing number of crimes in health care settings. The Sentinel Event Database contains reports of assault, rape, and homicide (which are suspected to be much higher due to under-reporting). Health care facilities must now maintain a written plan describing security measures along with conducting risk assessment to evaluate potential for violence (OSHA, 2015). Failure to have a formal system to address the behavior is indirectly promoting such occurrences.

The Center for American Nurses (2008 states that there is no place for bullying among nurses or health care providers and issued a "Zero Tolerance for Abuse." Sherman (2014) stated "learning to work with difficult people is both an art and a science" and identifies four types of difficult personalities: the volcano who makes personal attacks and has temper tantrums; the sniper who demonstrates passive-aggressive behavior and is prone to sabotage; the chronic complainer who blames others but does not offer solutions; and, the clam who simply shuts down and refuses to be a team member. She suggests focusing on the behavior and urges individuals to remember that the only behavior you can control is your own.

BOX 24-3	**Types of Workplace Violence**
Type 1. Violence by a stranger with criminal intent	These violent acts are not committed by employees; rather criminals are strangers without relationship to organization or employees. Robbery most common motive.
Type 2. Violence by customer or client	Patients or customers become perpetrators of violent acts.
Type 3. Coworker (worker to worker)	Employee or prior or disgruntled employees threaten or commit violence against current employees and/or management. This is referred to as vertical or horizontal violence.
Type 4. Violence by someone in a personal relationship	Individuals who have a relationship with a current employee commit a violent act in the health care environment.

Wild Iris Medical Education (2014). *Workplace violence.* http://www.nursingceu.com/courses/455/index_nceu.html#top. Accessed August 15, 2014.

INTUITION

A nurse walks into a patient's room and senses something is wrong, and even though the data shows nothing has changed, the patient confirms feeling anxious. The nurse stops to use all her senses to observe and assess the situation. She is using intuition. McEwen and Willis (2011) define intuitive knowledge as feelings and hunches. Intuition is not guessing, but a nonconscious pattern of recognition and experience. Green (2012) states nursing intuition is a legitimate form of knowledge. Benner (1984) described intuition as the function of an expert nurse—or that intuition develops over time as nurses move from novice to expert.

STRATEGIES TO EASE TRANSITION

When interviewing for their first positions, novice nurses should determine philosophies of the agencies and how orientation programs assist new nurses to enter the profession. There are many opinions on the best way to accomplish a smooth transition, and each nurse should evaluate the orientation options available.

The National Council of State Boards of Nursing developed an evidenced-based model for transitioning novice nurses to practice. The care of patients with complex health needs and a gap in practice readiness was the stimulus for the Transition to Practice Model. This model prescribed that a graduate will have the same preceptor for 6 months. In some settings, a team of preceptors is used for ongoing support for an additional 6 months. The Quality and Safety Education for Nurses (QSEN) competencies comprise the five modules used in this model: patient-centered care, teamwork and collaboration, evidence-based practice, quality improvement, safety, and informatics. Feedback and reflection are elicited from the novice nurses throughout the 6-month period.

One nurse said of her transition from student to professional nurse, "Take in every experience that you can during orientation, take the sick patients while there is someone to hold your hand, ask many questions, and read everything that interests you" (Hilton, 2012).

Biculturalism

Biculturalism is the joining of two contradictory value systems; in this context, those of school values with those of the workplace. Biculturalism is designed to enhance a positive self-image and help novice nurses set realistic goals for practice. This strategy, if accepted in the workplace, allows the new nurse to introduce ideas or values brought from nursing school and integrate them into the work environment. Kramer (1974) suggests that the novice nurse apprise both sides of an issue, determine how his or her behavior will have an effect on other members of the interprofessional health care team, and single out accessible objectives.

Role Models and Mentors

Mentoring and role modeling are often considered to be the same, but in fact they are different. Mentoring is a personal relationship with a more experienced person willing to guide a novice or inexperienced person. It is a voluntary, ongoing two-way partnership of at least 2 years (Smith-Trudeau, 2014). She suggests that the entire nursing profession will benefit from mentoring by retaining nurses. Mentoring is an interactive, mutual, and personal experience (Sullivan and Decker, 2012), whereas role modeling is usually not an interactive process (Stone, 2000). Mentoring has been shown to be a key strategy for increasing the diversity of the nursing workforce when faculty are mentored by culturally competent faculty-thus retaining more diverse students. Sullivan and Decker (2012) suggest that choosing the correct mentor is one of the most important tasks for the novice nurse.

Mentors are experienced nurses who must be willing to commit to a relationship with novice nurses to help them recognize their weaknesses and strengths. Mentors help novice nurses set and reach realistic goals by reinforcing and recommending appropriate courses of action and providing emotional support. Mentors help novice nurses develop confidence and organizational skills, and to validate intuitive notions (Smith-Trudeu, 2014). The benefactor of mentoring is termed a *protégé*. Smith-Trudeau (2014) lists the characteristics of both the mentor and protégé in Box 24-4. Rose Sherman (2013), a contributor to the website www.nursetogether.com, describes five steps to find a nurse mentor who will guide and lead you to success. See characteristics of a mentor who will help grow a nursing career in Box 24-5.

Some mentoring programs are aimed specifically at pairing male students and male novice nurses with male mentors. One resource for this is www.minoritynurse.com. Just as women face special challenges when entering a predominantly male profession, so do men entering the predominantly female profession of nursing. Networking with other male nurses helps with the socialization and integration of men into the profession (Turner, 2014).

Preceptorships

Another popular orientation program is the use of preceptors during the final semester of nursing school and on entering the workforce. Preceptor programs have gained popularity as a means to socialize the novice

BOX 24-4 Characteristics of Mentor and Protégé

Mentor	Protégé
Empathy and nonjudgmental	Intelligence
Advanced personal, social, and professional skills	Self-starter
	Curious
Ethical and moral integrity	Hard worker
Welcomes change	Risk taker
Excellent communicator (both listener and feedback)	Sense of humor
	Open to new ideas
Commitment to excellent in nursing practice	Has a vision both personally and professionally
Sensitivity to others' needs	
Positive outlook	Embraces challenges
Uses situations to teach	Possesses interpersonal and communication skills
Living example of the values, ethics, and practices of the nursing profession	

From Smith-Trudeau (2014). Will you be my nurse mentor? *Vermont Nurse Connection*, April-June 2014, 3.

BOX 24-5 Guidelines for Identifying Mentors

About Careers (2013)	Nurse Together (Rose Sherman)
Experience in specialty in nurse's area of interest	Determine what you want from the mentor and the experience
Lives nearby (preferably in your own organization)	Identify your strengths and weaknesses
Balances out similarities and differences for your own strengths and weaknesses	Identify what qualities you want in a mentor—someone you admire and is an excellent role model
No formal arrangement needed	Consider geographic proximity
	Identify potential mentors based on criteria listed above

nurse into the profession and to ease the tension of transition from student to nurse. Preceptor programs often are incorporated during the senior nursing student's final practicum, but they also may be used as part of the orientation program in the first work experience. Preceptors orient the novice nurse to the specific nursing area, aid in socialization, and teach skills that are deemed necessary. Recently, it has been shown that preceptors can help new graduates develop critical thinking skills, bridging the gap between theory and knowledge (Kaddoura, 2013). Preceptor programs reduce economic cost by reducing turnover of new graduates and assisting novice nurses in meeting the expectations of their employers and peers.

Self-Mentoring

Ultimately no one is as responsible for the transition into the nursing profession as the novice nurses themselves. Mentors and preceptors can ease the transition, but novice nurses can also help by using self-mentoring when preceptors or mentors are not available. Novice nurses must be willing to learn appropriate resources, develop problem-solving skills, and ask questions. Novices should reflect back over times when they were self-reliant and believed in themselves.

Residency Programs

Residency programs are one innovative way to ease the transition from academia to practice and also may be an incentive for graduates when selecting that first job. Residency programs often provide didactic or program activities as well as one-to-one preceptor experiences for an extended time, with 12 months being typical. Although residency programs differ, they all focus on retention and increased satisfaction of the new nurse with the added bonus of improved patient outcomes and safety. The University HealthSystem Consortium (UHC) and the American Association of Colleges of Nursing (AACN) established criteria for a 1-year nurse residency program to expand the capacity of baccalaureate nursing programs. These residency programs have increased retention rates of new graduates to 95.6% compared to turnover rates of 30% (AACN, 2015).

Preprofessional and Professional Organizations

Students who join preprofessional organizations, such as the National Student Nurses Association (NSNA), gain leadership opportunities and meet not only other students from across the nation and internationally but also leaders in nursing, whom they thought they would only read about. Students participating in the NSNA leadership university network learn how to "work in cooperative relationships with peers, faculty, students in other disciplines, community service organizations, and the public in a service learning environment" (NSNA, 2014). The NSNA Foundation provides scholarships and mentors future registered nurses into the profession. The NSNA publishes a magazine with information on job opportunities and legislative issues that affect nursing practice. Participation in preprofessional organizations develops leadership skills that are useful in professional organizations and for potential employers after graduation. The American Nurses Association (ANA) and some state specialty organizations offer reduced rates for new graduates and student nurses and continue with the above-mentioned benefits after graduation. In addition to lobbying efforts, access to current information on standards of practice, certification, and networking opportunities are also benefits of involvement in the ANA.

Self-Confidence and Self-Esteem

"Do you ever feel like an imposter, masquerading as a confident oncology nurse?"

Deborah Christensen

The Clance Imposter Phenomenon Scale can be used to identify the presence of this phenomenon in new graduates. Take a moment and rate yourself to determine if you are an imposter: http://paulineroseclance.com/pdf/IPTestandscoring.pdf. A relationship woven with encouragement can inspire self-esteem and self-confidence. It is easy to become discouraged and disillusioned when reality does not quite match our dreams and fantasies. Self-esteem, or belief in oneself, comes as the novice nurse passes through the stages of reality shock and into a career in nursing.

Self-esteem = Self-confidence + Self-respect

Individuals with high self-esteem can critically problem solve, tackle obstacles, take sensible risks, believe in themselves, and take care of themselves (Positive Way, 2012). Nurses with good self-esteem are effective and respond to themselves and others in healthy ways (Figure 24-2). They can accomplish more because they feel comfortable with themselves. Take the self-esteem questionnaire in Box 24-6; then visit the Create Positive Relationships website. If your score is low, visit the Positive Way website to learn how to stop your inner critic (http://positive-way.com/stopping%20your%20inner%20critic.htm).

So far, we have discussed ways that the employer and novice nurse can use to ease the transition period—implementing biculturalism, preceptorships, mentoring, and self-mentoring. However, each new nurse must begin by evaluating his or her own self-esteem. In addition, the novice nurse must realize his or her uniqueness and rely on instinct and past experiences when maturing and moving to a higher level of responsibility. The new nurse should remember to seek a role model or mentor for guidance through the transition. It is important to remember that it is difficult to be successful if one's personal and social lives are not kept in balance (e.g., in high school it was great to solve all the chemistry equations on an examination, but if "personal chemistry" was neglected, a void was felt that could plague future attempts at maturing).

Violence Prevention

Because new graduates are frequently victims of horizontal violence in their first year of practice, preceptors with zero tolerance for such activities are invaluable. It is also suggested that having nurses remember when they were a new nurse. Carlson (2012) suggests having nurses remember their first job: did they feel prepared

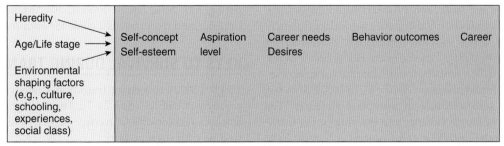

FIGURE 24-2 Behavior Model. (From Schutz C, Decker PJ, Sullivan EJ: *Effective management in nursing: an-experiential/skill building workbook,* Menlo Park, CA, 1992, Addison-Wesley.)

BOX 24-6 Self-Esteem Questionnaire

Answer yes or no to the following questions:

_____ Do you have a hard time nurturing yourself?

_____ Have you ever turned down an invitation to a party or function because of the way you felt about yourself?

_____ Do you get your sense of self-worth from the approval of others?

_____ Are you supportive of others who berate you?

_____ When things go wrong in life, do you blame yourself?

_____ Do you react to disappointment by blaming others?

_____ Do you begin each day with a negative attitude?

_____ Do you feel undeserving?

_____ Do you ever feel like an impostor and that soon your deficiencies will be exposed?

_____ Do you have an inner critic who is disparaging or demeaning?

_____ Do you believe that being hard on yourself is the best motivation for change?

_____ Do your good points seem ordinary and your failings all important?

_____ Do you feel unattractive?

_____ Have you ever felt that your accomplishments are due to luck but that your failures are due to incompetence or inadequacy?

_____ Have you ever felt that, if you are not a total success, then you are a failure and that there is no middle ground and no points for effort?

_____ Do you feel unappreciated?

_____ Do you feel lonely?

_____ Do you struggle with feelings of inferiority?

_____ Do other people's opinions count more to you than your own?

_____ Do you criticize yourself often?

_____ Do others criticize you often?

_____ Do you hesitate to do things because of what others might think?

The more yes answers you have, the greater the opportunity exists for improving your self-esteem.

From The Positive Way. (1996-2014). *Self-Esteem Questionnaire*. http://www.positive-way.com/self-est1.htm. Accessed June 10, 2015.

or did they feel like they had ten thumbs? Novices who practiced "cognitive rehearsal" (Griffin, 2004) responses to horizontal violence were better equipped to successfully defend against horizontal violence (Embree et al, 2013). Lorenz (2014) suggests that advancing collegiality is key to avoiding incivility: listen to understand and offer a solution rather than telling a novice nurse what to do. If incompetence of the novice is apparent, leave this issue to management to resolve. Perhaps most important is making horizontal violence transparent. Novice nurses entering the workforce will find the Occupational Safety and Health Administration (OSHA) book *Guidelines for Preventing Workplace Violence for Health Care and Social Service Workers* helpful (www.osha.gov/SLTC/etools/hospital/hazards/workplaceviolence/viol.html) along with the *Framework Guidelines for Addressing Workplace Violence in the Health Sector* (www.osha.gov/SLTC/etools/hospital/hazards/workplaceviolence/viol.html#violenceprevention). In fact, OSHA has called for zero tolerance of workplace violence. "The incidence of lateral violence and bullying in the workplace is on the rise" (Center for American Nurses, 2008; Center for American Nurses and AzNA, 2009). Due to this increase in workplace violence and conflict, The

Joint Commission (2008) introduced standards requiring health care organizations to construct a code of conduct that clearly defines "acceptable, disruptive, and inappropriate behavior" (TJC). Novice nurses can also access the ANA website for continuing education resources regarding conflict competence for help with conflict management and should review the ANA position statement for recommended strategies to help eliminate lateral violence (www.centerforamericannurses.org/positions/lateral_violence.pdf). Chapman and colleagues (2010) suggest that nurses can predict the risk of workplace violence instigated by patients by using the acronym STAMPEDAR (staring, tone of voice, anxiety, mumbling, pacing, emotions, disease process, assertive/nonassertive behavior, and resources) as a guide for assessment.

KEYS TO SURVIVAL DURING TRANSITION

Tingle (2000) suggests a transition strategy using the acronym NURSES (Box 24-7). The College of Health Sciences Jacksonville University suggests the following to cope with stress at work:

1. Breathe slowly, deeply, and easily to release endorphins
2. Be organized—awake earlier and leave for work earlier

Never fail to ask for help.
  If you do not ask, you may never receive help. The
  best way to get help is to ask.
Use available facility resources.
  Use other experienced staff, policy, and procedure
  manuals and staff development personnel.
Reenergize with professional associations.
  This helps to keep the novice nurse from losing
  sight of the profession in favor of the job.
Stay in contact with friends.
  Join the alumni association at your nursing school,
  and find out what your peers are doing.
Evaluate your growth realistically.
  Develop short-term goals (e.g., open all charts by
  9 AM), and then long-term goals (e.g., gain certifi-
  cation in your field).
Stay focused on your goals.
  Remember: Climbing the hill of professionalism is
  hard, but the pure "pride" becomes your armor.

3. Stay hydrated and eat regularly
4. Exercise to stay in good physical shape
5. Develop a sleep schedule that allows uninterrupted sleep
6. Use humor and laughter to reduce tension
7. Avoid negative people and think positive
8. Engage positive thinking friends, family, and coworkers
9. Take a break

Hilton (2014) suggests taking time to consider these important issues before accepting your first nursing job: ask about first-year turnover rates (if greater than 20%, this is a concern); ask about clinical, social, and emotional support for new nurses; don't just tour the unit, stay for a few hours and start on a specialty unit because it is more homogeneous; and consider accepting a "non-nursing" position prior to graduation to become familiar with the culture.

MEETING SPECIAL NEEDS OF THE NOVICE NURSE

It is important to review some common problems perceived by novice nurses and to offer suggestions to ease the transition period.

Organizational Skills

Lack of organization is common when the novice nurse's assignment becomes much heavier than that of a student nurse. The use of a report sheet can enable the novice nurse to note important information received during the shift report and from other members of the interprofessional health care team as the day progresses. The report sheet can also be used to document occurrences during the shift. Another suggestion for the novice nurse is to contact a former nursing instructor. Most students have developed a special rapport with one or two instructors. Novice nurses might telephone one of their former instructors to discuss the challenges they face during transition so that the instructor can help with problem solving.

The basic report sheet (Box 24-8) also can be transformed into a unit-specific sheet. For instance, if the novice nurse is on a telemetry floor, there might be a section for "rhythms." The orthopedic nurse could include "traction." This form also can be used to establish and set priorities. Once the care has been prioritized, the nurse can begin these critical interventions. However, it also may be possible to delegate tasks to ancillary staff if the tasks are within their scope of practice. This requires the novice nurse to become familiar with the job descriptions of other nursing personnel, such as licensed professional nurses, nursing assistants, or unlicensed personnel, so delegation will be within their defined roles. Remember that the RN cannot do everything.

Clinical Skills

According to Benner's model (1984), the graduate nurse must be allowed to develop clinical skills based on experiences. The novice nurse can develop competence with clinical skills during the orientation phase by asking to observe an experienced nurse perform those skills with which the novice nurse is less familiar. The novice nurse also can provide the nurse manager and mentor with a list of skills that need further practice. The unit's policy and procedure book is a valuable asset. It should describe in detail the steps to follow when performing a procedure. Spend time reviewing the manual before observing the procedure being performed, and then ask questions. Take into consideration that there is more than one correct way to perform a skill; remember though, it is not acceptable to take shortcuts that jeopardize the safety of the patient.

Interpersonal Skills

Developing interpersonal skills may be achieved by attending unit meetings, volunteering to serve on

---

BOX 24-8 Worksheet

Patient's Name _____	**Patient's Name** _____
Room # _____	Room # _____
Diagnosis _____	Diagnosis _____
Diet _____	Diet _____
Activity status _____	Activity status _____
Lab ordered/time _____	Lab ordered/time _____
IV fluids _____	IV fluids _____
INTAKE/OUTPUT	**INTAKE/OUTPUT**
Urine _____ Stools _____	Urine _____ Stools _____
Other _____	Other _____
IV primary _____	IV primary _____
IV secondary _____	IV secondary _____
Other _____	Other _____
Patient's Name _____	**Patient's Name** _____
Room # _____	Room # _____
Diagnosis _____	Diagnosis _____
Diet _____	Diet _____
Activity status _____	Activity status _____
Lab ordered/time _____	Lab ordered/time _____
IV fluids _____	IV fluids _____
INTAKE/OUTPUT	**INTAKE/OUTPUT**
Urine _____ Stools _____	Urine _____ Stools _____
Other _____	Other _____
IV primary _____	IV primary _____
IV secondary _____	IV secondary _____
Other _____	Other _____

committees on the unit or within the agency, and taking an active interest in the nursing unit. These activities aid in socialization into the unit and profession. It is important for all nurses, regardless of their experience, to take part in professional organizations at the local, regional, state, or national level. Specialty organizations often provide valuable information and continuing education pertinent to the nurse's area of practice.

As the nurse becomes more confident in his or her nursing abilities and is less stressed by performing tasks, he or she can develop positive relationships with physicians and other members of the interprofessional team. Various methods that may be used to develop professional relationships should be emphasized during the orientation period. Nurses in staff development positions can be key players in assisting the novice nurse in developing professional communication skills. Making rounds with physicians and assisting them with procedures opens the door for communication. Asking pertinent and relevant questions ensures that the door remains open.

Delegation Skills

Another important skill that novice nurses need to learn is delegating. First, nurses should consider how others have delegated to them. Body language is important when delegating. Look at the person, be pleasant, and leave room for suggestions from the delegatee; however, do not allow the delegatee to resist or intimidate you so that you end up completing the task yourself. After communicating face to face, give a list of tasks in writing, or post it at the nurses' station. This leaves little room for misunderstanding. Be willing to change the assignment if there are changes in a patient's condition, new patients are admitted, or you realize that the time needed to perform a task was underestimated. If time allows, it is always good to help those to whom you have delegated tasks. For example, if a nurse passes by a door and the attendant is trying to turn a very large patient, she should enter the room and ask, "How can I best help you turn the patient?" Always take time to give sincere positive reinforcement and say thank you.

Priority-Setting Skills

Now consider the best way to prioritize. How did you prioritize in nursing school? What worked then will probably work now with a few modifications. Remember: If it is not written down, it probably will be forgotten. Keep a notepad and pen in your pocket. Jot down reminders of things to be done, and place a number next to each indicating its importance. For example, assume that you have already written the following list:

＿＿＿ Start the IV for Mr. B. in room 211
＿＿＿ Check the IV site for Mrs. C. in room 300
＿＿＿ Call the laboratory and check on blood sugar for Mrs. M. in room 215

Now a call is received from the LPN that Mr. T.'s IV line is not dripping in room 212. Next the dietary worker calls to say that when she took the food tray to the patient in room 217, the patient vomited. Then the emergency light goes off in the bathroom of an older, confused patient. Now prioritize. What needs to be done first? First, answer the emergency light; do not even take time to write down this one. Now it is time to reprioritize. The new tasks have been added to the bottom of your previous list. Look over your list below. How would you prioritize these tasks?

＿＿＿ Start the IV for Mr. B. in room 211
＿＿＿ Check the IV site for Mrs. C. in room 300
＿＿＿ Call the laboratory and check the blood sugar for Mrs. M. in room 215
＿＿＿ Check Mr. T.'s IV line that is not dripping
＿＿＿ Assist the patient in room 217 who is vomiting

Now try out your delegating skills. Place a *D* next to any tasks that can be delegated in the list below.

＿＿＿ Start the IV for Mr. B. in room 211
＿＿＿ Check the IV site for Mrs. C. in room 300
＿＿＿ Call the laboratory and check on blood sugar for Mrs. M. in room 215

＿＿＿ Check Mr. T.'s IV in room 212 that is not dripping
＿＿＿ Assist the patient in room 217 who is vomiting

What had to be considered when you prioritized the tasks? First you needed to consider how much time was required for each task. It usually takes longer to start a new IV line than to check an existing IV site. It also requires less time to determine why an IV is not dripping. However, this is insignificant if the patient needing the IV line started is critical and needs the medication to reduce his or her blood pressure. Delegation may be needed. What tasks can other members perform? The unit secretary can call the laboratory to check on lab results, and a licensed practical nurse or nursing assistant can assist the patient who is vomiting, provided that you follow up very soon to assess the patient's condition. A nurse must know how to prioritize. Think through each situation. Change the priority as needed or as situations change throughout the shift.

Now that you know ways to develop organizational skills, refine clinical and interpersonal skills, delegate tasks, and set priorities, take time to remember other important areas of your life. Remember the people you may have neglected during school, and make it a priority to reestablish special relationships with friends, family, and loved ones.

Experienced RNs should consider the following to help ease the transition of the novice nurse to the profession of nursing: The novice nurse should not be expected to enter the work environment and be as productive as experienced staff members. It is important for experienced nurses serving on agency committees to serve as advocates for novice nurses by reminding nurse managers and administrators that it is not possible for nursing students to learn everything necessary for professional practice during school. Also remind other members of the nursing unit about this fact. If a novice nurse develops initiative, autonomy, and a desire to become a team member, he or she will succeed.

■ SUMMARY

The period of transition from novice to competent practitioner is critical. New skills must be learned and refined, professional relationships established, and autonomy gained in nursing practice. Knowledge and skills must be refined over time. The transition from student to RN can be compared with that of butterflies as they emerge from the cocoon. It is unfair to judge them while still nymphs; therefore, the nursing profession must withhold scrutiny until novice nurses fly with their beautiful wings spread.

REFERENCES

AACN: *Nurse residency program*, 2015. (website). http://www.aacn.nche.edu/education-resources/nurse-residency-program. Accessed June 10, 2015.

ANA: *ANA Nurse CE: Conflict competence*, 2011. (website). https://ananursece.healthstream.com/Pages/Category.aspx?category=SubjectConflictCompetence&cat=ANA&orderby=DisplayName&dir=ASC. Accessed June 10, 2015.

Anno L, Nuechterlein A, Dyette A, Bonie J: Eating their young: Prevention of horizontal violence in acute care nursing, *Nevada RNformation* 16:19, 2013.

Babble S: *Compassion fatigue*, 2013. (website). http://www.psychologytoday.com/blog/somatic-psychology/201207/compassion-fatigue. Accessed August 30, 2014.

Benner P: *From novice to expert*, Menlo Park, CA, 1984, Addison-Wesley.

Caliskan A, Ergun YA: Examining job satisfaction burnout and reality shock amongst newly graduated nurses, *Procedia-Social and Behavioral Sciences* 47:1392–1397, 2012.

Carlson K: *A soft landing for new nurses*, 2012. (website). http://digitaldoorway.blogspot.com/2012/08/a-soft-landing-for-new-nurses.html. Accessed September 15, 2014.

Center for American Nurses: *Lateral violence and bullying in the workplace*, 2008. (website). http://centerforamericannurses.org/associations/9102/files/Position%20StatementLateral%20Violence%20and%20Bullying.pdf. Accessed September 30, 2014.

Center for American Nurses and AzNA: *A collaborative approach, Arizona Nurse*, 2009. (website). http://www.aznurse.com. Accessed June 10, 2015.

Chapman R, Styles I, Perry L, Combs S: Examining the characteristics of workplace violence in one non-tertiary hospital, *Journal of Clinical Nursing* 19(3-4):479–488, 2010.

Christensen D: Are you masquerading as a confident oncology nurse? *ONC Connect Blog*, 2014. http://connect.ons.org/ons-connect-blog/are-you-masquerading-as-a-confident-oncology-nurse. Accessed September 15, 2014.

Compassion Fatigue Awareness Project: 2013. http://www.compassionfatigue.org. Accessed August 1, 2014.

Dahlby MA, Herrick LM: Evaluating an Educational Intervention on Lateral Violence, *The Journal of Continuing Education in Nursing* 45(8):344–350, 2014.

Duchscher JE: Transition shock: the initial stage of role adaptation for newly registered nurses, *Journal of Advanced Nursing* 65(5):1103–1113, 2009.

Embree JL, Bruner DA, White A: Raising the level of awareness of nurse-to-nurse lateral violence in a critical access hospital, *Nursing Research and Practice* 2013(207306): pp. 1–6, 2013. doi:10.1155/2013/207306.

Fearon C, Nicol M: Strategies to assist prevention of burnout in nursing staff, *Nurs Stand* 26(14):35–39, 2011.

Feng R, Tsai Y: Socialization of new graduate nurses to practicing nurses, *Journal of Clinical Nursing* 21:2064–2071, 2012.

Figley CR: *Compassion fatigue: an introduction*, 2001. (website). http://www.giftfromwithin.org/html/cmpfatig.html. Accessed December 2006.

Fink JL: Keeping nurses safe: Nursing is one of the most dangerous professions, 2013. (website). Healthcare Traveler. http://healthcaretraveler.modernmedicine.com/healthcare-traveler/news/keeping-nurses-safe-0?page=full. Accessed September 30, 2014.

Flanagan L, editor: *What you need to know about today's workplace: a survival guide for nurses*, Washington, DC, 1997, American Nurses Publishing.

Florida Nurses Association: Horizontal violence and bullying creating an equal and opposite reaction, *Florida Nurse* 62(2):18, 2014.

Green C: Nursing intuition: A valid form of knowledge, *Nursing Philosophy* 13:98–111, 2012.

Griffin M: Teaching cognitive rehearsal as a shield for lateral violence: an intervention for newly licensed nurses, *J Contin Educ Nurs* 35(6):257–263, 2004.

Hilton L: *Six tips to survive your first year as a hospital RN*, 2014. (website). http://career-advice.monster.com/in-the-office/workplace-issues/six-tips-to-survive-your-first-year-rn/article.aspx. Accessed September 15, 2014.

Hilton S: *How to Become a Nurse ©2006-2015:* 1-6. (website). http://www.hackcollege.com/guides/how-to-become-a-nurse. Accessed October 10, 2014.

Horsburgh D, Ross J: Care and compassion: The experience of newly qualified staff nurses, *Journal of Clinical Nursing* 22:1124–1132, 2013.

Hubbard P: What can be done about horizontal violence? *Alberta RN* 69(4):16–18, 2014.

Huber D: *Leadership and nursing care management*, ed 5, Philadelphia, 2013, Saunders.

Iheduru-Anderson K: Educating senior nursing students to stop lateral violence in nursing, *Australian Nursing & Midwifery Journal* 22(1):15, 2014.

IOM (Institute of Medicine): *The Future of Nursing: Leading Change, Advancing Health*, Washington, DC, 2011, The National Academies Press.

Kaddoura M: The effect of preceptor behavior on the critical thinking skills of new graduate nurses in the intensive care unit, *The Journal of Continuing Education in Nursing* 44(11):488–495, 2013.

Khadjehturian RE: Stopping the culture of workplace incivility in nursing, *Clinical Journal of Oncology Nursing* 16(6): 638–639, 2012.

Kramer M: *Reality shock: why nurses leave nursing*, St. Louis, 1974, Mosby.

Kramer M, Brewer BB, Maguire P: Impact of Healthy Work Environments on New Graduate Nurses' Environmental

Reality Shock, *Western Journal of Nursing Research* 35(3):348–383, 2013.

Laschinger HK, Wong CA, Grau A: The influence of authentic leadership on newly graduated nurses' experiences of workplace bullying, burnout, and retention outcomes: A cross sectional study, *International Journal of Nursing Studies* 49(10):1266–1276, 2012.

Longo J: *Navigating the work environment: Embracing zero tolerance for bullying*, 2011. ANA Nurse CE. (website). http://ananursece.healthstream.com/Pages/Product. aspx?ID=970a8bf6-fab6-e011-8fb9-001517135721. Accessed June 10, 2015.

Lorenz JM: *Building collegiality*, 2014. (website). http://nursing. advanceweb.com/Continuing-Education/CE-Articles/ Building-Collegiality.aspx. Accessed September, 2014.

Maguire D: Progressive learning: structured induction for the novice nurse, *British Journal of Nursing* 22(11):645–649, 2013.

Martin K, Wilson CB: Newly registered nurses' experience in the first year of practice: A phenomenological study, *International Journal for Human Caring* 15(2):21–27, 2011.

Mayo Clinic: *Job burnout: How to spot it and take action*, 2012. (website). http://www.mayoclinic.org/healthy-living/adult-health/in-depth/burnout/art-20046642. Accessed September 30, 2014.

McEwen M, Wills E: *Theoretical basis for nursing*, Philadelphia, 2011, Lippincott Williams & Wilkins.

National Council State Boards of Nursing: *Transition to Practice*, 2015. (website). http://www.ncsbn.org/ transition-to-practice.htm. Accessed June 10, 2015.

Nelson JL: Helping new nurses set priorities, *American Nurse Today* 5(5):39–40, 2010.

Norris T: Lateral violence: Is nursing at risk? *Tennessee Nurse* 73(2):1, 7, 2010.

NSNA: *Giving credit where credit is due*, 2014. (website). http://www.nsna.org/Membership/LeadershipUniversity. aspx. Accessed June 10, 2015.

Occupational Safety and Health Administration: *Guidelines for preventing workplace violence for health care and social service workers*, 2015. (website). https://www.osha.gov/ Publications/osha3148.pdf. Accessed June 10, 2015.

Olin J: *Compassion fatigue: Nurses need to take care of themselves as well as others*, Januray 5, 2012. (website). http:// www.rncentral.com/blog/2012/compassion-fatigue-nurses-need-to-take-care-of-themselves-as-well-as-others/. Accessed October 9, 2014.

Perkins DEK: My practice evolution: An appreciation of the discrepancies between the idealism of nursing education and the realities of hospital practice, *Creative Nursing* 16(1):21–24, 2010.

Pfaff K, Baxter P, Jack S, Ploeg J: An integrative review of the factors influencing new graduate nurse engagement in interprofessional collaboration, *Journal of Advanced Nursing* 70(1):4–20, 2014.

Positive Way: *Self-esteem questionnaire*, 2012. (website). http://www.positive-way.com/self-est1.htm. Accessed June 10, 2015.

Profit J, Sharek PJ, Amspoker AB, et al: Burnout in the NICU setting and its relation to safety culture, *BMS Quality and Safety* 23:806–813, 2014.

Sherman R: Dealing with difficult people, *American Nurse Today* 9(5):61–62, 2014.

Sherman R: *5 steps to finding a nurse mentor who will lead you to success*, 2013. Nursetogether.com. (website). http:// www.nursetogether.com/find-nurse-mentor-lead-success. Accessed September 15, 2014.

Smith ME: From student to practicing nurse, *American Journal of Nursing* 107(7):72A–72D, July 2, 2007.

Smith-Trudeau P: Will you be my nurse mentor? *Vermont Nurse Connection* 17(2):3, April, May, June 2014.

Stone S: Mentoring and modeling for the millennium, *Dean's Notes* 21(4):1–2, 2000.

Sullivan EJ, Decker PJ: *Effective leadership and management*, ed 8, Menlo Park, CA, 2012, Addison-Wesley.

The Joint Commission: *Sentinel Event Alert, Issue 40. Behaviors that undermine a culture of safety*, 2008. (website). http://www.jointcommission.org/SentinelEvents/ SentinelEventAlert/ sea_40.htm.

Tingle CA: Workplace advocacy as a transition tool, 2000. Retrieved December 2007 from http://www.lsna.org/ newpage12.htm.

Turner J: *Avoiding workplace fatigue*, 2014. (website). http:// www.minoritynurse.com/article/avoiding-workplace-fatigue. Retrieved September 1, 2014.

Turner J: *Men in nursing school*, 2014. MinorityNurse.com. (website). http://www.minoritynurse.com/article/ men-nursing-school. Accessed September 15, 2014.

University Alliance: *How to relieve stress in nursing*, 2014. http://www.jacksonvilleu.com/blog/nursing/how-to-reduce-stress-in-nursing/#.VDINbfldV8E. Accessed September 15, 2014.

Wild Iris Medical Education: *Workplace violence*, 2014. http:// www.nursingceu.com/courses/455/index_nceu.html#top. Accessed August 15, 2014.

Zerwekh J, Claborn JC: Role transitions. In Zerwekh J, Claborn JC, editors: *Nursing today: transition and trends*, ed 7, St Louis, 2013, Saunders.

25

Managing Time: The Path to High Self-Performance

Patricia Reid Ponte, DNSc, RN, FAAN, NEA-BC,
Genevieve J. Conlin, DNP, MEd, MS/MBA, RN, NEA-BC

Our lives revolve around time; use it as a way to ensure high performance, positive energy, and focus in all aspects of your life.

ⓔ Additional resources are available online at: *http://evolve.elsevier.com/Cherry/*

PROFESSIONAL/ETHICAL ISSUE

Karen is a busy staff nurse working on a medical-surgical unit at the local community hospital. She has just returned to work from her vacation and is getting report for her patient assignment. While she was away, there were some significant updates made to the clinical documentation system. Karen wasn't able to attend the training session to review the changes and is not familiar with the changes. Her manager told her she needed to attend the training before she could return to practice. She wasn't concerned, as she feels she has strong computer skills and she'd figure it out. "I mean, really, how hard can it be?" Karen said. One of her colleagues offered to take a few minutes to show her some of the new workflows in the system, but Karen brushed her off, stating, "I don't have time to review this, I need to get my meds passed so I can go to the uniform sale in the café before it closes."

Karen soon discovers there are some big differences in how to document medications, as well as some of the procedures. She quickly falls behind in her documentation and starts writing things on a piece of paper.

Karen has plans after work to meet friends for dinner. She's eager to finish her shift and get on with her evening. She has missed some important pieces of documentation, though she did give a thorough hand-off to the next nurse at shift change report. The oncoming nurse asked about a patient's response to a pain medication given. Karen said, "I need to remember to note that; I'll just deal with it next time I work. . . . Hopefully I'll remember everything I did!" She laughs it off as she leaves the unit at the end of her shift.

You're the nurse receiving report from Karen, and you realize her documentation isn't complete. What do you do? What systems could have been put in place to ensure that Karen didn't return to work before completing the new documentation system training? What could Karen have done when she realized the enormity of the gap in her knowledge and skills in using the new documentation system? What are the ethical considerations involved in this situation? Are they at the organizational as well as individual clinician levels?

VIGNETTE

Approximately 4 months ago, Susan Kenny transferred to a position as a staff registered nurse (RN) at an ambulatory cancer treatment center. Today Susan arrived at the chemotherapy infusion room 15 minutes before the start of her shift. She knew it was going to be a busy day, and given her lack of experience in this work setting, she thought she should get a head start on her assignment. She was heading toward the workstation when one of her colleagues stopped her to discuss a holiday party, and they both spoke fervently about how much fun it would be.

434

Ten minutes later, Susan resumed her trek to the workstation. Just as she arrived, the phone rang, and Susan answered it. A patient was seeking information about her appointment time. It took Susan quite a while to open up the computer screen, log in, and find the information, which she communicated to the patient. By now many of her colleagues were on-site, already starting to work on their assignments. Susan looked at her assignment and realized that in addition to her other assigned patients, one of her patients would be receiving the first treatment of a new chemotherapy protocol. She knew that given the time necessary to work with the patient and family, triple-check orders with her physician and pharmacist colleagues, and administer the premedication and chemotherapy, all while monitoring this very ill patient, she would be very busy all day.

While reviewing the new chemotherapy protocol, one of Susan's primary patients came in unexpectedly with a fever and low blood pressure, needing hydration and platelets. The physician gave Susan orders to stabilize the patient and arrange for transfer to the inpatient unit. The hospital was full, so the transfer would take some time. Susan began to get very anxious about being able to complete all of her assigned duties while giving her patients the specialized care and attention they needed. Unfortunately, this anxious feeling was becoming a common occurrence in Susan's workday.

Meanwhile, Maura Callahan, a staff RN who had been working on the inpatient oncology floor for just less than a year, was passing out 10 AM medications when she received a call from Susan to take report before accepting the patient later in the day when a room became available. Maura was already behind in passing medications because of the new barcoding system now in use for medication administration. Despite the fact that this system would be safer and more efficient, using the new application took more time in the first few weeks. The training was great, but medication administration took longer. Maura asked the charge nurse if she could take report for her, but the charge nurse said she was in the midst of transferring another patient to the medical intensive care unit.

Maura took the report from Susan and agreed to accept the patient at 1 PM, when another patient's discharge would be completed and the room cleaned. Maura thought, "How will I ever get finished in time to pick up my daughter from daycare by 4 PM?" Her day was lining up like so many before, not being able to finish her work before the end of the shift. She would have to call her mother to help out again by picking up her daughter.

Both Susan and Maura were working frantically to ensure that patients' needs were met in a timely way, but it seemed impossible to both of them before they decided to call their respective managers and seek assistance.

Questions to Consider While Reading this Chapter:

1. When Susan arrived on duty, what are some strategies she could have used to be sure she made the most of her early arrival?
2. What factors should Susan and Maura consider when deciding how to prioritize their patient care assignment?
3. What strategies could Maura and Susan consider when deciding how to manage their learning needs and the need to be patient and family focused?
4. What are some strategies that Maura and Susan can use to ensure balance between their work and personal lives?

KEY TERMS

Energy management: Ensuring that the right amount of effort matches the right task to optimize an outcome while gauging the amount of personal energy expended or taxed to achieve the desired result.

Goal: A tangible, measurable, and attainable act in a specific period of time. It has broad-term results, experiences, or achievements toward which someone is willing to work.

Novice to expert: Five stages of proficiency in the development of skill acquisition and performance within the domain of clinical nursing practice that frames a transition from reliance on abstract principles of the new learner to becoming an involved performer who is engaged in a situation—the expert performer (Benner, 2001).

Objective: An identifiable, measurable act that implements one's goal and is typically short-term.

Prioritizing: The act of deciding what should be done first and what activities should follow sequentially; establishing an ordered list or ranked items based on importance or urgency; method used to determine what actions need to be accomplished ahead of others; represents the execution of ranked items.

Procrastination: The act of intentionally and/or habitually putting off doing something that should be done.

Technology management: Application of information systems and equipment to enhance work and life activities to maximal benefit.

Time management: The development of processes and tools that increase efficiency and productivity within the set standard of time.

LEARNING OUTCOMES

After studying this chapter, the reader will be able to:

1. Understand the unique demands of complex health care environments in today's fast-paced world of high technology and communication transfer and its effects on personal time management.
2. Describe the relationship between personal performance and time management.
3. Articulate one's own time-management preferences and style.
4. Create an action plan to manage procrastination, distraction, and anxiety.
5. Describe how individual learning and communication styles interact with the ability to manage time effectively.
6. Adopt into daily practice a time-management strategy plan unique to one's own style to ensure high-level personal performance in work and home life.
7. Articulate the impact of personal time related choices made by individuals to the risk of patients and the organizations

CHAPTER OVERVIEW

The previous scenarios are typical of what happens daily in the lives of busy professionals. Managing multiple priorities during a particular workday and integrating personal and work-related demands is the constant dilemma of so many men and women today. Additionally, performing well in both arenas is not only a goal of most working professionals but more importantly an obligation to ensure quality and safety in care delivery. To accomplish the important goals in life, it is necessary to understand your own preferred style of managing priorities, recognize your typical distractions, identify a personal performance approach, and consistently use strategies and tools to make the most of every minute. This chapter is designed to assist students and busy professionals in implementing self-management strategies to better use their time and energy to ensure a highly productive, focused life.

HEALTH CARE TODAY

Health care environments are fraught with incredible complexities: high-acuity patients, vigilant and knowledgeable family members, ever-growing information technology geared toward supporting staff in the care of patients, often tight quarters in which to deliver high-tech and high risk care and little time to interact with patients on an interpersonal therapeutic level. Interprofessional practice models demand collaborative teamwork, when in reality disciplines often function in parallel work processes. The need to move patients quickly from one site of care to another on a constantly growing continuum that reaches into patients' homes is the norm in today's health care environment. Fast-paced clinics, high-tech ambulatory care practice settings, and quaternary care in high-intensity critical care units and operating rooms are typical. The nature of the intimate human element inherent in the delivery of health care makes it like no other work.

As health care continues to evolve and the nation is focused on major health care reform to improve access and quality and reduce costs, efficiency has become a critical component when considering the cost and quality of health care delivery (Larkin, 2009). Managing time, organizing care, and maintaining personal health and balance between work and home settings become much more demanding—and essential. Therefore, it becomes critical for each professional working in these dynamic settings to receive education and coaching in managing time, energy, balance, and focus to ensure high performance. Florence Nightingale's words resonate: "Knowing how you manage when you are there [at work] . . . impacts how your work should be done when you are not there" (1969).

PERSPECTIVES ON TIME

Each person has a specific perspective of time, which is based on his or her own experiences, values, education, socioeconomic factors, age, personality, culture, and genetic makeup. To understand an individual's own perspective on time and the resulting behaviors, it is necessary to create opportunities to think introspectively and examine personal preferences, traits, habits, and tendencies. This is the critical first step in achieving an individualized time-management strategy and plan.

In her book, *Time Management from the Inside Out*, Julie Morgenstern (2004) presents "10 psychological obstacles" that influence one's ability to create and sustain focused and productive work habits. As the following 10 obstacles are reviewed, carefully consider how they might affect your own ability to develop productive, energetic work habits.

1. **Unclear Goals and Priorities.** Within a particular work shift or within your life as a whole, if you lack clarity about purpose and expected outcomes, the ability to manage time to meet your desires becomes a futile task.
2. **Conquistador of Chaos.** If you are constantly overburdened with tasks, events, urgent requests, and last-minute cancellations, you are a better crisis manager than manager of time.
3. **Fear of Downtime.** Some individuals fear the possibility of standing still too long. They feel guilty with timeouts or time off. Often this is a result of not wanting to address the larger issues in life. Staying too busy to think keeps long-term planning and personal introspection at bay.
4. **Need to be a Caretaker.** In professions such as nursing, the need to be a caretaker is a common devotion and can be very gratifying. However, when this need becomes unbalanced, it can cause you to feel resentful, unappreciated, and overwhelmed.
5. **Fear of Failure.** When you are unable to get to the things that are important to you and are unable to meet your personal goals, it may mean you are afraid of failure. It can be very upsetting to go after your dreams and find out you cannot reach them. Sometimes it is easier to avoid making the effort. Take time to understand what your fears are and to openly address them.
6. **Fear of Success.** You may have been given a message somewhere in your life that you do not deserve to be a success. Therefore, it can be anxiety provoking to garner success and stand apart from others who may distance themselves from you. Take time to think through whether or not this is playing out in your life.
7. **Fear of Disrupting the Status Quo.** Not pursuing your goals for fear of the reactions of those around you is very common. Your family, coworkers, or supervisors may be critical of what you want to pursue. Gradually approaching changes gives you and those around you time to acclimate.
8. **Fear of Completion.** If you are afraid of completing a project that is creative and fun because you are fearful that another similar project will not find its way to you or the project may no longer be important to you, take the time to understand why you are not completing a routine task or a major project that has been with you for some time.
9. **Need for Perfection.** If you are a perfectionist and feel that everything should be completed with the same level of excellence, you are not keeping things in perspective. If you demand extremely high standards for every single task you undertake, you simply will not get everything done.
10. **Fear of Losing Creativity.** Many creative people think that by creating an organized time-management structure or approach to life their creative natures or tendencies will be squelched. However, creating a framework to manage priorities will allow more freedom and time to enhance one's creative juices.

Following are some of the benefits that will result if you take the time to uncover your own tendencies, fears, strengths, and weaknesses (Childre, 2008; Reid Ponte, 2008):

- Improved patient outcomes by implementing a collaborative structure in the work environment
- Increased satisfaction with your work accomplishments as a result of applying something new in your setting
- Improved interpersonal relations because of your ability to be fully present and engaged to do your best work
- Better future direction because there is more attentiveness to proactively managing and engaging in the environment
- Improved personal health because of decreased anxiety and a restoration of emotional balance

It is more crucial than ever that you strive to understand what you value, recognize your purpose in life, and determine strategies to ensure that your focus and energy are geared toward your major goals in life. Whether you are trying to organize how to approach a particular workday or trying to balance your personal and work life, the strategies that you will learn and integrate into your daily activities now will play out the rest of your life. Managing energy to ensure high performance is the first step.

ENERGY MANAGEMENT

According to Loehr and Schwartz (2003), "Energy, not time, is the fundamental currency of high performance." Striving to be more efficient and more organized or to manage time and priorities better is all in the interest of becoming a better performer either in one's work or personal life. Loehr and Schwartz (2003) also state that only when we are fully engaged do we perform our best. This requires drawing on four separate but related sources of energy: (1) physical, (2) mental, (3) spiritual, and (4) emotional.

Just as we build physical capacity through disciplined exercise and strengthening routines, we can also strengthen our emotional, spiritual, and mental capacities.

Consider Susan from our earlier vignette. Her decision to transfer to the chemotherapy infusion center, her third transfer in 18 months, came only after sheer frustration of not being able to feel in control of her work life and home life. At work, Susan felt overwhelmed, underappreciated, and unprepared physically for the daily challenges of 12-hour shifts. She was exhausted every morning, and she fell into bed as soon as she got home. Her energy level was poor. She felt dissatisfied with her inability to spend more time with friends on weekends. Susan could not bear the thought of getting out of bed early another day, even if it was for something fun. Because of this, she gained weight over the past 6 months, and the only thing that seemed to make her happy was to visit her sister on Sunday afternoons for shopping and dinner. Getting to work the next day often proved difficult because her motivation was low and her energy level even lower. With this new job, Susan was attempting to get back on track. "It's going to be different this time," she said to herself.

Physical Energy

This scenario is not uncommon as novice professionals begin the rigors of full-time work after spending time in college and working part time. Key components of successful transition to a productive, highly energizing experience include paying attention to physical energy through a routine of proper eating, adequate sleep and exercise, frequent breaks during long shifts (about every 90 minutes), drinking plenty of water, and focusing on one activity while collecting thoughts about what to prioritize next. Once the physical capacity of your holistic self is working well, then attention can be paid to your mental, spiritual, and emotional capacities.

Mental Energy

The mental energy that is most potent in ensuring full engagement and high performance is that of realistic optimism. Realistic optimism is seeing the world as it is, but always working toward an optimal solution or goal. Mental energy is the ability to maintain sustained concentration on a task, move flexibly between broad and narrow issues, and be internally and externally focused as needed by the situation. It includes mental preparation, visualization, positive self-talk, effective time management, and creativity. Susan has begun to identify this mental energy in her desire to get back on track. She realizes that change is necessary. To move in this direction, Susan needs to spend some time to reflect on the following: (1) What are my major goals in life, and (2) what is my purpose?

Spiritual Energy

Often we do not take the time to reflect about what is important to us. Being in a quiet place helps us identify our vision of life—our purpose and direction in life. Susan has yet to determine her life vision given her frequent job changes and her lack of clarity about how she wants to spend her personal time. Having direction and purpose is the key factor in one's spiritual capacity.

Peter Senge (2006) has identified "personal mastery" as the discipline of continually clarifying and deepening one's personal vision, focusing one's energies, developing patience, and seeing reality objectively. People with a high level of personal mastery live in a continual learning mode, uncovering their personal growth areas.

Emotional Energy

Physical, mental, and spiritual energy provide fuel for building our emotional capacity. Managing emotions skillfully in the service of high positive energy and full engagement is called *emotional intelligence*. Goleman (2006) suggests that self-confidence, self-control, and interpersonal effectiveness are all key to emotional intelligence. Striving to increase one's emotional capacity—which includes improving one's self-confidence, self-control, self-regulation, social skills, interpersonal effectiveness, empathy, patience, openness, trust, and enjoyment—will result in a more positive, invigorating work experience and personal life.

Understanding how the four energies—physical, mental, spiritual, and emotional—contribute to a fully engaged individual who is productive and happy will help you use the time-management skills and strategies described in the following sections of this chapter.

TIME DISTRACTIONS AND ENERGY DISTRACTIONS

We are all subject to distractions in our work and personal lives that may influence our propensity to procrastinate or not reach our goals. Nurses experience stress and distraction when they assume unplanned responsibilities while simultaneously conducting their planned work. This is referred to in the literature as "complexity compression" (Krichbaum et al, 2011). It is important to recognize and understand the distractions or complexities that inhibit our ability to complete tasks and to meet our objectives and goals in a planned way. Box 25-1 lists many common internal and external time

BOX 25-1 Time and Energy Distractions	
External Distractions	**Internal Distractions**
Interruptions	Procrastination
Socializing or visitors	Inadequate planning
Meetings	Ineffective delegation
Excessive paperwork	Failure to set goals and
Understaffing	priorities
Lack of information	A cluttered desk or
Ineffective communication	mind
Lack of feedback	Personal disorganization
Travel	Inability to say no
Inadequate policies and	Lack of self-discipline
procedures	Responding to crises
Incompetent or	Haste
uncooperative	Indecisiveness
coworkers	An "open-door" policy
Poor filing systems	Shifting priorities without
Looking for misplaced	sound rationale
files, and so on	Leaving tasks unfinished
Personnel or coworkers	Not setting time limits
with problems	Daydreaming
Lack of teamwork	Attempting too much
Duplicating efforts	at once
Confusing lines of	Overinvolvement in
authority, responsibility,	routine detail
and communication	Making numerous
Bureaucratic red tape	errors
Junk mail	Surfing the Internet
Waiting, meeting delays	Not listening

distractions and energy distractions that each of us may experience in a typical day. It is critical to be aware of the time distractions that affect us. The following section provides specific examples of how to strategically avoid these common time distractions.

TIME-MANAGEMENT STRATEGIES

It is easy to apply the perspectives-on-time concept to nurses because many nurses have type A personalities, which means they are oriented toward high achievement. As a result, they are more likely to encounter stress when they mismanage themselves and do not use time appropriately. The reason for this phenomenon becomes clear when some of the common characteristics of high achievers are examined. Nurses tend to go above and beyond for their patients, colleagues, and families and they set a high bar of achievement for themselves (Lee, 2004).

As high achievers, nurses are often attracted to activities that are challenging, difficult, and even risky. In most cases, the activities are complex and time-consuming, which forces the person to use self-management to meet the goals and gain internal satisfaction. When these people mismanage themselves in relation to time, it results in frustration and stress. To assist nurses in improving their self-management and time management, many different management strategies have been outlined for review including planning, implementing, and organizing.

Planning is the most important step in time management.

Planning, Organizing, and Implementing to Control the Use of Time

Planning, organizing, and implementing are the key actions a person can use to optimize the use of time. These three actions are sequential and build on each other for successful time management.

Planning for Control

Planning is the most important step in time management. Unfortunately, few people expend as much energy planning as they should. Some shy away from planning because they believe it is too time-consuming and never leads to closure. In reality, planning allows people to better use their time and can lead to closure in relation to those goals that will produce the most internal satisfaction. For example, 1 minute of planning can transfer to at least 10 minutes of productivity, proving to be a great return on the investment of taking the time to review and plan for the day. If you arrive 10 to 15 minutes early for your scheduled shift and map out the day's priorities, your likelihood of executing those priorities is far greater than had you not taken the time to plan up front.

Having a priority-planning list with you as you work is useful in keeping you on track to accomplish those tasks by the end of the shift or day. Those who plan well also tend to encounter fewer problems when Murphy's law becomes a reality: *If anything can go wrong it will.* Thus it is important to plan before beginning any task, project, or day's activities. Planning involves (1) setting goals and establishing priorities, (2) scheduling activities, and (3) making to-do lists.

Setting Priorities

Prioritizing is about making choices of what to do and what not to do. To prioritize effectively, you need to be able to recognize what is important, as well as to see the difference between urgent (must be done immediately) and important (must be done, but there may be flexibility as to when the task can be accomplished). A major component of planning is deciding what should be done first and what activities should follow sequentially. The factors that influence how to establish priorities include the following:

- Urgency of a situation
- Demands of others
- Closeness of deadlines
- Existing timeframe
- Degree of familiarity with the task
- Ease of the task
- Amount of enjoyment involved
- Consequences involved
- Size of the task
- Congruence with personal goals

Unfortunately, not all of these factors carry the same weight when considering the use of time. Factors that are most likely to assist in meeting your goals need to be given more consideration. Setting SMART goals (**s**pecific, **m**easurable, **a**chievable, **r**easonable, and **t**ime-based) may also provide the structure needed to manage these compounding factors we negotiate in our lives

(Skillpath Seminars, 2011). Several processes have been proposed to assist people in setting priorities, including the ABC approach, the Pareto principle, and the continuum approach.

The ABC approach is advocated by Lakein (1989) and Mancini (2003). In this approach, a person lists every task that needs to be done. An A is assigned to the high-value items, a B to the medium-value items, and a C to the low-value items. The A items should stand out from the other items because of their worth to the person making the list. Also the A items are likely to require more energy and time, but they should be completed before any of the B or C items. As the A items are completed, you may find that the C items were of such low value that they did not need to be done at all. It is also possible that Monday's C item could become an A item on Friday, reflecting a change in values. Of course this is an arbitrary system that is based on a person's estimation of the value of activities within his or her own life. It allows for reflection and change while maintaining focus.

The Pareto principle is another process that is suggested for setting priorities. This principle is also referred to as the 80-20 rule, suggesting that 80% of the time expended produces 20% of the results, and 20% of the time expended produces 80% of the results (Koch, 2004). The essence is in determining the "vital few" activities that should be done and eliminating the "trivial many." Focusing on one or two tasks at a time supports this concept (Skillpath Seminars, 2011). This principle emphasizes selecting the most productive activities, eliminating trivia, and learning to say no.

The continuum approach to setting priorities encourages a person to select priorities by categorizing or ranking items according to four continuums. As you read about the four continuums, think about Susan's assignment in the opening vignette and consider which of her tasks would have been priorities based on this approach.

- **Intrinsic importance**: very important and must be done; important and should be done; not so important and may not be necessary, but may be useful; or unimportant and can be eliminated entirely
- **Urgency:** very urgent and must be done now; urgent and should be done soon; not urgent and can wait; time is not a factor
- **Delegation:** must be done by me because I am the only one who can do it; can be delegated to A or B; can be dumped because task does not need to be done or delegated
- **Visitations and conferences:** people I must see each day; people to see frequently but not daily; people to see regularly but not frequently; people to see only infrequently

Obviously these continuums have varying usefulness, depending on the activity being scrutinized.

Overall it does not matter which method is used to establish priorities as long as priorities are established using a sound rationale. Fortunately, setting priorities becomes easier with practice. If Susan had established her priorities for the day, it is unlikely that talking about the holiday party or calling the inpatient unit to give a report on a patient that would not transfer for several hours would have taken precedence over reviewing the new chemotherapy regimen protocol she would be administering to a patient. Setting priorities would have allowed Susan to better use her time and decreased her anxiety about not managing her assignment appropriately.

Scheduling Activities

Scheduling activities is an important component of planning. It is one way to control Parkinson's law, which states that work will expand to fill the time that is available. By scheduling activities, a person determines how much time is spent on a specific activity. Such time delineations tend to focus attention and activity so that the task gets completed more efficiently and effectively. A schedule of activities can be constructed using a variety of different methods, including hourly time schedules, which are not new to most people because they tend to be used throughout life. Everyone has used an hourly schedule for appointments, classes, or leisure activities. In addition, nurses become adept at using hourly time schedules to administer medications appropriately. Unfortunately, most people, including nurses, do not use time schedules frequently or consistently enough.

The process of scheduling activities is an important part of planning to use your time more efficiently. However, scheduling needs to be done appropriately to ensure adherence. Remember to schedule activities so that they coincide with your internal "prime time," when you concentrate best, and your external "prime time," when you deal best with other people. Typically the first 2.5 hours of the workday are the most productive, so plan important tasks according to your most productive time in the day (Skillpath Seminars, 2011). As a general rule, 15 minutes of focused time and energy toward a project equates to 1 hour of productivity. Be sure to include some flexible time just for yourself. In addition, schedules have proven to be most useful when they are written down in ink; a written schedule tends to motivate people, particularly high achievers, because they are averse to deviate from whatever challenges them in black and white.

Establishing a To-Do List

Writing something on paper often is the first step to accomplishing it. A to-do list tends to keep people on track and focused on specific activities. Thus the list should be reflective of your priorities and goals. To-do lists should be made and revised daily to be the most useful in managing your time. Sometimes they require revision more frequently, even hourly, when priorities shift for valid reasons. The list should be legible and easily accessible to review throughout the day. It is helpful to review the list at the end of the shift or day to assess how you achieved or did not achieve your goals. This is an opportunity to reflect on the distractions you experienced so that you can make note of what not to do when the next situation arises. This will also provide you the opportunity to reevaluate your tasks to see what needs to be carried over to the next day. Some people find it useful to construct their lists on notecards, in day-planner calendars, on pocket calendars, in electronic recall devices, on computers, and myriad other ways. There is no right or wrong way to make a to-do list, but it should always be available to you.

Organizing for Control

Organizing yourself and your environment is an important component of time management. Such organization requires that you be able to deal effectively with the following:

- The stacked-desk syndrome
- The art of "no detourism"
- The art of "wastebasketry"
- E-mail and memo mania

The Stacked-Desk Syndrome

This syndrome is exactly what the label implies—a cluttered desk stacked with papers, books, and other things. The syndrome can also apply to the mind when it is cluttered with many thoughts and ideas. Both situations are distractions to accomplishing your goals and will divert your attention sufficiently so that you do not know where to begin. When you lose your concentration, you will again become distracted by the clutter. To deal effectively with this syndrome, you must clear both your work area and your mind. To effectively organize or clear a work area, you should do the following:

- Remove everything from the work surface that does not directly relate to the project at hand; only things you need every day should be on your desk.
- Place the telephone out of sight, but within reach.
- Remove all personal items, such as calendars, clocks, or photographs, if they are distractors.
- Close the door to the work area when possible, but communicate to colleagues that you may be interrupted in the case of an emergency (Emmett, 2009).

For a nurse, this usually means eliminating clutter from a patient's room so that care can be delivered effectively and efficiently. Keep out in the open only things you need to use to carry out the task at hand (e.g., if you are doing a dressing change, you do not need the catheter kit for your next patient in your immediate work space). Another desk management strategy is to assign a work location at the nurses' station for each staff person working on a given shift. This allows the nurse to have a dedicated space to keep schedules and patient charts available, in addition to having computer access, a critical resource for care delivery in today's health care environment.

The Art of "No Detourism"

To effectively organize, or clear the mind, you must practice the art of "no detourism." This requires complete concentration on one activity or task until—with no detours—it is completed. It mandates that only one activity at a time be undertaken and that it should be completed before moving to a different task. This method also implies that the task should be completed correctly the first time so that you do not waste time redoing it. Inherent in the concept of "no detourism" is the fact that the tasks undertaken are directly related to personal goals and objectives; thus completing them will result in internal satisfaction. Maura may have benefited from practicing "no detourism." Perhaps she would not have become distracted by the telephone call from the infusion unit if she had been focused on passing the medications via the barcoding system.

The Art of "Wastebasketry"

Perfecting the art of "wastebasketry" is mandatory for better use of time. The art of physical wastebasketry involves "circular filing" (in the trash can or with the delete key on the computer) of any documents, including e-mails or other paperwork that has limited use or needs no response. The goal is to handle a paper (or e-mail) only once, then either act on it (do it), send it along to another appropriate person (delegate it), or throw it away (dump it). Some also refer to this as the TRASH approach: Throw it away, Refer it to someone else, Act on it, Save it, or Halt it (e.g., stop junk mail from coming to you) (Skillpath Seminars, 2011). This art involves being sufficiently knowledgeable and skilled to ascertain which documents, e-mails, and paperwork are appropriate candidates for the "circular file" and then daring to follow through. Practicing this art daily will also help in managing the stacked-desk syndrome by reducing much of the clutter.

The art of mental wastebasketry also involves organizing your mind to deal with the established priorities. This requires using selective perception to attend only to those tasks at hand. It also assists in discarding useless information. Mental wastebasketry is a valuable skill to perfect in relation to affecting a better use of time.

E-Mail and Memo Mania

Keep electronic mail brief and to the point. Do not procrastinate in responding. Use correct form and proper etiquette, and be accurate. Also keep in mind that a telephone call may be a sufficient and more efficient means of response and often more appropriate. The consensus regarding e-mails is that too many of them are generated unnecessarily, which may constitute a major time distraction. It is beneficial to allot specified periods throughout the workday to review, filter, and respond to e-mail, as appropriate. Taking 10 minutes every morning to review your e-mail messages will allow you to prioritize those activities that may be time-sensitive. Make sure to review your e-mail inbox at least once again around the lunch hour or midday, and then again at the day's end to wrap up unfinished business.

E-mail has become the primary method of communication for the majority of individuals in professional, health care, and academic settings. It is an expedient route to contact people, regardless of their location. It is also a useful way to conduct business with a group of people concurrently, when appropriate, because of the ability to share information with many parties at once. Keep in mind, however, that e-mail is a professional channel of communication, and messages should contain a greeting, a clear body of text, specific and clear requests for information, and an acceptable closing to the message. Messages should also be free of grammatical and typographic errors. Chapter 19 provides additional information about how to use e-mail effectively.

Implementing for Control

Implementing for control refers to carrying out activities that assist people in managing time use. Further exploring these activities in the following sections clarifies how they can be easily implemented in daily life.

Attacking the Priorities

It is important to attack the priorities early to gain control of your time. Delay in beginning tasks will only result in crises when deadlines or personal goals are not met. One of the most cited reasons for delaying this process is fear—a very real symptom of procrastination—usually fear of failure, although it could be a fear of something else. Regardless, it is important to analyze your fears to be able to identify the source and to determine whether the fear is valid or exaggerated in order to manage it to obtain the results you established (Emmett, 2009; Vestal, 2009). If the priority is a big project or large task, it can be successfully approached by examining how the project can be divided up into smaller, more manageable tasks.

Finding "Extra" Time

The concept of finding extra time seems paradoxical because in reality everyone has the same amount of time. The concept actually relates to how people choose to use their time. In some cases, a different use of time may result in additional time for accomplishing goals. A few ways to produce extra time are as follows:

- Using commuting time and coffee breaks to relax so that designated working hours are more productive
- Instituting working lunches periodically, such as twice a week

Certainly there are other ways individuals might choose to alter their use of time. The key is knowing which activities can be altered without being detrimental to overall functioning. For example, perhaps giving up 30 minutes of television watching or reading each evening would work for some, but not if that is the only relaxation time that is available daily. Sacrificing down-time for more work may decrease overall productivity. It may be a case of working longer, but not smarter, so less actually gets accomplished.

Handling E-Mail and Paperwork Appropriately

The rule regarding paperwork is to handle it only once. Decide to act on the paperwork, delegate it, or toss it. Shuffling papers or e-mails, filing, and retrieving are time wasters. Plan to prevent becoming mired in paper-work. Perfecting the art of wastebasketry will assist in handling paperwork and e-mails appropriately. Another tip is to set aside a specific time each day for dealing with all e-mail and paperwork.

Avoiding Procrastination

Procrastination is a bad habit that ranks high on the list of time wasters. It has been referred to as an obstacle to suc-cess, "the cat burglar of time management," and a "hidden fear of conflict" (Mancini, 2003). It can wear many dis-guises, including fear, laziness, indifference, overwork, and forgetfulness. Procrastination most frequently is evident when a person is faced with an unpleasant task, a difficult task, or a difficult decision. Usually procrastination is easily recognizable because it involves doing low-priority rather than high-priority tasks, and it always welcomes interrup-tions. Procrastination is the art of "never doing today what can be put off until tomorrow." The result is less productiv-ity, less internal satisfaction, and more stress.

The first step in avoiding procrastination is being able to recognize when it is occurring. The second step is being able to admit that what is occurring is procras-tination. Once those two steps are accomplished, the work of overcoming procrastination can begin. Follow-ing are mechanisms for overcoming procrastination (Emmett, 2009):

- Identify the tasks that are being put off.
- Ask why the task is being avoided.
- Determine whether the task could or should be done by someone else.
- Identify consequences of the procrastination.
- Set priorities in relation to the task.
- Establish deadlines and adhere to them.
- Focus on one aspect at a time.
- Do not strive for perfection if 95% or 98% will be just as effective.

The last item is clearly one in which good clinical discernment must be exercised, because there are clearly instances when providing nursing care that is anything less than 100% could cause harm. It also helps if you can eliminate those tasks that make up the procrastination. For example, if rearranging the desk, the furniture, or even the medication cart is part of how a person pro-crastinates, then eliminate that activity by changing the work location or environment. Most important, em-phasize the benefits that are to be gained by completing the task and accomplishing the goals that will provide internal satisfaction.

Delegating Appropriately

Most simplistically, delegation is the art of giving other people tasks to be accomplished. In reality, however, there is nothing simple about delegation. It usually re-quires considerable time and energy to delegate, but the rewards are greater in the overall context of accomplish-ing goals. Mancini (2003) and Skillpath Seminars (2011) identify the following important benefits of delegation:

- Extends the results that can be accomplished from what one person can do alone to what he or she can manage through others
- Frees time for more important tasks
- Assists in developing the initiative, skills, knowledge, and competence of others
- Maintains the responsibility and decision level
- Is often more cost-effective

With these potential benefits, it would seem that ev-eryone would want to use delegation. Unfortunately this is not the case. Many barriers, internal and external, can hinder the delegation process.

A brief exploration of those barriers may clarify why delegation is such a problem for some people. The internal barriers to delegating include: a personal pref-erence for how tasks are accomplished, demanding that everyone know all the details, believing that no one else can complete the task as well, lack of experience in delegating, insecurity, fear of being disliked, lack of confidence in others, perfectionism resulting in over-control, lack of organizational skill, failure to delegate authority commensurate with the responsibility dele-gated, indecision, poor communication skills, and lack of commitment to the development of others.

The external barriers to delegating are either inher-ent in the situation or in the person to whom something is being delegated. External barriers within the situation may include stringent policies that mandate who can do what, low tolerance of mistakes, the criticality of the decisions, implementation of a management-by-crisis style, confusion regarding responsibilities and authority, and understaffing. External barriers to delegation that reside within the person to whom tasks are being delegated include lack of experience, lack of competence, avoidance of responsibility, overdependence on others, disorganization, procrastination, work overload, and immersion in trivia and clutter (Mancini, 2003). When the barriers are identified and overcome, the delegation process can proceed. Implementing the following steps will facilitate appropriate delegation (also see Chapter 20 for a complete discussion of delegation in the clinical setting):

- Identify exactly what is to be delegated and why.
- Select the best person for the task; this may be the person most qualified or it may be the person whose development the delegator chooses to contribute to.
- Communicate the assignment in detail, perhaps even including written instructions.
- Involve the delegatee in establishing the objectives and deadlines for the task.
- Have the delegatee repeat the details of the task.
- Give the delegatee the authority for accomplishing the task.
- Provide adequate resources and support as needed.
- Schedule regular meetings for progress reports.
- Establish controls, and monitor the results.
- Evaluate the process and progress of the delegatee.
- Let the delegatee do the job.
- Enjoy the results of having the delegated task completed and being able to accomplish other tasks simultaneously (Mindtools, 2006).

It is not prudent to take shortcuts when delegating tasks because the results might be different than what was originally intended. Avoiding delegation shortcuts is an important consideration because the nurse who does the delegating also retains accountability for the task.

Delegation would have been useful to Susan in the opening vignette. It could have helped her meet her patient care goals and decrease her anxiety. Unfortunately Susan was overwhelmed, and she could not identify those things that needed to be done or direct someone else to do them. In addition, Susan had not established any priorities, so it was difficult for her to plan for appropriate delegation. Ignoring the availability and influence of other colleagues can perpetuate a rather self-critical and individualist perspective of time

management (Waterworth, 2003). As seen in the vignette, this can lead to a failure to address problems in the organization of work and in the coordination of patient care within the health care team.

Controlling Interruptions

To focus on your priorities, it is important to establish uninterrupted blocks of time. Frequent causes of interruptions are telephone calls, meetings, and visitors, particularly the drop-in type. Learning how to control such interruptions will assist in accomplishing more in less time. One of the easiest ways to manage incoming calls is to not answer them during time that is scheduled for other activities. An answering machine, voicemail service, or an assistant can take the message to be responded to later. "Later" should refer to the time that was pre-established for returning telephone calls. A good example of controlling interruptions in the opening vignette would have been for Susan to ask the unit secretary to assist the patient requesting information about an appointment.

Most people schedule callbacks for times when their productivity level is lower or during their downtime. Also telephone calls can be controlled by the tone and verbiage used. If a person chooses to invite conversation and ensure a longer call, using a vague, open-ended greeting will accomplish that purpose. If a person chooses to focus the call specifically on its purpose, a specific, factual, informative greeting will enhance the productivity of the call and shorten its length. For example, "Hi, Bill, how are you? How are things going?" definitely invites the person to reply at length, whereas, "Hi, Bill. I have two questions that I need for you to answer" tends to condense the telephoning session. Also, being prepared for the conversation with all of the pertinent facts readily available helps to focus the conversation and to shorten the call.

Meetings can become a major time waster if they are poorly managed and nonproductive. The first step in controlling this interruption is deciding whether to attend. Such a decision should be based on an evaluation of the potential productivity of the meeting. For example, is the meeting absolutely necessary? Does the agenda contain items that you should be informed about? Is it necessary for you to contribute to the discussion? Will decisions be made that will affect you and your functioning? Are you conducting the meeting? These questions should guide the decision (Mancini, 2003). Once a person is committed to attending a meeting, he or she is responsible for helping to ensure that the meeting remains focused and productive. The person conducting the meeting not only shares these same responsibilities but also has a more direct role in effecting the outcome.

Visitors, particularly unplanned visitors, also create interruptions. One way to decrease the number of visitors is to seclude yourself during specific times by closing the door to others, physically and mentally. Managing visitors in today's health care environment can be difficult, given the fact that family members are able and welcome to accompany their ill members for extended periods and in a variety of settings. Educating family members can be a time-consuming task in a nurse's day. It is important to ensure that this time is factored into one's schedule because communicating with family members is an inevitable and important occurrence.

Learning the Art of Saying No

"No" is such a small word, but it is sometimes more difficult to say than any 14-syllable word. The first step in learning the art of saying no is determining when to say it. The cost-benefit ratio of each opportunity must be evaluated in relation to the overall goals. If the activity will be a benefit overall, obviously it must be given careful consideration. If it will not be a significant benefit, decline gracefully but emphatically. There isn't a need to provide an elaborate qualifier to your "no" response; a clear, succinct reply is acceptable (Patterson et al, 2011). For example, when asked to review a clinical guideline, do not refuse based on the fact that you are overworked and do not have a free minute for 3 weeks. The person requesting the review is likely to agree on the later timeframe, in which case you'll find yourself committed to doing something that has low benefit unless you create another excuse. Instead be polite and gracious in the refusal, but do not allow leeway to be manipulated into saying yes. Always consider the opportunity that "no" offers in terms of your overall goals.

Rewarding Yourself

All people function more productively when they are motivated. The sources of motivation vary from person to person. A person needs to identify his or her motivators and use them as rewards for accomplishing goals. It is important to identify long- and short-term rewards so that they can be implemented appropriately.

Most people are familiar with rewarding themselves in exchange for doing something, and they do it frequently. For some it is a way of life. It usually amounts to bargaining with yourself to facilitate the completion of a task. For example, "If I finish reading these two work-related articles, then I can read my novel for 30 minutes," or "If I complete this paper, I will treat myself to ice cream." You should know which rewards work best and use them appropriately to accomplish long-term goals.

Using Technology

Many of today's technologic advances can be used to improve time management. Most health care settings have adopted more uses of technologic resources to better improve the use of time and enhance patient care. Many health care organizations use electronic health records (EHRs), which allows for multiple users to access a patient's record at the same time to document and to review information. There are also electronic order entry systems now in place, in which clinicians enter orders and activate orders that are then transmitted to the pharmacy to fill the medication request. Patient acuity rating systems are now completed online and used by admitting departments to send patients to the appropriate units for care.

Just about every workplace has a professional office system that supports e-mail and scheduling activities. The scheduling features available can be very useful for staff in the planning phase of time management. However, there are advantages and disadvantages to most of the new technologic devices. If it takes longer to look up a telephone number in a computer system than using a traditional phonebook, for example, it makes sense to review that process for efficiency before determining which system would provide a best practice.

Many people today use smartphones to synchronize their personal and professional calendars. The PDA also becomes a valuable resource in the clinical setting when programmed with drug information and lab value databases, which allow a nurse to have a wealth of information at her or his fingertips without having to carry or look for resource manuals. However, when considering the many technologic devices available, keep in mind that the tools and devices should improve workflow and processes, not hinder them or create cumbersome ones (Brafman and Beckstrom, 2008). Also remember that taking time to learn to use new technology correctly will pay off in the long run by increasing effective use of time. Once the strategies have been implemented, it is important to continue to use them to achieve your goals and gain internal satisfaction.

CONTINUING TO SUCCEED

Improving time management to enhance self-performance and accomplish goals is a lifelong process. The process becomes easier the longer you engage in it, but time management still requires continual attention and energy. Obviously, time management does not just happen—it requires a strong personal commitment. Lakein (1989) suggests that it is important to continue doing the following to succeed:

- When feeling overwhelmed, always stop and plan activities.
- Keep focused on priorities, and act accordingly.
- Avoid favorite forms of procrastination.
- Maintain a positive attitude about the established goals, or revise them so that they coincide with your value system.
- Do something for yourself every day.
- Continue to work on overcoming your fears.
- Resist doing the easy but unimportant tasks.

In addition, delete the words "if only" from your vocabulary. Regret is a luxury and a great time waster. Significant time is expended rehashing mistakes or determining how to make something perfect when it was a one-time occurrence that is now over. Such time usually is not productive unless you will encounter similar situations in the future. It is more productive to admit mistakes, accept responsibility for them, and move on. Thus the words "if only" should be replaced with "next time," and the incident itself should be filed in the mental circular file to leverage for the future (Skillpath Seminars, 2011). The reader is encouraged to review the tips for continuing success in managing time presented in Box 25-2.

> **BOX 25-2   Tips for Successful Time Management**
>
> 1. Clarify objectives, put them in writing, and establish a priority list to work from.
> 2. Focus on objectives, not on activities.
> 3. Set at least one major objective for each day and achieve it.
> 4. Record a time log periodically to analyze how time is used and to document bad habits.
> 5. Analyze everything in terms of objectives.
> 6. Make a to-do list every day that includes daily objectives and priorities and time estimates to accomplish them.
> 7. Schedule time every day to ensure that the most important things are accomplished first.
> 8. Make sure the first hour of every workday is productive.
> 9. Set time limits for every task undertaken.
> 10. Take the time to do the task right the first time so that time will not be wasted doing it over.
> 11. Institute a quiet hour of uninterrupted time each day to work on the most important tasks.
> 12. Develop the habit of finishing whatever task is started.
> 13. Conquer procrastination and learn to do tasks now.
> 14. Make better time management a daily habit.
> 15. Never spend time on less important things when it could be spent on more important things.
> 16. Take time for yourself—time to relax, time to live, time to just be.
> 17. Develop a personal philosophy of time that is consistent with your values.
> 18. Know how you currently spend your time.
> 19. Identify your "prime productive time."
> 20. Do tomorrow's planning tonight.
> 21. Ask yourself often, "Why am I doing what I am doing right now?"
> 22. Handle each piece of paper only once.
> 23. Delegate whenever possible and delegate wisely.
> 24. Identify your high payoff items (80-20 principle).
>
> Source: Skillpath Seminars: Managing multiple projects, objective and deadlines, Mission, KS, 2011.

■ SUMMARY

This chapter has focused on how to better manage your energy to control one of our most precious and seemingly scarce resources—time. Time management is important to achieving any personal or professional goals, and it helps decrease frustration and anxiety in high achievers. Without time management, most professionals could never achieve their established goals, and for nurses many patient care activities would never be completed, perhaps resulting in poor patient outcomes. Susan's and Maura's experiences in the opening vignette are an example of what your life could be like in nursing, unless strategies for better self-management are implemented. Thus it is important in your professional career to initiate habits related to time management that will continue throughout the years. Start asking Lakein's question frequently throughout the day: "What is the best use of my time right now?" (Lakein, 1989). You may be surprised to learn that the answer does not coincide with your current activity. When that occurs, stop and implement the strategies for self-management to better control your time. You will become more productive and gain internal satisfaction as a result.

REFERENCES

Benner P: *From novice to expert: excellence and power in clinical nursing practice*, Upper Saddle River, NJ, 2001, Prentice-Hall.

Brafman O, Beckstrom RA: *The starfish and the spider*, New York, 2008, Penguin Group.

Childre D: *De-stress kit for the changing times*, Boulder Creek, CA, 2008, Institute of Hearthmath.

Emmett R: *Manage your time and reduce your stress: a handbook for the overworked, overscheduled, and overwhelmed*, New York, 2009, Walker.

Goleman D: *Emotional intelligence 10th anniversary edition: why it can matter more than IQ*, New York, 2006, Bantam Books.

Krichbaum K, Peden-McAlpine C, Diemert C, et al: Designing a measure of complexity compression in registered nurses, *Western Journal of Nursing Research* 33:7–25, 2011.

Koch R: *Living the 80/20 way: work less, worry less, succeed more, enjoy more*, Boston, 2004, Nicholas Brealey.

Lakein A: *How to get control of your time and your life*, New York, 1989, Signet.

Larkin H: Will we make history? *Hosp Health Netw* 83(2): 20–25, 2009.

Lee F: *If Disney ran your hospital: 9½ things you would do differently*, Bozeman, MT, 2004, Second River Healthcare Press.

Loehr J, Schwartz T: *The power of full engagement*, New York, 2003, Free Press.

Mancini M: *Time management*, New York, 2003, McGraw-Hill.

Mindtools: *How to: delegating work to other people*, 2006. (website). http://www.mindtools.com. Accessed January 15, 2015.

Morgenstern J: *Time management from the inside out*, New York, 2004, Henry Holt.

Nightingale F: *Notes on nursing: what it is and what it is not*, New York, 1969, Dover.

Patterson K, Grenny J, McMillan R, et al: *Crucial conversations: tools for talking when the stakes are high*, ed 2, New York, 2011, McGraw-Hill.

Reid Ponte P: Nurse executive: the four principles of management. In Adams LT, O'Neil EH, editors: *Nurse executive: the purpose, process, and personnel of management*, New York, 2008, Springer.

Senge P: *The fifth discipline*, New York, 2006, Doubleday.

Skillpath Seminars: *Managing multiple projects, objective and deadlines*, Mission, KS, 2011, Skillpath.

Vestal K: Procrastination: frustrating or fatal? *Nurs Leadersh* 7(2):8–9, 2009.

Waterworth S: Time management strategies in nursing practice, *J Adv Nurs* 43(5):432–440, 2003.

26

The career path for nurses is long and wide.

Contemporary Nursing Roles and Career Opportunities

Robert W. Koch, DNS, RN

e Additional resources are available online at: *http://evolve.elsevier.com/Cherry/*

PROFESSIONAL/ETHICAL DILEMMA

Ashley Burton was excited to begin her new job in a small home care agency in a rural area some 30 miles from her city home. Although she had been a medical-surgical nurse for several years, she decided to try home care nursing after completing her population-focused community health course in her RN to BSN program. She was sure she could be a positive asset to the meet the growing needs of this rural community.

Ashley made an initial evaluation home visit to see 78-year-old Mr. Horace Brown, who lives with his granddaughter, Megan, and her three preschool children. He is being monitored after hospital discharge for complications of congestive heart failure. His blood pressure is elevated, and Ashley assesses some edema in his lower extremities. She also notes that Mr. Brown's room is littered with newspapers and paper plates of half eaten food. Ashley asks about his intake and finds out that he is not eating a low-sodium diet. Megan states that she tries to fix food that everyone can eat and

struggles to keep the house clean while working a part-time job. She tells Ashley that she does not know how they would make it without Mr. Brown's social security check each month. Mr. Brown keeps the children while Megan works, but she admits he has spent more time in bed the last week. Ashley considers how to address the fact that the money from Mr. Brown's check should be used for low-sodium foods. She also worries that the children are not being properly supervised by Mr. Brown when he is in bed and not well. The home situation is not optimal for Mr. Brown nor his grandchildren. Should Ashley chart what she sees or call her supervisor for advice? Should she discuss her concerns with Megan first? Is the situation one that should be reported to the Department of Human Services or maybe referred to the home care agency social worker? As a home care nurse, does she have the right or obligation to critique this home situation? This is so different from the hospital setting where she previously practiced.

VIGNETTE

When Eric Sanders graduated 15 years ago, he thought he would work in the hospital his entire career. However, with so many changes in the economic forces affecting health care and the resulting shift of clients outside acute care, more opportunities exist for him. Eric can take his skills and seek new ones to have a choice of practice roles and settings. Being a registered nurse now gives him more options for practice than he ever thought possible.

Questions to Consider While Reading this Chapter:

1. What practice opportunities exist for graduate nurses?
2. How can a new nurse gain knowledge about the role of the faith community nurse, forensic nurse, or other unique nursing roles?
3. What special skills do nurses working in community settings need?

KEY TERMS

Advanced practice nursing: Based on knowledge and skills acquired through basic nursing education, with licensure as a registered nurse (RN) and graduate education and experience that includes advanced nursing theory, physical assessment, psychosocial assessment, and treatment of illness. Includes nurse practitioners (NPs), certified nurse-midwives (CNMs), certified registered nurse anesthetists (CRNAs), and clinical nurse specialists (CNSs).

Interprofessional team: Health care team composed of professionals from different disciplines including chaplains, nurses, dietitians, pharmacists, physical therapists, physicians, respiratory therapists, social workers, and speech-language pathologists who cooperate, collaborate, communicate, and integrate care to ensure that care is continuous and reliable.

Nursing roles: (1) Traditional duties and responsibilities of the professional nurse, regardless of practice area or setting, such as the roles of care provider, educator, counselor, client advocate, change agent, leader and manager, researcher, and coordinator of the interprofessional health care team. (2) Duties and responsibilities of the professional nurse that are guided by specific professional standards of practice and usually carried out in a distinct practice area (e.g., flight nurse, forensic nurse, occupational nurse).

LEARNING OUTCOMES

After studying this chapter, the reader will be able to:

1. Evaluate the effect of the current health care environment on the future role of nurses.
2. Analyze the influence of current demographic characteristics of RNs in the United States on contemporary nursing roles.
3. Differentiate among various innovative nursing practice roles today.
4. Differentiate between the roles of advanced practice nurses and other RNs in various settings.

CHAPTER OVERVIEW

The health care system continues to change as social and economic factors create a state of constant evolution. Professional nurses respond by creating innovative alternatives to traditional nursing practice to meet these new challenges. As nurses proactively define solutions to today's health care challenges, multiple career opportunities emerge.

In the past, most nurses considered acute care hospitals the main practice setting available upon graduation. Few other career choices were available. Public health nursing was one of the exceptions, providing some variety in the nursing job market. As health care moves from inpatient treatment to outpatient and home care, and acute care shifts to health promotion and disease prevention, the U.S. culture seeks alternative options to meet this growing need. This shift in health care settings creates a variety of choices for nurses exploring career opportunities.

Nurses today have more liberty to explore and create job opportunities. Nurses may continue to select the hospital acute care setting or venture into less traditional nursing roles. Nurses must claim ownership of nontraditional roles as they emerge in the health care job market. As professionals, they should exercise their influence to develop and support new nursing roles.

This chapter presents an overview of some key opportunities available for RNs today in the United States. Included are demographics of today's nurses, in addition to implications for the future. This chapter examines the traditional and less traditional options available and the current and future issues for roles in professional practice.

NURSING—MUCH THE SAME, BUT BIGGER AND BETTER

In the past, describing the role of the RN was simple because there were few opportunities for variation. Today, exploring job opportunities for RNs is more complicated because nurses can practice in literally hundreds of diverse settings with a broad variety of clients. The proliferation of career opportunities for nurses is growing. Although nursing roles have expanded, the traditional functions of the nurse remain intact. Box 26-1 summarizes the roles nurses assume in any employment role or setting.

Care Provider

The role of care provider is basic to the nursing profession. The nurse assesses client resources, strengths and weaknesses, coping behaviors, and the environment to optimize the problem-solving and self-care abilities of the client and family. The nurse plans therapeutic interventions in collaboration with the client, physician, and other health care providers. In addition, the nurse takes responsibility for coordination of care that involves other health care professionals or resources, providing continuity and helping the client deal effectively with the health care system. Caring is always central to nursing interventions and is an essential attribute of the expert nurse.

Educator and Counselor

Multiple factors increase the need for nurses to serve as educators. Today, the emphasis is on health promotion and health maintenance, in addition to management of disease conditions. The role of nurse counselor has been elevated to new heights. Nurses encourage clients to look at alternatives, recognize their choices, and develop a sense of control in a rapidly changing health care environment.

BOX 26-1 **Professional Nursing Roles**
Care provider
Educator and counselor
Client advocate
Change agent
Leader and manager
Researcher
Coordinator of the interprofessional health care team

Client Advocate

Professional nurses find that the role of client advocate is essential in various situations with a multitude of client populations. Promoting what is best for the client, ensuring that the client's needs are met, and protecting the client's rights remain important responsibilities of the professional nurse.

Change Agent

When nurses first adopted the role of "change agent," few individuals anticipated to what extent nurses would fulfill this role. However, nurses have expanded their role as change agents in many ways. The profession continues to identify client, patient safety, and health care delivery problems; assess individual and organizational motivation and capacity for change; determine alternative and explore possible outcomes of the alternatives; and assess cost-effective resources in infinite health-related situations.

Leader and Manager

The leadership role of the professional nurse is paramount to the health care system. Nursing leadership varies according to the level of application and includes the following:

- Improving the health status and potential of individuals or families
- Ensuring that safe, high-quality care is provided across all health care settings
- Increasing the effectiveness and level of satisfaction among professional colleagues providing care
- Managing multiple resources in a health care facility
- Elevating citizens' and legislators' attitudes toward and expectations of the nursing profession and the health care system

The management role of the nurse has become more important. Nursing management includes planning, giving direction, and monitoring and evaluating nursing care of individuals, groups, families, and communities.

Researcher

During the past decades, nursing has taken its place among other disciplines in the production and use of research specific to its profession. Although the majority of researchers in nursing are prepared at the doctoral and postdoctoral levels, an increasing number of clinicians with master's degrees are participating in research as part of their advanced practice role. Nurses prepared at the baccalaureate and associate degree levels are also participating in research. These nurses may be assisting with data collection, critiquing research findings, and using these findings in practice. More nursing interventions are based on nursing research than in the past.

Coordinator of the Interprofessional Health Care Team

Interprofessional teams consist of collaborative practice relationships among several disciplines of health care professionals. These disciplines may include nursing, medicine, pharmacy, nutrition, social work, case management, and other allied health professionals, such as physical therapists, respiratory therapists, occupational therapists, and speech therapists. Chaplains or pastoral care representatives also serve a valuable role on the interprofessional health care team. These teams are found in all health care delivery settings and function most effectively when their focus revolves around the needs of the client.

Interprofessional teams are valuable because professional members bring in-depth and specialized knowledge and skills to the interaction process. In an age of rapidly expanding information, the roles of interprofessional team members complement one another. Through the formal and informal communication of ideas and opinions of team members, health care plans are determined. A plan of care developed by the interprofessional team is considered a valuable health management tool.

Interprofessional teams refer to coordination between and among disciplines involved in providing client care. The collaborative process involved in interprofessional health care transcends a single health profession to create comprehensive work outcomes. This team process can improve the quality of care, enhance client satisfaction, strengthen nursing satisfaction, and reduce hospital costs by decreasing hospital length of stay and increasing nurse retention.

Successful health care team models that use concepts related to interprofessional health care include pain management, nutritional support, skin care, rehabilitation, mental health, and hospice. Discharge planning, a major focus of health care delivery in the 1980s, involves developing a plan of treatment that ultimately results in the discharge of the client from the health care facility. This practice is built on the concept of interprofessional care, with each discipline involved in developing the discharge plan.

Client education is another area in which collaboration of disciplines is absolutely essential. Health care professionals must understand one another's contributions to client education and ensure that the information clients and families receive is consistent and complete. This will produce the best possible health outcomes for clients and families.

Box 26-2 lists some common roles of interprofessional health care team members with the website of

---

BOX 26-2   Interprofessional Health Care Team Members

Nurse (RN): Often the coordinator of the team. RNs take licensure examinations after completing associate degree, diploma, or baccalaureate degree preparation from an accredited school of nursing. RNs are able to obtain specialty certification for advanced skills and/or advanced degrees. RNs use the nursing process in client care in any health care setting.
American Nurses Association
www.nursingworld.org

Physician (MD or DO): Often the leader of the team, the physician diagnoses and prescribes treatment interventions for clients. Medical doctors (MDs) or doctors of osteopathy (DOs) complete 4 years of medical school and board examinations. Physicians can complete postgraduate training, including internship, residency, and fellowship training in a specialty area. Physicians also complete state licensing examinations and function in all health care arenas.
American Medical Association
www.ama-assn.org

Pharmacist (RPh or PharmD): Responsible for providing drug therapy for positive client outcomes; activities include drug information services, client and health care staff education, dispensing medications and client monitoring, adverse drug reaction reporting, research, concurrent drug use evaluation, and consultative services in areas such as pain management and nutritional support. Pharmacists complete baccalaureate preparation, an internship period, and licensing board examinations. Pharmacists can complete additional specialized training, certifications, and/or advanced degrees. In some states, the PharmD, or doctor of

BOX 26-2   Interprofessional Health Care Team Members—cont'd

pharmacy degree, is now the educational requirement for entering practice.
American Pharmaceutical Association
www.pharmacist.com

Physician assistant (PA): Works under the supervision of the MD or DO and performs assessments, procedures, or protocols approved by the physician. PAs complete a baccalaureate degree with specialized PA training (usually 2 years) and state licensure.
American Academy of Physician Assistants
www.aapa.org

Dietitian (RD or LD): Provides nutritional therapy and support to ensure that the nutritional needs of the client are met. Activities include involving both client and family in dietary assessment and teaching, identifying resources for food purchase and preparation, and identifying areas of food-drug interactions. Dietitians complete a baccalaureate degree from an accredited nutrition or food service administration program and national board examinations and may also complete state licensure and advanced educational preparation.
American Dietetic Association
www.eatright.org

Physical therapist (PT): Attends to the client's needs for movement. Activities include assessing physical strength and mobility needs and developing a plan of strengthening exercises for the client with movement dysfunction, maintaining range of motion and muscle tone, and identifying assistive devices that may be needed. A physical therapist may also be expert in the area of wound care. The basic educational requirement is a baccalaureate degree in a physical therapy program and completion of a national certifying examination. Advanced degrees are available.
American Physical Therapy Association
www.apta.org

Speech-language pathologist (SLP): Assists clients who are communicatively impaired by intervening in speech, language, and/or swallowing disorders related to receptive language, expressive language, speech intelligibility, voice disorders, alaryngeal speech, or prosody and cognitive impairments; plays an important role in evaluation and treatment of swallowing disorders. Therapists complete a master's degree from an accredited school, a 1-year fellowship, and a national certifying examination.
American Speech-Language-Hearing Association
www.asha.org

Occupational therapist (OT): Plans activities that assist and teach clients with physical disabilities to become independent in activities of daily living, such as dressing, grooming, bathing, and eating. Once self-care goals have been met, the OT can help the client perform daily

responsibilities of caring for a home and/or returning to work. Educational requirements include completion of an occupational therapy program of study at the baccalaureate, graduate certification, or master's degree level. Graduates must complete a period of supervised clinical experience and state licensure examinations.
American Occupational Therapy Association
www.aota.org

Respiratory therapist (RT): Responsible for assessment and maintenance of the client's airway and respiratory equipment used for diagnosis and therapy of respiratory disorders. Activities include client assessment, aerosolized medication administration, sputum sampling, arterial and mixed venous blood sampling, pulmonary function testing, cardiopulmonary stress testing, and sleep studies; may also be involved in conducting pulmonary rehabilitation programs. RTs complete a program of study and take a national certifying examination. If the program of study is completed in an associate or bachelor's degree program, the level of credentialing examination is different.
American Association for Respiratory Care
www.aarc.org

Social worker: Uses skills to help clients, families, and communities address psychosocial needs. Activities include educating clients, families, and staff about community resources; discharge planning; financial counseling and identifying financial resources; crisis intervention; referring to community resources; abuse and neglect reporting; completing advanced directives; assisting with resolving ethical dilemmas; evaluating behavior and mental disorders; and conducting support groups. Social workers complete a minimum of baccalaureate preparation in the field and may pursue advanced degrees.
National Association of Social Workers
www.naswdc.org

Chaplain or pastoral representative: Attends to the spiritual and emotional needs of the client and family. Activities include providing pastoral counseling and support and sacramental ministry and liturgical celebrations; not all pastoral representatives share the same religion as the client or family members but must be able to acknowledge the differences among religions and help assist the person with spiritual needs. Basic education requirements vary based on the setting and religious affiliation. The Association for Clinical Pastoral Education is a multicultural, multifaith organization devoted to improving the quality of ministry and pastoral care offered by spiritual caregivers of all faiths.
Association for Clinical Pastoral Education
www.acpe.edu

their associated professional organization. These team members are involved in client care to varying degrees, depending on client needs for the specific talents and knowledge of each team member. This list contains selected professional roles, which contribute to the interprofessional health care team approach, but there may be more in a given team.

Case Study 26-1 provides an excellent example of the role of various members of the interprofessional health care team. Multiple professional caregivers provide health care within the limits of each provider's expertise. The joint efforts of all professionals provide the opportunity for a better overall outcome.

CASE STUDY 26-1

John was discussing a problem with a coworker over his cell phone as he approached the intersection. He did not notice the truck approaching on his left side, so he did not see the STOP sign. After evaluation in the emergency department, John was diagnosed as post–motor vehicle accident with multiple trauma, closed head injury, several rib and leg fractures, lacerations, and internal injuries. His physician ordered multiple diagnostic tests, laboratory tests, medications, and treatments. John's nurse monitored his physical status and carried out the orders written by the physician. The nurse organized the tests and procedures and managed his pain. The pharmacist reviewed and supplied the medications ordered and analyzed potential interaction effects of the multiple pharmaceutical agents. A respiratory therapist was consulted to perform breathing treatments to facilitate lung expansion and prevent respiratory complications. After surgical repair of his fractured leg, physical therapy was consulted to assess John's condition and his need for physical reconditioning. A plan of care was established to enhance his mobility. His long recuperation led to mild depression and spiritual distress. The nurse who assessed these symptoms made arrangements for the chaplain to visit John and discussed the possibility of pharmacotherapy for depression with the physician and pharmacist. Throughout John's period of care, all involved practitioners communicated their assessments and worked together to provide collaborative interventions for holistic care. In addition, all interprofessional team members collaborated in medical rounds and discharge planning meetings to plan and coordinate John's care.

NURSES TODAY: WHO ARE THEY, AND WHAT ARE THEY DOING?

The phrase "a typical nurse" became a misnomer as the profession entered the twenty-first century. Nursing roles are so diverse that no typical role or practice setting exists. Nurses are the largest component of the health care workforce, holding some 2.7 million jobs, with 61% working in a hospital setting. Projections state that nursing jobs will grow faster than other occupations due to the focus on preventive care, chronic disease, and increased demand for services by the aging baby boomer population. More specialties and diverse work options emerge as care shifts to outpatient settings for surgery, chemotherapy, and rehabilitation. Overall, jobs for nurses are projected to expand 19% between 2012 and 2022. Nurses can specialize in basically four ways: work or treatment setting, disease category or condition, organ or body system, or population. Some nurses specialize in more than one of these. Examples of specialization in work or treatment settings include ambulatory care nurses, critical care nurses, trauma or emergency nurses, home care nurses, holistic care nurses, medical-surgical nurses, hospice nurses, perioperative nurses, transplant nurses, psychiatric nurses, and rehabilitation nurses. Examples of nurses who specialize in disease category or condition are oncology nurses, addictions nurses, ostomy and wound care nurses, developmental disabilities nurses, diabetes management nurses, HIV-AIDS nurses, and genetics nurses. Organ or body systems can differentiate nurses as cardiovascular nurses, dermatology nurses, urology nurses, orthopedic nurses, nephrology nurses, gastroenterology nurses, gynecology nurses, ophthalmic nurses, or respiratory nurses. Nurses can be recognized by the population they serve, such as neonatology nurses, pediatric nurses, or gerontology nurses. Nurses such as CNSs, nurse anesthetists, nurse-midwives, and NPs have more direct patient contact, whereas case management nurses, infection control nurses, forensic nurses, legal nurses, nurse educators, nurse administrators, and nurse informaticists have little or no contact with patients. Truly, these diverse opportunities are increasing in the world of health care.

Demographics for Registered Nurses

In April 2013, the U.S. Health Resources and Services Administration (HRSA) issued a report defining trends in the nursing workforce. These trends are important in developing programs and policies to allow access to the health care. *The U.S. Nursing Workforce: Trends in Supply and Education* estimated 2.8 million RNs in the United States as of 2010. The study showed that some 55% of the RN workforce has a minimum of a bachelor's degree or higher. The RN workforce is becoming more diverse, with about 25% of the RNs being nonwhite and 9.1% being men. Although the RN workforce continues to age, the average age is now 44.6 years, with about one third older than 50. However, the RNs age 30 and younger have increased to about 15% of the workforce (HRSA, 2013).

Changes also are occurring in the educational preparation of RNs. The Institute of Medicine (IOM) nursing report *Future of Nursing: Leading Change, Advancing Health* recommended higher levels of education for nurses to prepare nurses for more complex care needed by sicker patients coupled with increased and sophisticated technologies. The IOM goal was to increase the proportion of nurses with a bachelor's degree to 80% by 2020. Currently about 55% of the RN workforce hold a bachelor's or higher degree. In 2011, some 28,000 nurses received their BSNs and about 26,200 achieved their master's or doctoral degrees. This represents an 86% increase in RN-BSN graduates annually and a 67% increase in nurses receiving graduate degrees over the past 4 years. The production of doctorally prepared nurses has tripled during the last 4 years (HRSA, 2013). The number of advanced practice registered nurses (APRNs) has continued to grow. Nurse practitioners (NPs) lead this group in numbers, followed by CNSs, nurse anesthetists, and nurse-midwives (HRSA, 2013). Nurse practitioner numbers have increased 69% over the past 11 years with some 154,000 documented in 2012. About 96% work in direct patient care with one third in hospitals and half in ambulatory care settings (HRSA, 2012). The Health Resources and Services Administration (HRSA) is part of the U.S. Department of Health and Human Services. The Bureau of Health Professions, a division of the HRSA, provides national information on the health professions workforce in this country. You can explore demographic changes in nursing online at http://bhpr.hrsa.gov/healthworkforce/reports/nursingworkforce/nursingworkforcefullreport.pdf.

Hospital Opportunities

Despite enormous changes in health care, jobs in the hospital environment will be available for a long time.

In the hospital, a nurse provides direct care for people who are ill and unable to care for themselves. Another function of the direct-care role is to help the client and family in managing the illness event. Hospital positions can range from staff nurse to administrator and may entail any of the clinical specialties and most of the nursing roles identified in Table 26-1. Determining the area of clinical interest depends mainly on personal preferences.

Depending on the region of the United States, the new graduate's degree of choice in the clinical setting is highly variable. However, if the desired arena for work in hospital-based acute care is not available, it may be wise to accept an alternate position, watchful of an opportunity to transfer when a position becomes available in an area of clinical preference. Such an approach is perceived as a willingness to be flexible and to learn. Accepting assignments in an open, cooperative spirit provides more opportunities for the novice nurse to learn about the organization and gain important experiences. Furthermore, working as a staff nurse offers diverse learning opportunities in addition to the immediate client-centered ones.

If the choice of the clinical setting has been based on experiences as a student, the new graduate needs to be prepared to have different perceptions in a new role. Experiences that are highly enjoyable on the limited-time basis of a student schedule may feel different when the new graduate functions in that role full time. It is good to have a mix of experiences and learning opportunities before making a definitive decision.

TABLE 26-1 **Trends in Health Care Delivery Systems**	
From	**To**
Acute inpatient care	Lifespan care
Focus on the individual	Focus on aggregates or populations
Product of care orientation	Value of care orientation
Number of hospital admissions	Number of lives covered (capitation)
Managing organizations	Managing networks
Managing departments	Managing markets
Coordinating services	Documenting quality and outcomes

Misleading perceptions about functioning in various clinical arenas are not limited to new graduates. Often a person perceives or believes that one clinical area is the ideal choice, only to find that it is not what he or she wanted. For example, Jane Patrick, RN, wanted to work with sick children and successfully landed a position on the pediatric unit after a couple of years of experience as a staff nurse on an adult surgical wing. Despite her eagerness for the position, Jane found it difficult to adjust to the unit. The distress of the children in the unit was painful to her, and she found herself depressed and unhappy. She began to dream about the children for whom she was caring and was increasingly unable to provide nursing intervention that entailed discomfort for the child. Jane was not in the right practice setting.

Nurses must stay attuned to their reactions and respond in a constructive manner to self-discovery. Internal transfers in large hospitals and health care organizations offer a continuum of care; the probability is high that the nurse will find a position that is deeply satisfying in another area.

In addition to clinical emphasis, nursing within hospitals offers almost endless opportunities for diversity. Staff level positions in a hospital can be on many different units, and working different shifts on those units, presents different work environments, approaches to work, and priorities for client care. Some examples follow.

Infection Control

The infection control nurse assesses the total incidence of infections within the hospital. Clients who suffer an infection while in the hospital are comprehensively reviewed to ensure prompt and accurate treatment and timely containment of the client's infection so that it is not passed to other clients or staff. The infection control nurse must also conduct a thorough analysis to determine the source of the infection and its onset. If the infection is determined to have been contracted during hospitalization, an investigation is initiated to assess the sequence of events leading up to the infection. An action plan is developed to prevent future occurrences. A position such as this enables the nurse to have hospital-wide interactions and functioning. Knowledge of epidemiology and outstanding interpersonal skills foster full participation in the infection assessment process. Infection control nurses may work in community settings and hospitals.

Quality Management

Although the parameters of a position in quality management may vary from setting to setting, the basic premise is to ensure that outcomes in client care services are consistent with established standards. Benchmarking activities to establish such standards have been under way on a national level for the past few decades. Quality management nurses assess the compliance of the agency or institution with established standards and explore variations from these established standards. Chart reviews and ongoing interaction with the staff of the agency are integral components of a quality management position. Chapter 22 provides a more in-depth overview of the quality management process.

Specific Client Services

An almost endless list of specific client services can be found in hospitals, depending on the hospital's size and function within the community. Some nursing positions might be self-evident, such as the intravenous team on which the nurse provides support and interventions with the insertion and maintenance of intravenous therapies. Other services might relate to ostomy care, counseling, support groups, or health education related to a specialty area.

Coordinator Positions

Some hospitals have various coordinator positions, such as trauma nurse coordinator. The nurse in this position is responsible for the coordination and integration of the clinical and administrative requirements of the trauma victim. Consisting of equal parts of program and case management, the trauma nurse coordinator role involves overseeing the care of the client from the point of injury through acute care to rehabilitation and back to home. Maintenance of a comprehensive database on the management of trauma victims is an important part of this position. Another example of a coordinator position for a highly specialized area is the organ donor coordinator, who procures organs and oversees the transplantation program. Coordinators require considerable experience in the specialty in which they practice.

Variations on Traditional Roles in Nursing

As clients shift from hospital to ambulatory and home care, the role of the community nurse has evolved beyond the traditional public health nurse concept.

Although still based in the framework of the traditional public health nurse concept, nurses today transfer their critical care skills from the acute care setting into the home, where clients recover from illness and surgery. Pharmacologic and technologic advances make the care of chronic and critically ill clients in their homes a cost-effective option. For example, therapies such as dobutamine administration or chemotherapy were once considered too risky for home administration. Today, adequate teaching of the client and family members and careful monitoring make these therapies a daily occurrence in clients' homes.

Clients can be monitored through home visits by RNs, expanded technology, radiographs, or telemetry at home. Uterine monitoring for high-risk obstetric clients is common as vital signs of the mother and baby are recorded and sent for review by nurses or doctors at a separate location by telephone modem. All of these changes increase the need for home health care nurses who are expert clinicians and client educators.

Hospice Nurse

As more clients with terminal illness choose to stop aggressive treatment, hospice nursing has flourished. About 5800 hospice programs exist in the United States. This estimate includes both primary locations and satellite offices. Hospices are located in all 50 states, the District of Columbia, Puerto Rico, Guam and the U.S. Virgin Islands. The growth of hospice was seen by the 1.5-1.6 million clients receiving these services in 2013. The growth of hospice was seen by the 1.5-1.6 million clients receiving these services in 2013 (NHPCO Facts and Figures, 2014).

Hospice and palliative care nurses treat the symptoms of those with progressive terminal disease. These nurses work holistically with clients and families to maximize quality of life rather than focus on the quantity of life remaining. To learn more about the hospice concept, visit the NHPCO website at http://www.nhpco.org/about-nhpco.

Informatics Nurse Specialist

As health care systems face the inevitable need for enhanced data management for decision making in diverse practice settings, another nursing role has emerged—the informatics nurse specialist. Nursing informatics (NI) focuses on management and processing of health care information. The American Nursing Information Association (ANIA) describes the specialty's charge as "integrating nursing science, computer science and information science to manage and communicate data, information, knowledge and wisdom in nursing and informatics practice." The organization claims the logo tagline "Where caring and technology meet" (ANIA, 2014).

The Joint Commission (TJC) recognized the increased need for information management in the clinical client care settings. The 1994 Joint Commission standards define information management as critical to organizational success. Nurses are well positioned to assume these roles because they best understand client care processes. The American Nurses Credentialing Center (ANCC) has developed a certification examination for nurses who demonstrate beginning levels of competency to become certified as informatics nurses. The American Nurses Association (ANA) *Scope and Standards of Nursing Informatics Practice* states:

> *"Nursing informatics is a specialty that integrates nursing science, computer science, and information science to manage and communicate data, information, knowledge and wisdom in nursing practice. NI supports consumers, patients, nurses, and other providers in their decision making in all roles and settings. This support is accomplished through the use of information structures, information processes, and information technology."*
> **American Nurses Association (ANA), 2008**

Emerging roles for informatics nurses include working as researchers, consultants, managers, educators, and product and web designers. More information is available on the ANA Informatics Association website https://www.ania.org/.

Occupational Health Opportunities

Nursing within the framework of specific occupational groups (e.g., automobile manufacturing, textile plants) has long been a career option for nurses. Within these settings, the nurse designs and implements a program of health promotion and disease prevention for employees and assists with immediate health needs as necessary. In this primary care milieu, the nurse assesses the need for programs about specific topics of importance to the health of the employees. Some examples of these might be breast-screening programs for female employees and information on early identification of prostate cancer for male employees. Other programs might revolve around the management of developmental events such as empty nest syndrome, menopause, care for aging parents, or retirement.

In addition to services related to maintaining the health of employees, the occupational nurse is responsible for the assessment of the work environment to ensure the safety of the employees. Examples of significant environmental improvements in the health of U.S. workers are clean air programs, anti–smoking-on-the-job campaigns, and eliminating the use of asbestos in heating or insulation of buildings. All these activities pose special challenges to the occupational health nurse. The nurse in this setting develops procedures to be followed in the event of illness at work, including the management of health care emergencies.

Opportunities also exist in specific industries. For example, within the airline industry the nurse is responsible for airline safety through maintaining the health of employees. Protection of the employee's health is a component of the role, as is the effect of the health of the employee on the safety of the airline and its passengers. The nurse must be vigilant in the assessment of employee health problems that could affect overall airline safety. An obvious function is alcohol and drug screening. Protocols for the maintenance of employee health programs in the airline industry must be strictly followed and enforced as required by government regulation.

Nonetheless, the heart of this nursing position still lies with providing care to people, which sometimes can place the nurse in a difficult position. In the ongoing monitoring of the health of the employees, the nurse often is the first to spot a deviation from health that could affect the career and livelihood of an employee. Such an example is hypertension. If an employee is developing high blood pressure, which will affect his or her employment status, that employee may encourage the nurse to "hear" the blood pressure in the qualifying range.

Occupational health and employment screening activities are entwined with urgent care and travel assistance for passengers. Although occasionally an emergency situation develops with a passenger or an employee, most of the client problems are neither -emergency nor travel related. For example, international travel to some countries requires comprehensive precautions regarding immunizations and inoculations. Airport nurses were critical in screening passengers on international flights during such times as with the severe acute respiratory syndrome (SARS) crisis in 2003 or the Ebola crisis in 2014. Also, passengers may forget prescribed medications, or medications may be lost in baggage. Short-term problems, such as fear of flying, are also managed.

Another form of transportation provides a career opportunity: cruise ship nurse. In general, when people think of taking a cruise, they do not plan on getting sick—nor do nurses usually consider career possibilities in the industry. However, many cruise ships are as large as small cities. The role of the nurse in this setting is similar to that of the airline nurse with respect to the health of the employees and the safety of the passengers. The unique elements of the ship relate to special sanitation requirements, such as testing and culturing the water supply, and managing the total health needs of the passengers. The nurse is responsible for instructing the staff on the basic elements of emergency care and transport. The nurse should be proficient in Basic Life Support (BLS) and Advanced Cardiac Life Support (ACLS). Primary patient care needs are similar to those found in an emergency department. Cruise ships also offer opportunities for nurse practitioners. Additional career information can be found at www.cruiseshipjob.com/medical.htm.

Quality Manager

Another role that is attractive to nurses is that of quality manager. This reflects the need for health care providers to assess opportunities for process improvement, implement changes, measure outcomes, and then start the improvement process over again. Quality management nurses research and describe findings and look for opportunities to improve care. The result of quality assessment studies may produce critical pathways or algorithms defining care and expected client outcomes. Basic and advanced knowledge of quality management tools is essential, although practice may vary from setting to setting. For instance, in the inpatient setting, the quality management nurse needs strong clinical skills, such as those that might be acquired in medical-surgical practice, intensive care units, or the operating room. Experience in home care would be an advantage for a quality management nurse if employed in that setting. Interpersonal skills are important because to be successful in this role, the nurse must build relationships and rapport with people and groups across the organization. The role of quality manager is one that promotes improved care for health care recipients in a variety of settings. For more information, visit the quality management websites and see Chapter 22.

Case Manager

This role has had a rich tradition in community and public health nursing and now has gained more prominence in acute care. Case managers coordinate resources to achieve health care outcomes based on quality, access, and cost. The complexity of case management practice is obvious in the era of chaotic systems caused by changes in the health care market, in which providers, services, and coverage details are constantly changing. Case managers identify the best resources at the lowest cost to achieve the optimal health outcome for the client. Case managers are often nurses but can also be other professionals such as medical social workers.

Flight Nurse

Flight nursing is a specialty for nurses who desire autonomous practice and the opportunity to use advanced clinical skills. Practice is diverse because clients are all ages and from all backgrounds with different health problems. Critical care experience, with certification in advanced cardiac life support, is necessary. Most programs prefer experienced nurses in critical care and/or emergency department nursing. The two types of flight practice available are military, such as in the Air Force Reserves or active duty, and civilian flight nursing. To learn more, visit the website titled "So, you wanna be a flight nurse?" Nurses who enjoy a fast-paced diverse practice in an unstructured setting may find this role a good fit. For more information, call the Air and Surface Transport Nurses Association, formerly known as the National Flight Nurse Association, at 1-800-897-NFNA (6362), or visit their website at www.flyingnurse.com.

Telephone Triage Nurse (Telehealth nurse)

Another career option is that of telehealth nurse. Telehealth uses technology to provide health services by various telecommunication tools. With a shortage of nurses and increased aging population with chronic diseases, telehealth can be a cost-effective way to reach more patients and monitor patient health in a timely way. The many opportunities to use telehealth are increasing with the expanding world of technology.

Telehealth nurses interact with clients through telephones, video devices, or computers to assess needs, intervene, and evaluate patient care. Telehealth nurses work in a variety of settings, including home telehealth care where patients who are homebound, have debilitating disease, or live in remote areas can be monitored. Patient education can be provided using telehealth with online videos, podcasts, MP3s, and webcasts or webinars.

Telephone triage nurses utilize physician-approved protocols to guide clients to the most effective and cost-efficient level of care while educating and supporting the client to relieve anxiety. This position requires excellent communication and assessment skills, in addition to problem-solving and crisis management skills. Telephone triage is used in a variety of settings, including emergency departments, physician practices, crisis centers, and health maintenance organization (HMO) health plans (McGonigle and Mastrian, 2012).

Forensic Nurse

Forensic nursing may well be one of the fastest-growing nursing specialties in the twenty-first century. This is likely caused by the epidemic increase in violence and resulting trauma in the United States. The ANA and the International Association of Forensic Nurses 2009 report, *Forensic Nursing: Scope and Standards of Practice*, serves as a professional guide for nurses working in or entering this evolving specialty. Forensic nursing applies nursing science to public or legal proceedings in the scientific investigation and treatment of trauma and/or death of victims of violence, abuse, criminal activity, and traumatic accidents. The forensic nurse may provide direct services to individual clients and consult with and/or be an expert witness for medical and law enforcement. To learn more about this exciting practice, visit the International Association of Forensic Nurses (IAFN) website http://www.forensicnurses.org/. The American Forensic Nurses', Inc. offers distance-learning programs through the Internet.)

School Nurse

Most registered professional nurses employed in school health are generalists prepared at the baccalaureate level who function as consultants or coordinators. The newer role for school nurses is school health manager or coordinator and includes functions, such as policy-making, case management and program management activities, and health promotion and protection activities. The National Association of School Nurses defines the role as "a specialized practice of professional nursing that advances the well-being, academic success, and life-long achievement of students. To that end, school nurses facilitate positive student responses to normal development; promote health and safety; intervene with actual and potential health problems; provide case management services; and actively collaborate with others to build student and family capacity for adaptation, self-management, self-advocacy, and learning" (National Association of School Nurses, 2012).

Travel Nurse

For the person who wants to travel and still work as a nurse, travel nursing may be an answer. This role is expanding as the demand for nurses grows nation-wide. Benefits and company programs vary, but many include travel reimbursement allowance for assignments, in addition to free housing, free insurance, travel money, free phone card use, and other benefits. Sign-on bonuses may also be offered. If these benefits are not important to the nurse, higher wages may be available. Some companies allow nurses' pets to travel with them. Assignments are usually for a minimum time, such as 12 weeks, but others may last as long as 1 year. For more information, visit http://healthcaretraveler.modernmedicine.com.

Faith Community Nurse

The role of faith community nurse (FCN), known previously as the parish nurse, is a recognized specialty in a growing professional practice. In 1998 the ANA, in collaboration with the Health Ministries Association (HMA), established the scope and standards of this professional practice. This role addresses holistic health promotion for oneself, others, and the community within the beliefs, values, and practices of various faiths, countries, and cultures. This professional practice focuses on the intentional care of the spirit as the client seeks wholeness in mind, body, and spirit (Church Health Center, 2014). In these contexts, health is seen as a sense of physical, psychological, social, and spiritual well-being. Health is further viewed as being in harmony with self, others, the environment, and God. "Nurses have long observed that when illness and brokenness occurs, health care consumers—whether individually or with their family and friends—may turn to their source of spiritual strength for reassurance, support, and healing" (ANA and HMA, 2012). "The

primary focus of the FCN is the intentional care of the spirit, differentiating this specialty practice from the general practice of the registered nurse" (ANA and HMA, 2012)

A faith community nurse is a registered professional nurse who is actively licensed in a given state and who serves as a member of the staff of a faith community. The FCN promotes health as wholeness of the faith community, its groups, families, and individual members through the practice of nursing as defined by that state's nurse practice act in the jurisdiction in which the FCN practices and the standards of practice set forth in the ANA/HMA Scope and Standards of Practice for Faith Community Nursing (2012).

The faith community nurse functions in either a paid or unpaid position as counselor, teacher, referral agent, volunteer coordinator, and integrator of spiritual care and health. Although all communities do not have a hospital or clinic, most have a faith community, providing an exciting setting in which to teach disease prevention and health promotion.

The late Granger Westberg (1990), founder of this role in the mid-1980s, proposed that clergy can and already do more in the field of preventive medicine than traditional physicians. Westberg's efforts focused on getting the medical establishment to recognize faith communities as partners in keeping people well. He stated that churches, even though they may not realize it, are in the health business. In this role, faith community nurses participate in joint ministry with other staff members, helping to integrate faith and health for healing and wholeness. For more information on this practice, visit the website http://www.churchhealthcenter.org/fcnhome of the International Parish Nurse Resource Center, a ministry of the Church Health Center.

Nursing Educator

Preparation for nurse educators occurs at the graduate level and doctoral level. Nursing educators should be competent in clinical practice either at the advanced generalist or specialist level. They should be prepared in the specialty area in which they teach and match the needs of the institution that hires them. Nursing educators assume leadership in curriculum development, instruction, and evaluation. Knowledge of the learning process and classroom and clinical teaching methods that include engagement and "virtual teaching" is essential. Educators need to have a commitment to lifelong learning and to stay current in their practice. The role of faculty or nursing educator can be rewarding for those nurses who enjoy lifelong learning and mentoring. Individuals who assume these roles usually are expected to have not only teaching responsibilities, but evidence of scholarship and service to the community.

Other Unique Roles

Career opportunities described in this chapter should not be considered an exhaustive list of possibilities. Nurses now have selections for practice areas never before considered. Nurses should adopt an attitude of openness, an attitude of creativity, and a willingness to take a chance to explore these different possibilities. Nurses can allow their imaginations to take them to unknown settings or explore uncharted waters. To do this, they must develop confidence in their abilities and talents and be willing to venture outside the norm. Many websites have been developed to portray nursing as an attractive career with endless opportunities—one lists more than 50 categories of roles for nurses, with links and discussion areas. For those interested in public health, Pfizer offers a free online document called *Advancing Healthy Populations: The Pfizer Guide to Careers in Public Health* (http://www.soph.uab.edu/isoph/pfizer/PHCareerGuide.pdf).

There are those in the nursing profession who would limit the possibilities for the profession, claiming that many of the aforementioned alternatives are not really "nursing." However, this mindset severely diminishes the expansion of professional nursing in a changing health care environment. For nursing to thrive, new roles need to be defined and refined for future success of the discipline.

One way to settle this dispute within the nursing profession is to evaluate new nursing roles through the definition established by the ANA in nursing's social policy statement (2010):

> "Nursing is the protection, promotion, and optimization of health and abilities, prevention of illness and injury, alleviation of suffering through the diagnosis and treatment of human response, and advocacy in the care of individuals, families, communities and population."

Therefore, evolving nursing roles should be evaluated based on the ability of the new role to fit this accepted definition. Does the newly created role require assessment, diagnosis, planning, implementation, or evaluation to human responses? Does the newly created role require the knowledge and expertise of a professional nurse? By answering these questions, nurses can see that nursing is now more encompassing than "traditional" nursing.

ADVANCED PRACTICE NURSING

Much is written in the professional and lay literature about **advanced practice nursing**. Although new roles in advanced nursing may be forthcoming, the term *advanced practice nurse* (APN) includes nurse practitioners (NPs), certified nurse-midwives (CNMs), certified registered nurse anesthetists (CRNAs), and clinical nurse specialists (CNSs).

Each specialty of APN has unique differences, although they share key elements. All APNs make independent and collaborative health care decisions and engage in active practice as expert clinicians. APNs are educationally prepared through master's-level education to assume responsibility and accountability for the health promotion, assessment, diagnosis, and management of client problems, including the prescription of medication.

The Patient Protection and Affordable Care Act (PPACA) authorized a grant program that funds community-based Nurse-Managed Health Centers. These centers can be operated and managed by advanced practice nurses that meet the qualifications of the law.

Nurse Practitioner

Nurse practitioners engage in advanced practice in a variety of specialty areas, such as family, adult, pediatric, geriatric, women's health, school health, occupational health, mental health, emergency, and acute care. Typically, NPs assess, diagnose, and manage medical and nursing problems. Health promotion and maintenance, in addition to disease prevention, are the emphases of their practice. Some NPs diagnose and manage acute and chronic diseases of their selected population. NPs play a key role in the expansion of health care services under the PPACA. Almost half of the states in the United States allow NPs to practice without physician oversight. This means NPs may set up individual practices. In most states, the NP collaborates with a physician at least weekly. The volume of people needing primary care under the PPACA means more opportunities for expanded practice by NPs (Nurse Practitioner Schools, 2013).

Job responsibilities of NPs include taking client histories; conducting physical examinations; ordering, performing, and interpreting diagnostic tests; and prescribing pharmacologic agents, treatments, and therapies for the management of client conditions. Frequently the NP serves as a primary care provider and consultant for individuals, families, or communities.

NPs have advanced education, with specific emphasis on pathophysiology and pharmacology. Certification is achieved via written examination after the completion of a master's-level program. Several professional organizations offer certification for NPs. For example, the National Certification Board of Pediatric Nurse Practitioners certifies pediatric NPs; adult NPs or family NPs may be certified by the American Academy of Nurse Practitioners. NPs achieve registration and licensure by state boards of nursing or other designated agencies. The state boards of nursing regulate NP practice and prescriptive authority and can vary from state to state.

Clinical Nurse Specialist

Clinical nurse specialists are APNs who possess clinical expertise in a defined area of nursing practice for a selected client population or clinical setting, such as oncology, pediatrics, geriatrics, psychiatric-mental health, adult health, acute-critical care, and community health. This practice specialty emphasizes the diagnosis and management of human responses to actual or potential health problems.

The CNS functions as an expert clinician, educator, consultant, researcher, and administrator. The CNS monitors the care of clients and collaborates with physicians, nurses, and other members of the interprofessional health care team. The emphasis of this advanced nursing practice is to provide clinical support that improves client care and client outcomes.

CNSs are educated in graduate nursing programs. Their expertise is acquired from combining graduate study with clinical experience. The educational program for CNSs features an intense study of nursing theories and knowledge from other disciplines. Programs emphasize advanced scientific concepts, research methodologies, and supervised clinical practice.

CNSs practice within a systems model paradigm, which means that in performing their role CNSs evaluate each client in the context of his or her social environment. These APNs view clients as individuals who are part of a larger society entering a complex health care delivery system. This practice philosophy prompts the CNS to use a comprehensive approach to client care.

As consultants, CNSs are called on for expert clinical advice within and outside the clinical setting. Their consultation function frequently consists of problem solving with a client who may be a colleague, an individual, family, group, agency, or community. Problems may be related to provider competence, equipment, facilities, or health care delivery systems.

CNSs contribute to research in their area of specialization, generating and refining research questions, interpreting research findings, applying them to clinical practice, and educating other nurses about research findings. As teachers, CNSs educate clients, families, and communities. The CNS functions as a role model or preceptor for nurse generalists and students in a variety of clinical settings (AACN, 2006; ANA, 2010).

Certified Registered Nurse Anesthetist

Established in the late 1800s, nurse anesthesia is recognized as the first clinical nursing specialty. Nurse anesthesia practice developed in response to requests from surgeons seeking a solution to the high morbidity and mortality attributed to anesthesia at that time. The most famous nurse anesthetist of the nineteenth century, Alice Magaw, called the "mother of anesthesia," worked at St. Mary's Hospital in Rochester, Minnesota. Magaw was instrumental in establishing a showcase of professional excellence in anesthesia and surgery. In 1909, the first formal educational programs preparing nurse anesthetists were established.

Since World War I, nurse anesthetists have been the principal anesthesia providers in combat areas of every war in which the United States has been engaged. Although nurse anesthesia educational programs existed before World War I, the war sharply increased the demand for nurse anesthetists and, consequently, the need for more educational programs.

Founded in 1931, the American Association of Nurse Anesthetists (AANA) is the professional association representing about 47,000 nurse anesthetists nationwide. The AANA promotes education, practice standards, and guidelines and affords consultation to private and governmental entities regarding nurse anesthetists and their practice.

The AANA developed and implemented a certification program in 1945 and instituted mandatory recertification in 1978. The association established a mechanism for accreditation of nurse anesthesia educational programs in 1952.

The educational preparation of CRNAs occurs at the graduate level or in association with traditional institutions of higher education, most commonly in schools of nursing or health sciences. The educational curriculum in the anesthesia specialty ranges from 24 to 36 months in an integrated program of academic and clinical study. The academic curriculum consists of a minimum of 30 credit hours of formalized graduate study in courses such as advanced anatomy, physiology, pathophysiology, advanced pharmacology, principles of anesthesia practice, and research methodology and statistical analysis. All programs require approximately 1000 hours of hands-on clinical experience. Students gain experience with clients of all ages who require medical, obstetric, dental, and pediatric interventions.

Admission requirements to a nurse anesthesia educational program include a bachelor of science degree in nursing, licensure as an RN, and a minimum of 1 year of acute care nursing experience. Nurse anesthetists are required to successfully complete a written examination for certification as a CRNA.

Recertification, which includes practice and continuing education requirements, must be met every 2 years. CRNAs are qualified to make independent judgments relative to all aspects of anesthesia care based on their education, licensure, and certification. CRNAs provide anesthesia and anesthesia-related care on request, assignment, or referral by a client's physician, most often to facilitate diagnostic, therapeutic, or surgical procedures. In other instances, CRNAs perform consultation or assistance for management of pain associated with obstetric labor and delivery, management of acute or chronic ventilatory problems, or management of acute or chronic pain through the performance of selected diagnostic or therapeutic blocks.

The laws of every state permit CRNAs to work directly with a physician or other authorized health care professional, such as a dentist, without being supervised by an anesthesiologist. TJC does not require anesthesiologist supervision of CRNAs, nor does Medicare. In some cases, a provider, payer, or medical staff bylaws may require anesthesiologist supervision. However, these decisions are not based on legal requirements (AANA, 2009).

Certified Nurse-Midwife

According to the American College of Nurse-Midwives (ACNM), certified nurse-midwives are primary care providers of women's health care, focusing particularly on pregnancy, childbirth, the postpartum period, care of the newborn, and the family planning and gynecologic needs of women (ACNM, 2010). This practice occurs within a health care system that provides consultation, collaborative management, or referral, as indicated by the health status of the client.

The ACNM is educated in the two disciplines of nursing and midwifery and possesses evidence of certification according to the requirements of the ACNM. The ACNM has successfully completed prescribed studies in midwifery and has met the requisite qualifications to be certified. The ACNM is legally qualified to practice in one or more of the 50 states. The ACNM supports educational programs for CNMs at the certificate and the degree level but opposes mandatory degree requirements for state licensure.

The ACNM claims that mandatory degree requirements would limit access to maternity and gynecologic services for women. Several national reports specifically recommend placing greater reliance on CNMs to increase access to prenatal care for underserved populations. These reports also recommend that state laws be supportive of nurse-midwifery practice.

The entry-level nurse-midwife is a primary health care professional who independently provides care during pregnancy, birth, and the postpartum period for women and newborns within their communities. Therefore, the CNM is an individual who has successfully completed an ACNM-accredited educational program in nurse-midwifery and passed the national certification examination administered by the ACNM Certification Council. Midwifery care occurs within a variety of settings, including homes, birthing centers, clinics, and hospitals. The nurse-midwife works with each woman and her family to identify their unique physical, social, and emotional needs. Services provided by the CNM include education and health promotion. With additional education and experience, the nurse-midwife may provide well-woman gynecologic care, including family planning services. When the care required extends beyond the CNM's abilities, the midwife should have a mechanism for consultation and referral.

CNMs are an expanding group of professionals. In 2008, midwives in the United States numbered 18,492 as compared with 9232 in 2000 (Bureau of Health Professions, 2010). In 2010, there were 39 accredited nurse-midwifery education programs in the United States. Approximately 50.3% of CNMs have a master's degree. Nurse-midwifery practice is legal in all 50 states and the District of Columbia and is reimbursed by Medicaid in all 50 states. They can prescribe medications in 49 states. Areas of practice include care to women from puberty through menopause, including gynecologic and wellness services, family planning and contraception care, preconception counseling, prenatal care, labor through childbirth and afterbirth care, and menopause counseling and care.

Nurse Administrator or Nurse Executive

Although not formally considered an APN, the nurse administrator or nurse executive has an important advanced role within nursing. It is vital that individuals be knowledgeable about the business of the health care system and the profession of nursing. Nursing administration unites the leadership perspective of professional nursing with the various aspects of business and health administration. The practice of nursing administration focuses on the administration of health care systems for the purpose of delivering services to groups of clients.

Individuals who assume a nurse executive role typically hold a master's degree. Master's-level and doctoral-level programs that offer degrees in nursing administration are available, although some nursing executives are educated in additional disciplines such as business.

Nursing administration research focuses on organizational factors and management practices and their effect on nurses, health care delivery systems, and client outcomes. Nursing administration is concerned with establishing the costs of nursing care and examining relationships between nursing services and quality client care. Nurse executives view problems of nursing service delivery within a broader context of policy analysis and delivery of health care services.

Nursing administration is an integral part of any organization that provides health care. Nurse administrators lead and direct large groups of nurses and ancillary personnel. They manage large budgets and are responsible for provision of quality care at reasonable cost.

They serve at all management levels in health care organizations and in the community.

WHAT ABOUT THE FUTURE?

The future of nursing is brighter than ever. Many new jobs will result from continuous change in the health care environment. Growth of the nursing profession will be prompted by technologic advances in client care, which allow an increased number of health problems to be detected early and managed quickly. A greater number of sophisticated health-related procedures are already performed not only in hospitals but also in a variety of settings such as clinics and physicians' offices. Health maintenance organizations, ambulatory surgical centers, and church health centers are only a few of the places where the public receives health care. Nursing can be a vital component of the alternative setting movement that is part of health care reform.

As the focus of health care shifts to disease prevention and lifestyle modification, the opportunities for nurses will follow. Nursing also can benefit from the increased emphasis on primary care because prevention is the only true mechanism to reduce health care expenditures. Professional nursing services should be viewed as a cost-effective way to provide disease prevention and health promotion activities in multiple areas of the community, including industry, business, and commerce. Wellness and disease prevention, historically fundamental to the nursing profession, are becoming more meaningful and revitalized concepts within the larger health care system.

The need for the traditional role of the hospital nurse will always exist. In fact, with a shift to more community services, the intensity of hospital nursing care is likely to increase because only those in most need are treated there. Increases in client acuity will expand the need for professional nursing within the hospital setting. However, the most rapid growth for nursing employment is expected in outpatient facilities such as same-day surgery, rehabilitation, and chemotherapy infusion centers.

Nurses also will see job opportunities continue to develop in home health care. Many factors contribute to this phenomenon. The increasing numbers of older persons with disabilities require nursing care to minimize their functional loss and optimize their quality of life. Another factor that promotes home care is the consumer's preference for care in his or her own home.

Home care is a feasible option with recent technologic advances. Complex health care treatment that was once thought only possible in the hospital setting is now a reality in the home. Professional nurses who are able to perform complex procedures and comprehensive client assessments are invaluable to the home care industry.

Financial pressures on hospitals to discharge clients as soon as possible are producing increased admissions to nursing homes, skilled nursing facilities, and long-term rehabilitation units. In addition, because more individuals are living into their ninth and tenth decades, the number of people entering nursing homes or assisted-living facilities is increasing. The opportunity for nursing is tremendous in the long-term care arena because no other discipline can offer the multiple skills that nursing has to offer to the aging population.

Despite this bright outlook, the nursing profession must heed the old cliché that "opportunity only knocks once." If nurses fail to seize their opportunities, other less-qualified health care providers may attempt to move into this advantageous position. Nursing professionals must demonstrate their contributions to health care and publicly market their potential. Throughout history the nursing profession has requested a chance to prove its worth in producing cost-effective, quality health care—more than ever before, now is the time.

SUMMARY

This chapter has explored the various roles available to professional nurses today. Social and economic trends influencing the development of new nursing roles in innovative practice settings have been discussed. Nurses who are interested in developing new roles should be encouraged by the examples provided by nurses who first envisioned and created new roles. Traditional, nontraditional, and advanced practice nursing roles offer many exciting opportunities for professional growth and satisfaction. The diversity and challenge available to professional nurses today are unparalleled.

REFERENCES

American Association of Colleges of Nursing (AACN): *AACN statement of support for clinical nurse specialists*, 2006, Washington, DC. (website). http://www.aacn.nche.edu/publications/position/CNS.pdf. Accessed Oct 1, 2014.

American Association of Nurse Anesthetists: *Qualifications and capabilities of the certified registered nurse anesthetist*. (website). http://www.aana.com/ceandeducation/becomeacrna/Pages/Qualifications-and-Capabilities-of-the-Certified-Registered-Nurse-Anesthetist-.aspx. Accessed September 7, 2015.

American College of Nurse Midwives (ACNM): *Become a midwife*, 2010. (website). http://www.midwife.org. Accessed September 7, 2015.

American Nurses Association (ANA): *Scope and standards of nursing informatics practice*, Washington, DC, 2008, American Nurses Publishing.

American Nurses Association (ANA): *Nursing's social policy statement*, Washington, DC, 2010, American Nurses Publishing.

American Nurses Association (ANA): *Nursing: scope and standards of practice*, ed 2, Washington, DC, 2010a, American Nurses Association.

American Nurses Association (ANA) and Health Ministries Association (AHM): *Scope and standards of practice: Faith community nursing*, ed 2, Silver Spring, MD, 2012, Nursesbooks.org.

American Nurses Association (ANA) and the International Association of Forensic Nurses (IAFN): *Forensic nursing: scope and standards of practice*, Washington, DC, 2009, American Nurses Association.

American Nurses Informatics Association (ANIA): *About Us*, (website). https://www.ania.org/about-us. Accessed September 7, 2015.

Church Health Center: *What is Faith Community Nursing*, 2014. (website). http://churchhealthcenter.org/whatis-faithcommunitynursing. Accessed Oct 1 2014.

Bureau of Health Professions, Division of Nursing, Health Resources Services Administration: *The registered nurse population: findings from the 2008 National Sample Survey of Registered Nurses*, Washington, DC, 2010. (website). http://bhpr.hrsa.gov/healthworkforce/rnsurveys/rnsurveyfinal.pdf.

Health Resources and Services Administration (HRSA): *National Sample Survey of Nurse Practitioners*, 2012. (website). http://bhpr.hrsa.gov/healthworkforce/supplydemand/nursing/nursepractitionersurvey/index.html. Accessed October 3, 2014.

Health Resources and Services Administration (HRSA), Bureau of Health Professions National Center for Health Workforce Analysis, The U.S. Nursing Workforce: *Trends in Supply and Education-Results in Brief*, 2013. (website). http://bhpr.hrsa.gov/healthworkforce/supplydemand/nursing/nursingworkforce/. Accessed October 1, 2014.

IOM (Institute of Medicine): *The Future of Nursing: Leading Change, Advancing Health*, Washington, DC, 2011, The National Academies Press. (website). http://thefutureofnursing.org/sites/default/files/Front%20Matter%20%28R1-R26%29.pdf. Accessed Oct 1, 2014.

Lathrop B, Hodnicki D: "The Affordable Care Act: Primary Care and the Doctor of Nursing Practice Nurse", *OJIN: The Online Journal of Issues in Nursing* 19(2), March 31, 2014. http://www.nursingworld.org/MainMenuCategories/ANAMarketplace/ANAPeriodicals/OJIN/TableofContents/Vol-19-2014/No2-May-2014/Articles-Previous-Topics/Affordable-Care-Act-Doctor-of-Nursing-Practice.html?css=print. Accessed October 4, 2014.

McGonigle D, Mastrian K: *Nursing informatics and the foundation of knowledge*, ed 2, Burlington, MA, 2012, Jones and Bartlett.

National Association of School Nurses: *Planning a career in school nursing*, 2014. (website). http://www.nasn.org/RoleCareer/PlanningaCareerinSchoolNursing. Accessed Oct 1, 2014.

NHPCO Facts and Figures: *Hospice Care in America*, 2014, NPHCO. (website). http://www.nhpco.org/sites/default/files/public/Statistics_Research/2014_Facts_Figures.pdf. Accessed September 7, 2015.

Nurse Practitioner Schools and Degree Program Guide: *Nurse Practitioners and Their Role in the Affordable Care Act*, Feb 27, 2013. (website). http://www.nursepractitionerschoolguides.org/nurse-practitioners-and-their-role-in-the-affordable-care-act/. Accessed October 1, 2014.

Westberg GE: *The parish nurse: Providing a minister of health for your congregation*, Minneapolis Minnesota, 1990, Augsburg Fortress Press.

27

Finding the right match can be exciting.

Job Search:
Finding Your Match

*Susan R. Jacob, PhD, MSN, RN ***

ⓔ Additional resources are available online at: *http://evolve.elsevier.com/Cherry/*

PROFESSIONAL/ETHICAL ISSUE

Alice and Renardo had just finished their senior seminar class in which the nursing recruiters from the local hospital held a session on job interviewing. The recruiters told the class about potential job opportunities at their hospital and described their intensive 3-month orientation process for new graduates. The recruiters discussed the high cost of orienting one new nurse and told the class that it was well worth the investment to have the assurance that the new graduates would be skilled and comfortable in their new positions. The recruiters added that once the hospital made an investment in a new nurse, they expected a commitment of at least 2 years. Alice told Renardo she planned to apply at this hospital because it was likely there would be positions available, but she also planned to apply at the other local hospital closer to her home,

where she really wanted to work, even though there were currently no openings for new graduates. Renardo said, "I may hold out for the hospital I really want because I would hate to take a position and start orientation and then find out there were openings in the hospital that is my first choice." Alice responded, "Not me! I will take the first position I am offered, because I can always quit if I get a better offer." "Even if you have already started orientation?" asked Renardo. "Yes sir," Alice said. "I need to do what is best for me and my family."

What are the professional and ethical issues involved in Alice's plans to take a job and quit if a better offer comes along? What are the implications for the hospital and for other new graduates if Alice quits a job at the hospital after only a few weeks or months?

VIGNETTE

"For 2 years I've struggled to meet deadlines for term papers, nursing care plans, and examinations," sighed Leslie. "Now that graduation is almost here, I'm scared that I don't know enough to be a 'real nurse.' And I'm confused about where to begin and what kind of nursing position I should seek. This first job seems so important."

Questions to Consider while Reading this Chapter:

1. How should the new graduate in the scenario decide where to apply for that first position?
2. What kinds of questions should the applicant ask about a prospective position?
3. How can the applicant demonstrate knowledge, skills, and experience to the recruiter?

*We thank Kathryn S. Skinner, MS, RN, CS, and Laura H. Day, MS, BSN, RN, for their contributions to this chapter in the 4th edition.

KEY TERMS

Orientation: Activities that enhance adaptation to a new environment.

Portfolio: A collection of evidence demonstrating acquisition of skills, knowledge, and achievements related to a professional career.

Professional objective: Occupational position for which one aims.

Résumé: Summary of a job applicant's previous work experience and education.

LEARNING OUTCOMES

After studying this chapter, the reader will be able to:

1. Use the interview process to evaluate potential employment opportunities.
2. Prepare an effective résumé and nursing portfolio.
3. Compare and contrast various professional nursing employment opportunities.
4. Summarize the employment process.

CHAPTER OVERVIEW

This chapter helps student nurses prepare to successfully negotiate their first employment as professional nurses. They learn the importance of networking, researching available opportunities, and examining their personal aptitudes, interests, lifestyle priorities, and long-term goals to find the best job fit.

Readers are shown how to create and use cover letters and résumés to market themselves in written introductions and how to prepare for and actively participate in a recruitment interview. The chapter describes what can be expected from a recruiter and how to obtain the information needed to make thoughtful and rewarding job choices. Putting these recommendations into practice will ensure the new graduate of the best chance for finding a good job match as an entry-level nurse, practicing in a suitable work environment.

EXPLORING OPTIONS

The job market for graduate nurses is extensive. There are many opportunities in urban as well as rural areas. Health care economics ride a roller coaster from robust to lean times, but the high demand for the skills of professional registered nurses (RNs) remains constant, and the potential for finding suitable employment is good. Trends in health care delivery direct today's health care providers to change their orientation from disease to health and from inpatient to outpatient services, which leads to a growing need for professional nurses in nonacute community-based care settings, such as primary care clinics, ambulatory surgery centers, and home, school, and work environments. However, although rapid changes in health care delivery systems continue to create new and varied opportunities outside the acute care settings where nurses have traditionally practiced, hospitals remain the most likely starting place for new graduates to acquire general experience helpful in opening career path doors. In fact, with a nursing shortage there is an increased demand for nurses to work in acute care settings.

Numerous marketing strategies have been tried in an effort to aggressively attract bright, energetic new graduates in times of demand and short supply. For some institutions in selected areas of the country, cost seems irrelevant. Sign-on bonuses, expense-paid weekends to visit institutions in other parts of the United States, promises of tuition reimbursement for continued education, student loan repayment, and low-interest loans for new cars, just to name a few, have been offered as enticements. However, in other areas of the country, for the first time in several years, it is taking graduates longer to find employment than in the past, when it was common for new graduates to have promises of employment prior to graduation. Ultimately, being aware of one's own qualities and taking advantage of networking opportunities are more important keys to finding just the right match in today's job market.

Knowing Oneself

The choice of a first nursing position deserves careful study. For some, the opportunities seem to be a smorgasbord of possibilities, all of them attractive. The neophyte nurse should carefully explore any job under consideration and its responsibilities in light of his or her own personal qualities. Some students find it helpful to consult an instructor, job counselor, or a trusted nursing mentor for objective input and perspective. An experienced nurse can see the pros and cons that may not be visible to a new nurse. A thoughtful review of general interests, abilities, and strengths (especially those pointed out by clinical instructors) as well as awareness of the types of patients who have provided the greatest emotional reward are essential.

Other important considerations are one's physical and emotional stamina, energy level, and responsibilities to others—spouse, children, and other family members; volunteer commitments; and social activities—all of which make legitimate demands on one's schedule. Long-term goals must be factored into the first job choice as well. Is the first job a stepping-stone to an advanced degree, to a narrowly specialized area of nursing, to a traveling nurse position, or to a management role? Selection of a position that fits the nurse's abilities, lifestyle, and career aspirations will affect job satisfaction, career advancement, and overall sense of success and happiness.

Finding the right practice environment is essential to long-term success and job satisfaction. The American Association of Colleges of Nursing (AACN) developed a white paper titled *Hallmarks of the Professional Practice Environment,* which can be accessed at http://www.aacn.nche.edu/publications/hallmarks.pdf. Based on this paper, a brochure for nursing school graduates was developed, titled "What Every Nursing Student Should Know When Seeking Employment." This brochure identifies eight key characteristics, or hallmarks, of the professional practice setting and suggests that applicants ask the following questions about the employer they are considering. Does the potential employer:

- Manifest a philosophy of clinical care emphasizing quality, safety, interdisciplinary collaboration, continuity of care, and professional accountability?
- Recognize the value of nurses' expertise on clinical care quality and patient outcomes?
- Promote executive-level nursing leadership?

- Empower nurses' participation in clinical decision making and organization of clinical care systems?
- Demonstrate professional development support for nurses?
- Maintain clinical advancement programs based on education, certification, and advanced preparation?
- Create collaborative relationships among members of the health care team?
- Use technologic advances in clinical care and information systems?

Box 27-1 provides other statistics and information to request from a potential employer. The numbers of hospitals seeking and receiving Magnet hospital credentialing are growing, and where these work environments are available, the nurse may wish to consider these organizations. Generally, hospitals with Magnet status have demonstrated excellence in areas such as low RN turnover rates, adherence to standards of nursing care as defined by the American Nurses Association (ANA), and mechanisms in place for staff participation in decision making. A recent study by Kelly and colleagues (2011) found that Magnet hospitals had a more positive nurse work environment and outcomes, were more likely to have specialty certified nurses, and a higher percentage of baccalaureate-prepared nurses. The American Nurses Credentialing Center (ANCC) lists all Magnet hospitals

---

BOX 27-1 Statistics and Information That Applicants May Request from a Potential Employer

RN vacancy rate and RN turnover rate
Patient satisfaction scores (preferably a percentile ranking)
Employee satisfaction scores
Average tenure of nursing staff
Education mix of nursing staff
Percentage of registry or travelers used
Key human resources policies (e.g., reduction in workforce; tenure versus performance criteria)
Copy of the most recent TJC report and the number of contingencies cited
Information about whether the nurses are unionized
Copy of contract

From American Association of Colleges of Nursing: *What every nursing school graduate should consider when seeking employment,* Washington, DC, 2002, American Association of Colleges of Nursing.

on its website at www.nursingworld.org/ancc/magnet/getall.cfm.

Many graduate nurses have discovered that working in an environment that did not match well with their personal attributes and long-term goals not only made them unhappy but also damaged their future employment options. Poor job fits lead to frequent job changes, which could lead to poor references and the attachment of the label "job hopper."

Appropriate job choice is critically important and can be costly to the new graduate. Accordingly, an ineffective hiring decision can also be expensive for the employer. Hospitals routinely pay for drug testing and criminal background checks. The pre-employment costs alone can tally close to $2,000 before the person even steps in the hospital door to begin employment. Classroom and hospital orientation includes the salary of the graduate nurse (GN) and the nursing instructors. Additionally, various other paid employees teach mandatory classes, such as infection control and fire safety, and the GN gets an official welcome from the CEO.

Following the classroom orientation is one full month of classroom instruction before the nurse arrives on the patient care unit. This month of one-on-one instruction to review basic nursing skills incurs the cost of not only the graduate nurse's salary, but the salaries of nursing educators.

Subsequently, assignments are made for the graduate nurse to follow a preceptor for the next 4 to 6 months, depending on how quickly the nurse achieves competency in each area. This phase of the training process costs the hospital the graduate nurse's salary and the preceptor's salary.

In addition, the clinical nursing instructor, who follows the nurse through completion of orientation to eventual competency, is also paid for the duration of the process. The additional time it takes to teach is another consideration when adding up cost, a cost to which it is difficult to assign a dollar value. Other non specific cost considerations include the cost of provision of space required for the education of new staff. Included in this category would be building utilities, engineering staff that support the operation, housekeeping costs, and general administration costs associated with the procurement of new graduate nurses.

Some estimate the cost of recruiting, placing, and orienting a new nurse to be from two to two and a half times the average RN salary—but the costs are more than financial. It causes hard feelings between employers and the school of nursing and the recruit when a new nurse orients and then leaves (Arnold, 2012).

Critical to effective selection is high-level nurse leader competency in resource management processes and attention to creation of an effective healthful practice environment. A great decision on the part of the new graduate and the nurse leader will have better outcomes for the individual nurse in areas of job satisfaction and retention and overall organizational outcomes, employee engagement and retention, and patient outcomes.

Networking

The investigative process of researching potential employers begins with networking at school, in the community, and within student nurse organizations. One may question other nurses, employees, and former employees, especially alumni of one's own school, who have worked in various settings. Faculty will have pertinent observations based on their experiences with clinical sites in the community. It is also valuable to listen to neighbors, friends, and family members who have been patients.

Employment sections of newspapers, particularly Sunday editions, contain advertisements for job openings and provide names to contact for further information. Some employers now offer "phone-a-thons" inviting nurses to speak directly with recruiters or nursing department supervisors. Websites, open houses, health care job fairs and virtual online career events are great places to pick up information about institutions. Recruitment materials and brochures often contain interesting facts about the organization, such as the mission, vision, and values statements and goals, available services, and information about associate benefits.

The Internet offers links to actual jobs and information on career planning. Most hospital and large health care systems maintain websites to post their employment needs and invite applications online. The Internet is a cost-effective recruiting method, and larger health care systems expect early communications to take place by fax and e-mail. Applicants who use this method to follow-up on a job posting should pay particular attention to the application and résumé that is sent electronically, being sure to follow the online prompts correctly, making sure there are no errors before submitting materials online. To make sure your online information is secure, do not share your username or password with anyone. If there is no response to Internet inquiries within a week, applicants should follow up with a telephone call. Internet sites are helpful in exploring job opportunities, writing résumés, and preparing for employment interviews. If a new graduate is seeking a position in a large community with multiple job choices available, this informal research will help to narrow the list to the best place to begin the job application process. Later in the interview, the applicant may wish to describe to the recruiter how his or her search resulted in this employer being the number-one choice over others for the graduate's first job. This process of researching potential employers will continue through the interview process. Assessing the climate of the work environment is a valuable tool in "finding a match" and is discussed more thoroughly later in this chapter.

WRITTEN INTRODUCTIONS

Three of the most important steps in a job search are writing a cover letter, preparing a professional résumé, and assembling a professional portfolio. These tools introduce the applicant to a prospective employer. The first impression should be persuasive; there may not be a second chance. Presenting oneself on paper can make a difference, perhaps the difference between getting a desired interview and being passed over in favor of someone else. These written introductions should present a conscientious, mature, competent, committed professional who would be an asset to an agency that prides itself on its nursing services.

How to Write a Cover Letter

The cover letter (Box 27-2) is a chance to sell oneself and make the recruiter look forward to meeting an attractive candidate. A convincing cover letter will show how this candidate is different and convey to the recruiter why he or she is the best fit for the position. The letter should also address why this institution is the applicant's first choice.

A cover letter should reflect the nurse's own style of writing, should never appear to have been copied from a book, and should be tailored to the particular job. Like any business document it should be clean, direct, and

---

BOX 27-2 Cover Letter

April 8, 2015
Ms. Donna Henderson, MS, RN
Director of Nurse Recruitment
Charleston Memorial Hospital
1600 Beckley Avenue
Memphis, TN 38104
Dear Ms. Henderson:

I would like to apply for a new graduate position on a cardiology nursing unit at Charleston Memorial Hospital. After graduating from Smith College with a BSN on June 6, I will be ready to start work immediately. I plan to take the RN licensing examination in early July.

Through reading about your hospital and my own personal experience in a recent clinical rotation at Charleston Memorial, I have learned that your institution is a modern, professional one with an emphasis on quality patient care. For this and many other reasons, I am convinced that Charleston Memorial is where I want to work as a nurse.

I will be in Memphis from April 20 to April 25 and will call to schedule an appointment to see you then. My home phone number is 555-912-3120; my cell phone number is 555-200-9999.

I look forward to meeting you and discussing how I can contribute to Charleston Memorial Hospital.
Sincerely,
(Sign your name here in pen)
Bonnie McCray Pino
Enclosure

---

letter perfect. It should be attractive and effortless to read. There must be no obvious erasures, no typing errors, and no grammar or spelling mistakes. Everything should fit on a single page of 8.5 by 11-inch white heavyweight bond paper with ample margins on the top, bottom, and sides.

The letter should be addressed to a specific person. If the person's name or title is unknown, refer to a marketing brochure or call the recruitment office to ask for correct title and spelling of the appropriate person's first and last names.

If spelling is not your strength, use the spell-check tool on the computer, but do not depend on its accuracy. Using a dictionary and asking a competent friend to proofread the final copy is also a good idea. Poor typists would be well served to pay someone to type for them. A sloppy letter will cast doubt on one's abilities to practice as a professional.

The body of the letter should be single-spaced, three or four block paragraphs long, with a blank line between paragraphs, and organized as follows:

- Paragraph 1 should be a statement of purpose that tells the recruiter what kind of position is being sought, the writer's expected date of graduation, state licensing status, and the date the writer will be ready to begin work.
- Paragraph 2 should emphasize the writer's suitability. The implied message should be "I'm just the person for the job" without going into all the details that will be included in the résumé. A sentence should describe past work or educational experiences that relate to the agency's particular needs and philosophy. The more homework the nurse has done in learning about the institution, the more convinced the recruiter will be. Finally, refer to the enclosed résumé.
- Paragraph 3 should request an interview appointment and give a range of dates of availability. It is a good idea for the writer to promise a telephone call "next week" or "soon" to schedule a meeting time and provide a telephone number where the writer can be reached, if the number is different from the permanent telephone number listed on the résumé.
- The letter can end with a "written handshake," such as, "I look forward to meeting with you to discuss available nursing positions in your institution"—a cautiously optimistic note.
- The letter closes with "Sincerely," and after four lines of space for a signature, the writer's name is typed. A line is skipped, and "Enclosure" is typed on the left margin to indicate that a résumé is enclosed.

The letter should be proofread carefully, signed, and copied; and the copy filed. If the nurse has chosen to use different approaches with different institutions, it would be wise to review the cover letter before the interview.

One week later the writer should follow up by telephone to be sure the letter was received. This attention to detail and follow-through will impress the recruiter or personnel office and improve chances of getting an interview soon. These telephone calls usually become mini-interviews, and the applicant should be extra courteous, aware that it usually is the secretary who controls the interview schedule. By keeping a written list of all contacts made, the new graduate will be able to add the flattering personal touch of acknowledging previous telephone contacts when meeting them for the first time during the interview process.

The cover letter serves as the foundation on which all other follow-up is built: résumé, call for appointment, and interview. What is presented in the letter should prompt the person responsible for hiring to take a close look at the enclosed résumé.

How to Prepare a Résumé

A résumé is a short account of one's career or professional life (Box 27-3). The résumé is different from a curriculum vitae (CV), which is a chronologic account

---

BOX 27-3 Résumé

Bonnie McCray Pino
416 Melody Avenue
Bristol, TN 37620
555-912-3120 (Home)
555-200-9999 (Cell)
E-mail: bpino@xyz.com

Professional objective:	**Staff nurse position (cardiology)**
Licensure:	Eligible to take NCLEX® examination after June 6, 2015
	Anticipated date of NCLEX®: July 2015

Education:

2011 to 2015	Smith College School of Nursing Bristol, TN BSN, June 6, 2015
2009 to 2011	Oakview High School Nashville, TN Diploma, June 2011

Experience:

May 2011 to August 2011, St. Mary's Hospital, Knoxville, TN

Patient Care Assistant: Assisted RNs in providing basic nursing care including feeding, bathing, assisting with ADLs, and patient teaching in a pediatric setting

June 2012 to August 2012, Drs. Smith and Jones OB/GYN office, Bristol, TN

Office Assistant: Accompanied patients to treatment area; weighed patients and recorded vital signs

Honors:	Sigma Theta Tau International, 2014 *Who's Who Among American High School Students*

Professional Organizations:
Tennessee Student Nurses Association, 2012-2015
References: Provided on request

of one's entire educational and professional work experience, usually required by academic institutions for educator positions. The résumé is the most appropriate format for the new graduate and will complement the cover letter by filling in important details about educational and work experiences. It is important to provide accurate information because inaccurate information on a résumé or application can lead to dismissal later. An effective résumé should compress education and employment history into an attractive, easy-to-read one-page summary. A wealth of valuable information can be communicated simply and straightforwardly by saying more with less. The key is writing concisely. For example, "BSN with high honors" speaks for itself. Citing exact grade point average or "dean's list" standing adds little. Succinct ways to convey a message will be found by experimenting with phrases and word choices. Avoid pompous language and use of the passive voice. Instead use active verbs, such as *improved, established, trained, administered, prepared, wrote,* and *evaluated.* Pepper the résumé with such words, and it will read easily.

A basic résumé contains three essential sections: (1) identifying information; (2) education; and (3) work experience. In addition, optional information may include professional objectives, honors, achievements, and memberships in professional organizations. A well-designed résumé will mark the writer as a career-minded professional, just what recruiters are seeking. A succinct, well-organized résumé indicates that the applicant is focused and organized in other areas as well.

The first section of the résumé, the identifying information, contains the applicant's name, address, and home and work telephone numbers, followed by licensure information. The states of licensure and license numbers are listed. Graduating students should indicate when and where the National Council of Licensing Examination (NCLEX®) was taken or will be taken.

If the résumé writer opts to include a professional objective, it should come next. Some interviewers like to see this because it shows that the nurse has put some thought into career planning. Keep in mind, though, that it is limiting to put forth a singular objective that ties the nurse to only one particular clinical area. If there is no such opening available in that department, the recruiter will consider the applicant an unlikely candidate to pursue. It is better to have an objective statement that is broad and general.

The second section should include details about education, including degrees and diplomas awarded, names and locations of schools, and graduation dates, starting with the most recent graduation and degree in reverse chronologic order.

The third section will present the information apt to be the greatest help in obtaining a job: work experience and employment history. Many recruiters are nurses themselves, so a detailed description of what a routine job entails is not needed. Instead efforts should be directed toward illustrating any special knowledge or contributions. The new graduate's résumé might reflect student accomplishments or elaborate on jobs in which he or she has demonstrated skills also applicable to nursing responsibilities, such as organization of tasks, time management, delegation to subordinates, and ability to work well with others. Start with current or most recent position and work backward, including place of employment, job title, dates worked, and responsibilities. List accomplishments while employed, including number and type of patients cared for, any special techniques used, or any participation in the development of programs, policies, or forms pertinent to the position.

This section closes with optional information, such as seminars attended, honors received, and memberships in professional organizations. It is not advisable to list community activities or activities from more than 5 years ago unless it can be clearly shown that they are pertinent to a nursing career. Similarly, exclude personal information, such as marital and health status, age, number of children, and hobbies. This information is not job related and should not be used by the employer to screen applicants.

References do not need to be included in the résumé, but should be ready for presentation in a neatly typed, photocopied list when requested from any future employer. Simply state, "references provided on request" or "references available." When someone agrees to be listed as a reference, take time to discuss what prospective employers may want to know. Former instructors or former employers may require written permission before releasing information. As the job search continues, keep references informed of the names of employers who may be inquiring.

Produce the résumé neatly and inexpensively, on a computer, because a good résumé will be used repeatedly with revisions, and the nurse will want to be able to produce an up-to-date version without completely rewriting it. Production methods should be kept as simple as possible. There are many tools and templates available on most word processing software programs for resume building and formatting. It is not necessary to go to the added trouble and expense of having the résumé professionally typeset and printed. Having it neatly typed and reproduced using good-quality photocopying services suffices. These resources as well as laser/color printers are available at public or university libraries. are available at To make the text easy to read, use one style of serif font throughout, in 11- or 12-point size. Again have someone review the final copy for typing errors, then use a photocopying service for "quick copying" onto good-quality white or ivory paper. It is important to remember that when it comes to résumés, appearances do count. A well-formatted résumé that is properly organized and neatly typed makes a great first impression.

How to Prepare a Portfolio

The nursing portfolio contains more information than a résumé and provides documentation to support the résumé. As health professionals, nurses are responsible for staying abreast of current professional knowledge and managing their own career, professional growth and development, and ideally, practices to support these activities should start during their student years. Professional development is a lifelong and continuous process, which is essential to the maintenance of clinical skills and knowledge essential in today's ever-changing health care environment. By creating a professional portfolio, a professional may showcase personal and professional development, practice excellence, and clinical leadership. Portfolio compilation provides an opportunity to assess abilities, identify learning goals, and devise a plan for further personal and professional development. In addition to validating accomplishments and highlighting milestones, this tool may illustrate a professional's progression along the continuum from novice to expert.

The portfolio introduces the professional nurse to recruiters, employers, admissions committees, and potential supervisors in a visual and tangible way. It includes traditional documents, such as a résumé, license to practice and certifications, educational documents (e.g., diplomas, transcripts), and examples of significant professional, community, and student activities (Box 27-4).

The simplest way to build a portfolio is to start with an attractive three-ring binder. A table of contents gives interviewers a map to guide their review of the information. Dividers can separate sections, each with its own cover page, and plastic sleeves or pocketed pages work

---

> **BOX 27-4 Documents For Professional Portfolio**
>
> **Professional Credentials**
> Résumé
> Licenses
> Certifications
> Specialty practice certifications
> Basic cardiac life support (BCLS)
> Advanced cardiac life support (ACLS)
>
> **Educational Credentials**
> Diplomas
> Transcripts
> Continuing education certificates
> Honors and awards (including program from awards ceremony, letters regarding awards, newspaper articles)
>
> **Research and Scholarly Activity**
> Publications
> Teaching materials for patients, staff, handouts
> Case studies
> Photo of poster sessions, classroom presentations
> PowerPoint outline of presentation
> Student papers and projects
>
> **Professional Activities**
> Membership cards
> Evidence of service as an officer or leader in student organizations
> Community involvement and volunteer activities
> Performance evaluations
> Letters of recommendation

well to hold loose items. Appropriate documents are assigned to each section. Make copies of important originals, such as diplomas, certifications, and licenses that would be difficult to replace. Include samples of letters from grateful patients, congratulations from peers, and complimentary notes from supervisors. Highlight sentences in longer letters or performance appraisals that address the information considered to be most important for the reader to note. The graduate nurse may want to include supervisor evaluations from non-nursing positions to demonstrate leadership qualities, dependability, and attention to detail, characteristics also relevant to the nursing work setting.

Interest in electronic or e-**portfolios** is gathering momentum as a strategy for fostering lifelong learning and enhancing on-going personal and professional development. The e-portfolio can represent an authentic means of assessing cognitive, reflective and affective skills. Furthermore, the e-portfolio provides a means through which nurses can record and provide evidence of skills, achievements, experience, professional development and ongoing learning, not only for themselves, but for the information and scrutiny of registration boards, employers, managers and peers (Green et al, 2014).

Graduation is the perfect time to create a career portfolio, one that will be easy to build on and update as your nursing career evolves. If documents are created on the computer, updates and revisions will be easy when the nurse pursues new and different professional roles and responsibilities. Many baccalaureate educational programs require students to create such a portfolio as part of their preparation for graduation and entry into the first job. Nurses who present portfolios to the recruiter may have a competitive edge over nurses who do not; increasingly, boards of nursing and many specialty organizations are making portfolios (or other methods for documenting evidence of competency) mandatory for relicensure and recertification. Continuing education and testing provide a limited picture of an individual's knowledge and/or skill acquisition in a limited area at one point in time. However, portfolios promote critical thinking, self-assessment, and individual accountability. A portfolio is a portable mechanism for evaluating competencies that may otherwise be difficult to assess.

HOW TO INTERVIEW EFFECTIVELY

No matter how qualified and self-confident a person may feel, sitting across the desk from an interviewer can be intimidating. One's conduct in the recruiter's office may determine whether a job offer is made. Being a little anxious is normal, but panic is not. When the applicant has made a good first impression in the cover letter and résumé, he or she can expect to be called for an interview. The graduate's task then becomes to enter the interview prepared to answer and ask questions that will help determine whether this organization, with its available job opportunities, is a good match.

Every agency has its own hiring and interviewing policies. Generally the smaller the organization and the more decentralized the nursing department, the more involved the lower-level manager is in the recruitment and hiring process. The same person who interviews nurse applicants also may be the manager, staff development instructor, quality assurance director, employee health nurse, or chair of the product standards committee. A large organization with many employees may have a separate human resources department with a nurse recruiter on staff. Within such large organizations, the hiring process becomes more complicated and more formal; applicants are more tightly screened, and the hiring decisions are further removed from the actual work position.

Increasingly hospitals are conducting panel interviews. A panel interview can be more efficient because several people can be in the room together and all have the same experience. The interviewers learn from the responses to each other's questions. Some organizations find this to be the easiest way to reach consensus on job candidates. If you know this is a possibility find out what you can about the panel members and the departments they represent (Bauer, 2013).

Not all "nurse recruiters" are nurses themselves, which may make a difference in the kind of information exchanged in the interview. A non-nurse is not likely to be able to fully discuss questions that pertain directly to a nurse's job description, patient care workload, and nursing responsibilities. The applicant does not have to answer questions that are not job related. In fact some questions are not legally allowed to be asked (Box 27-5).

BOX 27-5 Legal and Illegal Areas of Questioning

Some questions are inappropriate to be asked of an applicant before a job offer is made.

Legal	Illegal
Educational preparation	Race
Licensure status	Creed
Work experience	Color
Reasons for leaving previous jobs	Age
	Nationality
Reasons for applying to this institution	Marital status
	Sexual preference
Qualifications for this job	Religious beliefs
Strengths and weaknesses	Number of children or dependents
Criminal convictions	Financial or credit status

After a job offer is made, certain non–job-related questions may be asked, but not before. They should not be a part of deciding whether the applicant is offered a position.

How to Prepare: Planning Ahead

It is recommended that interview appointments be made as early as possible and that senior students not wait until graduation day. Ideally interviews should be scheduled at least 2 months prior to graduation. Job-hunting takes time, and appointments are not easily scheduled near nursing school graduation dates because these tend to be busy weeks for recruiters.

How to Prepare: Self-Talk

As the day approached, Mary obsessed about the interview, thinking to herself, "What if they ask me something I cannot answer, and I go blank like I used to do in clinicals when the instructor quizzed me about my patient's medicines? I will look like an idiot, and maybe even start to cry." The night before the appointment, Mary could not sleep.

Your thoughts dictate your reality. Nurses, especially new nurses, should be aware of what they are saying to themselves. The applicant who thinks, "Why would anyone want to hire a graduate nurse with no practical experience like me?" will project a lack of self-trust that may be interpreted by the recruiter as a lack of enthusiasm or even incompetence. However, a confident graduate's self-talk may be something like this: "I have successfully completed a difficult nursing course of study. I am now ready to take on the responsibilities of a professional. With orientation, on-the-job training, and the support of experienced nurses, I can succeed as an RN. I have everything I need to begin practice." This reality-based self-talk is an important internal dialogue for establishing feelings of confidence before the job interview.

The reality is that all graduates have met the criteria for graduation from a nursing education program and have been deemed ready by that credentialing body for an entry-level position as an RN. The final test of competence to practice, the NCLEX® examination, will provide further proof. Graduate nurses who fear failure of this final test must remind themselves of those now successfully practicing who preceded them from the same educational program with the same preparation.

How to Prepare: Rehearse

A simple visualization of how the graduate wants to appear to the recruiter can bring about the self-assurance needed to create an attractive candidate. It is helpful to mentally review and be prepared to describe pride in any past work experiences, especially the parts of any job that relate to what is required of a nurse. Even baby-sitting jobs can validate a worker as a responsible adult if that person worked consistently for the same family and showed stability and good judgment as a trusted caretaker for children. Applicants tend to discount minimum-wage, part-time, adolescent, or summer employment, but these experiences often reveal a great deal about the applicant: Would attendance records attest to the worker's dependability? Was the worker given greater responsibility over time? Was the worker allowed to open or close the business? Handle the cash receipts? Consider Case Study 27-1.

Remember that it is not only the graduate's academic standing or honors and awards that measure success as a student. Perhaps the student was not in the top 10% of the class, but was active in student affairs. Perhaps the student was chair of a student government committee or a contributor to the campus newspaper. The graduate should be prepared to describe other areas of student accomplishments.

Unfortunately, many nurses are not accustomed to selling themselves and are uncomfortable in situations in which they need to discuss their best attributes and market their qualifications. Therefore, after rehearsing in your own mind how to present these qualifications to interviewers, it would be wise to rehearse with another person, role-playing the expected interview dialogue. Role-play with another student or an experienced nurse (even better), rehearsing answers to questions the interviewer is expected to ask. Practice descriptions of the key points of past employment. A few minutes spent in rehearsing with another person will

---

CASE STUDY 27-1

The only job Sam had before nursing school had been working at the customer service desk at a large children's toy store, where he scheduled and supervised the cashiers. His title was "designated key carrier," which he listed on his résumé. The interviewer reasonably interpreted this to be a position that demonstrated the employer's trust in Sam.

contribute to composure and self-confidence in the actual situation.

Finally, it is important for the graduate to remember that the job interview is not an examination to pass or fail, nor is it an interrogation. It is an exchange of information—the recruiter hoping to find a potential employee to fill a staff vacancy and the applicant hoping to find employment as a nurse in this organization. Each has responsibilities for informing the other, and each has rights to obtain information from the other (Box 27-6).

How to Prepare: The Interview Itself
Dress Appropriately

Business-appropriate clothing, such as a neat dress, suit, or pantsuit, projects a professional attitude. Casual attire projects a casual attitude. Jeans are not acceptable, nor are shorts or any clothes that are too short, too tight, too revealing, or too trendy. Conservative and simple are always best. "Dressing for success" influences not only the impressions others have, but also the wearer's own behavior. When people are dressed to look their best, attitudes improve and levels of self-confidence increase. Facial makeup should be light, and the use of perfume or cologne should be avoided. Many institutions are fragrance free because of patients' and employees' allergic reactions to perfumes. Large, distracting jewelry should be avoided.

BOX 27-6 Applicants' Rights

Applicants have the right to:
- Be informed of available positions at an institution and the minimal qualifications required.
- Apply for any available position for which they are qualified.
- Be seriously and fairly considered for any available position for which they are qualified.
- Be interviewed, be shown a job description, and be made aware of the requirements and expectations of the job.
- Have the work schedule discussed.
- Be informed of the benefits package.
- See the nursing unit and meet the manager if they are being seriously considered.
- Be made aware of the orientation program.
- Be given an expected time by which a decision will be made.

Arrive on Time

Arriving late for a job interview creates a poor first impression. Be considerate of the interviewer's time and agenda. If delayed, call to reschedule. To arrive too early can make the interviewer feel rushed or the applicant appear overanxious; however, 10 to 15 minutes early is a reasonable target.

Bring a Résumé

Even if a résumé has already been submitted, the applicant should bring extra copies. The recruiter may have routed the mailed copy to a manager for review. Applicants probably will be asked to complete an employment application, and the résumé is a ready reference for past employers and dates of employment. A Social Security card, driver's license, and nursing license, if available, also will be requested as necessary parts of the identification process. Some agencies request that a current cardiopulmonary resuscitation card be made available to photocopy. These documents will be easy to produce if the applicant has also brought a professional portfolio folder.

The Telephone Interview

Telephone interviews are becoming a standard first step to narrowing down the applicant pool, and they minimize travel expenses for out-of-town applicants. The purpose of the telephone interview is to screen applicants and determine which ones to invite for a face-to-face interview. The applicant should be prepared for the interview just as if it were an in-person interview. Many job applicants have found it helpful to dress in business attire for the interview because it makes them feel and act more professionally. Control your surroundings by eliminating distracting background noise. Whether the interviewer is calling you, or vice versa, be ready before the appointed time, anticipate any time zone differences and respect the employer's time constraints. Eliminate any possible distractions from your phone room. Make sure kids and pets are quiet, put a "do not ring or knock" sign on your door, and turn off call waiting, cell phones, music, and television sets. Print out your résumé and have a pen and paper ready for note-taking. Have a glass of water nearby in case you get a dry throat. Standing may make you sound more confident, and smiling can be heard in your voice (Pagana, 2012).

In preparation for a telephone interview or a call from a potential employer, it is wise to make sure your voicemail message sounds professional. Although your friends may enjoy listening to your favorite band or sarcastic message, the potential employer might find it unprofessional (Pagana, 2012). The same caution goes for social media. It is important to remember that the messages and pictures posted on YouTube, MySpace, Facebook, Twitter, or other Internet websites are generally not private. Potential employers often research applicants' social media presence during the screening phase of the employment process.

The Face-to-Face Interview

The interview is the most time-consuming and subjective part of the employment process. For professionals, it is appropriate for interviews to be unstructured, using open-ended questions; both recruiter and applicant will have questions. The initial interview can be expected to last 30 minutes to 1 hour. Being prepared is the key, and planning answers to the questions most likely to be asked is the best way to prepare. Nine of the most frequently asked questions follow.

1. What Positions Interest You?

The interviewer needs to know whether there are positions available in the applicant's area of interest and whether the applicant has the required qualifications to fit the vacant positions. If there is no fit in interest or qualifications with jobs available, neither applicant nor recruiter needs to waste more time in the interview.

Because titles and position names vary from organization to organization, it is better to answer the question with favorite clinical experiences. Applicants might share short- and long-term goals and how they visualize laying the groundwork today for tomorrow's professional roles. A good response might be, "I'm interested in a position that will help me grow as a professional and give me opportunities to develop greater competency as a nurse. Ultimately, I would like to work as a critical care clinical nurse specialist." If interest, qualifications, and the available positions match, the interviewer will want to start planning secondary interviews and tours.

2. Tell Me About Your Work History

Even if previous jobs were not nursing related, the applicant can highlight the responsibilities carried out, the skills acquired, and how these skills can transfer to the professional nursing role. This is the point at which the interviewer will get an idea of motivation, drive, energy level, and reliability. No new graduate will be expected to have all the knowledge and skills of an experienced RN; however, when answering, the graduate may stress other aptitudes, such as verbal skills or interpersonal skills. It is best to start with the current or most recent job and proceed backward. A new graduate might discuss student clinical experiences, which clinical areas were favored, and why.

3. How Did You Choose to Apply for a Job Here?

Any previous investigative homework done on the institution is useful and helps to form honest responses. For example, an applicant might say, "This hospital has a reputation for its quality care, and I like that," or "I am interested in research and have heard you have a nursing research committee for staff nurses."

4. Do You Want a Full-Time or Part-Time Position, and Which Shift Do You Prefer?

If there is a need or desire for a particular schedule, the nurse should be honest and ask for that schedule. If the recruiter does not have that schedule available, ask what is available so that a decision can be made. Can the nurse be flexible to accept an undesirable shift until a preferred one becomes available? Part of one's investigation of an institution should include looking at a current list of posted positions. Particularly with smaller agencies, if what the nurse desires is not posted, it may be beneficial to ask for a particular schedule but, if willing, express an interest in working a schedule that is posted. For example, "I'm willing to work the evening shift posted for the medical-surgical unit; however, I'm most interested in moving into a day position in labor and delivery."

5. What Are Your Strengths and Weaknesses?

Sometimes this question may be asked in less direct ways, such as, "What are some of the areas you know you need to improve?" or "How have your skills developed in your advanced nursing courses?" Honesty always is best. By asking this question, the interviewer may only be trying to pinpoint the special skills and preferences of the nurse. For example, with what kind of patients has the nurse been most effective, and which ones proved most difficult? The clearer the applicant can be in articulating specific talents and deficiencies, the more closely the recruiter will be able to match the candidate to a position suited to his or her abilities. The closer these match, the more likely the employee will flourish and be able to use special talents.

6. It Is Not Advisable to Avoid the Issue of Weaknesses

Everyone has them. It is better to admit them, but to present them in a positive way. In addition, it may be helpful to tell the interviewer what is being done to correct weaknesses. For example, "Sometimes I tend to see the big picture and have to remind myself to pay more attention to the details. I've started keeping lists, and they seem helpful." Another suggestion might be, "I have limited bedside nursing experience, but I am excited about building on the clinical skills I have learned in school."

7. What Would You Do If . . .?

The recruiter probably will ask some situational questions related to decision making and critical thinking skills. The nurse will be asked to explain how to assess a particular situation, set priorities, decide what should be implemented first for a patient, and what can be delegated. Rather than fabricate an answer about unfamiliar circumstances, one can honestly say, "I've never been in that situation, but I think I would . . ." or "I was in a similar situation in which . . . occurred, and this is what I did in that circumstance."

When an interviewer says, "Tell me about a time when . . ." or "Give me a specific example of . . .," you're experiencing a behavioral interview. You need to be prepared to respond to these questions because many employers use a behavioral interview as part of the hiring process for nursing positions (LeMaster and Larson, 2010). This type of job interview is based on the logic that past behavior predicts future behavior and seeks previous experience of required job-related behaviors. If the job requires the ability to analyze and find solutions to problems, then the candidate may be asked to provide an example of when they previously found solutions to a difficult problem. The question might be: *"Tell me about a time when you faced a difficult problem. What steps did you take to solve that problem?"* Examples may be taken from any context as long as they include the required behavior. Remember, there are no right or wrong answers.

8. Why Should We Hire You?

This is an opportunity to share the special assets that the applicant would bring to the employer's institution. Without embellishment or selling oneself short, it is important to convey pride in being a nurse and conviction that one has something special to offer.

9. What Questions Do You Have?

Usually the interview ends with the interviewer asking whether there are any questions. This is an opportunity for the applicant to demonstrate initiative, and one should take advantage of it, although not to excess. In an effective interview with an experienced interviewer, most questions regarding salary, benefits, and human resource policies will have been addressed (Box 27-7). If they have not been addressed, this is the time to ask. Should a tour of the nursing unit and a meeting with the supervisor be arranged, many concerns will be answered then. Box 27-8 presents a list of suggested questions.

Mentally reviewing practiced responses to these questions will give the applicant confidence. The more information gathered, the easier it will be to make a decision, and the more likely it is that the nurse will be happy in the long term.

BOX 27-7 What to Expect a Recruiter to Communicate

Recruiters should inform applicants of basic human resource policies regarding job descriptions, compensation, benefits, and staff development, including:

- Conditional period
- Job descriptions
- Shift rotation
- Weekend rotation
- Salary
- Staff development
- Parking
- Security
- Health insurance and other insurance benefits
- Pre-employment physical examinations
- Credit union
- Overtime
- Scheduled paydays
- Paid time off
- Leaves of absence
- Employee discounts
- Transfer and promotion policies
- Resignation policies
- Preemployment policies
- Pay increases

BOX 27-8   Appropriate Questions for the Applicant to Ask

1. May I see the job description for the position we are discussing?
2. What is the nurse-to-patient ratio?
3. What support staff are available on the unit to assist nurses?
4. What about clerical help and support services? What nursing care delivery systems or models are practiced here (e.g., team nursing, primary nursing, centralized, decentralized)?
5. How available are physicians? Admitting physicians and house staff?
6. How often are nursing care conferences held on this unit?
7. What type of nursing documentation is used?
8. How long is the orientation program? What does the program include? What continuing education programs are available after my initial orientation?
9. How will my performance be evaluated? How often, and by whom?
10. What exact schedule or shift will I be working in this position?
11. What will my salary be? Is there a shift differential?
12. Are there differentiated practice levels or roles and differentiated pay scales for nursing congruent with differences in educational preparation, certification, and other advanced nursing preparation?
13. How are pay increases decided?
14. What other benefits are there (e.g., health, life insurance, vacation time, tuition reimbursement, retirement plan)?
15. What input do staff nurses have in decision making about nursing practice?

THE APPLICANT'S TASKS

Assess the Climate of the Work Environment

As mentioned in the discussion of researching potential employers, there are ways other than direct questioning to learn a lot about the institution. Every organization has its own personality and atmosphere. The first impression probably came from the secretary who answered the telephone when the applicant called for an appointment with the recruiter, followed by the greeting on arrival at the recruiter's office. A tone of respect and pride in being associated with the organization may have been communicated in the first encounter. Every subsequent encounter builds on the first.

In the hallways of the agency, how do people acknowledge each other? A visit to the employee cafeteria to buy a cup of coffee or a sandwich at mealtime can be enlightening. Are nurses eating there? Does it seem that the staff members are enjoying themselves? Pick up for later reading any available in-house publications, such as employee newsletters or bulletins.

Ask for a Tour

If the interviewer does not automatically offer a tour of the unit, the applicant can request to see it and will certainly want to meet with the person who would be the immediate supervisor. Some employers will arrange for the recruit to actually shadow a staff nurse for part of a shift. To get an accurate feel for the unit, the applicant should pay close attention to the pace, the tone of the staff interaction, and the morale. Is this a group the prospective employee would like to join? Are the manager's philosophy and management style similar to the applicant's own?

The astute applicant can get an accurate feel for the nursing unit's culture and personality if the manager's interactions with staff are observed. Is the manager accessible to the staff and supportive in response to them? How are telephone calls and other interruptions handled? How well do people seem to be getting along? Pay attention to the way people on the unit relate to each other—nurses to physicians, nurses to families, nurses to nurses. How are the patients responded to on the intercommunication system? Notice the efficiency with which staff work. How rushed are they? Also, note bulletin boards and any public displays of staff recognition (e.g., "employee of the month" plaques or brag boards). Even a second visit to the unit might be requested before a final decision is made. The more information gathered, the easier it will be to make a decision (DeLuca and DeLuca, 2010).

Some managers offer opportunities for the applicant to meet with staff, and formal interviews with staff nurses may be scheduled as a routine part of the hiring process. This gives the applicant a closer view of the actual work organization and gives representative staff members a chance to have a voice in selecting new coworkers. Staff nurses provide bedside care to patients and best understand the qualities appreciated in a good team member. Whether the introduction to staff is a formal interview or a casual conference room encounter, the applicant can be made to feel welcome and wanted, while learning about the real work and the real workers of the agency. Now that firsthand knowledge has been obtained, if the applicant confers again with these employees and former employees are consulted before applying, he or she can ask more informed questions.

Follow-up

Thank-You Letter

A follow-up letter thanking the recruiter is a courtesy and a reminder of the nurse's interest in receiving a timely response (Box 27-9). If the nurse does not hear from the employer within a reasonable length of time (1 to 2 weeks) after the interview, it is appropriate to inquire by telephone about the status of a hiring decision.

Avoid Impulse Decisions

If offered a position and time is needed to make a decision, the applicant should postpone a decision and should not feel pressured into acceptance while still unsure. An offer to telephone the recruiter with an answer within an agreed-on time is appropriate.

If there are other job opportunities, certainly comparisons need to be made by weighing the pros

---

BOX 27-9 **Interview Follow-up Letter**

April 24, 2015

Ms. Donna Henderson, MS, RN
Director of Nurse Recruitment
Charleston Memorial Hospital
1600 Beckley Avenue
Memphis, TN 38104

Dear Ms. Henderson:
It was a pleasure meeting with you on Monday. I now have a clear picture of what I might expect as a new graduate nurse in your hospital. Everyone on the units I visited was very friendly.

I look forward to hearing from you with good news about a position at Charleston Memorial. I can be reached in the afternoons at 555-912-3120 or on my cell, 555-200-9999.

Thank you again for your time and interest.

Sincerely,
(Sign your name here in pen)

Bonnie McCray Pino

---

and cons of each position and each organization. How do benefits compare? What are the possibilities for movement within the systems laterally and vertically? How available are continuing education opportunities to staff nurses? How do observations of the work culture fit with the nurse's ideas of what is needed to support professional success? Does the schedule that is offered fit the applicant's lifestyle? When a decision has been reached, a telephone call should be made promptly to the recruiter, whether the answer is yes or no.

Weighing Options

Applicants should take time to weigh options, especially if they have applied to several different organizations. It is not professional to accept a position while knowing you will resign if a more appealing offer comes along. Employers invest significant resources in orienting a new nurse and should expect a commitment rather than the casual attitude of "I'll keep this job until the job I really want becomes available." What questions might be asked of oneself while weighing the merits of one position against others? Remembering that no job is perfect, the following four questions should be considered.

Does the Position Match the Nurse's Qualifications?

Although it is flattering to receive a job offer for a position for which a nurse has little or no preparation, one should not be influenced by such a compliment. When there is a nursing shortage, a position that is beyond an applicant's present skills and experience may sound wonderfully challenging, when in actuality it may be overwhelming and a disastrous beginning for a new graduate. Being overzealous, overconfident, and over-eager to please can only lead to feelings of guilt and inadequacy if the job is not appropriate. It is wiser to accept a position in which adequate orientation and clinical support exist, which would allow the graduate to gain the experience and preparation necessary to accept a position requiring more skills at a later time.

What Are the Actual Responsibilities of the Job?

The newly hired nurse has the right to completely understand what will be expected in the position offered, including the overall and daily responsibilities and the length and nature of on-the-job training that will be provided. What will be the supervisory responsibilities? How many and what skill level of employees will be under the RN's leadership? What orientation is planned to prepare the RN for practicing independently? Are there arrangements for a preceptor to guide the graduate through the difficult transition of entering a first nursing job? Reality shock can be anticipated, and the more assistance a new graduate receives in adjusting to the new role of the nurse, the more likely the beginner is to be successful and satisfied.

Does this Position Lead the Nurse in the Direction of Projected Career Goals?

Is the offered job a step toward meeting long-term career objectives? For example, a graduate who wants to be a nurse-midwife would be wiser to accept a position in postpartum if labor and delivery is not available, rather than accepting a position in neurosurgery just because it offers a slightly higher salary or a few more weekends. No position or job change should be accidental or the result of a snap decision. Wise career moves result from deliberate planning and purposeful preparation.

How Will the Work Be Compensated?

Experienced nurses often advise novices that money, although important, is not the only reward associated with a job. However, money does matter, especially to a new graduate who may have subsisted on a limited income while in school. It is common for loans to have accumulated, along with unpaid bills. Inadequate salary can be a real source of job dissatisfaction, of course, but with 24-hour responsibilities, nurses traditionally have basic salaries that include other income-contributing factors, such as shift differentials, weekend differentials, holiday pay, paid vacation days, and expected salary increases over time. Compensation comes in other packages besides paychecks. There are policies that allow for maternity leaves, medical leaves, tuition reimbursement, sick days, discounts on prescriptions and health insurance, retirement benefits, and malpractice insurance coverage, all of which affect income in indirect but important ways. As is true in other areas of consideration, the better the total compensation package fits one's needs, the greater the likelihood that one will remain satisfied with the job.

Well-prepared job applicants will have listed those benefits they consider essential, and these vary with individual circumstances. For example, the essentials for

---

> **BOX 27-10** **Assessment Tool for Decision Making**
>
> When weighing options for employment, consider those measures of a professional work climate that are evident in written documentation and visible in the patient care areas. The following observations should guide the new graduate in making an informed decision.
> - Standards of nursing practice are evident and are an integral part of patient care.
> - Nurse-to-patient ratio is adequate and adjusted for patient acuity.
> - Orientation is structured, individualized, and adequate for new graduates.
> - Opportunities for horizontal transfer and advancement exist within the system.
> - The salary is competitive and reasonable.
> - Benefits are competitive.
> - Continuing education is available, and staff members are encouraged to attend.
> - A nurse administrator is responsible for delivery of nursing services.

someone who is the sole family breadwinner probably include health insurance, paid time off, and an employer-provided retirement plan. Available child care would be especially important for parents of preschool children. Box 27-10 further helps applicants evaluate potential employment opportunities.

THE EMPLOYER'S TASKS

In any agency providing nursing services, its nurses are the indispensable employees. The selection of new nurse employees is a critically important responsibility, and it is the recruiter's duty to make sure the best selection is made.

First, the nurse must meet the minimal requirements for the position desired. For example, 1 year of experience might be required for a nurse to work a weekender program or in a critical care area. Operating room (OR) experience may be required for OR nursing positions, and perinatal nursing experience may be required for labor and delivery positions. A secondary consideration is the nurse's suitability for contributing to the mission of the health care delivery system. The recruiter is selling the organization to the applicant and measuring the skills and aptitudes the applicant would bring to the organization.

The bottom line for any employer who provides health care services to the public is to ensure that its nursing staff practices safely. Recruiters are looking to uncover anything that would impair a nurse applicant's ability to provide safe nursing care, such as incompetence, unprofessional conduct, unreliability in attendance, chemical dependency, or record of criminal activity. For screening, recruiters have four primary sources of information: the application, interview impressions, test results, and references.

Applications are validated. Work history and references are checked to ensure accuracy. Previous supervisors are asked about attendance, dependability, performance, attitude, ability to get along with others, integrity, and eligibility for rehire. The applicant's stated reason for termination is compared with information obtained from work references. The employer has a right to obtain reasonable information about the people who are hired. Most employment applications ask whether the applicant has ever been convicted of a crime other than a minor traffic violation. The question is about convictions, not arrests, and the response is verified by a background or criminal record check. Response to this or any other question in the application process must be honest and truthful. Each institution has its own policies regarding convictions, but most are vitally concerned about their responsibilities regarding negligent hiring. The applicant is rejected if he or she committed a crime that, if repeated while in the employ of the institution, would cause harm to patients, families, other employees, or the institution.

A physical examination is often required. This usually is done on-site and at the employer's expense. It may involve obtaining the applicant's full medical history and vital signs, routine blood tests, a urine drug screen, and sometimes a chest radiograph. The purpose of the examination is to ensure protection for patients and to ensure that the caregiver can carry out the necessary physical responsibilities of the job. For example, are illegal mood-altering substances evident that would impair the nurse's abilities and judgment? Are there physical limitations the institution should know about to determine whether any special accommodations are necessary to allow the candidate to perform the usual duties associated with the position?

Even with a job offer made and a date for employment set, actual start dates are contingent on receipt of documentation of these final screenings, plus a reference check to verify the résumé; these items establish the practitioner's safety and reliability. Other parts of screening for safety might include paper-and-pencil testing, such as skills tests, pharmacology tests, and, in some cases, personality testing and psychological testing for specialty areas.

Although a preemployment pharmacology test is becoming less common than in past years, many institutions still give such a quiz to determine basic knowledge of routinely administered medications, their purposes, and side effects. Simple dosage questions and calculation methods may be asked. Some questions may be situational ones, such as, "What would you do in this case?" or "The first nursing action in this scenario should be . . . ."

A few larger institutions also may administer a clinical skills test. This might be conducted in a simulated laboratory setting, where frequently-used patient care equipment is set up. Usually a staff development instructor accompanies the nurse through a series of stations where the nurse would be asked to plan and perform the appropriate nursing actions. Examples might be starting cardiopulmonary resuscitation on a simulated patient, demonstrating the proper procedure for starting an intravenous line, or talking through an assessment of a patient.

It is far better to be prepared and even better to be proactive and offer to produce some of the documentation required. For instance, the nurse may be able to get a written reference from a former employer or a statement from a physician sooner than the institution can. The employment start date depends on the receipt of all necessary information, so it will expedite the process if the candidate volunteers to initiate some of the documentation gathering or even has references in hand with other documentation at the time of interview.

Once an applicant is selected, the agency has committed itself to costly training, orientation, and additional benefits that may cost as much as 30% to 40% of the employee's salary. A major element of control, which any organization possesses, is its ability to choose its employees. When the selection process is thorough, it is a sign to the committed professional that this is a reputable employer.

SUMMARY

If not offered a position, the new graduate should still feel good about himself or herself. There may have been several candidates for that same position. Perhaps it was not the best match for one's skills or preferences. There is victory in having had an opportunity to practice interview skills. Preparation, practice, and perseverance will reward the nurse with a job that is better suited to his or her personality, values, qualifications, and skills. New graduates have internalized standards of practice from their nursing education experience. On graduation, they must decide where to begin to put these standards to work in real-life terms handling real responsibilities with real patients. The question becomes, "Can school and work values be reconciled in this nursing environment?" When adequate groundwork in pursuit of a job has been laid, the answer should come easy.

REFERENCES

Arnold J: *Cost of hiring new nurses: In this tight economy, does it pay for hospitals to invest in graduate nurses?* http://nursing.advanceweb.com/Features/Articles/Cost-of-Hiring-New-Nurses.aspx. Accessed January 31, 2012.

Bauer, J: *The essential interview handbook*, Prompton Plains, New Jersey, 2013, Career Press.

DeLuca M, Deluca N: *Stand out and get hired: Best answers to the 201 most frequently asked interview questions*, ed 2, New York, 2010, The McGraw Hill Companies, Inc.

Green J, Wyllie A, Jackson D: Electronic portfolios in nursing education, *Nurse education in practice* 14(1): 4–8, 2014.

Kelly LA, McHugh MD, Aiken LH: Nurse outcomes in Magnet and non-Magnet hospitals, *J Nurs Adm* 41(10): 428–433, 2011.

LaMaster MA, Larsen RA: Prepare for a behavioral interview, then ace it! *Nursing 2014* 40(1):8–10, 2010.

Pagana K: Ten tips for handling job interviews by phone, *Am Nurse Today* 7(1):40–41, 2012.

ADDITIONAL RESOURCE

American Journal of Nursing: *2010 Career Guide* 40(Suppl 1):1, 2010, Nursing Career Directory, Philadelphia, Lippincott.

28

The NCLEX-RN® Examination

Tommie L. Norris, DNS, RN

Adequate preparation for the NCLEX-RN® examination can reduce panic and ensure success.

Ⓔ Additional resources are available online at: *http://evolve.elsevier.com/Cherry/*

PROFESSIONAL/ETHICAL ISSUE

Jamie Wilcox, senior nursing student, just left a meeting with the director of her BSN program. Jamie was devastated. She just learned that she would not graduate in a few weeks as planned because her score on the final standardized exam was not high enough and, according to the program director, was a predictor that she might not pass the NCLEX. Jamie did not realize there was so much at stake when she took the standardized exam, and she admitted to herself that she really did not prepare or take the exam seriously. After all, she had passed every course in the nursing program; her grades were not outstanding, but they were passing. She wondered, can this be fair? Was this high-stakes testing even ethical?

Over the next week Jamie learned more about standardized exams. She learned they were used at various points throughout the nursing school curriculum to provide students and faculty with insight into how a student's performance compares with other schools. These exams also provide individual assessment by noting a student's strengths and weaknesses and are used to develop remediation plans. Standardized exams are often used by nursing schools to predict the chance for being successful on the NCLEX-RN exam and to determine whether a student will graduate, so they are considered "high stakes." However, she also learned that standardized exams are just "predictors," or at best an estimate of future performance. Standardized exams lack the sophistication of computerized adaptive testing, thus comparing them to the NCLEX may prevent qualified students from graduating or taking the NCLEX. While Jamie was determined to be successful in completing her remediation plan and performing well on the next standardized exam, she still had many questions about such "high-stakes" testing.

- What responsibility belongs with the nursing program that progressed a student through the program but then deemed a student ineligible to graduate because of his/her performance on a standardized exam?
- What responsibility lies with the student who had poor performance on a standardized exam?
- Should standardized exams become the "standard" that determines whether a student should graduate from nursing school? Why or why not?

VIGNETTE

Consider for a moment how nursing and licensure examinations have changed as society has changed. Nursing is a reflection of society's values, knowledge, and needs. Test items or questions found on the NCLEX-RN examination today have little resemblance to questions asked on state board examinations administered during the early part of the twentieth century. The examinations of that era dealt with practical issues and consisted mainly of knowledge-based questions that had little to do with assessment, application, evaluation, or need. Consider, for instance, the following questions taken from the 1919 state board questions and answers for nurses (Foote, 1919):

- What are the advantages of fireplaces?
- How would you sterilize silkworm-gut and silk sutures?
- What care regarding nourishment would you give a gynecological patient to prevent a common discomfort?
- Give some general rules for preparing meats.

- Give three common complaints that the public makes about graduate nurses.

Questions to Consider While Reading this Chapter:
1. What is the purpose of the NCLEX-RN examination?
2. What type of questions can I expect on today's NCLEX-RN examination?
3. What is the best way to prepare for the examination?

KEY TERMS

Compulsory licensure: Requirement that must be met to legally practice or work as a registered nurse (RN). Licensure is a prerequisite to practice in each state and U.S. territory.

Computer adaptive testing (CAT): A type of testing taken on a computer, in which a person is given a test question to answer, followed by a subsequent question that is leveled based on the whether the candidate correctly answered the first question.

National Council of State Board of Nursing: An independent not-for-profit organization that

supports boards of nursing by monitoring trends in nursing practice and develops the licensing examination for both registered and practical nursing.

NCLEX-RN examination: NCLEX stands for National Council Licensure Examination, an examination taken by qualified graduates of approved schools of nursing. Graduates successfully taking the NCLEX-RN® examination are granted a license to practice as RNs.

LEARNING OUTCOMES

After studying this chapter, the reader will be able to:

1. Explain the purpose of the NCLEX-RN examination.
2. Evaluate various methods of preparation for the NCLEX-RN examination.
3. Create a personal plan for preparing for the NCLEX-RN examination.

4. Analyze the relationship between the nursing process and client needs as they relate to NCLEX-RN® test items.
5. Compare various review courses designed to aid in review for the NCLEX-RN examination.
6. Use the NCLEX-RN test plan to plan review and remediation strategies.

CHAPTER OVERVIEW

This chapter helps student nurses prepare to successfully pass the NCLEX-RN® examination. The purpose of the NCLEX-RN® is discussed, and an overview of the format

and content is given. Various strategies for preparing for the examination are given, and students are encouraged to develop a personal plan of study.

ARE YOU PREPARED FOR THE NCLEX-RN EXAMINATION?

You are pursuing a degree in nursing and plan to take the NCLEX-RN licensure examination after graduation. Do you know what to expect on the examination itself?

Do you feel you have the knowledge necessary for NCLEX-RN examination success? If not, you should be interested in this chapter, which offers an overview of the format and content you can expect on the test and strategies for success.

THE NCLEX-RN EXAMINATION

The NCLEX-RN examination and licensure to practice nursing go hand in hand. To receive a license to practice as an RN in the United States and its territories, candidates must furnish evidence of competency to provide safe and effective nursing care by successfully completing the NCLEX-RN examination (National Council of State Boards of Nursing [NCSBN], 2014a).

There are three types of RN programs: (1) 2-year associate degree programs usually found in community or junior colleges, (2) hospital-based diploma programs, and (3) baccalaureate degree or higher programs found in 4-year colleges and universities or academic health centers. Graduates from all programs take the same NCLEX-RN examination. The examination content common to all of these programs is job related and reflects current entry-level nursing practice (NCSBN, 2013). Individuals taking the examination must have graduated from approved schools of nursing.

In January 2015, the NCLEX-RN became the licensure/registration examination for Canadian provinces and territories (NCSBN, 2014b). The NCSBN has released the Transitional NCLEX Candidate Bulletin for Canadian Candidates. Candidates from Canada should contact their regulatory body regarding reciprocity of licensure.

Purpose of the NCLEX-RN Examination

The purpose of the NCLEX-RN examination is to:
1. Safeguard the public from unsafe practitioners.
2. Assist state boards of nursing in determining candidates' capabilities for performing entry-level RN positions.

To keep the NCLEX-RN examination current, the NCSBN conducts a practice analysis on a 3-year cycle by investigating current practice that entry-level nurses are performing in various health care settings in the United States. In the most current practice analysis completed in 2011, newly licensed nurses (n=2,832) were asked to prioritize 141 nursing care activities and state how often they perform them (NCSBN, 2012). The survey was sent by either paper version or Internet-based survey with participants evaluating half of the activities. The greatest amount of time was spent in management of care (17.6%), psychological adaptation (15.2%), and pharmacological and parenteral therapies (13.1%), with the least amount of time spent on health promotion and maintenance activities (10.7%). Most care was provided for clients with acute conditions between the ages of 18 to 85 with the majority working in hospitals (76.2%). These results varied slightly on all categories from the 2008 survey. Based on the results of this practice analysis, the NCSBN revised and implemented the current test plan in April 2013.

A panel of nine RNs serving as subject matter experts (SMEs) helped to create the practice analysis survey; nurses on this panel worked with or supervised RNs within the first six months of practice or were themselves new RNs (NCSBN, 2012). The SMEs created a list of activities performed by newly licensed nurses using job descriptions, activity logs kept by newly licensed RNs, performance evaluation documents and their own knowledge of newly licensed RN practice. This list of activities eventually became the 141 items used in the practice analysis survey. To view the latest practice analysis, visit https://www.ncsbn.org/12_RN_Practice_Analysis_Vol53.pdf.

Characteristics of the NCLEX-RN Examination

The NCLEX-RN examination is a pass-fail examination and has been computerized since 1994. Before that time, it was a paper-and-pencil examination requiring 2 days to complete. Today the NCLEX-RN examination is offered at Pearson Professional Centers throughout the United States, American Samoa, Guam, Northern Mariana Islands, and U.S. Virgin Islands. International scheduling is also available. It can be taken at the candidate's convenience and can be completed in 6 hours or less, which includes examination instructions and breaks. The official results of the examination are sent to candidates within 6 weeks after they have taken the examination. Unofficial results are available on the NCLEX candidate website at www.pearsonvue.com/nclex after 48 business hours. Candidates may also check the state board website for licensure verification.

Computer Adaptive Testing

The NCLEX-RN examination uses computer adaptive testing (CAT), which is a test-administering technique that uses computer technology and measurement theory. As a candidate answers questions on the examination, CAT adapts to the level of the candidate's knowledge, skills, and ability. After a candidate answers a question at a particular level of difficulty, the computer then selects the next item that the candidate should have a 50% chance of answering correctly. All examinations are consistent with the NCLEX-RN examination test plan, which controls inclusion of nursing content. Candidates have ample opportunity to demonstrate their competence because the examination does not end until stability of the pass or fail result is certain or time runs out (NCSBN, 2013).

Candidates taking the examination answer a minimum of 75 questions to a maximum of 265 questions. The NCSBN (2013) advises that the length of an NCLEX-RN examination be based on the performance of the candidate on the examination and has established a goal to be 95% sure of pass-fail decisions. The computer determines whether a candidate passes or fails based on the following three rules:

1. 95% confidence interval rule: 95% certainty that the candidate's ability is obviously above or below the passing standard.
2. Maximum-length examination rule: When the candidate is very close to the passing standard, the computer continues to give test items until the maximum number of items is reached; at this point, the computer disregards the 95% confidence rule and considers only the final ability estimate.
3. Run-out-of-time rule: The candidate runs out of time, and the 95% confidence interval has not been determined. If the candidate has not answered the minimum number of questions, then he or she fails; if the candidate has answered the minimum number of questions, the computer analyzes the last 60 questions to determine whether these questions were above or below the passing standard.

It is important for students to understand that the goal of CAT is to determine competency based on the difficulty of questions answered correctly rather than the number of questions answered correctly. The CAT is individualized, and two people taking the examination at the same time will not have the same questions. The candidate moves from easy to difficult questions and then defaults back to easy questions when a harder question is missed. The point where the candidate answers half the questions correctly is identified, and the competency level is determined based on the difficulty level where half of questions were answered correctly.

A tutorial is administered before the examination actually begins, providing candidates with experience in using the computer in CAT situations and explaining various question formats that may be presented in the exam. Candidates should carefully read an entire question and all possible answer options before selecting an answer. Candidates may request assistance regarding the use of the computer at any point, even during the NCLEX-RN examination. In addition, they may find it helpful to view the PowerPoint candidate tutorial before going to the testing center. This tutorial, provided by the NCSBN, may be accessed at the following website: www.ncsbn.org. A tutorial is also given at the beginning of the examination, which explains various formats that may be presented.

Skipping Questions and Changing Answers

Candidates taking the NCLEX-RN examination are not allowed to skip questions and return to them at a later time or to change answers to questions once an answer has been selected and entered into the computer. These actions would defeat the purpose of adaptive testing because CAT selects questions based on the examination taker's knowledge, skills, and abilities.

Question Format

All of the information needed to answer a particular question appears on one computer screen, so candidates do not need to see the previous or next screen for answer determination. Questions are presented in traditional top-down format, in which the question is presented, followed by the potential answers to it. Candidates will receive test items in a variety of formats which include traditional multiple choice, multiple response, ordered response, fill-in-the-blank calculations and/or hot spots. Recently items may also include charts, graphics, sound, video, tables, and multimedia.

Traditional Format: Multiple-Choice, One Option

With this type of format, the candidate is presented a question, followed by four possible responses. The candidate is asked to select the one option that best answers the question. Multiple-choice, one-option format is the style most commonly used on the examination. See the following example.

The nurse has received the following information about assigned clients. The nurse should first assess:

a) A 64-year-old client who had a total knee replacement 3 hours ago and has 15 mL of serosanguineous drainage in the collection device.

b) A 32-year-old client who had closed reduction of a fractured right malleolus 5 hours ago and has swelling of the right toes.

c) A 9-month-old client admitted 6 hours ago with vomiting; whose vital signs are temperature, 37.6° C (99.7° F); pulse, 124; respirations, 26.

d) A 6-week-old client who was admitted 2 hours ago with nasal flaring and has a pulse oximetry reading of 90%.

(Answer: d)

Alternate Item Format

Because of the nature of CAT, the type of item presented to the candidate will depend on the content area.

- **Hot spot (questions based on illustrations and charts).** With this type of item, the candidate is asked to identify one or more area(s) on a picture or graphic and answer using the mouse button when the cursor is over the area selected. See the following example:

    Identify the point of maximal impulse (PMI):

    1. a
    2. b
    3. c
    4. d

    (Answer: d)

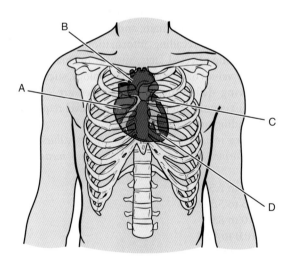

- **Multiple-response, multiple-choice questions.** The candidate is presented with a question, followed by five or more responses. The candidate is asked to check all responses that are correct; partial credit is not given. See the following example:

    A nurse is caring for a 47-year-old female client who has been diagnosed with hypothyroidism. Which of the following manifestations might the nurse expect the client to report? (Select all that apply.)

    a) Intolerance to heat
    b) Periorbital edema
    c) Weight loss
    d) Menorrhagia
    e) Constipation
    f) Fatigue

    (Answer: b, d, e, and f)

- **Fill-in-the-blank.** The candidate is presented with a question to which the answer must be typed, instead of selecting from among a set of four options. In some cases, candidates may be asked to calculate values, such as dosages. A drop-down calculator is available for the candidate to use. See the following example:

    A nurse is completing the intake and output record for a client who had a left total knee replacement 1 day ago. The client has had the following intake and output during the shift:

    Intake:

    3 oz apple juice
    ½ serving oatmeal
    8 ounces water
    1 cup fruit-flavored gelatin
    ½ cup beef broth
    800 mL of 0.45 sodium chloride (half-strength saline), IV

    Output:

    1200 mL of urine
    50 mL from the drainage tube

    How many milliliters should the nurse document as the client's intake?

    (Answer: 1490 mL)

- **Ordered response "Drag and drop" (prioritize).** The candidate is presented with a set of responses to a question and asked to place them in order or to prioritize. See the following example:

    A nurse is preparing to perform a sterile dressing change. In what order would the following steps be performed?

    1) Gather supplies.
    2) Set up the sterile field.
    3) Assess the wound.
    4) Explain the procedure to the patient.

5) Remove the soiled dressing.

6) Document the dressing change.

Type your answer in the box below (note: Do not use spaces or commas between the numbers in the answer.) Candidates may also be asked to click on the steps and drag items in the correct order.

(Answer: 1 4 5 3 2 6)

- **Chart exhibit.** The candidate is asked to seek additional information in a patient's chart to answer the question. See the following example in which the candidate must look in the chart to find pertinent information to report:

    A patient is ordered Lanoxin 0.25 mg daily. The nurse assesses the patient's heart rate as 48 beats per minute. Prior to calling the physician, what additional information is needed?

    a) Potassium 2.8 mEq/L

    b) Arterial blood gases (PaO_2), 95

    c) History of kidney stones

    d) Diet: 1800 calorie

    (Answer: a)

- **Audio.** Each candidate is furnished with earphones and listens to an audio clip. The candidate is asked to identify specific assessment findings. See the following example:

    Candidate listens to an adventitious breath sound such as crackles. Candidate will be asked to identify abnormal finding.

- **Graphic option identification.** The candidate is presented with options that are either pictures or graphic images rather than text.

    Candidates should note that any of the item formats, including standard multiple-choice items, may include tables, graphic images, or charts. Candidates can find additional information on alternate item formats in the NCLEX-RN® Examination Candidate Version (https://www.ncsbn.org/2013_NCLEX_RN_Detailed_Test_Plan_Candidate.pdf).

COGNITIVE DOMAINS AND THE NCLEX-RN EXAMINATION

NCLEX-RN examination questions use Bloom's original cognitive levels of knowledge, comprehension, application, and analysis; however, the revised taxonomy of remember, understand, apply, analyze, evaluate, and create (Anderson and Krathwohl, 2001; Bloom et al, 1956) can be applied. One primary

TABLE 28-1   Comparison of Original and Revised Bloom's Taxonomy

Original Bloom's Taxonomy	Revised Bloom's Taxonomy
Evaluation	Creating
Synthesis	Evaluating
Analysis	Analyzing
Application	Applying
Comprehension	Understanding
Knowledge	Remembering

difference between the two versions is that the original version uses nouns whereas the revised version uses verbs (Table 28-1). These levels may be viewed as consecutive steps, with knowledge (remembering) being the lowest, most fundamental step and analysis (analyzing) being the highest, most highly evolved of the steps. Because nursing requires application of knowledge, skills, and abilities, the majority of NCLEX-RN examination questions are written at the application or higher cognitive level and critical thinking skills (NCSBN, 2013).

Knowledge Questions (remember)

Knowledge is the lowest and simplest level of learning within the cognitive domain, and it is demonstrated by remembering or recalling information. This may include knowing selected facts, such as normal range of laboratory values or common terminology, such as dyspnea. Giving definitions and examples are common skills at this cognitive level because this level requires no understanding or judgment.

The nurse reviewing a patient's laboratory values realizes that the normal range for serum potassium measured in mEq/L is:

a) 0.5 to 2.5

b) 3.5 to 5.5

c) 6.0 to 8.0

d) 10.0 to 12.0

(Answer: b)

Comprehension Questions (understand)

Comprehension, the second level of Bloom's cognitive domain, is the fundamental level of understanding or the ability to grasp or summarize information or material or restate in one's own words. The following is an example of a comprehension level question:

A patient is ordered a clear liquid diet. The nurse can offer the patient which of the following on the food tray?

a) Orange juice
b) Lime Jell-O
c) Skim milk
d) Tomato soup

(Answer: b)

Application Questions *(apply)*

The third cognitive level, application, refers to the ability to use learned information in new situations. This level involves applying abstract theories and principles in new concrete or practical situations, solving mathematical problems, constructing charts and graphs, and making inferences. Information learned is applied to deliver safe and effective nursing care. The following is an example of an application level question:

*An adult patient with a history of alcoholism, 24 hours after gastric resection surgery, is complaining of pain rated as 9 on a scale of 1 to 10, with 10 being most severe. The nurse reviews the orders and prepares to administer morphine 2 mg intramuscularly. Before administration of pain medication, which assessment is a **priority** that must be completed by the RN?*

a) Bowel sounds and degree of nausea
b) Respiratory rate and level of consciousness
c) Heart rate and ambulatory status
d) History of addiction to narcotics and potassium level

(Answer: b)

Analysis Questions *(analyze)*

The highest cognitive level used on the NCLEX-RN examination, analysis, requires complex thought processes and includes the ability to reduce material into its fundamental parts so that relationships may be understood. Included in this level are questions of drawing conclusions, setting priorities, forming hypotheses, and creating something new. The majority of items are written at the application level or higher because the practice of nursing necessitates that nurses apply knowledge, skills, and abilities to problem solve. The following is an example of a question written at the analysis level:

A patient exhibits tetany and a positive Trousseau sign. The following lab values were reported: sodium 140 mg/dL, potassium 5 mEq/mL, calcium 8 mg/dL, and magnesium 3 mg/dL. These clinical manifestations and laboratory findings are consistent with which electrolyte disorder?

a) Hyponatremia
b) Hypomagnesemia
c) Hypocalcemia
d) Hypokalemia

(Answer: c)

COMPONENTS OF THE NCLEX-RN® EXAMINATION TEST PLAN

The test plan for the NCLEX-RN examination is based on the current nursing practice of entry-level RNs. According to the NCSBN (2013): "The NCLEX examination assesses the knowledge, skills and abilities that are essential for the nurse to use in order to meet the needs of clients requiring the promotion, maintenance or restoration of health." The NCLEX-RN examination test plan is framed by four major categories of client needs, which are further subdivided into a total of six subcategories (NCSBN, 2013):

1. Safe, effective care environment
   - Management of care
   - Safety and infection control
2. Health promotion and maintenance
3. Psychosocial integrity
4. Physiologic integrity
   - Basic care and comfort
   - Pharmacologic and parenteral therapies
   - Reduction of risk potential
   - Physiologic adaptation

Each of these will be examined individually, followed by a discussion of several processes that are fundamental to nursing and integrated throughout the client needs categories and subcategories.

Client Needs

The goal of nursing for client care in any setting is preventing illnesses and potential complications; alleviating suffering; protecting, promoting, restoring, and facilitating comfort and health; and dignity in dying (NCSBN, 2013). The organizing framework of the NCLEX-RN® examination is client needs, which is a broad component that "provides a universal structure for defining nursing actions and competencies across all settings for all clients" (NCSBN, 2013).

Safe and Effective Care Environment

This category pertains to the provision and direction of nursing care delivery to safeguard clients, their families or significant others, and health care providers. This category is further subdivided into two categories: management of care, from which 17% to 23% of the test plan is constructed, and safety and infection control, from which 9% to 15% of the test plan is constructed (NCSBN, 2013). Within this section, the nurse should have the knowledge, skills, and ability to meet the client's needs for a safe and effective environment.

Health Promotion and Maintenance

This category relating to client needs pertains to the provision and direction of nursing care that takes into consideration the projected growth and development principles, early detection and prevention of health problems, and plans to realize best possible health care outcomes. Six percent to 12% of NCLEX-RN examination questions are related to this category.

Psychosocial Integrity

In this category, "The nurse provides and directs nursing care that promotes and supports the emotional, mental, and social well-being of the client and family/significant others experiencing stressful events, as well as clients with acute or chronic mental illness" (NCSBN, 2013). Psychosocial integrity is addressed in 6% to 12% of NCLEX-RN examination questions.

Physiologic Integrity

This category entails the provision and direction of nursing care delivery to protect the client and family or significant others, in addition to health care providers. This category is further subdivided into four subcategories: (1) basic care and comfort, accounting for 6% to 12% of the test plan, is directed at the provision of comfort and assistance while performing activities of daily living; (2) pharmacologic and parenteral therapies, accounting for 12% to 18% of the test plan, is concerned with medication and parenteral therapies administration; (3) reduction of risk potential, accounting for 9% to 15% of the test plan, correlates with reducing the risk of clients developing complications related to their current conditions or treatments; and (4) physiologic adaptation, accounting for 11% to 17% of the test plan, is the management or coordination of care for clients with acute or chronic and life-threatening disease processes (NCSBN, 2013).

Integrated Processes

Processes that are fundamental to nursing are integrated throughout the previously noted client needs categories and subcategories (NCSBN, 2013):

- Nursing process
- Caring
- Communication and documentation
- Teaching and learning

For example, a question may be a health promotion and maintenance question that has to do with assessment or a psychosocial integrity question that also addresses implementation. All questions relate to some activity in which an entry-level nurse may engage when caring for or managing a patient. A more complete overview of these integrated processes follows.

Nursing Process

Success on the NCLEX-RN® examination relies on a sound working knowledge of the nursing process. The NCSBN (2013) defines the nursing process as "a scientific, clinical reasoning approach to client care that includes assessment, analysis, planning, implementation, and evaluation." The nursing process is applicable to all situations in which the nurse and patient interact and may be used with any theoretic framework.

Assessment. Assessment is the first step of the nursing process and establishes a database for the client. Just as the nursing process provides a foundation for nursing practice, assessment provides the foundation for the nursing process. Assessment includes gathering information or data about an identified client. Depending on the nurse's focus, the client may be a person, a family, a group of people, or a community.

Information about a client comes from a variety of sources, including the client, the family and significant others, laboratory or radiographic reports, physician records, hospital or clinic records, and other caregivers. Client data are typically classified as subjective and objective. Simply put, subjective data are the client's perception or understanding of a specific event or phenomenon. It is his or her opinion, such as the degree of pain experienced during an episode of angina. Objective data are observable and measurable by the nurse and come from various patient records. Blood pressure, heart rate, and the presence or absence of edema are examples of objective data.

Assessment also includes verification and communication of data. Seeking additional client-related information, such as laboratory work or talking with the family, may confirm data. Communication of data may be accomplished by verbal report to other health care workers or by written or computerized record.

Analysis. Analysis is the second step or phase of the nursing process. Client-related data gathered during assessment provide the basis for analysis. During this phase, the nurse classifies or groups assessment data and identifies actual or potential client problems. During classification, data also are validated and interpreted, and additional data may be required.

Planning. Planning is the third phase of the nursing process and includes setting realistic and measurable mutual goals, developing interventions to meet or resolve identified patient needs or problems, and modifying goals as necessary. Included in planning of care are ranking nursing diagnoses, documenting expected outcomes for each goal, and setting realistic target dates for the accomplishment of each goal. Goal setting should include the collaboration of members of the interdisciplinary health care team, the client, his or her family, and significant others as indicated. As with the previous phases of the nursing process, the plan must be communicated to other members of the health care team to ensure continuity of care.

Implementation. The fourth phase of the nursing process is implementation. This stage includes initiating and carrying out nursing interventions or nursing actions to achieve the goals set in the planning phase of the nursing process. The nurse implements interventions that will allow the patient to achieve goals and outcomes to support or improve the patient's health status (Potter and Perry, 2013).

Evaluation. To evaluate, data must be collected to document the progress the patient has made, or not made, in relation to the stated goal. Once data have been collected and analyzed, the nurse must decide what action to take or what modification to make regarding the goal. Using evidence, the nurse makes a judgment to determine whether the established outcome has met the actual response.

Caring

The NCSBN defines caring as "the interaction of the nurse and client in an atmosphere of mutual respect and trust. In this collaborative environment, the nurse provides encouragement, hope, support and compassion to help achieve desired outcomes" (NCSBN, 2013).

Communication and Documentation

The NCSBN defines communication and documentation as "the verbal and nonverbal interactions between the nurse and the client, the client's significant others and the other members of the health care team. Events and activities associated with client care are validated in written and/or electronic records that reflect standards of practice and accountability in the provision of care" (NCSBN, 2013).

Teaching and Learning

The NCSBN defines teaching and learning as "facilitation of the acquisition of knowledge, skills and attitudes promoting a change in behavior" (NCSBN, 2013).

PREPARING FOR THE NCLEX-RN® EXAMINATION

NCLEX is a "high-stakes" examination to evaluate nursing competence and protect the public. There is much debate concerning the use of similar high-stakes examinations used in nursing schools for progression, graduation, or eligibility to take the NCLEX. Because there are no universally accepted standards on using predictive test, schools are debating best practices. The National League for Nursing and The American Association of Colleges of Nursing have heard the concerns of the nursing community related to the use of standardized exit examinations and suggest a better understanding of this practice is needed.

There is no one best method for preparing to take the NCLEX-RN examination. Success depends on a candidate's nursing knowledge and ability to use that knowledge, test-taking skills, and confidence level. The best preparation any candidate can have is what the candidate brings from his or her nursing program.

Some measure of preparation for the NCLEX-RN examination after graduation from nursing school is a must for all candidates seeking success on the examination. Candidates should NOT convince themselves that they do not need to review because average or above-average grades were made in their academic and nursing coursework, nor should they decide that review will serve no purpose because average or below-average grades were made in their coursework.

In preparing for the NCLEX-RN examination, it is important to remember that review is a personal undertaking. What works for one candidate may not work for another and vice versa. Use study and review methods that have proven successful in the past. It is estimated that most students study 2-3 months prior to the examination. International students typically begin much earlier, studying for approximately 6 months prior to the examination.

Build Your NCLEX Study Plan

Use the following tips and strategies to build your own study plan and increase the likelihood of being successful on the NCLEX-RN examination:

- Review the NCLEX Candidate Bulletin (find the most current Bulletin at www.ncsbn.org).
- Become familiar with the test plan (find the most current Test Plan at www.ncsbn.org).
- Locate your test site early. Be sure to obtain an Authorization to Test (ATT). Remember you must apply to your board or nursing or regulatory body before registering with Pearson Vue (http://www.pearsonvue.com/nclex) to take the examination. Be certain you have acceptable identification. Acceptable identification can be found at https://www.ncsbn.org/1221.htm. You may need to order replacement identification before testing. If you have a name change, only a marriage license, divorce decree, or legal court name change documents are accepted.
- *Perform a needs assessment.* Determine content areas of strengths and weaknesses. Look at previous academic and nursing coursework, class notes and handouts, examination grades, and grades made on nursing care plans or process papers. If your school uses nationally normed assessment examinations, use the report to determine areas of strengths and weaknesses. The rationale provided when reviewing these exams provides a wealth of information and validates the correct answers. Talk with faculty in courses in which weakness or difficulty existed. Determine where the greatest amount of review is needed. Be honest in performing the needs assessment. The foundation for success or failure on the NCLEX-RN examination may be determined here.
- *Analyze standardized examinations.* If your school uses standardized examinations to compare your scores to your peers and nationally, look at where you rank compared to both. Again, do not be overconfident if you scored higher than your peers and nationally. This should give you positive affirmation that you have a high chance of successfully passing the NCLEX—not that you can delete your NCLEX-RN study plans. Even when students score at the highest level, many miss some questions. The "focused review" provided by the standardized examination describes the area of

the nursing process, and the specific content area should be used to remediate. Remember, these exams cannot test all content matter, so always consider you only received what is highly tested on the NCLEX-RN.

- *Determine the number of days or weeks necessary for review.* Candidates with a strong nursing knowledge base may need less time than candidates with weaknesses. As with the needs assessment, candidates should be realistic in planning the amount of review time needed.
- *Decide what method of review will be used.* Both Individual and group study have strong and weak points. Strong points of individual study include having total control over content and time spent in review. Weak points include having no immediate resources to explain or assist with understanding difficult concepts. Candidates with weakness in disciplining themselves may have problems sticking to review schedules and focusing on specific content with individual study. Strong points of group study include the support that members can give each other and learning from others in the group. Also, many minds working together are stronger than one working alone. Weak points of group study include a lack of preparation of some group members, weaker members of the group holding the rest back, and a tendency of the group to focus on topics that have more to do with socialization than review. Candidates using study groups should insist on members coming to sessions prepared to work.
- *Decide what materials or resources will be used during review.* Textbooks and class notes from nursing or nursing-related courses, such as anatomy and physiology, psychology, or nutrition, are helpful. It has been suggested that rereading your nursing school notes may not be the best use of time. Computer-assisted instructions used during the nursing program may be available. Numerous NCLEX-RN examination review books are available. Many review books include a computer disk or CD or online resources to be used during review. Make sure that these computer aids are compatible with the type of computer you will be using during review.
- *Structure review time.* Schedule review during times of peak performance. Learning is enhanced when reviewing for short blocks of time, around 50 minutes, instead of reviewing for several unbroken hours at a time. Candidates should remember that they are reviewing for an examination, not cramming for one.

- *Control the review environment.* Keep noise and distraction at a minimum. Have adequate space and lighting for review. Control the room temperature when possible; if not possible, dress for the environment. Have all materials needed for review, including soft drinks and snacks, close at hand so that time is not wasted gathering these items during review time. Make sure that friends and family know not to interrupt during review time.

- *Have a game plan for each review session.* Develop a review schedule complete with subject matter to be considered and specific tasks to be completed during each session. Stick to the schedule.

- *Learn concepts and principles, not isolated facts.* The NCLEX-RN examination tests a candidate's ability to apply, analyze, and evaluate nursing knowledge and does not focus on isolated events. Candidates whose past test-taking success has been based on memorization rather than actual learning have an increased risk for failure on the NCLEX-RN® examination.

- *Use learning techniques that have proven successful in the past.* Students have different learning styles and therefore benefit from different learning techniques. Students might choose to use flash cards or note cards, underscore key points, take notes or outline material, or record pertinent information for later playback. Students should quiz themselves or ask others to pose questions. Many students find downloading application software (i.e., an "app") to practice NCLEX-style questions is helpful. Examples include NCLEX Mastery found at http://www.nclexmastery.com.

- *Seek qualified help when reviewing information that is particularly difficult.* Faculty members are an excellent resource. If you invest in an external course review, ask for help during the question and answer sessions or determine whether an open forum to ask questions extends beyond the actual review class. Be cautious when asking peers for assistance because they may not understand the material as well as they think they do.

- *Practice taking NCLEX-RN–type examinations, paying particular attention to the rationales or reasons provided for correct and incorrect answers.* Successful test takers know why a specific option is correct or incorrect. Even though candidates may spend as much time as they want on a question when actually taking the examination, they should get into the habit of taking about 1 minute for each question. Poor time management may cause a candidate to not have enough time to complete the test and therefore

be unsuccessful on the NCLEX-RN examination. Practice also will help reduce test anxiety. NCLEX-RN–type examinations are commonly found in NCLEX-RN examination review books.

- *Use the Internet.* It provides numerous sources that may aid in preparation for the NCLEX-RN examination. *Avoid excessive stimulants (e.g., caffeine) to increase review time.* The best learning takes place when heads are clear.

- *Maintain a healthy, positive attitude toward reviewing and taking the NCLEX-RN examination.* Have confidence in your abilities to be successful on the examination. Remember that even practicing nurses with years of experience do not know everything there is to know about every aspect of nursing and that the goal on the NCLEX-RN examination is to demonstrate minimal competency for an entry-level RN position, not competency for an advanced RN position.

Food for Thought when Selecting an NCLEX-RN Review Course

Just as there is no one best method for preparing to take the NCLEX-RN examination, there is no one best review course for a candidate to take in preparation for the examination. The most important thing to remember is that a review course is exactly what it says it is—a review course. Such courses are designed to reconsider or reexamine content common to the three types of nursing programs.

The purpose of a review course is to enhance or polish what candidates already know from their nursing programs. Review courses are not intended to teach totally new concepts. If candidates have an extreme weakness in one or more content areas, the review course may not provide enough content to bring the candidate up to speed on the topic.

Numerous companies and people offer review courses. Each review offering has strong and weak points, and what appeals to one candidate may not appeal to another. Some offer financial discounts or other incentives if more than one candidate from a school of nursing registers for their course.

Review courses usually are expensive and last from 1 or 2 days to a complete week. Some courses provide books, CDs, or other written materials. Others may offer additional materials for a fee. Some courses will refund a part or all of the cost of the review if a candidate takes their review course and is unsuccessful in taking the NCLEX-RN examination.

Review courses may or may not be taught by competent people. Nurse educators who are teaching faculty at schools of nursing teach many review courses. However, people with no substantial background in nursing may teach some courses. A review course is no better than the person or people teaching it. Take the time to research who is teaching the review course.

The decision to take a review course in preparation for taking the NCLEX-RN® examination is a personal one. Some candidates find the structure and schedule of a review course helpful in preparation. Other candidates may find the structure and schedule restrictive and overly time-consuming.

Candidates seriously interested in taking an NCLEX-RN examination review course should look to the faculty at their school of nursing for guidance. Many faculty have had experience with review courses or may teach review courses. Candidates should also talk to peers who have recently graduated about recommendations for review courses. Serious candidates also should obtain written information from several different review course offerings and compare and contrast among

the offerings. Selection of a review course should be based on more than the cost of the review program—it should meet the candidate's unique needs.

The NCSBN's Review for the NCLEX-RN Examination course offers 3-, 5-, 8- and 15-week subscriptions. Student testimonials describe the course as extremely helpful in passing the NCLEX. New items are continually added, ensuring the review is current with the latest test plan. Alternate format items can be practiced. Immediate instructor feedback is available through the "Ask the Instructor" feature. The site offers a timeline for interested candidates; for example, if one registers for the 3-week subscription, 27 hours per week are need for review; by comparison, 5 to 6 hours are needed with the 15-week subscription. This is available at http://learningext.com/students/p/NCLEX-RN.aspx.

The NCSBN website offers tips for the actual examination date, such as dress comfortably, arrive 30 minutes early, and be prepared to provide your signature, photograph, and palm vein scan. Be sure to watch the "NCLEX Using CAT" video if you have any questions about how this type of testing works.

■ SUMMARY

Success on the NCLEX-RN examination is needed to obtain a license and practice as an RN. Most candidates taking the NCLEX-RN examination are successful. Of the 155,098 first-time, U.S.-educated candidates taking the examination during 2013, approximately 83.04% were successful (NCSBN, 2014c). The pass rate is somewhat higher for those testing for the first time in 2014, with 85.54% of the 89,032 candidates passing. The key to success on the NCLEX-RN® examination is sound preparation from the nursing program, adequate preparation for the examination, and confidence in oneself.

REFERENCES

Anderson LW, Krathwohl DR, editors: *A taxonomy for learning, teaching, and assessing: a revision of Bloom's taxonomy of educational objectives*, New York, 2001, Addison-Wesley.

Bloom BS, Englehart MD, Furst EJ: *Taxonomy of educational objectives: the classification of educational goals. Handbook I. Cognitive domain*, New York, 1956, David McKay.

Foote J: *State board questions and answers for nurses*, Philadelphia, 1919, Lippincott.

National Council of State Boards of Nursing: *NCLEX Examinations*, 2014a. (website). https://www.ncsbn.org/nclex.htm.

National Council of State Boards of Nursing: *Transitional NCLEX examination candidate bulletin for Canadian NCLEX candidates*, 2014b. (website). https://www.ncsbn.org/Transitional_NCLEX_Candidate_Bulletin_2014.pdf. Accessed September 2014.

National Council of State Boards of Nursing: *NCLEX pass rates*, 2014c. (website). https://www.ncsbn.org/Table_of_Pass_Rates_2014.pdf. Accessed September 2014.

National Council of State Boards of Nursing: *NCLEX-RN® examination test plan for the National Council Licensure Examination for Registered Nurses*, 2013. (website). https://www.ncsbn.org/2013_NCLEX_RN_Detailed_Test_Plan_Candidate.pdf. Accessed September 2014.

National Council of State Boards of Nursing: *2011 RN practice analysis: Linking the NCLEX-RN® examination to practice*, NCSBN Research Brief 53, 2012. (website). https://www.ncsbn.org/12_RN_Practice_Analysis_Vol53.pdf.

Potter PA, Perry AG: *Fundamentals of nursing*, St. Louis, Mo, 2013, Mosby Elsevier.

INDEX